THE OXFORD ENCYCLOPEDIA OF
AMERICAN POLITICAL AND LEGAL HISTORY

THE OXFORD ENCYCLOPEDIA OF AMERICAN POLITICAL AND LEGAL HISTORY

Donald T. Critchlow
Philip R. VanderMeer
EDITORS IN CHIEF

VOLUME 1

ABOR—MODE

OXFORD
UNIVERSITY PRESS

OXFORD
UNIVERSITY PRESS

Oxford University Press, Inc., publishes works that further
Oxford University's objective of excellence
in research, scholarship, and education.

Oxford New York
Auckland Cape Town Dar es Salaam Hong Kong Karachi
Kuala Lumpur Madrid Melbourne Mexico City Nairobi
New Delhi Shanghai Taipei Toronto

With offices in
Argentina Austria Brazil Chile Czech Republic France Greece
Guatemala Hungary Italy Japan Poland Portugal Singapore
South Korea Switzerland Thailand Turkey Ukraine Vietnam

Published by Oxford University Press, Inc.
198 Madison Avenue, New York, NY 10016
www.oup.com

The Library of Congress Cataloging-in-Publication Data

The Oxford encyclopedia of American political and legal history / Donald T. Critchlow and Philip R. VanderMeer, editors in chief.
p. cm.
Includes bibliographical references and index.
ISBN 978-0-19-975461-8
1. United States—Politics and government—Encyclopedias. 2. Political planning—United States—History—Encyclopedias. 3. Law—United States—History—Encyclopedias. I. Critchlow, Donald T., 1948- II. VanderMeer, Philip R., 1947- III. Title.

JK9.O94 2012
320.97303—dc23

2011032748

1 3 5 7 9 8 6 4 2

Printed in the United States of America
on acid-free paper

EDITORIAL AND PRODUCTION STAFF

Acquiring Editor	Grace Labatt
Development Editor	Eric Stannard
Editorial Assistants	Jenny Keegan Holly Seabury
Production Editor	Richard Johnson
Copyeditor	Heidi Yerkes
Proofreader	Heather Dubnick
Indexer	Katharyn Dunham
Compositor	Glyph International
Manufacturing Controller	Genieve Shaw
Interior Design	Fearn Cutler de Vicq
Cover Design	Brady McNamara
Managing Editor	Mary Araneo
Production Managers	Steven Cestaro David Ford
Executive Editor, Development	Stephen Wagley
Publisher	Casper Grathwohl
Editorial Director	Damon Zucca

CONTENTS

LIST OF ENTRIES

INTRODUCTION

The Oxford Encyclopedia of American History carries on a tradition of scholarly publishing by Oxford University Press that began in 1478, fourteen years before Christopher Columbus set out from Palos de la Frontera in Spain and sailed westward across the Atlantic. As for American history, Oxford's first contribution was John Smith's annotated *Map of Virginia,* published in 1612, five years after 104 English men and boys had founded the Jamestown settlement.

This tradition has continued over the centuries, including *The Oxford Companion to United States History* (2001), affectionately called "OCUSH," which I had the pleasure and privilege of editing along with a distinguished group of associates. To this long and noteworthy record, Oxford now proudly adds this new work. Building on the one-volume *Companion,* this twelve-volume set of six encyclopedias offers a far more capacious format, making it possible to include a greater number of entries and to provide more detailed, in-depth coverage than was possible in the briefer compass of the *Companion.*

The rationale for such a work is obvious. Awareness of, and interest in, our collective past is part of what makes us human, and the recording of history has characterized every great civilization. The case for this specific set of encyclopedias is equally compelling. From the time when the first human beings made their way from present-day Siberia across a now-vanished land bridge to what we call North America, the history of the peoples of this great geographic region has been rich in its diversity and interest. From the late sixteenth century onward, the various settlements in what Europeans called first the New World and then, after 1776, the United States have loomed large on the world stage—first in the realm of the imagination and then, increasingly, as unavoidable reality. The nation's political, social, economic, and cultural lives have always roused interest, sometimes as the target of criticism and ridicule, sometimes as an ideal to be envied and emulated. As Johann Wolfgang von Goethe wrote in an 1827 poem (in Daniel Platt's translation):

America, you've got it better
Than our old continent. Exult!
You have no decaying castles
And no basalt.
Your heart is not troubled,
In lively pursuits,
By useless old remembrance
And empty disputes.

The actual America of 1827, distracted by controversy over the tariff and by angry feuds within John Quincy Adams's unpopular and dysfunctional presidential administration, was, of course, irrelevant to Goethe. As others have done before and since, he was conjuring up a finer America of his dreams, a fresh, new society uncorrupted by the all-too-human flaws of tired, old Europe. (That strange reference to "basalt," some scholars believe, may be a metaphorical allusion to volcanoes as symbols of social unrest and revolutionary turmoil.) Of more substantive, less abstract interest has been America's global military, diplomatic, economic, and strategic role, which has grown steadily more significant and inescapable over the years. In short, for a variety of reasons, the case for a comprehensive reference work covering all of American history is clear.

But is such a work really needed in the twenty-first century, given the tsunami of "information" endlessly churning through the media, accessible at a keystroke? The answer is a decisive, "Yes." This set of encyclopedias arose from a core assumption shared by the editors at Oxford University Press, by the gifted scholars constituting the editorial teams, and certainly by me. In an era in which the production and dissemination of knowledge have become wholly diffuse, often anonymous and unsourced, and frequently idiosyncratic and unreliable, we are convinced that there is still a place—indeed, a vital necessity—for a historical reference work that is authoritative, carefully planned, analytically sophisticated, written by scholars familiar with the latest findings, and carefully edited for accuracy, clarity, and readability.

Grounded in these basic principles, *The Oxford Encyclopedia of American History* is chronologically comprehensive, from the earliest human settlements to the twenty-first century, from the Stone Age to the Computer Age. The work is topically comprehensive as well. This is a daunting task, particularly because the field of American history has expanded dramatically in recent decades: the field has come to include much more extensive coverage of social, cultural, scientific, medical, and demographic topics than was true in the past. Recent scholarship has vastly broadened our knowledge of the historical experience of all Americans of the past, not just the elite figures who once dominated the story. This set of encyclopedias fully reflects this broader understanding of the American past.

HISTORY: AN ANCIENT DISCIPLINE, YET EVER NEW

History is among the oldest of the scholarly disciplines, tracing its origins to West African griots, ancient Chinese chroniclers, and Mesopotamians who combined the skills of historian, elocutionist, scribe, and stonemason, celebrating the exploits of their rulers *in viva voce* orations and on steles and tablets for future generations to transcribe and wonder at. The Greek historian Herodotus, who lived in the fifth century

BCE, wrote an account of successive rulers of Persia, with whom Greece fought several wars. Filling his narrative with stories about the peoples and places he had heard about, he was an early practitioner of what is now called social and cultural history. Herodotus's younger contemporary Thucydides devoted his great talents to a history of the Peloponnesian war, the long conflict between Athens and Sparta. Focusing on battles and diplomacy and avoiding Herodotus's charming penchant for digression, Thucydides nevertheless recognized the importance of personality traits and social factors, such as the terrible plague that struck Athens in the midst of the war. In an authorial decision that would place him at odds with some participants in modern America's culture wars, Thucydides strictly excluded divine intervention from his causal forces, and he avoided suggesting that the gods favored one side or another in the conflict he was describing.

But history writing, this ancient pursuit, is also ever new, which helps account for its appeal to so many bright young scholars. It continually reinvents itself, not only because more things keep happening, but also because historians' understanding of their field, and of what merits their attention, is continually shifting and enlarging. In former times, the historian typically focused his attention (and it almost invariably was a "he") on politics, war, law, and diplomacy. Together with industrialization, finance, and other economic matters, these were considered history's driving forces, and thus the historian's proper subject matter.

But gradually a broader understanding emerged. George Bancroft, the prolific nineteenth-century historian, famously included a chapter on social history in his monumental ten-volume history of the United States (1834–1874). Henry Adams began his multivolume *History of the United States during the Administrations of Thomas Jefferson and James Madison* (1889–1891) with a chapter each on the "popular characteristics" of the American people, on "American ideals," and on the intellectual life of New England, the middle-Atlantic states, and the South. By offering new approaches to the history of ideas, Vernon L. Parrington's *Main Currents in American Thought* (1927) and Merle Curti's *The Growth of American Thought* (1943) helped create a new field, combining history and literature, that came to be known as American Studies.

Later scholars have vastly expanded these initiatives. The twenty-first century's historians recognize that the history of social groups, class conflict, sexuality, popular culture, ideas and ideology, religious belief, literature, music, and the arts, as well as developments in science, medicine, technology, and the economy, all lie within their purview and merit careful attention and study. The traditional areas of politics, the law, military history, and foreign relations remain central, of course, but these fields, too, have been enriched by attention to the broader sociocultural context within which elections, legislative battles, legal decisions, wars, and diplomatic maneuverings unfold.

Indeed, all these subfields are interconnected. One cannot understand the social and military history of colonial America, for example, without understanding the devastating effects of the bacteria and viruses that the European newcomers unwittingly brought with them: lacking the immunity to these bacteria and viruses that comes with long exposure, native peoples were decimated by disease. The history of slavery remains incomplete without attention to the changing technology of cotton production. One cannot grasp the full impact on America of World War I without also grasping the impact of the virulent influenza virus (the precise point of origin remains uncertain) that spread across the battlefields of Europe and home-front military bases, causing a global pandemic that took at least 50 million lives. The nation's military and political history is enriched by attention to the ways in which perceptions of wars, battles, elections, and political careers are shaped by the popular culture, from ballads and broadsides to cartoons, films, and television programs. Our picture of working-class America is enriched if we examine workers' families, leisure activities, religious lives, and consumption patterns, as well as their voting habits and participation in labor unions—important as voting patterns and unions obviously are. On and on the list could go, illustrating that American history, like all history, is really a seamless web, however we divide it into subfields for analytic and pedagogical purposes.

Along with the subject matter of history, the demographic profile of the profession of American history itself has changed. Once the domain of white males of British or northern European ancestry, in the twenty-first century the profession is far more diverse in terms of gender, race, and ethnicity. This has made for a livelier and more stimulating intellectual environment, as well as for a greater sensitivity to the diverse historical experience of the many subgroups within American society.

Historians' understanding of America's place in the world has evolved as well. In the past, U.S. historians tended to stress the uniqueness of the American experience. Underlying this view was the notion that America was not only different from, but superior to, other nations, and that it was somehow immune to the historical processes that could be seen in the rise and decline of other once-powerful civilizations and nation-states, from Babylon, Greece, and Rome to Spain, Portugal, Sweden, the Netherlands, and Great Britain. Sometimes, as in the writings of the New England Puritans, this view of America's uniqueness took on explicitly religious overtones. Even George Bancroft, a liberal Unitarian with a European education including a PhD from Germany's University of Göttingen, saw America as enjoying God's special favor. Such explicitly supernaturalist understandings of American history gradually faded, but notions of American exceptionalism survived, shaping historians' approach to their subject. This, too, has changed since the later twentieth century. U.S. historians now recognize that the forces shaping American history are hardly unique to the United States, but replicate processes also observable in other societies. This broader comparative dimension has both enriched American historical scholarship and added a chastening note of humility.

The heightened transnational awareness has not been only at the abstract level. American historians have vastly benefited from the work of foreign scholars, including the British historian E. P. Thompson, whose book on the making of the English working class was pathbreaking, and the French historians Lucien Febvre, Marc Bloch, Fernand Braudel, and Emmanuel Le Roy Ladurie, who did pioneering work in social history and founded the so-called *Annales* school, with its shift from providing a narrative of passing events to focusing on the *longue durée,* or long-term, processes that shape human societies over centuries.

Influential, too, has been the Italian historian Carlo Ginzburg, with his attention to the illuminating insights to be gained from "microhistory," the close analysis of specific events or small communities. Ginzburg's *Il formaggio e i vermi: Il cosmo di un mugnaio del Cinquecento* (1976; English trans., *The Cheese and the Worms: The Cosmos of a Sixteenth-Century Miller,* 1980), based on detailed Inquisition records that Ginzburg discovered in long-neglected archives of the Catholic Church, told of an obscure miller, Domenico Scandella, better known as Menocchio, burned at the stake in 1600 in the northeastern Italian town of Montereale for beliefs that he summed up this way:

> I have said that in my opinion, all was chaos . . . and out of that bulk a mass formed—just as cheese is made out of

> milk—and worms appeared in it, and these were the angels. There was also God, he too having been created out of that mass at the same time.

Such heresy shocked church authorities, and Menocchio went to his fiery death. In writing about this forgotten event in an obscure town, Ginzburg offered a wealth of fresh insights into the procedures and processes of the Inquisition, late medieval folk belief and oral culture, and the ramifications of the Counter-Reformation in Italy. Such scholarship proved appealing to American historians, who explored microhistories of their own to see what they would reveal. Laurel Thatcher Ulrich's Pulitzer Prize–winning *A Midwife's Tale* (1991) offered a biography of Martha Ballard, an obscure Maine midwife of the turn of the nineteenth century, based on Ballard's diary recording the unremarkable routines of her life. In the diary's "exhaustive, repetitive dailiness," Ulrich argued, lay its value as a historical document.

As this suggests, American historians' methodologies and sources have expanded as well. While retaining a strong sense of the value of their traditional text-based approaches, historians have learned from sociologists and political scientists the value of quantification in illuminating the past. Census records, voting data, tax lists, and many other forms of quantified information have yielded rich results. Such pathbreaking books using quantified data as Lee Benson's *The Concept of Jacksonian Democracy: New York as a Test Case* (1961) and Stephan Thernstrom's *Poverty and Progress: Social Mobility in a Nineteenth Century City* (1964) provided a means of testing cherished American myths about the "era of the common man," "rags to riches," and the United States as a "land of opportunity"—myths reinforced by Horatio Alger stories and the oft-told biographies of exceptional figures like Andrew Carnegie. (That Thernstrom's book was pathbreaking is indicated by its being relegated by the *American Historical Review* to a brief notice in a section called "Other Recent Publications" and by its being overlooked entirely by the *Journal of American History,* whose editor assumed that it was a work of sociology.)

Fully aware that statistically based findings must be interpreted for and presented in prose accessible to people who are not mathematicians, historians are in little danger of becoming computing automatons, spewing out numbers, statistics, and formulas. And the profession has learned that statistical data, like any other form of evidence, can be fudged and misrepresented and thus must be approached with due skepticism. Nevertheless, American historians have grown more conscious of the rich resources buried in the nation's vast repositories of quantified data. So, too, have they discovered the research value of material-culture products, visual materials, industrial designs, fashion shows, television commercials, and mundane everyday objects from toys, comic books, tombstones, and toilets to domestic structures. Approached with insight and imagination, such materials are invaluable historical sources.

To be sure, all this ferment and change within the profession of American history has raised troublesome questions. If historians focus too exclusively on subgroups within society, how can they formulate a larger conception of *American* history? Put another way, what meaning does the familiar phrase "one nation indivisible" from the original Pledge of Allegiance to the flag ("under God" was inserted later) retain in the twenty-first century, apart from the banal point that a second secession movement like that of 1861 would be unlikely to succeed? Or, again, if historians adopt a snapshot approach, documenting the experience of specific groups during one brief period of their history, how can they explain change over time? Other questions have been raised as well. As historians, from wholly laudable motives, turned their attention to the poor, disenfranchised, and disinherited—doing "history from the bottom up," as it was called—did they risk losing sight of the important role of powerful elites and interest groups in society? In abandoning the notion of American exceptionalism as self-serving and parochial, did they risk missing what might, in fact, be distinctive and unique about the American experience? At the practical level, could historians successfully integrate quantified statistical data and other new forms of evidence with the written sources upon which they have traditionally relied? Such questions have for decades energized the profession of American history, and echoes of these questions will be found in the pages of this set of encyclopedias.

THE OXFORD ENCYCLOPEDIA OF AMERICAN HISTORY: A REFERENCE WORK FOR THE TWENTY-FIRST CENTURY

All these trends—the greater diversity of the profession of American history, historians' broader understanding of the discipline's scope and available range of sources and methodologies, the greater openness to multicultural and transnational perspectives—have informed the planning and execution of *The Oxford Encyclopedia of American History.* This becomes immediately evident as one looks at the basic structure of the work. The effort to bring organizational and intellectual coherence to such a vast and unwieldy topic has been formidable indeed. We have been reminded more than once of Immanuel Kant's much-quoted observation: "Out of the crooked timber of humanity, no straight thing was ever made." Yet we have given it a try—with, we hope, some success. To make this set of encyclopedias of maximum benefit to its users, we have divided the sprawling, almost boundless field of American history into six topical subcategories, each comprising two volumes and each with its own editor or editors in chief. Here are these six subcategories, with the name of the editor or editors in chief and his or her academic affiliation:

The Oxford Encyclopedia of American Business, Labor, and Economic History
Editor in Chief
Melvyn Dubofsky
Binghamton University, State University of New York

The Oxford Encyclopedia of American Cultural and Intellectual History
Editors in Chief
Joan Shelley Rubin
University of Rochester

Scott E. Casper
University of Nevada, Reno

The Oxford Encyclopedia of American Military and Diplomatic History
Editor in Chief
Timothy J. Lynch
University of Melbourne

The Oxford Encyclopedia of American Political and Legal History
Editors in Chief
Donald T. Critchlow
Arizona State University

Philip R. VanderMeer
Arizona State University

The Oxford Encyclopedia of the History of American Science, Medicine and Technology
Editor in Chief
Hugh Richard Slotten
University of Otago

The Oxford Encyclopedia of American Social History
Editor in Chief
Lynn Dumenil
Occidental College

These editors, distinguished scholars all, have been assisted by teams of associate editors, ranging from prominent senior scholars to gifted younger scholars. Through extended discussions, these teams carefully formulated their entry lists to ensure comprehensive coverage of the core topics in their field, supplemented by mid-length and shorter entries on topics of interest. The editors then solicited entries from historians who had relevant expertise. This great project would be impossible without the participation of hundreds of scholars who welcomed the opportunity to offer an account of their work to a broader public, beyond the circle of colleagues who routinely review their books, evaluate their research proposals, and share panels at scholarly meetings. The specialization and compartmentalization of the profession of history can be rewarding, as one exchanges ideas with others who share one's specific interests, but it can also seem confining and a bit claustrophobic. Participation in a large-scale collaborative project like *The Oxford Encyclopedia of American History* provides an opportunity to move beyond one's professional comfort zone and to share one's research with an interested worldwide readership.

Incorporating the most recent research and interpretive approaches, the entries are designed to be of value to scholars, advanced students, and all those seeking high-level analytic treatment of key topics in American history. The entries include essential facts, of course—names, dates, and so on—but they go further, contextualizing the topic, conveying its human dimensions, suggesting its larger historical significance, and addressing matters of controversy or interpretive disagreement.

Along with matters of content, methodology, and scope, we have given high priority to the entries' organization and style. Historians have long hovered ambivalently between the social sciences and the humanities, unwilling to abandon the social scientists' commitment to methodological rigor, but also determined to retain the humanities' concern for clarity and persuasiveness of presentation. For all the changes since the days of Herodotus and Thucydides—and Edward Gibbon, Voltaire, Francis Parkman, George Bancroft, Henry Adams, and scores of other historians admired for their writing style—historians still take pride in writing lucid, accessible, even elegant prose. They pay attention not only to the information being conveyed, but to the manner in which it is conveyed.

In choosing our contributors, describing their assignments, and editing their entries, therefore, we have emphasized style as well as content. Lewis Mumford once rather cattily observed that reading John Dewey was like riding on the Boston subway: one eventually got to one's destination, but considerably the worse for wear. We have made every effort to ensure that such a criticism will not be leveled against the contributors to this set of encyclopedias. Acquiring historical knowledge should not be the intellectual equivalent of a visit to the dentist.

USING THE ENCYCLOPEDIA

Taken together, the twelve volumes of *The Oxford Encyclopedia of American History* include more than 3,500 entries, arranged in alphabetical order within each two-volume topical set, for ease of research. Composite entries gather together discussions of similar or related topics under one entry title. For example, under the entry "Internal Migration" in

The Oxford Encyclopedia of American Social History, the reader will find four subentries: "Colonial Era," "Nineteenth-Century Westward," "Twentieth Century and Beyond," and "African Americans." A headnote listing the various subentries introduces each composite entry.

A selective bibliography at the end of each entry directs the reader who wishes to pursue a topic in greater detail to the most important recent scholarly work. Most entries include references at the end that guide interested readers to related entries. Blind entries direct the user from an alternate form of an entry title to the entry itself. For example, the blind entry "Mormon Rebellion" tells the reader to look under "Utah War of 1857."

Throughout the planning and execution of this work we have been guided by a single goal: to make the full panorama of American history accessible and understandable to the maximum number of users. We hope that we have succeeded in this purpose.

Finally, the editors would like to extend sincere thanks to the professionals at Oxford University Press who aided immeasurably in the preparation of this work: Grace Labatt, who patiently and cheerfully oversaw the process of selecting the editors in chief; Stephen Wagley, executive editor, who shared his wisdom and experience and saw the project successfully launched; Damon Zucca, editorial director, and Alixandra Gould, senior editor, who aided us in thinking about the emerging world of online reference; Eric Stannard and Andrew Jung, the development editors, who with unfailing good humor moderated early discussions among the editors over where specific entries should go, dealt with problems as they arose, and gently prodded us to maintain the pace. Our thanks to one and all.

Paul S. Boyer
Merle Curti Professor of History Emeritus
University of Wisconsin–Madison
July 2011

PREFACE

Politics is a subject of great interest, complexity, and dispute. But beyond debates over the substance of politics, over what is desirable or right, is the larger question of defining the subject itself. The most inclusive definitions use the term to cover a vast range of topics, even something like interpersonal relationships. At the core of this approach is the notion that politics is about power, about "who gets what and how." Although every perspective on politics acknowledges that power is a central element of politics, a narrower, classic approach to politics uses the Aristotelian concept of *politikos*—pertaining to the city and state—to consider both theory and practice, institutions and behavior, principle and practice, justice and social order.

Modern scholars have broadened the approach of the classical political theorist to include a complication of additional factors. The emergence of the modern welfare and regulatory state; an expansive electorate; racial, gender, and class diversity within a democratic polity; the complexity of law within a constitutional government; and the pervasive role played by government in contemporary social and civic life presents a complexity to the meaning of politics not envisioned by the ancients, even in all their wisdom.

These theoretical considerations informed the editors as they thought about how to structure and define an encyclopedia of American political and legal history, but this volume is not a theoretical work, treatise, or text. It is, instead, an encyclopedia, and in completing it the editors confronted immediate and practical problems involving three questions.

First, how broadly should we define political history? This was a practical and immediate issue because this larger project, *The Oxford Encyclopedia of America History,* edited by Paul Boyer, includes separate volumes on social history, economic, business, and labor history; foreign relations and military history; and science, technology, and medical history. The obvious problem for the editors of this volume was that there is a political, judicial, and/or policy element in nearly every economic, social, cultural, intellectual, scientific and technological, and diplomatic topic. Our approach started, then, by determining the central character of a topic, and we worked with the editors of the other volumes, and the general editor, to lay out a flexible framework for inclusion and exclusion in our volume. The core topics for this volume, the most clearly "political," were presidential biographies, key political figures, important legislation and governmental institutions, and broad political trends relating to elections, voting behavior, party development, new constituencies within the electorate, and other topics directly related to American politics. The editors also believed that a useful approach to political history was to include various aspects of public policy and policy history. A third area of inclusion is legal history, because topics such as constitutional interpretation, key court cases, legal theories, and key figures in the history of America law are closely connected to political and policy history. The editors were greatly assisted by legal scholar Anders Walker in developing a list of important topics in these areas.

The second practical question we confronted—related to the first—was what is the audience for this volume? This seemed particularly crucial, given the array of printed sources and the even greater and easily accessible online sources. Answering this question proved less problematic than it first appeared and involved matters of focus and scope. The combined focus on political, policy, and legal history in this volume provides readers with coverage of a broad range of topics not found in most online resources. Using work by the best scholars working in their fields, this volume offers a quick, objective reference guide to important topics, as well as interpretative perspectives related to political, policy, and legal history. Informed by the latest scholarship, this volume reflects the advance of specialized research in the academy that has occurred over the past two decades, made accessible to the general reader and those seeking informed judgments about specific topics and general trends in American political, policy, and legal history over the course of American history from its roots in English and European political thought to today.

A final issue was how to avoid unnecessary duplication of excellent, relevant entries found in Paul Boyer's *Companion to American History,* which was the inspiration for this larger project. After closely reading the *Companion,* the editors for this new volume decided that some *Companion* entries had a specifically political focus and were of the desired length to be included in this more specialized volume. Some entries needed to be updated or extended to include the George W. Bush and Barack Obama administrations. After compiling the list of legal topics, the editors completed a similar review of Kermit L. Hall's excellent *Companion to the Supreme Court* and chose several essays from that volume. Although this encyclopedia does include some previously published essays, sometimes revised, the bulk of the volume comprises new essays written by scholars from across the country and abroad, many on topics not found in other volumes. The result, we believe, is a volume that includes familiar elements but that ultimately offers something different.

GENERAL PRINCIPLES INFORMING THIS VOLUME

In defining this volume, the editors began by addressing general principles that inform it. The editorial board and volume editors first looked at broad categories related to political and constitutional thought, American political institutions, critical legislation, party development, and key actors and movements that shaped American political and legal history. These categories were then broken down to specific topics. Members of the editorial board were asked to develop lists based on broad categories with specific topics under these categories. Paula Baker, a historian with expertise in gender and politics, was invited to contribute a list covering the colonial through the late nineteenth century. Vincent Cannato, an expert on immigration and urban history, developed topics covering the New Deal through the present. Alan Petigny, an intellectual historian with an interest in African American history, contributed topics related to race throughout American history. Political scientist Steve Thomas provided expertise on important interpretative trends in American political history and American political development. And, as noted earlier, legal scholar Anders Walker developed a list for legal history.

In this process, the editors and editorial board members understood that any volume addressing American political and legal history needed to capture the unique nature of the nation's founding principles embodied in the Constitution, the expansive nature of American democracy, political conflict and compromise, and the emergence of the modern welfare and regulatory state beginning in the late nineteenth century with the industrial revolution. Furthermore, the editors sought to capture the tension and contradiction manifested in American political and legal history. Thus, they suggest two primary themes for viewing the span of American history: first, fundamental changes to the nature of the state combined with the rise of influential nonprofit sector groups; and second, a shift in the nature of political involvement from parties and voting to a regard for consumerism and a focus on rights.

CHANGES IN THE STATE: PUBLIC POLICY AND THE RISE OF NONPROFITS

Those who drafted the U.S. Constitution, drawing from their deep understanding of ancient and modern history, English political and economic theory, and colonial tradition, constructed a government founded on principles of representative government, divided government, federalism, and the rule of law. In constructing this new order, the founders understood that no system of government is perfect, because human nature is imperfect. The founders feared centralized government, demagogues, and mob passion that could only undermine social order and liberty. For this reason, those involved in drafting the Constitution sought to create a stable political order that allowed for cautious change to accommodate future generations.

The fear of centralized government created a unique antistatist sensibility within the American political tradition, yet this faced expanding notions of democratic participation and a belief that government, mainly state and local government, had important responsibilities. The problems of the new industrial order in the late nineteenth and early twentieth centuries led Americans to create an enlarged role for government at all levels in regulating economic and financial corporations, protecting women and child labor, working conditions, and consumer products. Aspects of this regulatory state were further expanded by

Republican administrations in the 1920s and much more strikingly in the 1930s. At the same time the modern welfare state emerged with the enactment of the Social Security Act in 1934. Further growth came after World War II.

In the years between 1965 and 1980 the American social welfare state underwent a significant transformation. From 1965 through 1980, government spending on social welfare grew by 263 percent in inflation-adjusted dollars. While the federal government centralized social policy through congressional mandates, administrative and legislative regulations, and new funding arrangements, the delivery and implementation of these programs were placed in the hands of state and local governments and nonprofit organizations.

The result of this new welfare system blended public and private action. This "mixed" welfare state that emerged in the late 1960s and 1970s marked a creation unique to the United States, reflecting a deep-seated American tradition of associative enterprise that combines self-reliance and private voluntarism with communitarianism and government activity. An important feature of this second welfare state was the important role left to private, nonprofit organizations and to nongovernmental institutions in serving essentially public goals.

As this second welfare state emerged, the nonprofit sector was called upon to play a number of distinct roles. Nonprofit organizations served as funding intermediaries distributing funds to other parts of the nonprofit sector; service-providing organizations involved in health care, education, counseling, and adoption assistance; and political action agencies supporting particular pieces of legislation or candidates for political office. By providing public services, these nonprofit organizations developed a symbiotic relationship with the federal government.

The federal government relied on nonprofit service providers to implement social programs. In this way, the expansion of the welfare state in the 1960s and 1970s created a seeming paradox that remains apparent in the contemporary liberal regime: The rapid growth of the nonprofit, voluntaristic sector occurred at the same time as federal social policy became increasingly centralized and active. The parallel development of the centralized welfare state and the voluntary sector was no coincidence. The growth of federal social programs mobilized the nonprofit sector; in turn, the nonprofit sector, through policy innovation and program implementation, helped legitimize the modern welfare state.

Thus, as the traditional federal system, which had existed since the founding of the nation, eroded in the 1960s, when the federal government extended its powers at the expense of state power, the nonprofit sector was called upon to help design, implement, and administer social programs that had once been within the jurisdiction of the public sector. As a consequence, the nonprofit sector expanded in the 1960s at the very time that the federal government enlarged its powers over the states. The result produced an unusual phenomenon—government centralization produced greater nonprofit sector voluntarism. The proliferation of government and nonprofit institutions involved in public policy yielded a system that marshals expert against expert, testing the credibility of each and enriching the information environment in which policy discourse occurs and decisions are taken. On highly technical issues, opposing experts often cancel each other. Yet the growth of public and private agencies involved in collecting public knowledge allows for a more democratized policy process, much closer, in a sense, to the Jeffersonian–Jackson vision of an open, competitive democracy.

Still, two qualifications are in order: Neither Jefferson, nor Jackson, nor Teddy Roosevelt envisioned a world of competing experts representing various interests and ideological positions; and second, this contemporary world of competing institutional research is not equally open to all comers. Access to financing is one limitation and access to those in power is another, and the two are not necessarily reciprocal.

As government grew in size and power, greater reliance was placed on expertise to provide knowledgeable assessment about policy considerations, program implementation and assessment, and legal opinion. Already by the turn of the twenty-first century, the number of personal and committee staff of the Congress exceeded 11,000, with another 20,000 persons responding to the information needs of the legislature from the Congressional Budget Office, the Office of Technological Assessment, and the General Accounting Office. The executive branch commands far greater numbers. The scale of spending by the federal government was massive for the acquisition and application of public knowledge. In addition, a vast array of trade and professional organization and "public interest" groups conduct research in the areas of environmental policy, consumer affairs, civil rights, and foreign policy issues.

THE DECLINE OF POLITICS: FROM VOTING TO CONSUMERISM AND RIGHTS

Matching the serious, fundamental shifts in the nature of governance and the state were equally notable changes in the nature of American participation in politics. The first century of constitutional government saw the creation of political parties and a party system that provided crucial links between voters and government, between different levels of government, and between the different branches of government. Beside these various intergovernmental connections, by the 1840s parties also generated widespread and often intense loyalty among voters, and they provided the mechanisms by which nominations, campaigns, and elections were run. Changing notions of representation and suffrage were evident in an increasingly democratic system where the franchise was expanded and voters had greater influence in shaping the behavior of their representatives.

The passion that was evident in party affiliations, elections, and policy debates was not always kept in rational channels. This was most apparent in the continuous manifestation of conspiratorial fears among a large segment of the general population and the members of the political elite found early in American political history. As the Federalist Party declined, New England ministers such as Timothy Dwight and Jedidiah Morse alleged an international Masonic conspiracy at work. Anti-Masonic tendencies eventually found expression in the Whig Party that rose to challenge the Democratic Party. Conspiracy fears abounded in the volatile era of the 1850s that focused on nativist, anti-Catholic, and anti-Mormon sentiments. Similarly, conspiracies of the monied interests found political expression in the Greenback parties in states such as Indiana, Illinois, and Missouri in the 1870s. The 1890s saw even more forceful and widespread endorsements of conspiracies focused on anti-Catholic, anti-immigrant, anti-Semitic, and antimonied views. These were often but not only associated with Populist Party supporters.

Conspiracy theories followed the emergence of the second Ku Klux Klan in the 1920s, fears were widespread in the 1930s, and the Cold War encouraged anti-Communist worries that bordered on hysteria. The intense manifestation of conspiracy theories in recent years, especially after 9/11, is simply the most recent expression of this phenomenon. What should be said about a nation's political history that is filled with fears of puppet-masters and insidious inside interests? The least that can be said is that the prevalence of conspiracy beliefs in American history belies easy rational choice explanations and that placing these perverse theories into a paranoid style found in grassroots America is an inadequate explanation.

The prevalence of conspiracy theories in modern politics reflects another paradox in American political and legal history: As the electorate expanded to become more inclusive, especially for women and blacks, and as government grew to provide more welfare and services for people, Americans have grown increasingly distrustful of government and public officials. Since the 1960s, distrust of government and elected officials increased at alarming rates.

This suggests another paradox in American political history. While governmental powers and obligations to its citizens increased and democratic rights and civil protections were extended to new groups, the public's interest in electoral politics noticeably declined, with some slight renewal in more recent elections. Ironically, this disinterest in political life occurred at a time when the United States elevated its involvement in democratic state-building abroad. Thus, while the United States undertook efforts to bring democracy to other nations, at the same time insisting on the implementation of human rights, the American public appeared less ready to participate in the democratic process at home.

This lack of interest in electoral politics was readily evidenced in lower rates of voter participation throughout the twentieth century. Political scientists and historians attributed this decline to a number of causes, including the expansion of the electorate, a perceived failure of the two parties to represent the "real" interests of the voters, the breakup of party organizations, and the decrease in partisan loyalty along with a commensurate increase in independent voters. It is also very significant that this decline occurred at the same time that the nonprofit organizations and a wide range of interest groups were organizing to influence policy making. But in addition to these factors, Americans' declining interest in electoral politics paralleled the expansion of a vibrant consumer culture. Average Americans, it seemed, could more easily recognize movie and recording stars, distinguish brand labels, and discern new consumer trends than they could name their local state representatives, members of the Supreme Court, or U.S. Senators.

In stating this, two caveats are in order. First, the decrease in voter participation is not a new phenomenon; indeed, this decline first became noticeable with the election of 1896. Furthermore, there is no clear evidence that more voters knew who was on the Supreme Court in 1882 or 1928 or 1942 than in 1970. Thus, any distinction between voters' interest in electoral politics in the late nineteenth century and today is largely a matter of degree and intensity. What we do know is that voter participation rates are precipitously lower today than they were in the late nineteenth and early twentieth centuries. Moreover, we know that citizens (mostly white males) in the nineteenth century were intensely engaged in both national and local politics, party affiliation was higher, avid partisanship prevailed, and election days were festive occasions. The decline of interest in electoral politics that became apparent with the election of 1896 occurred exactly at the time when other modes of political participation emerged. Moreover, the nearly steady decline of interest in electoral politics corresponds with the steady expansion of a national popular culture, characterized by mass advertising, department stores, national brands, and growing disposable incomes among consumers.

Second, consumerism is not new to contemporary America. Victorian Americans, for example, became increasingly consumer conscious, and arguably this consumer consciousness replaced an early producer consciousness. And although it might be argued that voters in the late nineteenth century would not have been any more likely to name members of the Supreme Court than are voters today, Victorian Americans would know when to plant wheat, how to fix a broken harvesting machine, or how to repair a broken steam engine. Most Americans today would be at a loss to explain these things, but they are able to name designer labels and argue over the best automobile or stereo to buy or where the best places to shop are. Again, consumerism is a matter of degree and perhaps suggests a radical transformation in political consciousness. There is a marked difference from defining oneself as a producer (a farmer or laborer) to identifying oneself as a suburbanite with an income that allows the purchase of a four-bedroom house with four television sets, two stereos, a home entertainment center, and three cars.

Moreover, this pervasive and intensified consumer consciousness in postwar America helped restructure what the two parties stood for. Both the Democratic and the Republican parties proclaimed themselves the protectors of the middle-class consumer. Each party offered itself as the best agency to foster economic growth, job creation, and more efficiency in government. At the same time, although both political parties made general appeals to consumerism, the Democratic Party and the Republican Party staked out different claims on specific constituencies while trying to maintain support of the general middle-class voter (often ambiguously defined). For instance, the Democrats sought to appeal to those often at the margins of the consumer culture—lower income groups, ethnic minorities, the working poor, and those seen as most vulnerable to the fluctuations of the market economy. Republicans, too, sought to win these voters to the GOP banner; yet, at the same time, Republicans appealed directly to those groups distraught by the perceived breakdown of traditional values of family, religion, and sexual restraint—which the market appeared to subvert through self-indulgent consumption and hedonistic gratification. As a consequence, Republicans defined themselves as a party of conservatism, albeit a conservatism that understood the needs of the poor and the disfranchised.

Coinciding with the postwar growth of consumerism was the emergence of new groups that joined the urban workforce with aspirations of enjoying the benefits of an abounding economy. Most important in this regard was the entrance of African Americans who had migrated to the North during World War II for work. Their participation in the prosperity of the postwar economy laid the ground for the civil rights movement of the 1950s and 1960s that transformed race relations in the United States. A new black middle class demanded political rights, as well as equal opportunity to compete with whites for better jobs, admission to better colleges, and commissions in the armed forces. Women also experienced changes because of improvements in work and education. As women found new freedoms in the marketplace, they began to insist on individual rights as expressed in the feminist movement, the call for no-fault divorce, and "the right to control their bodies" through birth control and abortion.

The emergence of the civil rights movement and the woman's movement, as well as other ethnic-rights movements, led to a "rights" revolution in American society. This rights revolution laid the foundation for a realignment of the political parties. The Democratic Party captured for the most part those groups calling for new civil and social rights. As a consequence, however, the Republican Party was able to build a political base in the South, first evidenced in the Goldwater campaign in 1964 and gaining momentum under Nixon. By 1980, the Republicans had shifted their geographic base to the South and the Western Mountain states, as well as maintaining control of their traditional base in the Midwest, especially outside urban areas. These gains, however, were offset by a marked gender gap that emerged in the late 1980s as single women swung heavily toward the Democrats.

At the fringes of both parties stood certain constituents who criticized consumption in general. Within the Democratic Party, and to a lesser extent the Republican Party, were environmentalists who saw economic growth as destructive to the environment, disruptive of the balance of nature, and the cause of pollution, global warming, and environmental health hazards. Republicans attracted another anticonsumer faction, traditional moralists who saw in the consumer culture a destructive force of religious and family values. This group, it might be added, although critical of the culture, did not extend their critique to economic growth (or the market). Nevertheless, this critique of the culture created tensions within the conservative wing of the Republican Party, particularly the libertarian, free-market faction and the cultural Right.

The intensified consumer culture also generated changes in the electorate itself. The shift from a manufacturing economy to a rising service economy created anxieties with the electorate. Both parties tried to adjust to these changes in the economic structure, which led to different political calculations on the part of both political parties. Organized labor remained an integral part of the Democratic Party coalition, but the allegiance of rank-and-file members to the Democratic Party became increasingly tenuous as members of the industrial workforce became increasingly affluent, less dependent on government welfare programs, and open to Republican appeals for smaller government, lower taxes, and, in the case of Catholic blue-collar voters, moral and gender issues. Moreover, the globalization of the American economy that led manufacturing companies to move offshore threatened traditional blue-collar Democratic support. Because both parties remained free-trade proponents and internationalists, neither party was able to completely exploit labor's anxieties and thereby consolidate gains among labor. As a consequence, blue-collar voters, especially Catholics, emerged as part of a volatile swing vote that was essential to the success of both parties.

Contradiction and paradox can be found throughout this volume because they are endemic to American political and legal history. The volume also captures the importance of understanding change in American political history. Periodically, political upheaval swept aside the politics of old. Following the financial crisis of 2007, the Democrats under Barack Obama won control of the White House and both branches of Congress. It appeared that a time of great political change had occurred. In the midterm elections, however, Republicans made a political comeback, winning control of the House of Representatives.

Yet it was by no means certain where the nation was headed politically in a financial crisis that had taken on global proportions. The 2010 election raised ambitious expectations for Republicans to address the budget deficit and national debt, lower taxes, and reform entitlement programs such as Medicare and Social Security. Republicans held control of one chamber of Congress, which set the stage for a running battle with the White House and the Senate. From a larger perspective, the political landscape looked much like it did at the beginning of the decade. The nation was as divided along partisan lines as ever. Gridlock in government prevailed, although it had become clear that budget debts and the national debt were unsustainable. America, it appeared, was entering a new era marked by political and financial volatility.

If a new era was about to begin, it is the hope of the editors and the authors who have contributed to this volume that history will provide a guide to understanding what lies before us.

USING THIS VOLUME

We have sought to make this volume as user friendly as possible. There are nearly 550 entries in *The Oxford Encyclopedia of Political and Legal History,* arranged in alphabetical order letter by letter. A headnote listing the various subentries introduces each composite entry.

The contributors have sought to write in clear language with a minimum of technical vocabulary. The articles give important terms and titles in their original languages, with English translations when needed. A selective bibliography at the end of each article directs the reader who wishes to pursue a topic in greater detail to primary sources and the most important scholarly works in any language, plus the most useful works in English.

To guide readers from one article to related discussions elsewhere in the encyclopedia, end references appear at the end of many articles. Blind entries direct the user from an alternate form of an entry term to the entry itself. For example, the blind entry for "Penal Code, Model" tells the reader to "See Model Penal Code." Readers interested in finding all the articles on a particular subject can consult the systematic outline at the end of volume 2. A comprehensive index at the end of volume 2 lists all the topics covered in the encyclopedia, including those that are not headwords themselves. At the end of volume 2 are the topical outline (which shows how articles relate to one another and to the overall design of the encyclopedia), the directory of contributors, and the index.

The editors thank the authors who contributed to this volume. Special acknowledgment should be given to our Associate Editor, Cynthia Stachecki, who processed the entries, corresponded with the many contributors, and kept everyone on schedule. Throughout the process, the staff at Oxford University Press under the direction of Eric Stannard showed patience, humor, and efficiency. Paul Boyer, the Series Editor of *The Oxford Encyclopedia of American History,* provided wise counsel and able direction.

Donald T. Critchlow
Philip R. VanderMeer

COMMON ABBREVIATIONS USED IN THIS WORK

AD	*anno Domini,* in the year of the Lord
AH	*anno Hegirae,* in the year of the Hajj
b.	Born
BCE	before the common era (= BC)
c.	*circa,* about, approximately
CE	common era (= AD)
cf.	*confer,* compare
d.	died
diss.	dissertation
ed.	editor (pl., eds.), edition
f.	and following (pl., ff.)
fl.	*floruit,* flourished
l.	line (pl., ll.)
n.	note
n.d.	no date
no.	number
n.p.	no place
n.s.	new series
p.	page (pl., pp.)
pt.	part
rev.	revised
ser.	series
supp.	supplement
USSR	Union of Soviet Socialist Republics
vol.	volume (pl., vols.)

THE OXFORD ENCYCLOPEDIA OF
AMERICAN POLITICAL AND LEGAL HISTORY

A

ABORTION POLITICS AND POLICY

Abortion policy in the United States has been contentious for decades and continues to polarize the American electorate. The controversy over abortion began long before *Roe v. Wade* (1973), but the Supreme Court's landmark ruling on abortion rights escalated the political debate over the circumstances in which abortion should be legally permissible.

Abortion Policy before the 1960s. Prior to the early nineteenth century, there were no laws against abortion in either the United States or Britain. In the colonial era and the early republic, American jurists generally accepted the guidelines of English Common Law, which permitted abortion prior to "quickening" (that is, the moment at which a pregnant woman feels a fetus move), a stage that usually occurs during the second trimester of pregnancy. Many midwives performed abortions, and women who wanted to terminate their pregnancies commonly used herbal abortifacients.

In the early nineteenth century, physicians in both Britain and the United States led a campaign to regulate abortion and eventually prohibit it altogether because they were convinced, based on new studies using the microscope, that quickening was not a medically meaningful term in the life stages of the fetus and that fetal life began long before that point. In 1821, Connecticut, following Britain's lead, became the first state to pass an antiabortion statute, and by 1880, abortion was illegal in every state. A few states allowed abortion in cases where it was necessary to protect a woman's health, but most permitted it only when pregnancy endangered a woman's life.

Despite prohibitions on abortion, the practice remained widespread. Some abortions were self-induced, but many others took place in doctors' offices and hospitals, since many physicians quietly ignored the law. Women who sought out abortions were not prosecuted, since the laws did not criminalize their behavior, and physicians who performed abortions were usually prosecuted only if their practices resulted in a woman's death. Although abortions were common, the popular press depicted abortion as a dangerous procedure, usually performed by criminal abortion rings, and the last resort of "immoral" women.

The American Medical Association opposed abortion throughout the late nineteenth and early twentieth centuries, but in the 1930s, after many physicians began accepting the legitimacy of contraception, a few suggested that "therapeutic" abortion should be permitted as well. Although they did not advocate abortion on demand, they did suggest that the procedure might be permissible in cases in which pregnancy endangered a woman's health or in which the fetus was severely deformed. By the mid-twentieth century, medical advances, such as cesarean sections, had made the need for abortions in cases in which a woman's life was in danger extremely rare, yet women still requested abortions for other reasons, and a number of doctors performed these abortions despite their illegality.

The Campaign to Legalize Abortion. In 1959, the American Law Institute (ALI), responding to doctors' requests, proposed a model abortion law that would allow for abortion when a pregnancy endangered a woman's health or in the case of rape, incest, or fetal deformity. In 1961, California legislators introduced a bill modeled on the ALI guidelines, but the Catholic Church lobbied against it, and the bill was defeated. Catholic clergy had not participated in the nineteenth-century campaign against abortion, but by the mid-twentieth century, after waging a decades-long fight against the legalization of birth control, the Catholic Church had the political resources to launch a campaign against abortion law liberalization. However, public opinion polls showed that the Catholic Church was out of step with public opinion. By the mid-1960s, only 16 percent of Americans opposed abortions in cases where a woman's life or health was in danger.

An increasing number of Americans also believed that abortion was acceptable in cases of severe fetal deformity. In the early 1960s, an outbreak of rubella (German measles), which caused birth defects, resulted in an increased demand for therapeutic abortions, as did the discovery that thalidomide-based tranquilizers could likewise result in fetal deformities. Responding to popular pressure, legislators in several states introduced bills to allow for abortion in cases of suspected fetal damage.

In the spring of 1967, Colorado and California passed abortion laws modeled on ALI guidelines, allowing for abortion when a pregnancy endangered a woman's health and, in Colorado, in cases of fetal deformities. By 1970, twelve states had liberalized their abortion laws.

Although the Catholic Church strongly opposed abortion law liberalization, mainline Protestant churches generally supported it. In heavily Catholic states, such as New York and California, Catholic lobbying efforts succeeded in blocking abortion legalization efforts as long as Democrats controlled the state government. But when Republicans, who were less likely to be Catholics or represent Catholic districts, gained control, they were able to pass abortion reform bills that the Democrats had blocked.

In 1970, Republican Governor Nelson Rockefeller, who for years had advocated for population control and birth control distribution, signed into law the most liberal abortion bill in the nation, which allowed for abortion "on demand" up to the twenty-fourth week of pregnancy. Prior to 1970, abortion reform bills required a medical reason for women to obtain an abortion, but New York's law did not. Alaska and Hawai'i also adopted laws allowing for abortion on demand up to the twentieth week of pregnancy.

This new legislation reflected a national shift in thinking on abortion. Before the mid-1960s, the physicians and lawyers who had led the early campaign for abortion law liberalization had not advocated for unrestricted abortion rights, but only for abortion in a few circumscribed instances. But in 1967, the National Organization for Women stated that abortion was a fundamental human right that women deserved in the name of equality. The National Association for the Repeal of Abortion Laws (NARAL), founded in 1969, took the same stance. Women, they said, should have the right to choose whether to be pregnant.

The association of abortion legalization with the feminist movement resulted in a backlash against abortion liberalization in the early 1970s and bolstered the strength of the right-to-life movement. In 1972, referenda to liberalize abortion laws failed in Michigan and South Dakota, whereas legislatures in Maine and Connecticut likewise defeated abortion liberalization bills. President Richard Nixon, who had taken a moderately permissive stand on abortion in 1970 and 1971, backtracked in 1972 and endorsed the Catholic Church's campaign to repeal New York's abortion liberalization bill. The Democratic presidential candidate George McGovern backed away from his earlier hints that he might favor abortion rights and refused to allow his feminist supporters to include a pro-choice plank in the Democratic Party platform. By the end of 1972, nineteen states had adopted liberalized abortion laws, but the opposition movement was growing and was winning some unexpected victories.

***Roe v. Wade* and Its Aftermath.** In January 1973, the Supreme Court put an end to this legislative debate in its sweeping abortion rights ruling, *Roe v. Wade*. *Roe* declared that women had an unrestricted constitutional right to an abortion during the first trimester of pregnancy and that even during the second trimester states could restrict abortion only in the interest of protecting a woman's health, not preserving fetal life. Justice Harry Blackmun, the author of the decision, sided with abortion rights supporters largely because of his desire to protect physicians from prosecution, but he grounded the opinion in the language of women's rights. Women's right to an abortion, the Court declared, was based on their right to privacy, a right that the Court had first enumerated in the birth control case *Griswold v. Connecticut* (1965) and had further affirmed in *Eisenstadt v. Baird* (1972). States had a legitimate interest in protecting fetal life in the later stages of pregnancy, the Court said, but because fetuses were not persons "born or naturalized in the United States"—the Fourteenth Amendment's requirement for citizenship rights—and because the question of the personhood of the unborn was an issue of religious controversy in which the Court did not want to get entangled, a woman's right to privacy trumped any rights that the fetus might have in the early stages of pregnancy.

Roe required a thorough revision of American state abortion laws. At the time of the Court's decision, only four states had abortion laws that were liberal enough to meet the Court's guidelines, so forty-six states had to rewrite their laws in 1973. Before *Roe*, most states had abortion laws that were more restrictive than those of other non-Catholic industrialized nations, but *Roe* required them to adopt abortion legislation that was even more permissive than the laws in Britain, France, and most other Western European countries outside of Scandinavia. The American abortion rate rapidly escalated in the ensuing decade. By the end of the 1970s, the ratio of abortions to live births in the United States was nearly one to two, with approximately 1.5 million legal abortions performed each year. For some Americans, this was too much.

The Pro-Life Backlash against *Roe v. Wade*. Immediately after *Roe*, several members of Congress proposed constitutional amendments to either rescind *Roe* and return the power of abortion regulation to the states or ban abortion nationwide. In 1976, pro-life activists convinced the Republican Party, which until then had a strong pro-choice contingent, to endorse a constitutional amendment to "restore protection of the right to life for unborn children." The Democratic Party, by contrast, adopted a platform in 1976 that opposed antiabortion constitutional amendment proposals. In 1980, Democrats went even further by endorsing a woman's "right to choose whether and when to have a child." In response, much of the pro-life movement allied itself with the Republican Party, whereas pro-choice activists increasingly affiliated with the Democrats. After 1980, it became impossible for any Republican presidential aspirant to win the party's nomination without endorsing the party's opposition to abortion and its call for a constitutional amendment to ban the procedure. Conversely, every Democratic presidential nominee after 1980 supported a woman's "right to choose."

Conservative Republicans never gave the pro-life movement the antiabortion constitutional amendment that it wanted, but they did curtail federal funding for abortion. In 1976, Representative Henry Hyde (R-IL) introduced an amendment to a budget bill that prohibited Medicaid funding for abortions, an amendment that was renewed each year after that. Pro-choice advocates mounted a court challenge to the Hyde amendment, but the Supreme Court upheld its constitutionality in *Harris v. McRae* (1980). Although some states continued to pay for abortions for impoverished women, the number that did so rapidly declined in the late 1970s; by 1978, only sixteen states provided full funding for abortions.

Republicans also restricted the use of federal funds for abortion services overseas. In 1984, President Ronald Reagan introduced the "Mexico City policy," which denied federal funding to international family-planning agencies that provided abortion referrals or performed abortions. The Mexico City policy became a focal point of partisan debate in the ongoing controversy over abortion. President Bill Clinton rescinded the policy in 1993. President George W. Bush then reinstated it in 2001, only to have President Barack Obama rescind it once again in 2009.

State legislatures passed a wide variety of abortion restriction measures, almost all of which faced court challenges. In the 1970s and 1980s, the Supreme Court struck down laws that required minors to obtain parental permission before obtaining abortion, but upheld regulations that required only parental notification.

The election of President Ronald Reagan, an abortion rights opponent, gave the pro-life movement confidence that it could overturn

Roe v. Wade through either a constitutional amendment or a Supreme Court decision. In 1982, Senator Orrin Hatch (R-UT) proposed a constitutional amendment to overturn *Roe v. Wade* and return abortion policy to the states. But when only forty-nine senators voted for Hatch's proposal—eighteen short of the two-thirds majority needed to pass a constitutional amendment—proponents of the pro-life movement realized that they did not have sufficient congressional support to amend the Constitution.

The pro-life movement then embarked on a campaign to get the Supreme Court to overturn *Roe v. Wade,* a quest that seemed increasingly realistic after Reagan appointed several conservative justices. In *Webster v. Reproductive Health Services* (1989), the Court signaled a new willingness to uphold state abortion restrictions, and in *Planned Parenthood v. Casey* (1992), the Court came within one vote of overturning *Roe.* But after Bill Clinton's election to the presidency in 1992, pro-life activists realized that they were still years away from gaining the critical five-vote majority on the Court for their cause.

Having failed to win decisive victories in Congress or the courts, some members of the antiabortion movement became increasingly militant, and a few turned to violence. In 1987, Randall Terry's Operation Rescue began using civil disobedience to block access to abortion clinics and shut them down for a few hours. Terry remained committed to nonviolence, but other antiabortion activists did not. Some began bombing clinics, and in the 1990s, a few began killing abortion doctors. The violence prompted a public backlash against antiabortion extremism. In 1994, Clinton signed into law the Freedom of Access to Clinic Entrances Act, which made it a federal offense to block access to abortion clinics or intentionally damage an abortion facility. This act, along with lawsuits against Operation Rescue, largely curtailed Terry's operation.

The Continuing Controversy over Abortion Policy. In the mid-1990s, pro-life activists launched a campaign to ban a late-term dilation and extraction abortion procedure that they dubbed "partial-birth abortion." Public opinion surveys showed that 70 percent of Americans thought that the procedure, which involved puncturing the skull of a partially extracted fetus, should be illegal. Congress voted to ban the procedure in 1996, but Clinton vetoed the bill on the grounds that it did not allow for partial-birth abortion in cases in which it was necessary to protect a woman's health. Pro-life activists also lost ground when the Food and Drug Administration approved the sale of the abortion pill RU-486 in 2000.

President George W. Bush signed the Partial-Birth Abortion Ban into law in 2003, and the Supreme Court upheld the law in *Gonzales v. Carhart* (2007). Bush also issued a ban on using new embryonic stem-cell lines in stem-cell research, a victory for pro-life groups that believed in the full humanity of the embryo. He pushed the Supreme Court further to the right on the abortion issue with the appointment of two conservative justices, John Roberts and Samuel Alito. But pro-lifers in the Bush administration were unable to prevent the Food and Drug Administration from allowing the sale of the "morning-after" pill, dubbed "Plan B."

President Barack Obama's two appointments to the Supreme Court in 2009 and 2010 shored up the Court's slim majority in favor of preserving *Roe v. Wade.* Yet the election of a pro-choice president, along with Democratic majorities in Congress, did not make the abortion issue any less contentious. To pass Obama's health-care plan, congressional Democrats were forced to agree to an amendment from pro-life Representative Bart Stupak (D-MI) prohibiting federal funding for insurance plans covering abortion. Republican victories in the 2010 midterm elections led to increased efforts in several states to restrict abortions, with some states passing laws banning abortion after the twentieth week of pregnancy. Public opinion also seemed to be moving against abortion rights. A 2009 Gallup survey showed that for the first time a majority of Americans characterized themselves as "pro-life" rather than "pro-choice."

Today, the Supreme Court remains closely divided on abortion, but with a slight majority likely to uphold the general guidelines established in *Roe*, pro-life groups are not currently pushing for a test case to rescind that decision. Nor do they have much hope of passing a constitutional amendment banning abortion. Instead, they are tightening state abortion laws and preparing for court challenges that they hope will expand states' rights to restrict second-trimester abortions. Abortion remains one of the nation's most polarizing political issues, and it will likely continue to be a factor in future presidential elections and Supreme Court nominations.

[***See also Griswold v. Connecticut and Roe v. Wade.***]

BIBLIOGRAPHY

Critchlow, Donald T. *Intended Consequences: Birth Control, Abortion, and the Federal Government in Modern America.* New York: Oxford University Press, 1999.

Critchlow, Donald T., ed. *The Politics of Abortion and Birth Control in Historical Perspective.* University Park: Pennsylvania State University Press, 1996.

Garrow, David J. *Liberty and Sexuality: The Right to Privacy and the Making of* Roe v. Wade. Berkeley: University of California Press, 1998.

Glendon, Mary Ann. *Abortion and Divorce in Western Law.* Cambridge, Mass.: Harvard University Press, 1987.

Hull, N. E. H., and Peter Charles Hoffer. Roe v. Wade: *The Abortion Rights Controversy in American History.* Lawrence: University Press of Kansas, 2010.

Luker, Kristin. *Abortion and the Politics of Motherhood.* Berkeley: University of California Press, 1984.

McKeegan, Michele. *Abortion Politics: Mutiny in the Ranks of the Right.* New York: Free Press, 1992.

Reagan, Leslie J. *When Abortion Was a Crime: Women, Medicine, and Law in the United States, 1867–1973.* Berkeley: University of California Press, 1997.

Risen, James, and Judy L. Thomas. *Wrath of Angels: The American Abortion War.* New York: BasicBooks, 1998.

Rubin, Eva R. *Abortion, Politics, and the Courts:* Roe v. Wade *and Its Aftermath.* New York: Greenwood Press, 1987.

Daniel K. Williams

ABRAMS v. UNITED STATES

This 1919 Supreme Court case from the World War I era involved Russian-born anarchists convicted under the 1918 Sedition Act of distributing leaflets denouncing U.S. military intervention against Russia's new Bolshevik government. Writing for the majority, Justice John Clarke followed recent rulings by Justice Oliver Wendell Holmes Jr., in *Schenck v. United States* and *Debs v. United States* upholding the conviction of socialists for making antiwar statements on the grounds that such statements posed a "clear and present danger" in wartime America. The *Abrams* case involved the same principle, Clarke held, because the anarchists' leaflets created a clear and present danger of causing "the substantive evils that Congress has a right to prevent."

Justice Holmes, joined by Justice Louis Brandeis, dissented. Although Holmes denied that he was shifting ground, recent scholarship has shown that in his *Abrams* dissent, Holmes—stung by criticism from libertarian friends such as Zechariah Chafee of Harvard Law School and Harold J. Laski—did indeed seek to rework the *Schenck* and *Debs* test. In those cases, Holmes had linked the clear and present danger test to the broader claim that speech need not produce action to carry criminal liability. But in *Abrams,* he narrowed the clear and present danger test to make it more protective of First Amendment, free-speech rights. He hoped first that the courts would adopt it as a test of fundamental constitutional law and, second, that it might protect speech, such as that of the *Abrams* defendants, which had little likelihood of producing dangerous consequences. The *Abrams* dissent made Holmes a libertarian hero and propelled his clear and present danger test to the center of First Amendment discourse.

[*See also* **Bill of Rights; Brandeis, Louis; Censorship; Civil Liberties; Holmes, Oliver Wendell, Jr.; Sedition; Socialist Party of America;** ***and*** **Supreme Court, U.S.**]

BIBLIOGRAPHY

Polenberg, Richard. *Fighting Faiths: The Abrams Case, the Supreme Court, and Free Speech.* New York: Viking, 1987.

White, G. Edward. *Justice Oliver Wendell Holmes: Law and the Inner Self.* New York; Oxford: Oxford University Press, 1993.

Norman L. Rosenberg

ADAMS, JOHN

(1759–1826) served as a continental congressman, diplomat, vice president (1789–1797), and president of the United Sates (1797–1801).

Born and raised in Braintree, Massachusetts, Adams graduated from Harvard College in 1755 and become an attorney in 1758. During the 1765 Stamp Act crisis, his "Dissertation on the Canon and Feudal Law" maintained the importance of an educated citizenry in preserving public liberty. In 1770, at the behest of Patriot leaders, he defended the British captain and soldiers who had fired at the Boston Massacre and won the acquittal of all but two. A staunch and early believer that the colonists possessed the rights of Englishmen, Adams in 1770 won election to the Massachusetts House of Representatives.

Adams attended both the First and the Second Continental Congresses, where he became an early and forthright advocate for Independence. He served on ninety committees, twenty-five of which he chaired, the most important being the Board of War, tasked with provisioning the army. In 1775, he nominated George Washington to be Commander in Chief of the Continental Army. In 1776, while fellow Drafting Committee member Thomas Jefferson wrote the Declaration of Independence, the outspoken Adams led the fight on the floor of Congress for Independence.

In 1778, Adams sailed for France to help Benjamin Franklin negotiate the French Alliance, but upon his arrival found the treaty virtually finalized. Returning to Massachusetts, Adams drafted the state's 1780 Constitution, which created powerful executive and judicial branches to balance the legislature, as well as a bicameral legislature with a strong upper house to check sudden popular impulses from the lower house. He explained his constitutional theories in his *Thoughts on Government (1776)* and his *Defense of the Constitutions of Government of the United States of America (1787)*. Adams headed back to Europe in 1779, where he obtained Dutch loans before returning to Paris to help negotiate the 1783 Peace of Paris, securing American

Independence. Adams became the U.S. minister to Great Britain in 1785.

In 1789, George Washington was unanimously elected the first president of the United States. Coming in a distant second, Adams became vice president. Washington, who considered the vice presidency a legislative office, did not rely heavily on Adams for advice. Meanwhile, the Senate, over which Adams presided, viewed him as an executive officer and denied him the right to make speeches. Although bitter over his political impotence, Adams nevertheless cast more tiebreaking votes than any other vice president. Adams in 1791 authored the *Discourses on Davila,* arguing that the president should serve for life and be bolstered with the trappings of a king and that the Senate should represent wealth. Because of these views, Adams was unjustly labeled a monarchist.

Adams, a Federalist, was elected Chief Executive in 1796, and his 1797 inauguration marked the first transfer of presidential power. Jefferson, a Republican whom Adams narrowly defeated, became vice president and turned down Adams's overtures for a bipartisan copresidency. In the wake of the 1795 Jay Treaty with Great Britain, U.S. relations with France deteriorated into the Quasi-War, an undeclared naval conflict that convinced Federalists in Congress to expand the army and navy. When Republicans resisted these defense measures, Adams signed the 1798 Alien and Sedition Acts, giving the president the power to deport enemy aliens and making it a crime to falsely and maliciously criticize the president and Congress. The Federalists claimed the laws were national security measures, but they were in fact partisan political measures designed to silence the opposition party. Growing disillusioned with the military buildup, Adams—never one to cultivate popularity—outraged his own Federalist Party by negotiating the Convention of 1800, securing peace with France. After narrowly losing his reelection bid to Jefferson, lame duck Adams made several "midnight appointments" to the federal judiciary, including naming his own secretary of state, John Marshall, as Chief Justice. Adams surrendered executive power to Jefferson peacefully but boycotted the inauguration ceremony.

In retirement, Adams wrote many letters defending his political decisions, especially those of his presidency. Hard feelings remained over whether Jefferson had received credit for the Declaration of Independence that rightfully belonged to Adams. Fittingly, both men died on the same day, 4 July 1826, the fiftieth anniversary of the Declaration. As Adams correctly predicted, most interpretations of the era have favored the Jeffersonians at his expense. In the late twentieth and early twenty-first centuries, however, thanks largely to David McCullough's popular biography, as well as to a Home Box Office miniseries, Adams has been rehabilitated as a heroic and unfairly maligned statesman.

[*See also* **Alien and Sedition Acts; Continental Congress; Federalism; Franklin, Benjamin, Jefferson, Thomas; Marshall, John; Stamp Act;** *and* **Washington, George.**]

BIBLIOGRAPHY

Brown, Ralph A. *The Presidency of John Adams.* Lawrence: University of Kansas Press, 1975.

Ferling, John. *John Adams: A Life.* Knoxville: University of Tennessee Press, 1992.

Wood, Gordon, ed. *John Adams: Revolutionary Writings,* 2 vols. New York: Library of America, 2011.

Stuart Leibiger

ADAMS, JOHN QUINCY

(1767–1848), sixth president of the United States. Born in Quincy, Massachusetts, the son of John Adams and Abigail Adams, John Quincy Adams graduated from Harvard College in 1787. Apart from a brief interlude practicing law in Massachusetts, he spent almost his entire adult life in public service and politics. Beginning at age fourteen as the secretary to the U.S. minister to Russia, Francis Dana, he subsequently held overseas posts in England, the Netherlands, Prussia, Russia, Ghent, and again in England before becoming President James Monroe's secretary of state in 1817. A tough, belligerent negotiator, he seemed like "a bull-dog among spaniels," according to one English diplomat.

As secretary of state, Adams was an aggressive advocate of expansionism. He not only supported Andrew Jackson's invasion of Spanish Florida in 1819, but also used it to bully Spain into negotiating a transcontinental settlement, the Adams–Onís Treaty (1819), which gave Florida to the United States and ended Spanish claims to the Pacific Northwest. In 1823, when the British foreign secretary suggested a joint Anglo-American manifesto against further European intervention in Latin America, Adams successfully urged President Monroe to issue such a pronouncement unilaterally and wrote much of what became known as the Monroe Doctrine.

In the four-way presidential race of 1824, Adams finished second in both the popular vote and the Electoral College. Since none of the candidates received a majority of the electoral votes, the election went to the House of Representatives, where Henry Clay threw his support to Adams over the front runner Andrew Jackson. When President Adams subsequently made Clay secretary of state, Jackson denounced the appointment as a "corrupt bargain," resigned his Senate seat, and began organizing for the next election. Adams, never popular in the slave states, made Jackson's task easier by laying out a program of national planning that infuriated Thomas Jefferson's strict constructionist followers, violated the concept of states' rights, and thus drove virtually the entire South into Jackson's camp. With most of his nationalistic proposals mocked by the opposition and rejected by Congress, Adams was denied a second term in 1828—the same ignominy his father had experienced in 1800. Jackson defeated him handily, winning 92 percent of the electoral vote in the slave states and 49 percent in the free states.

In 1830, Adams won election to the House of Representatives from the Plymouth district of Massachusetts. Serving until his death in 1848, he led the long (1836–1844) fight against the "gag rule," a House rule that automatically tabled antislavery petitions and barred Congress from discussing the sensitive slavery issue. He also led the battle against the annexation of Texas (1836) and against the Mexican War (1846–1848). His sharp tongue and tactical dexterity made him a powerful figure in Congress and a folk hero to much of the North, earning him the sobriquet "Old Man Eloquent."

[*See also* **Adams, John; Amistad Case; Antislavery Movement; Clay, Henry; Federal Government, Executive Branch: Presidency, The; Federal Government, Executive Branch: State Department; Federal Government, Legislative Branch: House of Representatives; Jackson, Andrew; Jefferson, Thomas; Monroe, James; States' Rights;** *and* **Texas Annexation.**]

BIBLIOGRAPHY

Hargreaves, Mary W. M. *The Presidency of John Quincy Adams*. Lawrence: University Press of Kansas, 1985.

Richards, Leonard L. *Life and Times of Congressman John Quincy Adams*. New York: Oxford University Press, 1986.

Leonard L. Richards

ADKINS v. CHILDREN'S HOSPITAL

During the early twentieth century, Progressives sought to ameliorate the consequences of industrialization by enacting minimum wage laws. Conservatives and business groups challenged these laws in the courts. In *Adkins v. Children's Hospital,* the U.S. Supreme Court, by a vote of 5 to 3, struck down a 1918 congressional statute setting a minimum wage for women in the District of Columbia. The 1918 law, the Court held, violated the liberty of contract protected by the due process clause of the Fifth Amendment. Writing for the Court, Justice George Sutherland emphasized that under the Constitution, freedom of contract was the general rule and restraint the exception. Minimum wage laws, he argued, foisted on employers a welfare function that properly belonged to society as a whole. Moreover, Sutherland insisted, in light of the Nineteenth Amendment, women could not be more restricted in the exercise of contractual freedom than men.

Chief Justice William Howard Taft and Justice Oliver Wendell Holmes Jr., wrote dissenting opinions. Taft maintained that legislators could regulate the hours of work or minimum wages of women under the government's police powers. Holmes expressed doubt about the constitutional basis for the liberty-of-contract doctrine.

The *Adkins* decision stands as a classic expression of the Court's commitment to contractual freedom. It made clear the Court's determination to keep wages and prices free of regulatory interference. During the New Deal Era of the 1930s, however, the Supreme Court moderated its long-standing commitment to economic liberty and freedom of contract. *Adkins* was overruled in *West Coast Hotel v. Parrish* (1937) in which the justices, on a 5-to-4 vote, sustained a Washington State minimum wage law.

[*See also* **Bill of Rights; Nineteenth Amendment; Progressive Era;** ***and West Coast Hotel v. Parrish.***]

BIBLIOGRAPHY

Arkes, Hadley. *The Return of George Sutherland: Restoring a Jurisprudence of Natural Rights.* Princeton, N.J.: Princeton University Press, 1994.

Ely, James W., Jr. *The Guardian of Every Other Right: A Constitutional History of Property Rights.* 2d ed. New York: Oxford University Press, 1998.

James W. Ely Jr.

ADMINISTRATIVE STATE

The term "administrative state" entered the political science literature in Dwight Waldo's influential book of the same name in 1948. Waldo's work described the administrative state as the bureaucracy or administrative agencies that constituted the bulk of the executive branch of government in a democratic system like that of the United States. Although Waldo and his successors in the study of public administration intended the term for use in analyzing the United States and other developed-world bureaucracies, writers in history and law have used it in describing modern developments in government's ever-increasing involvement in almost all facets of present-day life.

The study of the administrative state has undergone significant changes as historians and political scientists contributed to an understanding of the unique trajectory of U.S. political history. Sixty-one years before Waldo coined the term, in 1887 Woodrow Wilson's seminal article in the *Political Science Quarterly,* "The Study of Administration," shifted the study of the administrative state from the question of why the United States has little to no bureaucracy to a description of how it acquired its own particular form of administrative state. Although the field is still divided among theorists who focus on institutional developments, comparativists who contrast practices with those of other polities, and specialists in legal developments, among others, a consensus has emerged that rather than being a state without a state, the United States has a rich, turbulent administrative history that can be placed into generalized periods.

From Origins to Spoils. The U.S. administrative state derived from three sources: the colonial inheritance, the revolutionary experience, and the political compromises of the early national period that began with the states' experiments and culminated in the ratification of the federal Constitution in 1789. The colonial inheritance included English legal, theoretical, and political traditions as well as familiarity with Britain's own imperial administration, such as the customs service, the vice admiralty courts, and the commissioners of Indian Affairs. The newly independent states also had a long history of administration, primarily in the form of local judicial officers and grand juries.

The process of waging a continent-wide war against the British Empire for independence brought with it its own lessons, but the states preferred to legislate rather than administer and to rely on committees of amateurs rather than career bureaucrats. The Constitution that emerged from the convention in Philadelphia, Pennsylvania, in the summer of 1787 established the means for creating an administrative state for the new nation, but it was the first Congress in 1789 and 1790 that actually oversaw the beginnings of that apparatus. Departments of the Treasury, State, War, and Navy had administrative duties, but divisions between President George Washington's secretaries of Treasury and State—Alexander Hamilton and Thomas Jefferson, respectively—demonstrated that there was no general agreement about how well developed a federal bureaucracy should be. Although Hamilton's more expansive view prevailed in the short term, it was Jefferson's view that was to substantially influence the shape of the administrative state through the early part of the nineteenth century.

Jefferson made a smaller, cheaper, less intrusive federal bureaucracy his goal. Although officials like Treasury Secretary Albert Gallatin (1801–1814) did not undo the work of Hamilton and others, Jefferson's Democratic–Republicans preferred what they called a strict construction of the Constitution, which limited the federal government's activities and agencies to a highly circumscribed area. Presidents James Madison and James Monroe subscribed to this philosophy. John Quincy Adams did not, but he failed in his reelection bid. When Andrew Jackson entered office in 1829, the so-called spoils system replaced the Jeffersonian gentlemen civil servants, eroding what remained of the colonial and early national system.

The spoils system—more of a practice than an actual system—found expression in land policy administered through the Land Office and the delivery of the mail through the Post Office Department. Administering an area roughly the size of Western Europe, the Land Office had considerable influence over the development of the United States. The Post Office performed a no less critical role with its ability to provide subsidized communications throughout the country as well as a center for community in the many remote areas. Democratic appointees (all federal administrative officers were presidential appointees at this time) filled these offices. With a few substantial additions such as the Interior Department, this slight, but important administrative state went about its business relatively undisturbed until the Civil War (1861–1865) upended this arrangement in several important ways.

From Civil War to New Era. Both the Union and the Confederate governments faced substantial administrative challenges in waging what became a staggeringly expensive, sanguinary, and logistically demanding conflict. The U.S. national government had considerably more resources at its disposal, but still had to create the sinews of a vast bureaucracy to prevail. Without the Jeffersonian philosophies of limited government of the seceding states' Congressional delegations, the Republican Party (later the Union Party) was free to enact its more expansive view of the national government's role, including the Homestead Act (1862), the Land Grant College or Morrill Act (1862), and a national banking law in 1863. Although many measures such as the newly introduced income tax ended after the conclusion of the hostilities, other programs and agencies survived and new ones were established.

The Bureau of Freedmen, Refugees, and Abandoned Lands, known as the Freedmen's Bureau, did not survive the Reconstruction Era (1865–1876) that followed the Civil War, but its influence cannot be underestimated. Schools, aid to the bereft, and its attempts to set up a new labor system in the states of the former Confederacy shaped the region for decades afterward. The Secret Service also had its start at roughly the same time and expanded its original mission of currency policing to become one of the first truly national law enforcement agencies. Of inestimable impact was the national government's foray into pensions and health care in the form of the Pensions Office, one of the largest federal programs in existence up to that point. Finally, the U.S. Congress fashioned a short-lived Department of Education (1867; later reduced to a bureau), the Department of Agriculture (1862) out of the Bureau of Agriculture, and a Department of Justice (1870). Although these three agencies did not fulfill the ambitions of those who favored them, they laid a foundation for further expansion.

Similarly, Congress in the late nineteenth century continued to reform and expand the administrative state through three important initiatives—the Pendleton Act for depoliticizing the civil service in 1883, the Interstate Commerce Commission for regulating railroads in 1887, and the Sherman Antitrust Act of 1890—although their full development would have to wait for further reforms in the Progressive Era. In the meantime, the Gilded Age U.S. Supreme Court began to weigh in against the administrative state in important ways. The Court was highly skeptical of most attempts at regulating aspects of American life, but the post-Reconstruction courts were particularly active in declaring Congressional as well as state regulations unconstitutional, such as the Civil Rights Act of 1875, anti–child labor laws, and minimum hours and wage restrictions. The Court also put severe limits on how much Congress could delegate to administrative agencies like the Interstate Commerce Commission.

The Progressive Era (1890–1920) saw a veritable explosion in the scale and scope of the national government. By the end of the period, the federal government was overseeing railroad rates and practices with the Interstate Commerce Commission, food and drug labeling, industrial and commercial combinations, fair trade practices with the Federal Trade Commission, the national banking system with the Federal Reserve Act of 1913, illegal drugs through the Bureau of Investigation in the Justice Department, and national security with the Espionage and Sedition Acts of 1917 and 1918, respectively.

During the New Era of the 1920s, the administrative state was further expanded with the enactment of Prohibition, as well as the establishment of new regulatory agencies. These agencies, such as the Civil Aeronautics Board for air travel and the Federal Communications Commission for radio, helped foster the grow of these industries. The collapse of the economy into the Great Depression in 1929 posed a severe test for this still relatively light form of government activity, but did not end it.

From New Deal to Cold War. Franklin D. Roosevelt became president in 1933 during one of the worst economic downturns in American history. His administration and a supportive Democratic majority in Congress created a permanent administrative expansion to help prevent such an event from recurring. The so-called first New Deal also introduced a host of temporary agencies, notably the Federal Emergency Relief Administration, the Public Works Administration, and the Civilian Conservation Corps. A large regulatory apparatus took shape to police the markets that had failed, including finance through the Glass–Steagal Act (separating commercial from investment banking), acts creating a central Federal Reserve Board and the Federal Deposit Insurance Corporation, and the Securities and Exchange Act of 1934 that created the Securities and Exchange Commission.

More controversial were the Roosevelt administration's agencies that engaged in government planning and support for industrial development, including the National Recovery Administration, the Tennessee Valley Authority, the Rural Electrification Administration, and the Resettlement Administration. Although the U.S. Supreme Court voided the National Industrial Recovery Act among others from the First New Deal, Roosevelt initiated what has become known as the Second New Deal. Its programs included the Wagner National Labor Relations Act (1935), which created the National Labor Relations Board governing collective bargaining or unions, the Social Security Act that provided old-age pensions, the Works Progress Administration, and a more steeply progressive and widely applied income tax through the Internal Revenue Service.

Although these programs failed to end the Great Depression, they vastly increased the scale and scope of the national administrative state. After World War II ended in 1945, Republican majorities in Congress dismantled the Depression relief agencies, but the expansion of government bureaucracy continued. The Cold War provided the impetus to expand the national security apparatus of the United States, featuring a united Department of Defense, the Central Intelligence Agency, and the National Security Agency. The post-Roosevelt reaction gave rise to the Administrative Procedures Act of 1946 to put procedural limitations on the administrative state, and a series of commissions starting with the Hoover Commission (1947–1949) advised a succession of presidents and Congresses on how to deal with the seemingly ever-expanding bureaucracy.

The fiscally conservative Eisenhower administration (1953–1961) expanded the Social Security program by expanding coverage and creating disability insurance. At the same time, federal spending increased for education and the creation of a federally built interstate highway system. Concerns about civil rights, poverty, consumer safety, and the environment all led to a new round of agency formation. The administrative state was about to take on additional responsibilities and complexity.

From the Great Society to the Crisis of Authority. In the 1960s and 1970s, national scandals concerning pollution, pharmaceuticals, nuclear power, automobile and work safety, and a host of other social problems prompted the creation of a number of new regulatory agencies including the Environmental Protection Agency, the National Highway and Traffic Safety Administration, a more powerful Food and Drug Administration, and the Occupational Safety and Health Administration. President Lyndon B. Johnson (1963–1968) added his Great Society programs, which included the Head Start program for early education, health insurance for the elderly and the poor in the form of Medicare and Medicaid, respectively, a revamping of federal housing programs that eventually became the Department of Housing and Urban Development, and a strong commitment to civil rights in the form of the Civil Rights Act of 1964 and Voting Rights Act of 1965, both of which provided for civil lawsuits as well as divisions in the Justice Department for federal enforcement.

President Richard M. Nixon (1969–1974) renewed initiatives such as the nation's "War on Drugs" to be waged by the Bureau of Alcohol, Tobacco, and Firearms and gave the Federal Bureau of Investigation new life. However, the crisis of authority stemming from the dispute over the Vietnam War and the Watergate scandal also led to a greater skepticism about the ability of the Congress and the president to control the now vast administrative state. Areas of substantive criticism included accountability, the capture of agencies by the industries they were regulating, and the ill effects of their regulations on economic growth and efficiency. The United States was seemingly on the edge of going to war against its own administrative state.

The War on Regulation. Influenced to an extent by the combination of rising prices and seeming economic stagnation, the political culture of the United States turned against regulation, and U.S. presidents from James "Jimmy" E. Carter (1977–1980) onward conducted what some called a "War on Regulation" regardless of whether they were Democrats or Republicans. Carter began the conflict with his deregulation of the airline industry and the establishment of boards of review within the White House to limit growth or impede regulation entirely—two practices his successors either endorsed or expanded. Although none of these efforts actually succeeded in eliminating a significant portion of the administrative state, they did add to its complexity and opened gaps in the regulatory frameworks. These gaps often led to market failures or scandals that then generated their own calls for regulation, including the savings and loan crisis of the 1980s, mining disasters, the near collapse of the financial services industry in 2008–2009, and the Deepwater Horizon oil rig disaster in the Gulf of Mexico in 2010.

The U.S. Supreme Court under Chief Justices Warren E. Burger, William H. Rehnquist, and John G. Roberts regarded the expansion of the administration state with concern, if not outright antipathy. Introducing doctrines like the "new" federalism and restoring strength to old doctrines like "nondelegation," the Court curtailed or ordered dismantling of administrative activities. The Court also supported substantial agency discretion in the performance of their duties, especially in areas of civil rights. A majority of justices frequently also found fault with or upheld agency decisions leading to a welter of legal decisions governing many aspects of the administrative state at all levels of government.

A Complex History. Altogether the United States has had a long, complex, and tumultuous relationship with its administrative state. Its growth from a relatively small operation to one of millions of employees administering a wide range of federal laws and programs running the gamut of activities was not a steady progression, but rather one of spurts and false starts. Given the popular support for federal programs and policing of a wide range of areas, this story and the debate over its nature are unlikely to be settled any time soon.

[*See also* **Freedmen's Bureau; Hamilton, Alexander; Jefferson, Thomas; Johnson, Lyndon B.; New Deal; Nixon, Richard M.; Prohibition; Reconstruction; Roosevelt, Franklin Delano; Supreme Court, U.S.;** ***and*** **Wilson, Woodrow.**]

BIBLIOGRAPHY

Bensel, Richard Franklin. *Yankee Leviathan: The Origins of Central State Authority in America, 1859–1877.* Cambridge, UK: Cambridge University Press, 1990.

Cooper, Phillip J. *The War against Regulation: From Jimmy Carter to George W. Bush.* Lawrence: University Press of Kansas, 2009.

Gould, Lewis L. *The Modern American Presidency.* Lawrence: University Press of Kansas, 2003.

Hays, Samuel P., in collaboration with Barbara D. Hays. *Beauty, Health, and Permanence: Environmental Politics in the United States, 1955–1985.* Cambridge, UK: Cambridge University Press, 1987.

Hoffer, Williamjames Hull. *To Enlarge the Machinery of Government: Congressional Debates and the Growth of the American State, 1858–1891.* Baltimore: Johns Hopkins University Press, 2007.

Ingraham, Patricia Wallace. *The Foundation of Merit: Public Service in American Democracy.* Baltimore: Johns Hopkins University Press, 1995.

Skocpol, Theda. *Protecting Soldiers and Mothers: The Political Origins of Social Policy in the United States.* Cambridge, Mass.: Belknap Press of Harvard University Press, 1992.

Skowronek, Stephen. *Building a New American State: The Expansion of National Administrative Capacities, 1877–1920.* Cambridge, UK: Cambridge University Press, 1982.

Williamjames Hull Hoffer

AFFIRMATIVE ACTION

This entry contains two subentries: Legal Aspects; and Politics of Affirmative Action.

LEGAL ASPECTS

Although the idea of antidiscrimination measures dates at least as far back as the New Deal, the term "affirmative action" was first articulated by President John F. Kennedy on 6 March 1961 in an executive memo requiring that employees be hired "without regard to race, creed, color, or national origin." Prompting Kennedy's directive was a growing awareness of racial discrimination in America brought to light largely by the Civil Rights Movement, which had begun to intensify with a wave of sit-ins across the American South in 1960. A string of movement victories from 1961 to 1965 further pressed the issue of ending discrimination in employment, spurring President Lyndon Johnson to revivify the concept of affirmative action in 1965 by issuing an executive order prohibiting federal contractors from taking race into account in hiring, a move that he expanded in 1968 with the inclusion of women.

Rather than end the federal push for affirmative action, Republican Richard Nixon's ascension to the White House intensified it because the conservative president articulated a vision for civil rights that was dependent less on forced integration and welfare transfers than on the inculcation of entrepreneurial initiative and black capitalism. Sympathetic to emerging calls for Black Power, Nixon endorsed affirmative action as the most effective means of ameliorating past discrimination, meanwhile targeting unpopular school busing programs aimed at achieving racial integration in schools. Indeed, affirmative action assumed its most aggressive posture in 1969, when Nixon official Arthur Fletchers recommended that "special measures" be taken to increase minority enrollment in the building trades. Such measures included the drafting of specific timetables, schedules, and quotas for minority hiring. Three years later, the Nixon administration expanded the scope of such measures, mandating that hospitals, banks, steel mills, and other institutions—including schools—adopt them, increasing the employment and enrollment of minorities and women.

Despite Nixon's enthusiasm, rifts broke out among conservatives as whites found themselves passed over for minorities, prompting charges of "reverse racism" as early as 1971, when Marco DeFunis filed a suit against the University of Washington Law School for being denied admission. More suits followed, leading to a string of major Supreme Court cases. In *Regents v. Bakke* (1978), the Court held that universities could consider race one of several factors in making admissions decisions but could not rely on quotas, with the ultimate goal of racial considerations being educational enrichment through exposure to a diverse student body. In *Richmond v. Croson* (1989) and *Adarand v. Peña* (1995), the Court reaffirmed this opinion, holding that any racial classification—even those designed to help minorities—must be subjected to strict scrutiny and could only survive if it served a compelling state interest. Although remedying past discrimination was initially considered a compelling state interest, the Supreme Court curtailed this rationale in *Shaw v. Hunt* (1996), holding that "past societal discrimination" could not be considered, meanwhile elevating interests such as diversity in *Grutter v. Bollinger* (2003). In 2007, the Supreme Court struck down a school assignment plan placing students in schools expressly to achieve racial balance. Meanwhile, in 2009, the Supreme Court ruled in *Ricci v. DeStefano* that the city of New Haven, Connecticut, could not jettison a promotion test inadvertently benefiting whites, marking a turn against even implicit efforts to improve minority hiring and promotion.

Barring a dramatic shift in public opinion, the prospects of affirmative action programs in the United States remain bleak. The Supreme Court conceded as much in 2003, when Justice Sandra Day O'Connor opined that "25 years from now, the use of racial preferences will no longer be necessary to further the interest approved today." Current judicial trends point to a rejection of all overt racial classifications as unconstitutional, regardless of intent.

[*See also* **Civil Rights; Johnson, Lyndon B.; Kennedy, John F.;** ***and*** **Nixon, Richard M.**]

Anders Walker

POLITICS OF AFFIRMATIVE ACTION

The term "affirmative action" first appeared in a legislative context in the 1935 National Labor Relations Act and was later written into state laws prohibiting racial discrimination in employment. But the phrase, implying simply that government agencies should try to prevent discrimination against African Americans, initially attracted little notice. Prior to the 1960s, virtually no one saw affirmative action as a way of giving minorities preferential treatment in hiring, promotions, and admissions.

More than anything else, the civil rights movement helped change the meaning of affirmative action. In 1964, after years of black protest, Congress passed the landmark Civil Rights Act, which among other things created new agencies run by officials eager to bring minorities into the mainstream of American life. By 1965, with the passage of the Voting

Rights Act, the legal barriers to integration began to crumble and government and civil rights leaders began to confront a new, more difficult issue: how to give underprivileged minorities a fair shot at economic and social equality.

One answer was affirmative action. In 1965 President Lyndon B. Johnson issued an executive order establishing the Office of Federal Contract Compliance, which, along with the Equal Employment Opportunity Commission, began requiring companies for the first time to set numerical racial hiring goals. The trend toward quotas, goals, and timetables continued into the late 1960s, as the Richard M. Nixon administration supported this new, more radical interpretation of affirmative action.

The nation's major institutions, under pressure from consumers, employees, students, and federal bureaucrats, and aware of recent U.S. Supreme Court decisions supporting race and gender preferences, quickly began devising their own affirmative action programs. By 1978, when the Supreme Court ruled in *University of California v. Bakke* that universities could use race as a plus factor in admissions, affirmative action had become deeply entrenched in American society.

By the late twentieth century, affirmative action had become a source of great controversy. Opponents tended to see racial preferences as unjust—an unfair government program that exacerbated an already large racial divide, harming whites while stigmatizing blacks as needing preferential treatment. Opponents also contended that affirmative action mainly aided more privileged African Americans and did little to help poor blacks.

In the 1990s, Republican Party politicians and activists lobbied hard against affirmative action, helping pass Proposition 209, a 1996 California initiative to abolish racial and gender preferences, and backing the Regents of the University of California who in 1995 voted to end affirmative action in hiring and admissions. That same year, President Bill Clinton tried to stake out a middle ground on the issue, arguing that affirmative action was a flawed although necessary response to centuries of discrimination against women, blacks, and other groups.

Many in the civil rights community went further in their defense of affirmative action, arguing that white males still held a disproportionate number of powerful positions in society and that laws and programs mandating preferences were one way to combat that imbalance. These supporters also argued that racism and sexism were still rampant and that affirmative action was a small but just part of national social policy.

The Supreme Court addressed the issue in two important 2003 cases involving the University of Michigan, *Grutter v. Bollinger* and *Gratz v. Bollinger*. On one hand, the high court by a 5-to-4 vote upheld the Michigan law school's admissions policy, which took race and ethnicity into consideration without using hard and fast quotas. On the other hand, the justices, 6 to 3, found that Michigan's undergraduate admissions system, favoring African Americans, Hispanics, and American Indians through an automatic point system, violated the equal-protection clause of the Fourteenth Amendment. The National Association for the Advancement of Colored People hailed the rulings as "a strong endorsement of the constitutionality of affirmative action with the proviso that institutions have to . . . structure these programs the right way."

[*See also* **Civil Rights Legislation; Fourteenth Amendment; National Association for the Advancement of Colored People;** *and* **National Labor Relations Act.**]

BIBLIOGRAPHY

Cahn, Steven M., ed. *The Affirmative Action Debate.* New York: Routledge, 1995.

Graham, Hugh Davis. *The Civil Rights Era: Origins and Development of National Policy, 1960–1972.* New York: Oxford University Press, 1990.

Matthew Dallek; updated by Paul S. Boyer

AFRICAN AMERICAN MAYORS SINCE 1960

In 1967 the mayoral victories of two African Americans, Carl Stokes in Cleveland, Ohio, and Richard Hatcher in Gary, Indiana, revolutionized American urban politics. In subsequent years, municipal voters elected African Americans chief executives of many of the nation's largest cities—so often, in fact, that by the 1990s this practice had become commonplace, particularly in the older industrial cities of the Northeast and Midwest. Urban electorates also chose African American mayors in cities located in the Old South (such as Atlanta, Birmingham, and New Orleans) and in cities with small black voting populations (Los Angeles and Denver, for example), as well as in communities with African American majorities or pluralities. In 2008, forty-five African Americans served as mayor of cities with populations exceeding fifty thousand. This electoral success, coupled with sweeping demographic changes whereby whites fled central cities and nonwhites predominated, has dramatically altered the balance of political power in urban America.

By the mid-1960s, demographic changes ongoing for many years had clearly altered the population makeup of America's urban areas. Although the percentage of African Americans nationally remained constant during the twentieth century, the proportion almost doubled in metropolitan areas and more than tripled in the central cities (where more than half of the black population resided by 1980). In the decade of the 1960s alone, the African American population of central cities grew by more than 35 percent, whereas the white population decreased by 9 percent. Also by the mid-1960s, the African American masses enjoyed legal protection allowing them to vote in greater numbers than ever before. The passage of civil rights legislation in 1957, 1960, 1964, 1965, 1968, and 1975 (especially the Voting Rights Act of 1965) led to increased black voter turnouts in the cities. Civil rights organizations shifted the focus of their efforts from demonstrations protesting racial segregation to voter education and registration. The increased activism of the 1950s and 1960s, culminating in a series of key courtroom and legislative triumphs, spilled over into electoral politics in subsequent decades. In many instances, the civil rights leadership produced a new cohort of politically active volunteers and office seekers who set their sights on city halls.

Almost without exception, black mayors were members of the Democratic Party. Indeed, in the two decades following the election of Carl Stokes and Richard Hatcher, none of the sixty-seven black mayors elected in cities of fifty thousand or more population was a Republican. Accelerating the electoral shift away from the Grand Old Party that began during the New Deal era, black voters increasingly supported Democratic candidates in the wake of a 1960s liberalism associated with civil rights advances, affirmative action, and Great Society programs especially beneficial to the black poor in cities. African American mayors hailed from a variety of socioeconomic backgrounds, but were almost always from the Democratic Party.

African American mayors encountered a series of nettlesome problems when finally ensconced in power. They often met resistance from entrenched white bureaucracies, and many top officials resigned rather than work in minority administrations. The new mayors encountered great difficulty filling vacant positions with qualified minority candidates, who had long been excluded from high-level managerial and technical positions in city government and industry. In Gary, for example, Richard Hatcher finally appointed African American schoolteachers to a number of high-level posts and endured much criticism as the appointees earned their experience on the job; in Detroit, Mayor Coleman Young recruited black civil servants from other cities. Having been barred from city government for so long, African Americans faced the handicap of inexperience once they attained positions of power.

The first African American mayors also frequently struggled with local law enforcement authorities. Escalating crime rates constituted a severe problem in the nation's large cities, where the majority of both criminals and victims were black, especially so because of the minority communities' long-standing distrust of overwhelmingly white police departments. Threatened by affirmative action hiring and promotion initiatives, white policemen and their professional associations frequently closed ranks against outside interference and resisted reform initiatives. New Orleans Mayor Dutch Morial clashed openly with the local police force, Maynard Jackson fired the obdurate white police chief in Atlanta, and Carl Stokes called his inability to transform the Cleveland police department his greatest failure.

African American mayors frequently found their dealings with city councils difficult. Some legislative bodies proved willing to work with black mayors, but others dug in their heels and refused to cooperate. In New Orleans the hostile "Gang of Five" dominated the seven-person city council during Dutch Morial's second term, frequently overriding his vetoes. No African American mayor suffered more than Harold Washington in Chicago. Virtually his entire first term slipped away with no legislation being passed because of the "Council Wars" in which twenty-nine recalcitrant whites composed an immutable barrier to action in the fifty-person council.

Most important, African American mayors encountered a host of intractable problems during the last decades of the twentieth century because they came to power during perilous times for American cities. The flight of the middle class, industry, and retail to the suburbs and the Sunbelt meant that African Americans achieved political power at the moment that America's cities were falling into rapid decline. Whereas the tax bases available to municipalities shrank, the same could not be said of the demand for public services. Rising costs for social services, law enforcement, maintenance of aging infrastructures, and the daily provision of municipal housekeeping services exacerbated the problems awaiting black mayors. A series of fiscal crises ensued in older industrial cities, and African American mayors faced the necessity of going hat-in-hand to lawmakers in state capitals and Washington, D.C., seeking financial aid. Increased reliance on federal dollars became all the more problematic as a series of presidential administrations beginning in the 1970s practiced a "new federalism" that was less generous to urban America. In short, African American mayors needed not only to secure scarce funds during a protracted period of fiscal belt-tightening, but also to do so while representing the interests of minority constituents to white power structures that frequently considered declining cities a low national priority. Thus, despite their undisputed success in local electoral politics, many African Americans lamented that urban decline made the mayoralty a "hollow prize."

[*See also* **African Americans in Politics** *and* **Civil Rights.**]

BIBLIOGRAPHY

Biles, Roger. "Black Mayors: A Historical Assessment." *The Journal of Negro History* 77 (1992): 109–125.

Colburn, David R., and Jeffrey S. Adler, eds. *African-American Mayors: Race, Politics, and the American City*. Urbana: University of Illinois Press, 2001.

Edsall, Thomas Byrne, with Mary D. Edsall. *Chain Reaction: The Impact of Race, Rights, and Taxes on American Politics*. New York: Norton, 1991.

Goldfield, David R., "Black Political Power and Public Policy in the Urban South." In *Urban Policy in Twentieth-Century America*, edited by Arnold R. Hirsch and Raymond A. Mohl, pp. 159–182. New Brunswick, N.J.: Rutgers University Press, 1993.

Roger Biles

AFRICAN AMERICANS IN POLITICS

The election of Barack Obama as president of the United States in 2008 was the culmination of an African American dream to achieve and exercise political rights that spanned more than two centuries.

Early Involvement. African American involvement in U.S. politics dates to the era of the Revolutionary War. Initially, most northern states and several southern states placed no racial restrictions on suffrage. Beginning in 1810, however, blacks lost the right to vote in those few southern states that had granted them suffrage. The extension of universal white manhood suffrage in the northern and western states generally coincided with restrictions on black suffrage. After 1820 most northern states either abolished black suffrage, or, as in the case of New York, retained property qualifications on black voters.

Despite these difficult circumstances, African Americans persisted in efforts to pursue their political interests. In New York they sometimes provided the margin in close elections, whereas during Dorr's Rebellion in Rhode Island blacks helped defeat the reformers' efforts to extend suffrage because it would disenfranchise African Americans. By the eve of the Civil War only five New England states allowed equal suffrage for blacks. Having lost the right to vote, most African Americans channeled their political efforts through various antislavery organizations. Frederick Douglass, the most prominent African American abolitionist, remained involved in party politics, first with the Liberty Party and then Free Soil Party, but most notably with the emerging Republican Party.

Emancipation. The emancipation of slaves during the Civil War did not immediately enfranchise African Americans. Few northern states rushed to extend suffrage to blacks, whereas in the former Confederate states the federal government utilized black suffrage to ensure the loyalty of southern governments as well as to provide a base for organizing the Republican Party in the South.

The Fourteenth Amendment, approved by Congress in 1866, contained provisions for reducing a state's representation in Congress if it denied suffrage to a significant percentage of its population. The Reconstruction Act of 1867 went further, requiring former Confederate states to extend voting rights to black males. State constitutional conventions that convened in 1867 and 1868 contained significant black representation, and the Loyal Union Leagues that were established across the South in support of the Republican Party mobilized black political participation in the elections that followed. The newly enfranchised African Americans overwhelmingly voted Republican—it was the party of Lincoln and emancipation. In turn the Republicans depended on the black vote to maintain power both in the South and in the nation. The importance of the black vote in the presidential election of 1868 led to the enactment of the Fifteenth Amendment. Black politicians used suffrage to gain access to political power—political offices, influence in the Republican Party, and civil service jobs.

Reconstruction. Following Reconstruction African Americans remained politically active in the South, mostly within the Republican Party but also with various third-party movements. They held office in state and local government and between 1868 and 1901 a total of twenty-one African Americans, all Republicans, served in Congress. Nevertheless, as Democrats resumed power in the South during the mid-1870s, African American political power began to fade.

The disfranchisement of blacks at the turn of the century and internal conflicts within southern state Republican organizations reduced and then eliminated blacks from meaningful political power in the South. As a result, in the early years of the new century African American office holders disappeared from the governments of the former Confederate states and from Congress. African American leadership, including Booker T. Washington and W. E. B. Du Bois, attacked racially based suffrage laws with little effect. As they lost power in state and local governments, African Americans continued to exercise some political influence at the national level. Booker T. Washington used his personal connections with presidents Theodore Roosevelt and William Taft in an effort to maintain the Republican Party's commitment to equal rights and, along with his political allies, dispensed patronage from the Republican Party to their supporters.

As southern blacks lost their political rights, northern blacks intensified their struggle for civil rights and began to emerge as a political force, led by African American scholar and activist W. E. B. Du Bois and the National Association for the Advancement of Colored People (NAACP), created in 1909 by white and black civil rights activists. The NAACP pursued a militant civil rights agenda and launched the initial legal challenges to disfranchisement. In the 1920s the organization's efforts spread to the antilynching campaign that coalesced around Missouri Congressman L. C. Dyer's unsuccessful attempt to make lynching a federal crime. African American involvement in northern politics was a natural outgrowth of the black migration that sent several hundred thousand northward during the second and third decades of the century. In the industrial cities where black migrants concentrated, their vote became a factor in local elections. Participation in electoral politics produced black candidates, first for local and state positions and then for Congress. In 1928 Republican Oscar De Priest won election to Congress from Chicago's south side. De Priest was the first African American elected to Congress from a northern state and the first elected following the disfranchisement of southern blacks at the end of the nineteenth century.

In the 1920s and 1930s African American political activity became more effective, although the number of elected black officials remained small. The NAACP took the lead, educating black voters about candidates who deserved their support or their opposition. In 1923 black voters began targeting congressmen who opposed the Dyer antilynching bill; in 1930 they organized to defeat the confirmation of John J. Parker to the U.S. Supreme Court because of racist statements attributed to him.

Change in Political Alignment. In this period African American political alignment began to change, as many blacks rethought their support of the Republican Party. Several factors contributed to the change. In an effort to build on their inroads in the South that they achieved in the 1928 presidential election, Republican leadership courted the support of white southerners, often at the expense of the disfranchised blacks. At the same time Democrats began to seek black political support and reward it with patronage. This was particularly evident during Franklin Roosevelt's administration, where his "black cabinet" of prominent African Americans advised him on race issues. Reflecting these changes, black Democrat Arthur W. Mitchell was elected to Congress to replace the retiring De Priest in 1934, and Democrat Adam Clayton Powell Jr., of Harlem became the second African American in Congress in 1945. Despite these developments many African Americans remained suspicious of Democrats because of Roosevelt's failure to confront the southern wing of his party on the race issue and their dissatisfaction with the level of discrimination in New Deal relief programs.

The Struggle for Civil Rights. In the 1940s as the struggle for civil rights intensified, the African American drift toward the Democratic Party accelerated. In 1941 President Roosevelt gave in to political pressure from A. Phillip Randolph and signed Executive Order 8802 to end discrimination in defense industries. In 1944 in *Smith v. Allwright* the NAACP won the first of a series of court decisions that weakened restrictions of black suffrage and created a growing number of registered black voters in the South. In 1947 Randolph launched a movement that threatened civil disruptions to pressure President Truman to desegregate the armed forces. In part the need to attract black voters prompted Truman and the Democratic Party to endorse a strong civil rights platform during the election of 1948. Although some white southerners temporarily bolted from the Democratic Party, the black vote aided Truman's reelection and signaled the increasing importance of this vote for the Democrats. In the 1950s these trends continued, although the black vote was not strong enough to offset Eisenhower's popularity. Neither party had a clear hold on the civil rights agenda. The *Brown v. Board of Education* decision, Eisenhower's use of troops to desegregate Little Rock's Central High School, his four-point proposal for civil rights in 1957, and the Civil Rights Acts of 1957 and 1960 strengthened the Republican's claim on the black vote, whereas Adlai Stevenson's ambiguous stand on civil rights and the southern Democrats hard line on segregation temporarily slowed the political shift away from the Republicans.

By 1960 the Civil Rights Acts of 1957 and 1960, the elimination of the white primary, and the registration of black voters in the border states gave blacks a greater political voice than they had had since Reconstruction. The civil rights movement mobilized this growing African American political potential and demanded political solutions to discrimination. In the election of 1960 Kennedy courted the black vote by carefully endorsing limited civil rights proposals; the black vote was critical in the key states that provided his narrow victory. The 1964 election consolidated this political realignment and tied the black vote to the Democratic Party for the rest of the century. In early 1964 President Johnson signed the Civil Rights Act of 1964. The enactment of the Twenty-Fourth Amendment that same year outlawed the poll tax. Following the conflict over seating delegates from the Mississippi Freedom Democratic Party in the 1964 Democratic Convention, the party outlawed segregated delegations in future conventions. After its landslide victory, the Johnson administration strengthened its hold on black political power with the 1965 Voting Rights Act.

The Voting Rights Act is central to understanding black political activity in the last half-century. As blacks began exercising their political rights, the number of black office holders increased rapidly across both the North and especially the South. The 2 black congressmen of 1945 had increased to 6 by 1965 and to 16, including Republican Senator Edward Brooke, by 1973. In 2011 a total of 42 African Americans served in Congress. In 1970, five years after the passage of the Voting Rights Act, over 1,400 African Americans held elected office in state, county, and local government. By 2002 that number had increased to 9,430, with 63 percent holding office in the 11 states of the old Confederacy. African Americans also began to enter higher ranks in government. A number of large cities, including New York, Los Angeles, Houston, and Chicago, elected black mayors in the late twentieth century, although they were not black majority cities. The 1967 civil rights attorney Thurgood Marshall became the first black to serve on the Supreme Court, and during the 1991 Gulf War Colin Powell served as the highest-ranking military officer, chair of the Joint Chiefs of Staff. Powell later served as national security advisor and secretary of state. Condoleezza Rice became national security advisor and secretary of state under President George W. Bush.

The Twenty-First Century. The nomination and election of Barack Obama as president of the United States in 2008 was the single most dramatic African American political achievement. Although many saw Obama's stunning victory as tectonic shift in American politics, there had been a steady growth of African American involved in presidential politics prior to this. Obama was certainly the most successful of over fifty African Americans who involved themselves in presidential politics by seeking or attaining nomination for president or vice president. Frederick Douglass briefly held the vice presidential nomination of the Political Abolition Party in 1856. Although the vast majority of these candidates were associated with minor parties or with fringe movements, more serious black candidates entered presidential races in the late twentieth century. The first of these was Shirley Chisholm, who participated in the Democratic primaries in 1972 and received over 400,000 votes. Chisholm, a congresswoman from New York, was the first African American to seek the presidency who actually held elected political office at the national level. Her candidacy was more pragmatic than quixotic. She used her campaign effectively to bring issues before the public and enhance her power within the Democratic Party. Jesse Jackson campaigned twice, in 1984 and again in 1988, and he surprised many political observers with his strong showing in the primaries, especially in 1984. Jackson likely saw himself as a potential vice presidential choice in 1988. The third candidate, and the only one with a serious chance to win the nomination and get elected, was Colin Powell. When Powell flirted with his candidacy in the summer and fall of 1995, polling data showed him outpacing all other potential Republican presidential candidates and leading President Clinton by 8 to 10 points. Powell, whose professional background held more in common with that of Dwight Eisenhower than Jessie Jackson or Shirley Chisholm, was considered electable and a serious threat to Clinton and the Democrats. However, in November 1995 he decided not to run.

It is not yet clear what the long-term impact of the Obama presidency will be on African

Americans in politics. Certainly black candidates will no longer be dismissed as unelectable. Both parties in the new century are bringing African Americans into high-level administrative positions in the government and in their party's leadership. Although African American senators and governors remain rare, a serious and competitive African American presidential candidate is no longer a dream.

[*See also* **Douglass, Frederick; Du Bois, W. E. B.; Emancipation Proclamation; Fifteenth Amendment; Fourteenth Amendment; Marshall, Thurgood; National Association for the Advancement of Colored People; Obama, Barack;** ***and*** **Washington, Booker T.**]

BIBLIOGRAPHY

Ali, Omar H. *In the Balance of Power: Independent Black Politics and Third Party Movements in the United States.* Athens, Ohio: Ohio University Press, 2008.

Bynum, Cornelius L. *A. Philip Randolph and the Struggle for Civil Rights.* Urbana: University of Illinois Press, 2010.

Davidson, Chandler, and Bernard Grofman, eds. *Quiet Revolution in the South: The Impact of the Voting Rights Act, 1965–1990.* Princeton, N.J.: Princeton University Press, 1994.

Glasrud, Bruce A., and Cary D. Wintz, eds. *African Americans and the Presidency: The Road to the White House.* New York: Routledge, 2010.

Goings, Kenneth W. *"The NAACP Comes of Age": The Defeat of Judge John J. Parker.* Bloomington: Indiana University Press, 1990.

Litwack, Leon F. *North of Slavery: The Negro in the Free States, 1790–1860.* Chicago: University of Chicago Press, 1961.

Reed, Adolph L., Jr. *The Jesse Jackson Phenomenon: The Crisis of Purpose in Afro-American Politics.* New Haven, Conn.: Yale University Press, 1986.

Sitkoff, Harvard, and Eric Foner. *The Struggle for Black Equality, 1954–1992.* New York: Hill and Wang, 1993.

Walters, Ronald W. *Freedom Is Not Enough: Black Voters, Black Candidates, and American Presidential Politics.* Lanham, Md.: Rowman & Littlefield, 2005.

Walton, Hanes, Jr. *Black Political Parties: A Historical and Political Analysis.* New York: Free Press, 1972.

Walton, Hanes, Jr. *Black Republicans: The Politics of the Black and Tans.* Meutchen, N.J.: Scarecrow Press, 1975.

Cary D. Wintz

AGNEW, SPIRO

(1918–1996) was the thirty-ninth vice president of the United States, from 1969 to 1973. Born in Baltimore, Spiro Agnew served in the Army during World War II, married Elinor "Judy" Judefind in 1942, and gained his law degree in 1947 from the University of Baltimore Law School. First a registered Democrat, Agnew switched to the Republican Party in 1946 and during the 1950s became active in local politics while practicing law in Towson, Maryland. Fifth in a 1960 five-candidate contest for a judgeship on the county circuit court, Agnew won election as county executive of Baltimore County in 1962. In 1966 he beat Democrat George Mahoney for the Maryland governorship as a moderate alternative to Mahoney's segregationism.

Characterized as a progressive, reform-minded Republican during his rapid political rise, Agnew responded in a more conservative manner to race-related unrest in 1968, stressing the need for order. Still largely unknown nationally when Richard Nixon selected him as his running mate, Agnew, whose father was a Greek immigrant, held electoral promise as a representative of the ethnic constituencies Nixon coveted and even more so of the nation's rapidly developing suburbs. Agnew was soon both celebrated and notorious for his campaigning, sometimes gaffe-prone.

The role Nixon assigned to his vice president was designed to harvest the promise of Agnew's flair for attention-grabbing speeches. Agnew sounded populist themes in speaking out against "permissiveness," antiwar protest, and elite liberalism; he became the administration's leading advocate of values-oriented cultural and social conservatism, which Nixon identified as a key element of his effort to build a "new majority" among disaffected supporters of the Democrats. Agnew's advocacy of conservatism achieved two high points. First, in November 1969 Agnew helped pioneer antimedia themes that would proliferate among subsequent conservatives when he attacked television news coverage of Nixon's "silent majority" speech about Vietnam policy. Second, the following fall he led an administration effort to boost Republican representation in Congress through attacks on the "radical liberalism" of opponents. Successful in generating enthusiasm among some, Agnew's rhetoric seemed shrill to others, encouraging Nixon to contemplate his replacement by another running mate in 1972.

Seeking at first as vice president to build a reputation for policy substance as well as to achieve political advancement, Agnew soon experienced disappointment in discovering that he was excluded from decision-making discussions in the Nixon administration. Assigned to an array of responsibilities (including intergovernmental liaison, space, and summer programs for youth) and to a number of White House bodies (including the domestic council and the cabinet committee on school desegregation), Agnew failed to use these opportunities to achieve the policy successes he had desired.

In 1973 an investigation of illegal campaign contributions and kickbacks in Maryland led to charges against Agnew. Following negotiations with federal prosecutors, Agnew pled *nolo contendere* (no contest) to a tax charge and resigned from the vice presidency on 10 October 1973. Taking up a business career, Agnew largely disappeared from the public eye, although he published a political novel, *The Canfield Decision* (1976), and an exculpatory memoir, *Go Quietly . . . or Else* (1980).

[***See also*** **Conservatism *and* Nixon, Richard M.**]

BIBLIOGRAPHY

Witcover, Jules. *Very Strange Bedfellows: The Short and Unhappy Marriage of Richard Nixon and Spiro Agnew*. New York: PublicAffairs, 2007.

Witcover, Jules. *White Knight: The Rise of Spiro Agnew*. New York: Random House, 1972.

Robert Mason

AGRICULTURAL ADJUSTMENT ADMINISTRATION

In 1933, American agriculture neared collapse as farm bankruptcies and foreclosures multiplied and agricultural prices fell below the cost of production. President Franklin Delano Roosevelt instructed his agricultural experts to draft legislation. The result was the Agricultural Adjustment Act (AAA) of May 1933. The law's fundamental goal was "parity": raising basic farm prices until they were in balance with the general economy. One way was to eliminate existing commodity surpluses by taking farm acreage out of production and inducing farmers to produce only what was needed for domestic consumption. The government paid benefits to farmers who contracted to reduce acreage and also offered parity payments on the crops actually grown. To finance these payments, the secretary of agriculture taxed the domestic processors of basic commodities—wheat, cotton, tobacco, corn-hogs, and milk products. Since pork and milk production could not be controlled effectively by reducing acreage, the government negotiated agreements among the meat packers and dairy companies to regulate markets and fix prices.

The law created the Agricultural Adjustment Administration to administer the new system. The first administrator was George N. Peek, a businessman and agricultural reformer. Because Peek assumed power in 1933 after crops had been planted and sows were bearing litters of pigs, his agency contracted with farmers to plow under nearly half of their crops and to slaughter baby pigs. Although calculated to increase prices and raise farm income, the destruction of crops and livestock stirred widespread dismay.

By late 1935, the AAA had enabled agriculture to approach a parity position. AAA payments especially benefited larger commercial farmers and southern planters. Acreage reduction, however, hurt tenant farmers and sharecroppers, many thousands of whom were evicted or received pitifully small payments.

The AAA saved agriculture from collapse, but as the crisis eased, constitutional questions arose. In 1936 the U.S. Supreme Court struck down the act for exceeding the government's interstate commerce powers. To keep the AAA operating, Congress passed a new law that preserved AAA programs under the pretext of soil conservation. In 1938 Congress passed a second AAA that emphasized price supports and subsidies. Congress ended the AAA during World War II as agricultural prices rose sharply and demand exceeded supply; the Department of Agriculture assumed many of the AAA's programs and implemented them as the core of post–World War II agricultural policy.

[*See also* **Agricultural Policy; Federal Government, Executive Branch: Agriculture Department; New Deal;** ***and*** **Roosevelt, Franklin Delano.**]

BIBLIOGRAPHY

Conrad, David E. *The Forgotten Farmers: The Story of Sharecroppers in the New Deal.* Westport, Conn.: Greenwood Press, 1965.

Nourse, Edwin, Joseph Davis, and John D. Black. *Three Years of the Agricultural Adjustment Administration.* Washington, D.C.: The Brookings Institution, 1937.

David E. Conrad

AGRICULTURAL POLICY

The American system of agriculture is a product of public policies that have sought to develop, protect, and regulate the agricultural economy. Before the 1930s, the federal government had established a steadily more important role in extending a farm economy built around national and world commodity markets. During the Great Depression in the 1930s, the federal government became more actively involved in regulating and subsidizing the farm sector. Since the 1980s, U.S. farm policy has lurched awkwardly between short-term safety-net actions and reduced forms of market control. More generally, American farm policies, especially in the twentieth century, have embraced conflicting goals as they have sought to sustain large numbers of independent farms while also transforming these farms into productive and efficient businesses.

For much of the nineteenth century, the United States encouraged agricultural development through land policies that sought the rapid transfer of public lands to private ownership. In addition, beginning at least with the creation of the U.S. Department of Agriculture (USDA) as a cabinet office in 1862, the United States has sought to develop its agricultural system through the public support of scientific research and other public goods necessary for an intensive system of crop and animal production. Supplemented by public subsidies for postal and road-building systems, what took shape was a public–private collaboration aimed at widening and deepening market activity. With its affiliated institutions such as the land-grant colleges, the experiment stations, and the cooperative extension system, the USDA was at the center of this system. Before 1930, this institutional network had acquired modest regulatory capabilities, but more generally it sought to facilitate biological and mechanical innovation and the integration of local and regional markets into national and international systems. The benefits were modest until 1930, but thereafter the cumulative effect achieved sustained productivity gains that lowered food costs and reduced the percentage of the labor force employed in agriculture from 41 to 1.9 percent in the years from 1900 to 2000.

Following World War I, deflationary shocks, low returns, unstable prices, and unfavorable terms of trade relative to the prewar era generated a widely held perception that the United States had a "farm problem." This perception provoked strong support for altering market outcomes, and there arose a highly politicized debate over how to bolster farm sector market power. The collapse of domestic and world commodity markets during the Great Depression opened the way for substantial forms of market intervention, and with the advent of the New Deal, the federal government assumed a major role in the farm economy. The Agricultural Adjustment Acts of 1933 and 1938, the expansion of the government-sponsored Federal Farm Credit System, and other policy innovations first began a massive rescue of farm assets and then vested the federal government with the ongoing responsibility for maintaining agriculture's economic and financial security. For major staple commodities, the New Deal put in place production controls, price support loans, conservation programs, import restrictions, and export subsidies that sought to reestablish price relationships for the years 1910–1014, what became known as parity prices. For dairy products and more specialized crops, it established marketing orders that enabled growers to organize to limit supplies and control the volume of sales. The New Deal interventions sought to balance between market expansion and market protections, but they sustained many farmers through the depression and also the decade's droughts and dust storms. Despite efforts to aid marginal farmers, the distributional effects favored more commercially advantaged land-owning producers who were able to invest in mechanized equipment and take advantage of innovations such as hybrid seeds.

During World War II, the combination of the need for abundant production and the enlarged political power of commercial farmers pushed commodity policy toward rigid marketing controls that boosted farm prices. The commitment to rigid price supports (measured by the parity index) remained in place until 1973, and it demanded extensive and costly market-limiting measures such as supply controls, export subsidies, tariff protections, marketing orders, and storage operations. This regime of high price supports achieved mixed results. It facilitated capital investment in postwar agriculture, sustained small-scale operators for commodities such as tobacco, and encouraged farm consolidation for other commodities. Along with agricultural policies worldwide (particularly Europe's Common Market), U.S. farm subsidies undercut American-led efforts to liberalize world trade through the General Agreement on Tariffs and Trade (GATT). Dissatisfaction with the heavy public costs and burdensome controls produced a series of farm bills beginning in 1965 that gradually shifted agricultural policy to more market-oriented policies with greater emphasis on income (rather than price) subsidies and soil conservation measures.

Since the 1970s, American farm policy has contended with conflicting pressures to sustain a farm safety net, reduce farm program costs, minimize market distortions, and open American agriculture to global markets. When the farm economy has been beset with price and liquidity shocks, as it was in the early and mid-1980s, Congress and (often grudgingly) presidential administrations have responded with massive rescue actions such as the Payment-in-Kind program of 1983 and the 1980s bailout of the Farm Credit System. At the same time, successive farm bills, culminating with the 1996 Federal Agricultural Improvement and Reform (FAIR) Act, have reduced the number of commodities and types of livestock covered by the farm programs, imposed caps on income payments, expanded conservation features, and eliminated supply management controls. These acts have also sought to conform to the trade rules established by the World Trade Organization (WTO).

Broadly speaking, there are two views of the historical legacy of American agricultural policy. Optimists contend that they transformed an overpopulated, inefficient part of the American economy into a highly productive sector capable of meeting the food needs of a growing population at relatively low costs. The decrease in the number of farms from over 6 million to about 1 million was a painful process, but was achieved with reasonable success. Pessimists see a history of interest group manipulation, environmental degradation, a tragic loss of rural culture, and unnecessary series of sacrifices born by the rural poor.

[*See also* **Agricultural Adjustment Administration** *and* **New Deal.**]

BIBLIOGRAPHY

Benedict, Murray. *Farm Policies of the United States, 1790–1950*. New York: Twentieth Century Fund, 1953.

Carpenter, Daniel P. *The Forging of Bureaucratic Autonomy: Reputations, Networks, and Policy Innovation in Executive Agencies, 1862–1928*. Princeton, N.J.: Princeton University Press, 2001.

Clarke, Sally H. *Regulation and Revolution in United States Farm Productivity*. Cambridge, UK: Cambridge University Press, 1994.

Cochrane, Willard W. *The Development of American Agriculture: A Historical Analysis*. Minneapolis: University of Minnesota Press, 1993.

Cochrane, Willard W., and Mary E. Ryan. *American Farm Policy, 1948–1973*. Minneapolis: University of Minnesota Press, 1976.

Dimitri, Carolyn, Anne Effland, and Neilson Conklin. *The 20th Century Transformation of U.S. Agriculture and Farm Policy*. Electronic Information Bulletin No. 3, Economic Research Service, USDA. June 2005. http://www.ers.usda.gov/publications/eib3/eib3.htm (accessed 17 March 2011).

Winders, Bill. *The Politics of Food Supply: U.S. Agricultural Policy in the World Economy*. New Haven, Conn.: Yale University Press, 2009.

David E. Hamilton

ALBANY CONGRESS

Representatives of seven American colonies meeting in Albany, New York, in the summer of 1754 drew up a plan to unite the American colonies under a federal government. The Albany Congress had initially been convened by the English Board of Trade, which was concerned about the weakness of intercolonial defense at the beginning of the Seven Years' War, as well as about growing friction between the colonists and the Iroquois.

The plan, derived largely from the ideas of Benjamin Franklin and Governor William Shirley of Massachusetts, provided for a chief military executive and a commissioner for Indian affairs, both to be paid by the Crown. A grand council of delegates would be drawn from the thirteen mainland colonies, with the size of each colony's delegation being proportional to its share of taxes. The delegates, to be elected every three years and to meet every year, were charged with negotiating Indian treaties that would bind all the colonies and with providing for intercolonial defense to be paid for by indirect taxes. The proposed Grand Council would have had more powers than the provincial assemblies vis-à-vis the imperial executives, but fewer powers than Parliament enjoyed in relation to the king.

Nothing immediately came of the Albany Plan. It was not supported by the colonial assemblies, which distrusted one another. And it was never presented for authorization in Parliament because the English ministry hesitated to introduce a plan for an intercolonial assembly that might facilitate American resistance to imperial authority. An early blueprint for colonial union, the Albany Plan showed that, in the mid-1750s, intercolonial cooperation was not yet a viable option.

[*See also* **Franklin, Benjamin.**]

BIBLIOGRAPHY

Newbold, Robert C. *The Albany Congress and Plan of Union of 1754*. New York: Vantage Press, 1955.

Alison G. Olson

ALCATRAZ, OCCUPATION OF

The 1969 occupation of Alcatraz Island grew out of the civil unrest sweeping across the United States in the 1960s. The participants came from the Bay Area colleges and universities where young Indian students began demanding that their voices be heard. Among the Indian students at San Francisco State was a Mohawk Indian, Richard Oakes. In September 1969, he and other Indian students began discussing the possibility of occupying Alcatraz Island as a call for Indian self-determination.

In the early morning hours of 20 November 1969, eighty-nine American Indians landed on Alcatraz Island and claimed the island by right of discovery. The occupiers set the tone of the occupation and the agenda for negotiations during the nineteen-month occupation by demanding title to the island, a center for Native American Studies, a Center of Ecology, and a Native American Museum. The recognized leader was Richard Oakes. The casting of Oakes as leader on the island, a title he himself never claimed, quickly created a problem. There was no one "leader" as the decisions were made by an elected counsel and some felt that Oakes sought self-aggrandizement. Additionally, Oakes was often sought out and identified by the media as the leader, the "chief," and the "mayor of Alcatraz."

By the end of 1969 two groups rose in opposition to Oakes as the Indian students began returning to school. The final blow to the nascent student occupation occurred on 5 January 1970, when Oakes's twelve-year-old stepdaughter, Yvonne, fell three floors down a stairwell to her death. Following Yvonne's death, the Oakes family left the island, and the two remaining groups vied for leadership.

In the months that followed, thousands of protesters and visitors spent time on

Alcatraz Island. The months of occupation were marked by proclamations, news conferences, and calls for negotiations with federal officials. The federal government insisted that the Indian people leave and placed an ineffective coast guard barricade around the island. Eventually, the government agreed to the demands for formal negotiations. From the Indians' side, the demands were nonnegotiable.

Over time, the attention of the federal government shifted from negotiations with the island occupants to the restoration of navigational aids to the Bay Area—aids that had been discontinued as the result of a fire on the island. The federal government soon became impatient. On 11 June 1971, the message went out to end the occupation. Federal marshals removed the remaining protesters, nineteen months after Indians of All Tribes first occupied the island.

The success or failure of the Indian occupation of Alcatraz Island should not be judged by whether the demands for title to the island and the establishment of the various institutions on the island were realized. The underlying goals of the Indians on Alcatraz Island were to awaken the American public to the reality of the plight of the first Americans and to assert the need for Indian self-determination. In this they were indeed successful. As a result of the Alcatraz occupation the official government policy of termination of Indian tribes was ended and a policy of Indian self-determination was adopted.

In his address to Congress on 8 July 1970, in the midst of the occupation, President Nixon admitted that it was time that the federal government recognize and build upon the capacities and insights of Native American people. On that same day Nixon returned Taos Blue Lake to the Taos Pueblo Indians and acknowledged that it was important for Native American people to see this action as a symbol of his administration's new approach toward Indian affairs.

The Alcatraz occupation became a strong symbol of activism and self-determination. Following that occupation there were sixty-four occupations of other facilities across the United States. Those who participated in the subsequent occupations came from Indians of All Tribes or stated that the American Indians on Alcatraz Island provided their motivation and their inspiration.

[*See also* **Nixon, Richard M.**]

BIBLIOGRAPHY

Cobb, Daniel M. *Beyond Red Power: American Indian Politics and Activism since 1900.* Sante Fe, N.M.: School for Advanced Research Press, 2007.

Johnson, Troy R. *The American Indian Occupation of Alcatraz Island: Red Power and Self-Determination.* Lincoln: University of Nebraska Press, 2008.

Johnson, Troy, Joane Nagel, and Duane Champagne. *American Indian Activism: Alcatraz to the Longest Walk.* Urbana: University of Illinois Press, 1997.

Smith, Paul, and Robert Warrior. *Like a Hurricane: The Indian Movement from Alcatraz to Wounded Knee.* New York: The New Press, 1996.

Troy Johnson

ALIEN AND SEDITION ACTS

The term "Alien and Sedition Acts" refers to four controversial laws enacted by the Federalist-controlled Congress in 1798 in response to fears about imminent war with France and about the loyalty of pro-French Irish immigrants. The Alien Enemies Act empowered the president to restrain or expel any "alien enemy" immigrant from a nation with which the United States was at war; the

Alien Act authorized expulsion of any alien, without a hearing, considered "dangerous to the peace and safety" of the United States; and the Naturalization Act extended to fourteen years (from five) the waiting time required for immigrants to become citizens. The passing of the war scare rendered the first measure meaningless; President John Adams never invoked the second; and the third only encouraged many Irish immigrants, eager to vote for the Federalists' Jeffersonian-Republican opponents, to become citizens before the fourteen-year requirement went into effect.

The fourth of these measures, the Sedition Act, a national seditious libel law that was to expire automatically in 1800, targeted supporters of the Jeffersonian-Republican party by declaring it a crime to make defamatory statements about the government or the president. Although it permitted persons charged to plead truth as a defense and allowed juries to determine whether a statement was actually seditious, these safeguards proved meaningless when Jeffersonian critics appeared before Federalist judges and juries in more than a dozen libel prosecutions.

The Alien and Sedition Acts deepened partisan political passions. Whereas Federalists defended them as a measured, appropriate response to legitimate concerns about how disloyal aliens and licentious criticism might endanger the nation's safety, Jeffersonians claimed that all four laws exceeded the limited constitutional powers delegated to the national government. The Virginia and Kentucky Resolutions (1798–1779), secretly drafted by James Madison and Thomas Jefferson and passed by their respective state legislatures, contended that these acts upset the balance of power between the states and the national government and argued that the national union rested on a compact among the states. Jefferson's Kentucky Resolution even vaguely implied that an individual state could decide whether a national law invaded its sovereign rights.

Jeffersonians also charged that the Sedition Act muzzled legitimate political dissent in violation of the First Amendment. Government rightly rested on the opinion of the citizenry, they argued, and public discussion could not proceed in the face of the kind of legal obstructions posed by libel prosecutions such as those conducted under the Sedition Act. The Alien and Sedition Acts rebounded against the Federalists. Prosecutions for seditious libel failed to silence their Jeffersonian critics, and Adams lost the presidency to Jefferson in 1800. A decade later, the Jeffersonian-Republicans dominated national politics, and the Federalist Party was moribund.

Although the political passions of the late 1790s soon cooled, the Alien and Sedition Acts episode raised issues that would reappear over the course of U.S. history, including the regulation of immigration, determining the balance of power between national and state governments, and drawing the constitutional limits of political dissent.

[*See also* **Bill of Rights; Censorship; Federalist Party; Immigration Law and Policy: Before 1930; Nullification; Sedition; States' Rights;** *and* **Virginia and Kentucky Resolutions.**]

BIBLIOGRAPHY

Cornell, Saul. *The Other Founders: Anti-Federalism and the Dissenting Tradition in America, 1788–1828.* Chapel Hill: University of North Carolina Press, 1999.

Elkins, Stanley, and Eric McKitrick. *The Age of Federalism: The Early American Republic, 1788–1800.* New York: Oxford University Press, 1993.

Rosenberg, Norman. *Protecting the "Best Men": An Interpretive History of the Law of Libel.* Chapel Hill: University of North Carolina Press, 1986.

Norman L. Rosenberg

AMERICA FIRST COMMITTEE

When Germany invaded Poland in September 1939, thereby unleashing World War II, President Franklin Delano Roosevelt sought to aid the Allies by such means as cash-and-carry (September 1939) and the exchange of fifty American destroyers for eight British bases in the Western hemisphere (September 1940). In the summer of 1940, amid rumors of increased shipments of American ships, tanks, and aircraft to Britain, Yale law student R. Douglas Stuart Jr., organized the Emergency Committee to Defend America First, which late in August renamed itself the America First Committee (AFC). The AFC was the primary "isolationist" organization that led opposition to Roosevelt's interventionist measures during 1940 and 1941.

Chaired by Sears Roebuck executive Robert E. Wood, the AFC included such diverse members as journalist John T. Flynn, retired diplomat William R. Castle, former New Dealer Hugh Johnson, advertising executive Chester Bowles, textile manufacturer William H. Regnery, and Chicago financier Sterling Morton. Stuart became executive secretary. Aviator Charles Lindbergh, who joined the AFC national committee in April 1941, was its chief drawing card, although he dealt the committee a severe blow that September by publicly claiming that Jews as a group sought full-scale American participation in the war. A staff composed of socialists, pacifists, and liberals prepared its position papers. At its peak in 1941, the AFC had 450 chapters, a membership of 850,000, and an income of $370,000 donated by 25,000 contributors. Huge AFC rallies featured such speakers as Lindbergh, Flynn, Senator Burton K. Wheeler (D-MO), Senator Gerald P. Nye (R-ND), Representative Hamilton Fish (R-NY), and socialist leader Norman Thomas. Although unable to defeat Roosevelt on any specific issue, the AFC undoubtedly caused him to be more circumspect on such matters as extending terms for draftees and convoying British vessels. The AFC disbanded after Japan's attack on Pearl Harbor in December 1941.

BIBLIOGRAPHY

Cole, Wayne S. *America First: The Battle against Intervention, 1940–1941*. New York: Octagon Books, 1953.

Doenecke, Justus D., ed. *In Danger Undaunted: The Anti-Interventionist Movement as Revealed in the Papers of the America First Committee*. Stanford, Calif.: Hoover Institution Press, 1990.

Justus D. Doenecke

AMERICAN ANTI-SLAVERY SOCIETY

The American Anti-Slavery Society (AASS) was founded in 1833 by a small group of radicals calling for the immediate abolition of slavery. The leading spirit was William Lloyd Garrison, whose interaction with black abolitionists inspired him to reject colonization as a means of eradicating slavery. The founders of the AASS did not condone a violent overthrow of the slave system, but believed that moral suasion would convince slaveholders of its evils.

Abolitionists soon came to disagree over the necessity of violence, the position of women in the movement, and the role of politics and organized religion in the antislavery cause. These divisions reached a critical point in 1839 when a majority in the AASS voted to allow women to serve as delegates to antislavery conventions. Led by Lewis Tappan, opponents of Garrison's approach to abolitionism, with its exclusive emphasis on moral suasion and its interest in other reforms as well as antislavery, formed a new organization, the American and Foreign Anti-Slavery Society, in 1840.

The violence of the 1850s caused many AASS members to rethink their commitment to moral suasion. Frederick Douglass rejected Garrisonian abolitionism in favor of political abolitionism. By the eve of the Civil War, Garrison and others endorsed the Republican Party and supported John Brown's raid. Although some Garrisonians continued to oppose violence, most endorsed the war as a means to end slavery.

Garrison retired in 1865 after ratification of the Thirteenth Amendment ended slavery, but Wendell Phillips, Sallie Holley, and others maintained the AASS. As the interests of abolitionists fragmented, the AASS could no longer sustain its activities or newspaper, the *National Anti-Slavery Standard,* and it disbanded in 1870 after the Fifteenth Amendment extended the franchise to freedmen. The AASS had witnessed the abolition of slavery, but had not been directly instrumental in its demise. Nevertheless, its members recognized that racism and the exploitation of black labor remained problems, and their principal legacy was a strong commitment to racial equality.

[*See also* **Antislavery Movement; Brown, John; Douglass, Frederick;** *and* **Peace Movements.**]

BIBLIOGRAPHY

Quarles, Benjamin. *Black Abolitionists.* London; New York: Oxford University Press, 1991.

Yellin, Jean Fagan, and John C. Van Horne, eds. *The Abolitionist Sisterhood: Women's Political Culture in Antebellum America.* Ithaca, N.Y.: Cornell University Press, 1994.

Carol Faulkner

AMERICAN CIVIL LIBERTIES UNION

A nonprofit membership association devoted to the defense of individual rights under the U.S. Constitution founded in 1920 as a successor to the National Civil Liberties Bureau, which defended the rights of dissidents and conscientious objectors during World War I, the American Civil Liberties Union (ACLU) established a reputation as the defender of unpopular causes. Its most famous early case involved the defense of John T. Scopes, who was tried in 1925 for violating a Tennessee law prohibiting the teaching of the theory of evolution in public schools. During World War II, the ACLU challenged the federal government's program of placing Japanese Americans in internment camps. In the 1970s, the organization successfully defended the right of a domestic Nazi group to hold a demonstration in the heavily Jewish community of Skokie, Illinois—a controversial case that cost it some support.

Molded by Roger Baldwin, the organization's executive director from 1920 to 1950, the ACLU participated in an estimated 80 percent of the landmark cases on individual rights decided by the U.S. Supreme Court. The ACLU's agenda includes First Amendment rights of free speech and religious liberty, due process of law, equal protection of the law, and the right to privacy. The ACLU has traditionally relied on volunteer attorneys representing clients without charge. Beginning in the late 1960s, however, it began to employ full-time staff attorneys to handle cases in specialized areas such as prisoners' rights. The organization's membership grew from about 1,000 in 1920 to over 275,000 in the 1990s. The ACLU maintains a national office in New York City, a legislative office in Washington, D.C., and affiliate chapters in every state.

In the aftermath of the terrorist attacks of 11 September 2001, the ACLU vigorously defended civil liberties as the Department of Justice under Attorney General John Ashcroft enforced provisions of the USA Patriot Act that, in the view of civil libertarians, threatened citizens' constitutional rights.

[*See also* **Bill of Rights; Civil Liberties; Conscientious Objection;** ***and*** **Federal Government, Executive Branch: Department of Justice.**]

BIBLIOGRAPHY

Walker, Samuel. *In Defense of American Liberties: A History of the ACLU.* New York: Oxford University Press, 1990.

Samuel Walker; updated by Paul S. Boyer

AMERICAN COLONIZATION SOCIETY

In 1816, white Americans who wanted to transport black Americans from the United States established the American Colonization Society (ACS). Whereas some ACS supporters hoped to remove only free blacks and thereby strengthen slavery, most championed the gradual relocation of all black Americans, free and slave alike. To them, colonization was a politically moderate solution to the problems of slavery and race in America.

In 1817, Congress rejected an ACS memorial calling for the founding of a free black colony. The organization consequently had to obtain federal aid by more surreptitious means. Specifically, the ACS convinced President James Monroe to loosely interpret the Slave Trade Act of 1819. The statute, which concerned the disposal of "recaptives" (i.e., illegally imported African slaves), empowered the president to arrange for their "safe-keeping, support, and removal" beyond the United States. The 1819 Slave Trade Act became the pretext for President James Monroe to provide financial and military assistance to the ACS's settlement of Liberia, although the national government had few recaptives to send to the colony. As time passed, the ACS generated more controversy. Abolitionists insisted that the colonization movement fueled racism and perpetuated slavery. Proslavery Southerners, fretting that colonization was the Trojan horse of abolitionism, repeatedly thwarted efforts to expand the federal government's commitment to the enterprise.

In 1828, Andrew Jackson won the presidency and subsequently ended federal funding for the ACS. In the 1830s, some states supported colonization programs, but ACS leaders knew that only the federal government could marshal the resources to resolve what they considered a national problem. Beset by political and financial challenges, the ACS factionalized, with Northerners gaining control of the organization after 1839. The colonization crusade inched along thereafter. By 1847, the ACS had transported 5,500 black Americans to Liberia. That year, the colony, with the ACS's blessing, declared its national independence. As a black republic, Liberia altered the slavery debate in America.

Proslavery Southerners understood Liberia's significance and blocked attempts to establish diplomatic relations with the African nation. The United States recognized Liberia in 1862, during a period when Union leaders were pitching colonization proposals and effecting emancipationist measures. Although those wartime colonization proposals came to naught, thousands of black people moved to Liberia during the perilous days of Presidential Reconstruction (1865–1867). Likewise, "Liberia fever" swept through several Southern states when Congressional Reconstruction ended in 1877. Emigration to Liberia declined thereafter, and the ACS transported its last emigrant in 1904.

The colonization movement had unexpected and enduring ramifications. First, the ACS fostered political and sectional divisiveness. Second, although colonizationists rejected racial egalitarianism in the United States, they insisted on black people's capacity for uplift and self-governance elsewhere, and thus they espoused ideas that foreshadowed the "separate but equal" doctrine. Finally, the ACS helped create Liberia, a country that, despite external threats and internal turmoil, has maintained its national sovereignty since 1847. The ACS's political impact, in other words, has reverberated through time.

[*See also* **Jackson, Andrew; Monroe, James;** *and* **Slavery, Laws.**]

BIBLIOGRAPHY

Burin, Eric. *Slavery and the Peculiar Solution: A History of the American Colonization Society.* Gainesville: University Press of Florida, 2005.

Guyatt, Nicholas. "'The Outskirts of Our Happiness': Race and the Lure of Colonization in the Early Republic." *Journal of American History* 95, no. 4 (March 2009): 986–1011.

Staudenraus, P. J. *The African Colonization Movement, 1816–1865.* New York: Octagon Books, 1961.

Eric Burin

AMERICAN FARM BUREAU FEDERATION

In the history of institution building in American agriculture, the most successful example of a general-interest farm organization is the American Farm Bureau Federation (AFBF). Formed in 1919, the AFBF has committed itself to expanding agricultural markets and building public and private institutions that would advance innovation and productivity. During its early decades, AFBF benefited from the close ties of its local associations to the Department of Agriculture's cooperative extension service. In addition, its state units bolstered its influence by establishing successful insurance, cooperative marketing, and farm supply affiliates.

The founders of the AFBF believed that farmers were at a disadvantage in the early twentieth century in a political system increasingly dominated by organized groups. Older forms of agrarian organization such as fraternal orders or third political parties, they argued, were ill suited to represent modern farm interests. The creation in 1914 of the Extension Service spurred the formation of a network of local and state farm associations that were often known as "farm bureaus" committed to developing commercial agriculture. Following World War I, frustration at the lack of farmer representation in administering wartime and postwar national policies encouraged the county and state farm bureaus to form what became the AFBF.

In the 1920s, the strong grassroots base, especially in midwestern states, enabled the AFBF to establish a larger role for farm interests before Congress and federal administrative agencies. At the start of the Great Depression, the AFBF faced a sharp drop in membership, but it survived this crisis when Edward A. O'Neal, its president from 1931 to 1947, adroitly committed the AFBF to supporting early New Deal farm policies. Programs such as the Agricultural Adjustment Administration succeeded in rescuing many farmers from bankruptcy and also strengthened the extension system. As a result, AFBF membership steadily rose, and by the 1940s it could use its almost unprecedented influence with Congress to thwart New Deal initiatives that it feared might weaken the extension system while also securing approval of rigid wartime commodity price protections.

In the post-World War II era, AFBF critics, including competing farm organizations, charged that AFBF was committed primarily to the interests of large-scale farms and agribusiness corporations. Its leaders countered that it spoke on behalf of a market-based system of agriculture capable of steady gains in food and fiber production. Although the AFBF remained a powerful voice in farm debates, it could not sustain its almost exclusive influence with Congress. Its state organizations after the war divided along regional and commodity lines over the direction of agricultural price support programs. More generally, farm policy, especially since the 1970s, has been marked by the emergence of a complex array of environmental, trade, and fiscal issues that have made it impossible for a single association to unite diverse interests.

[*See also* **Agricultural Adjustment Administration** *and* **New Deal.**]

BIBLIOGRAPHY

Berger, Samuel R. *Dollar Harvest: The Story of the Farm Bureau.* Lexington, Mass.: Heath Lexington Books, 1971.

Block, William J. *The Separation of the Farm Bureau and the Extension Service: Political Issue in a Federal System.* Urbana: University of Illinois Press, 1960.

Browne, William P. *Private Interests, Public Policy, and American Agriculture.* Lawrence: University Press of Kansas, 1988.

Campbell, Christiana McFayden. *The Farm Bureau and the New Deal: A Study of the Making of National Farm Policy, 1933–1940.* Urbana: University of Illinois Press, 1962.

Hansen, John Mark. *Gaining Access: Congress and the Farm Lobby, 1919–1981.* Chicago: University of Chicago Press, 1991.

Howard, Robert P. and James R. *Howard and the Farm Bureau.* Ames: Iowa State University Press, 1983.

Kile, Orville Merton. *The Farm Bureau through Three Decades.* Baltimore: Waverly Press, 1948.

Truelsen, Stewart R. *Forward Farm Bureau: Ninety Year History of the American Farm Bureau Federation.* Washington, D.C.: American Farm Bureau Federation, 2009.

David E. Hamilton

AMERICAN INDIAN MOVEMENT

Since its founding in 1968 by a group of Anishinabe Indians in Minneapolis, the American Indian Movement (AIM) has sought to shape federal and state Indian policy and provide social programs for Native peoples. Widely seen as a radical activist organization and part of a larger Red Power movement, it continues to protect the rights of Native Americans in the United States.

The organization formally began with meetings organized by Pat Ballanger, Dennis Banks, Clyde Bellecourt, Harold Goodsky, George Mitchell, Mary Jane Wilson, and others who formed an "Indian Patrol" to prevent police misconduct in Minneapolis. Although not present at the beginning, Russell Means also helped shaped the movement in its infancy. Drawing on centuries of discontent and pan-Indian behavior, the organization participated in several public protests to attract national attention. They joined the occupation of Alcatraz Island in 1969, a protest led by the Indians of All Tribes. The following year, the AIM seized the replica of the *Mayflower* during a protest of Thanksgiving's 350th anniversary, and in 1971 the AIM occupied Mount Rushmore and Fort Lawton in Washington State. Protests continued across the country, as the AIM voiced objections to various movies and other public representations of Indians, conducted "fish-ins" to protest fish and game laws, and responded to various injustices within Native American communities. The AIM obtained national credibility in 1972 when it successfully forced local authorities to prosecute and convict white residents for the murder of Raymond Yellow Thunder (Oglala) in Gordon, Nebraska.

By 1972, the AIM had local chapters across North America, with forty-three in the United States and six in Canada. In October 1972 the organization led a "Trail of Broken Treaties" caravan from the West to Washington, D.C., occupied the Bureau of Indian Affairs headquarters, and presented the 20-Point Manifesto as demands for their surrender. In it, the AIM demanded that the United States respect Native American treaty rights and address the substandard living standards of Indians, among other things. Within the next year, the AIM occupied the Bureau of Indian Affairs office on the Pine Ridge Reservation, the location of the infamous Wounded Knee massacre in 1890.

In 1973 and afterward, AIM leaders faced several legal challenges from federal and state governments. Infiltrated by the Federal Bureau of Investigation and ultimately facing more than five hundred indictments, the AIM struggled financially with legal costs. Only a handful of AIM members were convicted, mostly of minor offenses, but the legal obstacles overwhelmed the organization. Rather than promoting a civil rights agenda, the AIM spent its energies defending its members in court. Most notably, the trial, conviction, and continued imprisonment of Leonard Peltier for the 1975 murder of two Federal Bureau of Investigation agents damaged the organization. Part of a larger Red Power movement, the AIM continues to fight for the rights of Native Americans in the United States. Its influence in recent years has declined with the victory of the general waning of the organized civil rights movement in the United States and the victory achieved by the Indian Self-Determination Act of 1975.

[*See also* **Bureau of Indian Affairs** *and* **Civil Rights.**]

BIBLIOGRAPHY

Johnson, Troy, Joane Nagel, and Duane Champagne, eds. *American Indian Activism: Alcatraz to the Longest Walk*. Urbana: University of Illinois Press, 1997.

Smith, Paul Chaat, and Robert Allen Warrior. *Like a Hurricane: The Indian Movement from Alcatraz to Wounded Knee*. New York: New Press, 1996.

Andrew K. Frank

AMERICAN LIBERTY LEAGUE

Founded in August 1934, the American Liberty League was for a time at the forefront of the conservative attack on the New Deal. Although it claimed to be nonpartisan and was led by conservative Democrats, the Liberty League was in fact dedicated to discrediting the New Deal and mobilizing opposition to it. Well funded and publicized, the American Liberty League attempted to replace the discredited and demoralized Republican Party as the focus of opposition to Franklin Roosevelt's administration.

The origins of the Liberty League lay in the campaign against national Prohibition. That fight was led by the Association against the Prohibition Amendment (AAPA), which received most of its funds from prominent DuPont and General Motors executives, including Pierre and Irénée du Pont and John J. Raskob. The AAPA's complaint against Prohibition ran much deeper than simply an argument over the right to drink; it attacked the Eighteenth Amendment as an improper extension of federal power over the lives of citizens with worrying implications not only for the proper scope of the federal government but also for the future of private enterprise. In 1919 liquor sales had been banned; what industry would be next?

The end of Prohibition coincided with the beginning of the New Deal, and soon the AAPA's leaders saw an even greater threat to American traditions of limited government, free enterprise, and individual freedom. Taking advantage of the donors and organizational skills that the AAPA had nurtured, the Liberty League undertook a lavishly funded publicity campaign through radio speeches, press releases, and pamphlets that were distributed to every major radio station, sixteen hundred newspapers, and millions of households. By the end of 1935 it claimed seventy-five thousand members and an annual budget of $500,000, nearly half of which came from members of the du Pont family and their associates.

The Liberty League's president, Jouett Shouse, led the AAPA, and its publicity head was Charles Michelson, who had orchestrated the Democrats' campaign against Herbert Hoover between 1929 and 1932. The Liberty League argued that the New Deal was unconstitutional, that its economic planning threatened free enterprise and individualism, that it was dividing the United States into classes, that it was a plot to use public funds to entrench Franklin Roosevelt and the Democrats in power, and that its taxation policies penalized the rich and hampered recovery.

Despite its large budget and intense publicity, the Liberty League failed to derail the New Deal. Its leaders were insensitive in parading their wealth during a time of economic distress, and they allowed their ideological protests against the New Deal to descend into a plutocratic revolt against high taxes and the supposedly dictatorial tendencies of Roosevelt and his recovery program. The American Liberty League was really the "American Cellophane League," Postmaster General James Farley joked in 1936, because "first, it's a Du Pont product, and second, you can see right through it." Discredited after Roosevelt's overwhelming victory in 1936, the Liberty League died an unlamented death in 1940.

[*See also* **New Deal; Prohibition;** *and* **Roosevelt, Franklin Delano.**]

BIBLIOGRAPHY

Craig, Douglas B. *After Wilson: The Struggle for the Democratic Party, 1920–1934*. Chapel Hill: University of North Carolina Press, 1992.

Wolfskill, George. *The Revolt of the Conservatives: A History of the American Liberty League, 1934–1940*. Boston: Houghton Mifflin, 1962.

Douglas B. Craig

AMISTAD CASE

In 1839, in violation of Spanish law, Spanish slave traders transported over 40 enslaved Africans to Cuba. Here they were transferred to another vessel, the *Amistad*. After a mutiny led by an African named Cinque from the Mendi tribe in Nigeria, the blacks seized the vessel and ordered the surviving crew members to return to Africa. Instead, a U.S. warship seized the vessel off Long Island and towed it to New London, Connecticut. Spain demanded the return of the mutineers to Cuba for trial; the *Amistad's* owners, citing Pinckney's Treaty of 1795 between the United States and Spain, demanded the return of the vessel and its cargo, including the Africans.

Abolitionists formed an *Amistad* committee and hired lawyer Roger Baldwin to defend the Africans. A federal judge in Hartford declared the blacks free, since the slave traders' action had been illegal, and instructed President Martin Van Buren to return them to Africa. Van Buren, however, who favored extraditing the slaves to Cuba for trial, did not comply. On appeal, the case went to the U.S. Supreme Court, headed by Chief Justice Roger B. Taney.

The former president, John Quincy Adams, arguing for the defense, declared that, based on the Declaration of Independence, the *Amistad* mutineers were free persons and justified in defending their freedom. In an 1841 decision written by Justice Joseph Story (*United States v. The Amistad*), the high court ruled for the defense, finding that Pinckney's Treaty did not apply and that since Spain had banned the slave trade, the Africans had been enslaved illegally. Abolitionists, although pleased, had hoped for a broader ruling based on natural law. Private contributions financed the slaves' return to Africa. Although the Taney Court in the 1857 *Dred Scott* decision eroded the impact of the *Amistad* verdict, it nevertheless stands as a historic milestone in the struggle against slavery and racial oppression.

[*See also* **Antislavery Movement; *Scott v. Sandford*; Story, Joseph; Taney, Roger B.;** *and* **Van Buren, Martin.**]

BIBLIOGRAPHY

Jones, Howard. *Mutiny on the Amistad.* New York: Oxford University Press, 1987.

Zeinert, Karen. *The Amistad Slave Revolt and American Abolition.* North Haven, Conn.: Linnet Books, 1997.

Carolyn Williams

ANARCHISM

Anarchist rejection of centralized government and preference for direct democracy and voluntary associations are deeply rooted in the American historical experience. Idealization of nature as an alternative to the depravity of modern civilization runs equally deep, as in the work of Henry David Thoreau, for example.

Most native-born, individualist anarchists of the nineteenth century shared the Jeffersonian preference for artisans and small farmers over an industrial economy. Some tried to supplant the state with utopian communities. Benjamin Tucker (1854–1939), whose journal *Liberty* (1881–1908) espoused total individual sovereignty, illustrates this tradition. Also an anarchist, Tucker rejected violence and favored education to spread his ideas.

The Haymarket affair of 1886 was a watershed event marking the shift from individualist to European-inspired collectivist and revolutionary anarchism associated with such figures as the Russian Mikhail Bakunin (1814–1876). The Haymarket affair, in which eight men (mostly German immigrants) were condemned on little evidence for complicity in the throwing of a bomb at an anarchist-sponsored labor rally that killed seven Chicago policemen, galvanized the anarchist movement. The Russian-Jewish immigrant Emma Goldman, editor of *Mother Earth* (1906–1917), dated her conversion to the cause from this event. The execution of labor organizer Joe Hill in 1915 and of Sacco and Vanzetti in 1927 furnished further martyrs for the movement. At the same time, these events, as well as Alexander Berkman's attempted assassination of Carnegie Steel executive Henry Clay Frick during the 1892 Homestead lockout and the assassination of President William McKinley in 1901, linked anarchism with terrorism in most Americans' minds. In 1903, Congress barred "persons opposed to all organized governments" from entering the United States.

The Industrial Workers of the World (IWW), founded in 1905, was part of a trend away from terrorism and toward organizing anarchist unions. The IWW enjoyed some success organizing miners and textile workers, but government repression during and after World War I took its toll. IWW leader Bill Haywood was imprisoned and in 1921 fled to Bolshevik Russia, following Goldman, Berkman, and others already deported as radicals.

The counterculture of the 1960s showed the persistence of many anarchist values: direct democracy, back-to-nature communalism, alternative education, sexual liberation, and opposition to war and the draft. After the 1960s, radical environmentalists such as Earth First! demonstrated anarchists' preference for direct action, and anarchafeminists exposed the patriarchal nature of power.

[*See also* **Sacco and Vanzetti Case.**]

BIBLIOGRAPHY

Avrich, Paul. *The Modern School Movement: Anarchism and Education in the United States.* Princeton, N.J.: Princeton University Press, 1980.

Avrich, Paul. *Anarchist Portraits.* Princeton, N.J.: Princeton University Press, 1988.

De Leon, David. *The American as Anarchist: Reflections on Indigenous Radicalism.* Baltimore: Johns Hopkins University Press, 1978.

Richard D. Sonn

ANTHONY, SUSAN B.

(1820–1906), women's rights activist. Born in Adams, Massachusetts, Susan Brownell Anthony was influenced by her father's Quakerism, as well as his independence in marrying Lucy Read, a Baptist. When his business failed in 1837, Susan became a teacher. She never married and was a lifelong believer in the importance of self-support for women. In 1851 she met Elizabeth Cady Stanton and became a passionate subscriber to Stanton's women's rights ideas. The partnership of Stanton and Anthony sustained American feminism for the next half a century. Starting in 1854 they focused on the denial of basic economic rights to married women. For six years, Anthony collected petitions to the New York state legislature, which in 1860 passed its comprehensive Married Women's Property Act. Simultaneously, she worked for the American Anti-Slavery Society, viewing women's rights and abolitionist sentiments as closely related. In 1863 she and Stanton collected nearly half a million women's signatures petitioning Congress to abolish slavery.

After the Civil War, following the lead of the antislavery movement, Stanton and Anthony concentrated on equal citizenship and political rights for women. They tried but failed to convince Congress to include women in the Fourteenth and Fifteenth Amendments. Now committed to a focus on political equality and on the Constitution as the source of such rights, they formed the National Woman Suffrage Association in 1869, precipitating a split with Lucy Stone and other women's rights activists who were not willing to break with longtime abolitionist and Republican Party allies. For the next half a decade, Stanton and Anthony advanced the argument that the Fourteenth Amendment included women when it bestowed federal citizenship on "all persons born or naturalized in the United States." Because the vote was, they contended, a fundamental right of citizenship, woman suffrage was already constitutional. Accordingly, in November 1872, Anthony performed the most famous act of her life: she convinced election officials to allow her to vote for president. For this the U.S. District Court found her guilty of illegal voting and fined her $100, which she refused to pay. Three years later, in 1875, the U.S. Supreme Court ruled against the suffragists' line of argument.

From this point on, Anthony realized the necessity of a separate woman suffrage amendment and dedicated herself to that goal. In 1876 she presented a militant women's Declaration of Rights at the Fourth of July ceremonies held at the Centennial Exposition in Philadelphia. In 1880 she began to compile and publish the multivolume *History of Woman Suffrage*, an act of historical consciousness unequaled in American reform. In 1890 she oversaw the unification of the suffrage movement, split since 1869, and the election of Stanton as the first president of the National American Woman Suffrage Association. In 1892, Anthony succeeded Stanton as president. Throughout the 1890s, despite advancing age, Anthony traveled to California, Kansas, South Dakota, and Colorado to work for state suffrage referenda, and she traveled to England and France to organize suffragists internationally. She retired in 1900. By the time the Nineteenth Amendment passed in 1920, no name was more identified with woman suffrage than that of Susan B. Anthony.

[*See also* **Antislavery Movement; Civil Rights; Constitution; Fifteenth Amendment; Fourteenth Amendment; Nineteenth Amendment; Stanton, Elizabeth Cady;** *and* **Woman Suffrage Movement.**]

BIBLIOGRAPHY

Barry, Kathleen. *Susan B. Anthony: A Biography of a Singular Feminist.* New York: New York University Press, 1988.

Sherr, Lynn. *Failure Is Impossible: Susan B. Anthony in Her Own Words.* New York: Times Books, 1995.

Ellen C. DuBois

ANTI-COMMUNISM

Anti-Communism was one of the most significant forces in twentieth-century American politics. Although its enemies saw anti-Communism as dictating U.S. foreign and domestic policy, anti-Communists viewed themselves as a derided minority ignored by decision makers dedicated to policies of coexistence and détente that legitimized Communist totalitarianism.

American anti-Communism emerged from the Palmer raids: the roundup of alien Communists organized in December 1919 and January 1920 by J. Edgar Hoover, then a 25-year-old Justice Department attorney, with the backing of Attorney General A. Mitchell Palmer. From these raids arose a tradition of countersubversive anti-Communism rooted in the conviction that a Red network linked the American reform movement to the Communist International in Moscow. Also thanks to the Palmer raids, all American anti-Communists, in a guilt-by-association process, were identified with conspiracy-hunting countersubversives eager to smear groups and ideas they hated.

In reality, anti-Communism reflected the diversity of American society; its activists brought to the movement the distinct and often antagonistic interests of the communities that produced them. Countersubversive anti-Communists like Hoover, Hamilton Fish, Martin Dies, Richard M. Nixon, Joseph McCarthy, and Robert Welch of the John Birch Society, who regarded Soviet espionage and government subversion as the essence of the Communist threat, were the most vocal. Far more numerous, however, were responsible anti-Communists possessing accurate knowledge about domestic and foreign Communism and sincerely concerned about the threat it posed to their own communities, the nation, and the world. This group included Catholics like Father Edmund Walsh of Georgetown University, Patrick Scanlon, editor of the *Brooklyn Tablet,* Francis Cardinal Spellman, and William F. Buckley Jr.; New Deal Era liberals like the theologian Reinhold Niebuhr and Arthur Schlesinger Jr.; Jewish anti-Communists of such varied political convictions as Louis Marshall of the American Jewish Committee, George Sokolsky of the Hearst newspaper chain, and Norman Podhoretz of *Commentary;* socialists like Abraham Cahan of the *Forward;* labor-union officials like Samuel Gompers, David Dubinsky, Sidney Hillman, George Meany, and Albert Shanker; and black anti-Communists such as the columnist George Schuyler. The press tycoon Henry R. Luce, publisher of *Time, Life,* and *Fortune* magazines, represented another powerful anti-Communist voice. Ex-Communists and ex–fellow travelers like Whittaker Chambers, Sidney Hook, Eugene Lyons, and Jay Lovestone were especially important for the insights and experience they brought to the movement. United only in their hatred of Communism, these individuals often warred as fiercely among themselves as against the common enemy.

American anti-Communism exerted its greatest influence during the late 1940s and early 1950s, when it provided the moral and intellectual basis for the containment policies that underlay the Western alliance against the Soviet Union and other Communist regimes. During those Cold War years, anti-Communists created a widespread grassroots movement that mobilized millions of Americans in opposition to Soviet policies. The mass base of American anti-Communism was weakened, however, by the collapse of McCarthy's irresponsible career in 1954. After that, outspoken anti-Communism was often equated with the right-wing extremism of demonized groups like the John Birch Society and blamed for the disastrous policies of the John F. Kennedy, Lyndon B. Johnson, and Richard Nixon administrations in Southeast Asia.

Moribund by the late 1970s, anti-Communism enjoyed a remarkable revival during the Ronald Reagan Administration, led by a president whose anti-Communist career began as a labor-union leader in Hollywood. Under Reagan, anti-Communists from Walt Rostow and Paul Nitze's Committee on the Present Danger directed an anti-Communist foreign policy aimed at dismantling what Reagan termed the Soviet Union's "Evil Empire." The collapse of that empire brought to an end the momentous history of American anti-Communism. The debate over its role in American history, however, showed no sign of abating.

[*See also* **Buckley, William F., Jr.; Communist Party USA; Hoover, J. Edgar; House Un-American Activities Committee; McCarthy, Joseph; Nixon, Richard M.; Reagan, Ronald;** ***and*** **Rosenberg Case.**]

BIBLIOGRAPHY

Haynes, John Earl. *Communism and Anti-Communism in the United States: An Annotated Guide to Historical Writings.* New York: Garland, 1987.

Haynes, John E. *Red Scare or Red Menace.* Chicago: Ivan R. Dee, 1996.

Heale, M. J. *American Anticommunism: Combating the Enemy Within, 1830–1970.* Baltimore: Johns Hopkins University Press, 1990.

Newsletter of the Historians of American Communism, 1982–present.

O'Reilly, Kenneth. *Hoover and the Un-Americans.* Philadelphia: Temple University Press, 1983.

Powers, Richard Gid. *Not without Honor: The History of American Anticommunism.* New York: Free Press, 1995.

Richard Gid Powers

ANTI-FEDERALISTS

The Anti-Federalists opposed ratification of the Constitution as it was written in 1787. They felt the Constitution transferred too much power to the federal government, that it did not explicitly protect citizen rights, and that it would not ensure adequate representation of the people. The depth and reasoning behind their objections varied greatly. The mildest Anti-Federalists were satisfied by the promise that amendments would be considered during the First Congress. The document's staunchest opponents believed that there was a conspiracy of the wealthy afoot that would destroy self-government in America.

Many important political leaders and average citizens opposed ratification. For instance, the ruling party in New York State, led by Governor George Clinton, adamantly disliked the document. Virginia was closely divided on ratification, with revolutionary stalwart Patrick Henry being its most prominent opponent. In Massachusetts Samuel Adams initially led opposition before bowing to the wishes of his Boston constituency. In general, coastal areas tended to favor the Constitution because it promised to limit trading barriers between states. The Constitution was frequently disliked in areas with high concentrations of small farmers who did not rely heavily on the coastal trade. There were exceptions, as in Rhode Island, which took the most adamant stance of any state against ratification.

Familiar understandings of political theory galvanized opposition. The French writer Montesquieu had written convincingly in *The Spirit of the Laws* that popular governments would operate more effectively in small republics with a common culture. Many other political and legal theorists warned against the concentration of political power and the need for a separation of powers. Anti-Federalists frequently cited these arguments. Interests were also involved in the positions taken. New York was financing its state government through import tariffs. The Constitution promised to nationalize that revenue stream. Southerners feared the North's ability to curtail slavery; Northerners disliked the concessions given to slave states.

The Anti-Federalists were more widely dispersed than the Federalists, few newspapers circulated where they were strong, and they suffered from seeming to defend the discredited Articles of Confederation. Ratification occurred quickly in several states where opposition to the Constitution was weak or clearly outnumbered. Beginning with Massachusetts, the process became more difficult. Federalists allowed recommended amendments to be approved there to secure ratification. Several other states followed this practice, including Virginia. Because of this concession a sufficient number of states agreed to ratify for the Constitution to become legally valid. Eventually New York Anti-Federalists engineered approval so they did not lose the national capital. However, they called for a second constitutional convention. Only after the new government was operational did North Carolina and Rhode Island agree to join the Union.

Former Anti-Federalists fared poorly in the first federal elections. The First Congress was tempted to ignore the suggested amendments from the ratification process, but James Madison insisted that those guaranteeing citizen rights be considered, shoring up the legitimacy of the new government. Thus the Anti-Federalists contributed indirectly to the shape of the Constitution through the addition of the Bill of Rights, although it did not address their structural concerns about the new government. Anti-Federalists remained active in politics and became an indispensible part of the Jeffersonian coalition that took control of the national government after the election of 1800.

[*See also* **Articles of Confederation; Bill of Rights; Constitution;** *and* **Jefferson, Thomas.**]

BIBLIOGRAPHY

Cornell, Saul. *The Other Founders: Anti-Federalists and the Dissenting Tradition in America, 1788–1828*. Chapel Hill: University of North Carolina Press, 1999.

Siemers, David J. *Ratifying the Republic: Antifederalists and Federalists in Constitutional Time*. Stanford, Calif.: Stanford University Press, 2002.

David J. Siemers

ANTI-MASONIC PARTY

The Anti-Masonic Party arose in New York in response to the 1826 disappearance of William Morgan, a Mason. His lodge was suspected of murdering him in revenge for his publication of the organization's secrets. When state and local officials, mostly proto-Democrats, procrastinated in the investigation, angry citizens formed a political party and in 1827 won several New York legislative seats. By 1829 Anti-Masonry had spread throughout much of the Northeast, with its greatest political impact in Pennsylvania. Between 1828 and 1838, Anti-Masons elected 76 candidates to Congress. In 1832, Anti-Masonic Party candidates won 10 percent of all House races, and the party's presidential candidate, William Wirt, carried Vermont and won almost 8 percent of the popular vote nationally.

Anti-Masons owed some of their popularity to the religious revivalism of the 1820s. The role of economic factors is more problematic. Whereas some studies show that the party had the support of the emerging middle class, others indicate that economically declining groups voted for it. By 1836, most Anti-Masons had joined the Whig Party because Democratic President Andrew Jackson had vigorously defended the Masonic order. In addition, Anti-Masons opposed his Sunday mail transportation policies. Anti-Masons gave the Whigs an evangelical, populist dimension, as well as gifted leaders and political operatives such as Thaddeus Stevens of Pennsylvania and Thurlow Weed of New York. Anti-Masonry inspired social policies favored by Whigs, such as liquor and sabbatarian legislation, funding of educational and reformatory institutions, and to some extent the antislavery impulse of the party's Northern wing.

[*See also* **Prohibition;** *and* **Whig Party.**]

BIBLIOGRAPHY

Goodman, Paul. *Towards a Christian Republic: Antimasonry and the Great Transition in New England, 1826–1836*. New York: Oxford University Press, 1988.

Holt, Michael F. *Political Parties and American Political Development from the Age of Jackson to the Age of Lincoln*. Baton Rouge: Louisiana State University Press, 1992.

Kutolowski, Kathleen S. "Antimasonry Reexamined: Social Bases of the Grassroots Party." *Journal of American History* 71 (1984): 269–293.

Lex Renda

ANTI-MISCEGENATION LAWS

Anti-miscegenation statutes (or "miscegenation laws") prohibited marriage, and in some cases cohabitation, between persons defined by the law as "white" or "Caucasian" and those identified by the law as members of other codified racial categories. The ways in which these laws constructed such racial categories changed over time, but the legal regime was consistently designed to promote white supremacy. Anti-miscegenation laws deprived relationships between whites and "nonwhites" of the basic legal protections afforded to marital relations between whites, including the inheritance of property and the legitimacy of the couple's children. Anti-miscegenation laws often combined such civil consequences with criminal penalties including fines, corporal punishment, and significant terms of imprisonment for both members of the prohibited relationship.

From the colonial period until the laws were declared unconstitutional in 1967, all but eight states had anti-miscegenation laws in some form at some time. The earliest such laws in the American colonies bolstered slavery. The first anti-miscegenation law, enacted in 1664, legalized permanent slavery in Maryland and also prohibited marriage between free Englishwomen and "negro" slaves. The definitions of prohibited racial groups in various states proliferated as immigration created a more diverse American population, encompassing Chinese, Filipino, South Asian, and Japanese. The enforcement of such laws generally favored the property rights of whites. For instance, bans against marriage between "Indians" and whites were not commonly enforced in frontier states until the late nineteenth century, after intermarriage between settlers and Native Americans had helped to transfer land ownership to whites.

For a brief period during Reconstruction, several former Confederate states repealed or declared unconstitutional their anti-miscegenation laws in the wake of the Fourteenth Amendment. However, in *Pace v. Alabama* (1883), the U.S. Supreme Court ruled that the Fourteenth Amendment allowed such laws, provided that the punishment was the same for each violator of the law, regardless of race. The development of this legal theory, known as "equal application," in combination with the loss of Republican political power, turned the tide. By 1894, all Southern states once again had anti-miscegenation laws. Over time, some states narrowed the definition of white, for instance, from less than one-fourth nonwhite ancestry to none at all (in the language of such laws, not "one drop" of "negro blood"). People who had been defined as white became "black" by a legislative *fiat* (decree) that also had the power to invalidate their marriage.

Anti-miscegenation laws began to lose their grip on American legal and political thought for the last time in the mid-twentieth century. Between 1948, when a landmark California Supreme Court decision struck down that state's anti-miscegenation statute, and early1967, anti-miscegenation laws were abandoned everywhere except in sixteen Southern states. The U.S. Supreme Court in *McLaughlin v. Florida* (1964) rejected the equal application theory by ruling that Florida's treatment of interracial cohabitation as a crime was itself "invidious discrimination forbidden by the Equal Protection Clause," but expressly reserved the question of whether bans on interracial marriage could be valid (379 U.S. 184, 192 (1964)). In 1967, the U.S. Supreme Court struck down the remaining anti-miscegenation laws. In that opinion, *Loving v. Virginia,* a unanimous court held that a restriction of marriage based on a racial classification violates both the equal protection and the due process clauses of the Fourteenth Amendment.

[*See also* **Reconstruction; Slavery, Laws;** *and* **Supreme Court, U.S.**]

BIBLIOGRAPHY

Pascoe, Peggy. *What Comes Naturally: Miscegenation Law and the Making of Race in America*. Oxford, UK: Oxford University Press, 2009.

Wallenstein, Peter. *Tell the Court I Love My Wife: Race, Marriage, and Law—An American History*. New York: Palgrave, 2002.

Rebecca Schoff Curtin

ANTINUCLEAR MOVEMENT

In 1953, President Dwight Eisenhower announced the "Atoms for Peace" program that heralded a national commitment to nuclear energy. By 1960, the first commercial nuclear reactor, Yankee Rowe in Massachusetts, went online. Despite safety concerns and a partial nuclear meltdown in Detroit in 1967, it was not until the 1970s that a strong antinuclear movement arose in the United States.

The antinuclear movement of the 1970s resulted from a growing national commitment to nuclear power in response to the energy crisis. The early opposition came from "legal interveners" such as Ralph Nader's Critical Mass '74, which challenged individual nuclear reactor projects before the Atomic Energy Agency (later the Nuclear Regulatory Commission). These legal challenges failed to stop the growth of the nuclear industry.

In 1974, Sam Lovejoy, a 1960s radical then living on a commune, brought direct action protest to the nuclear debate when he toppled most of a five-hundred-foot meteorological tower at the site of a proposed nuclear plant in Montague, Massachusetts. Lovejoy's trial became a rallying point for a local referendum to shut down the Montague plant. (Lovejoy was acquitted on a technicality.) Organized labor, wracked by unemployment, took the lead in support of the Montague plant, which voters supported 52 to 48 percent. The Montague plant was never built.

The antinuclear movement drew many of its arguments from John Gofman's influential book, *Poisoned Power*. Activists emphasized the dangers of low-level radiation, the threat of core reactor meltdown, the difficulty of evacuation, and the vulnerability of nuclear plants to terrorist attack. In 1976 antinuclear referenda were narrowly defeated in several states, including a fiercely contested vote in California.

The watershed event in the growth of the antinuclear movement was the founding of the Clamshell Alliance and the series of protests against the proposed nuclear plant at Seabrook, New Hampshire, culminating in the arrest of 1,414 activists in May 1977. The mass arrests taxed the state's infrastructure, and protesters were dispersed among six New Hampshire armories for two weeks.

The spectacular action at Seabrook generated national news coverage and soon antinuclear alliances modeled on the Clamshell Alliance sprouted up across the nation, such as the Abalone Alliance in California and the Oyster Shell Alliance in Louisiana. In 1979 the movement held a star-studded "No Nukes" concert at Madison Square Garden featuring Bruce Springsteen, Jackson Brown, and Bonnie Raitt.

The near meltdown at Three Mile Island in March 1979 intersected with growing public doubts to bring an end to the era of nuclear expansion. The burgeoning nuclear weapons freeze movement soon eclipsed the antinuclear energy movement. In the 1980s, New York governor Mario Cuomo successfully stopped the completed Shoreham Nuclear Power Plant from going online. Massachusetts governor Michael Dukakis was unsuccessful in a similar bid to stop the Seabrook nuclear plant.

The early twenty-first century has witnessed a rebirth of the antinuclear movement in the face of a "nuclear renaissance." The movement has been influential in Vermont, where the Senate voted against relicensing the Vermont Yankee plant in 2010.

[*See also* **Eisenhower, Dwight D.**]

BIBLIOGRAPHY

Bedford, Henry F. *Seabrook Station: Citizen Politics and Nuclear Power*. Amherst: University of Massachusetts Press, 1990.

Epstein, Barbara. *Political Protest and Cultural Revolution: Nonviolent Direct Action in the 1970s and 1980s*. Berkeley: University of California Press, 1991.

Price, Jerome. *The Antinuclear Movement*. Boston: Twayne Publishers, 1982.

Price, Jerome, and Robert Surbrug Jr. *Beyond Vietnam: The Politics of Protest in Massachusetts, 1974–1990*. Amherst: University of Massachusetts Press, 2009.

Wellock, Thomas R. *Critical Masses: Opposition to Nuclear Power in California, 1958–1978*. Madison: The University of Wisconsin Press, 1998.

Robert Surbrug Jr.

ANTI-SALOON LEAGUE

The Anti-Saloon League was the most successful Prohibition organization in the United States, playing the key role in the passage of the Eighteenth Amendment to the Constitution, which prohibited the manufacture and sale of beverage alcohol. Howard Russell, an Ohio Oberlin-educated Congregationalist minister, founded the Ohio Temperance Society in 1893. Two years later, in 1895, the organization merged with other prohibitionist organizations to form the Anti-Saloon League. Believing that the partisan efforts of the Prohibition Party could not have a significant impact, Russell envisioned a nonpartisan group that would adopt the organizational efficiency that characterized successful corporations. The League was a latecomer to the Prohibition effort in America, but in its structure and its methodology it represents one of the first modern political interest groups.

The Anti-Saloon League enlisted the support of sympathetic clergy and politicians, with little regard to denominational or partisan affiliations. Despite the importance of American women in the temperance movement throughout the nineteenth century, the League did not welcome women into leadership roles. Russell and his colleagues supported local option efforts, statewide Prohibition referenda, and politicians sympathetic to their cause; however, they did not make a case against personal use of alcoholic beverages. Instead, their focus on the evils of the saloon as an institution rather than on individual behavior provided the League with a broad base of support. Even Americans who drank could be enlisted in a campaign against the saloon, with its associations with poverty, crime, and vice.

Under the leadership of Wayne Wheeler, a veteran of the Ohio campaigns, the League compiled voter rolls, recruited sympathetic clergy, and lobbied and campaigned for and against politicians at every level of government. These efforts paid off in the first decade of the twentieth century, as states, particularly those in the South and Midwest, began to adopt strict local option restrictions on the sale of alcohol. Statewide Prohibition was enacted in the new state of Oklahoma in 1907, after effective lobbying from the League. Eighteen more states adopted statewide Prohibition before 1917.

On the national level, the League's first major lobbying success came with the passage of the 1913 Webb–Kenyon Act, which made it a federal crime to import alcohol into any state in violation of that state's prohibition statutes.

That same year the leadership of the League announced their support of a federal Prohibition amendment. This marked a policy shift for the Anti-Saloon League because national Prohibition certainly would have an impact on individual drinking choices. The Congress elected in 1914 did not include a sufficient number of supporters, so the League redoubled its efforts in advance of the 1916 elections. The new Congress included a greater number of dry members, and with the increasing support for Prohibition after America's entry into the World War, Congress submitted the Eighteenth Amendment to the states on 18 December 1917. Ratification was accomplished on 16 January 1919. Wayne Wheeler, popularly known as the nation's "dry boss," was instrumental in drafting the legislation that became the Volstead Act, which provided the enforcement mechanism of the amendment until 1933, with the ratification of the Twentieth Amendment and the repeal of Prohibition. Despite the abandonment of Prohibition, the Anti-Saloon League remained a model for lobbying efforts in the decades that followed.

[*See also* **Prohibition.**]

BIBLIOGRAPHY

Blocker, Jack S. *American Temperance Movements: Cycles of Reform*. Boston: Twayne Publishers, 1989.

Kerr, K. Austin. *Organized for Prohibition: A New History of the Anti-Saloon League*. New Haven, Conn.: Yale University Press, 1985.

James Ivy

ANTISLAVERY MOVEMENT

The American antislavery crusade was a multifaceted, long-term social reform movement that persisted from the mid-eighteenth century through emancipation in 1864. Over the years, the movement evolved from religious protest and colonization efforts to political organization, abolitionism, violent protest, and, finally, emancipation.

Beginnings of Antislavery Agitation. Antislavery originated as a moral and religious issue. Various Protestant denominations—Mennonites and Amish, Presbyterians, Congregationalists, Baptists, and the Society of Friends (Quakers)—all contributed, with Quakers the early leaders. Eighteenth-century Quakers George Keith, John Woolman, and Anthony Benezet each attacked slavery on the basis of moral principle: namely, the equality of all persons before God. Among Baptists, local associations resolved to oppose the extension of slavery; some writers even called for its abolition. By the second decade of the nineteenth century, religious activists had formed antislavery societies that held public meetings and distributed literature to raise consciousness about the moral issues involved.

An early effort to achieve the progressive elimination of slavery was the African colonization movement. As a "gradualist" compromise between the moral issue of human bondage and the racial prejudices of white society, national leaders like Bushrod Washington, Thomas Jefferson, James Monroe, and Henry Clay advocated manumitting (freeing) slaves and returning them to Africa, with the costs—including compensation to the owners—to be paid from a combination of public and private funds. The American Colonization Society, established in 1817, founded Monrovia (later Liberia) on the West African coast in 1822 as a colony for freed slaves. By 1860, some 12,000 African Americans had returned to Africa. The colonization movement stirred hostility, however, from Southerners opposed to manumission, from those who disapproved of spending public monies on the project, and from persons truly interested in the slaves' well-being, who saw repatriation to Africa as simply a further injustice to persons of color.

By the late 1820s, rising public indignation in the North, called by some "ultraism," strengthened antislavery sentiments. Local societies began to appear, particularly in New England. Leaders like Lewis and Arthur Tappan in New York City, William Lloyd Garrison in Boston, and Theodore Dwight Weld in Ohio founded a national organization, the American Anti-Slavery Society (AAS), in 1833. Garrison, regarded as a fanatic by some and, worse yet, an incendiary by others, brought to the cause a sense of urgency, a genuine threat to slaveholders, and an uncompromising periodical, *The Liberator,* founded in 1831. An organizational genius, Garrison created a system whereby paid AAS agents fanned out across the North to lecture, debate, distribute tracts, sell *Liberator* subscriptions, and assist free blacks and fugitive slaves wherever possible. Through the AAS, the antislavery leadership combined careful planning and organization with the zeal of an evangelical religious crusade. Among the most effective AAS lecturers were the Grimké sisters of South Carolina, Sarah and Angelina, who had embraced Quakerism and moved to the North. In 1839 the Grimkés and Weld (whom Angelina had married) published *American Slavery as It Is,* a powerful documentary record of brutal abuses.

The religious dimension of antislavery found expression as well in the ministry of the Charles G. Finney and at two Ohio schools founded in 1833: Lane Theological Seminary in Cincinnati and Oberlin College. Lane, a Presbyterian school, was situated in close proximity to a large population of free blacks. Its faculty and students included many antislavery firebrands, and a series of public lyceum debates soon gave Lane such a reputation as a hotbed of activism that in 1834 the trustees forbade further discussion of the matter. Fifty-one Lane students, called "the Rebels," withdrew and enrolled at Oberlin, an antislavery center where Finney was professor of theology. Through various forms of ministry and activism, Oberlin students and faculty infused the antislavery cause with new energy and momentum, making the college one of the movement's major leadership resources.

The Turn to Politics. In 1840, Theodore Dwight Weld, the Tappan brothers, and other antislavery leaders turned to political organization. They were encouraged by the British Parliament's abolition of slavery throughout the British Empire in 1833. Forming the Liberty Party (also known as the Human Rights Party), they nominated James G. Birney, a slaveowner turned abolitionist, for president. In part a reaction against Garrison (who was displaying increasingly radical and anarchist tendencies), the Liberty Party stressed natural rights and political action. In 1840, too, these same individuals founded the American and Foreign Anti-Slavery Society, which challenged Garrison for leadership of the movement. (The issue of equality for women in the antislavery campaign, which Garrison supported and more conservative antislavery leaders opposed, figured in this split as well.) Although Birney received only about 7,000 votes, his candidacy brought national attention to the antislavery cause—and sharpened the proslavery defenses of Southern whites. Running again in 1844, Birney received 62,300 votes.

Congress's defeat in 1846 of the Wilmot Proviso (a resolution barring slavery in any territories other than Texas acquired in the Mexican War), coupled with the failure of either national party to take an unequivocal stand against slavery, further energized the effort to oppose slavery at the ballot box. In 1848 the Free Soil Party took up the antislavery banner, nominating former president Martin Van Buren on a platform opposed to the expansion of slavery into the territories, summed up in the slogan "Free Soil, Free Labor, Free Men." Although Van Buren ran third behind the Whig Party candidate Zachary Taylor (who won) and the Democrat Lewis Cass of Michigan, he did garner nearly 300,000 votes. Within a few years, many Free Soil voters would join the new Republican Party, a coalition of antislavery enthusiasts, religious leaders, and former Whigs.

Abolitionism. Meanwhile, "abolition" had become the cry of the more ardent antislavery advocates and "action-men." Radical activity ensued. Abolitionists flooded the South with inflammatory pamphlets. Free Northern blacks and escaped slaves like Frederick Douglass, William Wells Brown, and William and Ellen Craft played an important role in the movement. Douglass became a major abolitionist spokesman, particularly with the publication of his *Narrative of the Life of Frederick Douglass, an American Slave* (1845). Abolitionists organized and operated the so-called Underground Railroad, a complex network of antislavery households that spirited runaway slaves to the North and West, the Caribbean, and Canada. The 1850 Fugitive Slave Act, a victory for slaveholders, heightened abolitionist fervor and directly inspired the most famous of all antislavery works, Harriet Beecher Stowe's 1852 novel *Uncle Tom's Cabin.* The Kansas–Nebraska Act (1854) and the Supreme Court's Dred Scott (*Scott v. Sandford*) decision (1857), representing further victories for the Slave Power, added fuel to the abolitionist cause. Most radical of all were the ultraists like John Brown, who were prepared to wage armed conflict to achieve their objectives. Brown's career of antislavery violence, first in Kansas and then at Harpers Ferry, Virginia, in 1859, won the support of Douglass and other prominent abolitionist leaders. Within two years the Civil War, which would finally end slavery in America, was underway.

From its inception, the antislavery movement benefited greatly from the evangelical energies unleashed in the Second Great Awakening and from the many voluntary associations generated within the Protestant community. Countless antislavery leaders and supporters had roots in the evangelical missionary and revivalist traditions, and many also participated in other reform arenas, from Anti-Masonry and adventism to the temperance and women's rights movements. Such leading women's rights advocates as Lucretia Mott, the Grimké sisters, and Elizabeth Cady Stanton got their start in the antislavery movement. Antislavery was the first great human rights crusade in American history. A sustained campaign lasting more than a century, it not only helped bring about the emancipation of the slaves, but also inspired a long tradition of social reform.

[*See also* **American Colonization Society; Anti-Masonic Party; Brown, John; Clay, Henry; Douglass, Frederick; Emancipation Proclamation; Free Soil Party; Fugitive Slave Act; Jefferson, Thomas; Kansas–Nebraska Act; Liberty Party; Monroe, James;** ***Scott v. Sandford;*** **Van Buren, Martin;** ***and*** **Wilmot Proviso.**]

BIBLIOGRAPHY

Abzug, Robert. *Passionate Liberator: Theodore Dwight Weld and the Dilemma of Reform.* New York: Oxford University Press, 1980.

Friedman, Lawrence J. *Gregarious Saints: Self and Community in American Abolitionism.* Cambridge; New York: Cambridge University Press, 1982.

Kradotir, Aileen S. *Means and Ends in American Abolitionism: Garrison and His Critics on Strategy and Tactics, 1834–1850.* Chicago: Ivan R. Dee, 1989.

Perry, Lewis, and Michael Fellman, eds. *Antislavery Reconsidered: New Perspectives on the Abolitionists.* Baton Rouge: Louisiana State University Press, 1979.

Staudenraus, P. J. *The African Colonization Movement, 1816–1865.* New York: Octagon Books, 1961.

Stewart, James B. *Holy Warriors: The Abolitionists and American Slavery.* New York: Hill and Wang, 1976.

Walters, Ronald G. *The Antislavery Appeal: American Abolitionism after 1830*, 1978.

Wyatt-Brown, Bertram. *Lewis Tappan and the Evangelical War against Slavery.* Cleveland: Case Western Reserve University Press, 1969.

Yellin, Jean Fagan. *Women & Sisters: The Antislavery Feminists in American Culture.* New Haven, Conn.: Yale University Press, 1989.

William H. Brackney

ANTITRUST LEGISLATION AND LAW

Opposition to concentrated corporate power occupies a noteworthy if ambiguous place in American history. Ever since Congress passed the Sherman Antitrust Act of 1890, public consensus supported antitrust values in principle, even as repeated disputes arose over their application in particular cases. Such inconsistency paralleled the nation's unfolding experience with big government and managerial capitalism; the shifting significance of small business and organized labor; the growing importance of economic experts; and the central policy-making role of lawyers and courts, particularly the U.S. Supreme Court. A popular faith in competition governed antitrust development. What "competition" meant, however, and who benefited, were subject to change.

Gilded Age Beginnings. The antitrust movement originated as managerial capitalism burgeoned near the end of the nineteenth century. Following the Civil War, technological innovation and mass marketing fostered the development of large-scale corporate combinations, leading to a separation between owners and managers. In this new form of corporate enterprise, managers increasingly acted as the principal decision makers. The rise of big business spawned corporate mergers as well as loose cartel arrangements and other trade restraints. (A cartel is a secret agreement among supposedly competing businesses to establish a monopoly by price fixing or other means.) Although some states successfully limited both forms of combination, New Jersey enacted a law in 1889 permitting the formation of holding companies and facilitating the formation of corporate combinations controlled by managers. Because the New Jersey law conflicted with other states' laws, its critics demanded federal action.

The Sherman Act was a product of countervailing market and political pressures. Small business and farm groups, eager to limit the growth of large corporate combinations, supported federal action in principle. Big business interests and their lawyers, by contrast, were divided over the possible results of a more uniform national antitrust policy. Fearing that federal power might be used against it, organized labor opposed federal antitrust legislation. Popular opinion, at the time and ever since, reflected these divergent sentiments. Americans profoundly distrusted giant concentrations of corporate wealth and power, although at the same time they yearned for the consumer benefits that bigness often seemed to facilitate; people were also anxious about the apparent lack of legal accountability of huge, "soulless" corporations. Congress responded to those conflicting desires and interests with a law embodying several general provisions: Section 1 of the Sherman Act banned "[e]very contract, combination or conspiracy" that restrained interstate or foreign trade of commerce; Section 2 prohibited individual firms from monopolization and attempted monopolization. The act's enforcement relied upon the state and federal courts. Federal or state prosecutors, as well as private litigants, could win treble damages by proving violations of the law.

The Sherman Act's general provisions invited diverse interpretation. During the first decade of the law's operation, the Supreme Court encouraged corporations to adopt the holding company approach. (A holding company is a corporation that owns a controlling share of the stock of one or more other firms.) In 1895 the high court held that the E. C. Knight Company, a holding company that monopolized sugar production in the United States, did not violate the antitrust law. The Supreme Court and state courts also decided, however, that loose cartel practices were illegal under both the Sherman Act and state laws. The Court's simultaneous enforcement of rules against cartel practices and its toleration of holding companies facilitated a great turn-of-the-century merger wave. By 1903 most of the nation's largest firms were holding companies in which decisions were generally left to managers. Meanwhile, the Supreme Court and lower federal judges increasingly applied the Sherman Act against organized labor, enabling employers to defeat strikes and boycotts.

The Progressive Era. After 1900, demands for stricter antitrust enforcement increased. In the Northern Securities Case (1904), Theodore Roosevelt's administration became the first to successfully prosecute a holding company. This victory brought an end to the first merger wave. Federal officials, corporate leaders, economists, Wall Street lawyers, and Supreme Court justices soon concluded that a more flexible "rule of reason" should govern merger cases. Adopting a rule of reason as the basic doctrine governing merger cases, the Supreme Court in 1911 struck down predatory pricing practices that Standard Oil and American Tobacco were using to crush smaller firms.

Louis Brandeis, a prominent lawyer who championed small business and opposed big corporations, favored employing the rule of reason to allow for loose collusion among small enterprises, while urging the breakup of giant corporations. In taking this position, Brandeis adopted an Americanized version of European cartel policy. But in 1911 the Supreme Court frustrated Brandeis's hopes, outlawing loose cartel arrangements even among smaller companies.

Woodrow Wilson's victory in the 1912 presidential election brought the enactment of two new antitrust laws. The Federal Trade Commission Act of 1914 created an administrative agency with broad powers to prevent "unfair methods of competition." The terms "unfair" and "competition" remained sufficiently general, however, that judicial interpretation was inevitable. Similarly, the 1914 Clayton Act included provisions condemning the anticompetitive implications of price discrimination, exclusive arrangements, interlocking directorates, and stock-purchase mergers, particularly holding companies. The Clayton Act also contained language that seemed to prohibit injunctions against labor. However, the Supreme Court construed both laws so narrowly that the advocates of more vigorous antitrust enforcement grew frustrated. The Justice Department prosecuted single-firm monopolies; oligopolistic competition among a few managerially centralized big corporations characterized most leading industries. Still, the federal government's persistent prosecution of price-fixing violations did enhance competitive opportunities for small businesses. Farmer cooperatives and exporters, by contrast, benefited from antitrust legislation.

The New Deal Era and Beyond. As the twentieth century progressed, antitrust legislation achieved mixed results. The Norris–LaGuardia Anti-Injunction Act of 1932 decisively exempted labor organizations from the antitrust laws. Yet following the early New Deal's unsuccessful experiment with federally authorized cartelization under the National Recovery Administration, antitrust enforcement became more vigorous. Small business benefited from various fair-trade laws. In antitrust cases heard by the Supreme Court under Chief Justice Earl Warren (1953–1969), the Court favored smaller business as it curtailed many horizontal and vertical mergers. Simultaneously, however, corporate managers created conglomerates of competitively unrelated firms joined together primarily for investment purposes. The Hart–Scott–Rodino Act of 1976 added antitrust provisions that permitted the Justice Department's Antitrust Division to pursue a more proactive policy against mergers with antitrust implications. The Supreme Court's and the Antitrust Division's embrace of free-market theories during Ronald Reagan's administration in the 1980s, however, turned the Hart–Scott–Rodino Act to the benefit of new forms of financially driven vertical mergers. The court, moreover, expanded the application of the rule of reason to permit what previously had been treated as clear-cut violations of the antitrust laws. By the 1990s a reaction against the more extreme free-market enthusiasm of the 1980s arose, creating new possibilities for the future of antitrust enforcement.

Bringing antitrust law into the computer age, the Department of Justice won a landmark case against the software giant Microsoft in 2000. Microsoft appealed, however, and the final outcome remained uncertain.

[*See also* **Brandeis, Louis; Federal Government, Executive Branch: Department of Justice; Federal Trade Commission; National Recovery Administration; New Deal; Northern Securities Case; Progressive Era;** ***and*** **Supreme Court, U.S.**]

BIBLIOGRAPHY

Fligstein, Neil. *The Transformation of Corporate Control.* Cambridge, Mass.: Harvard University Press, 1990.

Freyer, Tony. *Regulating Big Business: Antitrust in Great Britain and America, 1880–1990.* Cambridge; New York: Cambridge University Press, 1992.

May, James. "Antitrust in the Formative Era: Political and Economic Theory in Constitutional and Antitrust Analysis, 1880–1918." *Ohio State Law Journal* 50 (1987): 257–395.

McCraw, Thomas K. *Prophets of Regulation: Charles Francis Adams, Louis D. Brandeis, James M. Landis, and Alfred E. Kahn.* Cambridge, Mass.: Belknap Press of Harvard University Press, 1984.

Peritz, Rudolph J. R. *Competition Policy in America, 1888–1992.* New York: Oxford University Press, 1996.

Sklar, Martin J. *The Corporate Reconstruction of American Capitalism, 1890–1916: The Market, the Law, and Politics.* Cambridge; New York: Cambridge University Press, 1988.

Tony A. Freyer

ANTIWAR MOVEMENTS

Organized opposition has accompanied most American wars. Sometimes dissent came from broader peace movements, which sought to supplant national wars with internationalism and nonviolent resolution of conflict, but peace advocates often supported particular wars. Sometimes war resistance derived from pacifism, understood as the repudiation of organized violence, but pacifists in that sense usually dissented as individual conscientious objectors (COs) or withdrew into sectarian communities. Sometimes opposition came from political, class, or sectional interests that were reinforced by broad principles.

In the nineteenth century, an organized and growing peace movement called for the arbitration of international disputes, but opposition to particular wars primarily reflected sectional and class interests. Thus, New Englanders who belonged to the Federalist Party, motivated by economic and political interests, challenged the constitutional legitimacy of the War of 1812. Similarly, the Mexican War was challenged in the North, where interest in western expansion reinforced antislavery principles. Opposition to the Civil War in the border states and the Ohio River valley fused local economic and cultural interests with a principled defense of states' rights. Finally, the U.S. subjugation of the Philippines in 1899–1901 was opposed mainly by members of a cultural elite who believed that the war was eroding the anticolonial foundations of U.S. foreign policy. A few absolute pacifists resisted all those wars, but regional interests or class-based opposition predominated.

This pattern changed during World War I. During the period of U.S. neutrality, 1914–1917, a principled opposition formed against any increase in military budgets and against any intervention in the European struggle. The strongest, most political antiwar group, the American Union against Militarism (1915), mobilized progressives to challenge both Woodrow Wilson's preparedness budget and his subsequent break with Germany. After U.S. entry into the war, opposition continued among many religious COs, progressive pacifists, and antiwar socialists like Eugene V. Debs, as well as within some ethnic communities, especially Irish Americans. The ostracizing and persecution of dissenters only strengthened their organizational ties, so that the principle of war resistance emerged from the war upheld by such groups as the Fellowship of Reconciliation (FOR, 1915) and the War Resisters League (WRL, 1923). Some, like the American Friends Service Committee (1917), had a progressive orientation, and all of them, especially the Women's International League for Peace and Freedom (1919), were related to international networks. Thus, the organizational base was created for a recurrent antiwar movement.

Given the prevailing antiwar mood of post–World War I society, these organizations found ready constituencies for political activism against military spending and military training in the schools, as well as for constructive internationalism. In the 1930s they spearheaded support for legislative measures calling for strict neutrality and, after 1939, lobbied against so-called collective-security programs. They were joined and eventually led by the socialist leader Norman Thomas in the Keep America Out of [the European] War Organization. From the political right came support from the isolationist America First movement and from the far left (until Germany invaded Bolshevik Russia in June 1941) the Communist Party. Organized opposition to war virtually dissolved after the attack on Pearl Harbor.

The institutional framework of war resistance remained, however, and the WRL especially came to harbor a number of COs who objected to both war and conscription. Steeped in Gandhian principles, they experimented with nonviolent direct action in the prisons and Civilian Public Service (CPS) camps housing conscientious objectors. Nonviolence was also applied to race relations during and after World War II. Further developed in both the civil rights movement and the antinuclear protest movements of the 1950s, nonviolent direct action and civil disobedience were frequently employed tactics among opponents of the Vietnam War after 1965.

Opposition to the Vietnam War, scarcely visible during the period of initial involvement and escalation, eventually became widespread. Antiwar activism was often spontaneous and local. Nonetheless, shifting national coalitions also provided focal points for public antiwar information and agitation. The most visible forms of activism were mass demonstrations, large-scale civil disobedience, and countercultural images; less public, but at least as important, was quiet, hard work in electoral and legislative politics. The Vietnam Veterans against the War organization (1967) helped to legitimize antiwar activism. By 1970 antiwar sentiment pervaded national institutions, including Congress; by 1972 it was dominant.

Adopting similar strategies in the post–Vietnam War era, a Latin American Solidarity movement helped to check the Ronald Reagan Administration's support of the "Contras" in Nicaragua and of military regimes elsewhere in Central America. An effective Washington lobby mobilized legislative opposition to the U.S.-sponsored Contra war. Simultaneously, a decentralized, grassroots citizens' movement made contact with Nicaraguans and Salvadorans and publicized their causes. The Persian Gulf War of 1991 stirred considerable opposition, which was ultimately ineffectual and aborted, given the brevity of the campaign.

There was considerable opposition to the 2001 Afghanistan War in the United States and the United Kingdom. Opposition was organized in the United States and internationally in the form of protests by various antiwar organizations that went on to organize much larger protests against the 2003 Iraq War.

The antiwar position gained renewed support and attention in the buildup to the 2003 invasion of Iraq by the United States and its allies. Many people staged mass protests across the world in the immediate prelude to the invasion, and demonstrations and other forms of antiwar activism have continued throughout the occupation. The primary opposition within the United States to the continued occupation of Iraq has come from the grassroots level. Opposition to the conflict, how it had been fought, and complications during the aftermath period divided public sentiment in the United States. Antiwar groups protested during both the Democratic National Convention and the 2008 Republican National Convention held in St. Paul, Minnesota, in September 2008. After the election of Barack Obama in 2008, the antiwar movement appeared to die down, although American involvement in Iraq and Afghanistan continued.

In summary, recurrent antiwar activism—grounded in a continuous peace movement; marked by ever shifting organizational bases, tactics, and philosophies; and growing or waning in relation to prevailing issues—has frequently been a factor influencing foreign and military policy making, especially in twentieth-century America.

[*See also* **Conscientious Objection; Debs, Eugene; Peace Movements;** ***and*** **Thomas, Norman.**]

BIBLIOGRAPHY

Chatfield, Charles. *The American Peace Movement: Ideals and Activism.* New York; Toronto: Twayne Publishers; Maxwell Macmillan Canada, 1992.

DeBenedetti, Charles. *The Peace Reform in American History*. Bloomington: Indiana University Press, 1980.
DeBenedetti, Charles, and Charles Chatfield. *An American Ordeal.* Syracuse, N.Y.: Syracuse University Press, 1990.
Early, Frances. *A World without War: How U.S. Feminists and Pacifists Resisted World War I.* Syracuse, N.Y.: Syracuse University Press, 1997.
Howlett, Charles. *The American Peace Movement: References and Resources.* Boston: G. K. Hall, 1991.
Morison, Samuel Eliot, Frederick Merk, and Frank Freidel. *Dissent in Three American Wars.* Cam bridge, Mass.: Harvard University Press, 1970.
Wittner, Lawrence. *Rebels against War: The American Peace Movement, 1933–1983.* Philadelphia: Temple University Press, 1984.

E. Charles Chatfield and Pearson Bramblett

ARMY–McCARTHY HEARINGS

On 22 April 1954, a huge crowd packed the Senate Caucus Room for the opening session of the Army–McCarthy hearings. At least 40 million people followed the action on radio and television. In a narrow sense, the hearings focused on two distinct questions: First, did Republican Senator Joseph McCarthy of Wisconsin and his top aide, Roy M. Cohn, exert improper pressure on the U.S. Army to win preferential treatment for Private G. David Schine, a part-time member of McCarthy's staff who had been drafted the previous year? Second, did army officials use Schine as a "hostage" in an effort to sabotage McCarthy's ongoing investigation of "Communist influence" in the armed forces?

In a larger sense, however, the issues ranged from the threat of domestic subversion to the constitutional separation of powers, from the integrity of the military to McCarthy's political future. As chairman of the Senate Committee on Government Operations and its powerful Subcommittee on Investigations, McCarthy had generated enormous publicity by charging that Communists infested the government, including the U.S. Army. In response, military officials claimed that Cohn had threatened to "wreck the army" through reckless investigations if his close friend Schine did not receive special favors, such as extra weekend passes and an assignment near Washington.

The controversy infuriated President Dwight D. Eisenhower, a five-star general, who deeply resented McCarthy's public assaults upon army personnel. It was Eisenhower who convinced Senate Republicans to televise the hearings, thereby bringing the senator into the living rooms of millions of Americans who had never seen his behavior at close range. McCarthy's day-to-day performance, marred by petulant outbursts and crude personal attacks, amply confirmed his critics' portrait of him as a bully and a fraud. The highlight of the hearings occurred on 9 June, when army counsel Joseph Welch berated the senator—"Have you no sense of decency, sir?"—to thunderous applause. The hearings ended on 17 June. In December, the Senate censured McCarthy for bringing that body "into dishonor and disrepute." Although McCarthy remained in office until his death in 1957, the Army–McCarthy hearings effectively ended his political career.

[*See also* **Anti-Communism; Eisenhower, Dwight D.;** *and* **McCarthy, Joseph.**]

BIBLIOGRAPHY

Oshinsky, David M. *A Conspiracy So Immense: The World of Joe McCarthy*. New York; London: Free Press, Collier Macmillan, 1983.
Straight, Michael. *Trial by Television*. Boston: Beacon Press, 1954.

David M. Oshinsky

ARTICLES OF CONFEDERATION

On 7 June 1776, Richard Henry Lee of Virginia moved in the Second Continental Congress that the 13 American colonies declare their independence from Great Britain and that Congress establish a committee to draft articles of confederation to bind the colonies together. Five days later, Congress created such a committee composed of one delegate from each colony with John Dickinson of Pennsylvania as chair. Congress approved the final version of the Articles of Confederation on 15 November 1777 and sent the document to the states for ratification. On 9 July 1778, delegates from eight states signed the Articles. Maryland, the last state to ratify, did so on 1 March 1781, at which time Congress declared "the Confederation of the United States" completed and perpetual.

The Articles provided for a unicameral Congress with no separate executive or judiciary. Congress, which could act only on the states, not on individuals, was to be elected annually in a manner determined by each state legislature. States could send up to seven delegates, with a minimum of two delegates needed for a state to be represented officially. Despite wide differences in population, each state had but one vote.

Congress had the sole power of determining war and peace, sending and receiving ambassadors, negotiating treaties, settling boundary disputes between states, regulating coinage, borrowing money, managing affairs with Indians, establishing and regulating a post office, regulating the army and navy, appointing courts for the trial of piracy and felonies on the high seas, and dealing with cases concerning captured ships. The vote of nine states was required for most important matters. Congress did not have the power to regulate foreign or interstate commerce, to levy and collect taxes, or to raise an army. It could only request the states to pay their share of federal expenses and supply soldiers for the Continental army.

Canada was specifically allowed to join the confederation, but all other colonies needed the approval of nine states to enter. Every state was to abide by the determination of Congress on questions delegated to Congress by the Articles, and the Articles were to be inviolably observed by every state. Amendments to the Articles had to be ratified by the legislature of every state.

Even before adoption of the Articles, Congress observed most of their provisions. The British military danger encouraged the states to meet their obligations to Congress. After peace returned, however, the Articles' inherent weakness became apparent and, after several attempts to strengthen Congress by amending them failed because of the unanimity requirement, a Constitutional Convention was called in 1787 to revise the Articles. In one of its first acts, the Convention voted to abandon the Articles altogether and draft a new constitution.

Congress under the Articles had three great successes: it obtained an advantageous peace treaty ending the Revolutionary War, it acquired a huge public domain from state cessions of their western lands, and it enacted the Northwest Ordinance, which established the pattern for the administration of federal territories.

[*See also* **Constitution; Constitutional Convention of 1787; Federalism; Northwest Ordinance; States' Rights;** *and* **Taxation.**]

BIBLIOGRAPHY

Jensen, Merrill. *The Articles of Confederation: An Interpretation of the Social-Constitutional History of the American Revolution, 1774–1781.* Madison: University of Wisconsin Press, 1940.

Morris, Richard B. *The Forging of the Union, 1781–1789*. New York: Harper & Row, 1987.
Rakove, Jack N. *The Beginnings of National Politics: An Interpretive History of the Continental Congress*. New York: Alfred A. Knopf, 1979.

John P. Kaminski

ASIAN AMERICANS

From governors and U.S. senators to city council members and state supreme court chiefs, Asian Pacific Americans are becoming more visible actors in the grand theater of American politics. Along with a growing number of elected officials, Asian Pacific Americans have also greatly enhanced their political infrastructure in recent years with increased numbers of registered voters, more campaign donors, and an array of advocacy and civil rights groups. Their future political impact is highly promising.

The Growth of Asian American Political Participation. Large-scale immigration from Asia since the Immigration Act of 1965 has dramatically influenced politics on the local, state, and national levels. From a predominantly U.S.-born group of 1.5 million in 1970, Asian Pacific Americans have grown and diversified and become a largely foreign-born population of over 16 million in 2011. Projections estimate that the number of Asian Pacific Americans will continue to increase to over 20 million by 2020.

Political scientists and commentators have speculated about whether Asian Pacific Americans will become a major new force in American electoral politics, perhaps akin to Jewish American, because of their dramatic demographic growth and concentration in certain key electoral states like California, New York, Texas, and New Jersey. Many believe that if Asian Pacific Americans, like Jewish American voters, come to represent a proportion of the electorate that is comparable to, if not greater than, their share of the total population then they could become a highly influential "swing vote" in critical local, state, and presidential elections. In California, for example, if the nearly 5 million Asian Pacific Americans, who are one in eight residents of the state, also became one in eight voters, they could play a strategically important role in national and local elections. Indeed, their voting potential, coupled with other attractive dimensions of their political infrastructure like their campaign fund-raising capabilities and their extensive network of community-based organizations, could elevate Asian Pacific Americans to the status of important actors in American electoral politics.

During the past three decades, there has been an unmistakable increase in the representation of Asian Americans in electoral politics. In 1978, for example, when the first edition of the *National Asian Pacific American Political Almanac* was published, it listed several hundred elected officials, who held offices primarily in Hawai'i, California, and Washington. Almost all were second- and third-generation Asian Americans, with the vast majority being Japanese Americans. In contrast, the 2011–2012 edition of the political almanac lists over three thousand Asian Pacific American elected and major appointed officials in thirty-nine different states, as well as the federal government. Although most continue to be second or third generation like former Hawai'i Governor Ben Cayetano and current South Carolina Governor Nikki Haley, a growing number of recently elected politicians have been immigrants and refugees. Examples include the former Franklin Township, New Jersey, Mayor Upendra J. Chivukula, who became the first Asian American and Indian American elected to the New Jersey State Assembly; City Councilman

Tony Lam of Westminster, California, who was the first Vietnamese American elected to public office; and City Councilman Chanrithy Uong of Lowell, Massachusetts, who was the first Cambodian American elected official.

These increasing levels of electoral participation and representation are all the more remarkable when they are considered in the context of the historical legacy of disenfranchisement of Asian Pacific Americans in relation to the American electoral system. Early Asian immigrants in the nineteenth and twentieth centuries were disenfranchised and excluded from fully participating in key sectors of American life because of a plethora of discriminatory laws and policies ranging from the Chinese Exclusion Act of 1882 to *Ozawa v. United States* (1922), which forbade Asian immigrants from becoming naturalized citizens. These legal barriers prevented early Asian immigrants from participating in electoral politics of any form and substantially delayed the development of electoral participation and representation by Asian Pacific Americans until the second and subsequent generations during the post World War II period. Although the national news media have oftentimes touted Asian Pacific Americans as America's "model minority"—a label that Asian Pacific American leaders and scholars have disputed because of its simplistic implication that other minority groups can overcome racial and other discriminatory barriers by following their example—this reputed success has disguised their historic lack of access and influence in the nation's most significant political and social decision-making arenas and institutions.

Asian Pacific Americans in American and International Politics. Electoral politics has become an increasingly significant focus of attention, but it represents only one of several major forms of political participation that have been and continue to be pursued by Asian Pacific Americans. First, Asian Pacific Americans have long been concerned about and affected by events, issues, and relationships, which are international in nature, particularly as they relate to their ancestral homelands or countries of origin. They have been active transnational participants in major revolutionary, nationalistic, and independence movements that have emerged in Asia and the Pacific Islands and have sought to contribute to subsequent national development efforts in their homelands. They also have been affected to a greater extent than other American immigrant groups by the dramatic shifts in bilateral relations between the United States and their homelands like the World War II internment of 120,000 Japanese Americans or the thwarting of leftist activities among Chinese and other Asian Pacific Americans during the McCarthy era and other "Cold War" periods in American history.

Asian Pacific Americans, like other American racial groups, have engaged in an array of nonelectoral political activities to advance or protect their group interests. Asian Pacific Americans have been active participants in labor-organizing efforts in the Far West, Hawai'i, New York, and the Rocky Mountain states and indeed were at the forefront of creating labor unions for agricultural workers in California and Hawai'i. Like other racial minorities, Asian Pacific Americans also have a long history of seeking social justice and equal treatment by continuously engaging in legal challenges against discriminatory laws and practices in education, employment, housing, land ownership, immigration, and other significant public policy issue areas, and many of their legal cases such as the *Lau v. Nichols* (1974) bilingual education law suit have become landmark U.S. Supreme Court civil rights decisions.

Impact of the Number and Diversity of Asian Pacific Americans on Politics. The Asian Pacific American population has undergone dramatic demographic transformations during the past four decades, which have greatly augmented their numbers and led to their increased internal heterogeneity. These demographic trends have had and will continue to have a significant impact on their political participation.

Asian Pacific Americans are the country's fastest growing group, having nearly doubled during each of the past four decades from 1.5 million nationally in 1970 to 3.5 million in 1980 to 7.2 million in 1990 and 12 million in 2000. In 2011, there were 16 million Asian Pacific Americans, representing about 5 percent of the nation's population.

Asian Pacific Americans also dramatically shifted from being largely American born to predominantly foreign born, as a result of an upsurge in international migration. Sixty-three percent of all Asian Pacific Americans in 2000 were foreign born, with 80 percent of the Vietnamese, 73 percent of the Koreans, 64 percent of the Filipinos, 75 percent of the Asian Indians, and 69 percent of the Chinese having been born outside the United States. Only the Japanese Americans, with 27 percent foreign born, had more native born. In contrast, 40 percent of the Hispanic/Latino population and 11 percent of all residents of the country were foreign born. Recent population projections estimate that the percentage of foreign-born Asian Pacific Americans will remain in the majority for several decades to come.

There have also been significant changes in the relative representation of different ethnic and national groups within the rapidly evolving Asian Pacific American population. For example, in 1970, Japanese Americans were the largest Asian American ethnic group and represented 40 percent of all Asian Americans. By 1980, both Chinese Americans and Filipino Americans surpassed Japanese Americans; other Asian Pacific American groups such as Asian Indian Americans, Korean Americans, and Vietnamese Americans grew rapidly through immigration. By 1990, both Chinese American and Filipino American populations had grown to be nearly twice as large as that of Japanese Americans, who experienced relatively little immigration from Japan and a gradually declining birth rate. The other three major Asian Pacific American groups—Asian Indian Americans, Korean Americans, and Vietnamese Americans—also recorded substantial population gains by 1990. By 2000, Japanese Americans fell further down the population rankings, with all other major Asian Pacific American groups outnumbering them. Chinese Americans were the largest group, followed in order by Filipino Americans, Asian Indians, Vietnamese Americans, Korean Americans, and then Japanese Americans. By 2008, Asian Indians surpassed Filipino Americans to become the second largest group after the Chinese Americans.

California has the largest population of Asian Pacific Americans, numbering 5 million in 2011, or greater than 30 percent of the Asian Pacific Americans in the United States. They now outnumber the state's African American population and are second to the rapidly growing Latino populace, which continues to be California's single largest population of color. New York and Texas now have the second and third largest Asian Pacific American populations, with Hawai'i being fifth. By 2009, New Jersey had the fourth largest Asian Pacific population, surpassing Hawai'i, which had the largest Asian Pacific American population in 1970.

The Asian Pacific American population should not be conceptualized as a single, monolithic group. It has become an extremely heterogeneous population with respect to ethnic and national origins, cultural values, generations, social classes, religions, and other socially differentiating characteristics. According to the 2000 U.S. Census, the term "Asian and Pacific Islanders" encompasses over twenty-five different ethnic groups, all with their unique cultures and histories of migration and settlement in the United States. At the same time, within any particular Asian Pacific American group like Chinese Americans, the internal, within-in group differences can be quite pronounced, reflecting different historical waves of immigration, major social class sectors, and religious and other significant differentiating preferences like religion.

The combination of unprecedented demographic growth, along with extraordinary internal diversification, has a number of implications for Asian Pacific American electoral participation. Asian Pacific Americans have come to represent an increasingly sizable proportion of the population in certain states, most notably California. With this population increase, specific urban areas like Los Angeles, New York, and San Francisco have become critical policy areas for Asian Pacific Americans, whereas previously such areas were seldom able to consider political issues and concerns requiring the support of large population groups that could make claims for fair political representation through redistricting and other remedies. This population growth has also spurred a number of campaigns organized by grassroots organizations and the major political parties to encourage Asian Pacific immigrants and refugees to exercise their right of franchise by becoming naturalized citizens, registering to vote, and finally casting their votes during elections. In this manner, the proportion of Asian Pacific American voters may approach or exceed their share of the overall population nationally, as well as in different states and municipalities.

Their unusual internal heterogeneity will continue to challenge the different Asian Pacific American sectors and communities to find common ground on key policy issues, to cope with the uneven political development and maturation of different ethnic groups, and to seek effective mechanisms for pursuing their shared interests in a unified manner on both a continuous and ad hoc manner. Although this may appear visionary, there are a number of examples from the past four decades, be it in terms of their concerted lobbying activities against university admissions quotas, anti-Asian violence, or unfair immigration policy legislation, to illustrate the reality and necessity of such collective endeavors. Finally, it is highly likely that the pan-ethnic concepts of "Asian American" or "Asian Pacific American," which have been imbued with constantly changing strategic, ideological, and tactical connotations since they were first articulated in the 1960s, will undergo further reconsideration in the future.

[*See also* **Immigration Law and Policy: After 1930.**]

BIBLIOGRAPHY

Aoki, Andrew, and Okiyoshi Takeda. *Asian American Politics*. Cambridge: Polity, 2008.

Chang, Gordon. *Asian Americans and Politics: Perspectives, Experiences, Prospects*. Washington, D.C.: Woodrow Wilson Center Press, 2001.

Lien, Pei-Pliyoshi Takeda, M. Margaret Conway, and Janelle Wong. *The Politics of Asian Americans: Diversity and Community*. New York: Routledge, 2004.

Nakanishi, Don T., and James S. Lai. *Asian American Politics: Law, Participation, and Policy*. Lanham, Md.: Rowman & Littlefield, 2003.

Nakanishi, Don T., and James Lai (eds). *National Asian Pacific American Political Almanac*, 14th ed. Los Angeles: The Center, 2011.

Don Toshiaki Nakanishi

ASSISTED SUICIDE POLICY

Assisted suicide, the act of aiding or abetting a person to kill himself or herself, did not emerge as an issue of policy debate in the United States until the second half of the twentieth century. In the wake of their war of independence from British rule, most of the former American colonies ended criminal penalties for suicide, but over the next 150 years state courts and legislatures criminalized the act of helping someone to commit suicide.

In the first half of the twentieth century, a small group of U.S. social reformers launched a movement in favor of legalizing euthanasia—taken from the Greek word for "good death"—but they tended to seek freedom from legal penalties for physicians who administered lethal injections to dying or disabled patients, not the decriminalization of assisted suicide. To euthanasia supporters it was more important to empower physicians treating the chronically ill and dying than patients who might wish to put themselves out of their own pain and misery.

A series of significant events and trends during the Cold War transformed assisted suicide into a contentious policy issue. More and more Americans were becoming aware that they stood to live longer than their ancestors because of improvements in public health and the introduction of life-sustaining medical technologies. Longer life expectancy, however, raised the prospect of Americans enduring prolonged pain and infirmity as they aged. A groundswell of support for patients' rights to determine end-of-life care began in the 1960s, coinciding with similar campaigns to win rights for African Americans, gays, and other minorities. The women's health movement overlapped the emerging patients' rights movements as women activists demanded franker, less authoritarian relationships with their doctors, as well as shared decision making when it came to treatment. The U.S. Supreme court decisions in *Griswold v. Connecticut* (1965) and *Roe v. Wade* (1973), striking down state laws against contraception and abortion, respectively, also established that there was a constitutional right to privacy, which in the eyes of many Americans ought to extend to death and dying.

The shift in emphasis to expanded rights for patients led to the 1967 introduction of the living will, an advance directive specifying what kinds of treatments a dying patient would want. Invoking the right to privacy, ethicists advocated freedom from unwanted end-of-life medical care, reflected in the hospice movement that arose in the 1950s and implemented spiritual counseling and better pain management for terminally ill patients. In 1972 the U.S. Senate Special Committee on Aging held hearings that conveyed the impression that the dying process at the hands of organized medicine diminished patient dignity and quality of life.

In the face of these fast-moving events, the euthanasia movement reorganized and began endorsing physician-assisted suicide (PAS), in which a doctor provides the suicidal patient with lethal drugs. The first group in U.S. history to openly back PAS was the Hemlock Society, a grassroots, mainly West Coast organization founded in 1980. Poll after poll in the 1980s and 1990s showed that a majority of Americans agreed with Hemlock's position that the legalization of voluntary PAS expanded patients' privacy and choices.

In the 1980s acquired immune deficiency syndrome (AIDS), a deadly, disfiguring disease that tended to kill slowly and painfully, wreaked havoc among young gay men, whose rates of assisted suicide were much higher than average. Public sympathy for AIDS sufferers helped to persuade some Americans that PAS should be legalized.

The 1990s proved to be a tumultuous decade in the history of assisted suicide. Jack Kevorkian, stripped of his license to practice medicine in 1991 by the state of Michigan, gained notoriety for helping dozens of his patients kill themselves, although some were not terminally ill. In 1994 Oregon became the first state to enact legislation permitting PAS, but by then PAS faced concerted opposition from various groups, including the Right-to-Life Movement. Defeats of the pro-PAS movement in Michigan, California, Maine, Hawai'i, Wyoming, and Vermont reflected the political clout of the anti-euthanasia forces. In 1997 President Bill Clinton prohibited the use of federal funds to cause a patient's death. Perhaps most importantly, in 1997 the U.S. Supreme Court ruled that there was no constitutional right to die, although it also ruled that individual states were free to pass their own end-of-life legislation. Denied a sweeping court decision in their favor, PAS supporters were faced with the daunting task of fighting campaigns state by state.

In the early twenty-first century, the policy debate over assisted suicide has steadily become enmeshed in bitter partisan politics. In 2006 a U.S. appeals court blocked an attempt by President George W. Bush's administration to prohibit Oregon doctors from helping terminally ill patients commit suicide. In 2008 Washington became the second state to permit PAS, and in 2009 the Montana Supreme Court ruled that PAS was not "against public policy" in Montana, although it declined to state that PAS was a constitutional right guaranteed by Montana's constitution. Meanwhile polls indicated that the American public was now split fairly evenly over PAS. This stalemate in public opinion suggested that as the twenty-first century unfolded the debate over PAS would prove to be as divisive and heated as ever.

[*See also* **Bush, George W.; Clinton, William J.; Constitution;** ***Griswold v. Connecticut; Roe v. Wade; and*** **Supreme Court, U.S.**]

BIBLIOGRAPHY

Dowbiggin, Ian. *A Merciful End: The Euthanasia Movement in Modern America*. New York and Oxford: Oxford University Press, 2003.

Dowbiggin, Ian. *A Concise History of Euthanasia: Life, Death, God, and Medicine*. Lanham, Md.: Rowman & Littlefield, 2006.

Filene, Peter G. *In the Arms of Others: A Cultural History of the Right to Die in America*. Chicago: Ivan R. Dee, 1998.

Lavi, Shai J. *The Modern Art of Dying: A History of Euthanasia in the United States*. Princeton, N.J.: Princeton University Press, 2005.

Lewis, Milton J. *Medicine and Care of the Dying: A Modern History*. New York and Oxford: Oxford University Press, 2007.

Ian Dowbiggin

ATOMIC ENERGY COMMISSION

The Atomic Energy Commission (AEC), made up of five members appointed by the president of the United States, was created by Congress in 1946. Establishing the principle of civilian control of atomic energy, Congress assigned the new agency responsibility for developing and testing nuclear weapons and for encouraging peaceful uses of the new technology. David E. Lilienthal (1899–1981), a former director of the Tennessee Valley Authority, became its first chairman. As the Cold War progressed, the agency focused its resources on weapons, expanding the U.S. stockpile, and, after January 1950, undertaking a crash program to build a hydrogen bomb. The agency's military emphasis proved a source of frustration and disappointment for

Lilienthal, whose interests lay in the nonmilitary uses of atomic energy. But Cold War tensions and the still-rudimentary state of the technology prevented major strides in civilian applications.

Although the AEC stood at the center of numerous controversies in its early years, the most divisive occurred in 1954 when it stripped J. Robert Oppenheimer, leader of the scientific effort to build the atomic bomb during World War II, of his security clearance for alleged Communist associations. The chairman of the AEC, Lewis L. Strauss, took the lead, for both personal and political reasons, in ending Oppenheimer's career as a scientific adviser to the AEC. At about the same time the AEC's atmospheric testing of nuclear weapons set off a major public debate over the health effects of the radioactive fallout they produced. The AEC's claims that fallout posed no significant health hazard aroused much dissent, permanently undermining the agency's credibility.

By the mid-1960s, the AEC was devoting increasing attention to promoting the peaceful uses of atomic energy. Its encouragement of the nuclear power industry helped stimulate a boom in reactor construction. But public faith in the AEC was further shaken by its dual mandate to promote and regulate nuclear power. By the early 1970s, controversies over reactor safety, radiation standards, environmental protection, waste disposal, and nuclear weapons proliferation had severely damaged confidence in the AEC. In response to widespread criticism, Congress abolished the AEC in 1974, dividing its functions between the Energy Research and Development Administration (later a part of the Department of Energy) and the Nuclear Regulatory Commission.

[*See also* **Federal Government, Executive Branch: Other Departments; Nuclear Power;** *and* **Nuclear Regulatory Commission.**]

BIBLIOGRAPHY

Hewlett, Richard G., and Francis Duncan. *Atomic Shield, 1947–1952.* University Park: Pennsylvania State University Press, 1969.

Hewlett, Richard G., and Jack M. Holl. *Atoms for Peace and War, 1953–1961.* Berkeley: University of California Press, 1989.

J. Samuel Walker

B

BACON'S REBELLION

This 1676 Virginia uprising, beginning with vigilante actions by frontier residents who opposed Governor William Berkeley's Indian policy, quickly escalated into a struggle that left Berkeley disgraced and the colony tightly in the grip of the Stuart monarchs. The leader, 29-year-old Nathaniel Bacon, a well-born English immigrant with substantial property holdings and close ties to Berkeley, mobilized disgruntled frontier planters, small property holders, white servants, and African slaves against both Indians and the governor.

Although granted a council seat by Berkeley, Bacon shared his wealthy neighbors' conviction that the governor's policies left them vulnerable to Indian attack and excluded from the Indian fur trade. The large planters' discontents, worsened by falling tobacco prices, might have remained confined to name-calling, lawsuits, and duels had not the small property holders also decried Berkeley's alleged failure to protect them from Indians. Under Bacon's leadership, a frontier force disobeyed Berkeley's orders and in April 1676 brutally attacked a nearby settlement of peaceful Susquehannock Indians.

Under challenge, Berkeley called the first election in fifteen years. Bacon won election to the burgesses, Virginia's upper house, but was arrested when he tried to take his seat. Soon released and commissioned by Berkeley to fight Indians, he rallied a force of some 1,300 men for more attacks that killed hundreds of

Indians along the Potomac and Rappahannock Rivers. When Berkeley reversed himself and declared Bacon a traitor, Bacon's army marched on Jamestown, the capital, which they burned on 19 September. As Berkeley raised his own force, the conflict became colonywide, with combatants gutting their opponents' houses and seizing their property.

Bacon's followers complained of overtaxation, political exclusion, religious persecution, and economic restrictions. A handful of influential white women supported Bacon's cause, as did many servants and some 400 slaves who, promised their freedom by the rebels, were the last to surrender to Berkeley's troops. With Bacon's death from dysentery on 26 October and the arrival of a royal commission to investigate the rebellion, the uprising dissipated, leaving Virginia under tighter royal control and in the grip of a conservative reaction that restricted both the public influence of white women and the de facto freedom of enslaved people. Although scholars continue to debate the significance of this short-lived rebellion, there is agreement that this upheaval came just as Virginia fully embraced slavery. Thus might the political wounds left by Bacon's Rebellion have been partially healed, inadvertently or intentionally, by the racial imperatives of slavery.

[*See also* **Indian law, Federal.**]

BIBLIOGRAPHY

Morgan, Edmund. *American Slavery, American Freedom: The Ordeal of Colonial Virginia.* New York: W. W. Norton, 1975.

Washburn, Wilcomb. *The Governor and the Rebel: A History of Bacon's Rebellion.* Chapel Hill: University of North Carolina Press, 1957.

Kathleen M. Brown

BAKER v. CARR

In this 1962, 6-to-2 decision, the U.S. Supreme Court established that the federal courts could decide cases involving the malapportionment of state legislatures. Previously, in *Colegrove v. Green* (1946), the Court held that matters relating to the fair apportionment of state legislative seats were a "political question" that should be considered only by elected officials.

Baker v. Carr involved the wide discrepancy in the numbers of voters living in different state legislative districts in Tennessee, which had ignored a state constitutional provision requiring periodic redistricting. Voters in the less populous rural districts enjoyed disproportionate political power, whereas those in larger urban districts had their voting power diluted and were thus denied the equal protection of the law guaranteed by the Fourteenth Amendment.

By taking the case, and thereby overruling the *Colegrove* decision, the Supreme Court opened the door to litigation to equalize the size of constituencies for all elective offices and established the principle of "one person, one vote." In *Wesberry v. Sanders* (1964), the Court held that U.S. congressional districts within a state must consist of roughly equal populations. The same year, the Court in *Reynolds v. Sims* extended the ruling to both the lower and the upper houses of state legislatures.

[*See also* **Equality; Federalism; Fourteenth Amendment;** ***and*** **Supreme Court, U.S.**]

BIBLIOGRAPHY

O'Brien, David M. *Storm Center,* 2d ed. New York: W. W. Norton, 1990.

Urofsky, Melvin I. *The Continuity of Change*. Belmont, Calif.: Wadsworth, 1991.

Ross K. Baker

BALLINGER–PINCHOT CONTROVERSY

The main actors in this bitter Progressive Era dispute over the future of conservation policy during the presidency of William Howard Taft (1909–1913) were Secretary of the Interior Richard A. Ballinger and Chief Forester Gifford Pinchot. At issue was the federal government's role in overseeing natural resources. From his post in the Department of Agriculture, Pinchot wanted to continue the forest management and coal-land policies of Theodore Roosevelt that involved a large role for the federal government. Under Roosevelt, Pinchot had enjoyed wide discretion in setting priorities about western land, water, and mining issues. Ballinger, a westerner from Seattle, Washington, sought to shift power back to the states and to allow localities to develop their own resources. He also believed that Pinchot had often failed to follow the letter of government policy or to observe appropriate legal procedures.

The resulting controversy spilled into the press in the fall of 1909. Taft's critics argued that he and Ballinger had repudiated the conservation goals of Roosevelt. Spurred by overblown charges against Ballinger provided by Louis Glavis, a Department of the Interior official, Pinchot pressed his case in the newspapers with sensational, exaggerated allegations that Ballinger had approved the sale of valuable coal lands in Alaska to a consortium of Seattle businessmen, who had in turn sold the land to J. P. Morgan and other New York bankers. When Pinchot in January 1910 wrote a public letter criticizing Ballinger to a U.S. senator, Taft fired him. In the congressional inquiry that followed, the Republican majority exonerated Ballinger, and the Democrats sided with Pinchot.

A discredited Ballinger left office in the spring of 1911. The controversy became a decisive element in the split between Roosevelt and Taft that led Roosevelt to challenge Taft for the Republican presidential nomination in 1912 and then to launch his independent candidacy on the Progressive Party ticket.

[*See also* **Federal Government, Executive Branch: Agriculture Department; Federal Government, Executive Branch: Other Departments; Land Policy, Federal; Progressive Era; Progressive Party of 1912; Roosevelt, Theodore; States' Rights;** ***and*** **Taft, William Howard.**]

BIBLIOGRAPHY

Hays, Samuel P. *Conservation and the Gospel of Efficiency: The Progressive Conservation Movement, 1890–1920*. Cambridge: Harvard University Press, 1959.

Penick, James L., Jr. *Progressive Politics and Conservation: The Ballinger–Pinchot Affair*. Chicago: University of Chicago Press, 1968.

Lewis L. Gould

BARUCH, BERNARD

(1870–1965), venture capitalist, investor, and government official. Born in Camden, South Carolina, and reared in New York City, Bernard Mannes Baruch graduated from the City College of New York in 1889. His first job on Wall Street, at the brokerage firm of A. A. Housman & Co., paid $3 a week, but he became a millionaire by the time he was thirty. He was a governor of the New York Stock Exchange, a leader in mining finance, and an occasional investor in properties controlled by the Guggenheim family. Although he did not sell out just before the stock market crash of 1929, as legend has it, he did salvage the bulk of his fortune.

Bernard Baruch's government service came in World War I and World War II. In March 1918, President Woodrow Wilson named him chairman of the War Industries Board. Granted sweeping powers, he effectively marshaled the U.S. economy for war. In 1919, he served in a senior capacity with the U.S. peace delegation at Versailles. During World War II he performed a variety of services, including the drafting of an influential report on rubber rationing. In 1946, President Harry S. Truman named the 75-year-old Baruch to present to the United Nations the U.S. plan for the international control of atomic energy drafted by Dean Acheson and David E. Lilienthal. Despite a dramatic opening speech by Baruch, the negotiations came to naught.

Six feet four inches tall, Baruch was a prototypical twentieth-century celebrity, cultivating his press image as "adviser to presidents" and "park bench statesman." In fact, the advice he eagerly offered a succession of presidents was only selectively accepted. His mastery of public relations is suggested by the fact that the *New York Times* devoted a paragraph-length news story in 1947 to his sprained ankle.

[*See also* **Atomic Energy Commission; Nuclear Power; Truman, Harry S.;** *and* **Wilson, Woodrow.**]

BIBLIOGRAPHY

Grant, James. *Bernard M. Baruch: The Adventures of a Wall Street Legend.* New York: John Wiley & Sons, 1997.

Schwartz, Jordan A. *The Speculator: Bernard M. Baruch in Washington, 1917–1965.* Chapel Hill: University of North Carolina Press, 1981.

James Grant

BILL OF RIGHTS

Dating from 1791, the first ten amendments of the Constitution. Although elements of the Bill of Rights can be traced back to ancient Greece, the Roman Republic, the Bible, medieval Germany, the Reformation, the Renaissance, and the Enlightenment, its more immediate origins are found in English history and in the colonial and revolutionary experiences of Americans themselves. Magna Carta (1215) proclaimed a commitment to limited government and legal process. The seventeenth-century Whig ideology that developed during the struggles against Stuart absolutism in England was revived in the political literature of the American revolutionaries a century later to warn against governmental abuse of power. Both eras ended in monumental enunciations of rights.

Background. English and colonial American rights were rooted in the unwritten doctrines of the Common Law. On rare occasions, usually in response to specific violations of rights by the monarch, Englishmen specified some rights in documents such as Magna Carta, the Petition of Right (1628), the Nineteen Propositions (1642), the Habeas Corpus Act (1679), and the Bill of Rights (1689). Americans in every colony, however, codified their rights in detail in dozens of documents limiting government. The fullest such assertion of rights appeared as early as 1641, in the Massachusetts Body of Liberties. In both England and America, written statements were viewed as tangible manifestations of rights already in existence.

As the movement toward independence advanced, Americans added the natural-rights philosophy to their Common Law foundation of liberty. The Declaration of Independence abandoned the Common Law and based liberty exclusively upon natural rights by stating "these truths to be self-evident, that all men are created equal, that they are endowed by their Creator with certain unalienable Rights, that among these are Life, Liberty and the pursuit of Happiness."

When they created their state constitutions, Americans either prefaced these documents with a bill of rights or incorporated various protections within the body of their constitution. The Massachusetts Declaration of Rights (1780), for example, declared "All men are born free and equal, and have certain natural, essential and unalienable rights." Interpreting this fundamental tenet, the state supreme court declared an end to slavery in Massachusetts.

On occasion, state legislatures protected specific rights thought to be endangered, confirmed earlier enactments of rights, or even enacted full-fledged bills of rights as statutes. All of these guarantees were based upon the social-compact theory in which people surrendered some rights to government but retained certain rights essential to liberty. Government was supposed to protect these retained rights, but frequently during the Revolutionary Era, state legislatures violated their bills of rights with impunity.

Because the Confederation Congress acted directly only on states and not on people, the Articles of Confederation contained no bill of rights. The Northwest Ordinance (1787, reconfirmed in 1789), however, contained a limited bill of rights because Congress could indirectly act on people through its appointed territorial governor, secretary, and judges.

The Constitutional Convention of 1787 included a limited number of specific protections of rights in its draft constitution. Near its conclusion, however, the Convention by a vote of ten states to none defeated a motion to appoint a committee to draft a bill of rights. This omission, which Anti-Federalists asserted endangered liberties, proved to be the single most powerful argument raised against ratifying the Constitution. Federalists maintained that a bill of rights was unnecessary because the federal government would have only delegated powers that would not threaten liberties. In fact, they suggested, an incomplete bill of rights would be dangerous since it would imply the abandonment of rights not listed. Furthermore, the Constitution itself was said to be a bill of rights, especially Article I, Sections 9 and 10, which specifically prohibited the state and federal governments from actions violating rights. Only with the Federalists' promise that amendments to the Constitution, including a bill of rights, would be advocated in the first Congress was ratification achieved.

Despite their promises, most Federalists ran for election to Congress opposed to any immediate amendments. Therefore, although President George Washington endorsed a bill of rights in his inaugural address and James Madison vigorously advocated a bill of rights in the House of Representatives in June 1789, most members of Congress opposed even discussing the matter. Madison, however, persevered and obtained the necessary two-thirds vote to send draft amendments to the Senate. The Senate modified the amendments and eliminated some key provisions, particularly limitations on the states. On 25 September 1789, Congress agreed to twelve amendments, and by 15 December 1791, two years later, the necessary three-quarters of the states had ratified ten of these amendments, which have become known as the Bill of Rights.

Contents of the Bill of Rights. The first eight amendments in the Bill of Rights protect freedom of religion, speech, and the press and the right to petition the government, to assemble, to bear arms, and to be entitled to a jury trial in civil cases. Quartering troops in peacetime and unreasonable searches and arrests are prohibited. Common Law protections are provided in criminal cases including "due process of law" and the right to counsel. Excessive bail and fines and cruel and unusual punishments are forbidden.

The Ninth Amendment provides that the enumeration of certain rights in the Constitution or in subsequent amendments does not deny the existence of other rights that remain with the people. The Tenth Amendment explains that powers not delegated to the federal government by the Constitution are reserved to the states or to the people.

Later Court Rulings and Controversies. In *Barron v. Baltimore* (1833) the U.S. Supreme Court ruled that the Bill of Rights applied only to the federal government, not to state or local governments. The Fourteenth Amendment (1868) added language that allowed later courts, beginning with *Gitlow v. New York* (1925), to apply the federal Bill of Rights to restrict the powers of state and local governments (the doctrine of incorporation). How far this incorporation extends the Bill of Rights is still a matter of debate.

Certain of the amendments in the Bill of Rights have proven particularly contentious and have generated much litigation, judicial interpretation, and public discussion. The First Amendment's ban on an "establishment of religion," coupled with its prohibition against any restrictions on the "free exercise" of religion, has been the basis of many court challenges involving the separation of separation of church and state. Similarly, the First Amendment's guarantee of freedom of speech and freedom of the press has led to numerous judicial pronouncements on issues relating to censorship, obscenity, and attempts to silence political dissidents or to curtail publications deemed seditious or dangerous, particularly in wartime. The Second Amendment's guarantee of "the right of the people to keep and bear Arms" remains deeply controversial, pitting gun-control advocates against individuals and groups such as the National Rifle Association suspicious of any governmental restraints in this area. The Fifth Amendment's "due process" protections, including protection against self-incrimination, have inspired many civil liberties battles and was the basis of the Supreme Court's landmark 1966 decision, *Miranda v. Arizona,* spelling out the rights of persons in police custody. The Tenth Amendment, reserving to the states or to the people "all powers not delegated to the United States by the Constitution," has often been invoked by opponents of "big government" alarmed over what they see as the unwarranted expansion of federal power.

The Fourth Amendment's protection against unreasonable searches and seizures (along with other amendments) has been interpreted by the Courts to protect the right to privacy in cases involving birth control, abortion, and homosexuality.

[*See also* ***Abrams v. United States;*** **Alien and Sedition Acts; Civil Liberties; Civil Rights; Constitution; Constitutional Convention of 1787; Declaration of Independence; Federalist Party; Fourteenth Amendment; Holmes, Oliver Wendell, Jr.; Madison, James; Northwest Ordinance; Sedition; Virginia Declaration of Rights;** ***and*** **Washington, George.**]

BIBLIOGRAPHY

Brant, Irving. *The Bill of Rights: Its Origin and Meaning*. Indianapolis: Bobbs–Merrill, 1965.

Conley, Patrick T., and John P. Kaminski, eds. *The Bill of Rights and the States: The Colonial and

Revolutionary Origins of American Liberties. Madison, Wisc.: Madison House, 1992.

Hall, Kermit L., ed. *By and For the People: Constitutional Rights in American History.* Arlington Heights, Ill.: Harlan Davidson, 1991.

Levy, Leonard W. *Origins of the Bill of Rights.* New Haven, Conn.: Yale University Press, 1999.

Murphy, Paul L. *The Historic Background of the Bill of Rights.* New York: Garland Science, 1990.

Schwartz, Bernard. *The Great Rights of Mankind: A History of the American Bill of Rights.* Expanded ed. Madison, Wisc.: Madison House, 1992.

John P. Kaminski

BIRTH CONTROL

Americans have practiced birth control throughout their history. Women in the Colonial Era, relying on centuries-old techniques, used sponges and suppositories to prevent pregnancy. Traditional folk medicine offered recipes for abortifacient brews of aloes, pennyroyal, and extracts from wild juniper bushes that so poisoned or irritated the system that miscarriages occurred as a side effect. Mechanical abortions, performed without anesthesia or antibiotics, were rare, painful, and dangerous.

The Nineteenth Century. In the nineteenth century, the fertility rate of American women fell from around 7 children per mother in 1800 to 3.5 in 1900. This decline can be attributed to periodic abstinence from sexual intercourse, coitus interruptus (male withdrawal before ejaculation), placing objects in the vagina to create a barrier between the sperm and the uterus, and inducing abortion through drugs or mechanical means. Although all such methods violated official standards of sexual conduct, a few free thinkers began in the 1830s to argue for family limitation to restrict the labor supply and ease the economic burdens of the poor. Also contributing to changing attitudes was the fact that marriage began to be seen as an expression of romantic love rather than merely an economic alliance.

As the century wore on, the declining fertility of native-born white women alarmed social leaders. Francis A. Walker, director of the 1870 U.S. Census, in noting the higher fertility of immigrant newcomers compared with native-born couples, called for restriction on immigration. Concerns about "race suicide" and exhortations to native-born couples of Anglo-Saxon origins to have more children persisted into the Progressive Era. This preoccupation, in turn, affected attitudes toward abortion. Prior to 1840, U.S. law, drawn from English Common Law, generally allowed abortion before quickening (the first fetal movement felt by the mother). At mid-century, however, physicians campaigned successfully to outlaw all induced abortions. This campaign allowed the medical profession to extend its authority while also addressing disturbing demographic trends. By the 1880s, most states had outlawed induced abortion except for therapeutic purposes. The 1873 Comstock Law, a federal obscenity law named for Anthony Comstock (1844–1915) of New York's Society for the Suppression of Vice, prohibited the mailing of abortifacients, contraceptives, or information about abortion or contraception.

From 1900 to World War II. The modern American family-planning movement emerged from three distinct although overlapping forces: the early twentieth century birth control advocacy of Margaret Sanger and other feminists; a Progressive Era eugenics campaign; and a post–World War II population-control movement. Sanger, a nurse active in New York's socialist and radical labor movements, became increasingly concerned about the plight of working-class mothers who bore the burden of uncontrolled fecundity. Her 1914 pamphlet "Family Limitation" forced her to flee to Europe to avoid prosecution under the Comstock Law. Upon her return she launched the *Birth Control Review* (1917), organized the American Birth Control Conference (1921), and otherwise devoted herself to the cause. Meanwhile, Sanger's rival Mary Ware Dennett (1872–1947) had formed the Voluntary Parenthood League, which campaigned for the repeal of federal laws against birth control. In 1925, Dr. Robert Latou Dickinson (1861–1950), concerned that birth control was acquiring a "bad name," organized the Committee on Maternal Health to sponsor research on fertility and sterility. In 1939, facing financial difficulties, these three groups merged to form the Birth Control Federation of America. Renamed the Planned Parenthood Federation in 1942, it pursued the cautious goal of providing contraceptive services to married women in physician-directed clinics.

By 1937, Americans spent $38 million on condoms and more than $200 million on "feminine hygiene" (contraceptive douching). Despite liberalization by some state and lower federal courts, however, contraceptives—many unsafe and defective—could still be purchased only with a prescription and at inflated prices. Through the efforts of Clarence J. Gamble, an heir to the Ivory Soap fortune, the Food and Drug Administration (FDA) began to test condoms and other contraceptive devices in the late 1930s. The birth control movement took heart from federal judge Augustus Hand's 1937 ruling in *United States v. One Package* that Congress in enacting the Comstock Law had lacked crucial information about the risks of pregnancy and the usefulness of contraceptives. Nevertheless, complete birth control bans remained in effect in Connecticut and Massachusetts into the 1960s. In a landmark victory for reproductive rights, the Supreme Court in *Griswold v. Connecticut* (1965) struck down the Connecticut law banning the distribution of contraceptive devices or information as a violation of married couples' right to privacy. The same principle, extended to unmarried persons in *Eisenstadt v. Baird* (1972), later formed the basis for *Roe v. Wade* (1973), which established a constitutional right to abortion.

Post–World War II Developments. Meanwhile, the post–World War II concerns about overpopulation led philanthropic foundations and activist organizations, including the Population Council, the Ford Foundation, and the Population Crisis Committee, to join Planned Parenthood in calling for federal support for international and domestic birth-control programs and reproductive services. In 1951, the chemist Carl Djerassi and his team at Syntex, a small Mexico City chemical company, synthesized a drug that would prove effective as an oral contraceptive. The endocrinologist and biotechnology entrepreneur Gregory Pincus (1903–1967) of Worcester, Massachusetts, and others conducted the experiments that established the drug's effectiveness and appropriate use. Thanks to Pincus's research, financed by Sanger and Katharine Dexter McCormick, the drug gained FDA approval and was marketed in 1960 by G. D. Searle and Company. The "pill," along with effective intrauterine devices (IUDs), transformed contraceptive practices in the United States.

By linking birth control to the War on Poverty, the Lyndon B. Johnson administration initiated federally supported family-planning programs in the mid-1960s. The Family Planning Service and Population Research Act of 1970 gave legislative support for such programs. The Roman Catholic hierarchy opposed federal involvement in family planning, however, favoring instead the "rhythm method" by which married couples abstained from sexual intercourse during the fertile period of the woman's menstrual cycle. Pope Paul VI's 1968 encyclical *Humanae Vitae* indicated the divisiveness of the issue even within the Catholic Church, however.

The family-planning debate was transformed in the late 1960s as feminists defined abortion as a women's rights issue. The abortion-reform movement, led by women's groups and such organizations as Planned Parenthood, Zero Population Growth (founded 1968), and the National Abortion and Reproductive Action League (known as NARAL), secured liberalized legislation in many states. The landmark *Roe v. Wade* decision, however, also mobilized the antiabortion forces. Congress restricted Medicaid funds for abortion, and many states placed stringent restrictions on abortion procedures. Although the federal courts overturned many of these state regulations, others were upheld. Although most antiabortion activists confined themselves to rallies and peaceful demonstrations, a few violence-prone loners on the movement's fringes bombed abortion clinics and even murdered physicians and other providers of abortion services.

By the 1990s, about 60 percent of American women used artificial contraception, with little difference among Protestants, Catholics, and Jews, and the federal government was spending $700 million annually on family-planning programs that included oral and mechanical birth control, sterilization, and abortion. Although the abortion controversy raged on, the debate over contraception appeared largely settled as the twentieth century ended.

[*See also* **Censorship; Feminism;** ***Griswold v. Connecticut;*** **Johnson, Lyndon B.; Medicare and Medicaid; NARAL Pro-Choice America; Population Policy; Progressive Era;** ***and Roe v. Wade.***]

BIBLIOGRAPHY

Chesler, Ellen. *Woman of Valor: Margaret Sanger and the Birth Control Movement in America.* New York: Simon & Schuster, 1992.

Critchlow, Donald T. *Intended Consequences: Birth Control, Abortion, and the Federal Government.* New York: Oxford University Press, 1999.

Garrow, David. *Liberty and Sexuality: The Right to Privacy and the Making of "Roe v. Wade."* New York; Toronto: Macmillan; Maxwell Macmillan Canada, 1994.

Gordon, Linda. *Woman's Body, Woman's Right: Birth Control in America.* New York: Grossman, 1976; rev. ed. 1990.

Kennedy, David M. *Birth Control in America: The Career of Margaret Sanger.* New Haven, Conn.: Yale University Press, 1970.

Mohr, James. *Abortion in America: The Origins and Evolution of National Policy.* New York: Oxford University Press, 1978.

Reed, James. *From Private Vice to Public Virtue: The Birth Control Movement and American Society since 1830.* New York: Basic Books, 1978.

Donald T. Critchlow

BLACK, HUGO

(1886–1971), associate justice of the U.S. Supreme Court (1937–1971). A police court judge and attorney in his native Alabama, Black served as a U.S. senator from 1925 to 1937, strongly supporting President Franklin Delano Roosevelt's New Deal. For this loyalty, Roosevelt selected Black as his first Supreme Court nominee in 1937.

Black's appointment was marred by reports that he had belonged to the Ku Klux Klan. While admitting past Klan involvement, Black repudiated the Klan's racism and religious bigotry. Known as one of the Court's greatest civil libertarians, Black participated in the unanimous desegregation ruling, *Brown v. Board of Education* (1954). Yet he also wrote—and never renounced—the majority opinion in *Korematsu v. United States* (1944), which sustained the federal government's forcible relocation of Japanese Americans during World War II on grounds of national security.

Black contended that judges should strictly follow the original intention behind the Constitution's provisions. Most strikingly, Black concluded that the First Amendment protects virtually all forms of speech and press, including obscenity, libel, and seditious utterances, which must be protected from government censorship. This constitutional absolutism was rooted in his affinity for Populism, the nineteenth-century agrarian movement (especially strong in Alabama) that emphasized the need to combat government's tendency to serve powerful interests at the expense of the less fortunate.

[***See also*** **Bill of Rights;** ***Brown v. Board of Education;*** **Civil Liberties; Japanese American Internment; Ku Klux Klan; New Deal; Populist Era; Populist Party; Roosevelt, Franklin Delano; Sedition;** ***and*** **Supreme Court, U.S.**]

BIBLIOGRAPHY

Black, Hugo L. *A Constitutional Faith*. New York: Alfred A. Knopf, 1968.

Hockett, Jeffrey D. *New Deal Justice: The Constitutional Jurisprudence of Hugo L. Black, Felix Frankfurter, and Robert H. Jackson*. Lanham, Md.: Rowman & Littlefield, 1996.

Jeffrey D. Hockett

BLACKMUN, HARRY A.

(1908–1999), associate justice, 1971–1994. Blackmun grew up in St. Paul, Minnesota, where his father owned a small store. He was educated at Harvard College, where he majored in mathematics, and at Harvard Law School. His early interest in medicine was reflected in his service as counsel for the Mayo Clinic. In 1959, President Dwight D. Eisenhower appointed him to the U.S. Court of Appeals for the Eighth Circuit to fill the seat vacated by John Sanborn, for whom Blackmun had clerked.

The "third man" after the defeated nominations of judges Clement Haynsworth and C. Harrold Carswell, Blackmun was appointed to the Supreme Court by President Richard Nixon. He was at the time a little-known federal judge, and it was thought he would bring to the Court the same values as his friend Chief Justice Warren E. Burger, playing his part in Nixon's effort to reorient the Court in a conservative ideological direction. Initially, Blackmun's voting was quite close to Burger's—something Burger may have taken for granted—and they were sometimes referred to as the "Minnesota Twins." He was quiet, even diffident, and a slow writer, which limited his influence within the Court. As he became more sure of himself, however, he moved away from Burger toward the liberal end of the Court, becoming outspoken and explicit in his efforts to keep an increasingly conservative Court on center.

Blackmun's early opinions reflected conservatism, support for law enforcement, and a general deference to government and social institutions. Later he came to demonstrate a growing skepticism about those institutions' effectiveness in relation to the common person. By the mid-1980s, Justice Blackmun, giving a high level of support for civil liberties claims, had become a regular voting partner of Justices William J. Brennan and Thurgood Marshall. His judicial transformation manifested itself even on matters of criminal procedure, where his initial conservatism had lasted longest. He questioned the Court's search-and-seizure positions and disagreed with the Court's haste in upholding death-penalty convictions, thus bringing his votes into line with his early statement, in *Furman v. Georgia* (1972), of "distance, antipathy, and . . . abhorrence" for the death penalty, which for him "violated childhood's training and life's experience" (p. 405).

Blackmun made a number of major contributions to Supreme Court jurisprudence. He was a key player on the question of whether Congress, through the Commerce Clause, could impose requirements on state and local governments, and he wrote for the Court in *Garcia v. San Antonio Metropolitan Transit Authority* (1985) in holding local governments subject to minimum wage requirements, saying that their representation in Congress provided states and localities with adequate protection. He also showed he could be the states' friend by allowing them to impose nondiscriminatory, properly apportioned franchise taxes and by supporting state economic policy making if it was not narrowly parochial.

His changing views on judicial federalism paralleled his changes on civil liberties. At first he was unwilling to let state courts provide greater federal constitutional protection than did the U.S. Supreme Court, and he took a restrictive view of federal courts' use of habeas corpus to redress state defendants' claims. Later, however, Blackmun wished to make habeas more available for those pressing federal constitutional claims, and he also gave a broad reading to Title 42, Section 1983, of the U.S. Code, the primary federal civil rights statute. In his Madison Lectures at New York University Law School in 1984, Blackmun argued strongly that federal courts should work actively to uphold individuals' federal rights asserted in Section 1983 cases.

Blackmun's major civil liberties contributions concerned commercial speech, aliens' rights, and abortion. On the question of First Amendment protection for "commercial speech" such as lawyer advertising, he opposed the states' paternalistic position of denying access to information that advertising would provide and argued that consumers ought to have more, not less, information. He took the side of aliens denied welfare benefits without satisfying long residence requirements or barred from holding public jobs. His key opinions opposed states' denying aliens the right to be civil servants, public school teachers, or probation officers; however, he was willing to allow a ban on their being police officers.

Blackmun's best-known contributions are his abortion opinions, particularly those for the Court in *Roe v. Wade* and *Doe v. Bolton* (1973), in which, respectively, the justices invalidated criminal penalties for performing abortions and established the basic trimester framework for evaluating whether and when the state could impose restrictions on a woman's freedom to obtain an abortion. He was committed to any woman's right to obtain an abortion and reacted strongly against the Court's upholding the government's refusal to provide Medicaid funding of abortions. The strength of his commitment continued through the many cases in which the Court dealt with states' efforts to limit abortion and was nowhere clearer than in his dissent in *Webster v. Reproductive Health Services* (1989). There he attacked his colleagues for dismantling *Roe v. Wade* and for "cast[ing] into darkness the hopes and visions of every woman who had come to believe that the Constitution guaranteed her the right to exercise some control over her unique ability to bear children," creating "inevitable and brutal consequences" with the government again able to intrude improperly into women's lives (pp. 3077–3078).

When Blackmun took his seat on the Supreme Court, few would have expected him to be a spokesperson for those on whom the hand of government weighed heavily. His service on the Court signified the possibility, and actuality, that a justice can change views when confronted with situations that call deeply held beliefs into question. Blackmun will also remain the symbol of one of the nation's most divisive issues—abortion.

However, he stood out most as a thoughtful justice representing centrism laced with compassion.

[*See also* **Abortion Politics and Policy; Burger, Warren; Civil Liberties; Jurisprudence; Marshall, Thurgood; Nixon, Richard M.;** ***Roe v. Wade; and*** **Supreme Court, U.S.**]

Stephen L. Wasby

BLACK PANTHERS

Founded in Oakland, California, in 1966 by Huey P. Newton and Bobby Seale, the Black Panther Party for Self-Defense soon became the best-known revolutionary, nationalist organization of the Black Power era. Rejecting the civil rights movement's integrationist goals and nonviolence, Panthers advocated self-help, community control, and armed defense against police brutality. The party's youthful, urban constituency organized citizens' patrols in black neighborhoods; wore paramilitary uniforms featuring black berets and leather jackets; and operated health clinics, food pantries, "liberation schools," and children's breakfast programs. Newton's 1967 imprisonment after his conviction (later reversed) for killing a policeman spurred a nationwide "Free Huey" campaign.

Addressing African Americans' specific problems, party leaders freely modified classical Marxism-Leninism, moving from a black nationalist stance to revolutionary socialism to intercommunalism. In this revolutionary vision, a Black Power vanguard would overcome the tyrannies of race and class; lead the masses in seizing the means of production; and redistribute wealth, technology, and political power. To this end, the Panthers forged alliances with nonblack leftists and established trade-union caucuses.

Black Panther militance frightened white America and many black moderates. The Federal Bureau of Investigation (FBI) and local police targeted the Panthers in a campaign against so-called black nationalist hate groups. A joint FBI–police raid in Chicago in 1969 left dead the head of the Illinois Black Panthers, Fred Hampton, and an associate, Mark Clark. Other Black Panthers died in police shoot-outs, and many were imprisoned. Bobby Seale was among the "Chicago Eight" radicals tried for conspiracy in 1969. The party's minister of information, Eldridge Cleaver, fled the United States to Cuba and then to Algiers. Bitter internal division and ideological disputes with other nationalist groups further weakened the party. Fading by 1972, the Panthers nevertheless inspired latter-day activists by proving that class consciousness and the concept of black self-rule need not be mutually exclusive.

[*See also* **Civil Rights;** ***and*** **Radicalism.**]

BIBLIOGRAPHY

Newton, Huey P. *To Die for the People.* New York: Random House, 1972.

Seale, Bobby. *Seize the Time: The Story of the Black Panther Party and Huey P. Newton.* New York: Random House, 1970.

Van Deburg, William L. *New Day in Babylon: The Black Power Movement and American Culture, 1965–1975.* Chicago: University of Chicago Press, 1992.

William L. Van Deburg

BLACKSTONE, WILLIAM, INFLUENCE OF

(1723–1780), English author of a highly influential treatise on English Common Law, practiced as a barrister in London, briefly served as a Member of Parliament, and for ten years occupied a seat on the royal Court of Common Pleas. Blackstone left no significant mark as a lawyer or politician, and his tenure on the bench is noted chiefly for his pedantic approach and bad temper. It is unlikely that Blackstone would be remembered at all had he not written his four-volume *Commentaries on the Laws of England*, originally published between 1765 and 1769, yet that treatise made him perhaps the most famous jurist in the history of the Common Law. The first professor to hold a university chair in English Common Law, Blackstone published the *Commentaries* as a written counterpart to his Oxford lectures, having seen his academic income shrink while his students earned a profit by selling their notes. Because the *Commentaries* originated as lectures, they were ideally suited for self-study. Early reviewers praised the first edition as a straightforward and careful exposition of the English Ccommon Law that made the subject accessible to gentlemen without prior legal training. American colonists embraced Blackstone's creation, purchasing at least a thousand copies of the first English edition and prompting a Philadelphia printer to publish a popular American edition in 1771. Subsequent American editions added citations to American authorities, further broadening the work's appeal. Even Thomas Jefferson, who came to consider Blackstone and his work a potential threat to jurisprudence and American liberty, once acknowledged the *Commentaries* to be an important component of a new lawyer's education. Scholars have compared the role of Blackstone's *Commentaries* in the development of an American legal tradition to the contribution of Noah Webster's *American Spelling Book* toward the promotion of literacy.

Blackstone's early reputation as an enemy of the cause of American independence stemmed partly from his support of the Stamp Act in Parliament and partly from his opinion, expressed in the *Commentaries,* that the American colonists were not entitled to the liberties of Englishmen except as specifically granted by the king. St. George Tucker, a professor of law at the College of William and Mary, alleviated this concern in his 1803 edition of the *Commentaries,* which began with a preface explaining how the *Commentaries* could help foster understanding of the law in the United States and thus promote republican government. Tucker also added appendices with references to the laws of Virginia and the United States that brought the *Commentaries* up to date for his readers. Other American editors followed a similar approach. Thomas M. Cooley, a professor of law at the University of Michigan and judge on the Michigan Supreme Court, produced an annotated version beginning in 1870 that saw multiple successive editions. The University of Chicago Press published the first paperback edition in 1979, with each volume including an introduction by a distinguished legal historian. New editions continue to appear in the twenty-first century.

Despite the popular success that the *Commentaries* achieved, or perhaps because of it, certain American scholars have criticized the work for its purportedly formalistic and idealized vision of the law. Other scholars have come to Blackstone's defense, arguing that the *Commentaries* have been misinterpreted or mischaracterized, as in the case of his supposedly absolutist conception of property rights. Although Blackstone did refer to property as a "despotic dominion," the

Commentaries contain many specific examples of limitations on property rights that seem to soften or contradict that bold assertion. In keeping with eighteenth-century literary fashion, Blackstone attempted to frame his discussion of national law in universal terms, but the significance of this may be overstated. Blackstone's attempt to situate English law within a broader framework of natural-law principles helped the work gain acceptance in the United States. In the nineteenth century, however, lawyers tended to cite the *Commentaries* not for lofty jurisprudential theory, but for the explication of technical details that would otherwise be obscure and because the addition of Blackstone's name could lend some gravitas to a list of more recent American authorities. Blackstone's *Commentaries* earned their place in American legal history by introducing generations of American pioneers to their English Common Law heritage.

[*See also* **Stamp Act.**]

BIBLIOGRAPHY

Alschuler, Albert W. "Rediscovering Blackstone." *University of Pennsylvania Law Review* 145 (1996): 1–55.

Blackstone, William. *Commentaries on the Laws of England*. 4 vols. Oxford: Clarendon Press, 1765–1769 (and subsequent editions).

Kadens, Emily. "Justice Blackstone's Common Law Orthodoxy." *Northwestern University Law Review* 103 (2009): 1553–1605.

Nolan, Dennis R. "Sir William Blackstone and the New American Republic: A Study of Intellectual Impact." *New York University Law Review* 51 (1976): 731–768.

Prest, Wilfrid. *William Blackstone: Law and Letters in the Eighteenth Century*. Oxford: Oxford University Press, 2008.

Schorr, David B. "How Blackstone Became a Blackstonian." *Theoretical Inquiries in Law* 10 (2009): 103–126.

Joshua C. Tate

BLAINE, JAMES G.

(1830–1893), Republican party leader. Blaine was born in Pennsylvania but moved to Maine in the mid-1850s, where he edited a newspaper before entering politics. His service in the U.S. House of Representatives (1863–1876) included three terms as speaker (1869–1875). A moderate on Reconstruction policy, Blaine was known for his support of the gold standard and of international reciprocity agreements to promote trade. A contender for the Republican presidential nomination in 1876, he lost his bid because of accusations that as speaker he had facilitated the award of a land grant to a railroad and then profited financially from his action. Blaine served in the Senate from 1876 until he became secretary of state in 1881 under President James Garfield—a brief tenure that ended in December 1881, three months after Garfield's assassination. Blaine won the Republican presidential nomination in 1884 but narrowly lost to Grover Cleveland. As secretary of state under President Benjamin Harrison, 1889–1892, he worked for a Pan American Union, or reciprocal trade area, and for trade agreements with other nations. These efforts proved largely unsuccessful, but they did establish an important precedent for the future.

Blaine was a charismatic politician known to his admirers as the "Plumed Knight" and the "Magnetic Man." Despite his ability to galvanize his followers, however, he could never overcome the suspicions of political reformers within and outside his party, who questioned his financial dealings and his internationalism. He presciently understood that the Republican Party needed to address the new industrial order, especially by promoting international trade, as the issues relating to the Civil War and Reconstruction faded. In this sense he was a politician of the future more than of his time. He left an indelible imprint on his followers, who saw him as a foresighted leader and a constructive party guide.

[*See also* **Cleveland, Grover; Federal Government, Executive Branch: State Department; Federal Government, Legislative Branch: Senate; Federal Government, Legislative Branch: House of Representatives; Garfield, James; Reconstruction; Harrison, Benjamin; Republican Party;** ***and*** **Tariffs.**]

BIBLIOGRAPHY

Crapol, Edward P. *James G. Blaine: Architect of Empire.* Wilmington, Del.: Scholarly Resources, 2000.

Keller, Morton. *Affairs of State: Public Life in Late Nineteenth Century America.* Cambridge, Mass.: Belknap Press of Harvard University Press, 1977.

Muzzey, David Saville. *James G. Blaine: A Political Idol of Other Days.* New York: Dodd, Mead & Company, 1934.

H. Wayne Morgan

BONUS ARMY

In 1932, with the nation mired in depression, thousands of unemployed World War I veterans traveled to Washington, D.C., to petition Congress for the immediate payment of thousand-dollar bonuses that 1924 legislation had promised to pay them in 1945. Styling themselves the "Bonus Expeditionary Force" (a takeoff on the American Expeditionary Forces of 1918), these protestors, many with their families, set up camp in vacant federal buildings and in shacks on the Anacostia Flats a few miles from the Capitol.

The House approved the Bonus Bill, but in June the Senate decisively rejected it. Yet many members of the "Bonus Army" stayed in Washington. In July, the Herbert Hoover administration ordered the veterans' eviction from the federal buildings. During this operation, police gunfire killed one veteran. Hoover sent in troops under the command of General Douglas MacArthur to restore calm. Exceeding his orders, MacArthur employed his forces, complete with a machine-gun squadron and several tanks, to drive the veterans out of the District of Columbia entirely. Using tear gas and bayonets, the troops cleared the petitioners and their families from their makeshift homes, which were then burned.

The spectacle of U.S. troops forcibly driving from the nation's capital peaceful, unarmed citizens who were themselves veterans illustrated the gap that had opened between the government and Great Depression victims by the end of Hoover's presidency. MacArthur insisted that the "mob" was "animated by the essence of revolution" and bent on taking over the government. In fact, the rout of the nonresisting Bonus Army demonstrated that government officials were more fearful of a revolution in 1932 than the unemployed were interested in fomenting one.

[*See also* **Hoover, Herbert; MacArthur, Douglas;** ***and*** **New Deal.**]

BIBLIOGRAPHY

Daniels, Roger. *The Bonus March.* Westport, Conn.: Greenwood Press, 1971.

Lisio, Donald J. *The President and the Protest.* Columbia: University of Missouri Press, 1974.

Robert S. McElvaine

BRANDEIS, LOUIS

(1856–1941), attorney, reformer, and associate justice of the U.S. Supreme Court. Born in Louisville, Kentucky, Brandeis graduated from Harvard Law School in 1877 and for thirty seven years practiced law in Boston. His eminent reputation in commercial practice rested on his mastery of facts and spacious vision of law. Drawn to many of the reform causes of the Progressive Era, he became a confidant and adviser to President Woodrow Wilson, shaping much of Wilson's "New Freedom" program. Brandeis spoke for the strand of Progressivism that feared corporate bigness and concentration and put its faith in local forms of self-government as "laboratories of democracy." In *Muller v. Oregon* (1908), Brandeis pioneered the "Brandeis brief," an argument relying more on facts and social science evidence than on legal precedent or syllogism. In 1914, Brandeis espoused Zionism and became a leader of the American wing of the movement.

In 1916, Wilson nominated Brandeis to the Supreme Court. Despite unprecedented conservative and anti-Semitic attacks on Brandeis, he was confirmed and served for twenty-three years. He advocated judicial self-restraint in cases involving state economic regulation, urging deference to legislative policy judgments. Usually in dissent during the chief justiceships of William Howard Taft (1921–1930) and Charles Evans Hughes (1930–1941), he repeated his Brandeis-brief technique, amassing facts and statistics to demonstrate that the legislative judgment was reasonable. Believing that the diversity-of-citizenship jurisdiction of the federal courts permitted large corporations to evade state regulation, Brandeis required federal judges to follow state substantive law in *Erie Railroad Co. v. Tompkins* (1938).

On issues of personal liberty, however, Brandeis was a vigilant judicial activist, hostile to laws that inhibited speech and press. His demand for a speech-protective reading of the "clear and present danger" test articulated by Justice Oliver Wendell Holmes Jr., in *Schenck v. United States* (1919) eventually prevailed in *Brandenburg v. Ohio* (1969). His eloquent call in the *Whitney v. California* (1927) concurrence for civic courage in defense of First Amendment rights similarly gained canonical status in *Dennis v. United States* (1951). In a seminal 1890 law-review article, Brandeis had developed the concept of a right of privacy protected by the Bill of Rights, a position he adopted in his *Olmstead v. United States* (1928) dissent. This, too, the Court later affirmed in *Griswold v. Connecticut* (1965) and *Roe v. Wade* (1973).

Although critical of the use of judicial power to frustrate state economic regulation, Brandeis had a profound reverence for the Supreme Court and for the rule of law. He therefore strenuously opposed President Franklin Delano Roosevelt's 1937 court-packing plan as an assault on both.

[*See also* **Censorship; Civil Liberties; Court Packing; *Muller v. Oregon*; Progressive Era; Supreme Court, U.S.; *and* Wilson, Woodrow.**]

BIBLIOGRAPHY

Strum, Philippa. *Louis D. Brandeis: Justice for the People*. Cambridge, Mass.: Harvard University Press, 1984.

Urofsky, Melvin I. *A Mind of One Piece: Brandeis and American Reform*. New York: Scribner, 1971.

William M. Wiecek

BROWN, JOHN

(1800–1859), Northern white abolitionist whose attempt to start a slave uprising at Harpers Ferry, Virginia (now West Virginia), helped bring on the Civil War. Brown, a businessman with a checkered career, joined the antislavery movement in the 1830s. He helped fugitive slaves escape via the Underground Railroad; befriended black leaders, notably Frederick Douglass; and eventually quit business to take up arms against the "Slave Power." In 1855–1857, Brown fought against proslavery militia in the guerrilla war for control of Kansas territory, winning a national reputation for courage but local notoriety for the "Pottawatomie massacre" (23–24 May 1856), in which he supervised the lynching of five proslavery men.

In 1857–1859, his focus shifted to the South and to inciting servile insurrection. With the secret support of prominent abolitionists, he organized an interracial "army" of twenty-one men and led them in an assault on the federal arsenal at Harpers Ferry (16–17 October 1859), expecting to seize weapons and arm the slaves. Instead, state and federal troops (the latter commanded by Lieutenant Colonel Robert E. Lee) crushed his force. Brown himself was captured; hastily tried for treason in a Virginia court; convicted; and, on 2 December 1859, hanged. The bravery of the "old man" during this ordeal, as well as his eloquence in defending his actions, made a powerful impression on the country. Many Northerners hailed him as a martyr for freedom, whereas white Southerners excoriated him as the embodiment of Northern aggression. In this charged political atmosphere, compromise between the sections became increasingly impossible.

[*See also* **Antislavery Movement; Douglass, Frederick;** *and* **Kansas–Nebraska Act.**]

BIBLIOGRAPHY

Boyer, Paul O. *The Legend of John Brown: A Biography and a History*. New York: Alfred A. Knopf, 1972.

Oates, Stephen B. *To Purge This Land with Blood: A Biography of John Brown*. New York: Harper & Row, 1970.

Dean Grodzins

BROWN v. BOARD OF EDUCATION

Decided on 17 May 1954, *Brown v. Board of Education* remains one of the most important U.S. Supreme Court cases of the twentieth century. Prior to 1954, public schools across the American South were segregated by law, part of a much larger system of racial segregation known euphemistically as Jim Crow, sanctioned by the Supreme Court in *Plessy v. Ferguson* in 1896. Initially supported by southern moderates to reduce racial violence, Jim Crow quickly joined a project of political disfranchisement that sapped both money and power from black communities, effectively reducing African Americans to second-class caste status. Although individuals like Homer Plessy challenged this system in court, organized legal resistance did not emerge until the formation of the National Association for the Advancement of Colored People (the NAACP) in 1909. Initially determined to guarantee equal accommodations, the NAACP began to focus on schools in the 1930s, winning a challenge to segregated law schools in Missouri in 1938 (*Missouri ex. rel. Gaines v. Canada*) and continuing with challenges to unequal higher education in *Sipuel v. Board of Regents* (1948), *Sweatt v. Painter* (1950), and *McLaurin v. Oklahoma Board of Regents* (1950). Southern attacks on black soldiers in the aftermath of World War II contributed to antisegregationist sentiment as President Harry Truman appointed a special civil rights commission to investigate racial abuses in the South, ultimately concluding that segregation and disfranchisement had to end. Truman adopted his committee's recommendations and issued in a 1947 report entitled "To Secure These Rights," even as he desegregated the District of Columbia and the armed forces in 1948, prompting a sudden revolt by the southern wing of the Democratic Party, or "Dixiecrats." Two years later, NAACP lawyer Thurgood Marshall decided to target segregated schools directly, arguing that racially separate education damaged the psychological development of African American children by instilling a sense of racial inferiority, thereby violating the equal protection clause of the Fourteenth Amendment. To establish this point, Marshall mounted five separate cases in Delaware; Virginia; South Carolina; Washington, D.C.; and Kansas; the last of which would come to be styled *Brown v. Board of Education, Topeka*. Marshall relied on psychological data to prove that the psychological development of African American youth was harmed by Jim Crow, engendering a sense of racial inferiority.

Others joined, including President Truman's Justice Department, which declared the invalidation of segregation necessary to win the Cold War. This point emphasized the ugly contrast between America's self-proclaimed ideals of democracy and the South's repressive regime of disfranchisement and repression. Sympathetic to such claims, along with the NAACP's social science evidence, Chief Justice Earl Warren worked diligently to achieve unanimity on the Court against the South, a goal that he achieved in May 1954, when all nine justices joined to rule that racial segregation in public schools was per se unconstitutional. In a concise, fourteen-page opinion, the Supreme Court held that few governmental functions were more important than education and that segregated education irreparably harmed minority children by excluding them from majority white "values" and instilling in them a sense of racial inferiority.

Almost immediately, signs of resistance surfaced in the former Confederacy, as white officials argued that the Court's focus on sociological data ignored precedent and embodied an unconstitutional usurpation of local rule and states' rights. The Supreme Court unwittingly accelerated such critiques in 1955 by ruling that southern states could employ "all deliberate speed" with which to integrate, prompting segregationists to pursue two lines of attack on the Court. In the first, extremists focused on eighteenth-century theories of constitutional nullification, or interposition, to endorse "massive resistance," a position that culminated in the decision of Arkansas Governor Orval Faubus to employ National Guardsmen in a desperate effort to block black students from integrating a public high school in Little Rock in 1957. Although initially popular among white voters, massive resistance fell to federal bayonets when President Dwight D. Eisenhower ordered the 101st Airborne to Arkansas to protect black students from white mobs—a bold move that spurred the Court to declare its supremacy and condemn defiance in *Cooper v. Aaron* in 1958. Undeterred, southern moderates advanced a second strategy, not as overt as massive resistance, which replaced racial classifications with more nuanced signifiers, including moral and sociological background, to keep black students out of white schools. While the Supreme Court tacitly endorsed such a campaign in 1959, African American college students rebelled, removing the process of desegregation from the courts to the streets by sitting down at white lunch counters across the region. For the next five years, waves of direct action protest rocked the South, eventually pressuring Congress to intervene by enacting a robust 1964 Civil Rights Act demanding desegregation and a subsequent Voting Rights Act in 1965, restoring the black franchise. By 1968, campaigns of southern subterfuge dissipated as violence moved north, prompting acts of terrorism and mob rule in cities as disparate as Boston and Denver.

Driving northern outrage was busing, a program to achieve racial balance that hinged on transporting public school students long distances to schools where they were otherwise underrepresented. As popular opposition to this policy grew, the Court backed down, curtailing the ability of busing programs to cross district lines and prompting families across the country to escape urban school districts. Following several decades of such "white flight," school districts across the nation resegregated, leaving *Brown*'s promise, to the minds of many, unfulfilled. Yet, others rejoiced as the Court adopted a rigid adherence to colorblindness, striking down ambitious racial balancing plans in places like Seattle and Louisville in 2007, potentially tolling the bell on over half a century of struggle over segregated schools.

Ostensibly a case about public schools, *Brown v. Board of Education* ultimately symbolized America's tortured struggle with race, underscoring the manner in which formal proclamations of racial equality become hopelessly trapped in larger discourses of resource allocation, local autonomy, child development, and demographic shift.

[*See also* **Civil Rights; Civil Rights Legislation; Eisenhower, Dwight D.; Marshall, Thurgood; Supreme Court, U.S.; Truman, Harry S.;** *and* **Warren, Earl.**]

BIBLIOGRAPHY

Walker, Anders. *The Ghost of Jim Crow: How Southern Moderates Used Brown v. Board of Education to Stall Civil Rights.* Oxford: Oxford University Press, 2009.

Anders Walker

BRYAN, WILLIAM JENNINGS

(1860–1925), populist leader, presidential candidate, secretary of state. A powerful orator first elected to Congress from Nebraska in 1890, Bryan won the Democratic Party's 1896 presidential nomination after delivering his electrifying *Cross of Gold* speech at the party convention in Chicago. The Populist Party also nominated him, and he ran on a platform endorsing free silver and other reforms. He personified the agrarian values of individualism, equality, and Protestant morality in an urban-industrial era of deepening class and ethnic divisions. His opposition to corporate power mirrored the spirit of discontent pulsing through the nation's heartland, but he failed to rally the urban working class and lost to the Republican William McKinley.

In foreign affairs, Bryan opposed overseas expansionism after the Spanish–American War as dangerous to republican institutions. Although losing again to McKinley in 1900, he retained national visibility through his newspaper, the *Commoner,* advocating trust control, Prohibition, and political reform. Again the Democratic candidate in 1908, he lost to William Howard Taft.

President Woodrow Wilson named him secretary of state in 1913. Bryan sought to keep America out of the European war that began in August 1914. Considering Wilson's notes to Germany protesting the sinking of the British liner *Lusitania* in 1915 too hostile, he resigned. In the 1920s, Bryan promoted Florida real estate, supported the fundamentalist movement, and battled the theory of evolution. At the celebrated 1925 Scopes trial, he testified as a prosecution witness. To the end, Bryan represented an America of small towns and consensual values—an older American under assault in the new industrial age.

[*See also* **Democratic Party; Federal Government, Executive Branch: State Department; Free Silver Movement; McKinley, William; Populist Era; Populist Party; Prohibition; Taft, William Howard;** *and* **Wilson, Woodrow.**]

BIBLIOGRAPHY

Cherny, Robert. *Righteous Cause: The Life of William Jennings Bryan*. Boston: Little, Brown, 1985.

Coletta, Paolo. *William Jennings Bryan*, 3 vols. Lincoln: University of Nebraska Press, 1964–1969.

H. Wayne Morgan

BUCHANAN, JAMES

(1791–1868), fifteenth president of the United States. Born in Lancaster County, Pennsylvania, the son of a storekeeper and farmer, Buchanan was a successful lawyer who soon turned to politics. Originally a Federalist, he became a Jacksonian Democrat, serving successively as a state legislator, congressman, minister to Russia (1832–1834), U.S. senator (1834–1845), secretary of state under James Knox Polk (1845–1849), and ambassador to Great Britain (1853–1856). Like other antebellum Democrats, Buchanan distrusted federal power, favored popular sovereignty, and remained largely indifferent to slavery. Elected president in 1856 with significant southern backing, Buchanan faced a sectional crisis inflamed by the struggle for control of the Kansas territory and the Republican Party's emergence as a Northern party opposed to slavery's expansion. Despite his efforts at conciliation, tensions intensified throughout his presidency. Buchanan's pro-Southern tilt on the Kansas issue, based on his hatred of the Republicans and his sympathy for Southern fears, provoked a split with the powerful Illinois senator Stephen A. Douglas, who believed that Buchanan and his Southern-dominated cabinet had leaned too far to placate the South. This split and the bloodshed in Kansas increased both northern resistance to southern demands and the South's determination to preserve the slave system.

Buchanan did not seek renomination in 1860 (nor would he have succeeded had he tried). As the Democratic Party fragmented, the election of the Republican Abraham Lincoln led seven southern states to secede and to seize federal property within their borders. Buchanan, still president, opposed secession and insisted on federal rights, but he did not believe that he could compel the seceding states to return, and his term ended in futility. His distinguished career of public service irretrievably tarnished by a failed presidency, Buchanan consistently ranks low in scholarly assessments of presidential greatness. A Jacksonian in outlook who lacked Old Hickory's willingness to use the presidency to accomplish great ends, he is remembered primarily for weakness and ineffectiveness.

[*See also* **Antislavery Movement; Democratic Party; Douglas, Stephen A.; Federalist Party; Jackson, Andrew; Kansas–Nebraska Act;** *and* **Popular Sovereignty.**]

BIBLIOGRAPHY

Klein, Philip S. *President James Buchanan*. University Park: Pennsylvania State University Press, 1962.

Smith, Elbert B. *The Presidency of James Buchanan*. Lawrence: University Press of Kansas, 1975.

Joel H. Silbey

BUCKLEY, WILLIAM F., JR.

(1925–2008), conservative journalist and intellectual. Buckley grew up in Sharon, Connecticut, one of ten children of William Frank Buckley and Aloise Steiner Buckley. The father had grown wealthy in the oil business, and both parents had strong Roman Catholic loyalties. After service in World War II and graduation from Yale University, Buckley won notoriety with his book *God and Man at Yale* (1951), an attack on his alma mater's liberal economic thinking and religious agnosticism. Buckley inherited much of his conservatism from his father, particularly the anti-Communism. He befriended Whittaker Chambers, a protagonist in the Alger Hiss case, and published their letters in *Odyssey of a Friend* (1964). With L. Brent Bozell, Buckley wrote *McCarthy and His Enemies* (1954), a defense of Joseph McCarthy's anti-Communist investigations.

Founding the *National Review* magazine in 1955, Buckley brought together the disparate strands of American conservatism—free-market and libertarian, religious and traditionalist, elitist and populist. It became America's leading conservative journal. Buckley also became known through his long-running National Public Television program *Firing Line*. There and in his writings, Buckley displayed his wit and sarcasm, his ample lexicon, and his erudition. Buckley himself did not develop a consistent intellectual conservatism; his opinions could reflect any of the varieties he welcomed in his magazine. Usually, however, he saw American conservatives as a beleaguered minority standing against a dominant and privileged liberal establishment. Against this ascendancy, Buckley defended a conservative counterculture and its tribal loyalists. Through his longevity, sustained productivity, and public visibility, Buckley served the conservative intellectual movement as a paterfamilias.

[*See also* **Anti-Communism; Conservatism; Liberalism;** *and* **McCarthy, Joseph.**]

BIBLIOGRAPHY

Judis, John B. *William F. Buckley, Jr.: Patron Saint of the Conservatives.* New York: Simon and Schuster, 1988.

Winchell, Mark Royden. *William F. Buckley, Jr.* Boston: Twayne Publishers, 1984.

J. David Hoeveler

BUDGET, FEDERAL

In Federalist No. 30 (1787), Alexander Hamilton asserted, "Money is, with propriety, considered as the vital principle of the body politic; as that which sustains its life and motion and enables it to perform its most essential functions." Over the next two centuries and beyond, the budget was a battleground for political actors holding different views about the federal government's scope, who should bear its costs, and whether to defray these costs to the future through operation of a deficit.

Until the 1920s budgeting was predominantly a legislative rather than an executive function. Possessing the constitutional power of the purse, Congress engaged in haphazard budgeting that lacked planning mechanisms. It set tariffs, the main revenue source, largely to protect industry, and its consideration of executive spending requests was unsystematic. In the pre-1861 era of small government, this *modus operandi* (mode of operating) still delivered balanced budgets aplenty—except in war and recession. Reinforcing fiscal responsibility, the Jeffersonian tradition reviled public debt as the anti-Republican harbinger of excessive federal power.

High protective tariffs underwrote the longest surplus sequence in fiscal years (FY) 1866–1893. Facing agrarian protest that duties should only have revenue-raising purposes, congressional Republicans expanded federal spending, notably on veterans' pensions and internal improvements, to reduce the surplus. This practice peaked during the "Billion Dollar Congress" of 1889–1891.

Increased spending, particularly on national security, coincided with fourteen deficit budgets in FY 1894–1915. Tariffs now generated insufficient revenue because industrialization had reduced dependence on imports. To many Democrats and Republicans, the efficient and equitable solution was a progressive tax on personal and corporate income. The Sixteenth Amendment of the Constitution (1913) duly empowered Congress to levy taxes on income "from whatever source derived." However, the elite focus of personal taxes meant that America's World War I costs were largely financed from borrowing, resulting in public debt expansion from $1.2 billion in FY 1916 to $25.4 billion in FY 1920.

The need for fiscal planning to retire debt inspired budget reform. The Budget and Accounting Act of 1921 mandated an annual presidential budget plan to guide congressional budget deliberations. Under its aegis, presidents could henceforth set the agenda of national government. The measure also created the Bureau of the Budget (BoB), initially located in the Treasury but transferred to the newly created Executive Office of the Presidency in 1939 in recognition of its technocratic importance to presidential budgeting.

The deficit budgets of the Great Depression were initially considered an emergency necessity. Anxious to restore business confidence, Franklin D. Roosevelt desisted from massive stimulus spending. Meanwhile, cyclical revenue growth and new taxes acted as a fiscal drag on recovery. Fiscal tightening in FY 1938 in premature anticipation of full recovery precipitated a new recession. Roosevelt's liberal advisers consequently persuaded him to implement British economist John Maynard Keynes's theory that expansive fiscal measures would boost private purchasing power. However, conservative influence in Congress limited the scope of spending expansion in 1939–1940. Mammoth wartime deficits, peaking at 30.3 percent of the gross domestic product (GDP) in 1943, eventually validated Keynesianism in restoring full employment and strong economic growth.

World War II's fiscal legacy shaped postwar budgeting. The personal income tax's transformation into a mass tax in 1943 provided ample revenue for outlay expansion. In FY 1960 expenditure and receipts each constituted 17.8 percent GDP compared with 9.8 percent and 6.8 percent, respectively, in FY 1940. Spending composition now prioritized defense over domestic programs. With the Cold War necessitating a huge military establishment, national security averaged 56 percent of outlays in FY 1955–1961. Reinforced by the Employment Act of 1946, which mandated federal maintenance of purchasing power, the budget also became the primary instrument of economic policy.

Post-1945 Democratic and Republican administrations operated countercyclical deficits and surpluses to manage aggregate demand. The fiscal revolution that started in the 1930s culminated with the Kennedy–Johnson tax cut of 1964 that embodied expansionary rather than compensatory intent. However, aggregative fiscal policy failed to cure Vietnam-Era inflation and 1970s stagflation. Monetary policy consequently eclipsed it as an instrument of economic management in the late 1970s.

Loss of budgetary suppleness resulting from entitlement growth also undermined fiscal demand management. Because of the postwar expansion of Social Security (created in 1935), development of new entitlements in the 1960s—notably Medicare and Medicaid—-and index-linking of many benefits to inflation in the 1970s, automatic payments to individuals rose from 26 percent of total outlays in FY 1960 to 59 percent in FY 2000. With debt interest accounting for 10 percent, discretionary domestic and defense programs constituted just 30 percent of the budget.

The federal government operated its longest sequence of deficits in FY 1970–1997. Policy makers prioritized their program goals over fiscal responsibility. Budget politics consequently reached new levels of polarization. Most Democrats wanted domestic programs safeguarded and tax levels maintained for deficit-control purposes, whereas Republicans favored defense expansion, tax reduction, and domestic outlay retrenchment. A balanced budget remained an ideal, but Democrats wanted to achieve it at a high revenue level that protected spending and Republicans at a low revenue level that necessitated economizing.

The post-1968 trend of divided party control of government, compared with Democratic ascendancy in mid-century, enhanced budgetary politics fragmentation. Institutional budget reform had the same effect. Richard Nixon's reorganization of the BoB as the Office of Management and Budget in 1970 drew it deeper into the president's political family. Meanwhile, his impoundment of domestic appropriations prompted the Democrat-controlled legislature to enact the Congressional Budget and Impoundment Control Act of 1974. Among other provisions, this act mandated a congressional budget plan, established new budget committees, and created the Congressional Budget Office to monitor the president's budget. The effect was to complicate and lengthen the budget process. Habitual congressional failure to adopt a budget by the start of the fiscal year (moved from 1 July to 1 October) necessitated Continuing Resolutions to fund government until one was agreed upon.

The Reagan administration overcame budget process inertia to enact the largest tax reduction in American history in 1981 and the largest defense expansion since Korea, but domestic retrenchment was small by comparison. The deficit consequently averaged 4.3 percent GDP during its tenure, nearly double the 1970s figure. This expansion resulted in efforts to mandate fiscal responsibility.

In the late 1970s, a grassroots movement persuaded thirty state legislatures to petition Congress for a constitutional convention to write a balanced budget amendment. Concerned that such a measure was unworkable and that the untried convention method could produce wholesale constitutional reform, the Carter administration counterorganized to stall the campaign four states short of the three-quarters majority required for Congress to act. In 1982, the Reagan administration itself proposed a balanced-budget amendment that won a two-thirds majority in the Republican Senate but not in the Democratic House. Seeking a legislative solution, Congress then enacted the Balanced Budget and Emergency Deficit Control Act of 1985 to eliminate the deficit in annual installments and mandate spending sequestration if targets were not met. Requiring re-enactment in amended form in 1987 following Supreme Court invalidation of its proposed sequestration enforcement, the measure was routinely circumvented through presidential and congressional legerdemain.

The 1990s saw growing engagement with the deficit problem but little consensus initially about its solution. George H. W. Bush alienated conservative Republicans by agreeing to tax increases for high earners in a bipartisan deficit-reduction deal with congressional Democrats that laid foundations for the eventual restoration of fiscal responsibility. In 1993 Bill Clinton secured enactment of a broad-based deficit reduction program that particularly benefited from post–Cold War defense retrenchment, but its tax increases aroused Republican opposition. In 1995 the new Republican Congress fell short by one Senate vote to enact a balanced-budget amendment. It then approved a five-year deficit-elimination plan that featured massive domestic retrenchment and large tax cuts. Clinton's refusal to approve this provoked two partial shutdowns of government, but the public blamed this on Republican intransigence. With national elections looming,

Republican leaders accepted compromise largely on the president's terms.

Anxious to develop a legacy, Clinton negotiated a five-year spending-control and tax-reduction balanced-budget plan in 1997. However, the revenues from a booming economy and rampant stock market eliminated the deficit within one year. Amid expectations of surpluses far into the future, Clinton and the Republicans then clashed over whether these should be invested in public debt reduction and Social Security trust fund enhancement or tax cuts.

Stock market collapse precipitated a recession in 2001 that wiped out the projected surpluses. However, the newly elected George W. Bush pressed ahead with large tax cuts in 2001 and 2003, defense expansion to fights wars in Afghanistan and Iraq, and domestic program expansion under the aegis of "big-government conservatism." The budget swung from the surplus cycle of FY 1998–2001 to a new sequence of deficits. Bush promised to halve the imbalance in his second term, but financial crisis and recession intervened. The Trouble Assets Relief Program of 2008 prevented financial system collapse but massively expanded federal liabilities. Bush's Democratic successor, Barack Obama, thereafter promoted the $787 billion three-year American Recovery and Reinvestment Act of 2009, the largest stimulus measure in American history. However, the cyclical combination of high spending and declining revenues drove the FY 2010 deficit to 10.6 percent GDP, a peacetime high.

The prospect of another decade of continuously high deficits intensified political divisions about deficit control. America also faces eventual debt explosion from the steady growth of entitlements as the post-1945 baby-boom generation reaches retirement and health care costs rise inexorably. The Congressional Budget Office has projected that the public debt to GDP ratio, currently 64.5 percent, may surpass its World War II–Era peak of 109 percent in 2025 and reach 185 percent in 2035. Fiscal course correction is essential to avoid this unsustainable trajectory that will threaten America's twenty-first-century power and prosperity.

[*See also* **Employment Act of 1946; Income Tax, Federal; Sixteenth Amendment;** ***and*** **Taxation.**]

BIBLIOGRAPHY

Ippolito, Dennis. *Why Budgets Matter: Budget Policy and American Politics*. University Park: Pennsylvania State University Press, 2003.

Morgan, Iwan. *The Age of Deficits: Presidents and Unbalanced Budgets from Jimmy Carter to George W. Bush*. Lawrence: University Press of Kansas, 2009.

Stein, Herbert. *The Fiscal Revolution in America: Policy in Pursuit of Reality*, 2d rev. ed. Washington, D.C.: AEI Press, 1996.

Iwan Morgan

BUNCHE, RALPH J.

(1904–1971), political scientist, diplomat, and the first African American to win the Nobel Peace Prize. Born in Detroit, the son of a barber, Bunche graduated summa cum laude from the University of California at Los Angeles in 1927 and went on to earn a PhD in government from Harvard in 1934. His dissertation, "French Administration in Togoland and Dahomey," won an award as the best political science dissertation produced at Harvard that year. Bunche founded the political science department at Howard University, where he taught from 1928 to 1950. His book *A World View of Race* (1936) saw racial conflict as a product of class conflict. He was an influential adviser to the Swedish social scientist

Gunnar Myrdal on his classic 1944 study of U.S. race relations, *An American Dilemma.* Bunche married Ruth Ethel Harris, a Washington, D.C., schoolteacher, in 1930. They had three children.

During World War II, Bunche served in the Office of Strategic Services, heading the Africa section of its Research and Analysis Branch. As a State Department specialist in postwar planning (1944–1946), he helped draft the United Nations (UN) charter. Turning to international diplomacy, Bunche served from 1946 to 1971 as a high-ranking UN official, concentrating on international peacekeeping. He won the Nobel Peace Prize in 1950 for negotiating armistice agreements between Israel and its Arab neighbors.

Bunche's achievements brought many accolades but also controversy. Accused in 1954 of having been a Communist in the 1930s, he was publicly cleared after an investigation. He actively supported the early civil rights movement, marching with Martin Luther King Jr., in 1965, but in 1967 he criticized King's anti–Vietnam War position.

[*See also* **Civil Rights.**]

BIBLIOGRAPHY

Keppel, Ben. *The Work of Democracy: Ralph Bunche, Kenneth B. Clark, Lorraine Hansberry and the Cultural Politics of Race.* Cambridge, Mass.: Harvard University Press, 1995.

Urquhart, Brian. *Ralph Bunche: An American Life.* New York: W. W. Norton, 1993.

Ben Keppel

BUREAU OF INDIAN AFFAIRS

The federal agency responsible for dealing with American Indians, the Bureau of Indian Affairs (BIA) was created within the War Department in 1824. In 1832, Congress authorized a commissioner of Indian affairs to direct it. The BIA shifted to the Department of the Interior when that department was established in 1849. The creation of area offices (eventually 12 in number) decentralized the bureau in 1949, and in 1977 an assistant secretary of the interior for Indian affairs replaced the commissioner.

As the nation's relations with Indian tribes grew more complex, the bureau's responsibilities multiplied. The Washington, D.C., office directed the work of Indian superintendents and Indian agents in the field, arranged treaty negotiations, and distributed annuity goods and money mandated by the treaties as payment for land cessions and handled claims of white citizens for depredations by Indians. Later, the BIA organized a national Indian school system, provided health services, and directed forestry and irrigation projects. The BIA held tribal lands in trust and managed the assets of individual Indians held in trust by the federal government.

Although sharply criticized for mismanagement and inefficiency and for perpetuating Indian dependency by dominating Indians' lives, the BIA survived. Indians denounced it but were unwilling to see it disappear, because it provided a special connection with the federal government. Moreover, under preferential hiring practices, the BIA's staff by the end of the twentieth century was nearly all Indian. Since 1966, every BIA head has been of Indian heritage.

From the mid-twentieth century on, many of the BIA's operations were assumed by other federal departments, by the states, or most important, by the tribal governments themselves. By the 1990s, the BIA, once the controlling force in reservation life, had become a service agency for the increasingly autonomous tribes while still remaining the chief federal agency concerned with federal trust responsibility.

[*See also* **Federal Government, Executive Branch: Other Departments; Indian Law: Federal;** ***and*** **Indian Law, Tribal.**]

BIBLIOGRAPHY

Berthrong, Donald J. "Nineteenth-Century United States Government Agencies." In *Handbook of North American Indians*, edited by William C. Stuyvesant. Vol. 4, pp. 255–275: *History of Indian–White Relations*, edited by Wilcomb E. Washburn. Washington, D.C.: Smithsonian Institution, 1988.

Nash, Philleo. "Twentieth-Century United States Government Agencies." In *Handbook of North American Indians*, edited by William C. Stuyvesant. Vol. 4, pp. 255–275: *History of Indian–White Relations*, edited by Wilcomb E. Washburn. Washington, D.C.: Smithsonian Institution, 1988.

Francis Paul Prucha

BURGER, WARREN

(1907–1995) chief justice, 1969–1986. Burger, the fifteenth chief justice, was a self-made man. Of Swiss and German ancestry, he grew up in modest circumstances. While selling insurance during the day, Burger attended school in the evening: two years at the University of Minnesota and four at St. Paul College of Law (now William Mitchell College of Law), where he graduated in 1931 magna cum laude.

Burger practiced law with Boyesen, Otis & Fancy in St. Paul from 1931 to 1953, primarily handling corporate, real estate, and probate matters. He was also involved in civic and political activities, most notably as a backer of Minnesota Governor Harold Stassen's presidential bids. Burger served as Stassen's floor manager at the 1948 and 1952 Republican conventions, where he won the respect of national Republican leaders. When Dwight Eisenhower became president in 1953, Attorney General Herbert Brownell named Burger assistant attorney general in charge of the Claims Division (later the Civil Division).

From 1956 to 1969 Burger served on the U.S. Court of Appeals for the District of Columbia Circuit, among America's most influential courts. As a circuit judge, he attracted national attention from the bench and bar for his judicial administration and for his jousts with the civil libertarians on that talented but badly divided court. Moderately conservative in most matters, Burger led the wing of the court that opposed extending the rights of criminal defendants and modernizing the insanity defense, preferring instead to give considerable leeway to police, prosecution, and trial judges.

Burger's appointment as chief justice by Richard Nixon became possible after Lyndon Johnson's nominee, Associate Justice Abe Fortas, failed to win confirmation. By the time Nixon focused attention on the vacancy (May 1969), Fortas had resigned from the Court following accusations of improprieties. Burger was chosen because of his judicial experience, his opposition to decisions of the Warren court on criminal procedures, and his criticism of judicial activism, as well as because his career was free of ethical blemishes.

Contrary to expectations, while Burger served as chief justice, the Supreme Court consolidated most of the major initiatives of the Warren court (such as civil rights and reapportionment), although the pace of change became more moderate. The Court recognized new rights and opened to judicial exploration such areas as gender discrimination, abortion, affirmative action, and welfare rights. Burger was among the least enthusiastic of the justices regarding these trends, but was at the forefront when the Court reversed direction in the criminal area, cut back access of litigants to the federal courts, and demonstrated more sensitivity to traditional principles of federalism than had Warren's court.

Among twentieth-century chief justices, Burger appears to have been considerably less successful in guiding the other justices to jurisprudential results he favored than either Earl Warren or William Howard Taft had been. His colleagues William J. Brennan Jr., and William H. Rehnquist were far more influential with their fellow justices, and Lewis Powell Jr., in a different way, left a greater imprint on constitutional jurisprudence. Burger was unable to take advantage of his allies within the Court, the relatively quiescent political environment, or the absence for much of his tenure of problems caused by aging or cantankerous justices. Within the Court, he appears to have been more pugnacious than conciliatory. Throughout his tenure, there were leaks to the press—some clearly from his colleagues—indicating dissatisfaction with his leadership. He does not seem to have been successful in managing the conference of the justices, and individual statements of opinion proliferated to an extent not seen since before 1800. Burger himself was less willing than any chief justice except Harlan F. Stone to suppress his own dissents to preserve the appearance of harmony.

As a judge, Burger was not of the first rank, but his work was much better than contemporary critics allowed and not recognizably different in craftsmanship from that of most of his colleagues. Not a man given to inner agonies, Burger usually was quite clear as to what he thought the law was. His opinions were generally short, fact-oriented, straightforward, and clearly written.

Burger's opinions of greatest importance are those dealing with separation of powers. His opinion for the unanimous Court in *United States v. Nixon* (1974) rejected Nixon's claim of executive privilege and ordered him to turn over tapes of conversations with aides for use in a criminal trial, but also recognized a presumptive privilege for presidential conversations. Generally, Burger's approach to separation of powers was formalistic, stressing the separateness of each branch and the supremacy of each within its own assigned sphere. He wrote the opinion in *Immigration and Naturalization Service v. Chadha* (1983), invalidating the legislative veto. His final opinion, *Bowsher v. Synar* (1986), held the Gramm–Rudman–Hollings budget-cutting law to be unconstitutional because it assigned executive functions to the comptroller-general, who is removable by Congress.

Personally critical of the media and extremely sensitive to press criticism, Burger wrote a number of important opinions upholding First Amendment claims. Among them were *Nebraska Press Association v. Stuart* (1976), in which the Court held that the protection against prior restraints makes the use of "gag" orders in a criminal trial a last resort, and *Miami Herald Publishing Co. v. Tornillo* (1974), which invalidated a Florida statute requiring newspapers that had assailed the character of a political candidate to afford free space to the candidate for reply. However, Burger rejected the view that the First Amendment guarantees the press a right of access to sources of information broader than that accorded to members of the general public, the right not to divulge sources to a grand jury, or immunity from police searches.

Burger was by no means antagonistic to the civil rights heritage of the Warren court, but he was far more cautious in employing judicial power to force integration. He spoke for a unanimous Court in *Swann v. Charlotte–Mecklenburg Board of Education* (1971), which affirmed a district court order to redraw attendance zones and to bus students to achieve a racial mix at each school approximating the racial composition of the entire district. In *Bob Jones University v. United States* (1983), he rejected a position of the Reagan administration by holding that the Internal Revenue Service has the authority to deny tax exemptions to private schools—even schools run by religious organizations—that discriminate on the basis of race. On the other hand, writing for a closely divided court in *Milliken v. Bradley* (1974), he held that although the Detroit school system was unconstitutionally segregated, the judiciary had no power to order an integration plan that would include suburban schools absent proof that interdistrict segregation was the product of race-conscious gerrymandering. No enthusiast where affirmative action was concerned, Burger still wrote the opinion in *Fullilove v. Klutznick* (1980) upholding congressional power to require 10 percent of the funds in a public works job bill to be set aside for awards to minority businesses.

The nonjudicial aspects of the office of chief justice were well suited to Burger's abilities and temperament, and to this dimension of his role he brought enormous energy, forcefulness, tenacity, and the willingness to risk controversy. Like Taft, Burger saw his office as a place to promote reform in the administration of justice, and, like Taft, he was a conservative reformer, primarily concerned with the traditional agenda of limiting high costs and long delays. Burger also saw his office as a "bully pulpit" from which to call attention to the problems of state courts. He had much to do with the founding of the Institute for Court Management, the National Center for State Courts, and the annual Brookings Seminars at which leaders of the three branches meet to discuss problems of judicial reform. He pressed hard but with limited success for reforms in the corrections process but made somewhat more headway in pressing for upgrading the quality of trial attorneys.

During Burger's tenure, new technologies, from copying machines to computers, were installed in the Court's offices, its personnel practices were overhauled, and a small central legal staff was created. The Court was also made more accessible to scholars and the public. Burger was unsuccessful in persuading Congress either to create a temporary national court of appeals to offer some relief to the Supreme Court or to increase federal appellate capacity. Although the time spent on these efforts and the ceremonial aspects of his office may have undermined Burger's leadership on the Court, no one could gainsay the deep commitment he brought to his work, his profound desire to measure up to his predecessors, or the fondness with which he was regarded by his staff. Deeply concerned about the importance of educating the public about the Constitution, Burger retired as chief justice in 1986 to give full time to his position as chairman of the Commission on the Bicentennial of the U.S. Constitution. He undertook no further judicial work after he left the bench.

[*See also* **Blackmun, Harry A.; Constitution; Executive Privilege; Federalism; Nixon, Richard M.; Supreme Court, U.S.;** *and* **Veto Power.**]

BIBLIOGRAPHY

Lamb, Charles M., and Stephen C. Halpem, eds. *The Burger Court: Political and Judicial Profiles.* Urbana: University of Illinois Press, 1991.

Schwartz, Bernard. *The Ascent of Pragmatism: The Burger Court in Action.* Reading, Mass.: Addison–Wesley, 1990.

Jeffrey B. Morris

BURR, AARON

(1756–1836), political leader, vice president, and conspirator. Best remembered for his duel with Alexander Hamilton and the failed attempt to create a separate empire in the western United States, Burr remains one of the more enigmatic figures in a generation of revolutionaries and nation-builders. Born in Newark, New Jersey, the son and namesake of a prominent Presbyterian minister and grandson of Jonathan Edwards, Burr graduated from the College of New Jersey (Princeton) at the age of sixteen and began legal studies. In 1775, he joined the Continental Army, serving with distinction under Benedict Arnold and George Washington. After the Revolutionary War, he practiced law in New York and entered politics, holding office as the state's attorney general and a U.S. senator (1791–1797). His long-term rivalry with Hamilton crystallized in the presidential election of 1800. When Burr tied Thomas Jefferson in the Electoral College presidential vote, throwing the election into the House of Representatives, Hamilton influenced Federalist congressmen to vote for Jefferson, making Burr vice president. In 1804, during Burr's unsuccessful campaign for governor of New York, Hamilton portrayed him as "a dangerous man, and one who ought not be trusted with the reins of government." This led to a duel at Weehawken, New Jersey, on 11 July 1804, in which Burr killed Hamilton.

In 1805–1806, Burr plotted with General James Wilkinson, Jonathan Dayton, and others to create an empire encompassing the Mississippi Valley, Mexico, and the American West. The nebulous scheme disintegrated, and Burr was indicted for treason. The 1807 trial, presided over by Chief Justice John Marshall in the U.S. Circuit Court in Richmond, Virginia, ended with Burr's acquittal on the grounds that he had not committed overt treasonable acts. Nevertheless, Burr's political influence faded and he lived in European exile for several years before resuming his New York law practice. His 1833 marriage to a younger widow, Eliza Jumel, soon ended in divorce. His beloved daughter, Theodosia, the child of an earlier marriage, had died in 1813.

[*See also* **Federalist Party; Hamilton, Alexander; Jefferson, Thomas; Marshall, John;** *and* **Washington, George.**]

BIBLIOGRAPHY

Abernathy, Thomas Perkins. *The Burr Conspiracy.* New York: Oxford University Press, 1954.

Lomask, Milton. *Aaron Burr: The Years from Princeton to Vice President, 1756–1805.* New York: Farrar, Strauss, and Giroux, 1979.

Nicholas Casner

BUSH, GEORGE H. W.

(1924–), forty-first president of the United States. George Herbert Walker Bush was born in Milton, Massachusetts, to Dorothy Pierce Bush and Prescott Bush Sr., a businessman and later (1953–1963) a U.S. Senator from Connecticut. After graduating from Philips Andover Academy, Bush served as a naval pilot in the Pacific, flying fifty-eight missions during World War II. On his return, he married Barbara Pierce of Rye, New York, and then attended Yale College, playing on the baseball team and graduating in 1948.

Rejecting a career on Wall Street (where his father was a partner in the brokerage firm of Brown Brothers Harriman), Bush moved to West Texas, where he formed a successful oil-exploration company before moving to Houston and entering politics. Running as a Republican, he campaigned unsuccessfully to unseat incumbent Senator Ralph Yarborough in 1964. Two years later, Bush was elected to the U.S. House of Representatives from Texas's Seventh District. After losing another Senate race to Democrat Lloyd Bentsen in 1970, Bush served as the U.S. Ambassador to the United Nations during the Richard M.

Nixon Administration and then as chair of the Republican National Committee during the Watergate scandals and Nixon's resignation in August 1974.

Under President Gerald Ford, Bush headed the U.S. Liaison Office in Beijing, China, before returning to Washington to run the Central Intelligence Agency (CIA). As CIA director, Bush helped to revive the agency's morale, which had been damaged by embarrassing exposés of its covert operations. Leaving the CIA in 1977 when Democrat Jimmy Carter became president, Bush launched his campaign for the White House. After unsuccessfully contesting Ronald Reagan for the Republican presidential nomination in 1980, Bush accepted the vice-presidential slot. Following the landslide Republican victory that fall, Bush served President Reagan loyally and participated in the secret arms-for-hostages trade with the Islamic fundamentalist government of Iran. Attempting to minimize damage to his political career, Bush alleged that he had been "out of the loop" during the most intense dealings of the so-called Iran-Contra affair.

Bush won the presidency in 1988 by defeating his Democratic opponent, Governor Michael Dukakis of Massachusetts, with a sweep of forty states and 53.4 percent of the popular vote. Facing Democratic majorities in both houses of Congress, the George H. W. Bush administration achieved its most notable successes in foreign affairs, the area of Bush's primary interest and preparation. Bush worked skillfully with President Mikhail Gorbachev during the collapse of the Soviet Union, and he responded forcefully to Iraq's invasion of Kuwait in August 1990 by organizing economic and military resistance through the United Nations and the Arab League. In early 1991, a U.S.-led coalition ejected Saddam Hussein's forces from Kuwait, thereby preserving a favorable balance of power in the oil-rich Persian Gulf. Bush also promoted U.S. interests in Central America by overseeing an end to Sandinista control in Nicaragua following free elections and by forcibly removing dictator Manuel Noriega from power in Panama and extraditing him to the United States to face drug-smuggling charges.

The Bush domestic record proved less impressive. The president's few achievements included the Americans with Disabilities Act (1990) and a bipartisan five-year budget agreement (1991) that attempted to tame the spiraling federal deficits of the 1980s. The budget agreement forced Bush to renounce his "Read my lips: No new taxes" pledge. That, combined with a lingering economic downturn, contributed to his reelection defeat in 1992. A favorable public opinion rating of 89 percent reached during of the Persian Gulf crisis could not be sustained, as Bush faced the additional complication of Texas billionaire H. Ross Perot's independent candidacy and the skillful campaigning of his Democratic opponent, Governor Bill Clinton of Arkansas. The distribution of the popular vote—Clinton 43 percent, Bush 38 percent, Perot 18 percent—demonstrated the significance of the third-party candidate in the final outcome.

Highly popular at its peak, George H. W. Bush's administration made an effective transition to what Bush called "a new world order," and, despite the prolonged recession, contributed to long-term stability at home.

Of the Bushes' five surviving children, two entered politics. John E. ("Jeb") Bush (1953–) won the Florida governorship in 1998, whereas George W. Bush (1946–) was elected Texas governor in 1994 and reelected in 1998. In 2000, in a very close and disputed election, George W. Bush defeated Democrat Al Gore to win the presidency with running mate Dick Cheney, resulting in the first father–son presidential succession since John Adams and John Quincy Adams.

[*See also* **Bush, George W.; Clinton, William J.; Ford, Gerald R.; Iran-Contra Affair; Nixon, Richard M.; Perot, Ross; Reagan, Ronald;** ***and*** **Watergate.**]

BIBLIOGRAPHY

Bush, George W., and Brent Scowcroft. *A World Transformed*. New York: Alfred A. Knopf, 1998.

Mervin, David. *George Bush and the Guardianship Presidency*. Basingstoke: Macmillan, 1996.

Parmet, Herbert S. *George Bush: The Life of a Lone Star Yankee*. New York: Scribner & Sons, 1997.

Herbert S. Parmet

BUSH, GEORGE W.

(1946-), forty-third president of the United States (2001–2009). He also has the distinction of being the son of President George Herbert Walker Bush, only the second father-and-son combination to hold the presidency. He served as governor of Texas from 1995 to 2000 and was a businessman, owner of the Texas Rangers baseball club and of an oil drilling company in western Texas.

George Bush was born on 6 July 1946 in New Haven, Connecticut, the first son of George Herbert Walker and Barbara Bush. His father was a World War II Navy veteran and aviator and the son of Connecticut senator Prescott Bush. After George H. W. Bush graduated from Yale University, the young family moved to Odessa, Texas, where he entered the oil business. In 1948 they moved to Midland, where George W. Bush spent his childhood. He was the oldest of five siblings. His brother Jeb Bush served as governor of Florida from 1999 to 2007.

George W. Bush attended Andover Academy and matriculated at Yale University, where he majored in history. After graduating from Yale in 1968, Bush joined the Texas Air National Guard and trained as a pilot. In 1972 he left the Guard to join the campaign of Red Blount, a Republican running for Congress, in Alabama. Years later when he ran for president in 2000, there was speculation that he had been away from the Guard without leave and that he had received shoddy recommendations from superiors. All of the accusations proved false, especially after it was revealed that one memo—reported on by Dan Rather of CBS News—was typed with a modern computer printer, rather than a typewriter.

After leaving the National Guard, Bush drifted, spending a summer on an oil rig, before finally deciding to pursue a master's degree in business administration at Harvard University. He joined a friend in the oil business and moved back to Midland, Texas. Like many young bachelors, Bush hung out with friends, drank heavily—which he continued to do until his fortieth birthday when he quit—and met his future wife, a librarian named Laura Welch. The couple married on 5 November 1977. A turn toward religion in the mid-1980s helped him quit drinking.

His path to politics was unconventional. He ran for a congressional seat from Midland in 1978 and lost. His father's career was more important to him, and Bush supported his father's candidacy for the Grand Old Party (GOP) nomination in 1980 and his later presidential administrations and candidacies in 1988 and 1992. Bush became an owner of the Texas Rangers, but he was still restless; in 1993, after his father's defeat to Bill Clinton, George decided to run for Texas governor. With his friend Karl Rove and political consultant Karin Hughes, they pulled an upset victory over Democrat Ann Richards.

As governor, Bush pursued and sought consensus with Democrats in the legislature and with Democratic lieutenant governor Bob Bullock. He worked to revamp education and sought input from Hispanics (he spoke fluent Spanish). He proved popular and easily won re-election. In 1999 he decided to run for president, hoping to campaign and run on the bipartisanship that had made Texas a growing and prosperous state.

Bush defeated a large field of candidates seeking the GOP nomination in 2000. Bush depicted himself as a compassionate conservative and won the evangelical Protestant vote in the primaries. He faced Vice President Al Gore in the campaign. On election night television networks declared the election for Gore after it appeared he had won Florida (polls in the northwest section of the state had not yet closed). A few hours later they reversed the call and declared for Bush. Gore called Bush to concede, yet a few hours later returns kept coming in that showed a narrowing Bush lead. Gore called to take back his concession and lawyers from both camps rushed to Florida for a 36-day contest decided finally by *Bush v. Gore,* a 5-to-4 Supreme Court decision invalidating the Florida Court decision allowing a statewide mandatory recount. Bush had been elected president.

Bush's presidency got off to a slow start. He secured a promised tax cut but spent most of his time advancing his education initiatives. That changed on the morning of 11 September 2001 when two hijacked airliners flew into New York's World Trade Center Twin Towers, causing them to collapse. Hijacked planes also attacked the Pentagon, and one was commandeered by passengers before crashing in a field in Shanksville, Pennsylvania. The culprits were twenty-six Islamic hijackers who were traced back to al-Qaeda, a terrorist group led by Osama bin Laden. Over 3,000 Americans were killed in the attack.

Bush reacted swiftly, invading Afghanistan to remove the Taliban government, which had provided cover for al-Qaeda operations, from power. Bush also focused attention on nations that supported terrorism, enunciating the Bush Doctrine, a strategy of preemptive war to ward off and destroy potential threats before they could harm the United States.

Most of his focus was on Saddam Hussein's Iraq, which, the administration claimed, possessed weapons of mass destruction (WMD) in violation of several United Nations (UN) sanctions. After many months of diplomatic wrangling Secretary of State Colin Powell presented evidence of Iraq duplicity regarding WMD and received UN Security Council condemnation of Iraq. Bush warned Hussein that he faced imminent invasion if Iraq did not comply with UN mandates. On 17 March 2003, the United States, Great Britain, and a coalition of smaller nations invaded Iraq, forcing the regime out of power.

Planning for the occupation of the country proved problematic and within a year's time the nation was embroiled in an insurgency between rival Shiite and Sunni Muslims. Al-Qaeda developed a presence in Iraq and support for the war at home crumbled.

Still, Bush was able to defeat Democrat John Kerry for the presidency in 2004, a narrow win that gave Bush a second term. With Iraq still dividing the nation, Bush faced the worst natural disaster in the country's history, Hurricane Katrina, which devastated the Gulf Coast of Alabama, Mississippi, and Louisiana, flooded New Orleans, and caused over 3,000 deaths. Bush was blamed for government inaction and the impression of incompetence helped deepen public distrust of the administration.

In 2006, the Democrats took control of Congress. Bush rejected the official report of a commission designed to investigate the Iraq War and pushed for a surge of additional troops into Iraq. The additional troops, commanded by General David Petraeus, made the difference in defeating the insurgents.

In 2007 Iraqis voted for a new government, and the number of Americans killed dropped precipitously after the surge.

Bush was a controversial president, one unafraid to make tough decisions. In domestic matters, he was conservative in some ways, cutting taxes for ten years and prohibiting additional use of stem cells from aborted fetuses in research. In other ways, he expanded government spending and borrowing tremendously, securing an expansion of Medicare (prescription drug program), creating a massive new federal bureaucracy (Department of Homeland Security), fighting wars to expand democracy abroad, and expanding the federal government's control over public schools.

Expansion of the federal purse came in his last few months in office. The economy had grown under Bush, but much of the growth was based on an inflated housing market, the classic speculative bubble. That bubble burst in 2008 when Wall Street imploded and the capital of huge, historic firms, like Bear Stearns and Lehman Brothers, was exposed to risk. The collapse of the housing market fueled a crash of proportions not seen since the 1970s. The Dow Jones collapsed from a high of 14,000 to a low of 6,800 in less than a year. Most Americans lost substantial retirement money and investments and home foreclosures rose.

Bush signed onto a plan, called the Troubled Asset Relief Program (TARP), to buy the toxic assets of banks. Congress voted against the plan until prompted by Treasury Secretary Henry Paulson and Federal Reserve Chairman Ben Bernanke of what would happen if troubled firms were not bailed out. Congress narrowly passed the bill. Some firms disappeared, whereas others received money from government. Even General Motors received a bailout, as TARP's budget was set at $800 billion.

The collapse of the economy further weakened the public's view of Bush and the GOP. In November 2008, Democrat Senator Barack Obama defeated John McCain for the presidency. Bush retired from an active role in politics, concentrating on writing his memoirs, *Decision Points* (published in 2010), and developing the George W. Bush library and center to promote democracy and education.

[***See also* Bush, George H. W.; *Bush v. Gore*; *and* Gore, Albert A., Jr.**]

BIBLIOGRAPHY

George W. Bush, *Decision Points*. New York: Crown Publishers, (2010).

Gregory L. Schneider

BUSH v. GORE

Bush v. Gore, still the subject of heated controversy, was the 5-to-4 U.S. Supreme Court opinion that decided the 2000 presidential election. The razor-thin race between then Governor George W. Bush and Vice President Albert A. Gore Jr., came down to who would win Florida's votes in the Electoral College. After many networks called the race for Bush, they backtracked, saying it was too close to call. By the morning after the election it was clear that there would be a recount of Florida's votes. The proper standard for recounting votes eventually became the subject of the litigation that would lead to *Bush v. Gore.*

Bush v. Gore was actually the final of three interventions of the Supreme Court into the Florida recount. In the first, *Bush v. Palm Beach County Canvassing Board,* the Supreme Court vacated a Florida Supreme Court ruling that interpreted the power of the Florida legislature under the Florida Constitution. Because the Supreme Court was uncertain about the basis for the Florida court's ruling, it remanded the case and asked the state court to clarify its ruling. The Supreme Court declined, at that point, to review "the federal questions asserted to be present."

The Supreme Court would later be more aggressive in asserting its role. The first time *Bush v. Gore* was presented to the Court, it issued a stay of the Florida recount. Justice Scalia, in a brief concurrence to the stay, justified it on the grounds that counting questionable votes first and ruling on their legality afterward was "not a recipe for producing election results that have the public acceptance democratic stability requires." Foreshadowing the line-up in the final *Bush v. Gore,* Justices Stevens, Souter, Ginsburg, and Breyer dissented from the order for the stay.

The opinion in *Bush v. Gore* was issued on 12 December 2000, nearly a month after the election. The majority opinion (which won five votes) rested on the claim that the lack of uniform standards governing the counting of votes represented a violation of the Equal Protection Clause of the Fourteenth Amendment. Florida's use of an ambiguous "intent of the voter standard" did not, the Court ruled, "satisfy the minimum requirement for non-arbitrary treatment of voters." The Court also concluded that there was not time enough to conduct a recount that would meet equal protection standards before the statutorily mandated deadline of 12 December. In a concurring opinion, Justices Rehnquist, Scalia, and Thomas found further reasons to favor Bush: the Florida Court, in ordering a recount, had usurped the state legislature's role provided under Article II of the U.S. Constitution.

Justices Stevens, Ginsburg, Breyer, and Souter dissented. Justices Breyer and Souter, who agreed in principle with the equal protection rationale, would have remanded the case back to Florida for a recount. Justice Stevens, in a charged dissent, asserted that although "we may never know with complete certainty" the winner of the 2000 election, "the loser is perfectly clear. It is the Nation's confidence in the judge as an impartial guardian of the rule of law."

Bush v. Gore is still widely attacked as a political decision, with the evidence (in part) being the fact that those in the majority had been appointed by Republican presidents. Some, conceding it might have been politically motivated, have sought to justify the decision on pragmatic grounds. The decision itself has been repeatedly condemned as poorly reasoned.

At least two legal issues still linger. The first is the implications of the equal protection rationale presented in *Bush v. Gore.* There have been several lawsuits subsequent to *Bush,* which have argued that disparities both in counting methods and in voting machinery represent a violation of the Equal Protection Clause. What does equal protection require in these contexts?

Second, and relatedly, there is the question of the precedential value of *Bush v. Gore.* The opinion, notoriously, stated that it was "limited to the present circumstances," suggesting that the equal protection rationale might merely apply to the facts of *Bush v. Gore.* Some courts have been reluctant to apply *Bush v. Gore* and, indeed, the Supreme Court has not cited *Bush* since it was decided. Whether *Bush* is dead or will live to be used another day is an open question.

[***See also* Bush, George W.; Fourteenth Amendment; Gore, Albert A., Jr., *and* Supreme Court, U.S.**]

BIBLIOGRAPHY

Ackerman, Bruce, ed. *Bush v. Gore: The Question of Legitimacy*. New Haven, Conn.: Yale University Press, 2002.

Dworkin, Ronald, ed. *A Badly Flawed Election: Debating Bush v. Gore, the Supreme Court, and American Democracy*. New York: New Press, 2002.

Hasen, Rick. "The Untimely Death of *Bush v. Gore*." *Stanford Law Review* 60 (October 2007).

Sunstein, Cass. R., and Richard A. Epstein. *The Vote: Bush, Gore & the Supreme Court*. Chicago: University of Chicago Press, 2001.

Chad W. Flanders

BUSING, SCHOOL

Busing is the controversial policy that involves the transportation of children across district lines for the purpose of promoting racial integration. As a widespread practice, busing began during the late 1960s in response to the slow pace of desegregation that was occurring in the South. Within a few years, however, busing would become one of the most divisive issues in the country.

In the 1971 case of *Swann v. Charlotte-Mecklenburg Board of Education*, the U.S. Supreme Court unanimously upheld the constitutionality of busing as a means of dismantling a system of dual schools. In handing down its ruling, the court allowed busing for the purpose of altering the makeup of racially homogenous schools that had arisen as a result of state action. However, in a more controversial move, the decision also allowed busing to be used to alter the composition of schools whose racial homogeneity had been the result of residential patterns. Beside ensuring the use of busing in communities both inside and outside the South, the ruling likely accentuated the move to the suburbs among middle-class urbanites—a process commonly referred to as "white flight." As a result of such outmigration, by the end of the 1970s the population of students attending public schools in most large U.S. cities had become majority black and/or Hispanic.

From the perspective of its critics, busing undermined neighborhood schools and punished people who had neither promoted nor sanctioned the segregation of the races; but from the standpoint of its supporters, busing was necessary to bring an end to the last remnants of segregation. With some notable exceptions, conservatives tended to oppose and leading liberals tended to support busing initiatives.

During the 1970s and beyond, surveys consistently showed that a clear majority of Americans were against the practice of busing. According to a 1971 Gallup Poll, for example, only about one in five Americans (18 percent) approved of busing for the purpose of racial integration. Within the African American population, the issue was more evenly divided, with 45 percent of black Americans favoring busing. Although leading civil rights organizations, such as the National Association for the Advancement of Colored People (NAACP) and the Congressional Black Caucus, were quick to support the policy of busing, other groups that were influenced by the Black Power movement expressed fierce opposition. For example, one of the resolutions that came out of the 1972 National Black Political Convention denounced busing as "a bankrupt, suicidal method of desegregating schools." The same resolution took issue with what it characterized as "the false notion that black children are unable to learn unless they are in the same setting with white children."

Given the strong sentiments surrounding the issue, busing became one of the great controversies of the early 1970s. During his first term in office, President Nixon adopted a strong stance against busing. As he stated in a televised address to the nation in March of 1972, court-ordered busing had left in its wake "anger, fear and turmoil in local communities and worst of all agonized concern among hundreds of thousands of parents for the education and the safety of their children who have been forced by court order to be bussed miles away from their neighborhood school." That same year, the former Alabama governor, George Wallace, adopted a similar approach, making his opposition to busing one of the cornerstone issues of his bid for the Democratic presidential nomination. In the 1972 Democratic primary in Florida, the issue had generated such intense opposition that the Washington senator Henry "Scoop" Jackson and former vice president Hubert Humphrey—two candidates for the Democratic nomination for president—joined Nixon and Wallace in expressing serious reservations about the practice of busing.

In the 1974 case of *Milliken v. Bradley*, the nation's suburbs became largely insulated from the practice of busing when the U.S. Supreme Court, in a 5-to-4 decision, ruled against cross-district busing. In its decision, the court maintained that in the absence of misbehavior on the part of the suburban school districts, it would not be a legitimate exercise of government power to compel the majority-white suburbs outside of Detroit to participate in an integration plan involving the overwhelmingly black public schools in the city of Detroit itself.

As a way of blunting opposition to busing, some urban schools districts in the 1970s began experimenting with magnet schools. The idea was to create a specialized, high-quality program (often in mathematics or the sciences) to which middle-class students would be eager to apply. Since the magnet school would typically be attached to a larger public school whose students came from lower socioeconomic backgrounds, the effect of the magnet school would be to ensure greater racial diversity by attracting large numbers of middle-class white students to public schools that would otherwise be overwhelmingly black and/or Hispanic. Throughout the 1980s and 1990s, magnet schools became a prominent feature of the public school system in cities across the nation.

Notwithstanding the popularity of magnet schools, support for busing continued to erode in the decades following the *Swann* decision. With increasing frequency, federal courts either lifted or refused to reissue decrees that extended the practice of busing. During the 1990s, for example, Denver, Dallas, Buffalo, Cleveland, Wilmington, Savannah, and numerous other cities were permitted by the courts to terminate their policy of busing. In 2001, the Fourth Circuit Court of Appeals brought an end to the policy of busing on the part of the Charlotte-Mecklenburg School District—the very community whose integration plan thirty years earlier had led to the landmark *Swann* decision.

[*See also* **Humphrey, Hubert; Nixon, Richard M.;** ***Swann v. Charlotte-Mecklenburg Board of Education; and*** **Wallace, George C.**]

BIBLIOGRAPHY

Lassiter, Matthew D. "The Suburban Origins of 'Color Blind' Conservatism." *Journal of Urban History* (May 2004), 549–82.

Orfield, Gary, and Susan E. Eaton. *Dismantling Desegregation: The Quiet Reversal of Brown v. Board of Education*. New York: New Press, 1996.

Alan Petigny

C

CALHOUN, JOHN C.

(1782–1850), politician and states' rights champion. For over a generation John Caldwell Calhoun dominated politics both in his native South Carolina and the entire South and exerted a powerful national influence. Born near Abbeville on the South Carolina frontier, Calhoun graduated from Yale in 1804, entered the bar in 1807, served in the state legislature, and in 1810 was elected to Congress. Marriage to his cousin Floride in 1811 brought him a large plantation. Early in his congressional career Calhoun exhibited strong nationalism, ranking as a leading "war hawk," supporting the War of 1812 and thereafter advocating federal internal improvements, a national bank, and the protective tariff of 1816. As James Monroe's secretary of war (1817–1825), Calhoun reorganized and modernized the department. By the time he served as vice president (under both John Quincy Adams and Andrew Jackson), Calhoun had shifted to a states' right position. His influential South Carolina Exposition and Protest (1828), an attack on the tariff of 1818, argued that protective tariffs were unconstitutional and that states retained their sovereignty when they entered the Union. The rise of antislavery sentiment and Northern voting power profoundly influenced his thinking; realizing that white Southerners lacked the votes to override the North, he hoped to find a mechanism to preserve southern rights and interests within the Union. His theories of nullification and state interposition offered a third path between unconditional unionists and secessionists. During the

Nullification Crisis of 1828–1833, Calhoun resigned the vice presidency (1832) and took a seat in the U.S. Senate to advocate his state's views. Briefly serving as secretary of state under John Tyler (1844–1845), Calhoun helped secure the annexation of Texas as a slave state. Returning to the Senate in 1845, he vigorously opposed the Compromise of 1850, seeing it as a thinly veiled attack on slaveholders, and came ominously close to advocating secession in the days preceding his death.

[*See also* **Adams, John Quincy; Compromise of 1850; Federal Government, Executive Branch: State Department; Federal Government, Legislative Branch: Senate; Jackson, Andrew; Monroe, James; States' Rights; Tariffs; Texas Annexation;** *and* **Tyler, John.**]

BIBLIOGRAPHY

Meriwether, Robert L., Clyde Wilson, eds. *The Papers of John C. Calhoun,* 23 vols. to date. Columbia: University of South Carolina Press, 1959– .

Niven, John. John C. *Calhoun and the Price of Union.* Baton Rouge: Louisiana State University Press, 1988.

Eric H. Walther

CAMPAIGN FINANCE REFORM

The marriage of money and politics is one of the most enduring and controversial topics in American law and public policy. Throughout the history of the United States, campaigns for public office have been financed primarily by private funds donated by individuals to the politicians they favor. For some, this arrangement is a testament to democratic participation. For others, private money threatens to breed corruption. Since the early 1900s, the debate over what constitutes corruption and how it should be prevented has shaped federal campaign finance policy.

Early Historical and Theoretical Evolution. Particularly at the federal level, current campaign finance policy began in the late nineteenth century. Alleged or actual exchange of official actions for campaign contributions first drew congressional attention during the Civil War, when influence-peddling among some government contractors was alleged. Attention to the issue again arose during the late 1800s and early 1900s amid concerns about questionable fund-raising by some presidential campaigns. Anticorruption themes and the demand for greater transparency continued to shape regulation for the next century.

One of the first and most prominent references to federal campaign finance policy appeared in President Theodore Roosevelt's 1907 annual message to Congress—delivered in writing then but which, today, would be equivalent to a State of the Union message. Roosevelt—some observers argued in response to controversies over his own campaign fund-raising—proposed that Congress appropriate funding for the national parties to support their presidential candidates' campaigns. In exchange, parties would have to accept limits on the individual contributions they received.

Roosevelt conceded that his proposal was controversial. Indeed, public financing of presidential campaigns did not become a reality until the 1970s. Nonetheless, Roosevelt's initial proposal for public financing embodied key principles in the debate over various campaign finance issues during the next century.

What role should individuals, corporations, and labor unions play in financing campaigns?

What information should be disclosed to the public and regulators? What should the regulatory structure be? What does campaign finance mean for representation and free speech—and for and by whom? All these questions have been central to the debate over money in politics. Most have no definitive answer but continue to shape campaign finance policy. More importantly, campaign finance policy is more than a technical set of requirements about documenting and limiting the flow of money. Rather, it represents one of the most crucial ways in which individuals and groups participate in the electoral process and how their elected officials represent their interests.

Limiting Corruption: Ongoing Concern and Controversy. Just as in Theodore Roosevelt's day and before, limiting the potential for what is known as "quid pro quo" corruption—namely, official actions in exchange for contributions—was central to campaign finance policy throughout the twentieth century. Limiting real or potential corruption remains a cornerstone of campaign finance policy in the early 2000s. Over time, however, disagreement among policy makers and activists has emerged about what constitutes corruption and which policy solutions are reasonable responses.

Anticorruption concerns continued throughout the 1900s, but perhaps because campaigns were largely party-run affairs until mid-century, serious legislative attention to the issue was rare. As campaigns became more candidate centered in the 1950s and 1960s, instances of alleged corruption from contributors seeking influence with individual candidates became more prominent. The anticorruption narrative reached its zenith in the 1970s, particularly following the Watergate scandal. Although the episode is today remembered primarily as a case of presidential disregard for the rule of law, its roots began with questionable fund-raising during Richard Nixon's 1972 reelection campaign. Watergate was the most prominent fund-raising scandal to date, but it nonetheless followed other instances of large and minimally documented contributions—some in cash—during presidential campaigns throughout the 1960s. In response, Congress sought to document and limit the flow of campaign contributions and spending.

For some, these requirements were reasonable measures to limit dangerous and demonstrable corruption of representative democracy. Critics, however, countered that corruption concerns were overblown. In particular, they argued that cases of quid pro quo corruption were rare and that regulating campaign contributions and spending inhibited the ability of contributors and candidates to engage in constitutionally protected free speech. Debate over the proper scope of regulation, as well as the extent to which corruption is a valid concern, continues to shape campaign finance policy in the early twenty-first century.

Foundations of Modern Campaign Finance Policy. Amid the anticorruption concerns of the 1960s and 1970s, Congress considered a variety of policy options. These options ranged from tax incentives and tax credits to encourage smaller individual contributions, to public financing of campaigns, to various reporting requirements and limits on amounts and sources of contributions. Indeed, documenting the flow of money has been the most common approach to campaign finance regulation since the 1970s. In particular, the Federal Election Campaign Act (FECA) remains the cornerstone of the nation's federal campaign finance law. FECA was enacted in 1971, but substantial post-Watergate amendments enacted in 1974,

1976, and 1979 are the primary source of modern law.

FECA and its principal amendments seek to prevent potential corruption through two major approaches. First, FECA requires reporting (known in campaign finance parlance as "disclosure") of contributions to, and spending by, candidate campaigns, political action committees (PACs), and political party committees (e.g., the Democratic National Committee and Republican National Committee). Disclosure surrounding some independent political advertising is also required. Generally, monthly or quarterly reporting is required depending on the type of filer and timing. Second, FECA limits the amounts and sources of political contributions. FECA initially limited individual contributions to no more than $1,000 per candidate, per election, meaning that a person could contribute no more than $2,000 total to a candidate's primary and general-election campaigns. The 2002 Bipartisan Campaign Reform Act (BCRA), also known as "McCain–Feingold" for its principal Senate sponsors, raised the individual contribution limits to $2,000 per candidate, per election, and indexed these amounts for inflation. Limits for the 2010 election cycle were $2,500 per candidate, per election.

By incorporating federal law enacted in the 1910s to the 1940s, FECA prohibits corporations, unions, and national banks from making contributions from their treasuries. Federal Election Commission (FEC) interpretation of FECA has, however, permitted these entities to establish legally separate PACs that may raise voluntary contributions from employees or members. The corporate or union parent may not dictate the PAC's activities, although media accounts and popular wisdom often suggest that PAC activity and corporate or union activity are one and the same. FECA limits PAC contributions to $5,000 annually, the same amount an individual may contribute to a PAC. Separate limits apply to contributions to political parties.

FECA also attempted to limit campaign spending. In its landmark *Buckley v. Valeo* decision, the U.S. Supreme Court held those limits unconstitutional and found that they inhibited protected political speech. At the same time, however, the Court determined that disclosure requirements were a reasonable means of providing information to voters and helped prevent corruption.

With *Buckley,* the Supreme Court also permitted limits on spending for candidates who voluntarily participate in public financing of campaigns. Public financing of presidential campaigns has been in effect since 1976, although declining program revenues and candidate participation have placed the program in jeopardy in the early 2000s. In 2008, Barack Obama became the first president elected without any participation in the public financing program since its inception—a development that some have argued marked the death knell for the program. Others have argued that public financing is antiquated but needs modernization to provide an option for nonwealthy candidates to pursue the nation's highest office.

The 1990s and Beyond. Congress made occasional amendments to FECA throughout the 1980s and 1990s. Momentum for amending the act became especially strong in the mid-1990s amid concerns about largely unregulated "soft money" contributions to national party committees, controversial "issue advertising" that skirted campaign finance law by criticizing or praising lawmakers but stopping short of calling for their election or defeat, and controversial fund-raising during the 1996 presidential election cycle. In response, Congress enacted BCRA in 2002. The act amended FECA and, among other things, banned soft money in federal elections, restricted issue advertising, and raised most contribution limits (except for PACs).

A series of developments has challenged BCRA's effectiveness, although the soft-money ban—one of the act's primary elements—remains in effect. Nonetheless, unlimited contributions may still flow to tax-exempt organizations that became prominent following BCRA, particularly those organized under Sections 501(c) and 527 of the Internal Revenue Code. These groups are largely outside the scope of federal campaign finance law. Corporations and unions also gained substantial new abilities to participate in campaign politics following Supreme Court rulings in 2008 and 2010. In particular, the 2010 *Citizens United v. FEC* decision permits corporations and unions to use their treasury funds to explicitly call for election or defeat of federal candidates (known as "express advocacy"). Some observers also contend that the FEC has been lax in implementing and enforcing parts of BCRA. On the other hand, the commission's bipartisan, six-member structure (which Congress designed) can make finding agreement on the most contentious regulatory issues difficult. As these developments show, although particular aspects of the debate over campaign finance policy have changed since the early 1900s, major issues of contention remain consistent.

DISCLAIMER

This entry represents the views of the author. It does not necessarily represent the views of the Congressional Research Service, Library of Congress, or any other institution with which the author is affiliated.

[*See also* **Elections, Election Law; Elections, Presidential Elections; Nixon, Richard M.; Obama, Barack;** *and* **Roosevelt, Theodore.**]

BIBLIOGRAPHY

Corrado, Anthony, et al. *The New Campaign Finance Sourcebook*. Washington, D.C.: Brookings Institution Press, 2005.

Garrett, R. Sam. *The State of Campaign Finance Policy: Recent Developments and Issues*. Washington, D.C.: Congressional Research Service, 2011.

Herrnson, Paul. *Congressional Elections: Campaigning at Home and in Washington*. Washington, D.C.: CQ Press, 2008.

La Raja, J. *Small Change: Money, Political Parties, and Campaign Finance Reform*. Ann Arbor: University of Michigan Press, 2008.

Mutch, Robert E. *Campaigns, Congress, and the Courts: The Making of Federal Campaign Finance Law*. New York: Praeger, 1988.

Samples, John. *The Fallacy of Campaign Finance Reform*. Chicago: University of Chicago Press, 2006.

R. Sam Garrett

CANNON, JOSEPH

Joseph "Uncle Joe" Cannon embodied the established traditional wing of the Republican Party during the Gilded Age and Progressive Era. He represented his Danville, Illinois, U.S. Congressional District almost continually for fifty years, from 1873 to 1922, and during the fifty-ninth to the sixty-first Congresses, 1903–1910, he served as Speaker of the House, controlling the chamber with a proverbial iron fist. Criticism of his near-dictatorial leadership would result in new House rules that diminished the Speaker's authority.

Events of his youth shaped the future congressman's political philosophy and defined the values he unflinchingly defended. Born in Guilford, North Carolina, in 1836, young Joseph moved north to Indiana with his Quaker family to escape the influences of slavery. This and his family's other abolitionist activities cemented his connection to the Republican Party's free labor ideology. Every American, Cannon believed, should have an equal opportunity to succeed, or fail, based solely on his or her work ethic. The nation owed its success to the collective efforts of such men and women who sought to make their way in what Cannon believed to be an egalitarian milieu, and he distrusted those who sought to move the nation from its traditional moorings.

Such convictions led Congressman Cannon to distinguish himself as an opponent of progressive reform, particularly those associated with President Theodore Roosevelt and Wisconsin Senator Robert La Follette. During his reign as Speaker, Cannon and his like-minded confederates stymied the progressives' efforts to pass legislation intended to grant the Interstate Commerce Commission (ICC) more authority to regulate business, lower the tariff rates, conserve natural resources, and end the use of injunctions against labor. Ultimately, in 1910, Cannon's opposition to reform—specifically to tariff adjustment—would lead to his downfall as Speaker and to a revision of House rules.

Cannon's despotic behavior likely thwarted one of his few unfulfilled ambitions. In 1908, he failed in his efforts to secure the Republican presidential nomination, which ultimately went to William Howard Taft, President Theodore Roosevelt's hand-picked successor. Political customs of the era precluded overt campaigning for party endorsement, but Cannon actively sought support of delegates to the Republican National Convention. He garnered some votes, but growing frustration with what many saw as his obstructionist bent, coupled with Taft's endorsement from the popular Roosevelt, insured his defeat.

He played a key role in creating the 1907 Dillingham Commission for the investigation of immigration, as a substitute for a proposed literacy test intended to restrict alien entrance, and he supported women's suffrage. Cannon himself took pride in having been part of a generation that had harnessed technology and engendered economic growth. Yet, more often than not, he left a legacy of having stood in the way of those who sought to use the very government of which he was a key part to alleviate distress and bring about social betterment.

[*See also* **Civil Rights;** *and* **Progressive Era.**]

BIBLIOGRAPHY

Busbey, L. White. *Uncle Joe Cannon: The Story of a Pioneer American*. New York: H. Holt, 1927.

Bolles, Blair. *Tyrant from Illinois: Uncle Joe Cannon's Experiment with Personal Power*. New York: Norton, 1951.

Zeidel, Robert F. "Hayseed Immigration Policy: 'Uncle Joe' Cannon and the Immigration Question." *Illinois Historical Journal* 88 (Autumn 1995): 173–188.

Robert F. Zeidel

CAPITAL PUNISHMENT

Since George Kendall's execution in Jamestown in 1608, about 20,000 people have been legally put to death in America—more than 7,000 of them in the twentieth century. All thirteen colonies mandated public hanging for certain crimes against the state, person, or property. When the Bill of Rights was adopted in 1791, the Eighth Amendment's prohibition against "cruel and unusual" punishment was understood to outlaw torture and the intentional infliction of pain, not the death penalty itself. Over the next two centuries, however, the criminal law gradually reduced the number of crimes punishable by death while introducing other reforms that lowered the number of executions. In 1793, for example, Pennsylvania introduced a distinction between murder and manslaughter and limited the death penalty to offenders convicted of the former. By the 1830s, five states (Pennsylvania, New York, New Jersey, Rhode Island, and Massachusetts) had outlawed public executions, and in the 1840s states began to grant juries the discretion to impose life imprisonment in capital cases. In the early twentieth century, states further restricted capital statutes, eliminating horse thievery, cattle rustling, assaults, and, finally, rape. By 1977, only murder could result in capital punishment.

The number of executions began to drop in the 1950s, and the years from 1968 to 1976 saw a moratorium on executions. Executions resumed thereafter, although the average time served under the death sentence grew to more than ten years, owing mainly to the expanding role of federal appellate courts. In 1990, the Supreme Court limited appeals to the federal courts by death row inmates.

The issue of deterrence long dominated the debate concerning capital punishment. By the late twentieth century, concerns about arbitrariness, racial discrimination, costs, and conviction of the innocent had taken center stage. In the 1972 case *Furman v. Georgia,* the Supreme Court temporarily ended the death penalty in America, deeming its application arbitrary and capricious. In response, thirty-eight states and the federal government enacted new capital punishment laws designed to pass constitutional muster. These laws typically separated the guilt-or-innocence phase of the trial from the sentencing phase, mandated a statutory list of "aggravating" and "mitigating" factors to guide juries in capital trials, and required automatic review by state courts of all death sentences and convictions. Many scholars, however, believed that these reforms failed to eliminate arbitrariness and that the administration of the death penalty remained no less inconsistent and arbitrary in the mid-1990s than it had been in 1972.

Some scholars contended that capital punishment involved racial discrimination. In *Equal Justice and the Death Penalty* (1990), David C. Baldus and his associates demonstrated that the victim's race was a significant factor in predicting which convicted murderers received the death penalty. Killers of whites were 4.3 times more likely to be sentenced to death than killers of African Americans. In *McCleskey v. Kemp* (1987), however, the Supreme Court held that such statistical patterns were insufficient to prove violation of the Fourteenth Amendment's equal protection clause in specific cases; proof of intentional discrimination against a particular defendant had to be provided.

The cost of death-penalty cases became an important issue as well, as the "super due process" requirements made the prosecution of capital cases extraordinarily expensive. In New Jersey, for example, capital trials cost about $750,000 in the 1990s, whereas non-capital murder trials cost around $50,000. Since only 15 percent of capital trials end in a death sentence, in 85 percent of the cases taxpayers pay the cost of both a capital trial and life imprisonment. Consequently, the cost of sending a single person to death row in New Jersey in the 1990s was a staggering $7.3 million.

Finally, the conviction of the innocent became an important issue in the late twentieth-century debate over capital punishment. According to one study (Bedau and Radlet, 1987), 350 people in the twentieth century were wrongly convicted of offenses punishable by death, and 25 were actually executed. Further, this study found that many of the wrongful convictions were not good-faith errors but resulted from conspiracies by the police, prosecutors, defense attorneys, judges, witnesses, and even jurors. The problems of human fallibility and malfeasance, neither of which can be effectively remedied, remained central in the continuing capital punishment debate as the twenty-first century dawned. The use of newly developed DNA techniques to exonerate a number of prisoners, including several on death row, deepened concerns about erroneous convictions and executions. In *Atkins v. Virginia* (2002), the Supreme Court barred the execution of a mentally retarded person. In 2004, the high court agreed to hear a case involving a young man sentenced to die for a murder committed when he was a minor. In such a case, the defense claimed, the death penalty violated the constitutional prohibition on cruel and unusual punishment.

[*See also* **Crime Policy, Federal; Fourteenth Amendment; Jurisprudence;** ***and*** **Supreme Court, U.S.**]

BIBLIOGRAPHY

Baldus, David, Charles Pulaski Jr., and George G. Wentworth. *Equal Justice and the Death Penalty: A Legal and Empirical Analysis.* Boston: Northeastern University Press, 1990.

Bedau, Hugo Adam. *The Death Penalty in America.* New York: Oxford University Press, 1997.

Bedau, H. A., and Michael L. Radlet. "Miscarriages of Justice in Potentially Capital Cases." *Stanford Law Review* 41 (November 1987): 161–170.

Bowers, William J., Glenn L. Pierce, and John F. McDevitt. *Legal Homicide: Death as Punishment in America, 1864–1982.* Boston: Northeastern University Press, 1984.

Johnson, Robert. *Death Work: A Study of the Modern Execution Process.* Belmont, CA: Wadsworth, 1990.

Zimring, Franklin E., and Gordon Hawkins. *Capital Punishment and the American Agenda.* Cambridge; New York: Cambridge University Press, 1986.

Richard Moran; updated by Paul S. Boyer

CARSON, RACHEL

(1907–1964), nature writer, environmentalist. Raised on a farm in western Pennsylvania, Carson attended the Pennsylvania College for Women and earned a master's degree in zoology from Johns Hopkins University. In 1935, she went to work at the U.S. Fish and Wildlife Service, producing numerous publications for the agency until she left in 1953 to write independently.

Carson's *The Sea Around Us* (1951), a hugely successful book about the oceans, was at once scientifically knowledgeable and compellingly lyrical. She is best known for *Silent Spring* (1962), an impassioned defense of unspoiled nature for its own sake and a powerful warning that the chemical despoliation of the environment, especially by the insecticide DDT, threatened human health. An international best-seller, the book eloquently popularized the idea that human beings must recognize themselves as part of nature rather than purely as masters of it.

In *Silent Spring,* which first appeared in the *New Yorker* magazine, Carson lucidly explained the intricate interconnectedness of nature and how chemical herbicides or insecticides applied by spraying the earth or the air could diffuse through the local soil, be carried through ground and surface water to distant areas, and accumulate in the wild food chain. Her book roused a barrage of ridicule and denunciation from the chemical industry, parts of the food industry, academic scientists allied with both, and some powerful sectors of the media. However, *Silent Spring's* carefully documented analyses were reviewed and endorsed by the President's Science Advisory Committee, and Carson's views helped inspire the environmental protection movement that began in the 1960s.

[*See also* **Environmentalism; Environmental Policy: An Overview;** *and* **Environmental Protection Agency.**]

BIBLIOGRAPHY

Brooks, Paul. *The House of Life: Rachel Carson at Work, with Selections from Her Writings Published and Unpublished.* Boston: Houghton Mifflin, 1972.

Freeman, Martha, ed. *Always, Rachel: The Letters of Rachel Carson and Dorothy Freeman, 1952–1964.* Boston: Beacon Press, 1995.

Daniel J. Kevles

CARTER, JIMMY

(1924–), thirty-ninth president of the United States. James Earl Carter Jr., was born in Plains, Georgia, the son of a conservative agribusinessman and a liberal nurse. Growing up in a prosperous but demanding family, Carter graduated from the U.S. Naval Academy at Annapolis in 1946. The high point of his naval career was service in the nuclear submarine corps under Admiral Hyman Rickover (1900–1986), who reinforced Carter's commitment to self-discipline and efficiency. Returning to Plains following his father's death in 1953, Carter established himself as a civic leader and was elected to the Georgia State Senate in 1962. Defeat in the 1966 Democratic gubernatorial primary plunged him into a brief depression that ended with a spiritual rebirth. He won the governorship in 1970 and attracted national attention by repudiating racial segregation in his inaugural address. Winning the Democratic presidential nomination in 1976, he narrowly defeated the Republican Gerald Ford by courting diverse constituencies and by emphasizing different sides of himself: farmer, fiscally conservative small businessman, nuclear engineer, and "born again" Baptist. In the aftermath of the Watergate scandal, he insisted on his honesty.

Carter entered the presidency with two major handicaps. First, he not only lacked experience dealing with Congress but also, viewing himself as an ethical "outsider" untainted by Washington corruption, doubted the propriety of making any deals. Second, whereas most congressional Democrats wanted to expand the welfare state, Carter stressed efficiency and limited government instead.

Nonetheless, Carter did record several major achievements. In keeping with his relatively conservative economic philosophy, he deregulated the airline and trucking industries and took steps to decontrol the prices of natural gas and oil. An advocate of civil rights, he appointed many African Americans to federal office. His campaign to protect human rights abroad, which he considered both sound national policy and a personal Christian duty, placed the issue firmly on the American agenda. At great political cost, he secured ratification of treaties returning the Canal Zone to Panama, mediated the Camp David Accords between Egypt and Israel, and rejected military intervention in both the Nicaraguan civil war and the Iranian revolution.

In 1979–1980, Carter's presidency was disabled by deteriorating economic conditions, the collapse of Soviet–American détente, and his decision to allow the exiled Shah of Iran into the United States for medical treatment. The oil shortages and rising fuel prices that accompanied the Iranian revolution worsened the "stagflation" (a combination of stagnation and inflation) already afflicting the economy.

Carter's unsuccessful effort in July 1979 to rally the country with an inspirational address was ridiculed as a lamentation over the nation's "malaise." The Shah's arrival in November provoked Islamic militants to seize the U.S. embassy in Iran and take American hostages. Soviet–American relations, acrimonious from the start of Carter's term, plummeted when the Soviets invaded Afghanistan in December 1979 and remained there despite the sanctions Carter imposed. Similarly, neither negotiations nor an inept rescue attempt in April 1980 managed to free the Americans held hostage in Iran. Having satisfied neither liberals nor conservatives, Carter narrowly won renomination but then lost the 1980 election to Ronald Reagan. In a final blow, Iran released the hostages hours after Carter left office.

Carter returned to Plains depressed and facing financial insecurity. He recuperated quickly by pursuing diverse activities with his customary discipline. Establishing the Carter Center at Atlanta's Emory University as his base, he continued to mediate Arab–Israeli differences, supervised foreign elections, focused attention on disease and starvation in poor and unstable nations, and volunteered with Habitat for Humanity, a program to build houses for the poor. In 1994, he defused a confrontation between the United States and North Korea and helped arrange the peaceful end of Haiti's military dictatorship. Although critics still questioned his diplomatic judgment and administrative style, Carter's post-presidential years largely restored his reputation. He was awarded the Nobel Peace Prize in 2002 for his work as a mediator and head of the Carter Center in Atlanta.

[*See also* Civil Rights; Federal Government, Executive Branch: Presidency, The; Energy Crisis of the 1970s; *and* Panama Canal.]

BIBLIOGRAPHY

Bourne, Peter. *Jimmy Carter: A Comprehensive Biography from Plains to the Presidency*. New York: Scribner & Sons, 1997.

Kaufman, Burton I. *The Presidency of James Earl Carter, Jr.* Lawrence: University Press of Kansas, 1993.

Strong, Robert A. *Working in the World: Jimmy Carter and the Making of American Foreign Policy*. Baton Rouge: Louisiana State University Press, 2000.

Leo P. Ribuffo; updated by Paul S. Boyer

CARTOONS, POLITICAL

Benjamin Franklin was first to draw a political cartoon for an American newspaper, in 1754. In "Join, or Die," calling for unity during the French and Indian War, each piece of a severed snake represented a colony. The cartoon was based on a superstition that a snake returns to life if the pieces are put together before sunset. The ubiquitous Franklin was also the first American politician to be ridiculed in a cartoon, in 1764.

Cartoons, laboriously engraved on copper or cut into wood, were a rare event until lithography lowered the cost of production. There were only seventy-eight known political caricatures issued as broadsides before 1828. The most famous of the early nineteenth century cartoons was "The Gerry-mander," 1812, in which Elkanah Tisdale used the shape of a voting district designed by Massachusetts governor Elbridge Gerry to create a monster and a new word for the American language.

The first lithographed political cartoon appeared in 1829, just in time for Andrew Jackson to take office and to begin a line of controversialist presidents whose features were destined to bring joy to cartoonists, notably Lincoln, Theodore Roosevelt, and Nixon. The most famous lithography firm, Currier &

Ives, founded in 1835, produced political cartoons for all sides and then sold them to party headquarters at bulk rates.

National symbols, such as "Uncle Sam," began to take shape. He was first seen in 1834 and started to look more like today's representation during the Civil War, partly influenced by the lanky and bearded Lincoln. There was always some figure to stand for the "common man." Major Jack Downing, a fictional Yankee peddler, was there in the 1830s and 1840s, renamed "John Q. Public" in the next century. The first Democratic donkey came from an anonymous artist in 1837; the Republican elephant was invented by Thomas Nast in 1874.

Nast was born in Germany in 1840, arrived in the United States at age six, and joined *Harper's Weekly* in 1862. For the next quarter century, his name would be inextricably joined with the magazine, becoming the most important political voice in postbellum publishing. Nast's fame rested mainly on some fifty drawings attacking "Boss" Tweed and New York City corruption in 1871. His centerfold cartoons—measuring 14 by 20 inches—are unsurpassed for raw power.

As Nast's popularity began to wane, his place at center stage was captured by Joseph Keppler, son of a Viennese baker, who started a German language weekly called *Puck* in 1876, adding an English edition the next year. If Nast's artistic weapon was the broadsword, Keppler's was the rapier, often cartooning in vivid color with a touch of Viennese gaiety. It is hard to overestimate the political influence of *Puck* and rival *Judge* during the century's last two decades. *Judge,* with Bernard Gillam as its chief cartoonist, was Republican; *Puck* was Democratic.

In the great newspaper war between Joseph Pulitzer's *World* and William Randolph Hearst's *Journal* in New York, some analysts contend that a massive front-page cartoon on 31 October 1884 caused James G. Blaine to lose New York and hence the presidency. In Homer Davenport, Hearst employed the most powerful cartoonist of his generation. Pulitzer and Hearst cartoonists ended the century successfully promoting war with Spain.

World War I generally displayed mainstream cartoonists as cheerleaders. The government helped the process by starting a weekly *Bulletin for Cartoonists* in 1918, offering "win the war" suggestions. The exceptions were a talented group on the left, including Robert Minor, Art Young, and Boardman Robinson, whose work mainly appeared in *The Masses*. The government tried the magazine's antiwar staff, including art editor Young, under the Espionage Act, but two trials ended in two hung juries.

The period between the wars featured several outstanding cartoonists' campaigns: Rollin Kirby challenged "Mr. Dry" (representing the Prohibition amendment) in the *New York World;* Edmund Duffy took on the Ku Klux Klan in the *Baltimore Sun;* and Daniel Fitzpatrick warned of Hitler's march through Europe in the *St Louis Post-Dispatch*. More often, newspaper cartoonists, reflecting their employers, ducked racism and civil rights and were unenthusiastic about Franklin Roosevelt's New Deal. Oliver Harrington produced moving cartoons for the African American press, but he was never invited into the mainstream.

What was unprecedented about World War II cartooning was the *Stars and Stripes* work of Bill Mauldin, who joined the army in 1940 at nineteen and showed what war looked like through the day-to-day travails of Willie and Joe, two battle-weary soldiers. War from this angle was not noble, and Mauldin became the youngest cartoonist to win a Pulitzer Prize.

Postwar challenges catalyzed American newspaper cartooning starting in the early 1950s when Herbert Block (Herblock) stood up to Senator Joseph McCarthy and his hunt for domestic Communists. For Herblock, this was a marker in a remarkable sixty-year record as the voice of liberalism at the *Washington Post*. Paul Conrad brought liberalism to the West Coast, where his cartoons on Watergate in the *Los Angeles Times* earned the honor of being the only cartoonist on Nixon's "enemies list." Pat Oliphant arrived in the United States in 1964 from Australia and won the Pulitzer Prize in his first year with the *Denver Post*. Bill Mauldin in civilian life at the *St. Louis Post-Dispatch* and the *Chicago Sun Times* is best remembered for his iconic obituary cartoon of Lincoln grieving for the murdered John Kennedy. Herblock, Mauldin, Conrad, and Oliphant were the masters of this period. But importantly, Walt Kelley's *Pogo* and Garry Trudeau's *Doonesbury* also brought tough political comment to the comic pages; Jules Feiffer in the *Village Voice* brought cartooning into a realm of political psychology or sociology; and David Levine in *The New York Review of Books* revived caricature that could be bitingly political.

The new century continued the sharp decline of traditional in-print newspapers, where most cartoonists earned a living. The Internet could offer an expanded audience and opportunities to experiment with new techniques. The Pulitzer Prize was awarded to an Internet animator in 2010. With journalism in transition, how to profitably adjust to technological change was an industry-wide problem of which cartooning was a part.

[*See also* **Franklin, Benjamin; Jackson, Andrew; Lincoln, Abraham; Nixon, Richard M.;** *and* **Roosevelt, Theodore.**]

BIBLIOGRAPHY

Fischer, Roger. *Them Damned Pictures: Explorations in American Political Cartoon Art*. North Haven, Conn.: Archon Books, 1996.

Hess, Stephen, and Milton Kaplan. *The Ungentlemanly Art*. New York: Macmillan, 1975.

Hess, Stephen, and Sandy Northrop. *American Political Cartoons: The Evolution of a National Identity, 1754–2010*. Edison, N.J.: Transaction Publishers, 2010.

Nevins, Allan, and Frank Weitenkampf. *A Century of Political Cartoons: Caricature in the United States from 1800 to 1900*. New York: C. Scribner's Sons, 1944.

Stephen Hess

CENSORSHIP

From the Colonial Era to the present, struggles over censorship have loomed large in American life, figuring in the history of antislavery and abolitionism, labor movements, antiwar protests, radical politics, gay rights advocacy, public education debates, controversies over sex and reproduction, and many other issues.

Although John Peter Zenger's 1735 acquittal did not eliminate seditious libel from American jurisprudence, it did make government censorship attempts more difficult. Although the founders' commitment to wholly unfettered speech remains in dispute, the First Amendment's guarantee of free speech and freedom of the press erected a strong barrier against censorship, and Americans of the era clearly valued free political discourse. Although common-law ideas of libel, blasphemy, sedition, and obscenity persisted, radical ideas of free expression thrived as well, as groups and individuals asserted their interests in the public arena. But although the Bill of Rights seemed a bulwark in defense of free speech, the 1798 Alien and Sedition Acts revealed its continued vulnerability.

Like the Federalist Party in the 1790s, subsequent leaders during the Civil War, the two world wars, and the Cold War would insist that the nation's fate depended on the government's capacity to censor its critics. Confronted with antiwar and pro-South agitation during the Civil War, President Abraham Lincoln suspended the writ of habeas corpus in 1863 and authorized the arrest of southern sympathizers, war opponents, and persons engaged in "any disloyal practice." In World War I, under the 1917 Espionage Act and the 1918 Sedition Amendment, the Woodrow Wilson Administration suppressed antiwar periodicals and arrested numerous war critics, including the socialist leader Eugene V. Debs. During the 1918–1920 Red Scare, officials imprisoned and deported many labor activists and radicals. During World War II and the early Cold War the government again engaged in censorship, monitoring wartime movie scripts and, later, removing books by politically suspect authors from United States Information Agency libraries abroad.

But anticensorship sentiment remained strong. The Wilson Administration's abuses led Roger Baldwin and others in 1920 to found what became the American Civil Liberties Union (ACLU). The Supreme Court Justice Oliver Wendell Holmes's dissent in *Abrams v. United States* (1919) sharply criticized censorship, as did the Harvard Law professor Zechariah Chafee in his critique of wartime censorship, *Freedom of Speech* (1920). The ACLU–Holmes–Chafee approach insisted that the First Amendment was meant primarily to serve the social good, by assuring a hearing for unpopular political views, not to protect individual liberty. This approach gave short shrift to traditional libertarianism, represented by Theodore Schroeder of the National Free Speech League, for example, which insisted on the individual's freedom of expression, political, sexual, or otherwise. In a tactically shrewd move, Progressive Era intellectuals offered their socially based argument for free speech in an era not particularly receptive to libertarian ideas. However, this argument made it harder to defend nonpolitical forms of expression, such as "obscene" books, "indecent" movies, and birth control information.

Following Holmes's lead, the Supreme Court in *Near v.* Minnesota (1931) overturned governmental efforts to impose prior restraint on a newspaper. In *New York Times v. Sullivan* (1964), the high court rejected a libel suit against the *Times* for a political ad, although the ad contained certain inaccuracies. In 1971, the justices turned back President Richard M. Nixon's efforts to prevent publication of the Pentagon Papers. The liberalizing trend gradually extended to sexually explicit material in such cases as *United States v. Ulysses* (1933); *Roth v. United States* and *Alberts v. California* (1957); and a 1966 case involving John Cleland's *Memoirs of a Woman of Pleasure*. Signaling a conservative turn, however, the Supreme Court in *Miller v. California* (1973) made it somewhat easier for local authorities to suppress sexually explicit material deemed obscene by local community standards.

Throughout American history, censorship battles have unfolded within a larger cultural context. For example, the expansion of First Amendment protection reflected the efforts of successive generations of artists, writers, and "sex radicals," from nineteenth-century advocates of "free love" to twentieth-century proponents of abortion and gay rights. Conversely, in times of rapid social change, threatened social groups have used censorship as an instrument of social control. Amid the social upheavals of the Gilded Age, elite groups like the New England Watch and Ward Society and Anthony Comstock's New York Society for the Suppression of Vice, relying on local statutes and on an 1873 federal law barring obscene material from the mails, sought to suppress dime novels, crime magazines, books deemed indecent, and contraceptive information. In the early twentieth century, as immigrants transformed urban America, as women surged into the workplace and the voting booths, as Victorian sexual mores eroded, and as movies and other new amusements captivated mass audiences, reformers condemned the stage, the press, and motion pictures for corrupting the young.

Would-be censors especially targeted motion pictures. As local and state censorship boards pressured studios to produce more decorous movies, the Supreme Court in *Mutual Film Co. v. Industrial Commission of Ohio* (1915) denied the film industry First Amendment protection. Catholic pressure forced Hollywood to accept a production code under Will H. Hays in 1930, and a Catholic censor, Joseph Breen, in 1934. Although the code was technically voluntary, Hollywood understood that the alternative was consumer boycotts and censorship. As oligopolies controlling production, distribution, and exhibition, the studios could enforce self-censorship. The comic-book industry, accused of promoting juvenile delinquency, copied the Hollywood model, adopting an almost identical code and enforcement mechanism. The movie-censorship tide turned in 1952, however, when the Supreme Court in *Joseph Burstyn, Inc., v. Wilson* (a case involving Roberto Rossellini's film *The Miracle,* denounced by New York's Francis Cardinal Spellman) reversed its 1915 position and gave the film First Amendment protection. Local and state censorship boards disbanded, and Hollywood abandoned the production code in 1966, adopting a rating system instead.

Censorship pressures revived, however, amid the culture wars of the late twentieth century. Evangelical Christians and conservative politicians defending "family values" demanded legal measures against sexually explicit movies, TV shows, rock lyrics, and Internet websites. The 1996 Communications Decency Act (CDA), which barred "indecent" materials from the Internet, was challenged by the ACLU and others, and in 1997 the Supreme Court struck it down on First Amendment grounds. Congress responded with the Child Online Protection Act (dubbed CDA-II), requiring public libraries receiving federal funds to install antipornography software on computers available to minors. The Supreme Court upheld the constitutionality of this law in 2003. At the local level, conservatives sought to purge objectionable books from school libraries and curricula. On the political left, meanwhile, activists and feminists called for legal action against "hate speech" denigrating ethnic or racial groups and against pornography considered degrading to women. Issues of censorship and free speech, in short, once again loomed large as a new century began.

[***See also Abrams v. United States;* Alien and Sedition Acts; American Civil Liberties Union; Anti-Communism; Bill of Rights; Christian Coalition; Conservatism; Debs, Eugene; Education Policy: Education in Contemporary America; Feminism; Hoover, J. Edgar; Jurisprudence; Lesbian, Gay, Bisexual, and Transgender Rights Movement; Lincoln, Abraham; Radicalism; Sedition; Socialism; Socialist Party of America; Wilson, Woodrow; *and* Zenger Trial.**]

BIBLIOGRAPHY

D'Emilio, John, and Estelle B. Freedman. *Intimate Matters: A History of Sexuality in America.* New York: Harper & Row, 1988.

Dickerson, Donna Lee. *The Course of Tolerance: Freedom of the Press in Nineteenth-Century America.* New York: Greenwood Press, 1990.

Levy, Leonard W. *Emergence of a Free Press.* New York; Oxford: Oxford University Press, 1985.

Neely, Mark E., Jr. *The Fate of Liberty: Abraham Lincoln and Civil Liberties*. New York: Oxford University Press, 1991.

Rabban, David M. *Free Speech in Its Forgotten Years*. Cambridge; New York: Cambridge University Press, 1997.

Walker, Samuel. *In Defense of American Liberties: A History of the ACLU*. New York: Oxford University Press, 1990.

Walsh, Frank. *Sin and Censorship: The Catholic Church and the Motion Picture Industry*. New Haven: Conn.: Yale University Press, 1996.

Francis G. Couvares; updated by Paul S. Boyer

CENSUS, FEDERAL

The decennial population census originated in the 1787 federal Constitution as a mechanism for determining each state's political representation in the House of Representatives and Electoral College. The Constitution (Article 1, Section 2) specifies that representatives and direct taxes are "apportioned among the several States which may be included within this Union, according to their respective Numbers" and goes on to require a census every ten years to determine those numbers. The census counted everyone in the country, except "Indians not taxed." The Constitution reduced the slave population count in each state to three-fifths of the total before adding it to the free population count for purposes of representation (the Three-Fifths Compromise). These provisions embedded race classifications in the census. The United States thus became the first nation to conduct a regular population census and use it to apportion legislative seats.

The nation successfully managed the allocation of political representation as it grew from thirteen states with 3.9 million people in 1790 to fifty states with over 300 million people in 2010. From 1790 to 1840, the State Department conducted the census, sending U.S. marshals' assistants to all households to tally the number of persons in the household, in broad demographic categories of age, sex, and social status. The number of questions on the census was expanded in later years. From 1850 to 1900, a Census Office in the Interior Department conducted the census. In 1850, Congress mandated an individual-level count that collected detailed information on Americans' demographic, social, and economic situations. Since 1910, the Bureau of the Census, housed in the Commerce Department, has taken the census. In 1890, a system of machine tabulation automated much of the work. UNIVAC, the first nondefense computer, tabulated the 1950 census. Today, the census is taken primarily by mail. In 1990, the bureau introduced the TIGER (Topologically Integrated Geographic Encoding and Referencing) system to provide maps and a list of every address in the United States.

Government, the private sector, and scholars use census data for planning; market forecasting; and social, economic, and political analysis. By the late twentieth century, these uses were as important as the original political functions, and congressional interests still shaped the questions asked and the data reported.

At times, the census became enmeshed in political controversies of such magnitude that it was challenged. When the Thirteenth Amendment to the Constitution abolished slavery, it also abolished the Three-Fifths Compromise and gave southern states full representation for the newly freed African American population in Congress. After the Civil War, Northerners realized that white Southerners would not permit the freed slaves to vote unless further federal protections were put in place. Hence, Congress wrote provisions to guarantee voting rights into the Fourteenth and Fifteenth Amendments of the Constitution. In 1920, members of Congress from rural states that were slated to lose representation to states with growing urban populations attacked the census. For the first and only time, Congress did not reapportion itself after the 1920 census. Starting in the late 1960s, big-city mayors and civil rights leaders charged that the census undercounted minorities and the poor. As the 2000 census loomed, partisan wrangling erupted over the Census Bureau's proposal to use statistical sampling techniques to supplement traditional counting techniques, and the Supreme Court ruled in 1999 that the census statute barred the use of sampling to determine the apportionment counts. The court acknowledged that adjusted data could be used for redistricting, but to date, the Census Bureau has not produced adjusted data in the official redistricting file, arguing that they could not certify that the block-level data would be improved by adjustment. As the census became politicized, ironically, this mechanism designed to defuse the contentiousness surrounding the allocation of political representation itself became embroiled in broader controversies about the distribution of power in American society. In 2010, the Census Bureau removed the detailed questions that had been on the "long form" questionnaire to a new continuous measurement rolling sample survey, the American Community Survey, which produces detailed demographic data annually for local areas. The 2010 census was, as the bureau advertised, ten questions that took ten minutes to complete.

[*See also* **Civil Rights; Constitution; Federal Government, Executive Branch: Other Departments; Federal Government, Executive Branch: State Department;** *and* **Federal Government, Legislative Branch: House of Representatives.**]

BIBLIOGRAPHY

Anderson, Margo. *The American Census: A Social History*. New Haven, Conn.: Yale University Press, 1988.

Anderson, Margo, Constance Citro, and Joseph Salvo, eds. *Encyclopedia of the U.S. Census*, 2d ed. Washington, D.C.: CQ Press, 2011.

Anderson, Margo, and Stephen E. Fienberg. *Who Counts? The Politics of Census Taking in Contemporary America*. New York: Russell Sage Foundation, 1999.

Choldin, Harvey. *Looking for the Last Percent: The Controversy over Census Undercounts*. New Brunswick, N.J.: Rutgers University Press, 1994.

Margo A. Anderson

CHARLES RIVER BRIDGE v. WARREN BRIDGE

An 1837 Supreme Court ruling relating to corporate development. In 1650, the Massachusetts legislature gave Harvard College an exclusive right to operate a ferry from Boston across the Charles River to Charlestown. Under acts of 1785 and 1792, Massachusetts transferred all rights of Harvard's monopoly to the Charles River Bridge Company and gave that company a seventy-year charter to operate a toll bridge between Charlestown and Boston. In 1828, the legislature chartered the Warren Bridge Company to build a new bridge that would revert to the state within six years after its completion. The stock owners of the Charles River Bridge complained that the charter for the new Warren Bridge violated its contract with the state. The Charles River Bridge Company argued that its original monopoly to operate the ferry included the bridge and that, in effect, the state had granted the company an exclusive right to operate a bridge between the two cities. The Charles River Bridge Company sued, citing the contracts clause of the U.S. Constitution (Article 1, Section 9), which bars states from "impairing the Obligations of Contracts."

By a vote of 4 to 3, the U.S. Supreme Court in 1837 upheld Massachusetts's right to charter the Warren Bridge. Writing for the Court, Chief Justice Roger B. Taney ruled that the charter granted to the Charles River Company should be read strictly; it did not include the promise of a monopoly, and therefore the state had the power to charter a new company.

This ruling allowed new industries to develop alongside—and even to supplant—existing technologies and companies. It gave states flexibility in developing public policy toward industries and utilities. It encouraged more competitive enterprise yet allowed states to grant monopolies to enterprises that served the public interest. Adhering to the logic of *Charles River Bridge,* however, states often included contract clauses enabling them to revoke all or some of the charter rights.

[*See also* **Economic Development;** *and* **Taney, Roger B.**]

BIBLIOGRAPHY

Kutler, Stanley I. *Privilege and Creative Destruction: The Charles River Bridge Case.* Baltimore: Johns Hopkins University Press, 1971.

Monroe, Elizabeth B. "Abridging Vested Interest: The Battle of the Massachusetts Bridge." In *Historic U.S. Court Cases: 1690–1990,* edited by John Johnson, pp. 174–181. New York: Garland, 1992.

Paul Finkelman

CHASE, SALMON

(1808–1873), chief justice, 1864–1873. After being raised an orphan, Salmon P. Chase graduated from Dartmouth (1823) and then read law in Washington, D.C., where he began practice in 1829. Moving to Cincinnati, Chase was thrice married (1834–1846), with his wives predeceasing him, and the father of six children. He compiled The Statutes of Ohio (1835), defended runaway slaves and their abettors in court, and was Ohio's senator (1849) and then governor (1855–1861).

An early Republican critic of the 1850 Fugitive Slave Act and an advocate of "freedom national" constitutionalism, Chase emerged as a would-be presidential candidate in 1860. The nomination and the election went to Abraham Lincoln, and Chase then became treasury secretary. He ably administered wartime tax, greenback, and banking laws; commerce with occupied southern areas; rebels' confiscated properties including slaves; and educational, agricultural, and industrial experiments for displaced bondsmen. Chase influenced Lincoln and Congress toward military emancipation in wartime state reconstruction, toward nationwide emancipation by constitutional amendment, and, by early 1865, toward equal legal and political rights for African Americans. Succeeding Roger B. Taney as chief justice in 1864, Chase tried but failed to convince either President Andrew Johnson or most of the justices that the Thirteenth Amendment incorporated the Declaration of Independence and Bill of Rights against national and state officials as well as private persons. He also failed in his argument that the amendment created a new federalism not of interstate diversity in laws and rights but of intrastate, race- and gender-blind equality.

Republican congressmen sharing his perception enacted the 1866 Civil Rights Act, providing federal alternatives to racially prejudiced state justice in matters of private rights as well as public law. On circuit in Maryland, Chase in *In re Turner* (1867) entertained a former slave's plea for discharge from her work contract with her former master and current employer. Affirming the constitutionality of the Civil Rights Act, Chase held that the Thirteenth Amendment clothed black citizens with full federal rights to litigate and testify, that private contracts existed only with state sanction, and that Turner's private contract, whose terms were inferior to those of contracts given to white apprentices, reduced her to involuntary servitude.

Encouraged by President Johnson, the white South resisted such policies. Overturning vetoes, Congress's various military Reconstruction laws required biracial electorates to ratify the Fourteenth and Fifteenth Amendments before southern states rejoined the Union. However, although Lincoln had appointed four other justices along with Chase, the chief justice was unable to form a majority on race equality. In *Ex parte Milligan* (1866), for example, Chase joined three other dissenters in opposing the Court's holding that Congress could impose military justice. The 5-to-4 Test Oath decisions, *Ex parte Garland*, and *Cummings v. Missouri* (1867) voided federal and state loyalty requirements for officeholders and licensed professionals as punitive ex post facto laws, bills of attainder, and denials of presidential pardons for rebels. Chase and the other dissenters insisted that the oaths were proper qualifications and questioned federal court jurisdiction. These decisions prevented the democratization of Southern officialdom and political leadership, impelling Congress toward military Reconstruction.

Chase retained influence among the justices, although not consistent leadership, a condition evident when Mississippi and Georgia petitioned the Court to enjoin military Reconstruction. Chase, for a unanimous Court in *Mississippi v. Johnson* (1867) and *Georgia v. Stanton* (1868), declined to politicize injunctions. In *Ex parte McCardle* (1869), a racist Mississippi editor arrested by military authorities for incendiary articles appealed to the Court based on the 1867 Habeas Corpus Act, key jurisdictional portions of which Congress had repealed.

The Court affirmed Congress's power over its appellate jurisdiction, but Chase noted that the 1867 law did not touch the Court's independent habeas corpus power. In *Texas v. White* (1869), Chase reasserted basic Republican constitutional principles that the Union and states were indissoluble, holding that Congress and not the Court had the sole authority to recognize state governments.

Chase presided ably over the impeachment trial of Andrew Johnson in early 1868. Ever ambitious, Chase sought unsuccessfully to become a presidential nominee. On the bench, his influence over his fellow justices oscillated. He dissented from their validation of prewar slave-purchase contracts in *Osborn v. Nicholson* (1873), their rejection of Thirteenth and Fourteenth Amendment claims by a qualified white woman to practice law in *Bradwell v. Illinois* (1873) and, above all, their Slaughterhouse decision (1873). The last consigned the fate of blacks seeking federally protected access to job markets to the same white state authorities who oppressed them by limiting the Thirteenth Amendment to the abolition of formal slavery and reducing the Fourteenth Amendment's privileges or immunities clause to inconsequentiality. Although a frequent dissenter, Chase helped "his" Court to exercise a full measure of governance by avoiding dangerous policy confrontations.

[*See also* **Antislavery Movement; Bill of Rights; Civil Rights; Civil Rights Legislation; Constitutionalism; Declaration of Independence; Equality; Federal Government, Judicial Branch; Johnson, Andrew;**

Lincoln, Abraham; Presidential Impeachment; Slaughterhouse Cases; Slavery, Laws; *and* Taney, Roger B.]

BIBLIOGRAPHY

Blue, Frederick J. *Salmon P. Chase: A Life in Politics.* Kent, Ohio: Kent State University Press, 1987.

Donald, David, ed. *Inside Lincoln's Cabinet: The Civil War Diaries of Salmon P. Chase.* New York: Longmans, Green, 1954.

Harold M. Hyman

CHENEY, RICHARD

(1941–), born in Lincoln, Nebraska, Richard Cheney began his political career in 1969 as an aide to a Wyoming congressman. He joined the White House staff during the Richard Nixon administration and eventually served as Chief of Staff to President Gerald Ford. Cheney became a congressman from Wyoming in 1978 and then Secretary of Defense under President George H. W. Bush eleven years later. He played a central role in planning and executing the 1991 war that drove the Iraqi army out of Kuwait. The success of that operation cemented Cheney's reputation as a shrewd, effective executive. Following Bush's defeat in the 1992 election, Cheney worked at the American Enterprise Institute and the Council on Foreign Relations. In 1995, he became head of Halliburton, a large energy corporation. Six years later, Cheney became vice president of the United States and served two terms under George W. Bush.

Uninterested in becoming president, Cheney instead was one of the most powerful vice presidents in United States history. Signs that he would not be a typical vice president were evident as the outcome of the 2000 election was being decided in a lengthy recount of votes in Florida. Cheney acted as if Bush would win and moved quickly and quietly to assemble an administration. Cheney took office determined to boost the power of the presidency. Congress, the courts, and the federal agencies, he believed, had since the 1970s usurped authority that belonged to the executive branch. Bush's leadership style left Cheney, a focused man with considerable knowledge about how the federal government worked, a great deal of room to maneuver. Cheney had little interest in politics or conservative social issues, such as abortion or gay rights. Instead, he played a central role in advancing the president's economic agenda regarding tax cuts, energy and the environment, and deregulation of business. He preferred to operate with as much secrecy as possible. Although detractors charged that this approach undermined democracy and enriched Republican supporters, including the vice president himself, Cheney saw it as essential for achieving the administration's goals.

Cheney made a larger imprint on the Bush administration's foreign policy. The 11 September 2001 terrorist attacks in the United States by al-Qaeda, a fundamentalist Islamic group, convinced him that the nation faced a new security threat. This conflict would, he said, force the United States to fight "in the shadows" rather than through large armies on a battlefield. Insisting there were few limits on the authority of the president to protect the nation, Cheney oversaw the development of policies that included unprecedented government surveillance within the United States and, he acknowledged, "robust interrogation" of enemies. Critics charged the administration with engaging in torture and thereby violating U.S. and international law as well as undermining the moral authority of the nation abroad.

Cheney believed that Iraqi leader Saddam Hussein was working with al-Qaeda and would soon be able to attack the United States with biological weapons or a small nuclear device. Cheney helped persuade Bush to launch an invasion of Iraq in March 2003 to eliminate an imminent threat, spark transformation in the Middle East, and send a warning to other potential adversaries. U.S. forces toppled Hussein quickly but remained in Iraq for several years afterward. Critics regarded the war as a catastrophic blunder, and later intelligence revelations strengthened their claims that Cheney had misinterpreted or ignored evidence and overstated the danger. Cheney, however, remained convinced it was a just and necessary endeavor.

[*See also* **Bush, George H. W.; Bush, George W.;** *and* **Ford, Gerald R.**]

BIBLIOGRAPHY

Gellman, Barton. *Angler: The Cheney Vice Presidency.* New York: Penguin Press, 2008.

Montgomery, Bruce. *Richard B. Cheney and the Rise of the Imperial Vice Presidency.* Westport, Conn.: Praeger, 2009.

Timothy N. Thurber

CHENEY v. U.S. DISTRICT COURT

This Supreme Court decision was an important part of a larger story that began soon after the first George W. Bush administration took office in 2001. The president formed a National Energy Policy Development Group (NEPDG). Headed by Vice President Cheney, the Group was composed of senior members of the government charged with developing legislative and regulatory proposals. Having consulted a variety of individuals both in the government and in the private sector, the NEPDG released its report and recommendations to the public on 17 May 2001.

The NEPDG sparked immediate controversy from environmentalists and Democrats, who controlled both the Senate and the House until the 2002 elections. In the spring of 2001, the initial challenge came not from the litigants who later appeared in *Cheney v. U.S. District Court,* but from the General Accounting Office (GAO) and its Comptroller General. Two House committee chairmen asked the GAO to investigate the Group's composition and deliberations; they wanted the names of the private sector groups and individuals who had participated. Cheney and his lawyers repeatedly refused the disclosure sought by the GAO, citing executive confidentiality and the separation of powers. Relying on a 1980 statute granting the GAO the power to take judicial action, the Comptroller General was reported to be prepared to sue the vice president when the 9/11 attacks occurred.

Democrats and environmentalists opposed the vice president's approach to energy policy. Cheney had disparaged some forms of conservation and favored expanded exploration of fossil fuels. The GAO eventually sued, but then dropped the case after the Republicans won control of the House in the 2002 election. Before the GAO withdrew, the controversy and suspicions once associated with the GAO's skirmishes with the vice president expressed themselves in separate litigation brought by the Natural Resources Defense Council, the Sierra Club, and Judicial Watch (a putatively conservative group favoring "transparency" in government). They sued under the Federal Advisory Committee Act (FACA), claiming that Cheney had an obligation to disclose the minutes of the Group's meetings, the names of attendees, and all working documents. The NEPDG was a federal advisory group, they argued, not a privileged executive body exempt from FACA, since outside members had through their participation become "de facto" members. It was these cases, consolidated, that found their way to the Supreme Court.

The Supreme Court case bears the name it has because Cheney was appealing a ruling of the trial court, the District Court for D.C. That court refused to dismiss the case and created a discovery process, including document-by-document assertions of executive privilege, which Cheney argued was contrary to the separation of powers. Determined to protect White House–level policy deliberations, Cheney was not content with earlier interpretations of executive privilege. When the D.C Circuit failed to agree, Cheney and the NEPDG went to the Supreme Court.

The Supreme Court's 7-to-2 ruling (Ginsberg and Souter dissenting) was a victory for the vice president's overall effort. (Producing an amusing memorandum, Justice Scalia declined to recuse himself, despite a duck-hunting trip that included the vice president.) The majority did not embrace the government's most ambitious claims for executive power, however, instead remanding the case to the Circuit Court to reconsider a procedural ruling. Eleven months later the Circuit Court unanimously ruled that forcing the executive branch, in a noncriminal case, to comply with FACA would violate the president's constitutional powers.

Cheney v. U.S. District Court ruled on a fraught matter, which began with Congressional oversight claims (plus Freedom of Information Act [FOIA] requests) seeking to limit the efforts, consistently associated in these years with the vice president and his counsel, to strengthen the executive against undue interference under a toughened doctrine of the separation of powers. The Bush administration's response to 9/11 made Cheney's defense in this litigation one of several claims of expanded executive power, which took the story beyond the "politics-by-other-means" scuffles of the pre-9/11 era. The Supreme Court proceeded cautiously in considering those claims.

[*See also* **Freedom of Information Act.**]

BIBLIOGRAPHY

Coffin, Shannen W. "An Examination of Cheney vs. U.S. District Court." *The Federalist Society*, 1 June 2004. http://www.fed-soc.org/publications/detail/an-examination-of-cheney-vs-us-district-court (accessed 11 August 2011).

Montgomery, Bruce P. "Congressional Oversight: Richard B. Cheney's Executive Brance Triumph". *Political Science Quarterly*, vol. 120 (Winter 2005): 581–617.

Schroeder, Chris. "Cheney v. U.S. District Court: Liberal Discovery Rules versus the Separation of Powers". *Duke Law/Supreme Court Online*. http://www.law.duke.edu/publiclaw/supremecourtonline/commentary/chevuni (accessed 11 August 2011).

Stephen R. Thomas

CHINESE EXCLUSION CASES

A series of disputes settled by the Supreme Court during the 1880s and 1890s: *Chew Heong v. United States*, 112 U.S. 536 (1884), argued 30 October 1884, decided 8 December 1884 by a vote of 7 to 2, Harlan for the Court, Field and Bradley in dissent; *United States v. Jung Ah Lung*, 124 U.S. 621 (1888), argued 9 January 1888, decided 13 February 1888 by a vote of 6 to 3, Blatchford for the Court, Harlan in dissent; *Chae Chan Ping v. United States* (also recorded as The Chinese Exclusion Case), 130 U.S. 581 (1889), argued 28 March 1889, decided 13 May 1889 by a vote of 9 to 0, Field for the Court; and *Fong Yue Ting v. United States*, *Wong Quan v. United States*, and *Lee Joe v. United States*, 149 U.S. 698 (1893), argued

10 May 1893, decided 15 May 1893 by a vote of 6-to-3, Gray for the Court, Brewer, Field, and Fuller in dissent. These decisions scrutinized congressional legislation designed to prevent Chinese immigration.

In 1882 Congress passed the first of a series of Chinese exclusion acts. It prohibited Chinese laborers and miners from entering the United States. An 1884 amendment required all Chinese laborers who lived in the United States before 1882 and who left the country with plans to return to have a reentry certificate. Six years later, the Scott Act (1888) became law. This statute prohibited Chinese laborers abroad or who planned future travels from returning. Over 20,000 Chinese were stranded. The Scott Act did allow merchants and teachers to return if they had proper papers. This loophole began the "paper names" industry whereby Chinese created new identities to return.

Congress passed a second exclusionary act, known as the Geary Act (1892). This law continued the ban on Chinese laborers and added the denial of bail to Chinese in habeas corpus proceedings and the requirement for all Chinese to have identification certificates or face deportation. The McCreary Act (1893) further defined laborers to include merchants, laundry owners, miners, and fishers. Finally, the Chinese Exclusion Act of 1902 permanently closed the door on all Chinese immigration.

The government of China, Chinese living in the United States, and Chinese Americans challenged the constitutionality of these anti-Chinese laws. The first case to reach the Supreme Court was *Chew Heong v. United States* (1884). In this case a Chinese laborer who resided in the United States in 1880 but left in 1881 was denied reentry in 1884 because he did not have a certificate. In a habeas corpus proceeding, he was denied a writ by Justice Stephen Field; on appeal Justice John Harlan led a divided Court in a reversal of Field's decision. Harlan determined that Chew Heong had befallen a statutory glitch, leaving before the 1882 act and returning after the 1884 amendments. Field and Justice Joseph Bradley dissented.

In 1888 the Court decided *United States v. Jung Ah Lung*. The defendant, a Chinese laborer, had been an American resident before 1882, and he had left to return to China in 1883 with a reentry certificate. When Jung tried to return in 1885, he did not have his certificate and was denied reentry. He sued for a writ of habeas corpus, which was issued. Once again a divided Court, this time led by Justice Samuel Blatchford, upheld the challenge of the Chinese to the enforcement of the Exclusion Act of 1882 as amended in 1884. The government argued that Chinese challenges through writs of habeas corpus were not allowed. Had the Court accepted this argument, Chinese rights would have been seriously curtailed. Once again Justice Field dissented, but he was gaining followers, including Justice Harlan.

After Jung Ah Lung, Congress passed the Scott Act, and the Supreme Court was quickly asked its interpretation in *Chae Chan Ping v. United States* (1889). Under the Scott Act, reentry certificates were abolished. Instead, an outright prohibition of reentry was established. Chae, a San Francisco Chinese laborer, left the United States to visit China before the Scott Act was passed but after the 1884 amendment. Although he had a reentry certificate, he was prevented from reentry and denied a writ of habeas corpus. The Supreme Court in an opinion written by Justice Field unanimously found the Scott Act constitutional.

The final Chinese attempt to challenge the Exclusion Acts came in 1893. In 1892 Congress renewed the Exclusion Act of 1882 for another ten years, and it added a new requirement that all Chinese laborers had to have certificates of residence or face deportation. Three Chinese were subsequently found guilty of not having residence papers, and they appealed. In the 1893 cases the Court completed the closing of the door to Chinese immigration and the restriction of basic freedoms of Chinese Americans by holding that Congress had the power retroactively to require Chinese to have residential certificates and allowing those without certificates to be deported.

After initially offering narrow holdings to protect Chinese reentry to the United States, the Supreme Court eventually succumbed to the anti-Chinese hysteria of the era and ratified far-reaching restrictions on basic rights for Chinese under American law.

[*See also* **Constitution; Constitutional Interpretation; Harlan, John Marshall; Immigration Law and Policy: Before 1930;** *and* **Supreme Court, U.S.**]

Konvitz, Milton R. *The Alien and the Asiatic in American Law*. Ithaca, N.Y.: Cornell University Press, 1946.

John R. Wunder

CHRISTIAN COALITION

Emerging from the failed bid of Pat Robertson (1930–), a prominent television evangelist, for the Republican Party's 1988 presidential nomination, the Christian Coalition by the early 1990s had become the flagship institution of the religious right. Much of its success was attributable to Ralph Reed, who was hand-picked by Robertson in 1989 to establish a new organization of political conservatives dedicated to mobilizing opposition to abortion, homosexuality, and pornography and supporting tax cuts, "parental rights," and prayer in schools. Learning from and building upon the Reverend Jerry Falwell's defunct Moral Majority, Reed created a politically savvy organization with strong grassroots support. By 1997 the coalition claimed 1.9 million members. But Reed enjoyed less success in constructing a broad-based conservative coalition: white Protestant charismatics, fundamentalists, and evangelicals dominated his organization.

The Christian Coalition waged many campaigns at the local level in school board, city council, and mayoral elections. But it also wielded substantial clout nationally by helping boost the arch-conservative victory in the North Carolina senatorial election in 1990 and mobilizing public support for the confirmation of Clarence Thomas to the Supreme Court in 1991. The Christian Coalition's most visible success came in 1994, when it contributed much to the Republican sweep of congressional elections.

Reed stepped down in 1997 to launch his own political consulting firm. Whatever the Christian Coalition's future, its key role in the political maturation of the religious right is indisputable.

[*See also* **Conservatism; Lesbian, Gay, Bisexual, and Transgender Rights Movement; Moral Majority; Reagan, Ronald;** *and* **Religious Right.**]

BIBLIOGRAPHY

Martin, William. *With God on Our Side: The Rise of the Religious Right in America*. New York: Broadway Books, 1996.

Watson, Justin. *The Christian Coalition: Dreams of Restoration, Demands for Recognition*. New York: St. Martin's Press, 1997.

William Vance Trollinger Jr.

CHURCH AND STATE, SEPARATION OF

The separation of church and state in the United States is a constantly evolving ideal that emerged out of struggles for disestablishment of established churches in the new states during the era of the Revolutionary War. The concept reflected the thought of the eighteenth-century Enlightenment, which in turn was influenced by the Protestant Reformation. Americans like Thomas Jefferson and James Madison considered religious influence in politics to be divisive and potentially repressive.

Not an end in itself, separation of church and state is a means of protecting religious liberty, securing the freedom of individuals in their choice, practice, and support of religious affiliation or nonaffiliation. The ideal has reflected the religious diversity of the American people and has adapted itself to vast changes in American society.

Separation was originally mandated by the religious-freedom provisions of the early state constitutions and in the First Amendment, which declares, "Congress shall make no law respecting an establishment of religion, or prohibiting the free exercise thereof." Scant evidence exists regarding the framers' intentions. At a minimum they clearly meant to preclude the federal government from interfering in religious matters, but equally clearly they did not intend to disestablish state churches or authorize the federal government to do so. This, however, is the narrowest possible reading of the framers' intent—a reading that perforce ignores two centuries of national experience.

Nineteenth-century struggles over religious policy merely identified problems of separation, rather than providing solutions for them. Litigation over schisms in the Congregational churches; prosecutions for blasphemy and Sabbath-breaking; persecution of Mormons for polygamy; efforts of Catholic prelates to obtain public funds for religious education; and the Kulturkampf waged by mainline Protestant clergy to "Americanize" the new Roman Catholic, Jewish, and Christian Orthodox immigrants from eastern and southern Europe all fueled religious controversy without clarifying any definitive meaning of the separation of church-and-state principle.

In the twentieth century, the federal judiciary, particularly the U.S. Supreme Court, assumed responsibility for defining and enforcing separation. In *Cantwell v. State of Connecticut* (1940), the Court interpreted the religion clause of the First Amendment as a restriction on state power. Thenceforth, the content of separation became largely a matter of judicial debate.

The "free exercise" principle developed without much controversy at first. Numerous cases in the 1940s involving Jehovah's Witnesses, most notably the second case involving Witnesses' refusal to salute the American flag, *West Virginia State Board of Education v. Barnette* (1943), imposed severe constraints on the states' abilities to dictate or prohibit religious observance. But in *Employment Division v. Smith* (1990), a case involving the sacramental use of peyote by members of the Native American Church, the Court determined that states could enforce laws of general applicability no matter how drastically such laws inhibited an individual's religious practice. Recognizing that the *Smith* principle could lead to discrimination and impermissible state interference with religious practices, especially those of minority groups, Congress in 1993 passed the Religious Freedom Restoration Act, repudiating *Smith*'s permissive approach to state authority. The Court responded to this unusual initiative by holding the statute unconstitutional as an intrusion on its powers of judicial review (*Boerne v. Flores* (1997)).

Issues involving the "establishment" clause generally proved more controversial, however, evoking efforts for constitutional amendments to overturn Supreme Court rulings. Questions of state aid to parochial schools and released time for religious education ignited the controversy. In *Everson v. Board of Education* (1947), Justice Hugo Black adopted a strict interpretation of separation and imposed Jefferson's metaphor of "a wall of separation" as a canonical reading of the First Amendment. Establishment controversies nevertheless continued, involving school prayer (*Engel v. Vitale* (1962), *Abington School District v. Schempp* (1963)), federal and state financial subventions for religious schools, and, finally, the constitutional flashpoint, cases involving the display of religious symbols such as crèches and menorahs on government property. In *Lemon v. Kurtzman* (1971), the Supreme Court tried unsuccessfully to resolve establishment-clause controversies by adopting the so-called three-part *Lemon* test, requiring a secular legislative purpose for government involvement in religious matters, forbidding governmental promotion or inhibition of religion, and barring excessive government entanglement with religion.

Chief Justices Warren Burger and William H. Rehnquist articulated the principal alternative to the Black–Jefferson view of strict separation, calling for a policy of "accommodation" of religious practice and rejecting impartial neutrality between religion and secularism (*Lynch v. Donnelly* (1984)). As the twentieth century ended, strict separation and accommodation vied for dominance in public debate. As religious practice became both more pervasive and more diverse in American society, issues of separation of church and state seemed likely to continue to roil understandings of the First Amendment.

[*See also* **Bill of Rights; Black, Hugo; Burger, Warren; Federalism; Jefferson, Thomas; Madison, James; Rehnquist, William;** *and* **Supreme Court, U.S.**]

BIBLIOGRAPHY

Ahlstrom, Sydney E. *A Religious History of the American People.* New Haven, Conn.: Yale University Press, 1972.

Feldman, Stephen M. *Please Don't Wish Me a Merry Christmas: A Critical History of the Separation of Church and State.* New York: New York University Press, 1997.

Howe, Mark De Wolfe. *The Garden and the Wilderness: Religion and Government in American Constitutional History.* Chicago: University of Chicago Press, 1965.

Kauper, Paul G. *Religion and the Constitution.* Baton Rouge: Louisiana State University Press, 1964.

Levy, Leonard W. *The Establishment Clause: Religion and the First Amendment.* Chapel Hill: University of North Carolina Press, 1994.

Tribe, Laurence H. *American Constitutional Law,* 2d ed., pp. 1154–1301. Mineola, N.Y.: Foundation Press, 1988.

William M. Wiecek

CITIZENS' COUNCILS

See **White Citizens' Councils.**

CIVILIAN CONSERVATION CORPS

Created on 31 March 1933, during President Franklin D. Roosevelt's (FDR's) first 100 days in office, the Civilian Conservation Corps (CCC) drew on a variety of federal agencies to provide employment on emergency conservation projects. Designed to address the Great Depression's crisis of mass unemployment, at first the CCC focused on providing work to young men (the unemployment rate for males between the ages of fifteen and twenty-four was at least 50 percent in 1933). The program's focus on rural conservation work stemmed in no small part from FDR's enthusiasm for the moral benefits of outdoor activity.

As Roosevelt once declared, "The forests are the 'lungs' of our land, purifying our air and giving fresh strength to our people."

Initially, the CCC enrolled unemployed young men between the ages of eighteen and twenty-five who were willing to volunteer for a six-month term of employment. The Department of Labor screened applicants to the CCC and then placed them into rural work camps in companies of 200 men. The Department of War used Army officers to administer the camps, whereas the Departments of Agriculture and the Interior supervised and selected various projects for CCC workers to perform. Although enrollees were eligible to reenlist in the CCC and serve for a maximum of two years, eligibility requirements and regulations were adjusted as time passed. For example, 14,000 Native Americans and 250,000 veterans of World War I, many much older than twenty-five, were allowed to join the CCC.

To ease objections from organized labor over the program's low wages, as well as worries about the specter of military control over working people, FDR appointed Robert Fechner, the former head of the American Federation of Labor's (AFL) machinists division, to run the CCC. (Fechner's AFL colleague James J. McEntee served as the program's deputy director.) In administering the CCC, Fechner maintained a policy of strict racial segregation in the program's camps and limited African American enrollment by their ratio in the nation's population (10 percent), rather than by their unemployment rate, which was several times higher. Although the CCC provided some limited vocational training and created a literacy program that ultimately taught 35,000 enrollees to read and write, Fechner avoided providing CCC workers with any additional training or skills that might eventually make them more competitive with union members in the labor market.

With the coming of World War II and the revival of the nation's economy, Congress voted in 1942 to abolish the CCC. During its existence, the CCC employed about 2.5 million men (of whom 200,000 were African American), planted over 2 billion trees, and built 800 new state parks. The CCC's focus on reforestation earned it the nickname "Roosevelt's Tree Army," but the program also improved and developed campgrounds and hiking trails, worked to combat soil erosion, built dams and irrigation systems, and helped fight forest fires.

[*See also* **Roosevelt, Franklin Delano;** ***and*** **National Park System.**]

BIBLIOGRAPHY

Maher, Neil M. *Nature's New Deal: The Civilian Conservation Corps and the Roots of the American Environmental Movement.* Oxford, New York: Oxford University Press, 2008.

Salmond, John A. *Civilian Conservation Corps, 1933–1942: A New Deal Case Study.* Durham, N.C.: Duke University Press, 1967.

Jason Scott Smith

CIVIL LIBERTIES

The term "civil liberties" refers to those individual freedoms protected by the Constitution, particularly by the Bill of Rights. These are liberties that, when the Constitution was adopted, had come to be seen as natural rights.

Revolutionary War through the Civil War. In the years leading up to the Revolutionary War, the colonists began voicing their opposition to British policies in the language of natural rights. Having earlier based their rights claims on royal charters and the

English common law, they now asserted, in the language of John Locke's *Two Treatises on Civil Government* (1690), that government could not infringe on certain natural, inalienable rights. This new natural-rights view of civil liberty later inspired both the Declaration of Independence and the Bill of Rights.

As a public-policy issue, civil liberties rarely surfaced prior to World War I. Throughout the nation's first 130 years, few occasions arose for suspension of the habeas corpus privilege, press censorship, regulation of the right of assembly, or the imposition of loyalty oaths. Consequently, the law regarding civil liberties remained ill-defined until well into the twentieth century.

During America's Quasi-War with France in 1798, the Federalists in Congress enacted the Alien and Sedition Acts, which, under the guise of war-justified controls, criminalized seditious libel and sought to suppress the activities of the Jeffersonian Republican political opposition. These laws also aimed to subdue the violent political partisanship that threatened the Federalists' vision of a stable society. But the Federalist Party's unpopularity doomed it, and with Thomas Jefferson's electoral victory in 1800, the politics of civil liberty remained quiescent until 1861.

When the Civil War began, President Abraham Lincoln imposed a series of measures (e.g., suspending the writ of habeas corpus and barring all "treasonable correspondence" from the mails) aimed at silencing opponents of the war. Using a rationale that would often be employed in the next century, Lincoln insisted that restrictions on civil liberties were needed to address the perceived threat of disloyal activities.

World War I through World War II. As these instances illustrate, attacks on civil liberties have usually coincided with periods of turmoil and insecurity. During World War I and its aftermath, civil liberties were subjected to greater restrictions than ever before in American history, typified by the repressive Espionage and Sedition Acts passed by Congress in 1917–1918 and emulated by many states. In the immediate postwar period, an economic depression and a surge of strikes threatened the economy, creating problems that many Americans blamed on radicals and aliens. The 1917 Bolshevik Revolution in Russia and increasing radicalism among certain immigrant groups in the United States spawned a Red Scare that led to the notorious Palmer raids of 1919–1920. These raids, led by President Woodrow Wilson's attorney general, A. Mitchell Palmer, and the young J. Edgar Hoover of the Justice Department's countersubversion division, resulted in the arrest of hundreds of suspected communists and radicals and the deportation of 249 Russian-born aliens. The American Civil Liberties Union (ACLU) was founded in 1920 to protest these violations of First Amendment protections.

In ruling on the constitutionality of the wartime espionage and sedition acts, the U.S. Supreme Court for the first time interpreted the First Amendment as a limitation on governmental power. Although the Court in two noteworthy 1919 cases, *Schenck v. United States* and *Abrams v. United States,* did not adopt a pro–civil liberties stance, these cases remain landmarks in the development of First Amendment doctrine, in part because of the eloquent dissent by Justice Oliver Wendell Holmes Jr. in the *Abrams* case.

As the Red Scare subsided, federal measures directed against dissenters faded as well. During the New Deal Era, as tyrannical governments assaulted individual freedom elsewhere in the world, the Supreme Court expanded the constitutional protection of civil liberties. Incorporating the Bill of Rights into the Fourteenth Amendment, the Court thereby applied these restraints to the states as well as to the federal government. The 1930s Supreme Court also downgraded the traditional primacy of property rights in the constitutional hierarchy. For instance, under then-existing law, picketing by union members could be outlawed because of its harmful effect on private property. But in *Senn v. Tile Layers Protective Union* (1937), a majority of the justices, recognizing the free speech aspect of this activity, prohibited any outright bans on picketing. Furthermore, by protecting the civil liberties of political dissidents, the Court encouraged the atmosphere of social experimentation central to the New Deal.

Even America's entry into World War II did not disrupt the Supreme Court's focus on enlarging the scope of individual liberty. The great exception, of course, involved the relocation and detention of 125,000 people of Japanese ancestry, most of whom were citizens of the United States. The Supreme Court did not seriously intervene. In *Hirabayashi v. United States* (1943), it upheld a curfew ordinance against Japanese Americans in Seattle on the grounds that wartime conditions sometimes justified measures that "place citizens of one ancestry in a different category from others." In *Korematsu v. United States* (1944), the Court upheld the evacuation of Japanese Americans, but added, in *Endo v. United States* (1944), that the War Relocation Authority should attempt to separate "loyal" internees from "disloyal" ones and release the former.

Cold-War Era Retrenchment. The early postwar era saw considerable retrenchment in the area of civil liberties. The conservative mood in the country brought a shift in political priorities from a concern for individual freedom to a desire for stability, order, and security. This mood found its way into the Supreme Court's civil-liberties decisions. The notions of "judicial restraint" and "balancing individual and community rights" facilitated this retrenchment. Under this new approach, First Amendment liberties no longer had an absolute or preferred position in constitutional adjudication, but had to be balanced against other concerns, such as public safety.

The most difficult civil-liberties questions of this period involved the Cold War crusade against domestic Communism. With the nation in the grip of McCarthyism, the federal government used the 1940 Smith Act to prosecute Communist Party officials. At the same time, loyalty programs directed at federal employees were implemented by both the Harry S. Truman and the Dwight D. Eisenhower administrations. Congress also passed a series of anti-Communist measures, including the McCarran Internal Security Act (1950) and the Communist Control Act (1954). In addition, the House Committee on Un-American Activities embarked on its notorious investigation of persons suspected of a Communist taint. For the most part, the Court supported this postwar anti-Communist crusade. In *Dennis v. United States* (1951), for instance, the Court upheld the conviction of eleven Communist party officers under the Smith Act for advocating (rather than actively planning) the overthrow of the U.S. government; in so ruling, the Court weakened the "clear and present danger" test established in *Schenck*.

A similar retrenchment occurred in the Court's approach to a variety of other civil-liberties questions. On the issue of picketing, for instance, the Court pulled back from its 1937 position that peaceful picketing represents a form of speech enjoying First Amendment protection. In *International Brotherhood of Teamsters v. Hanke* (1950), the Court held that picketing could also be a tool of economic coercion and restraint of trade and hence could be regulated.

After this period of postwar retrenchment, however, the pendulum soon swung in the other direction. The rise of the civil rights movement and the anti–Vietnam War crusade of the 1960s brought a dramatic expansion of civil liberties that, in turn, helped fuel the era's political activism. In *Shelton v. Tucker* (1960), for instance, the Court struck down restrictions aimed at discouraging membership in the National Association for the Advancement of Colored People.

The Warren Court and Beyond. A series of precedent-breaking Supreme Court decisions under Chief Justice Earl Warren (1953–1969) created a powerful body of libertarian-oriented constitutional law in the field of civil liberties. In *Albertson v. Subversive Activities Control Board* (1965), for example, the Court overturned the registration requirements aimed at the Communist Party and, for the first time, the Warren court consistently supported the First Amendment rights of those protesting U.S. involvement in a foreign war (Vietnam). In so doing, the justices recognized a social interest in free speech. More than simply an individual right, free speech was now seen as essential to the open debate needed for the maintenance of democracy. Long viewed as a threat to social stability, civil liberties were now seen as making a positive social contribution.

The Warren court also reformed the law dealing with the civil liberties of criminal defendants. The Sixth Amendment guarantee of counsel was now interpreted to mean that the states must provide lawyers for indigent defendants. And in *Miranda v. Arizona* (1966), the Court ruled that the Fifth Amendment privilege against self-incrimination required police to inform all suspects of their right to remain silent and to have an attorney present during interrogation.

The Warren court's civil-liberties activism also led it to carve out a new constitutional right of privacy. In *Griswold v. Connecticut* (1965), the Court used this privacy right to strike down state legislation prohibiting the use of contraceptives and the dispensing of birth control and family planning information to married couples.

This judicial activism was significantly tempered during the tenure of Chief Justice Warren Burger (1969–1986), named to that position by President Richard M. Nixon. The Burger court shifted rightward in its treatment of some civil-liberties issues. The Court's law-and-order stance, for instance, weakened certain criminal-procedure protections, including the *Miranda* precedent. Yet most of the First Amendment protections and privacy rights articulated by the Warren court were sustained. Indeed, it was the Burger Court, in *Roe v. Wade* (1973), that used the constitutional right of privacy to guarantee abortion rights.

The Court's commitment to First Amendment and privacy rights continued through the presidency of Ronald Reagan. During the 1980s and 1990s, however, calls for censorship came from political liberals advocating speech codes and advertising restrictions on "politically incorrect" speech. Perhaps the most heated and controversial of civil-liberties issues in the 1990s were ones involving the First Amendment's establishment-of-religion clause, such as crèches on public property, secular books for parochial school students, and prayer at public events. Yet despite public pressures, the strict church–state separation laid down by the Warren court survived.

The end of the twentieth century brought one significant change in the area of civil liberties. Whereas dissent in wartime and national-security concerns had previously produced the disputes and conflicts, technology now became the First Amendment battleground, involving such issues as free speech on the Internet and World Wide Web and the privacy of information relating to citizens' genetic profiles.

The federal government's response to the terrorist attacks of 11 September 2001 raised important civil-liberties issues and stirred the ACLU and other organizations to vigorous protest. Hundreds of persons were detained without trial and the USA Patriot Act gave the government vast investigative powers, including secret surveillance of telephone and email communications, that had serious implications for citizens' constitutional rights. As the public and the government understandably focused on forestalling future terrorist attacks, the defense of civil liberties became more challenging, and more pressing, than ever before.

[***See also Abrams v. United States;* Alien and Sedition Acts; American Civil Liberties Union; Anti-Communism; Bill of Rights; Censorship; Burger, Warren; Church and State, Separation of; Communist Party USA; Constitution; Debs, Eugene; Declaration of Independence; Fourteenth Amendment; Goldman, Emma; *Griswold v. Connecticut;* Japanese American Internment; Lincoln, Abraham; McCarthy, Joseph; *Miranda v. Arizona;* Patriot Act, The; Prayer in School; *Roe v. Wade; and* Supreme Court, U.S.**]

BIBLIOGRAPHY

Bailyn, Barnard. *The Ideological Origins of the American Revolution.* Cambridge, Mass.: Belknap Press of Harvard University Press, 1967.

Chafee, Zechariah. *Free Speech in the United States.* Cambridge, Mass.: Harvard University Press, 1948.

Frankel, O. K. *The Supreme Court and Civil Liberties.* New York: Oceana Publications, 1960.

Hall, Kermit L., ed. *Civil Liberties in American History.* New York: Garland, 1987.

Hentoff, Nat. *The First Freedom: The Tumultuous History of Free Speech in America.* New York: Delacorte Press, 1980.

Levy, Leonard. *Legacy of Suppression: Freedom of Speech and Press in Early American History.* Cambridge, Mass.: Belknap Press of Harvard University Press, 1960.

Murphy, Paul L. *World War I and the Origin of Civil Liberties in the United States.* New York: W. W. Norton, 1979.

Pfeffer, Leo. *Church, State and Freedom.* Boston: Beacon Press, 1967.

Stevens, John. *Shaping the First Amendment.* Beverly Hills, Calif.: Sage Publications, 1982.

Patrick M. Garry; updated by Paul S. Boyer

CIVIL RIGHTS

The concept of civil rights has changed dramatically since it first became a central idea in political discussions in the nineteenth century. Initially referring to a limited class of rights to which all people were entitled, the term has come to refer to a general guarantee against differential treatment in all areas of social life on the basis of what society deems to be arbitrary grounds.

The Revolutionary War and Antebellum Eras. The idea of natural rights played an important role in the Revolutionary War Era. Natural rights were those rights people enjoyed in a state of nature, independent of any organized society: the right to life and liberty and the right to attempt to procure property. Civil rights were the rights people possessed once they organized a society. The idea of civil rights came into its own during the abolitionist campaign against slavery. For abolitionists, one fatal characteristic of slavery was that slaves were denied civil rights. They could not own property, enter into contracts, or testify in court. These and a few other rights were what abolitionists understood to be civil rights. Typically the justification was that these rights distinguished organized—civil—society from the state of nature: People organized society so that they could have stable property holdings and secure contractual agreements, and a person's property and contracts could not be protected unless the person could testify about them.

Through the mid-nineteenth century, political activists and theorists sharply distinguished between civil rights on the one hand and political and social rights on the other. Civil rights were associated with all organized societies, whereas political rights were rooted in the particular arrangements of specific societies. Abolitionists believed that freed slaves had a right to own property, but they did not think that emancipation automatically entailed the right to vote or to serve on juries. They could imagine societies in which voting played a small role and in which juries played no role at all; it followed, they believed, that the rights to vote and to serve on juries were political rather than civil rights. The point was perhaps clearest in connection with women, who generally had the right to own property and make contracts, but the view that women had the right to vote was far from mainstream in the mid-nineteenth century.

The Reconstruction Era through the 1930s. Congress's first venture into the area of protecting civil rights came with the Civil Rights Act of 1866, passed to enforce the Thirteenth Amendment's abolition of slavery. The act granted all citizens equal rights to sue and testify; enter into contracts; and purchase, sell, or inherit property. The act was adopted over President Andrew Johnson's veto, in which he expressed concern that the Thirteenth Amendment did not give Congress the power to enact it. In part because of that concern, Congress proceeded to propose, and the states to ratify, the Fourteenth Amendment, which guaranteed "equal protection of the laws." To the extent that the Fourteenth Amendment was designed to place the 1866 Civil Rights Act on a secure constitutional footing, it protected core civil rights but did not deal with political rights such as the right to vote. The importance of the distinction was driven home by the perceived need to adopt the Fifteenth Amendment, securing the right to vote against efforts to restrict it on the basis of race.

The distinction between civil rights and political rights came under increasing pressure toward the end of the century. The Supreme Court held that the Fourteenth Amendment barred states from denying African Americans the opportunity to serve on juries (*Strauder v. West Virginia,* 1880). An amendment designed primarily to protect civil rights was thus interpreted to protect one of the central political rights. The increasing activism of woman-suffrage advocates further strained the distinction between civil and political rights.

In contrast, the distinction between civil rights and social rights survived. In a sense, the category of social rights was simply residual: everything not encompassed within civil or political rights implicated social rights. In part, the category identified the ways in which politically organized societies arranged their nonpolitical institutions. The Supreme Court in *Plessy v. Ferguson* (1896), upholding a state statute mandating racial segregation on privately owned railroads, asserted that the statute's challengers were claiming that they had a right to associate with whomever they chose. But that claim was mistaken, the Court's holding implied, because the right to associate was a social right, subject to regulation by ordinary legislative decision making.

Advocates for African Americans continued to press the claim that racial segregation and discrimination denied their civil rights. The core of their claim was that civil rights were denied whenever race discrimination affected any activity that society deemed fundamental, including education and employment. The National Association for the Advancement of Colored People (NAACP), organized in 1909, proved particularly effective in promulgating this broadened notion of civil rights, through political advocacy and support of legal challenges to segregation.

By the 1930s, the older distinctions among civil, political, and social rights had largely been obliterated. For the next decades, civil rights activists struggled to obtain legal protection for civil rights as they had come to be understood. Challenges to state-mandated segregation culminated in *Brown v. Board of Education* (1954), which repudiated the idea that education was not a civil right. During World War II, the national government created a Fair Employment Practices Committee, which attempted, without much success, to ensure that defense contractors refrained from discriminating in employment on the basis of race. Civil rights statutes enacted in 1957 and 1960 made modest efforts to overcome race discrimination in voting practices in the South.

The Era of the Civil Rights Movement and Beyond. The full transformation of the idea of civil rights occurred in the 1960s. Civil rights acts adopted in 1964 and 1965 banned race discrimination in employment and in public accommodations such as restaurants and hotels and responded to persistent discrimination in voting by displacing the authority of southern states to adopt voter-qualification standards. The effects of these two statutes were dramatic. Voter registration in the South expanded, and African Americans became important participants in politics there. Gains in employment were achieved more slowly because employers resisted hiring and especially promoting workers they believed to be unqualified.

Beyond the 1960s, the idea of civil rights underwent further development. It expanded past the realm of race discrimination to include a significant number of other "protected" classes. Since the early twentieth century, some women's rights activists had pressed for a ban on gender-based discrimination in employment. That proposal met with resistance from organized labor and from some other women's rights activists, who thought it important to ensure the survival of state laws that they believed protected women against exploitative employment practices. In part to divide the liberal coalition supporting the proposed Civil Rights Act of 1964, the Virginia representative Howard Smith introduced an amendment that would expand the coverage of the proposal's ban on employment discrimination to include discrimination based on gender. This portion of the 1964 act became one of the most important vehicles for gender equality over the following decade. Similar expansions of the notion of civil rights occurred as older Americans obtained protection in the Age Discrimination in Employment Act (1967), and the physically handicapped established their right to accommodation of their disabilities through the Americans with Disabilities Act (1990) and other statutes. The list of protected classes continued to increase as gays and lesbians sought and sometimes obtained protection against discrimination in employment and housing.

By the late twentieth century, the expanded notion of civil rights had begun to develop new elaborations. From the early years of the civil rights movement, activists had divided over whether they sought treatment for African Americans as individuals or as members of a distinctive social group. In employment, this produced strategic divisions over whether to seek a legal regime of nondiscrimination or one of proportional hiring. The strategic disagreements mattered little until the civil rights movement began to succeed. After the adoption of the 1964 and 1965 Civil Rights Acts, however, the differences became important. Proponents of affirmative action and race-conscious apportionment of election districts contended that their approaches were the best way to ensure that African Americans would obtain fair treatment and the resources to which they were entitled and that they were effective ways of securing a stable, self-determining African American community. Their opponents argued that race-conscious approaches undermined the focus on individual rights that had been the hallmark of previous struggles for civil rights.

The expansion of the concept of civil rights generated concern among some observers. Critics suggested that the discourse of civil rights produced an escalation of rhetoric that made it increasingly difficult to reach accommodations among competing interests. Others expressed concern that the concept had come to cover such a wide range of social life that its moral force had become diluted. Those who supported expanding the understanding of civil rights drew upon international human rights law to urge changes in U.S. law. These concerns, plus persistent conflicts over affirmative action and continued efforts to claim civil rights by groups that believed themselves to be disadvantaged, ensured that the concept of civil rights would continue to evolve as a new century began.

[*See also* **Affirmative Action: Legal Aspects; Antislavery Movement; *Brown v. Board of Education;* Civil Rights Legislation; Constitution; Fair Employment Practices Committee; Fourteenth Amendment; Lesbian, Gay, Bisexual, and Transgender Rights Movement; National Association for the Advancement of Colored People; *Plessy v. Ferguson;* Republicanism; Segregation; Supreme Court, U.S.;** *and* **Woman Suffrage Movement.**]

BIBLIOGRAPHY

Glendon, Mary Ann. *Rights Talk: The Impoverishment of Political Discourse.* New York; Toronto: Free Press; Collier Macmillan, 1991.

Graham, Hugh Davis. *The Civil Rights Era: Origins and Development of National Policy, 1960–1972.* New York: Oxford University Press, 1990.

Kluger, Richard. *Simple Justice: The History of Brown v. Board of Education and Black America's Struggle for Equality.* New York: Alfred A. Knopf, 1976.

Kull, Andrew. *The Color-Blind Constitution.* Cambridge, Mass.: Cambridge University Press, 1992.

Rodgers, Daniel T. *Contested Truths: Keywords in American Politics since Independence.* New York: Basic Books, 1987.

Mark Tushnet

CIVIL RIGHTS LEGISLATION

America's first civil rights legislation came during Reconstruction. The Fourteenth and Fifteenth Amendments extended citizenship to all persons born or naturalized in the United States, granted all citizens equal protection of the laws, and outlawed the denial of citizens' rights on the basis of race. Empowered by these amendments, Congress passed a civil rights act in 1870 providing remedies against state officials who violated citizens' constitutional rights and another in 1875 requiring equal treatment of all individuals in places of public accommodation. The Supreme Court interpreted the 1870 act narrowly, however, and in the *Civil Rights Cases* (1883) held the 1875 act unconstitutional, ruling that Congress's power did not extend to cases of private discrimination.

More than eighty years would pass before Congress again addressed the issue of civil rights. As African Americans became part of the New Deal coalition, they increasingly pressed for more effective civil rights legislation, but southern white politicians blocked all such bills until the enactment of the Civil Rights Act of 1957. Prodded by northern Republicans, the Dwight D. Eisenhower administration proposed a civil rights bill designed in part to divide the Democratic Party's liberal and southern wings. Senate Majority Leader Lyndon B. Johnson, viewing the bill as a vehicle for his presidential ambitions, maneuvered to get a watered-down version enacted. The act created a Civil Rights Commission to investigate and report on civil rights issues and set up a cumbersome method of enforcing federal voting-rights guarantees. A modest extension of the act in 1960 did not increase its effectiveness.

The Civil Rights Act of 1964, by contrast, inaugurated a new era of civil rights legislation. John F. Kennedy had made civil rights an issue during his presidential campaign, but as president he was reluctant to expend substantial political capital on the issue. His successor, Lyndon Johnson, however, forcefully pushed a comprehensive civil rights bill and used his influence to break a Senate filibuster. The act's major provisions banned racial discrimination in public accommodations and prohibited discrimination by employers and unions. The act also authorized the federal government to deny public funds to segregated schools.

The Supreme Court ruled the 1964 act constitutional, finding that Congress could use its power to regulate interstate commerce to ban racial discrimination. Desegregation of many restaurants and hotels followed quickly. The threatened loss of federal funding sped the pace of school desegregation.

The Voting Rights Act of 1965 dramatically expanded federal power over voting, invalidating literacy tests and other practices used to exclude African Americans from the franchise. It also required southern cities and states, and some northern ones, to secure permission from the Justice Department or a federal court for changes in their voter-registration laws. The 1965 act dramatically expanded the numbers of African American voters. Originally in effect for a limited period, it was regularly extended and eventually made permanent. Under the act, some states created race-based electoral districts designed to increase blacks' legislative representation—a practice that became intensely controversial in the 1990s.

The Civil Rights Act of 1968 banned race discrimination in housing, including renting. To prevent acts of violence against civil rights advocates, the act also expanded federal laws making interference with a citizen's civil rights a federal crime. Responding to urban upheavals, the act also made it a federal crime to cross state lines to incite a riot.

As the political climate became more conservative after 1970, the Supreme Court became increasingly skeptical of expansive applications of civil rights legislation. A series of decisions in the late 1980s narrowing the scope of civil rights laws provoked counterefforts in Congress to extend the laws' scope. President George H. W. Bush vetoed a civil rights bill in 1990, asserting that it permitted racial quotas in hiring to increase minority representation in business and education. Extended negotiations produced a bill with some cosmetic changes, which Bush then signed as the Civil Rights Act of 1991.

By the 1980s, a comprehensive set of civil rights laws was in place, producing a general culture of civil rights. The 1964 Civil Rights Act included a provision, long sought by women's rights advocates, outlawing employment discrimination on the basis of sex. Later statutes applied the nondiscrimination principle to older citizens (the Age Discrimination in Employment Act, 1967) and the handicapped (the Americans with Disabilities Act, 1990). Although proposals to extend the principle to homosexuals stirred controversy, the civil rights culture had transformed the embattled proponents of minority rights into powerful interest groups capable of placing their concerns at the center of public debate.

[*See also* **Affirmative Action: Legal Aspects; Civil Rights; Fifteenth Amendment; Fourteenth Amendment; Johnson, Lyndon B.; Lesbian, Gay, Bisexual, and Transgender Rights Movement; New Deal;** *and* **Segregation.**]

BIBLIOGRAPHY

Burk, Robert F. *The Eisenhower Administration and Black Civil Rights.* Knoxville: University of Tennessee Press, 1984.

Graham, Hugh Davis. *The Civil Rights Era: Origins and Development of National Policy.* New York: Oxford University Press, 1990.

Mann, Robert. *The Walls of Jericho: Lyndon Johnson, Hubert Humphrey, Richard Russell, and the Struggle for Civil Rights.* New York: Harcourt Brace, 1996.

Stern, Mark. *Calculating Visions: Kennedy, Johnson, and Civil Rights.* New Brunswick, N.J.: Rutgers University Press, 1992.

Mark Tushnet

CIVIL SERVICE REFORM

Early nineteenth-century Americans, with the widest suffrage in the world and many offices to be filled by election, invented mass-based political parties to nominate and elect candidates. Since electioneering required time and money that few Americans could spare, political leaders recruited civil servants (or would-be civil servants) to perform party work and contribute to the party a percentage of their salary (called a political assessment). Local, state, and federal civil officers accepted this arrangement, because not to do so would jeopardize their jobs. If reelected, the patron could replace a recalcitrant civil servant; if the patron was defeated, his victorious opponent would distribute the spoils of office (the patronage) among his party workers. This spoils system, critics maintained, had a deleterious effect on the civil service and on politics. Government service suffered from frequent turnover and low morals among workers more loyal to their patron than to their agency, and the patronage system enabled political bosses to control party machinery and determine the fate of aspiring politicians.

After the Civil War, merchants angered by customhouse irregularities and corruption, urban professionals in the Northeast, and intellectuals (especially editors and writers) embraced civil service reform. Leaders of the National Civil-Service Reform League included such figures as Carl Schurz (1829–1906), a Republican senator and journalist; Edwin L. Godkin (1831–1902), editor of *The Nation;* and George William Curtis (1824–1892), editor of *Harper's Weekly.* These reform-minded Republicans deplored their party's crassness and corruption in the era of Ulysses S. Grant and James G. Blaine.

Civil service reformers advocated open, competitive examinations for government work and a ban on political assessments. Since this reform was modeled on British experience and would deprive the political parties of money and workers, politicians of both parties attacked it as antidemocratic and monarchical. Supporters claimed that this reform would introduce efficient business practices in the civil service and raise the level of party politics. Although civil service reform was introduced in the New York Customhouse (the nation's largest office) in 1879 during the Rutherford Hayes administration, it was the shocking assassination of President James Garfield in 1881 by a mentally deranged disappointed office-seeker that spurred reform on the federal level. After the Republican Party lost the midterm election of 1882, a lame-duck Congress passed the 1883 Pendleton Civil Service Reform Act. Although that act initially applied to (classified) only 10 percent of federal workers, to freeze their partisans in office outgoing presidents gradually extended the ranks of classified workers. By the Progressive Era, most important non-policy-making positions were classified.

Civil service reform profoundly affected American society and politics. By laying the base for professional bureaucracies, it enabled twentieth-century government on all levels to play a larger role in American society. But this innovation, by depriving political parties of a dependable source of funds and workers, also forced politicians to rely on, and become beholden to, corporations and political-action committees to finance soaring campaign costs in the age of television.

[*See also* **Hayes, Rutherford B.; Jackson, Andrew; Roosevelt, Theodore;** *and* **Spoils System.**]

BIBLIOGRAPHY

Hoogenboom, Ari. *Outlawing the Spoils: A History of the Civil Service Reform Movement, 1865–1883.* Urbana: University of Illinois Press, 1961.

Ari Hoogenboom

CLAY, HENRY

(1777–1852), statesman and Whig Party leader in the second-party system. Born in Virginia, Clay read law and in 1797 moved to Lexington, Kentucky. After serving in the Kentucky legislature and teaching law at Transylvania University, he won election in 1810 to the U.S. House of Representatives, where he served, apart from brief intervals, until 1825, usually as speaker. An unsuccessful presidential candidate in 1824, he participated in the congressional maneuvering that brought John Quincy Adams to the White House. When Adams appointed him secretary of state, the supporters of Andrew Jackson charged a "corrupt bargain." After two early appointive terms in the U.S. Senate (1806–1807 and 1810–1811), he won election to the Senate in 1831, serving until 1842 and again from 1849 until his death. A perennial presidential candidate, Clay ran four more times between 1832 and 1848, but it was as a master legislator, eloquent orator, and the West's magnetic "Prince Hal" that his reputation lives.

While speaker of the House in 1812, Clay was among the "War Hawks" who favored declaring war on Britain, but he also served as a peace negotiator at Ghent (1814) and thereafter pursued conciliation in both domestic and foreign affairs. He became known as "the Great Compromiser" for his role in the Missouri Compromise of 1820, the Tariff Compromise of 1833, and the sectional Compromise of 1850. Coming from the border state of Kentucky, Clay hoped desperately to avoid a civil war. Although a slaveholder, he favored the slaves' gradual emancipation and their removal to Africa. He argued in vain for the right of Native Americans to retain their lands in the Southeast. He warned, correctly, that the 1845 annexation of Texas would worsen sectional tensions and lead to war with Mexico.

As a Whig leader, Clay battled for national economic development through a program he called "the American System." This included protective tariffs, a national bank, and federal subsidies to "internal improvements" (transportation projects like highways and canals). His Democratic Party opponents, fearing the expansion of federal power at the expense of the states, frustrated the plan's adoption. Although Clay ended on the losing side of many controversies, the Republican Party that arose after his death implemented much of his economic program.

[*See also* **Adams, John Quincy; Calhoun, John C.; Federal Government, Legislative Branch: House of Representatives; Federal Government, Legislative Branch: Senate;** ***and*** **Political Parties.**]

BIBLIOGRAPHY

Peterson, Merrill. *The Great Triumvirate: Webster, Clay, and Calhoun*. New York: Oxford University Press, 1987.

Remini, Robert. *Henry Clay*. New York: W. W. Norton, 1991.

Daniel Walker Howe

CLEVELAND, GROVER

(1837–1908), twenty-second and twenty-fourth president of the United States. Born in Caldwell, New Jersey, Cleveland spent most of his early life in Buffalo, New York, where he practiced law and held minor offices. (He also fathered a child out of wedlock, an indiscretion that his political opponents would later use against him.) In 1881, running as a Democrat, he won election as mayor of Buffalo. The following year he was elected governor of New York, establishing in both positions a reputation for honesty and courage. Elected president in 1884, narrowly defeating James G. Blaine, he became the first Democrat to serve in that office since the Civil War. As president, he worked for civil service reform and tariff reform. Seeking to restrain governmental expansion, he vetoed over two-thirds of the bills passed by Congress, more than all his predecessors combined.

Losing a close reelection race to the Republican Benjamin Harrison in 1888, Cleveland returned to his legal practice. He regained the presidency in 1892, defeating Harrison and the Populist Party candidate James B. Weaver, thereby becoming the only president to serve two nonconsecutive terms. In response to a devastating depression that began in 1893, Cleveland persuaded Congress to repeal the Sherman Silver Purchase Act of 1890, which he believed undermined the government's economic stability. In 1894, he vetoed a compromise silver measure, led an inept attempt at tariff reform, and sent federal troops to Illinois to put down the Pullman railroad strike. Leaving office under a cloud of unpopularity, he retired to Princeton, New Jersey, where he died in 1908.

Cleveland's stature rose posthumously, boosted in 1932 by Allan Nevins's *Grover Cleveland: A Study in Courage,* which praised his honesty and forthrightness. Although historians in 1948 and 1962 ranked him "near great," subsequent scholarly assessments, dwelling on his ineffective handling of the crises of the 1890s, placed him in the "average" category.

If not a great president, Cleveland was nonetheless an important one. In initiatives like the repeal of the Tenure of Office Act in 1887 (an act, passed in 1867, that prohibited a president from removing appointed officials without the approval of the Senate), his brisk use of the veto power, reforms in federal land and Indian policy, and efforts at tariff reform, he recaptured for the presidency some of the powers it had lost during Reconstruction. Although not closely involved with its passage, Cleveland signed into law the Interstate Commerce Act of 1887, a pioneering federal regulatory measure. Establishing important precedents, he used a sweeping court injunction to end the Pullman strike and sent federal troops to Illinois without a request from the governor. Cleveland also asserted presidential authority in foreign policy, giving it a moral dimension akin to Woodrow Wilson's. He tried unsuccessfully to reverse the 1893 revolution that overthrew the Hawaiian monarchy, citing wrongful involvement by U.S. officials and business interests in Hawai'i. In settling an 1895 border dispute between Great Britain and Venezuela, he gave the Monroe Doctrine additional force in U.S. foreign policy.

Cleveland, however, showed little understanding of the large forces of industrialization and urbanization unfolding in the late nineteenth century. Following the Democratic philosophy of states' rights and limited government, he devoted himself principally to maintaining the gold standard. His actions during the depression of the 1890s split the Democratic Party, heightened the influence of its agrarian wing, and strengthened the Republican Party.

[*See also* **Civil Service Reform; Federal Government, Executive Branch: Presidency, The; Free Silver Movement; Indian Law, Federal; Monetary Policy; Populist Era;** ***and*** **Tariffs.**]

BIBLIOGRAPHY

Hollingsworth, J. Rogers. *The Whirligig of Politics: The Democracy of Cleveland and Bryan*. Chicago: University of Chicago Press, 1963.

Marszalek, John F., ed. *Grover Cleveland: A Bibliography*. Westport, Conn.: Meckler, 1988.

McElroy, Robert. *Grover Cleveland: The Man and the Statesman*, 2 vols. New York; London: Harper & Brothers, 1923.

Merrill, Horace Samuel. *Bourbon Leader: Grover Cleveland and the Democratic Party*. Boston: Little, Brown, 1957.

Morgan, H. Wayne. *From Hayes to McKinley: National Party Politics, 1877–1896*. Syracuse, N.Y.: Syracuse University Press, 1969.

Tugwell, Rexford G. *Grover Cleveland*. New York: Macmillan, 1968.

Welch, Richard E., Jr. *The Presidencies of Grover Cleveland*. Lawrence: University Press of Kansas, 1988.

R. Hal Williams

CLINTON, HILLARY RODHAM

(1947–), Secretary of State, U.S. Senator, and wife of President Bill Clinton. Hillary Rodham Clinton, wife of former president Bill Clinton, emerged as a dominant political figure, winning election to the U.S. Senate in 2000 and later becoming the Secretary of State in the Barack Obama administration. Her strong stands and memorable phrases have shaped gender relations, domestic affairs, and foreign affairs.

Born a baby-boomer in Chicago, Illinois, on 26 October 1947, Hillary Rodham matured from "Goldwater Girl" in 1964 to leading student radical at Wellesley College class of 1969, then at Yale Law School class of 1973. At Yale, Rodham met Bill Clinton. After helping the House of Representatives Judiciary Committee draw up articles of impeachment against Richard Nixon, she moved to Arkansas.

After marrying Clinton in 1974, Hillary Rodham developed a national reputation as a corporate lawyer and children's rights activist. She became the first female head of the Legal Services Corporation in 1978 and Rose Law Firm's first female partner in 1979. Best known as Arkansas's polarizing First Lady from 1979 to 1981 and 1983 to 1993, Hillary Rodham—who initially kept her maiden name—was attacked as too feminist and too powerful.

When Bill Clinton ran for president, Hillary Rodham Clinton again engendered gender controversy. In January 1992, refuting adultery charges against Bill Clinton, she said, "You know, I'm not sitting here like some little woman standing by my man like Tammy Wynette." Two months later, she dismissed corruption allegations by snapping, "I suppose I could have stayed home and baked cookies and had teas. But what I decided to do was pursue my profession."

As First Lady, Mrs. Clinton led Clinton's health care reform initiative, which failed. Criticizing China during a 1995 visit there, she said "human rights are women's rights, and women's rights are human rights." Her unique partnership with the president enmeshed her in the Travelgate and Whitewater scandals. Trying to appear more traditional, Clinton wrote the 1996 bestseller *It Takes a Village,* which popularized the African phrase "It takes a village to raise a child."

When the Monica Lewinsky scandal broke in January 1998, Mrs. Clinton blamed the "vast right-wing conspiracy." That August, her husband admitted his guilt—to her and the nation. Still, even as he was impeached, Hillary Clinton stood by her man.

A pioneer of highs and lows, Hillary Clinton was the first First Lady subpoenaed and the first First Lady to enter electoral politics. Running for Senate in 2000, she became the first woman to win statewide office in New York. She easily won reelection in 2006.

In 2008, she almost won the Democratic presidential nomination, losing to Barack Obama. One campaign commercial coined a cliché to define leadership, asking, "It's 3 a.m. and your children are asleep. Who do you want answering the phone?" When conceding she said, "Although we weren't able to shatter that highest, hardest glass ceiling this time, thanks to you it's got about 18 million cracks in it." In January 2009, Hillary Clinton surprised many by joining Obama's administration as America's sixty-seventh Secretary of State.

[*See also* **Clinton, William J.**; *and* **Obama, Barack.**]

BIBLIOGRAPHY

Clinton, Hillary Rodham. *Living History*. New York: Simon & Schuster, 2003.

Troy, Gil. *Hillary Rodham Clinton: Polarizing First Lady*. Lawrence: University Press of Kansas, 2006.

Gil Troy

CLINTON, WILLIAM J.

(1946–),"Bill" Clinton's election as president in 1992 was a product of political acuity and good fortune. Clinton benefited from a recession and a third-party undertaking by maverick Ross Perot, which damaged the reelection bid of George Herbert Walker Bush. Also helping Clinton's bid for the White House, in an age largely dominated by the conservative ideology of former president Ronald Reagan, was his careful strategy of defining himself as a New Democrat, not a Great Society liberal. As a five-term governor of Arkansas, he brought to the Democratic primaries a record of having governed a border state. He was more conservative with respect to issues such as crime and welfare reform than many Democrats. This helped him defeat in the primaries five rival candidates: Jerry Brown, Paul Tsongas, Bob Kerrey, Tom Harkin, and Douglas Wilder. In the general election, Clinton and his running mate Al Gore Jr. won 43 percent of the popular vote to George H. W. Bush's 37 percent of the popular vote. Ross Perot, running as a third-party candidate, received 19 percent. Clinton decisively won the Electoral College, winning 370 electors to Bush's 168. Clinton and Gore came into the White House with high hopes of initiating a fresh beginning for their party.

As President Clinton prepared his domestic agenda in 1993, he focused on the reform of the health system and appointed Hillary Clinton, his wife, to propose a legislative package that would serve as a template for change. Her efforts were blocked by the Republicans in Congress, which gave them a major issue to use in their effort to take control of Congress in the 1994 midterm election. This Republican success forced Clinton to modify his approach to policy initiatives and to adopt new political tactics preparatory to the 1996 election.

Clinton moved deftly to triangulate his policy options in Congress along lines suggested to him by Dick Morris, an old advisor from his Arkansas days. Although his commitment to a North American Free Trade Agreement and his support of welfare reform angered many congressional Democrats, Clinton's tactic of consolidating a more centrist approach to policy freed him of more liberal alternatives and gave him room to maneuver in a Congress controlled by Republicans. On the other hand, Republicans, led by House Speaker Newton Gingrich, overreached their mandate and played into Clinton's hands by shutting down the government, which angered many voters who agreed that the Republicans were responsible for this unwanted action.

Clinton went into the 1996 election year with a stronger hand than could have been imagined after the Democratic debacle of 1994, thanks to the reopening of government and an improving economic outlook. A major issue confronting him was welfare reform. Republicans had twice passed welfare reform legislation that Clinton had vetoed, declaring it was too punitive. Dick Morris told him that his election prospects might depend on whether he accepted a more moderate bill, which still divided Democrats. Clinton nevertheless signed it and thereby denied his election opponent, Senator Robert Dole, the Senate majority leader, the opportunity to exploit the issue. With things now going his way, Clinton won a decisive victory, yet the Republicans kept control of Congress.

Becoming the first Democrat to win two terms since Franklin Roosevelt, Clinton pursued policies that carried over from his first term. He pushed hard for opening markets for American goods and employed American forces against Serbs to prevent their pursuing a policy of ethnic cleansing against Muslims living in Bosnia. At the same time, he benefited from an economic surge that lowered the unemployment rate to 4 percent of the work force. But reflecting the new economic era that had since taken hold, he also signed a bill overturning the Glass–Steagall Act that had separated commercial and investment banking since 1933.

Clinton's second term was marred by the dramatic events that that led to his impeachment by the House of Representatives and a subsequent trial in the Senate. The case against him grew out of his affair with Monica Lewinsky, a White House intern, which was spelled out in a report by independent counsel Kenneth Starr. He condemned Clinton's behavior, indicating that what followed from it was a serious compromise of his office. Supported by Starr's report and driven by ideology and politics, House Republicans passed an impeachment resolution against Clinton on a party line vote. The Senate, reflecting the strong opposition in the country to Clinton's impeachment, rejected the House's action in a bipartisan vote.

Clinton remained resilient and worked hard to recapture the middle of the political spectrum. He sought to protect the Social Security system from Republican efforts to privatize it. Although Clinton earlier had proclaimed that the era of big government was over, he was not about to scuttle a key program that had provided a basis of political support for Democrats from middle-class and working-class Americans, which was a reflection of his modus operandi. Clinton was not a liberal reformer per se, but rather a centrist-minded progressive politician who sought to achieve a working balance among competing interest groups inside the American political system. Where he could improve existing programs, such as food stamps or tax benefits for the working poor, he acted accordingly.

As the Clinton presidency wound down, the election of 2000 was the dominant event that decided whether Vice President Albert Gore, the Democratic presidential nominee, would be in a position as president to protect and extend the Clinton legacy on matters such as the budget, the environment, and global markets. But because he lost by the narrowest of margins to Texas Governor George W. Bush, Gore's defeat spelled the end of the Clinton era, along with its mix of incremental solutions and programs designed to advance the interests of corporate America and workers alike.

In his last weeks as president, Clinton worked to find a solution to the intractable conflict between Israel and the Palestinian Authority, but his efforts were, sadly, frustrated. Still, Clinton in leaving office was lucky. Despite the lasting embarrassment of his impeachment, in retrospect his second term was a period of prosperity and economic growth, and his hands had not been tied down in a massive foreign policy adventure. His future reputation as president might well rest on the fact that he did not change very much or put his stamp on major policy initiatives in the manner that Franklin Roosevelt or Ronald Reagan had earlier.

[*See also* **Bush, George H. W.; Gore, Albert A. Jr.;** *and* **Perot, Ross.**]

BIBLIOGRAPHY

Berman, William C. *From The Center to the Edge: The Politics and Policies of the Clinton Presidency.* Lanham: Roman & Littlefield, 2001.

Clinton, Bill. *My Life*: New York: Alfred Knopf, 2004.

Harris, John. *The Survivor: Bill Clinton in the White House.* New York: Random House, 2005.

Patterson, James. *Restless Giant: The United States from Watergate to Bush v. Gore.* Oxford, New York: Oxford University Press, 2005.

William C. Berman

COMMITTEE OF CORRESPONDENCE

Throughout the eighteenth century, colonial assemblies designated some of their members as committees of correspondence to communicate with their agents in Britain and with other assemblies. Merchants used similar bodies to keep in touch and to lobby politicians. The most significant committee of correspondence, however, had different purposes and a more crucial impact.

In 1772, at the urging of Samuel Adams and others, Boston's Town Meeting created a committee of correspondence to maintain contacts with the selectmen of every Massachusetts town and, through them, with every town meeting. Its goals were to defeat Governor Thomas Hutchinson's efforts to create a pro-administration faction, to rally support for Boston's resistance to imperial taxation, to educate townspeople about their constitutional rights and the threats to those rights, and, finally, to habituate the townspeople to concern themselves with larger political and constitutional issues. The committee's efforts proved spectacularly successful. Even before the 1774 crisis over the Coercive Acts, many Massachusetts towns were becoming more unified in resistance to

Britain and had developed a nascent republicanism that would animate the populace as the revolutionary crisis unfolded. As Samuel Adams exulted in 1776, the Boston Committee of Correspondence had "raised the Spirits of the People, drawn their attention from *picking up pins*, and directed their Views to great objects."

Loyalists such as Hutchinson claimed that the Boston Committee of Correspondence tricked gullible country folk into rebellion, but the reality was quite different. Encouraged to express their own ideas, the towns developed more radical democratic ideals than Boston itself. The committee of correspondence diffused and decentralized thought about the nature and structure of government, producing by late 1774 in the critical colony of Massachusetts a more unified and fiercer resistance to Britain and a more sophisticated ideology of republicanism than had hitherto existed.

[*See also* **Republicanism.**]

BIBLIOGRAPHY

Brown, Richard D. *Revolutionary Politics in Massachusetts: The Boston Committee of Correspondence and the Towns, 1772–1774*. New York: W. W. Norton, 1976.

John L. Bullion

COMMITTEE ON PUBLIC INFORMATION

The Committee on Public Information (CPI) was the leading U.S. government news and propaganda agency during World War I. Established shortly after America's declaration in 1917, the CPI was created by executive order. It was headed by George Creel (1876–1953), a veteran journalist, reformer, and longtime Wilson supporter.

Wilson provided the agency only a vague mandate to promote the "absolute justice of America's cause" at home and abroad through publicity in any media. Creel claimed that the CPI was not a propaganda organization. Building on his experience as a progressive muckraker, he insisted that the CPI—true to its name—provided wartime information to a discerning public rather than seeking to manipulate opinion. In practice, however, the CPI operated as a propaganda and censorship agency, limited by its annual budget of just under $10 million (nearly half of it raised through private donations).

The CPI had two major sections—domestic and foreign—each with multiple divisions. The CPI is best known for the news division's management of the wartime American press. The Wilson administration asked newspaper editors to limit the publication of sensitive military information and give prominent place to official war news. The CPI had little power to enforce its requests, but by controlling press access to government officials and cooperating with other federal agencies that administered draconian laws such as the Espionage and Sedition Acts, CPI officials effectively wielded great power.

The CPI's domestic section sponsored a media barrage to mobilize the nation. The speaking division's Four Minute Men gathered 75,000 volunteers across the country to deliver brief speeches on war aims, food conservation, draft registration, and bond sales in public parks and movie theaters. More than 9 million people attended CPI public fairs and exhibitions; the posters of the pictorial publicity division created some of the war's most memorable images. The civic and educational cooperation division circulated some 75 million copies of CPI publications authored by an array of cooperating writers. Many were translated by the division of work with the foreign born, which disseminated them to foster a sense of "100 percent Americanism" among America's immigrant communities.

The CPI's smaller foreign section conveyed American support for its allies, lobbied neutral nations to join the cause, and expressed official American war aims. The film division distributed American films and materials overseas. By requiring Hollywood studios and foreign exhibitors to participate in the agency's export licensing system, the CPI indirectly laid the groundwork for the postwar American dominance of global film markets.

The CPI closed most of its operations after the Armistice in November 1918. In the war's aftermath, critics attacked CPI propaganda techniques—and Creel's outsize personality—and the CPI came to symbolize the excesses of wartime repression. But the organization's achievements reflected a broad consensus among the CPI, the American press, and much of the general public. The CPI's legacies were enduring: CPI propaganda techniques fostered the nascent field of public opinion research and also served as a model for the Office of War Information during World War II, whereas Creel's mix of advertising and politics contributed to the emergence of the mass-mediated politics that would dominate the rest of the twentieth century.

BIBLIOGRAPHY

Axelrod, Alan. *Selling the Great War: The Making of American Propaganda.* New York: Palgrave Macmillan, 2009.

Creel, George. *How We Advertised America.* New York; London: Harper & Brothers, 1920.

Vaughn, Stephen. *Holding Fast the Inner Lines: Democracy, Nationalism, and the Committee on Public Information.* Chapel Hill: University of North Carolina Press, 1980.

Christopher Capozzola

COMMON SENSE

A 1776 Revolutionary-Era pamphlet. American independence had not yet been publicly discussed when on 10 January 1776 the Philadelphia printer Robert Bell published a forty-seven-page pamphlet whose title page only hinted at its explosive contents: *COMMON SENSE: addressed to the inhabitants of AMERICA, on the following interesting subjects: I. Of the Origin and Design of Government in general, with concise Remarks on the English Constitution. II. Of Monarchy and Hereditary Succession. III. Thoughts on the present State of American Affairs. IV. Of the present ability of America.* Ominously, the epithet proclaimed: "Man knows no Master save creating Heaven, or those whom choice and common Good ordain." The author, Thomas Paine, had only recently immigrated from England and initially remained anonymous. An expanded second edition went through at least thirteen printings; total sales, estimated at 150,000 copies within three months, eventually reached half a million. A German translation was published in February by the Philadelphia printers Melchior Steiner and Carl Cist. This wide distribution, together with newspaper excerpts, made *Common Sense* the single most influential pamphlet of the Revolutionary War.

In rousing agitator's rhetoric, Paine dispelled as a myth the "balanced," liberty-protecting character of the British constitution. Hereditary monarchy and aristocracy were absurd, Paine argued, and irreconcilable with the natural equality of human beings. The colonists could not seriously hope for a permanent reconciliation with "the Royal brute of Britain." The day had arrived for them to declare their independence. Paine did not specify how the future republican American government should be organized, nor did he advocate social leveling. He argued only that Americans had good reason and the material resources to assert their independence, if only they would join in support of "the rights of mankind and of the FREE AND INDEPENDENT STATES OF AMERICA." Public and private reaction to *Common Sense* was overwhelming. The taboo had been broken, and debate did not cease until independence was declared.

[*See also* **Declaration of Independence;** ***and*** **Republicanism.**]

BIBLIOGRAPHY

Claeys, Gregory. *Thomas Paine: Social and Political Thought*. Boston: Unwin Hyman, 1989.

Paine, Thomas. *Collected Writings*, edited by Eric Foner. New York: Library of America, 1995.

Willi Paul Adams

COMMUNIST PARTY USA

Two American Communist parties were founded in 1919: one by non-English-speaking immigrants and the other by the journalist John Reed (1887–1920), author of an admiring history of the Bolshevik Revolution, *Ten Days That Shook the World* (1919). Forced to unify by the Communist International, the Communist Party USA (CPUSA) spent the 1920s as a marginal force in American life. Dominated by Finnish, Slavic, and Eastern European Jewish immigrants, the party was torn by factional warfare between Charles Ruthenberg and Jay Lovestone on the one hand and William Z. Foster, a radical trade union leader, on the other. Frequent Comintern mediation culminated in 1929 with Lovestone's deposition as party leader through Joseph Stalin's personal intervention.

In the early 1930s, the CPUSA led militant strikes and protests from Gastonia, North Carolina, to California's Imperial Valley. The party's ultrarevolutionary posture did not lead to substantial membership growth, however; in 1934, after five years of economic depression, it had only 26,000 members. Membership grew once the Comintern adopted the Popular Front against fascism in 1935, reaching nearly 100,000 by 1939, many of them native-born Americans. The CPUSA became a political force in several states, notably New York, Minnesota, and California. Communists were influential in several of the newly organized CIO unions, as well as in groups representing African Americans, immigrants, writers, and intellectuals.

The Nazi-Soviet Pact of 1939 reduced Communist influence, but the CPUSA rebounded during the American–Soviet alliance of World War II. In 1945, however, party leader Earl Browder was deposed after Moscow denounced his policy of cooperation with American capitalism. Party members rallied behind Henry Wallace's 1948 Progressive Party presidential campaign. As the Cold War gathered momentum and American Communists faced legal attack and became pariahs, the party created an underground organization and sent many members into hiding. Events abroad completed the party's decimation. Revelations of Stalin's crimes, Soviet anti-Semitism, and the Russian invasion of Hungary in 1957 reduced the CPUSA to fewer than 3,000 members by 1958. The crisis of Communism in the Soviet Union led to still another factional war in 1989 that left Gus Hall, party leader since 1959, head of an organization with barely 1,000 members.

[*See also* **Anti-Communism; Federal Bureau of Investigation; McCarthy, Joseph; New Deal; Progressive Party; Rosenberg Case; Socialism;** ***and*** **Wallace, Henry A.**]

BIBLIOGRAPHY

Howe, Irving, and Lewis Coser. *The American Communist Party*. Boston: Beacon Press, 1957.

Klehr, Harvey, and John Haynes. *The American Communist Movement.* New York; Toronto: Twayne; Maxwell Macmillan Canada, 1992.

Harvey Klehr

COMPROMISE OF 1820

In 1817, Missouri became the first territory within the boundaries of the Louisiana Purchase, apart from Louisiana itself, to apply for statehood. Subsequent congressional consideration of the issue led to the first major national debate between free and slave interests. Although the resulting compromise lasted for several decades, the dispute served as an omen of future sectional tensions, one that an aging Thomas Jefferson described with remarkable prescience as "a fireball in the night" and "a [death] knell for the Union."

In February 1819, Congressman James Tallmadge of New York introduced an amendment to the Missouri statehood bill requiring that no further slaves be allowed into Missouri and that children of slaves already in the state (over 10,000 in 1820) be freed at age 25.

Tallmadge's amendment, coupled with a similar one banning "slavery in the adjacent Arkansas Territory," sparked impassioned debate. The House of Representatives, on votes falling almost entirely along sectional lines, narrowly approved both amendments. The Senate, by a wider margin, rejected them and imposed no restrictions on slavery, present or future, in Missouri. When the next Congress convened in early December, Senator Jesse B. Thomas of Illinois proposed a compromise that, despite initial rejection in the House, passed in March 1820 when each provision was voted on separately. Under its terms, Maine, whose bid for statehood had been blocked by southern senators, was admitted as a free state; Missouri came in as a slave state; and, most significantly, Missouri's southern border, the 36°30' parallel, was extended westward as the boundary north of which slavery would not be permitted within the Louisiana Purchase.

The significance of the Missouri controversy became fully apparent only in hindsight. It provided the impetus for the first full-scale debate on what would emerge by mid-century as the central issue of the gathering sectional crisis: the territorial expansion of slavery. It also revealed the power of sectional interests to overwhelm partisan loyalties when this issue arose and set a precedent for congressional authority in determining the limits and conditions of slavery's expansion. The Missouri Compromise defined the terms and the dynamics of a sectional crisis that would reemerge with even greater intensity in the later 1840s in the wake of the territorial gains resulting from the Mexican War.

[*See also* **Antislavery Movement, Compromise of 1850; Jefferson, Thomas; Kansas–Nebraska Act; Louisiana Purchase;** ***and Scott v. Sandford.***]

BIBLIOGRAPHY

Freehling, William W. *The Road to Disunion: Secessionists at Bay, 1776–1854,* chapter 8. New York: Oxford University Press, 1990.

Moore, Glover. *The Missouri Controversy, 1819–1821.* Nashville, Tenn., 1937.

John C. Inscoe

COMPROMISE OF 1850

A series of laws passed by Congress to settle issues arising from the deepening sectional conflict over slavery. Although enacted separately, the laws followed a tradition of complex federal compromises over slavery's expansion designed to obtain concessions from all parties.

A tough new Fugitive Slave Act, designed to stop interference by northerners with the capture and return of fugitive slaves, empowered federal marshals to deputize bystanders to assist in seizing runaways and permitted the settlement of cases without jury trials. Legislation to organize the new territories of New Mexico and Utah permitted the settlers to introduce or ban slavery when they sought statehood. (This legislation also permitted suits directly to the Supreme Court over the status of slaves in the territories, thereby laying the groundwork for the 1857 *Scott v. Sandford* case. California was admitted as a free state over the protests of southerners fearful of a free-state majority in the Senate. Congress also banned public slave trading in Washington, D.C., a compromise between antislavery forces demanding total abolition in the district and southerners who viewed any restriction as unconstitutional. Finally, the slave state Texas relinquished its claims on much of neighboring New Mexico territory in exchange for the federal government's assumption of Texas's pre-annexation debts.

The final shape of the legislation was hammered out during months of rancorous congressional debate. Although each element of the compromise garnered a majority vote, the entire package never attracted a solid majority in either house. Arguing for a comprehensive compromise were leaders of the aging Jacksonian generation, including Henry Clay of Kentucky and Daniel Webster of Massachusetts, joined by a group of younger politicians like Stephen A. Douglas of Illinois, who drew upon party loyalty to forge agreements on individual bills. Opposing compromise were powerful militants from both sections, including the Northerners William Seward of New York and Salmon P. Chase of Ohio, and the Southerners John C. Calhoun and Jefferson Davis.

The Compromise of 1850 briefly muted sectional antipathies and delayed civil war for a decade. But the controversial enforcement of the Fugitive Slave Act proved deeply divisive, and the settlement finally unraveled in 1854, when an overconfident Douglas, in the Kansas–Nebraska Act, engineered the reversal of the 1820 Missouri Compromise and opened Kansas to slavery on the basis of the local-option principle. Northerners, furious at this use of one compromise to overturn another, abandoned the Democratic Party in droves and flocked to the new Republican Party.

[*See also* **Antislavery Movement; Clay, Henry; Douglas, Stephen A.; Fugitive Slave Act; Kansas–Nebraska Act; *Scott v. Sandford*; Texas Annexation;** *and* **Webster, Daniel.**]

BIBLIOGRAPHY

Freehling, William W. *The Road to Disunion*, vol. 1, *Secessionists at Bay, 1776–1854*. New York: Oxford University Press, 1990.

Hamilton, Holman. *Prologue to Conflict: The Crisis and Compromise of 1850*. Lexington: University of Kentucky Press, 1964.

Potter, David M. *The Impending Crisis, 1848–1861*, compiled and edited by Don E. Fehrenbacher. New York: Harper & Row, 1976.

Stegmaier, Mark J. *Texas, New Mexico and the Compromise of 1850: Boundary Dispute & Sectional Crisis*. Kent: Ohio: Kent State University Press, 1996.

Peter B. Knupfer

COMPROMISE OF 1877

One of four nineteenth-century political compromises designed to hold the states together without resort to force, the Compromise of 1877 was the last and in some respects the most successful. Unlike the previous compromises, that of 1877 was framed in secrecy. The occasion was the disputed presidential election of 1876 in which each candidate—the Republican Rutherford Hayes and the Democrat Samuel J. Tilden (1814–1886), the governor of New York—claimed a majority of electoral votes. The traditional account by historians told of a last-minute bargain in which the Republicans agreed to abandon the two remaining Republican state governments in the South and their protection of freedmen's rights in exchange for a pledge by southern Democrats to support Hayes.

In reality, negotiations had gone on for months and involved many more interests than electoral politics. The Democratic Party in the South and the Republican Party in the North had both fallen under the dominance of conservatives, often former Whigs. Negotiations between these two groups were conducted by the nonpartisan Western Associated Press, to which belonged all important newspapers of the Mississippi Valley, South and North. Confederate Colonel Andrew Jackson Keller of the *Memphis Avalanche* and Union General Henry Van Ness Boynton of the *Cincinnati Gazette* did most of the bargaining. They found a South battered first by the war and then by severe depression, desperately demanding federal subsidies for new or deteriorated railroads, fallen bridges, destroyed public buildings, and blocked harbors. Bills for such subsidies flooded Congress, supported in large measure by powerful corporate lobbies. Hayes, working closely with Keller and Boynton, promised that "to restore peace and prosperity to the South," he would be "exceptionally liberal" about internal improvements. As expected, enough Southern Democratic congressmen opposed the pro-Tilden filibuster plan of northern Democrats to thwart it. The electoral commission ruled in favor of Hayes, who was peacefully inaugurated.

Although Hayes's promise of federal subsidies went largely unfulfilled, disappointing southern capitalists, the principal losers in the compromise were the ex-slaves, abandoned by the Republican Party. But Radical Reconstruction was already on the wane, and Tilden would probably have wiped out what remained of it even more quickly than did Hayes.

[*See also* **Hayes, Rutherford B.; Radicalism; Reconstructionism;** *and* **Whig Party.**]

BIBLIOGRAPHY

Polakoff, Keith Ian. *The Politics of Inertia: The Election of 1876 and the End of Reconstruction.* Baton Rouge: Louisiana State University Press, 1973.

C. Vann Woodward

CONFEDERATE STATES OF AMERICA

When Abraham Lincoln was elected president in November 1861, many Southern whites feared that their economic security and cultural identity, especially as represented by the institution of slavery, would be threatened by a government dominated by the Republican Party. Between 20 December 1860 and 1 February 1861, seven Southern states—South Carolina, Mississippi, Florida, Alabama, Georgia, Louisiana, and Texas—seceded from the Union in protest. On 4 February, their representatives met at Montgomery, Alabama, to form the Confederate States of America (CSA). Four additional states—Virginia, Tennessee, Arkansas, and North Carolina—joined the Confederacy in April and May after Lincoln called for troops to quell the rebellion, and the Civil War began. This doubled the white population of the would-be new nation, to 5.5 million (plus 3.7 million blacks, mostly slaves), and enabled the Confederacy to fight for its independence. Kentucky and Missouri sent representatives to the Confederate Congress, but these two states' legislatures never officially recognized the new government.

The CSA's capital was moved to Richmond, Virginia, in July 1861.

The most rabid secessionists, known as "fire-eaters," had been agitating for a separate Southern nation for years, but with secession now accomplished, these radicals gave way to more moderate leaders like Jefferson Davis, who became president of the Confederacy. Initially, all Confederates agreed that the government should adhere to a doctrine of states' rights. However, Davis soon realized that his government must wield more power, even at the expense of the states, if it hoped to win independence. His decision to institute military conscription (a first in American history), suspend habeas corpus, and nationalize segments of the economy angered both powerful state political leaders and many common folk. In addition, perhaps as many as 40 percent of white Southerners had opposed secession. Thousands of these "unionists" created turmoil by enlisting in the U.S. Army, organizing peace movements within the South, and resisting Confederate authority. As casualty lists grew, hope of foreign intervention faded, and inflation drove down the value of the Confederate dollar, even many loyal rebels became alienated from the government.

A revolutionary political experiment in many respects, the Confederacy finally collapsed in April and May 1865, with the fall of Richmond, the surrender of the CSA's armies, and the capture or flight of its political leaders. Some Southern whites would long romanticize the "Lost Cause" of the Confederacy, but its legacies were chiefly involuntary; slavery was abolished and secession was decisively discredited as a viable political option.

[*See also* **Antislavery Movement; Davis, Jefferson;** *and* **Lincoln, Abraham.**]

BIBLIOGRAPHY

Rable, George C. *The Confederate Republic: A Revolution against Politics*. Chapel Hill: University of North Carolina Press, 1994.

Thomas, Emory M. *The Confederate Nation, 1861–1865*. New York: Harper Perennial, 1979.

Daniel E. Sutherland

CONGRESS OF RACIAL EQUALITY

The Congress of Racial Equality (CORE), one of the most important national organizations of the post–World War II African American freedom movements, was founded by an interracial group of pacifists in 1942. Committed to nonviolent direct action and interracial activism, CORE first launched protests against racial segregation in public accommodations in the North. In 1947, CORE activists undertook the Journey of Reconciliation, riding buses into the South to test a recent U.S. Supreme Court decision outlawing segregation in interstate travel facilities. Although mob violence stopped the trip in Chapel Hill, North Carolina, the project served as a model for CORE's 1961 Freedom Rides.

Initially a mostly white organization in the Northeast and Midwest, CORE expanded into the South after the Montgomery Bus Boycott of 1955–1956. The charismatic leadership of James Farmer, appointed national director in 1961, and increased media attention surrounding the Freedom Rides enabled CORE to launch a wide range of campaigns in the South during the 1960s. The experience of CORE organizers, the influence of southern blacks, and the impact of black nationalists like Robert F. Williams and Malcolm X led to a growing radicalization. In 1966, under the leadership of Floyd McKissick, CORE endorsed the "Black Power" slogan and the following year deleted the term "multiracial" from its constitution, forcing whites from the organization. In 1968, new national director Roy Innis promoted black separatism and "black capitalism." Although CORE had lost most of its national influence and vitality by the end of the 1960s, it had for nearly three decades played an influential role in the struggle to topple America's formal racial caste system and to create a new black sense of self.

[*See also* **Civil Rights**; *and* **Segregation.**]

BIBLIOGRAPHY

Bell, Inge Powell. *CORE and the Strategy of Nonviolence.* New York: Random House, 1968.

Farmer, James. *Lay Bare the Heart: An Autobiography of the Civil Rights Movement.* New York: Arbor House, 1985.

Meier, August, and Elliot Rudwick. *CORE: A Study in the Civil Rights Movement.* Urbana: University of Illinois Press, 1975.

Van Deburg, William L. *New Day in Babylon: The Black Power Movement and American Culture, 1965–1975.* Chicago: University of Chicago Press, 1992.

Simon Wendt

CONSCIENTIOUS OBJECTION

Conscientious objection—the principled refusal to bear arms—was brought to England's North American colonies by pacifist Protestant sects, especially Mennonites, Brethren, and the Society of Friends (Quakers), who believed that biblical commandments and Jesus's teachings prohibited them from engaging in war or any violence against other human beings. Since these religious faiths were comparatively small, economically productive, and otherwise law abiding, most colonial governments eventually exempted them from bearing arms.

Some objectors were forced into militia service during the Revolutionary War, but several of the new states recognized religious conscientious objection. Indeed, James Madison sought to include protection for religious objectors in the Bill of Rights, but this amendment, after passing in the House of Representatives in 1790, failed in the Senate.

Both North and South adopted national conscription in the Civil War, and some objectors suffered severely, but ultimately both sides recognized the objectors' sincerity and determination. The Abraham Lincoln administration eventually allowed conscripted pacifists to assist wounded soldiers and former slaves.

The Selective Service Act of 1917 recognized only members of the historic peace churches as "conscientious objectors" (COs), the first official use of the term, and required them to serve in the military in non–arms-bearing roles. Some 64,700 men, including many who were not members of the historic peace churches, claimed CO status on religious or political grounds in World War I, and 20,900 COs were inducted into the army. The military treated many harshly, and 450 "absolutists," who refused any cooperation, went to military prisons.

More liberal, the Selective Service Act of 1940, on the eve of World War II, authorized CO status for all religious objectors and allowed them to choose either non–arms-bearing military service or alternative civilian service. Of the 50,000 COs drafted in 1940–1945, most served in the army's medical corps; 12,000 performed alternative work in Civilian Public Service (CPS), and 5,000 absolutists were imprisoned.

Of the 35,000 COs who performed alternative service between 1951 and 1965, the

Cold War's peak, most worked in hospitals or mental institutions, with the CPS camps having been abolished. During the Korean War, nearly 1.5 percent of inductees were exempted as COs compared with 0.15 percent in each world war.

In the Vietnam War, large numbers of young men, both secular and religious, applied for CO status or simply refused to cooperate with the Selective Service System. These new COs received support from mainline religious bodies as well as antiwar and antidraft groups. The Supreme Court, in the *Seeger* (1965) and *Welsh* (1970) decisions, expanded the criteria for CO status to include secular ethical beliefs. More than 170,000 registrants were classified as COs between 1965 and 1970, and CO exemptions soared from 8 percent of actual inductions in 1967 to 43 percent in 1971. Additionally, between 1965 and 1973, 17,500 members of the armed forces applied for noncombatant status or discharge as COs.

Conscription ended in 1973, but even in an all-volunteer military, conscientious objection remained an issue. In 1990–1991, during the Persian Gulf War, between 1,500 and 2,000 persons in military units applied for discharge as COs. Tensions between the freedom-of-conscience principle and America's citizen-soldier tradition continue to define the evolution of conscientious objection in America.

[*See also* **Conscription; Lincoln, Abraham; Madison, James;** ***and*** **Peace Movements.**]

BIBLIOGRAPHY

Moskos, Charles C., and John Whiteclay Chambers II, eds. *The New Conscientious Objection: From Sacred to Secular Resistance.* New York: Oxford University Press, 1993.

Schlissel, Lillian, ed. *Conscience in America: A Documentary History of Conscientious Objection in America, 1757–1967.* New York: Dutton, 1968.

Tollefson, James W. *The Strength Not to Fight: An Oral History of Conscientious Objectors of the Vietnam War.* Boston: Little, Brown, 1993.

John Whiteclay Chambers II

CONSCRIPTION

Known in the United States as "the draft"; the act of compelling citizens into military service. Long used in Europe as a means of raising armies quickly and cheaply, it was not employed in the United States until the Civil War, when both sides introduced conscription to fill their manpower needs. In the North, the Conscription Act of March 1863 exempted men who could hire a substitute or pay a $300 fee. These provisions stirred growing protest that culminated in the New York City Draft Riots of 13–16 July 1863. For four days, until federal troops restored order, rioting Irish immigrants targeted the city's elite as well as African Americans, whom they blamed for the war. As a result, the Conscription Act was amended to limit exemptions to conscientious objectors opposed to military service on moral or religious grounds. The Confederacy experienced analogous problems with its conscription law, adopted in April 1862, which favored wealthy slave owners.

Upon U.S. entry into World War I, Congress passed the Selective Service Act of 1917, which required all male citizens between twenty-one and thirty years of age (later changed to eighteen and forty-five) to register for military service. Over 2.8 million males were drafted in 1917–1918. Only men with a verified family hardship, the physically disabled, and conscientious objectors were exempt.

Conscription was again imposed on the eve of World War II, with the Selective Service Act of 1940. Although not initially popular, this first peacetime draft facilitated rapid military mobilization after the U.S. declaration of war in December 1941. More than 10 million males were drafted between 1940 and 1947. Once again, the only exemptions were for family hardship, disability, or conscientious objection to war. Because of the manpower needs of U.S. occupation forces in Germany and Japan and the beginnings of the Cold War, conscription continued after the war's end. It was further extended by the Universal Military Training and Service Act of June 1951, a congressional response to the Korean War, which was periodically extended thereafter. The Vietnam War prompted passage of the Military Selective Service Act of 1967, which differed from its predecessors in permitting educational deferments for males between the ages of eighteen and twenty-six. The social inequality of this provision, combined with the growing unpopularity of the war, caused riots and demonstrations. This act expired in 1973, and in 1974 President Gerald Ford granted clemency to many thousands of Vietnam-Era draft resisters, provided they took an oath of allegiance and performed two years of public service. Draft registration resumed in 1980 for all males when they reached the age of eighteen, but at least through the end of the century no inductions were needed.

[*See also* **Confederate States of America; Conscientious Objection;** *and* **Ford, Gerald R.**]

BIBLIOGRAPHY

Flynn, George Q. *The Draft, 1940–1973*. Lawrence: University Press of Kansas, 1993.

Christopher Clark

CONSERVATION MOVEMENT

Launched in 1908 as a national crusade, the conservation movement involved the wide range of concerns later embraced by the environmental movement. Its intellectual origins date to the western land surveys of the nineteenth century, but it belongs to the realm of politics as much as to science. In the Progressive Era, two main branches, utilitarian and preservationist, emerged. Gifford Pinchot (1865–1946), a wealthy Pennsylvania forester who in 1898 became head of the federal government's small division of forestry (renamed the U.S. Forest Service in 1905), led the utilitarian wing. He advocated multiple-purpose use of the national forests. An astute strategist, he won the support of industries and interest groups eager to exploit the forests for profit by proposing a system of government regulation that eliminated wasteful competition and conflict. Close to President Theodore Roosevelt, Pinchot spearheaded an expanding program focused on "wise use" of natural resources, coordinated with other departments and agencies concerned with federal lands. The National Reclamation Act of 1902, establishing a federal agency to oversee irrigation projects in the Southwest, exemplified this objective.

Opposition to these policies arose in the western states most affected by them, and congressional opposition soon followed. The "conservation movement" was, in effect, Pinchot's public-relations crusade to create broad popular support for policies that until then had been promoted by narrow interest groups and bureau chiefs like himself—policies that western opponents identified with eastern corporations and elitist eastern bureaucrats. Through magazine articles and a 1908 White House conference, Pinchot crafted a public constituency for conservation.

The forest service's timber doctrine—of continual yield management (cutting no more timber than annual growth replaced)—became the foundation for a wildlife-preservation policy and the central doctrine of the U.S. Fish and Wildlife Service. A former forest service ranger, Aldo Leopold, carried over from forestry the notion that game populations were an agricultural crop to be harvested periodically to prevent overpopulation and preserve their range and food supply. Leopold also learned from Pinchot to cultivate an interlocking coalition of support groups constituting an effective wildlife lobby.

The preservationist wing of the movement, originally a part of Pinchot's grand concert of interests, split off after the Hetch Hetchy controversy (1913). This conflict focused on whether the Hetch Hetchy Valley, a part of Yosemite National Park, should be used as a water reservoir for San Francisco—the position Pinchot supported—or preserved for its natural beauty, as advocated by John Muir, a nature writer and activist well known to readers of mass-circulation magazines. Although the Hetch Hetchy Valley became a reservoir, disappointed preservationists helped in 1916 to establish the National Park Service, a federal bureau that rivaled the utilitarian forest service. The first director, Stephen Mather, proved as adept as Pinchot at buttressing his agency with the support of friendly industries and interest groups whose managers understood the commercial benefits awaiting those who helped meet the leisure needs of a rapidly growing urban middle class.

[*See also* **Ballinger–Pinchot Controversy; Environmentalism; National Park System; Progressive Era;** *and* **Roosevelt, Theodore.**]

BIBLIOGRAPHY

Dupree, A. Hunter. *Science in the Federal Government: A History of Policies and Activities to 1940.* Cambridge, Mass.: Belknap Press of Harvard University Press, 1957.

Penick, James Lal, Jr. "The Progressives and the Environment: Three Themes from the First Conservation Movement." In *The Progressive Era,* edited by Louis L. Gould, pp. 115–131. Syracuse, N.Y.: Syracuse University Press, 1974.

James Lal Penick Jr.

CONSERVATISM

American conservatism has no distinctive date of origin and scholars of political and intellectual history are divided as to the details of the conservative movement's development. Most histories of conservatism focus on the movement that developed after World War II, which finally achieved political success with the election of Ronald Reagan as president in 1980. However, this focus is too narrow and neglects the wide range of conservative ideas and personalities that had little to do with politics or public policy.

In this broader framework, conservatism in America owes its origins to the defense of constitutional liberty embodied in the founding era. It found its best expression in the development of a tradition of free-market capitalism and the distrust of a powerful federal government impinging on the market and on individual liberties. Combined with the defense of western civilization and the order of Judeo-Christian religion, conservatism proved an amalgam of shifting ideological viewpoints until conservatives began to shape their own movement and to narrowly define their views after World War II.

Conservatism Before World War II. With the onset of the Industrial Revolution and the concentration of power in the hands of individuals like Andrew Carnegie and John D. Rockefeller, conservatives became even more defensive of private property rights. Legal conservatism, especially the jurisprudence of Supreme Court Justice Stephen Field, helped preserve private property rights of capitalists by granting corporate monopolies due process rights embodied in the Fourteenth Amendment of the Constitution. This allowed business conservatives to defend their power and property and crush challenges to it from labor unions and reformers.

Yet for all their influence within American life, in terms of both their economic power and their support for politicians who defended their prerogatives in office, conservatism was by no means a political movement during the first half of the twentieth century. At best, it represented a faction of probusiness and *laissez-faire* politicians within the Republican Party and limited government and states-rights southerners within the Democratic Party. Conservative politicians battled against progressive reformers and sought support for Great Britain in World War I, but did not represent the dominant faction within either political party and did not develop themselves as a political movement.

At the colleges and universities, however, conservatism was in vogue, especially during the early twentieth century. The new humanists, Irving Babbitt at Harvard and Paul Elmer More at Princeton, influenced generations of undergraduates, including the poet Thomas Stearns Eliot and essayist Walter Lippmann, by their focus on standards in literature, in the cultivation of a true humane way of living, and by their derogation of fake humanitarianism in politics. Other prominent conservative thinkers worried over the rise of mass democracy and the threat of Bolshevism during the 1920s, including Spanish political philosopher Jose Ortega y Gasset, whose *Revolt of the Masses* (trans. 1930) sold well in the United States. Architect Ralph Adams Cram, who led a Gothic revival in architecture, looked with disdain on the masses and on democratic leadership. He equated the majority of people with Neolithic Man and argued against the promotion of mass democracy.

Such fare was hardly the stuff by which to reach a political majority and it assured any who accepted such ideas a minority status in politics. Yet at the same time as intellectuals and writers looked with disdain and fear on the masses, the people elected conservative Republicans Warren Harding and Calvin Coolidge into office. With economic policies promoting the return to business and to *laissez-faire* after the progressive expansion of government, the 1920s boomed economically and conservatives reaped the rewards.

Yet they were easily blamed when prosperity ended and the Great Depression began. In opposition to Franklin Roosevelt's New Deal policies and his expansion of government, conservatives organized. Some, such as Sun Oil chairman J. Howard Pew, continued to focus on the idea revolution, supporting books and scholarship dedicated to capitalism and free-market economics. Pew organized the wide distribution of F. A. Hayek's *The Road to Serfdom* (1944) and sponsored organizations dedicated to the cause of free-market economics. Others mobilized business interests in groups like the National Association of Manufacturers and the National Chamber of Commerce to fight against antibusiness and prolabor union New Deal policies. When Roosevelt himself went too far and attempted to pack the Supreme Court, a conservative coalition in Congress resisted the expansion of government programs and helped usher in an effective conservative political response.

Many conservatives during the 1930s had opposed the drift toward war with Nazi Germany and had joined in the antiwar America First Committee when it was formed in September 1940. Although America First was a polyglot organization with a variety of ideological perspectives, its financiers were generally midwestern business conservatives, including William Regnery, Sears chairman Robert Wood, and Sterling Morton of Morton Salt.

Young conservatives such as William F. Buckley Jr. and Henry Regnery gained their political start in America First. Although it was a short-lived organization, disbanding after the Japanese attack on Pearl Harbor in December 1941, America First had a profound impact on the debate over war with Germany and helped solidify connections conservatives employed in the postwar years.

Building Principles: Conservatism from 1940s–1960s. Although the war years were good for conservatives—much of the New Deal was rolled back and business regained its lost social status as a result of building Franklin Roosevelt's arsenal for democracy—conservatism still had to define what it stood for in the public arena. In 1944, a group including Felix Morley, Frank Hanighen, and Henry Regnery began publication of *Human Events,* a newsletter propagating a return to the principles of the old Republic, including a return to prewar isolationism. Within a few years the weekly would become a vehicle propagating a new Cold War anti-communism, antagonizing many conservatives like Morley who felt the old principles had been betrayed.

Human Events was just one such effort on behalf of the propagation of conservative ideas. Books like Hayek's *Road to Serfdom,* Richard Weaver's *Ideas Have Consequences* (1948), Whittaker Chambers' *Witness* (1953), Russell Kirk's *The Conservative Mind* (1954), and numerous publications and pamphlets all helped develop conservative ideas and beliefs. During the early years of the Cold War against the Soviet Union, conservatives turned away from their isolationism and by the time of the Korean War (1950–1953) were hawks favoring a global war against Communism. At home, many conservatives supported investigations into communist subversion, with some supporting the antics of Wisconsin Senator Joseph McCarthy during the early 1950s.

William F. Buckley Jr., a Yale alumnus, came to national attention by writing an expose of his alma mater, *God and Man at Yale* (1952), which catapulted the young Buckley into national prominence. The son of an oil man, the Catholic Buckley attended prep schools and Yale, where he was editor of the *Yale Daily News* and leading member of the debate team. Buckley was interested in forming a magazine to stand for conservative principles. There were several liberal publications in the mid-1950s, but not one that represented the ideas of conservatism. Buckley sought investors and put together a prospectus, which he sent to hundreds of conservatives. In the end he used his own money to start *National Review;* the first issue came out on 19 November 1955.

The Plunge into Politics. *National Review* helped to develop the principles of conservatism even further, forming a place for free-market libertarians, traditionalists, and anti-Communists. Before, the journal conservatives were divided, with Hayek insisting that he was a classical Whig and not even a conservative. Two of the editors, James Burnham and Frank Meyer, were former Communists; Meyer played a crucial role in providing ideological coherence to the conservative idea, finding a way to balance those who believed in individual rights and free markets with those who preferred religious order and tradition. Called fusion, Meyer's balance allowed conservatives to unify against enemies like communism and opponents like liberalism. It moved the conservative movement into politics.

By 1960 conservatives had built organizations, such as the Intercollegiate Studies Institute (ISI), which mobilized college students on campus, founded magazines and publishing houses, and connected through a series of foundations and grassroots organizations. Young conservatives in particular longed to become active in politics and challenge the dominant liberalism of the day. They found their inspiration in Senator Barry Goldwater (R-Arizona), who published a collection of speeches, *Conscience of a Conservative,* in March 1960. Conservative students fought for the draft of Goldwater as vice president at the Republican convention in 1960. After Goldwater failed to secure the slot, they moved on to form Young Americans for Freedom (YAF), which became crucial for channeling the political activism of young people.

YAF fought for Goldwater, supported the Vietnam War, protested against communist countries, and later combated the New Left on campus in the 1960s. Many YAF members became involved in political campaigns and some played a crucial role in the Goldwater presidential campaign in 1964. Their membership peaked at around 80,000 in 1969 before they declined in influence within the conservative movement.

The Goldwater campaign of 1964 proved to be one of the defining moments of conservative political organizing. A group of conservative businessmen and activists drafted the reluctant Goldwater, who did not relish running against Lyndon B. Johnson (LBJ) after John F. Kennedy's death in November 1963. Conservative activists employed direct mail fund-raising to secure donations. Grassroots activists like Phyllis Schlafly got involved writing and speaking on behalf of the *Goldwater,* writing the bestselling book *A Choice, Not an Echo,* which articulated the differences between the candidates and between liberalism and conservatism. Yet Goldwater himself was not a good campaigner and liberalism was still riding strong in the country in 1964. Goldwater and the Grand Old Party (GOP) suffered an astounding defeat, with LBJ securing 60 percent of the popular vote.

Conservatism and the Exhaustion of Postwar Liberalism. Two important developments helped contribute to further political revival for conservatives after 1964. One was the fracturing of liberalism. LBJ's Great Society programs and the War on Poverty split the liberal coalition as the civil rights movement became more interested in contesting urban areas through confrontational strategies like Black Power. The white ethnic and union base of the Democrats looked toward politicians like George Wallace, Richard Nixon, and Ronald Reagan in future elections. Conservative on social and religious issues, many New Deal liberals found themselves disconnected from a party that emphasized feminism, antiwar radicalism, and multiculturalism as norms.

Conservatives also learned that they needed to embrace public policy. During the 1964 presidential campaign Goldwater discussed ending Social Security, but he did so without data concerning the efficacy of the program. With the fracturing of liberalism, a group of former radicals and liberals called the neoconservatives moved to the right because of the problems of Great Society liberalism and Democratic softening on the necessity of waging the Cold War against Communism.

Irving Kristol, editor of *The Public Interest* and an essayist who published regularly in the *Wall Street Journal,* represented the first faction to change sides in the 1970s. Kristol criticized liberal social policy, but did so using data and social science arguments. Norman Podhoretz, editor of *Commentary* magazine, moved to the right over conservative support for the Cold War and growing liberal antipathy with Israel in its wars against its Arab neighbors. The neoconservatives had important connections to both New York intellectuals and publishers as well as to important politicians, such as Democrats Henry Jackson (D-WA) and Daniel Patrick Moynihan (D-NY).

Conservatives also developed and supported their own think tanks. The Heritage Foundation was founded in 1972 in Washington and the libertarian CATO Institute in 1977. Both advocated for conservative and free-market policy solutions and supported a network of activist Capitol Hill staffers and politicians who used their policy studies to support or oppose legislation.

Conservative activists mobilized at the grassroots level during the 1970s as well. A growing cultural permissiveness combined with an active Supreme Court, which passed decisions like *Roe v. Wade* legalizing abortion, helped move evangelical Christians into politics. Christian activists had long been involved in grassroots efforts against Communism, but now they moved to defend the culture from assault by secular activists. Christian women were crucial in securing the defeat of the Equal Rights Amendment, with long-time activist Phyllis Schlafly organizing thousands of women to fight against it. They were also important in awakening the public to concerns about sex education and played prominent roles in the pro-life movement emerging in America.

By 1980 conservatives had the necessary organizations and grassroots network to win the presidency behind Ronald Reagan. Reagan campaigned on rebuilding America's military and revitalizing the dormant economy. He did both, securing passage of a tax cut, cutting regulations, and pushing for free-market economic reforms, which helped the economy grow. He also challenged the Soviets through support for anti-Communist groups in the Third World, increasing the defense budget and pushing for a strategic missile defense shield. After the emergence of Mikhail Gorbachev as leader of the Soviet Union, Reagan began to negotiate. In the end, his policies hastened the collapse of the Soviet economy and brought about the collapse of the Soviet empire in Eastern Europe.

Conservatism from Reagan to the Present. Since the 1960s conservatism has been more focused on political issues and policy, which led to the development of a more politicized conservatism of inside-the-beltway operatives and media. In 1994 conservatives scored a stunning triumph by winning control of Congress. Texas Governor George W. Bush ran and won a controversial election in 2000 as a compassionate conservative. After the terrorist attacks on New York and Washington on 11 September 2001, Bush proposed a new strategy of preemptive war, which was unleashed in the invasion of Iraq in March 2003. Conservatives were divided over the Iraq War and Bush's penchant for what Fred Barnes called "big government conservatism," using government programs to promote efficient outcomes in areas such as education, health care, and other programs.

Since the election of Barack Obama, the older constitutionalist and small government conservatism has returned. The bailout of Wall Street and the massive increase in the national debt under a Democratic Congress, as well as the passage of a massive new entitlement in health care, prompted grassroots organizing of the Tea Party, which had a huge impact on allowing the GOP to take back the House of Representatives in 2010.

Conservatism in the new millennium continues as the protean ideology. Conservatives have consistently shown themselves capable of changing their basic political posture while staying true to their beliefs in limited government, support for Constitutional order, and a strong defense.

[*See also* **Buckley, William F., Jr.; Bush, George W.; Conservatism, Legal; Conservative Movement; Goldwater, Barry; Obama, Barack; Reagan, Ronald; Schlafly, Phyllis;** ***and*** **Young Americans for Freedom.**]

BIBLIOGRAPHY

Allit, Patrick. *The Conservatives: Ideas and Personalities throughout American History*. New Haven, Conn.: Yale University Press, 2009.

Critchlow, Donald. *The Conservative Ascendancy: How the GOP Right Made Political History*. Cambridge, Mass.: Harvard University Press, 2007.

Farber, David S. *The Rise and Fall of Modern American Conservatism*. Princeton, N.J.: Princeton University Press, 2010.

Nash, George H. *Reappraising the Right: The Past and Future of American Conservatism*. Wilmington, Del.: ISI Books, 2009.

Regnery, Alfred S. *Upstream: The Ascendance of American Conservatism*. New York: Threshold Editions, 2008.

Schneider, Gregory L. *The Conservative Century: From Reaction to Revolution*. Landham, Md.: Rowman & Littlefield, 2009.

Gregory L. Schneider

CONSERVATISM, LEGAL

Legal conservatism is an approach to jurisprudence that emphasizes fixed rules about how to interpret constitutional provisions, resolve disputes between parties, and provide justice. Genuine legal conservatives argue that such rules transcend historical and sociological contingencies. Indeed, conservatives believe that rules must ultimately be fixed for law to retain its authority and moral force. To believe otherwise, they argue, substitutes the passing whims of present-day judges for the "rule of law."

For this reason, American legal conservatives object to the idea that the United States has a "living constitution" that must periodically evolve to better meet the challenges of the present day. Conservatives also reject several schools of legal thought—including sociological jurisprudence, legal realism, and critical legal studies—that seek to expose transcendent legal principles as a form of social power or class domination. Legal conservatives view such critiques as a sort of nihilism—an implicit rejection of the very possibility of justice.

Varieties of Legal Conservatism. American legal conservatives can nevertheless disagree about the source of transcendent legal rules and their application to specific controversies. One major camp of legal conservatives is made up of "textualists" and "originalists." Textualists maintain that judges should be bound by the specific text of laws and constitutional provisions, which were created and formally endorsed by electorally accountable branches of government. Justice Antonin Scalia of the U.S. Supreme Court considers himself a textualist.

When the text of the law is vague or contradictory, many textualists turn to history for further guidance. For example, some textualists look to the "original intention" of people who wrote a statute or framed a constitutional provision, for example, by reading the accounts of constitutional conventions or information entered into the *Congressional Record*. Others, including Justice Scalia, insist that the "original public meaning"—that is, how the text would have been generally understood at the time it became law—is the only context that should have legal force.

A second camp of legal conservatives is composed of advocates of "natural law." These thinkers believe that law exists prior to, and transcends, the Constitution or statutory law.

Some proponents of natural law believe that the foundation of American law can be found in Judeo-Christian religious texts. Others believe that secular philosophy has provided sufficient principles of right and wrong, responsibility and obligation, fair play and equal justice that must serve as the basis for any just regime. Natural law has fewer explicit adherents in the U.S. judiciary than originalism, although Supreme Court Justice Clarence Thomas has written admiringly about the concept.

A third camp of legal conservatives are marked more by temperament than by any specific theory of jurisprudence. Such conservatives tend to defend established precedent—that is, the accumulated decisions of past courts—and are skeptical of attempts to rethink first principles or engage in excessive "judicial activism."

Legal Conservatism and Political Conservatism. Legal and constitutional ideas have played a significant role in the electoral and intellectual mobilizations of the American right since the early twentieth century, when expansions of the federal government championed by progressives and liberals challenged some of the prerogatives of property owners, businesses, and local government. For example, the leading conservative congressman of the 1960s, Senator Barry Goldwater of Arizona, included an originalist critique of the Supreme Court's decision in *Brown v. Board of Education* (1954) in his manifesto *The Conscience of a Conservative* (1960). Although personally opposed to racial segregation, Goldwater believed that the Framers intended to leave education to state and local government. Goldwater later voted against the landmark Civil Right Act of 1964 on the grounds that its ban on racial discrimination by private businesses violated property rights and principles of federalism. At the grassroots level, activists put up lawn signs and billboards reading "Impeach Earl Warren," a reference to the Chief Justice who authored *Brown*.

The conservative electoral mobilization against the courts grew in the 1970s, when conservative politicians successfully ran against unpopular decisions, especially those mandating the "busing" of students to integrate public schools, reforms of criminal procedure that restricted law enforcement, and the use of affirmative action to remedy racial inequalities. At the same time, activists in an emerging Christian right mobilized around related legal issues. For example, religious conservatives challenged the authority of the Internal Revenue Service to deny the tax-exempt status to Christian academies that sprung up in the post-*Brown* era. They also lobbied for the repeal of *Roe v. Wade*, a 1973 Supreme Court decision that invalidated most restrictions on abortion.

The electoral successes of the right—especially the Republican domination of the presidency from 1968 to 1992—gave conservatives an opportunity to remake the courts. Republicans appointed ten consecutive Supreme Court justices and a host of federal trial and appellate court judges. But some Republican-appointed justices turned out to be relatively moderate, even liberal, on the bench. Others failed to win confirmation, most prominently the prominent originalist Robert Bork, whose nomination to the Supreme Court by President Ronald Reagan was rejected by the U.S. Senate in 1987.

Conservatives and Legal Institutions. One response to the failure of greater electoral conservatism to produce greater legal conservatism was an increased interest in the role of institutions—such as law firms, law schools, and professional associations—in maintaining the hegemony of legal liberalism.

In the early 1970s, conservatives began to build a network of nonprofit law firms intended to do for the right what attorneys like Thurgood Marshall had done for the civil rights movement: use litigation to achieve better outcomes or change legal precedent. These firms—including the Sacramento-based Pacific Legal Foundation and the Denver-based Mountain States Legal Foundation—could be mercenary in their use of any available legal tools, but they staked out a conservative claim to represent a "public interest" in certain outcomes. More recently, libertarian-leaning public interest groups such as the Center for Individual Rights and the Institute for Justice have brought important precedent-setting cases on affirmative action, school vouchers, and eminent domain.

In the law schools, conservatives challenged the hegemony of liberalism and left-wing thinking among law faculties. From the late 1970s through the 1990s, the right-leaning John M. Olin Foundation subsidized a discipline of legal studies known as law and economics. Devoted to bringing microeconomic analysis to bear on issues and justice and judging, law and economics showed how many commonly accepted legal principles resulted in suboptimal outcomes. Not all advocates of law and economics are legally or politically conservative, but some of the leading scholars of the field—including the University of Chicago's Richard Posner and Richard Epstein—used economic logic to question the efficacy and justice of the post–New Deal regulatory state. Epstein, in particular, connects his strong defense of property rights to an originalist understanding of the U.S. Constitution.

Legal conservatives also created their own professional organizations, most importantly the Federalist Society for Law and Public Policy Studies. Founded in 1982 by a group of law students, the Federalist Society became a hub of conferences, speaking events, and debates among like-minded lawyers and law students. These meetings helped push a once-dormant debate over originalism back into the public eye and served as an intellectual "farm team" for many jurists and intellectuals of the contemporary right.

[*See also* **Conservatism; Conservative Movement;** *and* **Goldwater, Barry.**]

BIBLIOGRAPHY

Arkes, Hadley. *Beyond the Constitution.* Princeton, N.J.: Princeton University Press, 1990.

Calabresi, Steven G., ed. *Originalism: A Quarter-Century of Debate.* Washington, D.C.: Regnery, 2007.

Epstein, Richard A. *Takings: Private Property and the Power of Eminent Domain.* Cambridge, Mass.: Harvard University Press, 1985.

Scalia, Antonin. *A Matter of Interpretation: Federal Courts and the Law.* Princeton, N.J.: Princeton University Press, 1997.

Teles, Steven M. *The Rise of the Conservative Legal Movement: The Battle for Control of the Law.* Princeton, N.J.: Princeton University Press, 2008.

Jefferson Decker

CONSTITUTION

The Constitution of 1787 is the basic governing document of the United States.

Intellectual Antecedents. The origins of the Constitution extend back centuries into Judeo-Christian culture, drawing upon the Bible (the Hebrew scriptures far more than the Christian); the political culture of the classical world, particularly the 500-year history of the Roman republic; natural law and natural rights doctrines formulated by ancient, medieval, and early modern writers; the rhetoric and philosophy of the Renaissance, Reformation, and Enlightenment; social contract theory; and English constitutional history, including Common Law, Whig libertarian tradition, and the formal enunciations in the Magna Carta (1215), Petition of Right (1628), Habeas Corpus Act (1679), and Bill of Rights (1689). Writers cited during the debate over the ratification of the Constitution included first and foremost the Baron de Montesquieu, followed by Sir William Blackstone, John Locke, Sir Edward Coke, Jean Louis DeLolme, James Harrington, Thomas Hobbes, David Hume, Richard Price, and Algernon Sidney. Frequently mentioned ancient writers included Aesop, Horace, Polybius, Socrates, Tacitus, and Virgil. The three most widely cited literary writers were Alexander Pope, William Shakespeare, and Jonathan Swift.

Historical Background. Despite the impressive breadth of these antecedents, the founders drew most heavily on their own experiences in America as colonists, rebels, and constitution writers. Beginning with their colonial charters, the New World settlers had embodied their English Common-Law rights in over two hundred written documents. Only on rare occasions in England, and after repeated abuses by the monarch, had rights been asserted in writing. In America, however, as a matter of course, colonists wrote charters and sometimes adopted statements of rights based on English Common Law. In some colonies these guarantees were offered willingly by the crown or benevolent founders or proprietors, as in Rhode Island, Pennsylvania, New Jersey, and the Carolinas. In others, rights had to be wrested from arbitrary or incompetent governors who tried to preserve the prerogatives of the crown or proprietors.

During the Colonial Era, governments developed in each colony with a governor, judiciary, and (usually) bicameral legislature. Governors controlled appointments to the judiciary and to their council, which often served as the upper house of the legislature. Largely left to develop on their own before 1764, colonial governments had come to an accommodation in which assemblies, the lower houses of the legislatures, developed a degree of self-government through their control over all tax measures and appropriations, including the salaries of governors and the rest of the civil list. Assemblies effectively used this fiscal authority as a check on their governors.

After the end of the Seven Years' War in 1763, Parliament pursued a new activist imperial policy toward its American colonies. One tax after another provoked vehement responses from colonial dissenters. When Parliament repealed the Stamp Act in response to colonial protests, the Declaratory Act (1766) unequivocally asserted Parliament's undisputed authority to pass any legislation for the colonies: self-government was a grant, not a right. The colonists never accepted this absolutist position, and after a decade of friction, Americans declared their independence and embarked on an unprecedented period of constitution writing at both the state and the national levels.

Between 1776 and 1780, Americans drafted and adopted state constitutions that, with few exceptions, created similar governments. Structurally the new state governments resembled their colonial predecessors with governors, bicameral legislatures (except for Pennsylvania, Georgia, and the self-proclaimed republic of Vermont), and judiciaries. Despite the commitment to the concept of separation of powers, real political power shifted almost exclusively to the assemblies. Assemblymen were elected annually. Governors, often elected by the legislatures for one-year terms, were denied the veto, and senates (the new upper houses) were not allowed to amend money bills. Most appointments, including the judiciary, were made annually by the assemblies. Judicial review of legislative acts hardly existed.

At the national level, the Continental Congress, after more than a year of deliberation, submitted a draft constitution, the Articles of Confederation, to the state legislatures for the requisite unanimous ratification. The Articles created a unicameral Congress in which each state had one vote, and delegates to Congress could serve only three years in any six-year period. Congress could act only on the states, not directly on the people. The Articles did not provide for a separate executive or judiciary, and according to Article II, the states retained their "sovereignty, freedom and independence" and Congress possessed only those powers "expressly delegated" to it. Lacking the power to regulate foreign or interstate commerce or levy taxes, Congress raised revenue by asking the states for money. Most important matters needed the approval of nine states in Congress. Amendments to the Articles required the approval of Congress and the unanimous ratification of the state legislatures.

Repeated efforts to strengthen Congress by amending the Articles or by persuading the states to grant specific additional powers failed. Congress could not pay its wartime debt and the states failed to pay their congressionally apportioned requisitions. When a postwar economic depression began in late 1784, most of the state legislatures enacted debtor-relief measures that sometimes violated the property rights of creditors. Sporadic violence by debtors, such as Shays's Rebellion in Massachusetts, erupted in several states. Unable to address adequately these economic, political, social, and diplomatic crises, Congress on 21 February 1787 called a Constitutional Convention to meet in Philadelphia in May "for the sole and express purpose of revising the Articles of Confederation" so they would be "adequate to the exigencies of government and the preservation of the Union."

In fact, when the Constitutional Convention of 1787 convened, the delegates voted immediately to abandon the Articles of Confederation and to draft a new constitution that would create a national government. The Virginia Plan, based mainly on the ideas of James Madison, served as the Convention agenda. After four months, thirty-nine delegates signed the document on 17 September 1787. Every part of the new Constitution was found in a state constitution, the Articles of Confederation, or the Northwest Ordinance (passed two months earlier by Congress). Despite this apparent lack of originality, the new Constitution was unique in the way it married the concepts of separation of powers, checks and balances, and federalism.

Provisions of the Constitution. The Constitution consisted of seven articles introduced by a preamble setting forth the aims of the American people. The first seven words of the preamble heralded a profound change: "We the People of the United States." The people—not the states—entered into this new compact to "form a more perfect Union, establish Justice, insure domestic Tranquility, provide for the common defence, promote the general Welfare, and secure the Blessings of Liberty to ourselves and our Posterity."

The first article—half of the entire document—dealt with the legislative branch of the new government. All legislative power was given to a bicameral Congress composed of a Senate and House of Representatives. Each state was to have two senators elected for a six-year term by the state legislatures. The vice president of the United States served as the Senate's president and could vote only to break ties.

Members of the House of Representatives, elected for two-year terms, were to be apportioned among the states on the basis of population, counting each slave as three-fifths of a person. Individuals qualified to vote for the lower house of their state's legislature were eligible to vote for that state's federal representatives. Every ten years a federal census would be taken, after which Congress would reapportion representatives among the states. All revenue bills had to originate in the House but the Senate could offer amendments.

The regulations for electing Congress were left to each state legislature, but Congress could alter such rules. Congress had to assemble at least once a year. Each house elected its own officers, adopted its own rules, kept its own journals, and judged the elections and qualifications of its members. Recall and mandatory term limits were eliminated. Members' salaries were to be set by law and paid by the federal Treasury. No member could hold another federal office.

Congress was specifically empowered to lay and collect taxes, borrow money, regulate foreign and interstate commerce, establish rules for naturalization and uniform bankruptcy laws, coin money, fix the standard of weights and measures, punish counterfeiters, establish a post office, grant copyrights and patents, create inferior judicial courts, define and punish piracy and crimes at sea, declare war, raise and maintain an army and navy, provide rules for the state militias, exercise complete jurisdiction over the federal capital and other federal properties, and "make all Laws which shall be necessary and proper for carrying into Execution the foregoing Powers." The president had veto power over any bill passed by Congress, subject to a congressional override by a two-thirds vote of each house.

The Constitution specifically prohibited Congress from passing bills of attainder, ex post facto laws, and export duties; granting titles of nobility; suspending the writ of habeas corpus except in emergencies; and prohibiting the foreign slave trade before 1808. The states, too, were prohibited from passing bills of attainder, ex post facto laws, and laws impairing the obligation of contracts; coining money; issuing paper money; declaring anything but gold and silver legal tender; entering into treaties or alliances; or laying import or export duties without the consent of Congress.

Article II vested the executive power of the federal government in a president and vice president, both elected for four-year terms by specially chosen electors. The electors themselves were to be elected in a manner decided by each state legislature. The president, who had to be a natural-born citizen of the United States, was to be commander-in-chief of the military and the state militias when brought into federal service. He or she could grant pardons and reprieves, and, with the advice and consent of the Senate, make appointments and enter into treaties, subject to the approval of two-thirds of the senators present. The president, vice president, and all civil officers of the United States are removable from office on impeachment by the House of Representatives and conviction by the Senate for "Treason, Bribery, or other High Crimes and Misdemeanors." When the president is impeached, the Chief Justice of the United States presides over the trial in the Senate.

The third branch of government—the judiciary—is the least defined in the Constitution. Article III provides for one Supreme Court and such inferior courts as Congress shall create. Federal judges hold their appointments during good behavior and their salaries cannot be diminished during their tenure. The jurisdiction of the federal judiciary extends to all cases of law and equity arising under the Constitution, federal laws, and treaties, as well as to cases involving the United States, cases between citizens of different states, and other cases where a national venue was considered important. The original jurisdiction of the U.S. Supreme Court was spelled out; in all other cases the Court could exercise appellate jurisdiction in law and fact, with such exceptions as Congress might by law direct.

Jury trial was guaranteed in all criminal cases (except impeachments) and these trials had to be held in the state where the crime was committed. Treason was defined narrowly as waging war against the United States or adhering to, or giving aid and comfort to, the enemies of the United States. Conviction for treason needed the testimony in open court of two witnesses to the same overt act. Punishment for treason could not extend to family or friends of the guilty party.

Article IV provided that each state give "full faith and credit" to the public acts, records, and judicial proceedings of every other state. Citizens of each state were to be entitled to all of the "privileges and immunities of Citizens in the several States." States were required to extradite persons wanted for crimes in other states, and slaves who escaped to another state could not be freed. Congress was authorized to make rules and regulations for federal territories and to admit new states into the Union. The United States guaranteed every state a republican form of government, protection from foreign invasion, and (upon application of the state legislature or executive) assistance against domestic violence.

Unlike the Articles of Confederation, the Constitution provided for a realistic (although difficult) method of amendment. According to Article V, amendments to the Constitution could be proposed by two-thirds of both houses of Congress or by a constitutional convention that Congress must call at the request of two-thirds of the state legislatures. Proposed amendments could be adopted by the agreement of three-fourths of either the state legislatures or the state ratifying conventions, whichever method Congress directs.

Article VI validated all debts and engagements entered into by the United States before the adoption of the Constitution and declared the Constitution, all laws made in pursuance of it, and all treaties to be the supreme law of the land, notwithstanding anything in the constitution or laws of any state. Article VI also required all federal and state officials to take an oath to support the Constitution, but prohibited any religious test for federal officeholding.

Ratification. Unlike the Articles of Confederation, unanimous ratification by the state legislatures was not required to adopt the Constitution. Article VII provided that the ratification of nine state conventions would be sufficient to establish the Constitution among the ratifying states.

The Constitutional Convention sent the engrossed manuscript Constitution to Congress, which transmitted the new form of government to the states for their ratification in specially elected conventions. An intense public debate over the Constitution raged for almost a year. In June 1788 New Hampshire became the ninth state to ratify, followed quickly by Virginia and New York. A key issue in this debate focused on the kind of government to be created by the Constitution: Did Article I, Section 8, grant Congress power to do anything necessary to promote the general welfare and national defense, or did it grant to Congress only limited, enumerated powers? In other words, would the new government be a consolidated national government that would eliminate the sovereignty of the states or would it be a limited government of specified powers that would leave the states sovereign and free to act in all other matters? Coupled with this issue was the debate over the omission of a federal bill of rights, which supporters of the Constitution argued was unnecessary because the Constitution's internal checks on government would prevent any violation of rights.

In several states, ratification was achieved only with a promise that amendments to the Constitution, especially a bill of rights, would be proposed in the first Congress. Largely through the efforts of James Madison, the first Congress in September 1789 proposed a Bill of Rights, which was adopted with little public debate in December 1791.

A Living Document. The debate over the breadth of federal power was renewed soon after the establishment of the new federal government. In essence, the question was how to interpret the "necessary and proper" clause. Should the Constitution be broadly or strictly interpreted? The followers of Alexander Hamilton advocated a broad interpretation, which President George Washington endorsed. The election of Thomas Jefferson as president in the "Revolution of 1800" heralded a shift to a stricter interpretation that circumscribed the actions of the federal government. The Civil War and the three constitutional amendments adopted in its aftermath, particularly the Fourteenth Amendment, allowed the federal government in the twentieth century to expand the protections embodied in the Bill of Rights to include actions by state and municipal governments. Over the years, ebbs and flows occurred in how the branches of the federal government viewed their constitutional powers and responsibilities. Not until the New Deal Era and World War II did the expansion of federal power through a broad reading of the Constitution's national defense, commerce, and general-welfare clauses overwhelmingly change the nature of the relationship between the states and the federal government. As the twentieth century ended, the debate over federalism continued.

[*See also* **Albany Congress; Articles of Confederation; Bill of Rights; Constitutional Convention of 1787; Constitutional Interpretation; Constitutionalism; Constitutionalism, Popular; Continental Congress; Eighteenth Amendment; Elections: Suffrage; Federal Government, Executive Branch: An Overview; Federal Government, Executive Branch, Presidency, The; Federal Government, Judicial Branch; Federal Government, Legislative Branch: An Overview; Federal Government, Legislative Branch: House of Representatives; Federal Government, Legislative Branch: Senate; Federalism; Fifteenth Amendment; Fourteenth Amendment; Hamilton, Alexander; Jefferson, Thomas; Judicial Review; Madison, James; Northwest Ordinance; Republicanism; Second Amendment; Shays's Rebellion; Sixteenth Amendment; State Governments; States' Rights; Supreme Court, U.S.; Taxation;** *and* **Washington, George.**]

BIBLIOGRAPHY

Adams, Willi Paul. *The First American Constitutions: Republican Ideology and the Making of the State Constitutions in the Revolutionary Era.* Chapel Hill: University of North Carolina Press, 1980; expanded ed., 2000.

Conley, Patrick T., and John P. Kaminski, eds. *The Constitution and the States: The Role of the Original Thirteen in the Framing and Adoption of the Federal Constitution.* Madison, Wisc.: Madison House, 1988.

Jensen, Merrill, John P. Kaminski, and Gaspare J. Saladino, eds. *The Documentary History of the Ratification of the Constitution,* 15 vols. to date. Madison: State Historical Society of Wisconsin, 1976– .

McDonald, Forrest. *Novus Ordo Seclorum: The Intellectual Origins of the Constitution.* Lawrence: University Press of Kansas, 1985.

Morris, Richard B. *The Forging of the Union, 1781–1789*. New York: Harper & Row, 1987.

Rutland, Robert Allen. *The Ordeal of the Constitution: The Antifederalists and the Ratification Struggle of 1787–1788*. Boston: Northeastern University Press, 1966.

Schwartz, Bernard. *The Great Rights of Mankind: A History of the American Bill of Rights*, expanded ed. Madison, Wisc.: Madison House, 1992.

Wood, Gordon S. *The Creation of the American Republic, 1776–1787*. Chapel Hill: University of North Carolina Press, 1969.

Wood, Gordon S. *The Radicalism of the American Revolution*. New York: Alfred A. Knopf, 1992.

John P. Kaminski

CONSTITUTIONAL CONVENTION OF 1787

By late 1786, only three years after the end of the Revolutionary War, most Americans had concluded that the Confederation Congress was too weak to deal with the social, economic, political, and diplomatic problems confronting the nation. Minimally, Congress needed power to tax through a tariff and to regulate foreign and interstate commerce. Repeated attempts to amend the Articles of Confederation or to persuade the states to grant Congress special powers had failed to obtain the required unanimous approval of the state legislatures. Finally, on 21 February 1787, Congress called for a convention in Philadelphia to revise the articles.

Fifty-five delegates from twelve states attended at one time or another between May and September 1787. Only Rhode Island refused to send delegates. Prominent Revolutionary leaders among the delegates included George Washington and George Mason of Virginia, Benjamin Franklin and Robert Morris of Pennsylvania, Roger Sherman of Connecticut, and Delaware's John Dickinson. James Madison and Edmund Randolph of Virginia, Alexander Hamilton of New York, James Wilson and Gouverneur Morris of Pennsylvania, and South Carolina's Charles Pinckney also played crucial roles. Absent were Confederation Secretary for Foreign Affairs John Jay and Secretary at War Henry Knox, Thomas Jefferson and John Adams (both on diplomatic assignment in Europe), Patrick Henry and Richard Henry Lee of Virginia (both refused appointments), and governors George Clinton of New York and John Hancock of Massachusetts. Indeed, only two sitting governors served as delegates. The delegates were generally far wealthier and better educated than the average American of the day. The convention rules granted each state one vote. Sessions were held in Pennsylvania's state house (now Independence Hall), and delegates were sworn to secrecy.

Ignoring their instructions only to amend the Articles of Confederation, the delegates planned a completely new national government. James Madison's "Virginia Plan," reflecting the interest of the three largest states (Virginia, Massachusetts, and Pennsylvania), proposed a bicameral legislature, with representation in each house proportional to population. The smaller states rallied around the "New Jersey Plan," which preserved the unicameral Congress of the Articles, with equal state representation. After the convention rejected this plan in mid-June, a consensus formed around the "Connecticut Compromise," providing for a bicameral system, with equal state representation in the upper house and proportional representation in the lower house.

A five-man Committee of Detail organized the agreed-upon provisions into a draft constitution, which, after further revision, was put in final form by a five-man Committee of Style, appointed on 8 September. Gouverneur Morris was the primary author. As adjournment neared, the convention considered and rejected both a Bill of Rights and a follow-up convention to consider amendments. Jacob Shallus prepared a four-page engrossed Constitution on parchment, and thirty-nine delegates signed it on 17 September 1787. Three delegates in attendance—the Virginians Randolph and Mason and Elbridge Gerry of Massachusetts—refused to sign.

The proposed Constitution radically changed the federal government's structure and its relationship with the states and the people, transferring many powers from the states to the central government. Abandoning the forbidding amendment procedure of the Articles of Confederation, the document provided that adoption by nine state conventions would establish the Constitution among the ratifying states. After almost a year of intense public debate, eleven states ratified the new Constitution.

[*See also* **Articles of Confederation; Constitution; Franklin, Benjamin; Hamilton, Alexander; Madison, James;** *and* **Washington, George.**]

BIBLIOGRAPHY

Farrand, Max, ed. *The Records of the Federal Convention of 1787*, 3 vols. New Haven, Conn.: Yale University Press, 1911; reprint 1966.

Van Doren, Carl. *The Great Rehearsal*. New York: Viking Press, 1948.

John P. Kaminski

CONSTITUTIONAL INTERPRETATION

Constitutional interpretation is both the process by which the American Constitution is construed and the study of that process. The latter is principally an academic activity, whereas the former art is practiced daily by government officials, private lawyers, and ordinary citizens. Constitutional interpretation is the process by which the meaning of the Constitution is determined. Constitutional adjudication is the process by which justices enforce the Constitution. Courts have no roving commission to strike down all government actions thought unconstitutional. A justice may exercise the power of judicial review only in an appropriate case or controversy, when the constitutional issue is justifiable, and when the constitutional violation is sufficiently clear to warrant judicial invalidation.

The Constitution as Law. Although usually taken for granted, the fact that the ways in which the American Constitution may be legitimately interpreted are similar to the ways in which lawyers and judges construe legal documents is significant. This is partly a consequence of the U.S. Constitution being a written document, indeed the first modern written constitution of a nation-state. The important American innovation was not the writing per se, but rather the political theory whereby the state was objectified and made a mere instrument of the sovereign will that lay in the people. The distinction between the sovereign and the organs of state, which seemed so absurd to minds before the eighteenth century, was an indispensable premise for a comprehensive, written constitution that conveyed limited powers. By this means, the United States put the power of the state under law. A written constitution made constitutional interpretation along customary legal modes of thinking feasible. A limited government, put under the written constraints of a superior legal instrument, will inevitably introduce the modalities of legal reasoning and argument into decisions affecting the legitimate power of the state.

One way of understanding the centrality of having a text to construe is to look at the role of texts in other legal contexts. A written constitution is like a trust agreement. It specifies what powers the trustees are to have and endows these agents with certain authority delegated by the settlers who created the trust. Because the American Revolution and the Declaration of Independence put sovereignty in the hands of the people, the "trustees" in the constitutional scheme (the government) are not identical with the "settlor" (the sovereign) and therefore are not at liberty to alter the trust agreement and change the limits of their authority. From this agreement must come decisions about the extent of that authority. A written constitution is not only a set of rules; it is also a way of creating rules. Like the trust agreement, the governing text will constrain the agents that it creates only if the methods of interpretation compel such constraints. When Thomas Jefferson wrote that "Our peculiar security is in the possession of a written constitution," he meant that the constraints manifest in a written charter would act as safeguards against a governmental usurpation of powers that belonged to the people. Because Jefferson, as principal drafter of the Declaration of Independence, believed that the state was the creation of sovereign power, not the other way around, he insisted on a written Constitution and a written Bill of Rights. The phrase "inalienable rights" that appears in the Declaration means that the people cannot alienate—that is, sell or trade—their rights because to do so would render the people less than sovereign.

By relying on a written instrument to perfect the constitutional understanding, the framers of the Constitution introduced the habits and style of Anglo-American legal argument into the politics of the state. This determined the foundation for constitutional interpretation in the United States. Since the Constitution was the supreme law, its terms had to govern; since it was a comprehensive law, it would be implicated in every legal decision; since it was written law, it had to be construed, both to give it supreme effect and to apply it in situations not explicitly anticipated in the text. And because it was law, this was to be done according to the prevailing methods of legal construction. The ways in which Americans interpret the Constitution could have been different; indeed, the forms of constitutional discourse are very different in other societies. For Americans, however, these ways have taken the forms of Common-Law argument, largely those forms prevailing at the time of the drafting and ratification of the U.S. Constitution. Thus the methods hitherto used to construe deeds, wills, contracts, and promissory notes, methods familiar to the mundane subjects of the Common Law, became the methods of constitutional construction once the state was put under law.

Modalities of Constitutional Argument. These methods of reasoning and ways of making arguments determine the ways in which constitutional propositions are characterized as valid from a legal point of view. These methods might be divided or recategorized in different ways, but the following six forms or modalities of constitutional argument are widely accepted: (1) historical—relying on the intentions of the framers and ratifiers of the Constitution; (2) textual—looking to the meaning of the words of the Constitution alone, as they would be interpreted by an average contemporary American today; (3) structural—inferring structural rules from the relationships that the Constitution mandates; (4) doctrinal—applying rules generated by precedent; (5) ethical—deriving rules from those moral commitments of the American ethos that are reflected in the Constitution; and (6) prudential—seeking to balance the costs and benefits of a particular rule. A modality is the way in which a proposition is characterized as true.

History. May a state validly enforce a law that makes it a crime to procure an abortion? Constitutional arguments from a historical perspective are as follows: the framers and ratifiers of the due process clause of the Fourteenth Amendment intended to prohibit such legislation because the ratification debates of the period demonstrate a concern to protect previously disfranchised persons from debasement by the state; or the framers and ratifiers did not intend to do so because blacks, not women, and voting, not the intimate acts of private persons, were the subjects of their debates; or we cannot ascertain what their intention was regarding the state's coercive power to compel women to bear children because the debates, although broad in subject matter, are fragmentary in detail. Arguments that rely on this interpretive modality might also approach the abortion question as follows. Did the framers and ratifiers of the Fourteenth Amendment intend to countenance extant state laws forbidding abortions? Because these statutes were unmentioned in the debates, were they thus tacitly tolerated? Or did they intend to overturn them by means of the amendment? Or are their intentions unclear? Because the framers made general references to an evolving standard of protection from state intrusion, did they mean to delegitimate such statutes? Or is the historical record simply unclear as to those anti-abortion laws that were on the statute books at the time of ratification? In any case, determinations of constitutionality will be made on the basis of historical evidence about the intentions of the framers and ratifiers of the relevant clauses of the Constitution.

Often the historical approach is confused with textual argument because historical argument usually refers to a specific text of the Constitution. Historical or "originalist" approaches to construing the text, however, are distinctive in their reference to what a particular provision is supposed to have meant to the ratifiers. What matters is the public meaning of the constitutional text at the time the provision was ratified, not private understandings between particular framers or what that constitutional language might mean at the present. When Chief Justice Roger B. Taney in *Scott v. Sandford* (1857) construed the scope of the diversity jurisdiction in Article III to determine whether a slave could seek freedom through a diversity suit before a federal court, he wrote,

> We must inquire who, at that time (1787–1788), were recognized as the citizens of a state, whose rights and liberties had been outraged by the English government; and who declared their independence, and assumed the powers of Government to defend their rights by force of arms. . . . We refer to these historical facts for the purpose of showing the fixed opinions concerning that race, upon which the statesmen of that day spoke and acted. (pp. 407–409)

Justices Antonin Scalia and Clarence Thomas are the leading proponents of originalism on the contemporary Court. "When interpreting" constitutional provisions, Thomas wrote in *McIntyre v. Ohio Elections Commission* (1995), "we must be guided by their original meaning, for 'the Constitution is a written instrument'" (p. 359). Justice Scalia in that case agreed that the Constitution bears its original meaning and is "unchanging" (p. 371). Justices Scalia and Thomas in that case, however, disputed whether the persons responsible for the Constitution had intended to protect anonymous pamphleteering. Similar historical disputes have taken place in other contemporary cases. Justice John Paul Stevens's majority opinion in *U.S. Term Limits, Inc., v. Thornton* (1995) concluded that the framers had not intended to allow states to add to the qualifications stated in Article I for members of Congress. Justice Thomas in dissent claimed otherwise.

Scott demonstrates other limitations of historical argument. Although the decision—which denied diversity jurisdiction to slave litigants and repudiated the Missouri Compromise—is regarded with shame by many constitutional scholars, there is nothing erroneous about Taney's historical argument. Perhaps, however, the framers and ratifiers did not intend that their contemporary opinions on every subject should govern every subsequent argument. More importantly, it is anachronistic and presumptuous to assume that we can determine what the framers and ratifiers of a particular provision, drafted a century or two before the present, would have preferred to happen in a world they could no more anticipate than we can successfully imagine theirs. We assume that Jefferson would be opposed to the intrusiveness and scope of the federal government today because he opposed Federalist policies so vehemently in his own day. But it is not clear whether he would have opposed the expansion of federal authority to eradicate the effects of slavery, an evil he also opposed but despaired of ever correcting.

Text. One of the constitutional questions in the *Scott* case—who are the "citizens" for purposes of diversity jurisdiction—provides an example for the textual modality. The text of the Constitution provides that "The judicial Power shall extend . . . to Controversies . . . between Citizens of different States" (Article III, Section 2). Does this text of the Constitution, to the average person at present, appear to declare that a former slave can bring suit in federal court (because the text's use of the word citizen is not qualified by race)? Or does the text appear to deny this jurisdiction (because the text's use of the word citizen rather than person implies a distinction by race)? Or is the language simply too vague to say whether a suit between a black American in one state and his former employer, a white American resident in another state, is a "controversy . . . between Citizens of different States"?

Textual approaches are not inevitably more progressive than originalist approaches. Sometimes the text can be a straitjacket, confining the judge within language that would have been different had its drafters foreseen later events. Is twentieth-century wiretapping prohibited by the Fourth Amendment, which guarantees "[t]he right of the people to be secure in their persons, houses, papers, and effects, against unreasonable searches and seizures"? Chief Justice William Howard Taft engaged in textual argument in a case where federal prohibition officers obtained incriminating information by intercepting telephone conversations of defendants:

> The amendment itself shows that the search is to be of material things—the person, the house, his papers or his effects. The amendment does not forbid what was done here for there was no seizure. The evidence was secured by the sense of hearing and that only. The language of the amendment cannot be extended and expanded.
>
> —(***Olmstead v. United States,*** 1928, p. 464)

Textual argument is associated with the dominant figure of the postwar Supreme Court, Justice Hugo Black and his frequently voiced assertion that the Constitution contained various "absolutes." Black cited the

First Amendment's provision that "Congress shall make no law . . . abridging the freedom of speech" as an example of a textual absolute on the grounds that if he read such a provision to the average citizen, it would be interpreted to mean "no law" whatsoever could constitutionally be applied to abrogate speech. To the objections that such an interpretation would strike down virtually all obscenity laws and a great many defamation, conspiracy, and anti-incitement statutes, Black simply interposed the text without further argument. Textual argument is thus often juxtaposed against judicial balancing tests that would concede, for example, that a particular regulation limits speech but requires the circumstances and necessity of the regulation to be taken into account.

Structure. Can a Congressional committee issue a subpoena for the disclosure of the president's working notes and diaries? Structural modes of argument would argue that the institutional relationships promulgated by the Constitution provide such power because Congress must have full information to fulfill its statutory function; or deny it because the president must be able to preserve the integrity of his deliberations free from the self-consciousness that follows from the anticipation of private debate that will be made public; or speak equivocally because in some contexts the need for public information outweighs the damage to the executive process of policy formulation. Recent examples of structural arguments in separation of powers cases include *Clinton v. Jones* (1997), permitting the president to be a defendant in a civil lawsuit; *Morrison v. Olson* (1988), upholding the appointment of a special prosecutor despite her ambivalent status as an executive officer with responsibilities to the judicial branch; and, most importantly, *Immigration and Naturalization Service v. Chadha* (1983), which struck down the legislative veto.

The second part of *McCulloch v. Maryland* (1819), the principal foundation case for constitutional analysis, relied almost wholly on structural approaches. In determining whether a Maryland tax on the federally chartered Bank of the United States could be enforced, Chief Justice John Marshall refused to specify what particular text supported his argument and explicitly rejected reliance on historical arguments, preferring instead to state the rationale on inferences from the structure of federalism. A federal structure could not be maintained, he concluded, if the states, whose officials are elected by a state's constituency, could tax the agencies of the federal government present in a state and thereby levy a tax on a nationwide constituency. By taxing a federal agency the state would be able to manipulate directly the choices made by the federal government—effectively prohibiting some choices by making them expensive—without the check of being answerable to affected constituents. The constitutional structure would not tolerate such a practice although the text and the ratification debates did not explicitly condemn it.

Structural arguments are less intuitively obvious than arguments from the text or history of the Constitution. Arguments in this modality usually follow a pattern: first, an uncontroversial statement about a constitutional structure is introduced; second, a relationship is inferred from this structure; third, a factual assertion about the world is made; and finally, a conclusion is drawn that provides the rule in the case.

Thus in *Printz v. United States* (1997), Justice Scalia addressed the question of whether a state officer may be required to implement a federal handgun law. He reasoned the following: (1) the Constitution sets up a federal system, that is, a system in which state and national officers are independent of each other (structure); (2) if the national government could control the actions of state and local officials, we would cease to have a federal system (relationship); and (3) requiring local officials to help implement national law would effectively make those officials agents of the national government and thus be incompatible with a federal system (conclusion).

Prudence. Can a state require mandatory testing for the AIDS virus antibodies? One might argue that it is wise because an epidemic can only be controlled by public health measures; or that it is unwise because of the distress caused to those who will falsely test positive and because the intrusiveness of testing an overwhelmingly virus-free population outweigh the benefits of locating a few victims; or that it is unclear on the present facts whether it is wise to permit such testing because the efficacy of the tests and the scope of the epidemic are subject to inconclusive debate. These questions propose an evaluation from a prudential point of view.

In the first half of the twentieth century, the prudential mode of constitutional argument was associated with doctrines that sought to protect the political position of the courts, although it had long been a staple of constitutional argument in the other branches. The national crises of depression and world war provided reason for the courts to consider the practical effects of constitutional doctrine as elements in the rationales underpinning doctrine. One such case arose when, in the depths of the midwestern farm depression, the Minnesota legislature passed a statute providing a moratorium from foreclosure for those unable to pay a mortgage. On its face, this statute seemed to vindicate the fears of the framers that state legislatures would compromise the national credit market by enacting debtor relief statutes and also seemed to violate the contracts clause of Article I that was the textual product of such concerns. Nevertheless, the Court upheld the statute, observing that an emergency existed in Minnesota that furnished a proper occasion for the exercise of the reserved power of the state to protect the vital interests of the community (*Home Building & Loan Association v. Blaisdell*, 1934). The Court, by a 5-to-4 vote, recognized the political expediency of the state's action and acquiesced in it.

The prudential approach is not confined to problems a nation encounters in emergencies. Prudential argument is based on facts because these play into political and economic policies. From a prudential point of view, the legal rule to be applied is derived from a calculus of costs and benefits, after the facts are taken into account. Often this calls for a balancing of costs and benefits since more than one policy will be at stake. Sometimes the pragmatic problem may be the costs of protecting a particular constitutional right and may require abandonment of essential constitutional commitments. Justice Lewis Powell advanced such a prudential view in *McCleskey v. Kemp* (1987) when rejecting a claim that statistical evidence of racial bias required a judicial decision striking down the procedures Georgia used to impose capital punishment. "McCleskey's claim," his majority opinion declared,

> taken to its logical conclusion, throws into serious question the principles that underlie our entire criminal justice system. The Eighth Amendment is not limited in application to capital punishment, but applies to all penalties. . . . Thus, if we accepted McCleskey's claim that racial bias has impermissibly tainted the capital sentencing decision, we could soon be faced with similar

> claims as to other types of penalty. Moreover, the claim that his sentence rests on the irrelevant factor of race easily could be extended to apply to claims based on unexplained discrepancies that correlate to membership in other minority groups, and even to gender. Similarly, since McCleskey's claim relates to the race of his victim, other claims could apply with equally logical force to statistical disparities that correlate with the race or sex of other actors in the criminal justice system, such as defense attorneys or judges. (pp. 314–317)

Doctrine. When a judge states that a neutral, general principle derived from the case law construing the Constitution should apply (that a particular precedent is on "all fours" with the instant case) or that it does not apply (the present case is one of "first impression") or that it may apply (the precedents are divided, with authority for competing positions), such arguments are made in a doctrinal mode. Doctrinal arguments are not confined to arguments originating in judicial or administrative case law; there are also precedents from other institutions, such as the practices of earlier presidents or Congress.

This mode of argument is the stuff of Common-Law legal reasoning. First-year law courses are devoted to its mastery, and it is not unique to constitutional law. Consider as an example the question: To what extent can a state constitutionally provide financial aid to parochial schools? Suppose, for example, that parochial school students are given a cash allowance by the state to subsidize their education. Does this offend the establishment clause of the First Amendment because the state is bearing costs that would otherwise be born by church members?

A judge confronting such a case might begin, not by reading the text of the First Amendment that states a rule in rather general terms, but by turning to precedent to find similar cases providing authoritative decisions. In the area of establishment clause jurisprudence a great deal of constitutional doctrine has been developed in numerous cases. The standards these cases develop and apply can be stated as legal rules. The case "on point," whose facts are similar in relevant aspects, is *Zelman v. Simmons-Harris* (2002), which sustained the power of local authorities to provide vouchers for children attending private and parochial church-related schools. In *Zelman* the Supreme Court treated the provision of vouchers as a form of public welfare legislation, noting that "public funds were made available to religious schools only as a result of numerous, private choices of individual parents of school-age children" (p. 650). The majority further reasoned that vouchers benefited the child in the same way as did police protection at crossings near the church school, fire protection for the school building, connections to the building for sewage disposal, and public highways and sidewalks by which one traveled to a parochial school.

Applying these principles to the illustrative question, the judge might write, "*Zelman* can be distinguished from the instance case because the program in *Zelman* provided vouchers for all students, whereas here only some students, the parochial ones, are given cash allowances. While doubtless the legislature had a secular purpose in mind, the effect of these allowances was in fact to make the parochial schools more attractive to parents than their secular counterparts and thereby advance the cause of religious institutions. Accordingly, the program must be held unconstitutional."

Or the judge might write, "*Zelman,* which also involved vouchers for parochial school students, governs this case. Here as there, the state's program provides aid to students and their parents and not—as in cases that have struck down state assistance in this area—direct assistance to church-related schools. Its secular purpose, to expand school choice for parents of children in failing schools, is apparent. Like school lunches, public health services, and secular textbooks, the vouchers provided here confer a benefit on the parochial student that is at parity with what the secular student receives."

In either case, the judge has applied a rule derived from the relevant case law. The rule is neutral as to the parties; that is, it applies equally to Catholic, Jewish, and atheist claimants and does not vary depending on who is bringing or defending the suit. And the rule is general; that is, it applies to all cases in which the state is giving assistance to religious institutions and is not confined to the facts of the original case that gave birth to the rule.

The commitment to neutral, general principles does not mean that cases cannot be overruled. A particular precedent may be overruled because it does not comport with a persuasive reading of the cases on which it relied or those from a competing line of doctrine originating in wholly distinct facts but progressively encroaching on the area of its operation. More significantly, doctrinal argument is not confined to the application of stare decisis, that is, the strict adherence to cases previously decided, because one of the assumptions of American doctrinalism is that the Supreme Court may reverse precedent. This would appear to follow from the family of modalities—which provide alternative legal rules—and the supremacy of the Constitution to the acts of government (including its judicial branch). The Court is empowered, indeed obligated, to overrule itself when it is persuaded that a particular precedent wrongly construed the Constitution. The justices in *Lawrence v. Texas* (2003) overruled *Bowers v. Hardwick* (1986) on the ground the former decision sustaining a ban on sodomy was constitutionally wrong when handed down and had been undermined by subsequent judicial and legislative precedents. By comparison, the plurality in *Planned Parenthood v. Casey* (1992) refused to overrule *Roe v. Wade* (1973) partly because the shaky constitutional foundations of the constitutional right to abortion had been buttressed by subsequent judicial precedents and social developments.

Ethos. Ethical arguments denote an appeal to those elements of the American ethos that are reflected in the Constitution. The fundamental American constitutional ethos is the idea of limited government, which presumes that all residual authority remains in the private sphere. Thus when we argue that a particular constitutional conclusion is required, permitted, or forbidden by the American ethos that has allocated certain decisions to the individual or to private institutions, we are arguing in an ethical mode.

Ethical arguments arise as a consequence of the fundamental constitutional arrangement by which rights, in the American system, are largely defined as those choices beyond the power of government to compel. Some constitutional commentators insist that elected officials have a constitutional duty to provide the economic and social conditions under which individuals can flourish, but few insist that such constitutional responsibilities are judicially enforceable in the absence of a violation of clear constitutional rights.

Structural and ethical arguments share some similarities. Each is essentially an inferred set of arguments. Structural argument infers rules from the powers granted to governments; ethical argument, by contrast, infers rules from the powers denied to government. The principal error regarding ethical argument is the assumption that any statute or executive act is unconstitutional if it causes effects that are incompatible with some preferred elements of the American ethos. Such an assumption equates ethical argument, a constitutional form, with moral and political argument generally. The American constitutional ethos is largely confined to the reservation of powers not delegated to a limited government.

A hypothetical example shows the basic pattern of ethical argument. Suppose a state judge offers a choice of a thirty-year prison sentence or impotence-inducing medical treatment to a convicted sex offender. The defendant accepts the latter option and is released on probation on terms that require that this pledge be fulfilled by systematic drug-induced impotence. If the probationer were to cease taking the prescribed drug and his probation were to be revoked, a constitutional challenge to the terms of his probation might take the following form.

First, there is no express constitutional power in federal courts to implement a program of eugenics. Indeed, the reservation to the individual of the decision whether to have children is deeply rooted in the American belief in the integrity of the individual conscience, which is reflected in several parts of the Constitution. Second, eugenics programs are not an appropriate means ancillary to any express power that is allocated to government; therefore, there is no federal power to assume this otherwise private authority. Third, those means denied the federal government are also denied the states. And, fourth, the hypothetical sentence would compel a man to comply with a eugenics scheme that rendered him ineligible to procreate.

The element of the American ethos at stake is the reservation to individuals and families of the freedom to make certain kinds of decisions. Similar arguments are found in cases in which a state criminalized particular forms of sexual behavior between consenting adults (*Lawrence v. Texas,* 2003); banned the use of birth control and abortion (*Griswold v. Connecticut,* 1965; *Roe v. Wade,* 1973); attempted to bar schools from teaching foreign languages (*Meyer v. Nebraska,* 1923); in which a state passed a compulsory education act requiring every school-age child to attend public school, which implicitly outlawed private schools (*Pierce v. Society of Sisters,* 1925); in which a local zoning ordinance intended to exclude communes was applied to prohibit a grandmother from living with her grandchildren (*Moore v. East Cleveland,* 1977); and in which parents sought to end the artificial nutrition of their severely brain-injured daughter (*Cruzan v. Director, Missouri Department of Health,* 1990). Each of these examples can be stated in the form of an ethical argument. For example, the *Lawrence* arguments could be framed thus: (1) there is no express constitutional power to regulate sexuality; (2) a statute outlawing consensual sexual behavior between adults is not an appropriate means associated with any express power (such as regulating commerce or providing for armed forces); (3) decisions about sexuality are reserved to individuals; and (4) a statue banning sodomy amounts to a scheme to mandate prescribed forms of intimate behavior and family life.

Academic and Political Commentary. Commentary on these modes of constitutional argument by scholars and critics constitute the field of constitutional interpretation outside the courts and legislatures. From the mid-1950s onward, the interpretation of the American Constitution has assumed a central place in American public life. Racial segregation, abortion, the powers of the presidency, and impeachment have all been made to turn on these methods of construction. At the same time, constitutional interpretation has become a rich academic field in its own right.

The seminal works in the academic field were Charles Black's *Structure and Relationship in Constitutional Law* (1969) and Alexander Bickel's *The Least Dangerous Branch* (1962). Black's remarkable study isolated one particular form of argument, the structural and established criteria for the making and assessing of such arguments. Bickel did much the same for prudential argument, tracing its lineage to Justice Louis D. Brandeis and demonstrating a family of related judicial techniques. John Hart Ely's *Democracy and Distrust* (1980) was the first sustained effort to answer the countermajoritarian objection to judicial review (the argument that overturning a legislative decision by a court amounts to a reversal of democratic, majoritarian choices) by relying on one of the classic forms of argument as preeminent. Ely divided the forms of argument into the interpretivist, that is, historical, textual, and structural forms, and noninterpretivist, that is, ethical, prudential, and doctrinal forms. Paul Brest, in an important series of articles and an influential casebook, wrote about interpretation as argument and isolated some of the paradigmatic forms of argument. *Constitutional Fate* (1982), by Philip Bobbitt, identified and elaborated the six forms of argument described here. Bobbitt argued that there could be no hierarchy of arguments. He maintained that the countermajoritarian objection was fundamentally nonsensical since legitimacy was conferred not by majoritarianism but by following accepted conventional forms, which could not be genuinely applied in the absence of judicial review. At the same time, questions of interpretation came to the forefront of literary criticism, and the influence of semiotics, especially the school of deconstruction associated with Jacques Derrida, Paul de Man, Michel Foucault, and others, was felt in the field of constitutional interpretation.

Constitutional interpretation outside the courts also became a field of academic study. Sandy Levinson and Walter Murphy challenged common notions that courts had the ultimate authority for determining constitutional meanings. Louis Fisher detailed how constitutional interpretation typically involved a dialog between courts and elected officials. Keith Whittington's *Constitutional Construction* (1999) detailed how elected officials resolved constitutional questions that were hardly ever adjudicated by courts.

In the political arena, attention also was focused on the methods of constitutional interpretation. The inspired but methodologically problematic opinion in *Brown v. Board of Education* (1954) invited such scrutiny. Perhaps the most influential member of the judiciary, Judge Learned Hand implicitly criticized Chief Justice Earl Warren's opinion in lectures published as *The Bill of Rights* (1958). With this controversy, the countermajoritarian objection was revived and with it the debate about the proper methods of constitutional interpretation. Controversial Warren court human rights and criminal process cases in the 1960s fueled this controversy, which erupted with new vehemence when the Supreme Court decided the abortion case *Roe v. Wade*. The debate was framed in terms of the legitimacy of judicial review itself rather than in terms of its various methods.

More fuel to these fires was added by a series of Rehnquist court decisions limiting the power of the national government to regulate firearms (*Printz v. United States*, 1997; *United States v. Lopez*, 1995), punish violence against women (*United States v. Morrison*, 2000), and adopt affirmative action programs (*Adarand Constructors, Inc., v. Peña*, 1995). By the turn of the twenty-first century, liberals were increasingly likely to argue that the constitutional powers of government should be broadly construed and courts should defer to legislative judgments on constitutional issues, whereas conservatives championed judicial review and the constitutional limits of government power. Many of the most salient questions of constitutional interpretation at present have been debated almost entirely outside the courtroom. These matters include whether lying about a sexual affair under oath is an impeachable offense and whether congressional approval is constitutionally necessary for a president to initiate combat abroad.

Originalism is presently at the center of many constitutional controversies. Edwin Meese, attorney general of the United States in the second Reagan administration, insists that justices should be confined to "strict construction" of the Constitution. He and other officials associated with the conservative wing of the Republican Party hold that only historical, textual, and structural arguments provide a legitimate basis by which to evaluate statutes and practices for their constitutionality. Justice Brennan throughout his career took a more expansive view, stressing the prudential and ethical modalities of judicial review. Such modalities underlie such judicial opinions as *Lawrence v. Texas*.

Nowhere was this conflict more clearly and dramatically presented than in the Senate hearings on the nomination of Robert Bork to the Supreme Court. To the question of how a judge should go about finding the law, Bork testified that the only legitimate way "is by attempting to discern . . . the intentions of . . . those . . . who ratified our Constitution and its various amendments." Repeatedly, Bork denied that there was "any legitimate method of constitutional reasoning" that would support controversial holdings that he opposed, but he was scrupulous about not criticizing them as policy. His rejection by the Senate may be taken as an affirmation of the legitimacy of the decisions that, as Bork argued, cannot be rationalized on strict constructionist grounds. All successful Supreme Court nominees in the wake of the Bork hearings have at a minimum indicated an open mind on the legitimate forms of constitutional argument.

Each of the various forms of argument can be used to construct an ideology, a set of political and practical commitments whose values are internally consistent and externally distinct from those of competing ideologies constructed around other modalities. Some persons believe that one particular modality represents the only legitimate means of interpreting the constitution (e.g., historical argument) since it is verifiable by a resort to materials (e.g., the evidence of the intentions of the framers) that are legitimated according to a particular political theory of interpretation. This has led some commentators to argue that the modalities of argument are no more than instrumental, rhetorical devices to be deployed in the service of the political ideologies of which they are a subsidiary part. Other critics have concluded that the modalities must be ranked in priority. In either case, some standard external to constitutional interpretation is imported into the decision making.

According to the latter argument, everyone agrees that the Constitution is law. Therefore, the Constitution does not merely mean what particular people want it to mean. If it did, it would not be law. The problem is that it is not always clear what the Constitution means and how it is to be applied or interpreted. Reasonable people disagree about what it means. Some think that a Constitution that guarantees "the equal protection of the laws" requires race-conscious affirmative action policies to remove the effects of past and present discrimination (a prudential argument); others think that a state that engages in affirmative action is violating that same guarantee (a textual argument). In hard cases, two or more legitimate modalities will conflict.

Since the Constitution itself does not direct how it is to be interpreted—does not say which modality is to be used—those who interpret the Constitution have to look to something other than the various legitimating forms of argument. This means that the interpretation of the Constitution must inevitably be based on principles that are external to the words of the Constitution itself. Those principles have to be created rather than found; the Constitution does not contain instructions for its own interpretation.

This does not mean that the Constitution could mean anything at all, that it is "indeterminate" regarding its appropriate interpretation. Sometimes the resort to interpretive principles admits of only one answer. Additionally, what various constitutional authorities think, and what they will say about questions not yet decided but likely to arise soon, can be predicted with some accuracy. Moreover, some interpretations are better than others; that is, only some correspond to the various legitimating modalities. Some interpretations of ambiguous provisions will produce an unacceptable increase in judicial discretion (prudential); others will leave politically weak groups at the mercy of the state (structural); others will make liberty too fragile (ethical); and others will be insufficiently respectful of the claims of original intent (historical). Hence, constitutional interpretation is not indeterminate although it does not always yield unique answers.

How shall we choose, however, among good interpretations? What is the legal basis for this and why is it legitimate? Perhaps importing an external standard to govern such choices—say, a preference for liberty or equality or efficiency, which would allow us to justify our decisions—sacrifices their legitimacy, since it requires a rule that is not generated by the legitimating modalities of argument. Perhaps we cannot, in fact, give good reasons that explain our choice of one legitimate outcome over a different, equally legitimate outcome if, by "good" reasons, we mean legitimate reasons. This, at any rate, is the most important question confronting the field of constitutional interpretation.

[*See also* **Affirmative Action: Politics of Affirmative Action; Articles of Confederation; Bill of Rights; Black, Hugo; Brandeis, Louis; *Brown v. Board of Education*; Constitution; Constitutionalism; Constitutionalism, Popular; Constitutional Law; Declaration of Independence; Due Process: Procedural Process; Eighteenth Amendment; Federalism; Fifteenth Amendment; Fourteenth Amendment; *Griswold v. Connecticut;* Jefferson, Thomas; Judicial Review; Jurisprudence; Marshall, John; *McCulloch v. Maryland;* Nineteenth Amendment; Obscenity and Pornography; Political Science; Popular Sovereignty; Rehnquist, William; *Roe v. Wade;* Scalia, Antonin; *Scott v. Sandford;* Second Amendment; Sixteenth Amendment; Supreme Court, U.S.; Taft, William Howard; Taney, Roger B.; Taxation; *and* Warren, Earl.**]

BIBLIOGRAPHY

Bickel, Alexander. *The Least Dangerous Branch: The Supreme Court at the Bar of Politics.* Indianapolis, Ind.: Bobbs-Merrill, 1962.

Black, Charles. *Structure and Relationship in Constitutional Law.* Baton Rouge: Louisiana State University Press, 1969.

Bobbitt, Philip. *Constitutional Fate.* New York: Oxford University Press, 1982.

Brest, Paul, Sanford Levinson, J. M. Balkin, and Akhil Reed Amar. *Processes of Constitutional Decision-Making,* 4th ed. Gaithersburg, Md.: Aspen Law and Business, 2000.

Ely, John Hart. *Democracy and Distrust.* Cambridge, Mass.: Harvard University Press, 1980.

Fisher, Louis. *Constitutional Dialogues: Interpretation as Political Process*. Princeton, N.J.: Princeton University Press, 1988.

Hand, Learned. *The Bill of Rights*. Cambridge, Mass.: Harvard University Press, 1958.

Levinson, Sanford. *Constitutional Faith*. Princeton, N.J.: Princeton University Press, 1988.

Murphy, Walter F. "Who Shall Interpret? The Quest for the Ultimate Constitutional Interpreter." *Review of Politics* 48 (1986): 401–423.

Whittington, Keith F. *Constitutional Construction: Divided Powers and Constitutional Meaning*. Cambridge, Mass.: Harvard University Press, 1999.

Philip Bobbitt; revised by Mark A. Graber

CONSTITUTIONALISM

Constitutionalism is a form of political thought and action that seeks to prevent tyranny and to guarantee the liberty and rights of individuals on which free society depends. This definition, drawn mainly from English and American political history, may be compared with a more formalistic view that regards constitutionalism as the conduct of politics in accordance with a constitution. The import of this definition depends on the meaning of constitution, a term that has been variously interpreted in western political thought. During the American Revolution, Americans conceived of a constitution as the permanent, binding, and paramount political law of the polity. Although this theoretical innovation did not end all controversy over the meaning of the concept, it generally caused constitutionalism to be defined thereafter as the forms, principles, and procedures of limited government.

Constitutionalism addresses the perennial problem of how to establish government with sufficient power to realize a community's shared purposes, yet so structured and controlled that oppression will be prevented. In the absence of any means of assuring statesmanship in rulers, two approaches to the problem of government have been employed. One approach proceeds through the ordering of political and governmental institutions. From ancient to modern times the idea of the mixed regime, juxtaposing properly balanced institutions of monarchy, aristocracy, and democracy and the social orders they represent, illustrates this way of limiting government. A second approach to the problem is through the rule of law. Historical examples of this tradition are the Roman idea that the law of nature provides a standard of justice for evaluating the legitimacy of government enactments and the English practice, beginning with Magna Carta, of subjecting the monarchical power to legal limits and Common-Law rules protecting the liberty and property of subjects.

Although analytically distinct, these approaches are historically related in the institutional arrangements and practices that provide the basis for defining constitutionalism. In modern political science a constitution is an authoritative text possessing legal force that prescribes the structure and principles of limited government. The constitutional text is normative, stipulating how government shall be organized, the ends it may pursue, and the means to be employed in pursuit of those ends. In premodern political thought constitution had a descriptive connotation, referring to the ordering of the polity or the way institutions had evolved and assumed their present form. It is important to note that this concept of constitution was also thought to have a normative aspect. The English writer Lord Bolingbroke, for example, defined the English constitution in the early eighteenth century as "that assemblage of laws, institutions, and customs, derived from certain fixed principles of reason, directed to certain fixed objects of public good, that compose the general system, according to which the community hath agreed to be governed." Bolingbroke said a good government exists when the administration of affairs is wisely pursued "and with a strict conformity to the principles and objects of the constitution."

In Roman and medieval times the word *constitutio, constitutiones,* of which the term constitution is a transliteration, referred to enactments, decrees, or regulations of a ruler or sovereign. (In Latin, *constituere* means "to cause to stand" or "to fix, set, or make" a thing.) It has been suggested that the enactments of the Roman emperor implied the idea of limited government insofar as they collectively defined the scope of state action. Subsequently, constitution was superseded by statute with respect to government enactments providing rules of action for the community.

The word constitution entered political discourse as a term describing the structure of the polity or the arrangement of governmental institutions in the seventeenth century. This usage was analogous to that employed in describing the constitution of the human body. Although in the nineteenth century the term constitution was proposed as a translation of the Greek word politeia, before that time *politeia* was translated as government, regime, or policy. The tradition of political science deriving from Aristotle did not require use of the word constitution.

A form of American constitutionalism began in the seventeenth century as voluntary associations of settlers founded colonies under royal charters conferring on a person or corporate group governmental powers for specific purposes. As the basis of local government, the colonists wrote and adopted covenants, compacts, combinations, ordinances, fundamental orders, and other instruments of mutual consent. Through these documentary agreements they constituted themselves as a political community, defined their purposes, affirmed the principles of a way of life, specified the rights of citizens, and organized governmental institutions.

In the imperial conflicts of the 1760s and 1770s, Americans gained a new understanding of what the constitution of a free state was and how it functioned to guarantee liberty. They rejected the idea that a constitution described the governmental order of the polity. American critics of English policy argued that a constitution was a deliberately framed agreement among the people that imposed effective limits on government to protect community and individual liberty. If Parliament was a component of the English constitution and could change the fundamental law by its enactments, they concluded, then England did not have a real constitution. The important distinction was that although a constitution conferred power, it was not the simple equivalent of a mandate to legislate or govern. The Massachusetts General Court in 1768 pointed the direction of modern American constitutionalism in declaring, "in all free States the Constitution is fixed; & as the supreme Legislative derives its Power & Authority from the Constitution, it cannot overleap the Bounds of it, without destroying its own foundation."

During the Revolution Americans wrote constitutions of liberty, the distinctive feature of which was their legal superiority to legislative enactments and other sources of ordinary law. This supremacy was more theoretical than actual in the early years of written constitutions, when state legislatures framed the documents and often exercised power despite their provisions. Constitutions took on greater authority when popularly elected conventions wrote them and the people ratified them. The Massachusetts constitution of 1780 and the New Hampshire constitution of 1784 were modeled in this way. In employing the constitutional convention device the framers of the federal Constitution established it as the norm for modern constitutionalism.

Unlike the state constitutions, which expressed the idea of forming political communities out of the state of nature, the original U.S. Constitution contained no bill of rights and only a brief preamble stating the nation's basic principles and ends. In effect, the Declaration of Independence is the preamble to the Constitution. Accordingly, the framers wrote a document that was less a social compact for a cohesive, like-minded community than a contractual specification of the powers, duties, rights, and responsibilities among the diverse people that constituted the American Union. Reacting against state encroachments on liberty and property, the framers emphasized protection of individual rights rather than promotion of virtue and community consensus.

In the political context of the 1780s, the founders' constitutional reforms signified the creation of energetic government to fill the vacuum of power under the Articles of Confederation. In the perspective of western political thought, the Constitution of 1787 marks the emergence of modem constitutionalism as a political theory combining limited government for the protection of individual rights with the principles of the people as constituent power.

Constitutionalism requires that the primary rules for the conduct of government be impartially maintained against the demands of political passion, interest, ideology, and ambition. It is remarkable therefore that the founders provided for enforcement of the Constitution by the political branches of the government as well as by the judiciary. Each of the coordinate departments was responsible for applying and interpreting the provisions of the constitutional document that defined or regulated the performance of its duties and responsibilities.

Asserted by Presidents Andrew Jackson and Abraham Lincoln in the nineteenth century, the departmental theory of constitutional decision making has never been effectively repudiated or expunged from the American political tradition. Yet it has in the twentieth century been obscured by the legalistic approach to constitutional interpretation, institutionalized in judicial review, which confers a monopoly of power on the judiciary with respect to the settlement of constitutional disputes. In *Marbury v. Madison* (1803), Chief Justice John Marshall asserted the power of judicial review in judiciary cases concerning individual rights, while adhering to the departmental theory in regard to political questions or public policy matters. In later cases dealing with federalism and the contract clause, however, Marshall employed a legalistic method of constitutional decision making based on the application of Common-Law rules of interpretation to the text of the Constitution. In this approach the Constitution became supreme ordinary law susceptible to judicial adaptation and emendation in a way that blurred the distinction between questions of a judiciary nature and policy matters properly subject to determination by the political branches of government. The Constitution was transformed from fundamental political principles into supreme ordinary law. A consequence was the steady expansion of judicial power into the sphere of public policy making. By the beginning of the twentieth century, constitutionalism in the United States was considered mainly a body of legal doctrines and rules that enabled the courts to play an active role in government and politics.

Constitutionalism in twentieth-century America continued to be largely juridical and increasingly policy oriented. Limited government constitutionalism, grounded in natural rights principles and protective of entrepreneurial liberty and property, persisted until 1937. Political demands for a more socially responsive rule of law that were first asserted in the Progressive Era came to fruition in the New Deal Era. The consequence was a general questioning of the nineteenth-century view of limited government and the expansion of government activism in social and economic regulation.

From 1937 until the 1980s, the Supreme Court generally approved governmental activism as a means of guaranteeing positive liberty or the provision of material support as the basis of individual autonomy and self-expression. To some extent the idea of liberty against government (negative government) persisted as the Court nationalized the Bill of Rights as limitations on the states. In other respects the Court confirmed the activist government tradition by transforming civil rights into group- and class-based claims to public benefits and entitlements.

The expansion of government under the concept of positive liberty raised the question of whether the Constitution was the binding political law that limited government or a rhetorical abstraction or symbol used by government officials, including the Supreme Court, to justify policy decisions. Did the Constitution control the government, or did the government control the Constitution?

From the eighteenth century to the mid-twentieth century, the essential element in modern constitutionalism was the doctrine of limited government under a written fundamental law. Postmodern constitutionalism in the second half of the twentieth century challenged this outlook by creating activist government to achieve social justice and positive liberty. Tension between these two conceptions of constitutionalism was a prominent feature of American politics as the third century of constitutional government began in the 1990s.

[*See also* **Bill of Rights; Civil Liberties; Civil Rights; Constitution; Declaration of Independence; Federalism; Jackson, Andrew; Judicial Review; Lincoln, Abraham;** ***Marbury v. Madison;*** **Marshall, John; New Deal; Progressive Era;** *and* **Supreme Court, U.S.**]

BIBLIOGRAPHY

Casper, Gerhard. "Changing Concepts of Constitutionalism: 18th to 20th Century." *Supreme Court Review* (1989): 311–332.

Lutz, Donald S. *The Origins of American Constitutionalism.* Baton Rouge: Louisiana State University Press, 1988.

Snowiss, Sylvia. "From Fundamental Law to Supreme Law of the Land: A Reinterpretation of the Origins of Judicial Review." *Studies in American Political Development* 2 (1987): 1–67.

Stourzh, Gerald. "Constitution: Changing Meanings of the Term from the Early Seventeenth to the Late Eighteenth Century." In *Conceptual Change and the Constitution,* edited by Terence Ball and J. C. A. Pocock, pp. 35–54. Lawrence: University Press of Kansas, 1988.

Herman Belz

CONSTITUTIONALISM, POPULAR

Popular constitutionalism holds that "the People Themselves"—not the judiciary or any branch of government—have active and final control over constitutional interpretation, as well as exclusive authority to make new constitutional law. Popular constitutionalism is law-like in accepting that legal interpretation imposes constraints different from those that exist in politics: whoever is doing the interpreting is bound by the Constitution's legal content and must ascertain and enforce whatever limits the text imposes on political action. It assumes, however, that the process of authoritative legal interpretation is not confined to courts and can be undertaken equally well in the political branches and by the community at large. Popular constitutionalism thus rests and relies on a political culture in which public officials, community leaders, and ordinary citizens believe in the distinction between law and politics, respond to different arguments in each setting, and treat questions of constitutional interpretation as legal problems that can be settled only by resort to the "law" as understood through interpretive norms like text, history, and precedent.

Popular constitutionalism is a concept—it is the idea that final authority to control the interpretation and implementation of constitutional law resides at all times in the community in an active sense. There are countless different institutional arrangements by which to make this sort of popular control meaningful. These include everything from the rowdy mobs of eighteenth century England and America to the Madisonian system of "departmentalism," the British system of Parliamentary supremacy, and many more that have existed or could be imagined.

[*See also* **Constitution; Constitutional Interpretation;** ***and*** **Constitutional Law.**]

BIBLIOGRAPHY

Kramer, Larry D. *The People Themselves: Popular Constitutionalism and Judicial Review*. Oxford; New York: Oxford University Press, 2004.

Larry D. Kramer

CONSTITUTIONAL LAW

In 1822 Thomas Sergeant of Philadelphia published the first compilation of cases and commentary focused exclusively on American constitutional law. *Constitutional Law: Being a View of the Practice and Jurisdiction of the Courts of the United States, and of Constitutional Points Decided* was, he confessed, a "novel" undertaking, one without a single precedent that he could find. It seems to have found favor with the bench and bar, his intended audiences, by the fact that a second, expanded edition appeared as early as 1830. The purpose of the text, Sergeant explained to his readers, was to trace the "principles and practice" of what he called the "national jurisprudence" to their "constitutional source" and to exhibit "the general origin and uniform harmony of the whole." It is no wonder that Sergeant's work was so successful (it was widely recommended as required reading for students of the law and was also invoked to bolster the arguments of advocates before the U.S. Supreme Court), only that it took so long for someone to produce such a volume.

Constitutional Treatises. By the time the second edition of Sergeant's *Constitutional Law* appeared, John Marshall had been the third U.S. Chief Justice for twenty-nine years. Such early seminal cases as *Marbury v. Madison* (1803) were well-settled law; and even such controversial later decisions as *McCulloch v. Maryland* (1819) and *Cohens v. Virginia* (1821) were already long on the books. The reporter of the official decisions of the Supreme Court, Richard Peters, was the fourth person to hold that post. Yet amid the old and the settled there were fresh constitutional stirrings, not least in the emergence of a vibrant treatise tradition of constitutional commentators. Peter DuPonceau's *A Dissertation on the Nature and Extent of the Jurisdiction of the Courts of the United States* appeared in 1824; William Rawle's *View of the Constitution of the United States* was published in 1825; the four volumes of James Kent's *Commentaries on American Law* began to appear in 1826; and in

1833 would come the magisterial three-volume *Commentaries on the Constitution of the United States* by Supreme Court Justice Joseph Story (who also served simultaneously as Dane Professor of Law at Harvard University). Preceding all these were the provocative and learned states' rights treatises of John Taylor of Caroline, not least his *An Inquiry into the Principles and Policy of the Government of the United States* (1814), *Construction Construed, and Constitutions Vindicated* (1820), and *New Views of the Constitution of the United States* (1823). Thus did Sergeant's *Constitutional Law* join the continuing jurisprudential and political struggle over what, precisely, was the true nature and proper extent of the national government under the Constitution. That most basic issue was still very much alive.

Federalism and the Separation of Powers. American constitutional law emerged from the constitutional ambiguity of the federal structure of the Constitution of the United States. That ambiguity stemmed from the way the founders had to accommodate their new nationalistic constitutional thinking to existing political facts—that is to say, to the presence of preexisting sovereign states and a vague but persistent commitment to the confederal form as the most appropriate to those states. On the eve of the Constitutional Convention, on 16 April 1787, James Madison wrote to George Washington expressing his view that "an individual independence of the states is utterly irreconcilable with their aggregate sovereignty" but that also any "consolidation of the whole into one simple republic would be as inexpedient as it is unattainable." His solution, Madison confessed, was to find "some middle ground, which may at once support a due supremacy of the national authority, and not exclude the local authorities wherever they can be subordinately useful." Later, in *The Federalist,* he would put it more simply, arguing that the Constitution in fact "is in strictness neither a national nor a federal constitution; but a composition of both." Early in the twentieth century Felix Frankfurter and James M. Landis in *The Business of the Supreme Court* (1928) could still argue that the "happy relation of States to Nation" was nothing less than the country's "central political problem," the resolution of which was "to no small extent dependent upon the wisdom with which the scope and limits of the federal courts are determined."

Federalism was not the only fundamental principle of the Constitution that vexed future interpreters and helped to define the contours of American constitutional law. So, too, was the scheme of separated powers that was put into place by the founders that would also equally depend upon the "wisdom with which the scope and limits of the federal courts are determined." These were the most basic principles drafted into the fundamental law, principles that together were intended, as Madison said in *The Federalist,* to provide a "double security . . . to the rights of the people." The power originally delegated by the people in their sovereign constitutive capacity would "first be divided between two distinct governments" and then "the portion allotted to each, subdivided among distinct and separate departments." The lines and limits of those allotments of power, spelled out as they were in a written constitution, would be determined in practice, many assumed, by the resolution of the concrete cases and controversies over constitutional meaning that would come before the federal courts for decision.

The Courts and Constitutional Review. The presumption that the federal judiciary had the power of what would in the twentieth century come to be called "judicial review" was not without its own troubling ambiguities.

After all, nowhere in the Constitution is such a power explicitly given to the courts. Although there is evidence that some in the Constitutional Convention understood such a power as simply the logical outgrowth of the more fundamental notion of an independent judiciary, there is nothing concretely given. Surely it was not too much to expect that such an extraordinary and ultimately undemocratic power would at least be explicitly spelled out. But there is not a single word to that effect. Thus some argued that by the Constitution's original design it fell to each of the three branches of the government—the legislature and the executive as well as to the judiciary—to determine for itself the true meaning of the Constitution. In his famous seventy-eighth essay in *The Federalist* Hamilton sought to assuage concerns and dismiss that argument by insisting that under a "limited constitution" it was "peculiarly essential" that the independent judiciary would have the power "to pronounce legislative acts void, because contrary to the constitution."

It was ultimately upon Hamilton's sturdy theoretical ground that Chief Justice Marshall in *Marbury v. Madison* would make clear what the Constitution merely implied and judicially create the institutional foundation of American constitutional law and sketch its likely contours. Although there had been earlier cases of constitutional adjudication, it was not until *Marbury* that the Court undertook to establish as unambiguously as possible the power of constitutional review to be wielded by the federal courts, the power that would become the engine of American constitutional law. The judicial power to "say what the law is" would not be some airy abstraction, but would actually empower judges to make the meaning of the Constitution concrete and legally binding as a real and enforceable law.

***Marbury v. Madison* and Constitutional Law.** Marshall's seminal opinion begins from a single premise, that the idea of a written constitution is nothing less than "the greatest improvement on political institutions." It is the simple fact of a constitution's being written that constitutes the enduring distinction between a government of limited powers and a government of unlimited powers. Because the Constitution of the United States was understood to be a document in which powers of the government were seen to be "defined and limited," it was essential that those powers and their limitations be "committed to writing" and that what was written be respected by those who would be called upon to interpret those words of the fundamental law. This all derived from the founders' political appreciation for, and philosophical commitment to, the natural rights roots of modern constitutionalism. Marshall put it this way in *Marbury:*

> That the people have an original right to establish, for their future government, such principles as, in their opinion, shall most conduce to their own happiness is the basis on which the whole American fabric has been erected. The exercise of this original right is a very great exertion; nor can it, nor ought it, to be frequently repeated. The principles, therefore, so established, are deemed fundamental. And as the authority from which they proceed is supreme, and can seldom act, they are designed to be permanent.

It is thus the obligation of the judges when cases and controversies about constitutional meaning come before them to take seriously the Constitution as the "paramount law" and seek to make clear the intentions and purposes behind the words used. The judges are thus charged to take the Constitution seriously as being at once both "fundamental" and "permanent" and not to be treated by them, to borrow Thomas Jefferson's words, as a "mere thing of wax . . . which they may twist and shape into any form they please."

Interpretation and Constitutional Law. At the heart of constitutional law is the science—or perhaps the art—of interpretation. What has been clear from the beginning is that constitutional interpretation and the constitutional law it produces is, perhaps more than any other branch of the law, inherently political. This is so because the Constitution, as the fundamental law, has always been understood to have as its primary function the ordering of the nation's politics—a sorting out of what each of the branches of the national government may or may not do as a matter of legitimate power and a clear statement of what the states may not do as a matter of course. No small part of constitutional law has come to be focused especially on individual rights and civil liberties.

Constitutional interpretation in particular is fraught with complexities. What do the words in the text mean? Are they to be construed in the sense in which they were originally understood by those who drafted and ratified the original Constitution and by those who designed and approved the subsequent amendments? Or are current generations free to seek the most just outcome of a case or controversy based on the most politically generous meaning one might import into the text of the fundamental law? That is to say, is the fundamental law to be considered at once fixed and knowable or is it to be understood as an evolutionary document, the meaning of which is more of a matter of theoretical judicial speculation? Put more simply, is the task of the judge or justice to keep the times in tune with the Constitution or to keep the Constitution in tune with the times? These questions have been at the heart of the debates over the nature and extent of judicial power since the earliest years of the republic.

Four Great Ages of Constitutional Law. Plotting this history of American constitutional law poses its own difficulties. One approach that has always been popular is to render the business of the Supreme Court according to the tenures of the chief justices over time—thus we speak of the Marshall Court, the Warren Court, the Rehnquist Court, and so on. Yet another is to sort the cases according to their substantive legal concerns, such as federalism, separation of power, individual liberties, and so forth. What follows is an effort to render the history of constitutional law according to what might arguably be seen as four rather well-defined epochs divided according to iconic and direction-changing decisions by the highest court.

The first historical period runs from the ratification of the Constitution and the beginnings of the new government to 1857 when the Supreme Court handed down the case of *Dred Scott v. Sandford,* only the second time since *Marbury* fifty-four years earlier that the Supreme Court struck down as unconstitutional a law duly passed by Congress. This stretch of constitutional history is notable for the concerns raised about the nature and extent of the federal scheme, the lines and limits of national power, limitations on the states, and the convulsive issue of chattel slavery under the Constitution.

The second period begins with *Dred Scott* and the discovery by Chief Justice Roger Taney (who had replaced John Marshall in 1836) of a "vested" right of private property as an element of what was meant by "due process of law" and the protection that doctrine accorded to life, liberty, and property as such. This was the first appearance of what would develop into the doctrine of substantive due process (a doctrine that is still regularly invoked and defended by most justices.) This notion eventually takes juridical flight and comes to inform the creation of a so-called "liberty of contract" as part of the due process clauses of the Fifth and Fourteenth Amendments. From the last quarter of the nineteenth century to the first third of the twentieth century, this notion of "liberty of contract" routinely undermined progressive political and legislative efforts to impose economic and social reforms both at the national level and within the states. This period extends to 1937 and the Court's decision in the case of *West Coast Hotel v. Parrish,* in which the justices refused to extend the doctrine of substantive due process but left it still very much alive and available for future judicial uses.

The third period begins that same year when the Court in a famous footnote to an otherwise obscure case, *United States v. Carolene Products Co.* (1938), insisted that the primary focus of constitutional protections must not be economic liberties and liberty of contract but rather a sharper judicial focus on, and attention to, what the Court described as "discrete and insular minorities." This epoch, with its explicit concern about minority rights and liberties, lasted until 1965 when the Supreme Court in *Griswold v. Connecticut* discovered an unwritten and general right to privacy by drawing loose inferences from particular constitutional protections in the Bill of Rights. This new right, Justice William O. Douglas famously argued, is the result of penumbras formed by emanations from those rights spelled out in the text.

In time, this fourth epoch of privacy rights, which remains dominant in the early twenty-first century, would lead to the controversial cases dealing with the right to abortion in *Roe v. Wade* (1973) and its progeny, homosexual behavior in such cases as *Bowers v. Hardwick* (1982) and *Lawrence v. Texas* (2003), and—it seems almost certain—eventually to same-sex marriage as an allegedly fundamental, albeit unwritten, constitutional right. What characterizes this period of constitutional law is the fact that the decisions are bereft of any reliance on clear textual provisions of the Constitution itself or the original intentions behind those provisions. This in turn has inflamed political passions and spawned tumultuous reactions to the Court's decisions; it has also rendered the confirmation process for those nominated to be justices to the highest court as nothing less than all-out, scorched-earth political battles. The political stakes are very high; in constitutional law, personnel is usually everything.

[***See also*** **Constitution; Constitutional Interpretation; *Marbury v. Madison; McCulloch v. Maryland; and Roe v. Wade.***]

BIBLIOGRAPHY

Bauer, Elizabeth Kelley. *Commentaries on the Constitution, 1790–1860.* New York: Columbia University Press, 1952.

Gunther, Gerald, ed. *John Marshall's Defense of McCulloch v. Maryland.* Stanford, Calif.: Stanford University Press, 1969.

Hobson, Charles F. *The Great Chief Justice: John Marshall and the Rule of Law.* Lawrence: University Press of Kansas, 1996.

Kramer, Larry D. *The People Themselves: Popular Constitutionalism and Judicial Review.* Oxford; New York: Oxford University Press, 2004.

O'Neill, Johnathan. *Originalism in American Law and Politics: A Constitutional History.* Baltimore, Md.: Johns Hopkins University Press, 2005.

Sergeant, Thomas. *Constitutional Law: Being a View of the Practice and Jurisdiction of the Courts of the United States, and of Constitutional Points Decided.* Philadelphia: P. H. Nicklin and T. Johnson, 1830.

Gary L. McDowell

CONTINENTAL CONGRESS

(1774–1776). The ten years between the Stamp Act crisis and the closing of the port of Boston in 1774 saw an erosion of British authority throughout the thirteen mainland colonies. In particular, the colonists' efforts to avoid British taxation led to a fatal crisis within the imperial order. When neither rioting nor royal petitions won for the colonists the political settlement they wished, provincials inspired by members of the Boston Whig movement began to systematically destroy taxed tea or otherwise impede its sale. The resulting crisis led Parliament to pass the Boston Port Bill (Coercive Acts), which in turn led to the calling of the First Continental Congress. This body, drawn from the provincial gentry, was primarily a last-ditch effort to seek legal redress and reform within the empire. Meeting in Philadelphia on 5 September 1774, the fifty-five delegates from all the colonies except Georgia elected Peyton Randolph of Virginia president of the congress; denounced the Coercive Acts; toyed with the Pennsylvanian Joseph Galloway's "Plan of Union," which would have kept the colonies in the empire; and formulated an address to George III. Adjourning on 26 October, the delegates agreed to reassemble the following year to set a course of action.

The Second Continental Congress, which convened in May 1775, contained both a conservative element, headed by John Jay of New York and Pennsylvania's John Dickinson (1732–1808), and a radical group leaning toward independence. The Battles of Lexington and Concord, in April 1775, and the subsequent siege of the British army in Boston by a provincial militia army, drove the majority of congressional delegates into the radical camp, where John Adams, Thomas Jefferson, Richard Henry Lee (1732–1794), and others advocated the end of the imperial relationship. In mid-June 1775, Congress voted to raise an army and named George Washington to lead it. In July 1776, the delegates issued the Declaration of Independence, proclaiming the colonies free from Great Britain, a move widely celebrated across America. By the Articles of Confederation, debated for months and finally adopted on 15 November 1777, the delegates constituted themselves as a unicameral legislative body that functioned as the central authority of the new nation until 1788. These representatives faced a host of domestic, military, and diplomatic problems. Foremost among these were raising and maintaining a Continental Army to fight the Revolutionary War, finance and money-supply issues, and launching overseas diplomatic initiatives. Factional fighting magnified these issues. Although the Continental Congress provided sufficient political leadership for the colonists to win the war, the financial and diplomatic problems faced by the new nation ultimately led to the Constitutional Convention of 1787 and a new government.

[*See also* **Adams, John; Albany Congress; Articles of Confederation; Committee of Correspondence; Constitution; Constitutional Convention of 1787; Jay, John; Jefferson, Thomas;** *and* **Stamp Act.**]

BIBLIOGRAPHY

Jillson, Calvin, and Rick K. Wilson. *Congressional Dynamics: Structure, Coordination, and Choice in the First American Congress, 1774–1789*. Stanford, Calif.: Stanford University Press, 1994.

Rakove, Jack. *The Beginnings of National Politics: An Interpretive History of the Continental Congress*. New York: Alfred A. Knopf, 1979.

Brendan McConville

CONTRACT, LAW OF

Histories of American contract law come in two varieties. One view comprehends contract enforcement under the Common Law as a continuous and slowly evolving enterprise, fluidly ongoing for hundreds of years. According to this view, the law of contract has been subject to gradual, piecemeal refinements over the course of five centuries or more, but at its core is a bargain instantiated by contractors' promises. This core remains identical as society changes, and although even the participants may not have perceived it clearly at all times, contract should be viewed as the often misunderstood but finally perfected art of enforcing promises. The second view of contract claims that contract law is not characterized by continuity, but rather by a transformative break somewhere in the nineteenth century. In this view, contract before the break was an embedded institution with an important role for equality in exchange, where benefit and reliance were seen as bases of enforcement, and customarily determined relations yielded the content of the parties' obligations. After the break, modern contract became an institution based on formal exchange. The new vision of contract assumed parties with purely subjective valuations and courts that facilitate whatever arrangement of obligations the parties create for themselves as private law.

These two historical views in turn may be linked to two opposed understandings of developments in twentieth-century American contract law. The first understanding points to the emergence and development of equitable doctrines that soften rigidities of formal or classical contract law. These are sometimes characterized as the socialization of contract or its equitable modification. In this view, contract law's piecemeal development up until the twentieth century (or for some well into the twentieth century) generated a law of contract appropriate for a simpler economy populated by small farmers and entrepreneurs doing business for themselves with like parties. However, as economic concentration toward the end of the nineteenth century led large corporations controlling vast amounts of wealth, their relationships with employees and consumers were no longer appropriately viewed through the lens of contract law as it had developed for the yeoman and the small businessman. Disproportionate bargaining power on the one hand and the complete control of standardized contract terms necessitated by production and distribution in a mass market on the other made the formal equality assumed by contract law seem merely formal. Judges and legislators responded by injecting mechanisms with the goal of ensuring substantive fairness of exchange, at least in the most egregious cases of abuse of asymmetrical power. Importantly, many observers who agree on this view of the historical evolution of the system disagree intensely when evaluating whether those developments were beneficial or detrimental.

The opposing view of twentieth-century developments is not a claim about whether socialization or equitable modification was good or bad, but rather a rejection of the thesis of socialization as a description of law's development. According to this view, contract law, alongside not only private law but also public law fields more generally, is an arena of conflict, the site of a constant play of forces where economic, political, and cultural battles are waged. Particular legal outcomes may be victories and defeats in these battles, but they are local; they do not combine into any general, coherent picture of how equitable or socialized an institution contract is.

The Claim of Socialization. The difficulty in the claim of socialization is twofold: first, the consequences of any particular rule change are often unpredictable. What seems like a victory for one group at the time of litigation may be undermined by new contracting practices, by new areas of application of the new rule, or by legislation dealing with that particular rule. But the second difficulty is more challenging: even if the consequences of changes in particular rules were predictable and stable in themselves, assessing the overall socialization of contract would require a much more encompassing inquiry including not only particular contract rules, but also all the surrounding legal, economic, and political institutions through which substitution or supplementation of the rule's effects might come about. In other words, to present a claim about the socialization of contract, one would need to present concurrent stories about the state of and changes in antidiscrimination law, family law, marital property law, corporate law, and a host of adjoining fields. All of these fields would be in play in trying to account for the state of contract, and no account of the socialization of contract on the basis of changes contract doctrine alone could maintain descriptive coherence.

The Development of Contract Law. Frameworks for evaluating the development of contract in America are multiple and will yield different judgments. To some extent, the evaluative frameworks impact not only normative assessment and explanation of events, but also their description. Nonetheless, certain elements of the development of contract form a degree of common ground in describing changes since the colonial period.

Some scholars view common law contract as a smoothly developing institution over the course of many centuries, whereas others understand modern contract as the product of a major shift during the nineteenth century. At the beginning of the nineteenth century in the United States, contract played a minor role in the study of law, especially when compared with other private law subjects, especially the law of property. Blackstone's *Commentaries* (1765–1769) included only a minor discussion of contract generally, among a much more developed discussion of particular relationships, some of which were also contractual. Although some systematic writing on contract preceded Blackstone, the treatise-writing tradition flowered in the nineteenth century, both in England and in the United States. Perhaps a dozen major treatises on contract were published over the course of the century, many of them in multiple editions. For common lawyers generally, the treatises provided an opportunity for systematic thought and, importantly, for the importation of a view of contractual obligation generally based on civilian jurisprudence.

Nineteenth-Century Contract Law. If eighteenth century common lawyers were most likely to learn about contracts through the typical relational pairings in the most prevalent relationships (bailor–bailee, master–servant, vendor–purchaser, principal–factor, etc.), nineteenth-century lawyers were likely to get at least some of their contract training through an understanding of contract as a general category. This trend intensified during the course of the century. Meanwhile, the early nineteenth century in the United States witnessed a rapid increase in commercial activity, termed by some historians a market revolution. Thus, alongside a shifting understanding of contract from within legal learning, the importance of contract as an economic institution was certainly on the rise.

In the 1870s, Christopher Columbus Langdell pioneered the case method of law teaching at Harvard Law School, beginning with the first case book, his *Selection of Cases on Contracts* (1871). The professionalization of law teaching that Langdell ushered in and symbolized had a significant impact on the field of contract. Langdell and the legal scholars who followed him developed the law review article genre, and a great deal of scholarly energy was devoted to contracts as well as other private law subjects. This proved to be an important innovation, allowing scholars to rationalize and refine scholarly statements of contract law by debating both general questions and the fine points of doctrine using arguments from history, analogy, comparative law, and, at times, even policy. Scholars were thus constantly in touch with developments in case law, although the extent to which the influence went the other way as well is less clear.

Twentieth-Century Contract Law. Scholarly refinement of doctrine as an institutional movement reached a peak in 1923 with the establishment of the American Law Institute (ALI), which combined judges, lawyers, and academics in an effort to rein in American law's diversity, complexity, and uncertainty. The ALI's first project was a set of restatements of major legal subjects. The first restatement to be published (1932) dealt with contracts and was reported by Samuel Williston of Harvard, with the assistance of Arthur Corbin at Yale School of Law, who also bore primary responsibility for the section on contract remedies. Williston had published his important and instantly influential treatise, *The Law of Contracts* (1920). Corbin's long-awaited treatise was published in parts through the 1950s. The restatements purported to restate existing law, but they were also devoted to extrapolating a principled understanding of the law in its entirety. Accordingly, the restatement advanced certain positions on the content and operation of legal rules that were not simple descriptions of the current state of the law, but rather preferences for particular solutions to existing uncertainties. Although the restatements have no binding authority, they have been extensively used in law teaching and widely referenced by courts and have thus formed one salient source for the law's continued development. The restatements themselves, including the Restatement of Contracts, have undergone multiple revisions, often occupying the revising committees for many years. The Restatement (Second) of Contract was published in 1981, after nearly two decades of drafting and revision.

The Restatements of Contracts centered contractual liability on the combination of promise with consideration, but they also include the principle of promissory estoppel, allowing for liability when a promise not backed by consideration induces reliance. The idea of reliance-based liability in contract attracted a great deal of attention from contracts scholars, some of whom believed it heralded an era when contractual liability generally would be swallowed up by tort principles. The impact of promissory estoppel on actual litigation has been significant, but far from revolutionary.

The ALI was also instrumental in the major legislative initiative in contracts in the twentieth century. In conjunction with the National Conference of Commissioners on Uniform State Laws (NCCUSL), the ALI helped to organize the drafting of the Uniform Commercial Code (UCC), published in 1952. The UCC was subsequently legislated, as a piece of (almost) uniform law, independently in each of the United States over the course of more than a decade. Article 2 of the UCC, governing the sale of goods, was chiefly drafted by leading contracts scholar Karl Llewellyn and has been an influential source of contract law well beyond the category of sales. The goal of harmonizing contracts and commercial law across jurisdictions extends beyond national boundaries, and in 1988 the United States adopted the United Nations Convention on the International Sale of Goods (CISG), which governs sales in transnational contracts of parties doing business in more than seventy signatory countries. Its provisions mirror the UCC in many areas, but its coverage is not identical.

The UCC included a number of features that many observers understood as innovations and that have been a focus of debate among contracts scholars for several decades. First, the UCC took the emphasis off the process of offer and acceptance and defined the contract as the parties' agreement in fact. In addition, although the code stopped short of eliminating the requirement of consideration, it did limit its importance and applicability, noting specifically that agreements to modify contracts may be valid without consideration. The provision on unconscionability, although touching on a concept that had been known (but little used) in contract law for at least a century, was considered a wide-ranging reform. On the topic of contract interpretation, the UCC placed emphasis on the context of the transaction, the parties' course of performance, the usages of trade, and the concept of commercial reasonableness. These elements had been recognized in sales law previously, but they gained wider recognition and heightened general status as a result of their inclusion in the new legislation. The UCC included a provision governing the possibility of "curing" certain contractual breaches, and some of its clauses seemed to soften the perfect tender rule. Perhaps most significantly, the UCC included a general obligation of good faith in the performance and enforcement of contracts. The Restatement (Second), following on the heels of the UCC, also adopted a general duty of good faith in performance and enforcement of contracts. The extent to which any of these innovations was actually new or rather already a part of contract law has exercised scholars since the adoption of the code, as have debates over whether the innovations constitute improvements over the common law.

The Impact of Change on Contract Law. The impact of changes on internal aspects of contract doctrine is difficult to gauge. Doctrines such as expanded excuses, unconscionability, or the duty of good faith apply to contracting parties generally, meaning that such developments need not, as is sometimes supposed, support weaker rather than stronger parties. Other twentieth-century developments, however, were geared specifically toward changing the balance of power between producers and sellers on the one hand and consumers on the other. Consumer protection legislation in fields ranging from truth in lending to workplace safety and product safety combined with doctrinal developments in products liability (limiting, in some instances, the ability of producers to shield themselves from liability for defective products) were geared toward limiting the types of contractual freedom thought to lead to exploitative relationships. Antidiscrimination legislation was also geared, in part, toward changing the setting for contractual practice among a wide range of parties. Legislation and common law developments on issues such as these change the background of entitlements that shape the bargaining situation between contractual parties. To the extent they succeed, they have more direct effects on many more parties than any molecular shift in internal doctrines of contract law. On the other hand, internal developments spur big changes. For example, the products liability revolution of the twentieth century had its beginnings in a weakening of the doctrine of privity of contract.

The conflict over the two visions of the history of contract is generally recognized, with some students of contract supporting the continuous view and others favoring the view of a transformation in the nineteenth century. The question of whether the socialization narrative is tenable is less well understood.

Late twentieth-century scholarship often dealt with doctrinal changes as if they had direct societal implications regarding individualism as opposed to communal control, and a conservative conception of contract was championed as a bulwark of individualism. As it had periodically through history, the idea of contract took on intense political connotations. Among scholars, this type of debate would generate discussions of the possibility of replacing societally supplied structures such as products liability law or bankruptcy law by contract. More generally, the rhetoric of contract could bleed easily into discussions ranging from trust in politicians (as one party's election slogan declared a "contract with America") to the privatization of social services. Many commentators seemed to believe that the development of contract doctrine itself could impact directly on the broad social questions. Extended reflection on changes in contract and on the state of American society generally, however, yield a far less decisive picture.

BIBLIOGRAPHY

Atiyah, P.S. *The Rise and Fall of Freedom of Contract*. Oxford; New York: Clarendon Press; Oxford University Press, 1979.

DiMatteo, Larry. "Equity's Modification of Contract: An Analysis of the Twentieth Century's Equitable Reformation of Contract Law." *New England Law Review* 33 (1998): 265–364.

Gilmore, Grant. *The Death of Contract*. Columbus: Ohio State University Press, 1974.

Gordley, James. *The Philosophical Origins of Modern Contract Doctrine*. Oxford; New York: Clarendon Press; Oxford University Press, 1991.

Hamburger, Philip A. "The Development of the Nineteenth-Century Consensus Theory of Contract." *Law and History Review* 7 (1989): 241–329.

Horwitz, Morton J. *The Transformation of American Law, 1780–1860*. Cambridge, Mass.: Harvard University Press, 1977.

Horwitz, Morton J. *The Transformation of American Law 1870–1960: The Crisis of Legal Orthodoxy*. New York: Oxford University Press, 1992.

Ibbetson, David. *A Historical Introduction to the Law of Obligations*. Oxford; New York: Oxford University Press, 1999.

Kennedy, Duncan. "Form and Substance in Private Law Adjudication." *Harvard Law Review* 89 (1976): 1685–1778.

Kennedy, Duncan. "From the Will Theory to the Principle of Private Autonomy: Lon Fuller's 'Consideration and Form.'" *Columbia Law Review* 100 (2000): 94–175.

Kreitner, Roy. *Calculating Promises: The Emergence of Modern American Contract Doctrine*. Stanford, Calif.: Stanford University Press, 2007.

Scheiber, Harry, ed., *The State and Freedom of Contract*. Stanford: Stanford University Press, 1998.

Simpson, A. W. B. *Legal Theory and Legal History: Essays on the Common Law*. London; Ronceverte, W. Va.: Hambledon Press, 1987.

Teeven, Kevin M. *A History of the Anglo-American Common Law of Contract*. New York: Greenwood Press, 1990.

Roy Kreitner

COOLIDGE, CALVIN

Calvin Coolidge served as the thirtieth president of the United States from 1923 to 1929. Coolidge was born on 4 July 1872 at Plymouth Notch, Vermont. He attended Amherst College. In 1904 he married Grace Anna Goodhue. Following college he read the law and went into private practice, opening an office in Northampton, Massachusetts, where he began his political career. He worked his way through the ranks of the Republican Party, serving as a Massachusetts state legislator, as mayor of Northampton, and as lieutenant governor. In 1918 he was elected governor of Massachusetts. He gained national fame when, in 1919, he intervened in the Boston police strike declaring that the police had no right to strike against the public safety. In 1920 there was talk of Coolidge running for president, but convention leaders selected Warren G. Harding of Ohio. Party leaders had selected another candidate for vice president when Coolidge's name was shouted and the delegates reacted favorably. Coolidge was nominated for vice president by acclamation.

As Warren Harding's vice president, Coolidge had few responsibilities, as was typical at the time. Harding did invite Coolidge to attend cabinet meetings, making him the first vice president to do so. Coolidge was visiting his father at Plymouth Notch, Vermont, when word reached him that Harding had died. As a notary, Coolidge's father administered the oath of office (it was later administered again). Coolidge assumed the presidency as emerging scandals tarnished the reputation of Harding and the "roaring twenties" began. Coolidge continued Harding's policies while acting to begin cleaning up the scandals, gradually removing Harding's associates tainted by scandal. In 1924 Coolidge ran for the presidency in his own right on the basis of Coolidge prosperity and his record as a small-government, honest president. Coolidge's campaign was not harmed either by the Harding scandals or by Robert LaFollette's break with the Republican Party to form a Progressive Party. Coolidge's 1924 campaign was subdued in part because it fit his reputation as "Silent Cal" and in part because his son, Calvin Jr., had died unexpectedly in July.

As president, Coolidge was known for his support for limited government and probusiness policies. He cut government expenditures and supported Secretary of the Treasury Andrew Mellon's policies of cutting taxes in the Revenue Acts of 1924 and 1926. Secretary of Commerce Herbert Hoover actively pursued probusiness policies. Coolidge has been criticized for not being more proactive in dealing with the issue of German reparations and the stock market bubble that developed late in his administration. He also twice vetoed farm relief bills and the Veteran's Bonus Act of 1924 passed over his veto. He signed the Immigration Act of 1924 that restricted immigration from Southern and Eastern Europe. His foreign policy was, by and large, isolationist although he did sign the Kellogg–Briand Pact of 1928 denouncing war. Coolidge was popular and could have run again, but abruptly declared "I do not choose to run for President in 1928."

[*See also* **Harding, Warren G.**]

BIBLIOGRAPHY

Ferrell, Robert H. *The Presidency of Calvin Coolidge.* Lawrence: University of Kansas Press, 1998.

Murray, Robert K. *The Politics of Normalcy: Governmental Theory and Practice in the Harding–Coolidge Era.* New York: Norton, 1973.

Sobel, Robert. *Coolidge: An American Enigma.* Washington, D.C.: Regnery, 1998.

Phillip Payne

COOPER v. AARON

In 1954, in *Brown v. Board of Education,* the U.S. Supreme Court declared that race-based segregation of public schools violated the Equal Protection Clause of the Constitution. *Brown II,* which followed in 1955, directed school boards to desegregate "with all deliberate speed."

The decisions met significant opposition. In the Southern Manifesto, 101 Southern members of Congress condemned them as "an unwarranted exercise of power by the Court, contrary to the Constitution." Nonetheless, many school boards drew up integration plans. In Little Rock, Arkansas, the plan called for nine African American students to enter Central High on 4 September 1957. Governor Orval Faubus and the Arkansas legislature opposed integration, and when the students arrived, they were turned away by Arkansas National Guardsmen acting at Faubus's direction.

A federal district court in Arkansas issued an order enjoining such interference, and the Arkansas Guard withdrew. Protected by local police, the students entered the school on 23 September, but the police proved unable to control the large numbers of demonstrators. On 25 September, President Dwight Eisenhower sent the 101st Airborne to Little Rock, and the students entered school under the escort of the U.S. Army.

Subsequently, the school board sought court approval to suspend its desegregation plan on the grounds that public hostility, created by the visible and public opposition of state officials, had made implementation a practical impossibility. In *Cooper v. Aaron,* the Supreme Court refused to accept this argument. In an opinion signed, unusually, by all nine Justices, the Court pronounced that the case boiled down to the question of whether state officials could, as the Arkansas governor and legislature sought, nullify Supreme Court decisions with which they disagreed. The answer the Court gave was a resounding no: "[T]he interpretation of the Fourteenth Amendment enunciated by this Court in the *Brown* case is the supreme law of the land, and Art. VI of the Constitution makes it of binding effect on the States 'any Thing in the Constitution or Laws of any State to the Contrary notwithstanding.'"

In practical terms, *Cooper* signaled the beginning of active enforcement of *Brown*'s desegregation command. The Court would no longer tolerate delay, and the president would use force to support its orders. Theoretically, it presented one of the perennial questions of American constitutional law: whose interpretation of the Constitution is authoritative? Nothing in the document's text gives a clear answer. (Government officials all swear an oath to support the Constitution, but that oath is to the document itself and not necessarily the Court's interpretation.)

The *Cooper* Court asserted its own preeminence: "[T]he federal judiciary is supreme in the exposition of the law of the Constitution." Federal supremacy over the states makes some obvious sense, since one authoritative interpretation is preferable to fifty competing ones. Judicial supremacy within the federal government is less clearly correct. In modern practice, *Cooper*'s view prevails. In academic circles, departmentalists argue that interpretive authority should be spread among the three branches and popular constitutionalists posit that it should rest with the people themselves.

[*See also* ***Brown v. Board of Education; Constitution;*** **Constitutional Interpretation; Constitutional Law; Fourteenth Amendment;** ***and*** **Supreme Court, U.S.**]

BIBLIOGRAPHY

Freyer, Tony. *Little Rock on Trial: Cooper v. Aaron and School Desegregation.* Lawrence: University of Kansas Press, 2007.

Klarman, Michael. *From Jim Crow to Civil Rights: The Supreme Court and the Struggle for Racial Equality.* Oxford; New York: Oxford University Press, 2004.

Kermit Roosevelt III

COURT PACKING

This practice involves a concerted effort on the part of a U.S. president to use his power to appoint Supreme Court justices and lower federal court judges, with the advice and consent of the Senate, to secure in the law a particular ideological understanding of the Constitution. The purpose of court packing is distinguishable from, although compatible with, other motives that inform presidential appointments to the judiciary, including considerations of merit, patronage, and group representation.

In 1937, Franklin Roosevelt initiated what would become the most famous court packing attempt when he asked Congress to give him the authority to appoint a new judge for every member of the federal judiciary over the age of 70 who declined to retire. Roosevelt stated that the purpose of his legislative proposal was to improve the efficiency of the judiciary. The Supreme Court had declared unconstitutional a number of New Deal programs, so Roosevelt sought the six appointments to the body that the bill stood to provide him. Subsequent decisions in which a majority of the justices revealed a willingness to uphold legislative reforms of the economy, Roosevelt's disingenuousness in the initial characterization of his bill, and the unseemliness of a president lashing out at an independent branch of government that Americans believe should be above politics all contributed to the unwillingness of Congress to bring the president's bill to a vote.

Ronald Reagan followed a shrewder court-packing strategy in an effort to roll back the liberal jurisprudence of the Warren Court and to counter the Burger Court's abortion rights decision, *Roe v. Wade* (1973). By establishing a Committee on Federal Judicial Selection composed of top White House and Justice Department officials, deemphasizing the merit ratings of the American Bar Association's Committee on the Federal Judiciary, and pressuring relevant senators when their patronage considerations conflicted with presidential choices for district court vacancies, Ronald Reagan was more successful than any preceding president at elevating ideology above other factors in the selection of federal judges. Presidents George H. W. Bush and George W. Bush employed a similar method of judicial selection.

Defenders of court packing contend that the life tenure of federal judges, the indeterminacy of constitutional language, and the increased importance of the judiciary in American life warrant the efforts of representatives of a political majority to affect the direction of constitutional law. But even if one sets aside the objection that majority sentiment is not an appropriate standard for controversies involving minority rights, one should consider that court packing also provides a method for the leader of a political party in transition to entrench a view of the Constitution that has proved unpopular and unworkable. Court packing also might foster the perception that the process of judicial selection is largely political. Should the pursuit of ideological purity damage the public's confidence in judicial impartiality and fairness, critics of court packing contend, the executive branch will have compromised the primary source of the prestige and authority of the federal courts.

[*See also* **Bush, George H. W.; Bush, George W.; Constitution; Reagan, Ronald; Roosevelt, Franklin Delano;** *and* **Supreme Court, U.S.**]

BIBLIOGRAPHY

Abraham, Henry J. *Justices, Presidents, and Senators: A History of the U.S. Supreme Court Appointments from Washington to Bush II*. Lanham, Md.: Rowman & Littlefield, 2007.

Shesol, Jeff. *Supreme Power: Franklin Roosevelt vs. the Supreme Court*. New York: W. W. Norton, 2010.

Jeffrey D. Hockett

CRIME POLICY, FEDERAL

Crime policy in American history reflects a core of common Republican values that is constantly evolving. Over the past few centuries, three general trends emerge. The first is a gradual shift toward increasingly greater freedom in matters of individual morality and lifestyle choices. The second is an equivalent shift toward greater regulation over individual actions that may impact public welfare, but do not encroach on individual morality. And the third, which is most evident during the twentieth century, is a shift from local to federal priorities in developing and implementing criminal codes. These trends reflect larger phenomena in American policy, wherein the locus of political action has shifted away from local and state government toward more centralized federal administration and oversight.

Divisions of American Law. American law is divided into four main divisions: contracts, torts, family law, and criminal law. The first three categories involve questions of mutual obligation, good faith and breach of expectations, individual and corporate liability, familial dependency, and custody and inheritance issues. The penal code is the only category of laws enforced by the state to protect the safety, health, and welfare of the general public. Each generation redefines specific definitions for offenses that threaten public health and safety, which necessarily reflect moral sensitivities of their time. As a rule, legal policies written into the penal code set forth the basic elements and thresholds necessary to define the specific criminal act (*actus reus*), the degrees of severity and culpability as indicated by criminal intent (*mens rea*), and recommended punishments. In most cases, penal codes stipulate that the criminal act and guilty intention occur simultaneously. Rare exceptions exist when a law considers only the intention to act and not the intention to produce a specific outcome. For example, modern environmental regulations impose penalties for certain violations regardless of whether the individual intended public harm. These instances of absolute liability bridge the divide between torts and criminal law and often reflect the unique sensitivities of a given generation.

Types of Criminal Law. Criminal laws can be divided into two types. Some laws forbid acts that are naturally wrong, regardless of whether a government exists to recognize it (*mala in se*). Other laws forbid acts that are wrong only because a legislative body deemed them to be so (*mala prohibita*). Most direct or participatory offenses against individuals and property, as well as those actions resulting in culpable death, fall under *mala in se*. Examples of *mala prohibita* include most regulatory crimes and some lesser forms of personal and property offenses such as prostitution and personal alcohol or drug use.

The specific line between *mala in se* and *mala prohibita* is not always easy to distinguish. In the seventeenth century, the American colonies' criminal code grew out of English Common Law and was enforced by local constables and magistrates guided mostly by principles of religious conviction and common custom. The bulk of codified offenses were deemed to be *mala in se*, and the number of *mala prohibita* codes was small and localized. Over the course of several centuries, the locus of American crime policy shifted toward more federal guidance rendering a more complex criminal code, which requires more specialized training for enforcement. Consequently, the twenty-first-century criminal code includes a greater proportion of *mala prohibita* offenses to support the proportionately larger federal state. At the same time, the code has adopted a more neutral stance on individual morality to accommodate its increasingly pluralistic constituency.

The Evolution of Crime Policy. During the colonial period, American communities relied heavily on religious proscriptions that included expectations of hierarchy, self-restraint, and communal conformity. Individuals had greater latitude outside of urban centers, but at the village level penal codes were sometimes highly customized. In addition to traditional laws against theft, assault, and murder, local communities might also include ecclesial decrees against blasphemy, failure to attend church, or regulations about dress and public decency. The close connection between religious and civic governances within each community meant that most laws were considered *mala in se.* Punishments were handled locally and swiftly and ranged from public shaming, whipping, and branding to death. There was little call for imprisonment except as a holding place for awaiting due process.

The American Revolution weakened the tight relationship between ecclesial and civil authority in setting the penal code. Political discourse emphasizing individual liberty and freedom of expression reinforced greater flexibility in defining those actions that undermine public moral health. Local churches, although still influential, assumed a more advisory role with less legal oversight. At the same time, the rush of westward expansion thrust Americans into regions with few legal or religious authority figures. By the middle of the nineteenth century, vast areas of American soil were patrolled by locally elected sheriffs, relying on locally elected judges to enforce local ordinances with little dependence on state or federal oversight. In economic terms, the nineteenth-century crime policy might be categorized as a "*laissez-faire*" approach to criminal justice. The penal code applied rules of basic public safety, whereas private individuals were expected to assume the primary responsibility for maintaining civic order.

Toward the end of the nineteenth century, geographic differences began to even out as a newly nationalized industrial economy produced an influx of technologies in communication and transportation. Telegraphs and mail trains created new criminal opportunities and the federal government responded with its first mail and wire fraud laws in 1872 to deal with crimes spanning state lines. Similarly, national social organizations, like temperance and purity movements of the late 1800s, focused particular pressure on the federal government to enact legal codes aimed at protecting the public's moral health. In 1873, Congress modified its fraud laws to include prohibitions against obscenity, making it a felony to sell, publish, or otherwise distribute pornography, including contraceptive manuals. The new law was popularly known as the "Comstock" law after its major advocate, Anthony Comstock, who led the New York City Society for the Suppression of Vice. He and other advocates for the purity movement pushed for federal legislation to guide state legislatures in passing their own codes. Similar pressure from social reformers resulted in the Mann Act of 1910, which forbade the transportation of women over state lines for immoral purposes. The federal law targeted organized prostitution rings and was a direct response to pressures from the Federated Council of Churches, Christian temperance groups, and woman suffrage organizations.

The Comstock Law and the Mann Act were mostly symbolic because few resources were devoted to national enforcement. Local authorities pressured bordellos into less centralized neighborhoods (known as "red light districts"), where the local communities were more willing to ignore enforcement. These new federal laws laid the foundation for greater national coordination of crime policy, but throughout the early decades of the twentieth century the vast majority of law enforcement facilities remained localized and actual enforcement heavily reflected local, and not federal, priorities.

By 1919, the purity movement produced its most far-reaching law in the Eighteenth Amendment, which prohibited the manufacture and sale of alcohol. The Prohibition Amendment and its accompanying Volstead Act required significant behavioral changes in all levels of American society, yet it relied on local law enforcement for implementation. Social movements to limit the consumption of alcohol first emerged in the 1840s and gradually gained momentum after the influx of new immigrants and culturally diverse urban centers seemed to challenge the moral order that had dominated the nineteenth century. By 1907, Georgia passed a statewide prohibition law, which was imitated by seventeen states in the decade that followed. The eventual Prohibition Amendment of 1920 in part reflected anti-German sentiments that followed World War I. Broad support existed in rural areas, but most large urban districts had little sympathy for prohibition. Local police complained that they were being asked to enforce a measure that a majority of their residents did not support. Like the Comstock and Mann Acts that preceded it, the Volstead Act faced the problem of selective enforcement almost immediately after passage.

Prohibition and Crime Policy. During the 1920s, Prohibition served as a primary manifestation for the first national debate over crime policy. Other issues emerged related to the unique frustrations of law enforcement confronting modern industrial technologies in dense urban populations. Of particular concern was the emergence of what appeared to be more organized criminal activity. Following the business model of vertical integration, local criminal gangs emerged to organize their abilities to avoid detection and apprehension through multilevel coordination, bribes to local law enforcement officials, and negotiated agreements over territorial operations.

Prohibition did not create criminal gangs, but the ambiguity between *mala in se* and *mala prohibita* created a cultural environment that tolerated certain levels of unlawfulness. Often, otherwise respectable citizens expended money to support illegal bootlegging operations because they did not see alcohol as morally wrong. The result was a voluntary transfer of wealth from the traditionally law-abiding sector of society over to criminal enterprises. In the process, these criminal gangs also increased their other operations—extortion and racketeering, gambling and loan sharking, kidnapping, and murder. The increase of violent crimes led to great public pressure from community leaders to more proactively confront crime as a state and national problem. The murder rate doubled between 1920 and 1921, and it continued to rise throughout the decade. The Chicago beer wars of 1925 and 1926 left more than 350 dead. Most sensational among these crimes were the 1926 assassination of Chicago's assistant district attorney, Bill McSwiggin, the 1929 St. Valentine's Day massacre, and the 1932 Lindbergh kidnapping.

Machine guns, automobiles, and telephones forced police departments to develop equally advanced technologies in law enforcement. No longer were police officers hired for their size, strength, or relationship to local political leaders. Modern police academies trained their officers in forensics, systematic evidence gathering, and science-driven investigative techniques. Academics lent their expertise with new departments in police science at the University of Chicago and University of California at Berkeley. Throughout the 1920s, local crime commissions pressed for statewide investigations to assess the effectiveness of existing legislation in deterring crime. Crime reports from Illinois and New York eventually found their way to Washington lawmakers.

President Herbert Hoover called the first national crime commission in 1929 to investigate what the federal government could do to support local efforts against rising crime rates. After two years, the Wickersham Commission reported that crime was a significant national problem and recommended that the federal government either significantly increase money and manpower devoted to national enforcement or consider repealing the national Prohibition laws. Hoover was opposed to repealing Prohibition, but he was faced with a strong public sentiment that associated the ban on alcohol with rising crime rates. The 1932 presidential candidate Franklin D. Roosevelt promised to not only repeal Prohibition, but also more actively dedicate federal resources to the national crime problem. The Eighteenth Amendment was fully repealed by the Twenty-First Amendment in 1933.

The Prohibition experience defined the national crime policy for the next forty years. A few Congressional voices following repeal of Prohibition called on President Roosevelt to form a national police force to combat the growing crime problem, but they were a distinct minority. The majority sentiment was that Prohibition demonstrated the impracticality of national enforcement of local activities. Key policy makers, like the Federal Bureau of Investigation's (FBI) Director J. Edgar Hoover and Attorney General Homer Cummings also concluded that any effort to enforce moral proscriptions on an increasingly diverse national population was futile. By 1935, the federal Department of Justice established a new policy framework that set the FBI up as a resource of local law enforcement officials who had access to advanced forensic labs, a national fingerprint database, and other training facilities and workshops. This model of federal expertise augmenting local law enforcement agencies remained firm until the 1970s.

The Federal Government's Role in Local Enforcement. Although the federal government deliberately limited its jurisdiction over local enforcement in the 1930s and 1940s, its position as a central source of expertise nevertheless stirred public debate. The FBI was not a police agency, but its role in establishing federal standards created unsettling comparisons in the aftermath of World War II. Particular concern was voiced by civil liberties groups who viewed the rise of European police states during the 1930s as a dangerous warning for America. The national security fears that accompanied the origins of the Cold War provoked further sensitivity for more transparent rights of due process. Throughout the 1950s, lawmakers and litigators reexamined the meaning of the First, Fourth, Fifth, and Sixth Amendments in the context of modern criminal procedures.

Beginning with concerns for the rights of communists in the 1950s and ending with the fear of racially based enforcement inequities in the 1960s, the Supreme Court under Chief Justice Earl Warren delivered a series of landmark decisions that redefined criminal due process in America. Cases such as *Mapp v. Ohio* (1961), *Gideon v. Wainwright* (1963), *Miranda v. Arizona* (1966), *Katz v. United States* (1967), and *Terry v. Ohio* (1968) all used the Fourteenth Amendment's guarantee of constitutional due process to require local law enforcement officials to adhere to basic federal guidelines. Of particular importance was the "exclusionary rule" established by *Mapp v. Ohio,* which compelled judges to throw out evidence obtained contrary to established procedures of due process. This ruling provided the enforcement tool necessary to ensuring that federal standards of criminal process were applied directly to local jurisdictions. Each subsequent due process case helped to clarify specific rules and local procedures.

In the late 1960s and early 1970s, local enforcement agencies became bound by a series of court-mandated procedures. As the distinction between federal and local procedures became blurred, the historical demands for local primacy in law enforcement also faded. Beginning with the 1968 Safe Streets Act and followed by the 1970 Organized Crime Control Act, Congress passed a series of new laws authorizing federal enforcement of crimes committed in local jurisdictions. Throughout the 1970s and 1980s, the multijurisdictional task force replaced the Hoover/Cummings model by establishing federally directed law enforcement groups to combat major crime problems. The result was a rapid expansion in the number of federal law enforcement agencies. By 2004, more than 100,000 federal law enforcement officers were authorized to carry weapons and make arrests. That same year, the ratio of federal agents to local agents was 1 to 6, with trends suggesting continued increases in federal enforcement.

One of the consequences of an increased role of federal law enforcement is that crime policy more closely follows national interests. Events such as the Oklahoma City bombing of the Alfred P. Murrah Federal Building in 1995 or the terrorist attacks on the World Trade Centers and the Pentagon on 11 September 2001 led to major changes in national crime policy. The Patriot Act, which Congress passed immediately following the 9/11 attacks, increased the powers of federal law enforcement and created entire agencies dedicated to national security. The omnibus crime package significantly impacted the size and scope of federal enforcement, yet it was merely an increase in the order of magnitude. The more significant change in crime policy occurred earlier following the Court-led due process revolution and the emergence of federal task force enforcement models. Local crime waves may impact changes in implementation and practice, but most major policy decisions come from federal and then state leadership.

Additionally, national coordination means that crime policy must take into account the wide diversity of America's pluralist society. As a result, moral issues have largely been removed from crime policy, leaving individuals with greater freedom to make personal lifestyle choices. At the same time, however, the decrease in common presumptions of moral behavior results in an increase in the number of regulatory laws (*mala prohibita*) to account for "risky" behaviors rather than stipulate "wrong" behaviors. Given the constant rate of growth in technological development and federal leadership, there is little reason to suggest that these historic trends are likely to change in the near future.

[*See also* **Eighteenth Amendment; Fourteenth Amendment; Hoover, Herbert; Hoover, J. Edgar;** ***Katz v. United States; Miranda v. Arizona;*** **Patriot Act, The; Roosevelt, Franklin Delano; Tort, Law of;** *and* **Warren, Earl.**]

BIBLIOGRAPHY

Berman, Harold Joseph. *Law and Revolution: The Formation of the Western Legal Tradition.* Cambridge, Mass.: Harvard University Press, 1983.

Calder, James D. *The Origins and Development of Federal Crime Control Policy: Herbert Hoover's Initiatives.* Westport, Conn.: Praeger, 1993.

Friedman, Lawrence. *Crime and Punishment in American History*. New York: Basic Books, 1993.
Hall, Kermit L., et al. *American Legal History: Cases and Materials*. Oxford; New York: Oxford University Press, 2005.
Horwitz, Morton J. *The Transformation of American Law, 1870–1960: The Crisis of Legal Orthodoxy*. New York: Oxford University Press, 1992.
Johnson, David R. *American Law Enforcement: A History*. St. Louis, Mo.: Forum Press, 1981.
Pestritto, Ronald. *Founding the Criminal Law: Punishment and Political Thought in the Origins of America*. DeKalb: Northern Illinois University Press, 2000.
Schlegel, John Henry. *American Legal Realism and Empirical Social Science*. Chapel Hill: University of North Carolina Press, 2011.
Schur, Edward M. *Our Criminal Society: The Social and Legal Sources of Crime in America*. Englewood Cliffs, N.J.: Prentice Hall, 1969.
Walker, Samuel. *Popular Justice: History of American Criminal Justice*, 2d ed. New York: Oxford University Press, 1998.

Aharon Zorea

CROLY, HERBERT

(1869–1930), political philosopher and editor. Croly was born in New York City, the son of two prominent journalists. Entering Harvard College in 1886, he studied intermittently for fourteen years but eventually left without earning a degree. He worked for the *Architectural Record,* a New York trade journal, until 1906. A close and thoughtful observer of politics, he was moved by the early stirrings of American Progressivism to write his most important book, *The Promise of American Life* (1909). The work criticized the Jeffersonian ideal of a weak central government and advocated an expanded government role in social reform and business regulation. Theodore Roosevelt's praise of the book established Croly's reputation as an insightful analyst of American political culture. His second work of political commentary, *Progressive Democracy,* appeared in 1914.

Two wealthy admirers, Dorothy and Willard Straight, provided Croly with funds to found and edit the *New Republic,* a weekly magazine of political and cultural commentary. From 1914 until he suffered a debilitating stroke in 1928, Croly—together with a remarkable collection of editors and writers, including Walter Lippmann, John Dewey, and Randolph Bourne—produced a literate, highly influential journal of liberal opinion and commentary on foreign affairs, domestic policy, literature, art, politics, and religion.

Painfully bashful, reticent, and modest, Croly nevertheless gathered a circle of admiring friends who respected his intelligence, integrity, and seriousness of purpose. He was one of that group of American intellectuals who transformed American liberalism at the turn of the century.

[*See also* **Progressive Era;** *and* **Roosevelt, Theodore.**]

BIBLIOGRAPHY

Levy, David W. *Herbert Croly of the New Republic: The Life and Thought of an American Progressive*. Princeton, N.J.: Princeton University Press, 1985.
Stettner, Edward A. *Shaping Modern Liberalism: Herbert Croly and Progressive Thought*. Lawrence: University Press of Kansas, 1993.

David W. Levy

D

DALEY, RICHARD J.

Richard J. Daley was the last of the big-city bosses and mayor of Chicago from 1955 to 1976. He autocratically guided the Second City's fortunes during the critical years that spanned the post–World War II "urban renaissance" and the "urban crisis"—the years of urban renewal, race riots, fiscal crisis, suburban flight, and Sunbelt boom. An Irish Catholic native of a working-class neighborhood bordering the Chicago's Union Stockyards, Daley attended parochial schools and received a law degree from DePaul University after attending night classes for eleven years. He served in the state legislature from 1938 to 1946, rising to the post of senate majority leader, and in 1949 returned to the state capital as Governor Adlai Stevenson's director of revenue. In 1955 Daley ousted the incumbent mayor in a bitterly contested Democratic primary and then narrowly defeated Republican Robert Merriam in the general election. He won reelection five times, the last in 1975.

During his early years in city hall, Daley won national acclaim as a reformer who reshaped Chicago's landscape. He presided over an unprecedented building boom that fashioned a spectacular downtown skyline, completed an extensive expressway system, enlarged Chicago–O'Hare International Airport, and constructed the University of Illinois at Chicago. The efficient delivery of services under his leadership made Chicago famous as "the city that works," and his success in balancing the city's books during the 1970s when countless big cities teetered on the verge of bankruptcy earned him the reputation of a financial wizard. Based in part upon his legendary machinations on behalf of John F. Kennedy in the 1960 presidential election, Daley became a powerful force in the Democratic Party nationally and an influential spokesman for urban interests in the 1960s and 1970s.

Despite his consistent popularity with voters and many successes as a manager, Daley became an increasingly controversial figure by the 1960s. Because of the brutal suppression of dissent at the 1968 Democratic National Convention and his infamous "shoot to kill" order during the rioting following the assassination of Martin Luther King Jr., he became widely regarded as a symbol of law and order and an intractable defender of the establishment. As growing numbers of whites left for the suburbs and Chicago's black population increased rapidly, the mayor consistently aligned himself politically with the conservative white ethnics who remained in the city. He resisted residential desegregation, defended the public schools' racially exclusionary policies, refused to implement affirmative action procedures in municipal agencies, and used federal funds to construct massive high-rise public housing projects that confined black Chicagoans in existing ghettos. At a time of metropolitan decentralization, increasing numbers of working class residents questioned the mayor's single-minded determination to revitalize the central business district at the expense of the neighborhoods. His death in 1976 and the disintegration of the Democratic machine over which he had long presided subsequently resulted in the election of Chicago's first black mayor, Harold Washington, in 1983. Richard Daley's son, Richard M. Daley, served as mayor from 1989 to 2011.

BIBLIOGRAPHY

Biles, Roger. *Richard J. Daley: Politics, Race, and the Governing of Chicago.* DeKalb: Northern Illinois University Press, 1995. This political biography pays particular attention to Daley's key role in the development of Chicago and to his place in urban history.

Royko, Mike. *Boss: Richard J. Daley of Chicago.* New York: New American Library, 1971. The author relied substantially on interviews to describe Daley's upbringing, rise to political power, and early mayoral years. This is a lively journalistic account by a persistent critic of the mayor.

Roger Biles

DARTMOUTH COLLEGE CASE

In *Dartmouth College v. Woodward* (1819), the U.S. Supreme Court extended the scope of the contract clause of the Constitution (Article 1, Section 10). In 1769, the royal governor of New Hampshire, acting in the name of the English crown, granted Dartmouth College a charter to operate as a private institution under the administration of a group of trustees. In 1816, however, the New Hampshire legislature passed several laws that transformed Dartmouth from a private to a public college, subject to inspection by the state.

The college, claiming that its charter rights had been violated, took the case to court, with Daniel Webster, a Dartmouth graduate, as its chief attorney. At this time, it was understood that state legislatures could regulate corporations, but that private property could not be taken from individuals by state action without proper compensation. Writing for the majority, Chief Justice John Marshall ruled that the college was a "private eleemosynary institution" and that the 1769 charter was a valid contract between the state and the original donors to the institution. By voiding the legislation that had transformed Dartmouth into a public institution, Marshall not only strengthened the contract clause of the Constitution, but also expanded the federal judiciary's role in overseeing state legislative action affecting property rights.

[*See also* **Marshall, John;** *and* **Webster, Daniel.**]

BIBLIOGRAPHY

White, G. Edward. *The Marshall Court and the Culture of Change, 1815–1835*. New York: Macmillan, 1988.

Paul G. E. Clemens

DAVIS, JEFFERSON

Jefferson Davis, a political leader from Mississippi and President of the Confederate States of America, embodied the contradictions and myths of the slaveholding South. He proved to be a bold and controversial executive but later became a symbol of state rights and the Lost Cause.

Davis was born in Kentucky in 1808, but his large family moved to Mississippi in 1812. There a wealthy older brother, Joseph Emory Davis, helped young Jefferson receive superior schooling. He attended Transylvania University in Kentucky and in 1824 matriculated at the U.S. Military Academy at West Point.

Graduating in the bottom half of his class, Davis entered military service in 1828. Assigned to frontier infantry units, he saw limited action in conflicts with Indians, but in 1835 he resigned his commission to marry the daughter of then Colonel Zachary Taylor. Within a few months Sarah Knox Taylor Davis had died of malaria. Stricken, Jefferson Davis retired to the isolated life of a slaveholding cotton planter, working fertile river-bottom land made available by his brother, with whom he read and discussed political works. During this period he prospered, purchased slaves, and completed the one-generation transition into an aristocratic planter that was common in the Deep South.

In 1844 Davis entered political life, winning election as a Democrat to the U.S. House of Representatives, and in 1845 he married Varina Howell, with whom he would have six children. The Mexican War interrupted, but ultimately aided, Davis's political career. He resigned from Congress, raised a regiment called the Mississippi Rifles, and fought near Monterrey and at the Battle of Buena Vista, where Davis distinguished himself and was wounded in the foot. Returning to Mississippi as a war hero, he was rewarded by political leaders with a seat in the U.S. Senate. Quickly Davis established a reputation as a tendentious defender of state rights, a fierce advocate of the South's interests, and an admirer of John C. Calhoun. Davis opposed the Compromise of 1850, arguing that at a minimum all lands won from Mexico and south of thirty-six degrees sixty minutes should be open to slavery. By this time he had established a typically Southern reputation for touchiness about his honor, engaging in a number of quarrels that almost ended in duels.

To aid his party in Mississippi, Davis resigned his Senate seat in 1851 and ran, unsuccessfully, for governor. Soon, however, he was appointed secretary of war by incoming Democratic President Franklin Pierce. He discharged his duties in that Cabinet position well and supervised a survey of possible railroad routes to link California with the rest of the nation. Davis favored the more southerly routes, but sectional conflict derailed all such bills. In 1854 Davis contributed to the intensification of sectional conflict when he played a leading role in convincing President Pierce to support Stephen

Douglas's Kansas–Nebraska Act. Northern anger over that law gave rise to the Republican Party, which Davis viewed as a threat because its "vital element" was antislavery.

After reelection to the Senate in 1856, Jefferson Davis accused the Federal government of violating state rights and argued aggressively that slaveholders had a right to take slavery into any region while it remained a territory. Only states, he insisted, possessed the sovereignty necessary to decide that they would not allow human bondage. Although insisting on southern interests, he hoped that the Union might be preserved. Yet he also emerged as a leading opponent of Stephen Douglas's desire to win the Democratic nomination for president in 1860. Davis's Resolutions on the Relations of States (1860) reiterated his territorial theories and fortified southern opposition to Douglas, who had supported the majority of Kansas settlers when it became clear that they favored a free state.

As the 1860 Democratic convention approached, Davis hoped that the Northern and Southern wings of his party could unite behind some candidate without a platform. However, the party split, and in the national election the Republican Party dominated northern states and gave Abraham Lincoln an Electoral College victory. Deep South states, led by South Carolina, began to secede. Davis counseled against immediate action, hoping a united South could compel a compromise. But when Mississippi seceded, he resigned his seat in the Senate and returned home, expecting to command Mississippi troops. Instead, the seceded states chose him to be provisional president of the Confederate States of America, and in November 1861 he was elected to a six-year term as president.

Jefferson Davis proved to be a bold, intelligent, and unpopular president beset by problems. The wealthy slaveholders who dominated Congress were overconfident and reluctant to sacrifice, especially in ways that affected slavery or taxes. The nonslaveholders suffered greatly from the immense demands that war made on the rural, nonindustrialized South. Many women became disaffected, and the slave population worked to advance its freedom. Davis saw that strong, often drastic steps needed to be taken to wage war, and the Confederate Constitution—which had been modeled on the U.S. Constitution—gave the government substantial powers. Consequently he pushed for strong measures, including conscription, military impressment, suspension of the writ of habeas corpus, higher taxes, a tax-in-kind on foodstuffs, subsidies for industry and railroads, controls on shipping, and finally a plan to arm and free slaves.

Often Davis got his way, particularly with conscription, but the refusal to tax spawned uncontrollable inflation, and Congress delayed action even on arming slaves until it was too late to matter. Davis's unexpected measures angered many, especially the elite, whereas privations and failures in defending the home front undermined support from ordinary southerners. By building a powerful but unpopular government, Davis kept the Confederacy in the war until defeat in 1865.

Ironically, the unpopular president later became a Southern hero. His imprisonment for two years won him sympathy, and in 1881 Davis published a turgid state-rights justification for the Confederacy that assailed the North and defended the virtue of the white South. Before his death in 1889 Jefferson Davis had become celebrated as a noble leader in the Lost Cause.

[*See also* **Confederate States of America; Conscription; Douglas, Stephen A.; Kansas–Nebraska Act; Pierce, Franklin; Slavery, Laws;** ***and*** **States' Rights.**]

BIBLIOGRAPHY

Cooper, William J. *Jefferson Davis, American*. New York: Alfred A. Knopf, 2000.

Escott, Paul D. *After Secession: Jefferson Davis and the Failure of Confederate Nationalism*. Baton Rouge: Louisiana State University Press, 1978.

McCurry, Stephanie. *Confederate Reckoning: Power and Politics in the Civil War South*. Cambridge, Mass.: Harvard University Press, 2010.

Thomas, Emory M. *The Confederate Nation, 1861–1865*. New York: Harper & Row, 1979.

Paul D. Escott

DAWES SEVERALTY ACT

An important 1887 law relating to Indian affairs. Sponsored by Senator Henry Dawes of Massachusetts, its central purposes included ending tribal title to land in favor of individual holdings, transforming Native Americans into farmers, and assimilating Indians into white society. The ideological roots of the legislation lay in the post–Civil War public faith in *laissez-faire,* private property, citizenship, and the "Americanization" of immigrants and minorities. The Women's National Indian Association, the Indian Rights Association, and the Lake Mohonk Conferences, important eastern reform groups, were largely responsible for passage of the legislation. Western settlers and economic interests had little influence on passage, although they benefited greatly afterward.

The Dawes Severalty Act applied to all Indians except a few groups in New York, Nebraska, and Indian Territory. Major provisions included assignment of 160 acres to each family head, 80 acres to unmarried Indians over eighteen years of age and to orphans, and 40 acres to those under eighteen. Title to allotments was held in trust by the government for twenty-five years, during which time the land could not be sold or encumbered. Citizenship was granted to all allottees and to others who adopted the "habits of civilized life." Unallotted land was declared surplus and could be purchased by the federal government for subsequent settlement by non-Indians.

The act proved disastrous to Native Americans. Legislation approved in 1891 permitted the leasing of allotments, and by 1916 over one-third of such land was rented to non-Indians. Other measures, most notably the Burke Act of 1906, allowed Indians to sell their allotments. The checkerboarding that resulted when allotments became intermingled with non-Indian holdings on reservations created major obstacles to proper land management and produced serious jurisdictional problems that persisted more than a century later. Many arid reservations were allotted that should have been left in common title to permit ranching. Allotments commonly became so fractionalized by heirship that they were virtually worthless except for leasing. Most importantly, the sale of surplus land and allotments reduced Indian land holdings from 156 million acres in 1881, when allotment of individual tribes started, to 53 million acres in 1933. The Indian Reorganization Act of 1934 prohibited further allotment, but did little to restore Indian land holdings. Allotment and citizenship did not "free the Indian" as promised, but led to increased federal control, poverty, and reduced agricultural production. What started as well-intended legislation produced a major disaster.

[*See also* **Homestead Act;** ***and*** **Indian Law, Federal.**]

BIBLIOGRAPHY

McLaughlin, Michael R. "The Dawes Act, or Indian General Allotment Act of 1887: The Continuing

Burden of Allotment. A Selective Bibliography." *American Indian Culture and Research Journal* 20, no. 2 (1996): 59–105.

Otis, D. S. *The Dawes Act and the Allotment of Indian Lands*, edited by Francis Paul Prucha. Norman: University of Oklahoma Press, 1973.

Donald L. Parman

DEBS, EUGENE

(1855–1926), labor leader, socialist, and presidential candidate. The son of Alsatian immigrants, Eugene Victor Debs became a railroad worker at age fourteen in his native Terre Haute, Indiana. After four years as a railway fireman, he took a job as a clerk but remained active in the Brotherhood of Locomotive Firemen, becoming its secretary-treasurer and editor of its journal. In 1893 he broke with the craft-union tradition by helping found the American Railway Union, which organized both skilled and unskilled workers. The following year, he led a boycott of the Pullman Palace Car Company, which tied up the nation's railroad system but ultimately failed.

After six months in jail for his role in the Pullman boycott, Debs began a career as a lecturer and journalist. Embracing socialism, he ran as the Socialist Party's candidate for president five times, beginning in 1900. His best showing came in 1912 when he won nearly 6 percent of the popular vote. In 1905 Debs helped found the Industrial Workers of the World, a radical alternative to the American Federation of Labor. Debs served two years in prison (1919–1921) for a 1918 speech denouncing the federal government's repressive wartime policies. Even behind bars, he polled nearly 920,000 votes in the 1920 presidential election. Afterward, he returned to Terre Haute, still committed to socialism but hampered by ill health.

Debs looms large in American labor history as an eloquent spokesperson for workers' rights and an early advocate of industrial unionism. Later, he became the most influential socialist in the nation's history. A spellbinding orator, he used the language of Christianity and American radicalism to argue for revolutionary change, widening socialism's appeal beyond the immigrant circles where it first won favor. Even after government repression and factionalism crippled the Socialist Party, Debs remained a popular symbol of dissent and egalitarianism.

[***See also* Debs, In re; Socialist Party of America; *and* Thomas, Norman.**]

BIBLIOGRAPHY

Ginger, Ray. *The Bending Cross, A Biography of Eugene Victor Debs*. New Brunswick, N.J.: Rutgers University Press, 1949.

Salvatore, Nick. *Eugene V. Debs: Citizen and Socialist*. Urbana: University of Illinois Press, 1982.

Joshua B. Freeman

DEBS, IN RE

158 U.S. 564 (1895), argued 25–26 March 1895, decided 27 May 1895 by vote of 9 to 0, Brewer for the Court. By refusing to grant a writ of habeas corpus to Eugene Debs, president of the American Railway Union, the Supreme Court sanctioned the use of injunctions against striking labor unions. During the depression of the 1890s, the Pullman Company, while still paying dividends, reduced its workers' pay literally to the starvation level. The laborers went on strike and were soon adopted by the newly formed American Railway Union. The union pursued a strategy of boycotting railroads using

Pullman cars. Members refused to handle trains with the cars; if dismissed by the road, then all the company's union members would strike. This plan was a direct challenge to the General Managers Association, a group of twenty-six Chicago railroads. Claiming that their contracts required them to use Pullman cars, they provoked strikes throughout the Midwest and nation by firing trainmen who refused to handle Pullman cars. Contending that the strikers were interfering with interstate commerce and the mails, the association urged federal intervention. Attorney General Richard Olney, fearing the violence of a large strike, came to the association's aid. Although wanting to send in the army, Olney settled initially for lesser measures. He created more than 5,000 special deputies to preserve order, prepared a case of criminal conspiracy against the union leaders, and sought an injunction in federal circuit court that would prohibit interference with the railroads' businesses. Not surprisingly, these actions and the activities of strikebreakers provoked rioting. To suppress violence, blown out of proportion by an alarmist press, the government sent in troops.

The federal circuit court, reasoning that the strike was a combination in restraint of interstate commerce, granted a sweeping injunction. The decree applied to the leaders of the union, all those who combined with them, and any persons whomsoever. It commanded such individuals to cease hindering the railroads, including by means of persuading employees, from carrying the mails and engaging in interstate commerce. Within a week of his arrest for criminal conspiracy, Debs and his fellow officers were again arrested for contempt of court for violating this injunction. While they were in jail the strike folded and the new union crumpled. Although the criminal trial collapsed, the contempt of court charge netted Debs six months' imprisonment. He sought release by writ of habeas corpus to the Supreme Court, arguing that he was tried for a criminal act in a court of equity and thus denied his constitutional right of trial by jury.

Justice David J. Brewer, speaking for a unanimous Supreme Court, rejected Debs's plea. Refusing to rest the decision on the narrow ground of a conspiracy in restraint of trade, he based the ruling on broad principles. Brewer asserted that the government of the United States, although a government of enumerated powers, had full attributes of sovereignty within those powers. It could forcibly remove any obstructions to commerce or the mails, either by military power or through an appeal to the federal courts' equity power. He labeled the union's action a public nuisance, which like a private nuisance was subject to equity jurisdiction. That Debs's acts violated the criminal law did not bar equitable relief. The actions also threatened the property rights of the railroads, which were protected under equity jurisdiction. Therefore, no matter what occurred on the criminal side of the law, the equity side could also be utilized. To preserve their authority in such equity proceedings courts needed the power to punish through contempt. Thus, Brewer rejected the argument that Debs had been denied jury trial. Brewer touted the use of federal tribunals as a better method than armed force in settling labor troubles; it met the potential mob violence not with force but with the rule of law. For the next thirty years, corporations faced with labor troubles turned to the federal courts; the Pullman injunction proved the model for many others. Not until the New Deal era did such labor injunctions fade away.

[*See also* **Debs, Eugene;** *and* **Supreme Court, U.S.**]

Richard F. Hamm

DECLARATION OF INDEPENDENCE

When the Second Continental Congress met in Philadelphia in May 1775, only a minority of delegates favored independence from Great Britain. Just a year later, however, sentiment for complete separation was strong enough to make a movement toward independence politically feasible. By that time George III had declared the colonies to be in rebellion, and Parliament had pronounced them beyond the protection of the Crown and forbidden all trade with them. Thomas Paine's *Common Sense,* published in January 1776 and widely circulated, forcefully and convincingly argued for a complete political and emotional break with the mother country.

By the spring of 1776 the delegates to the Continental Congress from the two largest colonies, Massachusetts and Virginia, strongly advocated independence. On 15 May, the delegates adopted John Adams's radical resolution that the colonies assume full powers of self-government and that all exercise of British authority be suppressed. On 7 June, Richard Henry Lee moved (and Adams seconded) that the colonies were "and of right ought to be, free and independent States." Four days later, Congress appointed a committee consisting of John Adams, Benjamin Franklin, Thomas Jefferson, Robert R. Livingston (1746–1813), and Roger Sherman (1721–1793) to draft a preamble to Lee's resolution. This preamble is what we know as the Declaration of Independence.

Jefferson, the youngest member of the committee and, according to John Adams, one with "reputation of a masterly pen," was chosen to prepare the document. Influenced by George Mason's draft of the Virginia Declaration of Rights and using the opening of his own first draft of the Virginia Constitution, Jefferson prepared a rough draft of the Declaration of Independence. He submitted it first to Adams and then to Franklin and other members of the committee for suggestions. They proposed some stylistic alterations and on 28 June the revised version was presented to Congress. On 2 July the Congress meeting as a committee of the whole adopted the Lee resolution, declaring independence without a negative vote (the New York delegation, waiting for new instructions, abstained). Between 2 and 4 July the committee's preamble, the Declaration, was debated. The congressional delegates, again meeting as a committee of the whole, further revised the document. The preamble was changed only in minor stylistic ways but major deletions were made in the list of grievances (see below). The Declaration was adopted on 4 July, and on 15 July, Congress directed that the word "Unanimous" be added to the document's official title, "Declaration of the Thirteen United States of America." After the official engrossed parchment copy was signed on 2 August, broadsides were distributed throughout the country.

Seeking not to set forth a new theory of government but to justify and publicize the American cause and to provide a philosophical rationale and political justification for independence, Jefferson turned to ideas that were the conventional wisdom of the day. He sought consensus, not originality. Among the ideas upon which he drew were those of natural law philosophy, the British Whig revolutionary tradition, and the Scottish enlightenment. Among these were the writings of John Locke, Algernon Sidney, John Trenchard, and Thomas Gordon. The Declaration proclaimed "self-evident truths": that all men are created equal and that they possess certain God-given rights by virtue of being human beings. Among these natural, "unalienable" rights are "Life, Liberty, and the pursuit of Happiness." The corollary of

Jefferson's premise was that government is instituted only to secure these rights and that whenever government fails in this duty, the people have the right "to alter or to abolish it" and institute a new one. Such a change, however, is not to be undertaken "for light and transient Causes."

The longest section of the document offered a catalog of grievances leveled not against Parliament but directly and personally at the Crown, to which, the colonists maintained, their loyalty was exclusively owed. These "facts submitted to a candid world" were systematically enumerated to demonstrate how patient the colonists had been in the face of repeated injury. Most of the accusations had been anticipated in earlier documents that Jefferson penned or contributed to (*A Summary View of the Rights of British America, Declaration of the Causes and Necessity for Taking Up Arms,* and the Preamble to the Virginia Constitution). Nineteen grievances, one of which is divided into eight parts, were included in the final version of the Declaration of Independence. Among the offenses of the king were refusing his assent to laws necessary for the public good, dissolving properly elected legislatures, creating a multitude of new offices "to harass our People," quartering armed troops in the colonies, imposing taxes without the consent of the people, ravaging coasts and burning towns, and inciting "domestic Insurrections." The repetition of the phrase "He has" before each of George III's misdeeds made a rhetorically powerful summary of "repeated Injuries and Usurpations" that could serve as useful propaganda for attracting support from other countries.

Most of the revisions that Congress made to the document tightened and improved the prose in this list of grievances. The most notable excision was a lengthy paragraph condemning the slave trade and holding George III responsible for its continuation by opposing all legislative efforts to halt it. Congress also softened Jefferson's strident criticism of the British electorate for failing to object to the abuses being heaped upon their compatriots in North America.

In the immediate postrevolution period, little attention seems to have been paid to the Declaration or its authorship. In the 1790s, a period of intense partisanship, however, the Republicans were eager to establish a connection between their party leader, Jefferson, and the nation's founding document. Federalists understandably played down the association. John Adams insisted that Jefferson had merely put a collaborative effort on paper.

Contemporary scholars tend to emphasize the social and cultural context of the document rather than the evolution of its text and the political ideas expressed in it. Criticized today for excluding blacks and women from its ringing assertion of equality, the Declaration of Independence nonetheless inspired the language and ideology of later social and political reform charters, including the declaration of the 1848 Seneca Falls woman's rights convention, which Elizabeth Cady Stanton explicitly modeled on the 1776 document.

[*See also* **Adams, John; Committees of Correspondence; *Common Sense*; Constitution; Continental Congress; Equality; Franklin, Benjamin; Jefferson, Thomas; Republicanism; Seneca Falls Women's Rights Convention of 1848;** *and* **Whig Party.**]

BIBLIOGRAPHY

Becker, Carl. *The Declaration of Independence: A Study in the History of Political Ideas.* New York: Harcourt Brace, 1922.

Boyd, Julian P. *The Declaration of Independence: The Evolution of a Text,* rev. ed. Charlottesville, Va.: International Center for Jefferson Studies at Monticello, 1999.

Fliegelman, Jay. *Declaring Independence: Jefferson, Natural Language and the Culture of Performance.* Stanford, Calif.: Stanford University Press, 1993.

Maier, Pauline. *American Scripture: Making the Declaration of Independence.* New York: Alfred A. Knopf, 1997.

McDonald, Robert M. S. "Thomas Jefferson's Changing Reputation as Author of the Declaration of Independence: The First Fifty Years." *Journal of the Early Republic* 19 (Summer 1999): 169–195.

Wills, Garry. *Inventing America.* Garden City, N.Y.: Doubleday, 1978.

Barbara B. Oberg

DEMOCRACY IN AMERICA

Democracy in America is an extended inquiry into the causes and effects of democracy in the modern world, with a focus on its operation in the United States. Written by a young French aristocrat, Alexis de Tocqueville (1805–1859), published in Paris in four volumes—two each in 1835 and 1840—translated in those same years by the Englishman Henry Reeve, and admiringly reviewed by John Stuart Mill in his *London and Westminster Review,* the work caused an immediate sensation. "Why, it seems you have written a masterpiece!" exclaimed Tocqueville's publisher, Gosselin, who followed a strict policy of not reading his authors' books (Lamberti, 1989, p. 121). The distinguished politician and judge John C. Spencer issued the first American edition in 1838, and so the work began its protracted American career as an often misunderstood classic.

In what we now call Volume I (the first two tomes), Tocqueville examined the consequences of building a political system on the principle of the sovereignty of the people. In the second volume (tomes three and four), he attended to the intellectual and emotional effects, as well as the characteristic patterns of social and political interaction, that resulted or could be anticipated to result from a democratic political culture.

In the 1835 volume, Tocqueville first investigated America's original "social state," with its historically peculiar combination of religiosity and political freedom; and then went on to describe local and state governments, the judiciary, the federal constitution, and the crucial role of political associations and newspapers. He considered the causes of democracy's endurance and concluded with a long, dark essay on the triangular relations among America's "three races"—the black, red, and white. Often scintillating in its observations contrasting aristocratic France with the boisterously democratic United States, the work delighted contemporary readers.

The next volume, published five years later, contains both superficial and profound research findings and reflections on what the author called "the influence of democracy." Tocqueville focuses on four areas: intellectual life, the emotions or sentiments, mores (the habitual intellectual and emotional states as they are manifest in collective behavior), and politics. As contemporaries noticed immediately, this second volume is distinctly more "abstract" than the first. The second volume seeks to explain general features of democratic eras and nations, with the United States often presented as an illustration of the ways in which the worst effects of democracy's evils might be either circumvented or moderated.

In *Democracy* Tocqueville introduced such key terms of modern political discourse as tyranny of the majority, individualism, and self-interest properly understood. Two themes of particular salience and enduring importance in the work are first that of the tension (not opposition) between equality and freedom; and second that of the different political trajectories taken by a democratic nation like France, in which democracy was introduced as a result of violent revolutionary upheaval, and the United States, where some degree of broad-based political freedom was evident from the earliest days of colonial settlement.

BIBLIOGRAPHY

Drescher, Seymour. "Tocqueville's Two Démocraties." *Journal of the History of Ideas* 25 (1964): 201–216.

Lamberti, Jean-Claude. *Tocqueville and the Two Democracies*. Translated by Arthur Goldhammer. Cambridge, Mass.: Harvard University Press, 1989.

Mancini, Matthew. *Alexis de Tocqueville and American Intellectuals: From His Time to Ours*. Lanham, Md.: Rowman & Littlefield, 2006.

Schleifer, James T. *The Making of Tocqueville's Democracy in America*. Indianapolis, Ind.: Liberty Fund, 2000.

Matthew J. Mancini

DEMOCRATIC PARTY

No certain date marks the beginning of the Democratic Party, but its intellectual heritage can be traced to Thomas Jefferson and James Madison, both of whom shunned parties even as they shaped the policies and sensibility of the so-called Democratic-Republican political movement during the 1790s. Opposing the centralizing programs of the secretary of the treasury Alexander Hamilton, who urged a revenue system based on tariffs, excise taxes, a federal bank, and funding of the national debt, Jefferson and Madison established enduring party themes. Champions of the common people, especially small farmers, they spoke for small and frugal government, of states' rights, and the people's sovereignty. In their presidential administrations from 1801 until 1817, the two Virginians sought to retire the national debt, remove the government from the nation's economic life, and rely on state militias rather than a federal army.

Although the Democrats had leaders, a program, and an ideology, they had no organization or loyal following until after 1828 when Andrew Jackson was elected president. The Democrats, who now embraced the name their enemies had employed to tarnish them as radicals, held national presidential nominating conventions beginning in 1832, making this the world's oldest continuing political party. Coalescing around the popular Jackson, they started campaign newspapers, organized local and state committees, and built support through barbecues and partisan clubs.

Jackson, in turn, using presidential patronage to solidify support, defined national issues—especially in his opposition to a national bank and to federally funded internal improvements. These positions linked Democrats throughout the country to an organization with a national identity distinct from the Whig Party (and later the Know-Nothing and Republican parties) in a competitive two-party system. By 1836 when master party-builder Martin Van Buren won the presidency, nearly 80 percent of white males were voting in national elections, with the Democrats the majority party controlling Congress and many state legislatures.

From 1840 to 1860, the Democrats displayed considerable resiliency. Although they elected presidents James Knox Polk, Franklin Pierce, and James Buchanan in this period, they faced a bitter sectional crisis. Recruiting urban German and Irish immigrants into their ranks, they achieved a nationwide constituency, only to see it shattered in the 1850s by congressional divisions over slavery in the territories and the emergence of a powerful Republican party in the North. On the eve of the Civil War, as party realignments shuffled the support of all political parties, the Democrats' power and programs tilted toward the South.

From 1860, when a divided Democratic Party offered the electorate two sectional candidates—Stephen A. Douglas of Illinois and Kentucky's John Breckinridge (1821–1875)—until the end of Reconstruction in 1877, the Democrats were a minority party. During the Civil War many leaders and supporters joined the Confederacy, and the majority Republicans tarred northern Democrats as disloyal copperheads. Still, even as Democrats opposed Emancipation and such popular Republican legislation as the Homestead Act and support for higher education, they continued to hold a third of the voters as well as a few northern governorships and legislatures.

After the war, Democrats came to embody white racism as they opposed the Reconstruction amendments granting freedmen citizenship and voting rights. White southerners' disproportionate power in the party was perpetuated by a party rule that presidential nominations must be approved by two-thirds, not just a majority, of convention delegates. Using voting-precinct surveys and door-to-door leafleting (a campaign strategy developed by New York's Samuel Tilden), Democrats captured the House of Representatives in 1874, stunningly demonstrating their durability. As Reconstruction collapsed and the South returned to white domination, the party's future was assured, albeit with a dependence on the South and the increasingly Democratic border states that lasted until after World War II. Urban ethnic voters and white southerners formed the party's core constituencies. Although failing to win the presidency apart from Grover Cleveland's two victories in 1884 and 1892, the late nineteenth-century Democratic Party elected significant numbers of congressmen and senators who, given seniority rules, dominated important committees.

From 1896 to 1932, Republicans overwhelmingly controlled the federal government. Even William Jennings Bryan, who sounded like a Jacksonian with his agrarian appeals and complaints about monopolies, could not win the presidency in 1896, 1900, or 1908. But Bryan marked a watershed in party thinking when he championed an activist government. The 1908 Democratic platform espoused regulation of trusts and railroads, a federal income tax, and a national health bureau. In keeping with the party themes of equal rights and opportunities for all, liberal Democrats came to accept government intervention as a necessity for the well-being of citizens in an industrial society.

Woodrow Wilson, in his successful presidential campaign of 1912, picked up on these themes with his New Freedom concept grounded in individual freedom achieved with the aid of the national government. Although Wilson won in 1912 primarily owing to a split in Republican ranks, he pursued a popular legislative agenda that included child-labor reform, aid to agriculture, federal income taxes, corporate regulations, and banking reform. In his second term (until incapacitated by a stroke in 1919) he identified the Democratic Party with an internationalist perspective sustained by party leaders throughout the remainder of the twentieth century.

The Democrats' long electoral drought in the 1920s ended in 1932 with the election of Franklin Delano Roosevelt. As the Republicans failed to meet the challenges of the Great Depression, the Democrats, led by the masterful coalition-builder Roosevelt, used the government to alleviate economic and social problems. For the first time, the party became popular among African Americans, historically attached to the party of Lincoln. The New Deal coalition of urban ethnic voters, blacks, farmers, union members, and (increasingly restive) white southerners enabled Roosevelt's successor Harry S. Truman to win election in his own right in 1948, sustained Democratic strength in Congress in the 1950s even as the Republicans regained the presidency, and undergirded the 1960s administrations of John F. Kennedy and Lyndon B. Johnson.

On foreign affairs, Democrats had historically differed widely, from Polk's expansionism to Bryan's pacifism and anti-imperialism to Wilson's internationalism. From the late 1930s through the Cold War, the party firmly espoused internationalism, military strength, and America's mission to resist totalitarianism of the right or left. Roosevelt stiffened the nation's resolve to battle fascism, and the Truman administration embraced America's postwar global role in the struggle against communism in Europe, Korea, and elsewhere. By the 1960s, the party's Cold War liberalism focused on Asia, as President Johnson, while championing social welfare and civil rights at home, also plunged the nation into full-scale war in Vietnam.

The late 1960s and 1970s brought a broad-based reaction against the Democrats, not only because of the Vietnam War's bitter legacy, but also because of the party's identification with welfare spending, school busing, racial preferences, and a series of volatile social issues from abortion to gay rights unpopular with conservatives. The party struggled to represent the interests of various minority constituencies while simultaneously offering a national vision, but Republican Richard M. Nixon defeated the liberal stalwart Hubert Humphrey in the 1968 presidential race and crushed the 1972 Democratic candidate, liberal senator George McGovern (1922–) of South Dakota. The southern Democrat Jimmy Carter narrowly won in 1976, in the aftermath of Watergate, but by the 1980s, as many white middle-class and working-class voters concluded that the party had abandoned "mainstream" values, millions of Roosevelt Democrats became Reagan Democrats.

As the twentieth century ended, Democratic and Republican leaders alike struggled to adapt in an era of diminished party loyalty, voter fractiousness, personalized overorganized politics, and the dominance of television. Divided government became the pattern: Democrats in the 1980s generally controlled Congress, the Republicans the presidency; in the 1990s, the situation was reversed.

Amid growing voter cynicism and apathy, Democratic neoliberals in Congress, organized as the Democratic Leadership Council, sought to erase the party's identification with big government and deficit spending. Adopting a centrist approach, Arkansas governor Bill Clinton proved a charismatic campaigner, returning the Democrats to the White House in 1992. Embracing deficit reduction and welfare reform, and aided by a buoyant economy, Clinton won reelection in 1996—only to endure the ignominy of an impeachment trial on charges arising from his efforts to conceal an affair with a White House intern. In the Cold War's aftermath, Clinton continued the tradition of Democratic internationalism, focusing now on regional peacekeeping, combating threats from rogue states, and promoting world trade.

Al Gore's narrow loss to George W. Bush after winning the popular vote in the disputed 2000 presidential election outraged and energized Democrats. But the party's 2004 presidential candidate, Massachusetts senator John Kerry, faced a challenge as he sought to uphold the party's liberal tradition, dating to the New Deal and Lyndon Johnson's Great Society, without alienating an increasingly conservative electorate hostile to big government, tax increases, and expansive social-welfare programs. As the Democratic Party continued to evolve 170 years after its founding, the question of what it fundamentally stood for still remained unresolved. After the defeat of its candidate Senator John Kerry in the 2004 presidential election, under the leadership of its national chairman Howard Dean, the Democratic Party began a controversial strategy to contest Republicans everywhere, even in the latter's safe districts. Meanwhile, the dissatisfaction of Americans with politics narrowed the base of both parties. More Americans identified themselves as independents amid an increasingly strident partisan atmosphere. In 2006 Democrats became the majority party in both the House and the Senate, and in 2008, Democrats won the presidency by seven percentage points, led by the charismatic Barack Obama, the first African American president in American history. In control of the legislature and executive, the Democrats enacted reforms in health care, the regulation of business, and, amid an economic recession and rising unemployment, a stimulus package. But two years later the party lost control of the House, as the political volatility of twenty-first-century American politics continued.

[*See also* **Affirmative Action; Bryan, William Jennings; Buchanan, James; Carter, Jimmy; Cleveland, Grover; Clinton, William J.; Compromise of 1877; Douglas, Stephen A.; Federal Government, Executive Branch: Presidency, The; Federal Government, Legislative Branch: House of Representatives; Federal Government, Legislative Branch: Senate; Gore, Albert A., Jr.; Jackson, Andrew; Jefferson, Thomas; Johnson, Lyndon B.; Kennedy, John F.; Kerry, John; Lesbian, Gay, Bisexual, and Transgender Rights Movement; Liberalism; Madison, James; New Deal; Obama, Barack; Party System; Pierce, Franklin; Political Parties; Polk, James Knox; Popular Sovereignty; Populist Era; Populist Party; Progressive Era; Progressive Party of 1912; Progressive Party of 1924; Progressive Party of 1948; Roosevelt, Franklin Delano; States' Rights; Truman, Harry S.; Van Buren, Martin;** *and* **Wilson, Woodrow.**]

BIBLIOGRAPHY

Cohn, David. *The Fabulous Democrats*. New York: Putnam, 1956.

Fisher, Murray, ed. *Of the People: The 200-Year History of the Democratic Party*. Los Angeles: General Publishing Group, 1992.

Goldman, Ralph. *The Democratic Party in American Politics*. New York: Macmillan, 1966.

Grantham, Dewey. *The Life and Death of the Solid South*. Ph.D. diss, University of Cincinnati, 1979.

Kovler, Peter, ed. *Democrats and the American Idea*. Washington, D.C.: Center for National Policy Press, 1992.

Rutland, Robert. *The Democrats: From Jefferson to Carter*. Baton Rouge: University of Louisiana Press, 1979.

Wade, Richard. "The Democratic Party, 1960–1972." in *History of U.S. Political Parties*, edited by Arthur Schlesinger, Jr., pp. 2827–2868. New York: Chelsea House, 1973.

Ware, Alan. *The Breakdown of the Democratic Party Organization*. Oxford; New York: Clarendon Press, 1985.

Jean Harvey Baker

DISASTER POLICY, FEDERAL

Whether caused by humans or nature, a disaster is an acute, unexpected event that inflicts serious harm on people or environments. Social scientists have argued that there really is no such thing as a purely natural disaster. Rather, disasters are a combination of human decisions and natural conditions that contribute to the risk for, and consequences of, all disasters. A massive flood in an uninhabited region is part of nature's cycle of renewal; when humans build a city in a floodplain, the deluge becomes a disaster. Disaster policy can be defined as what a government chooses to do, or not to do, about disasters.

Twentieth-Century Disaster Policy. Disasters in the contemporary United States are public problems that citizens want government to address. This was not always the case, however. U.S. federal disaster policy was mostly ad hoc and disjointed from its founding to the early 1900s. Congress provided some financial relief after major disasters, but left the responsibility for disaster preparation, response, and recovery to states and localities.

Eventually, a number of factors led to a greater federal government role in disaster relief and recovery in the twentieth century. These factors included a newly assertive post–Civil War state, major disasters that earned national attention, such as the San Francisco earthquake and the Galveston hurricane, and politicians' realization that constituents gave them credit for delivering disaster aid.

After the destructive Mississippi Flood of 1927, federal agencies offered loans for flood recovery, and Congress and the president centralized federal government disaster management. Many of the earliest federal disaster management agencies focused on civil defense or protection against a nuclear attack following World War II. These agencies included the Federal Civil Defense Administration and the Office of Defense Mobilization, which were combined in the Office of Civil Defense Mobilization in 1958. While participating in drills to prepare for attack, state and local officials sometimes used civil defense programs to bolster defenses against natural disasters by building evacuation routes or shelters.

Following a period of intense hurricane activity along the East Coast during the 1950s and 1960s, the Kennedy administration created the Office of Emergency Preparedness inside the White House to oversee federal disaster response. More hurricane activity and severe flooding led to passage of the National Flood Insurance Act of 1968, which established a program to offset the costs of disaster recovery. Congress further expanded the federal role when it passed the Disaster Relief Act of 1974, which specified the conditions under which federal agencies could intervene in disaster preparations and response. Disaster programs remained scattered among dozens of federal agencies until 1979, when President Jimmy Carter issued an executive order to merge many existing disaster programs into the new Federal Emergency Management Agency (FEMA), which became a single point of contact for states seeking disaster assistance.

Although there were few major disasters during the 1970s and 1980s, there were other significant changes in policy driven by congressional, state, and local demands to better organize federal assistance. The Stafford Act of 1988 gave the president authority to issue a disaster declaration that would open a wide range of federal assistance to states and localities. The act also established a disaster relief fund as part of the federal budget that agencies could use to manage relief operations from year to year, although Congress continued to appropriate additional monies for assistance following major disasters.

The Politics of Disaster. Over time, disaster policies have given politicians new tools to reward favored constituencies. From 1953 to 1969, Presidents Eisenhower, Kennedy, and Johnson averaged about 1.3 major disaster declarations per month; from 1989 to 2005, George H. W. Bush, Bill Clinton, and George W. Bush averaged 3.9 major disaster declarations per month. Economists Thomas Garrett and Russell Sobel (2003) have argued that from 1991 to 1999 states politically important to a president had a higher rate of disaster declaration by the chief executive and that disaster expenditures were higher in states that had congressional representation on FEMA oversight committees.

During periods of poor performance or scandal, disaster agencies have been lightening rods for criticism. Under the Reagan and George H. W. Bush administrations, FEMA drew criticism for its slow and sometimes bungling response to disasters and for its heavy emphasis on civil defense and national security programs. In 1993, President Bill Clinton appointed James Lee Witt as the FEMA director and gave the agency cabinet-level status. The agency promptly reversed course, from being vilified in Congress and the media to becoming a trusted brand name. The agency's improved reputation was associated with a number of factors: it reduced its national security programs, emphasized its natural disasters mission, was lucky not to experience a devastating event, and added experienced emergency managers, a new field that emerged after civil defense.

The Witt-era FEMA also embraced a new all-hazards, all-phases concept developed by emergency managers to guide disaster policy at all levels of government. The all-hazards concept means that disaster organizations would use much the same personnel, plans, and equipment to prepare for and respond to many kinds of disasters, rather than rely on stovepiped, disaster-specific programs. The all-phases idea means that disaster organizations would be responsible for the full timeline of a disaster, from preparation for an event, to response, helping communities recover, and mitigation. The all-hazards, all-phases idea caught on, and it helped to break down the silos of national security and civil defense programs in FEMA.

After the terrorist attacks of September 2001, a reorganization grafted FEMA into the newly formed Department of Homeland Security (DHS). FEMA lost its cabinet-level status and renewed its focus on terrorism. In the April 2005 version of National Planning Scenarios issued by the DHS to guide state and local planning, only two of the fifteen scenarios were natural disasters. The DHS took credit for preventing terrorist attacks, but many of the agencies responsible for intelligence gathering and interdiction were outside the department.

In 2004 hurricanes wreaked havoc along the Florida coast—one of the most active seasons on record. The following year, Hurricanes Katrina and Rita devastated the Gulf Coast, leaving approximately 1,800 people dead and causing more than $100 billion in property damage. Most of the fatalities occurred in and around New Orleans, which had not been evacuated prior to the hurricane's landfall. Congress authorized $62 billion in supplemental funding within two months of the disaster, and it appropriated billions more for extended rebuilding operations in the Gulf region.

Federal agencies, state and local officials, and private citizens failed to implement plans that could have saved lives and property in Louisiana and Mississippi. News reports focused on the inexperience of FEMA director Michael Brown and a lack of coordination among government agencies. Although states and localities were responsible for incomplete evacuations and poor planning and land use, FEMA's reputation suffered the most, and Brown resigned shortly after the storm.

Post-Katrina Policy. The criticism of the federal government following Katrina resulted in two significant changes. First, confusion among levels of government about who is in charge during a disaster led to efforts to clarify when federal government and military intervention is appropriate. The federal government can intervene in a natural disaster only at the request of a governor. After the governor's request, the president decides whether to issue a formal disaster declaration. Post-Katrina reforms retained state and local primacy in disaster response, but added tools for the federal government to cooperate with subnational governments before, during, and after disaster.

Second, Katrina exposed the vulnerability of urban populations living in hazardous areas. Reforms after the hurricane focused on building resiliency among high-risk communities so that they could evacuate or recover themselves. Other reforms emphasized better planning so that, for example, it was clear who would evacuate nursing home patients before a storm.

Yet the degree to which these new policy changes incorporate the lessons learned after a disaster remains unclear. For example, following Katrina reformers recommended redesigning New Orleans as a resilient community, but most of the reconstruction has focused on rebuilding the same areas that were devastated by the hurricane. And the levees, which failed after the storm, are only being rebuilt to Category 3 levels although Katrina was a Category 5 hurricane. Flood insurance reforms have also stalled in Congress in recent years, despite the fact that Katrina increased the National Flood Insurance Program's debt by over $16 billion—an amount it will likely never repay.

The Deepwater Horizon oil spill of 2010 reminded the public that industrial accidents were also subject to disaster policy. Since the spill's initial explosion occurred in federal waters, federal agencies and particularly the Coast Guard took responsibility for containing the fire aboard the rig, containing the spill, and cleaning up the surface oil. However, the long-term environmental impacts of the spill and its impact on federal disaster policy remain in question, and the spill exposed tensions among states, localities, private industry, and the federal government.

[*See also* **Homeland Security, Department of;** *and* **Oklahoma City Bombing.**]

BIBLIOGRAPHY

Birkland, Thomas. *After Disaster: Agenda Setting, Public Policy and Focusing Events.* Washington, D.C.: Georgetown University Press, 1997.

Daniels, Ronald, Donald Kettl, and Howard Kunreuther, eds. *On Risk and Disaster: Lessons from Hurricane Katrina.* Philadelphia: University of Pennsylvania Press, 2006.

Garrett, Thomas A., and Russell S. Sobel. "The Political Economy of FEMA Disaster Payments." *Economic Inquiry* 41 (2003): 496–509.

Mileti, Dennis. *Disasters by Design: A Reassessment of Natural Hazards in the United States.* Washington, D.C.: Joseph Henry Press, 1999.

Platt, Rutherford. *Disasters and Democracy: The Politics of Extreme Natural Events.* Washington, D.C.: Island Press, 1999.

Roberts, Patrick S. "FEMA and the Prospects for Reputation-Based Autonomy." *Studies in American Political Development* 20 (Spring 2006), 57–87.

Andrew F. Coffey and Patrick S. Roberts

DISTRICT OF COLUMBIA v. HELLER

The Second Amendment of the U.S. Constitution reads, "A well regulated Militia, being necessary to the security of a free State, the right of the people to keep and bear Arms, shall not be infringed." Despite the amendment's brevity, its purpose and meaning have been the focus of an ongoing and at times bitter cultural, political, and legal debate.

Interpretations of the Second Amendment's precise meaning and scope vary widely, but generally fall into two broad camps. The first views the amendment as protecting the state militia from disarmament by the federal government. This is often referred to as the "militia-based" or "collective rights" view of the amendment, and it arguably held sway in law and scholarship for most of American history. The second camp sees the Second Amendment as focused on the individual's right to keep and bear arms to defend him- or herself from private violence or to deter or fight off a tyrannical government. This is often called the "individual rights" approach, and it has been ascendant in scholarly and popular opinion since the 1980s.

The central issue in 2008's *District of Columbia v. Heller* involved which of these interpretations is correct. A five-justice majority came down squarely on the side of the individual rights view. Relying heavily on the method of constitutional interpretation known as originalism—an approach that gives special weight to the "original" understanding of a constitutional provision—Justice Antonin Scalia wrote for the majority that the Second Amendment guaranteed an individual the right to keep and bear arms whether or not that individual was associated with a state militia.

Four justices dissented in two separate opinions. Justice John Paul Stevens's dissent presented originalist and other evidence in an effort to demonstrate that the majority's interpretation of the amendment was simply incorrect. Justice Stephen Breyer's dissent criticized the majority opinion from a different angle, arguing among other things that it did not give sufficient weight to the government's interest in gun control and failed to provide workable rules for evaluating the constitutionality of gun control.

Heller left open at least two large questions. The first was whether the Second Amendment applied to gun control laws passed by the states. In 2010's *McDonald v. Chicago,* the Court answered that question in the affirmative, again in a splintered set of opinions.

The second question left unanswered by *Heller* was what types of gun control are constitutional. The regulation struck down in *Heller* was effectively a ban on the possession of handguns in the District of Columbia. The Court noted, however, that its holding should not be read to cast doubt on other long-standing gun regulations, such as bans on possession by felons or the mentally ill or on dangerous and unusual weapons. The next wave of Second Amendment cases has already begun to test the constitutional validity of these and other restrictions. How the Supreme Court will handle that wave, whenever it crests, remains to be seen.

[*See also* **Constitutional Interpretation; Gun Control;** ***and*** **Second Amendment.**]

BIBLIOGRAPHY

Levinson, Sanford. "The Embarrassing Second Amendment." *The Yale Law Journal* 99 (1989): 637–659.

Joseph Blocher

DIXIECRATS

The Dixiecrats were white southerners whose opposition to civil rights reform led them to disaffiliate from the Democratic Party and form the splinter States' Rights Democratic Party in 1948. President Harry Truman had aroused the enmity of southern Democrats with a series of initiatives intended to promote racial equality, including the appointment of a Committee on Civil Rights and the issuing of executive orders that desegregated the armed forces and guaranteed fair employment practices in the civil service. Tensions between southern and northern Democrats resulted in dramatic confrontation when the party held its convention at Philadelphia in July 1948. When southerners failed to soften the strong civil rights plank adopted as part of the party platform, all of the Mississippi delegates and half of those from Alabama stormed out of the convention. With the exception of a small number of party loyalists, the remaining southern delegates tried unsuccessfully to secure the nomination of Senator Richard Russell of Georgia. Southern dissenters reconvened in Birmingham, Alabama, where they established the breakaway States' Rights Democratic Party. Its members nominated Governor Strom Thurmond of South Carolina and Governor Fielding Wright of Alabama as their respective presidential and vice presidential candidates.

The States' Rights Democratic Party (or Dixiecrats) did not expect to win the presidential election but still hoped to influence its outcome. Securing the 127 electoral votes of the southern states would ensure that neither the Republican nor the Democratic presidential candidate could win an overall majority. With the election thrown into the House of Representatives, the Dixiecrats hoped to use their position as power brokers to demand concessions on the civil rights issue in return for their support.

Southern voters nonetheless proved reluctant to abandon their traditional loyalty to the Democratic Party. The Dixiecrat ticket won only four southern states: Alabama, Mississippi, Louisiana, and South Carolina. The failure of the Dixiecrat revolt was the result of several factors, including a lack of clarity about how it intended to resist civil rights reform. Its emphasis on states' rights also alarmed the emerging entrepreneurial and professional classes who benefited from the federal investment that transformed the southern economy after World War II.

Despite its failure, the Dixiecrat revolt had important repercussions. First, it represented the potential for electoral realignment in the South as white voters abandoned the Democrats for the Republicans. Second, it delineated the battle lines in the civil rights struggles of the 1950s and 1960s. Most of the support for the Dixiecrats came from the Black Belt, the plantation counties where whites were a minority of the population. It was there that the decline in the traditional rural economy and the increasing politicization of African Americans most threatened white supremacy and stimulated massive resistance to civil rights reform.

[*See also* **Civil Rights; States' Rights; States' Rights Party;** *and* **Truman, Harry S.**]

BIBLIOGRAPHY

Fredrickson, Kari. *The Dixiecrat Revolt and the End of the Solid South, 1932–1968*. Chapel Hill: University of North Carolina Press, 2001.

Garson, Robert A. *The Democratic Party and the Politics of Sectionalism, 1941–1948*. Baton Rouge: Louisiana State University Press, 1974.

Clive Webb

DOUGLAS, STEPHEN A.

(1813–1861), U.S. senator, presidential candidate. Arriving in Illinois as a young man from his native Vermont, Stephen A. Douglas practiced law and played a key role in building the state Democratic Party. Serving in the U.S. House of Representatives (1843–1847) and the Senate (1847–1861), he attained a party leadership role and a command of the legislative process unsurpassed in his generation. Called "the Little Giant" for his short height and lowering reputation, he worked indefatigably to promote his region's interests, especially geographic expansion and railroad construction. Reluctantly addressing the issue of slavery in the territories, Douglas adopted the formula known as "popular sovereignty"—that is, leaving the issue to local control—as he engineered passage of the Compromise of 1850.

If Douglas adopted popular sovereignty as an expedient, he embraced it thereafter as a principle, with ironic effects. His application of the doctrine in the Kansas–Nebraska Act (1854), which abandoned the geographic restraints on slavery written into the Missouri Compromise (1820), led directly to the creation of the Republican Party. His use of the doctrine to block Kansas's admission as a slave state alienated the South and hastened the sectional split of the Democratic Party. His defense of popular sovereignty in his famous debates with Abraham Lincoln in the 1858 Illinois senatorial race, although securing his reelection, served mainly to boost the fame of his Republican rival. Douglas won the presidential nomination of the northern Democrats in 1860, but was defeated by Lincoln and the Republicans, which in turn triggered secession. Although Douglas venerated the Union, he figured prominently in many of the events leading to its disruption.

[*See also* **Compromise of 1850; Democratic Party; Federal Government, Legislative Branch: House of Representatives; Federal Government, Legislative Branch: Senate; Kansas–Nebraska Act; Lincoln, Abraham; Lincoln–Douglas Debates;** ***and*** **Popular Sovereignty.**]

BIBLIOGRAPHY

Johannsen, Robert W. *Stephen A. Douglas*. New York: Oxford University Press, 1973.

George B. Forgie

DOUGLAS, WILLIAM O.

(1898–1980), associate justice of the U.S. Supreme Court. A native of Minnesota, Douglas graduated from Columbia Law School in 1925 and later taught at Yale Law School. A New Deal Democrat, he served on the Securities and Exchange Commission from 1935 to 1939, the final years as chairman. President Franklin Delano Roosevelt appointed him to the Supreme Court in 1939. Douglas promoted the causes of human dignity and individual liberties, most often grounding his decisions in the Bill of Rights. His judicial positions sought, in the words of a 1968 opinion, "to take the government off of the backs of the people." For Douglas, that meant full constitutional protection for all, including the despised and defenseless. His 1953 stay of execution for the convicted spies Julius and Ethel Rosenberg triggered one of four congressional impeachment efforts. His most famous opinion, in *Griswold v. Connecticut* (1965), established a constitutional right to privacy and laid the foundation for the controversial *Roe v. Wade* decision (1973) upholding a woman's constitutional right to an abortion.

Douglas wrote more than a dozen books, providing lively narratives of his world travels and wilderness expeditions and promoting his cherished causes, particularly environmentalism and protection of civil liberties. He was married four times and his freewheeling lifestyle coupled with his outspoken libertarianism outraged conservatives. Even his supporters sometimes found the willful, irascible Douglas easier to admire than to like. But for them, he stood as a symbol of the unwavering belief that individuals could improve the nation and the world.

[*See also* **Bill of Rights; Civil Liberties; Environmentalism;** ***Griswold v. Connecticut;*** **New Deal;** ***Roe v. Wade;*** **Roosevelt, Franklin**

Delano; Rosenberg Case; ***and*** **Securities and Exchange Commission.]**

BIBLIOGRAPHY

Douglas, William O. *The Court Years.* New York: Random House, 1980.

Douglas, William O. *Go East Young Man.* New York: Random House, 1974.

Simon, James F. *Independent Journey: The Life of William O. Douglas.* New York: Harper & Row, 1980.

James F. Simon

DOUGLASS, FREDERICK

(1818–1895), abolitionist, reformer, author. Born Frederick Bailey in rural Maryland to an enslaved woman and her master, he spent his youth alternately as a field hand and household servant in Baltimore, where his mistress gave him an aborted education. Returned to farm labor when his Baltimore master died, he attempted to flee, resulting in an often recounted showdown with the slave breaker Edward Covey, whom he vanquished. Douglass recorded his slave experiences in three autobiographies: *Narrative of the Life of Frederick Douglass* (1845), *My Bondage and My Freedom* (1855), and *Life and Times of Frederick Douglass* (1881).

In 1838 he fled North, married a free black, and worked on the docks in New Bedford, Massachusetts. He met the abolitionist leader William Lloyd Garrison in 1839; in 1841, after an impromptu antislavery speech in Nantucket, Massachusetts, he became an agent of the Massachusetts Anti-Slavery Society. He lectured widely, and his *Narrative* sold more than any other autobiography by a former slave. Only *Uncle Tom's Cabin* rivaled its impact. After two years in the British Isles (1845–1847), Douglass broke with Garrison over the latter's rejection of political means to end slavery. Purchasing his freedom and settling in Rochester, New York, he edited a series of antislavery periodicals: *North Star* (1847–1851), renamed *Frederick Douglass' Paper* (1851–1860), and *Douglas' Monthly* (1859–1863). His writings, urging the nation to return to first principles and warning of the dangers of apostasy, exemplify the jeremiad (an allusion to the biblical prophet Jeremiah), a literary genre stretching from Cotton Mather to Martin Luther King Jr. His autobiographies embody another long American literary tradition extolling the individual's capacity for self-fashioning and social mobility through the cultivation of moral virtue. His thought never represented a consensus, however. His advocacy of racial assimilation, his rejection of black nationalism as impractical, and his support for the woman suffrage movement all roused criticism, as did his 1884 marriage to a white woman.

Douglass viewed the Civil War as a millennial struggle between liberty and tyranny. Through his wartime writings and his role in recruiting two black regiments (the Massachusetts Fifty-fourth and Fifty-fifth), he sought to transform a war to preserve the Union into one to abolish slavery—a goal achieved with the Thirteenth Amendment (1865). Douglass continued his journalistic efforts with the *New National Era* (1870–1874), but the promise of the postslavery era quickly faded as reformers encountered entrenched racism in the Reconstruction Era South. As the North's commitment to biracial democracy gave way to efforts at sectional reconciliation, Douglass's faith in the nation waned. As race relations reached their nadir, he consoled himself with a series of minor government posts: U.S. marshal (1877–1881) and recorder of deeds (1881–1886) in Washington, D.C., and consul general in Haiti (1889–1891). Like many of his generation, he had attributed the evils of racism to the institution of slavery. The post–Civil War Era exposed the fallacy of that view as well as the limits of his self-help ideology as a vehicle for racial equality and African American social mobility.

[*See also* **Antislavery Movement;** *and* **Woman Suffrage Movement.**]

BIBLIOGRAPHY

Blight, David W. *Frederick Douglass' Civil War: Keeping Faith in Jubilee.* Baton Rouge: Louisiana State University Press, 1989.

McFeely, William S. *Frederick Douglass.* New York: W. W. Norton, 1991.

Patrick Rael

DRUG CONTROL POLICY, OFFICE OF NATIONAL

The White House Office of National Drug Control Policy (ONDCP), a component of the Executive Office of the President, establishes policies, priorities, and objectives for the U.S. drug control program. Its primary aims are to reduce the illegal use, manufacturing, and trafficking of drugs as well as drug-related crime, violence, and health consequences.

The ONDCP was created by a provision of the Anti–Drug Abuse Act of 1988 to develop and manage a national drug control strategy and to certify all federal drug control budgets. The ONDCP was built on the precedent established when the first White House drug chief was named on 17 June 1971 and then solidified with the creation of the Special Action Office for Drug Abuse Prevention (SAODAP) in 1972. The termination of SAODAP on 30 June 1975 led to a series of novel administrative formats that continued the White House Drug Office from 1975 until the creation of ONDCP in 1988.

Over the course of this time, the primary focus on drug policy changed from the heroin epidemic of the 1970s and its relationship to crime to the crack cocaine epidemic in the late 1980s. In 1989 William J. Bennett was named the first director of ONDCP, a position that required confirmation by the U.S. Senate.

Each year ONDCP publishes the National Drug Control Strategy, which establishes a program, budget, and guidelines for cooperation among federal, state, and local organizations and agencies. The ONDCP director evaluates, coordinates, and oversees all of the international and domestic antidrug efforts of the executive branch. The director advises the president on drug policy and of the activities of the federal agencies that could affect U.S. antidrug efforts. The director also oversees the federal agency compliance with their obligations under the national strategy.

Before the creation of ONDCP, early White House drug policy leadership roles varied in title and in office. These positions, like that of ONDCP Director, have been termed "Drug Czar." The following individuals served in this role under the president with three serving in Cabinet positions, indicated by an asterisk:

1971–1973	Jerome H. Jaffe, MD (Richard M. Nixon)
1973–1977	Robert L. DuPont, MD (Richard M. Nixon, Gerald R. Ford)
1977–1978	Peter G. Bourne, MD (James E. Carter, Jr.)
1978–1981	Lee I. Dogoloff, LCSW (James E. Carter, Jr.)
1982–1984	Carlton E. Turner, PhD (Ronald W. Reagan)
1984–1989	D. Ian MacDonald, MD (Ronald W. Reagan)
1989–1990	William Bennett, PhD (George H. W. Bush)
1991–1993	Bob Martinez (George H. W. Bush)

1993–1995	Lee Brown* (William J. Clinton)
1996–2001	General Barry McCaffrey* (William J. Clinton)
2001–2009	John Walters* (George W. Bush)
2009–Present	R. Gil Kerlikowske (Barack H. Obama)

[*See also* **Drugs, Illicit;** *and* **Federal Government, Executive Branch: Presidency, The.**]

BIBLIOGRAPHY

35th Anniversary of the White House Drug Czar. 16 June 2006. Symposium conducted at the University of Maryland, College Park. Center for Substance Abuse Research and the Institute for Behavior and Health, Inc.

Acker, C. J. *Creating the American Junkie: Addiction Research in the Classic Era of Narcotic Control.* Baltimore: Johns Hopkins University Press, 2002.

Campbell, N. D. *Discovering Addiction: The Science and Politics of Substance Abuse Research.* Ann Arbor: University of Michigan Press, 2007.

Courtwright, D. T. *Dark Paradise: A History of Opiate Addiction in America.* Cambridge, Mass.: Harvard University Press, 2001.

Courtwright, D. T. *Forces of Habit: Drugs and the Making of the Modern World.* Cambridge, Mass.: Harvard University Press, 2002.

Musto, D. F., ed. *One Hundred Years of Heroin.* Westport, Conn.: Auburn House, 2002.

Musto, D. F., and Korsmeyer, P. *The Quest for Drug Control: Politics and Federal Policy in a Period of Increasing Substance Abuse, 1963–1981.* New Haven, Conn.: Yale University Press, 2002.

Robert L. DuPont

DRUGS, ILLICIT

In the beginning there were no illicit drugs. From the seventeenth through the early nineteenth centuries, narcotics were simply part of medical practice. A few patients—and doctors—exhibited symptoms of opium addiction, but they were never numerous and posed no threat to the social order. The main problems were overdose and adulteration. Imported from the Middle East, opium often contained sand, fruit pulp, flour, beeswax, lead, and the like. Indeed, the first national drug law, enacted in 1848, was intended to bar adulterated foreign drugs, not drugs per se.

In the later nineteenth century, narcotic addiction took on a more visible and sinister aspect. Morphine, the principal alkaloid of opium, came into wide use with the spread of hypodermic medication in the 1860s and 1870s. Morphine injected hypodermically was more addictive than opium taken orally. By the mid-1890s, perhaps as many as many as 220,000 Americans were addicted to morphine or another medicinal opiate. Contrary to legend, most were not Civil War veterans, but rather ailing women introduced to morphine by physicians or through patent medicines, which often contained narcotics and alcohol.

Habitual opium smokers, mostly Chinese laborers and members of the white underworld, were less common, numbering at most 90,000 by the mid-1890s. Regarded far less sympathetically than medical addicts, they inspired restrictive local and state legislation, typically designed to outlaw public opium dens. The possibility of sexual relations between white women and Chinese men in the dens stirred fears, although in fact Chinese smokers usually kept to themselves.

Nonmedical cocaine use inspired similar sexual anxieties. Like morphine, cocaine began its career as a promising new alkaloid drug. In the mid-1880s Parke, Davis, its leading U.S. manufacturer, promoted cocaine for a range of illnesses, from hay fever to alcoholism. Cocaine's outstanding therapeutic property, the local anesthesia first noted in

1884, helped to revolutionize surgery and dentistry. But overdose cases soon appeared in the medical literature along with, as early as 1886, warnings of addiction resulting from medical treatment.

In the 1890s, the popular press chronicled the growing use of cocaine in the underworld, where prostitutes, pimps, and gamblers added cocaine to their repertoire of cigarettes, alcohol, and opium. In 1900, half the prostitutes jailed in the Fort Worth, Texas, were said to be cocaine addicts. By then cocaine was sufficiently cheap that ordinary laborers, including African Americans working on southern plantations and construction sites, could afford occasional use. A racially charged folklore sprang up, linking African American cocaine use to violent rampages and "increased and perverted" sexual desires.

Alarmed city councils and state legislatures passed laws restricting cocaine's purchase to those holding a prescription from a licensed physician—a provision increasingly applied to opiates as well. But economic and competitive considerations tempted physicians, particularly older and marginal practitioners, to continue to prescribe liberally. Conscientious pharmacists criticized such practices and found catering to addicts distasteful. But they knew that spurned customers would take their lucrative business to rival druggists or, if necessary, to street dealers, middlemen who resold drugs acquired from unscrupulous pharmacists or manufacturers. Their customers included teenage boys in slums and vice districts who snorted "decks" of cocaine and heroin, a powerful derivative of morphine. Opium smokers also enjoyed a ready supply, courtesy of smugglers and illegal manufacturers who dodged the heavy customs duty. The cliché that the 1914 Harrison Narcotic Act created the black market and drug subcultures of twentieth-century America is a political myth. Illegal sales, smuggling, and underworld use flourished decades before 1914. Drug abuse and trafficking spawned legislation, not the other way around.

The catalyst for national legislation, however, was the diplomatic situation in East Asia. American missionaries had long deplored the British opium trade in China. In 1905 they helped secure a policy of suppressing opium smoking in the Philippines, which had become a U.S. possession. In 1906 Bishop Brent asked for President Theodore Roosevelt's help in setting up an international opium conference, which finally convened in Shanghai in February 1909. But although the U.S. government was calling for suppression of the Asian opium traffic, it continued to tolerate (and tax) opium smoking at home. To refute charges of hypocrisy, Roosevelt's secretary of state, Elihu Root, persuaded Congress to prohibit imports of opium prepared for smoking. This legislation, signed into law a week after the opening of the 1909 Shanghai conference, represented the first nationwide ban on a particular type of drug. In this sense, smoking opium was America's first "illicit drug."

The next major piece of legislation, the 1914 Harrison Narcotic Act, required dealers in opiates and cocaine to register, pay a nominal tax, and keep accurate records of their transactions. Unregistered dealers faced prosecution. Thus, narcotic distribution would be confined to legitimate medical channels and made a matter of public record.

The Harrison Act skirted a key issue: whether registered doctors and pharmacists could legally maintain a supply of drugs for those who were addicted. In 1919 the U.S. Supreme Court, in the 5-to-4 Webb decision, ruled that they could not. The federal antimaintenance policy, for which Webb provided the key precedent, had lasting implications, particularly after the Treasury Department quickly closed more than thirty experimental municipal clinics designed to provide a legal supply of drugs for addicts, forcing them into the black market.

In the 1920s, street drugs, mostly diverted from surplus European manufactures, were still relatively pure. However, international agreements in 1925 and 1931 made the large-scale diversion of legally manufactured drugs more difficult. Smuggled and adulterated heroin became the mainstay of the black market, which centered on New York City, home to approximately half the nation's nonmedical narcotic addicts. In 1924 Congress effectively outlawed heroin, which, like smoking opium, was associated with vice and crime.

The Bureau of Narcotics, under the direction of Harry J. Anslinger from 1930 to 1962, vigorously suppressed the illicit drug traffic. Anslinger wanted traffickers behind bars and addicts in jail or in institutions like the federal prison hospitals in Lexington, Kentucky, or Fort Worth, Texas. Anslinger also worked to increase the scope and penalties of drug laws. He played a key role in the passage of the 1937 Marijuana Tax Act, which added a national ban to state and local legislation. Practically unknown before 1910, marijuana smoking was introduced by Mexican immigrant laborers and by Caribbean and South American sailors visiting New Orleans. By the 1930s it had spread to New York, Chicago, and other cities. Popular among jazz musicians and urban hipsters, marijuana offered a cheap high, 15 cents for a "reefer" in a Harlem "tea pad." At first, Anslinger and other authorities condemned marijuana for inciting wild violence. Later they emphasized its role as a stepping-stone drug. Over half of young heroin addicts had started with marijuana, Anslinger testified in 1951. "They took to the needle when the thrill of marijuana was gone."

Although most young addicts had smoked marijuana, the most important precursors of heroin addiction were social and geographic. The typical postwar addict was a young man living in a ghetto or barrio near a heroin trafficking areas in New York, Chicago, Los Angeles, or another large industrial city. He had come from a single-parent family, dropped out of high school, and had poor job prospects and few conventional aspirations. He aspired instead to a hipster lifestyle centered on jazz, drugs, and "hustling"—criminal activity that accelerated the flight of longtime residents and businesses, feeding a lethal cycle of isolation, poverty, and depopulation. "Heroin," as historian Eric Schneider put it, "was a city-killing drug." Increasingly, it was also an African American drug. The older white and Chinese narcotic addicts, who had been addicted before World War II, were either burning out or dying off. In the early 1930s only one of every four Detroit addicts known to officials was African American. By 1951, four of five were.

Concern over the post–World War II resurgence of heroin trafficking and addiction prompted Congress to enact the 1951 Boggs Act and 1956 Narcotic Control Act, which provided progressively stiffer mandatory sentences, all the way up to the death penalty for selling heroin to minors. States followed suit. Texas made marijuana possession punishable by life imprisonment. The prison-mindedness of drug policy provoked a reaction among those who viewed addiction as a public health problem. In 1958 a joint committee of the American Bar Association and the American Medical Association criticized the police approach and suggested the possibility of a controlled legal supply. In the 1960s, two physicians, Vincent Dole and Marie Nyswander, showed that heroin addicts could be maintained indefinitely on oral methadone, a synthetic narcotic. Their work challenged both the antimaintenance policy and the reigning explanation of addiction, which held that addicts suffered from defective, often psychopathic, personalities. But for Dole and Nyswander, addicts were more or less normal persons whose drug use triggered a permanent metabolic change. They needed narcotics the way a diabetic needed insulin. Methadone maintenance satisfied that need and kept them out of the illicit market.

Methadone maintenance proved to be a cost-effective treatment for narcotic addiction. Methadone patient rolls expanded rapidly during the heroin epidemic of the late 1960s and early 1970s, when the country had an estimated half-million narcotic addicts. After 1974, however, methadone's star faded because of more onerous federal regulations, local resistance to clinics, and its therapeutic irrelevance to marijuana, cocaine, lysergic acid diethylamide (LSD), and other drugs popular in the youthful counterculture.

The efflorescence of that counterculture and the rapid spread of illicit drug use among middle-class youth had no precedent in American history. Critics blamed lax parental discipline, a commercialized ethos of self-gratification, antiwar protest, and proselytizing gurus like poet Allen Ginsberg, novelist Ken Kesey, and one-time Harvard psychologist Timothy Leary, whose psychedelic gospel attracted widespread media attention. Public health experts noted the growing consumption of alcohol and tobacco, which served as social and pharmacological "gateways" to illicit drug use; the military buildup in drug-rich Vietnam; new sources of illicit supply from Asia and Latin America; and the entry of tens of millions of baby-boomers into their teens and twenties, the prime drug-experimenting years. (This wave of "susceptibles" also helps explain why youthful drug use increased throughout the world in the 1960s and 1970s, the postwar baby-boom being a global phenomenon.) Complicating matters further, amphetamine, a stimulant introduced in the mid-1930s, had spread outside medical circles by way of soldiers, athletes, long-haul truckers, cramming students, bohemians, and even prisoners who cracked open Benzedrine inhalers. By the 1960s diverted amphetamines ("uppers"), as well as barbiturates and tranquilizers ("downers"), had become part of a complex and fast-growing recreational drug scene.

Worried by military and youthful drug use and pledged to reduce crime, the Richard M. Nixon administration launched a multifront drug war. Federal agents stepped up international enforcement efforts, with some notable successes in Turkey and France. In 1971 the White House created the Special Action Office for Drug Abuse Prevention, which became the foundation for the National Institute on Drug Abuse. The administration funded methadone and other new treatment approaches, including therapeutic communities modeled on California's Synanon Foundation. All told, federal antidrug spending increased from $80 million in 1969 to $730 million in 1973. Legislatively, the 1970 Controlled Substances Act rationalized six decades of piecemeal statutes and court decisions. The law sorted drugs into five schedules, depending on their abuse potential and therapeutic value. Schedule I drugs, including heroin, marijuana, LSD, peyote, and other hallucinogens, were illicit in that the sense that they were off limits to everyone, including physicians. Drugs in schedules II through V could be used therapeutically, but with varying restrictions. The further down the schedule, the less onerous the restrictions.

The emergence of new patterns of abuse prompted later changes in the list, such as the addition of the amphetamine-based hallucinogen MDMA (Ecstasy) to Schedule I in 1985. Congress also enacted significant punitive amendments in 1986 and 1988, in the midst of a crack epidemic and a renewed, bipartisan drug war. Crack was a cheap, smokable form of cocaine that spread rapidly in inner cities in the mid-1980s, adding an exclamation point to a sustained, fifteen-year increase in national cocaine consumption. Like heroin, crack was associated with rapid addiction, prostitution, sexual degradation, and violence. Although the 1986 and 1988 legislation increased penalties generally, crack offenders received the stiffest sentences. Possessing just five grams of crack with intention to distribute brought a mandatory minimum sentence of five years, the same penalty prescribed for 500 grams of powder cocaine. Federal penitentiaries began filling with crack dealers, virtually all of whom were African American or Latino. (Congress partially rectified the disparity in the 2010 Fair Sentencing Act, although crack dealers continued to receive stiffer sentences than those caught with equivalent amounts of powder cocaine.)

In international perspective, the rightward shift of American drug policy was unusual. The intensification of hard-drug use and the spread of HIV/AIDS in the 1980s and 1990s prompted many European nations to move toward harm-reduction policies. Better to provide medical care, clean needles, injection rooms, or even a legal heroin supply, the thinking went, than to turn addicts into infectious outcasts. Politicians in America, however, proved indifferent or hostile toward public-health approaches. At both the federal and the state levels, they preferred to increase sanctions for drug abuse.

The explanation lay in the way in which America's culture war shaped electoral calculations. Reaction against permissiveness and the liberal policy failures that allegedly fostered it became a significant force in American politics in the late 1960s, in the wake of race riots, campus protests, the expansion of the youthful counterculture, and the breakdown of order and civility in American cities. Moral conservatives took out their anger against the Democrats, whom they identified as the party of permissiveness, especially after Senator George McGovern (tarred with the brush of "acid, amnesty, and abortion") won the nomination in 1972. Republicans seized the opportunity, exploiting moral backlash, particularly in the South, where the party became competitive for the first time since Reconstruction. But it was easier to run for office as a moral reactionary than to govern as one. If Republicans had tried to deliver the full program of moral reaction, including outlawing abortion and repressing homosexuals, they would have run the risk of losing majority support in a society that was, at least sexually, becoming more libertarian. The solution was to appease conservative activists in a way that did not alienate moderate and independent voters.

In practice that meant attacking street crime, welfare dependency, and drug abuse, issues linked to anxieties about race, lower-class disorder, and threats to the young. Cracking down on illicit drugs, the safest of safe issues, reassured moral conservatives, middle-class parents, and anyone else worried about the drumbeat of bad drug news. Democrats knew that they had to compete with Republicans on drug policy or play fatally to the permissive stereotype. The costly and punitive 1986 and 1988 legislation was essentially a "who's toughest" bidding war between congressional Democrats and the Reagan White House. Like reinstituting the death penalty—another criminal-justice contrast between late twentieth-century Europe and the United States—stiffer penalties for drug abuse and trafficking offered a politically efficient means of satisfying aroused voters.

As in the 1950s, the punitive turn provoked a reaction. Libertarians proposed "controlled legalization," a regulated adult market in psychoactive drugs, as an alternative to the drug war. Liberals and public-health advocates espoused harm-reduction measures, notably needle-exchange programs, which spread during the 1990s despite a ban on federal funding. Drug courts, which diverted nonviolent drug offenders into mandatory treatment, also became more common. Even so, federal policy remained basically unchanged during the Bill Clinton administration (1993–2001). Clinton knew that liberalization invited attacks from Republicans allied with moral conservatives and worried parents who wanted the government to lock up dealers, clean out the schools, warn kids about drugs, and shun anything that smacked of toleration.

Whatever its political advantages, the drug war failed to diminish the supply of illicit drugs. Prices fell and potency rose as prosecutions mounted. Drugs poured into the country, notably from Mexico, where rival drug cartels battled one another and such police and military officials who were not themselves complicit in the traffic. Domestic marijuana and methamphetamine production also expanded, particularly in remote and impoverished rural areas. By 2006 marijuana was reportedly the most valuable cash crop in the United States. That same year, 11,000 Americans lost their lives through accidental overdoses with opiate analgesics—up from 4,000 in 2001. OxyContin, a long-acting synthetic opiate, was only the most notorious of the potent analgesics and tranquilizers diverted into the black market.

Law enforcement had some deterrent effect. "Every time we have a helicopter go up on a mission," remarked a pot-hunting DEA agent, "there's someone down below who sees it and thinks, 'Maybe I better not.'" But could such deterrence be achieved at less cost, particularly in view of successful European experiments with harm reduction and decriminalization? Marijuana, the drug that generated the most arrests, but that also benefitted cancer and AIDS patients battling nausea and appetite loss, became the reform lightning rod. In 1996 California and Arizona voters passed initiatives that allowed physicians to authorize patients to smoke marijuana. Despite conservative insistence that medical marijuana was a stalking horse for legalization, fifteen states and the District of Columbia enacted similar measures by the end of 2010. The growing dissensus over marijuana's status as a Schedule I drug represented a breach in drug-war solidarity and a rare instance of states openly defying federal policy. In other respects, however, little had changed since the 1980s. In the early twenty-first century, illicit drug use continued to be defined, suppressed, and managed principally by criminal statutes and law enforcement.

[*See also* **Clinton, William J.; Crime Policy; National Institutes of Health; Nixon, Richard M.; Poverty; Progressive Era; Reagan, Ronald, Roosevelt, Theodore;** *and* **Supreme Court, U.S.**]

BIBLIOGRAPHY

Burnham, John C. *Bad Habits: Drinking, Smoking, Taking Drugs, Gambling, Sexual Misbehavior, and Swearing in American History*. New York: New York University Press, 1993. Describes the vice "constellation" that included illicit drug use.

Courtwright, David T. *Dark Paradise: A History of Opiate Addiction in America*, expanded ed. Cambridge, Mass.: Harvard University Press, 2001.

Courtwright, David, Herman Joseph, and Don Des Jarlais. *Addicts Who Survived: An Oral History of Narcotic Use in America, 1923–1965*. Knoxville: University of Tennessee Press, 1989.

Jonnes, Jill. *Hep-Cats, Narcs, and Pipe Dreams: A History of America's Romance with Illegal Drugs*. New York: Scribner & Sons, 1996.

MacCoun, Robert J., and Peter Reuter. *Drug War Heresies: Learning from Other Vices, Times, and Places*. Cambridge: Cambridge University Press, 2001. Provides historical and international perspectives on American drug policies.

Massing, Michael. *The Fix*. New York: Simon & Schuster, 1998. Late twentieth-century drug wars.

Musto, David F. *The American Disease: Origins of Narcotic Control,* 3d ed. New York: Oxford University Press, 1999. Policy-oriented study that is especially strong on the early twentieth century.

Rasmussen, Nicolas. *On Speed: The Many Lives of Amphetamine.* New York: New York University Press, 2008.

Schneider, Eric C. *Smack: Heroin and the American City.* Philadelphia: University of Pennsylvania Press, 2008.

Spillane, Joseph. Cocaine: *From Medical Marvel to Modern Menace in the United States, 1884–1920.* Baltimore: Johns Hopkins University Press, 2000.

David T. Courtwright

Du BOIS, W. E. B.

(1868–1963), African American scholar, polemicist, activist, and intellectual. Born and reared in Great Barrington, Massachusetts, Du Bois graduated from Fisk University in 1888. Enrolling as a junior at Harvard, he remained to earn a Ph.D. in history in 1895, with two years of study (1892–1894) at the University of Berlin. In 1896, Harvard published his dissertation on the suppression of the African slave trade. That same year, during a brief teaching stint at Wilberforce University in Ohio, he married a student, Nina Gomer; they had two children. A fellowship at the University of Pennsylvania (1896–1897) resulted in a path-breaking sociological study, *The Philadelphia Negro* (1899). From 1897 to 1910, he taught sociology at Atlanta University.

At this time, most southern blacks could not vote and faced racial segregation in public facilities; scores were lynched each year. Before 1900, Du Bois tended to agree with Booker T. Washington, who advised blacks not to protest social and political inequality but instead to focus on vocational training and economic advancement. However, in *The Souls of Black Folk* (1903), a collection of essays on race that included one on Washington, Du Bois rejected accommodationism and sided with the growing ranks of Washington's opponents. He soon emerged as leader of the Niagara Movement, an organization that opposed Washington and promoted political activism. When this organization broke up, Du Bois in 1910 joined with a group of liberal whites to form an organization with similar aims, the New York–based National Association for the Advancement of Colored People (NAACP). As editor of its journal, *The Crisis,* Du Bois exerted great influence as the NAACP's public voice. In monthly unsigned editorials he demanded social, economic, and political equality for all blacks and an end to lynching; promoted his idea of a "talented tenth" of liberally educated black leaders; and encouraged the development of African American arts and the preservation of black folk culture.

During the 1920s, Du Bois focused increasingly on Pan-Africanism, socialism, and economic issues while questioning the NAACP's exclusive focus on legal challenges to segregation. Increasingly at odds with the NAACP leadership, he resigned in 1934 and returned to Atlanta University. He rejoined the NAACP staff in 1944, but his increasingly radical politics ran counter to the postwar climate of anti-Communism and led to his resignation again, in 1948. He ran unsuccessfully for the U.S. Senate in New York in 1950 on the Progressive Party ticket and the following year stood trial on charges of acting as an unregistered agent of a foreign power in connection with his activities in a peace organization. Although acquitted, Du Bois was banned from traveling abroad (1952–1958). Upon retrieving his passport, he visited Eastern Europe, China, and the Soviet Union, where he received the Lenin Peace Prize. In 1961, having officially joined the Communist Party, Du Bois left the United States for good.

He spent his remaining years in Ghana, assembling an "Encyclopedia Africana."

The author of seventeen books, including five novels and one masterpiece of American literature, *The Souls of Black Folk,* Du Bois contributed significantly to many fields as an activist, scholar, critic, sponsor of African American letters, and, above all, spokesman for African American rights. At a time when Booker T. Washington's accommodationism seemed the most viable response to systematic racial oppression, Du Bois eloquently and persuasively described an alternative. He became the leading advocate of racial justice in the early twentieth century, helping to assure the victory of militant protest over accommodationism.

Yet Du Bois's legacy is complicated by the complexity of his thought and his later radicalism. Some historians characterize Du Bois's thinking as riddled with contradiction. Indeed, he championed the NAACP's campaign for integration, equality, and colorblind institutions while also promoting black cultural nationalism and even positing racial essentialism, most strikingly in his 1897 essay "The Conservation of the Races." His 1934 break with the NAACP came after he had begun to promote economic nationalism for blacks. Some see this break, and his increased interest in racial separatism, Pan-Africanism, and Marxism, as at odds with his earlier liberal integrationism. Yet through most of his career, Du Bois was attracted to socialism, grappled with ideological dilemmas, and sought to balance competing ideas and approaches, taking intermediate positions between idealism and pragmatism, integration and separation, self-help and demands for reparation, liberal education and vocational training. He often concluded that such dilemmas could never be fully resolved. As he put it in a much-quoted statement on African American identity in an 1897 *Atlantic Monthly* essay reprinted in *The Souls of Black Folk:* "One ever feels his two-ness—an American, a Negro; two souls, two thoughts, two unreconciled strivings; two warring ideals in one dark body, whose dogged strength alone keeps it from being torn asunder."

[*See also* **Antislavery Movement; Civil Rights; Communist Party USA; Equality; National Association for the Advancement of Colored People; Progressive Party of 1948; Segregation; Socialism;** ***and*** **Washington, Booker T.**]

BIBLIOGRAPHY

Horne, Gerald. *Black and Red: W. E. B. Du Bois and the Afro-American Response to the Cold War, 1944–1963.* Albany: State University of New York Press, 1986.

Jordan, William. *"Getting America Told": Black Newspapers and America's War for Democracy, 1914–1920.* Chapel Hill: University of North Carolina Press, 2001.

Lewis, David Levering. *W. E. B. Du Bois: Biography of a Race, 1868–1919.* New York: H. Holt, 1993.

Lewis, David Levering. *W. E. B. Du Bois: The Fight for Equality and the American Century, 1919–1963.* New York: H. Holt, 2000.

Marable, Manning. *W. E. B. Du Bois: Black Radical Democrat.* Boston: Twayne, 1986.

Rampersad, Arnold. *The Art and Imagination of W. E. B. Du Bois.* Cambridge, Mass.: Harvard University Press, 1976.

Rudwick, Elliott. *W. E. B. Du Bois: A Study in Minority Group Leadership.* Philadelphia: University of Pennsylvania Press, 1960.

William Jordan

DUE PROCESS

This entry contains three subentries: Legal Cases; Procedural Process; and Substantive Process.

LEGAL CASES

The due process of law is the essential characteristic of laws that are properly enacted and fairly applied to a person or situation according to the appropriate procedures to achieve purposes that are compatible with the basic ideals of the legal system. These ideas, that law must be performed according to some processes and must pursue some goals, distinguish an act performed through the power of the state that is done by law from an act that is done according only to the will of an official. The due process of law is the single doctrine in the U.S. Constitution that most embodies the ideal of the rule of law.

In the constitutional law of the United States, no conduct or interests in a person's life, liberty, or property can be burdened by the state without appropriate procedures and a reasonable cause. Moreover, due process of law requires equal treatment under the law and, when necessary, equal protection of the laws is implied as a matter of due process.

Ancient Sources. Many of the political leaders of the American Revolution and of the early republic were strongly influenced by the political history of the ancient world, particular ancient Greece and Rome, in which the ideas that underlie due process were central. Ancient law has many illustrations of such principles, requiring fair officials using established procedures to apply preexisting laws to decide disputes and adjudicate offenses. Aristotle argued this point in *Politics,* claiming that it mattered less if a state was governed by a democracy, an oligarchy, or a monarchy than that the people who governed did so according to laws. Early Roman law, in Table Nine of the Twelve Tables, required any person who might be condemned to be convicted by law, and it made a judge subject to death for taking a bribe in reaching a decision. Indeed, the great jurist Cicero went briefly into exile for violating the prohibition on due process while serving as consul.

The works of Aristotle, Cicero, and similar ancient authors were central to what became known as the republican understanding of law and the state, a complex set of ideas about the role of law and government that was reflected in much of the vocabulary and ideas of Thomas Jefferson, John Adams, James Madison, and other framers of the Declaration of Independence and the U.S. Constitution. These works, and the laws that persisted in direct influence from them in Roman law and the canon law of the Roman Church, also had a direct influence on early English law.

English Law. The idea that the monarch of England should act according to law was established long before the Norman invasion in 1066. Alfred the Great and others had relied on their councils to announce laws, according to which crimes were punished and disputes were settled. Indeed, William of Normandy's claim to rule England was based on a legal argument of inheritance (although the argument was settled by force of arms with his cousin Harold). The French overlords of England accepted the idea that the force of the state was governed by laws, and the early English law book attributed to Roger de Bracton noted in 1225 that "To rule well a king requires two things, arms and laws, that by them both times of war and of peace may rightly be ordered," and even more famously, "The king must not be under man but under God and under the law, because law makes the king. For there is no rex where will rules rather than lex." Early kings, especially Henry I and Henry II, spent considerable energy in organizing the laws.

During this age, the constitutional settlement of King John with the English barons and the church in England in 1215 resulted in one of the most enduring expressions of the requirements of legal procedure. Magna Carta stated that "No free man shall be seized or imprisoned, or stripped of his rights or possessions, or outlawed or exiled, or deprived of his standing in any other way, nor will we proceed with force against him, or send others to do so, except by the lawful judgment of his equals or by the law of the land." The early history of the Magna Carta is complicated, and only in Edward I's reign, eight decades later, did the Magna Carta become English law. The phrase "law of the land" was closely associated with a phrase by which the principle was further refined in the reign of Edward II, in the Liberty of the Subject Act of 1354, declaring that "no man, of what estate or condition soever, shall be put out of land or tenement, nor taken, nor imprisoned, nor disinherited, nor put to death, without being brought in answer by due process of law." This prohibition was apparently taken seriously by the Parliament, which passed a statute a generation later granting immunity for the lords of manors who had punished rebels without due process of law (*sanz due proces de loye*). The apparent interchangeability of "law of the land and judgment of one's peers" with "due process of law" was endorsed by Sir Edward Coke in his commentary on Magna Carta published in the 1650s. Both Magna Carta and the Liberty of the Subject Act remained in force in England and were enacted from time to time into colonial charters and statutes. As elements of English Common Law, they were received into the laws of the early U.S. states after independence.

The procedural safeguards of Magna Carta were recurrently violated by English monarchs, although they were usually reasserted in the courts or legislature, resulting in restatements such as the Petition of Right in 1628, by which Parliament reminded King Charles that "in the eight-and-twentieth year of the reign of King Edward III, it was declared and enacted by authority of parliament, that no man, of what estate or condition that he be, should be put out of his land or tenements, nor taken, nor imprisoned, nor disinherited nor put to death without being brought to answer by due process of law." A failure to abide by these terms was one reason Charles and Parliament fought a civil war in England from 1642 to 1651, which directly affected the English colonies, and the memory of which was a powerful influence on the American revolutionaries a century later.

Due Process of Law in the Early United States. The requirements of due process of law, as well as its apparent restatement in requiring respect for the law of the land, were written into the statutes and constitutions of several of the early states. It was not always clear whether these requirements limited the powers of legislatures or only the powers of the courts. When in 1787 Congress passed the Northwest Ordinance, the restriction was not framed as a limit on one branch or another of a territorial or state legislature but as a right of the individual against both. Article 2 provided, "No man shall be deprived of his liberty or property, but by the judgment of his peers or the law of the land."

In 1789, James Madison proposed a draft of a Bill of Rights to the first Congress, part of the commitments made by the Federalists needed to secure ratification of the Constitution. The Fifth Amendment adopted from his original list of twelve adopted language like that of the Northwest Ordinance, although with familiar substitution, "No person shall… be deprived of life, liberty, or property, without due process of law."

In 1819 Justice William Johnson's Supreme Court opinion in *Bank of Columbia v. Okely*, 17 U.S. (4 Wheat.) 235 (1819), equated the "law of the land" language of Maryland's declaration of rights with the "due process" language for the federal amendment but found neither to be violated by a state allowance of a summary procedure for the collection of debts, although each is "intended to secure the individual from the arbitrary exercise of the powers of government." That this security was sufficient to bind the Congress was clear in 1855, when Justice Curtis declared, "The article is a restraint on the legislative as well as on the executive and judicial powers of the government, and cannot be so construed as to leave congress free to make any process 'due process of law,' by its mere will" (*Murray v. Hoboken Land & Imp. Co.,* 59 U.S. (18 How.) 272 (1855)).

Federal Due Process and the States. Following the Civil War, Congress passed a series of statutes and constitutional amendments to ensure that each of the states secured a national standard of justice according to law to each of their citizens. Although the abolition of slavery and the fair treatment of freed slaves were matters of compelling concern, members of Congress then recognized that these were not the only arenas in which states had failed to ensure the civil liberties of their citizens. Among the provisions enacted that now bound the states to federal assurances of individual rights were two clauses of Section One of the Fourteenth Amendment, ratified in 1868: "nor shall any state deprive any person of life, liberty, or property, without due process of law; nor deny to any person within its jurisdiction the equal protection of the laws." Thus, the due process of law became a federal constitutional requirement on every state and local government in the United States.

The period of Reconstruction following the Civil War ended with a restriction on the applications of due process to prevent unjust or unequal treatment on individuals under the law. This process involved two different strains of interpretation of due process. Perhaps the more enduringly significant was the decision of the U.S. Supreme Court, in *The Civil Rights Cases,* 109 U.S. 3 (1883), to limit the effects of the due process clause of the Fourteenth Amendment to state action. Under this view, over Justice John Marshall Harlan's powerful dissent, the actions of private corporations or individuals that had a legal *significance or social effect in the public sphere* were barred from federal review.

The other strain of interpretation was initially a step intended further to restrict states from interfering with commerce but that eventually led to a wider scope of the doctrine as a basis of individual rights. Beginning in 1897, the Court began to use the due process clause to limit state legislation favoring consumer's and worker's rights. The most famous example of this line of cases was *Lochner v. New York,* 198 U.S. 45 (1905), in which Justice Rufus Peckham interpreted the Fourteenth Amendment's due process of law to require states to honor the protection of contracts that was required of the national government, barring states from interfering with the liberty of contract. This doctrine was then applied to strike down New York's wage and hour law, as a burden on the workers' rights to enter into contracts for dangerously long work days and weeks. Justice John Harlan, again, and Justice Oliver Wendell Holmes Jr., dissented, suggesting that the due process of law did not give employers' rights to exploit their workers.

Despite this initially restrictive reading, the due process of law was expanded throughout the twentieth century through a process of "incorporating" the substantive limits of many prohibitions of the U.S. Bill of Rights. In a process that has taken case by case the question of which federal rights limit the states, the Court has adopted into due process those rights necessary to a scheme of ordered liberty, in Justice Cardozo's language from *Palko v. Connecticut,* 302 U.S. 319 (1937). This process has bound the states from restricting the rights to speech, religion, the press, assembly, to bear arms, to be free of unreasonable search and seizure and arrest without a valid warrant, to be free from self-incrimination, to receive a public and speedy trial by an impartial judge and jury, and not to forfeit one's property for public use without just compensation.

Contemporary Due Process—Procedural and Substantive. What process is due remains the central question of the due process of law. To some extent the answer turns on what the laws are: that the laws enact rules that are—at least—not inappropriate for the place and time they govern. This is the idea of substantive due process. To a larger extent, the answer turns on how laws are made and how they are applied, so that they are made appropriately and applied fairly. These are the ideas of procedural due process.

Procedural due process requires that no person's interest in life, liberty, or property be taken by the state unless the taking is performed according to duly enacted laws applied in a pre-established procedure; such procedure must accord that person fair notice of the pending taking and an opportunity to be heard by a fair and impartial decision maker before the taking is complete. Accordingly, a law enacted by Congress, a legislature, or other legislative assembly by their procedures is procedurally valid, as is a regulation or rule enacted by an executive agency according to authority validly delegated to it. However, when powers that are authorized by such statutes or rules are applied in a given case to a particular person, the requirements of due process are specific to that situation.

In a criminal matter, due process requires that a person be accorded the procedural assurances of a valid basis for arrest, which is assured either by a valid arrest warrant or by a police officer with probable cause to make the arrest. Likewise, searches must be by valid warrant or inherently reasonable. A person may not be compelled to give self-incriminating evidence and is entitled to a competent attorney. The person may only be tried by an impartial jury and by an impartial judge; the punishment must not be cruel or unusual nor can a fine be unreasonably harsh.

In civil matters, a person may not be deprived of a property or liberty interest without reasonable notice of the impending deprivation and an opportunity to make a case that the proposed deprivation is unwarranted by the facts or unjustified under the law. The person is entitled to a fair hearing or trial before an unbiased magistrate, and all of the court rules and proceedings that apply in a given jurisdiction must be reasonably observed. Procedural due process does not limit a government from a taking, even when there is no wrongdoing. Due process does, however, require that a taking of private property that is for public use be given just compensation.

Substantive due process persists in three forms. One is the continued vitality of federal due process as a means of ensuring state fidelity to fundamental federal rights. A second is in the federal context: the recognition that part of due process incorporates the assurance of equal protection of the laws by the federal government. The third is the continuing force of a broad requirement of fairness and reasonableness in the law that forbids legislation that creates a burden on individual liberty unless the burden is rationally related to a legitimate or appropriate purpose of government.

Ultimately, the due process of law is one of the most essential aspects of judicial review in the United States. Thus, it is a controversial doctrine by which the actions of the executive branch or legislative branch may be stayed or reversed by the judiciary. Such a power on the bench strikes some observers as dangerously broad judicial discretion. Yet it is also essential to the American concept of separation of powers. Judges may give oversight both to the ultimate legislative wisdom of those laws that affect our most important notions of national and personal identity and to the daily executive activities that affect the individual. Both aspects of governance are shared among officials independent of one another and, ultimately, are subject to the branch that is itself expert in the law of the land.

[See also Bill of Rights; Civil Liberties; Civil Rights; Constitution; Constitutional Law; Harlan, John Marshall; Holmes, Oliver Wendell, Jr.; Judicial Review; *Lochner v. New York;* Northwest Ordinance; *and* Reconstruction.]

BIBLIOGRAPHY

Breyer, Steven. *Active Liberty: Interpreting Our Democratic Constitution.* New York: Alfred A. Knopf, 2005.

Denning, Baron Alfred Thompson. *The Due Process of Law.* New York: Oxford University Press, 2005.

Labunski, Richard E. *James Madison and the Struggle for the Bill of Rights.* Oxford; New York: Oxford University Press, 2006.

Lewis, Anthony. *Gideon's Trumpet.* New York: Vintage Books, 1989.

Nelson, William E. *The Fourteenth Amendment: From Political Principle to Judicial Doctrine.* Cambridge, Mass.: Harvard University Press, 1998.

Orth, John V. *Due Process of Law: A Brief History.* Lawrence: University of Kansas Press, 2003.

Steve Sheppard

PROCEDURAL PROCESS

The concept of due process derives from the Magna Carta (1215), the great charter of English liberties whereby the nobles limited the king's authority. Its phrase "law of the land" was transformed over the years to "due process of law," a phrase included in 1692 in a Massachusetts statute. The Fifth Amendment of the Constitution (ratified 1791) requires that the federal government not deprive any person of "life, liberty, or property without due process of law." The same language is included in the Fourteenth Amendment (ratified 1868) as a constraint on the states.

The central aim of due process doctrine is to assure fair procedure when the government imposes a burden on an individual. The doctrine seeks to prevent arbitrary government, avoid mistaken deprivations, allow persons to know about and respond to charges against them, and promote a sense of the legitimacy of official behavior.

Procedural due process does not prevent the government ultimately from making a deprivation. The notion of substantive due process does place substantive limits on official power, whereas procedural due process is concerned solely with the manner in which the government acts. This distinction appears in *Londoner v. City and County of Denver* (1908) and *Bi-Metallic Investment Co. v. State Board of Equalization* (1915). Taken together, these cases distinguish between the situation in which government singles out an individual for a deprivation based on the facts of a case, which triggers procedural due process requirements, and a broad rule affecting large numbers of people, which does not. In the former cases, the government must provide the procedural protections of notice and hearing; as the Supreme Court held in *Grannis v. Ordean* (1914), "[t]he fundamental requisite of due process of law is the opportunity to be heard" (p. 394).

A governmental deprivation of an individual's property will implicate due process. Property has a Common-Law meaning, including land

and personal property. In the 1970s, the Court articulated a "new property" concept, which includes government-provided benefits, licenses, or statuses (such as that of public employee) that have value, are relied upon by individuals, and can be called statutory, regulatory, or contractual entitlements. A statutory benefit such as welfare (*Goldberg v. Kelly,* 1970), a driver's license (*Bell v. Burson,* 1971), the expectation of continued employment as a tenured professor (*Board of Regents v. Roth,* 1972), and the status of a civil servant protected from at-will dismissal (*Arnett v. Kennedy,* 1974) are examples of such new property interests. The Court held in *Roth* that the mere hope or unilateral expectation of some property interest is not enough.

The term "liberty" has its own history. In the Fourteenth Amendment, liberty has been held to incorporate major protections of the Bill of Rights. Liberty also has an independent meaning in, for example, the criminal context. Basic freedom from incarceration, as well as a parolee's interest in staying on parole (*Morrissey v. Brewer,* 1972), are liberty interests. Liberty in the civil context includes certain personal interests in privacy, which were recognized in a series of substantive due process cases, notably *Roe v. Wade* (1973). In civil cases involving procedural claims, several interests have been recognized as liberty—such as the interest in parental status (*Lassiter v. Department of Social Services,* 1981) or a school child's interest in being free from corporal punishment (*Ingraham v. Wright,* 1977).

The Court in *Cleveland Board of Education v. Loudermill* (1985) separated the issue of whether due process is triggered from the question of how much process is "due." A court is to weigh the extent of an individual's interest in additional procedure, as well as its value and cost. *Mathews v. Eldridge* (1976) held a posttermination evidentiary hearing to be sufficient due process in a disability-benefit termination case. *Mathews* gives courts much leeway. Sometimes, a fairly full, trial-type hearing is required. At other times, a court simply requires basic notice and opportunity to speak.

The many due process cases that come before the federal courts—involving prisons, schools, social security, and public employment, among other areas—testify to the continuing centrality of this area of law and the undiminished controversy surrounding it. Increasingly, two opposing visions dominate: a personal participation model, which stresses dignitary values and greater procedure, and a bureaucratic model, which stresses efficient and cost-effective decision making. This tension is likely to persist.

[*See also* **Due Process: Legal Cases; Due Process: Substantive Process;** *and* **Fourteenth Amendment.**]

Thomas O. Sargentich

SUBSTANTIVE PROCESS

The constitutional doctrine of substantive due process can be traced back to the English idea of a fundamental but unwritten constitution and flows forward to modern constitutional guarantees of privacy. Although its antecedents include basic notions of republican government and individual civil rights, our modern notions of substantive due process are founded upon Justice Stephen J. Fields's dissent in the Slaughterhouse Cases (1873). Behind the spare language of the due process clause of the Fourteenth Amendment that barred Louisiana's statutory conferring of a monopoly upon a single slaughterhouse, Field discerned inalienable individual liberties:

> Clearly among these must be placed the right to pursue a lawful employment in

> a lawful manner, without other restraint than such as equally affects all persons ... The equality of right, with exemption from all disparaging and partial enactments, in the lawful pursuits of life, throughout the whole country, is the distinguishing privilege of citizens of the United States. (pp. 97, 109–110)

Free-Labor Ideology. Field brought to his dissent the powerful free-labor ideology of the victorious Republican Party. Before the Civil War, he had been a leading Republican jurist and judge; after the war he transformed this notion of equality into constitutional opinions. In his dissent in the Slaughterhouse Cases and in *Munn v. Illinois* (1877), Field clung to his own personal version of this free-labor ideology. He admitted that states had the right to regulate the economic activity of public enterprises, like the grain elevator companies in Munn, when that regulation was even-handed and served a genuine public need. But regulation of public businesses and private enterprises had no natural stopping place; it might, Field wrote in Munn, "justify an intermeddling with the business of every man in the community, so soon, at least, as his business became generally useful" (p. 141).

Although not a major theme in substantive due process scholarship, which instead focuses on the doctrine as a defense of property, it is apparent that Field's concern was the protection of free-labor ideology. Ironically, Field's antebellum Republican views better fit the Gilded Age than they did the Reconstruction Era. His view of the due process clause gained ground in the almost entirely reconstituted Court of the late 1880s and 1890s. Field was never as comfortable with giant corporations as newer members of the Court, such as Justices David Brewer and Rufus Peckham, but his ideal of liberty of enterprise became the orthodoxy of the Court in the late nineteenth century. Field's concurrence in *Butcher's Union Co. v. Crescent City Co.* (1884), a direct descendent of the Slaughterhouse Cases, expressed this vision: the "liberty of the individual to pursue a lawful trade or employment" was a "common right," one of the "certain principles of morality ... without which society would be impossible, ... [one of the] certain inherent rights [that] lie at the foundation of all action." "[U]pon them alone," Field wrote, "can free institutions be maintained" (p. 756).

For the Court, substantive due process was the wedge by which states were barred from abridging freedom of contract and liberty of enterprise. Substantive due process would take on a life of its own, but at its heart it remained a vision not of constitutional law but of a good society whose free marketplaces were managed by a benevolent, invisible hand. Equality of opportunity would be undermined by class legislation. Too much state intervention would pervert and destroy the natural relationships by which the United States had become an economic giant. One may say with much truth that freedom of contract theory was as responsible for the formulation and continuing vitality of substantive due process as substantive due process was for the legitimation of freedom of contract.

The Court expanded its jurisdiction by holding the states to a substantive due process standard. Potentially, every state regulatory statute had to pass muster as a valid exercise of health, welfare, morals, or police power. Most went untouched, but whenever a statute was found unconstitutional under substantive due process review a furor invariably ensued. In *Allgeyer v. Louisiana* (1897), the Court overturned a Louisiana law requiring all corporations doing business with Louisiana residents to pay fees to the state. In *Lochner v. New York* (1905), the Court found a maximum-hours statute unconstitutional.

In *Adair v. United States* (1908) the Court voided a federal law barring dismissals of interstate common carrier workers because they were members of unions. In *Coppage v. Kansas* (1915) the Court invalidated a state law barring yellow dog contracts. In *Adkins v. Children's Hospital* (1923) the Court struck down the minimum wage–setting powers of a District of Columbia employment commission. The Court relied on substantive due process grounds to void price regulation in non-public industries and licensing of nonpublic enterprises and the prevention of German-language teachers and parochial school teachers from earning a living at their trade.

The Reasonableness Standard. Throughout these cases, the Court asked itself whether the state economic regulations were reasonable—that is, did they fit the legitimate objectives of state intervention in the economy? The public/private enterprise distinction Chief Justice Morrison Waite employed in *Munn* was one attempt to elucidate a standard of reasonableness, as was the Court's weighing of evidence on the health of bakers in *Lochner*. The alternative—simple and uniform deference to the popularly elected representatives in state legislatures and Congress—was unpalatable to the majority in these substantive due process cases. The search for an appropriate and supple test of reasonableness—a rule of reason—in substantive due process cases nevertheless bedeviled the Court.

Meanwhile, progressive critics of substantive due process, notably James Thayer, Louis D. Brandeis, Roscoe Pound, and Theodore Roosevelt, accused the Court of setting itself up as a "super legislature." The same criticisms were voiced even more stridently by a new generation of reformers in support of New Deal programs. Recognizing that the line between public enterprises and private business and labor had become blurred in an administrative state and conceding that the legislatures had far greater ability to find and weigh facts than did the courts, Progressives on the Supreme Court, including Chief Justice Charles Evans Hughes and Justices Owen J. Roberts, Harlan Fiske Stone, and Benjamin N. Cardozo, began to lead the Court away from the freedom of contract version of substantive due process.

In *Nebbia v. New York* (1934), the Court, speaking through Roberts, found that a New York statute establishing a commission to fix milk prices was a reasonable health and welfare measure. The Court could only ask that state regulation not be unreasonable or arbitrary and that the regulation have a real relation to the object of the legislation. Free-market forces had failed to accommodate themselves to the needs of the community. There was nothing sacred about commodity prices that would prevent their regulation in the public interest.

The Court tackled minimum wage laws, the second major object of the Court's scrutiny under the regime of substantive due process, in *West Coast Hotel v. Parrish* (1937). A much-divided Court, with the majority clinging to a strict version of substantive due process, validated a Washington State minimum wage law for women. Chief Justice Hughes wrote that the "Constitution does not speak of freedom of contract" (p. 391). Hughes signaled that Field's logic of free labor, which *laissez-faire* advocates had gilded with their own ideal of free markets, no longer influenced the majority of the Court. He did not strike at the doctrine of substantive due process per se, but at the freedom of contract faith hidden within the older economic version of substantive due process. As Hughes wrote, "The liberty safeguarded [by the due process clause] is liberty in a social organization which requires the protection of law against the evils which menace the health, safety, morals and welfare of the people" (p. 391). The state could protect the liberty of a class of workers who were in an unequal bargaining position and were relatively defenseless against inadequate wages. The state could insure liberty as well as curtail it, a conception quite opposite Field's and one more appropriate to the New Deal than the antebellum free-labor ideology. After *West Coast Hotel,* economic due process review went into an eclipse from which it has not emerged.

If economic due process cases no longer absorbed a major portion of the Court's energies, substantive due process challenges to state and municipal regulations thrived in a new setting. Although recent Courts have generally observed a deferential policy toward state economic regulations, it has exempted from that approach state laws that discriminated against groups unable to gain the ear of the legislature; groups discriminated against by reason of race, gender, or other suspect categorization; and groups whose private lives were unduly invaded by the state.

Challenges to Segregation. In particular, the deferential approach to state economic regulations was not extended to state restrictions on the right to vote in primary elections or state-sponsored or state-condoned segregation of education, public facilities, or employment. These decisions remade private worlds as well as public places, ending widespread patterns of segregation. Critics of *Brown v. Board of Education* (1954) claimed that its sweeping language had no textual basis in the Constitution and, like economic due process, it merely rested upon the external, private social, and philosophical beliefs of the justices. Given the great differences in the regional, political, and educational background of the justices on the *Brown* court, their unanimity could not have arisen from a consensus of personal values, but the critics are right in one respect: *Brown* and its sister cases do reflect deeply felt aspirations that reach behind the text of the Constitution.

Privacy. Beginning in the 1960s, a new class of "social" substantive due process suit issues arrived on the Court's docket. These tracked our society's heightened concern for expressive individualism and the right to practice distinct family and personal lifestyles. The "new" social substantive due process rested on the recently articulated freedom of personal choice and privacy that the justices found in the "penumbras" of the Bill of Rights in *Griswold v. Connecticut* (1965) and imposed upon the states through the due process clause of the Fourteenth Amendment. The right to exercise those choices in the private spaces of one's life sustained the legality of abortion in *Roe v. Wade* (1973) but did not protect homosexuals or adulterers from prosecution, permit policemen to violate departmental personal-appearance regulations, deny states the right to collect and store information on drug prescriptions, or prevent state and local governments from releasing employees without explanation. In this group of cases the deferential policy of the Court proved that the freedom of contract doctrine is alive and well, for the government employer and the dismissed employee were hardly equal in bargaining power, particularly when the employee could not force the employer to divulge the reasons for the dismissal.

Despite the Court's retreat, under Chief Justice William H. Rehnquist, from earlier social due process decisions, substantive due process retains its protean ability to adapt constitutional law to changing social mores. In tandem with claims based on the equal protection clause, due process challenges to state laws restricting individual choice will continue to make their way to the Supreme Court.

[*See also* ***Adkins v. Children's Hospital;*** **Brandeis, Louis;** ***Brown v. Board of Education;*** **Civil Rights; Fourteenth Amendment;** ***Griswold v. Connecticut; Lochner v. New York;*** **New Deal; Privacy; Rehnquist, William;** ***Roe v. Wade;*** **Roosevelt, Theodore; Slaughterhouse Cases; Stone, Harlan; Supreme Court, U.S.;** *and* ***West Coast Hotel v. Parrish.***]

BIBLIOGRAPHY

Friedman, Lawrence. *The Republic of Choice, Law, Authority, and Culture.* Cambridge, Mass: Harvard University Press, 1990.

Hovenkamp, Herbert. "The Political Economy of Substantive Due Process." *Stanford Law Review* 40 (1988): 379–447.

Nelson, William E. *The Fourteenth Amendment.* Cambridge, Mass.: Harvard University Press, 1988.

Phillips, Michael J. "Another Look at Economic Substantive Due Process." *Wisconsin Law Review* (1987): 265–324.

Peter Charles Hoffer

E

ECONOMIC DEVELOPMENT

Economists define economic development as a sustained increase in per-capita income. Although this definition is a good starting point, historians generally conceive economic development as a broader set of social and political changes. In the context of U.S. history, those changes include the settlement of a capacious frontier, the growth of large cities, a vast influx of immigrants, and the rapid spread of new technology. The complexity of these changes notwithstanding, the course of U.S. development can be traced through three major periods: the extensive growth of the colonial and revolutionary periods; the expansion of commerce during the first half of the nineteenth century; and the emergence of "managerial capitalism" after the Civil War.

The Colonial and Revolutionary Periods. The economy of colonial America grew rapidly because of sustained population growth and profitable cultivation of staple crops. Massive free and unfree immigration from Europe and Africa—coupled with a moderate climate, relatively high nutritional levels, and high fertility rates—resulted in extraordinarily rapid population growth. Between 1650 and 1770, the population of Britain's mainland North American colonies increased from 55,000 to more than 2.2 million. Most colonists participated in a vibrant agricultural economy. High prices for wheat and tobacco—British North America's two main staples—encouraged the particularly rapid settlement of the middle and southern colonies in the eighteenth century. White colonists in the slave South—benefiting from slave labor and high staple prices—ranked as the wealthiest of the colonists.

Rapid population growth produced substantial economic development. Because no sweeping technological or organizational advances dramatically stimulated productivity, per-capita income grew quite modestly by modern standards, increasing anywhere from 0.3 to 0.6 percent per year. Yet colonists built an increasingly sophisticated commercial infrastructure that resulted in the growth of towns and cities. Such development was particularly important in New England and the Middle Colonies, where cities became major market centers. By 1770 such cities as Boston, New York, and Philadelphia provided an impressive array of mercantile services that induced future economic growth.

Government policy, both in Britain and in the colonies, also aided colonial development. Unlike France or Spain, British authorities did not seek to regulate overseas migration, thus abetting the population explosion in the North American colonies. British mercantilist policies, designed to further the interests of the imperial center, sometimes impeded colonial trade with other nations. Colonists, however, successfully evaded the most onerous regulations, whereas the British mercantile system enabled American merchants to export grains, lumber, livestock, and other goods. The Revolutionary War, in fact, initially had devastating economic consequences because American merchants lost many of the trading privileges they had enjoyed under the British Empire.

Expansion of Commerce between the Revolution and the Civil War. Most export agriculture in the colonial and revolutionary period was confined to areas with access to water transportation. Transporting bulky crops over the nation's rutted and muddy roads was prohibitively expensive. In the period from 1800 to 1820, private turnpike companies—which improved roads to collect tolls—alleviated the worst problems of overland transport, but grains and other bulky commodities remained too expensive to ship over roads. Hence, proponents of economic development avidly improved rivers and built canals to extend the nation's system of waterways. The Erie Canal, completed in 1825, was by far the most important of these improvements. Built through the gently rolling landscape of upstate New York, the Erie Canal connected the Great Lakes to the Hudson River. It transformed such cities as Buffalo, Rochester, and Syracuse into major transport, mercantile, and manufacturing hubs. Canal systems in Ohio and other Midwestern states extended the reach of the Erie system, providing farmers throughout the Middle West with an all-water connection to New York City. The steamboat, meanwhile, facilitated trade on the Mississippi and Ohio River systems, providing yet another avenue of commerce.

Steam power soon had an even larger impact when applied to overland carriage. Areas in which water transportation was either unavailable or prohibitively expensive turned to the railroad. First built in the late 1820s, railroads rapidly spread across the county. By 1860, Americans had built approximately 30,000 miles of track, with four separate roads penetrating the Appalachian Mountain barrier. Railroads not only accelerated the growth of cities on the eastern seaboard, but also transformed Pittsburgh, Chicago, and other midwestern cities into major marketing and manufacturing centers.

Although historians have discarded the view that the railroad single-handedly accounted for American industrialization, it nevertheless contributed to the dramatic expansion of commerce in everyday life. In the North and Midwest, the expansion of the railroad network created a self-reinforcing cycle of growth. As transportation improved, farmers produced more grains, dairy products, and other produce for urban centers. With more cash to spend on consumer goods, farm families demanded textiles, shoes, furniture, and other manufactured products. Manufacturers and merchants, responding to the larger agrarian market, increased their output and improved productivity. Firms producing such goods as ready-made apparel, hats and caps, and boots and shoes, for example, increased productivity through specialization and greater division of labor. Incremental technological advances—usually the result of tinkering by rather ordinary mechanics—further increased manufacturing productivity.

The South lagged far behind in inventive activity and other measures of economic development. Its slave-based economy, to be sure, produced enormous profits for many planters and farmers. The southern economy did especially well in the 1850s, when the price of cotton, tobacco, and other staples soared. Yet in almost every other measure of development—urbanization rates, inventive activity, manufacturing output, population growth—the North far outstripped the South. As the Civil War approached, the regional disparities grew. In 1860, the value of manufactured goods produced in New York City alone exceeded the combined production of the eleven southern states that would form the Confederacy. Underlying the South's failure was a lack of adequate demand to spur industrialization. Plantation slavery restrained population growth among free farmers and an unequal distribution of rural income undermined the earnings and consumption habits of farm families that had provided northern entrepreneurs with lucrative markets. However profitable it was to southern planters, slavery seriously impeded southern industrial development.

The limitations of southern development notwithstanding, the U.S. economy grew impressively between 1800 and 1860. Historians debate to what extent federal and state government action contributed to this remarkable economic expansion. State governments frequently intervened in the economy in the early nineteenth century, especially when, as in New York and Pennsylvania, they operated their own canal systems. Although New York's Erie Canal succeeded, most other state-owned canals failed. State and federal governments provided engineering expertise, land grants, and other subsidies to the railroads, but private investors supplied most of the capital. The most important government intervention was enforcing a stable set of property rights (including a patent system) that encouraged economic expansion and technological innovation. State governments made it easier for entrepreneurs to obtain corporate charters for banks, factories, and other enterprises, whereas the federal courts protected interstate commerce and used law to validate corporate charters and contracts. With a strong legal foundation in place, national markets and national enterprises came to dominate the economy.

Managerial Capitalism and the Modern Economy. The post–Civil War expansion of the railroad network—including the construction of the first transcontinental lines—enabled entrepreneurs to establish national corporations. Although a few large firms had flourished earlier during the market revolution, especially in the New England textile industry, these firms paled compared with the corporate giants of the late nineteenth and early twentieth century. By 1910, Standard Oil, U.S. Steel, Armour and Co., and the American Tobacco Company were among the firms with assets in excess of $200 million. Another round of technological change soon added such newer businesses as Ford Motor Company and General Motors to the list of industrial giants. These enterprises tended to be capital intensive, using their large size to forge substantial economies of scale. Technological advances became even more important. Many large firms organized research divisions and departments that institutionalized technological change.

Borrowing from the experience of the railroads, these large industrial firms also developed complex administrative bureaucracies heavily stocked with middle managers and upper-echelon executives. Entrepreneurs such as John D. Rockefeller and Andrew Carnegie used these new administrative forms to ascertain precise production costs, enabling them to identify and then to eliminate expensive bottlenecks. Rockefeller's Standard Oil Company, in particular, ruthlessly cut production costs, enabling the company to buy out or destroy less efficient competitors. By 1890, Standard Oil—which owned 20,000 oil wells, 4,000 miles of pipeline, and 5,000 specialty railroad cars—controlled more than 90 percent of the American oil and kerosene market. Whereas large corporations tended to dominate industries with relatively homogenous output (oil, steel, and tobacco), smaller firms thrived in sectors that produced specialty goods, ranging from complex machinery to such consumer goods as furniture. By the early twentieth century, America's combination of large and small firms encouraged the birth of new industries, including automobiles and electrical manufacturing.

Mass production made the marketing and distribution of consumer goods extraordinarily important. To insure a constant demand for their products, businesses invested heavily in advertising, first in print publications and later in radio and television. Innovative retailers devised new ways of selling both basic necessities and luxury goods. Department stores, fashionable retail districts, and eventually supermarkets as well as shopping centers and malls indelibly shaped the American landscape. By the early twentieth century, a number of firms expanded the scale of consumer borrowing (especially through installment plans) that allowed a broad range of families to purchase automobiles and other consumer durables.

By 1900, the United States possessed the basic elements of a developed economy: growing per-capita income, rapidly evolving technologies, increasingly efficient industrial producers, and sophisticated marketing and distribution channels. Although certain regions of the country—most notably Appalachia and other parts of the South—continued to lag, rapid economic development made the United States the world's largest economy for much of the twentieth century and laid the material foundations for what publisher Henry Luce called "The American Century."

Because economic development is so complicated, scholars continue to debate the ultimate source of U.S. success. Some stress the availability of such abundant natural resources as fertile soils and rich supplies of iron, coal, and oil. Others underscore the emergence of a national, integrated market that encompassed most of North America. Although political and geographic barriers hindered development elsewhere, these scholars argue, U.S. businesses grew in tandem with an expanding home market. Finally, many scholars have emphasized the importance of distinctive American cultural and political attitudes, including a devotion to private property and free enterprise and a corresponding suspicion of economic regulation that might hinder business success.

Despite widespread support of economic development, many Americans have nevertheless feared that the growing power of big business might subvert democracy. These fears, coupled with deep swings in the business cycle, have created important political movements, especially in the Populist, Progressive, and New Deal Eras, that raised important questions about economic development. Should the federal government encourage certain industries with tariffs and other subsidies? Should state and federal governments dissolve or regulate corporations that threaten to become monopolies? How should government mediate conflicts among labor, business, and consumers? What kinds and levels of taxation best encourage economic development while also promoting other social goods? These and similar questions relating to economic development remained divisive as the twentieth century ended.

The advent of the desktop computer in the 1980s and the Internet and World Wide Web in the 1990s opened a new era of U.S. economic development. The "information age" also exemplified many of the same characteristics of earlier changes, including the rapid adaptation of new technologies; a complex mix of both large corporation (including giants such as Microsoft and Intel) and smaller, more flexible firms; and attitudes and regulations generally favorable to free enterprise and hostile to government regulation. Yet despite these links to the past, the new economy also raised new questions. Would the rapid transmission of information make global markets the driving force of continued growth? Would the new information technologies transform consumer culture? How would new technologies affect the managerial structure of "old economy" stalwarts such as the steel, automotive, and chemical industries? Although these issues remained unresolved, the rapid emergence of "new economy" industries did once again illustrate the self-reinforcing nature of economic development. The earlier success of the U.S. economy created deep pools of capital, high levels of per-capita income, and a strong commitment to research and development that allowed new enterprises to flourish. Clearly the history of economic development remains unfinished, as it continues to influence society, politics, and culture.

[*See also* **Antitrust Legislation and Law; *Charles River Bridge v. Warren Bridge;* Economic Policy: Banking and Financial Regulation; Economic Policy: Medical Regulation; Economic Policy: Deregulation, 1970 to Present; Economic Policy: Regulation; Interstate Commerce Act; New Deal; Populist Era; Progressive Era; Property Rights; State Governments; Tariffs;** *and* **Taxation.**]

BIBLIOGRAPHY

Balleisen, Edward J. *Navigating Failure: Bankruptcy and Commercial Society in Antebellum America.* Chapel Hill: University of North Carolina Press, 2001.

Bruchey, Stuart. *Enterprise: The Dynamic Economy of a Free People.* Cambridge, Mass.: Harvard University Press, 1990.

Chandler, Alfred D. *The Visible Hand: The Managerial Revolution in American Business.* Cambridge, Mass.: Belknap Press, 1977.

Engerman, Stanley L., and Robert E. Gallman. *The Cambridge Economic History of the United States, Volume I: The Colonial Period.* Cambridge: Cambridge University Press, 1996.

Fogel, William Robert. *Without Consent or Contract: The Rise and Fall of American Slavery.* New York: W. W. Norton, 1989.

Lindstrom, Diane. *Economic Development in the Philadelphia Region, 1810–1850.* New York: Columbia University Press, 1978.

McCusker, John J., and Russell R. Menard. *The Economy of British America, 1607–1789.* Chapel Hill: University of North Carolina Press, 1985.

Taylor, George Rogers. *The Transportation Revolution, 1815–1860.* New York: Harper & Row, 1951.

Scranton, Philip. *Endless Novelty: Specialty Production and American Industrialization, 1865–1925*. Princeton, N.J.: Princeton University Press, 1997.

John Majewski

ECONOMIC POLICY

This entry contains four subentries: Banking and Financial Regulation; Medical Regulation; Regulation; and Deregulation, 1970 to Present.

BANKING AND FINANCIAL REGULATION

Commercial banking was suppressed in the colonies by Great Britain, but the Bank of North America was created during the Revolution to provide funding for the Continental army. It was overseen by Robert Morris, the "financier" appointed by the Continental Congress. After the Revolution, state legislatures began chartering banks, including the Bank of New York in 1784 (now the Bank of New York Mellon Corp.). This chartering process was a crude form of regulation because it restricted bank activities to those specified in the charter. Gradually, however, the executive branches of state government took over the chartering and regulation of state banks and began demanding financial reports and examinations, as well as licensing.

The Bank of the United States (BUS) was chartered in 1791 by the federal government for the purpose of collecting and holding government funds, as well as engaging in private banking. The BUS acted as an informal regulator of the state banks until its charter expired in 1811. A second BUS was created in 1816, but lost its federal charter in 1833. Thereafter, in 1846, independent federal subtreasury offices were established to hold federal funds. However, it was not until 1913 that Congress enacted the Federal Reserve Act that established a true central bank, the Federal Reserve System.

The National Banking Act of 1863 (NBA) created national bank charters for private banks. This led to a "dual" banking system in which national banks were regulated by the Office of the Comptroller of the Currency in the Treasury Department and the state banks by state authorities. National banks initially enjoyed a number of advantages over their state counterparts, but those advantages were mostly lost over the years as the states acted to loosen restrictions on their banks.

National and state banks were both initially restricted in their ability to open branch offices, a restriction that was memorialized in the McFadden Act in 1926. This effectively prevented commercial banks from operating outside narrowly defined geographical boundaries. Other legislation proscribed banks from engaging in nontraditional banking activities. For example, the Glass–Steagall Act of 1933 prohibited banks from underwriting stocks.

The Bank Holding Company Act of 1956 sought to prevent banks from being associated with commercial businesses. This was another manifestation of a widespread view that banks should be confined to a narrow range of traditional banking activities. In contrast, other commercial enterprises are allowed by state laws to engage in "any lawful business."

The inflation that began in the 1960s had a debilitating effect on the profits of commercial banks. Competition also appeared in the form of money market funds and other products being offered by broker-dealers in the securities industry. Congress then sought to make banks more competitive by loosening regulatory restrictions and widening the permissible activities of commercial banks. Restrictions on savings and loan association (S&Ls) activities were also reduced.

Unfortunately, much fraud and waste then occurred at S&Ls, resulting in the passage of the Financial Institutions Reform, Recovery, and Enforcement Act of 1989 (FIRREA). It provided a structure for liquidating failed S&L banks.

Congress, nevertheless, continued to loosen restrictions on banking. The Riegle–Neal Interstate Banking and Branching Efficiency Act of 1994 removed most barriers to interstate banking, leading to the development of large nationwide banking operations. Congress also repealed the Glass–Steagall Act in 1999 through the Gramm–Leach–Bliley Act (GLB). This act created "financial holding companies," which could engage, through subsidiaries, in nearly every range of financial activity, including previously prohibited securities and insurance underwriting.

Financial holding companies were subjected to "functional" regulation, which meant that their securities and other nontraditional banking activities were regulated by nonbank regulators such as the Securities and Exchange Commission. Traditional banking activities continued to be supervised by multiple state and federal bank regulators. This regulation included capital requirements adopted in the so-called Basel II accord. This regulation was thought necessary to protect the Federal Deposit Insurance Corporation (FDIC), which insures bank deposits. Banks were also subject to various consumer protection statutes, including the Truth in Lending Act, the Equal Credit Opportunity Act, and the Community Reinvestment Act.

After Gramm–Leach–Bliley, commercial banks competed directly with investment banking firms in the securities industry. That competition proved costly to both when the subprime mortgage market collapsed in 2007. Several large commercial and investment banks suffered massive losses, touching off a global financial crisis. Congress bailed out the banking system in 2008 by enactment of the Troubled Assets Relief Program (TARP).

Congress also enacted the Dodd–Frank Wall Street Reform and Consumer Protection Act of 2010 (Dodd–Frank). This legislation created the Financial Stability Oversight Council (FSOC), which is composed of banking and other financial services regulators. FSOC is tasked with identifying and mitigating risks to the financial system that could arise from the failure of large bank holding companies and nonbank financial companies.

Dodd–Frank imposed other regulations on banks, including restrictions on their proprietary trading and investments in hedge funds and private equity groups; it added regulatory supervision over payment, clearing, and settlement systems; and it imposed restrictions on mortgage originations. Dodd–Frank also created a Bureau of Consumer Financial Protection (BCFP) that will regulate the offering and provision of consumer financial products.

[*See also* **Federal Deposit Insurance Corporation; Federal Government, Executive Branch: Treasury Department; Federal Reserve Act; Federal Reserve System;** ***and*** **Securities and Exchange Commission.**]

BIBLIOGRAPHY

Broome, Lissa L., and Jerry W. Markham. *Regulation of Bank Financial Service Activities, Cases and Materials*, 4th ed. St. Paul, Minn.: West, 2010. A detailed examination of bank regulation in the United States and its history.

Markham, Jerry. "Banking Regulation: Its History and Future." *North Carolina Banking Institute* 4 (2000): 221–285. A survey of the history of banking regulation in the United States.

Meltzer, Allan H. *A History of the Federal Reserve (1913–1951)*. Chicago: University of Chicago Press, 2003. A classic description of the early years of the Federal Reserve.

Paulson, Henry M. *On the Brink*. New York: Business Plus, 2010. An insider's account of the governmental response to the banking crisis that began in 2007.

Jerry W. Markham

MEDICAL REGULATION

Despite some early experiments with regulation in colonial America and the early Republic, medicine in the United States was essentially unregulated by local, state, or federal governments before 1870. After 1870, states slowly began to debate and pass regulations that determined who could practice medicine. Physicians from competing medical sects ultimately collaborated with each other to pass laws that gradually established minimum educational requirements and sought to consolidate the control of American medicine into the hands of organized professional physicians. Most of these laws gave quasi-state powers to private organizations. These organizations often showed that they were incapable of adequately enforcing these medical regulations during the nineteenth and early twentieth centuries. During the first half of the twentieth century, the American Medical Association sought to impose standardized educational requirements across the country. It proved extremely difficult to create uniform standards in medicine until the 1930s. It was not until the 1970s and 1980s that the enforcement of medical licensing law moved fully from these private organizations to state medical boards.

Colonial and Early America. Although medicine had been regulated in parts of England since the sixteenth century, the practice of medicine in British colonies was essentially unregulated. Although various colonies, including Virginia, passed laws regulating physicians' fees in 1639, the colonies did not make any effort to define who could practice medicine. Strict regulatory laws would have made little sense for the colonies because American physicians were unable to pursue a formal medical education. Most American physicians were trained through apprenticeships, if they had been trained at all. The first formal medical school in the British colonies was not founded until 1765 in Philadelphia.

During the colonial period, organized medical societies began forming. During the years of the early republic, these colonial medical societies evolved into state medical societies. These private organizations provided the starting point for the first efforts to regulate physicians. After the Revolution, states such as Massachusetts (1781) permitted state medical societies to license physicians. By 1830, thirteen states had developed some type of licensing scheme, but these early statutes simply gave licensed physicians the right to sue for unpaid bills and were generally unenforceable. Some historians have argued that the public's perception of regular physicians declined after 1830 and this change in perception led to the elimination of these licensing statutes, but the fundamental political toward a more Jacksonian democracy may have been more decisive. By the 1840s, most of these laws were repealed as Americans became increasingly skeptical of interfering with the medical marketplace. By 1850, the number of states licensing physicians had fallen to two. Most physicians did not even bother to join their local or state medical society and they practiced outside of that system without any difficulty. Ultimately, this early regulatory wave floundered.

Nineteenth-Century Regulatory Efforts. As the early efforts to regulate medicine waned, the medical marketplace became increasingly chaotic. New medical sects arose to challenge traditional or regular medicine. Homeopathy and medical eclecticism presented the most formidable and organized challenges to the regular physicians. The medical practitioners of these sects, known as irregular physicians, emphasized the inability of regular physicians to successfully help their patients. Like their regular counterparts, the irregulars organized themselves into local, state, and national medical societies. As the irregular medical sects gained adherents, regular physicians became increasingly concerned that they were losing control of American medicine.

By the 1870s, regular physicians began lobbying state legislatures for new regulations designed to limit the ability of irregular physicians to practice medicine. Legislatures instead created licensing schemes that included and legitimatized irregular practitioners. Between 1870 and 1900, almost every state and territory would introduce some type of medical regulation act. These acts varied from state to state and they were not always effective at preventing unlicensed physicians from continuing to practice. Although their impact varied, these laws faced numerous legal and constitutional challenges from physicians. Despite some misgivings by the courts, these laws were almost universally upheld by the courts under a state's police powers. The U.S. Supreme Court in *Dent v. West Virginia* (1889) unanimously upheld an unusually restrictive medical licensing statute that permitted irregulars from practicing medicine. Although physicians continued to challenge these statutes on constitutional grounds, the Court in *Dent* essentially ended the debate regarding their constitutionality.

As the century came to a close, states began to enact more standardized medical licensing laws that created quasi-public medical licensing boards with the ability to create minimum standards for medical education, require tests for medical school graduates to practice medicine, judge medical school curriculums, prosecute unlicensed physicians, and revoke medical licenses for violating medical ethics. States began to model their regulations on the licensing schemes created in Illinois and California. Both of these states' medical regulatory schemes had proved to be more effective at eliminating unwanted medical practitioners. These laws forced all physicians to either pass a medical exam or graduate from medical school in good standing. Although these regulatory efforts were somewhat uneven, state medical boards were given powers that would be used more effectively in the twentieth century.

Twentieth-Century Regulation. As the medical sectarian crisis slowly faded at the beginning of the twentieth century, medical regulation had still failed to dramatically increase the quality of American medical education. State medical boards and societies became more aggressive in prosecuting unlicensed practitioners, but the medical regulations had not dramatically improved medical education. In 1906, the American Medical Association created a program that sought to grade the quality of American medical schools. In 1910, as a result of this program, Abraham Flexner published a searing report that lambasted the quality of medical schools. The report led to the closure of numerous schools and reignited efforts to both improve and standardize medical education.

Between 1920 and 1950, states sought to create more uniform and consistent educational standards for physicians. New state licensing laws provided state medical boards additional enforcement powers for effective medical regulation, but the medical boards still primarily relied on medical societies to enforce ethical standards. Starting in 1970, this practice changed dramatically as state medical boards responded to medical malpractice crisis by taking control from the private boards and consolidating all regulatory control under state authority. Instead of relying on medical societies, state medical boards created state bureaucracies that could regulate medicine more fully. Medical regulation had evolved from uneven state exercise to a complex mixture of regulation by state, federal, and professional associations.

BIBLIOGRAPHY

Kett, Joseph F. *The Formation of the American Medical Profession: The Role of Institutions, 1780–1860*. Westport, Conn.: Greenwood Press, 1968.

Latham, Stephan R., and James C. Mohr. "The Legal and Quasi-legal Regulation of Practitioners and Practice in the United States." In *The Cambridge World History of Medical Ethics*, edited by Robert Baker and Laurence McCullogh. Cambridge, UK; New York: Cambridge University Press, 2009.

Rothstein, William G. *American Physicians in the Nineteenth Century: From Sects to Science*. Baltimore: Johns Hopkins University Press, 1972.

Shryock, Richard Harrison. *Medical Licensing in America, 1650–1965*, Baltimore: Johns Hopkins Press, 1967.

Starr, Paul. *The Social Transformation of American Medicine*. New York, Basic Books, 1982.

Clinton M. Sandvick

REGULATION

The objectives of economic regulation are usually mixed: to achieve an appropriate balance between efficiency and equity, to steer acquisitive human urges into productive channels, and to strike reasonable trade-offs between economic growth and environmental protection. The United States has had an uneven history of regulation, one that was relatively good in comparison to that of many other countries. For most of its history, the United States featured the world's most entrepreneurially "free" economy with the least amount of public regulation. Such generalizations, however, disguise a more complex reality.

In the Colonial Era, religious considerations limited entrepreneurial impulses, yet the spread of a pervasive market economy in the eighteenth and nineteenth centuries worked a dramatic change. Although such old customs as the "just price" (the maximum allowable price for a basic necessity) ended, that did not preclude all regulation. The developing American capitalist economy still required a strong regulatory framework. Commercial transactions depended on a system of contract law enforced through courts. Other public and private regulatory mechanisms were essential as well.

The Monetary System and the Capital Markets. All cash-and-credit economies, including the American one, also require a monetary authority—typically a central bank—to regulate the supply and value of money. In colonial America, banks were almost nonexistent, but after independence Alexander Hamilton's First Bank of the United States (1791–1811) served some functions of a central bank until its twenty-year charter expired. The Second Bank of the United States (1816–1836) was even more successful, but it too fell victim to politics and its charter was not renewed. Thereafter, the United States had no central bank until the creation of the Federal Reserve System in 1913. During those three generations, the government generally maintained the gold standard, state authorities regulated banking haphazardly, and the nation experienced a chronically deficient money supply. All of these conditions changed under the Federal Reserve System. By the 1930s the "Fed," assisted by other bodies and officials such as state banking commissions and the Controller of the Currency, had become a modern regulatory agency overseeing the monetary system.

The nation's securities (stock and bond) markets, which developed during the nineteenth century and then blossomed in the twentieth, have benefited from one of the world's most modern and effective regulatory systems. A series of laws passed during the 1930s (including the Securities Act of 1933, the Securities Exchange Act of 1934, the Public Utility Holding Company Act of 1935, and the Trust Indenture Act of 1939) created a system in which regulation was overseen by the Securities and Exchange Commission and the federal courts, but implemented largely through third parties. These included hundreds of thousands of private lawyers and accountants, officials of the New York Stock Exchange and other exchanges, plus the National Association of Securities Dealers (NASD).

Labor Markets and Conditions of Work. Efficient, equitable, and flexible labor markets require systematic wage scales, rules for the number of hours and days to be worked, and numerous other regulations. In America, some of these had long been enforced through apprenticeship systems. With industrialization, however, the exploitation of factory labor became commonplace, and it lasted for many decades. During the Progressive Era, most states instituted workers' compensation laws and some enacted unemployment insurance, but effective national resolution of the labor question awaited the New Deal Era. The National Labor Relations Act of 1935 gave organized labor the power to bargain collectively; other laws passed during the 1930s ended child labor, set maximum hours, and established minimum wage levels.

By the 1990s some aspects of the American labor market were heavily regulated through antidiscrimination laws designed to protect women, minorities, the handicapped, and others. But in areas such as layoff policies and paid vacation time for employees, American practice granted fewer benefits to workers than those of some other countries, especially in Western Europe.

Product Markets and Competition. The United States has always had one of the world's most intensely competitive economies. There are many reasons why. For one thing, the entrepreneurial spirit of its ethnically mixed population has been remarkably vigorous. Also, for the first 150 years of the nation's history few countervailing forces existed to challenge business interests. The United States had no strong guild tradition, no established church, no hereditary aristocracy, and no powerful peacetime military. Until the mid-twentieth century, it had only a minuscule government. All of these conditions interacted to intensify business competition.

With the rise of "big business" in the 1870s and 1880s, state legislatures responded by enacting antitrust legislation. In 1890, Congress passed the landmark Sherman Antitrust Act, which outlawed cartels and monopolies. Since then, the Sherman Act, in combination with the Federal Trade Commission Act and the Clayton Antitrust Act (both passed in 1914), has had mixed results. But on balance, economists conclude that these antitrust measures have increased the level of competition within the American economy. Perhaps the truest index of the effectiveness of U.S. antitrust laws has been their widespread emulation by other nations since World War II.

The Economic Infrastructure. Active economic regulation has been most conspicuous in the areas of transportation, electric utilities, and telecommunications, where conventional competition seemed inadequate to achieve its usual function of automatically regulating prices and quality. The years from the 1870s through the New Deal saw a proliferation of state and federal commissions charged with regulating these industries. First railroads, then gas and electric utilities, streetcars, pipelines, telephones, trucking, and finally airlines came under regulation by public commissions, which oversaw prices and sometimes actually set them. Almost every state established a railroad and utility commission. The most prominent federal agencies were the Interstate Commerce Commission (created in 1887), which regulated first railroads, then pipelines and trucking; the Federal Power Commission (established in 1920, strengthened in 1930, and in the 1980s renamed the Federal Energy Regulatory Commission), which oversaw gas and electric utilities; the Federal Communications Commission (1934, radio, telephones, and television); and the Civil Aeronautics Board (1938, airlines). This complex regulatory structure proved controversial, however, in part because the "cost-plus" formula employed by regulators in some of these agencies provided little incentive for efficiency for cost cutting and in part because some of the industries regulated (trucking, for example) had few of the "natural monopoly" characteristics of early railroads and electric utilities. During the years after World War II, and particularly after the economic downturn of the 1970s, the cost-plus type of economic regulation began to be discredited.

Deregulation. The deregulation movement began in a serious way during the presidential administration of Jimmy Carter. It rapidly gathered force in many industries and spread to other countries as well. During the 1980s, the election of such "free market"–oriented politicians as Ronald Reagan in the United States, Margaret Thatcher in the United Kingdom, and Helmut Kohl in Germany underscored the apparent popularity of deregulation. "Privatization" schemes, moreover, marched alongside deregulation, as governments in Great Britain, Germany, Japan, and several other countries sold nationalized industries to private investors. In the United States, privatization often meant spinning off what had been public functions (such as garbage collection) to private contractors. Meanwhile, deregulation in the federal government included the outright abolition of several agencies, such as the Civil Aeronautics Board and the Interstate Commerce Commission. By the end of the twentieth century some of the industries mentioned above (railroads, trucking, airlines, radio, and television) were scarcely regulated at all, and others, such as electric power and telephones, were being moved toward deregulation.

Toward the end of the 1980s, as if to underscore the apparent triumph of free-market economics, the collapse of socialist economies and the breakup of the Soviet bloc seemed to complete the cycle of deregulation and privatization. This development, coupled with the superior growth performance of capitalist economies, seemingly demonstrated once and for all the virtues of minimal regulation.

Conclusion. But it would be a serious mistake to pronounce an end to the need for economic regulation, let alone regulation applying to health, safety, and the environment. At the end of the 1990s, experience with deregulated industries remained brief by historical standards, and economic history has a way of taking unexpected turns. Even so, several general conclusions concerning the history of economic regulation in the United States seem warranted:

First, the United States has regulated its economy less than most industrialized countries have done, although it has created large numbers of regulatory agencies. Second, the onset of regulation in America was usually associated with periods of political reform: the Progressive Era, the New Deal, and the New Frontier and Great Society Era of the 1960s.

Finally, and paradoxically, the enactment of consumer protection, health and safety, and environmental laws accelerated during the 1970s and 1980s, an era of economic deregulation. Regulatory bodies such as the Environmental Protection Agency (1970), the Occupational Safety and Health Administration (1970), and the Consumer Product Safety Commission (1972) were created during the Richard M. Nixon administration. These latter laws differed from traditional economic regulation despite their powerful economic impacts. In some respects they resembled Progressive Era legislation such as the Pure Food and Drug Act and the Meat Inspection Act (both passed in 1906) and similar measures having to do with forestry and other environmental concerns. They represented a nonpartisan consensus that people and the environment must be protected from the excesses of the unfettered market.

[*See also* **Antitrust Legislation and Law; Carter, Jimmy; Contract, Law of; Environmentalism; Environmental Protection Agency; Federal Communications Commission; Federal Reserve System; Great Society; Hamilton, Alexander; Interstate Commerce Act; Monetary Policy; National Labor Relations Act; New Deal; Nixon, Richard M.; Progressive Era; Pure Food and Drug Act; Reagan, Ronald; Regulatory Agencies, Federal;** *and* **Securities and Exchange Committee.**]

BIBLIOGRAPHY

Breyer, Stephen. *Regulation and Its Reform.* Cambridge, Mass.: Harvard University Press, 1982.

Derthick, Martha, and Paul J. Quirk. *The Politics of Deregulation.* Washington, D.C.: Brookings Institution, 1985.

Hawley, Ellis W. *The New Deal and the Problem of Monopoly: A Study in Economic Ambivalence.* Princeton, N.J.: Princeton University Press, 1966.

Hughes, Jonathan R. T. *Social Control in the Colonial Economy.* Charlottesville: University Press of Virginia, 1976.

Kahn, Alfred E. *The Economics of Regulation.* New York: John Wiley & Sons, 1971.

Keller, Morton. *Regulating a New Economy: Public Policy and Economic Change in America, 1900–1933.* Cambridge, Mass.: Harvard University Press, 1990.

McCraw, Thomas K. *Prophets of Regulation: Charles Francis Adams, Louis D. Brandeis, James M. Landis, Alfred E. Kahn.* Cambridge, Mass.: Belknap Press of Harvard University Press, 1984.

Vietor, Richard H. K. *Contrived Competition: Regulation and Deregulation in America.* Cambridge, Mass.: Belknap Press of Harvard University Press, 1994.

Wilson, James Q., ed. *The Politics of Regulation.* New York: Basic Books, 1980.

Thomas K. McCraw

DEREGULATION, 1970 TO PRESENT

The 1970s was a time of more federal regulation in the areas of environmental protection, consumer product safety, drugs, and worker safety—much of it bipartisan. Paradoxically, it was also a decade that saw the deregulation of several important industries. Deregulation of the airlines, railroads, trucking, and telecommunications sectors was largely completed by 1980, although the Reagan administration would be associated with deregulation. Deregulation of electric power, natural gas, and financial services had been initiated—again with bipartisan support and with considerable sustenance from the regulators themselves. The debates over "economic" deregulation were mainly technical. To a surprising degree, this was the politics of ideas, although conditions of "stagflation" certainly helped.

By the end of the 1970s, experts who had long studied the origins and conduct of regulatory regimes had to look again to explain the successful impulse toward deregulation. In these years, economists, policy analysts, political scientists, organizational behaviorists, historians, and administrative lawyers all contributed to a vast literature, theoretical and empirical, that concerned itself with economic regulation, principally prices and entry. These regulatory regimes were shown to shelter firms from competition; regulation encouraged inefficient operations and the overall misallocation of resources. Regulators had been "captured," it was said, and would be loath to scale back their power or their personnel. Often the same analysis that justified deregulation explained why it was unlikely to happen, given the patterns of concentrated benefits and diffuse costs of the regulatory status quo. But deregulation did happen, in varying degrees.

The purest examples of successful deregulation were airlines and trucking. In the "politics of deregulation," they most fully met the special conditions for reforming old Progressive and New Deal regulatory regimes, according to Martha Derthick and Paul Quirk's later (1985) analysis. Elite opinion, supported by broad academic consensus, converged on the value of reform. In both airlines and trucking, initiative by the commissions (Civil Aeronautics Board and Interstate Commerce Commission) was crucial, and their very commission form helped, since the effects of procompetitive policy decisions on actual behavior (prices and new entrants) were immediate. Changes in the rules did not require torturous implementation. At the same time, reformers in the commissions got strong support from Congress—for example, from Senator Edward Kennedy. (Working closely with Kennedy was future Supreme Court justice Stephen Breyer, whose later book, *Regulation and Its Reform,* became a standard source on the subject.) Eventually major deregulatory legislation followed, reinforcing what had begun as administrative action. The industries did not give up their preference for the old ways, but they could do little but retreat and adjust as best they could (sometimes issuing dire warnings about the future).

Telecommunications was more complex with a mixed outcome. The 1970s saw sweeping federal policy change regarding the industry, and a procompetition consensus emerged in Congress, yet no new statute passed. (Congress did refuse to *prohibit* competition.) Technological changes made matters difficult, even aside from the political leverage of AT&T. The deregulation that occurred was by way of administrative action by the Federal Communications Commission (FCC)—on "terminal equipment" and eventually (with the help of the courts) on long-distance service. The question of the structure of the industry—the question of AT&T—held up action by Congress, but was finally settled by the divestiture agreement with the Justice Department in 1982.

Deregulation had its limits. Political scientists Derthick and Quirk's, among others, studied examples in this period of much more limited departures from established regulatory regimes: natural gas pricing, milk pricing, and the application of the "locally prevailing wage" provisions of the Davis–Bacon Act. Their stories continued into the future, as the criticism of the bad effects of these policies encountered formidable pushback. Congress in 1978 did pass the Natural Gas Policy Act of 1978, a confusing and stopgap outcome for natural gas. Here, especially in the absence of expert consensus about problem definition, everybody agreed that the issue would have to be revisited.

At the end of our period, the deregulation of the savings and loan industry (S&L) illustrates how complex deregulation can be, with perplexing unintended consequences. The disaster that followed gave deregulation a bad name. Regulations fixed the interest that S&Ls could pay on their savings accounts and restricted their business to home mortgages. To keep them afloat, the government allowed the S&Ls to pay slightly more than larger banks. But competition from new money market mutual funds changed the game, while at the same time the decade's high inflation reduced the urge to save anywhere. Congress came to the rescue in 1980 and 1982 with two deregulatory statutes. The first lifted the lid on the interest rates that the "thrifts" could pay and raised federal insurance coverage from $40,000 to $100,000 per account. The second reform, the Garn–St. Germain Act, allowed the S&Ls to invest their funds beyond home mortgages. At the same time, the Office of Management and Budget and Congress reduced the amount of monitoring and supervision of the industry. The result was fraud, theft, bad management, and an eventual enormous federal bailout.

Enthusiasm for deregulation continued, after 1980, into the Reagan years and beyond, but became more partisan than it had been earlier. A strengthened Office of Information and Regulatory Affairs within the Office of Management and Budget was headed by lawyer Christopher DeMuth, a scholar and advocate who had been active in the deregulation movement. Benefit–cost analysis became formally a part of regulatory review. DeMuth was also the executive director of the Presidential Task Force on Regulatory Relief. When the Reagan Administration seemed to target the Environmental Protection Agency (EPA), support for its regulatory programs proved more resilient than had been the case in the airlines or trucking. The appointment of William Ruckelshaus as EPA administrator meant that regulatory "relief" would take more modest forms: "controlled trading" in the existing air program, for example, had long had support among economists on efficiency grounds. In general, "big government" regulations protecting health and safety proved more popular and much harder to reform or eliminate than the Progressive and New Deal era programs in economic regulation. Consumer reveled in lower prices and better service, but continued to worry about their drinking water and about smog alerts. Historian Robert M. Collins has noted that by the end of the second term, "Reagan's key achievement was not further deregulation but rather the prevention of re-regulation."

In recent years, the public debate about regulation has been very different from that of the 1970s. By the early twenty-first century, intense partisan debates over the proper role of the federal government were far removed from the largely technocratic arguments of the 1970s. Ordinary politics, after all, usually trumps pretences to possession of the right answers. The enduring interest of deregulation in the 1970s—the clearest examples are airlines and trucking—is that it showed that sometimes the policy "merits" are decisive; ideas can matter; government can shrink.

[*See also* **Federal Communications Commission;** ***and*** **Reagan, Ronald.**]

BIBLIOGRAPHY

Breyer, Stephen *Regulation and Its Reform.* Cambridge: Harvard University Press 1984.

Derthick, Martha, and Paul Quirk. *The Politics of Deregulation.* Washington, D.C.: Brookings Institution, 1985.

Collins, Robert M. *Transforming America: Politics and Culture during the Reagan Presidency.* New York: Columbia University Press, 2009.

Landy, Marc, Marc J. Roberts, and Stephen R. Thomas *The Environmental Protection Agency: Asking the Wrong Questions: From Nixon to Clinton* New York: Oxford University Press 1994.

Stephen R. Thomas

EDUCATION POLICY

This entry contains three subentries: An Overview; Education in Contemporary America; and Higher Education.

AN OVERVIEW

From the founding of Harvard College in 1636 and Massachusetts's public-school law of 1647 to America's vast and diverse modern-day educational system, education has been a central thread in the national experience, a focus of reform effort, and a subject of urgent public debate. The founders and early leaders of the new nation viewed an educated electorate as crucial to their republican experiment. As nineteenth-century municipalities expanded their public-school systems, religious bodies founded colleges to educate and nurture their young. Whereas some turn-of-the-century reformers looked to the public schools to "Americanize" the immigrant masses, the philosopher John Dewey viewed the schools as incubators of a more just and humane social order. In the same era, research universities arose to promote scientific inquiry, scholarly endeavor, and professional training. In the 1944 Servicemen's Readjustment Act, Congress granted generous educational benefits to returning World War II veterans. When the Russians launched the space satellite *Sputnik* in 1957, Congress responded with increased funds for education, especially in math and science. When the civil rights movement arose in the 1950s, schools became a prime battleground. *Brown v. Board of Education*, the Supreme Court's landmark 1954 civil rights decision, outlawed racial segregation in the public schools. Soon, women and other disadvantaged groups would also demand equal access to educational opportunities. As the twentieth century ended, politicians vied to propose strategies for improving American education. The underlying point is clear: there are few better ways to approach American history as a whole than to examine the nation's centuries-long effort to educate its citizens.

[*See also Brown v. Board of Education;* **Education Policy: Education in Contemporary America; Education Policy: Higher Education;** *and* **Servicemen's Readjustment Act.**]

Paul S. Boyer

EDUCATION IN CONTEMPORARY AMERICA

Few subjects generated more partisan rhetoric and less consensus in the 1990s than the fate of the public schools. The nation's schools have always had strident critics and impassioned defenders, but the demand for educational reforms echoed throughout the land as the twentieth century ended. Presidential hopefuls routinely aspired to become the "education president," although public schools were largely funded and controlled by state and local officials. Governors' task forces, big-city mayors, and local worthies all favored school reforms and improvements, from charter schools to high-stakes testing, from voucher plans to more funding for Head Start. In his final State of the Union message in January 2000, President Bill Clinton, proclaiming education central to the good life, called for a "twenty-first-century revolution in education, guided by our faith that every child can learn. Because education is more than ever the key to our children's future, we must make sure all our children have that key. That means quality preschool and after school, the best-trained teachers in every classroom, and college opportunities for all our children." What was at stake, he concluded, was the American dream.

The centrality of education in everyday life in 1990s America was nothing short of astounding. The nation made impressive emotional and financial investments in its schools. By 1997, more than 46 million pupils were enrolled in the public schools. In 1995, roughly 65 percent of public-school pupils were white, with 35 percent minority (including 17 percent African American and 14 percent Hispanic American), reflecting America's ethnic and racial diversity. The teaching force (86 percent white) numbered well over 2 million, and the country spent many billions of dollars on salaries, school construction and repair, and innumerable school-related services and programs, from school transportation to hot lunches to educating children with special needs. All this occurred in the Western world's most decentralized school system. Compared with European ministries of education, the U.S. Department of Education (created only in 1976) was relatively weak, poorly funded, and vastly less important in educational matters than state and local governments. Formal control over the nation's tens of thousands of schools resided in the hands of lay people elected or appointed to the school boards of more than 15,000 independent districts. The enormous reach and diversity of this vast educational enterprise, ranging from inner cities to suburbs and rural America, gave ample scope to critics and friends alike.

The schools most often attracted criticisms as numerous campaigns for educational reform gained popularity. As in the past, many stakeholders in the schools—parents, politicians, educators, teachers, and pundits—joined the debate. Characterizing the countless reformers of the 1990s is complicated by the willingness of so many people to voice their complaints and offer proposals for improvement. One large strand of reform reflected the broad influence of a seminal report, *A Nation at Risk* (1983), published by a national commission under the auspices of the U.S. Department of Education during the early years of Ronald Reagan's presidency. Despite the occasional insults they hurled at the department, Republicans effectively used this report as a catalyst for larger national debates on the public schools. Indeed, they set the terms of most subsequent educational debates.

Written at a time of national preoccupation with Japan's seemingly invincible economy and presumably superior educational system, *A Nation at Risk* blamed America's schools for the nation's economic woes and low industrial productivity. The sustained economic growth of the United States in the 1990s, in contrast, did not cause politicians to see public schools more favorably. Instead, Republicans and increasingly Democrats, too, chanted a familiar mantra: that the public schools were failing and test scores were unimpressive, reflecting permissive, liberal school policies and practices, leading to incivility and even violence in the classroom. Only more testing, accountability, and school choice could possibly save the beleaguered schools. Other interest groups agreed, while adding their own spin to school improvement. Evangelical Christians, among the strongest advocates of independent church schools and home schooling, lobbied conservative legislators to guarantee equal time for the teaching of "creation science" in biology classes and for voluntary prayer in the public schools. Back-to-basics zealots scrutinized textbooks for hints of anti-Americanism, whole-language teaching, and "secular humanism." Admirers of free markets and liberty, energized by the collapse of Communism abroad, pressed for public aid to private schools, whether through tuition tax credits or vouchers, whose constitutionality in pilot programs in Milwaukee, Wisconsin; Cleveland, Ohio; and other places remained unclear. Conservatives differed on the means but not the ends: to restore competitiveness, discipline, high achievement, and character training to the schools. That might mean ending social promotion, tightening graduation standards, and expunging the permissiveness widely perceived as the offspring of 1960s-era social turmoil. Jeremiads on the state of youth and the schools proliferated.

As Great Society liberalism became less influential within the Democratic Party and identity politics gained momentum, left-of-center activists lost political clout. Many eloquently defended the public schools, but Republican criticisms of education remained popular throughout the 1990s. To oppose higher standards, testing, discipline, and market solutions to school improvement seemed out of step with the times, whereas holding schools more accountable, weakening teachers' unions, and upgrading the curriculum and graduation requirements had considerable appeal. Like sporting events, the test scores of school districts were publicized by the local media, to applaud the high achievers and chastise the rest (usually the poorest, nonwhite districts). Schoolteachers had long been criticized for their failures, so much of this was familiar, but it was persistent. After all, the left had offered many of the same criticisms of the nation's schools in the 1960s, calling them racist, sexist, class biased, and unable to educate the poor and minorities well. By the 1980s and 1990s conservatives threw most of the stones and set the agenda for most policy debates.

More liberal or left-of-center educational activists remained on the defensive throughout the 1990s. Faculty who trained teachers on the nation's campuses had difficulty refuting attacks on teacher-certification programs. With few exceptions, schools of education were widely regarded as diploma mills. Teachers' unions faced considerable hostility in this age of accountability, although Albert Shanker of the American Federation of Teachers and other union leaders endorsed more teacher and student testing and tougher standards. Civil-rights and feminist leaders in turn divided on the issue of single-sex education, despite the long tradition of coeducation in the public schools, and liberals and activists similarly split on the question of racial integration, with a resurgence of support for racial separatism. African American parents in inner cities, whose children often faced the greatest educational hurdles, increasingly embraced the idea of "school choice," even voucher plans, in defiance of traditional black leadership.

Culture wars, debates over standards, and occasionally struggles for economic justice preoccupied many activists. In a seemingly endless battle over religion in the classroom, groups such as Americans United for the Separation of Church and State and the American Civil Liberties Union spent much time and money in court challenges to the teaching of "creation science" and the reestablishment of school prayer. Battle lines formed over attempts to frame national history standards; whereas white liberals and Afrocentrists debated academic content, Congress loudly rejected a more multicultural approach to social studies and history teaching. California residents reflected the conservative mood by voting down state-sponsored bilingual education programs, further alienating liberal elites from the masses of voters. As liberal groups filed lawsuits on behalf of poor districts, some states declared existing school-funding formulas unconstitutional; legislatures proved less diligent in sharing the public purse with poorer districts.

Despite splits within both conservative and liberal ranks, Republicans largely shaped late twentieth-century educational debates. Democratic aspirants for office realized that conservative times required more moderate approaches to educational and social issues. Reacting to the wholesale rejection of liberalism in presidential elections in the 1980s, a new generation of politicians like Arkansas governor Bill Clinton shifted the Democratic Party rightward. A leader in the moderate Democratic Leadership Council, Clinton joined with Republicans late in the decade to frame a series of national goals for America's schools for the year 2000. Less concerned with how to educate poor and minority children well or with difficult issues related to multiculturalism, economic inequality, and racial injustice than with standards, discipline, competition, testing, and accountability, the goals reflected the broader public mood. Although Democrats often resisted endorsing voucher or choice plans that included private and church-related schools, the two major parties had become nearly indistinguishable on most educational issues.

When President Clinton linked the fate of the public schools with the American dream in his 2000 State of the Union address, he tapped deep convictions about education's role in shaping the public good. To most students climbing the educational ladder, however, school seemed like a series of courses, tests, and quizzes on a wide variety of academic subjects. They often perceived the school as a social as much as an academic institution: a place offering sports teams, clubs, and peer groups. As a new century dawned, however, adults continued to argue, mostly about how to toughen standards, enhance competition, and tighten discipline in institutions that seemed forever in need of reform.

The administration of President George W. Bush strongly backed "school choice" plans that funneled tax dollars to private, usually church-related schools. In 2002 a closely divided Supreme Court upheld the constitutionality of Cleveland's tuition-voucher arrangement. The administration's showcase education bill, the No Child Left Behind Act, became law in 2002. Drafted by conservatives alarmed by the public schools' alleged academic failings, this measure, among other provisions, required every public school to administer standardized tests to all children from grades three through eight in reading, math, and science. Critics, including teachers, school administrators, and many state officials, charged that the measure represented an unprecedented level of federal meddling in public education, historically a local matter; forced instructors to "teach to the test"; discriminated against schools with large immigrant enrollments; and provided insufficient funds to pay for the new federal mandates.

President Barack Obama proclaimed that improving education was one of his top priorities. Early in his administration he undertook significant changes in the student loan program, which portended profound consequences. Educational institutions currently have two ways to offer federal loans to students. In the Federal Family Education Loan program, the government pays subsidies to banks and lenders to loan money to borrowers and reimburses companies up to 97 percent of the cost of any loan that is not paid back. The second way is the direct-loan program, created in 1993 as an alternate option, in which the government cuts out the middle man, lends money directly, and gets all the profits. When President Obama signed the Student Aid and Fiscal Responsibility Act (SAFRA), the approximately 4,500 colleges and universities that were signed up for the program had to abandon the prior program and start using the direct-loan option by 1 July 2010.

The new law eliminates fees paid to private banks to act as intermediaries in providing loans to college students and use much of the nearly $68 billion in savings over eleven years to expand Pell grants and make it easier for students to repay outstanding loans after graduation. The law also invests $2 billion in community colleges over the next four years to provide education and career training programs to workers eligible for trade adjustment aid after dislocation in their industries. The law increases Pell grants along with inflation in the next few years, which should raise the maximum grant to $5,975 from $5,550 by 2017, according to the White House; it will also provide 820,000 more grants by 2020. Students who borrow money starting in July 2014 will be allowed to cap repayments at 10 percent of their income above a basic living allowance, instead of 15 percent. Moreover, if they maintain payments, their balances will be forgiven after twenty years instead of twenty-five years—or after ten years if they are in public service, such as teaching, nursing, or serving in the military.

Mr. Obama portrayed the overhaul of the student loan program as a triumph over an army of lobbyists, singling out Sallie Mae, the nation's largest student lender, which he said spent $3 million on lobbying to stop the changes. With rising costs in student tuition fees found in both private and public institutions of higher education, student loans were expected to soar. Experts project that the average student on a per-capita basis will leave college approximately $40,000 in debt.

[*See also* **American Civil Liberties Union; Bush, George W.; Busing, School; Clinton, William J.; Education Policy: An Overview; Education Policy: Higher Education; Federal Government, Executive Branch: Other Departments; Great Society; National Education Association; Obama, Barack; Prayer in School; Reagan, Ronald;** *and* **Supreme Court, U.S.**]

BIBLIOGRAPHY

Ravitch, Diane, and Maris Vinovskis, eds. *Historical Perspectives on Current Educational Reforms*. Baltimore: Johns Hopkins University Press, 1994.

Urban, Wayne J., and Jennings L. Waggoner Jr. *American Education: A History*. New York: McGraw–Hill, 1996.

William J. Reese; revised and updated by Pearson Bramblett

HIGHER EDUCATION

Higher education in the United States has sought to strike a balance among ever-changing constituencies, balancing the needs of students, faculty, state and federal governments, and society more generally. This has manifested itself in a gradual shift from teaching-centered, undergraduate-focused, small, private colleges to large universities, both public and private, that try to balance teaching with research while also trying to assure the broadest possible access. Much of this gradual transformation has been the result of changes in sources of revenue that are often linked to shifts in public attitudes toward the purpose of higher education.

Colonial and Antebellum Era Colleges. Early American institutions of higher learning were patterned on European models, but they soon developed distinctive features. The nine colleges founded before the Revolutionary War were primarily private, denominational, and focused on training ministers and an American elite through a focus on the classics. Colleges in this period established what would become the tradition of drawing from multiple resources to finance their operations. Contributions came largely from the private sector at this time, but also from legislative bodies, fund-raising, and tuition.

As the nation expanded after the Revolution, so too did the college system. Religious denominations continued to splinter, with each creating its own college. New western communities founded colleges in imitation of more established cities. At the same time, and in response to questions about education's function in a meritocratic society devoted to progress, colleges began to move away from a strictly classical curriculum to one that included modern disciplines. Higher education became a vital component of professional preparation, as an education beyond an apprenticeship became essential to rapid upward progress in law, medicine, and theology.

The number of public colleges grew rapidly during this era as people began to accept the principle that states should support higher learning. Vermont chartered a state college in the 1791, the year it entered the union, and Michigan organized its first public college while still a territory. States also provided some support to private institutions in the form of cash or tax exemptions, especially where public institutions were slow to develop. Both public and private institutions were the beneficiaries of state land grants.

The Advent of Universities (1865–1940). Beginning after the Civil War, colleges, technical schools, and scientific schools began a period of rapid expansion. Higher education became necessary for a broader range of occupational groups as they worked to professionalize themselves. In addition to the established professions of law, medicine, and theology, colleges began creating schools of business, architecture, engineering, and agriculture as the idea that one had to be trained to enter these careers grew and these groups sought professional status.

Some colleges began to transform themselves into universities, emphasizing research, the discovery and codification of knowledge, and a commitment to the practical use of that knowledge, career preparation, and advanced study. A curricular shift began as natural sciences were introduced and classics were deemphasized. Fledgling universities created units specifically for scientific learning and advanced studies while leaving the collegiate structure in place for undergraduates. By 1900, research universities had become a distinctive type of higher education. They grew rapidly because of funding from private donors and the Morrill Land Grant Act, which allotted each state monies for the founding of at least one college that would teach subjects related to agriculture and the "mechanic arts." Debates arose regarding the relationship of colleges to the new universities, with some university presidents seeking to make their institutions places for advanced study only, but the collegiate idea proved durable. The new universities emerged as institutions with large faculties engaged in research, but also in undergraduate teaching and training future scholars. They proved popular and their growth outpaced that of other institutions.

Universities could not accommodate everyone who sought higher education, so different forms developed and existing forms adapted. Small liberal arts colleges expanded their professional programs and broadened their undergraduate curriculum. Few liberal arts colleges accepted African Americans, which led to the creation of separate institutions by philanthropists and, in the case of Howard University, by Congress. The Morrill Land Grant Act also contributed by denying appropriations to any state that refused college admission on the basis of race, unless separate but equal facilities were created. Women's colleges also appeared in this period, evolving from women's seminaries or endowed by philanthropists. Community colleges began as a way of separating students doing advanced work from freshman and sophomores doing basic coursework. They grew because of a demand for further education on the part of an increasing number of high school graduates. They prepared people for further study and for immediate entry into the workforce. State colleges also enjoyed success, especially in training teachers, nurses, accountants, and other professionals who did not need advanced studies.

Throughout this period, higher education continued to be funded primarily through philanthropic gifts and state appropriations, with students paying only a small percentage of the cost of their education. Endowments or charitable gifts were the only way universities had of funding new research, facilities, and equipment. This system reached its apogee between World War I and World War II. World War I had the effect of bringing together elite scientists, industry, and large foundations on the National Research Council (NRC), which was tasked with coordinating scientific resources and securing the cooperation of governmental, educational, and industrial agencies with research facilities at their disposal. The NRC set the precedent that a central organization designed to direct American science was a good idea, a notion interpreted by some to mean the government should play a larger role, especially as it became increasingly apparent during the Depression that private funding was unreliable and inadequate. But there was no general consensus on the appropriate role for government in advancing science and, relatedly, no administrative mechanisms for implementing such a role.

World War II and After. Scientists' contributions to military advances during World War II suggested that perhaps the government did have reason to invest in academic research. Over the first two decades of the Cold War, government funding of education, both through research grants and through tuition payment under the Servicemen's Readjustment Act, grew to be the primary source of revenue for universities. In general, this led to broader access, rapid expansion, and massive investments in facilities, but also gave government agencies substantial say in research agendas. After the protests against military-related research on campuses in the 1960s, the consensus on federal funding for research began to break down, leaving universities to find new ways to meet budgets for expanded facilities and government new ways of ensuring access to higher education.

The exigencies of World War II helped establish a new relationship between government and universities. During World War II, the Office of Strategic Research and Development (OSRD) oversaw both medical and defense research. University researchers studied nuclear physics, radar, rocket propulsion, new medical techniques, and basic science such as nonnuclear physics and chemistry. The government had a clear interest in continuing to fund research in projects with military applications, but its interest in basic research was less clear. This was problematic because basic science was central to academic inquiry, but practical applications were most important for government funding. In the near term, the government funded programs with clear military applications, largely through the Office of Naval Research (ONR). The National Institutes of Health (NIH) provided grants for medical research and the Atomic Energy Commission (AEC) funded ongoing nuclear studies. In 1950, largely in an attempt to limit the influence of the ONR, Congress created the National Science Foundation (NSF). The NSF was supposed to support basic science, as well as programmatic research that aimed to fulfill the needs of a certain agency, but tended to continue the tradition of funding projects with clearly defined outcomes.

At the same time that a financial relationship between research universities and government agencies was being institutionalized, access to higher education became more widely available. The program that had the greatest impact was the Servicemen's Adjustment Act (GI Bill), under which almost 2 million soldiers advanced their education at government expense. Enrollments ballooned in the late 1940s, swelling the coffers of both public and private institutions. By the mid-1950s, the GI Bill students had departed, but the Soviet launch of Sputnik in 1957 led to national soul-searching regarding how to improve American science.

One outcome was a recognition that American competitiveness in the sciences rested on the complex infrastructure of research universities that both supported current researchers and trained the next generation of graduate students. Ultimately this meant funding research and recruiting talent, which led, again, to a broadening of access. Another was the realization that the government had a substantial interest in basic, as well as programmatic, research. The result was a golden age of academic science in which several agencies, including the National Aeronautics and Space Administration (NASA), the NSF, and the NIH funded basic research.

Federal spending reached its height in 1967 and 1968. It began to decline partly in response to student protest movements that targeted military research on campuses around the country. The consensus of the time seemed to be that universities could best fulfill their social responsibilities when they remained apart from and above society in general. This notion was reinforced by the student protesters against military research. In response, Senator Mike Mansfield added a rider to the Military Authorization Act for 1970, forbidding the Department of Defense (DoD) from funding research that had no direct relationship to a specific military function, eventually ending the DoD's role as a supplement to the NSF.

The golden age of federal funding for research overlapped with a commitment to increasing access to higher education. Voters implemented policies at the local, state, and federal levels that increased the number of people attending college. Congress codified this commitment with the Guaranteed Student Loan program in 1965 and expanded it with the Education Amendments of 1972. These amendments created the Basic Educational Opportunity Grant (Pell Grant), authorized State Student Incentive Grants for states to create scholarships, and created the Student Loan Marketing Association to provide funds for student loans. Over time, the amount received by students as grants dropped, whereas the proportion of aid they received in loans increased. The result was a gradual increase in the amount of educational expenses borne by individual students.

This commitment to greater access created problems during the economic downturn beginning in 2008. A new institutional form, the for-profit career school, had arisen in response to this commitment. These schools offered practical training in business or technical fields, often on an accelerated basis. As unemployment rates in the United States rose after the collapse of the housing market, new graduates found it difficult to find entry-level positions. Consequently many of them deferred their loans or defaulted. They were not alone. Many students who attended four-year institutions did the same. By federal law, student debt is rarely dischargeable in bankruptcy, often leaving underemployed students with substantial debt burdens. The federal government responded to increasing default rates in 2010 by revamping student loan programs. It removed subsidies for private banks to make loans, lowered the percentage of income a graduate must devote to repayment, tied Pell Grant increases to inflation, and accelerated loan forgiveness. In the case of for-profit schools, the Department of Education proposed "gainful employment" rules that would curtail federal aid to programs that have a repayment rate of less than 35 percent or a high debt-to-income ratio.

By the beginning of the twenty-first century, American colleges and universities had become large, complex systems that sought to balance research and teaching, often in response to society's needs. Since World War II, they had become increasingly dependent on federal funding in the form of research grants and aid to students to accomplish this mission. The result was a system in which federal policy affected the direction of university growth, especially in terms of research agendas, and student access, especially in terms of the cost to each student for his or her education.

[*See also* **Atomic Energy Commission; Morrill Land Grant Act; National Aeronautics and Space Administration; National Institutes of Health;** ***and*** **National Science Foundation.**]

BIBLIOGRAPHY

Cohen, Arthur M. *The Shaping of American Higher Education: Emergence and Growth of the Contemporary System*. San Francisco: Jossey–Bass, 1998.

Geiger, Roger. *Research and Relevant Knowledge: American Research Universities since World War II*. New York: Oxford University Press, 1993.

Geiger, Roger. *To Advance Knowledge: The Growth of American Research Universities, 1900–1914*. New York: Oxford University Press, 1986.

Rudolph, Frederick. *The American College and University*. New York: Vintage Books, 1962.

U.S. Department of Education. http://www.ed.gov/ accessed 19 March 2011.

Veysey, Laurence R. *The Emergence of the American University*. Chicago: University of Chicago Press, 1965.

Wilkinson, Rupert. *Aiding Students, Buying Students: Financial Aid in America*, Nashville, Tenn.: Vanderbilt University Press, 2005.

Amy C. Wallhermfechtel

EIGHTEENTH AMENDMENT

The Eighteenth Amendment to the U.S. Constitution, instituting national Prohibition, was born out of temperance reformers' efforts to remove the blight of alcoholic drinks from society as they maneuvered within the intricacies of American federalism. In the 1880s and 1890s, prohibitionists in dry states struggled against the operations of a federal system that frustrated their efforts. Interstate commerce laws permitted liquor sellers from wet states to sell their products in dry territory. Also, the federal excise tax on liquor fostered a benign view of the liquor business as an economically vital industry. Drys (as Prohibition advocates were called) responded by formulating a policy of concurrent state and federal action against liquor. In the twentieth century, the Anti-Saloon League (founded in 1895) carried this strategy to new heights. Through league pressure, Prohibition spread to half the population of the United States by 1912, and Congress adopted laws, most notably the 1913 Webb–Kenyon Act, designed to aid Prohibition states.

In 1913, the league called for a national constitutional amendment. Exploiting division in their opponents' ranks, drys drafted the bill and pressured Congress to pass it. Capitalizing on concerns associated with World War I, including German-American dominance of the brewing industry and fears of diminished efficiency through alcohol consumption, the prohibitionists succeeded. Congress passed the amendment in December 1917 and sent it to the states for ratification, which occurred in January 1919. In January 1920 national Prohibition went into effect. The amendment banned the manufacture, sale, transportation, and importation of intoxicating liquors within the United States. It granted Congress and the states "concurrent power" of enforcement.

The Volstead Act of 1919 set up a specific federal enforcement apparatus.

The Eighteenth Amendment lasted only thirteen years before being repealed in 1933, the only time a constitutional amendment has ever been rescinded. Repeal was brought about by a number of factors, including the failure of enforcement. The concurrent-power provision let the states abdicate their enforcement responsibility to the federal government, which—although it expanded its efforts—could not fully curtail the illegal liquor trade. Although Prohibition significantly reduced the amount of liquor being consumed and improved the health of Americans, it also stimulated the growth of organized crime and corruption. A federal study, the Wickersham Report of 1930, documented the breakdown of enforcement, especially in the larger cities. Changes in cultural attitudes toward liquor consumption further eroded support for the policy. Anti-Prohibition editorial writers, newspaper cartoonists, and journalists like H. L. Mencken heaped ridicule on the Eighteenth Amendment and its supporters. Moreover, the strongest organization behind the amendment, the Anti-Saloon League, lost much of its influence, just as lobbying organizations favoring repeal gained strength. Finally, the Great Depression, by destroying the claim that Prohibition would assure national prosperity and by carrying predominantly "wet" Democrats into national office, assured the speedy demise of national Prohibition.

The Eighteenth Amendment produced long-lasting consequences for American law and constitutionalism. National Prohibition stimulated growth in the federal law-enforcement establishment, a process that did not disappear after repeal. The Eighteenth Amendment directly shaped the constitutional system by specifying a seven-year time limit for ratification. Such limits subsequently became customary, allowing amendment opponents to translate delay into defeat.

[*See also* **Anti-Saloon League; Constitution; Progressive Era; Prohibition;** *and* **Woman's Christian Temperance Union.**]

BIBLIOGRAPHY

Clark, Norman H. *Deliver Us from Evil.* New York: W. W. Norton, 1976.

Hamm, Richard F. *Shaping the Eighteenth Amendment.* Chapel Hill: University of North Carolina Press, 1995.

Merz, Charles. *The Dry Decade.* Garden City, N.Y.: Doubleday, Doran, 1931.

Richard F. Hamm

EISENHOWER, DWIGHT D.

(1890–1969), U.S. army general, Supreme Commander of Allied Forces in Europe during World War II, and thirty-fourth president of the United States. Dwight David Eisenhower was born in Denison, Texas, but spent his youth in Abilene, Kansas. After high school he spent two years working before entering West Point, from which he was commissioned in 1915. The following year he married Mamie Doud; they had one son, John.

Eisenhower remained in the United States during World War I. In the 1920s he served in Panama and attended both the General Staff School at Fort Leavenworth, Kansas, and the Army War College in Carlisle, Pennsylvania. From 1930 to 1935, he was assistant secretary of war and then chief of staff to General Douglas MacArthur in Washington, D.C. In 1936 he accompanied MacArthur to the Philippines, but returned to America when war broke out in Europe in 1939.

Eisenhower rose meteorically during World War II. His performance in the 1941

Louisiana Maneuvers earned him a summons to Washington to assist Army Chief of Staff George Marshall. In 1942 he was given command of American and Allied forces in North Africa; his rout of General Erwin Rommel's forces led President Franklin Delano Roosevelt to select him to lead the Allied invasion of Normandy (Operation Overlord). Eisenhower's key decision—to invade on 6 June 1944 (D-Day) despite bad weather—proved critical to the operation's success. Although he was criticized by second-guessers, most notably for allowing Russian troops to liberate Berlin, his strategic decisions have withstood retrospective scrutiny.

After brief service as army chief of staff, Eisenhower returned to civilian life in 1948 as president of Columbia University. In 1951, President Harry S. Truman appointed him as commander of the North Atlantic Treaty Organization (NATO) forces in Europe. A year later, moderate Republicans successfully pressed Eisenhower to run in the New Hampshire Republican presidential primary; he did well there and in other primaries. At the Republican Party convention in July, his forces outmaneuvered those of Senator Robert Taft to secure the nomination, thus launching the "nonpolitical" general's political career. With Senator Richard M. Nixon as his vice presidential runningmate, he easily defeated Democrat Adlai Stevenson in the general election.

As president, Eisenhower was less conservative than liberals feared, but more so than moderates hoped. A committed internationalist, he supported the United Nations and engaged in a series of historic summit meetings with Soviet leaders. His differences with extreme conservatives included opposition to the Communist-baiting Wisconsin senator Joseph McCarthy. Although criticized at the time for his seemingly passive role, Eisenhower worked subtly to undermine McCarthy even while remaining publicly neutral. In foreign policy, he successfully brokered an armistice ending the Korean War and presided over a military buildup (mostly airpower and nuclear weaponry) while holding the federal budget virtually constant. He refused to send American troops to aid the 1956 Hungarian uprising against Soviet military rule, but acted decisively in invading Lebanon in 1958 to stabilize its pro-Western government. His appeal across the political spectrum was reflected in his sweeping reelection in 1956, again defeating Stevenson.

Eisenhower sought to moderate American tendencies to overmilitarize the Cold War, defying public pressures to build up U.S. defenses after the Soviets launched the world's first space satellite, Sputnik, in October 1957. In domestic policy, he steered a moderately conservative course, opposing public power and direct support for farmers and labor, while compromising with a Democratic Congress. Although cool to the civil rights movement, he did send federal troops to Arkansas in 1957 when Governor Orval Faubus defined a court order to integrate a Little Rock high school. A dramatic confrontation with the Soviets over the downing of an American surveillance (U-2) plane in 1960 only increased Eisenhower's popularity. His January 1961 farewell address, warning against the military–industrial complex, proved to be one of his more enduring political contributions.

After leaving the White House, Eisenhower avoided partisan activities. In 1964 he disappointed Republican moderates by refusing until the last minute to support their efforts to stave off Barry Goldwater's presidential nomination.

A major figure of the twentieth century, Eisenhower was one of those rare American presidents whose reputation rests more on his prepresidential achievements than on his activities as president or afterward. His strategic decisions and political acumen are widely viewed as crucial to Allied victory in World War II. Still, his accomplishments as president were significant. As the first Republican to occupy the White House after the New Deal, he helped to legitimize the liberal political revolution it represented. He also introduced a staff system to the White House that became the model for succeeding presidents. Finally, the peace (after Korea), prosperity, and balanced federal budgets that characterized his White House years underscore the success of his moderate leadership.

[*See also* **Conservatism; Federal Government, Executive Branch: Presidency, The; Liberalism; MacArthur, Douglas; McCarthy, Joseph; New Deal; Nixon, Richard M.; Republican Party; Roosevelt, Franklin Delano; Stevenson, Adlai;** *and* **Truman, Harry S.**]

BIBLIOGRAPHY

Ambrose, Stephen E. *Eisenhower: Soldier and President.* New York: Simon & Schuster, 1990.

Brendon, Piers. *Ike: Life and Times of Dwight D. Eisenhower.* London: Martin Secker & Warburg, 1987.

Gary W. Reichard

ELECTIONS

This entry contains five subentries: Election Law; Nominating Systems; Presidential Elections; Suffrage; and Voting Systems.

ELECTION LAW

Election laws regulate who votes, when and how they vote, for whom they can vote, how campaigns are conducted and financed, and how votes are recorded, counted, and allocated. The development of these laws over the course of American history has been far less linear and progressive and far more subject to reversals, far less motivated by ideals, and far more driven by partisanship and self-interest than popular and even some scholarly accounts have contended. It is also far more currently contentious and unsettled than at any time since at least the 1960s. The last time the United States experienced a long period of bitter, ideological partisan divisions, during the Civil War, Reconstruction, and the post-Reconstruction Era, changes in election laws twice revolutionized the nation's politics. Similar although much dampened changes may be in process in the early twenty-first century.

Born Democratic. Even during the Colonial Era, America had the broadest electorate in the world: three to six times as high a percentage could vote here as in England at the time. White males could vote if they owned fifty acres of land or, in other colonies, property that would rent for forty shillings. Plentiful land in an overwhelmingly agricultural society meant that the vast majority of free males who lived long enough could meet those qualifications. During the Revolution, efforts to rally popular support loosened suffrage requirements, in some states enfranchising all "mechanics" or those with little property who paid a small poll tax (a tax of fixed amount on an individual) and terminating the disfranchisement of Roman Catholics and, in five states, of free African Americans. Lax enforcement of even these restrictions, especially during periods of intense factional or party competition, sometimes produced de facto universal white male suffrage.

Although the existing evidence is fragmentary, turnout in colonial elections for which we have accurate records varied from 10 to 50 percent of adult white males, and in the period from 1800 to 1824—before the onset of "Jacksonian Democracy"—peak turnout in state elections in seventeen of the twenty-two states in the Union at the end of the period exceeded 50 percent of white adult males. Over the first half of the nineteenth century, the remaining curbs on white male democracy gradually dissolved, although those on black suffrage increased, and the one state that had allowed propertied women to vote, New Jersey, ended that experiment in 1807. In the 1860 presidential election, over 80 percent of white male adults cast ballots.

The Struggles for Black and Woman Suffrage. Although voter registration laws and literacy tests succeeded in keeping some foreign-born, chiefly non–English-speaking immigrants from voting, and many American Indians and natives of China were disfranchised until the 1920s or even later, the largest exceptions to the democratic character of American suffrage were African Americans and women. Their contrasting experiences demonstrate the importance of partisan interests in suffrage extension and contraction.

Although blacks had been able to vote in 1860 in New England and, if they could meet a stiff property qualification, in New York, it took the Military Reconstruction Act of 1867 to enfranchise African Americans in the South and the Fifteenth Amendment of 1870 to prohibit voting discrimination against the race nationally. As the party of abolition and civil rights, the Republicans were sure to win the overwhelming majority of black votes, which they did until the 1930s. As the party of secessionists and discriminatory "Black Codes" and Jim Crow laws, the Democrats were sure to lose them. It was as natural, therefore, for the Republicans to act to enfranchise the largely illiterate freedmen shortly after emancipation as it was for Democrats to use a succession of tactics—horrific, carefully targeted violence; widespread fraud; gerrymandering, registration, secret ballot, and other restrictive statute laws; and finally, state constitutional disfranchisement through poll taxes and literacy tests, as well as whites-only Democratic primaries—to disfranchise them over the period from the 1870s through 1910. Republican efforts, most notably in the 1890 Lodge Fair Elections Bill, which was defeated by the longest filibuster in U.S. history up to that point, failed to stop vote fraud against blacks and to enforce the Fifteenth Amendment. In still shocking abdications of its constitutional responsibilities, the U.S. Supreme Court invalidated the most far-reaching law to protect black political activity in *United States v. Cruikshank,* 92 U.S. 542 (1876), and rejected legal efforts to block state disfranchising laws in *Giles v. Harris,* 189 U.S. 475 (1903). Between 1865 and 1900, not a single Democratic member of Congress voted for any civil rights or voting rights law, whereas almost all Republicans did.

By contrast, since women were never entirely identified with a single political party or cause and since white women's interests overlapped with those of white men, they were not enfranchised so quickly or suddenly, but there were never any serious efforts to withdraw suffrage rights from them once they had been granted, except in New Jersey. Because of their special role as mothers in Victorian America, women were granted the right to vote for school officials, beginning in Kentucky in 1838 and spreading to twenty-five other states by 1900.

Having failed to add female to black suffrage in several states and in the national Fifteenth Amendment, part of the woman suffrage movement became harshly anti-black and later, anti-immigrant. Beginning with adoption at the state level in Wyoming, Colorado, Utah, and Idaho in the 1890s, just as African Americans were being disfranchised in the South, woman suffrage spread to fifteen states by 1918. In nine other states, women could vote in presidential elections. Predominantly backed by Republicans, woman suffrage attracted growing support from Democrats, and majorities of members of Congress from both parties endorsed the Anthony Amendment by the time it passed in 1919.

Although the final achievement of women's suffrage in 1920 had relatively little immediate impact, because women initially turned out to vote at lower levels than men and voted for each political party in proportions similar to those of men, black suffrage revolutionized American politics because of the race's high participation rates and marked partisan leanings. In the 1860s, African American enfranchisement gave the Republican Party a southern wing, bringing schools to all children and vigorous governments that attempted to rebuild the war-ravaged region. In the 1890s and 1900s, the disfranchisement of blacks and poor whites created a one-party South that enshrined racial discrimination as government-sponsored policy and held back the region's, and therefore, the nation's socioeconomic development for a half century.

With the Supreme Court's dismantling of the white primary in *Smith v. Allwright* (321 U.S. 649 (1944)) and especially with the passage of the Voting Rights Act in 1965, the reinvigoration of black suffrage in the South revolutionized southern and national politics for a third time. Partisan competition was gradually reintroduced into the South and legally sanctioned segregation and most other discriminatory governmental policies very gradually faded in the face of Supreme Court decisions that restored the original intent of the framers of the Reconstruction Amendments. African American voices in state and national legislatures and administrations helped to reconstruct the American state a second time.

Amendments to the Voting Rights Act in 1982 that for the first time protected African American interests during a decadal redistricting and made possible a tripling of the number of black southern members of Congress in the 1992 elections produced another backlash in the Supreme Court. Suddenly, a five-person majority of the Court took notice of pro-black gerrymandering, although the courts had largely ignored anti-black and other gerrymandering for more than a century (*Shaw v. Reno,* 509 U.S. 630 (1993)). Since after 1965, nearly all African Americans voted Democratic, Republicans had a strong incentive to pass and strictly enforce "voter identification" and criminal disfranchisement laws that had racially disproportionate impacts on blacks. Republican surges in state legislative seats, particularly in the 2010 elections, allowed them to pass these laws.

An even more serious assault on minority political rights was the attempt by leading Republican lawyers to have part of the Voting Rights Act declared unconstitutional, which came very close to success in *Northwest Austin Municipal Utility District No. 1 v. Holder,* 557 U.S.__ (2009). Cases from Alabama and North Carolina that raised the same issues that the *Northwest Austin* majority had sidestepped were pending in lower federal courts in 2011, and one was on a fast track to the Supreme Court. Glimpses of a post–Voting Rights Act southern politics were visible in 2011 redistricting plans in areas containing just under the proportion of African Americans and Latinos that the Supreme Court ruled had to be protected during redistricting (*Bartlett v. Strickland,* 556 U.S.__ (2009)). Minority populations were split up and scattered into overwhelmingly Republican districts, where minority voters could have no political influence. The reshaping of minority rights by election laws, one of the major themes of American history, is far from over.

The Electoral College. The Founding Fathers designed the Electoral College to authorize wise men from each state to meet and select the best men to be president and vice president, but the Framers did not foresee political parties, which undermined the original intent of the college by 1800. By separating voting for the two offices, the Twelfth Amendment fixed the immediate problem, but the state-based nature of the Electoral College and its interaction with partisan and regional incentives continued to produce consequences that had not been envisioned.

Because representation in the Electoral College was based on the number of senators (two for every state) plus the number of representatives (based on population), the Electoral College gave small states power in the selection of a president disproportionate to their population. Because political parties quickly organized slates of electors in each state and because nearly all states assigned all of the electors to the candidates of the party that won a majority of the votes in the state as a whole, the state basis for political parties was strengthened and national parties quite early began to concentrate on states where the outcome was expected to be close and to ignore states that were solidly for one party or another.

Usually, the popular vote winner won the Electoral College vote as well, avoiding controversy, but the 2000 election produced a split in the two outcomes, as Florida's razor-thin margin, settled by a much-criticized 5-to-4 U.S. Supreme Court decision (*Bush v. Gore,* 531 U.S. 98 (2000)), threw the election to a man who lost the popular tally by a half-million votes. An effort to get states containing a majority of the electoral votes to commit to casting their individual electoral votes for the popular vote winner seemed close to success in 2011.

Reapportionment and Redistricting. Another election law issue that has been controversial from the beginning was the redistricting of legislative seats. The redistricting that gave a name to odd-shaped districts (the "gerrymander") took place in Massachusetts in 1812, and the unequal apportionment of seats between long-settled coastal areas and the burgeoning backcountry had flared tempers during the Colonial Era. Northern resentment over counting slaves as three-fifths of a person in the apportionment of members of the House and the Electoral College festered before the Civil War, and the specter of voteless ex-slaves bolstering the numbers of former Southern rebels in Congress hastened Republican efforts to enfranchise the freedmen after the war.

In the face of the urbanization and suburbanization of America, rural interests froze apportionments in some states during the first half of the twentieth century. For example, rural interests refused to reallocate state legislative seats in Alabama and Tennessee from 1900 to 1960. Farmers allied with anti–labor union urban interests in California to grant the smallest counties 425 times the representation of Los Angeles County in the state Senate. In the 1920s, struggles over reapportioning congressional seats between states became so heated that Congress simply failed to act for a decade.

The Supreme Court broke the logjam in *Baker v. Carr,* 369 U.S. 186 (1962)), which ruled reapportionment justifiable—that is, suitable for courts to rule on. Litigants, courts, and legislatures responded with startling rapidity: *Gray v. Sanders,* 372 U.S. 368 (1963), the case that announced the "one person, one vote" standard, was filed on the afternoon that *Baker* was announced; by 1964, *Reynolds v. Sims,* 377 U.S. 553, ruled that both houses of every state legislature had to be apportioned on a strict population basis; and by the end of the decade, almost every state legislature and most local legislative and administrative bodies had been completely reapportioned. Despite the fear of Justice Felix Frankfurter, in his dissent in *Baker,* that courts would be lost in a "mathematical quagmire," standards for judging population equality proved simple to formulate and apply. The confluence of interests in reapportioning between citizens in urban and suburban areas, the centers of Democratic and Republican strength, respectively, made the "reapportionment revolution" remarkably uncontroversial with the vast majority of the American public.

But many questions central to the allocation of political power remained, even fifty years after *Baker*. What, exactly, constituted "racial gerrymandering"? Did the shape of the districts matter, or was shape merely one indication of an intent to gather together like-minded voters? Why should racial "communities of interest" be treated differently under the equal protection clause than economic groupings, cities, regions, or the interests of incumbent officeholders or political parties (*Miller v. Johnson,* 515 U.S. 900 (1995))? Was partisan gerrymandering justiciable, and if so, exactly what practices were to be declared illegal (*Davis v. Bandemer,* 478 U.S. 109 (1986), *Vieth v. Jubilirer,* 541 U.S. 267 (2004))? As computer hardware and software developed and as election and population data became much more easily and quickly available, savvy redistricting consultants and even novice college and law students could design districting plans to disadvantage one group at the expense of another with astonishing ease and precision, all the while drawing districts with equal populations. Should courts withdraw from attempting to apply the vague equal protection clause to such difficult tasks of oversight, even if that meant implicitly blessing inequities in political power that began to approach those of the pre-*Baker* era? If not, what practical standards should be applied, and how could courts avoid the appearance and/or reality of judicial partisanship, an appearance that had shadowed the Supreme Court's reputation since *Bush v. Gore?*

Campaign Finance Regulation. In the nineteenth century, many campaigns for federal office were partly or largely financed by contributions from current or prospective federal employees. The Pendleton Act of 1883, which established a merit system and banned requiring federal employees to contribute to campaigns, might therefore be considered the first federal act regulating campaign finance. When the relatively small contributions by individual federal workers were replaced by huge ones from corporations, a movement to ban direct corporate contributions began, which resulted in the Tillman Act of 1907. Lacking a commission to oversee it or provisions to force candidates to disclose the sources of their funds, the act was at first largely ineffectual, but with amendments over the years it gradually shifted the principal source of contributions to federal political campaigns to wealthy individuals. Some, but by no means all states and localities adopted similar restrictions.

As labor unions burgeoned during the New Deal and World War II, they began to balance the influence of the rich in political campaigns, contributing largely to Democrats. It was hardly surprising, therefore, that the Republican sweep of the 1946 elections led to a ban on political contributions from union treasuries in the 1947 Taft–Hartley Act. Unions were allowed, however, to aggregate voluntary contributions from their members in "political action committees" (PACs), and over the years, many businesses and other groups also formed PACs, pooling individuals' resources to focus their messages and maximize their impact.

More comprehensive legislation, the Federal Election Campaign Act of 1971 (FECA) and the amendments of 1974 mandated disclosure of contributions, limited contributions and expenditures, set up a public financing system for presidential (but not congressional) campaigns, and established a Federal Election Commission (FEC) to oversee it all. In a 138-page opinion with 83 more pages of concurrences and dissents, the U.S. Supreme Court upheld most of FECA's contribution limits and disclosure requirements, as well as its public financing system, but struck down the sharing of nominations to the FEC by Congress and the president and, most importantly, vetoed the act's expenditure limits (*Buckley v. Valeo,* 424 U.S. 1 (1976)). In an age of campaigning by television ads, it took money to speak, so limitations on spending limited speech, contrary to the First Amendment, the justices concluded. The Court rejected the idea, which had been stressed by the lower court in *Buckley,* that too much money on one side would restrict the speech of other sides by drowning out their voices.

Buckley ruled that the only valid justifications for governmental limits on contributions were to diminish corruption or, since it was usually difficult to prove the connection between particular contributions and politicians' conduct, "the appearance of corruption." If an effort to equalize voters' influence was irrelevant to campaign finance regulation or even, as Chief Justice John Roberts implied during a 2011 oral argument, enough by itself to render the law unconstitutional, then restrictions on contributions to ballot measures in the states or to committees that were formally independent of particular candidates were invalid as well [*First National Bank of Boston v. Bellotti,* 435 U.S. 765 (1978); *Citizens United v. FEC,* 130 S. Ct. 876 (2010).]

Although the Court first approved the attempt by Congress in the 2002 Bipartisan Campaign Reform Act (BCRA) to regulate "soft money" (contributions to national political parties that were passed on to state-level parties, used for activities other than media ads, or employed to run "sham" issue ads that attacked candidates without urging a vote against them), the replacement of Justice Sandra Day O'Connor by Samuel Alito in 2005 shifted the Court's balance (*McConnell v. Federal Election Committee,* 540 U.S. 93 (2003)). *Citizens United* allowed corporations and labor unions to make unlimited contributions to independent committees, committees formed for the 2010 campaigns entirely skirted disclosure rules, the Court in 2011 invalidated an Arizona public campaign financing law, and longtime critics of any campaign financing regulation seemed poised, with an apparently sympathetic five-man majority on the Supreme Court, to shred the 120-year effort to regulate money in elections *Arizona Free Enterprise Club's Freedom Club PAC v. Bennett,* 131 S. Ct. 2806).

[***See also* Baker *v.* Carr; Bush *v.* Gore; Fifteenth Amendment; Smith *v.* Allwright; Taft–Hartley Act; *and* Woman Suffrage Movement.**]

BIBLIOGRAPHY

Issacharoff, Samuel, Pamela S. Karlan, and Richard H. Pildes. *The Law of Democracy: Legal Structure of the Political Process.* New York: Foundation Press, 2007.

Keyssar, Alexander. *The Right to Vote: The Contested History of Democracy in the United States.* New York: Basic Books, 2000.

Kousser, J. Morgan. *The Shaping of Southern Politics: Suffrage Restriction and the Establishment of the One-Party South, 1880–1910.* New Haven, Conn.: Yale University Press, 1974.

Lowenstein, Daniel Hays, Richard L. Hasen, and Daniel P. Tokaji. *Election Law: Cases and Materials.* Durham, N.C.: Carolina Academic Press, 2008.

Ratcliffe, Donald J. "Myths of the Lost Atlantis: Was Andrew Jackson Really the People's Choice in 1824?" www.common-place.org/pasley/?paged=16 (accessed 11 October 2011).

J. Morgan Kousser

NOMINATING SYSTEMS

The processes through which candidates for elective public offices in the United States are nominated have varied, depending partly on whether the would-be nominee is seeking to run as an independent candidate or as the representative of one of the two major parties.

In one important respect the Independent candidate in the early twenty-first century is in the same position as candidates in the preparty era at the beginning of the Republic: he or she nominates himself or herself. However, at the end of the 1780s candidates had to do little more than present themselves for election. Today, depending on the particular requirements of state electoral law, they must also obtain the signatures of a specified number of qualified electors who support their being placed on the ballot. In many states there are partisan aspects to this process, especially when the officials responsible for the conduct of an election, as well as local and state judges, owe their positions to a party. Their own party's interests can result in the scrutiny of a nominee's credentials being more intense or lax depending on where that party's interests are thought to lie. Frequently, Independent candidates must acquire far more signatures than the minimum stipulated to reduce the risk of failing to be listed on the ballot.

Once parties started to form and to contest elections—initially in the 1790s and then more permanently in the 1830s—nomination processes inevitably became more complex. Unlike parties in most countries that democratized subsequently, in the United States they were nominating candidates in the same year for many different levels of public office, often with different electoral boundaries. If those nominations were to include a wide range of supporters meeting for a selection, then more than one party gathering would be necessary. The single caucus meeting, of the kind that had been used in the early stages of party development, was insufficient; a ward-level meeting could nominate a candidate for an office at that level, but selection for an office at the city, county, or state level could be effected only if there were means of coordinating the activities of the various local party units. Thus was born the caucus-convention system, a multistage process of candidate selection. The initial stage was that of the caucus (although it was called the primary or primary election in some states). A ward or district caucus would make nominations for offices at that level and then select delegates to attend the conventions at "higher" levels, such as those for the city or county. At the apex of a state party was the state convention, which, in addition to making nominations for state-level offices, including the governorship, would also select delegates to the national convention in presidential election years. The system was certainly decentralized, although describing it as democratic would usually have been misleading. Local political elites were often able to outorganize any opposition they faced; participants in the process were never equally powerful. Moreover, the extent to which deliberation actually took place, even in the caucuses, was limited. Indeed, except in New England and a few other states, caucuses were never more than places to which party supporters would turn up to vote for the nominees of their choice and then depart, having done so.

The heyday of the caucus-convention arrangement lasted from the 1820s until the 1890s. However, a few counties in some states came to select their candidates by other means. In particular, in various Pennsylvania counties alternative nominating procedures were deployed. The most significant of these was the so-called Crawford County Plan, first introduced by Democrats in 1842. Its historical importance lies in it being the first known example of a direct primary in America. Such a primary eliminates multistage nominations and replaces them with just one stage that leads directly to the nomination of a candidate. Thus, there are no conventions; selection of nominees for offices at the county level, for example, is conducted through an election in which all party supporters present can participate. In a sense, therefore, such nominations resemble those made in a caucus for the lowest level of political office.

The direct primary moved beyond Crawford County during the second half of the nineteenth century, albeit rather slowly. There is evidence that during the 1890s it was being used by parties in some congressional districts, counties, or subunits of counties by about fourteen of the then forty-five states. It had also been introduced in one major city (by the Republicans in Cleveland) but the procedure there was soon abandoned as a failure. It had been spreading outside Pennsylvania for precisely the same reason that it would be adopted by most states in the first two decades of the twentieth century. The direct primary was believed to meet two objectives. It could provide a solution to the growing difficulties of managing the caucus-convention system effectively and do so without compromising a principle accepted since the Jacksonian era, that parties should not be able to formally exclude anyone who wished to participate in them. Consequently, many "regular" politicians, as well as reformers with hostile attitudes toward the parties, would end up supporting this method of selecting candidates. Furthermore, the demise of the old Republican ideal, that candidates should not "hustle" for a nomination but must be seen to have been recruited by others to run for office, was gradually weakening one possible defense of the old system.

The caucus-convention system had worked well earlier in the century because the relatively small populations of most counties meant that informal methods of controlling the nomination processes could be effective in face-to-face communities. Later the vastly increased number of people who came to live there and could then participate in party politics increased the likelihood of confusion and conflict arising over disputed nominations. Indeed, before the end of the 1880s, when the Australian ballot was rapidly introduced in most states, one such problem facing the parties had been a relatively high level of ticket-splitting that was evident farther down the party ballot. A would-be candidate who had failed to secure the party nomination for an office could obtain the party's ballot papers for the general election, "paste" his own name over that of the candidate who had supposedly been nominated by the party, and then distribute those ballots to voters. This was not illegal. Once responsibility for printing and distributing ballots was placed in the hands of governments, pasting was usually prohibited, with the result that in the 1890s split-ticket voting seems to have declined.

During the later nineteenth century emerging democracies, including Britain, had also moved toward taking control over ballot papers away from parties and placing it with governments. In the United States, however, public control was to be extended to the process of party nominations as well. Although this was a measure advocated by reformers outside the parties, evidence now suggests that it was also acceptable to many party politicians. There were two main reasons for this. First, as the experience of attempted reform of the caucus-convention system in the 1890s was to demonstrate, the parties' decentralized structures made their own effective management of reform difficult and often impossible. The autonomy enjoyed at the local level largely prevented state parties from regulating party processes at these other levels. Moreover, those counties most in need of reform—many of which were in highly populated urban areas—were often run by the party elites most resistant to reform. Within such decentralized parties, implementing party rules that were effective, both in combating chaos and in introducing fair procedures to prevent local party elites from stymieing challenges by their opponents, proved elusive. In fact, even a well-attended national conference (in 1898) focusing directly on the problems of party nominations failed to derive any prescriptions for reform of the caucus-convention system that could be used widely—either by the parties directly or through legislation.

Starting with Kentucky in the 1890s and then spreading rapidly in the early twentieth century, the subjection of party nominations to legislative control became the norm. Minnesota introduced the first state law to require the use of the direct primary in one of its counties (in 1899), whereas Wisconsin (in 1904) was the first state to mandate direct primaries statewide. The move to reform nominations in this way spread like wildfire. By 1915 all but three states employed it widely for nominations within their borders, and by the mid-twentieth century it had been adopted for candidate selections in all states. During this period parties generally kept firm control of these processes to protect their own interests. For example, most states used a closed primary—that is, one supposedly confined only to a party's supporters—rather than an open primary in which any registered voter could participate. Again, a few states (such as Colorado) used preprimary party conventions in which one candidate would be endorsed by the party and given the (advantageous) first line on the primary ballot. Consequently, the overall impact of primaries on party strength was not great, at least not before the 1960s, when changes in campaign technologies made it easier for candidates to circumvent party organizations in seeking a nomination. Prior to that, in the Eastern states direct primaries did relatively little to enhance the position of candidates not supported by those organizations. The situation appeared different in the West, but only because in many states a number of other reforms (including nonpartisan elections for local governments) had weakened party organizations to an extent not evident in the east. In the South the direct primary was introduced into a political system where party competition had collapsed (by the 1890s) and where the individual candidate, rather than the party organization, was now the prime actor in the nomination process. Certainly, in both the West and the South, the direct primary shaped how candidate competition developed, but in neither region had it been responsible for reducing the role of parties in candidate selection. However, one partial exception to this should be noted. California's cross-filing primary (used from 1913 to 1959) advantaged incumbents because they were in the best position to run in the primaries of both parties, and this practice did contribute to a reduced party role in the nomination process.

Party nominations of presidential candidates have had a somewhat different trajectory from candidate selection for other offices, partly because until the later twentieth century the national parties were really no more than the sum of all their constituent state parties.

At the beginning of the party era the congressional caucus of the Democratic-Republicans nominated their presidential candidate. One consequence of Andrew Jackson's defeat in 1824 was that his supporters moved toward the use of the caucus-convention system for the presidency as well. Thereafter party delegates from each state, previously selected in their state convention, attended their national convention at which the nominee would be chosen. With the introduction of direct primaries for other offices early in the twentieth century, proposals for selecting national convention delegates through a primary gained support. First used in 1912, presidential primaries were deployed in 20 states by 1920. Subsequently the number of states using them fell to about thirteen or fourteen in a typical year, with the vast majority of delegates still being selected in a process that involved caucuses and conventions within a state. This so-called "mixed" nominating system was characterized by power residing usually with a state's party organization, with governors often being able to control the votes of delegates. Consequently, displays of electoral appeal in primaries were not decisive in securing a presidential nomination; Estes Kefauver won every Democratic primary he entered in 1952 but failed to secure the nomination, for example.

The demise of the mixed system followed the report of the McGovern–Fraser Commission (1968–1972). The commission had been established by the Democratic Party after its disastrous national convention of 1968. The main thrust of the report was an attempt to ensure (a) more representation at future conventions of various social groups among the Democrats' supporters and (b) a better reflection of support for particular candidates within a state party in the composition of its delegation. Ensuring such proportionality within the caucus-convention system proved complex and was one of the main reasons why many state Democratic parties then adopted presidential primaries. State Republican parties followed suit in switching to primaries, although their party had not been afflicted by the problems of the Democrats. By 1976 the nomination process had been transformed to the current "plebiscitary" system, in which the great majority of convention delegates are selected in primaries. One consequence of this is that, with the partial exception of the Democrats in 2008, the person who will be formally nominated by the party is known well in advance of the convention itself. Before 1972 the nominee could be the product of bargaining in back rooms among state delegations after the convention had started. Rather than being a decision-making arena, the contemporary national convention has been transformed into a spectacle at which the nominee is formally endorsed.

Since 1971 the power of state parties over the presidential nominating process has generally declined. In the current era it is the candidates, and not state party organization leaders, who are the prime actors in the process. Moreover, since the mid-twentieth century the national parties have acquired the right to determine the rules to be applied in the selection of delegates; delegations will not be seated unless the party has conformed to them.

This is not the only nominating arena in which state party influence has been dissolving, albeit slowly, because the same is true of nominations for other offices. By the end of the last century the number of states employing closed direct primaries had decreased to twenty-six. Although closure could not entirely prevent those who were not really party adherents from participating in the primaries if they chose to do so sufficiently early, nonetheless it had tended to ensure that the primary electorate contained more party-oriented voters than did open primaries. Moreover, the nonpartisan blanket primary (NPBP) has also been introduced in a few states—first in Louisiana and then in Washington (where its constitutionality has been upheld in the Supreme Court)—and in 2010 it was approved by initiative referendum in California. Under this arrangement the candidates of both parties run in the same primary election; should no candidate receive at least half the votes cast, there is a run-off election between the two leading candidates, irrespective of their party. In effect, this arrangement denies a major party any legal standing in the nominating of election candidates. The NPBP could thus be interpreted as a reversion to the early, preparty procedures of the American Republic when candidates simply presented themselves for election, except that now they do not print their own ballots and they are likely to face a two-stage (rather than a one-stage) election. The candidates selected may be ardent supporters of one party but under this type of primary are in no real sense the formal representatives of that party.

[*See also* **Elections: Election Law.**]

BIBLIOGRAPHY

Hazan, Reuven Y., and Gideon Rahat. "Candidate Selection: Methods and Consequences." In *Handbook of Party Politics,* edited by Richard S. Katz and William Crotty, pp. 109–121. London; Thousand Oaks, Calif.: Sage, 2006.

Ranney, Austin. *Curing the Mischiefs of Faction: Party Reform in America.* Berkeley: University of California Press, 1975.

Reynolds, John F. *The Demise of the American Convention System, 1880–1911.* Cambridge; New York: Cambridge University Press, 2006.

Shafer, Byron E. *Quiet Revolution: The Struggle for the Democratic Party and the Shaping of Post-Reform Politics.* New York: Russell Sage Foundation, 1983.

Ware, Alan. *The American Direct Primary: Party Institutionalization and Transformation in the North.* Cambridge, UK; New York: Cambridge University Press, 2002.

Alan Ware

PRESIDENTIAL ELECTIONS

American presidential elections trace the history of the nation and of the personalities that have sought this high office. These elections highlight the different party systems that have shaped American political history from the Early Republic through the present time.

The Early Republic. America's Constitution of 1787 created a president who was both chief executive and commander in chief of the armed forces. The president would neither be chosen by Congress nor elected directly by the people. Instead, an Electoral College of members selected by each state would choose the president and vice president. Each elector would cast two votes. The candidate with the most votes and a majority of electors would be elected president; the candidate with the second largest number of votes would become vice president.

Three different systems for choosing electors developed in the early Republic: selection by the state legislature (the most common), winner-take-all by popular vote; and popular vote election by districts within the state. The selection of George Washington as the first American president was not contested. Washington refrained from openly soliciting the office, establishing a precedent. The members of the Electoral College unanimously voted for him as president, selecting John Adams, Washington's favored choice, as vice president. In 1796, after Washington's unanimous reelection, America experienced its first contested presidential election. John Adams, the candidate of Washington's Federalist Party, defeated Thomas Jefferson, who by this time had formed his own fledging party—the Democratic-Republicans, establishing America's first party system.

In a rematch in 1800, Jefferson narrowly defeated President Adams. Elections such as 1800 that threaten the established order tend to bring out the worst in campaigners. This election featured smear tactics far in excess of the modern negative campaign. Federalists attacked Jefferson for his alleged atheism, radicalism, and lack of moral standards. The Jeffersonians fought back by charging that Adams intended to marry one of his sons to the daughter of the king of England, start an American monarchy, and reunite America and England.

The election of 1800 produced major changes in national policy and established a precedent for the peaceful transition of power in the United States. It installed Jefferson's Democratic-Republicans as America's dominant party for another twenty years. The election also led to the reform of a flawed system for electing presidents. Jefferson and his running mate Aaron Burr each received seventy-three electoral votes, which tossed the election of the president into the lame duck House of Representatives, which was closely divided between Federalists and Jeffersonians. With each state constitutionally assigned one vote, it took thirty-six ballots for the House finally to elect Jefferson as president, with Burr becoming vice president. To avoid the problem of future tied votes, the Twelfth Amendment was added to the Constitution just before the presidential election of 1804. It created the modern presidential ticket system, with separate balloting for president and vice president in the Electoral College.

A twenty-year period of single-party competition followed the 1800 election, in which nomination by the congressional caucus of Democratic-Republicans became tantamount to election as president. The caucus system collapsed in 1824, when four candidates competed for the presidency: Secretary of the Treasury William Crawford (the nominal Caucus nominee), Secretary of State John Quincy Adams, Speaker of the House Henry Clay, and war hero Andrew Jackson. Jackson won a plurality of the national popular vote. With no candidate winning a majority of the Electoral Vote, the House selected Adams as president. When Adams appointed Clay as his secretary of state, Jackson's partisans charged that the speaker had entered into a corrupt bargain with Adams, engineering his election in the House in return for this prestigious cabinet appointment.

The Second Party System and Its Collapse. Jackson gained his revenge four years later, easily defeating Adams in a bitter presidential election marked by attacks on the character and integrity of both candidates. Jackson's election in 1828 established a second party system. Jackson's supporters founded the modern Democratic Party, which upheld limited government and state's rights. His opponents eventually coalesced into a Whig Party that backed federal intervention to protect domestic industries, promote education, build the nation's infrastructure, and enforce moral standards. The new parties were far better run and organized than the earlier Federalist and Democratic-Republican parties. In 1828, the number of popular votes cast had more than tripled since 1824, reflecting the rise of popular politics and the increasing number of states that chose electors by popular vote. In future elections candidates would also have to appeal to a broad electorate, although in deference to the Washington tradition, they would generally avoid personal campaigning. Jackson's Whig opponents successfully used new electioneering techniques in 1840, when they portrayed their presidential nominee, the aristocratic general William Henry Harrison, as the "log cabin and hard cider candidate," the champion of the common man.

Beginning in 1832, major party candidates would also be chosen in national nominating conventions. In 1844, the Democratic convention chose America's first "dark horse" presidential candidate, the little known James K. Polk of Tennessee. Polk won the presidency in a close contest against Whig candidate Henry Clay and added to American territory through negotiation with Britain and war with Mexico.

In the 1850s, the Whig Party collapsed under the pressure of controversy over slavery, and a new Republican Party emerged in its place, introducing the modern party system. The Republicans nominated Abraham Lincoln in 1860 and adopted a platform that opposed the expansion of slavery. Lincoln's election precipitated the secession of southern states and the onset of the Civil War. Republicans entered the election year of 1864 with no assurance that Union forces would prevail on the battlefield. To broaden his coalition, Lincoln dumped his vice president, Hannibal Hamlin, a former senator from Maine, in favor of Andrew Johnson, a "War Democrat"' from Tennessee. The fortunes of war turned in the Union's favor shortly before the election and Lincoln solidly prevailed over his Democratic opponent, General George B. McClellan. However, Lincoln's turnabout on the vice presidency had profound implications after his assassination on 15 April 1865. President Johnson spent nearly four years obstructing Republican efforts to secure civil and political rights for freed slaves.

Efforts to "reconstruct" the South by Republicans in Congress and President Ulysses S. Grant during his two terms ended with the disputed presidential election of 1876. Although Democrat Samuel J. Tilden won the popular vote, conflicting returns from Florida, Louisiana, and South Carolina put the Electoral vote in doubt. Eventually, a congressional commission of eight Republicans and seven Democrats decided all disputed returns in favor of Republican nominee Rutherford B. Hayes, who withdrew the last federal troops from southern states, effectively ending Reconstruction.

From the Gilded Age to the Progressive Era. During the "Gilded Age" from 1876 to 1892 a near stalemate prevailed between Republicans, who dominated the North, and Democrats, who controlled the South. White southerners disenfranchised African Americans to establish an all-white one-party system in most of their region. Democrats elected their first postwar president in 1884, when Grover Cleveland, the governor of New York, narrowly defeated Maine senator James G. Blaine. Cleveland lost his reelection bid in 1888, but won again in 1892, becoming the only American president elected to nonconsecutive terms. Cleveland's second term coincided with the severe depression of the 1890s, and his party nominated an anti-Cleveland Democrat, former representative William Jennings Bryan of Nebraska. With his candidacy endorsed by the Populist Party, Bryan embraced such reform proposals as the free coinage of silver to inflate the currency, a graduated income tax, arbitration of labor disputes, and stricter regulation of railroads—policies that challenged his party's traditional commitment to hands-off government. Despite his defeat by Republican William McKinley, Bryan vigorously stumped the nation, helping introduce the modern style of personal campaigns. In turn, the Republicans, who vastly outspent the Democrats, pioneered modern fundraising techniques.

Although McKinley won in a 1900 rematch with Bryan, his assassination in September 1901 elevated Vice President Theodore Roosevelt to the presidency. During two terms in office Roosevelt sustained McKinley's expansionist foreign policies and added a domestic progressive agenda, which developed his idea that government should operate in the public interest by steering a middle course between unchecked corporate greed and socialistic remedies.

After Roosevelt stepped down from the presidency, his hand-picked successor William Howard Taft thwarted Bryan's third attempt to win the presidency in 1908. When Roosevelt became disillusioned with the Taft administration, he challenged the president for the GOP nomination in 1912. About a dozen states had recently introduced primary elections and Roosevelt, Taft, and Republican senator Robert A. La Follette of Wisconsin fought the first primary battle in American history. Roosevelt swept the primary contests, but the majority of convention delegates were selected by state party bosses who favored the sitting president. Roosevelt then launched a third-party campaign, which split the Republican vote and elected Democrat Woodrow Wilson, the governor of New Jersey. Wilson prevailed in the Electoral College with just 42 percent of the popular tally. Roosevelt finished second in the popular vote, with 27 percent, compared with 23 percent for Taft. It was the largest vote ever tallied by a third-party candidate, before or since. His defeat, however, demonstrated the limitations of an independent or third-party presidential campaign in a nation wedded to the two-party system. President Wilson narrowly won re-election in 1916, serving two terms in which he became the first president of his party to advance an agenda of activist, progressive government. He also implicitly rejected the party's traditional isolationism and continued America's increasing involvement abroad, including U.S. participation in World War II.

The Rise and Fall of Conservative Presidents. In 1920, amid a wave of postwar disillusion, Republican Warren G. Harding promised a "return to normalcy" and won the presidency by the greatest landslide to date in American history, shattering the coalitions that had supported Wilson in 1912 and 1916. In just four years, the Democratic Party had shrunk to its southern base and isolated enclaves in the north. Republicans would also prevail in the presidential elections of 1924 and 1928 by landslide margins and maintain control of Congress throughout the 1920s. Republicans slashed taxes, deregulated industry, restricted immigration, enforced prohibition, and raised tariffs. The election of 1920 was the first in which the Nineteenth Amendment to the Constitution guaranteed women the right to vote. Although advocates of women's suffrage had argued that the woman voter would spearhead progressive reforms, women actually voted for Harding in greater proportion than men and would continue to vote conservatively throughout the 1930s and 1940s.

Democrat Franklin Roosevelt's victory over President Herbert Hoover in 1932, during the Great Depression, began a new era in American politics. Roosevelt shattered Washington's two-term tradition and won four consecutive presidential elections. He transformed the party loyalties of Americans by forging a new coalition of whites in the South; working-class Catholics, blacks, and Jews in the North; and reformers in mountain states. Democrats would control both the presidency and Congress from 1933 to 1953. Roosevelt's transformational New Deal program greatly expanded government responsibility for regulating the economy, controlling the abuses of business, and providing for the welfare of ordinary Americans. His leadership in World War II helped defeat Nazis in Germany and fascists in Japan and vastly expanded America's involvement in world affairs.

In 1944, Roosevelt followed Lincoln's precedent and dumped his vice president, the liberal visionary Henry Wallace, in favor of the reliable senator Harry S. Truman of Missouri. After Roosevelt's death on 12 April 1945, Truman filled most of Roosevelt's fourth term and won the presidency on his own in 1948, scoring a victory over the New York governor Thomas E. Dewey that surprised the pollsters and pundits of the time. As America's first Cold War president, Truman worked with Congress to expand America's national security apparatus, create the "invisible government" of the Central Intelligence Agency (CIA), and establish the policy of containing Communism. During Truman's presidency, the states ratified the Twenty-Second Amendment to the Constitution, limiting presidents to two terms. Although the amendment exempted Truman, he declined to seek a third term in 1952, leading to the election of Republican Dwight Eisenhower. Eisenhower remained personally popular during his two terms in office, but his "modern Republicanism," which steered a middle ground between America's right and left wings, failed to convert a majority to his Republican Party.

Democrats Return and Then Falter. When Ike stepped down in 1960, a Democrat, John F. Kennedy, became America's first Catholic president by defeating Vice President Richard Nixon. The 1960 election established important precedents for later campaigns. Both candidates energetically stumped the nation, and Kennedy became the first candidate to rely heavily on a pollster (Louis Harris) to identify issues and plan strategy. Kennedy also broke new ground using his own loyalists to direct the grassroots campaign traditionally conducted by the state and local parties. The campaign most prominently featured the first televised presidential debates in American history.

After Kennedy's assassination in November 1963, his vice president, Lyndon Johnson, extended liberal initiatives begun during Kennedy's time. In 1964, Republicans nominated the first genuine conservative since the 1920s in Senator Barry Goldwater of Arizona. In his reelection campaign, Johnson succeeded in branding Goldwater as a dangerous radical and read his landslide victory as a mandate for his Great Society program. It appeared that liberal Democrats would control American government for the indefinite future. However, the Johnson administration unraveled under pressure from a failing war in Vietnam and social unrest at home. After Johnson declined to seek another term, Richard Nixon, in a remarkable comeback, narrowly defeated Vice President Hubert Humphrey. Independent candidate George C. Wallace, the former segregationist governor of Alabama, benefitted from southern resentment against Johnson's sponsorship of civil rights legislation. Wallace won five Deep South states, but could not extend his appeal to the north.

Humphrey won the Democratic nomination without contesting primary elections. He then appeased his Democratic critics by authorizing a commission to reform the nominating process, headed by the liberal senator George McGovern of South Dakota. The McGovern Commission required that all delegates must be selected in open state caucuses or primaries. The Republicans soon followed suit, and conventions became largely irrelevant, as the state nominating contests essentially chose presidential nominees.

Although Nixon talked like a conservative, he governed more liberally than Eisenhower. Nixon signed pathbreaking environmental laws, backed affirmative action programs, opened relations with mainland China, and deescalated the Cold War. He sailed to a landslide victory over Democratic nominee McGovern, but the Watergate scandal and Nixon's resignation in 1974 dashed Republican hopes for 1976. Democrat Jimmy Carter, the former governor of Georgia, defeated sitting president Gerald Ford that year. Ford had become America's first appointed vice president in 1973 when Spiro Agnew resigned amid a bribery scandal from his years as governor of Maryland. Ford then became president when Nixon resigned.

The Conservative Resurgence. The Carter administration failed to protect its constituents from the ravages of stagflation—an improbable mix of slow growth, high unemployment, high inflation, and high interest rates. Carter also exhibited weakness in foreign affairs by failing to gain the release of American hostages seized by militants in Iran or to halting the resurgent expansionism of the Soviet Union. He lost the presidential election to conservative Republican Ronald Reagan, the former governor. Unlike in 1932, the 1980 election did not establish a new political era, dominated by a single party. Rather, it brought Republicans into near parity with Democrats, enabled Reagan to implement his conservative ideas in domestic and foreign policy, and moved the national conversation about politics to the right. Voter loyalties, however, remained fluid, and Democrats regained the presidency when the moderate Bill Clinton, the governor of Arkansas, thwarted President George H. W. Bush's bid for a second term in 1992. Although Clinton won reelection in 1996, he became embroiled in a scandal that led to his impeachment in 1998 and an acquittal by the Senate in 1999.

During the late twentieth century, the American electorate aligned along class, ethnic, and religious lines. The Republicans relied on affluent voters and white Protestants, especially evangelicals, whereas Democrats rallied working class voters, African Americans, Jews, and those with no religious affiliation. Devout Catholics generally voted Republican; secular Catholics typically backed the Democrats.

In 2000, Texas governor George W. Bush restored conservative Republican control of the presidency when he defeated Vice President Al Gore in the most hotly contested election since 1876. Although Gore won the popular vote, Bush prevailed in the Electoral College when the Supreme Court by a 5-to-4 decision along ideological lines on 8 December stopped a recount in Florida with Bush ahead by just 537 votes. After al-Qaeda operatives launched devastating attacks on the Pentagon and the World Trade Center in New York City on 11 September 2001, Bush dedicated his presidency to protecting the nation from terrorism attacks. By 2004, however, the public was growing disillusioned with the wars in Afghanistan and Iraq that Bush had launched after 9/11. Still, Bush narrowly defeated Massachusetts Democratic senator John Kerry in the 2004 election. Bush won every southern state in both 2000 and 2004, marking the transformation of the South from the most reliable Democratic to the most reliable Republican region of the nation.

Governing, Not Campaigning, Counts. President Bush encountered many difficulties during his second term, including a botched response to Hurricane Katrina on the Gulf Coast, a scandal in the Justice Department, and a financial meltdown shortly before the 2008 election. Given this subpar performance, Barack Obama, after a close nomination contest against former First Lady and New York senator Hillary Clinton, easily defeated the veteran Republican senator John McCain of Arizona. Obama became the first African American president in American history and the first liberal Democratic president since Lyndon Johnson in the 1960s.

As the 2008 and other elections demonstrated, governing counts more than campaigning in determining the outcome of presidential elections. Presidents who govern well earn second terms and usually pass on the presidency to a successor of their own party. It is bold and innovative presidents like Thomas Jefferson, Abraham Lincoln, Theodore Roosevelt, Woodrow Wilson, Franklin Roosevelt, and Ronald Reagan who have also been successful politically. In contrast, centrist, cautious presidents like Martin Van Buren, William Howard Taft, Jimmy Carter, and George H. W. Bush have been less successful at the polls.

[*See also* **Party System.**]

BIBLIOGRAPHY

Black, Earl, and Merle Black. *The Rise of Southern Republicans*. Cambridge, Mass.: Belknap Press of Harvard University Press, 2002.

Busch, Andrew. *Reagan's Victory: The Presidential Election of 1980 and the Rise of the Right*. Lawrence: University Press of Kansas, 2005.

Cole, Donald B. *Vindicating Andrew Jackson: The 1828 Election and the Rise of the Two-Party System*. Lawrence: University Press of Kansas: 2009.

Egerton, Douglas R. *Years of Meteors: Stephen Douglas, Abraham Lincoln and the Election that Brought on the Civil War*. New York: Bloomsbury Press, 2010.

Ferling, John E. *Adams vs. Jefferson: The Tumultuous Election of 1800s*. Oxford; New York: Oxford University Press, 2004.

Lawrence, David G. *The Collapse and Fall of the Democratic Presidential Majority: Realignment, Dealignment, and Electoral Change From Franklin Roosevelt to Bill Clinton*. New York: Westview Press, 1997.

Lichtman, Allan J. *The Keys to the White House*. Lanham, Md.: Rowman & Littlefield, 2008.

Stebenne, David L. *Modern Republican: Arthur Larson and the Eisenhower Years*. Bloomington: Indiana University Press, 2006.

White, Theodore. *The Making of the President, 1960*. New York: Atheneum Publishers, 1961.

Allan J. Lichtman

SUFFRAGE

Disputes over voting rights and the consequences of elections have been defining the dynamics of American history since the first American election in 1619. Following the English (and, more broadly, European) practice of legitimizing governmental actors and policies through electoral expressions of consent, those governing Virginia in 1619 summoned "the Inhabitants" of twelve parts of the colony to elect two representatives each to form a new colonial assembly, the House of Burgesses. Several Virginians contested their exclusion from participating in this first election, and it was determined that, notwithstanding any previous order, "the Polonians resident in Virginia" should also "be enfranchised, and made as free as any inhabitant there whatsoever."

When the first elected Virginia assembly convened on 30 July 1619, additional disputes arose over the credentials of four of the twenty-four elected representatives. Two burgesses were excluded and later readmitted, although all agreed they resided in Virginia without the proper legal documentation. Two other elected burgesses, however, were expelled because they refused to accept the legitimacy of the new assembly's authority to make binding legal decisions. A fifth elected burgess, Walter Shelley from Smyths Hundred plantation, died on the third day of the assembly's inaugural session.

American elections since this first one in 1619 have not always been as significant, contested, or consequential, but collectively they constitute what now can be seen as the American political tradition of electoral democracy. Not surprisingly, much of the interior and exterior elements of this American tradition have reflected the ways in which suffrage rights and the institutions and practices of voting have been defined and contested over the past four centuries.

The Colonial Era. As in Virginia, every British colony in North America established a colonial assembly composed of locally elected representatives. Suffrage rights in colonial elections followed British precedents, which prohibited several "dependent" classes of persons from voting, while prescribing freeholder voting rights to "free" individuals in possession of land, income, or property worth at least forty shillings annually. The political rationale driving these exclusionary and inclusionary distinctions turned on long-standing fears that democracy was an inherently unstable form of government and that popular rule had always resulted in the misappropriation of the property of the wealthy. Property thresholds, therefore, acted as proxies for demarcating individuals with what were deemed sufficient capacities for and a minimal stake in maintaining the material well-being of the society.

The precise terms and enforcement of voting rights varied across the American colonies and according to local circumstances. South Carolina, for example, did not employ the conventional definition of the freehold, granting voting rights instead to those who annually paid twenty shillings in taxes. Even the presumed and pervasive exclusion of women was contested vigorously but unsuccessfully as early as 1648 by Maryland businesswoman Margaret Brent, who demanded not only a vote in the Maryland assembly for herself, but a second vote (!) because of her status as executrix of the extensive properties of the recently deceased governor of Maryland. Throughout the eighteenth century, women still were widely prevented from voting, but the historical record also indicates that wealthy female property owners were permitted to vote in several localities in Massachusetts and New York. Minors, unnaturalized aliens, convicts, Roman Catholics, Jews, and free and enslaved nonwhites were other common classes of persons generally barred from voting and office holding in the American colonies. Interestingly, the racially based exclusions were American constructions without clear precedent in British law.

The breadth of these suffrage restrictions generally guaranteed that a surprisingly small proportion of the American colonial population voted—likely less than 5 percent. Other historians, however, estimate that in the late Colonial Era 50 to 80 percent of the American colonial adult white male population was eligible to vote, almost twice the number of eligible British voters. Several factors explain this relative difference. The most important factor was that colonial economic and social conditions were more equal and fluid, which made the freehold requirement relatively and increasingly less restrictive in the American colonies. Elections also were held more often in the colonies than in Great Britain, with annual or biennial elections customary in many colonies. Other factors (e.g., the oppositional role the colonial assemblies increasingly assumed as tensions with Great Britain escalated) likely also contributed to greater interest in the results of colonial elections and the collective actions taken by those elected.

Early National Era. American commitments to winning their independence from British rule in 1776 opened new constitutional possibilities for the development of suffrage rights and voting practices. These rights were not defined in a uniform manner by the new national government, but in the particular terms of each new state constitution subsequently drafted. Although suffrage terms were debated and contested in every state, colonial suffrage standards most often were adopted or slightly modified in the new state constitutions ultimately ratified. In several states, property ownership thresholds were reduced and in a few others taxpaying status was accepted as an equivalent threshold. As in the Colonial Era, the wide availability of land generally diminished the exclusionary effects of the freehold stakeholder standard as the wartime devaluation of currency did for the taxpayer standard. Colonial suffrage prohibitions against Roman Catholics also were abandoned in the new state constitutions written after 1776, although several state constitutions initially barred non-Christians from voting and public office. The latter restrictions, however, were superseded by subsequent state statutes, new state constitutions and amendments, and the U.S. Constitution ban on religious tests.

Given these developments, most historians concur that in most states 80 to 90 percent of adult white males met the eligibility thresholds for voting. Although more were able to vote, suffrage rights and voting practices were not radically extended by the American Revolution, especially when measured relative to the whole American population. No state, after all, guaranteed females the right to vote. The 1776 New Jersey constitution, it bears noting, did not explicitly bar women from voting; and some women there who met state property requirements clearly voted in elections before 1807, when a state constitutional amendment explicitly restricted voting to white adult males. Age, citizenship, and residency requirements also were included in the new state constitutions, making these restrictions more explicit than they had been before 1776. In addition, racial restrictions against voting were eased in several states; although enslaved persons were never granted voting rights, and the new constitutions of South Carolina and Georgia included new restrictions that barred voting by freedmen who were not "white."

The Nineteenth Century. Additional changes in the definition of voting rights occurred over the course of the nineteenth century. One of the more significant was the gradual abandonment of property and taxpayer qualifications for determining voter eligibility. This change clearly was hastened by the admission of new states, none of which employed the property stakeholder language inherited from the Colonial Era. Although the conditions for this fundamental transformation clearly are varied, they likely also reflect a deeper conceptual reconfiguration of the priority of the relationship between governmental authority and electoral expressions of consent. This much is certain: by 1860 every state constitution—including those of the original thirteen states—assigned voting rights to individual persons regardless of a demonstrable economic stake within the society.

As state constitutions shed their religious and then their property and taxpayer qualifications, states increasingly grafted racialist language into their definitions of voting rights. Before 1790, small numbers of African Americans had voted in thirteen of sixteen states, including five Southern states. By 1860, however, free African American adult males possessed the legal right to vote in only five of thirty-three states. Moreover, every new slave and free state admitted into the Union before the Civil War limited voting rights to the white population only. In fact, not only did a far western state like Oregon deem it constitutionally necessary to state "No Negro, Chinaman, or mulatto, shall have the right of suffrage," but also immediately after the Civil War, nine Northern states rejected constitutional changes designed to extend the suffrage to African American citizens of their own states.

With few advocates in the states, the national government became the champion for the first time of African American voting rights. Congress crafted several amendments to the U.S. Constitution that greatly altered the legal language of voting rights. The Thirteenth Amendment (1865) prohibits slavery, thereby making all potentially "free" to vote. The Fourteenth Amendment (1868) guarantees citizenship to all native-born or naturalized persons, which meant that these classifications could no longer be used by states to bar voter eligibility. The Fourteenth Amendment also guarantees equal protection of the law and provides a method for reducing a state's federal representation if it denied or abridged voting rights to any eligible males, thereby creating a fairness standard and a maximalist incentive to extend voting rights. The Fifteenth Amendment

(1870) prohibits states from denying or abridging the right to vote on account of race, color, or previous condition of servitude. Congress additionally enacted civil rights legislation and various Reconstruction policies that successfully created the conditions under which many new voters were registered in Southern states, including more than 800,000 African American males. As a result, many African Americans voted, were elected, and served in federal, state, and local offices for the first time, including the U.S. House and U.S. Senate.

Reconstruction advances were immediately resisted by white supremacist groups like the Ku Klux Klan and others, who shamelessly and ruthlessly employed violence, intimidation, and electoral fraud to reverse the political empowerment of African Americans. More invidiously, for the rest of the nineteenth century and well into the next, these racially motivated groups used their political influence to devise and administer new state and local policies and practices that imposed voting rights restrictions explicitly prohibited by the Fifteenth Amendment. These policies and practices included locally administered registration laws; literacy, understanding, and good character tests; poll taxes; criminal disenfranchisements; white party primaries; closed political party membership rules; racially skewed redistricting plans; and grandfather clauses that exempted white voters from restrictions imposed on potential nonwhite voters. As a result of these policies and practices, voting by African Americans declined precipitously, and nineteenth-century politics in Southern states ended the century where it began: with the long familiar image of a small, white electorate and one-party political domination by the Democratic Party.

Whereas the admission of new states spurred the abandonment of economic qualifications and the aftermath of the Civil War offered opportunities for (temporarily) abandoning racial qualifications of voting rights, the nineteenth century afforded no similar mechanism for extending voting rights to the largest class of persons still prevented from voting in the United States. Although organized efforts to achieve female voting rights were launched in the 1840s and sustained thereafter, these efforts garnered widespread attention but achieved very limited success for the remainder of the century. In 1861, only two states had permitted women voting rights in local school board elections. In the latter third of the century, the results also were less than spectacular. The Fourteenth Amendment explicitly recognized male voters, thereby constitutionalizing a gender standard that explicitly excluded females. Moreover, no fewer than seven states rejected state constitutional amendments and referenda for women's suffrage. Four territorial states, however, granted full voting rights to women. And by 1890, women also were permitted to vote in local school district and municipal elections in nearly one dozen states and territories. In addition, four new western states—Wyoming (1890), Colorado (1893), Utah (1896), and Idaho (1896)—granted women full voting rights.

The Twentieth Century. Women's suffragists persisted with their efforts in the twentieth century, winning over about one-third of the American states by 1915. Outside of the United States, five national democracies also recognized full women's voting rights: New Zealand (1893), Australia (1902), Finland (1906), Norway (1913), and Denmark (1915). Alliances with the Temperance Movement, the promising expectations associated with the end of World War I (1914–1920), and the 1917 Russian Revolution's declaration of the equality of women increased interest in women's suffrage and the political and social concerns of women. Canada, the United

Kingdom, the Russian Federation, and several other nations granted voting rights to women in 1917–1918; as did Belgium, the Netherlands, and Sweden in 1919. In the United States, women's suffrage organizations renewed their efforts with mass demonstrations and political lobbying of both Congress and President Woodrow Wilson. President Wilson initially remained uncommitted to amending the Constitution, but as his postwar visions came into focus, he became convinced that women's suffrage fit well with his ideas for establishing a League of Nations and a more peaceful and democratic world. Once President Wilson endorsed the idea, Congress followed by proposing the Nineteenth Amendment in 1919, which three-quarters of the states ratified by 1920. As a result, gender was removed as a classification used to exclude many from having their interests directly represented in the electoral process.

At the beginning of the twentieth century, new civil rights organizations like the National Association for the Advancement of Colored People (NAACP) emerged to work on advancing African American civil rights, including the right to vote. Unlike the women's suffrage movement, these organizations and others achieved several reforms using the judicial system to challenge the constitutionality of various state voting restrictions. In *Guinn and Beal v. United States* (1915), the U.S. Supreme Court held that the Oklahoma grandfather clause was an unconstitutional evasion of the Fifteenth Amendment. The Supreme Court also struck down all-white primary elections in 1944 and, in 1960, a redistricting plan that effectively excluded African Americans from the electoral process.

Other factors, especially the desegregation of the U.S. military during World War II, reengaged the U.S. Congress in the cause of voting rights reforms. In 1942, Congress exempted U.S. soldiers from state voter poll taxes, but additional legislative efforts were repeatedly frustrated by Southern members of Congress fearful that further involvement by the national government would be the undoing of the system of racial segregation and their political careers. Civil rights and voting rights reformers persevered nonetheless, mobilizing a network of supporters throughout the nation and peaceful public protests and civil rights demonstrations throughout the South.

Reformers within Congress succeeded in enacting civil rights acts in 1957 and 1960. Both acts lacked adequate enforcement provisions, but they created the U.S. Civil Rights Commission and empowered the U.S. attorney general to investigate and litigate voting rights violations. The Commission collected and published statistical evidence of the breadth of African American disenfranchisement. Congress remained unresponsive, proposing instead the Twenty-Third Amendment (1961), which allowed District of Columbia residents to vote in U.S. presidential elections. Interestingly, although Congress earlier had extended citizenship and thus voting rights to Native Americans in 1924 and Chinese Americans in 1943, it missed an opportunity when it proposed the Twenty-Third Amendment in 1960 to similarly enfranchise all American citizens in Puerto Rico and the other U.S. territories.

In 1961, under the more assertive leadership of the U.S. attorney general Robert Kennedy, the Department of Justice began to compile evidence to litigate against state voting rights discrimination. In 1962, Congress endorsed the Twenty-Fourth Amendment, which prohibited poll taxes in federal elections. Two years later, in 1964, Congress enacted a more expansive civil rights act and in 1965 a new voting rights act, which banned literacy tests and other racially discriminatory devices in both federal and state elections. The 1965

Voting Rights Act also guaranteed that the federal government would monitor and review voter registration, elections, and electoral procedures in all or parts of eight southern states, Alaska, and several non-southern localities with historically low rates of registration and voting. Under the authority granted in the 1965 act, the U.S. attorney general Nicholas Katzenbach successfully challenged the constitutionality of state poll taxes and in *South Carolina v. Katzenbach* (1966) and several subsequent decisions the U.S. Supreme Court upheld the constitutionality of the 1965 Voting Rights Act, including the broad federal review of state election practices required under Section 5 of the act. As a result of these decisions and of the 1965 Act reauthorizations in 1970, 1975, 1982, and 2006, race and ethnicity are no longer permissible classifications for denying the right to vote.

Additional Exclusions. Despite conventional references to universal suffrage, significant exclusionary classifications remain. Although almost every state bars incarcerated, probationary, and paroled persons from voting, nearly one-quarter of the states bars this class of individuals from voting after completing their sentence—most for several years—but several states provide no automatic or necessary rescission of their voting prohibitions. This excluded class exceeds 5 million persons. Age is another exclusion. Although the Twenty-Sixth Amendment (1971) lowers the minimum voting age to eighteen years, younger individuals remain the second largest category of persons excluded from voting. According to the 2010 Census, there are 74.2 million in this excluded class, which constitutes 24 percent of the U.S. population. The largest excluded category includes the approximately 80 million unregistered persons over the age of eighteen, which represents 26 percent of the U.S. population. Approximately 60 million of this group are unregistered citizens; the other 20 million are unregistered noncitizens. When assessed together, these excluded categories indicate that more than half of the U.S. population remains unable to vote, despite the tremendous expansion of the American electorate over the past four centuries.

[*See also* **Civil Rights; Elections: Election Law; Fifteenth Amendment; Fourteenth Amendment; National Association for the Advancement of Colored People; Nineteenth Amendment;** *and* **Woman Suffrage Movement.**]

BIBLIOGRAPHY

Bishop, Cortlandt F. *History of Elections in the American Colonies*, Studies in History, Economics and Public Law, Vol. III, Number 1. New York: Columbia College, 1893.

Carr, Louis Green. "Margaret Brent (ca. 1601–1671)." Archives of Maryland: Biographical Series. http://www.msa.md.gov/megafile/msa/speccol/sc3500/sc3520/002100/002177/html/bio.html#mpt/ (accessed 27 August 2011).

Davidson, Chandler, and Bernard Grofman, eds. *Quiet Revolution in the South: The Impact of the Voting Rights Act, 1965–1990*. Princeton, N.J.: Princeton University Press, 1994.

Dinkin, Robert J. *Voting in Provincial America*. Westport, Conn.: Greenwood Press, 1977.

Dinkin, Robert J. *Voting in Revolutionary America*. Westport, Conn.: Greenwood Press, 1982.

Engerman, Stanley L., and Kenneth L. Sokoloff. "The Evolution of Suffrage Institutions in the New World." *Journal of Economic History* 65, no. 4 (December 2005): 891–921.

Ewald, Alex C. *The Way We Vote: The Local Dimension of American Suffrage*. Nashville, Tenn.: Vanderbilt University Press, 2009.

Greene, Jack P. *Imperatives, Behaviors, and Identities: Essays in Early American Cultural History*. Charlottesville: University Press of Virginia, 1992.

Katz, Richard S. *Democracy and Elections*. New York: Oxford University Press, 1997.
Keyssar, Alexander. *The Right to Vote: The Contested History of Democracy in the United States*. Revised ed. New York: Basic Books, 2000.
Kousser, J. Morgan. *The Shaping of Southern Politics: Suffrage Restrictions and the Establishment of the One-Party South, 1880–1910*. New Haven, Conn.: Yale University Press, 1974.
Kromkowski, Charles. *Recreating the American Republic: Rules of Apportionment, Constitutional Change, and American Political Development, 1700–1870*. Cheltenham, UK; New York: Cambridge University Press, 2002.
Monahan, Arthur P. *Consent, Coercion and Limit: The Medieval Origins of Parliamentary Democracy*. Kingston, Ontario, Canada: McGill–Queen's University Press, 1987.
Porter, Nicole D. *Expanding the Vote: State Felony Disenfranchisement Reform, 1997–2010*. Washington, D.C.: The Sentencing Project, 2010. http://www.sentencingproject.org/doc/publications/publications/vr_ExpandingtheVoteFinalAddendum.pdf/ (accessed 28 August 2011).

Charles A. Kromkowski

VOTING SYSTEMS

The 2000 presidential election brought American ballot laws sharply to national and international attention. The vote in Florida, the outcome of which would determine the next president of the United States, revealed as never before the vulnerabilities associated with the vagaries of U.S. ballot design and the inadequacy of vote-counting technology. These twin deficiencies, products of the Constitution's highly decentralized authority over voting and the conduct of elections, converged in the 2000 presidential contest to cast doubt upon the legitimacy of the entire American electoral process.

Responses to this highly negative domestic and foreign perception are evident in the 5,295 pieces of election reform legislation that have since been introduced into state legislatures. At the federal level, the Help America Vote Act (HAVA) passed Congress after two years of contentious debate between those seeking a surer public connection with the electoral process and those focused on the threat of electoral fraud. In the end, a much amended bill found strong bipartisan support and HAVA was signed into law, perhaps ironically, by President George W. Bush on 29 October 2002.

This act brought the federal government into new levels of involvement in the conduct of federal elections, requiring each state to develop a single centralized and computerized voter registration list, provide for registration by mail, develop voter identification procedures, and create a system for provisional voting. It has facilitated the replacement of the punch card (and lever) voting machines that gave rise to the infamous "chads," those tiny pieces of cardboard that featured so largely in Florida's vote counting in the 2000 election. HAVA also established the Election Assistance Commission (EAC) to devise minimum voting system standards and to act as a resource assisting state and local authorities in the conduct of federal elections. Combined with the National Voter Registration Act of 1993—the "motor-voter act"—these institutional reforms promise, if adequately funded and rigorously enforced, significant steps toward the development of nationwide election standards for the first time in the United States. If this occurs, it will be at the expense of the long-standing allocation of significant autonomy to state and local governments in designing ballots and conducting elections. These reform measures draw attention to the historical importance of ballot law and may encourage more careful study of the implications of ballot design in U.S. political history.

The Preballot Era: Voting as a Public Act. Colonial voting was accomplished with instruments as varied as corn kernels, beans, balls, a show of hands, paper, and (to an extent largely unappreciated) the voice of the individual voter. In this varied history of the vote, there is one seldom- noted commonality: for most of American history, the vote of the individual was a public act.

Eighteenth- and nineteenth-century elections were conducted either by ticket or *viva voce* (by voice). *Viva voce* elections followed British (and some Continental) electoral law, requiring that an individual's electoral choices were spoken aloud prior to being transcribed into "poll books" by election clerks. Voting by ticket meant depositing in a ballot box the party-produced slate of candidates that the party wished to see elected. The voter could "scratch the ticket" by crossing off the name of the party's preferred candidate for a position and writing in an alternative, but the system encouraged the elector to "vote the ticket" and deposit the party-prepared roster in the ballot box.

Both forms of voting were public and all individual votes (bar the rare ticket scratching) were knowable. This was most unambiguously so in *viva voce* states. In this system, voters as well as nonvoters assembled around the election platform at each polling place. One by one, voters ascended the steps to the platform where the election officials were congregated. The individual voter was identified and the choice of each voter for each office was declared in an audible voice—by the voter, an election official, or the sheriff. Seven states still conducted their elections *viva voce* in the 1850s, casting about 10 percent of the national presidential vote.

The choices of voters in a ticket system were only slightly less public. Here too the crowd gathered around the voting platform; but voters first approached party officials, often housed in highly decorated booths, who handed out the party ticket listing the party's candidates for every office. These tickets were, as the Huntington Library's collection of nineteenth-century ballots demonstrates, brightly colored, differently sized and shaped, and distinctively patterned. As in the *viva voce* system, the voter ascended the steps of the voting platform, but with ticket in hand; election officials ascertained the legitimacy of the voter, who then deposited the party ticket in the ballot box. Identification obviously ran both ways: the distinctive markings and colors assisted the voter in identifying the party with which he was affiliated, just as the "color of his ticket" revealed to all observers the partisan choices of that voter. Local party officials often watched closely the tickets being deposited by individual voters and sometimes recorded the names of electors whom they recognized and their party choice.

A comparison of George Caleb Bingham's painting of a *viva voce* election, *The County Election*, 1852, with sketches of elections being conducted under the ticket system, published in *Leslie's Magazine* and *Harper's Weekly*, demonstrates the essential similarity of the two systems and their common theme: all votes, prior to the adoption of the secret ballot at the end of the nineteenth century, were public and knowable. Only in the poll books states, of course, was this public knowledge systematically preserved in official records.

The requirement to publicly reveal partisan choice did not suppress turnout, a rather remarkable feature of American electoral history. Open voting accompanied the enormous expansion of the nineteenth-century American electorate to include all adult white males and, facilitated by high levels of party organization in the electorate and the celebration of elections as festivals, is associated with the highest rates of political participation in America's history. Exactly the opposite features accompanied the move to secret voting.

Ballot Secrecy and Its Consequences. The central characteristics of the Australian or secret ballot reflect elements of the distinctive political culture of the nation that invented it: an obsession with privacy and a willingness to delegate to the state activities and functions performed elsewhere by nonstate associations and organizations. The fundamental features of the ballot form pioneered in Australia in the mid-1850s and adopted in the United Kingdom and Canada in the 1870s are readily summarized: a single ballot printed by the state at public expense, carrying all candidates for all offices, available only to qualified voters upon entry to a polling station, marked in secret, and deposited without those choices being seen or subsequently attributable to the individual voter.

Opponents of the secret ballot in England eventually included John Stuart Mill, the political philosopher, who observed that if the vote were private it would be used for private rather than public purposes. American advocates of open voting pronounced it the "manly" way of making a political choice while ensuring that, in this rapidly expanding electorate, those who could not read could still vote. Alexis de Tocqueville, the author of *Democracy in America,* appearing in 1835 before a British Parliamentary select committee on secrecy in voting, testified that in the America he knew, there was neither threat nor fear associated with individual electoral decisions being public and known.

A half century later, however, in a more industrial and urban America characterized by even more powerful political machines, increasing numbers of immigrants from southern and eastern Europe, and a newly enfranchised black male population, real and imagined electoral impropriety made de Tocqueville's political world no longer tenable. American experimentation with the Australian ballot began in 1883; Massachusetts adopted the secret ballot in 1888 and a majority of American states did so within four years. The intensity of the debates that followed reflects the fact that ballot reform had consequences for political party and citizen participation.

The state-printed ballot required the legal recognition of political parties and provided new opportunities for their regulation. Party interests were reflected in new controversies over the symbolism permitted on the state printed ballot (to assist—or not assist—illiterate voters), whether the ballot would be arranged by office or by party (really the old ticket system in new guise), the comprehensiveness of the ballot, and whether local elections would be by ward or at large. The system of presidential primaries and direct primaries (particularly the blanket and nonpartisan forms of the latter) challenged and diminished the power of party, particularly at the state and local levels, attesting again to the institutional consequences of ballot reform.

The participatory consequences were just as great. Historians have noted the eagerness with which the former Confederate states adopted the secret ballot and the explicitness of their interest in it as a means of disenfranchising poor whites and former slaves who could not read a printed ballot. To be sure, state control over the ballot made possible the Progressive Era's experiments in government, including alternative counting procedures (systems of preferential voting as in the Bucklin system), direct democracy (the initiative, referendum, and recall), primary elections, and even considerations of compulsory voting. Nevertheless, party organization, deprived of its ticket distribution function, largely disappeared from the polling place, as did election-day crowds. Officials who experimented with the new system reported enthusiastically that one would hardly know an election was being conducted. Shorn of its political drama and of uproarious and indeed riotous behavior, the polling place was quickly sanitized, reduced to quietude, and ultimately "sanctified." Turnout fell.

The secret ballot stands with many other reforms adopted between the 1880s and the 1950s, which depressed, and in many cases suppressed, turnout. Some of these devices, especially in the South, were explicitly designed to "purify" the electorate by limiting the suffrage. The electorate expanded as women gained the franchise but contracted with demands to reduce fraud by tightening electoral rules and creating complex registration systems that made enrollment the responsibility of the voter and allowed electoral lists to be closed long before election day. These requirements could be made effectively discriminatory and contrast with registration procedures in other nations that facilitate, rather than constrict, electoral participation. Some have argued that calls for "the more intelligent use of the vote" were code for suffrage restriction. A comprehensive democratic audit would help reveal the extent to which the outcome of the Progressive Era ballot initiatives was a voting public much less differentiated by sex but much reduced in extent and more sharply defined by race, class, education, and ethnicity.

The Contemporary Moment. The years since the 1960s have seen major reforms designed to enhance political participation, particularly the 1965 Voting Rights Act and the Twenty-Sixth Amendment lowering the voting age. As party competition has returned to the South, national party differentiation has increased, and with it turnout, especially as measured by the participation of age-eligible citizens. The 2000 presidential election, rather accidentally, thrust ballot laws into this generally expansionistic trend, raising the question of whether the emerging reforms will continue the participatory theme of recent years or facilitates a return to the restrictive participatory policies of the Progressive Era. HAVA and EAC, when combined with the 1993 National Voter Registration Act, define a moment of potentially significant reform. Not surprisingly, given that ballot laws shape in the most intimate way the interaction of the citizen with electoral process, the contemporary debate echoes that far older disagreement between those more determined to increase participation and those, alarmed by the risk of fraud, determined to constrain participation. Ballot reform, as its history suggests, can be shaped to serve either cause.

[*See also* **Constitution;** ***and*** **Elections: Election Law.**]

BIBLIOGRAPHY

Bensel, Richard Franklin. *The American Ballot Box in the Mid-Nineteenth Century.* Cambridge, UK; New York: Cambridge University Press, 2004.

Bourke, Paul F., and Donald A. DeBats. *Washington County: Politics and Community in Antebellum America.* Baltimore: Johns Hopkins University Press, 1995.

Fife, Brian L. *Reforming the Electoral Process in America: Toward More Democracy in the 21st Century.* Santa Barbara, Calif.: Praeger, 2010.

Gidlow, Liette. *The Big Vote: Gender, Consumer Culture, and the Politics of Exclusion, 1890s–1920s.* Baltimore: Johns Hopkins University Press, 2004.

Keyssar, Alexander. *The Right to Vote: The Contested History of Democracy in the United States.* New York: Basic Books, 2000.

Klinghard, Daniel. *The Nationalization of American Political Parties, 1880–1896.* New York: Cambridge University Press, 2010.

Wang, Tova Andrea, et al. *Balancing Access and Integrity: The Report of the Century Foundation Working Group on State Implementation of Election Reform.* New York: Century Foundation Press, 2005.

Ware, Alan. *The American Direct Primary: Party Institutionalization and Transformation in the North.* Cambridge; New York: Cambridge University Press, 2002.

Donald A. DeBats

EMANCIPATION PROCLAMATION

Issued by President Abraham Lincoln on 1 January 1863, the Emancipation Proclamation declared that all slaves, in states or portions of states in rebellion against the United States, "are and henceforward shall be free." The president thus freed slaves in Arkansas, Texas, Mississippi, Alabama, Florida, Georgia, South Carolina, North Carolina, and parts of Virginia and Louisiana. Lincoln exempted those states remaining loyal to the Union, such as Maryland, and portions of Confederate states occupied by U.S. troops. Lincoln justified the proclamation by citing military necessity.

The proclamation was the culmination of a gradual process. Although Lincoln had initially declared the preservation of the Union and not the abolition of slavery as his principal purpose in fighting the Civil War, the two goals had become intertwined as the conflict progressed. Northerners were divided over the issue of slavery, and many were hostile to fighting a war on behalf of slaves. Lincoln also knew that any hope of compromise with the Confederacy ruled out the abolition of slavery as a war aim. He also feared that slaveholding states still loyal to the Union would secede if slavery were threatened. But the course of war determined Lincoln's actions and ensured that the abolition of slavery would become a central focus of the conflict.

Slaves, free blacks, and white abolitionists had, of course, immediately recognized the war's potential to end slavery. As the Union army and navy moved into portions of the South, such as the Sea Islands of South Carolina, slaves sought freedom behind Union lines. In May 1861, General Benjamin F. Butler declared slaves who fled to the Union army headquartered at Fortress Monroe, Virginia, to be contraband of war—that is, enemy property open to confiscation by Union troops. Lincoln signed this policy into law as the First Confiscation Act on 6 August 1861. Other moves toward ending slavery followed. In April 1862, Republicans in Congress abolished slavery in the District of Columbia and in the territories. The Second Confiscation Act, passed 17 July 1862, freed all rebel-owned slaves who came behind Union lines, whereas the Militia Act of the same date freed slaves employed by the military. Lincoln and his military commanders recognized that undermining slavery would ultimately weaken the Confederacy and strengthen the Union. Military losses and the knowledge that reconciliation was unlikely also encouraged Lincoln to move toward emancipation. But his advisers encouraged him to refrain from issuing any proclamation until after a Union victory. On 22 September 1862, five days after Robert E. Lee's army withdrew following the Battle of Antietam, Lincoln released a preliminary proclamation announcing his intentions to free slaves in rebellious states on 1 January.

A crucial difference between the preliminary and the final proclamation was the latter's silence on the question of colonization—the repatriation of freed slaves to Africa. In the preliminary proclamation, Lincoln asserted his commitment to colonization, a measure that would appease loyal Southerners and Northerners who feared competition from free black labor. Lincoln's decision not to include a plan of colonization in the final proclamation bolstered its radical potential. In addition to freeing slaves in rebel states and recommending that able-bodied freedmen be "received into the armed service," Lincoln advised former slaves to immediately become free laborers by working "faithfully for reasonable wages."

The Emancipation Proclamation had several important consequences. Although freeing only slaves in areas outside the control of the federal government, it tied the abolition of slavery to the defeat of the Confederacy and ensured that northern victory would mean a reconstruction of southern society and economy. Before the Emancipation Proclamation, African American men and women had been employed by the Union army as servants, teamsters, laborers, scouts, cooks, and laundry workers. Although the proclamation did not directly state that African American soldiers would serve in combat, former slaves and their allies quickly interpreted it this way. Approximately 190,000 black men would serve in the army and navy during the Civil War. The enlistment of African Americans facilitated the abolition of slavery in border states and throughout the South. As black soldiers demonstrated their courage at Port Hudson, Louisiana; Milliken's Bend, Louisiana; and Fort Wagner, South Carolina, they gained Northern respect and support for emancipation increased. In joining the Union army or seeking its protection, former slaves denied the Confederacy their labor, thereby hastening the destruction of slavery.

Providing a precedent for the Reconstruction Era amendments to the Constitution, especially the Thirteenth Amendment abolishing slavery, the Emancipation Proclamation revealed what slaves had known from the beginning: slavery was the central issue of the Civil War.

[*See also* **Antislavery Movement; Confederate States of America; Lincoln, Abraham;** ***and*** **Reconstruction.**]

BIBLIOGRAPHY

Berlin, Ira, Barbara J. Fields, Steven F. Miller, Joseph P. Reidy, and Leslie Rowland. *Slaves No More: Three Essays on Emancipation and the Civil War*. Cambridge: Cambridge University Press, 1992.

Foner, Eric. *Reconstruction: America's Unfinished Revolution, 1863–1877*. New York: Harper & Row, 1988.

Franklin, John Hope. *The Emancipation Proclamation*. Wheeling, Ill.: Harper Davidson, 1995.

Litwack, Leon F. *Been in the Storm So Long: The Aftermath of Slavery*. New York: Alfred A. Knopf, 1979.

McPherson, James M. *Battle Cry of Freedom: The Civil War Era*. New York: Oxford University Press, 1988.

Quarles, Benjamin. *Lincoln and the Negro*. New York: Da Copo Press, 1991.

Carol Faulkner

EMBARGO ACTS

By 1807 the protracted war between Britain and Napoleonic France had reached a stalemate. The British navy had destroyed the Spanish and French fleets in October 1805, giving Britain control of the sea. But France dominated the European continent following Napoleon's victories over Austria, Prussia, and Russia. Without a military option, each side sought to starve the other into submission by depriving it of neutral trade. In this new war of Napoleonic Decrees and British Orders-in-Council, both sides preyed on American shipping.

President Thomas Jefferson and Secretary of State James Madison strongly believed in using commercial coercion to force England and France to rescind their offensive policies and to respect America's rights as a neutral nation. European economies, they reasoned, depended on American agricultural supplies, whereas the United States could easily survive without luxuries imported from the Old World. On 22 December 1807 Congress passed the Embargo Act, prohibiting all American exports.

The Embargo Act, amended several times in 1808 to tighten its enforcement, had disastrous effects for America. Neither France nor Britain altered its policy toward neutral trade. Instead, Napoleon seized American ships in European ports, claiming to believe that any ship trading under the American flag must be a British vessel in disguise. The U.S. economy plunged into a severe depression. Resentment against the embargo spread from merchants to farmers to urban workers and erupted into near rebellion in parts of New England and New York. Jefferson, however, ignored the act's diplomatic failure and the widespread suffering it caused at home, praising it as late as 1815 as "a wise and powerful measure." Grievances arising from neutral rights issues ultimately helped bring on the War of 1812.

[*See also* **Jefferson, Thomas; Madison, James;** *and* **Trade Policy: An Overview.**]

BIBLIOGRAPHY

Ben-Atar, Doron S. *The Origins of Jeffersonian Commercial Policy and Diplomacy*. New York: St. Martin's Press, 1993.

Spivac, Burton. *Jefferson's English Crisis: Commerce, Embargo, and the Republican Revolution*. Charlottesville: University Press of Virginia, 1979.

Doron Ben-Atar

EMPLOYMENT ACT OF 1946

This act created the Council of Economic Advisers as part of the White House staff, whose duty was to "formulate and recommend national economic policy" that would further the national goal of "maximum employment, production, and purchasing power." It reflected the conviction of many liberal policy makers that the greatest economic danger facing the United States after the war was a return to mass unemployment and that the surest way to avoid such a catastrophe was through economic growth. But the law provided no effective tools for achieving its goals, and its supporters soon became disillusioned.

The idea for the bill emerged from the National Resources Planning Board, the New Deal's official planning agency, which in the early 1940s promoted the idea of "full employment." It also reflected President Franklin Delano Roosevelt's call in 1944 for an "economic bill of rights," which included "the right to a useful and remunerative job." Progressive labor and farm groups were also actively lobbying for legislation to promote government-guaranteed full employment, as were leading Keynesian economists. When the bill was introduced in Congress in January 1945, it was titled the Full Employment Bill; it called for the president to adopt economic policies that would create jobs for all who wanted them. The government would spend money on job-creation programs if the private sector appeared unlikely to generate enough employment. President Harry S. Truman supported it after Roosevelt's death, as did most congressional New Dealers.

But by 1946, not enough New Dealers remained in Congress to enact the original bill. After strenuous opposition from employers, who feared that a full employment economy would drive up their labor costs, conservatives in Congress so diluted the legislation that many of its early supporters dismissed it as meaningless rhetoric. The phrase "full employment," which had resonated so strongly among liberals in the 1940s, disappeared from both the title and the body of the bill, as did all the specific policy requirements that were to have given the phrase meaning. But the Council of Economic Advisers created by the act did at times influence presidents to choose policies that promoted economic growth. Although the Employment Act did not guarantee full employment, it did help make fiscal policy an important lever of economic planning in the postwar era.

[*See also* **Federal Government, Executive Branch: Presidency, The; New Deal;**

Roosevelt, Franklin Delano; *and* Truman, Harry S.]

BIBLIOGRAPHY

Bailey, Stephen K. *Congress Makes a Law: The Story behind the Employment Act of 1946*. New York: Columbia University Press, 1950.

Alan Brinkley

ENERGY CRISIS OF THE 1970s

Energy issues have risen and fallen unpredictably on the national political agenda since the 1970s. Their visibility and agenda status reflect shifting conditions, particularly the level of political conflict in the Middle East, oil price spikes, economic upheavals, accidents at energy production facilities, and the choices political leaders make to exert leadership on energy problems. Despite the varying agenda status, energy issues only rarely have been of sustained interest to the American public and policy makers and few policy actions have led to major changes in the nation's use of energy resources.

The energy crisis of the 1970s reflects these patterns. Energy issues rose rapidly on the policy agenda and occupied the attention of three presidents, all of whom urged the necessity of seeking energy independence. Nonetheless, after four decades the United States has yet to deal effectively with the multiple challenges presented by its enormous appetite for energy resources, from continuing dependence on imported oil to the effects from use of fossil fuels on the world's climate.

The immediate cause of the energy crisis in the 1970s was the formation of the Organization of Petroleum Exporting Countries (OPEC), including the original founding nations of Iran, Iraq, Kuwait, Saudi Arabia, and Venezuela and later Qatar, Indonesia, Libya, United Arab Emirates, Algeria, and Nigeria. The formation of this cartel and its policy to drive up oil prices revealed the growing American dependence on imported oil.

In October 1973, members of OPEC initiated an oil embargo in retaliation for the U.S. decision to assist Israel by supplying it with weapons and other war material during the Yom Kippur war. That embargo lasted until March 1974, and it disrupted oil supplies in the United States and substantially raised the price of oil. Notable effects at the time included scarce gasoline supplies, which resulted in long lines at service stations and at least some short-term attempts at fuel rationing. In the end, the most memorable effect was a stark reminder of the risks associated with the nation's reliance on imported oil, particularly the portion coming from a politically volatile Middle East.

The longer-term impact of the 1973 embargo was the political leverage OPEC acquired by its capacity to set a world price for oil through its members' agreement on production levels. Industrialized nations relied heavily on OPEC for their oil, and oil price increases were a significant factor in high levels of inflation in the 1970s and the economic recession related to it. It would not be too much of an exaggeration to say that inflation and the recession were instrumental in President Jimmy Carter's loss to Ronald Reagan in the 1980 election.

During the 1970s, three presidents tried with only modest success to limit the nation's reliance on imported oil. Presidents Richard Nixon, Gerald Ford, and Jimmy Carter all sought to stabilize U.S. energy supplies out of concern for national security and economic implications, and all promoted the elusive goal of U.S. energy independence. Yet by 2011 the nation imported a far greater percentage of its oil, mostly used for transportation, than the level that prevailed during the 1970s energy crisis.

The United States produced most of the oil it used in 1950 (importing about 9 percent), but it imported 35 percent of it by 1973 and over 60 percent by 2011.

In 1975 Congress approved the Energy Policy and Conservation Act, which established the Corporate Average Fuel Economy (CAFE) standards for motor vehicles, extended domestic oil price controls, and authorized the U.S. Strategic Petroleum Reserve to stockpile oil for future emergencies. The CAFE standards pushed automobile companies to improve vehicle fuel efficiency, but the gains reached a plateau by the late 1980s and had only a small effect by the 1990s and 2000s. In 2007 Congress increased those standards in the Energy Independence and Security Act, the first significant change since the 1975 act.

In reaction to the events of the early to mid-1970s, President Carter made energy policy his chief domestic priority in his first two years in office, in 1977 and 1978, referring to the energy crisis as the "moral equivalent of war." In 1977 Congress established the new Department of Energy, consolidating previously independent energy agencies into a cabinet department, with the Nuclear Regulatory Commission remaining an independent agency charged with overseeing nuclear energy.

Carter's proposed National Energy Plan, developed by a task force headed by Secretary of Energy James Schlesinger and submitted to Congress in April 1977, emphasized a strong governmental role rather than continuing a pattern of relying on the private sector. It also looked more to energy conservation than to the traditional options of increasing domestic supplies of energy as the solution to the crisis. However, the complex plan, with 113 separate provisions on energy taxes, efficiency standards, utility rate reforms, and spending priorities, drew little support in Congress (especially in the Senate) as energy producers, industry, utilities, consumer groups, labor, and environmentalists all found something in the plan to dislike.

As a result of the political conflicts over energy policy, Congress approved some parts of the plan while rejecting many others; the surviving elements were collectively called the National Energy Act of 1978. Key components included partial deregulation of natural gas pricing, creation of a market for small energy producers using nonconventional sources such as solar and geothermal, and a series of measures that promoted energy conservation in homes and businesses, efficiency standards for home appliances, changes in power plant and industrial fuel use, and changes in energy taxes, including a new tax on so-called gas-guzzler cars.

The effects of the energy crisis of the 1970s extended well into the 1980s. Consumer groups and industry continued to demand more energy-efficient vehicles, buildings, lighting, motors, and appliances, with some success. By the late 1980s, American industry used only 70 percent of the energy needed in 1973 to produce the same goods. Appliances in the early 1990s were about 75 percent more efficient than they were in the late 1970s, and passenger automobiles in 1991 averaged about twenty-two miles per gallon compared with only fourteen miles per gallon in 1973. These gains were impressive, and yet the nation's growing population and economy, Americans' penchant for larger vehicles and homes, and use of an ever-expanding array of electronic devices translated into increased energy use over time.

In retrospect, the policy responses to the 1970s energy crisis proved to be clearly insufficient to wean the nation from what President George W. Bush characterized in 2006 as its continuing "addiction to oil." The limited policy actions of the 1970s did, however, set the stage for repeated efforts in subsequent decades to formulate and approve a diverse array of national energy and climate change policies.

Most of these proposals were as controversial as the parallel efforts in the 1970s, and they often bitterly divided the two major parties and the nation itself over the necessity of governmental action and the preferred direction for energy policy. Because they deal with fundamental questions related to economic growth, environmental protection, the role of government, and American lifestyles, these debates are likely to continue for some time.

[*See also* **Energy Policy;** *and* **Nuclear Regulatory Commission.**]

BIBLIOGRAPHY

Feldman, David Lewis, ed. *The Energy Crisis: Unresolved Issues and Enduring Legacies.* Baltimore: Johns Hopkins University Press, 1996.

Goodwin, Craufurd D., ed. *Energy Policy in Perspective.* Washington, D.C.: Brookings Institution, 1981.

Kraft, Michael E. "Congress and National Energy Policy: Assessing the Policy Process" In *Environment, Energy, Public Policy: Toward a Rational Future,* edited by Regina S. Axelrod. Lexington, Mass.: Lexington Books, 1981.

Marcus, Alfred A. *Controversial Issues in Energy Policy.* Newbury Park, Calif.: Sage, 1992.

Michael E. Kraft

ENERGY POLICY

In contrast to other industrialized nations, the United States has not developed a coherent national energy policy.

Energy policy intersects several policy narratives, including conservation and environmentalism, regulation and deregulation of private and public energy operations, federalism, and foreign policy. On a continuum between national planning at one end and promoting free market development at the other, U.S. energy policy has trended toward the latter. Policy making has promoted industry (guaranteed returns, tax breaks) and consumers (cheap energy, reliable service) and, for the most part, has been implemented on an industry-by-industry basis. Unlike in other industrialized nations, energy policy in the United States has evolved under a reality of abundance. The emergence of oil as a dominant fuel by the twentieth century brought perceptions of scarcity, but the reality of abundance enabled special interests, emphasis on low prices, and short-term perspectives to shape energy policy.

There is merit in dividing the history of energy policy into two chronological periods—the regulatory era and the era of deregulation—with the break coming in the 1970s, when shortages of imported oil and domestic natural gas forced policy makers to shift their views. Although interest group politics underlie both eras, there has been some progress toward taking a holistic approach since the 1970s. The period of deregulation has also been labeled the "long transition" from a reliance on abundance to the recognition that scarcity and sustainability can shape more effective energy policy.

The themes of conservation, regulation, and federalism have bridged the two eras. Conservation interests had little impact during the first era, although there was some success in national forests preservation, oil production regulation in the 1930s, and curtailing of natural gas flaring in the late 1940s. Regulation appeared within an industry-by-industry approach, with some thought but little action occurring to coordinate how each energy source best served the economy. Meanwhile, all conservation and regulatory policies floundered on the complex legal relationships between state and federal authorities. Special interests often took advantage of the Federalist tensions to prevent planning from taking hold.

The result of this century-long, fractured energy policy has been the enormous waste of natural (economic) resources, vast pollution of the environment, and reliance on foreign sources of oil, which in turn have affected foreign and military policies. Only in the past several decades have increased conservation, pollution regulations, and emphasis on renewable fuels brought some reversals of earlier trends. Even this success has been slowed by the continuing influence of special interests and federalism.

The Abundance of Energy Sources—The Economic Context. Americans have benefitted from an abundance of energy sources from the founding of the country in the eighteenth century (wood and water for heating and small-scale manufacturing), to the nineteenth and twentieth centuries (coal and water for steam engines and hydroelectric generators for manufacturing, illumination, home heating, and cooking), to the twentieth century (petroleum, oil for illumination and transportation; natural gas for heating and cooking). Other nations with fewer energy sources have increased the use of nuclear, solar (including wind), and ocean power systems. These energy systems have been slow to expand in America in part because of the abundance of coal and petroleum and in part because special interests have blocked long-term technical and economic development in favor of short-term policies.

There has always been a mix of energy sources, and that mix has changed over time because of the interaction of energy policy making with economics and ideology. Although petroleum has appeared to dominate the energy arena, the consumption of coal has increased throughout the twentieth century; in 2000, coal-fired plants generated over 50 percent of the electricity in the United States. On the other hand, the production of electricity from hydroelectric dams has declined since the 1980s. As the economy became more dependent on oil for transportation, manufacturing, and home heating and cooking, more imports from abroad filled in the gap created by diminishing national sources. Despite the increased reliance on imported oil, however, there is an abundance of energy sources in the United States in the form of coal, shale oil, potential hydroelectric, natural gas, solar, and wind power.

The Regulatory Era. In the 1920s and 1930s, local, state, and national governments established agencies to promote and control private and public electric and natural gas producers and distributors; most of these systems served urban areas. In the 1930s, the federal government promoted three programs to bring electricity to rural Americans: the Tennessee Valley Authority (TVA), hydroelectric dams in Texas and the West, and the Rural Electrification Administration (REA), which sponsored consumer cooperatives. Most Americans had access to electricity by the 1950s. But the "public power" agenda had elicited political protests from "private power" corporations and conservatives opposed to government programs. No more government-sponsored large-scale electricity projects were initiated.

Regulation of the natural gas industry, which boomed during the 1940s, evolved through an interest group–based politics that established a complicated federal system of control over natural gas production, transportation, and distribution. The failure of Congress and the executive branch to act effectively in the late 1940s and the 1950s resulted in the Supreme Court establishing the parameters of natural gas regulation for the Federal Power Commission (FPC) to enforce. During the 1950s and 1960s the federal regulatory agency failed to promote industry or protect consumers of natural gas.

In this period oil had begun to fuel the automobile age. State highway systems, supported by the tourist industry and automobile clubs, expanded across the nation, paid for in part by gasoline taxes. The synergy between the gasoline tax and highway building promoted the automobile culture, which undermined the rail passenger and freight systems and changed the urban landscape. Between the mid-1930s and 1960s, government policies (a Federalist system of control over oil production, generous "depletion allowances" to oil well drillers, support of inefficient oil wells to promote "small" producers, building of the interstate highway system) ensured low prices for gasoline, which discouraged conservation of the nation's nonrenewable resource.

By the 1950s, it was clear that the internal combustion–fueled automobile was an entrenched part of the American political–economic culture and that it could not survive solely on domestically produced oil. American and other oil firms expanded production abroad to Mexico, Venezuela, and the Middle East. Although the American government did not control this expansion, it shaped foreign and military policy to sustain the world oil market.

Crises in the 1970s. A two-pronged energy crisis rocked the political economy in the 1970s. Shortages of natural gas plagued the Midwest and Northeast; consumers in the Southwest had gas, but paid relatively higher prices. Beginning in the 1960s, oil-producing nations belonging to the Organization of Petroleum Exporting Countries (OPEC) gained control over the pricing of their oil from American and other oil firms. Exerting their new power in response to the West's support of Israel (1973) and the Iranian Revolution (1979), OPEC withheld supplies, which led to higher gasoline prices in the United States and elsewhere. These oil shocks, along with the shortages in natural gas supplies, prompted much discussion about energy policy. Although there was a shift in perspective, for the most part interest group politics, industry-specific approaches, and federalism continued to shape energy policy making.

Era of Deregulation and the Long Transition. Three concepts shaped energy policy making after the crises of the 1970s: energy independence, deregulation, and sustainability. Many politicians supported the idea of reducing America's reliance on foreign oil through increased drilling for oil offshore, in the Alaskan wilderness, and in oil shale deposits, all of which environmentalists opposed as too risky for too little payoff. Based in large measure on the FPC's failure to regulate natural gas and electric utilities effectively, but also tied to a wider movement to reduce government regulation, the states and Congress began in the 1980s and 1990s to deregulate energy systems. At the same time, the environmental movement supplanted the older progressive conservation movement. Activists championed the idea of sustainability, which included conservation (increased miles per gallon in autos, more efficient home insulation and construction or "green" policies, right-turn-on-red laws, etc.) and development of renewable sources of energy (wind, solar, synfuels, biofuels such as ethanol, and geothermal).

The era of deregulation and the long transition, which continues in the second decade of the twenty-first century, has brought mixed results. Energy independence remains a chimera, unless Americans are willing to discard the automobile culture in favor of a drastically different transportation system. America's interaction with the world oil market militates against independence because that relationship not only includes imports but also involves protecting oil supplies to Japan and Europe. If technical developments were forthcoming, theoretically coal could sustain much of the energy demand in the nation; "clean coal," however, awaits technological breakthroughs. Some "alternative fuels"—promoted by special interests—consume almost as much in fossil fuels as the energy they provide (ethanol). Deregulation of natural gas and electric power has not evolved evenly or with clear positive results. Although the national government has acted to loosen restraints on pricing, most of the deregulatory activity has taken place in the states, but a majority of states have not deregulated. The one clear failure of state deregulation—California (Enron)—has dampened enthusiasm for deregulation elsewhere.

Environmental politics have made a difference in energy policy making since the 1970s. Energy-related pollution has been reduced, and conservation and sustainability are more accepted and promoted in legislation (e.g., see the American Recovery and Reinvestment Act of 2009). For the foreseeable future, however, the economics of sustainable fuels will hinge on the price of coal and petroleum. Given the immense supplies, the interest group influences, and ideologically based politics, the long transition will continue for some time.

[*See also* **Energy Crisis of the 1970s;** ***and*** **Tennessee Valley Authority.**]

BIBLIOGRAPHY

Clark, John G. *Energy and the Federal Government: Fossil Fuel Policies, 1900–1946*. Urbana: University of Illinois Press, 1987.

Hirsh, Richard F. *Power Loss: The Origins of Deregulation and Restructuring in the American Electric Power Industry*. Cambridge, Mass.: MIT Press, 2000.

MacAvoy, Paul W. *The Natural Gas Market: Sixty Years of Regulation and Deregulation*. New Haven, Conn.: Yale University Press, 2000.

Melosi, Martin V. *Coping with Abundance: Energy and Environment in Industrial America*. Philadelphia: Temple University Press, 1985.

Vietor, Richard H. K. *Energy Policy in America since 1945: A Study of Business–Government Relations*. Cambridge, UK; New York: Cambridge University Press, 1984.

The White House. *Energy and Environment*. http://www.whitehouse.gov/issues/energy-and-environment (accessed 12 August 2011).

Yergin, Daniel. *The Prize: The Epic Quest for Oil, Money and Power*. New York: Simon & Schuster, 1991.

William R. Childs

ENGEL v. VITALE

A 1962 U.S. Supreme Court decision addressing the issue of school prayer. In the early 1960s some New York public school districts asked children to recite a state-composed prayer each day: "Almighty God, we acknowledge our dependence upon Thee, and we beg Thy blessings upon us, our parents, our teachers and our Country." Some non-Christian parents objected that the prayer, although supposedly not compulsory, was nonetheless required and that tax-supported facilities were used for a religious observance. While the American Civil Liberties Union and the American Jewish Committee came to the aid of the parents, the New York Board of Regents, twenty state attorneys general, and Porter R. Chandler, a lawyer with close ties to the Roman Catholic Archdiocese of New York, joined in defense of the prayer requirement.

The case produced one of the Supreme Court's most controversial decisions under the chief justiceship of Earl Warren. Justice Hugo Black's majority opinion assuming a high wall of separation between church and state, declared the prayer an unconstitutional violation of the First Amendment's Establishment Clause. Using public schools to encourage prayer, Black argued, was "a practice wholly inconsistent with the Establishment Clause." Justice Potter Stewart's lone dissent reasoned that the Establishment Clause only forbade government from establishing an official church and coercing religious beliefs.

President John F. Kennedy supported the Court by noting that Americans were still free to pray at home with their children. Yet fundamentalist religious groups charged that the Court in *Engel* had erected too high a barrier between church and state and had promoted atheism, agnosticism, and secularization.

[*See also* **Bill of Rights; Black, Hugo; Christian Coalition; Civil Liberties; Kennedy, John F.; Moral Majority; Supreme Court, U.S.;** *and* **Warren, Earl.**]

BIBLIOGRAPHY

Hall, Kermit L. *The Magic Mirror: Law in American History*. New York: Oxford University Press, 1989.

Kermit L. Hall

ENVIRONMENTALISM

Although its roots go back much earlier, the social movement known as environmentalism first appeared in the 1960s. It soon became one of the most successful movements in modern history, with a national and global impact on politics, economics, technology, design, and personal values. As the twentieth century ended, that impact seemed likely to endure, yet how truly profound it would be remained unclear. As it grew, the movement came to mean different things to different groups, although at its core it remained an effort to improve human relationships with the other-than-human world.

Roots of Environmental and Ecological Awareness. In the early twentieth century, the word "environmentalism" referred mainly to the effects of external social influences (as opposed to genetic endowment) on the individual. But increasingly after World War II, "environment" came to mean the natural world surrounding people, including flora, fauna, climate, water, and soil—the entire biosphere. At the same time, that natural world began to seem highly vulnerable to human activity; it was no longer an all-powerful Mother Earth providing boundless nourishment for her children but an endangered source of life. That sense of vulnerability inspired a social and political reform movement. Environmentalists called for a more responsible relationship between human beings and nature. Human survival was at stake, as was the stability and integrity of the whole fabric of life on the planet.

More and more citizens sensed that the human–nature umbilical link was itself under attack and that defending it required a radically new way of thinking. The environment had to be seen holistically, they insisted. For them, nature was not a realm set above and apart from human beings, like another country one visits from time to time, but instead is a vast, intricate community interacting all around us, a system of connections and interchanges to which we all belong. Human beings cannot move away from that condition, nor ignore it with impunity, they concluded, even in the midst of the largest metropolis.

A defining work in the emergence of environmentalism was Rachel Carson's *Silent Spring* (1962), which warned of the wholesale contamination of the environment by chemical pesticides such as dichlorodiphenyltrichloroethane (DDT). Like many others of her generation, Carson was shaken by the fear of all-out nuclear war and worried about radioactive fallout from weapons testing polluting food chains, even in the most remote parts of the planet. In 1967, a group of scientists and lawyers founded the Environmental Defense Fund, which sought to get dangerous pesticides banned by the courts as a threat to the health of both human beings and natural ecosystems.

The National Environmental Policy Act (1969) set up a federal regulatory agency, the Environmental Protection Agency, and required an "environmental impact statement" for any federally funded project that might cause damage to the earth. The 1963 Limited Nuclear Test Ban Treaty, a ban on DDT use in the United States, and the passage of many new laws (including the 1960 Clean Water Act and the 1963 Clean Air Act) all sprang from growing conviction that the human–nature relationship was more essential than Americans had generally realized and that what happened to one side of the relationship inevitably affected the other. Capping a decade of ferment, environmentalists in 1970 declared the first Earth Day, an event to celebrate human–nature interdependence. An estimated 20 million people, most of them North Americans and most under the age of thirty, participated, far outnumbering student demonstrations for the civil rights movement or for an end to the Vietnam War. The event became an annual, and eventually a truly international, ritual—an unprecedented global "holiday." More substantially, almost all nations passed laws similar to those enacted in the United States, and several nations surpassed the United States in cleaning up their rivers and atmosphere, recycling their wastes, reducing toxic emissions, improving energy efficiency, and preserving a critical habitat for biodiversity.

Within the United States, environmentalism was an amalgamation of several older strands of intellectual and political consciousness. Among them were nineteenth-century transcendentalism and the Romantic movement. Rachel Carson acknowledged her indebtedness to such figures as Henry David Thoreau and John Muir, both of whom had celebrated American nature in its wilder state and sought to recover a direct personal relationship with the nonhuman. Both looked for ways of getting outside the confine of civilization now and then and into primeval woods or mountains. Painters and poets had encouraged people to seek the sublime in nature, alone or in small groups, in such awe-inspiring landscapes as Yellowstone, Yosemite, and the Grand Canyon. Carson herself, a marine biologist with the U.S. Fish and Wildlife Service, was passionate about the sea; she found her wilderness in tidal pools along the Maine coast. But by the 1960s, in a highly urbanized nation of over 200 million people, with a far denser web of artifice obscuring the natural order, this kind of romantic quest had become increasingly difficult to satisfy by solitary, private excursions. Environmentalism, although inspired by romantic yearnings for contact with nature, could not be simply an individual act of reverence for or withdrawal from modernity; it must be a public project pursued collectively in the courtroom, the legislative chamber, and the corporate headquarters. Organization and lobbying were required to win passage of the 1964 Wilderness Act, which over the next three decades would protect 100 million acres and stand as one of the great successes of the American environmental movement.

A second strand was the Progressive Era conservation movement, which gained momentum in the early twentieth century under the leadership of Gifford Pinchot, chief forester during Theodore Roosevelt's presidency, and of Roosevelt himself. That movement supported the preservation of national parks and wildlife refuges, but even more importantly it set up a national forest system based on sustained-yield management principles and called for protecting the nation's soils and minerals from overrapid development. The core ideal was "wise use." For Pinchot and his allies, that ideal required the federal government to be permanently in charge of managing land and overseeing national development. American society could not endure, they felt, without a secure, continuing permanent supply of natural resources. Unregulated private exploitation, they feared, threatened the nation's long-term security. The post-1960 environmental movement shared that same concern about stopping waste and inefficiency and safeguarding resources for the future, but it went further, calling for an overhaul of the entire modern economic system to fit consumption patterns to the limits of the land.

A third source of modern environmentalism was a public health movement working for cleaner, safer factories and urban neighborhoods. By the mid-nineteenth century, physicians and other professionals in Europe and North America were agitating for better sanitation to prevent devastating outbreaks of cholera and typhoid fever. The early targets had been water supplies contaminated by human waste, slaughterhouse offal, and garbage. As coal replaced wood as the nation's chief energy source after 1870, public health concerns broadened to include air pollution, although clear medical evidence of the effects of such combustion on lungs and other body tissues was slow in coming. The urban environmentalist Alice Hamilton—a medical doctor, social worker at Jane Addams's Hull House in Chicago, and a sometime professor of industrial hygiene at Harvard University—pioneered in investigating the poisons that infected workplaces and tenement dwellings. Reformers found life in the modern city particularly degraded and unwholesome, but they soon extended their efforts into rural areas, including Indian reservations and sharecroppers' cabins, wherever poor people disproportionately bore the costs of progress. Not until Rachel Carson, however, did public health reformers generally begin to realize that the human body is a part of nature too and that its pollution by dangerous substances is one with the pollution of the earth.

Finally, the emergence of environmentalism owed something to a relatively obscure group of natural scientists and academics in such fields as ecology and geography who first perceived the environment as an interactive physical system connecting human beings and the rest of nature. Visualizing that system on a global scale, many of them dramatically transcended the nationalistic perspective of the Progressive conservationists or the localized concerns of urban health reformers. Their basic theories often came from abroad as well: from the Russian geologist V. I. Vernadskii, originator of the concept of the biosphere; from French andGerman geographers, who had long debated the question of nature as a limiting factor on human activity; and from a succession of English naturalists, including Charles Darwin, Charles Elton, and Arthur Tansley (who suggested the idea of the ecosystem). A key American figure in this emerging body of scientific thought was Aldo Leopold, a University of Wisconsin wildlife expert, who introduced many readers to the science of ecology through his *Sand County Almanac* (1948).

By the 1950s, these scientific ideas had come together in a new integrative and interdisciplinary point of view that united the natural and social sciences, a perspective that might be called human ecology. Avoiding the extremes of environmental determinism, which had tried to reduce cultures to their physical conditions, and of a technological optimism that was blind to all environmental limits, the new view insisted that human life must be lived within natural constraints, both physical and moral.

The concept of human ecology emerged on many fronts in the late 1940s and 1950s. The anthropologists Betty Meggers and Julian Steward—one working in Amazonia and the other in the American Southwest—laid the foundations for "cultural ecology." The historian James Malin argued for an ecological approach and applied it in his own studies of the relations of plants, animals, soils, climate, and human populations on the Great Plains. Among geographers, Carl Sauer produced influential essays and books exploring the effects of European colonialism on New World peoples and landscapes. Several of those scholars and others from diverse disciplines gathered in Princeton, New Jersey, in 1956 for a symposium on the deteriorating state of the human–nature relationship. The resulting publication, *Man's Role in Changing the Face of the Earth* (1956), dedicated to the nineteenth-century American conservationist George Perkins Marsh, played a major role in preparing the deeper intellectual ground for the environmental movement.

Among the symposium participants was Paul B. Sears, a botanist who chaired the conservation program at Yale University. In his short but prophetic paper, "The Processes of Environmental Change by Man," Sears reviewed the global impact of human population growth, the intensification of agricultural land use, and water and air pollution in industrial areas, noting that the United States, with less than a tenth of the world's population, was consuming more than half of its mineral production. Neither Sears nor the other conference-goers called themselves environmentalists, but their concern over the growing effect of human beings on global ecology helped give environmentalism a set of defining ideas and theories. In 1972, when environmentalists from many countries assembled in Stockholm to resurvey the global situation, they drew on the perspective worked out by those pioneering human ecologists. By the later 1990s, that same perspective had become widely popularized in the United States, and ecology (however shallow or profound) was part of the daily language of masses of people worldwide.

Growing Urgency and Backlash: Post-1960 Developments. What the environmentalist movement added to these fertile new ideas of human ecology was a growing sense of urgency, bordering at times on apocalyptic fear. By the 1960s, activists warned of an environmental "crisis." Rachel Carson's nightmare of a future springtime when no birds would sing, all dead from manmade poisons, introduced a tone of anxiety missing from the writings of Thoreau, Pinchot, Hamilton, Leopold, or Sears. Following Carson, another anxious biologist, Paul Ehrlich, warned in *The Population Bomb* (1968) of a demographic hazard that "keeps ticking," ready to explode. In *The Closing Circle* (1971), the Washington University biologist Barry Commoner alerted the country to the death of Lake Erie from pollutants and the death of people from radioactivity, smog, and ground-water contamination. Commoner explained that he had first been alerted to the environmental crisis by the activities of the Atomic Energy Commission (predecessor of the Nuclear Regulatory Commission), which during the 1950s had exposed Americans and others to deadly strontium 90 through nuclear-weapons testing and then failed to let the public know the full consequences of that exposure. The urgent need, in his view, was for an awakened public, led by informed scientists, to force the government and corporate America to develop less life-threatening technologies. The specter haunting each of these environmentalists was nothing less than death—the death of birds, of ecosystems, of nature itself, and, because of our dependence on nature, the death of human beings as well.

Only slightly less apocalyptic were those environmentalists who by the 1970s called for a reevaluation of the purposes and consequences of economic development. In their view, an economy expanding geometrically using ever more energy, land, minerals, and water must eventually encounter the limits of the earth's resources. The environment, they insisted, must be seen as more than a storehouse of commodities to be ransacked and consumed. Here the environmentalists confronted attitudes deeply engrained among economists, business leaders, politicians, and the public about the virtues of economic growth, attitudes underlying the modern economic system and indeed the whole materialistic ethos of contemporary culture. Although the popular response to this challenge was difficult to gauge, polls did show a growing tilt toward environmentalist views in all the industrial countries and a greater public willingness, at least in affluent societies, to make economic sacrifices to reduce pollution, preserve species, and consume less energy.

During the 1980s, as American politics turned conservative, a rising chorus of antienvironmentalists, led by President Ronald Reagan and Secretary of the Interior James Watt, insisted that the environment was neither fragile nor a real constraint on human ambition. The antienvironmental backlash continued during the presidency of George W. Bush (2001–2009). Closely linked to corporate interests and energy companies, the Bush Administration sought to roll back environmental regulations, promoted logging in national forests and oil drilling in the Arctic National Wildlife Refuge, and dropped investigations of more than 140 refineries and industrial sites suspected of Clean Air Act violations. The administration also withdrew from negotiations over the final terms of the 1997 Kyoto Accords, a United Nations–sponsored effort to reduce emissions contributing to global warming. Environmentalists responded by renewing their sense of mission and increasing their numbers.

The Sierra Club and other environmental organizations vigorously protested this retreat from a well-established bipartisan commitment to environmental protection. They countered opposition by seeking alliances with other groups demanding cultural change: among feminists, some of whom insisted that women were more attuned to ecological interdependencies than men; among ethical radicals, who wanted to extend rights to animals, trees, and the rest of nature; and among social-justice advocates at home and abroad, who demanded protection for the poor from the environmental damage and toxic dumping by the rich. Above all, environmentalists tried to temper their gloomier tendencies with a more hopeful, and more politically acceptable, emphasis on creating a new "green future" in which environmentally sensitive cities, economies, and technologies would all be reembedded in the tangled web of life.

[*See also* **Atomic Energy Commission; Carson, Rachel; Conservation Movement; Conservatism; Environmental Policy: An Overview; Environmental Policy: Clean Air Act; Environmental Policy: Clean Water Act; Environmental Policy: Endangered Species Act; Environmental Protection Agency; Feminism; National Park System; Nuclear Regulatory Commission; Progressive Era;** *and* **Roosevelt, Theodore.**]

BIBLIOGRAPHY

Dunlap, Riley E., and Angela G. Mertig, eds. *American Environmentalism*. Philadelphia: Taylor & Francis, 1992.

Fox, Stephen. *John Muir and His Legacy: The American Conservation Movement*. Boston: Little, Brown, 1981.

Gottlieb, Robert. *Forcing the Spring*. Washington, D.C.: Island Press, 1993.

Hays, Samuel P. *Beauty, Health, and Permanence*. Cambridge, UK; New York: Cambridge University Press, 1987.

Kempton, Willett, James S. Boster, and Jennifer A. Hartley. *Environmental Values in American Culture*. Cambridge, Mass.: MIT Press, 1995.

Paehlke, Robert C. *Environmentalism and the Future of Progressive Politics*. New Haven, Conn.: Yale University Press, 1989.

Taylor, Bob Pepperman. *Our Limits Transgressed.* Lawrence: University Press of Kansas, 1992.
Sale, Kirkpatrick. *The Green Revolution.* New York: Hill and Wang, 1993.
Worster, Donald. *Nature's Economy,* 2d. ed. Cambridge, UK; New York: Cambridge University Press, 1994.

Donald Worster; updated by Paul S. Boyer

ENVIRONMENTAL POLICY

This entry contains four subentries: An Overview; Clean Air Act; Clean Water Act; and Endangered Species Act.

AN OVERVIEW

It remains common practice to characterize U.S. environmental policy as the product of an "age of limits," an era of introspection that compelled a wholesale rethinking of national attitudes and actions affecting the natural world. If so, then the turn of the twentieth century duly qualifies as the age at issue. Haunted by the specter of dwindling resources, vanishing frontiers, urban-industrial malaise, and economic decline, an array of actors and interests looked to conserve the nation's environment as a means to salvage its heritage, society, and political economy.

Environmental Conservation. Concerns about environmental limits were not entirely new, of course. Political tradition in New England and elsewhere recognized protection of the "commons," be they fields, forests, or fisheries, as a legitimate, albeit contested, function of state and local government. Insuring democratic access to natural resources, however, became more difficult with the expansion of population, industrial production, and global markets. In *Man and Nature* (1864), the brilliant polymath George Perkins Marsh emphasized nature's intricate ecological interdependence and vulnerability to human activity, warning that historically, the environment and civilization declined together.

Marsh echoed the concerns of Gilded Age elites who were ill at ease with rapid industrialization and resource profligacy, but the depression of the 1890s intensified these anxieties. Although its deprivations extended everywhere, the once booming West fell victim to both economic and environmental reversals. Even as historian Frederick Jackson Turner eulogized the western frontier as the incubator of American democratic culture, drought-beleaguered homesteaders abandoned their failing farms in droves, viewing the arid lands beyond the ninety-eighth meridian as less demographically "closed" than ecologically inaccessible.

Prominent Progressive reformers responded to Turnerian concerns about scarcity with a redoubled effort to utilize natural resources even more intensely. They looked to science, technology, specialization, and top-down administration to ferret out waste and inefficiency in the service of material progress and democracy. As such, they turned confidently to the federal government to manage the public domain rather than simply distribute its bounty to private citizens in the traditional nineteenth-century mode.

National Conservation Efforts and Resource Management. Theodore Roosevelt personified these trends. Combining a love of rugged frontier wilderness, dismay at squandered western resources, and confidence in executive stewardship of the public interest, he also saw a link between the sustainable growth of a complex industrial economy and the rational exploitation of natural assets. To that end, he cultivated loyal administrators who treated resource management as the spur to reorganizing the executive branch and reconceptualizing the scale and scope of the American state. Gifford Pinchot (Forest Service), James Garfield (Interior), and Frederick Newell (Reclamation Service) all sought to transform oversight of the public domain's timber, grazing lands, and hydropower sites by replacing patronage-addled agencies, legislative interference, local politics, and judicial review with more independent, centralized, expert-driven bureaucracies. Pinchot's prolonged battle to transfer control of the nation's neglected forest reserves (established in 1891) from the Bureau of Land Management to the Department of Agriculture embodied the internecine conflict that accompanied the politics of conservation.

The Roosevelt administration enlisted independent investigations, personalized bureaucratic networks, and the rhetoric of science, democracy, and the market to advance the cause of national conservation. Roosevelt appointed Pinchot to various commissions studying public lands, inland waterways, country life, and executive efficiency, all of which argued for consolidating managerial authority in the hands of qualified federal planners. Pinchot solidified his own status as an expert forester on the basis of an abbreviated jaunt through the German university system, assembled a dedicated Forest Service cadre by building institutions (the Yale School of Forestry) and ties of loyalty based on reputation and interpersonal relationships, peddled scientific forestry as a profitable method for insuring sustainable timber yields, and cast conservationists with the people against monopolistic interests in the struggle to allocate resources equitably.

Pinchot's books were cooked, his professional credentials half-baked, his science backed less by supporting evidence than moral fervor, and his preference for utilitarian efficiency more often amenable to large corporations than to the little guy. Yet all served as successful state-building tools. The Forest Service soon employed a staff of 2,500. Meanwhile, Roosevelt trebled forest reserve acreage to 150 million between 1900 and 1909, encompassing 138 national forests in twenty-one states. He also set aside fifty wildlife refuges, hundreds of hydropower sites, 75 million acres of mineral lands, and five national parks.

Legalistic Mechanisms in Environmental Policy. Roosevelt's successor, William Taft, preferred legalistic mechanisms to the faith of Pinchot et al. in administrative discretion, slowing the conservationists' bureaucratic momentum. So, too, did pushback in Congress, particularly from westerners. Although Pinchot courted stockmen and other local interests to secure oversight of grasslands and dam sites within forest reserves, he never gained control of those elsewhere in the public domain. Congressional conservatives rejected most commission recommendations, including calls for executive reorganization and comprehensive river basin planning. Meanwhile, the Enlarged (1909) and Forest (1906) Homestead acts, together with outright land sales, continued to distribute broad swaths of federal acreage, while Roosevelt, eager to build Republican Party loyalty out West, did little to rationalize the nation's overlapping land laws.

The waxing political muscle of Western states helped place reclamation on the government agenda as well. Nevada Senator Francis Newlands's eponymous 1902 law set out to establish a self-liquidating federal irrigation program. It fused a Jeffersonian faith in independent yeoman farmers with the ecological pragmatism of nineteenth-century explorer-geologist John Wesley Powell in an effort to reopen Turner's democratic frontier to more sustained agricultural production. As with federal forestry, the moral zeal of administrators in the Bureau of Reclamation (BR) often outstripped sound technical knowledge or economic justification. Its first three lackluster decades subsidizing desert agriculture also confirmed that poor farmers made for fickle clients.

Prior to the era of big federal water projects, San Francisco's efforts to dam the scenic Hetch Hetchy Valley (1903–1913) exposed tensions among conservation-minded Progressives. The conventional retelling of the celebrated standoff between Gifford Pinchot and John Muir—featuring the former's utilitarian case for urban water supplies versus the latter's spiritual defense of "untouched" nature—exaggerates their differences. Pinchot appreciated the aesthetic rewards of the outdoors as much as the founder of the Sierra Club, who sought not pristine wilderness but a developed destination for urban tourists. The promise of publicly generated electrical power to challenge private utilities ultimately tipped the balance toward dam supporters, who characterized Muir as an elitist apologist for monopoly.

Aesthetics and Equity. Questions of aesthetics and equity likewise pervade the history of national parks. Beginning with Yellowstone (1872), park boosters sought to preserve the natural heritage of the frontier for the benefit of overcivilized urban dwellers. Muir, who tramped gaily through sublime landscapes his Transcendentalist forbearers could never stomach, had a hand in establishing six parks, including his beloved Yosemite (1890). His political acumen rivaled Pinchot's, and his connections with corporate power brokers helped secure support for large western parks—each enjoyed the backing of major railroads seeking tourist trade and the protection of watersheds adjoining their own extensive properties. Federal officials never hesitated to reconstruct the parks' "natural" environs to conform to the expectations of well-to-do patrons: building rustic lodges; shooting predators to cultivate charismatic moose, buffalo, and elk; and ejecting Native Americans from their ancestral hunting grounds. As well with state initiatives like New York's Adirondack Park (1892), every act of preservation—fixing boundaries and banning hunting and timbering—served to exclude poorer locals and limit traditional subsistence activities. The laudable efforts of elite sportsmen, outdoor enthusiasts, and women's clubs to conserve land and fauna nonetheless stirred class resentments.

Progressive Conservation. During the interwar years, the proliferation of automobiles rendered parks more accessible to the middle class, stirring controversy anew about their proper function. The National Parks Service (NPS, 1916), formed in the wake of the Hetch Hetchy hullabaloo, responded to growing demands for outdoor recreation with an aggressive campaign to expand parklands and build extensive roadways therein. But autotourism elicited a reaction from critics of mass consumption like Robert Marshall, Benton MacKaye, and Aldo Leopold. These founders of the Wilderness Society (1935) sought instead to preserve natural expanses absent the trappings and traffic of civilization. Thanks in part to its turf war with the NPS, the Forest Service accepted Leopold's recommendation to establish New Mexico's Gila National Forest (1924) for low-tech hiking and camping and, at Marshall's urging, strengthened internal regulations preserving millions of "primitive" forest acres, the precursors to even stricter protections established under the Wilderness Act (1964).

Progressive conceptions of conservation were clearly evolving, but never more so than during the Great Depression, when Franklin Roosevelt's (FDR's) New Deal placed concerns about nature at the center of its drive for economic recovery and reform. FDR's administration identified a link between rural poverty and mismanagement of natural resources, pitching conservation as the means to distribute them more equitably between country and city, raise rural income, and prevent future depressions.

New Dealers sought to remove marginal farmland from production, mend damaged landscapes, reserve more acreage for recreation, and modernize regional economies. The Taylor Grazing Act (1934) ended homesteading in the public domain, whereas the Agricultural Adjustment Act (1933) paid farmers not to grow glutted commodities, incentivizing mechanization and the eventual demise of southern sharecropping. The young, urban unemployed of the Civilian Conservation Corps (CCC, 1933–1942) planted 2 billion trees, took the lead in practicing soil conservation on public and private land (including the dust-stricken Plains), and built the infrastructure for hundreds of new state parks created with federal land purchases, benefiting residents of the urban East and rural South. In this way, the CCC touted the benefits of conservation to new geographic and demographic constituencies. The Tennessee Valley Authority (1933), meanwhile, envisioned rural electrification as the key to a more diversified, industrial, and consumer-based southern economy. In the West, Hoover, Grand Coulee, and dozens more "multipurpose" dams to follow also promised a more prosperous, democratic, and neotechnic rural future. Like in the South, however, agricultural production increased as the population and appeal of farms declined; as the BR jettisoned the Newlands Act's acreage limitations and embraced massive congressional appropriations, irrigated farms grew larger and more corporate. The other major beneficiaries of subsidized water and hydropower were western and Sunbelt cities, whose industry and populations mushroomed during and after World War II.

Postwar environmentalism grew out of a burgeoning suburban middle class that knew nature more through consumption and leisure than work—first as industrial efficiency veiled nature's role in mass production and later when urban deindustrialization detached such production from a young, educated, white, and white collar demographic. Pollution grew more unpalatable as concerns about health and quality of life turned clean air, pure water, and open space into desirable amenities worthy of government protection (indeed, sprawling suburbia often imperiled them). Writers like Aldo Leopold (1949), Rachel Carson (1962), and Barry Commoner (1970) introduced a popular ecological discourse that once more draped a moral message in scientific garb, articulating nature's nonanthropocentric value beyond the market and declaring its complexity, diversity, and "balance" vulnerable to unchecked technology, technocracy, or economic growth. The mass success of Earth Day testified to their cultural resonance by 1970.

Environmentalists spent much of their time attempting to circumscribe the administrative discretion Progressives and New Dealers coveted. Accordingly, the initiative for environmental policy making shifted from the executive branch to Congress and the courts. True, Richard Nixon centralized environmental regulation in the Environmental Protection Agency (EPA, 1970). But legislative entrepreneurs like Senator Edmund Muskie (D-ME) sponsored legislation like the Clean Air Act (1970) and the Clean Water Act (1972), deemphasizing cooperative federalism in favor of strict timetables and technology-based (and technology-forcing) standards. Like the Endangered Species Act (1973), they also included citizen suit provisions designed for new public interest litigants who trusted government less but relied upon its enforcement powers more than ever.

Environmental law evolved to render agency hearings boards and federal judges more solicitous of countervailing interests and information. In the 1950s, David Brower's Sierra Club had few options beyond political coalition building to prevent a BR dam inside Utah's Dinosaur National Monument. By 1965, courts had broadened legal standing to sue, and by 1969 Senator Henry Jackson's (D-WA) National Environmental Policy Act had institutionalized challenges to agency expertise. As a consequence, environmental politics became, and remain, more complex and contentious in the aftermath of the second "age of limits."

[*See also* **Environmental Policy: Clean Air Act; Environmental Policy: Clean Water Act; Environmental Policy: Endangered Species Act; Roosevelt, Franklin Delano; Roosevelt, Theodore;** ***and*** **Tennessee Valley Authority.**]

BIBLIOGRAPHY

Brooks, Karl Boyd. *Before Earth Day: The Origins of American Environmental Law, 1945–1970.* Lawrence: University Press of Kansas, 2009.

Milazzo, Paul Charles. *Unlikely Environmentalists: Congress and Clean Water, 1945–1972.* Lawrence: University Press of Kansas, 2006.

Phillips, Sarah. *This Land, This Nation: Conservation, Rural America, and the New Deal.* Cambridge, UK; New York: Cambridge University Press, 2007.

Pisani, Donald. "The Many Faces of Conservation: Natural Resources and the American State, 1900–1940." In *Taking Stock: American Government in the Twentieth Century,* edited by Morton Keller and R. Shep Melnick, pp. 123–155. Washington, D.C.: Woodrow Wilson Center Press, 1999.

Schulman, Bruce. "Governing Nature, Nurturing Government: Resource Management and the Development of the American State, 1900–1912." *Journal of Policy History* 17, no. 4 (2005): 375–403.

Summers, Gregory. *Consuming Nature: Environmentalism in the Fox River Valley, 1850–1950.* Lawrence: University of Kansas Press, 2006.

Wellock, Thomas R. *Preserving the Nation: The Conservation and Environmental Movements, 1870–2000.* Wheeling, Ill.: Harlan Davidson, 2007.

Paul Charles Milazzo

CLEAN AIR ACT

Enacted in 1963, the Clean Air Act seeks to protect the public from airborne contaminants. The act was amended in 1970, 1977, and 1990 to strengthen enforcement and regulatory oversight.

The first Clean Air Act of 1963 mandated enforcement of interstate air pollution standards and funding for monitoring studies and source inspections. In 1970, Senator Edmund Muskie (R-ME) drafted far-reaching amendments to the act, which greatly strengthened the regulatory powers of the federal government to enforce ambient air quality standards and hazardous emission standards. Amendments in 1977, 1990, and 1997 added regulatory requirements to control acid rain and additional toxic air pollutants, as well as to protect stratospheric ozone protection and to increase enforcement authority.

The Environmental Protection Agency (EPA) is the federal government's principle agency for the implementation of the act. The EPA works closely with state governments in drafting and enforcing regulations and in studying air quality. The powers of this agency through the Clean Air Act have increased over time. In early 2011 the EPA began to regulate so-called greenhouse gases.

The enforcement of Clean Air Standards through the EPA have created much political controversy, especially from industries related to toxic emissions such as the auto industry and the coal industry. Nonetheless, the air quality for Americans has greatly improved compared with the conditions in the nineteenth century through the 1950s. For example, the industrial revolution in the late nineteenth and early twentieth centuries introduced new problems, including toxic auto emissions and factory effluent including metals, ozone, sulfur, and nitrogen oxides. In the 1950s, smog was so bad in Los Angeles that television aerials disintegrated, houses needed repainting every year, and people were warned not to go outdoors.

Yet by every measure emissions of sulfur dioxide, nitrogen oxides, volatile organic compounds, and lead and carbon dioxide from fuel emissions from factories and automobiles had declined dramatically, falling to half in most cases, through the use of petroleum and coal containing less sulfur, the installation of scrubbers and cleaning devices in power plants, and the introduction of catalytic converters and other technologies in cars. For example, emissions of lead fell from close to 350,000 tons in 1970 to zero by 1995; carbon dioxide emissions fell from over 120,000 tons to a little under 100,000 tons. The world was not entirely safe, but immense progress had been made. Perhaps most dramatically, the world production of chlorofluorocarbons (CFC) has dramatically fallen through the efforts of voluntary restrictions by corporations such as DuPont and international agreements such as the Montreal Agreement in 1986. From 1986 through 2000, world production of CFCs has fallen from over 1,000 tons to 200 tons. CFCs have a half life of about fifty years, so they remain a danger to the atmosphere, but some environmentalists and scientists maintain, albeit with considerable controversy, that the ozone layer as a whole is safer in the early twenty-first century than two decades ago.

[*See also* **Environmental Policy: An Overview;** *and* **Environmental Protection Agency.**]

Donald T. Critchlow

CLEAN WATER ACT

Until the 1970s, the states and the courts played the leading roles in regulating water pollution. In 1972 Congress embarked on a major policy shift in combating this national problem when it enacted the Federal Water Pollution Control Act over the veto of President Richard M. Nixon.

This law established sweeping regulations to address water problems and articulated ambitious goals such as the elimination of all pollution from the nation's waters by 1985. The law nonetheless suffered from serious gaps that made the achievement of many of its goals difficult. Congress extensively amended the act, most notably in 1977 and in 1987.

The 1960s were a period of social change and environmental awareness. Rachel Carson's *Silent Spring* (1962) brought substantial public attention to the problem of environmental pollution. In 1969 a Union Oil Company blowout emptied some 200,000 gallons of crude oil into the Pacific Ocean and further revealed the enormity of environmental hazards. A thick layer of crude slick covered hundreds of square miles off the California coast, closing off thirty miles of beach and killing thousand of sea birds.

Increased toxicity in the nation's waters caused record fish kills at this time. There were alarming reports that pollution killed as many as 26 million fish in Lake Thonotosassa in Florida and that the country's shrimp harvest was decreasing precipitously.

Dangers to public health from industrial discharge were demonstrated in rising levels of pollutants in the river waters. The Detroit River, for example, exceeded the Public Service Health limit for mercury by six times. The level of pollution in other water bodies, such as Lake Erie, was so acute that many scientists believed the damages were irreversible. Less than half of the U.S. population was covered by sewage treatment plants.

In June 1969 the Cuyahoga River in Cleveland, full of industrial discharge and oil spills, caught fire. Water pollution thus became synonymous with industrial pollution. The media extensively covered sewer and industrial discharges that were polluting rivers, lakes, and bays around the country. Environmental groups disseminated information on the nation's worsening water pollution. The public soon understood that existing laws were ineffective.

By the time of the first Earth Day on 22 April 1970, experts such as ecologist Kenneth Watt and Harvard biologist George Wald predicted that without serious remedial action, widespread destruction and even mass starvation would follow. Public support grew for a stronger federal role in pollution control.

Congress put environmental pollution at the front of the national policy agenda when it enacted the National Environmental Policy Act (NEPA) in 1969. The following year Congress enacted the Clean Air Act (CAA) and created the Environmental Protection Agency (EPA). Within two years, Congress passed the landmark Federal Water Pollution Control Act. Certain key political developments resulted in the radical shift in policy in 1972.

A Democratic Congress and a Republican administration were at odds over how to combat environmental pollution. The chairman of the Senate Public Works Committee and the Subcommittee on Air and Water Pollution, Senator Edmund Muskie (D-ME), played the leading role in the development of national environmental policy. Furthermore, Ralph Nader's high-profile 1971 report, *Water Wasteland,* lent credibility to Muskie's efforts in Congress. Muskie warned that the threat to the nation's waters was so dire that without government action, life in lakes, rivers, and bays would end, and the oceans would no longer provide a sustainable food source.

William Ruckelshaus, the first administrator of the EPA, cautioned Congress against quick action as he claimed there was inadequate knowledge on the types and sources of pollution. He maintained that implementation of existing laws exposed the complexities of combating water pollution. Ruckelshaus asked Congress for more time to gather scientific data and conduct analyses.

Congress rejected Ruckelshaus's request. Muskie introduced a bill on 2 November 1971, which passed 86 to 0 in the Senate and 380 to 14 in the House. President Richard M. Nixon vetoed the bill as too costly. Both houses of Congress voted to override the veto.

Congress passed the Federal Water Pollution Control Act as an amendment to a 1948 clean water law. This action signified a major policy shift. The 1948 act and subsequent amendments to it had entrusted states with maintaining water quality within their borders and restricted the federal role to mainly navigable intrastate and interstate waters. The federal role had emphasized assistance to municipal and other dischargers. Yet these laws clearly were inadequate to address the problems of water pollution control. With the 1972 statute, Congress established national goals such as providing fishable and swimmable waters by 1983 and elimination of all pollutant discharges from the nation's waters by 1985.

Previous federal water pollution laws were mostly concerned with oil spills and treatment of sewage discharged into the rivers. The 1972 act defined pollutants so broadly that nearly all human activity that impacted the water could be defined as pollution. The act made a distinction between point source and non–point source (NPS) pollution. Effluents emitted directly into the waterways by factories, industries, or sewage treatment plants through conveyances—pipes, ditches, channels, conduits—are point sources because they discharge at a particular point along the waterway. NPS pollution is from diffuse sources such as agriculture, storm water runoff, farms, mines, or construction sites.

To achieve zero pollution discharge by 1985, Congress established technology-based standards according to which effluent limits were to be set for various pollutants. Congress rejected a water quality–based standard largely because of the failures in using a similar approach in the earlier Clean Air Act. The EPA set up the technological standards to be applied to all dischargers and polluters and regulated point source discharge with the National Pollution Discharge Elimination System (NPDES) permit program.

The primary focus of the 1972 act was limiting discharges from point sources. Congress's ambitious zero discharge goal was entirely unrealistic. Even Muskie admitted that the 1985 deadline was a policy ideal, but not achievable. In addition, Congress burdened the states with the unattainable responsibility of conducting studies to gather all necessary information regarding the nation's waters within a year.

The 1972 statute targeted the conventional pollutants generally found in polluted waters and include such agents as five-day biological oxygen demand (BOD), suspended solids, pH level, fecal coliform bacteria, oil, and grease. The NPDES permits issued in the first round of permitting from 1972 to 1976 required dischargers to apply effluent treatment according to the "best practicable technology currently available" (BPT) by 1 July 1977.

In drafting the law, Congress expected technological standards to improve and the costs associated with such advancements to diminish. In addition to the BPT requirement Congress also mandated that the "best achievable technology economically feasible" (BAT) be installed by 1 July 1983. However, in the absence of a uniform effluent limitation standard, EPA issued the NPDES permits according to "best professional judgment" (BPJ).

The 1972 act did not clearly define water quality standards or how to achieve them. Congress amended the law in 1977 to give the EPA authority to define water quality criteria for a new class of sixty-five "priority toxins" as listed in *Natural Resources Defense Council v. Train* (1976) by the end of 1979. The 1977 amendment, known as the Clean Water Act (CWA), shifted the focus from regulating conventional pollutants to include the new class of toxic pollutants, resulting in a second round of permitting. Congress modified the BAT requirement to include the group of toxic pollutants with an extension of the deadline to 1984. The EPA could add to or subtract pollutants from that list. Regarding additional toxic pollutants included by the EPA, the deadline for compliance became within three years of the issuance of effluent limitations.

Congress established yet another guideline, referred to as "best conventional pollution control technology" (BCT), for conventional pollutants regulated under the BPT standards. The EPA seldom made any distinction between BCT and BPT. To encompass any pollutants that did not fall under the conventional or toxic categories, the amendment provided for a new class designated as nonconventional pollutants subject to BCT standards (Salzman and Thompson, 2003).

A problem encountered even after the 1977 amendment was that in some cases technology-based (BCT, BAT) effluent limitations were unable to meet the water quality standards set by states. Further, the emphasis of both the 1972 act and the 1977 amendment had been point source pollution with the requirement of only state-level planning actions to address NPS pollution. With as much as half of water pollution caused by NPS runoff, Congress amended the CWA on 4 February 1987, which came to be known as the Water Quality Act of 1987 (WQA).

The focus of this amendment was combating post-BAT/BCT pollution. The amendment sanctioned programs to address NPS pollution. States were to identify water bodies that were not in compliance with designated water quality standards after the implementation of technology-based standards. Congress directed the states to formulate strategies to control NPS pollution and to reduce toxic pollution from both NPSs and point sources. Further, the law urged states to consider groundwater pollution while addressing pollution from NPSs. The amendment authorized federal financial assistance to the states. Congress extended the deadlines for BAT and BCT effluent limitations, with compliance targeted for 1989 (Department of Environmental Quality, n.d.).

In amending the law several times, Congress has in effect acknowledged that its initial ambitious goals have gone unmet. Instead of isolating the nature and source of water pollution, Congress initially adopted a uniform technology-based standard that was applicable to all dischargers, regardless of the existing water quality. In so doing, when this adopted standard failed to meet the goal of zero discharge, Congress enacted amendments to incorporate new information and knowledge on pollutants—the emphasis therefore shifted from conventional pollutants in 1972 to toxic pollutants in 1977 to NPS pollution in 1987.

[*See also* **Environmental Policy: An Overview; Environmental Policy: Clean Air Act; Environmental Protection Agency;** ***and*** **Nader, Ralph.**]

BIBLIOGRAPHY

Adler, Robert W., Jessica Landman, and Diane Cameron. *The Clean Water Act: 20 Years Later.* Washington, D.C.: Island Press, 1993.

Carson, Rachel. *Silent Spring.* New York: Fawcett Press, 1962.

Copeland, Claudia. "Clean Water Act: A Summary of the Law." *CRS Report for Congress,* 2002.

Copeland, Claudia. *Clean Water Act: Current Issues and Guide to Books.* New York: Nova Science Publishers, 2003.

Department of Environmental Quality. "National Pollutant Discharge Elimination System." http://www.michigan.gov/deq/0,1607,7-135-3313_3682_3713_10197--,00.html (accessed 22 November 2005).

Freeman, A. Myrick, III. "Environmental Policy since Earth Day I: What Have We Gained?" *Journal of Environmental Perspectives,* 16, no. 1 (Winter 2002): 125–146.

Freeman, A. Myrick, III. "Water Pollution Policy." In *Public Policies for Environmental Protection,* edited by Paul Portney, pp. 97–149. Washington, D.C.: Resources for the Future, 1990.

Graham, Mary. "Environmental Protection & the States: 'Race to the Bottom' or 'Race to the Bottom Line'?" *Brookings Review* (Winter 1998). http://www.brookings.edu/articles/1998/winter_environment_graham.aspx (accessed 5 November 2010).

Halpern, Richard A. "1491 and All That." *American Outlook* (November–December 2000).

Kubasek, Nancy, and Gary Silverman. *Environmental Law.* New York: Prentice Hall, 2002.

"National Water Quality Goals: An Overview of the 1977 Clean Water Act Amendments." *Environmental Reporter* Special Report No. 4 (May 1978).

Pedersen, William F., Jr. "Politics, Bureaucracy, and the Merits of the Clean Water Act." *Stanford Law Review* 33, no. 5 (May 1981): 967–977.

Salzman, James, and Barton Thompson. *Environmental Law and Policy.* New York: Foundation Press, 2003.

Stoner, Nancy. "Clean Water At Risk: A 30th Anniversary Assessment of the Bush Administration's Rollback of Clean Water Protections." National Resources Defense Council, October 2002. http://www.nrdc.org/water/pollution/cwa30/cwa30.pdf (accessed 5 November 2010).

Zwick, David, and Marcy Benstock. *Water Wasteland: Ralph Nader's Study Group Report on Water Pollution.* New York: Grossman, 1971.

Mark J. Rozell

ENDANGERED SPECIES ACT

The Endangered Species Act provides the most comprehensive endangered species protection under federal law.

Signed into law by President Richard Nixon in 1973, the Endangered Species Act reflected a century-long concern about disappearing species in the American environment. Ornithologists and sportsmen in the late nineteenth and early twentieth centuries warned that many animals and birds were under threat. As a result, the Lacey Act (1900) regulated commercial animal markets and prohibited interstate commerce of wild game. In 1929 the Migratory Bird Conservation Act was enacted, followed in 1940 by the Bald Eagle Protection Act. In 1965, Congress provided funds for the protection of lands to protect endangered species of fish and wildlife. The Endangered Species Preservation Act of 1966 required the secretary of the interior to list endangered domestic fish and wildlife, while providing funding to the U.S. Fish and Wildlife Service to buy habitat for listed species. This act was amended in 1969 to protect species threatened by worldwide extinction.

Drafted by scientists and lawyers, the Endangered Species Act represented landmark environmental legislation to protect species and the ecosystem upon which they depend. The Endangered Species Act is administered by the U.S. Fish and Wildlife Service and the National Oceanic and Atmospheric Administration.

The administration and implementation of this act created controversy at various times with private property owners, private industry, state governments, the courts, and the White House. Nonetheless, the Endangered Species Act has proved critical in protecting and restoring to abundance many species once listed as endangered. Recovery for an endangered species averages 30 to 50 years and 100 years for whales. Yet the record of recovery has been impressive for animals, birds, and plants. For example, there were an estimated 500 bald eagles when the legislation was passed. In the early twenty-first century there are over 8,000 bald eagles in America and they have been removed from the endangered list. In Ohio, river otters increased from about 500 in 1995 to 5,400 in 2005; beavers from 12,000 to 30,000; and Lake Erie water snakes from 2,000 in 1999 to 7,700 in 2006. Desert bighorn sheep increased from 7,000 in the 1960s to 19,000 in 1993. In North Carolina the number of wild turkeys grew from 2,000 in 1970 to 17,000 in 1988. International efforts by the United States, Russia, and Japan have saved the Aleutian Canadian goose from extinction. Similar international efforts have allowed several species of whales to recover, although this battle for preservation is not over. Many plants have also fared well. Once endangered, Robbins's cinquefoil, the large-flowered skullcap, and dozens of other plants are now thriving. All in all, the nonprofit Center for Biological Diversity found that 41 percent of the species on the Endangered Species list were stable and 93 percent were increasing in numbers. Still, three species were in decline.

[*See also* **Environmental Policy: An Overview; Environmental Protection Agency;** *and* **Nixon, Richard M.**]

Donald T. Critchlow

ENVIRONMENTAL PROTECTION AGENCY

Established by the Richard M. Nixon administration in October 1970, in the wake of the first Earth Day that April, the Environmental Protection Agency (EPA) became the agent and symbol of a vast expansion of the federal government's role in addressing a widely perceived environmental crisis. Initially proposed by a Nixon advisory committee seeking ways to streamline the federal bureaucracy, the EPA brought together under one institutional umbrella several long-standing federal programs aimed mostly at pollution control. Through existing and new legislation that it implemented and defended in court, including Clean Water and Clean Air Acts, the Toxic Substances Control Act, and laws regulating pesticides and hazardous wastes, the EPA spearheaded the most far-reaching federal intervention into the American economy since the New Deal.

During its first three decades, the EPA grew steadily in its size, responsibilities, and regulatory strategies, even as its fortunes fluctuated with the political climate. Although its founding laws and early administrators envisioned an "ecological" protection encompassing nonhuman as well as human life, the agency found its scientific footing by stressing environmental threats to public health. Initially quite decentralized, the EPA under President Jimmy Carter centralized and coordinated its programs, largely through quantitative risk assessments (starting with carcinogenic risks) and cost–benefit analyses. Early appointees in the Ronald Reagan administration assaulted the EPA's programs and damaged morale, but in the wake of the Love Canal exposé—a scandal involving long-term toxic pollution by the Hooker Chemical Company in Niagara Falls, New York—Congress mandated a new and ambitious EPA initiative to control industrial wastes. Friendlier Republican administrations of the later 1980s and early 1990s restored money and muscle to the EPA's older programs while expanding its regulatory tools. Experiments with dispute mediation and market-based incentives carried over into the Bill Clinton administrations. During the 1990s, the EPA tightened pollution standards and began monitoring and regulating the effects of pollution on nonhuman species. In response to the environmental-justice movement, the agency also moved to shed its white, middle-class image by attending more closely to the disproportionate share of environmental risk borne by minorities and the poor. In April 2008, the Union of Concerned Scientists said that more than half of the nearly 1,600 EPA staff scientists who responded online to a detailed questionnaire reported they had experienced incidents of political interference in their work. The survey included chemists, toxicologists, engineers, geologists, and experts in other fields of science. About 40 percent of the scientists reported that the interference had been more prevalent in the past five years compared with previous years. The highest number of complaints came from scientists who are involved in determining the risks of cancer by chemicals used in food and other aspects of everyday life.

In June 2005, a memo revealed that Philip Cooney, former chief of staff for the White House Council on Environmental Quality and former lobbyist for the American Petroleum Institute, had personally edited documents, summarizing government research on climate change, before their release. Cooney resigned two days after the memo was published in *The New York Times*. Cooney said he had been planning to resign for over two years, implying the timing of his resignation was just a coincidence. Specifically, he said he had planned to resign to "spend time with his family." One week after resigning he took a job at Exxon Mobil in their public affairs department.

In July 2005, an EPA report showing that auto companies were using loopholes to produce less fuel-efficient cars was delayed. The report was supposed to be released the day before a controversial energy bill was passed and would have provided backup for those opposed to it, but at the last minute the EPA delayed its release.

The state of California sued the EPA for its refusal to allow California and sixteen other states to raise fuel economy standards for new cars. EPA administrator Stephen L. Johnson claimed that the EPA was working on its own standards, but the move has been widely considered an attempt to shield the auto industry from environmental regulation by setting lower standards at the federal level, which would then preempt state laws. California governor Arnold Schwarzenegger, along with governors from thirteen other states, stated that the EPA's actions ignored federal law and that existing California standards (adopted by many states in addition to California) were almost twice as effective as the proposed federal standards. It was reported that Stephen Johnson ignored his own staff in making this decision.

After the federal government bought out General Motors and Chrysler in the automotive industry crisis of 2008–2010, the 2010 Chevrolet Equinox was released with a fuel economy rating abnormally higher than that of its competitors. Independent road tests found that the vehicle did not outperform its competitors, which had much lower fuel economy ratings.

Since its inception the EPA has begun to rely less and less on its scientists and more on nonscience personnel. The EPA has recently changed its policies regarding limits for ground-level ozone particulates, sulfur dioxide, nitrogen oxides, carbon monoxide, and lead. New policies will minimize scientist interaction with the agency and rely more on policy makers who have minimal scientific knowledge. On 12 March 2008, the federal government of the United States reported that the air in hundreds of U.S. counties was simply too dirty to breathe, ordering a multibillion dollar expansion of efforts to clean up smog in cities and towns nationwide. As of 2010, The EPA has a budget of $10.5 billion and employs over 18,000 people, with fewer than 10 percent of those employed as scientists.

[*See also* **Carson, Rachel; Carter, Jimmy; Economic Policy: Regulation; Environmental Policy: An Overview; Environmental Policy: Clean Air Act; Environmental Policy: Clean Water Act; Environmentalism; New Deal;** ***and*** **Nixon, Richard M.**]

BIBLIOGRAPHY

Russell, Edmund. "Lost among the Parts per Billion: Ecological Protection at the United States Environmental Protection Agency, 1970–1993." *Environmental History* 2 (1997): 29–51.

U.S. Environmental Protection Agency. *The Guardian: Origins of the Environmental Protection Agency.* Washington, D.C.: U.S. Environmental Protection Agency, 1992.

Christopher Sellers; revised and updated by Pearson Bramblett

EQUALITY

"We hold these truths to be self-evident, that all men are created equal." Although these words from the Declaration of Independence are among the most familiar in the American canon, much of American history challenges the principle they proclaim. From the nation's beginnings onward, certain groups of Americans were judged unequal, not according to their virtue, intelligence, or talent, but rather on the basis of race, religion, gender, or wealth. Nonwhites, women, some immigrants, and the propertyless were denied the privileges and obligations of citizenship, despite the nation's ostensible commitment to the principles of legal and political equality.

Yet Thomas Jefferson's ringing declaration, even if not fully observed in practice, nevertheless echoed long and loud. Successive generations of reformers—Jeffersonians and Jacksonians challenging economic privilege; abolitionists challenging slavery; women's-rights and woman-suffrage advocates challenging the subjugation of women; civil libertarians challenging the suppression of dissent; farmers and workers challenging the unchecked prerogatives of capital; and critics of intolerance challenging religious, ethnic, and racial injustice—invoked the principle of equality as one of their primary weapons. Protracted and sometimes bloody as their battles were, these crusaders prevailed: by the late twentieth century, legally imposed discrimination on the basis of religion, race, ethnicity, gender, income, or sexual preference had been outlawed in the United States. Given the nation's long record of exclusion and oppression, this achievement testifies not only to the activists' heroic efforts, but also to the protean power of the principle of equality.

In the economic and social spheres, the record has been more equivocal. Although most Americans' commitment in these areas was to equality of opportunity, not equality of outcome, even that more limited goal proved difficult to achieve. From 1913, when the quintessential progressive reform measure, the graduated income tax, was authorized, through the New Deal of the 1930s and the Great Society legislation of the 1960s, economic inequality diminished in the United States. Taxing the wealthy and regulating the economy to expand social and economic opportunities for the poor made a difference—albeit a less dramatic difference than that of the post–World War II rights revolution.

The trend reversed in the two decades after 1980, however, as the gap between the richest and poorest Americans widened steadily. The civil-rights and women's movements did not automatically assure equality of opportunity in the economic and social spheres. Many women, members of minority groups, and recent immigrants still in the late twentieth century faced barriers, and de facto racial segregation persisted in urban America. The quality of public schools and other governmental services varied widely among neighborhoods of different ethnic make up and income level, as did the employment opportunities available to different groups. The late twentieth-century prosperity of highly educated, technologically sophisticated computer specialists and information-service providers and of entrepreneurs in these fields was accompanied by the decline of industries that had lifted earlier generations from poverty, the eroding buying power of the minimum wage, and a proliferation of entry-level service-sector jobs leading nowhere. As a new century dawned, the goal of equality first promulgated in 1776 remained elusive.

[*See also* **Asian Americans; Antislavery Movement; Civil Liberties; Declaration of Independence; Economic Policy: Regulation; Equal Rights Amendment; Feminism; Hispanic Americans; Immigration Law and Policy: After 1930; Immigration Law and Policy: Before 1930; Jefferson, Thomas; Socialism; Taxation;** *and* **Woman Suffrage Movement.**]

BIBLIOGRAPHY

Pole, J. R. *The Pursuit of Equality in American History*, 2d ed. Berkeley: University of California Press, 1993.

Smith, Rogers M. *Civic Ideals: Conflicting Visions of Citizenship in U.S. History*. New Haven, Conn.: Yale University Press, 1997.

James T. Kloppenberg

EQUAL RIGHTS AMENDMENT

Passed by Congress in 1972, the Equal Rights Amendment (ERA) failed to be ratified by a three-fourths majority of the states. The struggle for ratification had substantial importance for American politics and the feminist movement. The amendment declared, "Equality of rights under the law shall not be denied or abridged by the United States or by any State on account of sex." The debate over the ERA proved as controversial at the time as any amendment to the Constitution, with the exception of slavery abolition, national prohibition, and women's suffrage.

The ERA was first promoted by militant feminist Alice Paul and the National Woman's Party in 1923 and introduced to Congress that year by U.S. Senator Charles Curtis (R-KS). Over the following years, the ERA failed to win the necessary support in Congress because progressive women were divided over the amendment. For example, the ERA was opposed by Florence Kelley and the National Consumers' League, prolabor Democrats, and other female activists. This female-labor protectionist view was evidenced in Senate hearings in 1929 and 1931. Eleanor Roosevelt, wife of President Franklin Roosevelt, remained an opponent of the ERA until after World War II.

Support for a modified ERA bill that preserved protective legislation gained support in the late 1930s when it won the endorsement of the General Federation of Women's Clubs, the National Association of Women Lawyers, and the National Education Association. The League of Women Voters, however, continued to oppose the amendment. In 1940 the Republican Party endorsed the ERA, although divisions within the party over the amendment were evident. Conservative Republican Senator James W. Wadsworth (R-NY) opposed the ERA, whereas Ohio Senator Robert Taft supported the bill. In the Senate debate over the ERA in 1950, Senator Carl Hayden (D-AZ) attached a rider stating "the provisions of this article shall not be construed to impair any rights, benefits, or exemptions conferred by law upon the persons of the female sex." Supporters of the ERA opposed this rider because it was too restrictive. As a result, the bill failed to even come to a House vote.

The second wave of feminism in the 1960s fostered the reemergence of this issue in the 1960s. In 1967, the newly formed National Organization for Women enthusiastically endorsed the ERA. After being blocked in the House by Emanuel Celler (D-NY), chair of the Judiciary Committee, Representative Martha Griffiths (D-MI) led her congressional colleagues to discharge the bill from the Judiciary Committee and brought it to the floor in 1970. The House passed the amendment 353 to 15. The ERA failed to win support in the Senate, but the House again passed the ERA in 1971 in a vote of 354 to 23. The Wiggins Amendment, exempting women from military service and preserving laws protecting women, was defeated at the time. This time the ERA overwhelming passed the Senate, although Sam Ervin (D-NC) attempted to amend the legislation to protect the traditional rights of women. The legislation granted seven years for the amendment to be ratified by three-fourths of the states.

The ERA was quickly ratified by thirty states, leaving only eight more states to make it part of the Constitution; but ratification stalled when opposition from antifeminists, led by Phyllis Schlafly and her STOP ERA organization, arose. STOP ERA drew support from evangelical Christians, Mormons, Orthodox Jews, and traditional Roman Catholic women. Supporters of the ERA found support in ERAmerica, an umbrella organization of labor leaders, feminists, and liberals, and the National Organization for Women. The battle over the ERA was waged in state capitols. Eventually thirty-five states ratified the ERA, although five states, including Nebraska, Tennessee, Idaho, Kentucky, and South Dakota rescinded their previous votes. Fifteen states never ratified the ERA, including Alabama, Arizona, Arkansas, Florida, Georgia, Illinois, Louisiana, Mississippi, Missouri, Nevada, North Carolina, Oklahoma, South Carolina, Utah, and Virginia.

When it became apparent that the ERA was not going to meet the deadline of 22 March 1979, Congress voted to extend the deadline to 30 June 1982. The battle for ratification centered on five states: Illinois, Florida, North Carolina, Missouri, and Oklahoma. These battleground states, especially the border and southern states, played to the strength of ERA opponents. At the same time, feminist promotion of abortion and lesbian rights alienated many legislators and the general public in these states. By 1982, the ERA had failed, although it had won the endorsement of Congress, three U.S. presidents—Richard Nixon, Gerald Ford, and Jimmy Carter—and major women and labor organizations. The defeat of the ERA marked a turning point in American politics as conservatism exerted itself with the election of Ronald Reagan in 1980.

[*See also* **Constitution; National Education Association; National Organization for Women; National Woman's Party; Roosevelt, Eleanor;** *and* **Schlafly, Phyllis.**]

BIBLIOGRAPHY

Critchlow, Donald T. *Phyllis Schlafly and Grassroots Conservatism*. Princeton, N.J.: Princeton University Press, 2005.

Kyvig, David E. *Explicit and Authentic Acts: Amending the Constitution, 1776–1995*. Lawrence: University Press of Kansas, 1996.

Donald T. Critchlow

EXECUTIVE POWER

Vested in the president by Article II of the Constitution, executive power has been a source of considerable controversy since the founding itself. In his book *The Strategy of Rhetoric: Campaigning for the American Constitution,* political scientist William Riker claims the power of the presidency was one of the most important sources of conflict between the Federalists and the Anti-Federalists. Rather than shrinking from this conflict by claiming the power of the presidency was not as great as the Anti-Federalists indicated, the Federalists openly defended the power or, in their words, "energy" as essential to a healthy republic. As Publius in *The Federalist Papers,* Alexander Hamilton writes, "Energy in the executive is a leading character in the definition of good government."

That the Federalists so openly defended a powerful executive power within the constitutional order, however, had been, to a certain degree, lost to history. Once Thomas Jefferson assumed the presidency from John Adams, he ushered in a theory of the constitutional order that was, at least ostensibly, much more centered on Congress. The Hamiltonian theory of the presidency had looked to the executive not just as the power that would preserve the country during difficult times, but also as the motive force of the government, even during normal times. Under Hamilton's leadership during Washington's administration, the executive branch took control of much of the initiation of legislation within Congress. The executive branch initiated the legislation on which Congress then deliberated. Once Jefferson assumed the presidency, however, the Hamiltonian theory disappeared from practice. Rather than looking to the executive for leadership in legislative matters, Congress formed more internal committees, which became responsible for the preparation of legislation. Because some features of the twentieth-century presidency are similar to the Hamiltonian conception, political scientists Edward Corwin and Clinton Rossiter claim that the modern theory of presidential power is the contribution of Alexander Hamilton.

However, the theory of the presidency that informed the way in which the office was understood for much of the nineteenth century was Jefferson's. Although recent scholarship has to some degree called into question Jefferson's true commitment to a weak presidency by showing the extensive role of "prerogative" in Jefferson's conception of the office, this argument does not change Jefferson's understanding of the proper constitutional power of the executive. Jefferson conceived of the presidency as a major locus of extraconstitutional agency and leadership. In seeing the leadership role of the presidency as primarily extraconstitutional, Jefferson maintains the executive power itself as modest and limited.

Because even Jefferson's invigorated presidency remains limited in its constitutional power, Jefferson's conception of executive power remains, in a certain manner, consistent with that of his friend and intellectual confidante, James Madison. Madison most fully articulated his conception of executive power in 1793 in the debate with fellow *The Federalist Papers* coauthor Alexander Hamilton. In the *Pacificus–Helvidius Debates of 1793–1794,* Madison worried that Hamilton's conception of executive power would lead to a presidency that would dominate and destroy the rest of the constitutional order. Arguing as Pacificus, Hamilton had used the difference in the constitutional language of the vesting clause between Article I and Article II, that is, "All legislative Powers herein granted shall be vested in a Congress of the United States" versus "The executive Power shall be vested in a President of the United States," to suggest that the Constitution intended to limit the legislative power to only those powers listed, whereas it intended a more general grant of executive power to the president—the powers listed only illustrate rather than exhaust the range of executive power. Although Madison agreed with the constitutionality of the action that Hamilton's argument aimed to justify, Washington's Proclamation of Neutrality, he disagreed vehemently with the constitutional principles on which Hamilton had justified that action. Madison worried both that Hamilton's principle of constitutional interpretation would eviscerate the clear landmarks of power in the document and that affording the executive power, in particular this kind of generality of power, would be especially dangerous because of the war-making resources at its disposal.

Madison's worry about the danger executive power poses to the constitutional order points to a theme that has been prominent in executive power since its creation in the Constitution and, even before, in the constitutional thought of those who created modern constitutionalism (i.e. Locke, and Montesquieu). The founders of modern constitutionalism were aware that executive power is both essential to and dangerous for the survival of constitutionalism. In other words, the deepest source of danger comes from the fact that it would be simply unwise for a constitutional republic wholly to foreclose the possibility of strong executive power. As Alexander Hamilton wrote in *The Federalist Papers,* "There is no nation which has not, at one period or another, experienced an absolute necessity of the services of particular men in particular situations, perhaps it would not be too strong to say, to the preservation of its political existence." If a constitutional republic could afford to foreclose a strong executive, then it would be easier to manage the danger. A good constitutionalist could always insist on the Constitution over and against strong executive power. Because, as John Locke wrote in *The Second Treatise of Government,* the laws themselves are sometimes in need of strong executive power—whether that power be understood as part of the constitutional order or outside it—the good constitutionalist must always be judging each act of executive power to determine whether it was a mere usurpation or conducive to the common good. And, more than that, as emphasized in *The Discretionary President: The Promise and Peril of Executive Power* (Kleinerman, 2009), the danger is even greater to the constitutional order because the immediacy and security offered by a powerful and benevolent executive are quite appealing, regardless of whether that power remains within the laws.

The American founders solved the problem of executive power partially by choosing to constitute a strong executive. Beginning with the claim that there is no way around the need for strength in the executive arm of government, they tried to control that strength by placing it within the Constitution. Hamilton understood that if a strong executive power were not integrated into the Constitution, it would break in "through the back door." Given the strength of the Constitution's executive, it made the alternative Jeffersonian solution constantly precarious. As Henry Adams, writing in the nineteenth century, showed in his history of the Jefferson presidency, as much as Jefferson might have disagreed in principle with a strong presidency, he was not able to resist availing himself of the powers at his disposal. Yet even if Jefferson was more amenable in theory to a strong president than Adams admits, Jefferson was opposed to a constitutionally strong presidency.

The argument that presidents have a considerable array of constitutional powers stands in opposition to much of the conventional wisdom about the power of the presidency in the past fifty years. Owing a great deal to the progressive critique not just of the presidency but of the whole system of separation of powers, scholars of the presidency have fairly consistently followed the argument of Richard Neustadt, whose book *Presidential Power and the Modern Presidents: The Politics of Leadership from Roosevelt to Reagan* remains one of the seminal books on presidential power. The claim has been that presidents must supplement their constitutional powers through the arts of persuasion and bargaining. In the first place, presidents must increase their constitutional powers through extraconstitutional practices because their constitutional powers are so limited. Neustadt's argument, which owes a great deal to Woodrow Wilson's argument, suggests that because the proverbial constitutional "deck" is stacked against presidential leadership, presidents can only become the leaders they want to be—and we expect them to be—by augmenting their constitutional powers through both their rhetorical and their bargaining skills.

In his important *The Rhetorical Presidency,* Jeffrey Tulis provides a crucial corrective to Neustadt's argument by showing not only that the founding design never intended presidents to act as rhetorical mouthpieces for the wishes of the people but also that, in seeking to become this, presidents are, paradoxically, in a weaker position than they were when their power depended on the constitutional resources of the office. And, although there is no turning back from the situation presidents now face, presidents would do better if they were aware of the competing tensions of the office. Tulis points to a phenomenon that has not yet been sufficiently studied: because of the considerable powers that lie in the executive power portion of the presidency, powers most fully elaborated upon by Alexander Hamilton in *The Federalist Papers* and further developed by him as Pacificus, presidents have turned to those powers when some of the modern "rhetorical" expectations of the office have failed them. Thus, presidents of both parties have often found in foreign wars the popularity that their domestic projects could not provide. Although the calculus reverses if the war lasts too long or does not go successfully, presidents who can fight limited and successful foreign wars find that this provides them with an important boost in their approval ratings. Relatedly, presidents have couched their domestic leadership projects in the terminology most suited to the executive power portion of their office. Thus, we have seen "wars" on poverty, drugs, and terror. Because presidential power is greatest in wartime, presidents look to rhetorical language that justifies their greatest range of powers.

A brief legal and political history of executive power would be incomplete if it did not include the constitutional and political controversies that now swirl around its exercise, especially since the advent of the "war on terror." At the center of this controversy is a question concerning the constitutional status of executive power in relation to the legislative power. Whatever range of powers is encompassed by the executive power within the Constitution—generally, Hamilton's claim concerning the generality of executive power has come to be accepted—do those powers preclude Congress from regulating or limiting them? Does the president have a range of independent powers so vouchsafed by the Constitution that they cannot be constitutionally impinged upon by Congress? The Bush administration consistently answered this question in the affirmative. The George W. Bush administration advanced this claim on behalf of the independent powers of the executive with an almost theological ardor that sometimes blinded it to its own political interests. This claim to a preclusive constitutional power, however, appears to have no support either in constitutional law or in practice. Whatever the executive power is—much of the struggle within American political history has been to define it—its necessarily extralegal character does not include the power to insist, as a matter of law, that Congress has no legal ability by which to limit it.

[*See also* **Constitution; Federalist Papers; Hamilton, Alexander; Jefferson, Thomas;** ***and*** **Madison, James.**]

BIBLIOGRAPHY

Adams, Henry. *History of the United States of America during the Administrations of Thomas Jefferson.* New York: Viking Press, 1986.

Bailey, Jeremy D. *Thomas Jefferson and Executive Power.* Cambridge, UK; New York: Cambridge University Press, 2007.

Barron, David, and Martin Lederman. "The Commander in Chief at the Lowest Ebb." *Harvard Law Review* 121 (2008): 689.

Binkley, Wilfred E. *President and Congress.* New York: A. A. Knopf, 1947.

Corwin, Edward. *The President, Office and Powers.* 5th ed. New York: New York University Press, 1984.

Flaumenhaft, Harvey. *The Effective Republic: Administration and Constitution in the Thought of Alexander Hamilton.* Durham, N.C.: Duke University Press, 1992.

Goldsmith, Jack. *The Terror Presidency: Law and Judgment inside the Bush Administration.* New York: W. W. Norton, 2007.

Hamilton, Alexander, James Madison, and John Jay. *The Federalist Papers.* New York: New American Library, 1961.

Hamilton, Alexander, and James Madison. *The Pacificus–Helvidius Debates of 1793–1794.* Indianapolis, Ind.: Liberty Fund, 2007.

Kleinerman, Benjamin. *The Discretionary President: The Promise and Peril of Executive Power.* Lawrence: University Press of Kansas, 2009.

Locke, John. *The Second Treatise of Government.* Mineola, N.Y.: Dover Publications, 2002.

Neustadt, Richard. *Presidential Power and the Modern Presidents: The Politics of Leadership from Roosevelt to Reagan.* New York; Toronto; New York: Free Press; Collier Macmillan Canada; Maxwell Macmillan, 1991.

Riker, William. *The Strategy of Rhetoric: Campaigning for the American Constitution*. New Haven, Conn.: Yale University Press, 1996.
Tulis, Jeffrey. *The Rhetorical Presidency*. Princeton, N.J.: Princeton University Press, 1987.

Benjamin Kleinerman

EXECUTIVE PRIVILEGE

Executive privilege has long been part of Anglo-Saxon jurisprudence and American constitutional history. In 1792, President George Washington, citing the constitutional separation of powers, denied a congressional request for access to papers relevant to General Arthur St. Clair's defeat by Indian forces in Ohio. Three years later, Washington withheld documents pertaining to the negotiations that resulted in Jay's Treaty. The nation's third president, Thomas Jefferson, used similar grounds to defy a subpoena issued by U.S. Supreme Court Justice John Marshall during the treason trial of Aaron Burr. More recently, Presidents Harry S. Truman and Dwight D. Eisenhower cited executive privilege—Truman in resisting a 1948 House resolution to turn over executive papers and Eisenhower in rejecting a Senate demand for access to Defense Department files.

Subsequent Supreme Courts, however, sharply limited the executive-privilege claim. In *United States v. Nixon* (1974), the Court rejected Richard Nixon's assertion of executive privilege, ruling that his refusal to turn over the Watergate tapes to Federal Judge John Sirica would "gravely impair" the judiciary's role under Article III of the Constitution. More recently, when President Bill Clinton claimed executive privilege in refusing to provide Congress with documents relating to activities of the White House Travel Office, the Supreme Court upheld a subpoena demanding the notes of relevant conversations between First Lady Hillary Clinton and White House attorneys. Moreover, in *Clinton v. Jones* (1997), a sexual-harassment case against the president, the Court unanimously required Clinton, while still in office, to answer civil lawsuits brought against him. As Justice John Paul Stevens noted, the president, like all other citizens, "is subject to judicial process in appropriate circumstances."

In 2004 President George W. Bush, citing executive privilege, initially refused to permit National Security Advisor Condoleezza Rice to testify in public and under oath before the bipartisan blue-ribbon panel investigating the intelligence failures preceding the terrorist attacks of 11 September 2001. Under growing pressure Bush relented and permitted Rice to testify, but insisted that this should not be considered a precedent for the future.

[*See also* **Bush, George W.; Clinton, William J.; Constitution; Eisenhower, Dwight D.; Federal Government, Executive Branch: An Overview; Federal Government Executive Branch: Presidency, The; Federal Government, Jefferson, Thomas; Judicial Branch; Jurisprudence; Truman, Harry S.;** ***United States v. Nixon; and*** **Washington, George.**]

BIBLIOGRAPHY

Berger, Raoul. *Executive Privilege: A Constitutional Myth*. Cambridge, Mass.: Harvard University Press, 1974.
Kutler, Stanley I. *The Wars of Watergate*. New York: Alfred A. Knopf, 1990.

Herbert S. Parmet; updated by Paul S. Boyer

F

FAIR EMPLOYMENT PRACTICES COMMITTEE

In June 1941, President Franklin Delano Roosevelt reluctantly created the Fair Employment Practices Committee (FEPC) to forestall a mass demonstration planned by the black labor leader A. Philip Randolph to protest discrimination and segregation in defense industries. Executive Order 8802 authorized the FEPC to investigate job discrimination in war industries and federal agencies. Led by Lawrence Cramer and black Chicago alderman Earl B. Dickerson, the committee and its interracial, interethnic staff, including appointees from business and labor, examined complaints of discrimination and held hearings. Howls of protest, particularly from southern politicians and editors, soon led Roosevelt to abolish the original committee.

The FEPC enjoyed strong support among blacks, liberals, religious groups, and labor unions, however, and in May 1943 Roosevelt created a new FEPC. The staff at the Washington headquarters, headed by the black law school dean George M. Johnson, oversaw thirteen regional offices. Significantly, the agency became the first in U.S. history to appoint blacks to policy-making positions. Dealing with other agencies often cool and even hostile toward its goals, the FEPC exposed the subterfuges used by private and federal employers to deny war-related jobs and upgrading to minorities. But the FEPC had little real power. By summer 1946 relentless congressional opposition led to its dismantling.

Many historians credit wartime labor shortages for decreasing job discrimination, not the parsimoniously funded FEPC. Others, however, cite the FEPC for establishing the principle that job bias constituted a denial of civil rights. Blacks indeed used the FEPC in tight labor markets to open up work opportunities, and in some regions the agency placed qualified minorities in skilled trades and professions ordinarily closed to them. In some ways a precursor of the postwar civil rights movement, the FEPC's symbolic and long-term significance seems unquestioned.

[*See also* **Roosevelt, Theodore;** *and* **Segregation.**]

BIBLIOGRAPHY

Neuchterlein, James A. "The Politics of Civil Rights: The FEPC, 1941–1946." *Prologue* X (1978): 171–191.

Reed, Merl E. *Seedtime for the Modern Civil Rights Movement: The President's Committee on Fair Employment Practice, 1941–1946*. Baton Rouge: Louisiana State University Press, 1991.

Merl E. Reed

FARMERS' ALLIANCE MOVEMENT

The Farmers' Alliance, the largest agricultural movement in American history, was triggered by worsening agricultural conditions in commercial crop-producing areas of the southern and Great Plains states, particularly the fall in agricultural prices after the Civil War and consequent loss of land by small farmers. To counter these conditions, the Texas Alliance appeared in the late 1870s and by 1884 was promoting cooperative ideas and antimonopoly politics.

A democratic organization centered around local suballiances and a system of lecturers, the Texas Alliance in 1886 began its spread into the Southeast and north into Kansas. Women were encouraged to join, but African American farmers could not, although the Southern Alliance did cooperate with the Colored Farmers' Alliance, organized in 1886. By 1889 Alliance cooperative enterprises, including statewide cooperative purchasing and marketing exchanges, had spread across the South. The state exchanges failed or did not live up to expectations, but local cooperative efforts often succeeded temporarily.

In the latter half of the 1880s the Farmers' Alliance movement, still incorporating the message of cooperation and antimonopoly politics, appeared in the tier of states from the Dakotas to Nebraska and in parts of the Middle West. Efforts in 1889 at St. Louis to combine all the organizations in the movement failed, but most joined the new National Farmers' Alliancc and Industrial Union on an antimonopoly platform calling for an end to large landholding; government ownership of the railroads and telegraph systems; the free and unlimited coinage of silver; the replacement of national bank notes with legal tender notes issued by the federal government; and the subtreasury plan, a sophisticated proposal developed by Charles Macune for using non-perishable crops as collateral for federal loans to farmers and as a way to increase seasonal currency flexibility.

Between 1889 and early 1892 much of the Farmers' Alliance movement entered independent politics. Until then, support for the Farmers' Alliance movement had been strong, even among nonfarmers. Its entry into third-party politics in 1892 with Populism—the Populist Party adopted the Farmers' Alliance St. Louis platform—produced opposition as well as many defections from the Alliance. Indeed, the Farmers' Alliance movement fell apart that year, a victim of internal dissension. By 1893 only a few local Alliances and Alliance cooperatives survived. Although the movement did pass the cooperative ideal to another generation of farm organizations, it proved less successful in transmitting its conviction that a democratic government should play an active role in the political and economic life of its citizens.

[*See also* **Agricultural Policy; Free Silver Movement; Granger Laws; Granger Movement; Monetary Policy; Populism; Populist Era;** *and* **Populist Party.**]

BIBLIOGRAPHY

Goodwyn, Lawrence. *Democratic Promise: The Populist Moment in America*. New York: Oxford University Press, 1976.

McMath, Robert C., Jr. *American Populism: A Social History, 1877–1898*. New York: Hill and Wang, 1993.

Bruce Palmer

FEDERAL BUREAU OF INVESTIGATION

The Federal Bureau of Investigation (FBI) is the principal investigative arm of the Department of Justice, with jurisdiction over more than 200 categories of federal crimes. Its major late twentieth-century priorities were counterterrorism, illicit drugs and drug-related crime, foreign counterintelligence, violent crimes, and financial malfeasance. The Bureau provides local police with training, fingerprint identification, and crime-laboratory services. Its National Crime Information Center compiles crime statistics. In 1997, with a budget of some $2.5 billion, the FBI employed 10,529 special agents and 15,398 support personnel in a network of field offices, special installations, and foreign liaison posts. The director, nominated by the president and approved by the Senate, is limited to a single ten-year term.

Founded in 1908, the FBI received its current name in 1935. Its earliest responsibilities included bankruptcy fraud, antitrust crimes, violation of neutrality regulations, and enforcement of interstate prostitution laws. Its jurisdiction expanded during World War I to include espionage, sabotage, sedition, and draft-law violation. The Bureau won the lasting enmity of radicals and civil libertarians during the 1919–1920 Red Scare when hundreds of aliens were arrested and deported. The Warren Harding–era Teapot Dome scandal further tarnished its reputation. To reform the Bureau, J. Edgar Hoover, with whom the FBI's history is inextricably entwined, was appointed director in 1924; he served until his death in 1972.

Committed to professionalizing law enforcement, Hoover during the later 1920s sought to make the Bureau an indispensable resource for local police. The activist New Deal administration unleashed the Bureau on John Dillinger, Pretty Boy Floyd, and other celebrity gangsters of the era. During World War II, the Bureau targeted homefront sabotage and espionage. Movies, radio programs, magazine features, and tours of the FBI's Washington headquarters enhanced the Bureau's reputation.

With the Cold War, the Bureau entered its most controversial phase as it allied with the House Un-American Activities Committee to purge alleged Communist sympathizers from unions, schools, and the entertainment industry. Despite notable successes in investigating Soviet espionage, especially in the Alger Hiss and Rosenberg cases, the Bureau became embroiled in partisan politics with Hoover feeding information to Red-hunting politicians like Richard M. Nixon and Joseph McCarthy.

During the 1950s and 1960s, the Bureau conducted surveillance of Martin Luther King Jr.;

assembled dossiers on thousands of citizens; and used infiltration and counterespionage techniques to disrupt the Communist party, then the Ku Klux Klan, the Black Panthers, civil rights organizations, and Vietnam War protesters. The Bureau's deep-dyed conservatism and hostility to social protest widely discredited it. Revelations of illegalities and excesses that emerged during House and Senate investigations of the intelligence agencies in 1975–1976 led to the creation of formal congressional oversight committees and other reforms.

During the 1980s the Bureau used the Racketeer Influence and Corrupt Organizations Act (RICO, 1970) and wiretapping authority granted it in 1968 to build devastating cases against organized crime figures. Under director Louis Freeh (appointed in 1993) it played a key role in international law enforcement, training foreign law officials at its Quantico, Virginia, academy and establishing FBI academies overseas. But the Bureau's disastrous handling of armed stand-offs with militant antigovernment groups at Ruby Ridge, Idaho (1992), and Waco, Texas (1993), coupled with revelations of slipshod laboratory procedures, complicated its efforts to restore its reputation as America's most professional, as well as most celebrated, law enforcement agency.

[*See also* **Anti-Communism; Black Panthers; Civil Liberties; Civil Rights; Communist Party USA; Conservatism; Crime Policy: Federal; Drugs, Illicit; Federal Government, Executive Branch: Department of Justice; Hoover, J. Edgar; House Un-American Activities Committee; Ku Klux Klan; McCarthy, Joseph; New Deal; Nixon, Richard M.; Rosenberg Case; Sedition; Teapot Dome Scandal.**]

BIBLIOGRAPHY

Kessler, Ronald. *The FBI.* New York: Pocket Books, 1993.

Powers, Richard Gid. *Secrecy and Power: The Life of J. Edgar Hoover.* New York; London: Free Press; Collier Macmillan, 1987.

Richard Gid Powers

FEDERAL COMMUNICATIONS COMMISSION

Created by the Communications Act of 1934, the Federal Communications Commission (FCC) grew out of the Federal Radio Commission (FRC) that from 1927 to 1934 had rationalized the regulation of radio broadcasting. By the beginning of President Franklin Roosevelt's New Deal, however, growing complexity in electrical communications led to calls for a more comprehensive independent regulatory agency. Incorporating the earlier FRC, the new FCC was expanded to seven commissioners (from five) to incorporate regulation of interstate telegraph and telephone "wire line" services in addition to radio and other users of electromagnetic spectrum. Commissioners were nominated by the president, confirmed by the Senate (their only requirements were to be citizens, and no more than four of the seven could be from the same political party), and served staggered seven-year terms. The new commission was organized around the different types of work it had to undertake—engineering, accounting, legal, and the like. All were to be regulated by the "public interest, convenience, or necessity" standard that was stated but not defined by the 1934 act.

The FCC's initial years were dominated by two investigations, the first one mandated in the 1934 law. Growing out of information developed while drafting that legislation, Congress funded an in-depth study of AT&T, then the dominant wire line company. A dedicated FCC team of attorneys and accountants gathered an immense amount of information and by 1938 produced an initial report calling for extensive changes in federal rules concerning the provision of telephone service. A final report in mid-1939 went to Congress, and a decade later it formed the basis of an antitrust suit brought against AT&T by the Department of Justice. The other study began in 1938 and investigated the operation of the country's national radio networks, then just a decade old. A mid-1941 study concluded that networks excessively dominated their affiliate radio stations. The result was a long list of rule changes that, on appeal, were upheld by the Supreme Court in 1943. They also raised the ire of some in Congress, which during World War II held extensive hearings on the administration of FCC chairman James Lawrence Fly. Both studies showed the developing importance of economic issues in telecommunications regulation.

On the eve of American entry into World War II, the commission authorized commercial FM radio service (1 January 1941) and the inception of regular television broadcasting (1 July 1941), although few stations in either service got on the air before wartime production priorities forced a halt in new station construction. During the war, the FCC operated the Foreign Broadcast Information Service, which monitored and recorded radio broadcasts from Axis and other nations. In the immediate aftermath of the war, spectrum issues took center stage as the FCC dealt with the complex problems of reducing interference in television station allocations, leading to a definitive decision in early 1952. This continued the use of a dozen channels for television in the traditional VHF band and added many more in the higher UHF frequencies. A year later the commission approved technical standards for color transmission, although the expensive service took another dozen years to achieve success. Dealing with the aftermath of these decisions remained a focus of FCC time and effort well into the 1960s. Cable television lacked any federal regulation from the appearance of the first cable systems in the late 1940s until the mid-1960s when the agency began to assert its regulatory authority. Dubbed a service "ancillary" to broadcast television, cable was pervasively regulated by the commission in 1972 rules, although court decisions and FCC deregulation over the following decade undid most of them.

FCC treatment of postwar radio involved the licensing of thousands of new AM stations, whereas its role with newer FM radio varied. In 1945, the commission shifted FM broadcasting from its 1941 42- to 50-MHz allocation to the present 88–108 MHz, providing more channels for expansion, but making existing receivers obsolete. Later decisions—including approval of multiplex FM technology to allow multiple transmissions (1955), stereo standards (1961), and requiring programming separate from that of AM stations (late 1960s)—helped the faltering medium to grow once again.

By mid-century, and partially at the bidding of Congress, the commission reorganized its operations around the services it regulated into bureaus focused on common carrier (telegraph and telephone), broadcasting, and special or private radio services. Regulation of communication common carriers saw little change before the late 1950s when, in a series of decisions, the commission slowly weakened AT&T's long dominance of those markets. The Hush-a-Phone court ruling (1956) and the FCC's *Carterfone* decision (1968) began to open the terminal device market to AT&T's competitors. Likewise, the commission's decisions on above 890-MHz spectrum allocation (1959), MCI service authorization (1969), and Specialized Common Carriers (1971) allowed the first limited service competition with the Bell System.

Growing complexity in the telecommunication industry and the resulting regulatory policy led to congressional efforts from 1976 to 1981 to first replace and then modify the 1934 act. Although these efforts failed, they helped to lay ground for 1984 and 1992 cable television and broader 1996 amendments. These efforts encouraged (and sometimes required) deregulation of both common carrier and broadcast services, an effort the agency had already begun. Worry about the costs of regulation and a growing realization that government could not control a fast-changing field better than marketplace competition underlay these initiatives. Action by Congress in 1983 reduced the number of FCC commissioners from seven to five, serving staggered terms of five years each.

By 2010, the FCC was an agency of about 2000 people with an annual budget approaching $400 million. Much of its cost was made up of regulatory fees and auctions of spectrum licenses authorized by Congress in the 1990s.

BIBLIOGRAPHY

Brinson, Susan L. *The Red Scare, Politics, and the Federal Communications Commission, 1941–1960.* Westport, Conn.: Praeger, 2004.

"Communications Act of 1934: 50th Anniversary," *Federal Communications Law Journal* 37 (1985): 71–170.

Paglin, Max D., et al., eds. *The Communications Act: A Legislative History of the Major Amendments, 1934–1996.* Silver Spring, Md.: Pike & Fischer, 1999.

Slotten, Hugh R. *Radio and Television Regulation: Broadcast Technology in the United States, 1920–1960.* Baltimore: Johns Hopkins University Press, 2000.

Sterling, Christopher H., Phyllis W. Bernt, and Martin B. H. Weiss. *Shaping American Telecommunications: A History of Technology, Policy, and Economics.* Mahwah, N.J.: Lawrence Erlbaum Associates, 2006.

Zarkin, Kimberley A., and Richard J. Zarkin. *The Federal Communications Commission: Front Line in the Culture and Regulation Wars.* Westport, Conn.: Greenwood Press, 2006.

Christopher H. Sterling

FEDERAL DEPOSIT INSURANCE CORPORATION

The Federal Deposit Insurance Corporation (FDIC) was established in a provision of the Banking Act of 16 June 1933, a law also known as Glass–Steagall. The creation of the FDIC was in response to the 5,000 bank failures that had occurred since the onset of the Great Depression in 1929. The FDIC was to provide a guarantee to bank customers of their first $2,500 in deposits at any member institution. This sum went up periodically over the years, beginning with a doubling in 1934. Assessments from banks on insured deposits, along with credit facilities from the Treasury and Federal Reserve, provided the initial capitalization of the FDIC.

Ten weeks prior to the passage of Glass–Steagall, President Franklin Roosevelt issued an executive order prohibiting the private ownership of gold. A chief reason bank depositors had been making cash withdrawals en masse since 1929 was the popular presumption that the official price of gold would soon be raised significantly, a move that happened in 1934. Thus the issuance of the executive order in April was a necessary step to ensure that the FDIC would not be overwhelmed with business after it was chartered in June. Indeed, the number of bank failures requiring disbursements from the FDIC over its first seven years, through 1941, was only 370, a far cry from the record set in the Great Depression years.

In the 1950s and 1960s, the FDIC was a sleepy affair, treating comparatively so few failures that at one point, an overseer in Congress wondered if this indicated an unhealthy lack of competition in the banking system. It was an objective of the FDIC to reduce bank competition and thus risk to depositors. This was addressed mainly though the FDIC's interest-rate policy. Member banks could charge no interest on checking account deposits, and interest on savings accounts was capped. Banks could not compete on price.

It was precisely this policy that played into the extreme volatility that the banking system, and thus the FDIC, experienced in the 1970s and 1980s. When inflation took off at upwards of 10 percent annual rates in the 1970s, it became untenable for depositors to keep assets in no-interest or capped-interest accounts. Yet as deposits fled for inflation hedges outside the banking system (such as commodities), providers of the hedges in turn presented large sums ("petrodollars") for deposit. This raised the ratio of aggregate deposits to insured deposits and led to uncommon risk taking on the part of banks. The FDIC had to cover large failures, such as that of Penn Square in 1982. In this period the FDIC was transformed into being a receiver as well as an insurer of failed banks.

In 1991, the FDIC swallowed the residue of a partner, the Federal Savings and Loan Insurance Corporation, which had served the residential housing market and had been hit even harder by the inflation contagion of the previous decades. The FDIC contribution to the bailouts of 2008 was to raise the depositor guarantee from $100,000 to $250,000.

[*See also* **Federal Government: Executive Branch: Treasury Department;** ***and*** **Federal Reserve System.**]

Brian Domitrovic

FEDERAL GOVERNMENT, EXECUTIVE BRANCH

This entry contains eight subentries: An Overview; Agricultural Department; Defense Department; Department of Justice; Other Departments; Presidency, The; State Department; and Treasury Department.

AN OVERVIEW

The fear that drove the delegates to the Constitutional Convention of 1787 was not the specter of monarchy but rather the anxiety created by a national Congress that was incapable of governing. For much of the convention, executive independence was threatened by a provision calling for election of the president by the legislature, but eventually the Electoral College compromise took the selection out of the hands of the legislature and laid the basis for the president's claim to popular support. In addition, the decision to give the president the power to appoint executive officers provided a foundation for the cabinet system that would be developed by George Washington and used by all subsequent presidents.

Still, the potential for a popularly chosen and independent executive was not immediately realized. In the 1790s, supporters of executive independence became increasingly suspicious of popular opinion, and defenders of popular government were hostile to executive power. It was the Federalists who initially encouraged the growth of the executive branch, but Thomas Jefferson helped solidify its power. Although Jefferson saw a powerful executive as a threat to democracy, in founding the Democratic Republican Party he established the role of president as a popular leader. Moreover, despite his distrust of executive power, he allowed for the continued expansion of the executive branch to handle the exigencies of government.

It was, however, Andrew Jackson who first embraced the idea of permanent political parties. Arguing that the president rather than Congress could best claim to represent the people, Jackson relied on that claim to defend extensive executive discretion. Jackson used the spoils system—giving federal jobs to one's political supporters—to tie the national government to the people through the party machinery and also to establish political control of the executive branch.

The Civil War proved a catalyst for further expansion of the executive branch. President Abraham Lincoln's exercise of emergency powers demonstrated the tremendous potential of an independent executive in time of war, a potential that would be exploited by presidents during the two world wars and the Cold War. Presidents from Lincoln to Woodrow Wilson saw the spoils system become a major threat to executive independence and energy. Although civil service reform in part arose from reformers' desire to clean up the corruption of the spoils system, presidential support for the reform was also motivated by the same goal that had moved Jackson to adopt the spoils system in the first place: increased control over the executive branch.

Since President Franklin Delano Roosevelt in the 1930s, presidents have sought greater control of an executive branch that grew from 239,476 civilian employees in 1901 to 2,482,666 in 1951. Twentieth-century presidents also relied on popular leadership skills to enhance their power. Theodore Roosevelt's concept of a "bully pulpit" and Franklin Roosevelt's "fireside chats" became the models for other great communicators such as John F. Kennedy and Ronald Reagan, who used the new medium of television very effectively. The increased reliance on popular leadership, however, weakened the president's ties to political parties and to Congress. Personal popularity proved an unreliable foundation for presidents from Lyndon B. Johnson through Jimmy Carter.

Nonetheless, presidents from Reagan to Obama have been able to wield broad influence over government through their control of the executive branch. Beginning with Reagan, the Office of Management and Budget became a major tool for setting the priorities of government. Reagan used the budget process to implement his political agenda, including tax cuts, increases in defense spending, and domestic spending cuts. George H. W. Bush and William J. Clinton used the budget process to establish and maintain limits on domestic spending. During George W. Bush's presidency, the powers of the executive branch were expanded in response to 9/11. The use of executive orders, signing statements, national security findings, and the expanded use of military tribunals each enhanced the president's power. Bush defended each of these practices under the theory of the "unitary executive"—the idea that under the Constitution the president has wide discretion and complete control over the executive branch. Although Barack Obama originally campaigned against these expanded powers, as president he has continued to exercise such powers. In both his response to the financial crisis and his health-care reform he has laid the groundwork for even greater executive branch control through the broad use of administrative rule-making procedures.

[*See also* **Bush, George W.; Constitution; Democratic Party; Federalist Party; Jackson, Andrew; Jefferson, Thomas; Republican Party; Republicanism; Spoils System; Veto Power;** *and* **Whig Party.**]

BIBLIOGRAPHY

Calabresi, Steven G., and Christopher S. Yoo. *The Unitary Executive: Presidential Power from Washington to Bush*. New Haven, Conn.: Yale University Press, 2008.

Dickinson, Matthew J. *Bitter Harvest: Presidential Power and the Growth of the Presidential Branch*. Cambridge, UK; New York: Cambridge University Press, 1999.

David K. Nichols

AGRICULTURE DEPARTMENT

The U.S. Department of Agriculture (USDA) was established in 1862. The first commissioner of agriculture, Isaac Newton, organized the department by scientific fields such as entomology and botany, each represented initially by one person and later by a division. Early contact with farmers was limited to the distribution of seeds for trial and the publication of advisory pamphlets. The USDA began with a small budget and an uncertain relationship to the land-grant universities in the development of agricultural science. In 1887 the Hatch Act established state agricultural experimental stations as institutions for basic research in agriculture-related fields.

In the late nineteenth century the USDA began reorganizing its research activities to focus on specific problems, such as livestock diseases. The first new unit was the Bureau of Animal Industry, created in 1884. With permanent status and funding, an approving interest group (cattle ranchers in this case), and regulatory power, this new bureau made rapid progress against livestock diseases and became the model for other problem-oriented bureaus. Harvey W. Wiley, head of the Bureau of Chemistry from 1883 to 1912, led a long campaign against food adulteration, culminating in the 1906 Pure Food and Drug Act. The high-visibility activist Gifford Pinchot ran the Bureau of Forestry (later Forest Service) from 1898 to 1910, pursuing a policy of sustained use that has remained largely unchanged.

Working in the Bureau of Plant Industry during the early twentieth-century period when the boll-weevil infestation began to devastate the southern cotton industry, Seaman A. Knapp started "demonstration farms" to persuade farmers to try new methods developed by agricultural scientists, particularly those in the Bureau of Entomology. Knapp's success led to the Smith–Lever Act of 1914, which formed the Extension Service as a cooperative program of the USDA and land-grant colleges.

The USDA became a cabinet-level department in 1889. Secretary James Wilson (1897–1913) oversaw the expansion of scientific work in the bureaus, the establishment of federal experiment stations in new territories such as Hawai'i and Puerto Rico, and the introduction of new crops and varieties by the "plant explorer" David Fairchild. Henry C. Wallace (1921–1923) increased the department's work in agricultural economics, recognizing that merely improving production did not guarantee prosperity for farmers. His son, Henry A. Wallace (1933–1940), implemented such New Deal programs as the Agricultural Adjustment Acts, which introduced crop reduction and agricultural subsidies to boost prices, policies that in some form would long remain in place.

Direct contact between department scientists and farmers declined over time. In 1954 the bureaus were abolished and their scientific work reorganized into the Agricultural Research Service. The Food and Drug Administration was removed from the department in 1940. By World War II, the department was emphasizing pesticides to the near exclusion of other methods of insect control, opening it to a storm of criticism by environmentalists after the publication of Rachel Carson's *Silent Spring* in 1962. The controversy reflected a long-standing ideological divide between advocates of maximum resource utilization in the USDA and preservationists in the Department of the Interior. During the late twentieth century, the USDA came under criticism for favoring large agribusinesses and big, rich, white farmers in its scientific research, economic policies, and regulatory actions. Since 2001, there have been four appointments for secretary of agriculture. Three of these secretaries were appointed by President George W. Bush; Ann M. Veneman (1/2001–1/2005),

Michael O. Johanns (1/2005–1/2007), and Ed Schafer (1/2007–1/2009). President Barack Obama appointed Tom Vilsack in January 2009. He was confirmed by unanimous vote in the U.S. Senate. There has been considerable debate over the USDA's subsidies on biofuels such as ethanol. The Energy Policy Act of 2005 increased the amount of biofuel (usually ethanol) that must be mixed with gasoline sold in the United States to 4 billion gallons by 2006, 6.1 billion gallons by 2009, and 7.5 billion gallons by 2012. In 2007, the biofuel industry received $3.25 billion in federal support.

[*See also* **Agricultural Adjustment Administration; Carson, Rachel; Homestead Act; New Deal; Pure Food and Drug Act;** ***and*** **Wallace, Henry A.**]

BIBLIOGRAPHY

Dupree, A. Hunter *Science in the Federal Government.* Baltimore: Johns Hopkins University Press, 1957.

Marcus, Alan I., and Richard Lowitt, eds. "The United States Department of Agriculture in Historical Perspective." *Agricultural History* 642, special issue (1990).

Richard C. Sawyer; revised and updated by Pearson Bramblett

DEFENSE DEPARTMENT

The Department of Defense, established in 1949, evolved from the National Military Establishment (NME), a hybrid organization created by Congress in 1947 to unify the previously separate War and Navy departments, dating from 1781 and 1798, respectively. Unification had its immediate origins in the experiences of World War II, which demonstrated the need for new organizational mechanisms to achieve more effective military coordination. As the war ended, attention turned to enacting permanent reforms. One plan, sponsored by the War Department and endorsed by President Harry S. Truman, called for a highly centralized defense organization, including a separate air force, under a single secretary of defense. A competing plan, advocated by the navy, urged closer coordination rather than outright unification.

The resulting legislative compromise under the National Security Act of 1947 borrowed from both plans. Desiring the savings and increased efficiency promised by unification but fearing that an overly centralized system would produce a "Prussian-style general staff," Congress therefore incorporated aspects of the navy concept by loosely unifying the services under the NME and granting the secretary of defense only qualified authority. Additionally, the 1947 act gave statutory standing to the Joint Chiefs of Staff (JCS), a body that had existed without a formal charter since 1942, and established two new organizations: the National Security Council to oversee high-level policy coordination and the Central Intelligence Agency to collect and analyze intelligence.

The first secretary of defense, James V. Forrestal (1947–1949), took office on 17 September 1947. As secretary of the navy during the unification debate, Forrestal had opposed service unification. Once installed in his new job he adopted a go-slow approach—"evolution, not revolution"—toward integrating service activities. Even so, he did not receive what he considered sufficient cooperation from the military services. Especially intense was interservice competition over roles and missions. Meanwhile, worsening relations with the Soviet Union intensified pressures to step up military preparedness, despite rigid budget ceilings imposed by President Truman for economic reasons.

Doing an about-face, Forrestal recommended that the secretary's powers and staff support be strengthened. In 1949 Congress removed the limitations on the secretary's authority and converted the NME into the

Department of Defense, a full-scale executive department. With unencumbered powers and a larger staff, the secretary of defense became the focal point of an increasingly centralized administrative system. During the summer and fall of 1949, opponents of unification fought back, as senior navy officers, reeling from recent budget cuts, openly attacked service unification for causing a shift away from sea power toward growing reliance on strategic nuclear bombing as the country's first line of defense. But following the across-the-board rearmament precipitated by the Korean War, money for defense became more plentiful and the stresses and strains of interservice relations eased.

The Korean War produced renewed complaints from Congress that the services continued to squander resources while unnecessarily duplicating activities. In 1953 and 1958, President Dwight D. Eisenhower addressed these problems through organizational reforms that took the unification process nearly as far as it could go without abandoning the concept of individual military services. In the Defense Reorganization Act of 1958, Congress authorized the secretary to reassign service functions and approved a new chain of command that bypassed the service secretaries. Instead of being separately administered, as in the past, the military departments were merely to be "separately organized," a gesture toward preserving service autonomy but a distinct departure from the preunification days when the departments had operated as sovereign entities.

The first secretary of defense to make full use of these increased powers was Robert S. McNamara (1961–1968). His initial task was to fulfill President John F. Kennedy's campaign promise to replace Eisenhower's *New Look* defense strategy, which had emphasized nuclear weapons, with a "flexible response" posture giving greater weight to general purpose forces. To control rising defense costs, McNamara introduced a variety of reforms, including mission-oriented budgeting with five-year expenditure projections, "systems analysis" techniques that used computer models to evaluate the cost-effectiveness of weapons and programs, and consolidation of service activities under defense-wide agencies. The net effect was an unprecedented degree of centralized civilian control.

McNamara's management successes contrasted sharply with the military debacle that developed in southeast Asia during his tenure. Secretaries of defense had customarily stayed out of the operational side of military affairs, leaving them to the professionals, but McNamara inserted himself directly into the details of running the Vietnam War. Initially a strong proponent of American involvement in Vietnam, he gradually became disillusioned and left office, counseling stepped-up negotiations and disengagement.

After McNamara came a reaction to centralized authority. Although the managerial and budgeting techniques he had pioneered generally survived, his use of civilians in roles traditionally reserved for military professionals aroused much resentment among the services and skepticism in Congress. By the mid-1980s, the question at issue was how to revitalize the Joint Chiefs of Staff, whose stature and effectiveness had diminished steadily since Vietnam. The Goldwater–Nichols Act of 1986 attempted to reverse this trend by giving the JCS chairman broader advisory powers and increased administrative authority over the Joint Staff (the JCS bureaucracy) and by mandating more "jointness" among the services. Although the performance of U.S. forces in the 1991 Persian Gulf War seemed to bear out the soundness of the new emphasis on joint doctrine, subsequent misadventures in Somalia and command-and-control problems in the Middle East suggested a need for further refinements.

During the 1990s the Department of Defense faced the challenge of an international environment that, although no longer dominated by the threat of a global thermonuclear war, continued to exhibit unstable tendencies. At the same time, a revolution in military affairs, driven largely by new technologies, augured major changes in the role and composition of future military forces. In the circumstances, the demands on the secretary of defense and the JCS chairman to work together in providing unified policy and programmatic guidance appeared unlikely to diminish. Unification, born of necessity after World War II, had become a fact of life throughout the defense establishment.

The war in Afghanistan began on 7 October 2001, as the U.S. Armed Forces launched Operation Enduring Freedom along with the British Armed Forces and Afghan United Front (Northern Alliance) in response to the 11 September attacks with the stated goal of dismantling al-Qaeda and ending its use of Afghanistan as a base for terrorist operations. The United States also promised to remove the Taliban regime from power and create a viable democratic state.

The preludes to the war were the 11 September attacks on the United States, in which almost 3,000 civilians lost their lives in New York City, Washington, D.C., and Pennsylvania, and the 9 September 2001 assassination of anti-Taliban leader Ahmad Shah Massoud two days prior. The United States identified members of al-Qaeda, an organization based in, operating out of, and allied with the Taliban's Islamic Emirate of Afghanistan, as the perpetrators of the attacks.

In the first phase of Operation Enduring Freedom, ground forces of the Afghan United Front working with U.S. and British Special Forces and with massive U.S. air support ousted the Taliban regime from power in Kabul and most of Afghanistan in a matter of weeks. Most of the senior Taliban leadership fled to neighboring Pakistan. The democratic Islamic Republic of Afghanistan was established and an interim government under Hamid Karzai was created, which was also democratically elected by the Afghan people in the 2004 general elections. The International Security Assistance Force (ISAF) was established by the UN Security Council at the end of December 2001 to secure Kabul and the surrounding areas. NATO assumed control of ISAF in 2003. ISAF includes troops from forty-two countries, with NATO members providing the core of the force.

The 2003 invasion of Iraq (19 March–1 May 2003) was the start of the conflict known as the Iraq War, or Operation Iraqi Freedom, in which a combined force of troops from the United States, the United Kingdom, and smaller contingents from Australia and Poland invaded Iraq and toppled the regime of Saddam Hussein in twenty-one days of major combat operations. This phase (March–April 2003) consisted of a conventionally fought war, which concluded with the fall of the Iraq capital Baghdad. This was considered a continuation of the Gulf War of 1991, prior to which Saddam Hussein had invaded Kuwait and after defeat by Coalition Forces had agreed to surrender and/or destroy several types of weapons, including SCUD missiles and weapons of mass destruction (WMD).

Since the Persian Gulf War in 1991 the United States and Britain had been keeping a tight rein on Saddam Hussein, waging an undeclared conflict against Iraq for twelve years. U.S. President Bill Clinton had maintained sanctions and ordered air strikes in the "Iraqi no-fly zones" Operation Desert Fox in the hope that Saddam would be overthrown by political enemies inside Iraq. Clinton also had signed into law H.R. 4655, the Iraq Liberation Act, which appropriated funds to Iraqi opposition groups. Four countries participated with troops during the initial invasion phase, which lasted from 19 March 19 to 9 April 2003: the United States (148,000), the United Kingdom (45,000), Australia (2,000), and Poland (194). Another thirty-six countries were involved in its aftermath. In preparation for the invasion, 100,000 U.S. troops were assembled in Kuwait by 18 February.

Coalition casualties from terrorist bombings and attacks by counterinsurgent forces averaged approximately 850 per year between 2003 and 2006. Secretary of Defense Donald Rumsfeld adopted a new strategy in 2006. By 2006, coalition casualties averaged only 150 per year.

The surge in Iraq has been one of the most impressive military accomplishments in recent years. Al-Qaeda in Iraq's campaign of terrorism and intimidation had turned its Sunni base of support against it. The result was the so-called Anbar Awakening in the late summer of 2006, followed by similar awakening movements across Iraq. From 2003 through 2006, U.S. military forces, under the leadership of General John Abizaid and General George Casey, inflicted huge losses on the Baathist and Qaeda leadership. Many thousands of insurgents, including the Qaeda chief in Iraq, Abu Musab al-Zarqawi, were captured or killed and proved difficult to replace. The Iraqi Security Forces had achieved cohesion, improved operational effectiveness, and critical mass. By December 2006, some 320,000 Iraqis had been trained, equipped, and deployed, producing the forces necessary to help hold difficult neighborhoods against the enemy. By 2007, the surge, for most Iraqis, could have an Iraqi face.

The political environment in Iraq had also shifted. Moktada al-Sadr, the firebrand cleric, declared a cease-fire in February 2007. The government of Prime Minister Nuri Kamal al-Maliki, seated in May 2006, moved against militias and Iranian-backed militias and has rejected narrow sectarian policies. In 2005, troop levels in Iraq were increased to numbers nearly equal to the 2007 surge, twice. But the effects were not as durable because large segments of the Sunni population were still providing sanctuary to insurgents, and Iraq's security forces were not sufficiently capable or large enough.

[*See also* **Eisenhower, Dwight D.; Federal Government, Executive Branch: An Overview; Kennedy, John F.; National Security Act of 1947; National Security Council;** ***and*** **Truman, Harry S.**]

BIBLIOGRAPHY

Art, Robert J., Vincent Davis, and Samuel P. Huntington, eds. *Reorganizing America's Defense.* Washington, D.C.: Pergamon-Brassey's, 1985.

Blackwell, James A., Jr., and Barry M. Blechman, eds. *Making Defense Reform Work.* Washington, D.C.: Brassey's, 1990.

Condit, Doris M. *History of the Office of the Secretary of Defense: The Test of War, 1950–1953.* Washington, D.C.: Historical Office, Office of the Secretary of Defense, 1988.

Rearden, Steven L. *History of the Office of the Secretary of Defense: The Formative Years, 1947–1950.* Washington, D.C.: Historical Office, Office of the Secretary of Defense, 1984.

Trask, Roger, and Alfred Goldberg. *The Department of Defense, 1947–1997.* Washington, D.C.: Historical Office, Office of the Secretary of Defense, 1997.

Watson, Robert J. *History of the Office of the Secretary of Defense: Into the Missile Age, 1956–1961.* Washington, D.C.: Historical Office, Office of the Secretary of Defense, 1997.

Steven L. Rearden; revised by Pearson Bramblett

DEPARTMENT OF JUSTICE

The Judiciary Act of 1789 established the U.S. attorney general's office as one of the earliest and most prominent within the executive branch. As the nation's chief legal officer, the attorney general joined the secretaries of Treasury, State, and War as a member of the cabinet.

Yet President George Washington's attorney general, Edmund Randolph, was assisted by only one clerk. Not until 1870 did Congress establish a Department of Justice headed by the attorney general. The new department was given responsibility for representing the U.S. government in all federal courts, providing legal advice to the White House and other executive agencies, prosecuting violations of federal law, and protecting the country from subversion.

During its early history, the Department of Justice primarily enforced antitrust legislation, prosecuted tax evasion cases, and monitored so-called "subversives" and "public enemies." The Federal Bureau of Investigation (FBI) was established in 1908 as the department's chief investigative arm. The department gained notoriety during the post–World War I Red Scare when Attorney General A. Mitchell Palmer mobilized a vast campaign against radicals allegedly planning "to rise up and destroy the Government at one fell swoop." Working with local law enforcement officials, Palmer coordinated massive dragnet raids in 1919 and 1920 that targeted members of socialist or Communist organizations, especially alien members. Not surprisingly, Congress placed the Immigration and Naturalization Service within the Department of Justice in 1940.

Sweeping civil rights reforms in the 1960s and after expanded the department's mission and functions dramatically. In particular, the Justice Department's Civil Rights Division was given responsibility for prosecuting violations of the Civil Rights Act of 1964, the Voting Rights Act of 1965, the Fair Housing Act of 1968, the Equal Educational Opportunities Act of 1974, and the Americans with Disabilities Act of 1990.

The post-1960 Justice Department also played a major role in presidential efforts to launch a "war on crime." Whereas President Lyndon B. Johnson's attorney general, Ramsey Clark, championed civil rights and due process, his successor John N. Mitchell embraced the Richard M. Nixon administration's call for "law and order." As Mitchell insisted, the Department of Justice "was an institution for law enforcement, not social improvement." Ironically, Mitchell himself was convicted in 1975 of conspiracy and obstruction of justice in the Watergate scandal. In the Clinton administration, Attorney General Janet Reno made the Department of Justice a key participant in debates over the 1994 crime bill and oversaw such varied departmental responsibilities as investigating violations of federal law, regulating immigration, policing narcotics trafficking, guarding domestic security from subversive attacks, assisting local law enforcement, providing legal advice to executive officials, and trying all government litigation before federal courts.

The Justice Department has long been authorized to name special prosecutors to investigate wrongdoing by executive branch officials. During the Nixon administration, for example, Archibald Cox was appointed to spearhead the Watergate investigation. Yet Cox's summary discharge for pursuing incriminating White House tapes highlighted dramatic limitations in how executive officials were policed. The Ethics in Government Act of 1978 established the office of independent counsel as well as formal procedures by which the attorney general is required to initiate independent investigations of high-level executive officials for malfeasance. Since then, various White House challenges to the independent counsel's broad discretion over witness selection, investigatory strategies, and indictment decisions have routinely failed in the federal courts. The independent-counsel process thus has generated fierce debate and considerable fine-tuning whenever the law has required congressional reauthorization. This was especially true of the 1999 reauthorization that followed the controversial investigation of President Clinton by independent counsel Kenneth Starr.

The Department of Justice became embroiled in controversy under Attorney General John Ashcroft, a deeply conservative former Missouri senator named to the post in 2001 by President George W. Bush. Forty-two senators voted against the nomination, but it narrowly carried. Ashcroft took a hard line on criminal-justice issues, pressing for tougher sentencing guidelines and strongly supporting the death penalty, for example. Under Ashcroft, the Justice Department opposed a series of gun-control measures as infringements of the Second Amendment and spent millions on an antipornography campaign. (To further protect the public's morals, the department covered in blue drapery a partially nude female statue representing "Justice" that appeared behind Ashcroft in his early televised news conferences.) Ashcroft's vigorous enforcement of the USA Patriot Act, passed in the aftermath of the terrorist attacks of 11 September 2001, led to accusations that the Justice Department was jeopardizing the civil liberties of American citizens. In 2004 Ashcroft faced heavy criticism from a blue-ribbon national panel investigating the 9/11 attacks for failing to make antiterrorism a top Justice Department priority earlier in 2001 despite urgent warnings from the Federal Bureau of Investigation of an imminent domestic attack.

The USA Patriot Act of the U.S. Congress was signed into law by President George W. Bush on 26 October 2001. The law was authored by the Justice Department in response to the terrorist attacks against New York City and the Pentagon on 11 September 2001. The title of the act is a contrived three-letter initialism (USA) preceding a seven-letter acronym (PATRIOT), which in combination stand for Uniting and Strengthening America by Providing Appropriate Tools Required to Intercept and Obstruct Terrorism Act of 2001. The act dramatically reduced restrictions on law enforcement agencies' ability to search telephone, email communications, medical, financial, and other records. It also eased restrictions on foreign intelligence gathering within the United States, expanded the secretary of the Treasury's authority to regulate financial transactions, particularly those involving foreign individuals and entities, and broadened the discretion of law enforcement and immigration authorities in detaining and deporting immigrants suspected of terrorism-related acts. The act also expanded the definition of terrorism to include domestic terrorism, thus enlarging the number of activities to which the USA Patriot Act's expanded law enforcement powers can be applied. President Barack Obama signed a four-year extension of the three key provisions in the act on 26 May 2011.

The dismissal of U.S. Attorneys controversy was initiated by the unprecedented midterm dismissal of seven U.S. Attorneys on 7 December 2006 by the George W. Bush administration's Department of Justice. Congressional investigations focused on whether the Department of Justice and the White House were using the U.S. attorney positions for political advantage. Allegations were that some of the attorneys were targeted for dismissal to impede investigations of Republican politicians or that some were targeted for their failure to initiate investigations that would damage Democratic politicians or hamper Democratic-leaning voters. The U.S. attorneys were replaced with interim appointees, under provisions in the 2005 USA Patriot Act reauthorization.

These dismissed U.S. attorneys had been appointed by George W. Bush and confirmed by the Senate four years earlier. Two other attorneys were dismissed in controversial circumstances in 2005–2006. Twenty-six or more U.S. attorneys had been under consideration for dismissal during this time period. The firings received attention via hearings in Congress in January 2007, and by March 2007 the controversy had national visibility. Attorney General Alberto Gonzales stated that the U.S. attorneys "serve at the pleasure of the president" and described the affair as "an overblown personnel matter." By mid-September 2007, nine of the highest-level officers of the Department of Justice associated with the controversy had resigned, most prominently Attorney General Alberto Gonzales.

A subsequent report by the Justice Department Inspector General in October 2008 found that the process used to fire the first seven attorneys and two others dismissed around the same time was "arbitrary" and "fundamentally flawed" and "raised doubts about the integrity of Department prosecution decisions." In July 2010, the Department of Justice prosecutors closed the two-year investigation without filing charges after determining that the firing was inappropriately political, but not criminal, saying "Evidence did not demonstrate that any prosecutable criminal offense was committed with regard to the removal of David Iglesias. The investigative team also determined that the evidence did not warrant expanding the scope of the investigation beyond the removal of Iglesias."

In 2008, President Barack Obama appointed Eric Himpton Holder Jr. to the cabinet post of Attorney General of the United States. Confirmed by the Senate on 28 January 2008, Holder became the first African American to this position. Prior to this he had worked for the Washington, D.C., legal firm of Covington and Burling and as a judge for the Superior Court of the District of Columbia. He brought to his position as attorney general a strong record as a progressive in favor of the Washington, D.C., ban on handguns and the closing of Guantanamo Bay, where prisoners involved in the war on terror were held. Once in office, he began to modify this position.

[*See also* **Anti-Communism; Antitrust Legislation and Law; Civil Rights Legislation; Crime Policy; Federal Bureau of Investigation; Federal Government, Executive Branch: An Overview; Federal Government, Judicial Branch; Immigration Law and Policy: After 1930; Judicial Review; Judiciary Act of 1789; Jurisprudence;** *and* **Patriot Act, The.**]

BIBLIOGRAPHY

Bledsoe, W. Craig, and Leslie Rigby. "The Cabinet and Executive Departments." In *Cabinets and Counselors: The President and the Executive Branch*, pp. 73–140. Washington, D.C.: Congressional Quarterly, 1997.

Burke, John P. *The Institutional Presidency*. Baltimore: Johns Hopkins University Press, 1992.

Fenno, Richard. *The President's Cabinet*. Cambridge, Mass.: Harvard University Press, 1959.

Hinsdale, Mary L. *A History of the President's Cabinet*. Ann Arbor, Mich.: G. Wahr, 1911.

Learned, Henry Barrett. *The President's Cabinet: Studies in the Origin, Formation, and Structure of an American Institution*. New Haven, Conn.: Yale University Press, 1912.

Moe, Ronald C. "The President's Cabinet." In *Understanding the Presidency*, edited by James P. Pfiffner and Roger H. Davidson, pp. 136–155. New York: Longman, 1997.

Patterson, Bradley H., Jr. *The President's Cabinet: Issues and Questions*. Washington, D.C.: American Society for Public Administration, 1976.

Daniel J. Tichenor

OTHER DEPARTMENTS

As the authority and sheer size of the federal government expanded over the course of American history, so did the number of cabinet-level departments within the executive branch. Since the creation in 1789 of three great executive departments (Treasury, State, and War), lawmakers have added twelve cabinet-level departments to address new problems, interest-group pressures, and functions that could not be met easily by the original departments. Nine of the current fifteen departments in the executive branch were created in the twentieth century, seven alone after 1960, and the most recent (Homeland Security) in 2003. Charged with broad responsibilities, cabinet-level departments are the largest units of the contemporary executive branch.

Department of the Interior (1849). Although a "home affairs" or "interior" department was proposed in the earliest days of the republic, Congress resisted until the administration of James Knox Polk. Polk's treasury secretary, Robert J. Walker, strongly supported an interior department, arguing that managing the public lands of an expanding nation was overly burdensome for his department. Walker was especially daunted by U.S. acquisitions of vast new territories following the Mexican War and the 1848 treaty with Britain ceding much of the Oregon Territory to the United States. After heated debate, Congress in 1849 approved an administration plan establishing the Department of the Interior. The measure shifted to the Interior Department the General Land Office from the Treasury, the Patent Office from the State Department, and the Bureau of Indian Affairs, and the Pension Office from the War Department.

For most of its history, the Department of the Interior's policies reflected the notion that the public lands and natural resources under its management were practically limitless and should be fully developed to promote national growth and prosperity. The environmental movement altered the politics and policies of the department, however. Stewart L. Udall, President John F. Kennedy's interior secretary in the early 1960s, forged closer ties with the environmental movement. Udall, a supporter of national parks and environmental preservation during his years as a congressman, fostered department initiatives for improving the national park system, resource planning, and outdoor recreation. After Udall's tenure, the Interior Department found itself drawn into heated political conflicts pitting environmental groups against mining, logging, and other development interests. Secretary Cecil D. Andrus (1977–1981) drew fire from corporate interests for championing new controls on strip mining, stronger protection of the Alaska wilderness, and new efforts to redress chemical contamination. His successor, Ronald Reagan appointee James G. Watt, faced withering criticism from environmental groups who protested his plans for private use of resources in the public domain, stronger state control over public lands, and the appointment of prodevelopment personnel.

Former Arizona governor Bruce Babbitt, secretary of the interior in the Bill Clinton administration, found himself at the center of tense struggles over grazing, mining, logging, and controlled-burn policies. The administration of his successor, Gale Norton, was plagued by allegations of improper contacts with lobbyists and using political rather than scientific standards as the basis of policy decisions.

By the early twenty-first century, the Department of the Interior was responsible for managing the nation's natural resources, including its wildlife and over 500 million acres of public lands. Among its 30 major bureaus and agencies were the Bureau of Land Management, the U.S. Fish and Wildlife Service, the U.S. Geological Survey, the Bureau of Indian Affairs, and the National Park Service.

Department of Commerce (1903). Amid rapid industrialization and economic development, a modest commerce agency was formed within the executive branch in 1888. After the

Panic of 1893, business interests such as the National Association of Manufacturers lobbied strenuously for a cabinet-level department of commerce. In 1903, courting both business and labor support, President Theodore Roosevelt won congressional approval for a Department of Commerce and Labor. With over 10,000 employees, the department's functions included regulating foreign and domestic commerce; the mining, manufacturing, shipping, and fishing industries; labor interests; and transportation. The 1913 creation of a Labor Department resulted in an independent Department of Commerce.

Departmental authority and resources expanded sharply under the ambitious leadership of commerce secretary and presidential aspirant Herbert Hoover (1921–1928). Under Hoover, the Department of Commerce's budget soared from $860,000 in 1920 to $38 million in 1928. When Hoover became president in 1929, the Department of Commerce remained powerful. But in the antibusiness climate of the 1930s, President Franklin Delano Roosevelt and the New Dealers did not look kindly at the Department of Commerce. Significantly reducing its budget and authority, they even considered dissolving the department altogether.

Although the Department of Commerce weathered New Deal–Era assaults, many of its traditional functions were subsequently taken over or shared by other executive agencies. Regulation of transportation was shifted to a new Department of Transportation in 1967. By the 1990s, responsibilities for commerce, trade, and economic analysis were shared with a host of other agencies, such as the Office of the U.S. Trade Representative, the Council of Economic Advisers, and the Treasury. Nevertheless, the Department of Commerce continued to play an important collaborative part in these areas and to manage various programs to aid American businesses, encourage technological innovation, and enhance U.S. fortunes in international trade. Commerce Secretary Ron Brown died in a plane crash in 1996 while leading a group of U.S. businesspeople on a trade mission to the former Yugoslavia. The Commerce Department also is responsible for conducting the federal census.

Department of Labor (1913). Labor activists lobbied vigorously in the 1880s for a cabinet-level department dedicated to the needs of organized labor. A small Bureau of Labor was created in 1884 within the Interior Department, followed in 1888 by an independent Department of Labor without cabinet rank. When a Department of Commerce and Labor was established in 1903, labor activists protested that it would be captured by business interests. In 1913, a Democratic Congress created a separate cabinet-level Department of Labor. During the New Deal–Era under Secretary Frances Perkins (1933–1945) the Department of Labor gained new prominence. The 1960s brought further expansion as Secretary W. Willard Wirtz forged close alliances with organized labor.

During the Reagan administration, the Labor Department faced budget cuts and charges of lax enforcement of worker-protection laws. President George Bush's first Labor secretary, Elizabeth H. Dole, revitalized the department, winning budget increases, making worker safety a key objective, negotiating an increase in the minimum wage, and pressing companies receiving government contracts to move more women and minorities into managerial positions. Labor Secretary Robert B. Reich (1993–1997) further restored departmental prominence, emphasizing education and training for unskilled workers in a global economy while overseeing the Department of Labor's responsibility for occupational health and safety, antidiscrimination in employment, worker's compensation, unemployment insurance, minimum wages and overtime pay, pension rights, and free collective bargaining. The department also maintains job training and manpower programs (such as the Job Corps) and collects labor statistics.

Department of Health and Human Services (1979). The roots of the Department of Health and Human Services date to the Federal Security Administration (FSA), formed in 1939 to coordinate various agencies responsible for health, education, and Social Security programs. The Federal Children's Bureau (1912) was transferred from the Department of Labor to the FSA a few years later. In 1953, President Dwight D. Eisenhower won legislative approval for making the FSA a cabinet-level department, the Department of Health, Education, and Welfare (HEW), which soon grew into one of the largest departments in the federal government. Social Security expanded steadily, providing disability insurance in 1956 and gradually increasing retirement benefits while easing eligibility standards. HEW responsibilities grew again in 1965 with new Medicare hospital insurance for the elderly and a Medicaid program to fund medical expenses of the poor.

With the creation of the Department of Education in 1979, HEW became the Department of Health and Human Services (HHS). HHS functions were reduced again when the Social Security Administration became an independent agency in 1995, thereby distancing the program from political pressures. Despite this streamlining, HHS retained a broad mandate, administering Medicare and Medicaid and overseeing the work of the Surgeon General, the Centers for Disease Control and Prevention (CDC), the National Institutes of Health (NIH), and the Food and Drug Administration (FDA). Despite reforms in the Clinton years shifting responsibility for welfare to the states, HHS continued to oversee numerous programs designed to promote the welfare of children, families, and the elderly. The department's importance increased amid growing concerns over medical costs and health insurance coverage, trends that resulted in the passage of the Patient Protection and Affordable Care Act (2010).

Department of Housing and Urban Development (1965). The Department of Housing and Urban Development (HUD), with the endorsement of both the Kennedy and the Johnson administrations, was created in 1965 to provide housing assistance for low-income citizens and to address a decline in the nation's urban infrastructure. Robert Weaver, the first African American cabinet member in history, served as the first secretary.

Controversial from the start, HUD administrated fair housing practices, rental supplements, public housing, and homebuyer assistance. During the Reagan years, HUD experienced budget reductions and corruption scandals. George H. W. Bush and Bill Clinton, however, presided over expansions of HUD programs. Bush's HUD secretary, Jack Kemp, spearheaded initiatives to revitalize the inner city. Congress and the Clinton administration furthered Kemp's ideas while expanding HUD oversight of housing discrimination. In 1992, HUD also began a controversial program to turn public housing projects into mixed-income developments.

American homeownership reached a historic high in 2000, but the burst of the U.S. housing bubble in 2008 brought HUD under close scrutiny. Thousands of homeowners with subprime mortgages underwritten by government-backed lenders discovered themselves saddled with loans far exceeding their home values. During the ensuing wave of foreclosures, HUD's role in encouraging higher risk lending garnered heavy criticism.

In response to the U.S. housing and global financial crises, Congress passed the American Recovery and Reinvestment Act (2009). The act contained $13.6 billion for HUD, including public housing modernization projects and community development grants. In an attempt to prevent additional foreclosures, HUD's Federal Housing Administration (FHA) also implemented reforms to make borrowers' mortgage payments more affordable.

Department of Transportation (1966). Established to coordinate the government's labyrinthine transportation policy, the Department of Transportation (DOT) in fact never received broad authority to manage the national transportation system. Various key agencies, such as the National Transportation Safety Board, were made independent of the department's secretary. Despite its narrow authority, DOT played an important role in deregulating the airline, railroad, and trucking industries in the late 1970s and in promulgating new rules for making public facilities handicapped-accessible. DOT oversees the Coast Guard, the Federal Aviation Administration, the Federal Railroad Administration, public mass transit systems, and the nation's highway system.

Department of Energy (1977). The immediate impetus for an energy department was the 1973 Arab oil embargo, which led to the creation in 1974 of two federal agencies, the Energy Research and Development Administration and the Federal Energy Administration, to design and implement a national energy policy. These agencies were consolidated into a Department of Energy in 1977. President Jimmy Carter gave the new department prominence, arguing that it should have broad discretion to address national energy problems. During the late 1970s, the Department of Energy promoted conservation by embracing solar power and other alternative technologies as well as new ways to burn fossil fuels. Federal regulation of energy markets was rolled back during the Reagan years, while Energy secretaries James B. Edwards and Donald P. Hodel promoted nuclear power. The Nuclear Waste Policy Act of 1982 placed the Energy Department at the center of political controversy by giving it responsibility for locating, constructing, and operating sites for the disposal of civilian and military nuclear waste. The department also monitors U.S. energy consumption and promotes new energy technologies.

Department of Education (1979). Given the decentralized structure of the U.S. educational system, the creation of a federal education department was relatively late in coming and highly controversial. When the Department of Education was formed in 1979 with strong backing from the powerful National Education Association, a teachers' union, Congress stipulated that the new department "shall not diminish the responsibility for education which is reserved to the states and local school systems." Lacking a broad mandate to shape education policy, departmental efforts to overhaul American education were routinely frustrated by Congress, and Republican leaders periodically called for dismantling the department altogether. The department administers federal funds to enhance preschool, elementary, and secondary schooling; to educate handicapped children and rehabilitate disabled adults; and to help young adults pay for postsecondary education. In the 1990s, the department became embroiled in debate over "school choice" plans, a proposed national examination for students, and merit standards for teachers.

Department of Veterans' Affairs (1989). Since the Revolutionary War, various government programs were established to assist veterans and their dependents. These programs were scattered among different federal agencies until Congress in 1930 placed them under the control of the Veterans Administration (VA). The VA's resources and functions expanded significantly after World War II, as the number of American veterans soared to 19 million. By the 1980s, more than 27 million Americans were veterans and roughly one-third of the population were dependents and survivors of veterans. Veterans groups lobbied vigorously for the VA's elevation to cabinet status, and the Reagan administration strongly agreed. Although a congressionally mandated report by the National Academy of Public Administration found "no compelling reason" to make the VA a cabinet-level department, lawmakers bowed to political pressure and established a Department of Veterans' Affairs in 1989. In the 1990s, the department won special benefits for Vietnam War and Persian Gulf War veterans suffering illnesses related to exposure to harmful chemicals. Its major responsibilities include oversight of an extensive veteran's health-care system, various benefits programs for veterans and their families, and the maintenance of 147 national military cemeteries.

[*See also* **Conservatism; Conservative Movement; Education Policy: An Overview; Education Policy: Education in Contemporary America; Education Policy: Higher Education; Energy Policy; Environmentalism; Federal Government, Executive Branch: An Overview; Housing Policy, Federal: An Overview; Housing Policy, Federal: Federal Housing Administration; Housing Policy, Federal: Public Housing; Indian Law, Federal; Land Policy, Federal; Medicare and Medicaid; National Education Association; National Institutes of Health; National Park System; Nuclear Power; Public Health: An Overview; Public Health: Surgeon General; Public Health Service, U.S.; Regulatory Agencies, Federal;** *and* **Social Security.**]

BIBLIOGRAPHY

Alexander, Yonah, and Don Musch, eds. *Terrorism and Homeland Security*. Madison: University of Wisconsin Press, 2004.

Bledsoe, W. Craig, and Leslie Rigby. "The Cabinet and Executive Departments." In *Cabinets and Counselors: The President and the Executive Branch*, pp. 73–140. Washington, D.C.: Congressional Quarterly, 1997.

Burke, John P. *The Institutional Presidency*. Baltimore: Johns Hopkins University Press, 1992.

Fenno, Richard. *The President's Cabinet*. Cambridge, Mass.: Harvard University Press, 1959.

Hinsdale, Mary L. *A History of the President's Cabinet*. Ann Arbor, Mich.: G. Wahr, 1911.

Learned, Henry Barrett. *The President's Cabinet: Studies in the Origin, Formation, and Structure of an American Institution*. New Haven, Conn.: Yale University Press, 1912.

Moe, Ronald C. "The President's Cabinet." In *Understanding the Presidency*, edited by James P. Pfiffner and Roger H. Davidson, pp. 136–155. New York: Longman, 1997.

Patterson, Bradley H., Jr. *The President's Cabinet: Issues and Questions*. Washington, D.C.: American Society for Public Administration, 1976.

David L. Herzberg, Daniel J. Tichenor, and Joshua H. Mather

PRESIDENCY, THE

The American presidency, the world's oldest continuous republican chief executive office, is the choicest prize in the nation's political system. It stands at the apex of national and international attention and power. When the framers of the Constitution introduced Article II with the words, "The executive power shall be vested in a President of the United States of America," the word "president" was readily acceptable to the public, having been the title of the presiding officer of the Continental Congress.

The office combines the political and symbolic functions that are ordinarily divided in other countries, so that the president is both chief of state and head of government. The executive function of the office, namely to see that the nation's laws are faithfully carried out, has expanded over the course of two centuries to include vast legislative, judicial, administrative, economic, and diplomatic responsibilities. The president serves also as the commander-in-chief of the armed forces. Since the early twentieth century, presidents have also functioned as the head of their parties, dispensing patronage and shaping party programs. In 1940 Franklin Delano Roosevelt created the Executive Office of the President to bring executive-branch activities under tighter control. Its many subunits, staffed by about 500 people by the 1990s, schedule the president's (and the first lady's) activities, deal with the media, and generally manage the far-flung activities of the office, including everything from advising on economics, scientific, and technological developments and maintaining cabinet records to drug control and safeguarding the codes for deploying nuclear weapons.

Shaping the Presidency in the Early Republic and Beyond. The shaping of the presidency was a troubling issue at the Constitutional Convention of 1787. Some of the delegates favored a plural executive, but James Wilson (1742–1798), a Scottish-born Pennsylvania lawyer and political theorist who deserves to be regarded as the father of the presidency, adamantly argued that only a single executive could give the necessary "energy, dispatch and responsibility to the office." Wilson also insisted that the office be independent of the legislature, have a veto power, and control foreign relations. He also pressed for the direct popular election of the chief executive—a novel idea at the time that continues to win advocates. Late in the Convention, a committee appointed to find an appropriate alternate solution invented a system of electors. Each state would have as many electors as the total number of its representatives and senators, to be chosen by any method on which the state legislature decided. Collectively known as the Electoral College, the arrangement plainly gave an advantage to the large states. Still, it was assumed that in many elections no aspirant would win the required Electoral College majority and that the election would be thrown into the House of Representatives, which would choose the president from the top five (later changed to three) names, with each state having one vote. In fact, only in 1800, 1824, and 1876 were presidential elections decided by the House. Despite the complexity of the Electoral College arrangement, the selection of the president almost from the beginning has been regarded as the equivalent of a popular election. Nevertheless, in the elections of 1876 and 1888, the candidates who polled the most popular votes failed to win the presidency in the Electoral College.

The presidential term was fixed at four years almost as an afterthought, with no limit on reelection. George Washington, Thomas Jefferson, and James Madison retired after two terms, establishing a precedent that stood until Franklin D. Roosevelt won a third term in 1940 and a fourth in 1944, although Ulysses S. Grant in 1880 and Theodore Roosevelt in 1912 had sought third terms. The Twenty-second Amendment (1951), in a kind of posthumous rebuke to FDR, limited presidents constitutionally to two terms. Other amendments have also modified the original presidency: the Twelfth (1804) required the Electoral College to vote separately for president and vice president to avoid the confusion that marred the election of 1800;

the Nineteenth (1919) altered the voter base by granting the ballot to women and the Twenty-sixth (1971) altered it further by enfranchising eighteen-year-olds; the Twentieth (1933) moved inauguration day from 4 March to 20 January; the Twenty-third (1961) gave electoral votes to the District of Columbia; the Twenty-fourth (1964) forbade the imposition of a poll tax on voters in presidential elections; and the Twenty-fifth (1967), in the aftermath of President Dwight D. Eisenhower's major illnesses while in office, set forth procedures to be followed in case of presidential disability. The recurring idea of a single fixed presidential term is of long standing. Andrew Jackson in his State of the Union messages repeatedly called for a single, six-year term.

The strong presidency provided for in the Constitution owed much to the expectation that George Washington would inaugurate the office. One delegate wrote, "I do [not] believe the [executive powers] would be so great had not many of the members cast their eyes toward General Washington as President; and shaped their Ideas of the Powers to be given a President, by their opinions of his Virtues." Washington, keenly aware that he was the first national president in history, knew that he would be setting precedents by almost everything he did, including choosing the heads of the executive departments—then state, treasury, war, and attorney general—and making of them a cabinet, an extraconstitutional institution. On formal occasions he received guests while standing on a raised platform and wearing a sword and did not shake hands during his time in office. Still, neither he nor the American people desired a monarchy. After considerable discussion in Congress and elsewhere as to how to address him, including one suggestion that he be called "His Highness the President of the United States of America and Protector of their Liberties," the simple phrase "President of the United States" was deemed sufficient. When Washington left office in 1797, he created the matchless tradition that an elected executive departs on schedule, and all of his successors have followed suit, so that the fact seems ordinary when in fact it is extraordinary. As his successor, John Adams, wrote to his wife on his inauguration day, "The sight of the sun setting and another rising (though less splendid) was a novelty."

The third president, Thomas Jefferson, although a slaveholder, brought to the office a democratic manner that seemed better befitting to a republic. He walked to his inauguration, shook hands freely, and forbade presidential birthday celebrations. In greeting people at the newly completed "President's House" (later called the White House), he took no account of differences in rank or prestige. His style, with many additions and variations, in time became the norm of presidential behavior. Democratization and responsiveness to public opinion constantly brought the chief executive closer to the public: Andrew Jackson was the first "man of the people," winning a national constituency with supporters in every section of the country; Abraham Lincoln was metamorphosed in affectionate parlance from "Honest Abe," when he was the Republican candidate, to "Father Abraham," when he became the embattled Union's war leader; and Theodore Roosevelt came to be "Teddy"—a nickname immortalized in the Teddy Bear. Franklin D. Roosevelt entered America's homes via radio "fireside chats." Dwight D. Eisenhower in the same spirit allowed his news conferences to be televised; James Earl Carter made himself officially Jimmy Carter; William Jefferson Clinton, known everywhere as Bill Clinton, opened the White House email address to the public. In the later twentieth century, however, the tight security imposed by the U.S. Secret Service (a division of the

Treasury Department), the trappings of what some called "the imperial presidency," symbolized by the giant presidential jet, Air Force One, and the vast entourage accompanying the president on every trip, tended to make these populist gestures more a matter of public relations than of participatory democracy.

The Presidency and Party Politics. Until 1824, presidential and vice presidential nominees were selected by congressional leaders meeting in secret—later public—sessions called caucuses. Attacked as undemocratic, "King Caucus" was replaced by national nominating conventions, introduced by the Anti-Masonic Party in 1831 and adopted by the two major parties in 1836. Now meeting quadrennially in the summertime, the conventions of the Democratic and Republican parties, consisting of 1,100 to 1,800 delegates chosen at the state level by primary elections, convention, or committees, nominate their candidates by majority vote. Until 1936, however, the Democratic Party required a two-thirds majority. Thus it took the Democrats 46 ballots to nominate Woodrow Wilson in 1912 and 103 ballots to agree upon John W. Davis in 1924. Not since 1952, however, has a major party proceeded past the first ballot to select a candidate, and the television networks no longer offer gavel-to-gavel coverage of the extravaganzas.

The parties have ranged widely in their selection of presidential nominees: from governors and former governors (the Democrats' Adlai Stevenson in 1952 and 1956 and the Republicans' Ronald Reagan in 1980 and George W. Bush in 2000) to war heroes (the Whig Party's William Henry Harrison in 1840 and Zachary Taylor in 1848 and the Republicans' Ulysses S. Grant in 1868 and Dwight D. Eisenhower in 1952) and the Senate (the Republicans' Warren G. Harding in 1920 and the Democrats' John F. Kennedy in 1960).

As presidential election campaigns moved to the center of national political attention, they became filled with hoopla that included catchy songs and slogans, parades with marching bands, election eve bonfires, and cruising sound trucks. Some rallying cries are embedded in the national memory: *Tippecanoe and Tyler Too* (1840), *The Full Dinner Pail* (1900), *He Kept Us Out of War* (1916), *Keep Cool with Coolidge* (1924), *No Third Term* (1940), *I Like Ike* (1952), and *Nixon's the One* (1972). When the twenty-first century dawned, there was growing public concern over the astronomical cost of presidential campaigns, the methods used to raise the required money, and the role of attack ads and superficial sound bites in television-dominated campaigns.

Presidential Succession; Impeachment; First Ladies. Eight vice presidents have succeeded to the presidency upon the death or assassination of the president: John Tyler (1841), Millard Fillmore (1850), Andrew Johnson (1865), Chester A. Arthur (1881), Theodore Roosevelt (1901), Calvin Coolidge (1923), Harry S. Truman (1945), and Lyndon B. Johnson (1963). When Richard M. Nixon resigned in the wake of the Watergate scandal—the first resignation in the history of the office—he was succeeded by Gerald Ford (1974). Ford in 1973 in accordance with the Twenty-fifth Amendment had been named by President Nixon—and confirmed by Congress—to succeed Vice President Spiro T. Agnew, who had been forced to resign amid bribery and tax-evasion charges. Ford, as president, selected Nelson A. Rockefeller to be vice president, giving the nation for the first time not only a president but also a vice president who were not elected. The line of succession to the presidency after the vice president was established by law in 1947: the Speaker of the House, the president pro tempore of the Senate, and the members of the cabinet in order of the creation of their department, beginning with the secretary of state. Under the constitutional provision for the removal of presidents, vice presidents, and other ranking federal officers by impeachment and trial, Andrew Johnson (1868) and Bill Clinton (1999) were impeached by the House of Representatives for "high crimes and misdemeanors" but found not guilty by the Senate.

The role of the president's wife—the designation "First Lady" was not used until the Civil War era—has sometimes made the presidency seem like a two-person position. Among the best known spouses have been Martha Dandridge Custis Washington, an involved helpmate of the General; Dolley Payne Madison, who served as Jefferson's hostess in the White House and subsequently her husband's as well; Sarah Childress Polk, whose political savvy was legendary; Edith Galt Wilson, the president's second wife, who jealously guarded his privacy and even took over some of his duties after he was incapacitated by a stroke in October 1919, so that she is sometimes regarded as the "first woman president"; Eleanor Roosevelt, whose constant travels made her FDR's "eyes and ears"; Jacqueline Bouvier Kennedy, whose grace and charm made her a national icon; Rosalynn Smith Carter, who sat in cabinet meetings and conducted diplomacy unofficially for the president; Nancy Davis Reagan, who was a dominant political force in the Reagan White House; and Hillary Rodham Clinton, whose powerful place in her husband's administration appeared to fulfill Clinton's campaign assertion that his election would give the nation "two-for-one" and in 2000 won election to the U.S. Senate from New York.

George W. Bush, elected in 2001, was only the second son of a president (his father was George H. W. Bush, who served from 1989 to 1993) to reside in the White House on his own. The first had been John Adams's, John Quincy Adams (1825–1829). Bush's opponent was the then Vice President Albert Gore, who won over half a million more votes than Bush. The final outcome of the election, resting on the assignment of Florida's electoral votes, was settled in a 5-to-4 decision by the Supreme Court. This was only the second presidential election handled outside the normal way. The first was the election of 1876 that brought Rutherford B. Hayes to office through the decision of a bipartisan commission. Bush is remembered most for the costly long war against Iraq, which he started in 2003 without the consent of Congress. His aim was to dethrone Saddam Hussein, the Iraq dictator, who he said he believed was secreting away weapons of mass destruction designed to dominate neighboring states. Bush did not deal effectively with the economy, which was in serious crisis before he left office. He departed with a low public judgment of his labors. His successor was Barack Obama, the first president of African American background. He aimed to stimulate the economy and reduce the rising rate of unemployment he had inherited. Through his involvement, and working closely with a Democratic-controlled Congress, a major overhaul of the health care system was undertaken, which drew major, although divided, public opposition. At the midterm election in 2010 he suffered a heavy defeat, losing Democratic control of the House of Representatives and Democratic seats in the Senate. A major question facing him and likely his successors is how to reduce the frighteningly high deficit of the U.S. government.

[*See also* **Clinton, Hillary Rodham; Constitution; Constitutional Convention of 1787; Elections: Election Law; Elections: Presidential Elections; Federal Government, Executive Branch: An Overview; Federal Government, Legislative Branch: House of Representatives; Federal Government,**

Legislative Branch: Senate; Political Parties; Presidential Assassinations; Presidential Debates; Presidential Impeachments; Presidential Primaries; Roosevelt, Eleanor; Veto Power; *and entries on individual presidents.*]

BIBLIOGRAPHY

DeGregorio, William. *The Complete Book of U.S. Presidents: From George Washington to Bill Clinton,* rev. ed. New York: Random House, 1993.

Graff, Henry F., ed. *The Presidents: A Reference History,* 2d ed. New York: Charles Scribner's Sons, 1996.

Hess, Stephen. *Organizing the Presidency,* 2d ed. Washington, D.C.: Brookings Institution, 1988.

Kunhardt, Philip B., Jr., Philip B. Kunhardt III, and Peter W. Kunhardt, eds. *The American President.* New York: Riverhead Books, 1999.

Levy, Leonard W., and Louis Fisher, eds. *Encyclopedia of the American Presidency,* 4 vols. New York: Simon & Schuster, 1994.

Neustadt, Richard E. *Presidential Power and the Modern Presidents: The Politics of Leadership from Roosevelt to Reagan,* 4th ed. New York: Free Press, 1990.

Pious, Richard. *The Presidency.* Boston: Allyn & Bacon, 1996.

Seale, William. *The President's House,* 2 vols. Washington, D.C.: White House Historical Association, 1986.

Schlesinger, Arthur M., Jr., et al., eds. *Running for President: The Candidates and Their Images,* 2 vols. New York: Simon & Schuster, 1994.

Henry F. Graff

STATE DEPARTMENT

The State Department began as something of an institutional anomaly. It was patterned on the British government's secretary of state for foreign affairs, but had no counterpart comparable to the British secretary for domestic affairs. The department's early history reflected the revolutionary generation's ambivalent attitude toward formal diplomacy. Only with great reluctance had the Continental Congress created a professional diplomatic corps. This meager political backing translated into a weak support structure for the conduct of early American foreign policy. Poor communication between the secretary of state James Monroe and U.S. diplomats in London helped bring on the War of 1812. Monroe's successor at the State Department, John Quincy Adams, lacking a clerical staff, had to transcribe three copies of the Adams–Onís Treaty himself. Later, Adams's uncertainty over whether to recognize Brazil was complicated by the fact that no one in his employ could translate Portuguese.

If ill-equipped to handle foreign relations, the State Department from the first became enmeshed in partisan politics, with the wars of the French Revolutionary Era providing an early flashpoint. Whereas the first secretary of state, Thomas Jefferson, favored the French, the Treasury secretary Alexander Hamilton advocated a pro-British neutrality. Hamilton's triumph in this dispute helped give rise to the first party system, while also anticipating the department's later struggles to control foreign policy. As revolutionary passions faded, the department evolved into something of an incubator for presidents. Three successive secretaries of states—James Madison, James Monroe, and John Quincy Adams—rose to the presidency.

Whereas Adams's appointment of the westerner Henry Clay as secretary of state in 1825 marked the end of the first cycle of American diplomacy, the election of Andrew Jackson in 1828 began an interval in which the State Department was weaker than at perhaps any other time in U.S. history. It also suffered appalling organizational deficiencies. During a diplomatic crisis with Peru in the early 1850s, for example, departmental staff took several months to find a crucial memorandum documenting an agreement the secretary of state Daniel Webster had reached with the Peruvians over offshore island guano rights.

Abraham Lincoln's appointment of William Seward as secretary of state in 1861 helped resolve these related problems of inefficiency and low prestige. Seward initiated an efficient indexing system, regional responsibilities for staff members, and the publication of diplomatic documents in the *Foreign Relations of the United States series.* Appointing a talented diplomatic corps, Seward pursued a risky but successful strategy of preventing European intervention in the Civil War. Seward's tenure, however, also saw the emergence of a pattern of congressional thwarting of State Department initiatives. Congress stymied Seward's attempts to purchase the Danish West Indies and the efforts of his successor, Hamilton Fish (1869–1877), to annex the Dominican Republic.

The State Department, meanwhile, had developed a two-tier culture in which the consular service endured low pay and poor working conditions, whereas top diplomats were appointed for patronage reasons or their social connections. With 80 percent of secretaries of state having served in Europe and most still coming from privileged backgrounds, the department became an inviting target for congressional critics who denounced its "elitism" and demanded less exclusionary recruitment policies. Their crusade culminated in the Rogers Act of 1924, which established a professional foreign service with improved pay, retirement benefits, and tenure provisions, while combining the diplomatic and consular services.

On substantive foreign policy issues, Secretaries of State James G. Blaine (1881, 1889–1892), John Hay (1898–1905), and Elihu Root (1905–1909) skillfully promoted the nation's turn-of-the-century emergence as a world power. President Woodrow Wilson pleased the Democratic Party's agrarian wing by appointing William Jennings Bryan as secretary of state in 1913, but the pacifist Bryan, unhappy over the belligerence of Wilson's protests of German U-boat attacks, resigned in 1915. His successor Robert Lansing proved ineffectual because Wilson, advised by Colonel Edward M. House, essentially acted as his own secretary of state, an approach imitated by other strong presidents.

Despite congressional criticism, the State Department regained prestige in the 1920s, but the freewheeling presidential style of Franklin Delano Roosevelt again lessened the department's influence, even as the number of State Department personnel swelled from under 2,000 in 1940 to more than 16,000 by 1950.

The lawyer and career diplomat Dean Acheson, secretary of state from 1949 to 1953, played a major role in shaping America's Cold War policy—a policy built upon the containment doctrine proposed in 1946 by U.S. diplomat George Kennan. But the department faced problems as well. Accusations of disloyalty against State Department officials, including Acheson and the respected George Marshall (secretary of state from 1947 to 1949), leveled by Wisconsin senator Joseph McCarthy and others, demoralized departmental personnel. Meanwhile, the department's policy-making role was challenged by such newly created entities as the Department of Defense, Joint Chiefs of Staff, Central Intelligence Agency, National Security Council, and the National Security Advisor. Indeed, during the presidencies of John F. Kennedy and Lyndon B. Johnson, each of these agencies exerted more influence than did the State Department under Dean Rusk (1961–1969), whereas Henry Kissinger exerted great influence as President Richard M. Nixon's national security advisor before himself becoming secretary of state in 1973.

In the post–Cold War Era, the State Department again became a target of congressional criticism, this time from nationalists who saw it as insufficiently tough in the war on terror. This period also brought a series of personnel breakthroughs. In 1997, President Bill Clinton appointed the first woman secretary of state, Madeleine K. Albright; four years later, President George W. Bush named the first African American secretary of state, Colin Powell. Powell's successor, Condoleezza Rice (2005–2009), helped restore the U.S. position internationally while proving an effective bureaucratic infighter against neoconservatives headed by the vice president, Richard Cheney.

After his election in 2008, President Barack Obama embraced the nineteenth-century precedent of secretaries of state who possessed independent political standing. He nominated as the nation's top diplomat the runner-up for that year's Democratic presidential nomination, New York Senator Hillary Clinton.

[*See also* **Adams, John Quincy; Blaine, James G.; Bryan, William Jennings; Clay, Henry; Clinton, Hillary Rodham; Jefferson, Thomas; Madison, James; Monroe, James; National Security Council;** *and* **Webster, Daniel.**]

BIBLIOGRAPHY

De Santis, Hugh. *Diplomacy of Silence: The American Foreign Service, the Soviet Union, and the Cold War, 1933–1947*. Chicago: University of Chicago Press, 1980.

Bemis, Samuel Flagg, ed. *American Secretaries of State and Their Diplomacy*, 10 vols. New York: Alfred A. Knopf, 1963.

Henrichs, Waldo. *American Ambassador: Joseph Grew and the Development of the United States Diplomatic Tradition*. Boston: Little, Brown, 1966.

Simpson, Smith. *Anatomy of the State Department*. Boston: Houghton Mifflin, 1967.

U.S. Department of State, Office of the Historian. http://history.state.gov (accessed 7 October 2011).

Robert David Johnson

TREASURY DEPARTMENT

Alexander Hamilton, the first secretary of the treasury, said that most of the important measures of the government are connected with the Treasury Department. That was as true at the beginning of the twenty-first century as it was in Hamilton's time. From its Revolutionary War beginnings to the present, the department has played a key role in the nation's development. The secretary of the Treasury is the president's senior economic adviser and supervises the operation of an executive department that has served the nation with distinction since 1789.

The demands of effective financial administration forced the Continental Congress and then the U.S. Congress to overcome their misgivings about delegating the power of the purse. Accordingly, on 2 September 1789, Congress created the Treasury Department under the direction of a secretary, to be aided by a Comptroller (the superintendent of accounts), an Auditor (the certifier of accounts), a Register (the keeper of accounts), a Treasurer (in charge of receiving and disbursing funds), and a general assistant.

On 11 September 1789, Alexander Hamilton began his tenure as secretary and instituted an economic program that included proposals for funding the nation's debt, establishing a central bank, augmenting internal revenues, and promoting domestic industry. Hamilton's program, which envisioned an urban-based, manufacturing economy, proved controversial, as did his penchant for wielding his power over the budgets of other government departments to influence their policies.

Hamilton's successor, Albert Gallatin—the longest-serving secretary (1801–1813) in Treasury history—was an active crusader for government economy, which brought him into frequent conflict with other department heads. (The Treasury's control over government estimates and expenditures under Hamilton and Gallatin anticipated the function of the Office of Management and Budget today.) Thanks largely to Gallatin's economies, the Treasury employed fewer people in 1826 than in 1801. Customs duties and land sales generated sufficient revenue to retire the national debt by 1834 and, in most years before the Civil War, to generate a surplus that was refunded to the states. A growing national economy and a budget-minded government combined to make possible the elimination of excise taxes on products like whiskey and jewelry, while reducing the size of the Treasury Department itself.

From the beginning, the Treasury Department spawned subsidiary agencies and functions. The Post Office Department, originally under Treasury supervision, gained autonomy in 1829; the General Land Office left the Treasury to become part of the new Interior Department in 1849. At one time or another, the Public Health Service, the Bureau of Narcotics, and the Supervisory Architect of the United States operated under the Treasury's umbrella.

The Treasury has always functioned as the collector of customs duties. From the fleet of ten small ships authorized by Hamilton to enforce the customs laws evolved the U.S. Coast Guard, the oldest seagoing branch of the military, whose functions were transferred to the Department of Transportation in 1967.

The National Currency Act of 1863, designed to end the chaos associated with the distribution of private bank notes and to help finance the Civil War, created an Office of the Comptroller of the Currency within the Treasury Department to administer a system of national banks authorized to distribute a uniform national currency. (The Treasury relinquished most of its monetary responsibilities to the newly created Federal Reserve System in 1913.) The U.S. Secret Service was founded in 1865 to protect the money supply against counterfeiters; later, the agency acquired responsibility for protecting the president and vice president and candidates for those offices. (In 2002, the Secret Service became part of the Department of Homeland Security.) Until the creation of the Federal Bureau of Investigation in 1935, the Secret Service was the government's principal general law enforcement agency.

The financial pressures of the Civil War led to a sweeping taxation program, including the first federal income tax, administered by a Commissioner of Internal Revenue under the secretary of the Treasury. Many these taxes lapsed after the war, but the Sixteenth Amendment to the Constitution (1913) authorizing a federal income tax brought the Internal Revenue Service back to life. Enforcement of the 1919 Volstead Act, prohibiting the sale of alcoholic beverages, also fell to the Treasury. The unit created to combat liquor trafficking eventually evolved into the Bureau of Alcohol, Tobacco, and Firearms.

The Great Depression caused hundreds of banks to fail and in 1933 led newly inaugurated President Franklin Delano Roosevelt to declare a bank holiday to stop the panic. The Treasury then supervised the reopening of the solvent banks and the orderly liquidation or reorganization of the others.

U.S. involvement in both World War I and World War II was partly financed by the sale of government bonds under Treasury supervision. The Defense Bond campaigns of World War II, modeled on the Liberty Bond drives of World War I, raised $211 billion, or about two-thirds of the war's total cost. (U.S. savings bonds, administered by the Treasury Department's Bureau of Public Debt, are a direct offshoot of the wartime bond program.) An influential function of the Treasury during both wars was the implementation of freeze orders on enemy assets under the 1917 Trading with the Enemy Act.

After the 1944 Bretton Woods Conference established a new international monetary system, Treasury secretary Henry Morgenthau Jr., was named chairman of the Board of Governors of both the International Bank for Reconstruction and Development (the World Bank) and the International Monetary Fund. In 1959, Treasury spearheaded the creation of the Inter-American Development Bank to promote economic development in Latin America.

Later, the Treasury assisted a succession of presidential administrations in addressing the problems of inflation, unemployment, negative trade balances, and rising federal deficits. In the early 1990s, the Treasury played an important role in the negotiations that led to the North American Free Trade Agreement (NAFTA), which advanced regional economic integration and growth.

During the final years of the twentieth century and the early years of the twenty-first century, the Treasury confronted episodes of acute financial and economic instability. The savings and loan crisis of the 1980s was followed by a crisis in commercial banking, with many financial institution failures. The end of the "dot.com" bubble and the terrorist attacks of 2001 roiled U.S. and global financial markets. The collapsing market for residential real estate triggered the economic crisis of 2008–2009 and a protracted global recession.

Working closely with Congress and the Federal Reserve, the Treasury helped stabilize the financial system. The Troubled Asset Relief Program (TARP) recapitalized shaky banks, whereas other programs helped ease the impact of home-mortgage foreclosures, provide jobs and infrastructure reinvestment, revive private-sector lending to businesses and consumers, and restructure the financial system. The Dodd–Frank Wall Street Reform and Consumer Protection Act of 2010, which toughened regulatory standards for financial institutions, created new mechanisms for detecting and correcting problems in the financial economy—an effort in which the Treasury Department will continue to play a key role.

[*See also* **Continental Congress; Economic Development; Economic Policy: Banking and Financial Regulation; Eighteenth Amendment; Federal Government, Executive Branch: An Overview; Federal Reserve Act; Federal Reserve System; Hamilton, Alexander; Income Tax, Federal; Land Policy, Federal; Monetary Policy; New Deal; North American Free Trade Agreement; Postal Service, U.S.; Prohibition; Public Health Service, U.S.; Roosevelt, Franklin Delano; Sixteenth Amendment; Tariffs;** *and* **Taxation.**]

BIBLIOGRAPHY

Katz, Bernard S., and C. Daniel Vencill, eds. *Biographical Dictionary of United States Secretaries of the Treasury*. Westport, Conn.: Greenwood Press, 1996.

The Department of the Treasury. Washington, D.C.: Office of Information, Department of the Treasury, 1969.

Taus, Esther Rogoff. *Central Banking Functions of the United States Treasury*. New York: Columbia University Press, 1943.

White, Leonard D. *The Federalists: A Study in Administrative History*. New York: Free Press, 1965.

Jesse Stiller

FEDERAL GOVERNMENT, JUDICIAL BRANCH

The American federal judiciary was authorized by Article III of the U.S. Constitution, which states that "the judicial Power of the United States shall be vested in one supreme court, and in such inferior Courts as the Congress may from time to time ordain and establish." The Judiciary Act of 1789 established a six-member Supreme Court and enough district courts to match existing state boundaries. Court justices were assigned in pairs to travel along regional circuits throughout the various states to hear trials with a local district judge. State courts shared jurisdiction and enjoyed considerable reserved powers. For the first half century, state judiciaries were held in greater esteem than their federal counterparts. The duties of the circuit court system were physically exhausting and the voluntary turnover was high. The Supreme Court went through three chief justices and five associates between 1789 and 1801, with average terms lasting less than five years.

The federal judiciary has experienced significant change since its origins in the 1790s, yet it also retains remarkable continuity. One reason for the continuity is the Court's independence from direct involvement in political debate. Article III specified lifelong tenures and guaranteed salaries for federal judges to ensure an independent judiciary. The Court has also intentionally limited itself to actual cases rather than get involved with "advisory opinions" that necessarily reflect political interests. In addition, the Court's primary authority of judicial review guarantees the Court's freedom from inappropriate pressures from Congress or the president's office. First articulated by Alexander Hamilton in Federalist No. 78 and later affirmed by the landmark case *Marbury v. Madison* (1801), judicial review empowers the Court with the right to declare acts of Congress unconstitutional and to compel compliance within the executive branch. The authority to rule state laws unconstitutional was affirmed by *Fletcher v. Peck* (1810), but like *Marbury,* the decision codified theories held by most legal theorists of the time.

The strong tradition of judicial independence does not mean that the federal courts are detached from political influences. The congressional power to impeach combined with the appointment privileges of governing parties ensures that the court is always bound by the general ebb and flow of political tensions. The combination of independence and political sensitivity has enabled the federal judiciary system to both echo the changing priorities of public discourse and still influence the course of those changes.

From its origins, the Supreme Court was embroiled in the political tensions. President John Adams's decision to support the Alien and Sedition Acts of 1798 plagued the first court. Jefferson charged the sitting justices with using the laws to squelch political dissent and he rallied the public in opposition leading to the first peaceful transition of power between parties in 1801. For a decade, Federalist justices faced repeated impeachment charges from the new president and his Congressional majority. Meanwhile, state legislatures in Kentucky and Virginia passed resolutions to limit the judiciary's ability to review state legislative acts. Other lawmakers sought to limit the Court's ability to handle cases between persons of multiple states, because that authority forced state judiciaries to follow outside rulings.

The Court survived these assaults under the leadership of its fourth chief justice, John Marshall. From 1801 to 1835, the Marshall Court elevated the power and authority of the court by carefully crafting an image of unanimity on the bench. Justices might disagree, but Marshall delivered all opinions. He used the Court to strengthen the union and protect the rights of individual property owners. Marshall's famous *Marbury* and *Fletcher* decisions affirming the doctrine of judicial review were followed by *McCulloch v. Maryland* (1819), which laid the foundations for federal supremacy in relation to state powers. *McCulloch* established the doctrine of implied powers with its interpretation of the final clause of Article I, Section 8, which authorizes Congress "to make all laws which shall be necessary and proper for carrying into execution the forgoing powers, and all other powers vested by this Constitution in the government of the United States." The framers held two views on this clause: Jefferson argued the word "necessary" should be strictly defined to mean only those laws that were indispensible for maintaining the enumerated powers. Hamilton adopted a broad interpretation, which allowed Congress greater latitude. The *McCulloch* decision allowing Congress the power to charter a federal bank despite the fact that such a power was not explicitly mentioned in the Constitution codified Hamilton's interpretation. This ruling not only opened a centuries-long debate among legal scholars over the extent of "implied powers," but also by ruling against a state government the *McCulloch* case established the primacy of federal action over state action. This authority was reaffirmed by *Gibbons v. Ogden* (1824), which interpreted the power to "regulate Commerce with foreign nations, and among the several States" clause as a justification for federal regulation over state affairs.

Marshall was arguably the greatest influence in the Court's history, but he was followed by another chief justice who was almost equally significant. Chief Justice Roger Taney was appointed by President Andrew Jackson and served for twenty-eight years. He was joined by four other Jackson appointees, resulting in a Southern-dominated Court right up to the final days of the Civil War. Taney articulated Jackson's vision of popular empowerment by promoting the public welfare over individual benefit and protecting state's rights. As Jackson's attorney general, Taney drafted the veto message killing the third national bank and he maintained a preference for state sovereignty throughout his tenure. Equally important was Taney's promotion of "community interest." Taney's decision against a private corporation in *Charles River Bridge v. Warren Bridge* (1837) argued that the community must prevail when the interests of the public competed with the interests of private property.

Despite the new ideological tendency, the power and prestige of the Court expanded with the physical dimensions of the union and was generally respected in much the same fashion as it had been under Marshall. Unfortunately, the Taney Court is forever tainted by his infamous *Dred Scott v. Sanford* decision of 1857. The landmark case not only deprived African Americans of all rights of constitutional due process, but also elevated the state's authority in determining property rights above those of Congress and other states (thereby nullifying any free state's prohibitions against slavery). Most significant is that Taney did not have to address the slavery issue in his disposition. The first conclusion of the Court held that blacks (free or slave) could never gain American citizenship and thus had no right to file a complaint in federal court. Nevertheless, in an attempt to resolve a paralyzing national issue, the Taney Court added other conclusions that held the Missouri Compromise forged by Congress thirty-seven years earlier to be unconstitutional because Congress had no power to regulate slaveholding in the territories. Rather than resolve the issue, the decision led to an increasingly bitter political climate. This assertion of the Court's power was a fundamental error that cost the Court every bit of prestige it had accrued since Marshall. For the next half century, *Dred Scott* was held up as a *prima facie* (legally sufficient) example for sitting justices for why the Court should remove itself from deeply controversial political questions.

After the Civil War unionist lawmakers threatened to reorganized the federal judiciary and strip it of specific jurisdiction, especially in connection with newly reconstructed territories. Part of the *Dred Scott* decision relied on Fifth Amendment protections of due process to guarantee slaveholders their property rights regardless of where they lived. It was in reaction to Taney and *Dred* that Republican lawmakers pushed for the ratification of the Thirteenth, Fourteenth, and Fifteenth Amendments abolishing slavery, guaranteeing citizenship and due process regardless of race, and mandating universal male suffrage. Fortunately for the independence of the Court, Taney died in 1864 and the new leadership under abolitionist Salmon Chase strongly supported the Congressional right to impose rigid requirements over the readmission of rebel states into the union. *Texas v. White* (1869) legitimized Reconstruction, and the Supreme Court was left untouched by Republican lawmakers. For its part, the Court voluntarily limited its reach during the next three decades.

The Civil War changed the nature of the federal judiciary at many levels. Beyond the obvious affirmation of equal rights regardless of race, the Fourteenth Amendment's guarantee of due process was critical in establishing the federal Court's authority to review state decisions and to compel compliance in a variety of regulatory issues. Originally drafted to compel state recognition of racial equity in the South during Reconstruction, the protection was quickly reverted back to a protection for federal commerce and private enterprise. During the White, Taft, and Hughes Courts, due process was used in several cases to oppose expansive state labor laws. It was not until after World War II that the Warren Court reclaimed due process guarantees as a tool for compelling massive changes in state and local jurisdiction with regard to race, free speech, and criminal due process. At the time of Reconstruction, however, the Court restrained its use of these added powers and generally maintained the primacy of state courts in deciding local matters.

The emotional fervor for Reconstruction gradually faded and the policy ended after the Hayes–Tilden Compromise of 1877. Most of the northern lawmakers shifted their attention to issues around the growing industrialized economy. The federal courts followed suit by easing prerogatives over Southern states' interpretations of civil rights. In 1883, the Court ruled in *Civil Rights Cases* that segregation in private facilities was outside the purview of federal regulation. This doctrine was more fully articulated a dozen years later in the now infamous *Plessy v. Ferguson* (1896), which asserted the "separate but equal" doctrine affirming legal segregation. With *Williams v. Mississippi* (1898) the Southern states successfully reasserted their autonomy over racial issues. On paper, the Court presupposed each state's good faith attempt to faithfully apply civil rights protections, even when the massive disenfranchisement rates among Southern blacks gave obvious evidence to the contrary. In practice, the Court refocused its attention to questions related to interstate corporations, labor relations, and the power to regulate monopolies and trusts.

The Civil War proved significant in other structural ways. The admission of each new western state greatly increased the demands on each justice, who were still expected to sit over circuit court trials. Congress earlier expanded the size of the court to seven members (1807) and then again to nine members (1837) to account for the new admissions, but each member was still expected to physically travel to hear circuit court cases. The admission of California prior to a reliable transcontinental railroad forced Congress to appoint additional circuit court judgeships, but justices were still required periodically to preside over trial. Many lawmakers feared that Supreme Court justices were gradually losing touch with the practical needs of the public. A physical presence at the district level helped tether the justices to political changes.

It was not until 1911, during the midst of the Progressive Era, that the Supreme Court finally shed its circuit court duties entirely. By that time, the Supreme Court had changed. The Marshall/Taney model of apparent unanimity on the bench was replaced by a new model of ideological balance. Dynamic tension between mild *laissez-faire* advocates (Chief Justices White and William Taft) and the progressive voices for labor, community welfare, and free speech (Oliver Wendell Holmes Jr., and Louis Brandeis) restored a more mature sort of relevance to the federal judiciary. The Court leaned mostly toward *laissez-faire,* but newly articulated dissenting opinions gained increasing relevance. For example, *Lochner v. New York* (1905) interpreted the due process clause to protect the rights of employers to establish their own work schedules, thereby stripping from states the power to regulate working conditions. Yet, Oliver Wendell Holmes's dissenting opinion soon became the primary reference cited by the Court for subsequent labor-relations cases.

The increase in federal cases involving minimum wage, maximum workloads, woman and child labor laws, and World War I antiespionage laws once again thrust the Court into politically charged issues. Progressive lawmakers often reacted strongly to *laissez-faire* preference for property rights and corporation. New plans emerged for a constitutional amendment allowing Congress to overturn Court decisions, as well as term limits and elections for federal judges. These measures were unsuccessful during the constant economic growth of the 1920s, but the political antagonism found greater force during the 1930s when the Court overturned several New Deal measures.

President Roosevelt faced Chief Justice Charles Evans Hughes and a majority of associates who had been appointed by his Republican predecessors, Warren Harding, Calvin Coolidge, and Herbert Hoover. The Hughes court struck two New Deal cornerstones (the Agricultural Adjustment Act and the National Industrial Recovery Act) and ruled against numerous labor issues. After his successful 1936 election, Roosevelt proposed a judicial reorganization plan that would allow the President to appoint additional judges for each sitting member over the age of seventy. Since six of the nine members of the Court were overage (including Chief Justice Hughes), the new plan would allow Roosevelt to appoint an entirely new majority to the Court.

Public reaction was decidedly negative. The federal government and its judiciary were significantly larger than they had ever been. Lawmakers and jurists from both sides of the aisle rejected the proposal as a court-packing scheme and the Court emerged slightly more powerful. Fortunately for Roosevelt, many of the Coolidge/Hoover era justices retired shortly thereafter and he was able to appoint his new majority after all.

An important turning point in extending power of the federal judiciary came after World War II when Earl Warren was appointed chief justice in 1953. The Warren court presided over a series of landmark cases that permanently altered the manner by which constitutional due process is interpreted at the state and local levels. Justice Warren was not particularly known for civil rights prior to his appointment—he was a former governor of California known for being tough on organized crime and was the principle proponent behind the evacuation of Japanese Americans during World War II. Yet as chief justice, Warren became better known for *Brown v. Board of Education* (1954), *Mapp v. Ohio* (1961), *Miranda v. Arizona* (1966), and *Griswold v. Connecticut* (1965), which modern historians sometime refer to as the "due process revolution."

What distinguishes the Warren Court from its predecessors is that so many of its landmark cases resulted in massive changes in practice and procedure and the local level. The *Brown* decision overturned *Plessy* and was one of several cases leading to the eventual elimination of segregation in the South. It symbolized the launch of a new generation of grassroots civil rights movements. Likewise, the *Mapp* decision was one of several to establish the "exclusionary" doctrine compelling judges to exclude evidence obtained through unconstitutional means—effective for the day-to-day evidence-gathering practices of law enforcement at all levels (local, state and federal). The *Miranda* case is famous for the "Miranda warnings," which every arresting officer must recite to ensure voluntary testimony. The *Griswold* case established an entirely new doctrine of substantive due process, which not only legalized contraceptives but also eventually led to the legalization of abortion under *Roe v. Wade* (1973). Since the 1970s, both political parties often define their positions on social issues based on their support or opposition to practical application of these cases.

The Warren Court's willingness to engage in controversial social issues was not without critics. New generations of political opponents argue that unelected federal judiciary should not decide issues that have not decided by publicly elected state and federal legislatures. Since the 1970s, lawmakers debate harm or value of "activist judges" but there are no calls for the dramatic plans of reorganization, which may have accompanied similar criticisms of the 1930s, or the 1860s, or the 1800s. The physical size of the federal judiciary was, by 1980, large enough to create its own bureaucratic constituency. In addition to the Supreme Court, the Circuit Courts of Appeal, the Circuit Trial Courts, and the District Court, Congress has also authorized the creation of the federal magistrate system to handle pretrial motions, a separate bankruptcy court system, and three separate administrative bodies: the Judicial Conference of the United States, the Administrative Office of the United States Courts, and the Federal Judicial Center. The federal judiciary supports thousands of judges, clerks, and support staff making any significant challenge to judicial political impractical.

Each successive chief justice since the Warren Court has presided over a court divided more or less equally between various ideological positions. In 1988, Congress eliminated all categories of mandatory appellate jurisdiction, which means that the Court bears the sole decision whether to hear or not hear a case. The independence of the federal judiciary remains relatively unchanged since its founding in 1789, but its practical influence in modern American policy making is unprecedented. Recent trends suggest that the Court will continue to be both a reflection and an agent of social change for foreseeable future.

[*See also* ***Brown v. Board of Education;*** **Constitution;** ***Gibbons v. Ogden; Griswold v. Connecticut; Lochner v. New York; Marbury v. Madison; McCulloch v. Maryland; Miranda v. Arizona; Plessy v. Ferguson; and*** **Supreme Court, U.S.**]

BIBLIOGRAPHY

Berman, Harold Joseph. *Law and Revolution: The Formation of the Western Legal Tradition.* Cambridge, Mass.: Harvard University Press, 1983.

Friedman, Lawrence, and Harry N. Scheiber, eds. *American Law and the Constitutional Order: Historical Perspectives.* Cambridge, Mass.: Harvard University Press, 1988.

Hall, Kermit, ed. *The Oxford Guide to United States Supreme Court Decisions.* Oxford; New York: Oxford University Press, 2009.

Leuchtenburg, William E. *The Supreme Court Reborn: The Constitutional Revolution in the Age of Roosevelt.* New York: Oxford University Press, 1995.

Nelson, William E. *The Fourteenth Amendment: From Political Principle to Judicial Doctrine.* Cambridge, Mass.: Harvard University Press, 1998.

Powe, Lucas, Jr. *The Supreme Court and the American Elite, 1789–2008*. Cambridge. Mass.: Harvard University Press, 2011.

Powe, Lucas, Jr. *The Warren Court and American Politics*. Cambridge, Mass.: Belknap Press of Harvard University: 2001.

Schwartz, Bernard. *A History of the Supreme Court*. New York: Oxford University Press, 1993.

White, G. Edward. *The Marshall Court and Cultural Change, 1815–1835*. New York: Oxford University Press, 1991.

White, G. Edward. *Patterns of American Legal Thought*. Indianapolis, Ind.: Bobbs-Merrill, 1978.

Aharon Zorea

FEDERAL GOVERNMENT, LEGISLATIVE BRANCH

This entry contains three subentries: An Overview; House of Representatives; and Senate.

AN OVERVIEW

The legislative branch of the U.S. government—the Congress—is a bicameral legislature composed of the House of Representatives, whose membership is based on proportional representation, and the Senate, made up of two members from each state. This arrangement resulted from a compromise at the Constitutional Convention of 1787 between the representatives of states with large populations and those from small states, who feared being automatically outvoted under a wholly proportional system.

The House of Representatives was modeled on the British House of Commons. Elected directly by the citizens, representatives serve two-year terms. The Senate, in contrast, was a new creation, designed not only as a body where each state would have an equal number of votes, but also as a check on the popular emotions that might sway House members. To this end, senators were to be older—at least thirty years of age as opposed to twenty-five for representatives—and thus presumably more mature. To insulate them from popular pressures, senators would serve staggered six-year terms and be elected by the legislatures of their states instead of directly by the citizens.

Together, the House and Senate are responsible for making all laws, with tax bills originating in the House. Congress also possesses the power to declare war, oversee and investigate the administration of programs initiated by the executive branch, and override presidential vetoes by two-thirds votes of both houses. In addition, the Senate has sole responsibility for reviewing and approving treaties and confirming presidential nominations.

The House has the power to impeach government officials who abuse their office, whereas the Senate acts as a court to try impeachment cases brought by the House. Conviction by the Senate brings removal from office. Each house also has the power to discipline its own members and to expel a member by a two-thirds vote.

Until 1794 the Senate met in closed session, whereas meetings of the House were always open to the public. Although the House had two standing committees as early as 1795, both bodies generally operated with ad hoc committees chosen for each piece of legislation or for a single term until the early 1800s, when both the House and the Senate established more permanent standing committees.

The basic structure of the legislative branch has generally remained stable, with only a few changes over time. As new states entered the Union, the membership of both bodies multiplied, from 26 senators in the first Congress to 100 after 1959 and from 65 representatives to 435 since 1911, when the total number of representatives was capped by statute. By the mid-1850s, the House and Senate had outgrown their chambers in the Capitol Building, leading to the addition of large north and south wings to provide spacious new chambers.

Down to the first decade of the twentieth century, representatives and senators had little or no office space or staff, but as staff members were hired and more working space was needed, both bodies erected office buildings.

As the twentieth century progressed, the role of the federal government expanded and became more complex, a trend accelerated by the New Deal and World War II. Legislative branch activities kept pace, leading to the hiring of additional staff, until by the 1990s the House had more than 10,000 staff members and the Senate more than 6,000, housed in seven congressional office buildings.

One structural change occurred with ratification in 1913 of the Seventeenth Amendment, which mandated that senators, like members of the House, be elected by direct popular vote. Also important, although less dramatic, was the Legislative Reorganization Act of 1947, which made such "housekeeping" changes as reducing the number of House and Senate committees, consolidating jurisdictions, and authorizing professional staff members for both members and committees.

Although most federal government agencies are part of the executive branch, the legislative branch has created several agencies to serve its particular needs. The Library of Congress, established in 1800, serves as a repository and disseminator of knowledge for the entire nation; the Government Printing Office, set up in 1860, publishes official congressional and other governmental documents; and the General Accounting Office, established by the Budget and Accounting Act of 1921, audits and reviews the actions of federal agencies. In 1974, Congress established its own Congressional Budget Office as an independent source of fiscal information. A congressional Office of Technology Assessment existed from 1972 until it was abolished in 1995.

By the early twenty-first century, continuing a long-term trend of growing political partisanship, deliberation in both houses of Congress was characterized by acrimony, jockeying for advantage, and a decline in bipartisan cooperation, mutual respect, and basic courtesy. In what some observers called "the perennial campaign," legislators spend much of their time raising money, courting special-interest groups, and delivering speeches and sound-bite comments to nearly empty House and Senate chambers for the benefit of TV cameras and voters back home.

[*See also* **Constitution; Constitutional Convention of 1787; Elections: Nominating Systems; Federal Government, Legislative Branch: House of Representatives; Federal Government, Legislative Branch: Senate; New Deal; Presidential Impeachment; Taxation;** ***and*** **Veto Power.**]

BIBLIOGRAPHY

Bacon, Donald C., Roger H. Davidson, and Morton Keller, eds. *The Encyclopedia of the United States Congress*, 4 vols. New York: Simon & Schuster, 1995.

Byrd, Robert C. *The Senate, 1789–1989: Addresses on the History of the United States Senate*, 4 vols. Washington, D.C.: U.S. Government Printing Office, 1989–1994.

Galloway, George B. *History of the House of Representatives*. New York: Crowell, 1961.

Josephy, Alvin M., Jr. *On the Hill: A History of the American Congress*. New York: Simon & Schuster, 1979.

Silbey, Joel H., ed. *Encyclopedia of the American Legislative System*, 3 vols. New York: Charles Scribner's Sons, 1994.

U.S. Congress, Senate. *Biographical Directory of the United States Congress, 1774–1989*. Washington, D.C.: U.S. Government Printing Office, 1988.

Wendy Wolff; revised by Pearson Bramblett

HOUSE OF REPRESENTATIVES

Of all the components of the federal government, the House of Representatives derives most directly from Great Britain, being closely patterned on the House of Commons and retaining many of that body's features, including a speaker as presiding officer.

Creating the House of Representatives. The decision to create a House of Representatives elected directly by the people was made by the Constitutional Convention of 1787 following earlier decisions establishing a three-part national government and a bicameral national legislature. The convention assigned eighteen specific powers to the legislative branch, including the power to levy and collect taxes, declare war, and regulate interstate and foreign commerce. The most divisive issue, and the one on which the convention might have foundered, was the manner in which seats in the House would be assigned to the thirteen states. Would the states be equally represented, or would they be given seats according to their populations? After lengthy debate, the convention decided that states should receive seats in proportion to their population of free citizens plus three-fifths of all others. (The latter provision, a concession to the Southern states, with their vast populations of slaves, would continue until nullified after the Civil War by the Thirteenth, Fourteenth, and Fifteenth Amendments to the Constitution.) The delegates next settled on a two-year term for members of the House; decided that revenue bills should originate in the House but be subject to modification by the other branch of the national legislature, the Senate; and set the qualifications for membership in the House: to be elected, a person must have been a U.S. citizen for at least seven years, must be a resident of the state, and must be at least twenty-five years of age.

The Nineteenth Century. The first House, which convened on 1 April 1789, elected Frederick A. C. Muhlenberg of Pennsylvania as speaker. As presiding officer of the House, the speaker is the only official of the chamber specifically mentioned in the Constitution. The need for strong leadership was paramount in a chamber destined to grow larger as the nation's population expanded. Beginning with only 65 members, the size of the house nearly tripled by 1830 to 186 members, and it increased to 435 by 1910, at which point the number was fixed by statute. Speakers have played a central role throughout the House's history, although the influence of individual speakers has varied widely.

In the early years of the republic, the House of Representatives, possessing the democratic legitimacy that came from its members' direct election by the people, was the dominant legislative chamber. (Senators were not directly elected until the ratification of the Seventeenth Amendment in 1913.) But equally important was the emergence of a forceful speaker in Henry Clay of Kentucky, who was elected speaker on his first day in the House, 19 January 1811, and served almost continuously until 1825.

Because of the rough balance between slave and free states in the Senate, that chamber beginning around 1820 became the principal forum for debating the divisive issues of slavery and tariffs; the House proved less able to conciliate these differences. After the Civil War, however, the House again became dominant because one party or the other usually had a clear majority, and a number of unusually strong speakers emerged, including Republicans James G. Blaine and Thomas Brackett Reed of Maine and Democrats John Carlisle of Kentucky and Charles F. Crisp of Georgia.

With the growth of the House came two important adaptations: legislative committees and an elaborate structure of rules that govern debate and the lawmaking process. Initially, House committees were "select" or "special committees," set up either for a brief period—such as a single two-year Congress—or to deal with a single bill. In the earliest period there were only two standing (that is, permanent) committees: a Committee of Elections and, to fulfill the House's constitutional role as the point of origin for revenue bills, the Committee on Ways and Means. The latter body, established in 1795, is the only early committee that survives under its original name.

Originally, the House was governed by a simple set of rules, one of which allowed the members to resolve themselves into "The Committee of the Whole House" to expedite action. By the legal fiction of reconvening under a different name, quorum requirements could be relaxed. At first, debate was unlimited. Filibusters, or interminable speech-making to purposely block consideration of a bill, were common. Only in 1811, as war with Britain loomed, did the House adopt a motion that allowed members to cut off debate by calling for the previous question, a parliamentary procedure requiring an immediate vote on whatever motion is on the floor. Denounced as a "gag rule," this initial effort to limit debate proved ineffective, and not until 1841 was a rule adopted limiting each member to one hour of debate on each question. Filibustering was further restricted in 1847 with the adoption of a rule that gave members only five minutes to introduce, explain, and advocate amendments to bills. Resourceful representatives, however, continued a form of filibustering by offering many amendments—a tactic that was restricted in 1860.

One of the most radical steps ever taken by a speaker came in response to members' practice of deliberately failing to respond to a roll call, so as to make it impossible to achieve a quorum. In January 1890, when minority Democrats refused to answer the roll call that would register them as present and prepared to vote, Speaker Reed ordered the clerk of the House to record as present all members who were actually in the chamber. By thwarting the "disappearing quorum" and other techniques used by the minority to obstruct the legislative process, Reed earned the enmity of Democrats, who denounced him as "Czar Reed," but he enabled the majority to work its will more easily and thereby moved the House closer to the majoritarian institution it would become.

Reforms and Changes in the Twentieth Century. Reed's six years as speaker (1889–1891 and 1895–1899) marked the beginning of a period of extreme dominance by House speakers. Joseph G. Cannon, an Illinois Republican who served as speaker from 1903 until 1911, ruled the House with an iron hand and greatly reduced the influence of individual members. Cannon inherited Reed's powers to appoint the standing committees and name their chairs. He also appointed all five members of the Rules Committee, the most important procedural committee in the House, which was responsible for forwarding bills to the entire chamber for action. As presiding officer of the House, Cannon would refuse to recognize those who had incurred his disfavor. His dictatorial reign ended in 1910 when a group of Progressive Republicans joined with the Democrats to strip the speaker of his membership on the Rules Committee (a position of vast influence that Speakers had enjoyed since 1858), denied him the power to appoint standing committees and their chairs, and restricted his discretion in recognizing or refusing to recognize members. Although the revolt against Cannon divested the speakership of certain autocratic features, the speaker retained an important core of powers that included the ability to influence—if not control—committee assignments and to interpret House rules.

One outgrowth of the limitations placed on Cannon was the principle that seniority would determine who would chair House committees. Ultimately, the seniority system meant that committee leadership was usually vested in those members—often conservative southern Democrats—from the safest districts. Reformers, strengthened by a large influx of younger Democrats in the election of 1974, succeeded in reducing the force of the seniority system in the 1970s when they required chairpersons of standing committees and of the powerful appropriations subcommittees to be approved by a vote of all the party's members (the Caucus). In 1975 the Caucus ousted three senior Democratic chairmen. Despite the reforms, however, there remained a presumption that seniority on a committee gave one a strong claim to the chairmanship. But even this presumption was eroded in the 104th Congress (1995–1997) when Republican Speaker Newt Gingrich of Georgia elevated some relatively junior members to committee chairmanships, most notably Bob Livingston of Louisiana as chair of appropriations and John Kasich of Ohio as chair of budget. As another by-product of dramatic Republican gains in the 1994 midterm elections, the Republican Conference (the counterpart of the Democratic Caucus) restricted chairs of standing committees to three two-year terms, altered the jurisdiction of committees, and changed the names of most of them.

Whereas changes in many House rules reflected action by the party in power, other reforms resulted from nonpartisan statutory action. These include the legislative reorganization acts of 1946 and 1970, which reorganized committees and improved their staffing, and the 1974 Budget Control and Impoundment Act, which established budget committees for both chambers.

Throughout its history, certain persistent tensions have existed within the House: between the need for strong leadership to process legislation efficiently and the desire of individual members to have a role in shaping bills and between the desire by party leaders to fashion comprehensive policies and the needs of the individual members to retain the support of their constituents or of special-interest groups.

Another source of tension that arose in the late twentieth century was that between the power of incumbency, which reinforced the overwhelming preponderance of white male representatives, and pressures to make the House more truly representative of the population as a whole. Because of the manner in which House districts are drawn by state legislatures, one party or the other often has disproportionate strength, making reelection all but certain for most members. Indeed, it is unusual for more than 25 percent of all House seats to be seriously contested. The resources available to incumbents further enhance their reelection chances. These factors contributed to the dominance of the Democrats between 1955 and 1995.

Efforts to promote racial diversity by redrawing district lines proved contentious. A succession of Supreme Court cases, beginning in 1964 with *Wesberry v. Sanders*, coupled with the Voting Rights Act of 1965 and its subsequent amendments, required state legislatures to maximize the chances that candidates who belonged to racial minority groups could win seats in the House. A generation later, however, Supreme Court decisions in the cases of *Shaw v. Reno* (1993) and *Miller v. Johnson* (1995) narrowed the role that race could play in redistricting. In 2011, forty-four African Americans served as voting members of the House; all but two were Democrats. African Americans, comprising 12 percent of the population, were slightly underrepresented in the House in the early twenty-first century, with about 10 percent of the membership. Women, who make up more than 50 percent of the population, constituted only about 13 percent of the House. Latinos, with 9 percent of the population nationally, claimed only 5 percent of House seats in 2011.

As the first decade of the twenty-first century ended, the House of Representatives continued to evolve, responding to the changing realities of American life while also reflecting the traditions and precedents deeply embedded in its more than 200-year history.

[*See also* **Blaine, James G.; Clay, Henry; Constitution; Constitutional Convention of 1787; Federal Government, Legislative Branch: An Overview; Federal Government, Legislative Branch: Senate; Fifteenth Amendment; Fourteenth Amendment; Interstate Commerce Act; Slavery, Laws; Tariffs;** ***and*** **Taxation.**]

BIBLIOGRAPHY

Brown, George Rothwell. *The Leadership of Congress.* Indianapolis, Ind.: Bobbs–Merrill, 1922.

Davidson, Roger H. *The Postreform Congress.* New York: St. Martin's Press, 1992.

Galloway, George B. *History of the House of Representatives.* New York: Crowell, 1961.

Josephy, Alvin M., Jr. *On the Hill.* New York: Simon & Schuster, 1979.

MacNeil, Neil. *Forge of Democracy.* New York: D. McKay, 1963.

Peters, Ronald M., Jr. "The History and Character of the Speakership." In *The Speaker*, edited by Ronald M. Peters, Jr. New York: CQ Press, 1995.

Sinclair, Barbara. *Majority Leadership in the U.S. House.* Baltimore: Johns Hopkins University Press, 1983.

Ross K. Baker

SENATE

The Senate forms the upper house of the bicameral Congress established by the U.S. Constitution. The earlier government under the Articles of Confederation had consisted of a Congress of one house, in which each state had a single vote. With no executive branch, all officials were responsible to Congress. The Constitutional Convention of 1787 was called because that government, a confederation of sovereign states rather than a union, did not meet the needs of the new nation.

After extensive discussions, the framers arrived at the so-called Great Compromise. They devised a House of Representatives in which a state's representation was proportional to its population and a Senate in which each state would be equally represented with two members, thus providing protection to the smaller states. The two senators representing each state would serve staggered, six-year terms, with only one-third of the Senate running in any election year. The Senate is thus a continuing body, unlike the House of Representatives whose entire membership is elected every two years. The Convention's members hoped the Senate would carefully review measures passed by the House, which, with frequent elections, would more likely be swayed by popular passions. With this goal in mind, they set the Senate's age requirement at thirty (in contrast to the House's twenty-five), and they provided for the election of senators by state legislatures rather than by popular vote.

To start the staggered terms, senators of the first Congress drew lots to determine who would have two-, four-, or six-year terms. The Senate continues to be divided into three "classes," depending on which year a member faces reelection. When a new state enters the Union, its senators are assigned to classes so that the number in each class remains nearly equal, with no class having more than one senator from any state.

Powers. The Senate shares with the House responsibility for making laws, declaring war, and appropriating funds to operate the federal government, as well as for instituting new programs and overseeing old ones. With the House, the Senate has the power to override presidential vetoes by a two-thirds vote. In addition, the Constitution assigned three powers exclusively to the Senate: reviewing and approving treaties, confirming nominations of judges and executive branch officials, and serving as the court for impeachment trials.

Under the Articles of Confederation, congressional agents negotiated treaties, which required approval by nine of the thirteen states. The U.S. Constitution, by contrast, gives the treaty-making power to the executive, with the requirement of Senate approval. Having the Senate review treaties, the framers thought, would provide counsel to the president, as well as place checks and balances on the executive power. Since all states have equal representation in the Senate, the arrangement would also protect the interests of the states.

In practice, the president submits the text of each treaty to the Senate, which reviews it first in committee. If the committee approves, it sends the treaty to the full Senate for a vote. Presidents have frequently found it useful to consult the Senate while negotiating a treaty or to include senators in the delegation conducting the negotiations. On only twenty-one occasions has the Senate formally rejected a treaty, the most famous being the Treaty of Versailles ending World War I. After President Woodrow Wilson failed either to consult the Senate or to accept reservations it had adopted, the body refused to approve the treaty in two votes in 1919 and 1920.

The requirement for Senate approval of presidential nominations to executive and judicial offices is another of the checks and balances written into the Constitution. Every year the Senate reviews thousands of military and civilian nominations, generally submitted to it in long lists, as well as the individual nominations of cabinet officers, federal judges, and ambassadors. Most of these nominees are confirmed, but occasionally the Senate objects. As of 1997, the Senate had failed to confirm a total of 27 Supreme Court nominees. Although it has formally rejected only nine cabinet appointees, the nominations of eight others have been withdrawn in the face of Senate opposition.

Fearing that the president might abuse his position, the Constitutional Convention included an impeachment provision similar to those many of the new states had included in their constitutions. After considering whether the Supreme Court should try impeachment cases, the framers foresaw a possible conflict of interest, since the Court's members were presidential appointees. They settled instead on having the Senate try impeachments. Through 1999, the Senate had conducted impeachment trials of two presidents (Andrew Johnson and Bill Clinton, both acquitted); one senator (William Blount, 1797, already expelled, so impeachment failed); one cabinet officer (William Belknap, 1876, already resigned); one Supreme Court justice (Samuel Chase, 1804, acquitted); and twelve federal judges (seven found guilty and removed from office).

Structure. Under the Constitution, the vice president of the United States is the president and presiding officer of the Senate. The Constitution also gives the Senate the power to choose a president pro tempore to preside in his absence, as well as authority over its own membership, including the power to expel a member by a two-thirds vote and to serve as judge in contested election cases. Empowered to select its officers, the Senate elects a chaplain, a secretary, and a sergeant at arms. For more than 200 years, these latter two officers have supervised the Senate's basic administrative structure. The secretary of the Senate, the body's chief administrative and financial officer, also oversees the official journals and records and the clerks who serve in the Senate chamber. The sergeant at arms is the chief law enforcement and protocol officer of the Senate and also manages most of the support services.

Many of the Senate's rules were originally based on English precedent, as well as on the rules of the Continental and Confederation congresses. The Senate has recodified its rules on seven occasions, most recently in 1979. Unlike the House, which strictly regulates the length of debate, the Senate prides itself on its right of extended debate as a protection for the rights of the minority. Through the delaying tactic known as the filibuster, a minority of senators can block action on a measure. Not until 1917 did the Senate adopt its first "cloture" rule permitting a vote by two-thirds of the senators to shut off debate and bring a measure to a vote. Subsequent refinements to the rule now allow a vote by sixty senators (three-fifths of the Senate) to close debate.

Since the first Congress, the Senate has assigned proposed legislation (bills) to committees for review. Initially, temporary committees handled specific legislation and then disbanded. Not until 1816, except for three housekeeping panels, did the Senate create permanent standing legislative committees. The number of standing committees grew steadily thereafter, reaching more than seventy by 1913. The Legislative Reorganization Act of 1946 reduced the number of committees to seventeen, while providing for professional staff members. A further restructuring in 1977 produced the approximately sixteen standing committees that existed in 1997.

In designing the Senate, the framers did not envision political parties, but party divisions began almost immediately and continued through the early nineteenth century. By 1860 the present Democratic and Republican parties were in place. Although Senate Democrats and Republicans elected chairs and secretaries in the late 1800s, not until the early twentieth century did the body adopt the modern system of party leadership. In the 1920s the party caucuses began electing floor leaders. These majority and minority leaders, assisted by party whips, manage legislation on the Senate floor.

Unlike the House of Representatives, which was open to the public from the beginning, the Senate initially met behind closed doors, not opening public galleries until 1795. Thus, in the early 1790s, newspapers reported the House debates but citizens knew little of what transpired in the Senate. Starting in 1802, the Senate admitted notetakers to record its debates, which were published initially by the newspaper the *National Intelligencer* and later in other private publications such as the *Register of Debates* and the *Congressional Globe*. The official *Congressional Record*, a government publication, began reporting in 1873, at which time the Senate also hired its own official reporters.

The Senate considers treaties and nominations in executive session. Until 1929, these executive sessions were generally closed to the public, although detailed information about the debates regularly leaked to the press. Recognizing that the sources of the leaks must be the members themselves, the Senate in 1929 opened all executive sessions except those involving national security.

Development and Growth. The Senate's relative importance within the federal government has fluctuated over its history. In the early years, because the House met in open session, its debates had more public visibility than the Senate's. By the 1830s, the Senate had entered what became known as its Golden Age, as intense debates raged over slavery and the very nature of the Union among such leaders as Henry Clay of Kentucky, Daniel Webster of Massachusetts, and John C. Calhoun of South Carolina. When Alexis de Tocqueville visited Washington in 1832, he deplored the rowdiness of the House of Representatives, while praising the Senate for its articulate statesmen (apparently unaware that many senators had previously served in the House).

Memorable Senate debates and bargaining produced the Missouri Compromise of 1820 and the Compromise of 1850, both dealing with slavery and the admission of new states to the Union, but only temporarily defusing deepening sectional conflicts. When the Civil War broke out in 1861, the Senate shrank temporarily from sixty-eight members to fewer than fifty, as senators from the seceding states withdrew or were expelled.

The dominance of radical Republicans in Congress during the Civil War and after set up a confrontation with President Andrew Johnson that culminated in the impeachment of Johnson, whom the Senate failed to convict by a single vote in 1868. For the rest of the nineteenth century, the Senate, still led principally by Republicans, dominated the federal government until its position was challenged in the early 1900s by the powerful presidencies of Theodore Roosevelt and Woodrow Wilson.

The turn of the twentieth century also saw growing public dissatisfaction with the method of electing U.S. senators. Political battles in state legislatures could lead to long vacancies in some Senate seats. This problem, combined with charges of corruption and purchased votes, led to adoption and ratification of the Seventeenth Amendment in 1913, directing that senators be elected by popular vote.

Influential during the 1920s, the Senate played a more subordinate role during the early New Deal Era as President Franklin Delano Roosevelt, enjoying overwhelming popularity and strong congressional majorities, proposed measure after measure that received prompt legislative approval. The Legislative Reorganization Act of 1946 streamlined the operations of both the Senate and the House to deal with the flood of postwar legislation. Joseph McCarthy's anti-Communist crusade of the early 1950s brought moments of high drama. The so-called Army–McCarthy hearings of early 1954 attracted a vast television audience. That December, resorting to a rarely used expedient just short of expulsion, the Senate voted to censure the Wisconsin Republican.

In the 1950s and 1960s, the Senate struggled with civil rights legislation before breaking a southern filibuster to pass the landmark Civil Rights Act of 1964, followed by President Lyndon B. Johnson's Great Society programs. As the Vietnam War absorbed the nation's treasure and manpower during the later 1960s and early 1970s, the Senate and House eventually balked and cut off funding for the war. They also adopted the War Powers Resolution of 1973, requiring the president to notify Congress and seek congressional approval when sending U.S. troops into combat. Again asserting its authority in early 1991, the Senate held an intense debate before approving the use of military force to repel Iraq's invasion of Kuwait.

Since the 1920s, the Senate has energetically exerted its right to investigate executive branch activities, supported by a Supreme Court decision (*McGrain v. Daugherty,* 1927) that established the power of Senate committees to compel testimony from witnesses. The Senate's high-profile investigations have included the Teapot Dome inquiry of 1923–1924, probing the leasing of government oil reserves in Wyoming; the "Truman Committee's" investigation of defense contracts during and after World War II; Tennessee Senator Estes Kefauver's investigation of organized crime in the early 1950s; and the Watergate Committee's inquiry into wrongdoing by the Richard M. Nixon administration.

For more than two centuries, the Senate has fulfilled its unique constitutional role as the deliberative arm of the legislative branch, using its power to review treaties and nominations and its right of extended debate to slow executive branch or House pressures for more precipitous action.

In recent times, some Americans have seen increasing polarization in the U.S. political system. Some point to Jim Jeffords's resignation from the Republican Party in 2001 because of his feelings that the party was becoming increasingly polarized and that moderate voices were getting shut out. Former President Bill Clinton said in an interview on 18 September 2006 that he thinks the Republican Party believes in polarization. In a typical two-party or multiparty system, the distribution of party power looks like a normal curve with a slight skew. Under such a condition, most of the country is moderate or moderate-leaning liberal or conservative. If the country becomes polarized, then the curve becomes one with two main humps and looks like a bimodal distribution, with the power at the far political left and right ends and a severe dip in the middle; one side will have more influence than the other, creating a strong trend to follow them. There is speculation that a nation with such a distribution, effectively having two highly separate approaches with no compromise positions in the middle, becomes difficult to govern.

Others take the view that the U.S. political parties themselves are actually quite close in terms of actual policy and party leadership. They say that political rhetoric is polarized to create some illusion of policy difference; however, in practice and action, both parties take a similar approach to government. Examples include vast bipartisan and popular support for one side of various supposedly controversial issues; a majority of both major parties in Congress voted to cut taxes in 2001, to authorize use of force in Iraq in 2002, and to ban partial-birth abortion in 2003. Additionally, since 1948, the Congress and the president—whether Democratic or Republican—have shown the same willingness to grow the size of the federal government. Supporters of this theory also say that public opinion has not gone to the extreme; rather, both parties have come closer to the center. Thus, for the average "centrist" voter, it is easier to decide which party/candidate is closest to them. This can be demonstrated in both the 2000 and the 2004 presidential elections, when the vote was virtually half and half between the two sides. Essentially, both parties are equally desirable to average Americans. However, the two parties do have their differences, such as the 2010 health care package. The health care bill was voted against by every Republican in the Senate, yet had greater Democratic support. However, many Democrats also opposed the bill. There is discussion in the literature about the nature and cause of polarization in the U.S. electorate. One side argues that polarization is almost purely elite, or "top-down" driven. The other side argues that it is a two-way street, but primarily a "bottom-up" phenomenon facilitated by the engaged partisans in the American electorate.

[*See also* **Articles of Confederation; Calhoun, John C.; Civil Rights Legislation; Clay, Henry; Compromise of 1820; Compromise of 1850; Constitution; Constitutional Convention of 1787; Continental Congress; Elections: Nominating Systems; Federal Government, Executive Branch: An Overview; Federal Government, Executive Branch: Presidency, The; Federal Government, Legislative Branch: An Overview; Federal Government, Legislative Branch: House of Representatives; Great Society; Johnson, Andrew; Johnson, Lyndon B.; McCarthy, Joseph; New Deal; Nixon, Richard M.; Presidential Impeachment; Political Parties; Roosevelt, Franklin Delano; Roosevelt, Theodore; Slavery, Laws; Supreme Court, U.S.; Teapot Dome Scandal; War Powers Act; Watergate; Webster, Daniel;** *and* **Wilson, Woodrow.**]

BIBLIOGRAPHY

Bacon, Donald, Roger Davidson, and Morton Keller, eds. *The Encyclopedia of the United States Congress,* 4 vols. New York: Simon & Schuster, 1995.

Baker, Richard A. *The Senate of the United States: A Bicentennial History*. Malabar, Fla.: R. E. Krieger, 1988.

Byrd, Robert C. *The Senate, 1789–1989: Addresses on the History of the United States Senate*, 4 vols. Washington, D.C.: U.S. Government Printing Office, 1989–1994.

Dole, Bob. *Historical Almanac of the United States Senate*. Washington, D.C.: U.S. Government Printing Office, 1989.

Silbey, Joel H. *Encyclopedia of the American Legislative System*, 3 vols. New York: Charles Scribner's Sons, 1994.

U.S. Congress, Senate. *Biographical Directory of the United States Congress, 1774–1989*. Washington, D.C.: U.S. Government Printing Office, 1988.

U.S. Congress, Senate. *Guide to the Records of the United States Senate at the National Archives, 1789–1989: Bicentennial Edition*, prepared by the National Archives' Center for Legislative Archives. Washington, D.C.: U.S. Government Printing Office, 1989.

U.S. Congress, Senate. *Guide to Research Collections of Former United States Senators, 1789–1995*. Washington, D.C.: Superintendent of Documents, U.S. Government Printing Office, 1995.

U.S. Congress, Senate. *Senators of the United States: A Historical Bibliography*. Washington, D.C.: U.S. Government Printing Office, 1995.

Wendy Wolff; revised by Pearson Bramblett

FEDERALISM

Federalism is the division of governing power between the national and state governments. Advocates of federalism assert that it allows states to experiment with new programs that other states can adopt or modify, protects against tyranny by imposing checks on the national government, and provides the citizens of a diverse nation with a way of governing locally to achieve their distinctive interests while creating a national government to serve truly national purposes. Federalism's critics believe that local diversity is much less important in the modern world than it was in the past and that a centralized government can encourage experimentation.

Conflicts over federalism have been a recurrent feature of U.S. history. Dividing power appropriately between the states and the nation was one of the central concerns of the Constitutional Convention of 1787. Anti-Federalists feared that a powerful national government might tyrannize the people and displace the important power of self-government they associated with state government. A key compromise resolved the controversy by giving the national government a list of enumerated powers in the Constitution and state legislatures the power to select senators.

Controversies over federalism in the Antebellum Era frequently arose from the conflict over slavery. Slavery's defenders were concerned that interpreting the Constitution expansively would ultimately authorize Congress to regulate slavery. They therefore opposed nationalist interpretations of Congress's power to regulate interstate commerce, as well as efforts by nationalist politicians to appropriate federal funds for the construction of roads and other elements of the national economic infrastructure.

The national government's reach grew during the Civil War, as it developed the machinery to conduct a large-scale military conflict. Constitutional theory, however, remained focused on ensuring a federalism that protected state government power. The constitutional amendments adopted after the Civil War authorized Congress to protect the newly freed slaves and individual rights more generally, but in the Slaughterhouse Cases (1873) the Supreme Court refused to give these new enumerated powers an interpretation that, in the Court's view, would allow Congress to exercise general governmental power.

As corporations operating in many states and internationally gained substantial influence, reformers took the position that the growth of private power made it impossible for any single state to regulate economic activity. From the late 1880s to the Progressive Era, Congress enacted statutes that occupied terrain previously left to state governments. The Supreme Court gradually endorsed this expansion of national power, although often with reluctance.

The New Deal's response to the Great Depression produced a dramatic growth in national power and a displacement of state authority, as most Americans concluded that only the national government could alleviate the national economic disaster. President Franklin Delano Roosevelt's administration developed programs of economic relief and reconstruction on a far larger scale than any earlier national efforts. The Supreme Court initially held that these programs invaded areas the Constitution reserved for the states, but in 1937 the Court changed course and held that the national government could, in effect, exercise general governing authority: Congress could enact any program that it believed to be in the public interest, despite the apparent limitations implied by the Constitution's enumeration of powers.

Even after the New Deal, states remained important arenas for the development of innovative policies, but the focus of governing authority had clearly shifted from state capitals to Washington, D.C. Although President Richard M. Nixon articulated a program he called the "New Federalism," the first real assault on the New Deal–Great Society centralization of power occurred during the Ronald Reagan Administration, which sought to reduce the scope of government generally, not simply the reach of national government.

In the mid-1990s the Supreme Court imposed some modest limits on congressional power. It struck down a federal statute making it a crime to possess guns near schools, saying that the connection between crime and interstate commerce was so tenuous that upholding the statute would imply that Congress could constitutionally pass any statute whatsoever (*United States v. Lopez,* 1995). The Court also invalidated the 1993 Religious Freedom Restoration Act as beyond Congress's power to protect individual rights under the Fourteenth Amendment (*City of Boerne v. Flores,* 1997). It protected the institutions of state government in two decisions denying Congress the power to "commandeer" either state legislatures or state executive officials to carry out national policy (*New York v. United States,* 1992; *Printz v. United States,* 1997). In 1999 the Court invoked the concept of a state's sovereign immunity from lawsuits seeking damages for copyright infringements and violations of national minimum wage law to expand the constitutional protection afforded state governments. As a group the decisions of the 1990s suggested that the Supreme Court might impose substantial limits on national power, but the decisions could be interpreted to make only modest revisions in the constitutional law developed through the twentieth century.

Even with these new limits on national power, the national government clearly remained vastly more powerful than state governments as the twentieth century ended and almost certainly more powerful than the Constitution's framers had envisioned.

[*See also* **Antislavery Movement; Constitution; Constitutional Convention of 1787; Great Society; New Deal; Nixon, Richard M.; Reagan, Ronald; Roosevelt, Franklin Delano; Slaughterhouse Cases; State Governments; States' Rights;** ***and*** **Supreme Court, U.S.**]

BIBLIOGRAPHY

Beer, Samuel H. *To Make a Nation: The Rediscovery of American Federalism.* Cambridge, Mass.: Belknap Press of Harvard University Press, 1993.

Elkins, Stanley, and Eric McKitrick. *The Age of Federalism.* New York: Oxford University Press, 1993.

Rubin, Edward, and Malcolm Feeley. "Federalism: Some Notes on a National Neurosis." *UCLA Law Review* 41 (1994): 903–952.

Shapiro, David L. *Federalism: A Dialogue*. Evanston, Ill.: Northwestern University Press, 1995.

Mark Tushnet

FEDERALIST PAPERS

The Federalist Papers (1787–1788) are the most important American contribution to political theory. Conceived by Alexander Hamilton and John Jay, this series of essays, written under the pseudonym "Publius," countered the political campaign mounted by opponents of the Constitution during the months after the adjournment of the Constitutional Convention of 1787. Planned as a modest series of essays to appear in New York City newspapers, the Federalist Papers grew to eighty-five numbers. Newspapers in others states reprinted the first numbers, but with the announcement in January 1788 that the essays would appear as a book, the out-of-state reprintings dwindled. Eventually the series filled two volumes published in March and May 1788. Hamilton wrote about fifty of the essays. Illness restricted Jay to only five, and James Madison (joining the consortium later) contributed the balance. Disagreement persists over whether Hamilton or Madison was the author of a handful of the essays. It was widely believed at the time that Hamilton and Madison were the primary contributors.

Written in a nonpartisan style, the Federalist Papers extolled the benefits of the union, demonstrated the inefficacy of the Articles of Confederation, explained and clarified the principles and provisions of the Constitution, and justified the exclusion of various provisions such as a Bill of Rights and a religious test for office-holding. Hamilton introduced the series on 27 October 1787 with an essay suggesting that Americans must "decide the important question, whether societies of men are really capable or not, of establishing good government from reflection and choice, or whether they are forever destined to depend, for their political constitutions, on accident and force." Conceding that the love of liberty could lead to an "illiberal distrust" of government, he nevertheless insisted that "the vigour of government is essential to the security of liberty."

Whereas Hamilton's essays emphasized the importance of an energetic federal government, Madison, especially in Federalist Nos. 39 and 51, stressed the restraints placed on that government by free and frequent elections, the checks and balances built into the government through the separation of powers, and the healthy tension created by the division of power between the states and the federal government. Federalist No. 10, also by Madison, is particularly celebrated for its argument that in a large republic like the United States under the proposed Constitution, conflicting interest groups—notably economic interests—would be sufficiently numerous and dispersed to counterbalance each other and thereby promote rather than endanger political stability, with no one interest group gaining complete dominance.

The original objective of the Federalist Papers was to convince New Yorkers to elect to their state ratifying convention delegates who would support the Constitution. In this the authors failed because two-thirds of New York's convention delegates initially opposed ratification unless the Constitution was first altered by amendments. But the series succeeded beyond the authors' expectations in other ways. Arguments espoused by "Publius" became the standard explanations used by other Federalists in the public debate waged in newspapers and pamphlets as well as in speeches in the state ratifying conventions.

Thomas Jefferson, writing to Madison, praised the Federalist Papers as "the best commentary on the principles of government which ever was written." To his son-in-law Jefferson observed, "descending from theory to practice there is no better book than the Federalist." Since the adoption of the Constitution, scholars, judges, and lawyers have elevated the Federalist Papers to a unique status as the most authoritative source for discerning the framers' original intent.

[*See also* **Articles of Confederation; Constitution; Constitutional Convention of 1787; Federalism; Hamilton, Alexander; Jay, John;** *and* **Madison, James.**]

BIBLIOGRAPHY

Cooke, Jacob E., ed. *The Federalist.* Middletown, Conn.: Wesleyan University Press, 1961.

Engeman, Thomas S., Edward J. Erler, and Thomas B. Hofeller, eds. *The Federalist Concordance.* Middletown, Conn.: Wesleyan University Press, 1980.

John P. Kaminski

FEDERALIST PARTY

By 1783 critics of the Articles of Confederation—those who thought the Continental Congress too weak and its powers insufficient—were using the word "federal" when discussing the powers and stature of Congress. In June 1783 George Washington, as commander-in-chief of the army, sent a circular letter to state governors discussing the need to add "tone to our federal government." The term federal was thus both a description of the central government and a shorthand method of describing the program for enhancing its authority. By 1786 Washington, James Madison, and their political friends were referring to those who opposed strengthening the Articles of Confederation as "anti-federal."

At the Constitutional Convention of 1787, the Federalists drafted a Constitution that greatly increased the powers of Congress and the executive, and the debate over ratification sharpened the lines of division. Washington, elected president in 1789, solidified the organization of the embryonic Federalist Party through the use of patronage. Although Washington's public criteria for federal offices were honesty and intelligence, in practice he found those qualities only in persons who agreed with him politically. Treasury secretary Alexander Hamilton took the next step in party development when he gave the new party a political creed. Hamilton's fiscal policy, which involved funding the national debt through the issue of bonds and the founding of a Bank of the United States to provide a national currency, advanced a Federalist political program that won the support of wealthy merchants and landowners. The outbreak of war in Europe in 1783 further polarized American opinion, and the political parties became associated with the contestants in Europe: the Federalists were regarded as pro-British and their "Republican" opponents, led by Thomas Jefferson, as pro-French. By means of the Alien and Sedition Acts, passed in 1798 as war with France loomed, the Federalist majority in Congress sought to silence their Republican critics.

By the middle of Washington's second term, he was an avowed partisan, and his successor John Adams was a staunch Federalist from Massachusetts. The election of Jefferson as president in 1800 ended Federalist rule, and the party never recovered control of the national government. The party's chief contribution was to convert the Constitution into a stable, relatively affluent government that they peacefully turned over to their electoral successors.

After 1800 the party's dwindling popular support was mainly confined to rural New

England and pockets of voters of German or Scots ancestry in the mountain valleys of the South. The Federalists ran Charles Cotesworth Pinckney of South Carolina for president in 1804 and 1808, and DeWitt Clinton of New York in 1812. The party's opposition to the War of 1812 and flirtation with disunion in the Hartford Convention of 1814 completed its ruin. In the presidential election of 1816, Rufus King of New York, the last Federalist presidential candidate, lost to Republican James Monroe. Most Federalists, such as Daniel Webster, who began his congressional career in 1814, became National Republicans in the 1820s and joined the Whig Party in the 1830s.

[*See also* **Adams, John; Alien and Sedition Acts; Articles of Confederation; Conservatism; Constitutional Convention of 1787; Federal Government, Executive Branch: Presidency, The; Federal Government, Legislative Branch: House of Representatives; Federal Government, Legislative Branch: Senate; Federalism; Hamilton, Alexander; Hartford Convention; Madison, James; Political Parties; Washington, George; Webster, Daniel;** *and* **Whig Party.**]

BIBLIOGRAPHY

Banner, James M., Jr. *To the Hartford Convention: The Federalists and the Origins of Party Politics in Massachusetts, 1789–1815*. New York: Alfred A. Knopf, 1970.

Elkins, Stanley, and Eric McKitrick. *The Age of Federalism*. New York: Oxford University Press, 1993.

Norman Risjord

FEDERAL RESERVE ACT

The Federal Reserve Act (1913) had its origins in the Panic of 1907, when the collapse of several loosely managed trust companies sparked a general financial crisis. Depositors frightened by the collapse of trust companies withdrew money from banks, which then called in loans and dumped securities on the market, contributing to a serious recession. Financier J. P. Morgan saved the day, using a fund created by bankers and the federal government to prop up threatened but basically sound financial institutions.

The crisis illuminated severe weaknesses in the American banking system. National banks around the country issued currency backed with U.S. government bonds. They kept their reserves either in cash or on deposit in several designated money-center banks. The system produced an inelastic currency—since it was tied to the availability of Treasury bonds, it could not expand with the economy. The problem became particularly acute at harvest time, when the demand for money rose as farmers sold their crops. Moreover, because reserves were dispersed throughout the system, mobilizing them during a crisis proved extremely difficult.

The panic inspired Congress in 1908 to create the National Monetary Commission, chaired by Senator Nelson Aldrich of Rhode Island, to study banking reform. A Republican stalwart with personal ties to the John D. Rockefeller family, Aldrich was in no sense a Progressive, yet in this case he was open to change. His commission toured Europe studying continental financial arrangements, but Aldrich made his most important contact in New York. There he met Paul Warburg, a member of the noted German-Jewish banking family and a partner at Kuhn, Loeb, who combined strong civic responsibility with wide financial experience.

In late 1910, Aldrich, Warburg, and several other leading bankers met secretly to hammer out a plan to create a central bank along European lines, but more decentralized. The group recommended the creation of fifteen regional banks, controlled by local bankers, to handle the issuance of currency. These institutions would issue money in exchange for either gold or "real bills"—short-term commercial paper backed by goods (inventories, for example). Such a currency would be "elastic," that is, able to expand with the economy. The regional banks would also hold the reserves of financial institutions in their region, permitting a concerted response to any crisis. Over the regional banks would stand a central board composed largely of representatives of business and finance but also including a few government appointees. Aldrich formally submitted the plan to Congress in January 1911.

Although Aldrich's proposals remained stalled in Congress for almost two years, the election of Woodrow Wilson in 1912 opened the way for financial reform. In December 1912, even before Wilson's inauguration, Senator Carter Glass of Virginia, chairman of the Senate Banking Committee, put forward his own plan. It closely resembled Aldrich's, except that Glass, a states' rights Democrat, sharply restricted the authority of the central board.

Glass quickly secured Wilson's support, but his plan horrified most congressional Progressives. Deeply suspicious of bankers, whom they believed manipulated the financial system for their own ends, Progressives feared that Glass's measure would increase bankers' power. Fortunately Wilson, who knew little about finance and had few convictions on the subject, made enough concessions to win over Progressive critics. In a key concession, Wilson agreed to strengthen the authority of the central board and to make all of its members presidential appointees, giving Washington a predominant voice in the new system.

The financial community opposed the final version of the bill, which it feared gave the federal government too much authority over the nation's banking system. As a result, Progressives rallied around the measure and gave the proposal a radical aura that it did not entirely merit. The bill, authorizing the creation of twelve regional banks and the Federal Reserve Board in Washington, became law in 1913. The Federal Reserve Act had one serious weakness, not rectified until the 1930s: It did not define precisely the relationship between the regional banks and the central board. Nevertheless, the Federal Reserve Act gave the United States a central bank able to pursue consistent monetary policies.

[*See also* **Economic Policy: Regulation; Federal Reserve System; Monetary Policy; Progressive Era; States' Rights;** *and* **Wilson, Woodrow.**]

BIBLIOGRAPHY

Chernow, Ron. *The House of Morgan.* New York: Atlantic Monthly Press, 1990.

Chernow, Ron. *The Warburgs.* New York: Random House, 1993.

Link, Arthur S. *Woodrow Wilson and the Progressive Era.* New York: Harper Stanley, 1954.

West, Robert C. *Banking Reform and the Federal Reserve.* Ithaca, N.Y.: Cornell University Press, 1977.

Wyatt C. Wells

FEDERAL RESERVE SYSTEM

Congress created the Federal Reserve System, the central bank of the United States, in 1913. It consisted of twelve regional banks and the Federal Reserve Board in Washington, which had ill-defined powers of oversight. Lawmakers expected the system to regulate the supply of money and credit (monetary policy), mitigating the effects of the business cycle; to oversee, in concert with other federal and state agencies, the operations of commercial banks; and to carry out the government's international financial transactions. Ideally, the system's decentralized structure would reduce the influence of New York City banks over the nation's credit system.

During World War I, the Federal Reserve financed government deficits by expanding the money supply, and it broke the postwar inflation by raising interest rates and sharply restricting credit. In the 1930s, however, the shortcomings of the Federal Reserve's decentralized structure became apparent. During the Great Depression, infighting between the regional banks and the central board prevented a coordinated response to the crisis. Incoherent monetary policy permitted the money supply to contract by a third, contributing mightily to the catastrophe.

Accordingly, President Franklin Delano Roosevelt and Marriner Eccles, his appointee as chair of the Federal Reserve Board, initiated reforms. Eccles persuaded Congress to enact new legislation confirming the board's authority over the regional banks, solidifying the position of its chair, and vesting in the Open Market Committee (a group consisting of members of the Federal Reserve Board and the presidents of the regional banks) control over monetary policy.

Despite its new organization, the Federal Reserve soon fell under the influence of the Treasury Department. Throughout World War II and for many years after, the central bank at the behest of the Treasury "pegged" long-term interest rates at a low level, permitting Washington to finance its debt cheaply. This policy became controversial after 1945 because, by accommodating every demand for credit, it threatened to fuel inflation. Surging prices during the Korean War forced the Treasury to relent and grant the Federal Reserve the authority to set interest rates as it saw fit. The subsequent increase in the cost of money, engineered by the central bank, helped stabilize prices.

Over the next twenty years, the Federal Reserve exercised its newfound autonomy carefully, following policies described as "leaning against the wind." Put simply, during recessions it cut interest rates to stimulate production, and when inflation threatened it increased rates to cool demand. But the stagflation of the 1970s—simultaneous inflation and recession—stymied the central bank. After years of vacillating between expansion and contraction, the Federal Reserve in 1979 under Chairperson Paul Volcker embraced a policy of fierce monetary stringency, driving interest rates to near 20 percent and triggering the worst recession since the 1930s. Hard times inspired calls for reforms to make the Federal Reserve more responsive to elected officials. Economic recovery after 1983, however, coupled with stable, low inflation, bore out the wisdom of Volcker's policy and garnered the Federal Reserve immense prestige. Subsequently, the central bank followed policies designed primarily to keep prices stable. Under the leadership of Alan Greenspan, the Federal Reserve continued this policy through the long boom of the 1990s.

When he retired in 2006, Alan Greenspan's policies appeared to be remarkably successful: low inflation, low unemployment, and long expansion periods. The 2008 financial collapse would erase this legacy. Instead of being viewed as the Wall Street Maestro, his policy of low interest rates were blamed for overexpansion in credit markets and his unwillingness to intercede in the housing market was seen as fueling the housing bubble.

Ben Bernanke, a Princeton economics professor, was selected to replace Greenspan. Bernanke had established himself as an economist of the Great Depression, pioneering studies on the gold standard and coining the term "financial accelerator" to describe the unique role banks play in processing credit information. His announcement originally sparked concern, with some arguing he would stray from Greenspan. This proved unfounded because Bernanke followed his predecessor's policies.

The first signs of crisis appeared in the housing market during 2006. The Fed received criticism for not responding quickly to the housing bubble, insisting that the crisis was "contained." As it became clear that the financial crisis was larger than expected, the Fed began cutting interest rates. Bernanke was determined that his Fed would not have the legacy of cautious action that plagued it during the Great Depression. Using the powers of "unusual and exigent circumstances," Bernanke and NY Fed Chief Timothy Geithner organized a $30 billion loan to save Bear Stearns in March 2008. The Fed worked with the Treasury Department to arrange bailouts for major banking institutions and create the Trouble Asset Relief Program. Bernanke, arguing that there were tools the Fed had to stimulate the economy even with interest rates at zero, instituted quantitative easing to increase money circulation. A second round, named QE2, was announced in 2010.

Bernanke and the Fed have received criticisms from the right and the left for the Fed's handling of the financial meltdown. Calls for more transparency and congressional oversight were codified into law in the Dodd–Frank Wall Street Reform and Consumer Protection Act, signed into law in July 2010. Despite these criticisms, President Barack Obama nominated Bernanke for a second term, which was confirmed in early 2010.

[*See also* **Economic Policy: Banking and Finance Regulation; Economic Policy: Regulation; Federal Government, Executive Branch: Treasury Department; Federal Reserve Act; Monetary Policy; New Deal; Progressive Era;** *and* **Roosevelt, Franklin Delano.**]

BIBLIOGRAPHY

Kettl, Donald F. *Leadership at the Fed.* New Haven, Conn.: Yale University Press, 1986.

Wessel, David. *In Fed We Trust: Ben Bernanke's War on the Great Panic: How the Federal Reserve Became the Fourth Branch of Government.* New York: Crown Business, 2009.

Wooley, John T. *Monetary Politics: The Federal Reserve and the Politics of Monetary Policy.* Cambridge, UK; New York: Cambridge University Press, 1984.

Wyatt C. Wells and Andrea Field

FEDERAL TRADE COMMISSION

An independent federal regulatory agency. Created in 1914, the Federal Trade Commission (FTC) was part of an antitrust settlement that included the Clayton Antitrust Act and congressional acceptance of a judicial "rule of reason," which tolerated aspects of business concentration. Consisting of five appointed commissioners, the agency inherited the investigatory powers of an earlier Bureau of Corporations and became the administrator of regulatory legislation outlawing "unfair methods of competition." Subsequently, it also became the administrator of laws under which it supervised export associations and enforced restraints on price discrimination, deceptive advertising, proposed mergers, and certain labeling, lending, packaging, and warranty practices.

The FTC's creation was supported both by antimonopolists seeking to halt the "unfair competition" involved in trust-building and by businessmen seeking "fairness" as a basis for greater order and stability. Differing definitions of "fairness" could serve differing ends, however, and in practice the FTC pursued contradictory policies. At times it fought industrial concentration, most notably in its investigations of the electrical power, iron and steel, and cement industries in the 1930s and in its actions against "shared monopoly" in the 1970s. But at other times, especially under chairs William E. Humphrey (1925–1933), Edward F. Howrey (1953–1955), and James C. Miller (1981–1985), it sponsored corporate collaboration and business stabilization schemes. In addition, its rulings tended to be more concerned with protecting complaining competitors than with encouraging competitive markets, especially in its enforcement of the Robinson–Patman Anti-Price Discrimination Act, which from 1945 to 1965 generated nearly 70 percent of the FTC's regulatory orders.

Historians generally regard the FTC as one of the least successful of America's regulatory commissions. It showed political staying power and conducted investigations of lasting importance for industrial policy. But it was more often characterized by contradictory impulses, unstable policies and standards, persisting organizational problems, and the squandering of its resources on relatively inconsequential matters.

[*See also* **Antitrust Legislation and Law; Federal Regulatory Agencies;** *and* **Progressive Era.**]

BIBLIOGRAPHY

Katzmann, Robert A. *Regulatory Bureaucracy: The Federal Trade Commission and Antitrust Policy.* Cambridge, Mass.: MIT Press, 1980.

Stone, Alan. *Economic Regulation and the Public Interest: The Federal Trade Commission in Theory and Practice.* Ithaca, N.Y.: Cornell University Press, 1977.

Ellis W. Hawley

FELLOW-SERVANT RULE (TORT)

Between the 1830s and the early 1900s, the fellow-servant rule was one of three defenses that could be invoked by a negligent employer to avoid paying compensation to workers injured in workplace accidents. The others were contributory negligence and assumption of risk.

Under the common law rules of negligence liability a worker who was injured in a workplace accident was eligible to receive compensation for his injuries if the worker could show that the accident had been caused by the failure of his employer to exercise due care in maintaining a safe workplace. Under the fellow-servant rule, however, the employer could avoid liability if a fellow worker had caused the accident. The legal argument implied that the injured worker should be seeking compensation from the fellow worker instead. Since fellow workers often did not have many financial assets, injured workers typically received little accident compensation from fellow workers when the fellow-servant defense was invoked.

Some scholars argue that the negligence rules and the three defenses evolved as judges sought to avoid slowing the industrialization process in the nineteenth century. Law and economics scholars argue that the fellow-servant defense can contribute to more efficient accident prevention in settings where workers can influence their fellow workers' accident prevention decisions more effectively than the employer can. For example, in a coal mine where workers work in isolated pairs throughout a large mine, the miners working together are far more effective at monitoring each other's accident prevention than a supervisor who visited once or twice a day would be.

The common law rules for workplace accident liability developed as the relations between masters and their servants in apprenticeship contracts were increasingly replaced by situations where employers hired workers for pay in industrial relationships. Legal scholars suggest that the key court decisions that began to establish the common law rules for negligence liability in workplace accidents were rulings in *Priestly v. Fowler* in 1837 in England and *Farwell v. Boston & Worcester R.R.* in 1842. The fellow-servant defense was invoked as part of the *Farwell* decision as one of reasons why the railroad was not obligated to compensate Farwell for his injuries, and the defense can be found in a significant number of decisions for the rest of the century.

In the late 1800s and early 1900s more than half of the states passed laws disallowing one or more of the three defenses. The Federal Employer Liability Acts in 1906 and 1908 restricted the fellow-servant defense for workers injured in railroad accidents. As each state adopted workers' compensation laws between 1911 and 1948, the employer became liable for all accidents "arising out of or in the course of employment." The fellow-servant defense was no longer allowed in those states, even when the employer opted not to participate in the workers' compensation system.

[*See also* **Tort, Law of.**]

BIBLIOGRAPHY

Fishback, Price, and Shawn Kantor. *A Prelude to the Welfare State: The Origins of Workers' Compensation.* Chicago: University of Chicago Press, 2000.

Friedman, Lawrence. *A History of American Law.* New York: Simon & Schuster, 1985.

Horwitz, Morton. *The Transformation of American Law, 1780–1860.* Cambridge, Mass.: Harvard University Press, 1977.

Landes, William, and Richard A. Posner. *The Economic Structure of Tort Law.* Cambridge, Mass.: Harvard University Press, 1987.

Schwartz, Gary T. "Tort Law and the Economy in Nineteenth Century America: A Reinterpretation." *Yale Law Journal* 90 (July 1981): 1717–1775.

Tomlins, Christopher. *Law, Labor and Ideology in the Early American Republic.* Cambridge, UK; New York: Cambridge University Press, 1993.

Price V. Fishback

FEMINISM

Throughout recorded history, some women have protested their exclusion from full participation in their society's educational, economic, social, cultural, sexual, and/or political life. But most have not described themselves as feminists or professed a belief in feminism. The historian Gerda Lerner has addressed this problem by defining feminist consciousness rather than feminism.

From "Feminist Consciousness" to Feminism. "Feminist consciousness" is especially useful for embracing all those women who, over the centuries, have struggled against patriarchal constraints, but have not acted or written as participants in a larger women's movement. In *The Creation of Feminist Consciousness* (1993), Lerner defined feminist consciousness as women's awareness "that they belong to a subordinate group; that they have suffered wrongs as a group; that their condition of subordination is not natural, but societally determined; that they must join with other women to remedy these wrongs; and finally, that they must and can provide an alternate vision of societal organization in which women as well as men will enjoy autonomy and self-determination." Even with this broad definition, most women—including those who have protested women's condition—have not identified themselves as feminists.

The actual word *feminism*, or *feminisme*, was coined by the French reformer Charles

Fourier (1772–1837) in his *Théorie des quatres mouvements et des destinées généralisés,* written sometime between 1808 and 1837. According to the historian Karen Offen, Alexandre Dumas the Younger first used the word *féministe,* pejoratively, in 1872. In 1882, Hubertine Auclert, a French advocate of woman suffrage, began to employ the term and even used it in a letter to the American suffragists Elizabeth Cady Stanton and Susan B. Anthony. By the early 1890s, the words had entered common political discourse in Europe; in the *London Daily News* (1894); and in Latin America, most notably in Argentina. About 1910, it appeared in the United States.

Most nineteenth-century American suffragists did not refer to themselves as *feminists* or espouse an ideology called feminism. Rather, they saw themselves as advocates of women's rights or as suffragists. In 1910, a group of young women in New York City formed a club they called Heterodoxy. In *The Grounding of Modern Feminism* (1987), the historian Nancy Cott describes their commitment to personal emancipation, unconventional behavior, and self-fulfillment. Although they supported suffrage and other formal rights, they emphasized the individual psychological and social emancipation of women and prefigured the many young women of the 1920s who similarly sought emancipation in personal realization rather than in any ideology or movement.

Shifting Views of Feminism, 1920–1970. After the Nineteenth Amendment was ratified in 1920, some women in Alice Paul's National Woman's Party called themselves *feminists.* Many of these women were independently wealthy and/or hostile to other progressive reforms. Some were stridently anti-Semitic or racist as well. By contrast, Progressive women of the Old Left, civil rights movement, and labor unions, who joined the fight against fascism or organized unskilled workers during the Depression of the 1930s, subsumed feminist issues under the Marxist phrase "The Woman Question." To them, the word *feminist* conjured up an image of a conservative, wealthy woman who voted Republican, rather than supporting the New Deal, the Communist or Socialist parties, or radical labor unions. During World War II, these same women continued to debate many issues subsumed under the Woman Question rubric, but without identifying themselves as feminists or espousing an ideology called feminism.

After the war, the very word *feminist* came to denote an unpatriotic woman who dared challenge the Cold War effort to contain Communism. Since women were expected to stay home and fight the Cold War as consumers for their families, feminists, like working women, emerged as major villains at the height of the anti-Communist hysteria. During the 1960s, women's rights activists did not commonly use the word *feminism.* Many of the women who founded the National Organization for Women (1966) and who fought legal discrimination against women had deep roots in the Progressive politics of the 1930s, 1940s, and 1950s. Furthermore, feminism still brought to mind images of bourgeois women unconcerned with issues of race, social class, or poverty.

To the younger women who created the highly publicized women's liberation movement in the late 1960s, the word feminism also seemed too tame. Having emerged from the civil rights or New Left movements, they viewed themselves as radicals who were unconcerned with bourgeois feminist issues. The press dubbed all these young activists "Women's Libbers," a term of disparagement that trivialized the movement and which activists consciously avoided.

Feminism since 1970. By the 1970s, as the various branches of the women's movement began to fragment and merge, new populations of American women embraced the women's movement and activists began to refer themselves as feminists—sometimes qualified as liberal, radical, socialist, or lesbian. To these activists, the term now expressed their determination to seek emancipation by challenging economic, political, sexual, cultural, and social traditions. In *The Politics of Women's Liberation* (1975), the political scientist Jo Freeman compared the difference between a "traditional" and a feminist view of society. Feminists, she argued, recognize the changing, artificial, and highly arbitrary ways that men and women are permitted or denied access to the educational, political, and economic institutions of their society. Traditionalists, by comparison, view the organization of gender in society as normal and natural.

Some feminists emphasized women's rights and demanded equality with men. Others argued that society needed to change to accommodate women and their capacity to bear children, rather than trying to squeeze women's experiences into a male life cycle. From this perspective came the feminist creation of "family-friendly" work policies that could embrace women both as workers and as mothers.

As women of various minority groups analyzed their own subordinate position within their communities, some resisted the word *feminism*, viewing it as a "family quarrel" among white, middle-class women. In 1983, the African American writer Alice Walker coined the term *womanism* to express the needs and aspirations of women of color. The word *womanist*, she explained, grew out of a black folk expression that mothers often used with their daughters. "You acting womanish," a mother would say, meaning that the youngster was engaging in outrageous, audacious, or willful behavior. Minority women, many of whom had never been schooled in learned helplessness, Walker felt, could better express their desire for equality and freedom with this term. Not all minority women agreed, but the phrase did gain some currency.

With the conservative backlash of the 1970s and beyond, the phrase "I'm not a feminist, but" became almost mandatory for women political candidates and other women entering the public arena, distancing them from media-generated stereotypes of man-hating superwomen, even as they worked for feminist goals.

By the 1980s and 1990s, many different populations of women—old, young, trade unionists, displaced homemakers—had reinvented feminism to address the specific realities of their lives. Four United Nations' World Women's Conferences convened in 1975 (Mexico City), 1980 (Copenhagen), 1985 (Nairobi), and 1995 (Beijing), further broadened the term, so that feminism no longer belonged to American women or indeed to any particular society. The *Platform for Action* adopted by the Beijing conference urged all nations to view all social, political, economic, cultural, and military policies "through the eyes of women." This meant thinking about development, population control, human rights, and other global issues *as if women mattered*. In Africa, for example, fuel and water and the ritual mutilation of the body became feminist issues. In other areas, feminist concerns included dowry deaths, domestic violence, child labor, and the traffic in sexual slaves.

With the spread of feminist perspectives to many nations, often referred to as "global feminism," these transnational feminist networks promoted the improvement of women's lives in countless ways. Although activists debated many issues, they all tended to emphasize that equality for women required an end to violence and poverty and access to education. That, in the end, constituted the broadest and most inclusive description of feminism as the twenty-first century began.

[*See also* **Anthony, Susan B.; Anti-Communism; Conservatism; National Organization of Women; National Woman's Party; New Deal; New Left; Progressive Era; Radicalism; Republican Party; Socialism; Stanton, Elizabeth Cady; Woman Suffrage Movement;** *and* **Women in Politics since 1920.**]

BIBLIOGRAPHY

Cott, Nancy. *The Grounding of Modern Feminism*. New Haven, Conn.: Yale University Press, 1987.

hooks, bell. *Ain't I a Woman: Black Women and Feminism*. London: Pluto Press, 1983.

Kauffman, Linda. *American Feminist Thought at Century's End*. Cambridge, Mass.: Blackwell, 1993.

Lerner, Gerda. *The Creation of Feminist Consciousness*. New York: Oxford University Press, 1993.

Offen, Karen. "Defining Feminism: A Comparative Historical Approach." *Signs* 14 (Autumn 1988): 119–157.

Offen, Karen. "On the French Origin of the Word Feminism and Feminist." *Feminist Studies* 8, No. 2 (Fall 1988): 45–61.

Rosen, Ruth. *The World Split Open: How The Modern Women's Movement Changed America*. New York: Viking, 2000.

Scott, Joan. *Feminism and History*. Oxford; New York: Oxford University Press, 1996.

Walker, Alice. *In Search of Our Mothers' Garden*. San Diego, Calif.: Harcourt Brace Jovanovich, 1983.

Warhol, Robyn R., and Diane Price Herndl, eds. *Feminisms: An Anthology of Literary Theory and Criticism*, 2d ed. New Brunswick, N.J.: Rutgers University Press, 1997.

Ruth Rosen

FERRARO, GERALDINE

(1935–2011) was the first female nominated to run for vice president by a major political party. In 1984, Democratic presidential nominee Walter Mondale selected Ferraro, a member of Congress representing New York, as his running mate.

Born in Newburgh, New York, Ferraro moved to New York City as a child. She married businessman John Zaccaro in 1960 and graduated from Fordham University School of Law that same year. She later was named assistant district attorney for Queens County, New York.

Ferraro launched her political career with a successful race for the U.S. House of Representatives from Queens in 1978. A Democrat, she served three terms in the House before Walter Mondale selected her to be his running mate for vice president in the 1984 presidential election. Ferraro became the first woman to be nominated on a presidential ticket by a major American political party. She also became the first Italian American to be nominated. Mondale had hoped that Ferraro would appeal to both women and working class "Reagan Democrats." Ferraro proved to be a determined campaigner, but she was dogged by questions regarding her husband's finances, as well as questions about her pro-choice stance on abortion, which contradicted the teachings of the Catholic Church, of which she was a member. In the end, the Mondale–Ferraro ticket garnered only 41 percent of the vote.

In later years, she remained active in politics and civic life, but never again won elective office. She lost races for the Democratic nomination for the U.S. Senate from New York in 1992 and 1998. In 1993, President Bill Clinton appointed her U.S. Ambassador to the United Nations Commission on Human Rights. She also served as co-host of the CNN political talk show *Crossfire*.

In 2008, Ferraro supported Hillary Clinton in the Democratic presidential primary. During the campaign, she created a minor controversy when she said of Barack Obama, "If Obama was a white man, he would not be in this position. And if he was a woman (of any color) he would not be in this position. He happens to be very lucky to be who he is." Ferraro died in March 2011 from multiple myeloma.

[*See also* **Clinton, Hillary Rodham; Clinton, William J.; Democratic Party;** *and* **Women in Politics since 1920.**]

BIBLIOGRAPHY

Ferraro, Geraldine A., with Linda Bird Francke. *Ferraro: My Story*. Evanston, Ill: Northwestern University Press, 2004.

Vincent J. Cannato

FIELD, DAVID DUDLEY

(1805–1894), law reformer. David Dudley Field's reputation rested on his advocacy of codification of the law, a process by which scattered court decisions and legislation were assembled into accessible codes. In 1846 Field was appointed to the New York state codification commission, over which he exerted enormous influence. Two years later, the commission produced the so-called Field Code and over the next two decades Field helped to frame additional political, civil, and penal codes. Several other states adopted his civil procedure and penal codes. In 1873 Field extended his scope to include international law, founding the Association for the Reform and Codification of the Law of Nations.

Field's legal career mixed high-profile constitutional cases and important business clients in ways that typified the most successful Gilded Age practitioners. Field, for example, persuaded the U.S. Supreme Court to reject the wartime practice of using military rather than civilian courts when the latter were still open. In 1869 he served as counsel to Jay Gould and James Fisk in the controversial Erie Railroad litigation. The New York City bar association accused him of unprofessional conduct, but its recommendations of censure were never adopted officially. Field's reputation also suffered because of his connections with William Magear Tweed, a codirector of the Erie Railroad and the archetypical late nineteenth-century political boss.

[*See also* **Jurisprudence.**]

Kermit L. Hall

FIFTEENTH AMENDMENT

The Fifteen Amendment (1870) to the U.S. Constitution declares that the right to vote shall not be denied or restricted by the federal or state governments on account of race. The amendment reflected both the egalitarian ideals of Reconstruction and the self-interest of the Republican Party.

Two developments led to the framing of the amendment: the northern state elections of 1867, in which voters rejected black suffrage, and the presidential election of 1868, which signaled future electoral trouble for the Republicans. Having enfranchised southern freedpeople in 1867, Republican leaders proposed the enfranchisement of African Americans—most of whom could be counted on to vote Republican—in those northern and border states that still prohibited black voting.

The Republican-controlled Congress approved the Fifteenth Amendment on 26 February 1869. In the brief but intense ratification struggle in the state legislatures, Democrats opposed and Republicans supported ratification. With the outcome uncertain, a combination of pressure and incentives brought about final ratification on 30 March 1870.

Upon ratification, adult black males in seventeen northern and border states became voters. With racist repression in the South, growing political indifference in the North, and federal inaction, however, most southern and border state blacks lost the franchise.

During the long retreat from egalitarian principles after 1867, federal courts often interpreted the amendment narrowly to deny federal authority to prosecute violations of federal voting rights. From 1941 onward, however, courts began to reverse this trend. The landmark Voting Rights Act of 1965 owed its constitutional underpinning to the Fifteenth Amendment.

[*See also* **Civil Rights Cases; Civil Rights Legislation; Fourteenth Amendment; Racism; Reconstruction;** ***and*** **Republican Party.**]

BIBLIOGRAPHY

Elliott, Ward E. Y. *The Rise of Guardian Democracy: The Supreme Court's Role in Voting Rights Disputes, 1845–1969*. Cambridge, Mass.: Harvard University Press, 1974.

Gillette, William. *The Right to Vote: Politics and the Passage of the Fifteenth Amendment*. Baltimore: Johns Hopkins University Press, 1969.

William Gillette

FILLMORE, MILLARD

(1800–1874), thirteenth president of the United States. The son of a tenant farmer in western New York, Millard Fillmore gained a minimal education before he was apprenticed as a clothier. After reading law with a local judge, he moved to Buffalo and gained admittance to the bar at the age of twenty-three. Capitalizing on the Anti-Masonic frenzy in New York, Fillmore won election to the state legislature in 1828. He joined the Whig Party in 1834 and served four terms in the U.S. Congress. A supporter of Henry Clay's American System, Fillmore helped craft the Tariff of 1842. After retiring from Congress in 1844, Fillmore lost a campaign for governor of New York, but his continued service to the party won him the vice presidency in 1848. Fillmore initially deferred to President Zachary Taylor, playing a small role in the new administration. As president of the Senate, he broke with Taylor to support the Compromise of 1850. When Taylor died unexpectedly that July, Fillmore became president. He signed the compromise measures into law, confident that the sectional crisis had finally been resolved.

Capitalizing on his presidential patronage power, Fillmore removed his intraparty opponents from office. The ensuing battle led to the Whigs' decision in 1852 to bypass Fillmore and give the presidential nomination to the Mexican War hero Winfield Scott, who subsequently lost to Democrat Franklin Pierce. Out of office and skeptical about the prospects of the Whigs, Fillmore in 1855 joined the new nativist Know-Nothing Party, which nominated him for president in 1856. Fillmore used the campaign to promote his own nationalist vision, largely ignoring the nativism that brought the party together. After his defeat, Fillmore opposed the Republican Party and Abraham Lincoln's administration, which were both controlled by his political foes. Although he continued to engage in politics in his later years, he exerted little influence, in part because of his personal vindictiveness.

[*See also* **Anti-Masonic Party; Antislavery Movement; Clay, Henry; Compromise of 1850; Federal Government, Executive Branch: Presidency, The; Know-Nothing Party; Tariffs; Taylor, Zachary;** ***and*** **Whig Party.**]

BIBLIOGRAPHY

Rayback, Robert J. *Millard Fillmore*. Buffalo, N.Y.: Buffalo Historic Society, 1959.

Smith, Elbert B. *The Presidencies of Zachary Taylor and Millard Fillmore*. Lawrence: University Press of Kansas, 1988.

Eric D. Daniels

FLAG, U.S.

The thirteen-stripe, fifty-star flag of the United States is one of the most recognized symbols of the nation. Often referred to as the Star-Spangled Banner, the Stars and Stripes, and Old Glory, the flag's early history is filled with myth and misinformation. It is not certain who designed the first flag, although many historians believe that it was Francis Hopkinson, a signer of the Declaration of Independence who also was an artist. Nor is it known who made the first flag, the widely told Betsy Ross story notwithstanding. No document exists explaining why the flag's designer chose the stars and the stripes or the red, white, and blue colors.

The flag came into being with the first Flag Resolution, enacted by the Second Continental Congress on 14 June 1777. It read, "Resolved, that the flag of the United States be thirteen stripes, alternate red and white; that the union be thirteen stars, white in a blue field representing a new constellation."

This resolution and the two subsequent Flag Resolutions (enacted in 1795 to add stars and stripes for each new state and in 1818 to go back to thirteen stripes and to add a star for each new state) did not include language specifying how many points the stars should have or the stars' arrangement in the canton. That situation was rectified on 29 October 1912 when President William Howard Taft signed an Executive Order that, for the first time, set out the flag's exact specifications.

The last three decades of the nineteenth century saw the rise of the "cult of the flag," the near-religious feelings many Americans had for the Stars and Stripes. During this time, the Pledge of Allegiance was written (1892) and recited in the public schools; the first movement toward a national Flag Day holiday was begun, and the first state flag protection laws were drawn up in reaction to the rampant use of the flag's image in packaging and advertising.

President Woodrow Wilson proclaimed the first 14 June Flag Day in 1916. In 1931, President Herbert Hoover signed a bill designating "The Star Spangled Banner"—written by Francis Scott Key during the September 1814 Battle of Baltimore—as the official national anthem. In 1942, Congress adopted the U.S. Flag Code, a series of flag-use guidelines drawn up at the first National Flag Conference in June 1923. On 4 July 1968, Congress passed and President Johnson signed into law the first federal Flag Protection Act, which outlawed flag desecration.

In 1989, in *Texas v. Johnson,* the U.S. Supreme Court ruled the federal law and all state flag protection measures unconstitutional on First Amendment grounds. The Court reaffirmed that ruling in 1990. Since then, Congress frequently has considered, but has not adopted, a Flag Desecration Constitutional Amendment.

In 1943, West Virginia instituted a policy requiring teachers and pupils to participate in the Pledge of Allegiance. The policy prompted a legal challenge from Jehovah's Witnesses after children were expelled from West Virginia public schools for refusing to recite the Pledge. On 14 June 1943, the U.S. Supreme Court, in *West Virginia State Board of Education v. Barnette,* ruled that schoolchildren could not be compelled to recite the Pledge. Despite that ruling, many state legislatures subsequently enacted variants of mandatory school Pledge laws.

In 1954, during the height of the Cold War, the phrase "under God" was added to the Pledge of Allegiance by a congressional act amending the U.S. Flag Code signed by President Dwight D. Eisenhower. The "under God" phrase has survived several legal challenges.

BIBLIOGRAPHY

Furlong, William Rea, and Byron McCandless. *So Proudly We Hail: The History of the United States Flag*. Washington, D.C.: Smithsonian Institution Press, 1981.

Guenter, Scot M. *The American Flag, 1777–1924: Cultural Shifts from Creation to Codification*. Rutherford, N.J.; London: Fairleigh Dickinson University Press; Associated University Presses, 1990.

Leepson, Marc. *Flag: An American Biography*. New York: Thomas Dunne Books/St. Martin's Press, 2005.

Moeller, Henry W. *Shattering an American Myth: Unfurling the History of the Stars and Stripes*. Mattituck, N.Y.: Amereon House, 1992.

Preble, George H. *Origin and History of The American Flag*, 2 vols. Philadelphia: N. L. Brown, 1917.

Marc Leepson

FORD, GERALD R.

(1913–2006), Leslie Lynch King was born in Omaha, Nebraska. His mother left an abusive marriage and took her newborn son back with her to her hometown, Grand Rapids, Michigan. She remarried, and her son took the name of his stepfather—Gerald R. Ford. Following service in the Navy from 1942 to 1946, young Ford returned to Grand Rapids to practice law and enter politics. Michigan was a solidly Republican state, and Ford gravitated to the internationalist wing of that party, led by his state's senior senator, Arthur Vandenberg. The internationalists rejected the calls of conservatives such as Ohio Senator Robert A. Taft for a postwar retreat into isolationism and instead supported the growth of the new United Nations and called for American monetary aid to rebuild Western Europe. In September 1948, Ford upset incumbent four-term congressman Bartel Jonkman, who had long been allied with the conservative wing of the party, and won the Republican primary in Michigan's Fifth Congressional district. That fall, Ford easily won the general election, defeating his democratic opponent, J. Fred Barr Jr.

Ford handily won reelection to the House of Representatives in each of the next thirteen elections, serving in that body until November 1973. While in Congress, Ford specialized in budgetary matters, was a member of the President's Commission to Investigate the Assassination of President Kennedy ("The Warren Commission"), and from 4 January 1964 to 6 December 1973 served as House Minority Leader. On 10 October 1973, Vice President Spiro T. Agnew resigned, pleading *nolo contendere* (no contest) to a charge of income tax evasion. The next day, under the terms of the Twenty-Fifth Amendment, President Richard M. Nixon offered Ford the nomination for vice president. Confirmed by both the House and the Senate, Ford was sworn in on 6 December 1973. He served as vice president until 9 August 1974, when he acceded to the presidency upon Nixon's resignation from that office.

Ford's presidency was highlighted by an 8 September 1974 pardon of Nixon for his Watergate-related offenses, a worsening economy, the final withdrawal of American troops from South Vietnam, and halting attempts to conclude a second strategic arms limitation treaty (SALT II) with the Soviet Union. On 20 November 1975, former California Governor Ronald Reagan announced that he would challenge Ford for the Republican nomination for president. A grueling primary campaign found Ford eventually winning the Republican nomination on 19 August with 1,187 votes to 1,070 for Reagan. In the fall election, Ford faced former Georgia Governor

Jimmy Carter. From having to fire his secretary of agriculture Earl Butz for telling a racist joke to a reporter to Ford's own insistence in the second debate with Carter that "there is no Soviet domination of Eastern Europe," Ford's campaign never got traction. On 2 November 1976, Carter defeated Ford, winning 49.9 percent of the popular vote to Ford's 47.9 percent and 297 electoral votes to Ford's 241.

Ford retired to California, only to reenter the political arena in 1980. That year, Reagan—now the frontrunner for the Republican nomination—explored the possibility of Ford being his running mate. The Ford camp, represented by former Secretary of State Henry Kissinger, suggested that Reagan and Ford create a "shared" presidency. Ford intended to accept the offer, but he carelessly violated Reagan's confidence by publicly discussing the proposal in a televised interview with CBS News's Walter Cronkite. A furious Reagan withdrew the offer; George H. W. Bush was named Reagan's running mate. This effectively ended Ford's political life. Ford once again retired to homes in Rancho Mirage, California, and Vail, Colorado. His death on 26 December 2006 made him the longest-lived U.S. president.

[*See also* **Carter, Jimmy; Nixon, Richard M.;** *and* **Reagan, Ronald.**]

BIBLIOGRAPHY

Cannon, James. *Time and Chance: Gerald Ford's Appointment with History*. New York: HarperCollins, 1994.

Greene, John Robert. *The Presidency of Gerald R. Ford*. Lawrence: University of Kansas Press, 1995.

John Robert Greene

FOUNDATIONS, PHILANTHROPIC

Foundations have long been important actors in U.S. public policy processes. Over many decades they have built and sustained an infrastructure of policy research institutions and advocacy groups. Foundations and the organizations they support wield influence in policy discussion and debate, generating new ideas, supplying policy analysis, funding litigation, and monitoring policy implementation, among other strategies. Foundations are also acted upon, the object of judicial decisions, legislative enactments, and executive agency regulations. Thus, their public policy role has boundaries.

Those boundaries are shaped in part by a rich and complicated legal inheritance. That legacy encompasses developments in the late Middle Ages that gave rise to last wills and testaments, secured property transfers to religious entities, and bestowed rights and privileges on corporate bodies. It includes Elizabethan statutes, most memorably the 1601 Statute of Charitable Uses that aimed to reform charitable activity, defining the roles of charitable trusts and creating mechanisms for overseeing charities. This venerable legal inheritance is significant but in the United States it is tax policy, primarily the Tax Reform Act of 1969, which has had the largest policy impact on American foundations.

Although charitable institutions are of ancient vintage, the large-scale general-purpose foundation is a twentieth-century invention. Some of the most prominent American foundations predated ratification of the Sixteenth Amendment and the Revenue Act of 1913, which established the income tax. A few more foundations came into existence before the 1917 legislation allowing charitable deductions from income and the 1919 legislation permitting charitable deductions from estates. Even in the absence of tax benefits, foundations attracted congressional attention and populist skepticism. The U.S. Commission on Industrial Relations, the so-called Walsh Commission, investigated their activities and reflected widespread suspicions that wealthy donors were using their new foundations to exert control over educational and social welfare organizations. Among other remedies, the Commission's 1916 report recommended that foundations be allowed to pursue only specific and narrowly defined purposes, possess endowments no larger than $1 million, be prohibited from accumulating income, and report routinely to the government about investments and expenditures. Congress did not take action on the recommendations, although the Commission's concerns foreshadowed future regulations.

Growing in numbers and size, foundations began to be viewed differently from other charitable organizations. Beginning in 1943, foundations were required to report annually on their receipts and distributions, a requirement that religious organizations, schools, and hospitals did not face. During the decade of the 1940s, complaints also surfaced about the use of private foundations as mechanisms for controlling business enterprises, thus exempting profits from business taxes and gaining an unfair competitive advantage over other businesses. Some foundations also retained their income and neglected to make distributions for charitable purposes. As early as 1950 the House Ways & Means Committee sought remedies that would restrict financial transactions between foundations and their donors, trustees, and other related parties, an issue that remained unresolved when the Senate Committee on Finance watered down House proposals.

Two congressional committees—one chaired by Representative Eugene Cox in 1952, the other by Representative B. Carroll Reece in 1953—also turned their attention to foundations, asking whether their activities were unpatriotic, subversive, and un-American. The Cox Committee, for the most part, absolved foundations of the charges and praised their contributions to American life. The Reece Committee, after abruptly truncated hearings, leveled charges against foundations that many contemporary observers found laughable. But both committees offered policy proposals that seemed to anticipate future developments: more extensive reporting, minimum charitable distributions, limitations on business holdings, and prohibitions on political activity.

Representative Wright Patman began his one-man inquiry into foundations in 1961 and over the next decade produced volume after volume about their role in the U.S. economy. Patman's data were often unreliable but his reports kept foundations in the legislative crosshairs. Abuses were discussed but not addressed in the Revenue Act of 1964. Congress wanted more information before it took action and the Treasury Department agreed to provide a thorough report on foundations. The Treasury's1965 report lauded foundations for the roles they were playing and offered an authoritative analysis of the issues. Although they were not considered widespread, misdeeds were uncovered and the report proposed a series of preventive measures, remedies, and enforcement strategies. Most of the Treasury Department's proposals found their way into the 1969 Tax Reform Act, creating a regulatory regime that, although amended several times, is largely unchanged. The framework included a strict prohibition on "self-dealing" transactions, a mandatory annual payout for charitable purposes (initially a fluctuating minimum of 6 percent of investment assets, which was later dropped to 5 percent), limitations on holding interests in businesses (no more than 20 percent in any one business), and provisions for a 4 percent excise tax on net investment income (later reduced to 2 percent and, in some circumstances, 1 percent).

The financial provisions of the 1969 Act had enjoyed a long gestation. Other features of the act were responses to more immediate political matters. Testimony about political uses of foundation funds in the late 1960s proved alarming. Foundation grants had been used to assist a political candidate in New York, had supported minority voter registration initiatives in Cleveland to the apparent benefit of mayoral candidate Carl Stokes, and had funded travel and study grants to the senatorial staff of Robert F. Kennedy following his assassination. The 1969 Act aimed to reinforce older provisions against lobbying and electoral activity. It created new provisions for assuring that grants to individuals were fairly and impartially awarded and used legitimately for educational and training purposes; it required foundations to exercise "expenditure responsibility" for grants made to other private foundations and to groups that were not public charities, thus assuring that charitable purposes were met. Enforcement would be bolstered by penalty taxes to be imposed not only on foundations but also on their trustees and senior administrators.

Regulations elaborated since the passage of the Tax Reform Act define terms such as "direct" and "grassroots" lobbying precisely and narrowly. Regulations always change but, generally speaking, foundations can employ a wide range of communications strategies, including mailings, television and radio advertisements, and documentary films. Adhering to guidelines about nonpartisanship, sound research, and "full and fair" discussion of particular legislation, they can communicate with legislators and their staffs. Following guidance about "calls to action," foundations also have latitude to communicate with the public on legislation and public referenda. There are even fewer restrictions of foundation interaction with the executive branch of government. Whether it is dealing with legislators, their staffs, executive agencies, or the broader public, there is wide scope for foundations to engage in policy-related activities.

[*See also* **Income Tax, Federal; Sixteenth Amendment;** *and* **Taxation.**]

BIBLIOGRAPHY

Anheier, Helmut K., and David C. Hammack, eds. *American Foundations: Roles and Contributions.* Washington, DC: Brookings Institution Press, 2010.

Condliffe Lagemann, Ellen, ed. *Philanthropic Foundations: New Scholarship and New Possibilities.* Bloomington: Indiana University Press, 1999.

Ferris, James M., ed. *Foundations and Public Policy: Leveraging Philanthropic Dollars, Knowledge, and Networks for Greater Impact.* New York: The Foundation Center, 2009.

James Allen Smith

FOURTEENTH AMENDMENT

Congress's first attempt to settle the issues of the Civil War and restore the former Confederate states to the Union (1868). The first of the amendment's five sections defined state and national citizenship, reversing the ruling in *Scott v. Sandford* that African Americans were not citizens of the United States. It also forbade states to deprive anyone of the rights of citizenship, infringe fundamental rights without due process of law, or deny equal protection of the laws. Other sections reduced the congressional representation of any state that denied voting rights to any class of men, disqualified many former government officials who had supported the Confederacy from holding public office, and guaranteed payment of debts incurred in suppressing the rebellion while barring payment of those incurred in support of it. Since the amendment appeared to sanction voting discrimination against women, some women's rights advocates opposed it. The fifth section authorized Congress to enforce the prior four sections.

Nearly all the states that had remained loyal to the Union quickly ratified the proposed amendment after Congress submitted it to the states for ratification in June 1866, but all the ex-Confederate states except Tennessee refused. Congress then passed the Reconstruction Act, which pronounced existing governments in the South provisional until they adopted new constitutions and ratified the amendment. With this prodding, the amendment was ratified on 9 July 1868.

In the decades following, the Supreme Court defined the amendment narrowly to maintain a clear distinction between the powers of the federal and state governments. In the Slaughterhouse Cases (1873), the Court distinguished the rights Americans held as state citizens from their rights as U.S. citizens. The Fourteenth Amendment, the Court held, guaranteed only the latter. In the Civil Rights Cases (1883), the Court held that Congress could enforce the amendment only against state actions and could not punish private citizens for violating civil rights. In *Plessy v. Ferguson* (1896), the Court ruled that racial segregation did not deprive African Americans of equal protection of the law. Other decisions held that the amendment did not require the states to adhere to the protections written into the Bill of Rights.

Although the Court narrowed the Fourteenth Amendment's guarantee of civil rights and civil liberties, it took an expansive view of the amendment's protection of property rights. From the 1880s to the later 1930s, in such cases as *Lochner v. New York* (1905), for example, the Court held that the Fourteenth Amendment's due process clause protected corporations from governmental regulation of such matters as workers' wages and working conditions and prices charged for goods and services. In the New Deal Era, when this *laissez-faire* interpretation of the Fourteenth Amendment hobbled governmental efforts to deal with the Great Depression, the Court reversed itself and ceased to overthrow economic regulation on constitutional grounds.

After World War II the Supreme Court began to use the equal protection clause of the Fourteenth Amendment to strike down state infringements of nonproperty civil rights and to sustain federal laws protecting such rights. Ruling that the Fourteenth Amendment "selectively incorporated" the most important provisions of the Bill of Rights, the court established a national body of rights that states cannot infringe. In *Brown v. Board of Education* (1954), the Court rejected the *Plessy* decision, ruling that the equal protection clause forbade racial segregation. By expanding the scope of the Fourteenth Amendment, the Supreme Court after the 1930s became a major influence on public policy issues relating to civil liberties and civil rights.

[*See also* **Bill of Rights; *Brown v. Board of Education;* Civil Rights; Civil Rights Cases; Civil Rights Legislation; Civil Liberties; Constitution; Federalism; *Lochner v. New York; Plessy v. Ferguson;* Reconstruction; *Scott v. Sandford;* Slaughterhouse Cases; States' Rights; Supreme Court, U.S.;** *and* **Woman Suffrage Movement.**]

BIBLIOGRAPHY

Cortner, Richard C. *The Supreme Court and the Second Bill of Rights.* Madison: University of Wisconsin Press, 1981.

Nelson, William E. *The Fourteenth Amendment: From Political Principle to Judicial Doctrine.* Cambridge, Mass.: Harvard University Press, 1988.

Michael Les Benedict

FRANKFURTER, FELIX

(1882–1965), an Austrian by birth, Felix Frankfurter immigrated to the United States in 1894.

He graduated from the College of the City of New York in 1902 and from Harvard Law School in 1906. He served on the faculty of the latter institution from 1914 until 1939 and was a pioneer in the field of administrative law. Frankfurter held a number of public positions before and during the Progressive Era, including assistant U.S. attorney for the southern district of New York (1906–1909); law officer for the Bureau of Insular Affairs in the War Department (1910–1914); assistant to Secretary of War, Newton D. Baker (1917); secretary and counsel of President Woodrow Wilson's Mediation Commission (1917); and chair of the War Labor Policies Board (1918). At this time, Frankfurter also helped found the Progressive magazine, the *New Republic,* and he served as a representative of the American Zionist movement at the Paris Peace Conference in 1919. Exhibiting a strong commitment to civil liberties and civil rights, Frankfurter helped found the American Civil Liberties Union in 1920, served as an advisor to the National Association for the Advancement of Colored People, and supported the campaign to overturn the death penalty convictions of the immigrant Italian anarchists, Nicola Sacco and Bartolomeo Vanzetti.

Although Frankfurter was a political independent, he informally advised President Franklin Roosevelt in the 1930s on matters of policy, and he recommended a number of his Harvard Law School students for positions in the New Deal. Roosevelt made Frankfurter his third nominee to the U.S. Supreme Court in 1939, after the death of Justice Benjamin Cardozo. Frankfurter served as an associate justice from 1939 to 1962.

On the Supreme Court, Frankfurter predictably exhibited judicial deference toward legislative and administrative decisions in cases that involved constitutional challenges to governmental efforts to regulate and redistribute property. But, much to the confusion of liberals, he appeared to abandon his civil libertarian convictions when he exercised the same restraint in the face of constitutional challenges to governmental actions that infringed upon noneconomic rights, including the First Amendment freedoms of speech and press. Frankfurter's decisions in both economic and noneconomic cases were in significant measure a product of his Progressive political background and of his study of administration. Like the Progressives, he emphasized the dangers of abstract judicial decision making, which he attributed to institutional deficiencies that prevented judges from recognizing and appreciating the complexity of an increasingly interdependent society. The phenomenon of social interdependence also inspired within Frankfurter considerable confidence in the fairness of American politics. The increased proximity and relatedness of individuals in an urban-industrial age, he believed, predisposed the elements of society toward harmony or integration in the same way that the parts of an organism tend toward cooperation and concert for the purpose of survival. Frankfurter characterized politics as the integrative task of adjusting the interests of diverse groups toward a comprehension of mutual understanding.

[*See also* **American Civil Liberties Union; Civil Liberties; Civil Rights; National Association for the Advancement of Colored People; Roosevelt, Franklin Delano;** *and* **Supreme Court, U.S.**]

BIBLIOGRAPHY

Hockett, Jeffrey D. *New Deal Justice: The Constitutional Jurisprudence of Hugo L. Black, Felix Frankfurter, and Robert H. Jackson*. Lanham, Md.: Rowman & Littlefield, 1996.

Parrish, Michael. *Felix Frankfurter and His Times: The Reform Years*. New York; London: Free Press; Collier Macmillan, 1982.

Jeffrey D. Hockett

FRANKLIN, BENJAMIN

(1706–1790), writer, scientist, statesman, and philanthropist. Born in Boston, Benjamin Franklin was apprenticed as a youth to his half-brother James, a printer. Largely self-taught and an avid reader, Benjamin at the age of sixteen published in James's *New England Courant* his *Silence Dogood* essays, the first essay series in American literature. At seventeen, he ran away to Philadelphia. Employed in Samuel Keimer's print shop, Franklin was befriended by Governor William Keith, who offered to lend him money to travel to London to buy a press, type, and printing supplies. After reaching England, Franklin learned that he had been deceived. Forced to make his own way, he worked briefly for two printing establishments in London.

Back in Philadelphia by 1726, Franklin soon became the city's premier printer. Shortly after he and Hugh Meredith purchased the failing *Pennsylvania Gazette* in 1729, they were chosen as the official printers for the province. In 1732 Franklin brought out the first issue of *Poor Richard's Almanac,* which quickly became the staple of his business. He also profitably printed the sermons and journals of the touring English revivalist George Whitefield. In 1730 Franklin and Deborah Read, whom he had courted before going to England, contracted a Common-Law marriage and raised in their home his illegitimate son, William. The couple also had two children of their own.

During his working years in Philadelphia, from 1726 through 1748, Franklin led the life of an involved urban citizen. He founded the Junto (1727), a self-improvement society for artisans, and joined the Masonic Order. He established America's first subscription library, the Library Company of Philadelphia (1731), and drafted the founding document of what became the American Philosophical Society, the nation's first learned society. He organized Philadelphia's first fire-fighting company and the nation's first mutual insurance company, the Philadelphia Contributionship (1752). He also contributed to the opening of an academy that would evolve into the University of Pennsylvania and to the creation of the Pennsylvania Hospital, the first permanent hospital in what became the United States.

Franklin earned lasting fame as one of the eighteenth century's most original scientists, or "natural philosophers." He conducted experiments demonstrating that electricity is a single fluid identical to lightning, publishing his findings in *Experiments and Observations on Electricity* (1751–1753). He also undertook important work on the Gulf Stream; conceived experiments on the conductivity of metals; and is remembered for several practical inventions, from the fuel-efficient Franklin stove and the lightning rod to the flexible catheter and bifocals.

Retiring from active management of his printing business in 1748, Franklin turned to politics. He sat in the Pennsylvania Assembly from 1751 to 1764. As Pennsylvania's delegate to the Albany Congress of 1754, called in response to the outbreak of the French and Indian War, he drafted a Plan of Union that anticipated the later Constitution of the United States. He undertook two missions to England (1757–1762 and 1764–1775) to represent Pennsylvania in its struggles with its proprietors, the Penn family. During his residence there he published numerous newspaper articles defending the American cause to the British government and people.

Between his missions to England, Franklin again immersed himself in Pennsylvania politics. The massacre of friendly Christian Indians by frontiersmen (the "Paxton Boys") and the movement for a petition to substitute royal government for the Penns' proprietorship prompted two of his most important polemical writings, *A Narrative of the Late Massacres* and *Cool Thoughts* (both 1764). His failure to win reelection to the Pennsylvania Assembly in 1764 was a bitter blow, but the new Assembly appointed him agent to England to petition the Crown for royal government in Pennsylvania.

The most pressing problem confronting Franklin upon his arrival in London in December 1764 was the Stamp Act, recently proposed by George Grenville. Franklin initially opposed it, but after its passage by Parliament in February 1765 he urged acceptance, underestimating the depth of American resistance to the measure. After helping secure repeal of the Stamp Act in 1766, Franklin stayed on in England, serving in effect as the ambassador from the American colonies as the imperial crisis deepened.

Once Franklin sailed for America in March 1775, he abandoned all efforts at reconciliation and vociferously championed the patriot cause. He was unanimously chosen a delegate to the Second Continental Congress, served on the committee that chose George Washington to command the revolutionary army, and was one of four commissioners on a failed mission to urge Canada to join the independence movement. He also sat on the committee that drafted the Declaration of Independence.

Named one of a three-person commission to seek diplomatic recognition and financial assistance from France, Franklin departed in October 1776 for an extended stay in France that brought him both diplomatic success and great personal satisfaction. He not only negotiated treaties of alliance, amity, and commerce with France (1778), but also, as minister plenipotentiary, raised substantial loans and gifts for the American cause from the French government, issued letters of marque for American privateers, and provided relief for American seamen held in English jails while he worked for prisoner exchanges. Lionized by Parisian society, he shrewdly played the role of the simple American democrat. With his colleagues John Jay and John Adams, Franklin negotiated the 1783 Treaty of Paris with Great Britain that ended the Revolutionary War and secured American independence.

Returning to Philadelphia in September 1785, Franklin, now nearing eighty, served as president of the Supreme Executive Council of Pennsylvania, represented his state in the Constitutional Convention of 1787, and presided over the Pennsylvania Abolition Society. Among his last writings was an attack on slavery and the slave trade published in the *Federal Gazette* in March 1790. His posthumously published *Autobiography* became the prototype of a classic American genre, the story of the self-made man. Although his historical reputation has fluctuated, Benjamin Franklin's status in the American pantheon seems secure.

[*See also* **Adams, John; Antislavery Movement; Constitution; Constitutional Convention of 1787; Continental Congress; Declaration of Independence; Jay, John; Stamp Act;** *and* **Washington, George.**]

BIBLIOGRAPHY

Dull, Jonathan R. *Franklin the Diplomat.* Independence Square, Philadelphia: American Philosophical Society, 1982.

Labaree, Leonard W., William B. Willcox, and Barbara B. Oberg, eds. *The Papers of Benjamin Franklin,* 3 vols. to date. New Haven, Conn.: Yale University Press, 1959– .

Lemay, J. A. Leo, ed. *Benjamin Franklin's Autobiography.* New York: W. W. Norton, 1981.

Lopez, Claude-Anne, and Eugenia W. Herbert. *The Private Franklin.* New York: W. W. Norton, 1975.

Van Doren, Carl. *Benjamin Franklin.* New York: Overseas Editions, 1938.

Barbara B. Oberg

FREEDMEN'S BUREAU

To assist the adjustment of newly freed slaves in the post–Civil War South, Congress in March 1865 established the Bureau of Refugees, Freedmen, and Abandoned Lands under the leadership of General Oliver Otis Howard and the auspices of the War Department. Given an initial life of one year, the agency provided food, clothing, fuel, and medical treatment to destitute and dislocated freedpeople and white refugees. It was also supposed to parcel out abandoned and confiscated lands in forty-acre plots to freedmen, but President Andrew Johnson, a staunch critic of the agency, undercut this effort by restoring most of the available land to its former white owners. Local agents of the bureau thus spent much time mediating labor contracts and disputes between the freedmen and intransigent white employers and attempting to secure economic and civil justice for the freedmen—even as they slipped into a debilitating sharecropping system.

More positive was the bureau's work with northern philanthropic groups to establish some three thousand freedpeople's schools by 1869. In July 1866, over Johnson's veto, Congress renewed the bureau for two years, and personnel reached a high of nine hundred, but as the former Confederate states rejoined the Union, Congress limited the agency's work to education and bounty payments to African American soldiers. Sharply reduced in personnel by 1869, the Freedmen's Bureau ceased operations in June 1872. Overall the bureau provided invaluable relief and educational aid for the 3.9 million former slaves, but its initial promise was limited by inadequate funding and manpower, excessively paternalistic leadership, and deeply embedded racial antagonisms.

[*See also* **Johnson, Andrew;** *and* **Reconstruction.**]

BIBLIOGRAPHY

Bentley, George R. *A History of the Freedmen's Bureau.* Philadelphia: University of Pennsylvania Press, 1955.

McFeely, William S. *Yankee Stepfather: General O. O. Howard and the Freedmen.* New Haven, Conn.: Yale University Press, 1968.

Terry L. Seip

FREEDOM OF INFORMATION ACT

The Freedom of Information Act (FOIA, 1966) provides any person—individual or corporate, regardless of nationality—with presumptive access to identifiable unpublished federal agency records. Certain categories of information may permissibly be exempted from the rule of disclosure. Disputes over requested records may be settled in federal court. The FOIA overturned a "need-to-know" policy, initially asserted by federal bureaucrats after World War II and based on the discretionary authority of agency heads to regulate the public availability of the records under their jurisdiction.

The product of years of deliberation in both houses of Congress, the FOIA was reluctantly signed into law by President Lyndon B. Johnson. It became operative in July 1967, one year after its enactment. Among those prominent in the development and passage of the statute were representatives John E. Moss and Donald Rumsfeld and Senator Edward V. Long. In subsequent amendments between 1974 and 1996, Congress modified the FOIA to clarify its provisions or otherwise improve its functioning. The 1996 amendments brought electronically maintained information within the scope of the statute.

The FOIA was not supported as legislation or welcomed as law by the executive branch. Despite its less than vigorous implementation, however, the statute has proven to be a useful tool for journalists, historians, writers, and ordinary citizens to gain access to millions of pages of records that otherwise might never have been disclosed.

[*See also* **Johnson, Lyndon B.**]

BIBLIOGRAPHY

Relyea, Harold C. "The Administration and Operation of the Freedom of Information Act: A Retrospective." *Government Information Quarterly* 11 (1994): 285–299.

U.S. Congress, House of Representatives, Committee on Government Reform and Oversight. *A Citizen's Guide on Using the Freedom of Information Act and the Privacy Act of 1974 to Request Government Records* (House Report 105–37). Washington, D.C.: U.S. Government Printing Office, 1997.

Harold C. Relyea

FREE SILVER MOVEMENT

Traditionally the United States had a bimetallic monetary system in which sixteen ounces of silver equaled one ounce of gold. As the world supply of silver became scarce by the 1850s, the value of silver rose and it was rarely used to coin money. In the 1860s, western miners discovered new supplies of silver, which decreased the commodity's value. By then more nations were adopting the gold standard. To maintain a stable currency, Congress passed a coinage act in 1873 that demonetized silver. At first there was little reaction, but as the price of silver fell, demands for the free and unlimited coinage of silver increased. To pacify the silver forces, Congress passed the Bland–Allison Act (1878) authorizing the Treasury to coin $2–$4 million in silver each month and the Sherman Silver Purchase Act (1890), providing for the monthly coinage of 4.5 million ounces of silver.

To this point, the silver issue had not been deeply divisive. In 1893, however, in response to the Depression of 1893–1896, President Grover Cleveland persuaded Congress to repeal the Sherman Silver Purchase Act, thereby again demonetizing silver. Many people then exchanged silver money for gold and the Treasury's gold reserve became seriously depleted. To bolster the reserve, the Cleveland administration sold bonds to New York bankers in return for gold bullion.

These developments revitalized the free silver movement. Within the Democratic Party, William Jennings Bryan assumed leadership of the silver forces, and in 1896 the Democrats nominated Bryan for president on a free silver platform, as did the Populist Party. The Republican Party, rallying behind William McKinley, endorsed the gold standard. In the ensuing campaign, the two sides offered competing visions. Silverites argued that instead of rigidly adhering to the gold standard, the government should devise a more flexible monetary system; Republicans insisted that gold be the sole basis for money. Silverites desired price inflation to combat depression; Republicans feared that inflation would worsen the economy. Silverites charged that eastern bankers used the gold standard to exploit farmers and the working class; Republicans responded that only the gold standard could ensure prosperity for all.

McKinley won the election, and the silver issue soon faded. Free silver appealed mostly to indebted farmers and mine owners and the movement failed to bridge the division separating agriculturists and wage laborers. After 1897, however, new discoveries of gold enabled the nation to enjoy economic expansion and moderate inflation while maintaining the gold standard.

[*See also* **Bryan, William Jennings; Cleveland, Grover; Farmers' Alliance Movement; Federal Government, Executive Branch:**

Treasury Department; Monetary Policy; Populist Era; *and* Populist Party.]

BIBLIOGRAPHY

Nugent, Walter T. K. *The Money Question during Reconstruction*. New York: W. W. Norton, 1967.

Ritter, Gretchen. *Goldbugs and Greenbacks: The Antimonopoly Tradition and the Politics of Finance in America*. Cambridge, UK; New York: Cambridge University Press, 1997.

William F. Holmes

FREE SOIL PARTY

As sectional tensions over slavery increased following the Mexican War, both the Whig and the Democratic parties experienced internal disputes. Antislavery members of both parties expressed disappointment in 1848 when their respective conventions nominated Zachary Taylor and Lewis Cass for the presidency. So-called "Conscience Whigs" in Massachusetts, led by Charles Francis Adams, the son of ex-president John Quincy Adams, joined with former Liberty Party supporters in calling for a new organization to oppose the growth of slavery. Their call attracted a faction of New York Democrats loyal to former President Martin Van Buren, called Barnburners, who had bolted the party the previous year. At a meeting at Buffalo in August, the Free Soil Party was born. The convention nominated Van Buren for president and Adams for vice president.

The party drew its strongest support from antislavery Whigs in the Northeast and Middle West, northern antislavery Democrats, and former Liberty Party backers. The party's 1848 platform, written by Benjamin F. Butler of Massachusetts and Salmon P. Chase of Ohio, called for an end to slavery in the District of Columbia and a halt to its extension in the territories. The rest of the party's planks, like its constituency, reflected a wide array of interests, including a high tariff, support for internal improvements, and a free homestead land policy. Although the party won no electoral votes in the subsequent election, its nearly 300,000 popular votes more than quadrupled the Liberty Party's support in 1844.

After a strong showing in state-level contests, many Free Soil politicians turned to coalition politics in the following years, joining whichever side would embrace their issues. With some success, coalition Free Soilers gained congressional seats and state offices. When Congress passed the series of measures known as the Compromise of 1850, the Free Soil coalition broke down. Calling itself the Free Soil Democratic Convention, the party at its national meeting in 1852 nominated Senator John P. Hale of New Hampshire as its presidential candidate. The party polled poorly in the election, but hoped in vain that the faltering Whig Party would offer a fresh influx of members. Outside of Ohio and Wisconsin, the party collapsed.

The passage of the Kansas–Nebraska Act in 1854 again thrust sectional tensions to the forefront of national politics. In the next two years, the Whig and Democratic parties fragmented, resulting in political realignments along sectional lines. In 1856, former Free Soilers Salmon P. Chase and Charles Sumner joined discouraged Whigs, antislavery Know-Nothings, and former Liberty Party men to form the Republican Party.

[*See also* **Antislavery Movement; Compromise of 1850; Kansas–Nebraska Act; Know-Nothing Party; Liberty Party; Political Parties; Republican Party; Van Buren, Martin;** *and* **Whig Party.**]

BIBLIOGRAPHY

Mayfield, John R. *Rehearsal for Republicanism: Free Soil and the Politics of Antislavery*. Port Washington, N.Y.: Kennikat Press, 1979.

Rayback, Joseph G. *Free Soil: The Election of 1848.* Lexington: University Press of Kentucky, 1970.

Eric D. Daniels

FUGITIVE SLAVE ACT

Drafted by Senator James Y. Mason of Virginia and the product of months of contentious debate in the Senate, the Fugitive Slave Act of 1850 was signed into law by President Millard Fillmore as part of the Compromise of 1850. Senator Charles Sumner of Massachusetts, an ardent critic, denounced the law as unconstitutional, but Daniel Webster, in a famous speech on 7 March, supported it as part of a larger political effort to preserve the Union. The southern senators John C. Calhoun and Jefferson Davis doubted that the law would achieve its purpose, but they did not oppose it. Organized opposition to the law in the North faded after the summer of 1851. The Supreme Court in *Ableman v. Booth* (1859) affirmed the law's constitutionality.

The Fugitive Slave Act authorized newly appointed fugitive slave commissioners to issue warrants for the arrest of runaway slaves. In a federal proceeding, before fugitive slave tribunals established by the act, the commissioner summarily ruled whether the person described in the warrant was indeed the person claimed by the slave owner or the owner's agent. (A court record taken in the state from which the slave had escaped was deemed sufficient proof of ownership.) This summary decision could not be appealed, nor could state courts issue writs of habeas corpus.

The law's historical significance lay in the white South's belief that it was not vigorously enforced, that northerners had acted in bad faith in passing it, and that the southern states were therefore justified in seceding from the Union. Of a total of 332 cases, federal tribunals remanded 157 slaves, 68 at government expense; 141 fugitive slaves were captured and returned without due process of law. The law was also of significance in inspiring Harriet Beecher Stowe's abolitionist novel *Uncle Tom's Cabin* (1852). Fugitive slaves were returned from Washington, D.C., to owners in the free states as late as June 1863, but Congress repealed the Fugitive Slave Act in 1864.

[*See also* **Antislavery Movement; Compromise of 1850; Fillmore, Millard;** *and* **Webster, Daniel.**]

BIBLIOGRAPHY

Campbell, Stanley W. *The Slave Catchers: Enforcement of the Fugitive Slave Law, 1850–1860.* Chapel Hill: University of North Carolina Press, 1970.

Stanley W. Campbell

G

GARFIELD, JAMES

(1831–1881), twentieth president of the United States. Born in poverty in a log cabin near Cleveland, Ohio, Garfield graduated from Williams College, taught at the Eclectic Institute in Hiram, Ohio (later Hiram College), in 1857–1861, and was a lay preacher in the Disciples of Christ church. Rising from colonel to major general in the Civil War, he helped create the forty-second Ohio Volunteer Infantry and saw action at Shiloh and Chickamauga. As a Republican congressman (1863–1880), Garfield, like his contemporary James G. Blaine, identified with the younger element of the party, oriented toward economic issues rather than residual matters from the Civil War. Although implicated in the 1873 Crédit Mobilier scandal, involving bribery of politicians by railroad interests, he survived politically. In 1880, he supported Ohio's favorite son, John Sherman, for the Republican presidential nomination, opposing a third term for Ulysses S. Grant. A deadlocked convention chose Garfield himself, however, with Chester A. Arthur as his running mate, to represent both factions in a bitterly divided party. Narrowly defeating the Democrat Winfield Scott Hancock in the popular vote, Garfield won overwhelmingly in the Electoral College.

The major issue confronting the new administration was the divisive matter of civil service reform, which Garfield generally favored, although he was preoccupied with distributing jobs to party loyalists. On 2 July 1881, at the Washington, D.C., railroad station, a delusional office-seeker, Charles J.

Guiteau, shot Garfield. Lingering in pain through the summer, the president died on 19 September. Guiteau's plea of not guilty by reason of insanity sparked much discussion of the nature of mental disorder. He was convicted and hanged on 30 June 1882. Although himself immersed in the politics of patronage, Garfield after his death was widely viewed as a martyr to a corrupt political system, and his assassination helped spur passage of the Pendleton Civil Service Act of 1883.

[*See also* **Blaine, James G.; Civil Service Reform;** *and* **Republican Party.**]

BIBLIOGRAPHY

Doenecke, Justus. *The Presidencies of James A. Garfield and Chester A. Arthur*. Lawrence: Regents Press of Kansas, 1981.

Peskin, Allan. *Garfield: A Biography*. Kent, Ohio: Kent State University Press, 1978.

H. Wayne Morgan

GARNET, HENRY HIGHLAND

(1815–1882), abolitionist, Presbyterian minister, civil rights activist, colonization proponent, and U.S. Minister to Liberia. Born a slave in Maryland, he escaped with his family to New York City in 1824. There he attended the African Free School No. 2. He went to sea briefly and afterward lost the use of his right leg, which later was amputated. He learned classics, theology, oratory, and abolitionist activism at the High School for Colored Youth in New York City and founded the Garrison Literary and Benevolent Association. He attended the Noyes Academy in New Hampshire and Oneida Institute in western New York, emerging as a fiery speaker and abolitionist agitator. He cofounded the American and Foreign Anti-Slavery Society and was the first African American to join the abolitionist Liberty Party. Garnet criticized nonpolitical abolitionists and worked to enfranchise black New Yorkers. Garnet took up his ministry in Troy, New York, married Julia Ward Williams, and embarked on missionary work. He cofounded the National Convention of Colored Citizens and Their Friends and in 1843 began to advocate violent slave uprisings. "Let your motto be resistance!" he famously urged.

Garnet attracted controversy in the late 1840s by advocating voluntary black emigration to Africa in the service of an African American national identity. In 1850, he traveled to Great Britain, Europe, and Ireland, speaking against slavery. He then undertook missionary work in Jamaica before returning to New York City, where he became minister of Shiloh Presbyterian Church in 1856. He held that position on and off for nearly the rest of his career. In 1858, Garnet founded the African Colonization Society for the "Evangelization and Civilization of Africa." In response to John Brown's hanging, Garnet preached violence against slavery. In 1861, during the Civil War, he returned to England to plead the Union cause and gather support for African colonization. Back in America, Garnet pushed for emancipation as a war aim and the use of African American soldiers to win it. Garnet commenced recruiting and was targeted in the draft riots of July 1863. His disability prevented him from becoming an army chaplain. Garnet delivered a memorial sermon in the U.S. House of Representatives in February 1865, praising the Thirteenth Amendment ending slavery.

After the war Garnet sponsored aid and education to freed people. Local Garnet Leagues organized, but his influence diminished because he was pulled in opposite directions by African colonization and advocacy of African American civil rights. In 1868, Garnet accepted the presidency of Pittsburgh's all-black Avery Institute and continued to agitate for black male suffrage. In 1870, he resigned and returned to New York City, where he struggled with church finances and his wife's death in 1871. He spoke for Cuban emancipation and U.S. civil rights and supported the Republican Party as the best hope of accomplishing both. After a brief second marriage, he was appointed U.S. minister and counsel general to Liberia in 1881, the highest diplomatic office occupied by an African American. Garnet died there in early 1882.

[*See also* **Antislavery Movement; Civil Liberties; Civil Rights;** ***and*** **Liberty Party.**]

BIBLIOGRAPHY

Marable, Manning, and Leith Mullings, eds. *Let Nobody Turn Us Around: An African American Anthology: Voices of Resistance, Reform, and Renewal.* Lanham, Md.: Rowman & Littlefield, 2009.

Ofari, Earl. *"Let Your Motto Be Resistance": The Life and Thought of Henry Highland Garnet.* Boston: Beacon Press, 1972.

Pasternak, Martin B. *Rise Now and Fly to Arms: The Life of Henry Highland Garnet.* New York: Garland, 1995.

Ripley, C. Peter, ed. *The Black Abolitionist Papers, Vol. V: The United States, 1859–1865.* Chapel Hill: University of North Carolina Press, 1985.

Schor, Joel. *Henry Highland Garnet: A Voice of Black Radicalism in the Nineteenth Century.* Westport, Conn.: Greenwood Press, 1977.

Calvin Schermerhorn

GAY RIGHTS MOVEMENT

See **Lesbian, Gay, Bisexual, and Transgender Rights Movement.**

GETTYSBURG ADDRESS

Union soldiers who died in the three fierce days of battle at Gettysburg, Pennsylvania (1–3 July 1863), were buried in a cemetery specially created by a corporation of northern states. The leading orator of the day, Edward Everett of Massachusetts, was asked to deliver the funeral oration at the cemetery's formal opening on 19 November 1863. President Abraham Lincoln, invited to make "remarks" on the same occasion, quickly accepted, since presidents had few occasions to deliver speeches at a time when the State of the Union address was sent to Congress in written form. Lincoln knew the power of his oratory and prepared very carefully all his formal statements as president. The myth that he scribbled his remarks on an envelope reflected a romantic ideal of "natural" inspiration, contrasting Lincoln's short (three-minute) speech with Everett's labored two-hour performance. In what became known as the Gettysburg Address, Lincoln distilled into 272 words a use of the Declaration of Independence he had developed over the preceding six years—putting the clause "all men are created equal" at the center of American government. This prompted some protest in the North that Lincoln was enforcing a nonlegislative document, the Declaration, instead of the binding Constitution. But Lincoln viewed the Constitution as a partial and developing document meant to put the ideals of the Declaration into practice.

The need for brevity made Lincoln pack a great deal into few words. His argument for union is contained in the triple invocation of "the people" in the last sentence—he and others had opposed secession on the grounds that "the people" as a whole had ratified the Constitution and only they, acting as a whole, could amend or dissolve the union formed by that document. He also drew on the idealistic, transcendental rhetoric associated with the rural-cemetery movement of the time.

Contrary to myth, both Everett's and Lincoln's speeches were successful with their original audience. Lincoln's was interrupted by applause five times and was widely reprinted. His assassination less than a year and a half following the address made it the most concentrated and memorable statement of his attitude toward the Civil War. It has become his legacy, one of the great informal charters of the nation, competing with and eventually displacing Washington's Farewell Address as a statement to rank with the Declaration and the Constitution as an expression of the spirit of American government.

[*See also* **Declaration of Independence; Equality; Lincoln, Abraham;** *and* **Republicanism.**]

BIBLIOGRAPHY

Mearns, David C., and Lloyd A. Dunlap. *Long Remembered: Facsimiles of the Five Versions of the Gettysburg Address in the Handwriting of Abraham Lincoln*. Washington, D.C.: Library of Congress, 1963.

Wills, Garry. *Lincoln at Gettysburg*. Boston: Doll & Richards, 1992.

Garry Wills

GIBBONS v. OGDEN

In 1798, New York State gave Robert Livingston an exclusive fourteen-year franchise to operate a steamboat "within the state." In 1808, the legislature extended this monopoly, now shared with Robert Fulton, until 1838. Chief Justice James Kent, speaking for New York's highest court in 1812, approved the monopoly. In 1815, Livingston and Fulton sold part of their franchise rights to Aaron Ogden of New Jersey, who began operating a steamboat between New Jersey and New York City. In 1819, Ogden's former partner Thomas Gibbons began operating his own boat between New Jersey and New York. Ogden sued Gibbons, and in 1820 the New York court again upheld the steamboat monopoly. Gibbons appealed to the U.S. Supreme Court, which decided the case in 1824. Daniel Webster, representing Gibbons, argued that his client had the right under federal law to "navigate freely" in all of the waters of the United States.

In one of his most important opinions, Chief Justice John Marshall struck down the monopoly as it applied to interstate commerce. The authority the Constitution granted the federal government to regulate interstate commerce, Marshall asserted, was a linchpin of the national government's power. Commerce, he declared, "is traffic, but it is something more; it is the commercial intercourse between nations and parts of nations, in all its branches." The Constitution, Marshall ruled, vested in Congress alone the complete power to regulate all commerce "among the states." The states could regulate "completely internal commerce," Marshall conceded, but all commerce that began in one state and entered into a second state fell exclusively within the federal government's regulatory power. In striking down an unpopular monopoly, Marshall also skillfully interpreted the Constitution's commerce clause to expand the power of the federal government. His decision was widely applauded by nationalists and states' rights advocates alike.

[*See also* **Constitution; Economic Policy: Regulation; Federalism; Marshall, John; States' Rights; Supreme Court, U.S.;** *and* **Webster, Daniel.**]

BIBLIOGRAPHY

Baxter, M. G. *The Steamboat Monopoly: Gibbons v. Ogden*. New York: Alfred A. Knopf, 1972.

White, G. Edward. *The Marshall Court and Cultural Change, 1815–35*. New York: Macmillan, 1988.

Paul Finkelman

GLORIOUS REVOLUTION IN AMERICA

Political principle and self-interest are the keys to understanding the American colonial rebellions of 1689. British imperial policy stiffened after the restoration of the monarchy in 1660. The Navigation Acts established a monopoly of the empire's commerce in England's favor. Admiralty courts and the Royal Navy with enlarged powers bore down on offenders. The rules of empire narrowed political freedom. New England, including New York and New Jersey, was consolidated into the Dominion of New England under a single governor, Sir Edmund Andros, vacating charters and eliminating representative assemblies. Marylanders struggled under a Catholic proprietary government that discriminated against the Protestant majority. The bishop of London, Henry Compton, encouraged Anglican churches even in dissenting colonies such as Massachusetts. The accession of James II in 1685 increased the threat of Catholicism, real and imagined. Between 1660 and 1689, the colonists' economy, governments, and religion all experienced more stringent control from London.

When news of the accession of William III and Queen Mary to the British throne in 1689—the so-called Glorious Revolution—reached America, it was welcomed as a release from James's arbitrary power, not just in England, but in the empire as well. The people of Massachusetts, hoping to reinstate their original charter, imprisoned Governor Andros and his close supporters. Rhode Island and Connecticut followed suit. In New York, Jacob Leisler, a merchant of German origin, led a rebellious group that brought down James's local government. Leisler's rebels carried on precariously under strong protest, hoping the new king would accept their rebellion. Led by John Coode, Maryland Protestants toppled the Catholic proprietary and begged King William to absorb Maryland as a royal colony. Throughout, these rebellions were both a struggle for equal rights and violent attempts to exploit England's constitutional and religious crisis for colonial purposes.

The success of the rebellions hung on skillful negotiation with the Crown. The agent, Increase Mather, Massachusetts's foremost Puritan, extracted a new charter guaranteeing many, but not all, of the colony's earlier privileges. Massachusetts became a royal colony but lacked protection against further royal or imperial regulation as well as the religious underpinnings of its original charter. Jacob Leisler's regime in New York was thwarted by a strong royalist faction that bested the colony's weak negotiators in London. When Leisler hesitated to recognize a new royal governor appointed by William III, he and his deputy were tried and hanged as traitors. Maryland's effort to shed the Catholic proprietor succeeded, although without the guarantees of Englishmen's rights the colony sought. As in New York, London repeatedly vetoed the attempts of Maryland's new assembly to attain such rights by legislation.

The Glorious Revolution in America laid bare two distinct interpretations of empire that had emerged after the Restoration. Despite differences among the colonies, they had all assumed the rights of Englishmen overseas were equal to the rights of those in England. The Glorious Revolution taught them differently: From London's perspective, colonies in America existed for the benefit of the realm; they were the king's dominions and would be dealt with accordingly. Despite the lesson of 1689, however, the American colonists in the early eighteenth century generally continued to assume equality of rights. When these assumptions were again challenged by the Crown and Parliament in the 1760s and 1770s, independence resulted.

[*See also* **Equality.**]

BIBLIOGRAPHY

Hall, M. G., L. H. Leder, and M. G. Kammen, eds. *The Glorious Revolution in America: Documents on the Colonial Crisis of 1689*. Chapel Hill: University of North Carolina Press, 1964.

Lovejoy, David S. *The Glorious Revolution in America*. Middletown, Conn.: Wesleyan University Press, 1972; 2d ed., 1987.

Sosin, Jack M. *English America and the Revolution of 1688*. Lincoln: University of Nebraska Press, 1982.

David S. Lovejoy

GOLDMAN, EMMA

(1869–1940), anarchist, social activist, free-speech advocate, spokesperson for women's freedom. Born in a Jewish ghetto in present-day Lithuania, Goldman moved with her family to Prussia and in 1881 to St. Petersburg, Russia. Fleeing provincialism and anti-Semitism, she migrated to the United States in 1885 with a half sister and settled in Rochester, New York, where she worked in a clothing factory. Her marriage to Jacob Kersner in 1887 ended in divorce. The Haymarket affair, coupled with harsh industrial conditions and violence against striking workers by government and business, propelled her toward anarchism and support of the eight-hour-day movement. Moving to New York City in 1889, she encountered such émigré radicals as Johann Most and Alexander Berkman. Goldman's involvement with Berkman's attempted assassination of the industrialist Henry Clay Frick and her alleged link to the 1901 assassination of President William McKinley (by an anarchist who claimed to have been inspired by her speeches) resulted in her public demonization by the press.

She reclaimed her voice in 1906 by founding a literary and political magazine, *Mother Earth,* and through her lively cross-country tours lecturing on anarchism, feminism, sexual radicalism, birth control, and new literary trends, especially modern drama. Liberals and radicals formed free-speech clubs to protest the suppression of Goldman's talks and Roger Baldwin attributed his founding of the American Civil Liberties Union to Goldman. Goldman had been a mentor to Margaret Sanger and in 1916 was arrested for advocating birth control. Along with Berkman, she was tried, convicted, and imprisoned in 1917 for protesting wartime conscription, and in 1919, amid the post–World War I Red Scare, she and Berkman were deported with several hundred other alien radicals to Russia. In *My Disillusionment in Russia* (1923, full text 1925), she exposed the hypocrisy of Russia's Bolshevik regime and protested its suppression of dissent. Criticized and isolated by the left and the right, Goldman found refuge in southern France while frequently visiting England and Canada. Her compelling biography, *My Life* (1931), precipitated a final visit to the United States in 1934. Bereaved by the suicide of Berkman, her longtime comrade, in 1936, Goldman plunged into propaganda work for the Spanish anarchists during the Spanish Civil War, basing herself in London and Barcelona (1936–1938). She died in Canada, championing the cause of Spanish refugees and maintaining her lifelong commitment to free expression.

[*See also* **American Civil Liberties Union; Anarchism; Feminism; McKinley, William; Progressive Era;** *and* **Radicalism.**]

BIBLIOGRAPHY

Falk, Candace, et al., eds. *The Emma Goldman Papers: A Microfilm Edition*, 69 reels. Alexandria, Va.: Chadwyck–Healey, 1991.

Falk, Candace, et al., eds. *Emma Goldman: A Guide to Her Life and Documentary Sources.* Alexandria, Va.: Chadwyck–Healey, 1995.

Wexler, Alice. *Emma Goldman in America.* Boston: Beacon Press, 1984.

Candace Falk

GOLDWATER, BARRY

Barry Goldwater served five terms in the U.S. Senate, representing the state of Arizona from 1953 to 1965 and then again from 1969 to 1987. In 1964 he was nominated by the Republican Party for president of the United States. Known for his strident anti-Communism and principled libertarianism, Goldwater—despite losing the 1964 presidential election in an epic landslide—is considered by many political observers and historians the father of modern American conservatism.

Barry Morris Goldwater was born on 2 January 1909 in Phoenix, Arizona Territory. His political awareness grew during the 1930s, at the height of the Great Depression, in direct opposition to Franklin D. Roosevelt's New Deal. During World War II, Goldwater served as a pilot with the Twenty-seventh Ferry Squadron of the Air Transport Command, flying missions in North Africa and the Middle East. He left the Army Air Corps in 1945 with a rank of lieutenant colonel. Following the war, he returned to Arizona and, in 1949, won his first election, earning a seat on the Phoenix City Council. In 1952, Goldwater won a stunning victory to the U.S. Senate, defeating Democratic Senate Majority Leader Earnest McFarland.

During the 1950s Goldwater supported Senator Joseph McCarthy's (R-WI) goal of ridding the nation of communist subversion. He was also a vocal critic of "modern Republicanism," or as he and others sometimes ridiculed it, "me-too Republicanism." In this context, Goldwater considered Dwight Eisenhower, Richard Nixon, and many of his Republican colleagues too moderate, particularly on issues related to domestic spending and bureaucratic growth, although he remained a strong party member and would support Nixon for his presidential races in 1960 and 1968.

By 1960, Goldwater was considered one of the nation's foremost conservative spokespersons. That year, Goldwater published *The Conscience of a Conservative,* in which he outlined his political and philosophical worldview. The book was received favorably by most conservatives and contributed to his popularity with his party's right wing.

Goldwater also delivered an important speech at the 1960 Republican National Convention. Prior to accepting the GOP nomination for president, Richard Nixon angered many conservatives for compromising with New York's liberal Republican governor, Nelson Rockefeller, on several key points in the GOP platform. Disparagingly referred to by conservatives as the "Compact of Fifth Avenue," Nixon's negotiation with Rockefeller destabilized his already tepid support among conservatives. Goldwater's speech was, in part, an effort to reunify the party and bring conservatives back into the Nixon fold.

However, Goldwater also exhorted conservatives to assert themselves more vigorously into the inner workings of Republican leadership. Although he did call on conservatives to unite behind Nixon, Goldwater's speech signaled an acceleration of right-wing influence within the GOP.

Goldwater's stature among conservative Republicans continued to grow in subsequent years. In 1964, thanks largely to the efforts of local conservative leaders and grassroots volunteers across the Sunbelt West, Goldwater was "drafted" into the race for the GOP's presidential nomination. Goldwater reluctantly entered the race and, in doing so, exacerbated deep factional divisions with the Republican Party, predominantly between western populists and northeastern moderates. After a bitter primary battle with several potential nominees, including Nelson Rockefeller, Goldwater accepted the GOP's presidential nomination in July 1964. During his acceptance speech, Goldwater famously declared, "Extremism in the defense of liberty is no vice."

Goldwater's comment about extremism remains one of the most controversial moments in major political convention history. Goldwater had been labeled an "extremist" by several of his opponents during the Republican primaries. Following Goldwater's nomination, the Democratic nominee, Lyndon Johnson, employed largely the same strategy of labeling Goldwater an "extremist." The 1964 presidential campaign is often remembered as one of the most brutally mean-spirited, in large part because of Johnson's negative campaign ads designed to reinforce the image of Goldwater as dangerous and extreme. The most famous of these ads was simply known as "Daisy," produced independently with the guiding hand of Bill Moyers in the Johnson White House, and insinuated that a vote for Goldwater was a vote for nuclear holocaust. Johnson also attempted to link Goldwater to the Ku Klux Klan. Goldwater, a former member of the National Association for the Advancement of Colored People and among the first small business owners in Phoenix to publicly support nondiscriminatory hiring practices, opposed the Civil Rights Act of 1964 on what he said were "constitutional reasons" unrelated to race. The implied connection further distanced Goldwater from independents and moderates, but did not hurt his efforts in the Deep South, where he carried five traditionally Democratic states.

Goldwater also hurt himself during the 1964 campaign by carelessly providing sound bites that only reinforced the perception that he was an extremist. For instance, Goldwater once told reporters that "sometimes I think this country would be better off if we could just saw off the Eastern Seaboard and let it float out to sea." Despite his popularity with conservatives, the divisions his candidacy exacerbated within the Republican Party, a political climate deeply affected by the assassination of John F. Kennedy less than a year earlier, and Johnson's effective antiextremist campaign, all worked together to ensure one of the largest landslides in American presidential election history. In November 1964, Goldwater was overwhelmingly defeated, losing to Johnson in the Electoral College 486 to 52 and in the popular vote 61 percent to 38 percent.

Having vacated his senate seat to run for the presidency, Goldwater regained that seat in 1968. He continued to serve as a Republican senator from Arizona until his retirement in 1987. During those years, Goldwater remained active and influential within the Republican Party. In the Watergate scandal in Nixon's second term, Goldwater played a critical role in forcing Nixon's resignation from the presidency in 1974. During the late 1970s and early 1980s, Goldwater emerged as a leading critic of the increasingly influential and politically mobilized Christian Right. Goldwater's pro-choice stand on abortion, as well as his support for homosexuals in the military, alienated many conservatives, despite Goldwater's position that such stands were consistent with a strictly libertarian worldview. Nonetheless, political observers and historians traditionally credit Goldwater with the popular emergence of several conservative political figures in the years following 1964, most notably Ronald Reagan.

Goldwater died on 29 May 1998 at his home in Paradise Valley, Arizona.

[*See also* **Anti-Communism; Conservatism; National Association for the Advancement of Colored People; Nixon, Richard M.;** ***and*** **Roosevelt, Franklin Delano.**]

BIBLIOGRAPHY

Critchlow, Donald T. *The Conservative Ascendancy: How the GOP Right Made Political History.* Cambridge, Mass.: Harvard University Press, 2007.

Goldberg, Robert Alan. *Barry Goldwater.* New Haven, Conn.: Yale University Press, 1995.

Goldwater, Barry. *The Conscience of a Conservative.* Shepherdsville, Ky.: Victor, 1960.

McGirr, Lisa. *Suburban Warriors: The Origins of the New American Right.* Princeton, N.J.: Princeton University Press, 2001.

Perlstein, Rick. *Before the Storm: Barry Goldwater and the Unmaking of the American Consensus.* New York: Hill and Wang, 2001.

Sean P. Cunningham

GORE, ALBERT A., JR.

(1948–), born in Washington, D.C., made the papers because his father, Tennessee congressman Albert Gore (1907–1998), had extracted a promise from the Nashville *Tennessean* to run the headline, "Well, Mr. Gore, Here He Is—On Page 1." His mother, Pauline LaFon Gore (1912–2004), was one of the first female graduates of Vanderbilt Law School and his father held degrees from Tennessee Teachers College and the YMCA Law School. His father started in politics as a school superintendent and became a Tennessee congressman in 1939 and then senator in 1953. Gore Sr., established himself as expert on atomic energy, earned acclaim for refusing to sign the Southern Manifesto, and won the label of a maverick and Southern progressive. In 1956 and 1960, Democratic leaders closely considered him as a vice-presidential nominee.

Al Gore Jr., lived with his family in the Fairfax Hotel throughout his formative years, traveling to the family farm in Carthage during the summers to work. He attended the prestigious St. Alban's School and later graduated from Harvard. In 1969, he volunteered for the U.S. Army and served one tour of Vietnam. Before shipping out, he married his high school sweetheart, Mary Elizabeth "Tipper" Aitcheson. He also personally campaigned for his father's reelection against Bill Brock. The elder Gore lost in 1970 because of his controversial positions on civil rights and opposition to the Vietnam War. The defeat left the younger Gore very disillusioned with politics.

After returning from Vietnam, Gore settled into a job at the *Tennessean* and took classes at the Vanderbilt Law School and Divinity School, seeking to better understand the world. In 1976, Gore sought his father's old congressional district, ultimately winning the crowded Democratic primary and then the general election.

Once in the House, Gore established himself as a hardworking legislator who often focused on arcane issues including the environment, technology, and consumer safety.

After easily winning three terms, he won a Senate seat vacated by Howard Baker, taking more than 60 percent of the vote. Once in the upper chamber, he continued concentrating on issues such as arms control, where he advocated cuts in multiple warhead delivery systems, pushed technology ideas including the groundwork for government support of the Internet, and became a leading advocate for environmental safeguards, publishing *Earth in the Balance: Ecology and the Human Spirit* in 1992.

Gore's stature in the Senate and family name led to an early attempt at the Democratic nomination for the presidency in 1988. Only thirty-nine, he jumped into the campaign, describing himself as a Southern centrist. He placed a great deal of hope on a Super Tuesday primary among southern states. Ultimately, he dropped out after mixed results and an association with former New York City mayor Ed Koch, who made some derogatory attacks on competitors including Jesse Jackson. During the New York primary campaign he also accused rival Michael Dukakis of being soft on crime, as evidenced when as governor of Massachusetts he allowed a prisoner, Willie Horton, to take a weekend deferral during which he brutally raped a woman in Maryland. The Willy Horton issue was picked by the George H. W. Bush campaign in the general election to attack Dukakis, who had won the Democratic nomination.

During the next four years in the Senate, Gore emerged as a leader of the Democratic Leadership Council (DLC), an organization dedicated to making the Democratic Party more mainstream and moderate. An accident involving his young son in 1989 partly caused Gore to retreat from a possible presidential run in 1992. However, when Bill Clinton emerged victorious in the Democratic primaries, he selected Gore as the vice presidential nominee. They successfully worked together to take the White House.

Gore established a reputation as an activist vice president who became the administration spokesperson on environmental issues and continued promoting the Information Superhighway as well as government efficiency. He also headed efforts to reduce regulation and bureaucracy within the federal government. In foreign policy, he pushed internationalist trade positions including a defense of the North Atlantic Free Trade Treaty in 1993 and intervention in the Balkans to stop the genocide. When Clinton stumbled during the Lewinsky scandal, Gore loyally supported the president.

As the 2000 presidential primary approached, Gore sought the Democratic nomination against Senator Bill Bradley of New Jersey. He battled his association with Clinton's scandals as well as accusations of his own on fund-raising and gaffes, including a claim that he invented the Internet. Nonetheless, he took the Democratic nomination and faced off against Texas governor George W. Bush in the general election. After selecting a conservative running mate, Senator Joe Lieberman (D-CT), he pushed for Social Security and health care reform and a continuation of the policies that created economic growth in the 1990s. In debates with the Texas governor, Gore struggled not to appear stiff, arrogant, or aggressive. When the final vote occurred, Gore took the popular vote by more than 500,000 votes and needed one more electoral vote, but a contested election in Florida impeded the victory (as well as the loss of his home state of Tennessee) as terms such as "hanging chads" and "butterfly ballots" entered the American lexicon. After much debate, the U.S. Supreme Court suspended the recount in Florida, and Gore conceded.

For a couple of years, Gore retreated from the limelight and focused on writing new books, starting a television network, and giving speeches on issues including the environment.

However, over time, he became a vocal critic of the Bush administration, particularly its rush to war in Iraq, its failure to adequately respond to Hurricane Katrina, and attacks on civil liberties and freedoms after 9/11, ideas he pushed in books including *The Assault on Reason* (2008). He made the biggest splash with his participation on the documentary "Inconvenient Truth," which outlined the dangers of global warming. For his environmental work, he received an Academy Award and ultimately a Nobel Prize. He has also participated in efforts to free American hostages held in North Korea and other international efforts to promote peace and democratic development.

[*See also* **Bush, George W.; Clinton, William J.;** *and* **Environmentalism.**]

BIBLIOGRAPHY

Longley, Kyle. *Senator Albert Gore, Sr.: Tennessee Maverick.* Baton Rouge: Louisiana State University Press, 2004.

Maraniss, David, and Ellen Nakashima. *The Prince of Tennessee: The Rise of Al Gore.* New York: Simon & Schuster, 2000.

Turque, Bill. *Inventing Al Gore: A Biography.* Boston: Houghton Mifflin, 2000.

Kyle Longley

GRAND ARMY OF THE REPUBLIC

The largest and most powerful post–Civil War organization of Union Army and Navy veterans. Founded on 6 April 1866, at Decatur, Illinois, by the former army surgeon Benjamin Franklin Stephenson (1823–1871), its proclaimed goals were "fraternity, charity and loyalty." Simultaneously a political club, pension lobby, fraternal lodge, charitable society, and patriotic group, the Grand Army of the Republic (GAR) was perhaps the most influential voluntary organization of the Gilded Age. Except for Grover Cleveland, every president elected between 1868 and 1900 was a member; the unprecedented Dependent Pension Act of 1890 (which cost $1 billion by 1907) was the product of GAR lobbying; and the nearly 7,000 local posts that ultimately dotted the northern landscape were important centers of sociability. Grand Army membership crossed class lines, and to some extent it was interracial, although black veterans usually were relegated to segregated posts.

Between 1866 and 1872, the GAR operated as a virtual wing of the Republican Party, boosting the careers of soldier-politicians such as Illinois senator John A. Logan (1826–1886), who served several terms as GAR president. After 1872, it entered a steep decline, reaching a low of fewer than 27,000 members in 1876. In the 1880s, the GAR was revived as a fraternal order, emphasizing its secret initiation ritual and the provision of charity to needy veterans. It also began focusing on pensions and, by the 1890s, on a conservative version of American nationalism that stressed the ideals of independent producerism and the citizen-volunteer. At its peak membership of 409,489 in 1890, the GAR enrolled about 40 percent of eligible Union veterans.

The GAR declined in influence after 1900, holding its last encampment in 1949 and officially expiring with the death of its last member in 1956. Its chief legacies to the twentieth century were a pension system that acted as the template for subsequent entitlement spending and a conservative political agenda that later veterans' groups (notably the American Legion) emulated.

BIBLIOGRAPHY

Dearing, Mary R. *Veterans in Politics: The Story of the G.A.R.* Baton Rouge: Louisiana State University Press, 1952.

McConnell, Stuart. *Glorious Contentment: The Grand Army of the Republic, 1865–1900.* Chapel Hill: University of North Carolina Press, 1992.

Stuart McConnell

GRANGER LAWS

A major goal of the Granger movement of the early 1870s was to bring about public regulation of railroads. Western farmers, who had applauded the rapid expansion of the rail system, now believed that rates were unreasonably high and fluctuated suspiciously, especially at noncompetitive points. These activist farmers also claimed that rail carriers discriminated between places and persons, formed illegal business combinations, and gave free passes to politicians and others who could serve the railroads' interests.

As the political power of organized farmers grew in the 1870s, agrarian representatives in the state legislatures, aided by spokesmen for certain business interests, pushed through legislation in Illinois, Iowa, Wisconsin, and Minnesota that collectively were known as the Granger Laws. These laws varied from state to state, but generally they sought to outlaw the widespread abuses by railroads, establish maximum rates in some instances, and create regulatory agencies to administer and enforce the laws. Beyond their immediate importance, the Granger Laws mark an early attempt by a previously rural nation to adjust to the conditions and challenges of an increasingly urban and industrial society.

The railroad corporations either ignored the Granger Laws or fought them in the courts. In due course, a case arising in Illinois found its way to the U.S. Supreme Court. In *Munn v. Illinois* (1877), the Court upheld the constitutionality of the Granger Laws. Rejecting the contention of a warehouse operator that the regulatory actions of the Illinois Railroad and Warehouse Commission (the agency established to administer the Granger Law in that state) deprived the company of property and thus violated the Fourteenth Amendment of the U.S. Constitution, the Court ruled instead that enterprises such as railroads and warehouses that substantially affected the public interest had to submit to some degree of public control. This, in turn, opened the way for state regulation of a variety of businesses.

In 1886, the issue of state regulation of railroads again came before the courts. The Wabash railroad, an interstate carrier in the Middle West, appealed a decision of the Illinois courts to the Supreme Court. In *Wabash v. Illinois* (1886), the Court found for the railroad, ruling that a state could not regulate interstate commerce, since the Constitution granted that power solely to the federal government. This decision led Congress to enact the Interstate Commerce Act in 1887. That measure assigned the task of regulating railroads to the newly created Interstate Commerce Commission, the nation's first independent regulatory agency.

[*See also* **Granger Movement; Interstate Commerce Act; Populist Era; Populist Party;** *and* **Regulatory Agencies, Federal.**]

BIBLIOGRAPHY

Buck, Solon J. *The Granger Movement.* Lincoln: University of Nebraska Press, 1913.

Miller, George H. *Railroads and the Granger Laws.* Madison: University of Wisconsin Press, 1971.

Roy V. Scott

GRANGER MOVEMENT

The Granger movement was the first stage of the agrarian crusade of the late nineteenth century in which farmers voiced their dissatisfaction with deteriorating economic conditions and agriculture's declining status in a rapidly industrializing nation. The Patrons of Husbandry, or the Grange, was founded in 1867 in Washington, D.C., by Oliver Hudson Kelley (1826–1913). A Minnesota farmer who became a government clerk, Kelley believed that a rural social organization modeled on the Masonic Order but admitting women to full membership could improve the intellectual life of farmers and overcome rural isolation. As secretary of the group, Kelley set out to form local Granges. He enjoyed little success at first, but beginning in 1869 the Grange grew rapidly. At its peak in the mid-1870s, with a network of county and state organizations, the national Grange claimed 775,000 members in twenty thousand local groups.

Although Kelley initially viewed the Grange as primarily a social organization, the order discovered other interests as it grew in strength. Its social role remained, especially at the local level, but the Grange also became an educational agency. Granges devoted a portion of each meeting to debate and discussion, thereby encouraging the members to read and to think about contemporary issues. Granges interested themselves in the one-room country schools, seeking to make the instruction more relevant to pupils' lives, and in the land-grant colleges, which they considered to be their institutions. The Patrons of Husbandry embraced economic cooperation as one way to improve farmers' economic condition, especially by reducing the role of middlemen. Members formed farmer-owned stores, elevators, and creameries, launched mutual insurance companies, and in a few instances established factories to manufacture farm machinery. Most of these enterprises failed because of inadequate capital and management, but they presaged the successful farm cooperatives of the twentieth century.

Although officially the Grange was nonpartisan, discontented farmers organized by the Grange often turned to political action. Railroad abuses especially concerned them, and in the four states of the upper Mississippi valley they successfully campaigned for the so-called Granger laws that sought to bring railroads under public control. These laws, in turn, laid the groundwork for the Interstate Commerce Act of 1887. By then, however, the Grange had lost most of its membership and influence, though the organization remained a voice of agriculture and a social institution for farmers in the northeastern states.

[*See also* **Granger Laws; Homestead Act; Interstate Commerce Act; Populist Era;** ***and*** **Populist Party.**]

BIBLIOGRAPHY

Nordin, D. Sven. *Rich Harvest: A History of the Grange, 1867–1900*. Jackson: University Press of Mississippi, 1974.

Woods, Thomas A. *Knights of the Plow: Oliver H. Kelley and the Origins of the Grange in Republican Ideology*. Ames: Iowa State University Press, 1991.

Roy V. Scott

GRANT, ULYSSES S.

Born 27 April 1822 in Point Pleasant, Ohio, the son of an antislavery Whig businessman and newspaper editor, Hiram Ulysses Grant entered the U.S. Military Academy at West Point in 1839, where a bureaucratic mixup resulted in rendering his name as Ulysses S. Grant. Graduating in the middle of the Class of 1843, Grant saw action in the Mexican-American War before marrying Julia Dent, daughter of a Missouri slaveholder (the couple would have four children). Resigning from the army in 1854, Grant attempted to eke out a living as a farmer and small businessman in the St. Louis area, but illness and poor economic conditions hampered his efforts, and he moved to Illinois in 1860 to work in his father's general store. His political views at this time leaned toward the Democratic Party after a brush with the Know-Nothing movement, although he had no firmly held political beliefs other than his opposition to secession.

When the American Civil War broke out in 1861 Grant volunteered his services, eventually landing a commission as a colonel of the Twenty-first Illinois. He skillfully networked with Illinois congressman Elihu B. Washburne, a Republican, who was responsible for Grant winning promotion to brigadier general within a few months. In February 1862 Grant became a household name when he directed the capture of Forts Henry and Donelson, for which he earned promotion to major general; he survived criticism for his performance at Shiloh that April, where a Confederate army surprised his command before Grant drove the attackers away in a costly battle. In 1863, after a stunning campaign, he captured Vicksburg, Mississippi, and followed that up with another triumph at Chattanooga, Tennessee, ending the year as the United States' most successful general in the conflict. Elevated to lieutenant general in 1864 and named general in chief, Grant directed operations that resulted in the collapse of the Confederacy by the spring of 1865, and he personally accepted the surrender of Confederate general Robert E. Lee at Appomattox Court House 9 April 1865.

During the war Grant came to embrace emancipation as a war aim, although he also favored efforts to build a peace based upon reconciliation with white Southerners. A skilled political networker who was well aware of establishing a solid working relationship with President Abraham Lincoln, Grant nevertheless showed no interest in following Lincoln as president. He soon found himself in opposition to President Andrew Johnson's Reconstruction policy, particularly the Tennessean's neglect of black civil rights and toleration of white supremacist terrorist violence. He sided with Republican congressional Reconstruction initiatives, supported Johnson's impeachment, and accepted the Republican nomination for president in 1868 in the belief that peacemaking should not be left to professional politicians. "Let us have peace," he declared upon accepting the nomination: his victory that fall over Democrat Horatio Seymour was taken as a sign that Reconstruction would soon come to an end, leaving the nation to address other political issues.

Grant became president at a time when both Republicans and Democrats confronted the possibility of realignment with what seemed to be the final settlement of wartime issues. Toward that end, the new president worked to secure the ratification of the Fifteenth Amendment and the readmission of the remaining former Confederate states. Republicans soon divided over a number of issues, including overseas expansion, foreign policy, fiscal policy, tariffs, and civil service reform. During his first term Grant presided over a forging of the Republican majority, complete with building support for administration measures in Congress, including efforts to protect southern blacks from terrorist violence. Many Republicans, dissatisfied with Grant's performance, joined the Liberal Republican movement, which drew support from a struggling Democratic Party during the election of 1872. Although Liberal Republican leader Carl Schurz warned that "anything to beat Grant" was a poor platform, the dissidents fell into disarray after they nominated newspaper editor Horace Greeley, and in the fall contest Grant won reelection by an overwhelming margin.

Grant's second term proved difficult. The panic of 1873 resulted in a major economic depression; revelations of corruption, first among congressional Republicans and then within the administration itself, damaged Grant's reputation. Support for Reconstruction collapsed, as public support for Grant's use of federal force to protect blacks in the South waned. By 1876 whatever hope some people had entertained of a third term for Grant had vanished. In the disputed election that followed, Grant's ability to balance the threat of force with a willingness to negotiate facilitated the settlement known as the Compromise of 1877 and the election of Rutherford B. Hayes.

After leaving the White House Grant embarked upon a tour around the world: foreign leaders welcomed him as a prominent statesman. That success fueled speculation that he would run for a third term in 1880, but his bid for the nomination failed. That fall Grant campaigned for Republican candidate James A. Garfield, but soon fell out of favor with the new president's administration, and he grew equally dissatisfied with the performance of Chester A. Arthur, once a loyal Grant supporter. Turning to business, Grant found himself the victim of a scam that ruined his family; the discovery that he had throat cancer further propelled him to compose his memoirs as a way to provide for his family. He completed the manuscript days before he passed away at Mt. McGregor, New York, on 23 July 1885.

[*See also* **Compromise of 1877; Emancipation Proclamation; Fifteenth Amendment; Lincoln, Abraham;** *and* **Reconstruction.**]

BIBLIOGRAPHY

Bunting, Josiah, III. *Ulysses S. Grant.* New York: Times Books, 2004.

Simpson, Brooks D. *The Reconstruction Presidents.* Lawrence: University Press of Kansas, 1998.

Smith, Jean Edward. *Grant.* New York: Simon & Schuster, 2001.

Brooks D. Simpson

GREAT SOCIETY

The Great Society has been incorporated into American political lore as the brand name for the social policies that distinguished the 1960s. For the political right, these policies exemplify the failures of American liberalism, particularly liberal tendencies toward government overreach and indulgence of the poor and African Americans. Indeed, for a time the term "Great Society" became virtually an epithet in the polemics of national Republican politicians, used to conjure up images of black misbehavior and liberal foolishness. A good many academic commentators have scarcely been kinder, treating the spate of new programs initiated in the 1960s as badly mistaken interventions.

The features of domestic policy that distinguish the Great Society era are widely agreed upon. First, a series of new federal programs were initiated, presumably to deal with social problems like juvenile delinquency (the Juvenile Delinquency and Youth Offenses Control Act of 1961), mental illness (the Community Mental Health Centers Act of 1963), poverty (the Economic Opportunity Act of 1964), or blighted neighborhoods (the Demonstrations Cities and Metropolitan Development Act of 1966). Second, these new programs were targeted to the big cities, especially to the inner-city populations that were increasingly black and poor. Third, as the number of programs increased, the state and local fiscal contributions customarily required by federal grant-in-aid programs diminished. Fourth, the new programs tended to bypass the state governments and even municipal governments, in favor of a range of new organizational participants, including neighborhood groups and nonprofit agencies. Finally, the federal programs permitted—and even seemed to rhetorically encourage—these new entities to wage campaigns to change the practices of established municipal agencies.

This was not the whole of it. A number of policies first initiated in the 1930s were revived, revamped, and expanded. The Food Stamp Program, later renamed the Supplemental Nutrition Assistance Program, has roots in the New Deal pilot program that permitted people on relief to receive surplus food, but it lasted only a few years. After the 1960 election, President John F. Kennedy revived a pilot food stamp program. Then the Food Stamp Act of 1964 made the program permanent. The Aid to Families with Dependent Children program, which was liberalized by regulatory changes and court rulings in the 1960s, had also been initiated in the 1930s as part of the Social Security Act. In 1972, programs to provide cash assistance to the impoverished blind, old, and disabled, also part of the Social Security Act, were replaced by a new and more generous program called Supplemental Security Income. And the main social security program that provided pensions to the aged became more generous.

Such a massive shift in federal social policy, the rapidity and even urgency with which it was implemented, the upheaval it created in federal–local relations as well as in local politics, and the forty-year backlash against safety-net policies all seem to argue that there must be a large political reason for the policies. After all, the troubles, particularly objections from the big-city mayors who were Democratic Party stalwarts, began almost immediately. Yet the basic model of the Great Society initiatives that targeted the inner city and limited state and local authority persisted and was repeated.

The Usual Political Explanations. Why? The familiar explanations seem weak. As usual, one of the favorites fastens on the aspirations of presidents, particularly in this case those of Lyndon Baines Johnson, who was given to proclaiming his vision of "an end to poverty and racial injustice," or who elsewhere said, "I wanted power to give things to people—all sorts of things to all sorts of people, especially the poor and the blacks." Another favored explanation points to "urban problems"—whether crime, mental illness, poverty, or substandard housing—and the inability of state and local governments to deal with these problems. "From the perspective of the Washington policy-maker," says Robert Reischauer, "these governments suffered from three major weaknesses. The first . . . was fiscal starvation. . . . The second . . . technical and administrative capacity." And the third was simply a lack of will.

None of this is adequate. True, Johnson spoke the words attributed to him; there were also urban problems, and there were deficiencies in the fiscal, administrative, and political capacity of state and local governments. These explanations, however, only push the question back a step. Why did Johnson, the wily politician whose career in the Congress revealed no such commitments, suddenly become preoccupied with poverty and racial discrimination? Similarly, although there are always "urban problems," few of these problems were new, and in any case, there were existing federal programs that provided vehicles to help the cities. Why did the problems of the cities suddenly loom so large as to demand action through entirely new programs?

Academic critics of the Great Society who see the policy initiatives as simply mistaken have even less satisfactory explanations. Margaret Weir, for example, thinks the emphasis of the programs ought to have been on what she calls the structural reform of labor markets and points to features of the internal politics of the national administration to explain why this did not happen (1992). The Harvard University sociologist and senator Daniel Patrick Moynihan (D-NY) blamed muddy and contradictory goals, which he attributed to the cloudy thinking of the academics who advised the policy makers. But if the policies were mistaken, can that reasonably be blamed on foolish academics who relied on "bankrupt" therapeutic and cultural interventions? Why were these particular academics influential, why these specific mistakes, on such a large scale, and why were they repeated and even enlarged from one program initiative to another? A satisfactory account must go beyond the good or mischief that can be wrought by a handful of not very powerful advisors. It must deal with politics, for the simple reason that the actors who initiated the programs, repeated them, and enlarged upon them were the leading politicians of the nation.

An Alternative. The 1960s policy initiatives, and their distinctive administrative features, were efforts to cope with major political disturbances in the Democratic base, particularly in the presidential electorate. The mass movement of American blacks from the plantations to the cities of the South had helped to set off the civil rights movement, which jeopardized white Southern support for the party. In short order, the migration of blacks to the ghettoes of the big cities of the north and the conflicts that ensued were jeopardizing the northern urban base of the party as well.

The swelling ghettos were encroaching on white neighborhoods, schools, and parks, setting off fierce conflicts between the newcomers and older residents. Recall, for example, the bitter and long-lasting battles over school desegregation. Confronted by apparently irreconcilable group demands, mayors generally favored their older white constituents. Federal funds for public housing had gone unused because the projects had come to be associated with the black poor and thus aroused adamant opposition. Meanwhile, urban renewal funds were actually used to displace blacks in favor of better-off whites and white businesses. Nor were big-city politicians attending to their new minority constituents. They were not working to mobilize black electoral participation, either in local or in national contests.

The 1960 election cast the problem in sharp relief. Kennedy owed his victory to the heavy Democratic vote in key northern cities, especially to the black vote. But his good showing in the ghettos could not be taken for granted. To the contrary, although urban blacks had been Democrats for almost a quarter century, there were clear signs of slippage. In 1952 blacks had voted 79 percent for Stevenson; in 1956 the black Democratic vote dropped to 61 percent. Kennedy won back some of these votes (69 percent in 1960) by taking a strong stand on civil rights. But to act on that platform would only cause further defections in the South. Other ways to strengthen the allegiance of urban blacks were needed.

The new federal programs directed to the inner city were adorned with legislative titles and rhetorical statements intended to win broad support. After all, everyone was in favor of doing something about juvenile delinquency or mental health or blighted communities. But proclamations notwithstanding, the programs were an effort to cope with the political problems set off by demographic upheaval, by incorporating the black newcomers into urban politics. No wonder that the activities funded by the programs recalled those of the old political machine. Local agencies were created, often in storefronts. Staff offered residents help in finding jobs and securing services, and neighborhood leaders were hired as "community workers" to dispense the new federal patronage, much as the old ward heelers had done. Whether the funds were appropriated for delinquency prevention or mental health or antipoverty or model cities, on the streets of the ghettos the programs looked very much alike.

Politics and Government Structure. Somehow, these federal interventions had to reach and incorporate the black newcomers despite the framework of the federal grant-in-aid system, which gave large discretion over programs to state and local government officials. This was no small challenge, given the intransigence of municipal governments and their white constituents. To be sure, the Great Society programs tried to coax municipal agencies into providing services for blacks with new monies. But they also did something quite different by establishing a direct relationship between the federal government and ghetto neighborhoods, bypassing both state and local governments. This appears to be evidence of the effort of the national administration to override the obstructions posed by state and local authorities to the political integration of black newcomers.

In fact, this was not the first time, nor was it to be the last, that electoral shifts prompted federal initiatives to restructure intergovernmental relations. The New Deal administration had bypassed recalcitrant state governments to channel grants-in-aid directly to the party's urban strongholds. And when the Nixon and Reagan administrations reversed the pattern of the Great Society, channeling program authority and funds back to the states and away from the older big cities, they were also acting on their distinctive electoral calculus. Politics has to do not only with the substance of policy, but also with the changes in the structure of government authority the policy dictates.

[*See also* Johnson, Lyndon B.; Liberalism; New Deal; Nixon, Richard M.; *and* Reagan, Ronald.]

BIBLIOGRAPHY

Kaplan, Marshall, and Peggy L. Cuciti, eds. *The Great Society and Its Legacy*. Durham, N.C.: Duke University Press, 1986.

Moynihan, Daniel Patrick. *Maximum Feasible Misunderstanding: Community Action in the War on Poverty*. New York: Free Press, 1969.

Patterson, James T. *Grand Expectations: The United States, 1945–1974*. New York: Oxford University Press, 1996.

Piven, Frances Fox, and Richard A. Cloward. *Poor People's Movement: How They Succeed, Why They Fail*. New York: Vintage Books, 1977.

Weir, Margaret. *Politics and Jobs: The Boundaries of Employment Policy in the United States*. Princeton, N.J.: Princeton University Press, 1992.

Frances Fox Piven

GREENBACK LABOR PARTY

The Greenback Labor Party represented a brief but potent Gilded Age expression of working-class antimonopoly sentiment. In the aftermath of the depression of 1873, the formation of the agrarian-based Greenback Party in 1874–1875, the railroad strikes of 1877, and the electoral success of local workingmen's parties in industrial states in 1877, 150 delegates assembled in Toledo, Ohio, in February 1878 to organize the National (or Greenback Labor) Party. Its labor-oriented platform called for shorter working hours, a ban on contract prison labor, immigration restriction, and government bureaus of labor statistics. The party attracted 1 million votes in the 1878 midterm election and elected fifteen congressmen across the East, South, and Midwest. In some localities, it took on a distinctly radical character; in the coal districts of Alabama, black Greenback Laborites exercised leadership among both black and white miners.

The party's 1880 platform included farmer-labor planks that foreshadowed the Populist

Party's 1892 Omaha Platform, calling for government control of transportation and communications, a graduated federal income tax, opposition to a standing army, and the lifting of all restrictions on suffrage. Despite the party's impressive start, however, its 1880 presidential candidate, the Civil War general James Weaver of Iowa, attracted only 3 percent of the vote, mostly in agricultural districts. The end of the depression in 1878 and the government's resumption of specie payments (the gold standard) in 1879 had sapped the party's fortunes. Nevertheless, hopes for an independent labor party revived with the rise to prominence of the Knights of Labor after another wave of national strikes in the 1880s.

[*See also* **Monetary Policy; Populist Era; Populist Party;** ***and*** **Taxation.**]

BIBLIOGRAPHY

Ritter, Gretchen. *Goldbugs and Greenbacks: The Antimonopoly Tradition and the Politics of Finance in America*. Cambridge, UK; New York: Cambridge University Press, 1997.

Sanders, Elizabeth. *Roots of Reform: Farmers, Workers, and the American State, 1877–1917*. Chicago: University of Chicago Press, 1999.

Shelton Stromquist

GRISWOLD v. CONNECTICUT

381 U.S. 479 (1965), argued 29 March 1965, decided 7 June 1965, by vote of 7 to 2; Douglas for the Court, Goldberg, Harlan, and White concurring, Black and Stewart in dissent. *Griswold* is a curious but important case in American constitutional history. It concerned an "uncommonly silly law" (as Justice Potter Stewart called it) that was technically difficult to challenge on constitutional grounds, as evidenced by the divergent positions of the justices concurring with the majority position. These opinions not only made *Griswold* one of the most significant decisions of the 1965 term but also fueled controversies both about the general character of constitutional lawmaking and about specific rights that have continued decades later.

Evolution of the Dispute. A Connecticut statute of 1879 made it a crime for any person to use any drug, article, or instrument to prevent conception. This statute had been challenged twice before, in 1943 (*Tileston v. Ullman*), where the Supreme Court held that the plaintiff lacked standing, and in 1961 (*Poe v. Ullman*), where the Court determined that the controversy was not ripe because the plaintiff had not been prosecuted.

By 1965, however, the Court determined to resolve the constitutionality of the statute. The suit was initiated by two members of the Planned Parenthood League of Connecticut. Its executive director and medical director had been convicted of violating the statute by giving information, instruction, and medical advice to married persons regarding means of preventing conception. The conviction was affirmed by the Supreme Court of Errors of Connecticut.

On appeal, the U.S. Supreme Court reversed by a 7-to-2 margin. The majority determined that: (1) the appellants had standing to raise the constitutional rights of people with whom they had a professional relationship; and (2) the statute was invalid because it infringed on the constitutionally protected right to "privacy" of married persons.

Implied Rights: The New Substantive Due Process? The majority holding in *Griswold* to a large extent was positioned within post-1937 constitutional theory. It protected basic constitutional rights and applied them against the states in conventional fashion under the Fourteenth Amendment, and it mandated a stricter scrutiny for laws that interfere with "fundamental personal rights" than for those that regulate economic relations. The Court's more controversial step of applying this logic to fundamental rights—here, of privacy—not expressly enumerated in the Bill of Rights likewise was hardly unprecedented. The Court previously had affirmed the unwritten rights to teach one's child a foreign language (*Meyer v. Nebraska,* 1923), to send one's children to private schools (*Pierce v. Society of Sisters,* 1925), to procreate (*Skinner v. Oklahoma,* 1942), to resist certain invasions of the body (*Rochin v. California,* 1952), and to travel abroad (*Aptheker v. Secretary of State,* 1964). What made *Griswold* a landmark case was the Court's willingness to explicitly justify at length this practice of investing such unenumerated rights with full constitutional status.

It is on this point that the justices were most divided. Indeed, four different lines of justification in defense of unenumerated fundamental rights were outlined by supporters of the majority decision. Justice William O. Douglas, writing for five members of the Court, referred to rights that are implicit in, or peripheral to, other express guarantees in the Bill of Rights. In his famous words, "specific guarantees . . . have penumbras, formed by emanations from those guarantees that help give them life and substance" (p. 484). Just as the Court earlier had found that First Amendment rights to freedom of speech implied a peripheral "right to freedom of association," he reasoned, so do the First, Third, Fourth, Fifth, and Ninth amendments imply "zones of privacy" that form the basis for the general privacy right affirmed in this case.

Justice Arthur Goldberg, joined by Chief Justice Earl Warren and Justice William Brennan, staked out a more expansive approach to justifying right of privacy. Although he found merit in the penumbra and emanations argument of Douglas, Goldberg argued further that "liberty protects those personal rights that are fundamental, and is not confined to the specific terms of the Bill Rights." The Fourteenth Amendment may not incorporate all of the first eight amendments Goldberg acknowledged. However, the specific "language and history of the Ninth Amendment" provide strong support for judicial incorporation of additional rights "so rooted in the traditions and conscience of our people as to be ranked fundamental" in our constitutional legacy (p. 487).

Justices John M. Harlan and Byron White advanced positions that, by contrast, severed altogether the link between the Fourteenth Amendment and the Bill of Rights. Harlan rejected the incorporation doctrine as a historically groundless and ineffective check on judicial discretion, while reproaching the "letter or penumbra" logic of Douglas as overly restrictive of future rights development. Instead, he affirmed a commitment to due process and liberty that "stands . . . on its own bottom," constrained only by the forces of history and cultural values that bind the court. By this logic, the Connecticut statute violated basic values "implicit in the concept of ordered liberty" (p. 500). Justice White rooted his argument in a similarly expansive interpretation of Fourteenth Amendment due process guarantees but focused his attention on the terms of strict scrutiny by which the Court should balance fundamental rights of individuals with compelling state interests in such cases.

The dissents by Justices Hugo Black and Potter Stewart expressed the same disdain for the Connecticut statute as had the majority. However, both denied that the state law infringed upon any fundamental constitutional right. In their view, such a right—whether rooted in the "implied rights" theories of

Douglas and Goldberg or in the "natural justice" positions of Harlan and White—lacked specific constitutional authorization and represented an arbitrary exercise of judicial power that threatened the American system of government. "Use of any such broad, unbounded judicial authority would make of this Court's members a day-to-day constitutional convention," argued Black. This would amount to a "great unconstitutional shift of power to the courts which . . . will be bad for the courts and worse for the country" (p. 520).

Scholarly debate has amplified these disagreements among members of the Court. In particular, many critics of the decision have elaborated Black's charge that the majority was simply offering a new and unwarranted version of the old "substantive due process" doctrine. Why, critics asked, is it less dangerous for Supreme Court justices to impose their personal preferences on legislators and society in matters of personal rights than in matters of economic relations? If the old *Lochner* logic was wrong, why is this new form of "Lochnerizing" not wrong as well? Moreover, are judges any more qualified to determine one form of rights than another? And is the legitimacy of a "government of laws" no less undermined by unrestrained, arbitrary judicial policy making in one sphere than in another?

Defenders of the majority have ranged even more widely in their arguments than did the justices. Some supporters have emphasized the decision's solid groundings in past judicial practice, theoretical logic, and constitutional text. Indeed, both Douglas and Goldberg explicitly declined the invitation to follow in the substantive due process tradition. "We do not sit as a super-legislature to determine the wisdom, need, and propriety of laws that touch economic problems, business affairs, or social conditions," wrote Douglas. The law in question, by contrast, "operates directly on an intimate relation of husband and wife" that long has received constitutional protection (p. 482).

Other supporters of the majority instead have affirmed Justices Harlan and White's unabashed rejection of formalist illusions about textual constraints upon judicial action. They argue that legal interpretation is always discretionary and that textual constraints on judges are far less important than cultural and political forces. Moreover, many scholars have defended the Court's zealous defense of personal rights as both within its institutional capacities and functionally necessary to maintaining liberty in our modern corporate society. Such arguments were sufficiently compelling that all nine justices, including Stewart, by 1973 had accepted the Court's role in giving the Fourteenth Amendment's due process clause a substantive content that exceeds the Bill of Rights, although considerable differences remained about how and when that authority should be exercised.

Privacy Rights: Subsequent Case Law and Theoretical Disputes. Controversies over the constitutional grounding of unenumerated rights have been paralleled by controversies over the range of practices and relations that such rights protect. Indeed, the majority in *Griswold* was far more expansive about legal justifications for a right of privacy than about its theoretical content and reach. And although the Court recognized that commitments to privacy have deep roots in American society and its laws, that legacy has provided a vague guide for determining the substantive scope of privacy rights in modern social relations. Not surprisingly, questions regarding conceptual coherence have continued to surround the doctrine.

Critics query whether the logic of "privacy" extends to all social relations—including the sale of contraceptives to unmarried individuals (*Carey v. Population Services International,*

1977), relations among homosexuals (*Bowers v. Hardwick,* 1986), and women's choices regarding abortion (*Roe v. Wade,* 1973). For example, is it really privacy that is most infringed by regulations restricting the sale and distribution of contraceptives? Do regulations of sales concern privacy more than those on solicitation, which was treated primarily as matter of free speech in *Bolger v. Youngs Drug Product Corp.* (1983)?

Moreover, the privacy doctrine has been increasingly attacked from both ends of the political spectrum. On the one hand, the doctrine as applied to abortion since *Roe* has continued to provoke the outrage of conservatives over both the expansion of judicial authority and its resulting protections for allegedly immoral individual actions. Ironically, conservatives have rejected the privacy doctrine because it limits state intervention into the lives of citizens.

On the other hand, the privacy doctrine has been assailed from the political left for advancing a far too truncated and archaic liberal understanding of freedom. Critics on the left condemn the *Griswold* decision for limiting the privacy protection for contraception use to persons bound in conventional marriage relations. This shield for contraception use was extended a few years later to unmarried persons in *Eisenstadt v. Baird* (1972), but the Court's repeated denial of protection for homosexual relationships has revealed privacy limits as a challenge to traditional norms regarding sexuality (*Bowers*). Moreover, although the privacy logic has been useful to limit at least some unwanted state intervention in intimate sexual matters, it has also been employed to preclude a positive state role in educating citizens and providing funding essential for the exercise of rights to use birth control and receive an abortion. Some critics thus argue for the need to replace the privacy logic with a more affirmative conception of autonomy rights that is more consistent with the goals of equality and empowerment.

Legacy. The legacy of the privacy rights doctrine thus points to the perennial problem of Court efforts to deal with changing social needs, values, and interests through invocation of traditional norms long supportive of quite different relationships. The right of privacy affirmed in *Griswold* still stands, but clearly is jeopardized by increasingly restrictive Court rulings on protections for abortion, its most important doctrinal application.

[*See also* **Bill of Rights; Black, Hugo; Civil Rights; Civil Rights Legislation; Douglas, William O.; Due Process: Legal Cases; Due Process: Substantive Process; Equality; Fourteenth Amendment; Harlan, John Marshall;** ***Lochner v. New York;*** **Privacy;** ***Roe v. Wade;*** **Supreme Court, U.S.;** *and* **Warren, Earl.**]

BIBLIOGRAPHY

Copelon, Rhonda. "Beyond the Liberal Idea of Privacy: Toward A Positive Right of Autonomy." In *Judging the Constitution: Critical Essays on Judicial Lawmaking,* edited by Michael W. McCann and Gerald L. Houseman, pp. 287–316. Glenview, Ill.: Scott, Foresman, 1989.

Dionisopolous, Allan, and Craig Ducat, eds. *The Right to Privacy: Essays and Cases.* St. Paul, Minn.: West, 1976.

Henken, Louis. "Privacy and Autonomy." *Columbia Law Review* 74 (1974): 1410–1433.

"Symposium on the Griswold Case and the Right of Privacy." *Michigan Law Review* 64 (1965): 197–282.

Michael W. McCann

GUN CONTROL

Gun-control laws first appeared in urban America during the early twentieth century.

They typically specified where and how firearms could be used and restricted the carrying of concealed weapons. The most sweeping early effort to regulate firearms, New York State's Sullivan Law (1911), strictly limited the sale, possession, and carrying of guns. By the late 1990s, some authorities estimated, more than 20,000 state and local statutes regulated firearms.

Federal gun-control laws were enacted in 1927, 1934, and 1938. These forbade mail-order pistol sales, regulated firearms dealers, and limited possession of "gangster" weapons. The Gun Control Act of 1968 tightened the earlier laws and prohibited some categories of persons from gun ownership. The so-called Brady Law of 1993 imposed a waiting period on handgun purchases and banned sales of some types of semiautomatic weapons. (This act was named for James Brady, a presidential press secretary who was shot and disabled in the 1981 attempted assassination of President Ronald Reagan, and a prominent gun-control advocate.) In 1972, enforcement of federal gun laws was assigned to the Treasury Department's Bureau of Alcohol, Tobacco, and Firearms.

Late twentieth-century gun-control strategies emphasized either selective or comprehensive policies. Selective policies regulate gun use in that they seek to keep firearms away from dangerous situations and people but to avoid inconveniencing owners. Examples include restrictions on carrying guns, prohibitions on ownership by felons and mental patients, and laws mandating longer prison sentences for crimes involving gun use. Selective policies proved difficult to enforce, because guns easily pass from legal to illegal uses.

Comprehensive policies limit general firearm possession. Such laws ban guns with high potential for misuse, such as military-style rifles, inexpensive handguns (also called "Saturday night specials"), or all handguns. Comprehensive policies raise problems of definition ("military-style" and "inexpensive" are imprecise terms), and they cannot stop persons bent on violence from substituting other types of firearms. Because they affected more owners, comprehensive policies also stirred greater opposition.

The effectiveness of gun-control laws remained an unresolved question as the century ended. Studies that examined a disparate set of laws in many areas usually concluded that the laws did not influence violence. However, studies focusing on the effects of a single law in one area often found that they did reduce violence. Gun control ultimately remained as much a political and cultural issue as a matter of public safety. Although polls regularly found strong support for stricter firearm laws, most proposals failed in referenda and legislatures. Commentators usually attributed this outcome to the efforts of the powerful National Rifle Association (NRA), a pro-gun lobbying organization that contributes heavily to the campaigns of sympathetic legislators. The NRA could not be successful, however, without support from millions of persons who view firearms access as a basic right under the Second Amendment to the Constitution. A late 1990s wave of multiple murders involving guns, some committed by schoolchildren, further energized the campaign for stricter gun-control laws.

In a particularly horrendous incident in 1999, two students at Columbine High School in Colorado methodically shot and killed twelve of their classmates before committing suicide. Such incidents intensified calls for tougher gun control.

Federal policy moved in the opposite direction under President George W. Bush, however, reflecting in part the more than $1 million contributed by the NRA to pro-gun candidates in the 2000 campaign. The Bush

Administration and many legislators resisted proposals to tighten rules governing gun sales and even sought to roll back some existing regulations. The administration, responding to NRA pressure, also opposed a United Nations treaty aimed at reducing the global traffic in small arms, including hand guns and shoulder-launched rockets of the kind used with deadly effect against U.S. helicopters in the violent aftermath of the Iraq War of 2003.

[*See also* **Bill of Rights.**]

BIBLIOGRAPHY

Anderson, Jervis. *Guns in American Life*. New York: Random House, 1984.

Bijlefeld, Marjolin, ed. *The Gun Control Debate: A Documentary History*. Westport, Conn.: Greenwood Press, 1997.

Kennett, Lee, and James LaVerne Anderson. *The Gun in America: The Origins of a National Dilemma*. Westport, Conn.: Greenwood Press, 1975.

Reiss, Albert J., Jr., and Jeffrey A. Roth, eds. *Understanding and Preventing Violence*. Washington, D.C.: National Academy Press, 1993.

Alan Lizotte and David McDowall;
updated by Paul S. Boyer

H

HAMILTON, ALEXANDER

(1755–1804), first secretary of the treasury and Federalist Party leader. Alexander Hamilton was born out of wedlock on the island of Nevis to Rachael Paucett Lavien and James Hamilton, a Scottish merchant. In 1765 the family moved to St. Croix. Abandoned by James, Rachel apprenticed Alexander to a merchant firm, where he remained after her death in 1768. In 1772, his employer paid Hamilton's way to New York, where he attended King's College (now Columbia University). Opposing British imperial policy, he joined a local militia and in March 1776 was appointed an artillery captain by the New York legislature. With George Washington's forces when the British attacked Long Island, he participated in the retreat across New Jersey late in 1776 and in the successful counterattacks at Trenton and Princeton. In March 1777 he became one of Washington's aides-de-camp, an experience that sharpened his criticism of the weak Articles of Confederation government. In March 1780 he married Elizabeth Schuyler, daughter of General Philip Schuyler, a wealthy and prominent New Yorker. They had eight children. Resigning as Washington's aide in 1781 and given command of a battalion at Yorktown, Hamilton fought in the Revolutionary War's final major battle.

Returning to New York, he entered the bar and embarked on a political career. After service in the Continental Congress (1782–1783), he helped establish the Bank of New York (1784) and in 1786 was elected to the state legislature.

At the Constitutional Convention of 1787, Hamilton unsuccessfully argued for a government modeled on the English system. Writing under the name "Publius," Hamilton—in collaboration with John Jay and James Madison—published a series of essays urging ratification of the Constitution. Collectively known as the *Federalist Papers,* they rank as classics of political thought.

As secretary of the treasury in the Washington administration, Hamilton prepared a set of influential reports on the nation's government and economy and how they might be strengthened. In *Report for the Support of Public Credit* (1790) he proposed that, to secure the credit of the new United States, the federal government should pay all foreign, domestic, and state debts remaining from the Revolutionary War. He also advocated an excise tax to supplement tariff revenues and the establishment of a mint and a national bank. His *Report on Manufactures* (1791), written with Tench Coxe (1755–1824), his assistant secretary, called for the protection and encouragement of nascent industries. Hamilton envisioned a powerful republic in which the national interest would be synonymous with the interests of the most economically successful and energetic citizens.

Most of Hamilton's proposals became law, but they also engendered mounting opposition. Clashes with Thomas Jefferson, Washington's secretary of state, over Hamilton's alleged meddling in foreign policy, as well as Jefferson's conviction that Hamilton was power-hungry and corrupt, splintered the administration. The violence of the French Revolution and the outbreak of war between Great Britain and France further polarized American politics. Washington, Hamilton, and their "Federalist" supporters backed neutrality and Jay's Treaty, which resolved outstanding differences with Great Britain; Jefferson, Madison, and a growing "Republican" interest, fearing monarchical plots, supported a more pro-French policy.

Hamilton resigned as treasury secretary in early 1795. Resuming his New York law practice, he remained immersed in the struggles between Federalists and Republicans. He substantially rewrote Madison's draft of Washington's Farewell Address, worked to assure that the Federalists would retain the presidency, and during John Adams's administration (1797–1801) offered advice to friends in the cabinet.

Personal setbacks and political blunders marked Hamilton's final years. A 1791 affair with Maria Reynolds became a public scandal in 1797. As inspector general of the army in 1798 he proved ineffective. In 1800 he attempted to prevent Adams's reelection by publishing a vitriolic personal attack on him. In 1801, his oldest son, Philip, died in a duel. In 1804, Hamilton attacked Aaron Burr, an old political enemy, when Burr ran for governor of New York. After the election, Burr challenged Hamilton to a duel. The two met at Weehawken, New Jersey, on 11 July 1804. Burr fatally shot Hamilton, who died the next day.

Despite contemporary suspicions of his motives, Alexander Hamilton played a monumental role in establishing the new nation, including his service as Washington's advisor and confidant, his brilliant collaborative defense of the Constitution in *The Federalist,* his shaping of the first national financial system, and his leadership of the Federalist Party. His political thought, often contrasted with that of Jefferson, continued to influence American political discourse well into the twentieth century.

[*See also* **Burr, Aaron; Conservatism; Constitution; Constitutional Convention of 1787; Continental Congress; Croly, Herbert; Economic Development; Federal Government, Executive Branch: Treasury**

Department; Federalism; Federalist Papers; Federalist Party; Jay, John; Madison, James; Monetary Policy; Tariffs; Taxation; *and* Washington, George.]

BIBLIOGRAPHY

McDonald, Forrest. *Alexander Hamilton: A Biography.* New York: W. W. Norton, 1979.

Stourzh, Gerald. *Alexander Hamilton and the Idea of Republican Government.* Stanford, Calif.: Stanford University Press, 1970.

Paul G. E. Clemens

HANNA, MARK

(1837–1904), central figure in the politics of the 1890s and early 1900s. Based in Cleveland, Ohio, Marcus Alonzo Hanna became rich as a shipper and broker serving the coal and iron industries, which developed as a result of Cleveland's strategic location. One of the few industrialists fascinated less by profits than by the machinations of politics, Hanna served as a key advisor for Ohio Republican governor William McKinley, who established himself as the outstanding Republican spokesman for high tariffs, high wages, and renewed prosperity in the face of the depression of the 1890s. Hanna helped to secure McKinley's presidential nomination in 1896 and to defeat William Jennings Bryan's free silver movement. Hanna nationalized the GOP campaign, raising $3.5 million, mostly from corporations fearful of Bryan's policies. Hanna's campaign reached millions of voters with a firm, insistent message of sound money, prosperity, and cultural pluralism. The Democrats caricatured him as an archvillain who put corporate interests ahead of the national interest. Serving as a U.S. senator (1900–1904), he emerged as a Republican leader in his own right. Hanna also worked with the National Civic Federation to conciliate labor strife. He sought to bring unions into the Republican fold and to avert major strikes that would be economically damaging as well as politically and socially divisive. Hanna's death at the peak of his power in 1904 ended a struggle with Theodore Roosevelt for control of the Republican Party.

[*See also* **Bryan, William Jennings; McKinley, William; National Civic Federation; Political Parties; Populist Era; Republican Party; Roosevelt, Theodore; *and* Tariffs.**]

BIBLIOGRAPHY

Croly, Herbert. *Marcus Alonzo Hanna: His Life and Work.* New York: Macmillan, 1912.

Marcus, Robert D. *Grand Old Party.* New York: Oxford University Press, 1971.

Richard Jensen

HARDING, WARREN G.

Warren G. Harding served as the twenty-ninth president, from 1921 to 1923. Harding is best known for restoring "normalcy," a word he coined, after World War I and for scandals. Harding was born in Blooming Grove, Ohio, on 2 November 1865. Prior to entering politics, Harding was a newspaper publisher and a civic booster, adopting the motto "Boost, don't knock." He was active in Ohio politics, serving as a state senator and as lieutenant governor. In 1910 Harding made an unsuccessful bid for governor. In 1912 Harding placed William Howard Taft's name in nomination at the Republican convention. In 1914 Harding won a seat in the U.S. Senate.

In 1920 Harding entered the presidential primary race as a long-shot favorite-son candidate, but secured the nomination at the deadlocked convention as a compromise dark horse candidate. Harding conducted a front porch campaign from his hometown to underscore his message of a "return to normalcy." Despite the nostalgic theme, the campaign made sophisticated use of advertising and celebrity endorsements to win a convincing landslide victory that ushered in a decade of Republican rule and limited government.

In the campaign, Harding had also promised to bring the "best minds" into his administration. He appointed notable leaders such as Charles Evans Hughes (State), Herbert Hoover (Commerce), and Andrew W. Mellon (Treasury). He appointed William Howard Taft as chief justice of the Supreme Court. However, other appointments went to political cronies whose actions resulted in scandal.

His successes include signing legislation to formally end the war, pardoning Eugene V. Debs, a socialist jailed in the First World War for sedition, and signing the Sheppard–Towner Maternity and Infancy Act of 1921. Harding cut taxes, reduced government expenditures, and established the modern executive budgeting system through the Budget and Accounting Act (1921). His administration undertook radio and transcable regulation, repeal of wartime profit taxes, and a reduction of railroad rates. He increased spending for highways. He appointed more women to government than any previous president. In addition, Harding signed the Emergency Quota Act of 1921, which set the stage for restrictionist immigration legislation in 1924. He proposed legislation to make lynching a federal crime, and he condemned segregation in the South. He pushed for the twelve-hour work day in the steel industry but his administration used a nationwide injunction to end strikes in the coal and railroad industries. After a major scandal in the Bureau of Veterans Affairs, the Harding administration undertook major reform and reorganization of the bureau. Secretary of State Hughes convened the Washington Naval Disarmament Conference that limited weaponry.

Harding died in office on 2 August 1923 in Birmingham, Alabama, on the cross-country "Voyage of Understanding." The economy was recovering from the postwar recession but scandals were also emerging, and charges of cover-ups and foul play unfolded within a climate of sensationalism and scandal. Charles Forbes embezzled funds from the Veterans' Bureau. In the Teapot Dome scandal, Secretary of the Interior Albert Fall was convicted of accepting bribes in exchange for no-bid contracts from oil executives. Attorney General Harry Daugherty allegedly operated the infamous "little green house on K Street" where influence was sold. Harding's personal life was also tainted by scandal, most famously with the 1928 publication of Nan Britton's book, *The President's Daughter.* Britton claimed to have been Harding's mistress and the mother of his child. By the end of the decade Harding's reputation as a failed president was secure and the scandals overshadowed the successes that had made him popular.

[***See also*** **Debs, Eugene;** ***Debs, in re;*** **Hoover, Herbert; Immigration Law and Policy: Before 1930; Taft, William Howard;** ***and*** **Teapot Dome Scandal.**]

BIBLIOGRAPHY

Ferrell, Robert H. *The Strange Deaths of President Harding.* Columbia: University of Missouri Press, 1996.

Murray, Robert K. *The Harding Era: Warren G. Harding and His Administration.* Minneapolis: University of Minnesota Press, 1969.

Payne, Phillip G. *Dead Last: The Public Memory of Warren G. Harding's Scandalous Legacy.* Athens, Ohio: Ohio University Press, 2009.

Russell, Francis. *The Shadow of Blooming Grove: Warren G. Harding and His Times.* New York: McGraw–Hill, 1968.

Stratton, David H. *Tempest over Teapot Dome: The Story of Albert B. Fall.* Norman: University of Oklahoma Press, 1998.

Phillip Payne

HARLAN, JOHN MARSHALL

(1833–1911), justice of the U.S. Supreme Court, 1877–1911. A native of Boyle County, Kentucky, John Marshall Harlan, during his thirty-four-year tenure on the Supreme Court, supported a strong national economy based on free trade among the states and expansive readings of the due process and equal protection clauses of the Fourteenth Amendment. Harlan's somewhat idiosyncratic perspective as a judge was most vividly articulated in his 361 dissenting opinions.

Harlan wrote famous civil rights dissents in the *Civil Rights Cases* (1883), *Hurtado v. California* (1886), and *Plessy v. Ferguson* (1896). In the *Civil Rights Cases,* he defended the constitutionality of the Civil Rights Act of 1875, which guaranteed "full and equal enjoyment" of public accommodations to all citizens. In *Hurtado,* Harlan became the first to espouse the theory that all the protections enumerated in the Bill of Rights should be considered part of the right of "due process" guaranteed by the Fourteenth Amendment, thereby making the Bill of Rights a protection against infringements by the states as well as by the federal government. He pressed this position with little success. In *Plessy,* Harlan dissented from the majority's support for the constitutionality of "separate but equal" transportation facilities for blacks and whites, insisting that state laws segregating the races on public transportation denied blacks equal protection of the laws.

Harlan's constitutional decisions on issues of political economy upheld what he considered important boundaries between the regulatory spheres of the federal government and the states. He believed in strong federal power to maintain the free flow of commerce, but he also upheld the police powers of the states in cases such as *Lochner v. New York* (1905), involving state regulation of the banking industry, so long as he did not find any commercial self-interest motivating the legislation.

Harlan's approach was opinionated, intractable, and impassioned. In the words of Chief Justice Edward Douglass White, "he could lead but he could not follow." Nevertheless, on issues involving racial discrimination and civil rights, his isolated views subsequently resonated with many late twentieth-century Americans.

[*See also* **Bill of Rights; Civil Rights; Civil Rights Legislation; Due Process: Legal Cases; Economic Policy: Regulation; Fourteenth Amendment; *Lochner v. New York; Plessy v. Ferguson;*** **Segregation;** *and* **Supreme Court, U.S.**]

BIBLIOGRAPHY

Beth, Loren. *John Marshall Harlan: The Last Whig Justice.* Lexington: University Press of Kentucky, 1992.

White, G. Edward. "John Marshall Harlan—The Precursor." In *The American Judicial Tradition,* 2d ed., edited by Edward G. White, pp. 129–145. New York: Oxford University Press, 1988.

G. Edward White

HARRISON, BENJAMIN

(1833–1901), twenty-third president of the United States. Born in North Bend, Ohio, Harrison graduated from Miami University in Oxford, Ohio, in 1852 and studied law in Cincinnati. He married Caroline Scott in 1853, and they moved to Indianapolis, Indiana, the following year. Leaders of the new Republican

Party recognized Harrison's political potential. His great-grandfather, also Benjamin Harrison, had signed the Declaration of Independence. His grandfather, General William Henry Harrison, had been elected president in 1840. After holding a succession of minor political positions between 1857 and 1862, Benjamin Harrison organized the Seventieth Indiana Regiment and commanded it as a colonel in the Civil War, winning promotion to brigadier general in 1865.

Resuming his legal practice after the war, Harrison became leader of the Republican Party in Indiana. Elected to the Senate in 1881, he quickly emerged as a possible presidential candidate. Harrison failed to win a second Senate term in 1887, but James G. Blaine, the most prominent Republican of the era, endorsed him for president in 1888. Harrison won the nomination and then the election, garnering 233 electoral votes to 168 for the incumbent Democrat, Grover Cleveland.

A contemporary said that Harrison "in his contempt for flattery seldom indulged in praise." Harrison has been rated an average president at best, based on perceived failures in domestic policy. He chose not to intervene when Congress passed two controversial laws in 1890, the McKinley Tariff, with record high rates, and the Sherman Silver Purchase Act, which undermined confidence in the gold standard. Exploiting the unpopular McKinley Tariff, the Democrats won control of the House of Representatives in a landslide in 1890.

Harrison, working closely with Blaine as secretary of state, pursued a more activist foreign policy. He agreed to participate in the nation's first protectorate, with Great Britain and Germany, over the Samoan Islands in the Pacific, and in 1889 he welcomed to Washington, D.C., the representatives of the nations of the Western hemisphere for the first Pan American Conference.

After losing to Cleveland in a rematch in 1892, having endured the death of his wife during the election campaign, Harrison returned to Indianapolis. He married the much younger Mary Lord Dimmick, the widowed niece of his first wife, in 1896. They had a daughter in 1897. He died in Indianapolis, a leader of the generation of Republican Party founders who fought in the Civil War and led the nation through the often chaotic years of the Gilded Age.

[*See also* **Blaine, James G.; Cleveland, Grover; Conservatism; Democratic Party; Federal Government, Executive Branch: Presidency, The; Free Silver Movement; Monetary Policy; Republican Party;** *and* **Tariffs.**]

BIBLIOGRAPHY

Sievers, Harry J. *Benjamin Harrison,* 3 vols. Chicago: H. Regnery Co., 1952–1968.

Socolofsky, Homer, and Allan Spetter. *The Presidency of Benjamin Harrison.* Lawrence: University Press of Kansas, 1987.

Allan Burton Spetter

HARRISON, WILLIAM HENRY

(1773–1841), ninth president of the United States. Born into Virginia's Tidewater elite, William Henry Harrison attended Hampden-Sidney College and in 1795 married Anna Symmes. Their ten sons and daughters included John Scott Harrison, father of President Benjamin Harrison. William Henry Harrison studied medicine briefly and then served in the Northwest Territory as a soldier, territorial secretary, congressional delegate, and territorial governor of Indiana (1800–1812). Despite his efforts to deal fairly with the Indians, friction over land cessions united area tribes under the Shawnee warrior Tecumseh, who allied with the British during the War of 1812. At the Battle of the Thames (5 October 1813), Harrison's Army of the Northwest killed Tecumseh, smashed his confederacy, and prompted the British to vacate the Northwest.

After retiring to his North Bend estate near Vincennes, Ohio, Harrison served briefly in local offices and in both houses of Congress. In 1836, as part of an ill-conceived strategy to deny Martin Van Buren an electoral majority, he sought the presidency as the favorite son of the Whig and Anti-Masonic parties in the West, winning seventy-three electoral votes. Harrison shrewdly kept his organization intact and in 1840 bested Henry Clay for the Whig nomination. That year the Whigs elevated the politics of popular amusement to unrivaled levels, eschewing a platform and avoiding positions on substantive issues to promote Harrison, the Virginia aristocrat, as a humble farmer partial to log cabins and hard cider. The "Tippecanoe and Tyler too" campaign (an allusion to Harrison's running mate, John Tyler) featured massive parades, rallies two and three days long, an extraordinary array of ephemera, including cologne, bitters, and whiskey in log-cabin bottles, and huge buckskin balls rolled hundreds of miles. Harrison defeated Van Buren, but succumbed to pneumonia a month after his inauguration.

[*See also* **Anti-Masonic Party; Clay, Henry; Federal Government, Executive Branch: Presidency, The; Northwest Ordinance; Political Parties; Tyler, John; Van Buren, Martin;** *and* **Whig Party.**]

BIBLIOGRAPHY

Goebel, Dorothy Burne. *William Henry Harrison, a Political Biography*. Indianapolis: Historical Bureau of the Indiana Library and Historical Department, 1926.

Gunderson, Robert Gray. *The Log-Cabin Campaign*. Lexington: University of Kentucky Press, 1957.

Roger A. Fischer

HARTFORD CONVENTION

The Hartford Convention (1814–1815) was a conference of twenty-six New England Federalists who met behind closed doors in the Connecticut state capital from December 1814 to January 1815 to channel opposition to the War of 1812. Rejecting extremist Federalist demands for resistance, nullification, and disunion, the convention pursued a moderate course.

The final report of the Hartford Convention echoed long-standing grievances of New England Federalists against ex-President Thomas Jefferson, incumbent James Madison, and the Republican congressional majority. Conceding their party's permanent minority status, the Hartford Federalists recommended constitutional amendments that would give a congressional minority a qualified veto over unwanted legislation and would check the Jeffersonian Republican party's rising ascendancy. Under the proposed changes, a two-thirds congressional majority would be required to approve all future embargoes, war declarations, and admission of new states; presidents would be limited to a single term; the three-fifths constitutional compromise that gave southern slave states additional congressman and electoral votes would be repealed; and commercial embargoes would be limited to 60 days. The convention also demanded that Congress allow the state governments to use federal taxes collected within their own boundaries for their own defense and recommended that states "interpose" their authority if a militia conscription proposal took effect.

Within New England, the Hartford Convention probably helped to quiet extremism.

Elsewhere it had no direct effect other than to discredit the Federalist Party as obstructionist. Fortuitously, news of the Treaty of Ghent, which officially ended the war, and of Andrew Jackson's victory at New Orleans, arrived simultaneously in Washington with the Hartford delegation, and the proposed amendments died.

Historian Henry Adams once implied that the Hartford Convention's real purpose was to promote New England's secession. In reality, the principal leaders were moderate Federalists whose purposes were to protest the war, advance constitutional proposals, protect the New England coast, and preempt radical acts by extremist Federalists.

[*See also* **Constitution; Embargo Acts; Federalism; Federalist Party; Jefferson, Thomas;** *and* **Madison, James.**]

BIBLIOGRAPHY

Banner, James M., Jr. *To the Hartford Convention: The Federalists and the Origins of Party Politics in Massachusetts, 1789–1815*. New York: Alfred A. Knopf, 1970.

Hickey, Donald R. *The War of 1812: A Forgotten Conflict*. Urbana: University of Illinois Press, 1989.

Roger H. Brown

HAYES, RUTHERFORD B.

(1822–1893), nineteenth president of the United States. Born in Delaware, Ohio, Hayes graduated from Kenyon College and Harvard Law School and became a successful attorney in Cincinnati, Ohio. Strongly antislavery and pro-Union, he led a company of volunteers in the Civil War, rising to the rank of major general. Severely wounded at the Battle of South Mountain in 1862, he recovered to fight in the 1864 Shenandoah campaign. After the war, he entered politics, serving a term in Congress (1865–1867) and three terms (1868–1872, 1876–1877) as governor of Ohio. Hayes won the 1876 Republican presidential nomination when the front-runner, Senator James G. Blaine of Maine, became enmeshed in a financial scandal. In the general election, the Democratic candidate, Samuel Tilden of New York, received 250,000 more popular votes than Hayes and appeared to win the electoral tally as well, but the Republican managers contested the result, challenging the returns in three southern states and Oregon. The ensuing controversy threatened to revive sectional conflict until a special electoral commission appointed by Congress awarded the presidency to Hayes by a single electoral vote. The bargaining that produced this outcome, the so-called Compromise of 1877, which involved Republican support for southern railroads and the withdrawal of federal troops from the South, marked the end of Reconstruction, opening the door to the restoration of white rule in the region and the suppression of freedpeople's rights.

As president, Hayes's unruffled, sometimes deceptively optimistic personality helped to calm national politics and to shift attention from the "southern question." Although Hayes did what he could to support the Republican Party in the South, he also focused on new issues, especially civil service reform, which he saw as essential to modernizing the federal government. He challenged Republican and Democratic leaders alike to implement his motto: "He serves his party best who serves his country best." Hayes asserted executive power through his appointments and in general upheld the authority of the presidency. Not personally popular even within his own party, he gained respect as his administration proceeded. His wife Lucy promoted the cause of temperance, whereas the Hayes family epitomized the Victorian ideal of piety and domesticity. Believing in a single presidential term, Hayes did not seek reelection in 1880. As an ex-president, he focused on higher education, philanthropy, and educational opportunities for African Americans. Although his presidency had few dramatic accomplishments, Hayes did maintain the dignity of the office and raise new political and social issues.

[*See also* **Antislavery Movement; Blaine, James G.; Civil Service Reform; Compromise of 1877; Education Policy: Higher Education;** *and* **Prohibition.**]

BIBLIOGRAPHY

Hoogenboom, Ari. *The Presidency of Rutherford B. Hayes.* Lawrence: University Press of Kansas, 1988.

Hoogenboom, Ari. *Rutherford B. Hayes: Warrior and President.* Lawrence: University Press of Kansas, 1995.

H. Wayne Morgan

HEALTH INSURANCE

The history of health insurance in America is largely a twentieth-century story. Well beyond 1900, paying for medical care, with few exceptions, remained a private activity between patients and their physicians and hospitals. Widespread interest in sickness insurance—as it was originally called—did not develop in the United States until the 1910s, and then attention focused on compulsory, not voluntary, insurance. Inspired by the rapid spread of government-sponsored sickness-insurance plans in Europe, the progressive American Association for Labor Legislation in 1912 set up a committee to prepare a model bill for introduction in state legislatures (on the assumption that the U.S. Constitution prohibited a federal plan). The model bill required the enrollment of most manual laborers earning $100 a month or less and provided for both income protection and medical care. Although many physicians greeted this plan enthusiastically, sentiment turned against the measure during World War I, and by 1920, when the American Medical Association (AMA) formally declared its opposition, the campaign for compulsory health insurance—or socialized medicine, as it was sometimes called—was dead.

The Great Depression, beginning in 1929, again brought health insurance to the fore. As hospital receipts and physician income plummeted, interest in voluntary health insurance grew. In December 1929, the Baylor University Hospital in Dallas, Texas, announced a plan to sell hospitalization policies to the city's school teachers for 50 cents a month. Other hospitals around the country adopted similar plans, and within a few years groups of hospitals were banding together to offer what came to be called Blue Cross insurance. The AMA, which urged Americans "to save for sickness" rather than purchase insurance, initially opposed this development "as being economically unsound, unethical and inimical to the public interests."

In 1937, however, in the face of a renewed push for compulsory health insurance, the AMA finally approved group hospitalization plans—as long as they left the payment of physicians out of the scheme. By this time the AMA was working on a physician-controlled plan to provide medical (as opposed to hospital) insurance. The resulting medical-society plans, which started in the Pacific Northwest, took the name Blue Shield. By 1952 over half of all Americans owned some health insurance, and although insurance benefits paid only 15 percent of private expenditures for health care, prepayment plans were being hailed by a presidential commission as "the medical success story of the past fifteen years."

With voluntary plans failing to protect so many Americans, the perennial debate over compulsory health insurance flared again. Pro-insurance reformers had been bitterly disappointed when President Franklin Delano Roosevelt failed to include health insurance in the 1935 Social Security Act. To remedy this omission, the Social Security Board in 1943 drafted a bill to provide health insurance to all persons paying Social Security taxes, as well as to their families. Despite the strong backing of President Harry S. Truman, neither this nor subsequent versions were enacted by Congress. The election of a Republican administration in 1952 temporarily ended the debate over compulsory health insurance.

The 1960 election of John F. Kennedy, a Democrat, revived discussion of the government's responsibility to provide adequate health care for its citizens. Despite strong opposition from organized medicine, Kennedy's successor, Lyndon B. Johnson, persuaded Congress in 1965 to include health insurance as a Social Security benefit (Medicare) and to provide for the indigent through grants to the states (Medicaid). Ironically, after years of warning that government health insurance would ruin the medical profession financially, physicians found that Medicare and Medicaid—by bringing in more patients, raising fees, and facilitating bill collecting—greatly increased their income.

The last third of the twentieth century witnessed numerous attempts to solve the twin problems of access to health care and its ever-increasing cost. In the private sector the most notable development was the rapid growth of health maintenance organizations (HMOs) after 1973, when Congress passed the bipartisan HMO Act. By 1990, the California-based Kaiser Permanente, which had pioneered in developing prepaid group-practice arrangements, had enrolled more than 6.5 million members. Proposals offered by different advocacy groups ranged from a national health service, on the left, in which medical workers would become salaried employees, to income-tax credits for the purchase of commercial health insurance, on the right. None of these efforts succeeded, including President Bill Clinton's ill-fated health security plan in 1993–1994, which would have covered all Americans through large health-insurance purchasing cooperatives, and the establishment in 1997 of Medicare Part C, also known as Medicare Advantage, as part of the Balanced Budget Act of 1997.

Under Medicare Advantage, beneficiaries had the option to receive their Medicare benefits through private insurance plans in the hope that such private plans would prove less expensive than traditional Medicare, although to date Medicare Advantage has been somewhat more expensive. To reduce Medicare spending further, the Balanced Budget Act enacted Medicare cuts and a reduction in hospital inpatient and outpatient payments. Congress restored some of those reductions through new legislation in 1999 and 2000. Instead of achieving some form of universal coverage, the United States continued its piecemeal response to health care coverage, with considerable experimentation occurring at the state level. By the end of the century, nearly 84 percent of Americans enjoyed health insurance coverage, but an estimated 44 million remained uninsured, some by choice (over 8 percent of the uninsured earned more than $75,000 annually), but most by necessity.

In 2006, President George W. Bush signed into law a new prescription drug benefit, Medicare Part D. To receive this benefit, the recipient must enroll in a separate Prescription Drug Plan or Medicare Advantage plan with prescription drug coverage. These plans are approved by Medicare but administered by private health insurance companies. Although critics lamented the high cost of the new prescription drug benefit, the Chief Actuary testified in 2008 the projected ten-year cost of the new benefit was 37 percent lower than estimated in 2003. Expansion of the Medicare program, however, did nothing to restrain the growth of health care costs in the United States.

In another attempt to restrain the growth of health care costs, President Barack Obama in 2010 signed into law the Patient Protection and Affordable Care Act. The act included numerous provisions to take effect separately from 2010 to 2018. Overall, the Act was estimated to reduce the number of uninsured persons in the United States by about 32 million people, a reduction financed by a variety of new taxes and fees, including a tax on Cadillac insurance plans, which provide significant benefits negotiated by unions for their workers in certain industries. To achieve health care cost reductions, the act contains a variety of pilot programs that include nearly every cost containment idea for health care advocated by experts except malpractice reform. Although the Congressional Budget Office estimated the act would reduce the federal budget by about $143 billion over 10 years and by about $1.2 trillion over the second decade, Republicans disputed those figures, arguing that the act would increase the deficit by anywhere from $562 billion to over $700 billion over the first decade of its existence. The attorneys general of several states filed suit, arguing the act was an unconstitutional violation of state sovereignty. Although legal experts disagree over the merits of such suits, it is possible that the Supreme Court may hand down a ruling on the constitutional merits of the act as early as 2012. No matter the outcome of such a ruling, health insurance appears likely to be a major and continuing concern in the twenty-first century as it had been in the twentieth century.

[*See also* **Bush, George W.; Clinton, William J.; Great Society; Johnson, Lyndon B.; Kennedy, John F.; Medicare and Medicaid; New Deal; Obama, Barack; Progressive Era; Public Health: An Overview; Public Health: Surgeon General; Public Health Service, U.S.; Social Security; Social Security Policy;** ***and*** **Truman, Harry S.**]

BIBLIOGRAPHY

Cunningham, Robert, III, and Robert M. Cunningham Jr. *The Blues: A History of the Blue Cross and Blue Shield System.* DeKalb: Northern Illinois University Press, 1997.

Hirshfield, Daniel S. *The Lost Reform: The Campaign for Compulsory Health Insurance in the United States from 1932 to 1943.* Cambridge, Mass.: Harvard University Press, 1970.

Numbers, Ronald L. *Almost Persuaded: American Physicians and Compulsory Health Insurance, 1912–1920.* Baltimore: Johns Hopkins University Press, 1978.

Numbers, Ronald L., ed. *Compulsory Health Insurance: The Continuing American Debate.* Westport, Conn.: Greenwood Press, 1982.

Poen, Monte M. *Harry S. Truman versus the Medical Lobby: The Genesis of Medicare.* Columbia: University of Missouri Press, 1979.

Starr, Paul. *The Social Transformation of American Medicine.* New York: Basic Books, 1982.

Ronald L. Numbers and Stephen E. Randoll

HEARST, WILLIAM RANDOLPH

(1863–1951), newspaper publisher and son of mining millionaire and California Democratic senator George Hearst. Privately educated, William Randolph Hearst attended Harvard for several years. Having worked briefly on Joseph Pulitzer's *New York World*, he used it as a model to remake his father's *San Francisco Examiner*. He made the paper successful by means of sensationalism, crusades against the Southern Pacific Railroad, and luring the best talent.

When his father died, Hearst's mother, Phoebe Apperson Hearst, gave him $7.5 million to buy the *New York Journal* in 1894. Raiding Pulitzer's staff, he launched a circulation war with the *World*, using crude sensationalism and crusades against "the money power." Accuracy was slighted in this "yellow journalism" and in the *Journal*'s exploitation of the Cuban revolution and the Spanish–American War.

An egomaniac burning with political ambition, Hearst served two terms in Congress (1903–1907), received 263 Convention votes for the Democratic presidential nomination in 1904, lost a third-party race for mayor of New York in 1905, and lost again as the Democratic candidate for governor of New York in 1906. After this he exercised his influence indirectly through his newspapers. By the 1920s he controlled a publishing empire of over twenty newspapers, several magazines, the International News Service, and the King Features Syndicate. But he spent more than he earned, collecting art and antiques; promoting the film career of his mistress Marion Davies; and building a palatial mansion, San Simeon, in California.

Hearst helped Franklin Delano Roosevelt secure the 1932 presidential nomination, but his early support of the New Deal ended in 1935 with attacks on business regulation, new taxes, and Roosevelt's foreign policy.

The Depression battered Hearst's fortune. By 1937 he was forced to sell some of his newspapers and art and antiques and to relinquish financial control of his publications. His papers prospered during World War II, and he recovered some of his control in 1945. At his death in 1951, his remaining properties passed to his five sons. His biographer W. A. Swanberg concludes that Hearst "was essentially a showman and propagandist, not a newsman." Orson Welles's classic 1941 film *Citizen Kane* was based on Hearst's career.

[*See also* **New Deal;** *and* **Roosevelt, Franklin Delano.**]

BIBLIOGRAPHY

Nasaw, David. *The Chief: The Life of William Randolph Hearst*. Boston: Houghton Mifflin, 2000.

Swanberg, W. A. *Citizen Hearst*. New York: Scribner & Sons, 1961.

James L. Crouthamel

HEPBURN ACT

The 1906 Hepburn Act, along with the Elkins Act of 1903 and the Mann–Elkins Act of 1910, strengthened federal authority to regulate the nation's railroads under the 1887 Interstate Commerce Act. Named for Republican congressman William Hepburn of Iowa, the law empowered the Interstate Commerce Commission (ICC) to set maximum railroad rates. Democratic congressmen and Progressive Republicans like Theodore Roosevelt played key roles in crafting the Hepburn Act. The passage signaled Congress's commitment to a bureaucratic form of railroad regulation that aimed to limit economic discrimination against rural and low-volume customers without undermining corporate power.

The Hepburn Act originated from the failures of the Interstate Commerce Act of 1887, which required that railroad rates be "reasonable and just" and prohibited rate discrimination. Congress established the ICC to monitor railroad practices and enforce the law. But the ICC's powers were substantially weakened by the Supreme Court. In 1897 the Court denied the ICC authority to set reasonable rates in place of those it had deemed exorbitant. Without additional legislation, the ICC had little influence over rates.

Congressional Democrats, federal bureaucrats, and President Roosevelt called for rate regulation. By 1900, railroad owners and managers had effectively created several giant, nationwide railroad combinations. With little competition, rates rose, and so too did public support for regulation. The Democratic Party made railroad regulation a key part of its platforms in 1896, 1900, and 1904. Members of the ICC urged Congress to grant the commission power to set rates "in view of the rapid disappearance of railway competition and maintenance of rates established by combination" (Sanders, 1999, p. 198). President Roosevelt made railroad regulation part of his 1904 campaign pledge to give Americans a "square deal."

Roosevelt pursued a middle-of-the-road solution that aimed to mollify antirailroad Congressional Democrats without alienating conservative Republicans. He supported Hepburn's bill, which granted the ICC power to establish maximum rates, oversee railroad bookkeeping practices, and expanded its jurisdiction to private cars. The bill passed the House. In the Senate, Democrats began a campaign to grant even greater powers to the ICC. Benjamin Tillman of South Carolina and Joseph Bailey of Texas backed an amendment to limit appellate courts' power to review the ICC's rulings. Conservative Republicans, supported by Roosevelt, defeated the amendment. The Senate nonetheless strengthened the Hepburn Act by adding provisions that included expanding ICC jurisdiction over oil pipelines and ancillary railroad facilities, eliminating a requirement that railroad rates be "fairly remunerative," and augmenting ICC power to solicit information from the railroads.

The Hepburn Act passed with the support of Democrats and moderate Republicans. Some conservative Republicans acquiesced to the bill, reasoning that the Supreme Court might strip the ICC of its rate-setting authority. But that did not happen. In 1910, the Court ruled it could not "usurp merely administrative functions [of government] by setting aside a lawful administrative order" (Ripley, 1913, p. 541) Thus, Congress had ensured that an expert commission, not a democratic assembly, would regulate the nation's railroads.

[*See also* **Interstate Commerce Act;** *and* **Roosevelt, Theodore.**]

BIBLIOGRAPHY

Martin, Albro. *Enterprise Denied: Origins of the Decline of American Railroads, 1897–1917*. New York: Columbia University Press, 1971.

Ripley, William. *Railroads: Rates and Regulation*. New York: Longmans, Green, 1913.

Sanders, Elizabeth. *Roots of Reform: Farmers, Workers, and the American State, 1877–1917*. Chicago: University of Chicago Press, 1999.

Joshua Salzmann

HISPANIC AMERICANS

In 2000, Hispanic or Latino Americans—persons of Latin American, Spanish, or Portuguese ancestry—in the United States numbered over 25 million, or about 10 percent of the population. This highly diverse group included recent immigrants and families whose U.S. roots extended back many generations. With more than 50 percent under the age of 25, Latinos were among the nation's youngest population groups, and, with high levels of natural increase, the most rapidly growing minority group. Relatively concentrated geographically, approximately 90 percent of Latinos lived in Arizona, California, Colorado, Florida, Illinois, New Mexico, New York, and Texas. Cities with major Latino concentrations included Los Angeles, Miami, New York, Chicago, and Houston. Most were Roman

Catholic, but many belonged to fundamentalist or charismatic Protestant churches.

Colonial Era to World War II. Hispanic colonists settled Florida, Louisiana, and New Mexico, and two of the oldest communities within the present-day United States—St. Augustine, Florida (1565), and Santa Fe, New Mexico (1610)—have had Latino inhabitants from the beginning. Cities that have had Latino residents for more than 200 years include San Antonio, Texas; New Orleans; and San Diego. Louisiana governor Bernardo de Galvez contributed money, arms, and supplies to the Continental Army during the Revolutionary War, and Captain Jorge Farragut from the Spanish island of Minorca served with distinction in the U.S. Navy in the Revolutionary War and the War of 1812 (and fathered the Civil War naval hero David Farragut). Commemorating New Spain's contributions to American independence, Mexicans contributed 1,000 silver pesos to help construct the first Catholic church in New York City. Spanish-speaking residents of Florida, Louisiana, Mexico's northern territories, and Puerto Rico became U.S. citizens as these regions were absorbed over the course of the nineteenth century. With citizenship came political participation. Joseph Marion Hernandez was elected to Congress from Florida in 1822. Miguel A. Otero served as governor of New Mexico from 1897 to 1906.

As Americans settled these Hispanic regions, they adopted Hispanic words, folkways, legal practices, mining and grazing laws, and agricultural and livestock methods. California retained women's community-property rights, derived from Hispanic law, when it became a state. California gold-rush miners utilized Mexican, Peruvian, and Chilean mining techniques and Mexican laborers experienced in silver and copper mining. Arizona's Bisbee Copper Mines, linchpin of the Arizona–New Mexico mining industry, recruited a Latino labor force. Early western songs and stories often derived from those of Latino vaqueros (literally, "cowmen"). Hispanic architecture, well adapted to the arid Southwest, was highly influential.

One of the more interesting individual Hispanic Americans of an earlier era was California's Doña Arcadia Bandini (1827–1912). Twice widowed and an astute investor, Bandini left an estate conservatively estimated at $8 million. The state's wealthiest woman, she contributed generously to schools, parks, and hospitals.

Latinos have fought in every American war. During the Civil War, New Mexico and Arizona volunteers, including Mexican-American cavalry under Manuel Antonio Chavez and Rafael Chacon, resisted Confederate efforts to separate the western states from the Union. At Gettysburg, Lt. Colonel Federico Fernandez Cavada fought on the Union side, whereas Colonel Santos Benavides fought for the Confederacy. Mexican Americans and other Latinos volunteered for service during the Spanish–American War. During World War I, many Puerto Ricans and Mexican Americans volunteered or were drafted.

In the twentieth century, many Mexicans migrated northward. The restrictive immigration legislation of the 1920s did not apply to Latin America, and many Latino immigrants arrived, becoming agricultural laborers in the Southwest and California or unskilled urban workers, living in the barrios of Los Angeles and other cities. During the Depression of the 1930s these migrants, earlier welcomed as cheap labor, faced hostility and deportation. In the 1930s Latino migrant workers in California's agricultural fields went on strike for higher pay and better working conditions. Many joined the Confederación de Uniones de Campesinos y Obreros Mexicanos (Confederation of Unions of Mexican Workers and Farm Laborers).

Since World War II. As described in Raul Morin's *Among the Valiant* (1963), as many as 400,000 Latinos fought in World War II, often with great distinction. Air Force hero José L. Holguin, a Los Angeles Mexican American, won the Distinguished Flying Cross, the Air Medal, and the Silver Star for his exploits. Despite this record, Latinos became a focus of wartime hostility, most notoriously in the Los Angeles "zoot-suit riots" targeting Mexican-American youths. More than 200,000 Latinos proudly served in the military from 1945 to 2000, including many in Korea and Vietnam and some 25,000 in the Persian Gulf War. Of some 100,000 Hispanics in the armed services in 2000, about 5,000 were women.

The post–World War II era brought continued growth of the Hispanic population through legal and illegal immigration and natural increase. Under the bracero program (1942–1965), Congress permitted the regular annual importation of Mexican farm laborers for seasonal work in the agricultural fields of California, Arizona, and Texas. The 1965 Immigration and Nationality Act set an annual ceiling of 120,000 on immigration from the Western Hemisphere, on a first-come, first-served basis, with special provisions for reuniting families. Later legislation permitted the immigration of Cubans fleeing Fidel Castro's Communist regime in Cuba, thousands of whom settled in Miami.

In many respects, the story of these years is one of achievement—economically, organizationally, politically, educationally, and culturally. In 1992, 85 percent of Latino men and 53 percent of Latina women were employed. Some 1.5 million belonged to labor unions. Latino business ownership surged in the 1990s, particularly in the Southwest, New York, Florida, Illinois, and Puerto Rico. By 2000 these enterprises had some 100,000 employees, and the total sales of the 500 largest Latino-owned businesses reached $20 billion. Many Latino businesspeople belonged to the United Hispanic Chamber of Commerce or some 200 state and local Latino chambers of commerce.

Latinas (Hispanic women) populated all sectors of the labor force in the 1990s. Linda Chavez-Thompson, executive vice president of the AFL-CIO, was one of many Latinas active in labor unions. Like their male counterparts, many Latina workers held unskilled or entry-level jobs. In 1996, Latinas working full-time had median earnings of $17,500. But their ranks also included many managers and professionals. The number of Latinas in managerial positions grew from 110,000 in 1980 to 300,000 in 2000, twice the growth rate for Latino males. The number of Latina professionals in fields ranging from urban planning, personnel relations, and health care to teaching, counseling, and library science consistently exceeded that of male Latinos. In 2000, 10 percent of Latina women over age 25 were college graduates. Changing career and educational patterns among Latinas were among the most significant developments in the Hispanic community in these years.

The growing Latino community in the twentieth century generated numerous civic organizations. The largest, the League of United Latin American Citizens (LULAC), founded in the 1920s, had some 100,000 members in 200 chapters nationwide by 2000. LULAC's program included antidiscrimination and equal-rights campaigns and promotion of education. The American G.I. Forum (1948) addresses Latino veterans' interests, encourages education and patriotism, and offers job-training services. The bipartisan National Association of Latino Elected Officials (1975) provides issue analysis and promotes information exchange, training for public service, and advocacy on matters of importance to Latinos. The Southwest Voter Registration Project, founded in 1974 by Willie Velasquez of San Antonio, with a small staff and a network of volunteers, focuses on increasing the Latino vote and electing Latino candidates nationwide. Other advocacy organizations include the National Council of La Raza, the National Council of Hispanic Women, and the Hispanic Association on Corporate Responsibility.

Twentieth-century Latinos continued to participate in politics and governance. Mexican-born Octaviano A. Larrazolo, governor of New Mexico in 1919–1923, in 1928 became the first Latino in the U.S. Senate when he was elected to complete the term of a deceased incumbent. In 2000, some 5,000 Hispanic Americans, including 1,500 women, held elective office nationwide. Five Latinos have served as cabinet members, 5 as governors, and over 25 as members of Congress. In the 1990s over 100 Hispanic Americans served in state legislatures.

On the education front, Latinos comprised 12 percent of public school students and perhaps 4 percent of the teachers in the 1990s. From 1982 to 1992, Latino college enrollment rose from 520,000 to 950,000. Some 40,000 Hispanic Americans graduated from college annually in the mid-1990s, and over 5,000 were college and university faculty members. The Spanish-born molecular biologist Severo Ochoa shared the 1959 Nobel Prize in Medicine and Physiology for his discovery of RNA. Dr. Alfredo Baños, a theoretical physicist at UCLA, did significant work in nuclear technology.

Latinos' late twentieth-century cultural contributions were too extensive to treat adequately in a brief essay. By 2000 the United States had some 250 Spanish language radio and television stations and over 1,000 Spanish or Spanish–English periodicals. Latinos were major players in the recording industry and were increasingly visible in films and on television. Indeed, Latino participation in films began with such silent-era performers as Myrtle Gonzales and Beatriz Michelena. In the later 1920s and 1930s came Dolores del Rio, Lupe Velez, and Ramon Novarro. Mid-century Hispanic stars included Rita Hayworth, Fernando Lamas, Desi Arnez, Rita Moreno, Anthony Quinn, and Ricardo Montalban. The late twentieth century brought stardom to Charlie Sheen, Emilio Estevez, Raul Julia, Rosie Perez, and many others.

Latinos' cultural visibility increased markedly after the 1960s, as many intellectual and creative activities intended for Latino audiences demonstrated broader appeal. Latino poets, playwrights, novelists, musicians, and dancers won a large following. A Latino ethnic theater movement provided experience for young performers. In music, the traditional Latin styles enjoyed continued popularity. Hispanic dance—folkloric, modern, and classical—attracted enthusiastic audiences. The long-established Hispanic mural tradition remained vital, including work not only in the classical Mexican tradition of public murals but also by iconoclastic individual artists adopting a full range of contemporary styles.

The national pastime for millions of Latinos was baseball. The long roster of Hispanic stars in the major leagues, beginning with the Cuban third-baseman Esteban Bellan in 1871, includes Roberto and Sandy Alomar, Jose Canseco, hitter Juan Gonzalez (Most Valuable Player in 1996), homerun champion Sammy Sosa, and pitcher Pedro Martinez, the 1999 Cy Young Award winner. The most beloved Latino player was the Pittsburg Pirates' great Puerto Rican right fielder Roberto Clemente, killed in a plane crash in 1972 at the age of 38 while on a humanitarian mission to aid Nicaraguan earthquake victims.

The late twentieth-century Hispanic-American experience included not only noteworthy achievement and economic and cultural progress, impressive as these were, but also poverty and social problems. Although many

Latinos continued to work as migrant laborers, great numbers also lived in the nation's inner cities, plagued by unemployment, social disorganization, illicit drugs, gang activity, and out-of-wedlock pregnancy. In the mid-1990s some 30 percent of Hispanics lived below the poverty line and a third of Latino children lived with a single parent, typically the mother. Lack of education, prejudice and discrimination, and a changing economy that required technical training and offered little to unskilled workers all contributed to the problem. Latinos in the United States illegally, perhaps 12 million in the early 1990s, faced special difficulties, working long hours for low wages and lacking health coverage or job benefits. But even at the lower economic ranks, family, community, and church ties remained strong, and Latino organizations and leaders mobilized to alleviate the problems of the poor. Cesar Chavez, founder of the United Farm Workers Union, led organizational campaigns and boycotts to improve the lot of migrant workers from the 1950s to his death in 1993.

Between 2000 and 2010 the Latino numbers increased over 40 percent and the total exceeded 50 million. In 2003, as the nation's Hispanic population reached 39 million—nearly four times the 1970 total—the Census Bureau reported that Hispanics had supplanted African Americans as the nation's largest minority. By 2050, demographers predicted, Hispanics would comprise one-quarter of the U.S. population. Thus, their needs and contributions can only be understated "minority." To be sure, as always, it must be pointed out that Latinos are not homogenous economically, socially, culturally, or ideologically. In terms of income earned and education achieved, a considerable gap occurs between the top 10 percent and the rest of the Latino demographics. Perhaps half of the Latino workforce earns $10.50 an hour to support a family of four. Latinos earn 68 percent that of whites and Latinas 77 percent that of white women. Latinos with decent wages in the past have been concentrated in job sectors hit by the economic slowdown, which occurred between 2005 and 2010: machinery, apparel, construction, furniture, electronic components, metal products, and primary metals. Moreover, approximately 50 percent of Latino workers have no health insurance and over 60 percent have no retirement benefits from their jobs. Comparing Latinos with whites in five areas of social life—economic status, social justice, civic participation, education, and health—Latinos score 72 percent compared with 100 percent for whites.

The number of Latino citizens is growing, but citizenship does not insure societal equality. Even with citizenship, material inequalities persist and, in many cases, Latinos do not and will not attain citizenship. Thus, full incorporation of Latinos remains a paramount goal for institutional and civic participation. Latino civic participation, at least on three levels, has increased: organizational sectorial advocacy, voter participation, and elected and appointed official designation. Although these are positives, questions contextualizing and marking inequality remain. The most salient electoral achievements of 2010 are the significance of the Latino vote for the to-date fragmented and ineffectual Democrats and the Latino Republican victories in the New Mexico governorship and Florida Senate contests. Both of these Latino electoral victories were obtained by decidedly conservative personalities.

A vibrant and diverse group that has been a significant part of American history, the Latino community was clearly poised to play an increasingly important role in the nation's social, economic, political, and cultural life as the twenty-first century unfolded.

[*See also* Agricultural Policy; Immigration Law and Policy: After 1930; Immigration Law and Policy: Before 1930; Louisiana Purchase; Poverty; *and* Texas Annexation.]

BIBLIOGRAPHY

Bean, Frank D., and Marta Tienda. *The Hispanic Population of the United States*. New York: Russell Sage Foundation, 1987.

Bureau of the Census. *Population Projections of the United States, by Age, Sex, Race, and Hispanic Origin: 1995 to 2050*. Washington, D.C.: U.S. Bureau of the Census, 1997.

Cockcroft, James D. *The Hispanic Struggle for Social Justice: The Hispanic Experience in the Americas*. New York: F. Watts, 1994.

Davis, Mike. *Magical Urbanism: Latinos Reinvent the U.S. City*. London; New York: Verso Press, 2000.

de Varona, Frank, ed. *Hispanic Presence in the United States: Historical Beginnings*. Miami, Fla.: National Hispanic Quincentennial Commission, 1993.

Fox, Geoffrey. *Hispanic Nation: Culture, Politics, and the Construction of Identity*. New York: Carol, 1996.

Kanellos, Nicolás. *The Hispanic Almanac: From Columbus to Corporate America*. Canton, Mich.: Visible Ink Press, 1995.

Kanellos, Nick, and Cristelia Perez. *Chronology of Hispanic American History*. New York: Gale Research, 1995.

Pew Hispanic Center. "Between Two Worlds: How Young Latinos Come of Age in America." Washington, D.C.: Pew Hispanic Center, 2009.

Shorris, Earl. *Latinos, a Biography of the People*. New York: W. W. Norton, 1992.

Singley, Catherine. "Fractures in the Foundation: The Latino Workers Experience in an Era of Declining Job Quality." Washington, D.C.: National Council of La Raza, 2009.

Suro, Roberto. *Strangers Among Us: How Latino Immigration Is Transforming America*. New York: Alfred A. Knopf, 1998.

Juan Gómez-Quiñones and Irene Morris Vásquez

HOLDEN v. HARDY

169 U.S. 366 (1898), argued 21 October 1897, decided 28 February 1898 by a vote of 6 to 2; Brown for the Court, Brewer and Peckham in dissent, Field retired. To challenge his conviction for violating a Utah statute that prohibited employment of workers in mines for more than eight hours a day, Albert F. Holden initiated this habeas corpus proceeding against the sheriff, Harvey Hardy. Holden contended that the statute deprived him of freedom to contract with employees and violated three provisions of the Fourteenth Amendment: privileges or immunities, due process, and equal protection. The Supreme Court rejected these arguments, treating them as a single contention.

Justice Henry Billings Brown accepted the importance of freedom of contract. He emphasized, however, that the right was subject to limitation by a state's police power to protect the health, safety, or morals of its citizens. The Fourteenth Amendment, in his view, was not intended to inhibit severely the evolution of the states' exercise of powers to protect their citizens, because law was "to a certain extent a progressive science" (p. 385). Obscured by that sweeping pronouncement was Brown's pivotal conclusion that there was a reasonable basis in fact to support the legislature's judgment about the danger of mining. Despite the opinion's recognition of state power, the real import of the decision lies in the implication that the Court would assess the reasonableness of any regulatory statute. The significance became apparent when the Court subsequently struck down a statute regulating the hours worked by bakers in *Lochner v. New York* (1905). Thus, despite its apparent support for state experimentation, Holden actually foreshadowed a period of active judicial supervision of economic legislation.

[*See also* **Contract, Law of; Due Process: Legal Cases; Due Process: Substantive;** ***and*** **Fourteenth Amendment.**]

Walter F. Pratt, Jr.

HOLMES, OLIVER WENDELL, JR.

(1841–1935), judge, legal scholar, and justice of the U.S. Supreme Court, 1902–1932. Oliver Wendell Holmes Jr. consistently ranks as one of the "great" justices to sit on the Supreme Court. Born in Boston, the son of the physician, poet, and man of letters Oliver Wendell Holmes Sr., Holmes graduated from Harvard College in 1861. He was wounded three times while serving in the Union Army during the Civil War. Graduating from Harvard Law School in 1866, he practiced law in Boston, edited a legal journal, and wrote several scholarly essays in legal history and jurisprudence. His work *The Common Law* (1881) ranks as one of the most important works of nineteenth-century legal scholarship. This work earned Holmes a professorship at Harvard Law School in 1882, but he left after six months to become an associate justice on the Supreme Judicial Court of Massachusetts; he became its chief justice in 1898. President Theodore Roosevelt appointed him to the U.S. Supreme Court in 1901.

In 1905, Holmes wrote one of his best known opinions, his dissent in *Lochner v. New York,* which argued that judges should defer to the wishes of legislators in most cases involving regulations of the economy. By the time of World War I, a group of "progressive" intellectuals had become attracted to the principle of judicial deference enunciated in Holmes's Lochner dissent and to Holmes himself. By the 1930s, judicial deference to legislatures in the economic arena had become orthodoxy, with Holmes lionized as a "progressive" and "liberal" judge. At his ninetieth birthday in 1931, when he was still active on the Court, he was honored in a nationwide radio broadcast. A second source of Holmes's attractiveness as a judge to early twentieth-century commentators was his increasingly protective attitude toward freedom of speech. In a series of decisions extending from the World War I era to his retirement in 1932, Holmes reversed his normal deferential stance toward regulatory legislation and insisted that even "freedom for the thought we hate" be given constitutional protection. Although his free-speech decisions resist being associated with any consistent doctrinal theory, in the main they affirmed the proposition that unfettered speech is indispensable to a democratic society.

Holmes's own views had little in common with the political radicals whose speech he protected or with the legislators who sought to alleviate market inequalities. He remained a nineteenth-century Brahmin, conservative in his social instincts and doubtful that economic tinkering did much good. But his eloquent pronouncements on behalf of free speech and judicial deference in the realm of political economy—propositions that remained jurisprudential orthodoxy from the 1930s through the 1970s—made him an attractive figure to commentators long after his death. So did his arresting prose style, his academic contributions, his philosophical insight, and the memorable length of his career.

[*See also* **Bill of Rights; Civil Liberties; Conservatism; Economic Policy: Regulation; Jurisprudence; Liberalism;** ***Lochner v. New York;*** **Supreme Court, U.S.;** ***and*** **Roosevelt, Theodore.**]

BIBLIOGRAPHY

White, G. Edward *Justice Oliver Wendell Holmes: Law and the Inner Self*. New York: Oxford University Press, 1993.

G. Edward White

HOMELAND SECURITY, DEPARTMENT OF

The creation of the Department of Homeland Security (DHS) was the largest government reorganization of people, agencies, and programs since the National Security Act of 1947. President George W. Bush initially opposed the creation of a new department after the terrorist attacks of 2001, but then the following year announced plans for a new department that included many agencies with little or no responsibility for protecting the nation against terrorism. The department consolidated customs, border, transportation security, and emergency preparation and response functions at the federal government level and issued grants to states and localities.

A cabinet-level department was not the government's first organizational response to the infamous attacks. On 20 September 2001, President Bush proposed the creation of the Office of Homeland Security, which began formal operations on 8 October. The president named Pennsylvania governor Tom Ridge to lead the new office, which would coordinate homeland security activities throughout government in cooperation with a new Homeland Security Council parallel to the National Security Council. Ridge assumed responsibility for setting budget priorities in four areas: emergency preparedness and response, protection against weapons of mass destruction, border and transportation security, and information analysis and infrastructure protection.

The new homeland security structure provoked conflict with Congress. Some members of Congress asked that the new homeland security advisor be subject to Senate confirmation and have statutory authority over budgets, rather than serving as merely a presidential advisor. During the 2001 anthrax attacks, confusion between Ridge and Health and Human Services secretary Tommy Thompson about who spoke on behalf of the federal government gave ammunition to critics. Meanwhile, in November 2001, Congress and the president created the Transportation Security Administration, which absorbed more than 40,000 new federal employees who replaced private security screeners at airports and transportation hubs.

A number of proposals for a new cabinet-level agency with a security mandate circulated among Capitol Hill legislators. Democratic Senator Joseph Lieberman introduced legislation to centralize homeland security functions in a new department, but the president responded coolly between December 2001 and early 2002. Lieberman's proposals gained support, however, and Republican Representative Mac Thornberry led a parallel effort in the House as the public continued to express concern about terrorism.

In March, White House aides gathered in closed meetings to craft a plan for a presidential proposal for a new cabinet-level department that could win support in Congress. Their plan formed the substance behind President Bush's announcement on 7 June that he wanted to create the DHS. Congress agreed, and the Homeland Security Act of 2002 incorporated twenty-two agencies into the DHS. At the Bush Administration's insistence, the act reformed civil service rules, giving the DHS secretary unusual control over hiring practices. The Act's authors explained that the department's emergency security functions required a new civil service system, but the rules reflected a longstanding administration agenda to increase presidential control over agency personnel.

The department's functions were divided into four directorates: Border and Transportation Security (by far the largest), Intelligence and Infrastructure Protection, Science and Technology, and Preparedness, formerly the Federal Emergency Management Agency (FEMA). Congress resisted changes that would weaken committee oversight power. For instance, the House Judiciary Committee transferred immigration law enforcement functions to the DHS, but kept citizenship functions in the justice department and under the committee's jurisdiction. DHS officials spent much of their time reporting to Congress. Secretary Ridge estimated that he had been called to appear before eighty different committees and subcommittees on the Hill. In early 2005, Michael Chertoff, a former U.S. attorney and federal prosecutor with experience prosecuting a convicted member of the September 11 plot, succeeded Ridge as secretary.

In August 2005, Hurricane Katrina struck the Louisiana and Mississippi Gulf Coast. Approximately 1,800 people died in the storm, and it was the costliest natural disaster in U.S. history. After-disaster reports found that the DHS was a bottleneck between FEMA and other parts of the federal government, including the White House. The media narratives blamed FEMA for shortcomings in protecting New Orleans, and FEMA's director, Michael Brown, resigned within weeks of the storm. Most scholars agree that the dominant narratives about the storm overemphasized the role of FEMA and neglected the failures of city and state government, other federal agencies, or even citizens themselves. Nevertheless, the federal government's apparent incapacity in the face of devastation called attention to the divide between the DHS's responsibility for preventing terrorism and its natural disaster functions. Some legislators revived calls to move FEMA out of the DHS and return it to its former status as an independent agency reporting directly to the president.

The department drew criticism also for the lack of objective criteria in its grant allocation process for antiterrorist programs. On 4 January 2006, however, Chertoff announced that the department would allocate homeland security grants according to a "risk-based" formula and not issue "party favors to be distributed as widely as possible." The new formula used secret calculations about terrorism risk and a more transparent list of urban areas deemed at high risk of attack to guide grant allocations. Rural states' power in the Senate ensured that some portion of DHS grants remained equally divided among states, however. Furthermore, rural areas claimed that they were vulnerable since no one knew where terrorists would strike next.

In 2009, President Barack Obama appointed former Arizona governor Janet Napolitano as department secretary. Napolitano took office in a department that made strides toward integration. Nevertheless, the DHS faced questions about whether it should further integrate homeland security functions or be merely a holding company for component agencies, especially as new issues such as immigration and pandemic disease entered the agenda.

[*See also* **Disaster Policy, Federal; National Security Act of 1947; National Security Council;** ***and*** **Terrorist Detention Policy.**]

BIBLIOGRAPHY

Cohen, Dara K., Mariano-Florentino Cuéllar, and Barry R. Weingast. "Crisis Bureaucracy: Homeland Security and the Political Design of Legal Mandates." *Stanford Law Review* 59 (2006): 673–760.

Kettl, Donald F. *System under Stress: Homeland Security and American Politics*. Washington, D.C.: CQ Press, 2004.

Moynihan, Donald P. "Homeland Security and the U.S. Public Management Policy Agenda." *Governance* 18 (2005): 171–196.

Roberts, Patrick S. "FEMA and the Prospects for Reputation-Based Autonomy." *Studies in American Political Development* 20 (Spring 2006): 57–87.

Patrick S. Roberts

HOMESTEAD ACT

The 1862 Homestead Act was an attempt to transform the settlement of the public domain in the West. Passed by Congress in 1862 and put into operation on 1 January 1863, it offered actual settlers free title to 160 acres (a quarter section) after they had established residence and improved the land for five years. The act also sought to bind the West to the North during the Civil War. It altered the historic policy of cash sale of the public domain since the first Land Survey Act of 1785. Potential settlers saw the Homestead Act as a great boon, but much of the available land was in regions of insufficient rainfall such as the midcontinent High Plains. In fact, farmers west of the 98th meridian (which passes through central Kansas, Nebraska, and the Dakotas) needed four to eight times the allotted acres for successful settlement. In the 1870s, of some 1.3 million new farms carved out of the public domain, only around 320,000 were actual homestead entries. In some areas, fewer than a quarter of the original entries actually completed the process and established homesteads. Farm families that did persevere described the initial five years as their "period of starvation." Homesteading was abused by fraudulent surveys and deceptive multiple claims by ranchers, lumbering interests, and other speculators. A series of legislative efforts between 1873 and 1916 to correct some of the problems resolved neither the climate realities nor the fraud. Dryland farming techniques, however, stabilized some High Plains settlement. Between 1863 and 1904, some 720,000 farms, totaling nearly 100 million acres, had been established under the Homestead Act. Homesteading of at least 3 million acres a year continued until the 1930s Depression.

[*See also* **Agricultural Policy; Land Policy, Federal; Northwest Ordinance;** *and* **Republican Party.**]

BIBLIOGRAPHY

Opie, John. *The Law of the Land: 200 Years of American Farmland Policy*. Lincoln: University of Nebraska Press, 1994.

Gates, Paul W. *History of Public Land Law Development*. Washington, D.C.: U.S. Government Printing Office, 1968.

John Opie

HOOVER, HERBERT

(1874–1964), thirty-first president of the United States. Born in West Branch, Iowa, of Quaker parents, Herbert Clark Hoover was orphaned at the age of nine and subsequently reared by relatives in Oregon, where he attended Friends Pacific Academy. After graduating from the newly founded Stanford University in 1895, he entered the employ of mining engineer Louis Janin. Hoover next joined the British firm of Bewick, Moering, initially as a manager in Australia, later as a company representative in China, and after 1901 as a partner. In business for himself after 1908, he specialized in reorganizing and refinancing "sick" mining enterprises. He married Lou Henry, a fellow Stanford graduate in 1899; they had two sons.

During World War I, Hoover achieved world stature as both an engineer and a humanitarian. His role in rescuing stranded Americans and feeding starving Belgians made him the "master of relief." As food administrator in the Woodrow Wilson administration he engaged in "Hooverizing" U.S. consumption habits to conserve scarce commodities and became the best known of America's wartime domestic managers. He remained in the limelight after the war, first as director of American relief abroad, then as a progressive leader of the engineering profession, and after 1921 as an active and highly visible secretary of commerce in the Republican presidential administrations of Warren Harding and Calvin Coolidge. In 1928 a legion of admirers helped him secure the Republican presidential nomination, and in November he easily defeated Democratic opponent Alfred E. Smith.

During his prepresidential government career, Hoover had launched regulatory and welfare agencies heavily reliant on private-sector resources and in the process had worked out a progressive social agenda to be realized through government-encouraged "associational action" rather than through public administration. In 1928 he spoke of a *New Day* to be ushered in by this "cooperative system." As president, Hoover made extensions of this ideology the basis of his reform agenda and his battle against the Great Depression, which set in after the stock market crash of October 1929. Rejecting laissez-faire prescriptions, including those of Treasury Secretary Andrew Mellon, he tried to raise spending levels through government-sponsored cooperative action by business leaders and through federalization of parts of the credit system, creating in 1932 the Reconstruction Finance Corporation, modeled on the federal lending agency of World War I, to extend credit to major economic institutions such as banks and insurance companies. But he rejected allegedly "dangerous" forms of federal investment, financing, relief, and market control. Perversely, his success in raising tariffs in 1930 and other taxes in 1932 worked at cross purposes with his economic recovery aims. Moreover, the Depression's persistence undercut most of the reform agenda he kept trying to implement. The construction of Hoover Dam on the Colorado River, begun in 1931, and passage of the Federal Home Loan Bank System Act in 1932, designed to help hard-pressed homeowners avoid foreclosure, were lasting achievements. But most of Hoover's attempts to promote cooperative, private-sector recovery and relief efforts, including those involving agricultural marketing associations, oil and timber conservation, and social-welfare organizations, eventually failed.

Abroad, Hoover's administration made only limited responses to the Depression's corrosive effects on international order. Disarmament initiatives produced only the ineffectual London Naval Treaty of 1930. Concerns about international debts brought only the one-year Hoover Debt Moratorium of 1931 and a renunciation of forced debt collection in Latin America. Japan's aggression in China produced only a policy of not recognizing Japan's puppet state in Manchuria. Proposals for war-debt cancelation, economic sanctions against aggressors, and the United States' becoming the international lender of last resort were all ruled out. These options were not only politically difficult but also beyond the limits of Hoover's internationalism.

Meanwhile, the deepening Depression was also sparking political realignment and a growing anti-Hoover national mood. The one-time "great engineer" and "great humanitarian" now became a national scapegoat. The floating communities of jobless men in the nation's cities were dubbed Hoovervilles. Making matters worse were such public relations fiascoes as Hoover's opposition to more generous drought relief, his continued support for Prohibition, and his administration's 1932 military action against a "bonus army" of veterans in the nation's capital. Hoover won renomination in 1932, but in the November election he carried only six states. In March 1933, after a four-month interregnum marked by governmental stalemate and collapse of the banking system, his presidency gave way to Franklin Delano Roosevelt's New Deal.

After leaving the White House, Hoover remained active in Republican Party politics and in debates concerning the New Deal. As World War II approached, he backed the noninterventionist cause and tried unsuccessfully to establish food relief programs in German-occupied countries. After the war, he gradually attained elder-statesman status, advising on postwar relief problems, heading commissions on governmental reorganization, and publishing his memoirs and other works. He is buried in West Branch, Iowa, near the Hoover presidential library.

A man of immense energy, a sincere commitment to public service, legendary organizational and administrative skills, and enduring Quaker sensibilities, Hoover served his nation well as a relief director, wartime food czar, commerce department secretary, and promoter of executive reorganization. But he lacked the political skills, charisma, and capacity for economic learning needed to lead a nation caught in the throes of the Great Depression. And although scholars now reject the older label of "do-nothingism" and see his presidency as activist, reformist, intellectually sophisticated, and in some ways anticipatory of the New Deal, most still judge it a failure overall.

[*See also* **Coolidge, Calvin; Federal Government, Executive Branch: Other Departments; Federal Government, Executive Branch: Presidency, The; Harding, Warren G.; New Deal; Prohibition; Reconstruction Finance Corporation; Republican Party; Tariffs; Taxation;** *and* **Wilson, Woodrow.**]

BIBLIOGRAPHY

Barber, William J. *From New Era to New Deal: Herbert Hoover, the Economists, and American Economic Policy, 1921–1933*. Cambridge, UK; New York: Cambridge University Press, 1985.

Burner, David. *Herbert Hoover: A Public Life*. New York: Alfred A. Knopf, 1979.

Fausold, Martin L. *The Presidency of Herbert C. Hoover*. Lawrence: University Press of Kansas, 1985.

Lloyd, Craig. *Aggressive Introvert: A Study of Herbert Hoover and Public Relations Management, 1912–1932*. Columbus: Ohio State University Press, 1972.

Nash, George H. *The Life of Herbert Hoover*, 3 vols. New York: W. W. Norton, 1983, 1988, 1996.

Wilson, Joan Hoff. *Herbert Hoover: Forgotten Progressive*. Boston: Little, Brown, 1975.

Ellis W. Hawley

HOOVER, J. EDGAR

(1895–1972), director, Federal Bureau of Investigation (FBI). Born in Washington, D.C., Hoover earned a law degree from George Washington University night school in 1917 and obtained employment in the Justice Department's alien enemy registration section. His administrative abilities, strategic mind, and diligence quickly won him promotion in 1918 to head the General Intelligence Division, in 1921 to assistant director of the Bureau of Investigation (formally renamed the FBI in 1935), and in 1924 to bureau director, a post he held until his death. A lifelong bachelor, he devoted himself to the FBI.

Inheriting a scandal-ridden operation, Hoover refurbished the bureau's image and turned it into a powerful and respected agency by instituting a series of administrative reforms and then capitalizing on public concerns, first about organized crime during the 1930s and then about spies during World War II and the Cold War. Indeed, Cold War anti-Communism became the catalyst of Hoover's unquestioned power and influence on national politics. Hoover also astutely cultivated presidents, members of Congress, and the media and promoted a public-relations campaign that successfully identified criticism of himself or the FBI with disloyalty. With Hoover's collaboration, the entertainment industry burnished the FBI's image, as in the radio program *The FBI in Peace and War.* The story of Herbert Philbrick, who infiltrated the Communist Party for the FBI, was recounted in a movie, *I Was a Communist for the FBI* (1951); Philbrick's own *I Led Three Lives* (1952); and a 1950s television series. The FBI's *Ten Most Wanted* lists, posted in post offices across the nation, further enhanced Hoover's reputation as a crime fighter.

After the 1930s, FBI investigations were not confined to law enforcement. FBI agents also collected (in some cases, as FBI officials themselves conceded, through "clearly illegal" means such as break-ins, mail opening, telephone wiretaps, and electronic bugs), and Hoover and senior FBI officials covertly disseminated, derogatory personal and political information. Such material went to Senator Joseph McCarthy and the House Un-American Activities Committee, for example, either to influence public opinion or to "harass, disrupt, and discredit" targeted individuals and organizations. The subjects of FBI investigations ranged from Communist Party activists to Eleanor Roosevelt, the actor Rock Hudson, the author Ernest Hemingway, the baseball star Mickey Mantle, the poet Allen Ginsberg, and the rock star John Lennon. Furthermore, Hoover authorized a series of programs that targeted civil rights and radical organizations for the explicit purpose of discrediting and neutralizing them. Hoover particularly sought to discredit Martin Luther King Jr., by circulating information about King's private life obtained through clandestine surveillance devices.

The scope and nature of these abuses first became known in the mid-1970s when Hoover's wall of secrecy immunizing FBI activities was first breached. The resultant disclosures tarnished Hoover's posthumous reputation and led to tighter administrative rules governing FBI operations.

[*See also* **Anti-Communism; Civil Rights; Federal Government, Executive Branch: Department of Justice; Federal Bureau of Investigation; House Un-American Activities Committee; King, Martin Luther, Jr.;** *and* **McCarthy, Joseph.**]

BIBLIOGRAPHY

Gentry, Curt. J. Edgar Hoover: *The Man and the Secrets.* New York: W. W. Norton, 1991.

Theoharis, Athan, and Cox, John Stuart. *The Boss: J. Edgar Hoover and the Great American Inquisition.* Philadelphia: Temple University Press, 1988.

Athan Theoharis

HOPKINS, HARRY

(1890–1946), social worker, New Deal relief administrator, and key advisor to President Franklin Delano Roosevelt. Born in Sioux City, Iowa, Harry Hopkins had a distinguished early career with various New York City social-work agencies. In the Depression year 1931, Roosevelt, then governor of New York, named him deputy director of the state's Temporary Emergency Relief Administration. With Roosevelt's election as president, he brought Hopkins to Washington, D.C., in

1933 to head the Federal Emergency Relief Administration, charged with providing assistance to the unemployed. Believing that most of the needy were not at fault, Hopkins pushed for government-created jobs rather than handouts. A dole keeps a person physically alive, but often destroys self-respect and undermines job skills, Hopkins argued, whereas work sustains spirit and mind, as well as body. This argument produced the short-lived Civil Works Administration (1933–1934) and the Works Progress Administration, which Hopkins supervised from its start in 1935.

From 1936 until Roosevelt's death in 1945, Hopkins was the president's closest confidant. He hoped to succeed Roosevelt as president in 1940, but his poor health and opposition from key Democrats blocked this ambition. Roosevelt sent Hopkins on critical missions to British Prime Minister Winston Churchill and Soviet dictator Josef Stalin in 1941. During World War II, Hopkins served as assistant to the president and became his alter ego.

A central figure during the nation's two largest twentieth-century crises, Hopkins brought to his varied assignments a combination of idealism and practicality summarized by his retort to the claim that a plan would work in the long run: "People don't eat in the long run—they eat every day."

[*See also* **New Deal; Roosevelt, Franklin Delano;** *and* **Works Progress Administration.**]

BIBLIOGRAPHY

McJimsey, George. *Harry Hopkins*. Cambridge, Mass.: Harvard University Press, 1987.

Sherwood, Robert E. *Roosevelt and Hopkins*. New York: Harper, 1948.

Robert S. McElvaine

HOUSE UN-AMERICAN ACTIVITIES COMMITTEE

The House Un-American Activities Committee (HUAC) was created in 1938 by legislators concerned about fascist groups in America and by conservative opponents of President Franklin Delano Roosevelt's New Deal. First chaired by Congressman Martin Dies of Texas, the committee created a sensation by charging that Communists dominated numerous federal agencies, including the Works Progress Administration. The raucous committee hearings drew attention to the prominent role of left-wing radicals in the political life of the 1930s and abetted the Republican Party's resurgence in the 1938 midterm elections.

The HUAC enjoyed its most dramatic hours in 1947 and 1948: the Hollywood hearings that resulted in the jailing of ten screenwriters and directors for contempt and led to a show-business blacklist that would linger for years, as well as the confrontation between the ex-Communist Whittaker Chambers and the former State Department official Alger Hiss that would send Hiss to jail for perjury and propel Representative Richard M. Nixon, a committee member, to national attention.

Much criticized for its bruising treatment of witnesses, its use of hearings as a weapon of repression, and its lack of legislative accomplishments, the committee did contribute to the 1950 Internal Security Act that called for the registration of Communist party members. Subsequent investigations—into atomic scientists, colleges, churches, and labor unions—did not stir much excitement as the loyalty–security issue began to ebb in the 1950s. Despite a foray against anti-Vietnam War protestors in the 1960s and the enduring support of Federal Bureau of Investigation director J. Edgar Hoover, the HUAC was abolished in 1975.

[*See also* **Anti-Communism; Communist Party USA; Hoover J. Edgar; Internal Security Act; New Deal; Nixon, Richard M.; Radicalism; Republican Party;** ***and*** **Works Progress Administration.**]

BIBLIOGRAPHY

Goodman, Walter. *The Committee*. New York: Farrar, Strauss, and Giroux, 1968.

Walter Goodman

HOUSING POLICY, FEDERAL

This entry contains five subentries: An Overview; Fannie Mae; Federal Housing Administration; Home Owners' Loan Corporation; and Public Housing.

AN OVERVIEW

Federal intervention in U.S. housing markets first occurred during World War I. Before then, housing was regulated through local police powers establishing minimum standards for construction and services like plumbing. However, the war led to housing shortages in critical industrial centers. Looking to the example of Britain, reform-minded architects and economists convinced Congress to develop high-quality, well-equipped housing for workers, to be sold off after the wartime emergency. After the war, residual housing shortages in Europe were met with robust new public action. U.S. reformers hoped for the same. Instead, the market returned to normalcy. By 1924 a private-sector housing boom was underway, and most Americans seemed to believe that further government action in housing was unnecessary.

Public Housing. The Great Depression generated new support for state-aided housing. When the Public Works Administration was established in 1933, a Housing Division was created to make loans to nonprofit builders. When sound proposals proved rare (only seven merited funding), leaders announced plans to develop projects directly. When the ability to do so was questioned in the courts, the program was altered to channel funds through local housing authorities. Between 1934 and 1937, when the Housing Division ceased operations, these new local agencies developed 49 complexes.

State-built housing was made permanent with the U.S. (Wagner–Steagall) Housing Act of 1937. The law was contentious. Especially difficult was the question of whom the program should serve: working families otherwise unable to afford spacious new housing or only the very poor. Additional debates centered on whether projects should sustain themselves or receive subsidies; whether housing should occupy low-cost suburban land or urban slum-clearance sites; and, in turn, whether construction should be contingent on the elimination of old substandard housing. Most proponents believed only suburban complexes for working families could be successful. Congress, however, felt that any appropriation should go to those most in need. In part because no operating funds were provided, the result was a system most historians believe was capable only of producing warehouses for the poor, doomed to rapid social and physical deterioration.

Modern Mortgages. The Depression also ushered in a second strand of housing policy: indirect aid for the private, middle-class housing market. Housing was a major component of the economy; policy makers hoped that by reviving it unemployment would fall. In late 1931, President Hoover convened the President's Conference on Home Building and Home Ownership, which brought together hundreds of members of the homebuilding and home-finance fields. Their main recommendation was for long-term, low-interest, self-amortizing mortgages. A first step in this direction came in 1932 with creation of the Federal Home Loan Bank. This body made mortgage money available by advancing funds to lenders at a time when deposits were scarce. Efforts were redoubled under President Roosevelt with the introduction of the Home Owners' Loan Corporation (HOLC) in 1933 and the Federal Housing Administration (FHA) in 1934.

HOLC protected homeowners against foreclosure by refinancing mortgages and extending new low-cost loans for repurchase of homes already lost. Of equal importance, HOLC demonstrated the viability of long-term, self-amortizing mortgages. Although rates of homeownership reached 40 percent by 1920 and 46 percent by 1929, mortgages were small (typically 50 percent of the value), short-term (five to seven years), and required repayment of the principal all at once. To process loans, HOLC established new standards for appraisals by surveying every neighborhood in metropolitan America. Information about the physical and economic characteristics of housing and the social and economic characteristics of residents, including race, were used to assign neighborhoods one of four grades. Although HOLC made loans to homeowners in all four zones, its color-coded maps were later used by private lenders, who often refused to do business in fourth-class "red-lined" districts, which included all areas with African Americans. Redlining of black areas remained a serious problem for decades.

FHA stimulated new construction of low-cost housing for working and middle-class families and encouraged long-term stability by imposing best practices pioneered in the early twentieth century by developers of high-class housing. Agency leaders, drawn mainly from real estate, established design standards for homes and neighborhoods. Conforming projects were insured, or guaranteed, by the FHA. If they defaulted, the FHA took full responsibility. The FHA also qualified homeowners for agency-insured mortgages. Similar to HOLC loans, buyers paid just 20 percent down and the balance (including interest and principle) in equal monthly installments over twenty years. Down payments were later reduced and the loans extended to thirty years.

To further encourage lenders to participate, Congress created the Federal National Mortgage Association (Fannie Mae) in 1938. This agency bought loans from banks, freeing them to use the money again for new customers. The FHA also made funds available for home improvement projects and for construction of apartments, both rented and owned. Although slow to take hold in the 1930s, these FHA programs brought new, modern, privately developed housing within financial reach of ordinary working families for the first time in U.S. history.

Suburbanization. During World War II, several emergency programs were established to stimulate production of housing—especially rental housing—in critical war areas while avoiding the extreme difficulties surrounding World War I. The Office of Price Administration, for example, imposed rent controls in all defense-related areas, including most major cities. These were extended into the early 1950s in many places. Of equal importance, the Servicemen's Readjustment Act of 1944 (GI Bill) offered veterans favorable loans through the Veterans Administration (VA) for houses and owned apartments. Wartime also saw many advancements in construction technology, which were incorporated into postwar policy guidelines.

After the war, federal housing programs helped facilitate a mass migration of the working and middle classes out of older housing stock into new houses and garden apartments, often in suburban areas. The largest new developments, including Levittown on Long Island, Lakewood in L.A. County, and Park Forest outside Chicago, accommodated tens of thousands of people. Between 1945 and 1956, nearly 17 million new homes were built. By 1956 one-third of all dwellings in the United States had been built since 1945. Of these 17 million, more than 4.5 million—including half of all apartments—were financed with federally insured loans. Of equal importance, 11 million houses were financed with "conventional" (non-FHA or VA) mortgages that mimicked FHA terms. The share of homeowners rose from 41 to 51 percent during World War II and then to 59 percent by 1956.

Limited efforts were made in the postwar era to furnish the poor with better housing. Under the New Deal, public housing started slowly; between 1937 and 1941, 130,000 units were completed. Advocates began a fresh campaign for funding in the mid-1940s. It was not until after the election in 1948, however, that Congress renewed the program as part of the National Housing (Taft–Ellender–Wagner) Act of 1949, which promised "a decent home and a suitable living environment for every American family." As in 1937, opposition resulted in many compromises. A strict income ceiling meant that only those who were very vulnerable qualified for leases, and insufficient funds forced housing authorities to build cheaply. Social and physical problems quickly followed. Chronic underfunding also meant that of 810,000 units initially authorized to funding by the mid-1950s, only 320,000 were built by 1962.

End of Public Housing. The 1960s and 1970s saw major changes in housing policy. As the baby boom matured, demand for houses stabilized and there was a shift to apartments, rented and owned. High interest rates and inflation meant that after decades of flat prices, the cost of housing rose rapidly. This era also saw new concerns about the negative impact of suburbanization on city centers, about the geographic concentration of public housing, and about racial discrimination in housing. Federal policy had condoned segregation in housing until the 1950s and early 1960s; only in 1968 did the Fair Housing Act outlaw discrimination in housing altogether.

In response to these trends, policy grew more complex, with smaller-scale programs offering low-interest subsidized loans for "middle-income" apartments, FHA insurance for condominiums, and assistance for master-planned new communities. To further improve opportunities for people of color, Congress also introduced programs specifically designed to bolster low-income homeownership, to disperse low-cost housing through metropolitan areas, and to direct housing investment to neighborhoods and borrowers once shunned by lenders. To help manage these programs, the various federal housing agencies were elevated to full cabinet status with the creation of the Department of Housing and Urban Development (HUD) in 1965. In concert with HUD and President Johnson's Great Society, Congress launched aggressive new goals for low-cost housing production. By the late 1960s and early 1970s, production of state-built and state-subsidized housing reached an all-time high.

After two decades of intense private-sector building the primary housing problem was no longer scarcity but cost. When a deep recession led to a spending freeze in 1973, President Nixon imposed a moratorium on public housing. In 1974 he canceled it permanently. Congress replaced public housing with the Section 8 housing voucher program under which tenants lived in private housing but paid only 25 to 30 percent of their income in rent. The balance was covered by federal funds dispersed through local housing authorities, which took responsibility for inspecting units and enforcing standards in maintenance. Section 8 also helped finance construction of qualifying housing, although by the early 1980s emphasis shifted toward subsidizing rents in existing buildings.

Neoliberalism. Since the 1970s and 1980s housing policy has been dominated by efforts to use the power of the private market to meet public goals. Section 8 vouchers remained the primary mechanism for furnishing well-equipped dwellings for those unable to pay market prices. Vouchers became yet more important as housing authorities began to demolish public units. To cope with deteriorating living conditions, HUD authorized demolitions on an experimental basis in the 1980s. In 1993, Housing Opportunity for People Everywhere (HOPE) VI made this program permanent by offering grants for the redevelopment of "severely distressed" public housing complexes with a mixture of public, moderate-rent, and market-rate homes, rented and owned. Renamed Choice Neighborhoods under President Obama, HOPE VI eliminated much of the nation's public housing, including the entire stock in several cities.

To generate new low-cost housing, the low-income-housing tax credit (LIHTC) was established in 1986. LIHTC made the entire cost of qualifying projects tax deductible. Because deductions were transferable, developers sold the credits for cash, allowing them to build with minimal financing. In its first twenty-five years, more units of low-rent housing were constructed (1.6 million) than had been done cumulatively after a half-century of public housing. A limitation of LITHC was that homes were released from low-cost requirements after fifteen years and could then be rented or sold at market rates.

In the arena of private, market-rate construction, lowering barriers to homeownership remained the primary policy goal. One way Congress did this was by strengthening the secondary mortgage market. In 1968, Fannie Mae was recast as a "government-sponsored enterprise": a private company subject to close federal oversight but permitted to buy any mortgage rather than only those insured by the FHA and VA. To fulfill Fannie Mae's old role, the Government National Mortgage Association (Ginnie Mae) was created. In 1970, a third body, the Federal Home Loan Mortgage Corporation (Freddie Mac) was chartered. It was owned by the 12 regional Home Loan banks until 1989, when Congress privatized it. In the 1970s, 1980s, and 1990s, special emphasis was placed on encouraging low-income homeownership, particularly among black and Latino families, as a way to help them build equity. New fair-housing and community-reinvestment initiatives targeted persistent discrimination in lending and encouraged banks to invest in underserved areas. With the collapse of the for-sale housing market in 2007 lawmakers began to question these goals, but deep support for the American dream of democratic homeownership remained.

[*See also* **Great Society; Housing Policy, Federal: Fannie Mae; Housing Policy, Federal: Federal Housing Administration;** ***and*** **Servicemen's Readjustment Act.**]

BIBLIOGRAPHY

Doan, Mason C. *American Housing Production 1880–2000: A Concise History.* Lanham, Md.: University Press of America, 1997.

Hirsch, Arnold R. *Making the Second Ghetto: Race and Housing in Chicago, 1940–1960.* Chicago: University of Chicago Press, 1998.

Hunt, D. Bradford. *Blueprint for Disaster: The Unraveling of Chicago Public Housing.* Chicago; London: University of Chicago Press, 2009.

Jackson, Kenneth T. *Crabgrass Frontier: The Suburbanization of the United States*. New York: Oxford University Press, 1985.

Schwartz, Alex F. *Housing Policy in the United States*. 2d ed. New York: Routledge, 2010.

Matthew Gordon Lasner

FANNIE MAE

Congress established the Federal National Mortgage Association (commonly known as Fannie Mae) in 1938 as part of New Deal efforts to strengthen the nation's housing market during the Great Depression. The purpose of Fannie Mae is to provide liquidity to the housing market by creating a secondary mortgage market. Fannie Mae purchases mortgages from lenders, who in turn are able to make more loans to homebuyers.

Prior to the 1930s, there were constant credit shortages and regional differences in mortgage rates, with credit often concentrating in large metropolitan areas. By creating a national secondary mortgage market, Fannie Mae allowed banks and other lenders to provide more credit to the mortgage market and lowered the cost of such mortgages.

Fannie Mae was originally a government agency, but in 1954 Congress rechartered it as a mixed private–public corporation. In 1968, Congress split it into two separate organizations: Fannie Mae would be again rechartered, this time as a "government-sponsored enterprise" (GSE). This meant that Fannie Mae, although congressionally chartered, would become a privately owned company with its own board of directors and its shares would be traded on the New York Stock Exchange (NYSE). The other part would become the Government National Mortgage Association (commonly known as Ginnie Mae), which would remain a government-funded agency within the Department of Housing and Urban Development (HUD). Ginnie Mae provides U.S. government guarantees of "mortgage-based securities" that consist of mortgages guaranteed or underwritten by government agencies such as the Federal Housing Administration, Rural Housing Services, or the Department of Veterans Affairs. In 1970, Congress created the Federal Home Loan Mortgage Corporation (commonly known as Freddie Mac). Originally a government-owned entity, Freddie Mac was created to provide competition to Fannie Mae and expand the secondary mortgage market. In 1989, Congress rechartered Freddie Mac into a GSE whose shares would also be publicly traded on the NYSE.

Fannie Mae creates a secondary mortgage market by purchasing mortgages from lenders, freeing those lenders to make even more credit available for homebuyers. After purchasing mortgages, Fannie Mae can either keep them on its books and make money directly from those loans or bundle together the mortgages and sell them to investors. This process is known as securitization.

For years, Fannie Mae enjoyed broad bipartisan support in Washington and was well known for its lobbying efforts and political campaign contributions. Defenders pointed to Fannie Mae's role in increasing homeownership rates by lowering the cost of mortgages. However, the organization saw its first major scandal in the mid-2000s. The Office of Federal Housing Enterprise Oversight (OFHEO), which as part of HUD had oversight over Fannie Mae, accused the organization of widespread accounting errors. Officials of Fannie Mae, including its then-CEO Franklin Raines, were accused of overstating earnings to inflate the bonuses of top executives. The scandal brought into focus the inherent conflicts of GSEs: they were private companies that reaped large profits while benefiting from government-granted privileges. Despite the scandal, congressional attempts to tighten regulatory oversight over Fannie Mae went nowhere.

The economic crisis of 2008–2009 highlighted the role of Fannie Mae in the creation of the housing bubble as well as the subsequent collapse of the housing market. Since the 1990s, Fannie Mae had been part of a broad coalition to extend homeownership, especially to low-income Americans. Critics accused Fannie Mae of inflating the housing bubble, lowering underwriting standards for mortgages, and taking on excessive risk.

For Fannie Mae, one benefit of being a GSE was that investors long believed that Fannie Mae and other GSEs had the implicit backing of the federal government. This allowed Fannie Mae to borrow money at rates lower than those of its private-sector competitors. Legally, there was never any explicit guarantee of Fannie Mae obligations by the federal government. However, in the economic crisis of 2008–2009, the federal government made explicit what investors had long assumed.

The housing market crash and subsequent rise in foreclosures severely affected the finances of Fannie Mae. By 2008, Fannie Mae and Freddie Mac held a combined $5.4 trillion in outstanding obligations. In September 2008, the Bush administration placed both Fannie Mae and Freddie Mac into government conservatorship. The government takeover cost taxpayers roughly $150 billion. In June 2010, Fannie Mae and Freddie Mac were delisted from the NYSE. For all of its troubles, Fannie Mae ironically played an even more important role after the housing market crash. With private lenders cautious about reentering the mortgage market, Fannie Mae and Freddie Mac, together with the Federal Housing Administration, were guaranteeing the vast majority of new mortgages, more than before the economic crisis.

By 2011, Congress was considering various plans to reform or abolish Fannie Mae, although no action had been taken at that time. There remained much uncertainty about the direction of the housing market and there was no clear consensus as to how to address the conflicts and contradictions inherent in a GSE such as Fannie Mae, while still providing support to the mortgage market.

[*See also* **Housing Policy: An Overview;** ***and*** **New Deal.**]

Vincent J. Cannato

FEDERAL HOUSING ADMINISTRATION

Congress created the Federal Housing Administration (FHA) under the National Housing Act of 1934. Its main role is to insure mortgages made by private lenders to homeowners. The agency was created during the Great Depression, a time of great economic crisis affecting both the housing and the banking sectors. Its creators hoped that the FHA would (1) expand homeownership, (2) strengthen banks and other lending institutions, and (3) provide a stimulus for employment in the homebuilding industry.

Prior to the 1930s, most mortgages were for short terms (around five years) and were not fully paid off at the end of the term of the mortgage. During the Depression, it became difficult to refinance mortgages that came due and many homeowners lost their homes to foreclosure. Banks were saddled with bad loans. The real estate market crashed and mortgage lending dried up. The FHA was an attempt to use the federal government to stimulate private markets. The FHA built no homes and provided no loans. Instead, it insured mortgages made by private lenders. In doing so, it helped restore confidence in the mortgage market and stimulate lending.

In doing so, the FHA (along with the Home Owners' Loan Corporation) helped to revolutionize the mortgage market in the United States. Now, homebuyers could access long-term twenty-year mortgages (within a few years that would be extended to thirty years) that would be fully repaid at the end of the loan. These new mortgages also required smaller down payments from homeowners, usually 20 percent or less. The government mortgage guarantee also helped lower interest rates for such loans. In short, FHA mortgage insurance helped reduce the risks of lending, made such lending more predictable, and thereby increased the supply of credit. The FHA also had its intended effect on the construction industry. With more credit available, new housing starts increased from 332,000 in 1937 to 619,000 in 1941.

Only lenders who met strict underwriting criteria set by the agency could make FHA-insured loans. Even more importantly, the FHA set minimum property standards for housing that it would insure. Homebuilders, homebuyers, lenders, and home improvement companies now had clear written guidelines setting out basic standards for housing. Such standards were enforced by on-site inspections and they soon became the industry norm, even for loans not backed by the FHA.

By 1943, the FHA was insuring 80 percent of all new housing units. The Servicemen's Readjustment Act of 1944 (also known as the GI Bill) also provided housing assistance to America's veterans. The effects of the FHA and the GI Bill helped boost homeownership rates from 43 percent in 1940 to 62 percent in 1960. By the 1950s, the private mortgage insurance (PMI) market had grown and FHA-backed mortgages declined. By 1970, roughly 25 percent of mortgages were backed by the FHA.

Despite its successes, the FHA has also encountered much criticism. The first was that the FHA favored single-family, detached homes outside of the city, thereby fueling the postwar suburban boom and causing a decline of urban neighborhoods. The second criticism is that the FHA underwriting principles discouraged lending in neighborhoods populated by African Americans. The FHA made it much easier and cheaper to borrow money for homes in predominantly white suburbs, rather than for homes in densely populated, racially diverse urban neighborhoods. The FHA not only made lending in urban areas more difficult, but also was not shy about tying its decisions to race and ethnicity. Black homeownership rates, although still lagging far behind those of whites, still increased steadily in the postwar years from 23 percent in 1940 to 38 percent in 1960.

With the creation of the Department of Housing and Urban Development (HUD) in 1965, the FHA came under the authority of the new cabinet department. The FHA began to direct its efforts to help expand homeownership to low-income Americans and racial minorities. In the wake of the urban riots of the 1960s, the FHA extended heavily subsidized FHA-insured mortgages with a nominal down payment to low-income urban residents. The program was poorly administered and fell prey to corrupt appraisers. Speculators and real estate agents engaged in "blockbusting" of white neighborhoods. Foreclosures under this program were high and many urban neighborhoods suffered. Although that specific program was discontinued, the question remained as to how to increase lending in urban neighborhoods, especially those that were largely poor and minority.

After the 1960s, however, the FHA began to play a less important part in the overall housing market. By 1993, FHA-backed mortgages had fallen to around 8 percent of the total market. But in 2008, as credit markets began to tighten, FHA stepped up and again began insuring an increasing number of mortgages. Oftentimes, the down payment on these loans was only 3.5 percent. In the ensuing economic crisis, which hit the housing market hard, defaults on FHA-backed mortgages increased, putting great stress on FHA finances. Although the FHA tightened its loan standards somewhat, it did not want to exacerbate an already weak real estate market by tightening credit too much. By 2011, the housing market had yet to fully recover and many questions remained about government housing policy.

[*See also* **Housing Policy, Federal: An Overview; Housing Policy, Federal: Home Owners' Loan Corporation; Housing Policy, Federal: Public Housing;** ***and*** **Servicemen's Readjustment Act.**]

BIBLIOGRAPHY

Jackson, Kenneth T. *Crabgrass Frontier: The Suburbanization of the United States*. New York: Oxford University Press, 1985.

Vincent J. Cannato

HOME OWNERS' LOAN CORPORATION

The Home Owners' Loan Corporation (HOLC) was created in 1933 as part of President Franklin D. Roosevelt's New Deal. During the Great Depression, the nation was in the throes of both a banking and a housing crisis. The HOLC was formed to protect homeowners from foreclosure and to protect banks that held mortgages on those homes. The parent organization for the HOLC was the Federal Home Loan Bank Board, created in 1932.

HOLC loans were only available for mortgages that were in default or held by troubled financial institutions. Only nonfarm, owner-occupied structures consisting of no more than four units and worth less than $20,000 were eligible. The HOLC loan could be no more than 80 percent of the appraised value of the property. Between 1933 and 1935, HOLC received over 1.8 million applications for aid. Not everyone who applied received a loan. In the end, HOLC provided over 1 million loans totaling $3.1 million. HOLC loans covered 10 percent of all nonfarm, owner-occupied homes and 20 percent of all mortgaged homes. The HOLC also provided loans to home owners to cover property taxes and home insurance.

Despite the mortgage assistance—and lenient terms—provided by the HOLC, around 20 percent of participating home owners still lost their homes. That meant that HOLC acquired nearly 200,000 homes during its lifetime. Although the HOLC stopped accepting new applications in 1935, it remained in operation until 1951, as it serviced borrowers and worked to manage and eventually sell its inventory of foreclosed homes. According to one estimate, HOLC closed its books in 1951 with a small profit.

The HOLC not only made it possible for many people to keep their homes during the Depression, but also changed the way in which homes would be purchased in the future. The HOLC, along with the Federal Housing Administration (FHA), helped usher in the use of long-term, self-amortizing mortgages, which would soon become standard practice among private lenders as well. Prior to the 1930s, home mortgages were generally for shorter periods of time (around five years) and the principal was often not paid off at the end of loan period. These new mortgages helped usher in the postwar housing boom.

Another important aspect of the work of the HOLC was standardizing real estate appraisals. Not only was it important to analyze the credit-worthiness of borrowers, but also lenders needed better tools for calculating the future value of the properties they might finance. Therefore, HOLC appraisers used a uniform set of standards that divided cities into distinct neighborhoods. These standards looked at income, housing age and quality, property values, and demographic factors such as the race and ethnicity of the population. The HOLC provided intensive training for appraisers in its methods.

These appraisals divided urban neighborhoods into four different "grades" rated A, B, C, and D, with corresponding color codes of green, blue, yellow, and red, respectively. Neighborhoods given an "A" rating were deemed "best," whereas "D"-rated neighborhoods were considered "hazardous." These appraisals were recorded onto color-coded "residential security maps." Neighborhoods receiving higher grades tended to be those strictly residential areas farther from the central city and populated by middle-class native-born whites. Neighborhoods receiving lower grades tended to be closer to the central city, more densely populated, containing mostly older housing stock, and populated by poorer residents, especially recent immigrants and their children and racial minorities.

Scholars have argued that these appraisal maps began to institutionalize a process known as "redlining," which made it difficult for residents of low-income, inner-city neighborhoods to receive loans from banks. These scholars argue that such policies hardened racial segregation and helped spur the decline of inner-city neighborhoods in favor of suburban development. They also argue that the HOLC maps had a great impact on the FHA in setting its own housing policies.

However, more recent scholarship has cast some doubt on these theories. The lending patterns of the HOLC show few discriminatory patterns; it provided loans to home owners at all appraisal grades. It is also not entirely clear that the FHA subsequently used the HOLC maps. The HOLC maps and the premises of the appraisals instead seem to have mirrored already existing ideas and prejudices regarding urban lending. Although there is no doubt that banks were much less likely to provide loans to poor, inner-city neighborhoods in the postwar years, the case against government programs such as the HOLC is overstated.

[*See also* **Housing Policy, Federal: An Overview; Housing Policy, Federal: Public Housing; New Deal;** *and* **Roosevelt, Franklin Delano.**]

BIBLIOGRAPHY

Jackson, Kenneth T. *Crabgrass Frontier: The Suburbanization of the United States.* New York: Oxford University Press, 1985.

Harriss, C. Lowell. *History and Policies of the Home Owners' Loan Corporation.* New York: National Bureau of Economic Research, 1951.

Vincent J. Cannato

PUBLIC HOUSING

Before the 1930s millions of poor urban Americans lived in tenements that lacked modern services such as central heat, private bathrooms, and hot water. Housing regulations passed in the Progressive Era had improved new low-cost construction, but reformers lacked sufficient power to challenge slum landlords. A few model tenements, built to high standards by philanthropists and limited-dividend housing corporations, failed to attract many investors.

The early twentieth century produced more dramatic housing reform programs in Europe. These large-scale, government-supported projects—incorporating the latest in modern design, open space, and amenities—impressed American visitors. Reformers such as Senator Robert F. Wagner of New York held up European housing as a model in the 1930s despite its obvious leftist pedigree. He and other advocates believed low-cost housing, like water or public education, could become a standard and uncontroversial municipal service.

The collapse of the private sector both economically and politically during the Great Depression opened the door to public intervention in the housing market. Most housing advocates, however, carefully framed the public housing initiative as equal parts employment and housing program.

The Housing Division of the Public Works Administration (established 1933) pioneered and closely supervised a small number of high-quality projects for working-class Americans. The Housing Act of 1937, championed by Senator Wagner, decentralized primary authority to local housing agencies to boost scale and efficiency. The new law also set tighter income limits, reduced unit costs, and mandated slum clearance. These mandates, the result of both good intentions and political compromise, had a number of long-term consequences: they reduced future rents, concentrated the poor in public housing, favored scale over beauty, and required slum clearance.

The government built temporary defense housing during the war, but public housing remained stalled postwar by conservative congressmen. The Housing Act of 1949 only passed as part of business-friendly plans to reshape American downtowns in what became known as urban renewal. Subsequent legislation in the 1950s and 1960s eventually created 1.3 million units nationally. Federal guidelines in the postwar era maintained the low income levels, low unit cost limits, and slum clearance requirements. Modernist architects eagerly pioneered elevator "tower in the park" superblocks to maximize air, open space, and a community ideal.

By the 1950s even public housing advocates disliked the institutional appearance and identified growing social issues. Cold War concerns about competition with private industry, for instance, isolated projects by restricting stores and purging higher-income tenants. White resistance and relocation for private-sector redevelopment in many cities created an alienating "second ghetto" adjacent to or inside existing minority ghettos. Efforts to disperse public housing, as well as economic and racial integration efforts within projects, also faltered.

Unsafe housing conditions at many projects often exceeded or equaled that in the slums they had replaced. Public housing turned out to be a complex social welfare program that required competence by local officials in a range of political and administrative tasks: drafting legislation and securing short- and long-term government funding; eminent domain and demolition; architectural design and construction; establishment of tenancy and admission standards; and long-term daily tasks such as maintenance, rent collection, and public safety. The difficulty of balancing complex government activities—in a local urban context dominated by deindustrialization, white flight, shifting politics, and corrupt political machines—made viable public housing exceptional.

As demand for public housing fell in the 1950s and 1960s, so did standards for admission and continued tenancy; poorer tenants, in turn, paid less in rent, often vandalized projects, and demanded more services. A few cities, such as New York City, leveraged stronger demand to maintain higher standards of admission and ran the day-to-day operations to a higher standard to keep working people in the projects. Tenants and associated advocates fought for improved services nationally and an end to discriminatory site placement, but these efforts met with limited success. The Brooke Amendment (1969), for instance, a well-meaning attempt to protect tenants by limiting rent increases sought by desperate local housing authorities, fatally undermined housing authority finances across the nation.

The liberal John F. Kennedy and Lyndon B. Johnson administrations expanded public housing and experimented with better design. President Richard Nixon, responding to both troubled projects and his own conservative political principals, imposed a moratorium on new public housing in 1973. Public housing starts never recovered and subsequent federal policy emphasized private-sector subsidy programs such as Section 8 vouchers. Inflation and rising fuel and personnel costs in the 1970s and 1980s, as well as inconsistent federal subsidies, worsened conditions and bankruptcy of housing authorities became common.

The reimposition of federal guidelines through a variety of Housing Opportunity for People Everywhere (HOPE) programs targeted dysfunctional projects in the 1990s. Although initial Republican plans called for selling units to tenants, the Hope VI program that began during the Clinton administration replaced some of the most distressed housing projects with tightly screened, mixed-use developments usually housing very few poor people. The dramatic problems in big-city public housing, to be fair, have obscured the better record of public housing in many small towns and cities across the country.

[*See also* **Housing Policy, Federal: An Overview.**]

BIBLIOGRAPHY

Biles, Roger, et al. *From Tenements to the Taylor Homes.* University Park: Pennsylvania State University Press, 2000.

Bloom, Nicholas Dagen. *Public Housing That Worked.* Philadelphia: University of Pennsylvania Press, 2008.

Hays, Allen. *The Federal Government and Urban Housing.* Albany: State University of New York Press, 1995.

Hirsch, Arnold. *Making the Second Ghetto: Race and Housing in Chicago, 1940–1960.* Cambridge; New York: Cambridge University Press, 1983.

Hunt, D. Bradford. *Blueprint for Disaster: The Unraveling of Chicago Public Housing.* Chicago; London: University of Chicago Press, 2009.

Nicholas D. Bloom

HOUSTON, SAM

(1793–1863), antebellum Texas leader. Born in Virginia, Sam Houston moved to Tennessee in 1807. A youthful runaway, he lived with the Cherokees from 1809 to 1812 and in 1813 enlisted in the U.S. Army. He left the army in 1818, moved to Middle Tennessee, became a lawyer, and launched a political career. A Jacksonian Democrat, Houston served in Congress from 1823 to 1827, when he was elected governor of Tennessee. He abruptly resigned the governorship in April 1829, following the breakup of his marriage, and went into exile with the Cherokees in present-day Oklahoma.

Three years later, Houston traveled to Texas as an agent of the United States to the Comanches. Although little involved in planning the 1835–1836 Texas revolution against Mexico, Houston became commander-in-chief of the Texan forces. After initial setbacks suffered by units not under his immediate command, including the fall of the Alamo in March 1836, Houston's army won Texas independence at the Battle of San Jacinto (21 April 1836), defeating the Mexican commander Santa Anna. Houston was president of the Texas Republic in 1836–1838 and again in 1841–1844. Following the U.S. annexation of Texas in 1845, which he actively supported, he served in the U.S. Senate from 1846 to 1859.

During the 1850s, Houston's staunch unionism reduced his popularity in Texas. He won the governorship in 1859 but was removed from office when the Civil War began in 1861 because of his opposition to Texas's secession and his refusal to swear loyalty to the Confederacy. He retired to Huntsville, where he died. Sam Houston, more than any other individual, had brought Texas into the Union that he loved.

[*See also* **Confederate States of America; Democratic Party; Jackson, Andrew;** ***and*** **Texas Annexation.**]

BIBLIOGRAPHY

Campbell, Randolph B. *Sam Houston and the American Southwest.* New York: HarperCollins, 1993.

Friend, Llerena B. *Sam Houston: The Great Designer.* Austin: University of Texas Press, 1954.

Randolph B. Campbell

HUMPHREY, HUBERT

(1911–1978), senator, vice president, and Democratic presidential candidate. Perhaps the most eloquent and forceful proponent of New Deal liberalism after World War II, Hubert Humphrey rose from mayor of Minneapolis (1945–1949), to the U.S. Senate (1949–1965), to vice president (1965–1969). Four times he sought the presidency and four times he was rejected. In 1968, amid bitter domestic divisions over the Vietnam War, he won the Democratic nomination but lost in a close election to Republican Richard M. Nixon. In 1971 he returned to the Senate, where he served until his death in 1978.

Humphrey's rise to national prominence coincided with a critical period in the evolution of American liberalism and the Democratic Party. During World War II, liberals and Communists had worked together for progressive causes, but growing U.S.–Soviet hostility after 1945 convinced Humphrey and many others that liberalism and Communism were incompatible. In 1947 he joined with theologian Reinhold Niebuhr, historian Arthur Schlesinger Jr., and others to organize the anti-Communist Americans for Democratic Action (ADA) and conducted a successful purge of communists from Minnesota's new Democratic-Farmer-Labor party. The following year he gained national attention at the Democratic national convention with a stirring speech in support of civil rights that established his reputation as one of the leading orators in American politics. Minnesota voters rewarded Humphrey by electing him to the Senate in 1948. Over the next fifteen years, he emerged as the Senate's most outspoken liberal and most effective lawmaker. He shaped some of the most important social legislation of his time, including the Civil Rights Act of 1964, which helped to erode racial segregation in the South.

In 1964, President Lyndon B. Johnson picked Humphrey as his vice-presidential running mate and the ticket won a landslide victory. But the administration's 1965 decision to escalate the war in Vietnam splintered the Democratic Party and destroyed Humphrey's 1968 presidential bid.

[*See also* **Anti-Communism; Civil Rights; Civil Rights Legislation; Communist Party USA; Democratic Party; Federal Government, Legislative Branch: Senate; Johnson, Lyndon B.; Liberalism;** ***and*** **New Deal.**]

BIBLIOGRAPHY

Solberg, Carl. *Hubert Humphrey: A Biography.* New York: W. W. Norton, 1984.

Thurber, Timothy. *The Politics of Equality: Hubert H. Humphrey and the African American Freedom Struggle, 1945–1978.* New York: Columbia University Press, 1999.

Steven M. Gillon

I

IMMIGRATION LAW AND POLICY

This entry contains two subentries: Before 1930; and After 1930.

BEFORE 1930

In America's colonial period migration occurred in the frames of British imperial policies and the interests of chartered company and proprietorial colonies. English, Scots, Irish, Dutch, Germans, Swedes, and others of several distinct religious confessions came. One-half to two-thirds of Europeans came as indentured servants under contracts of between three and seven years' duration, depending on the laws of the dynastic state of origin. Africans were brought in first under indentures, but soon legal changes made them slaves for life. They often arrived after a "breaking in" in the Caribbean. Religion, in Europe still a marker of identity, induced colonies to attract dissenters from Puritans to Mennonites or, in the case of Maryland, to provide refuge to Catholics. Some colonies actively recruited settlers or encouraged importation of chattel slaves.

At the inception of the American Republic, policies and politics as well as the new constitutional frame led to a mass refugee outmigration of "Tories" or "Loyalists"; some 60,000, including free and enslaved African Americans, left. The Age of Revolution's next French phase caused massive fears among U.S. "postrevolutionary" Federalist politicians. In 1798 the new Alien and Sedition Acts, a reaction to

American Democratic–Republican societies, aimed at critics of the administration and permitted exclusion and deportation of aliens. After repeal by the next administration, immigration remained unrestricted until 1875.

The "Open Door" Period. For three-quarters of a century governments kept the entry gates open. Regulations reduced overcrowding onboard immigrant ships and some states demanded bonds when poor immigrants seemed likely to become public charges. Forced immigration (i.e., slave transport) was ended by law as of 1 January 1808, but some traders smuggled slaves as late as the 1860s. Nativists expressed anti-immigrant sentiments from the 1840s, but the need for rural settler and urban craft and working families precluded policy and legal changes. Beginning in 1864, the responsibility for immigration shifted from the states to the federal governments, which, from 1891, had sole authority.

Given the conditions in Europe, state or federal governments did not have to actively recruit immigrants. With the newly emerging U.S. contacts in China and other Asian countries, the first Chinese migrants came beginning in the mid-1840s. The military annexation of about one-half of Mexico in 1848 involved moving the border over an estimated 150,000 men, women, and children who became part of the U.S. population—but not necessarily citizens with equal rights—without migrating or being consulted. Trading contacts to the Caribbean Islands established (shipping) connections that induced some African Caribbeans to migrate. At the same time U.S. citizens migrated to Mexico and the Caribbean without restrictions. The "opening" of Japan by the navy to U.S. trade in the 1850s and the annexation of the Philippines, Puerto Rico, and Hawai'i in 1898, as well as political interference in Cuba, created further connections and thus migratory routes for men and women, neither citizens nor aliens, from the latter territories.

By mid-century, self-sustaining migration did not fill all needs for labor forces and, in the prairies, for settler families. Under the open-door policy, railroad companies encouraged Mexicans to migrate northward and, through contractors, recruited southern Chinese as "credit-ticket" migrants, who worked off their passage. Some of the new Midwestern states sent recruitment brochures or even agents to Europe; some reintegrated Southern states tried to recruit white European labor to replace black men and women. When Congress established the Office of Commissioner of Immigration in 1864, immigration of contract labors could be permitted if contracts to work off the advance of the credit for passage lasted no longer than twelve months. Although none of the schemes involved sizeable numbers of immigrants, from 1862 the Homestead Acts successfully encouraged immigrants' and internal migrants' settlement in the West.

After anti-Irish and anti-German nativism, anti-Asian racism emerged on the Pacific Coast in the 1870s and, against the "new" immigrants, anti-East and South European sentiment on the East Coast in the 1890s. Although California did pass anti-Chinese measures, in the East the demand for industrial labor, men and women, precluded exclusionary governmental intervention against those southern and eastern Europeans who, in the racializing thought of the times, were inferior to Anglo-Saxons or Teutons. Passage, especially after the introduction of steamships in the 1870s, was cheap, and entry was easy given that states in the Atlantic world had not yet "invented" a passport system. This system would evolve from the late nineteenth century when fear of radicalism reached unprecedented heights. Race and gender sooner came to be factors for exclusion from the nation. Thus, economic conditions, stateside warfare and annexations, and new commercial relations were the main determinants of the volume and origin of migration until 1875. State and federal governments observed immigration rather than regulated it.

Control of Entry by Race, Ethnicity, Gender, Health, and "Immorality." The first steps toward immigration control reflected racist and sexist positions. In 1875 Congress passed a law, sponsored by Republican Horace F. Page, to prevent entry of "any subject of China, Japan, or any Oriental country" coming as "coolie labor" (bound by a contract, legal for immigrants from Europe) or coming for "lewd and immoral purposes" (prostitution). Thus, migrants summarily called "Orientals" and women, summarily suspected of being prostitutes if traveling unaccompanied, were singled out.

From 1882 policies for the Pacific ports bordered on total exclusion; those on the East Coast involved only a few designated classes. European immigrant admission was concentrated in Ellis Island from 1892. Land borders remained basically uncontrolled—but crossing of these borders by unwanted Europeans and small numbers of Asians would spark debates about further controls.

The Chinese were excluded from entry for 10 years beginning in 1882—although students and merchants could enter. This provision was continuously extended (1892, 1902). But the state bureaucrats' laws, a great (paper) wall, became permeable when the Chinese, in response, created "paper" relatives with assumed, but documented identities. Japanese, arriving in increasing numbers after 1900, faced racism too, and by 1907, the U.S. and Japanese governments negotiated treaties, called "Gentlemen's Agreements" (although they were not gentlemanly from the migrants' point of view), in which Japan agreed to stop the emigration of laborers. Small numbers of Punjabis (Sikhs by religion) came from British Columbia and Filipinos came from the annexed islands.

The anti-Chinese measures were trial runs for the exclusion of Europeans who, from 1885, in the discourse of the times, were mainly "dark," "swarthy," and "olive" ones from Europe's east and south. Restriction evolved step by step: criminals, paupers, mentally ill, and "other undesirables" (1882), and then contract laborers (1885, ten years after the Page Law), but domestics, professionals, and skilled workers did not fall under this provision. For migrants this created a legal frame in which a contract for a job, the best sign that a newcomer was not "likely to become a public charge," was prohibited for some but not for others. In 1891, impoverished migrants, those suffering from "loathsome and dangerous contagious" diseases, those convicted of a felony or guilty of "moral turpitude," and polygamists were excluded. In 1902, radicals, especially anarchists, and prostitutes were added to the list. In public, a wide debate on germ-carrying aliens emerged; among admission personnel fears of a "white slave trade" made women traveling alone potential prostitutes; in foreign relations, border control became extraterritorial since consuls and shipping companies could refuse embarkation in foreign ports.

From 1882, immigrants had to pay a fee ("head tax") of 50 cents, which was raised to $2 in 1903 and to $4 in 1907—at that time the poorest newcomers, East European Jews, came with just over $12 in savings and the "richest," the Germans, with about $41. Although around 1900 one-third of all European migrants returned, no emigration laws were ever debated. Of the land borders, the border with Canada drew attention because unskilled Europeans, especially Italian workers, crossed it in both directions; the Mexican border, given the demand for labor, remained open without discussion.

The racialized views on eastern and southern Europeans led to a congressional investigation and the Dillingham Commission's 41-volume report (1911) provided abundant and valuable data. But its recommendations considered the new immigrants morally, physically, and emotionally inferior to earlier Western and Northern Europeans. The racist position found harsh expression in Madison Grant's *The Passing of the Great Race, Or the Racial Basis of European History* (1916). But from August 1914 to 1918 World War I ended immigration from Europe. In 1917—with arrivals almost at zero—Congress passed an act requiring a literacy test: immigrants had to prove reading capability in English or their native language.

Closed Doors. The sustained racial and gender paranoia, acerbated by the radicalism of the Russian Revolution of 1917, led Congress to pass the Emergency Quota Act of 1921. It limited the number of immigrants to 3 percent of their ethnocultural group's share in the population of 1910 and thus weighted the new cap of 357,800 annually toward the "old-stock" groups. Next, the 1924 Johnson–Reed Act set an annual cap of 150,000 and lowered the national-origin quotas to 2 percent of the 1890 census. At that time few new immigrants had arrived; thus, Britain's quota was 65,000 compared with an Italian quota of 5,800 and a Jewish quota of 2,784. Because of extensive lobbying by western agribusiness, the "western hemisphere," meaning Mexico, was exempted from the provisions.

By 1929, when the 1924 law took full effect, the Great Depression drastically reduced migration and Mexicans, too, faced exclusion. Land border controls had begun in 1924 and, with a surplus of native migrant labor, including dust bowl refugees in the Southwest, agribusiness ceased to defend Mexican migration. The doors remained closed for 35 years until Congress abolished racial and ethnic quotas in 1965. In these decades the laws kept out Jewish refugees from fascist Europe after 1933, and a presidential order permitted nonquota entry of Europe's "Displaced Persons" from 1945 to 1952.

[*See also* **Homestead Act.**]

BIBLIOGRAPHY

Breitman, Richard, and Alan M. Kraut. *American Refugee Policy and European Jewry, 1933–1945.* Bloomington: Indiana University Press, 1987.

Daniels, Roger. *Guarding the Golden Door. American Immigration Policy and Immigration since 1882.* New York: Hill and Wang, 2004.

Kraut, Alan M. *Silent Travellers. Germs, Genes, and the "Immigrant Menace."* New York: Basic Books, 1994.

Ngai, Mae M. *Impossible Subjects: Illegal Aliens and the Making of Modern America.* Princeton, N.J.: Princeton University Press, 2004.

Spickard, Paul. *Almost All Aliens: Immigration, Race and Colonialism in American History and Identity.* New York: Routledge, 2007.

Tichenor, Daniel J. *Dividing Lines. The Politics of Immigration Control in America.* Princeton, N.J.: Princeton University Press, 2002.

Torpey, John. *The Invention of the Passport. Surveillance, Citizenship and the State.* Cambridge; New York: Cambridge University Press, 2000.

U.S. Immigration Legislation online. http://library.uwb.edu/guides/USimmigration/26%20stat%201084.pdf (accessed 15 August 2011).

Zolberg, Aristide R. *A Nation by Design. Immigration Policy in the Fashioning of America.* New York: Cambridge, Mass.: Russell Sage Foundation; Harvard University Press, 2006.

Dirk Hoerder

AFTER 1930

During the 1930s, the United States had highly restrictive immigration laws and relatively little immigration. The policies began to loosen somewhat during World War II. After the war, Congress passed major legislation regarding immigration. In 1965, the U.S. began to adopt policies that contributed to the arrival of the largest numbers of immigrants in American history. Undocumented immigration, as well as legal immigration, increased sharply from 1980 onward, and undocumented immigration became a major policy issue.

Immigration Policy before 1952: The Low-Immigration Period. During the late nineteenth and early twentieth centuries, the United States went through a great wave of immigration. In 1924, the U.S. Congress contributed to ending the historic immigration wave by establishing highly restrictive immigration laws, which especially limited the access of immigrants from areas outside northern and western Europe. The day-to-day oversight of immigration rested with the Bureau of Immigration, which operated under the Department of Labor. In 1933, an executive order of the president changed the name of the Bureau to the Immigration and Naturalization Service (INS). Seven years later, the government transferred the INS to the Department of Justice. Immigration to the United States during the 1930s was slight because of the contraction in economic opportunities of the Depression as well as the exclusionary immigration policy.

War and Immigration Law. World War II brought some broadening American immigration policy. China was a U.S. ally and the American government sought to support the Nationalist Chinese under Chiang Kai Chek. The Magnuson Act, also known as the Immigration Act of 1943, repealed the Asian exclusion policy that had been in effect since 1882 and that had been reaffirmed by succeeding legislation. The war also created a demand for workers in American fields that led the U.S. government to bring in temporary labor migrants from Mexico in 1942.

An estimated 150,000 to 200,000 European women married U.S. soldiers between 1944 and 1950. During the same period of time, 50,000 to 100,000 Asian women married U.S. servicemen. These marriages of military personnel led the U.S. Congress to pass the War Brides Act on 28 December 1945, waiving most of the immigration requirements for women who had married members of the American armed forces serving overseas.

The war had uprooted millions of people from their homelands and left many in desperate situations. In response to the urging of President Harry S. Truman, Congress passed the Displaced Persons Act of 1948. In 1950, with further encouragement of the president, Congress revised the Act and removed much of the apparent discrimination of the original version against Jewish refugees.

Immigration Policy from 1952 to 1965: The McCarran–Walter Act. Following World War II, the U.S. Congress began to develop a new immigration policy to replace the policies enacted in the 1920s. Some members of Congress were especially critical of the national quota system, which had set quotas for immigrants from European countries and largely banned immigration from the rest of the world. Others wanted simply to establish a general codification of immigration law and to continue to limit overall immigration and the access of non-European groups. Ultimately, Senator Patrick McCarran of Nevada and Representative Francis Walter of Pennsylvania succeeded in crafting a new overarching immigration law that retained the national quota system and limited the overall number of immigrants. McCarran–Walter added a series of preferences as means of selecting immigrants within the quotas. The first basis rested on the economic criterion, since immigrants with special skills were given first preference. Other preferences, however, rested on the social norm that family relationships enjoy a special status. Parents of U.S. citizens constituted the second preference, spouses and children of resident aliens the third, and other relatives the fourth.

President Harry S. Truman objected to several parts of the new bill and vetoed it, but the Senate and House voted to override his veto. Although the law continued many of the policies of the past, it also enacted a number of changes. The ban on Asian immigration, which had begun to loosen during the war, ended altogether. The new law also guaranteed that the right to become a naturalized citizen of the United States could not be denied or abridged because of race or sex. Addressing the problem of refugees, the McCarran–Walter Act, or the Immigration and Naturalization Act of 1952, created a special status for refugees. Although it was greatly altered by later amendments, especially the 1965 amendment, the McCarran–Walter Act continued to be the basic immigration law for the United States into the twenty-first century.

The Cold War and Immigration Policy. For much of the second half of the twentieth century, competition with Communist nations was an overriding geopolitical concern of the United States. Senator McCarran was a leading a anti-Communist and the law that bears his name reflected the anxieties of the Cold War. The Immigration and Naturalization Act contained measures intended to exclude Communists or individuals with Communist affiliations from settling in the United States.

Developing refugee policy, in particular, reflected the Cold War geopolitical environment. President Truman's appeal to Congress to help escapees from the Communist countries of Eastern Europe led to the passage of the Refugee Relief Act of 1953, which authorized over 200,000 new visas, not counted in the national quotas. The administration of President Dwight D. Eisenhower expanded opportunities for the admission of Hungarian refugees by defining them as parolees, allowed to remain in the United States temporarily for emergency purposes. In 1958, the Hungarian Refugee Adjustment Act changed the status of the over 30,000 Hungarian parolees in the United States to that of permanent resident aliens. When Fidel Castro took power in Cuba in 1959, the United States created the Cuban Refugee Program to provide welfare benefits and to assist in resettlement for the Cubans streaming into Florida. Until the fall of the Soviet Union at the beginning of the 1990s, most of those designated as refugees by the United States were fleeing from Communist countries.

Hart–Cellar and the Post-1965 Wave: A New Approach to Immigration. Thirteen years after McCarran–Walter, a new amendment to American immigration law pushed preference categories to the forefront and largely removed the national origins restrictions. The 1965 amendment to the Immigration and Nationality Act, known as the Hart–Cellar Act, after its sponsors, essentially eliminated the national quota system, by that time seen as unfairly discriminatory by President Lyndon Johnson and other supporters. In its place, it installed an overall ceiling of 290,000 immigrants per year, with admissions allocated by the preference system. Most preferences were for family members of citizens and residents, although occupational skills also counted.

The Great Wave. When Congress passed the 1965 Act, President Lyndon B. Johnson assured critics of immigration change that neither the numbers of immigrants nor their places of origin would change greatly. During the 1970s, however, migration to the United States began to increase rapidly. From 1971 to 1980, 4,493,000 immigrants were admitted into the country, an increase of 1,171,000 people from the decade 1961 to 1970. Admissions increased to 7,338,000 during the 1980s and 9,095,500 in the 1990s. In the first decade of the twenty-first century, over 10,500,000 people received admission to the United States as legal permanent residents. By 2009, over 38,500,000 foreign-born people resided in the United States, making up close to 13 percent of the total population. Whereas prior to 1965 most immigrants had come from Europe, during the late twentieth and early twenty-first centuries about half of all immigrants came from Latin America and about one-quarter came from Asia.

The high level of legal migration in the late twentieth and early twenty-first centuries led some to argue that post-1965 American immigration policy was in error. Some critics of immigration policy maintained that immigrants took jobs at lower wages than natives, driving down living standards. Others argued that the family preference system encouraged the entry of low-skilled workers, thereby increasing economic inequality by creating competition with Americans at the bottom of the labor pool.

Immigration proponents maintained that immigrant workers took jobs that were difficult to fill and that their energy and drive brought dynamism to the American economy. Further, proponents also argued that the aging population of the United States required the infusion of new and younger workers. Since many native-born Americans retained memories of immigrant forbears, they often tended to sympathize with new immigrants.

New Sources of Immigration: Refugee Resettlement. As regular immigrant admissions expanded rapidly, refugees provided another major source of newcomers to the United States. Geopolitics continued to shape U.S. refugee policy. In the spring of 1975, governments allied with the United States in South Vietnam, Cambodia, and Laos fell to Communist forces. On 18 April of that year President Gerald Ford authorized the admission of 130,400 refugees from those three countries, with most of the initial arrivals from Vietnam.

More Southeast Asian refugees entered under the parole authority of the U.S. attorney general, but numbers of refugees continued to increase, so Congress passed the Refugee Act of 1980. This placed refugees in a category separate from other immigrants, and it provided a definition of refugees as people fleeing their countries because of persecution on grounds of race, religion, nationality, or political opinion. Further, it gave the president authority to establish the number of refugees to be allowed into the United States. Massive arrivals occurred through the official refugee program.

The same period that saw extensive refugee resettlement from Southeast Asia also saw people attempting to flee to the United States from political and social disorder in Haiti and Central America. The United States categorized the Haitians as economic migrants, rather than political refugees, and established the practice of "interdiction" during the administration of President Ronald Reagan. This meant stopping boats with Haitians at sea, interviewing them, and returning most to Haiti. Among Central Americans, the United States generally did not recognize Salvadorans and Guatemalans as refugees and many entered the United States illegally. Some American religious and activist organizations sympathized with the excluded Central Americans and worked to provide sanctuary. The United States allowed some Nicaraguan refugees to remain in the United States temporarily, since the United States was opposed to the socialist government that ruled Nicaragua during the 1980s.

In the twenty-first century, the fall of Communism and American involvement in new world crises led the refugee policy created in the previous decades to turn to new national groups. In 2000, for example, Bosnia-Herzegovina, formerly part of Yugoslavia, was the single greatest source of refugees, sending nearly 20,000 people to the United States. In 2004 and 2005, the United States admitted about 50,000 refugees from Africa, half of them from Somalia. By 2008–2009, with American forces occupying Iraq, over 33,000 Iraqi refugees arrived.

Undocumented Migration. Undocumented immigrants have entered and lived in the United States throughout the nation's history and there has always been substantial unregulated movement across the nation's southern and northern borders. However, a dramatic rise in undocumented migration, especially from Mexico, at the end of the twentieth century produced new population flows and new policy responses. The estimated undocumented immigrant population grew steadily, from about 1 million in 1980 to nearly 12 million by 2008.

Undocumented migration raised serious questions about the power of immigration officials to detain those suspected of being in the country illegally and the rights of undocumented immigrants to legal protections and benefits. The U.S. Supreme Court attempted to deal with some of these questions by setting limits on the power of officials over undocumented immigrants. The Court has, for example, ruled that that immigration officials may not use roving patrols far from the border to stop vehicles without a warrant or probable cause (*Almeida-Sanchez v. United States,* 413 U.S. 266 (1973)) and that immigration officials may not use physical appearance or ethnic group membership alone as a justification for detaining suspects (*United States v. Brignoni-Ponce,* 422 U.S. 873 (1975)). Responding to a law in Texas, the Court ruled that the state could not deny public school education to children in the United States illegally and that the rights of the Fourteenth Amendment covered undocumented immigrants, as well as other residents of the nation (*Plyler v. Doe* 457 U.S. 202 (1982)).

The growing number of undocumented immigrants led Congress to enact the Immigration Reform and Control Act of 1986. This raised the annual ceiling on legal immigration to 540,000 to provide more opportunities to enter the United States through official means. To decrease the jobs drawing illegal immigrants into the country, the Act introduces stiff penalties for employers of those in the country illegally. The Act also offers amnesty to illegal aliens who can prove that they have resided in the United States since 1 January 1982.

Despite efforts to intensify border security, the undocumented populations continued to come. The responses of some states and localities with large undocumented populations provoked support, outrage, and legal scrutiny. In particular, Arizona, which had an undocumented population of about 560,000 by 2008, sparked controversy when it passed SB1070 in April 2010. This law would require noncitizens to carry papers at all times and allow local law enforcement officials to arrest undocumented immigrants. Critics maintained that the bill was an attempt by a state to rule on a matter restricted to the federal government and that it endangered the rights of both citizens and noncitizens. A judge blocked enforcement of key provisions of the law before just before it took effect.

Changes Immigration Laws and Policy Resulting from the 9/11 Events. American immigration policy came under increased scrutiny following the terrorist attacks on New York and Washington, D.C., on 11 September 2001. The U.S. government began to react almost immediately with new legislation. Public Law 107-56, or the Uniting and Strengthening America by Providing Appropriate Tools Required to Intercept and Obstruct Terrorism Act of 2001(USA PATRIOT Act), passed Congress on 26 October 2001. The Act included new reasons for denying entry into the United States, gave a broader definition to the concept of terrorist activity, and increased the causes for deporting visitors and immigrants. It also gave new and controversial powers to the U.S. attorney general, including the power to detain any person the attorney general would reasonably suspect of being connected to terrorist activity.

Congress passed the Border Security Act in November, authorizing more funds for immigration and customs staff, providing for the sharing of information on deportation cases among federal agencies, tracking foreign students, and tightening oversight in other ways. The Department of Justice also issued a variety of new directives and regulations in the months following 9/11, including interviews with recently arrived Middle Eastern men and provisions for detaining terrorist suspects.

The two individuals who flew airplanes into the World Trade Center were not only foreign-born residents, as were their accomplices, but also had both received change-of-status approval from the Immigration and Naturalization Service (INS), allowing them to remain in the country as students after entering as tourists. On 3 March 2003, as part of a general plan to improve national security, the INS became the U.S. Citizenship and Immigration Services (USCIS) and moved from the Department of Justice to the newly created Department of Homeland Security. Responses to undocumented immigration, issues of the rights of undocumented immigrants and their children, and overall levels and types of immigration continued to be divisive and controversial public topics.

[*See also* **Anti-Communism; Department of Homeland Security; Federal Government, Executive Branch: Department of Justice;** ***and*** **Fourteenth Amendment.**]

BIBLIOGRAPHY

Bakalian, Anny, and Mehdi Bozorgmehr. *Backlash 9/11: Middle Eastern and Muslim Americans Respond.* Berkeley: University of California Press, 2009.

Bankston, Carl L., III, and Danielle A. Hidalgo. *Immigration in U.S. History*. Pasadena, Calif.: Salem Press, 2006.

Foner, Nancy. *From Ellis Island to JFK: New York's Two Great Waves of Immigration.* New Haven: Yale University Press; New York: Russell Sage Foundation, 2001.

Mize, Ron, and Alicia Swords. *Consuming Mexican Labor: From the Bracero Program to NAFTA.* Toronto: University of Toronto Press, 2010.

Carl L. Bankston III

INCOME TAX, FEDERAL

The first U.S. income tax was introduced during the Civil War and collected through a newly established Bureau of Internal Revenue in the Department of the Treasury. It was designed less as a money-raiser (although, at its height, it accounted for one-fifth of Union revenues) than as a political diversion—conspicuously targeting the well-to-do to cloak the disproportionate burdens that higher tariffs and new consumer excise taxes placed on typical Americans. Phased out by 1872, it was politically resurrected in succeeding decades in response to sectional (western and southern), partisan (Democrat and Populist), and economic resentments against the power and wealth of the Republican-dominated industrial East. Congress again enacted an income tax in 1894, only to have it declared unconstitutional by the Supreme Court the following year.

The income tax was revived permanently in 1913, with the ratification of the Sixteenth Amendment of the Constitution and the passage by Congress of an income tax graduated up to a 7 percent rate but with exemption provisions that shielded all but the top 2 percent of households. Substantial tax increases in World War I (reaching a peak rate of 77 percent), reinforced by prosperous conditions that more than counterbalanced the Republican-sponsored income-tax cuts of the 1920s, transformed the individual income tax into a major federal revenue raiser. The tiny minority of income earners receiving over 50,000 dollars annually shouldered most of this burden, however. New Deal Era tax reforms heightened the class tilt of the income tax (including a new 79 percent top bracket applying only to John D. Rockefeller Jr.). Nevertheless, the erosion of incomes in the Great Depression, combined with new Social Security and consumer taxes, meant that the personal income tax accounted for under one-fifth of federal revenue collections in the 1930s.

Drastic rate increases and cuts in exemptions to finance World War II mobilization transformed the individual income tax into the federal government's primary revenue source (40 to 50 cents of every dollar collected from 1944 to today). Irving Berlin's "I Paid My Income Tax Today" became the theme music of the income tax's conversion from a class tax (only 5 percent of the public had filed taxable returns in the 1930s) to a citizenship-affirming mass tax, deducted directly from paychecks beginning in 1943 and applying to most American workers.

In 1963–1965, embracing the "New Economics" of the Council of Economic Advisors, the Kennedy and Johnson administrations subordinated the income redistributional potential of the federal income tax to an apparently successful "Keynesian" countercyclical strategy of using broad income-tax cuts and temporary budget deficits to stimulate economic growth, dropping the Eisenhower administration's 91 percent ceiling rate to 70 percent. In the 1980s, a conservative revolt lead by President Ronald Reagan demonized tax burdens and privileged business investment in the name of free market capitalist expansion, and the top income tax rate plunged to 28 percent. As budget deficits ballooned, Reagan's successor George H. W. Bush felt compelled to jack up that tax ceiling to 31 percent, and the Clinton administration, as part of a budget plan that yielded a rare budget surplus, hiked the top rate to 39 percent. But in the new century, George W. Bush revived the Reaganite tax logic, becoming the first American president to cut taxes on wealthy Americans in a time of war (the peak rate fell to 35 percent, where it remains today).

The mounting income inequality that has so distinguished the United States since the 1970s might have worked to advance the revenue domination of a tax imposed at escalating rates up the income scale. But plummeting upper-bracket rates, reduced further by more generous tax treatment of capital gains, countered that revenue windfall. Moreover, higher child and earned income tax credits allowed growing numbers of Americans to escape income taxes altogether; in fact, in the first decade of the twenty-first century, most wage earners paid out more in Social Security/Medicare payroll taxes than in income tax. But even if the fiscal significance of the income tax may be eclipsed, its role as a measure of what and who matters in American political life endures.

[*See also* **Federal Government, Executive Branch: Treasury Department; New Deal;** ***and*** **Sixteenth Amendment.**]

BIBLIOGRAPHY

Brownlee, W. Elliot. *Federal Taxation in America: A Short History*. 2d ed. Washington, D.C.; Cambridge, UK; New York: Woodrow Wilson Center Press; Cambridge University Press, 2004.

Hacker, Jacob S., and Paul Pierson. *Winner-Take-All Politics*. New York: Simon & Schuster, 2010.

Mark H. Leff

INDIAN HEALTH SERVICE

In 1873, amid growing national interest in social and public-health reforms, the Office of Indian Affairs in the Department of the Interior created a Medical and Educational Division, forerunner of today's extensive, multitasked Indian Health Service. At the time, only about half of the nation's seventy-four reservations employed physicians. Despite the subsequent construction of the first Indian hospitals, more rigorous hiring standards for medical personnel, and a late-1880s policy shift toward disease prevention, rampant epidemic disease and malnutrition persisted.

Throughout the nineteenth century, health care competed poorly with educational efforts for the Interior Department's meager resources. In the period 1900–1920, however, a number of bureaucratic changes and budgetary successes enhanced Indian health services. In 1908, the department created the position of chief medical supervisor to oversee the medical service. In 1911, the first congressional appropriation specifically for general health services to Indians resulted in the addition of dentists and public-health nurses.

A reorganization of the Indian Bureau in 1924 resulted in a separate Medical Division (in 1931 renamed the Health Division, later the Indian Health Service). In 1926, the medical division itself reorganized, expanded, and added supervisors detailed from the U.S. Public Health Service. The pre–World War II period brought expansion for the medical department. Its staff successfully treated trachoma, conducted sanitation surveys, and built more hospitals. Service hospitals were now the site of 80 percent of Indian births, reflecting the degree of native trust.

Yet federal studies of reservations, such as the 1928 Meriam Report, consistently found abysmal health conditions. Controversies over salaries and limited resources persisted as well. Reformers and the National Tuberculosis Association called for transfer of medical services from the Interior Department to the Public Health Service, and in 1955 Public Law 568 did just that: the Indian Health Service became part of the new Department of Health, Education, and Welfare (now the Department of Health and Human Services). In subsequent years, personnel, budgets, facility construction, and the numbers of patients served increased dramatically. Troubling discrepancies persisted, however, between health statistics for the 1.5 million Native Americans and those of the general population.

[*See also* **Bureau of Indian Affairs; Federal Government, Executive Branch: Other Departments; Public Health: An Overview;** ***and*** **Public Health Service, U.S.**]

BIBLIOGRAPHY

Benson, Todd. *Race, Health, and Power: The Federal Government and American Indian Health, 1909–1955*, PhD diss., Stanford University, 1994.

Trannert, Robert A. *White Man's Medicine: Government Doctors and the Navajo, 1863–1955*. Albuquerque: University of New Mexico Press, 1998.

Diane D. Edwards

INDIAN LAW, FEDERAL

Federal Indian law is the body of law that regulates the interactions among the United States, state governments, and American Indian tribes. Three foundational principles guide the area. First, the Constitution vests Congress with plenary power over Indian affairs. Second, Congress's plenary power is exclusive as to the states, sharply limiting state authority in Indian affairs. Third, Indian tribes retain sovereign authority unless divested through agreement, an act of Congress, or Supreme Court decree.

The Marshall Trilogy. Federal Indian law originated in what is known as the Marshall Trilogy of cases, each written by Chief Justice John Marshall. In *Johnson v. M'Intosh* (1823), the Court adopted the Doctrine of Discovery, ruling that Indian tribes and individual Indians do not possess full property rights to land. Instead, Indians have the right of mere occupancy of their lands, and that property interest may only be alienated to the United States, the successor to European "discoverers" of Indian land. The Court followed with the *Cherokee Nation v. Georgia* (1831), maintaining that Indian tribes are "domestic dependent nations," and *Worcester v. Georgia* (1832), holding that state laws generally have "no force" in Indian country because of tribal treaty rights and the Supremacy Clause.

The Treaty and Reservation Era. Federal Indian law and policy moved in overlapping cycles, beginning with the treaty and reservation era, loosely dating from the formation of the United States to the 1870s. Early federal policies toward Indian tribes favored trade and negotiation over violent conquest, and so the president began negotiating treaties with Indian tribes in the eighteenth century. From the 1770s until 1871, when Indian treaty making ceased, the United States executed over 400 treaties with Indian tribes. Key provisions in over 200 treaties remain extant. Indian treaties served as recognition of tribal sovereignty by the federal government and remain the source of key rights to hunting, fishing, water and other resources, and territory, as noted by the Supreme Court as early as *United States v. Winans* (1905). Early Indian treaties established reservations of land for Indian tribes in the east, a policy that continued throughout the middle part of the century in the western half of the United States. Beginning in the 1830s, however, the United States pursued a policy of "removal," using the treaty process, backed up by the Army, to force tribes to leave eastern portions of the United States for lands west of the Mississippi, especially in Oklahoma. In the mid-nineteenth century, the United States often used the treaty process to undermine the tribal land base and often unilaterally abrogated Indian treaties, a practice ratified by the Supreme Court in *Lone Wolf v. Hitchcock* (1903).

Allotment and Assimilation. Beginning in the 1870s, the United States adopted policies intending to break up the reservation land base and assimilate Indian people into the American mainstream. Federal officials forced Indian children into military-style boarding schools involving hard labor and violent coercion intending to undermine Indian culture and language.

In 1887, Congress entered the allotment era, during which two-thirds of all tribal landholdings (about 90 million acres) passed into non-Indian hands. Allotment largely eliminated Indian communal landholdings on many reservations and forced individual land ownership upon unprepared Indians, resulting in the loss of land in the face of concerted efforts by non-Indians to dispossess them of their property.

Reorganization and Termination. In 1934, Congress passed the Indian Reorganization Act (IRA), the first major legislation intending to establish modern Native nations, which also ended allotment. Nearly 200 Indian tribes "reorganized" into constitutional governments complete with tribal councils, later adding tribal judiciaries and separate business entities. Soon, however, Congress began to "terminate" Indian tribes, ending its political relationship with over 100 Indian tribes. Although treaty rights survived termination, as in *Menominee Tribe v. United States* (1968), terminated tribes generally suffered untold hardships because federal officials confiscated tribal assets and eliminated tribal governments.

Meanwhile, the Supreme Court upheld the authority of Indians and tribes to make their own laws and be governed by them in *Williams v. Lee* (1959), the first case in the modern era of federal Indian law.

Self-Determination and Treaty Rights. During the 1970s, Congress began to encourage tribal self-determination and restored many terminated tribes. During this period, American Indians began asserting rights guaranteed by treaty to hunt, fish, and gather both on- and off-reservation. In 1974, a federal court divided the Puget Sound region fishery 50–50 between Indians and non-Indians in *United States v. Washington,* a landmark precedent that was influential nationwide.

In 1978, the Supreme Court affirmed tribal sovereignty in *Santa Clara Pueblo v. Martinez,* protecting tribal immunity from suit, and in *United States v. Wheeler,* recognizing tribal prosecution authority over tribal members. That same year, however, the Court held that Indian tribes do not have the authority to prosecute non-Indians in *Oliphant v. Suquamish Indian Tribe.*

Native Nation Building. By the 1970s, Indian tribes and individual Indians had engaged in tobacco and motor fuel sales and gaming enterprises to generate desperately needed governmental revenue. Because of the unpredictability of the Supreme Court's Indian taxation cases, such as *Washington v. Confederated Tribes of Coleville Reservation* (1980), smoke shop and gas station operations have only been partially successful. In *California v. Cabazon Band of Mission Indians* (1987), however, the Supreme Court roundly affirmed the right of Indian tribes to engage in gaming operations. Congress followed with the Indian Gaming Regulatory Act, fostering a $25 billion industry. Additionally, Native nations have successfully retaken control over reservation natural resources such as oil, natural gas, and coal in recent decades.

During this era, Native nations have been developing their governance structures as well, enacting sophisticated civil rights, land use, and commercial laws, for example. Despite several Supreme Court decisions, such as *Montana v. United States* (1981) and *Strate v. A-1 Contractors* (1997), undercutting the jurisdiction of tribal governments and courts over nonmembers, tribal regulatory and justice systems have developed exponentially in recent years.

[*See also* **Bureau of Indian Affairs; Indian Law, Tribal;** ***and*** **Marshall, Thurgood.**]

BIBLIOGRAPHY

Getches, David H., et al. *Cases and Materials on Federal Indian Law,* 6th ed. St. Paul, Minn.: West, 2011.

Newton, Nell Jessup, et al. *Cohen's Handbook of Federal Indian Law*. Newark, N.J.: LexisNexis, 2005.

Pommersheim, Frank. *Broken Landscape*. Oxford; New York: Oxford University Press, 2009.

Wilkinson, Charles F. *American Indians, Time, and the Law*. New Haven, Conn.: Yale University Press, 1987.

Matthew L. M. Fletcher

INDIAN LAW, TRIBAL

Tribal law is the law of American Indian tribes, with origins in tribal constitutions, tribal statutes, and tribal common law as articulated in tribal courts. Indian tribes possess their own inherent sovereign authority, including the authority to establish governmental structures of their own design, establish membership provisions, and generally regulate Indian country activity.

Customary and Traditional Law. American Indian customary and traditional governance practices and justice systems were highly sophisticated but less formal than European structures. Government structures typically formed around extended family groups for local questions such as crime and property rights. Larger, more formal, government structures formed to address important region questions, such as intertribal warfare. Indian communities often passed on critical legal rules through stories, with the complexities of domestic relations, property rights, and criminal law, for example, finding nuances in the various tribal languages and dialects.

Traditional governance structures eroded greatly during the reservation era of the late nineteenth and early twentieth centuries, as the Bureau of Indian Affairs assumed control over reservation life. Federal officials enacted "law and order codes" that penalized Indian people for practicing their religions and instituting formalized justice systems, the so-called "Courts of Indian Offenses."

Tribal Constitutions and Codes. Although several Indian tribes had adopted a constitutional form of government in the nineteenth century, most notably the Cherokee Nation (1828) and the Seneca Nation of Indians (1848), most Indian tribes did not ratify a tribal constitution until Congress enacted the Indian Reorganization Act of 1934 (IRA). In the years following, nearly 200 tribes adopted tribal constitutions. These early constitutions, sometimes called "model IRA constitutions," are marked by their relative uniformity and limits on tribal government authority. For example, few early constitutions included provisions for tribal judiciaries. Also, nearly all included provisions requiring important tribal government actions to be approved by the Secretary of the Interior before they would be valid. Not all tribes adopted written constitutions during this period; most notably the Navajo Nation, which voted not to reorganize under the IRA and still has not adopted a constitution in the early twenty-first century.

The IRA-era constitutions survived, with amendment, into the modern era, and other tribes have adopted more and more indigenous constitutions. Tribal constitutions often include complex recitations of individual civil rights, separation of powers, and Federalism-style governance. Fewer and fewer tribal decisions remain under the approval authority of the Secretary of the Interior. Since the 1970s, as federal Indian policy has moved into the self-determination era, more and more tribes assert control over their resources, economies, and federal appropriations.

Tribal legislatures have enacted a wide variety of statutes to implement their police powers, including criminal codes, commercial codes, and even codes defining and protecting cultural property. Tribal ordinances and regulations implement rules on investment of federal housing and health appropriations, tribal trust funds, and other government assets. Tribal law regulates employee–employer relations, land use, and taxation, as well as the relationship of tribes, tribal members, and nonmembers within tribal territories.

Tribal Justice Systems. In a series of Supreme Court decisions and statutory enactments, the federal government activated tribal justice systems, establishing the legal and political encouragement for tribes to develop tribal court systems. In *Williams v. Lee* (1959), the Supreme Court held that tribal courts have exclusive jurisdiction in civil suits arising in Indian Country where the defendant is a tribal member. Congress later enacted the Indian Civil Rights Act in 1968 (ICRA), attempting to apply federal civil rights norms to Indian tribes. In *Santa Clara Pueblo v. Martinez* (1978), the Supreme Court held that civil rights suits under the ICRA may only be adjudicated in tribal courts.

In the 1960s, fewer than 100 Indian tribes had tribal courts, but by 2006, nearly 300 Indian tribes did. Indian communities with many nonmembers in their midst tended to develop tribal courts more inspired by state and federal courts, whereas more insular tribal communities retained significant ties to tribal customs and traditions. For example, the Mashantucket Pequot Tribal Court intentionally mirrors Connecticut courts, a result of the tribe's reliance on the hundreds of thousands of nonmember customers and vendors that do business with the tribes. Conversely, the Navajo Nation, in which most residents are tribal members, relies extensively on tribal common law in its judicial decisions. Many other tribal courts incorporate traditional dispute resolution values into the adversarial tribal court systems, often by liberalizing civil procedure and evidence rules to accommodate tribal member access to the courts.

Tribal courts have handled many of the most controversial and complicated cases arising in Indian country in recent years, including disputes involving the Cherokee Freedmen (*Nash v. Cherokee Nation Registrar,* 2011), cultural property (*Chilkat Indian Village, IRA v. Johnson,* 1993), land use and Indian religions (*Bugenig v. Hoopa Valley Tribe,* 1998), and Indian gaming (*United States ex rel. Auginaush v. Medure,* 2009). Tribal courts are not beholden to federal and state law; for example, some tribal courts have only reluctantly adopted the so-called Miranda warnings because those tribal communities have no tradition of using official coercion to pressure criminal suspects into confessing (*Navajo Nation v. Rodriguez,* 2004).

Peacemaker Courts and Other Traditional Justice Systems. The adversarial system often is not a good fit for Indian communities, where the winner-takes-all approach to litigation creates serious social consequences, as with more insular tribes. Following the lead of the Navajo Nation and numerous Alaskan Native villages, tribal courts have begun to develop alternative justice systems, such as peacemaker courts. Peacemaker courts often are not really courts at all, but diversion programs for certain kinds of cases and litigants. For example, minor juvenile criminal cases can be transferred to a peacemaker, a person trained and versed in tribal custom and tradition who can work with the defendant, victim, and other persons within the community affected by the alleged crime to obviate the need to criminally prosecute and punish a young person. Other tribes have drug court programs to divert nonviolent drug offenses from the criminal justice system.

[*See also* **Bureau of Indian Affairs; Federalism;** ***and*** **Indian Law, Federal.**]

BIBLIOGRAPHY

Austin, Raymond D. *Navajo Courts and Navajo Common Law*. Minneapolis: University of Minnesota Press, 2009.

Deloria, Vine, Jr., and Clifford Lytle. *American Indians, American Justice*. Austin: University of Texas Press, 1983.

Fletcher, Matthew L. M. *American Indian Tribal Law*. Austin, Tex.: Wolters Kluwer Law and Business, 2011.

Pommersheim, Frank. *Braid of Feathers*. Berkeley: University of California Press, 1995.

Matthew L. M. Fletcher

INITIATIVE AND REFERENDUM

These two institutions of direct democracy give American voters—acting most often through organized interest groups—the authority to propose new laws or constitutional amendments (the initiative) and to repeal laws passed by legislators (the referendum). Neither device may be used at the federal level. However, voters in twenty-four states possess the power to propose initiatives, and twenty-four states allow the referendum; these two sets of states overlap almost perfectly. Because thousands of local governments have adopted the initiative and referendum, 71 percent of Americans now live in a city or state that employs direct democracy. All of this has created a governing experiment across the United States; democracy is purely representative at the federal level, whereas nearly half of the states have combined both representative and direct democratic institutions to build a hybrid form of democracy.

Direct democracy has both ancient and modern roots. Athenians practiced direct democracy, and it was revived in Switzerland's canton governments during the late nineteenth century. Explicitly patterning themselves on the Swiss, many of America's Populist and then Progressive reformers at the turn of the century pushed state legislators and governors to give a direct vote to the people. Beginning with South Dakota's adoption of the initiative and referendum in 1898, a total of twenty states enacted direct democracy reforms by 1918. This shift was most pronounced in the West, where nascent governments proved more amenable to the democratic experiment, but the initiative also appears in states such as Florida, Michigan, and Maine and in a list of cities that includes Houston, Columbus, and New York City. Adoption was most likely where the Populist and Progressive movements were strong, where there was tight political competition, and where the electorates that would be empowered were relatively homogenous.

Initiative and referendum provisions differ in their crucial details, which leads to differences in their patterns of use and in electoral success. All states and cities require voter signatures to propose initiatives or to call referendums on laws, but they differ in the percentage of voters who are required to sign petitions.

Once one of these proposals reaches the ballot, it must receive broad voter support, but in some instances supermajority support is required. States and localities also vary in whether they allow elected lawmakers to amend successful initiatives. Because of these differences, initiative usage ranges from five to ten ballot measures per decade in Nebraska and Idaho to thirty-five to fifty measures per decade in Oregon and Colorado, and passage rates vary from 35 percent in California to 70 percent in Florida. Across the nation, use of the referendum to overturn existing laws is relatively rare.

The rationale behind giving voters a direct voice in government is consistent and clear. Direct democracy has been prescribed as a cure for the ills of representative government, because its use (or the mere threat of its use) should bring policy in line with what the average voter wants rather than what a legislature corrupted by interest groups favors. In the words of a Montana governor who was an early proponent of the initiative, "It is the sure weapon with which to put to flight the briber and the lobbyist, and drive them, like Hagar, to the wilderness."

Although modern studies of the effectiveness of direct democracy have yielded mixed findings, the weight of the evidence is that states with the initiative produce policies that are more closely aligned with voter sentiment than states with purely representative democracies. Voter turnout and engagement also appears to rise when voters possess and use the initiative. Yet critics point out that voters are often confused by long ballots filled with complex propositions. Also, moneyed interests now dominate direct democracy in the same way that they once controlled legislatures, spending $478 million on California's ballot measures in November 2008 alone. Some observers worry that direct democracy empowers a tyrannous majority to work against minority interests, and still others are concerned that the will of the voters is flouted when legislators and governors fail to implement initiatives faithfully. Over a century after its initial adoption in America, there are calls to reform this reform. Yet polls show that although many voters are uneasy about how direct democracy operates in practice, they are loathe to give up the power to make or reject laws themselves.

[*See also* **Populist Party; Progressive Party of 1912;** ***and*** **State Governments.**]

BIBLIOGRAPHY

Bowler, Shaun, Todd Donovan, and Caroline J. Tolbert. *Citizens as Legislators: Direct Democracy in the United States*. Columbus: Ohio State University Press, 1998.

Broder, David S. *Democracy Derailed: Initiative Campaigns and the Power of Money*. New York: Harcourt, 2008.

Gerber, Elisabeth R., Arthur Lupia, Mathew D. McCubbins, and D. Roderick Kiewiet. *Stealing the Initiative: How State Government Responds to Direct Democracy*. Upper Saddle River, N.J.: Prentice Hall, 2001.

Gerber, Elisabeth R. *The Populist Paradox: Interest Group Influence and the Promise of Direct Legislation*. Princeton, N.J.: Princeton University Press, 1999.

Goebel, Thomas. *A Government by the People: Direct Democracy in America, 1890–1940*. Chapel Hill: University of North Carolina Press, 2002.

Matsusaka, John G. *For the Many or the Few: The Initiative, Public Policy, and American Democracy*. Chicago: University of Chicago Press, 2004.

Piott, Steven L. *Giving Voters a Voice: The Origins of the Initiative and Referendum in America*. Columbia: University of Missouri Press, 2003.

Thad Kousser

IN RE DEBS

See **Debs, In re.**

INSTITUTE OF PACIFIC RELATIONS

Founded in 1925 by Stanford University president Ray Lyman Wilbur, the businessman Frank Atherton, and Merle Davis, who, like many others, was formerly linked to the Young Men's Christian Association (YMCA), the Institute for Pacific Relations (IPR) sought to advance understanding of Asia through conferences with Asian leaders, annual meetings, research, and publications. By 1939, eleven national IPR councils had been established in the United States, Canada, Australia, New Zealand, China, Japan, the Philippines, the Soviet Union, the Netherlands, Great Britain, and France. From the start, the American council exerted the greatest influence because of its size (nearly 1,400 members by 1939) and fund-raising abilities. In the 1930s, under Edward C. Carter, secretary of the American council and later secretary-general of IPR itself, IPR became the premier organization for the study of Asia. It published *Pacific Affairs* and *Eastern Survey;* gave scholarly research grants; and provided reliable information to scholars, the government, and the public at a time when such information was scarce. The respected Asian scholar Owen Lattimore, who edited *Pacific Affairs* from 1933 to 1941, brought to the post a wealth of experience; insatiable curiosity; and impressive language proficiency in Chinese, Mongolian, and Russian.

Despite its nonpartisan beginnings, IPR became embroiled in controversy in the 1940s, when some members resigned over what they considered its left-leaning slant. Principal among the disgruntled was the textile importer Alfred Kohlberg, who charged Lattimore and others with turning the organization into a front for Communist propaganda. Senator Joseph McCarthy picked up these charges in the early 1950s, particularly targeting Lattimore, who had moved to Johns Hopkins University. IPR never recovered; its membership declined, and it ended in 1960. In its heyday, however, IPR stood high among international nongovernmental organizations seeking to expand knowledge of Asia and to bring scholarly expertise to bear on the shaping of international relations.

[*See also* **Anti-Communism; Asian Americans;** ***and*** **McCarthy, Joseph.**]

BIBLIOGRAPHY

Newman, Robert P. *Owen Lattimore and the "Loss" of China.* Berkeley: University of California Press, 1992.

Thomas, John N. *The Institute of Pacific Relations: Asian Scholars and American Politics.* Seattle: University of Washington Press, 1974.

T. Christopher Jespersen

INSULAR CASES

In twenty-four cases decided between 1901 and 1922, the U.S. Supreme Court held that the Constitution does not apply automatically to territories acquired by the nation. Badly divided initially, the Court later unanimously held that the Constitution applied only after Congress had "incorporated" a territory into the United States.

Following the Spanish–American War, the United States acquired the islands of Puerto Rico and the Philippines (thus the name "Insular" cases). Almost immediately, a dispute arose over whether the national government could tax goods imported from its newly acquired territory. The dispute involved two sources. First, the Constitution required that duties be uniform throughout "the United

States"; second, tariff laws imposed tariffs on goods imported from "foreign" countries. If the island territories were part of the United States, goods imported from them could not be taxed. From that mundane problem emerged constitutional issues of great significance, in particular whether the Bill of Rights applied to the newly acquired territories. Behind the language lay issues of race and cultural hegemony: Were people in the territories "fit" for constitutional protections? Should the United States impose its constitutional values on other cultures?

In the most important of the early cases, *Downes v. Bidwell* (1901), the Court failed to agree on a rationale for its conclusion that a duty could be imposed on goods imported from Puerto Rico because it was not part of "the United States." In announcing the Court's conclusion, Justice Henry Billings Brown explained that a territory could not become a "state" until Congress said it was. Chief Justice Melville W. Fuller dissented, reasoning that the Constitution applied to every action taken by Congress. Between those two positions fell the concurring opinion of Justice Edward D. White, who proposed that the Constitution applied only to territories that had been "incorporated" into the United States and that incorporation could come only from an act of Congress. The entire Court eventually adopted White's interpretation, first in a majority opinion, *Dorr v. United States* (1904), and later in a unanimous decision, *Balzac v. Puerto Rico* (1922).

The Insular case decisions placed the Supreme Court's imprimatur on overseas expansion, allowing the president and Congress great flexibility in international affairs. Never having been overruled, the doctrine of the Insular cases has continuing vitality, especially in the efforts to enforce U.S. laws outside its borders and in the U.S. involvement in international organizations.

[*See also* **Bill of Rights; Supreme Court, U.S.;** *and* **Tariffs.**]

BIBLIOGRAPHY

Kerr, James E. *The Insular Cases: The Role of the Judiciary in American Expansionism*. Port Washington, N.Y.: Kennikat Press, 1982.

Walter F. Pratt Jr.

INTERNAL SECURITY ACT

Also known as the McCarran Act. Enacted during the early Cold War, shortly after the Soviet Union's detonation of an atomic bomb and North Korea's invasion of South Korea, the Internal Security Act of 1950 expressed the nation's growing fear of Communism, both at home and abroad, in the so-called McCarthy Era. Its main intention was to control the spread of domestic subversion. Title I—"The Subversive Activity Control Act"—required "Communist-action" organizations and "Communist front" organizations to register with the Justice Department. The original sponsors of this measure were Senator Karl E. Mundt (R-SD) and Representative Richard M. Nixon (R-CA). The act also contained provisions for the exclusion and deportation of, and the denial of passports to, Communists and other "subversives."

Title II—"The Emergency Detention Act"—provided for the detention of potential espionage agents and subversives whenever the president proclaimed an "internal security emergency." Sponsored by seven Democratic senators as a substitute for Title I, it was added to the Internal Security Act through the efforts of Nixon, Mundt, and Senator Patrick McCarran (D-NV), the bill's chief sponsor.

The measure became law on 23 September 1950, after Congress overrode a veto by

President Harry S. Truman. The registration and other measures of Title I were challenged in the courts until declared unconstitutional by the U.S. Supreme Court in *Aptheker v. Secretary of State* (1964) and *Albertson v. Subversive Activities Control Board* (1965). The "Emergency Detention Act" was repealed by Congress in 1972 during Nixon's presidency and the controversial Vietnam War protests.

[*See also* **Anti-Communism; Federal Government, Executive Branch: Department of Justice; McCarthy, Joseph;** *and* **Nixon, Richard M.**]

BIBLIOGRAPHY

Latham, Earl. *The Communist Controversy in Washington*. Cambridge, Mass.: Harvard University Press, 1966.

Tanner, William R., and Robert Griffith. "Legislative Politics and 'McCarthyism': The Internal Security Act of 1950." In *The Specter*, edited by Robert Griffith and Athan Theoharis. New York: New Viewpoints, 1974.

William R. Tanner

INTERSTATE COMMERCE ACT

An 1887 regulatory law. Railroads were the earliest major corporations whose interests transcended state boundaries. In some places, railroads competed for traffic, but over long stretches of their tracks they were monopolies. As common carriers, they were forbidden by their charters to discriminate among customers. Nevertheless, to lure traffic between competitive points, railroads offered larger shippers rebates—and charged less for a competitive long haul than for a monopolistic short haul. With their prosperity threatened by railroad pricing practices, farmers, merchants, communities, and even entire regions turned to politics for redress. Abandoning their free-market laissez-faire notions, protestors convinced several states to regulate railroads.

The U.S. Supreme Court upheld state regulation of railroads in *Munn v. Illinois* (1876) and then reversed itself in *Wabash v. Illinois* (1886), triggering demands in the West and the South for federal action. In 1887, Congress passed the Interstate Commerce Act (ICA), designed to prevent railroad rate discrimination. The only significant opposition came from the Northeast and California. Since divergent bills had passed the House and Senate, the ICA was a compromise measure that incorporated some provisions that railroads opposed and other features that reformers disliked. The ICA tried to eliminate price discrimination between long and short hauls, required railroads to charge their published rates, and established the Interstate Commerce Commission (ICC) to administer the law.

The ICC worked effectively until 1897, when the Supreme Court outlawed its power to set rates and to prevent the long-haul/short-haul abuse. During the Progressive Era, Congress amended the ICA through the Hepburn Act (1906), giving the ICC the power to set maximum freight rates and extending its jurisdiction to express companies and oil pipelines. In 1910, the Mann–Elkins Act again empowered the ICC to enforce the long-haul/short-haul clause. Following World War I, the Esch–Cummins Transportation Act of 1920 amended the ICA by granting the ICC enormous power to consolidate railroads into about twenty competing systems and to regulate minimum rates as well as maximum ones. The Motor Carrier Act of 1935 subjected the trucking industry to ICC regulation, and the Transportation Act of 1940 gave the ICC jurisdiction over water carriers, while ordering it to protect equally all modes of transportation.

Railroads declined after World War II, partly because minimum-rate regulation prevented them from competing successfully with motor and water carriers. In the Transportation Act of 1958, Congress attempted but failed to clarify minimum-rate policy by giving the ICC two contradictory tasks: preserving rail, motor, and water carriers while also promoting competition among them. That act also facilitated railroads' abandonment of passenger service, which had become unprofitable because of airline competition. By the 1970s and 1980s, critics declared the much-amended ICA a failure.

Presidents and Congress agreed. The Motor Carrier Act of 1980 deregulated the trucking business, and the Staggers Rail Act (1980) allowed railroads to compete with trucks. In 1982, Congress reduced the ICC from eleven to five members, and in 1985 the Office of Management and Budget proposed that the ICC be abolished. With budget-cutting mania sweeping Washington, that proposal was carried out, and the Interstate Commerce Act became a dead letter on 31 December 1995.

[*See also* **Economic Policy: Regulation; Granger Laws; Granger Movement; Hepburn Act;** *and* **Regulatory Agencies, Federal.**]

BIBLIOGRAPHY

Hoogenboom, Ari, and Olive Hoogenboom. *A History of the ICC: From Panacea to Palliative.* New York: W. W. Norton, 1976.

Ari Hoogenboom

INTERSTATE HIGHWAYS

On 29 June 1956, President Dwight D. Eisenhower signed the Federal-Aid Highway Act of 1956 into law. The act accomplished two goals that had eluded advocates of express highway construction for decades. Title I authorized $25 billion over thirteen years to build 41,000 miles of limited-access, high-speed routes as part of an interstate highway program. Title II created the Highway Trust Fund to finance the construction of this system. Federal Bureau of Public Roads (BPR) officials first designated rural portions of this system in 1944 to meet the needs of increased automobile travel, which had grown by 600 percent between 1921 and 1941. Although Eisenhower signed the bill unceremoniously while recovering from surgery at Walter Reed Army Medical Center, no one who had studied highway development could have doubted that the interstate system would have a decisive impact on the spatial geography and socioeconomic contours of American life.

Getting on the Interstate. Interstate highways were not a novel idea in 1956. Congress had considered a national interstate highway program as early as 1912, but such a centralized system was inconsistent with the exceptionally local and rural nature of early twentieth-century road-building practices. Most roads were then cared for under a labor tax assessed by towns and supervised by pathmasters, local officials responsible for the annual upkeep of short stretches of dirt roads. When Congress acted, it adopted a more cooperative approach, embodied in the Federal-Aid Highway Act of 1916. Under this legislation and its 1921 reauthorization, the federal government, still favoring rural areas, offered matching grants to states for farm-to-market roads and, later, intercity highways.

BPR chief Thomas H. MacDonald (1919–1953) closely guided the state highway departments responsible for this construction. But in 1937, when the Pennsylvania Turnpike Commission began work on the nation's first limited-access automobile toll road, MacDonald worried that a wave of state toll road construction would undermine the system of free roads built under his watch. A 1939 report, *Toll Roads and Free Roads,* made the case for a system of federally financed interstate highways, which was mapped and incorporated into the Federal-Aid Highway Act of 1944. Despite this legislative support, long-standing conflicts confined the interstates to paper. Truckers wanted more freight routes but resisted further taxation; automobile lobbyists sought an end to urban congestion; farmers prioritized rural roads; leaders of large and small states quibbled over federal apportionment formulas; and economists insisted that construction be tied to national economic growth. As bitter divisions persisted, toll road construction quickened and state highway officials contemplated road modernization plans should Congress fail to implement the interstate program.

Eisenhower had been a highway advocate since World War I, when his army convoy became bogged down on a cross-country journey. In 1954, he supported interstate highway construction as a long-term economic driver that would enjoy broad national support. Nonetheless, it took two years of negotiation to hammer out legislation that offered something to all parties. The measure relied on 90 percent federal financing for a national system of interstate and defense highways, accelerating construction of the interstate system as part of a national economic stimulus, while requiring continued attention to rural roads. The Highway Trust Fund (HTF) supported toll-free interstates with dedicated revenue from federal taxes on fuel, tires, and truck sales. This assured motorists and truckers—the groups who primarily financed interstate construction—that gas tax revenue would not be diverted to nonhighway uses. It also illustrated the depth of Americans' commitment to automobility and to the idea that mobility and freedom were synonymous terms, each served by maximizing the unfettered movement of people and goods by cars and trucks.

Interstate Highways and Their Critics. The Interstate Highway System was primarily constructed between 1956 and 1973. By the 1990s, all but a few segments had been completed, and the system, ultimately covering 42,795 miles, cost over $125 billion. Construction generated both immediate and long-term growth, particularly as economic sectors reorganized to take advantage of the cost savings afforded by safer, high-speed travel. Interstate supporters argued that these new corridors integrated marginal regions into the national economy, while rescuing cities' congested central business districts.

Critics quickly appeared on the scene. As state and federal engineers routed interstates through mountainsides and rural landscapes, they produced an unchecked monotony that troubled many observers. As novelist John Steinbeck declared, the interstate highway made it "possible to drive from New York to California without seeing a single thing." In the cities, this same triumphal engineering produced what critics described as a kind of architectural brutalism. Arterial highways and mammoth interchanges—walls of concrete and steel when viewed at street level—displaced hundreds of thousands of residents. The goals of traffic service and urban renewal provided city politicians with the opportunity to demolish working-class neighborhoods and to sharpen racial segregation, while redirecting land use toward high-end real estate development.

The sheer scale of destruction caused by routing expressways through neighborhoods, historic districts, parks, and waterfronts produced a wave of citizen backlash. A 1959 grassroots movement in San Francisco halted construction of the Embarcadero Freeway, and resistance increased throughout the 1960s. Congress lent support to Freeway Revolt activists with the Federal-Aid Highway Act of 1962, which made assistance for transportation projects in urban areas contingent upon a continuing, comprehensive, and cooperative planning process. Still, freeway opponents had only mixed success until 1967, when they gained a powerful ally in Alan S. Boyd, secretary of the newly created U.S. Department of Transportation (DOT). Sensing the public mood, Boyd broke with federal highway engineers and validated the protesters' concerns. A year later, the Federal-Aid Highway Act of 1968 mandated new safeguards, providing relocation assistance for those displaced by highways and securing protection for wildlife refuges, parks, and historic sites. The National Environmental Policy Act of 1969 and the Clean Air Act of 1970 further emboldened environmental activists to adopt a strategy of litigate and delay, slowing the tide of interstate construction in contested areas.

Although antifreeway activists achieved victory in several areas, the system steadily approached completion by 1973. At that point, Congress released a small fraction of HTF dollars to urban transit, allowing cities to use 90 percent federal funding for noninterstate purposes for the first time. The disparity between road and transit support remained enormous until 1991, when Congress passed the Intermodal Surface Transportation Efficiency Act (ISTEA). This legislation opened HTF money to a wide array of transportation initiatives from bicycle paths to airports. ISTEA also mandated that transportation planning decisions be made by metropolitan planning organizations rather than be dictated by state and federal engineers. This shift toward locally sensitive, multimodal transportation planning marked the end of the interstate highways' dominance in American transportation.

Even as interstate construction slowed, the highways continued to transform America. Contrary to its designers' intent, the system proved more adept at fostering urban flight and sprawl than at salvaging central business districts. The highways thus facilitated a tremendous demographic shift to the suburbs and exurbs, generating new patterns of decentralized living and working that intensified dependence on cars and trucks. Between 1960 and 1990, the number of people who worked outside their county of residence jumped from 9 million to 27.5 million, whereas the number of workers commuting by private vehicle leapt from 43 million to 101 million during the same period. In addition to the social costs of unchecked suburban growth, increased road use placed new pressures on the highway system itself. In 1998, Congress passed a $217 billion public works bill, the largest in its history, to repair, expand, or dismantle the crumbling roads. Despite federal support, the transport finance crisis remained so severe that some states turned to privatization schemes, leasing highways in exchange for multibillion dollar cash infusions.

In the twenty-first century, urban leaders continue to debate the future of interstate highways, with cities from Seattle to Providence tearing down (and often rerouting) urban segments of the interstates to reclaim city street systems. Boston's Central Artery/Tunnel, completed in 2006 at a cost exceeding $15 billion, included a massive highway teardown and a costly underground expansion, building 160 new lane miles through (and below) the city of Boston. The nation's costliest urban megaproject, it was also one of the last to receive federal aid under the interstate formula. Fifty years after Congress first funded the interstate program, this culminating project revealed Americans' essentially unaltered commitment to the automobile and to bearing its social, environmental, and economic costs. In 2009, U.S. DOT secretary Ray LaHood argued that, having completed work on the interstates, new transportation initiatives should serve "livable" communities that were no longer dependent upon automobiles. But absent political consensus, a long-range transportation plan, and a dedicated revenue stream, LaHood's vision lacked precisely the elements that made the Federal-Aid Highway Act of 1956 such transformative public policy.

[*See also* **Eisenhower, Dwight D.**]

BIBLIOGRAPHY

Guttfruend, Owen. *Twentieth-Century Sprawl: Highways and the Reshaping of the American Landscape*. Oxford; New York: Oxford University Press, 2004.

Ladd, Brian. *Autophobia: Love and Hate in the Automotive Age*. Chicago; London: University of Chicago Press, 2008.

Mohl, Raymond, "The Interstates and the Cities: The U.S. Department of Transportation and the Freeway Revolt, 1966–1973," *Journal of Policy History* 20 (2008): 193–226.

Rose, Mark. *Interstate: Express Highway Politics, 1939–1989*. Knoxville: University of Tennessee Press, 1990.

Seely, Bruce E. *Building the American Highway System: Engineers as Policy Makers*. Philadelphia: Temple University Press, 1987.

Michael R. Fein

IRAN-CONTRA AFFAIR

The Iran-Contra affair surfaced in 1986–1987 when evidence became public that President Ronald Reagan's National Security Council (NSC) staff had secretly sold arms to Iran, used the profits to provide aid to the Contra forces opposing Nicaragua's leftist government—aid expressly prohibited by Congress in 1984—and then concealed the truth by lying to Congress and destroying evidence.

The affair began in 1985 when, at Israel's urging, Reagan secretly approved selling TOW antitank (and later antiaircraft) missiles to Iran for use in its war against Iraq, which was viewed by Israel as its most dangerous enemy. Although Reagan had publicly vowed never to negotiate with hostage-takers, he hoped that the aid would encourage Tehran to facilitate the release of nine American hostages held in Beirut, including agents of the Central Intelligence Agency (CIA). Some hostages were indeed released, but others were taken. As Reagan continued to approve arms shipments to Iran in 1986, Secretary of State George Schultz and Defense Secretary Caspar Weinberger objected, arguing that the shipments contradicted administration policy and violated a U.S. embargo imposed on Iran in 1979 because of its anti-American policies.

In November 1986, a Lebanese journal embarrassed the administration by revealing the arms shipments. At the same time, Attorney General Edwin Meese informed Reagan that NSC staff, led by Lieutenant Colonel Oliver North, had illegally diverted the arms-sale profits to buy military supplies for the Contras. North, an embittered Vietnam War veteran, hated Communism and was determined to defeat Nicaragua's revolutionary government at any price. The diversion, however, was probably initiated by CIA Director William Casey, who died of a brain tumor just as the illegalities surfaced. Reagan appointed a review board led by the former senator John Tower of Texas. Its March 1987 report chastised the president for not controlling his administration and sharply criticized White House Chief of Staff Donald Regan, who resigned.

Later that spring, a joint House–Senate investigative committee uncovered crimes, including lying to Congress and destroying evidence, by North and his superiors, National Security Advisers Robert McFarlane and John Poindexter. The committee's televised hearing, especially the riveting testimony by Oliver North in full-dress Marine uniform, captured the nation's attention. The committee's report concluded that the actions had been concealed not for security reasons, as the administration claimed, but to circumvent the law to the detriment of America's democratic institutions. President Reagan was again judged an incompetent administrator, but he was found to have been unaware of the diversion of the arms' profits to the Contras. Meanwhile, independent prosecutor Lawrence Walsh, appointed by Attorney General Meese, charged 14 persons with crimes. Eleven pleaded guilty or were convicted. An appeals court overturned North's and Poindexter's convictions on technicalities. In 1992, President George Bush pardoned six others.

The Iran-Contra affair, the nadir of the Reagan presidency, formed a chapter in the long struggle between Congress and the executive branch over control of foreign policy. It also exemplified how officials could come to justify criminal activity in fighting what they considered righteous battles, even if a majority in Congress and the American public disagreed.

[*See also* **Anti-Communism; National Security Council;** *and* **Reagan, Ronald.**]

BIBLIOGRAPHY

Draper, Theodore. *A Very Thin Line: The Iran-Contra Affair*. New York: Hill and Wang, 1991.

Walsh, Lawrence. *Final Report of the Independent Counsel for Iran/Contra Matters*. Washington, D.C.: U.S. Court of Appeals for the District of Columbia Circuit, 1993.

Walter LaFeber

J

JACKSON, ANDREW

(1767–1845), seventh president of the United States, founder of the Democratic party. Born in Waxhaw, South Carolina, to Scotch-Irish immigrants, Jackson fought as a boy in the Revolutionary War, studied law, and in 1788 moved west to Nashville. In 1791, he married Rachel Robards, believing that her divorce had been finalized. When this proved incorrect, they were remarried in 1794. Malicious rumors relating to the contretemps followed Jackson throughout his career. After serving as a Tennessee prosecutor, judge, congressman, senator, and militia general, he won fame in the War of 1812 with smashing victories against the Creek Indians in 1814 and against the British at the Battle of New Orleans in January 1815.

His triumph at New Orleans, which eventually acquired an almost mythical coloring, gave Jackson a heroic stature unrivaled since George Washington. In 1818, he pursued Seminole Indians into Spanish Florida, creating an international incident. Appointed military governor of Florida (1821), he again served in the Senate in 1823–1825. In a confused, four-candidate presidential race in 1824, Jackson led the popular and electoral vote but lost in the House of Representatives to John Quincy Adams through the machinations of Henry Clay. Jackson challenged Adams again in 1828 and defeated him. The campaign introduced new vote-getting techniques but also exhibited a sectional pattern, with Jackson sweeping the South and West. In 1832, Jackson easily defeated Henry Clay.

Elected president more for his patriotic persona than for his largely unformed political views, Jackson carved out a policy while in office and in doing so shaped his diffuse electoral coalition into an organized political party. He replaced many government officials on partisan grounds, inaugurating the so-called spoils system. Serving his core southwestern constituency, he condemned abolitionism, advocated cheaper public lands, and strong-armed Indian tribes into moving west of the Mississippi. In a confrontation between Georgia and the Cherokee Nation, Jackson backed state authority against tribal sovereignty and refused to protect Indians' treaty rights despite a ruling by U.S. Supreme Court Chief Justice John Marshall.

Jackson's presidency defined itself in two central episodes: the nullification crisis and the "Bank War." Jackson took office amid mounting sectional acrimony over the American System, a program of fostering economic development through protective tariffs and transportation improvements, policies that many southerners condemned as promoting northern growth at their expense. Jackson curbed the American System by vetoing congressional transportation subsidies (most famously the Maysville Road in 1830) on constitutional grounds and urging a lower tariff. When South Carolina, led by John Calhoun, declared the 1828 tariff null and void in 1832 and prepared to resist its collection, Jackson acted quickly to uphold federal supremacy, by force if necessary. In a ringing proclamation he declared the country indivisible and nullification tantamount to treason. With Jackson's blessing, Congress lowered the tariff in 1833, and South Carolina backed down.

Another element in the American System was the Bank of the United States, a privately managed institution chartered by Congress to provide a stable currency and handle the government's finances. Following Thomas Jefferson, Jackson deemed a national bank dangerous and unconstitutional. In 1832, he vetoed a bill engineered by bank president Nicholas Biddle (1786–1844) to renew its charter, scheduled to expire in 1836. His veto message counterposed the virtuous plain people against the bank's privileged stockholders. The following year, he transferred the federal government's deposits to selected state-chartered banks, triggering a brief financial panic and prompting the Senate to censure him in 1834. Undeterred, Jackson launched a broader assault against all forms of government-granted special privileges, including corporate charters. His farewell address in 1837 warned of the insidious "money power." After his presidency, Jackson retired to the Hermitage, his cotton plantation near Nashville, where he died.

Jackson's Bank War and its populistic, egalitarian rhetoric provided the platform and vocabulary for the emerging Democratic Party. (His policies also arguably helped trigger the Panic of 1837, which deepened into a severe depression.) By casting himself as the people's tribune against the moneyed elite and their tools in government, he introduced an enduring theme in American politics. Jackson exercised executive powers vigorously, defying Congress, vetoing more bills than all his predecessors, and frequently reshuffling his cabinet.

Jackson's political philosophy adapted Jeffersonian precepts to a developing democratizing society. Combining energetic nationalism and attacks on privilege with laissez-faire and limited government policies, Jackson appealed simultaneously to the longing of many Americans for a purer republic and to their ambition for a more open future. Strong-willed and sharp-tempered, a fierce patriot and rabid partisan, Jackson himself was always controversial. For him, politics was personal, whether the opponent was Henry Clay, John Marshall, John Calhoun, or Nicholas Biddle. A cabinet crisis erupted in 1829 when the wife of Vice President Calhoun ostracized Peggy Eaton, the daughter of a Washington innkeeper and wife of Jackson's secretary of war. Jackson defended Peggy, and the resulting controversy helped push Calhoun into opposition and open the way for Martin Van Buren, Jackson's 1832 running mate, to win the presidency in 1836.

Andrew Jackson was both a champion and a symbol of democracy, the first westerner and self-made man to achieve the presidency, yet also a wealthy slaveholder. The preeminent public figure between Jefferson and Abraham Lincoln, he dominated and gave his name to an era.

[*See also* **Adams, John Quincy; Calhoun, John C.; Clay, Henry; Democratic Party; Federal Government, Executive Branch: Presidency, The; Jefferson, Thomas; Monetary Policy; Nullification; Spoils System; Tariffs; Van Buren, Martin;** ***and*** **Veto Power.**]

BIBLIOGRAPHY

Feller, Daniel. *The Jacksonian Promise: America, 1815–1840.* Baltimore: Johns Hopkins University Press, 1995.

Pessen, Edward. *Jacksonian America,* rev. ed. Urbana: University of Illinois Press, 1978.

Remini, Robert V. *Andrew Jackson,* 3 vols. New York: Harper & Row, 1977–1984.

Schlesinger, Arthur M., Jr. *The Age of Jackson.* Boston: Little, Brown, 1945.

Sellers, Charles. *The Market Revolution: Jacksonian America.* New York: Oxford University Press, 1991.

Ward, John William. *Andrew Jackson: Symbol for an Age.* New York: Oxford University Press, 1955.

Watson, Harry L. *Liberty and Power: The Politics of Jacksonian America.* New York: Hill and Wang, 1990.

Daniel Feller

JAPANESE AMERICAN INTERNMENT

Internment is the common (if imprecise) term for the mass removal and confinement of 120,000 ethnic Japanese from the Pacific coast during World War II. Although presented as a national security measure, internment reflected a history of prewar anti-Japanese prejudice. Japanese immigrants (Issei) were legally barred from land ownership in California, ineligible for citizenship, and ultimately excluded from further entry. Their children, the Nisei (second-generation U.S. citizens) faced educational and job discrimination.

During the 1930s, as relations between the United States and Japan grew strained, West Coast Japanese communities were subjected to official surveillance. In the days following the Japanese attack on Pearl Harbor in December 1941, hundreds of Issei previously marked as community leaders were detained and interned. Nevertheless, over the following weeks, military officials in California, led by West Coast defense commander general John DeWitt, became panicked over a potential Japanese invasion. Charging that Issei and Nisei were members of an "enemy race" and potential spies and saboteurs—although there were no documented cases of disloyal activity by Japanese Americans—Army officials demanded their expulsion from the West Coast. The campaign for removal was abetted by West Coast nativist and commercial groups anxious to eliminate their economic competitors and by opportunistic political leaders.

The pressure from the West Coast led President Franklin Roosevelt and his War Department chiefs to support "evacuation." On 19 February 1942, Roosevelt signed Executive Order 9066, which formed the legal basis for mass removal (a policy subsequently adjudged constitutional by the U.S. Supreme Court). West Coast Japanese Americans, irrespective of citizenship, were taken from their homes without charge and herded under military guard into "assembly centers," disused fairgrounds and racetracks where they were housed in stables and animal pens. After several months, the inmates were transported inland to a network of "relocation centers" operated by a new civilian agency, the War Relocation Authority. These were camps in remote desert and swamp areas, surrounded by barbed wire and armed sentries. The inmates were housed in hastily built tarpaper shacks, one room to a family. Health care and sanitary facilities were generally primitive, and food was limited and of poor quality until inmates were able to grow their own. Maximum salaries for inmate laborers were set at $19 per month. The hardships of camp life and stigma of arbitrary imprisonment led to widespread tension and sparked several inmate strikes and riots.

Government leaders soon recognized that their fears of widespread disloyalty by Japanese Americans were misplaced. To increase manpower and allow Japanese Americans to demonstrate their loyalty, Army chiefs created a volunteer (later conscript) all-Nisei combat battalion, the 442nd Regimental Combat Team, even as the WRA attempted to resettle inmates outside the West Coast by instituting a cumbersome and avowedly unconstitutional "parole" procedure involving "loyalty" examinations. However, their attempts to test the loyalty of the inmates led to further misery, and those deemed "disloyal" were segregated and locked in a high-security camp at Tule Lake. In the end, most Japanese Americans remained confined until the war's end. The camps were closed in 1946.

In 1944 the Supreme Court upheld the constitutionality of exclusion in *Korematsu v. United States* in a 6-to-3 decision, but in *ex parte Endo* unanimously declared that concededly loyal citizens, regardless of ethnicity, could not be detained without cause. In July 1948, Congress passed the Japanese Evacuation Claims Act allowing internees to apply for compensation, generally up to $2,500, for losses during removal. However, the former internees were required to furnish receipts or other proof of losses. This was impossible in many cases, especially as the Internal Revenue Service had destroyed most of the 1939–1942 tax records of internees. In 1988, President Ronald Reagan signed the Civil Liberties Act of 1988, providing each internee $20,000, up to $1.2 billion in total. In 1992, George H. W. Bush signed an amendment to this act providing an additional $400 million to compensate internees.

[*See also* **Roosevelt, Franklin Delano.**]

BIBLIOGRAPHY

Commission on Wartime Relocation and Internment of Civilians. *Personal Justice Denied: Report of the Commission on Wartime Relocation and Internment of Civilians.* Washington, D.C.: The Commission, 1982. Reprint, 1997.

Daniels, Roger, ed. *American Concentration Camps: A Documentary History of the Relocation and Incarceration of Japanese Americans, 1941–1945,* 9 vols. New York; London: Garland, 1989.

Hansen, Arthur, ed. *Japanese American World War II Evacuation History Project,* 5 vols. Westport, Conn.: Meckler, 1990–1992.

Taylor, Sandra C. *Jewel of the Desert: Japanese American Internment at Topaz.* Berkeley: University of California Press, 1993.

Greg Robinson

JAY, JOHN

(1745–1829), statesman, diplomat, first chief justice of the Supreme Court. Born to wealth in New York City, John Jay was a rather political lawyer until the eve of the Revolutionary War. In 1775, he became a member of the Second Continental Congress and a leader of the conservative faction that favored resistance to Britain but opposed independence. After independence, he drafted the constitution of the State of New York, served as president of Congress in 1779, became U.S. representative to Spain in 1780, and joined Benjamin Franklin and John Adams to negotiate peace with Great Britain.

Returning from Europe in 1783, Jay served Congress as secretary for foreign affairs for the next six years. Although not a member of the Constitutional Convention of 1787, he supported its efforts by helping Alexander Hamilton and James Madison write the *Federalist Papers* to defend the new Constitution. President George Washington rewarded Jay's efforts by appointing him the first chief justice of the U.S. Supreme Court. In 1794, Washington sent Jay to London to settle issues that threatened to drag the United States into war against Britain on the side of revolutionary France. The controversial concessions he made in the resultant Jay's Treaty produced a major party battle between Jay's Federalists and the Republican opposition. After two terms as governor of New York, Jay retired from politics. Overshadowed by more illustrious contemporaries, John Jay was a steady conservative contributor to the creation and survival of the new nation.

[*See also* **Adams, John; Constitution; Continental Congress; Federalism; Federalist Papers; Federalist Party; Franklin, Benjamin; Hamilton, Alexander; Madison, James; Supreme Court, U.S.;** ***and*** **Washington, George.**]

BIBLIOGRAPHY

Monaghan, Frank. *John Jay: Defender of Liberty*. New York; Indianapolis: Bobbs–Merrill, 1935.

Morris, Richard B. *John Jay, the Nation, and the Court*. Boston: Boston University Press, 1967.

Jerald A. Combs

JEFFERSON, THOMAS

At a 1962 dinner honoring fotry-nine Nobel Laureates, President John F. Kennedy identified the assembled guests as "the most extraordinary collection of talent and of human knowledge that has ever been gathered together at the White House—with the possible exception of when Thomas Jefferson dined alone." The tribute would seem hyperbolic did it not have the ring of truth. Jefferson has been called, with no little justification, the "Father of our national architecture" ("the only President of the United States who was also a great artist," Garry Wills tells us), the "founding father of American Anthropology" (he anticipated all of anthropology's major fields as well as a number of its strategies and methods, says David Hurst Thomas), and the Father of American Viticulture (he devised what one student of American pomology has called "the most comprehensive American vineyard plan that survives from the first half of the nineteenth century"). He simultaneously held the presidencies of the United States—a political office granted by the acclaim of democratic assent—and of the American Philosophical Society—a cultural and intellectual office bestowed by the assessment of an exclusive community of science, before which he presented a paper on megalonyx based on the latest fossil evidence from Virginia. Living in an age before specialization, Jefferson was as comfortable discussing natural history and mathematics as he was political theory, designing buildings as easily as he constructed the institutions that would inhabit them.

Jefferson often lamented the time he spent in public life as a distraction from these other passions and mourned the time lost for devotion to "my family, my books and farms." "Public service & private misery" he believed were "inseparably linked together," and he advised his grandson to avoid men with "a passion for politics" just "as you would from the infected subjects of yellow fever." Jefferson typically described his life in politics as a necessary, but perhaps regrettable, public obligation in terms familiar to the Virginia gentry among which he came of age: "Nature intended me for the tranquil pursuits of science, by rendering them my supreme delight. But the enormities of the times in which I have lived, have forced me to take a part in resisting them, and to commit myself on the boisterous ocean of political passions." But such assessments can deceive, as Jefferson's political enemies—many of whom underestimated his adroit understanding of the game of politics—found out. And we do not have to see such assertions as lies or evasions to wonder whether a life so devoted to politics was truly so ill suited to his deepest interests and enthusiasms.

Jefferson was born at Shadwell in what is now Albemarle County, Virginia, on 13 April 1743, the third child (and first son) of Peter Jefferson, a surveyor and public official, and Jane Randolph, through whom he was connected to one of the most prominent families of Virginia. After the death of his father in 1757, Jefferson attended the school of the Reverend James Maury, whom he called "a correct classical scholar," and he later considered himself "more indebted to [his] father" for this introduction to the classical languages "than for all the other luxuries his cares and affections have placed within my reach." Jefferson attended the College of William and Mary where he fell under the influence of mathematician William Small, from whom he later said he acquired his "first views of the expansion of science & of the system of things in which we are placed." This influence "probably fixed the destinies of my life." Jefferson read the law with George Wythe and began a successful legal practice in 1767.

Jefferson moved easily as a member of Virginia's gentry and married Martha Wayles Skelton in 1772, adding 11,000 acres of land and 135 slaves to his estate (as well as what would become an insurmountable debt) upon the death of her father the following year. Martha bore Jefferson six children in the 10 years of their marriage, only two of whom (Martha and Maria) survived to adulthood. Jefferson's 10 years with Martha, "the cherished companion of my life," were, he recalled, years of "unchequered happiness."

In 1769 Jefferson was elected to the House of Burgesses where he served until the Revolution closed it and he entered the Second Continental Congress as a delegate from Virginia. Jefferson was reticent in debate and public speaking. John Adams recalled that "during the whole time I sat with him in Congress, I never heard him utter three sentences together." But he was apparently effective in the close deliberation demanded of committees and became distinguished for his writing (Adams noted his "happy talent for composition" and the "peculiar felicity of expression" that characterized his pen), drafting many public papers for the Congress and, eventually, becoming the principal writer of the Declaration of Independence, words with which he will forever be associated.

During the Revolution, Jefferson served in the Virginia House of Delegates through 1779 when he was elected governor. He spent his years in the legislature as a member of the committee charged with revising those Virginia laws he considered "founded on principles heterogeneous to the republican spirit" of the Revolution. Among the bills he introduced as part of this reform, four of them (elimination of primogeniture and entail, public education, religious freedom, and emancipation of slaves) he considered a "system by which every fibre would be eradicated of antient or future aristocracy; and a foundation laid for a government truly republican." In all cases, the proposals sought to tear down artificial impediments to human freedom consistent with his later vow of "eternal hostility to every form of tyranny over the mind of man." The Statute for Religious Freedom, in particular, with its insistence that "the opinions of men are not the object of civil government, nor under its jurisdiction," encapsulates nicely Jefferson's libertarian commitment to preserving individual liberty and natural rights against the restraints of power, whether exercised by single tyrants or by democratic majorities.

Jefferson's two terms as governor (1779–1781) ended with a certain ignominy when Jefferson virtually abdicated his position after being forced to flee a British raid on Monticello. Jefferson was exonerated of all charges that he had failed to properly prepare the state for British invasion but the implications of personal weakness haunted him, inflicting "a wound on my spirit which will only be cured by the all-healing grave." During his brief retirement, Jefferson worked on the text of what would become his only book, *Notes on the State of Virginia,* the publication of which would bring him international fame as a philosophe and confirm his stature in the cosmopolitan republic of letters. In the *Notes,* among other things, Jefferson defended the integrity of American nature against the critique of the European scientific community, attacked slavery, praised independent farmers as the "chosen people of God," and identified economic autonomy as the foundation of American republicanism.

Jefferson returned to public life in 1783, partly in an effort to cope with the death of his wife, which plunged him into a debilitating grief. Martha's death (after the birth of their sixth child), he wrote, had "rendered me . . . dead to the world" and "left me a blank." During his brief stint in Congress, he authored the report that would be the template for the Northwest Ordinance, which paved the way for the indefinite expansion of the union of equal republics out of land in the national domain, probably the most significant achievement of Congress outside of winning the war. In December, Jefferson was appointed to assist Benjamin Franklin and John Adams in negotiating treaties of commerce with European powers. Upon Franklin's retirement in 1785, Jefferson was named American minister to France, where he remained until the autumn of 1789, witnessing the last days of the ancien régime and the opening of the French Revolution. Jefferson's years in France acquainted him firsthand with the degrading effects of monarchy and aristocracy and gave him a renewed appreciation for American republicanism. In France during most of the confederation period, Jefferson first read and evaluated the new Constitution from afar, objecting to the perpetual reeligibility of the president for election and the lack of a bill of rights, but otherwise approving the document as a significant improvement over the weak Articles of Confederation. His largely unsuccessful experience of negotiating treaties of commerce with European powers convinced him that a stronger central government with a unified and independent commercial and foreign policy would be essential to the survival of the new republic.

Shortly after ratification, Jefferson returned to Virginia to attend to his debts and reintroduce his daughters to Virginia society, but soon accepted President Washington's invitation to join his cabinet as secretary of state. Jefferson entered the administration hoping to strengthen the republican elements of the government. However, he was soon expressing shock over the "high tone" Secretary of the Treasury Alexander Hamilton had been setting for the Washington administration and the aristocratic pretensions of what he called "a sect" committed to replacing American republicanism with an "English constitution" of King, Lords, and Commons. The administration's "mimicry . . . of royal forms and ceremonies," he said, was "not at all in character with the simplicity of republican government," but instead looked "as if wishfully to those of European courts," the very European courts Jefferson had decried abroad. Jefferson's hostility to the style of the administration was soon compounded by several serious disagreements with Hamilton over policy. Jefferson urged commercial discrimination against Britain as a peaceable way to pry open European markets. But such a stance threatened to undermine Hamilton's financial program, dependent as it was upon the steady impost revenue that could only come from continued good commercial relations with Britain. In that sense, Jefferson came to believe, Hamilton's scheme went beyond favoring Britain and into subservience to a foreign government that could dictate American foreign policy, tendencies he believed confirmed by the passage of the Jay Treaty in 1795. Worse, the program seemed designed, Jefferson believed, to concentrate wealth and create a ministerial influence in the legislature that would sever the close relationship between the public and representatives demanded of republican government. Hamilton's "phalanx" in the legislature was full of "deserters from the rights & interests of the people," seeking only "to enrich themselves." Insofar as it sought to create an autonomous state with its own rationale, Hamilton's system, Jefferson told Washington, "flowed from principles adverse to liberty, & was calculated to undermine and demolish the republic."

Jefferson soon found himself identified as the head of a party opposed to many of the policies emanating from the administration, committed to federalism and a strict construction of the Constitution. Jefferson, along with his colleague Madison, began to act in some senses like a partisan leader, facilitating the publication of an opposition newspaper, coordinating the activities of legislators favorable to the "Republican" cause, and maintaining a network of Republican allies in various states. But, insofar as they were opposed in principle to the very concept of "party" politics, they kept their activities secret and justified them by identifying their beliefs with those of "the people" and characterizing their opponents—the Federalists—as a minority sect. The Republicans, then, would work to gain office only to return the Republic to its Constitutional purity, not to maintain their organization as a permanent institution. Jefferson's principles, after all, he believed, were "unquestionably the principles of the great body of our fellow citizens."

Following a brief retirement from politics (Jefferson left Washington's administration at the end of 1793), Jefferson ran second in the 1796 presidential contest and thus became vice president under John Adams (prior to the Twelfth Amendment, which distinguished votes for president and for vice president). Adams's administration soon found itself embroiled in international conflict, largely with France, in a "Quasi-War" that proved to have dangerous consequences for Republican partisans at home who resisted war. The war scare led in 1798 to electoral majorities in both houses of Congress for Federalists who prepared for military conflict and passed a series of Alien and Sedition Acts for the suppression of domestic opposition. The Sedition Act, which made criticism of the president or government a punishable crime, was particularly odious and Jefferson and Madison secretly penned resolutions that endorsed the right of states to resist (Jefferson's draft said "nullify") unconstitutional legislation coming out of Congress.

Although he kept his authorship of the Kentucky Resolutions secret, Jefferson made his political views known to key supporters who could do the work of spreading the news. A Congressional caucus of Republicans endorsed Jefferson as their candidate for president in 1800, which election he won as the result of superior organization, genuine popular enthusiasm for Jefferson's principles, and a split in the Federalist Party over Adams's controversial decision to send a peace delegation to France.

Jefferson eventually called his election the "Revolution of 1800" and exulted at the time that the people had reaffirmed American Revolutionary republicanism against Federalist efforts to "put everything into the hands of power & priestcraft." Such effusion seems confirmed somewhat less by his own close victory over Adams (and over running mate Burr) than by the majorities the Republicans gained in Congress and by his overwhelming reelection in 1804. His first inaugural address attempted to dispel the bitterness of the partisan struggle, encouraging his "fellow-citizens" to "unite with one heart and one mind" and suggesting that "every difference of opinion is not a difference of principle . . . We are all republicans, we are all federalists." True Americans were both and thus had "nothing to fear" from Jefferson's administration. Only the "incurables" among the Federalists would disagree and those could remain "undisturbed as monuments of the safety with which error of opinion may be tolerated where reason is left free to combat it." Majority rule was the "vital principle of republics," but "the minority possess their equal rights." The "State governments" were "the most competent administrations for our domestic concerns and the surest bulwarks against antirepublican tendencies," but the "General Government" would be preserved "in its whole constitutional vigor, as the sheet anchor of our peace at home and safety abroad." The "sum of good government" was simple: "restrain men from injuring one another" but "leave them otherwise free to regulate their own pursuits of industry and improvement." But this same government would also be "the strongest Government on earth" because it was "the only one where every man . . . would meet invasions of the public order as his own personal concern."

Historians have disagreed on whether Jefferson's presidency represented as stark a transformation as he implied, with some emphasizing the elimination of much of the ceremonial style admired by Federalists, significant reduction in federal spending and taxation (the government ran a budget surplus in seven of his eight years in office), trimming of the national debt, repeal of the Judiciary Act of 1801, and the purging of Federalists from the bureaucracy (and the officer corps of the Army). Others note that the administration largely maintained Hamilton's financial system and expanded the scope and power of the executive authority, eventually, in the eyes of a contemporary critic, "out-federalizing" the Federalists with more expansive readings of the Constitution than Republicans in opposition had championed. One way to reconcile these seemingly contradictory facts is to note that Jefferson's goal was always to Americanize the government. This goal was less about reduction of state power as an end than about an appropriately American confinement of government at all levels to its proper constitutional sphere and a renewed commitment to independent pursuit of the national interest. At crucial moments during his administration, then, Jefferson demonstrated a pragmatic flexibility with means toward the larger end of securing American republicanism and prosperity. Jefferson's reduction of government in some key areas and dramatic expansion of it in others, particularly in the area of foreign policy, is, by this reading, no paradox. Whether the reduction in government revenue and military readiness were appropriate to his expansive and aggressive foreign policy is another question.

The purchase of Louisiana from Napoleon in 1803—generally considered the great triumph of Jefferson's presidency—doubled the size of the United States, simultaneously removing the presence of a major European power from North America and securing a vast territory for indefinite expansion and the perpetuation of an American political economy of agrarian independence and commercial prosperity. But international conflict threatened to engulf the United States in European war as both Britain and France attacked American neutral shipping as a potential aid to their enemy. Jefferson's embargo, a grand experiment in economic coercion of the belligerents, failed to change policies abroad and nearly destroyed economy and morale at home. Enforcement of the embargo eventually required curtailment of civil liberties and a dramatic expansion of the police powers of the state beyond anything the Federalists had ever dreamed and witnessed Jefferson urging Congress to "legalize all *means* which may be necessary to obtain its end." Jefferson finished out his administration beleaguered by self-styled "Old Republican" critics who decried Jefferson's purported violation of the principles of the Republican Party and by Federalists revitalized by the embargo.

Jefferson entered his final retirement as "a prisoner, released from his chains," relishing his return to private life. He never left Virginia again. But he could not escape a sense of duty to the public as he continued an enormous correspondence; entertained friends, admirers, and the fascinated public at Monticello; and invested considerable energy in the establishment of the University of Virginia. Even the private life he idealized foundered on domestic troubles and an ever-present gloom of debt, which became debilitating when a friend, whose loan he had cosigned, defaulted. His family would lose Monticello to creditors after his death.

The problem of slavery dogged Jefferson in life and has pursued his reputation ever since. His criticism of slavery in the *Notes on the State of Virginia* and his early championing of a program of emancipation earned him the status of a progressive opponent of the institution. But his lifelong ownership of slaves, his shrinking from confrontation over the issue in later years, his racist assertions in the *Notes,* and his coupling of emancipation with colonization of free blacks on the assumption that blacks and whites could not live in the same political community have rendered his legacy on this issue a mixed one. He alternated between hope and despair over it and his sense—in darker moments—that the issue could destroy the union proved prophetic.

Jefferson died on 4 July 1826, fifty years to the day that Congress approved the Declaration of American Independence he had drafted. His final letter affirmed the world-historical significance of that moment. American republicanism would be "the signal of arousing men to burst the chains under which monkish ignorance and superstition had persuaded them to bind themselves, and to assume the blessings and security of self-government."

[*See also* **Adams, John; Declaration of Independence; Franklin, Benjamin; Hamilton, Alexander; Louisiana Purchase; Northwest Ordinance; Republicanism;** ***and*** **Washington, George.**]

BIBLIOGRAPHY

Bailey, Jeremy. *Thomas Jefferson and Executive Power.* Cambridge, UK; New York: Cambridge University Press, 2007.

Bailyn, Bernard. "Jefferson and the Ambiguities of Freedom," In *To Begin the World Anew: The Genius and Ambiguities of the American Founders,* pp. 37–59. New York: Random House, 2003.

Cogliano, Francis D. *Thomas Jefferson: Reputation and Legacy*. Edinburgh: Edinburgh University Press, 2006.
Cunningham, Noble. *The Jeffersonian Republicans*. Chapel Hill: University of North Carolina Press, 1957.
Cunningham, Noble. *The Process of Government under Jefferson*. Princeton, N.J.: Princeton University Press, 1978.
Gordon-Reed, Annette. *Thomas Jefferson and Sally Hemings: An American Controversy*. Charlottesville: University Press of Virginia, 1997.
Johnstone, Robert M., Jr. *Jefferson and the Presidency: Leadership in the Young Republic*. Ithaca, N.Y.: Cornell University Press, 1978.
Onuf, Peter. *The Mind of Thomas Jefferson*. Charlottesville: University Press of Virginia, 2007.
Onuf, Peter, and Leonard Sadosky. *Jeffersonian America*. Malden, Mass.: Blackwell, 2002.
Peterson, Merrill D. *Thomas Jefferson and the New Nation*. New York: Oxford University Press, 1970.
Sloan, Herbert. *Principle and Interest: Thomas Jefferson and the Problem of Debt*. New York: Oxford University Press, 1995.
Yarbrough, Jean. *American Virtues: Thomas Jefferson on the Character of a Free People*. Lawrence: University Press of Kansas, 1998.

Brian D. Steele

JOHN BIRCH SOCIETY

The John Birch Society was founded in 1958 by Robert H. W. Welch Jr. (1899–1985). Born in rural North Carolina, Welch became a prominent executive in the candy industry during the 1930s and a director of the National Association of Manufacturers. His political involvement began in 1950 with an unsuccessful run for office in Massachusetts as a Republican. His affiliation with the right wing of the GOP was evident in his book, *May God Forgive Us* (1952), which denounced President Harry Truman for firing General Douglas MacArthur. In 1956 Welch began to organize a network of like-minded activists around his periodical *One Man's Opinion*, which became *American Opinion*, the official organ of the John Birch Society, in 1958.

The John Birch Society was named for a Protestant missionary in China who served with U.S. military intelligence during World War II. Apparently murdered by Chinese Communists in 1945, Birch was viewed by Welch as a martyr in the crusade against Communism and the first casualty of the Cold War. Following the lead of Senator Joseph McCarthy, whom Welch lionized, the John Birch Society maintained that Vladimir Lenin had initiated an ongoing conspiracy to undermine the political, economic, and social systems of the United States. The plan to seize power from within the United States involved the active participation of covert Communists and traitors in the highest circles of government and society. In his book *The Politician*, circulated privately since 1957 and published in 1963, Welch accused President Dwight D. Eisenhower of "knowingly receiving and abiding by Communist orders, and consciously serving the Communist conspiracy for all his adult life." Although he later retracted this accusation, the Birch Society was tarred as an extreme right wing organization with paranoid views of Communist subversion in America.

Welch's anti-Communism drew scorn from the mainstream media along with the rebuke of William F. Buckley, Jr., who struggled against Welch to establish a respectable, ideologically coherent conservative movement to challenge the liberal hegemony of post–New Deal America. The extremism of the John Birch Society made it the watchword for the fringe right among the American public. Despite its radical positions, the society drew its leadership from prominent industrialists, financiers, retired military officers, and jurists. Among its directors were Colonel Laurence E. Bunker, aide-de-camp to Douglas MacArthur; Fred C. Koch, president of Rock Island Oil; and Clarence Manion, former dean of the Notre Dame Law School. By 1964 several hundred chapters of the John Birch Society had been established.

The society considered its major purpose educational; it strove to educate Americans about the dangers of Communism. Local chapters met regularly to discuss current affairs and reading rooms were founded in many cities to circulate Birch Society periodicals and books. Although chapters could be found in most states, the society was strongest in California, where it had some influence in politics. Conceiving his mission as warning the public, Welch became a tireless public speaker, pundit, and organizer. Even his foes never doubted the sincerity of his belief that America was already "60–80 percent" dominated by Communists or Communist ideology. Although the society opposed the spread of Communism anywhere in the world, it was chiefly preoccupied with what it regarded as the threat of internal subversion within the United States. Welch feared that Communism, which he considered a messianic secular ideology, was a threat to win converts in America by duping the uninformed. Some Communists, who were partners in the web of conspiracy, posed as patriotic Americans. Welch believed they had infiltrated the government, the media, and universities.

The civil rights movement netted the John Birch Society additional membership among segregationists. Welch avoided overtly racist rhetoric, but his message that the drive for African American civil rights was led by Communists appealed to militant opponents of the movement, as did his call to impeach U.S. Supreme Court Chief Justice Earl Warren for ruling that legal segregation was unconstitutional. Welch's assertion that the society numbered 60,000–100,000 members at its height in the mid 1960s cannot be supported. The estimate of 27,000 members made in 1965 by Gordon Hall, an independent researcher into extremist groups, probably represents the zenith of the society's strength.

Despite a relatively modest number of dues-paying members, the John Birch Society exerted an influence in the Republican Party through its support of Senator Barry Goldwater's 1964 presidential campaign. The society's influence also extended into the conservative wing of the Democratic Party. One of its members, U.S. Congressman Larry McDonald, was a passenger aboard the Korean Airlines plane shot down by a Soviet missile in 1983. In *None Dare Call It Treason,* Birch Society member John Stormer expounded the thesis that America's news media, schools, and churches were working to "condition" the American people to accept the triumph of Communist values. It reportedly sold over 7 million copies.

By the time of Welch's death, the John Birch Society's strength had waned, but the group continued to exist even after the collapse of the Soviet Bloc, arguing that the demise of Communism was a ploy by the Communists. Following his death, the society continued to propagate conspiracy theories and linked mainstream Republicans such as George H. W. Bush to an international Masonic conspiracy. Declaring itself as the voice of radical libertarianism, the Birch Society spread its views online through the Liberty News Network from its headquarters in Appleton, Wisconsin. It opposed the wars in Iraq and Afghanistan, warned against the advent of a world government, and advocated a limited role for the federal government in domestic life.

[***See also* Anti-Communism; Buckley, William F., Jr.; *and* Cold War.**]

BIBLIOGRAPHY

Broyles, J. Allen. *The John Birch Society: Anatomy of a Protest.* Boston, Beacon Press, 1964.

Webb, Clive. *Rabble Rousers: The American Far Right in the Civil Rights Era.* Athens, Ga.: University of Georgia Press, 2010.

Welch, Robert. *The Politician.* Belmont, Mass.: Robert Welch, 1963.

Glen Jeansonne and David Luhrssen

JOHNSON, ANDREW

(1808–1875), seventeenth president of the United States. Born in extreme poverty in Raleigh, North Carolina, Johnson in 1826 moved to Greenville, Tennessee, where he operated a tailor shop. Lacking formal education, he was taught to read and write by his wife, Eliza McCardle, whom he married in 1827, when she was 16. Johnson held a series of public offices, culminating in his election as governor in 1853 and U.S. senator in 1857. Throughout his career he stressed his plebian origins and claimed a special identification with ordinary people. Although he vigorously defended the South and slavery in Congress, he supported the Union in 1861 and was the only southern senator to refuse to resign when his state seceded. After Union troops occupied central Tennessee in 1862, President Abraham Lincoln named Johnson military governor. In 1864, he was elected Lincoln's vice president on the National Union (Republican) Party ticket.

Becoming president on 15 April 1865, following Lincoln's assassination, Johnson announced a program for reconstructing the postwar South. He built upon Lincoln's wartime policy of appointing provisional governors in the seceding states, offering amnesty to Confederates who professed future loyalty to the Union, and requiring constitutional conventions to reinstitute southern state governments. Johnson's plan required the new state governments to renounce slavery and secession, but by limiting the vote to adult white men, he assured the dominance of lawmakers unsympathetic to the rights of the free people. The reestablished governments passed legislation that denied black Southerners' political rights and circumscribed their civil rights by enacting "black codes" to replace the prewar slave codes.

The Republican-dominated Congress refused to recognize the southern state governments restored under Johnson's authority and in June 1866 responded to their racially discriminatory legislation by proposing the Fourteenth Amendment, which defined citizenship and guaranteed fundamental rights and equal protection to all. When all the Johnson-created governments but that of Tennessee rejected this amendment, Congress passed the Reconstruction Act of 1867 and supplementary legislation. These laws placed the recalcitrant states under military rule until they established new governments recognizing equal civil and political rights for all adult men regardless of race.

Supported by the Democratic Party and a few renegade Republicans, Johnson bitterly assailed Congress's civil rights and Reconstruction legislation, denying the constitutionality of these measures and using his influence and authority as president to obstruct their enforcement. His course threatened a dangerous confrontation over whether to count southern votes in the 1868 election. An initial House of Representatives effort to impeach Johnson, motivated in part by a desire to forestall the potential crisis, failed in December 1867. However, a second attempt succeeded in February 1868 after Johnson removed Secretary of War Edwin M. Stanton (1814–1869) in apparent violation of the 1867 Tenure of Office Act, which permitted removal of government officials only upon Senate confirmation of their successors.

The impeachment trial before the Senate revealed significant weaknesses in the House's case. Despite the overwhelming Republican majority in the Senate, the House managers of the impeachment narrowly failed in two key Senate votes (16 and 28 May 1868) to secure the two-thirds majority needed to convict. However, Johnson stopped obstructing the congressional Reconstruction program and served out the balance of his term without incident.

Despite opposition from former secessionists, in March 1875 a coalition of Tennessee Republicans and dissident Democrats again elected Johnson to the U.S. Senate, where he served until his death that July.

[*See also* **Civil Rights; Civil Rights Legislation; Confederate States of America; Democratic Party; Federal Government, Executive Branch: Presidency, The; Federal Government, Legislative Branch: House of Representatives; Federal Government, Legislative Branch: Senate; Fourteenth Amendment; Lincoln, Abraham; Reconstruction;** *and* **Presidential Impeachment.**]

BIBLIOGRAPHY

Benedict, Michael Les. *The Impeachment and Trial of Andrew Johnson*. New York: W. W. Norton, 1973.

Trefousse, Hans L. *Andrew Johnson: A Biography*. New York: W. W. Norton, 1989.

Michael Les Benedict

JOHNSON, HIRAM

Hiram Johnson (1866–1945) was the most important California politician in the first half of the twentieth century. He was born in Sacramento, the son a prominent California politician whose shady behavior and political invective shaped Hiram's intense devotion to honesty and his instinct for vituperative attack. After reading law and practicing with his father from 1888 to 1893, Hiram broke personally and politically with his father. Moving to San Francisco in 1902, Hiram quickly became one of the city's most prominent attorneys. Working after 1906 as a prosecutor in the city's corruption trials brought him fame and influenced his views on party politics.

After Progressive Republicans persuaded the legislature in 1908 to pass a primary election law, they convinced Johnson to run for governor in 1910. An effective speaker and clever political strategist, Johnson focused his campaign on ending the Southern Pacific Railroad's control of California politics. After his election, Johnson worked closely with the legislature in 1911 to pass strong railroad regulation plus regulation of utilities. Second, he won passage of direct democracy measures such as initiative and referendum and of laws reducing the influence of political parties. He supported various labor laws, including restricting child labor, regulation of hours and wages, and creating a system of workman's compensation, but he was silent on women's suffrage and on legislation restricting gambling and liquor. In the 1913 and 1915 legislative sessions he supported stronger labor laws, created various commission and a state water board, and backed important political changes, allowing candidates to "cross-file"—to run for the nomination of more than one party—and making nonpartisan elections for county and township offices.

By 1912 Johnson was a nationally prominent progressive leader. Supporting Theodore Roosevelt and morally outraged by President Taft's "theft" of the nomination, he ran as the Progressive Party's vice-presidential candidate. Over the next four years Johnson struggled to balance ideology and political realities: in

1914 he won reelection as a Progressive and Republican, and in 1916 he gained the Senate nomination in the Republican primary, which excluded Progressive voters.

As governor Johnson had reshaped the Golden State's political structure and culture. As a senator (1917–1945), Johnson worked mostly in opposition, a role he relished. Believing in American exceptionalism, he preached an isolationist foreign policy. Strongly opposed to the League of Nations and other international organizations, he condemned using American troops abroad and reducing the Navy, and he denounced the draft and Lend-Lease. During the 1920s Johnson remained progressive on some domestic issues, opposing tax cuts for the wealthy, supporting various labor measures, and endorsing public power and public works projects. With the onset of the Depression, Johnson pushed government action, especially on relief and banking reform, and he endorsed Franklin Roosevelt in 1932 and 1936. However, he grew increasingly unhappy with the president and with government spending and regulation. In 1937 his concerns about presidential power, sparked by the "court-packing plan," and labor militancy pushed him into open opposition to New Deal liberalism. In ill health by 1940 and suffering a stroke in 1943, Johnson spent his last years as a senator in feeble opposition to a larger federal government, a changing society, and America's expanded international role.

[*See also* **Progressive Party of 1912.**]

BIBLIOGRAPHY

Lower, Richard Coke. *A Bloc of One: The Political Career of Hiram W. Johnson.* Stanford, Calif.: Stanford University Press, 1993.

VanderMeer, Philip R. "Hiram Johnson and the Dilemmas of California Progressivism." Edited by Ballard C. Campbell. *The Human Tradition in the Gilded Age and Progressive Era.* Wilmington, Del.: SR Books, 2000.

Weatherson, Michael A. *Hiram Johnson: Political Revivalist.* Lanham, Md.: University Press of America, 1995.

Philip R. VanderMeer

JOHNSON, LYNDON B.

(1908–1973), thirty-sixth president of the United States. Lyndon Baines Johnson came from a moderately well-to-do family in the impoverished hill country of central Texas. After graduating from Southwest Texas State Teachers College in 1930, he spent a year teaching school before beginning his career in Democratic Party politics as a legislative assistant to a Texas congressman. In 1934, he married Claudia Alta ("Lady Bird") Taylor. They had two daughters.

Johnson returned to Texas in 1935 to head the state National Youth Administration office, a New Deal agency. Two years later, he won a special election to Congress, defeating a field of eight candidates by staunchly supporting the controversial programs of Franklin Delano Roosevelt, who became the first of Johnson's many powerful patrons. As a congressman, Johnson strongly supported rural electrification and won federal funding for a key dam in his district. In 1941, he lost a close race for the U.S. Senate. In a second Senate race in 1948, Johnson defeated former governor Coke Stevenson by 87 votes in an election marred by suspected voter fraud that gave rise to the nickname "Landslide Lyndon."

An extremely effective senator, Johnson moderated his New Deal liberalism without giving up his belief that the federal government should aid the less fortunate. He staunchly backed Presidents Harry S. Truman and

Dwight D. Eisenhower in waging the Cold War, making sure that Texas benefited from heavy defense spending. He continued to cultivate powerful leaders, notably House speaker Sam Rayburn (1882–1961) and Senator Richard Russell (1897–1971) of Georgia, to advance his career. In 1955, he became Senate majority leader. Criticized by liberal Democrats for his flexibility, Johnson prided himself on his ability to bargain with the Republican Eisenhower administration to secure needed legislation. Famous for his brand of personal persuasion, known as the "Johnson treatment," he helped in 1957 secure passage of the nation's first civil rights bill since Reconstruction.

LBJ, as he liked to be called, proved less successful in a 1960 presidential bid. Outmaneuvered and outspent by John F. Kennedy, Johnson finally agreed to become Kennedy's running mate to carry the South. When Kennedy won, LBJ virtually disappeared from sight as vice president. After Kennedy's assassination in November 1963, however, Johnson displayed both sensitivity and statesmanship by stressing the theme of continuity in carrying out the programs of the fallen leader. In 1964, he persuaded Congress to pass two of Kennedy's most controversial measures, a civil rights bill desegregating public accommodations and a major tax cut, as well as inaugurating his own War on Poverty. With the Minnesota liberal Hubert Humphrey as his running mate, he easily won a landslide victory over Republican Barry Goldwater, an outspoken conservative, in the 1964 presidential election.

President Johnson's greatest success in domestic policy came with the enactment of his Great Society program. Building on FDR's New Deal and Truman's Fair Deal proposals, LBJ persuaded Congress to enact more than sixty separate reform measures in 1965. The three most important Great Society achievements were greatly increased federal aid to education, the enactment of Medicare and Medicaid to provide health care for the elderly and the indigent, and a Voting-Rights Act that gave previously disenfranchised African Americans in the South the political power to protect and advance their interests. Johnson moved quickly to implement his Great Society program, capitalizing on the trauma of Kennedy's death as well as on the heavy Democratic majorities in Congress created by Goldwater's crushing defeat. Critics would charge that many of the programs were overly ambitious, inadequately funded, or carelessly administered. The Great Society, however, suffered most from LBJ's growing obsession with the Vietnam War.

Against Johnson's legislative success must be balanced his failure in foreign policy. Less sure of himself on diplomatic issues, LBJ relied on advisers he had inherited from Kennedy, who were committed to the defense of South Vietnam, a policy successively upheld by Truman, Eisenhower, and Kennedy. Instead of reassessing America's role in what was essentially a civil war, Johnson accepted the domino theory—the Cold War belief that a North Vietnamese victory would doom all of Southeast Asia to Communism. In 1964, after a presumed attack on American destroyers in the Gulf of Tonkin, he persuaded Congress to grant him unlimited power to use force to defend South Vietnam. In early 1965, U.S. warplanes began bombing North Vietnam; in July, Johnson authorized sending 50,000 American combat troops to Vietnam. Yet he refused to declare war, disguised the heavy cost of the fighting, and failed to justify the conflict to the American people. By 1968, despite the presence of more than 500,000 American troops in Vietnam, he had achieved only a costly stalemate. After the Tet offensive, a bloody setback for the enemy but a devastating blow to American confidence, Johnson rejected

Pentagon requests for an additional 200,000 troops. Instead, on 31 March amid mounting domestic protests and facing a challenge for the nomination from antiwar Democrats Eugene McCarthy and Robert Kennedy, he announced that he would not run for reelection in 1968 and would instead devote himself to peace negotiations with Hanoi. Humphrey won the nomination at a deeply divided Democratic Convention in Chicago but lost the general election to Richard M. Nixon.

Johnson spent his final years in retirement on his Texas ranch. He died of a massive heart attack on 22 January 1973, just a day before the Nixon administration signed the Paris Peace Accords ending America's direct combat role in the Vietnam War. Since that time, Johnson's reputation as president has been clouded by his failure in Vietnam. In many ways, he was a tragic figure. In Vietnam, he simply tried to carry out the policies of his predecessors. Yet his refusal to explain the war candidly to the American public, in part out of fear that it would reduce support for the Great Society, cost him dearly. At the same time, he received little acclaim for his more enduring domestic achievements. The Voting-Rights Act did help African Americans gain political office and influence; Medicare and Medicaid would give millions of elderly and impoverished citizens' access to health care. Despite later conservative counterattacks, the Great Society remained deeply embedded in modern American life. An ambitious, hard-driving politician with an outsized ego masking deep insecurities, particularly in his dealings with the wealthy, socially confident Kennedy clan, he could be devious, bullying, and crude while also displaying high idealism and great generosity of spirit.

[*See also* **Anti-Communism; Antiwar Movements; Civil Rights Legislation; Democratic Party; Education Policy: An Overview; Eisenhower, Dwight D.; Federal Government: Executive Branch: Presidency, The; Federal Government, Legislative Branch: Senate; Goldwater, Barry; Great Society; Humphrey, Hubert; Kennedy, John F.; Liberalism; Medicare and Medicaid; New Deal; Poverty; Roosevelt, Franklin Delano;** *and* **Truman, Harry S.**]

BIBLIOGRAPHY

Califano, Joseph A. *The Triumph and the Tragedy of Lyndon Johnson.* New York: Simon & Schuster, 1991.

Caro, Robert A. *The Years of Lyndon Johnson,* 2 vols. New York: Alfred A. Knopf, 1982–1990.

Conkin, Paul. *Big Daddy from the Pedernales: Lyndon Baines Johnson.* Boston: Twayne, 1986.

Dallek, Robert. *Flawed Giant Lyndon Johnson and His Times, 1961–1973.* New York: Oxford University Press, 1998.

Dallek, Robert. *Lone Star Rising: Lyndon Johnson and His Times, 1908–1960.* New York: Oxford University Press, 1991.

Johnson, Lyndon B. *The Vantage Point.* New York: Holt, Rinehart, and Winston, 1971.

Keams, Doris. *Lyndon Johnson and the American Dream.* New York: Harper & Row, 1976.

Robert A. Divine

JUDICIAL REVIEW

Judicial review is the power of a court to adjudicate the constitutionality of actions by the political branches, most controversially the legislature. Although scholars have identified possible precursors in imperial governance and English ideas of fundamental law, the practice of judicial review first clearly emerged in the United States in the early 1780s. Proponents argued that judicial responsibility to decline enforcement of unconstitutional laws followed from the republican principles on which the American Revolution was based: A constitution is law created by "the people" to govern their governors. It includes limited delegations to different agents to act on behalf of the polity—a legislature to enact laws, an executive to enforce those laws, and courts to interpret and apply the laws in particular cases. Because the people's agents can never act contrary to limits imposed by their principal, judges cannot enforce unconstitutional laws that come before them in the ordinary course of litigation. As James Iredell wrote in 1786,

> The judges . . . must take care at their peril, that every act of Assembly they presume to enforce is warranted by the constitution, since if it is not, they act without lawful authority. This is not a usurped or a discretionary power, but one inevitably resulting from the constitution of their office." "To the Public," in Griffith J. McRee, *Life and Correspondence of James Iredell,* 1857, p. 148

In this view, judges do not have any special responsibility to interpret the Constitution, nor do they have greater power than other government officials when they do so. They have, rather, the same duty and the same obligation to enforce the Constitution as every government agent. Known as "departmentalism," this approach posited coequal branches, each equally responsible to act in accord with its best understanding of the Constitution whenever a question of constitutionality arises in the course of its usual business.

The departmental understanding of judicial review was most famously expounded by the U.S. Supreme Court in the celebrated case of *Marbury v. Madison* (1803). Because the Constitution is "a superior, paramount law," Chief Justice John Marshall wrote, legislation inconsistent with it is void. A court called upon to interpret or apply an act of the legislature—"to say what the law is"—cannot ignore the Constitution: "Those who apply [a law] to particular cases, must of necessity expound and interpret that [law]. . . . Those then who controvert the principle that the constitution is to be considered, in court, as a paramount law, are reduced to the necessity of maintaining that courts must close their eyes on the constitution, and see only the law." Yet that would be absurd, Marshall concluded, because "courts, *as well as other departments,* are bound by that instrument."

In deciding *Marbury,* Marshall ignored a second, quite different, theory of judicial review that had developed in the 1790s. Fearful of what the French Revolution could portend for America, conservatives in the ruling Federalist Party sought in various ways to dampen democratic politics. As part of this strategy, they articulated what has subsequently come to be known as "judicial supremacy": the idea that the Constitution makes courts supreme in interpreting the Constitution, such that their decisions about constitutional meaning are superior to, and final and binding on, both the other branches of government and the people themselves. Political or popular authority to revise or supersede judicial interpretations, they said, is limited to formally amending the Constitution. Supporters of judicial supremacy justified the theory by arguing that the Constitution is a form of ordinary law and separation of powers reposes final interpretive authority over law in judges. Interestingly, *Marbury* is often misread to support this theory of judicial review, an ironic argument since Marshall deliberately avoided and abandoned it in drafting the opinion.

The difference between these two theories of judicial review plays out on a practical level, affecting when judicial decisions are likely to be politically resisted and the form such resistance takes. Opposition to judicial rulings is only partly a product of agreement or disagreement with a court's results. It is also affected by perceptions of the legitimate range of judicial authority. A public that accepts judicial supremacy—that accepts, in other words, that final authority to interpret the Constitution is *supposed* to reside in judges—will let courts go farther and do more than a public that does not. By the same token, accepting judicial supremacy limits the forms of legitimate opposition to amending the Constitution (something nearly impossible to achieve in the United States), urging judges to change their minds and using new appointments to reshape a court as members die or retire. Under the departmental view, in contrast, public backing may encourage the political branches to ignore judicial mandates or to push back by stripping the court's jurisdiction, slashing its budget, or changing its procedural rules or composition to produce faster change than would otherwise be possible. Political action meant to pressure or punish the court is, in this view, a legitimate part of constitutional politics and not a violation of judicial independence.

For most of American history, the departmental view prevailed, although proponents of judicial supremacy remained active among conservatives and in the profession. Of course, the difference between departmentalism and supremacy was difficult to spot because judges were careful not to buck strongly held public views on important constitutional issues. But controversies did erupt from time to time, such as during the fight over a national bank in the 1820s, over slavery in the territories in the 1850s, and over the creation of a social welfare system in the 1930s. At times like these, the question of judicial supremacy was thrown into sharp relief, and each time judicial authority was decisively repudiated.

Legal interpretation began to change only after the Supreme Court's decision in *Brown v. Board of Education* (1954), which struck down laws mandating segregated schools. In the years after *Brown,* the idea of judicial supremacy seemed gradually to find wide public acceptance. The Court's decisions were still often controversial, but beginning in the 1960s, resistance and noncompliance turned into a form of protest rather than a claim of interpretive equality. By the 1980s, most protests that touched on constitutional matters were being directed to rather than against the Court, and acceptance of judicial supremacy became the norm.

Legal progressives began to see the judiciary as a friend rather than a foe. As Warren court activism crested in the mid-1960s, a new generation of liberal lawyers and scholars discarded opposition to courts and turned the liberal tradition on its head by embracing a philosophy of broad judicial authority. Although familiar with the history of progressive resistance to courts, this new generation put aside misgivings about accountability, conceded that judicial review might be in tension with popular government, and justified any trade-off on the ground that courts could advance the more important cause of social justice.

Conservatives, for their part, had no problem with judicial supremacy. It was an idea they had always embraced, going all the way back to the eighteenth century, and they continued to do so after Chief Justice Warren took over. For them, the problem with the Warren Court was simply that its decisions were wrong, and their protests were thus directed at the substantive interpretations of the liberal justices, whom they saw as falsely using the Constitution as cover to deal with matters that constitutional law did not in fact reach or address.

The upshot was that, for the first time in American history, Conservatives and Liberals found themselves in agreement on the principle of judicial supremacy. People across the political spectrum now took for granted that judges were responsible for interpreting the Constitution and that their interpretations were final and should be binding on the rest of government and on the polity. Debate shifted from who had interpretive authority to how the text should be interpreted. Liberals offered a range of novel interpretive theories to justify efforts by courts to effectuate social change through constitutional interpretation—arguing that judges might act to correct flaws in the democratic process, to keep constitutional law current with the mores of society, to inject proper notions of morality into government action, and more. Conservatives opted for different principles of interpretation, urging narrow reading of the text or reliance on so-called original meaning to secure outcomes consistent with their beliefs. But both sides embraced judicial supremacy. The result has been that traditional devices for controlling courts are today deemed illegitimate because they are inconsistent with judicial independence, and every new appointment has become a moment of high political drama.

In the meantime, the practice of judicial review has spread internationally. Today, it is an essential part of the constitutional systems of all but a few democratic nations. Even Great Britain, long considered the paradigmatic example of a nation that has eschewed judicial review, has begun inching toward adopting the practice in connection with its European Union obligations.

There are, however, critical differences between judicial review as it is practiced in the United States and in most other nations. The central problem in engineering a democratic government is how to balance independence with accountability. On the one hand, the very definition of popular government is that public officials are responsive and accountable to the larger community. On the other hand, we want and need government agents to have a degree of independence: room to exercise leadership and to act for the benefit of society based on experience and superior access to information. When it comes to legislative and executive officials, the balance tends greatly to favor accountability, although we build in degrees of independence through devices like long terms in office, large electoral districts, and (particularly in the executive branch) indirect rather than direct popular control.

When it comes to judges, in contrast, the balance swings heavily in the direction of independence. Article III of the American Constitution presents an extreme version of this tilt, immunizing the compensation of federal judges and giving them life tenure. This is because judicial review was still in its infancy when the American Constitution was adopted, and no one fully recognized the powerful policy-making role it would give to courts. Judicial independence was thought of primarily in connection with the courts' ordinary law functions, and life tenure and salary protection were valued chiefly as devices to eliminate executive and legislative influence over garden-variety litigation. It was only as the judicial power expanded and its political importance became clear that Americans discovered a need to compensate for this gap in our Constitution, so political leaders scrambled to create a degree of control and accountability by turning to blunt political tools like jurisdiction stripping and court packing.

Recognizing that constitutional enforcement is not and never could be like ordinary legal interpretation, most of the post–World War II constitutions of Europe established special courts, not part of the ordinary legal system, whose sole function is to review constitutional questions. Given the high political station these courts occupy, additional safeguards were added to ensure an appropriate level of political accountability without needlessly compromising judicial independence. Appointment to the bench thus typically requires a supermajority in one or both houses of the legislature, guaranteeing that constitutional courts have a mainstream ideology and judges serve terms that are limited and staggered to ensure a regular turnover. In addition, the constitutions themselves are more easily amendable than that of the United States. The combined effect of these innovations is to relieve the pressure a doctrine of judicial supremacy creates by reducing the likelihood of serious breaches between the constitutional court and the other branches of government and by making political correctives easier to implement when breaches occur. Partly as a result, constitutional courts in Europe have managed successfully to mimic America's judicial activism without the same controversy, and the European model has provided the blueprint for most new democracies in structuring their judiciaries.

Constitutional engineering can only go so far, however, and recent developments suggest that European judges, too, may be approaching the limits of their authority. Rising friction in Europe and elsewhere over the role of courts reflects an inescapable fact about judicial review: to say that politically insulated judges will have final say over the meaning of the constitution can never be fully reconciled with saying that the government rests on popular sovereignty. Intellectual or ideological commitments can hold back the built-in tension for a time, but given the complexity and unpredictability of politics, they cannot thwart it permanently.

[*See also* **Brown v. Board of Education; Constitution;** ***and*** ***Marbury v. Madison.***]

BIBLIOGRAPHY

Bickel, Alexander M. *The Least Dangerous Branch: The Supreme Court at the Bar of Politics.* Indianapolis, Ind.: Bobbs–Merrill, 1962.

Dworkin, Ronald. *Freedom's Law: The Moral Reading of the American Constitution.* Cambridge, Mass.: Harvard University Press, 1996.

Ely, John Hart. *Democracy and Distrust: A Theory of Judicial Review.* Cambridge, Mass.: Harvard University Press, 1980.

Friedman, Barry. *The Will of the People.* New York: Farrar, Straus, and Giroux, 2009.

Hamburger, Philip. *Law and Judicial Duty.* Cambridge, Mass.: Harvard University Press, 2008.

Kramer, Larry D. *The People Themselves: Popular Constitutionalism and Judicial Review.* Oxford; New York: Oxford University Press, 2004.

Kramer, Larry D. "'The Interests of the Man': James Madison, Popular Constitutionalism, and the Theory of Deliberative Democracy." *Valparaiso Law Review* 41 (2006): 697.

Scalia, Antonin, and Amy Gutmann. *A Matter of Interpretation: Federal Courts and the Law.* Princeton, N.J.: Princeton University Press, 1998.

Larry D. Kramer

JUDICIARY ACT OF 1789

The framers of the Constitution provided that the new national government would be divided into three branches. The third was to be a court system, an institution that did not exist in the previous national government under the Articles of Confederation. However, the Constitution set out only the barest of outlines for the new judiciary, unlike the legislative and executive branches that were extensively detailed and circumscribed. Thus, the first Congress had to flesh out the Constitution by creating a court structure.

The Judiciary Act of 1789 ranks as one of the most important enactments Congress has ever undertaken, more akin to a constitutive act (like amendments to the Constitution) than to ordinary legislation. The task was arduous, given the weakness of the new government and the extreme political sensitivity of many features of the court system. Congress struggled with the problem during the whole of its long first session, and the act that finally emerged in September 1789 was thought by many to be a sound but temporary compromise. Yet, thanks to a combination of astute political foresight, hard work, and luck, most of the important features of the national judiciary established by the act are with us today.

Structure. The act's most enduring feature was also the aspect that most surprised contemporaries: a three-tiered hierarchical judicial structure. At the bottom were district courts, each with a single district judge, one in each state except Virginia and Massachusetts, which had two. (The remote Kentucky district of Virginia demanded its own court as the price of staying in the union, and the Maine portion of Massachusetts also received a court). At the top was a Supreme Court, staffed by five associate justices and one chief justice. In between were three circuit courts, the Southern (consisting at the time of South Carolina and Georgia; North Carolina was added in 1790 after it joined the union), the Eastern (containing New York, Connecticut, Massachusetts, and New Hampshire; Rhode Island was added in 1790 and Vermont in 1791, when they joined the union), and the Middle (comprising Virginia, Maryland, Pennsylvania, Delaware, and New Jersey). To reduce expenses for the nation and for poor litigants, the circuit courts were not staffed with their own judges. Rather, each district judge sat in the circuit court when it convened in his state, and two itinerant Supreme Court judges joined them during each of three twice-yearly circuits. Since the broad trial jurisdiction of the circuit courts included the most sensitive and disputed kinds of federal cases, decisions there would be made by the most respected federal jurists, making costly appeals less likely. (The circuit courts are now known as the Courts of Appeal, are solely appellate, and are staffed with their own judges, but the three-tiered arrangement has persisted.)

Both the hierarchy and the number of national courts surprised most Americans in 1789. All courts were trial courts at that time. No courts were confined to ruling on purely legal issues appealed from inferior courts, and an "appeal" might connote a new trial before a court containing more judges. However, opponents of the Constitution's ratification had feared that an "appellate" jury trial (or merely the Supreme Court sitting without a jury) might overturn facts found below by a local jury. To calm these fears and thus to reduce antagonism to the new centralized government, the Judiciary Act prohibited the Supreme Court from rehearing facts, thus limiting it to questions of law and coincidentally giving it hierarchical control over the lower federal courts in issues of law. Today all state and federal appellate courts follow this model, but it was a remarkable novelty in 1789.

If Americans had been polled in 1788, a large majority would probably have predicted that trials of cases coming within federal jurisdiction would take place in the various state supreme courts. Many Americans anticipated that the only federal courts would consist of a few admiralty judges scattered among seaports, dealing with maritime matters, and a single appellate Supreme Court. Such a scheme would have kept costs low while assuaging the fears of state judges and localistic opponents of the Constitution that federal courts would swallow up state court jurisdiction. Virginia Senator Richard Henry Lee and others supported this model in the first Congress, but nationalists led by Connecticut Senator (and later Chief Justice) Oliver Ellsworth beat back the challenge. They desired a highly articulated court system so that crucial cases could be tried before national judges (rather than state judges susceptible to strong antinational pressure) and so that the majesty and power of an otherwise small and distant, distrusted new national government might be brought closer to everyone's doorstep.

A second alternative model was also rejected by the first Congress. This system, known as *nisi prius*, was patterned on the extant court systems in England, Massachusetts, and New York, among other jurisdictions. It would have entailed a large Supreme Court that would have traveled in groups of two or three to try federal cases in the hinterlands and then would have periodically returned to the capital to decide difficult issues of law as a group. There would have been no other federal courts. If either the Lee plan or the *nisi prius* plan had been adopted, our judicial landscape (and probably our constitutional history) would have been vastly different than it has been.

Jurisdiction. The fear widespread in 1787–1789 that the federal courts might swallow up state court jurisdiction was rational. The Constitution used quite broad, inclusive, and vague language to describe the jurisdiction that the federal judiciary would exercise. Article III, Section 2, states in pertinent part that "the judicial Power [of the United States] shall extend to all Cases" arising under the Constitution or federal law or treaties, and to controversies "between Citizens of different States . . . and between . . . the Citizens [of a State] and foreign . . . Citizens or Subjects".

The political disputes that led James Madison and others to demand a national court system in the first place involved state court refusal to enforce ordinary debt contracts during the depression years of the 1780s. Hatred of the British impelled thousands of Americans to repudiate all or part of the debts that had been contracted with British merchants before the Revolution and that had remained unpaid when the courts closed on the eve of that bloody eight-year struggle. Despite prohibitions in the peace treaty with Great Britain, state legislatures continued to pass court-closing and debt-reducing acts that made collection of British debts difficult or impossible. They also enacted moratorium laws postponing, and legal tender laws allowing reductions in, the obligations Americans owed to domestic creditors, many of whom were speculators and many of whom, relative to the debtors, lived out of state. Many state courts respected the anticreditor message sent by the economically hard-pressed majority, enforcing this legislation and in some instances adding to its contract-repudiating effects.

Several provisions of the Constitution could bring ordinary contract cases involving such debts into the federal courts: such cases might be controversies between citizens of different states or between a citizen and a foreigner; they might involve a statute contrary to the peace treaty and thus "arise" under it; or they might involve a violation of the prohibitions in Article I, Section 10, against a state's "mak[ing] any Thing but gold and silver Coin a Tender in Payment of Debts" or passing "Law[s] impairing the Obligation of Contracts," and thus "arise" under the Constitution. Many opponents of the Constitution did not want these cases taken away from the state courts. The Constitution's opponents also objected to the breadth and vagueness of the Constitution's jurisdictional language. The framers' avowed purpose of greatly strengthening the national government portended the possible sweep of many other ordinary cases into federal court. Especially upsetting was the possibility that ordinary cases between citizens of different states involving small amounts might allow out-of-state plaintiffs to win by default against poor and middling defendants unable to travel or to bring their witnesses great distances to appear in federal court. The movement to amend the Constitution, which resulted in the adoption of the Bill of Rights in 1791, had a strong component of support from these opponents of the Constitution, who wished to restrict federal court jurisdiction severely (although nothing in the Bill of Rights as enacted directly accomplished such an objective).

The fears of the Constitution's opponents were partially neutralized by the Judiciary Act of 1789 because Congress adopted restrictions on the jurisdiction that might have been allotted to the federal courts under a full and broad reading of the Constitution. The least controversial types of jurisdiction—admiralty, petty crimes, collection of revenue—were lodged in the single-judge district courts.

Much more controversial were cases involving citizens of two or more states ("diversity" suits) and those involving a U.S. citizen on one side and a foreigner on the other ("alienage" suits). Although debt contract cases were the primary reasons for these types of jurisdiction, nothing in Article III prevented many other kinds of suits from being taken to federal court under them. Three judges, two of whom were members of the Supreme Court, would sit at the trial of such cases in the circuit courts, ensuring litigants more wisdom and care at their trials. Congress imposed an absolute amount-in-controversy limitation of $500—a large sum in 1789—on alienage and diversity cases, so that defendants involved in suits of less than that amount could not be taken to federal court by out-of-state or alien plaintiffs. Further, federal jurisdiction over diversity and alienage suits was made concurrent, giving such plaintiffs their choice of state or federal court. If the state court were chosen and the defendant decided at the beginning of the suit not to transfer the case to federal court, the case would remain in the state court, because no avenue of appeal to the Supreme Court from state courts in diversity or alienage cases was permitted. (These restrictions persist today, although the amount-in-controversy limitation now is $75,000.) A further amount-in-controversy limitation of $2,000 was placed upon appeal of alienage and diversity cases to the Supreme Court, lessening even further the likelihood that poor defendants would be twice subjected to expensive travel.

The most controversial type of jurisdiction was that over cases "arising" under the Constitution, treaties, or laws of the United States ("federal question" suits). Today we have comprehensive federal regulatory legislation that gives rise to many federal question suits. However, such legislation was nonexistent in 1789. Modern readers have difficulty understanding the fears that such an open-ended jurisdiction raised in the minds of opponents of the Constitution. Might "laws of the United States" encompass the laws of all the states? What state control over its domestic affairs could be wrested away by the federal negotiation of a treaty with a foreign power?

On the other hand, proponents of the Constitution saw this as the most important type of federal jurisdiction. They believed that the courts could use it to repel attacks upon the new Constitution. The most significant restriction in the Judiciary Act of 1789 gave the trial of federal question suits to the state courts. Only upon appeal to the Supreme Court after a final decision was had in the highest court of a state might a federal question actually reach a federal court. (Except for a brief interlude in 1801–1802, federal courts did not obtain general trial jurisdiction over federal questions until 1875.)

The restrictions astutely placed in the Judiciary Act of 1789 were successful in preventing any jurisdictional limitations or restrictions from being adopted as amendments to the Constitution. Proponents of the new government grumbled about these restrictions and about the undignified and arduous circuit riding that Supreme Court judges were forced to make and planned to enact appropriate changes. They eventually did so in the Judiciary Act of 1801, the famous "midnight judges' act," but Thomas Jefferson and the Republicans repealed this new law in 1802 as their first action after coming to power. The Judiciary Act of 1789 attained hallowed status as the enduring blueprint for America's judicial structure.

[*See also* **Bill of Rights; Constitution; Contract, Law of; Federal Government, Judicial Branch; Judicial Review; Madison, James; State Governments;** *and* **Supreme Court, U.S.**]

BIBLIOGRAPHY

Goebel, Julius, Jr. *History of the Supreme Court of the United States,* vol. 1, *Antecedents and Beginnings to 1801*. New York: Macmillan, 1971.

Holt, Wythe. "'To Establish Justice': Politics, the Judiciary Act of 1789, and the Invention of the Federal Courts." *Duke Law Journal* No. 6 (December 1989): 1421–1531.

Ritz, Wilfred J. *Rewriting the History of the Judiciary Act of 1789: Exposing Myths, Challenging Premises, and Using New Evidence*. Norman: University of Oklahoma Press, 1990.

Warren, Charles. "New Light on the History of the Federal Judiciary Act of 1789." *Harvard Law Review* 37 (November 1923): 49–132.

Wythe Holt

JURISPRUDENCE

The term "jurisprudence" technically means skill in the science of the law. That definition rests on the premise that law is a science, a premise deeply rooted in Anglo-American legal education since at least the eighteenth century, but one that came under severe assault in the twentieth century. The conception of law as a science presupposes its methodological and even substantive universality as a set of fundamental principles that can be analyzed and discerned in an unchanging fashion, akin to the traditional view of "the scientific method." Many conventional treatments of jurisprudence have been organized around these premises. However, jurisprudence can also be thought of as the cumulative history of ideas about the nature and cultural significance of law and legal institutions in a given nation. This essay takes the latter approach, emphasizing ideas about the law in successive periods of American history.

Fundamental to an examination of the stages in American jurisprudence is the assumption that a sea change in conceptions of the nature of law occurred over the course of the nineteenth century. Once thought of as a repository of essentialist, unchanging principles, akin to other fundamental causative forces in the universe, law came to be thought of as equivalent to the ideologies and policies of officials empowered to make legal decisions. Although this change in the meaning of law as a causative agent in society took place gradually, the view of law as essentialist and external to human will, dominant at the time of the framing of the Constitution, had by the 1930s been replaced by one that defined law as largely indistinguishable from the legal decisions of authoritative officials.

Nineteenth-Century Jurisprudence. This sea change in attitudes involved two fundamental stages, the "classical" (nineteenth-century) and the "modern" stage, each associated with certain jurisprudential movements. The jurisprudential issues contested in the classical period revolved around whether judges had correctly "discerned the course prescribed by law"—in other words, whether they had accurately adapted fundamental legal principles to emerging social issues. Thus, the struggles that produced the leading constitutional decisions of the nineteenth century—over the federal government's authority to supplant the authority of the states, the constitutional status of slavery, federal enforcement of the civil rights of former slaves, income tax, antitrust legislation, or states' efforts to regulate contractual relationships among employers and their employees—were not thought of as raising fundamental questions about the legitimacy of judges making law or entering into the domain of policy. They were thought of, instead, as raising questions of whether the judges deciding those cases had accurately discerned the course prescribed by law.

During the Gilded Age, some American legal commentators, influenced by the growing prestige of science and its secularized explanations for the flow of events in the universe, began to question the essentialist nature of law. This group of "modernist" commentators concluded that the distinction between the will of officials, including judges, and the "will of the law" was simply a fiction. Legal decision makers, including judges, were now characterized as "making" law. This characterization naturally raised issues that centered on the problem of separating politics from law and of checking the potentially tyrannical or arbitrary tendency of legal decisions by human actors in a society premised on the supremacy of a written Constitution and on democratic theory.

Early Twentieth-Century Developments. In response to these problems, three successive twentieth-century jurisprudential movements sought to erect constraints on legal decision makers, especially judges. "Sociological jurisprudence," an early twentieth-century movement, insisted that judicial decisions must be grounded in an empirical understanding of current social conditions. Legal realism, the next movement, abandoned the idea of essentialist legal principles altogether and proposed that judging be seen as the equivalent of policy making and that legal rules be frankly recast in a functional form. Some legal realists pressed the idea of judging as human will so insistently that, in the context of totalitarian threats to American democracy, it appeared frightening.

The next influential twentieth-century jurisprudential movement, "process jurisprudence," attempted to constrain the unsettling implications of the realist movement. Because process jurisprudence beliefs continued to be widely held by lawyers and judges of the late twentieth century, it merits a more extended treatment. Process jurisprudence attempted to justify a selective approach to judicial review, in which a degree of activism in common law judging and in certain constitutional realms—notably free speech—was combined with judicial deference to legislatures and to the federal administrative agencies that had proliferated from the 1930s on. Process jurisprudence correlated selective judicial review with a set of institutional spheres in "the legal process," each with its own set of competence requirements.

For its adherents, process jurisprudence "solved" the jurisprudence dilemma of activist judging in a constitutional democracy by providing criteria for determining whether a particular judicial decision had been grounded in institutional competence theory and was thus rational. Aggressive judicial review in the free speech area was seen as competent because the justifications for that review articulated the vital role of freedom of expression in a modern democracy. Deferential judicial review in the realm of political economy was equally viewed as competent because the collapse of orthodox capitalism had demonstrated that American democracy was not committed to an essentialist economic policy, but rather to experimentation, embodied in legislative solutions.

In an influential series of decisions highlighted by *Brown v. Board of Education* (1954), the Supreme Court expanded aggressive judicial review into areas beyond free speech, such as race relations, reapportionment, and criminal procedure. Process theorists insisted that these decisions be justified by a grounding in "neutral principles of law" that would demonstrate their rationality and competence. Eventually, after finding the Court's justifications inadequate, process theorists supplied their own justifications by formulating two additional essentialist policies to which the judiciary could subscribe: the policy of antidiscrimination on the basis of race or skin color, which justified the Court's desegregation decisions; and the policy of reinforcing the democratic principle of representation by ensuring that if a minority group was unrepresented or underrepresented in a legislature, the judiciary could invoke aggressive constitutional review on its behalf.

The Late Twentieth Century. In the late twentieth century, the governing assumptions that linked sociological jurisprudence, legal realism, and process jurisprudence were called into question. Specifically, a series of theoretical perspectives appeared in legal scholarship that collectively denied that modern scientific methodology actually amounts to a constraint on its practitioners, whether in law or in any other human "science." Critical legal studies, feminist theory, critical race theory, republicanism, and communitarianism all were openly normative perspectives that made no pretense of being a positive, objective "science." Their implicit jurisprudential theory appeared to be that no legal actors, including judges, are constrained in any meaningful fashion in their decision making. From this perspective, the effort of modern jurisprudence to substitute empirically derived and rationally justified essentialist policies for the essentialist principles of classical jurisprudence is simply incoherent.

Some commentators suggested that with the collective surfacing of these diverse perspectives, process jurisprudence had disintegrated, resulting in the dawn of a "postmodern" stage of American jurisprudence. This conclusion was perhaps premature. The problem of distinguishing the "will" of the law from the will of those who make legal decisions seems to transcend history, given that law, unlike economics or physics or literature, is assumed to be a regime that provides authoritative rules for governing human conduct. Unless "postmodern" jurisprudential perspectives devoted themselves to fashioning some techniques—whether derived from modern science or elsewhere—they were not likely to gain the lasting influence of their predecessors. The purported emergence of "postmodernism" in jurisprudence may have signaled not so much the collapse of modernist epistemology as the collapse of the idea, from which conventional treatments of jurisprudence had started, of law as a science. That is to say, law resists being analogized to a field with predictive universalistic rules; it is too grounded in human complexity. But at the same time, law's authoritative force, at least in democratic societies, derives from its ascribed ability to function as an alternative to tyranny and arbitrariness. Thus, at least in the United States, the subject of jurisprudence appears integrally bound to the recurrent dilemmas posed by law as both a facilitator of and a constraint upon human willfulness.

[*See also* **Antitrust Legislation and Law; *Brown v. Board of Education;* Civil Rights;**

Constitution; Federal Government, Judicial Branch; Income Tax, Federal; Judicial Review; Slavery, Laws; State Governments; States' Rights; *and* Supreme Court, U.S.]

BIBLIOGRAPHY

Duxbury, Neil. *Patterns of American Jurisprudence.* Oxford: Oxford University Press, 1995.

Kalman, Laura. *The Strange Career of Legal Liberalism.* New Haven, Conn.: Yale University Press, 1996.

Minda, Gary. *Postmodern Legal Movements: Law and Jurisprudence at Century's End.* New York: New York University Press, 1995.

Rodgers, Daniel. *Contested Truths.* New York: Basic Books, 1987.

Ross, Dorothy, ed., *Modernist Impulses in the Human Sciences.* Baltimore: Johns Hopkins University Press, 1994.

Ross, Dorothy. *The Origins of American Social Science.* Cambridge: Cambridge University Press, 1993.

White, G. Edward. *The American Judicial Tradition.* New York: Oxford University Press, 1988.

White, G. Edward. *Intervention and Detachment: Essays in Legal History and Jurisprudence.* New York: Oxford University Press, 1994.

White, G. Edward. *Patterns of American Legal Thought.* Indianapolis, Ind.: Bobbs–Merrill, 1978.

G. Edward White

K

KANSAS–NEBRASKA ACT

The 1840s brought a rising tide of foreign immigrants and internal migrants to the trans-Mississippi West, generating interest in promoting orderly settlement of the Great Plains. However, the Mexican Cession of 1848 became the focus of fierce sectional debates over the spread of slavery. Senator Stephen A. Douglas of Illinois played a crucial role in congressional adoption of the Compromise of 1850, which implicitly opened new southwestern territories to slavery on the principle of "congressional nonintervention" and "popular sovereignty," whereby the people of a territory, like those of a state, would decide the issue for themselves. To Douglas and his Democratic Party, this principle was superior to the 1820 Missouri Compromise's federal dictate that slavery could not exist in the Louisiana Purchase territory north of the 36°30′ line of latitude. Extending popular sovereignty to the still unorganized northern portion of the Louisiana Purchase, they believed, would represent a victory for local self-government; further, it would promote national political unity and economic development by securing the Democratic Party against the threat of sectional fracture and by expediting settlement and railroad construction on the Great Plains.

Hence, in January 1854, Senator Douglas's Committee on Territories reported a "Nebraska Bill" that, with subsequent amendments, became the Kansas–Nebraska Act. Bowing to pressure from his party's powerful southern wing, but fully expecting that climate would exclude slavery from the Great Plains, Douglas agreed that the act should explicitly repeal the Missouri Compromise line and provide for the organization of two territories, Kansas and Nebraska. The bill passed the Senate by a vote of 37 to 14 and the House of Representatives by a much closer vote of 113 to 100, with northern Democrats evenly split. President Franklin Pierce signed it into law on 30 May. Douglas hoped that the Kansas–Nebraska Act would settle the slavery issue in the territories, coalesce national Democratic support for popular sovereignty, and further his presidential aspirations. In reality, the law triggered a violent struggle in Kansas between pro- and antislavery forces; deepened antislavery sentiment in the North; and set the stage for a new Republican Party opposed to the expansion of slavery, whose 1860 presidential nominee, Abraham Lincoln, frustrated Douglas's bid for the White House.

[*See also* **Antislavery Movement; Brown, John; Compromise of 1850; Douglas, Stephen A.; Louisiana Purchase; Pierce, Franklin;** *and* **Popular Sovereignty.**]

BIBLIOGRAPHY

Morrison, Michael A. *Slavery and the American West: The Eclipse of Manifest Destiny and the Coming of the Civil War.* Chapel Hill: University of North Carolina Press, 1997.

Shearer Davis Bowman

KATZ v. UNITED STATES

389 U.S. 347 (1967), argued 17 October 1967, decided 18 December 1967 by vote of 7 to 1; Stewart for the Court, Harlan and White concurring, Black in dissent, Marshall not participating. *Katz* altered significantly the approach that courts must use in determining, under the Fourth Amendment, whether certain police conduct constitutes a "search" that is subject to the amendment's warrant and probable cause limitations. Illustrative of the pre-Katz approach is *Olmstead v. United States* (1928), where the Supreme Court held that it did not constitute a search for the authorities to place a tap on certain telephone wires and thereby eavesdrop on the defendant's telephone conversations. As the Court later put the matter in *Silverman v. United States* (1961), for there to be a Fourth Amendment search the police must have physically intruded into "a constitutionally protected area" (p. 682). Katz replaced the *Silverman* standard with a reasonable expectation of privacy test.

At his trial for transmitting wagering information by phone, the government introduced over Katz's objection evidence of his end of telephone conversations, overheard by federal agents who had attached an electronic listening/recording device to the exterior of a public phone booth habitually used by Katz. The lower court concluded there was no search because the wall of the booth had not been physically penetrated. The Supreme Court reversed, holding that "[t]he Government's activities in electronically listening to and recording the petitioner's words violated the privacy upon which he justifiably relied while using the telephone booth and thus constituted a 'search and seizure' within the meaning of the Fourth Amendment" (p. 512). This proposition was elaborated in Justice John M. Harlan's concurring opinion, later relied upon by lower courts and the Supreme Court itself in determining the meaning of *Katz.* Harlan stated that "there is a twofold requirement, first that a person have exhibited an actual (subjective) expectation of privacy and, second, that the expectation be one that society is prepared to recognize as 'reasonable'" (p. 516).

The first branch of the Harlan formulation should not be a part of any statement of what the Fourth Amendment protects. This is because the government could easily, either by edict or by systematic practice, condition the expectations of the general public in such a way that there would be no hope of privacy. Harlan later appreciated this, stating in *United States v. White* (1971) that analysis under *Katz* must "transcend the search for subjective expectations" (p. 786). The Supreme Court has seldom addressed this point in more recent cases, although some of its statements are legitimate cause for concern. Illustrative is *California v. Ciraolo* (1986), holding that it is not a search to make an aerial observation of marijuana plants growing inside a fenced backyard, where it was intimated that a defendant's 10-foot high solid wood fence would not provide a subjective expectation of privacy because the plants could be seen by "a policeman perched on the top of a truck or a two-level bus" (p. 211). A person is unlikely therefore to get by the first *Katz* hurdle unless he or she has taken steps to ensure against all conceivable efforts at scrutiny.

As for the second prong of the Harlan elaboration, he stressed in *White* that "those more extensive intrusions that significantly jeopardize the sense of security which is the paramount concern of Fourth Amendment liberties" are searches (p. 1143). Unfortunately, the Supreme Court has not interpreted *Katz* this way, as is evident from two cases: *United States v. Miller* (1976), holding that a person has no justified expectation of privacy in a bank's records of his financial transactions because those documents "contain only information voluntarily conveyed to the banks and exposed to their employees in the ordinary course of business" (p. 442); and *Ciraolo,* holding that it is not a search for police to look down from an airplane into one's solidly fenced yard because "any member of the public flying over this airspace who glanced down could have seen everything that these officers observed" (pp. 213–214). In these and other cases the Court has failed to appreciate, as Justice Thurgood Marshall put it in his *Smith v. Maryland* (1979) dissent, that "privacy is not a discrete commodity, possessed absolutely or not at all" (p. 749).

[*See also* **Harlan, John Marshall; Marshall, Thurgood; Privacy;** *and* **Supreme Court, U.S.**]

BIBLIOGRAPHY

LaFave, Wayne R. "The Forgotten Motto of Obsta Principiis in Fourth Amendment Jurisprudence." *Arizona Law Review* 28 (1986): 291–310.

Wayne R. LaFave

KEATING–OWEN CHILD LABOR ACT

Members of the anti–child labor movement viewed President Woodrow Wilson's signing of the 1916 Keating–Owen Act as a triumph. Cosponsored by Representative Edward Keating (D-CO) and Senator Robert L. Owen (D-OK), the vote was 337 to 46 in the House of Representatives and 50 to 12 in the Senate. President Wilson highlighted the legislation as part of his New Freedom agenda and evidence of his progressive credentials.

Nonetheless, some parents and children objected to child labor regulations as unwelcome interference in family life. Many business owners disliked efforts to end child labor. The Keating–Owen Act used the Constitution's interstate commerce clause to overcome possible legal arguments that such legislation was an overreach of federal authority. The act used fines to prohibit the sale and shipment of products from mines that employed children under age sixteen and goods produced in factories with employees younger than fourteen years old.

The U.S. Children's Bureau had the responsibility for enforcing the new law. Verifying the age of young workers would be a major problem. Few adolescents at the time had birth certificates, and physical standards left little room for individual differences. Poverty encouraged many parents and their children to devise ways to circumvent child labor laws. Most of all, the Children's Bureau hoped that the Keating–Owen Act would encourage states to tighten their laws beyond the federal minimums.

On 31 August 1917, however, one day before the Keating–Owen Act was to go into effect, a North Carolina judge ruled that the law was unconstitutional. Twenty days earlier, Roland H. Dagenhart filed suit enjoining the Charlotte district attorney, William C. Hammer, from enforcing the law. Dagenhart argued that the act violated the constitutional rights of his two sons, Ruben (fourteen) and John (twelve), and denied him as their father the right to his sons' wages. The editor of the *Southern Textile Bulletin,* an anti–child labor tool of the mill industry, urged Roland Dagenhart to bring the suit and probably paid the legal fees.

On 3 June 1918, in a five to four decision, the U.S. Supreme Court held the Keating–Owen Act unconstitutional. The *Hammer v. Dagenhart* decision held that Congress could not invoke the interstate commerce clause to prevent child labor. However, the court agreed that child labor was an evil in need of government regulation. Anti–child labor activists were disappointed at the ruling, but also encouraged that the court recognized a need to end exploitive child labor.

Congress passed another law imposing taxes rather than fines, but it was also declared unconstitutional by the U.S. Supreme Court (*Bailey v. Drexel Furniture Co.,* 1922). The next step was a constitutional amendment that passed Congress in 1924, but never received ratification by the necessary three-fourths of the states. With the onset of the Great Depression, a combination of adults seeking to push adolescent wage earners out of the work force, new technologies making child labor less profitable, and a growing belief that a high school education was essential for job security encouraged inclusion of child labor regulations in the 1938 Fair Labor Standards Act. This time the court upheld the law.

In a 1923 interview about the Keating–Owen Act, twenty-year-old Ruben Dagenhart said that he did not derive any benefit from winning the case. In fact, he lamented, "Look at me! A hundred and five pounds, a grown man and no education. . . . From 12 years old on, I was working 12 hours a day—from 6 in the morning until 7 at night, with time out for meals. And sometimes I worked nights besides. . . . It would have been a good thing for kids in this state if that law they passed had been kept."

[*See also* **Wilson, Woodrow.**]

BIBLIOGRAPHY

Hindman, Hugh D. *Child Labor: An American History*. Armonk, N.Y.: M. E. Sharpe, 2002.

Lindenmeyer, Kriste. *"A Right to Childhood": The U.S. Children's Bureau and Child Welfare, 1912–1946*. Champaign: University of Illinois Press, 1997.

Mellet, Lowell. "The Sequel to the Dagenhart Case." Reprinted in Robert H. Bremner et al., *Children and Youth in America: A Documentary History,* vol. 2, pp. 716–717. Cambridge, Mass.: Harvard University Press, 1970.

Sallee, Shelley. *The Whiteness of Child Labor Reform in the New South*. Athens, Ga.: University of Georgia Press, 2004.

Trattner, Walter. *Crusade for the Children: A History of the National Child Labor Committee and Child Labor Reform in America*. Chicago: Quadrangle Books, 1970.

Wood, Stephen B. *Constitutional Politics in the Progressive Era: Child Labor and the Law*. Chicago: University of Chicago Press, 1968.

Kriste Lindenmeyer

KENNEDY, EDWARD

Edward Moore "Ted" Kennedy (1932–2009) was a Democratic senator from Massachusetts and a liberal statesman. He entered the Senate in a special election in 1962 to replace his elder brother, President John F. Kennedy. He managed the 1968 presidential campaign of his other brother, Robert F. Kennedy. After Robert's assassination in June, Ted was briefly considered as a Democratic presidential nominee at the August convention in Chicago. He took his name out of contention on the grounds of his youth and inexperience. Handsome and charismatic, Kennedy appeared to be headed toward the presidency.

Tragedy struck Kennedy on 18 July 1969. Ted Kennedy drove his car off a bridge on Chappaquiddick Island. His passenger, twenty-eight-year-old Mary Jo Kopechne, was killed. Kennedy later claimed that he escaped the overturned vehicle and dived down to try to reach Kopechne. But he failed to call the police or ask neighbors for help until the next morning. He pled guilty to a charge of leaving the scene of an accident. The Chappaquiddick incident stalled Kennedy's political career. He lost his position as Senate majority whip and decided not to run for the 1972 Democratic presidential nomination. When his son was diagnosed with cancer, he sat out the 1976 race as well.

During the 1970s, Kennedy adopted the fight for single-payer national health insurance as his flagship cause. Kennedy rejected President Jimmy Carter's health care reform plan, which emphasized hospital cost containment and a guaranteed role for private providers. Although the high inflation of the late 1970s did not favor costly government programs, Kennedy thought the pragmatic Carter was too conservative. He declared a challenge for the Democratic presidential nomination on 7 November 1979. Initially, Kennedy led Carter in polls by margins of 2 to 1. But he ran a poor campaign and the press revisited the Chappaquiddick tragedy. The Iranian hostage crisis and the Soviet invasion of Afghanistan boosted Carter's popularity enough to help him win the Iowa caucus and the New Hampshire primary. As the economy worsened, Kennedy recouped with a landslide victory in the 25 March 1980 New York primary. He lost the nomination, but won twelve contests, including California, Pennsylvania, Michigan, and Arizona. He declined to run in 1984 and focused on building a legislative record in the Senate.

Many commentators have noted that Kennedy's failed presidential ambitions marked the end of the liberal era. However, scholar of the 1980 Democratic primary Timothy Stanley argues that Kennedy was undone by bad luck and enjoyed a rapport with blue-collar Reagan Democrats. Biographer Adam Clymer finds that Kennedy flourished in the Senate after his presidential campaign, helping to pass health care reform, federal funding for AIDS treatment, and No Child Left Behind. His endorsement of Barack Obama in the 2008 Democratic primaries, shortly before he died of brain cancer, was widely seen as passing the torch from one generation of liberals to the next.

[*See also* **Health Insurance; Kennedy, John F.;** *and* **Kennedy, Robert.**]

BIBLIOGRAPHY

Clymer, Adam. *Edward M. Kennedy: A Biography*. New York: Harper Collins, 2003.

Stanley, Timothy. *Kennedy vs. Carter: the 1980 Battle for the Democratic Party's Soul.* Lawrence: University Press of Kansas, 2010.

Timothy Stanley

KENNEDY, JOHN F.

U.S. respondents to polling data consistently rank John "Jack" Fitzgerald Kennedy among the most beloved U.S. presidents, although surveys of historians judge the thirty-fifth president as slightly above average. Kennedy's popular appeal reflects his ability to overcome obstacles of illness and religious prejudice, his family's wealth and education, and his dramatic speeches that challenged humanity to confront tyranny, racism, and the mysteries of outer space. The graphic video image of Kennedy's assassination in November 1963 etched his tragic death into a collective U.S., and even global, consciousness.

Irish Catholic Roots, Education, and World War II. On 29 May 1917, Kennedy was born in Brookline, Massachusetts, as the second of nine children to the Irish Catholic family of Joseph Patrick and Rose Fitzgerald Kennedy. Confronting the first of many health problems, young Jack suffered a near-fatal illness at age two. He attended several private schools prior to graduating in 1935 from the Choate School in Connecticut. In 1940, Kennedy received a bachelor's degree from Harvard University. His senior thesis examined the perceived failure of the British government to deter German expansion in the 1930s. Kennedy interviewed U.S. consuls and European leaders, thanks in part to the access provided by his father, who served as U.S. ambassador to the Court of Saint James in the United Kingdom from 1938 to 1940. The ambassador supported Kennedy's efforts to revise his work, which was published under the title *Why England Slept*.

World War II had a dramatic impact on Kennedy's future career. Just prior to the U.S. entry into the war in late 1941, Jack secured a naval commission. Joe Kennedy's former military attaché in the U.S. embassy ensured that navy doctors overlooked Jack's health limitations. Stationed in the Pacific Ocean, Jack captained a patrol-torpedo boat, PT-109. In August 1943, a Japanese warship collided with PT-109 near the Solomon Islands. Kennedy's heroism in rescuing several of his crew members earned him several medals, including the Purple Heart. A year later, in August 1944, Kennedy's older brother Joseph Kennedy Jr., a navy pilot, tragically died in a mid-air explosion over Europe on an extremely dangerous mission for which he had volunteered.

Massachusetts and National Politics. At the end of the war in 1945, Kennedy stood as the bearer of his Irish Catholic family's dreams for continued upward mobility in an English Protestant nation. Upon returning from the war, Kennedy briefly wrote articles for the Chicago-based Hearst newspapers. In 1946, however, he returned home to pursue election to the U.S. House of Representatives from Massachusetts's eleventh Congressional District, which included heavily Catholic wards such as Boston's Italian North End and Irish Charlestown. Kennedy's strengths included an impressive war record and a maternal grandfather, John Fitzgerald, who maintained a vast political network as former mayor of Boston. Members of the large Kennedy family worked hard to publicize his candidacy through direct voter contact and hosting tea parties. His father exploited business connections and spent hundreds of thousands of dollars, including purchasing and distributing 100,000 copies of a *Reader's Digest* excerpt on Jack's PT-109 heroism. Despite a year of many victories for Republicans, the Democrat Jack won the congressional contest. After successful reelection campaigns in 1948 and 1950, he won election to the U.S. Senate seat in 1952.

Although Kennedy never established a reputation as a skilled lawmaker, he attracted widespread media attention. In 1953, he married Jacqueline Bouvier, the elegant Catholic daughter of elite Newport, Rhode Island, and New York families. Despite continued health challenges—which may partially explain his failure to assume legislative leadership in Washington—Kennedy produced a book, *Profiles in Courage,* in 1956. Documenting the lives of eight senators who had voted their conscience despite the electoral consequences, *Profiles* won a Pulitzer Prize in 1957. Some of Kennedy's critics claimed that Kennedy aide Theodore Sorensen actually wrote the book, a charge Sorensen consistently denied.

Sorensen authored a 1956 memorandum to persuade Democratic presidential nominee Adlai Stevenson to choose Jack as his vice-presidential running mate. Following Stevenson's loss to President Dwight Eisenhower in 1952, Sorensen argued that Kennedy, as a Catholic, could contribute to the revival of the Democratic Party's popularity with Catholics and immigrants. Stevenson avoided making a choice by allowing convention delegates to select his vice-presidential nominee. Although Kennedy did not gain the nomination, Stevenson rewarded him with several high-profile roles in the convention. Kennedy's gracious acceptance of defeat positioned him for party leadership after Stevenson again fell to Eisenhower in the 1956 election.

1960 Presidential Campaign. In subsequent years, Kennedy sought to remove problems related to his Catholicism, youth, and inexperience. As a congressman, Kennedy had earned accolades from Catholic publications for securing government assistance to Catholic schools. Yet Senator Kennedy proposed a bill in 1958 that would exclude parochial schools from all federal aid to education. This change revealed Kennedy's anxiousness to demonstrate that he would not show favoritism toward his church. Overwhelming reelection to the Senate in 1958 enhanced Jack's credibility, as did his national speaking tours, frequent media features about him, and cover photographs in national magazines.

At a time when the endorsement of party leaders was of paramount importance, Kennedy worried that Democratic kingmakers would choose an older, more experienced, and Protestant nominee. He thus negotiated aggressively with party bosses and entered seven state primary elections to generate media attention and momentum for his candidacy. In the primaries, Kennedy again faced questions about his religion. Media analysis of his victory in Wisconsin's April 1960 primary contest focused on his strong showing in heavily Catholic districts. West Virginia's May primary, however, offered him a chance to prove that he could poll as well with non-Catholic voters. In that state, which had fewer than 5 percent Catholics, Kennedy openly addressed the "religious issue." Upon winning more than 60 percent of that state's primary voters, Kennedy's nomination appeared likely. Former President Harry Truman called a press conference in June to ask party leaders to resist the accelerating Kennedy bandwagon, but the Democratic Party hungered for a winner after having lost two straight presidential contests. Recognizing Kennedy's perfect record in the primaries he entered, the convention delegates selected him as the party's nominee on the first ballot in July.

During the presidential campaign, televised media proved more important than in previous elections. Few policy differences separated

Kennedy and the Republican nominee Richard M. Nixon; news reporters often emphasized Kennedy's youth, inexperience, and Catholicism. Kennedy's supporters denounced religious prejudice at every opportunity. In September, Kennedy explained his support for church–state separation in a televised meeting with Protestant ministers in Houston, Texas. Kennedy again denied that he would favor Catholic institutions. In subsequent weeks, the first ever televised presidential debates reached an even wider audience, and in this venue, Jack projected confidence that persuaded many Americans of his qualifications for leadership.

When Kennedy won by slightly more than 100,000 votes, many of his supporters blamed anti-Catholicism for the slim margin of victory. However, Kennedy's status as a member of a religious minority also might have helped him secure Catholic, Jewish, and African American votes. Democrats framed the election around an antibigotry theme, which may have resonated with racial and religious minorities. Seventy percent of African Americans, 80 percent of Jews, and more than 70 percent of Catholics endorsed the Catholic candidate. The geographic position of large minority populations in northeastern and midwestern cities also may have tipped the balance in many states with large numbers of electoral votes. These voters may thus have accounted for Kennedy's wider margin of victory in the Electoral College—303 to Nixon's 219. At age forty-three, Kennedy became the youngest president-elect in U.S. history.

Foreign Policy Crises. Kennedy's presidency proved much more eventful in foreign than domestic affairs. Historians have debated whether Kennedy prompted international crises or whether Soviet premier Nikita Khrushchev purposely tested the young president's resolve. Kennedy's inaugural address pledged that America would "pay any price" for freedom. Yet the new president appeared uncertain at first. In April 1961, only months into his presidency, he agreed to a covert effort to help Cuban exiles overthrow Fidel Castro's rule. Unwilling to provide air support, however, the president failed to salvage the mission. The Bay of Pigs, where the invading force landed, became an early symbol of Kennedy's initiation by fire into the role of commander in chief. Kennedy proved unable to deter the Soviet Union from building a wall in August to prevent refugees from fleeing communist East Berlin to the capitalist West. Nonetheless, the wall proved a much better outcome than a Soviet invasion of West Berlin. Since this pro-U.S. capital was geographically encircled by Soviet ally East Germany, the citizens relied on America's vigilance in protecting their sovereignty. Prior to the year's end, Kennedy had also escalated the U.S. commitment to defend South Vietnam, which stood opposed to communist North Vietnam, by more than doubling the number of U.S. military personnel in that country.

Public diplomacy would characterize the most successful initiatives of the Kennedy administration. Kennedy's Peace Corps, initiated by executive order in March 1961, sent young volunteers abroad to provide skills to individuals in need. More than 70 percent of Americans approved of the program. Kennedy was attentive to polling data that reported foreign publics overwhelmingly believed the Soviet Union had the world's strongest space program. In response, he captured the popular imagination by challenging U.S. scientists to place an astronaut on the moon by the decade's end. The president's weekly televised press conferences showcased to a wide audience his quick wit and command of statistics. By April 1962, polling data reported that nearly 75 percent of Americans had seen or heard the president in this venue. Formal speeches, often covered live on television, also allowed Kennedy to frame analysis of a particular issue. Kennedy's June 1963 address to a West Berlin audience, for example, inspired confidence that the United States would stand with West Germany if challenged by Soviet aggression. The speech ranked with his inaugural among the century's most remembered rhetorical moments.

In addition to projecting a positive image abroad, Kennedy's crisis management skills improved in his second Cuban challenge. After Kennedy's embarrassment in the Bay of Pigs fiasco, the Soviet Union installed nuclear missiles in Cuba. In October 1962, Kennedy addressed the nation and the administration provided photographic evidence of the missiles to the United Nations. The Joint Chiefs of Staff recommended a U.S. invasion of Cuba to seize the missiles. Their inclination for military action increased after antiaircraft weapons downed a U.S. espionage plane, killing its pilot. Most historians conclude that this Cuban missile crisis brought the United States and the Soviet Union closer to nuclear war than at any other time in the nearly 50 years of Cold War competition. Kennedy was acutely aware of the potential for rapid escalation to a nuclear war, and he proceeded cautiously. After implementation of a blockade of the island, Kennedy exchanged telegrams with Khrushchev. A negotiated solution resulted in the Soviet removal of the missiles and Kennedy's secret agreement to dismantle U.S. missiles in Turkey.

Domestic Challenges. Having resolved an intense international crisis, Kennedy now turned his attention to the domestic challenge of African American protests for equal rights. Assistance to a black minority population in the South risked alienating a southern, white majority, which had traditionally provided a solid electoral base to his party. Yet Kennedy had polled well in 1960 with African American voters in northern cities, and he wanted to maintain this trend. Media publicity about black–white divisions also had foreign policy implications as the United States pursued allies in African and other nonwhite majority nations.

Until 1963, Kennedy had shown only limited leadership on civil rights. In September 1962, the U.S. Supreme Court required the University of Mississippi to admit James Meredith, an African American air force veteran. To quell violent attempts to block Meredith's registration of the university, the president assumed legal authority over units of the Mississippi National Guard. In the spring of 1963, however, nonviolent activist Reverend Martin Luther King Jr. expanded black demands for civil rights by mobilizing marches against segregated facilities in Alabama. Video images and photographs appeared of police dogs attacking young black marchers. In June, Kennedy delivered a nationally televised speech to announce his proposal for congressional legislation on civil rights. The Kennedy administration subsequently decided to assist civil rights activists who organized a mass protest demonstration in the capital city. In August, Jack invited King and other leaders of this March on Washington to the White House.

Kennedy's ability to appear confident in front of the camera overshadowed his failure to persuade Congress to pass major legislation. None of his major proposals—tax reductions, Medicare, federal aid to education, and civil rights for African Americans—secured sufficient votes by the time of his assassination. His successor Lyndon Johnson showed far greater skill in shepherding these—and more far-reaching—proposals through the legislature. Kennedy's inability to negotiate compromise, such as his rigid refusal to include Catholic schools in the education bill, may have contributed to his lackluster record as a lawmaker.

Assassination and Assessment. On 22 November 1963, Kennedy traveled in an open car through the streets of Dallas, Texas. In 1960, he had won the state by a small margin, and white southerners opposed his aggressive approach to civil rights. The 1964 presidential election would test Kennedy's ability to maintain popular support. Aiming a mail-order Italian rifle at the president from the sixth floor of the Texas School Book Depository, Lee Harvey Oswald shot three times. The second bullet struck Kennedy's neck, but a brace for his weak back kept his torso erect, which allowed the third bullet to enter his cerebellum.

News of Kennedy's death, about an hour later, spread rapidly through radio and television. The common experience of shock, sadness, and fear unified Americans of different regions, religions, and ethnicity. Martin Luther King Jr.'s daughter returned home and lamented, "Oh, Mommy, we're never going to get our freedom now." Soviet premier Khruschev cried and inscribed condolences in an official book at the U.S. embassy in Moscow. Similar gestures by individuals in America's embassies around the world testified to the man's iconic power.

JFK's name came to adorn airports, space and art centers, streets, and schools around the world. U.S. Presidents Bill Clinton and Barack Obama cited Kennedy as an important inspiration for their career choice of public service. Kennedy's vigorous optimism and rugged good looks were complemented by the trappings of wealth and education. As an Irish Catholic in an English Protestant nation, his material success offered hope for outsiders everywhere. The Peace Corps, the space program, and his symbolic support for civil rights remain his most admired legacies. Perhaps most significantly, Kennedy's rejection of a military solution to the Cuban missile crisis helped prevent a nuclear confrontation that would have had unforeseen consequences.

[*See also* **Civil Rights; Nixon, Richard M.;** *and* **Stevenson, Adlai.**]

BIBLIOGRAPHY

Carty, Thomas J. *A Catholic in the White House? Religion, Politics, and John Kennedy's 1960 Campaign.* New York: Palgrave Macmillan, 2004.

Dallek, Robert. *An Unfinished Life: John F. Kennedy, 1917–1963.* Boston: Little, Brown, 2003.

O'Brien, Michael. *John F. Kennedy: A Biography.* New York: Thomas Dunne Books/St. Martin's Press, 2005.

Piereson, James. *Camelot and the Cultural Revolution: How the Assassination of John F. Kennedy Shattered American Liberalism.* New York: Encounter Books, 2007.

Rorabaugh, R. J. *Kennedy and the Promise of the Sixties.* Cambridge, UK; New York: Cambridge University Press, 2002.

Thomas J. Carty III

KENNEDY, ROBERT

(1925–1968), attorney general of the United States, senator from New York. Born in Brookline, Massachusetts, third son of Rose Fitzgerald Kennedy and Joseph P. Kennedy, a wealthy businessman and former ambassador to Great Britain, Robert Francis Kennedy served in the navy during World War II, graduated from Harvard in 1948, and received a law degree from the University of Virginia in 1951. He first came to public notice in the 1950s as a staff member of Senator Joseph McCarthy's Red-hunting Subcommittee on Investigations and later as the twenty-nine-year-old chief counsel to the so-called Rackets

Committee headed by Senator John McClellan, which publicized criminal activity in organized labor.

In 1960, he successfully managed his brother John F. Kennedy's campaign for the presidency. To the surprise and disapproval of many, President Kennedy appointed Robert attorney general, joking that he wanted his brother, who had never tried a case, to get some experience before he practiced law. In fact, Robert won high marks as attorney general, orchestrating a campaign against organized crime that resulted in the conviction of the teamster president James R. Hoffa, among others, and definitively entering the civil rights struggle on behalf of racial integration. The Kennedy Justice Department was widely criticized, however, for illegal wiretapping, supporting segregationist judges for federal judicial appointments, and tolerating the Federal Bureau of Investigation excesses of J. Edgar Hoover.

After President Kennedy's assassination in November 1963, Robert emerged from a season of despair and in 1964 won election to the U.S. Senate from New York. As a senator, he investigated the underside of American life, including hunger in the Mississippi Delta, joblessness in northern ghettos, and squalid conditions in the migrant labor camps of California. In 1968, he campaigned for president as a law-and-order candidate, a champion of the disadvantaged, and an opponent of the Vietnam War. The Kennedy charisma won enthusiastic support from the young, the poor, the alienated, members of minority groups, and others. Yet he was resented by some on the left as an opportunist and by others on the right as an integrationist.

On 5 June 1968, Robert Kennedy was shot to death in Los Angeles, having just won the California primary. The assassin was Sirhan Sirhan, a supporter of the Palestinian cause. Kennedy's murder shocked a nation already reeling from the assassinations of President Kennedy, Malcolm X, and Martin Luther King Jr. Robert Kennedy never got the chance to fulfill the possibilities he so eloquently described.

[*See also* **Anti-Communism; Civil Rights; Federal Bureau of Investigation; Federal Government, Executive Branch: Department of Justice; Federal Government, Legislative Branch: Senate; Hoover, J. Edgar; Kennedy, John F.;** *and* **McCarthy, Joseph.**]

BIBLIOGRAPHY

Navasky, Victor S. *Kennedy Justice*. New York: Atheneum, 1971.

Schlesinger, Arthur M., Jr. *Robert Kennedy and His Times*. Boston: Houghton Mifflin, 1978.

Victor S. Navasky

KENT'S COMMENTARIES

James Kent (1763–1847) was the nation's most influential jurist between Independence and the Civil War. His life spanned the American Revolution, constitution making, the formative years of the new nation, and its aggressive western expansion to the Pacific Ocean. As a lawyer, judge, and treatise writer, Kent participated directly and indirectly in several aspects of this crucial phase of American nation-building. He entered Yale College one year after the Declaration of Independence. The war repeatedly interrupted his studies, but he continued to read on his own. During one break, he devoured the fourth volume of Sir William Blackstone's recently published *Commentaries on the Laws of England*. The highlight of that volume is an essay on "the rise, progress, and gradual improvements of the laws of England." Kent accepted entirely Blackstone's thesis that English law was constantly improving, and he believed that English law was the bedrock of American law. For the rest of his life he sought to participate in what he called a transatlantic "republic of letters" and to contribute to a common Anglo-American project of articulating the best legal principles. "Best," for Kent, meant those legal principles that integrated the states together as a nation, and the nation into the surrounding Atlantic world.

Kent served on the New York Supreme Court from 1798 to 1813, the last seven years as its chief justice, and then became the state's chancellor, its highest judicial officer, from 1814 to 1823. During that quarter century on the bench he published hundreds of opinions in more than twenty volumes of reports. When the state's first official reporter failed to meet his standards, he nominated the replacement, a friend who served alongside Kent for twenty years. Upon his forced retirement at age sixty, Kent began lecturing at Columbia, something he had first tried briefly in the 1790s, and he commenced a national consulting practice. His son suggested that Kent publish his Columbia law lectures, and they became the core of his *Commentaries on American Law,* undoubtedly the best-selling law book—and one of the best-selling books of any sort—in nineteenth-century America. The first edition appeared in four volumes between 1826 and 1830. Kent was editing the sixth edition at the time that he died. It served as a civics text for college students, a primer for law students, and a handy resource for practitioners. Consequently, American judges cited the *Commentaries* regularly. In time, so too did judges in the common law world outside the United States because Kent became the most-cited American judge in the courts of nineteenth-century Great Britain.

In many ways Kent's treatise fit the model of national legal institutes published in early modern Europe. Institutes served several goals. One was to forge a national law that reduced gaps and inconsistencies among regions within the nation. Another, international dimension was to distinguish the nation's law in some areas while tracing its common European heritage in others. In addition, these works served as introductions to legal training for law students and others seeking some education in the law. Finally, the books served as reference works for legal practitioners. Blackstone's *Commentaries* was a type of institute and the most immediate model for Kent's work.

Kent's *Commentaries* served all these purposes. In addition, and unlike many European institutes, Kent devoted a substantial part of his first volume to the law of nations, a decision explicitly designed to suggest that the United States was part of a larger community of nations. "When the United States ceased to be a part of the British empire," he wrote in the first sentence of the first chapter, "and assumed the character of an independent nation, they became subject to that system of rules which reason, morality, and custom had established among the civilized nations of Europe, as their public law." Kent's next section then celebrated the national achievement symbolized by the Constitution. These dual aims of integrating the nation into the larger world while distinguishing some of its unique characteristics served the classic goals of an institute but did so in an unprecedented structure. Another distinguishing characteristic of Kent's work was the amount of material on personal property, or commercial law. A full third of his four volumes was devoted to commercial law subjects like negotiable instruments, marine insurance, freight contracts, and maritime law. These areas of law were relevant to interstate and international trade, which Kent and many of his generation believed marked the highest stage of civilization. Blackstone had covered none of them. Finally, although Blackstone devoted one volume to criminal law ("pleas of the crown"), Kent barely touched on the subject. Implicitly, criminal law was not "American law" but rather just state law.

The *Commentaries* were an enormous success in all ways. The work brought immense wealth to the family for two generations, was used in many college classrooms and law offices, and was cited in hundreds of published opinions in the nineteenth century. It also made a mark in Britain, where one treatise writer paid what Kent would have considered the highest compliment by calling him "a Transatlantic Chancellor."

[*See also* **Blackstone, William, influence of.**]

BIBLIOGRAPHY

Horton, John T. *James Kent: A Study in Conservatism.* New York: D. Appleton–Century, 1939.

Hulsebosch, Daniel J. *Constituting Empire: New York and the Transformation of Constitutionalism in the Atlantic World, 1664–1830*, pp. 274–302. Chapel Hill: University of North Carolina Press, 2005.

Hulsebosch, Daniel J. "An Empire of Law: Chancellor Kent and the Revolution in Books in the Early Republic," *Alabama Law Review* 60 (2009): 377–424.

Langbein, John H. "Chancellor Kent and the History of Legal Literature," *Columbia Law Review* 93 (1993): 547–594.

Daniel J. Hulsebosch

KERRY, JOHN

John Forbes Kerry is a Democratic U.S. senator from Massachusetts first elected in 1984. In 2004 he was his party's nominee for president but was defeated by incumbent George W. Bush. Kerry's lifetime ratings from Americans for Democratic Action and the American Conservative Union place him as one of the most liberal members of the Senate.

Kerry commanded a Navy swift boat in Vietnam, earning three Purple Hearts, a Silver Star, and a Bronze Star. He first came to national attention as an activist with Vietnam Veterans against the War. Kerry famously asked during 1971 testimony before the Senate Foreign Relations Committee, "How do you ask a man to be the last man to die in Vietnam? How do you ask a man to be the last man to die for a mistake?" He participated in a protest wherein veterans tossed their medals into a trash bin near the Capitol, although Kerry apparently threw his ribbons and not his medals. His experience in Vietnam has informed his career in government and interest in foreign relations.

Kerry lost his first general election race for a congressional seat in 1972. He then went to law school and upon graduation became an assistant district attorney in Middlesex County, rising to the position of first assistant. Upon leaving that office in 1979 he began his own practice and stayed visible politically.

In 1982 Kerry won the office of lieutenant governor of Massachusetts, serving with Governor Michael S. Dukakis. In early 1984 Senator Paul Tsongas announced that he would not run for reelection because of poor health, and Kerry sought the Democratic nomination. He defeated Congressman James Shannon in a tough primary and coasted to victory in the general election.

He became a critic of the Reagan administration's foreign and military policy, especially its support for the Nicaraguan contras. Kerry investigated evidence of drug running against contra operatives; his suspicions that Panamanian dictator Manuel Noriega was involved in drug trafficking led him to investigate and help bring down the Bank of Credit and Commerce International, a corrupt institution favored by drug dealers, arms merchants, and dictators.

When the U.S. Senate faced the issue of authorizing President George H. W. Bush to intervene militarily after Iraq's invasion of Kuwait, Kerry urged continued sanctions rather than invasion. He voted against the resolution authorizing the president to use military force against Saddam Hussein. Later Kerry helped lead a select committee that concluded that no American servicemen were still alive in Vietnam. In 1995 he stood with fellow veteran Senator John McCain as President Clinton announced the opening of diplomatic relations with Vietnam. In 1996 he faced a very serious challenge to his Senate seat from the highly regarded Governor William Weld and was reelected.

In the wake of the terrorist attacks against the United States on 11 September 2001, Kerry supported President George W. Bush's use of force in Afghanistan. In October 2002, after months of expressing doubts about President Bush's foreign policy, Kerry joined in support of a resolution that would permit the administration to intervene forcefully against Iraq.

Kerry easily achieved reelection in 2002 but was already preparing to run for president. His Iraq vote exposed him to liberal critics in the party and his nomination candidacy foundered. He fell behind former Vermont governor Howard Dean in the first-in-the-nation Iowa caucuses and New Hampshire primary. Yet Dean peaked early and Kerry surged, winning Iowa and New Hampshire and capturing the nomination.

Voters seemed disappointed in the performance of President George W. Bush in 2004, but Kerry was unable to convince them he would be a marked improvement. In the wake of 9/11, terrorism loomed as an important issue, and voters favored Bush over Kerry on that topic. Swift Boat Veterans for Truth, an independent group loosely allied with the Bush campaign, accused Kerry of lying about his record in Vietnam. The attacks hurt his campaign despite the fact that the accusations were falsehoods. Bush prevailed by 286 to 252 in the Electoral College although he led Kerry by only 120,000 votes in Ohio, where a minor shift toward the Democrat would have given him the state and the presidency.

Kerry returned to the Senate and contemplated another campaign for the presidency in 2008, but decided not to run. He became chairman of the Senate Foreign Relations Committee. In that capacity he has been especially vigorous in oversight of the war in Afghanistan. He was a strong advocate for ratification of the new Strategic Arms Treaty with Russia in 2010.

[*See also* **Bush, George W.**]

BIBLIOGRAPHY

"John Kerry." http://kerry.senate.gov (accessed 18 August 2011).

Kranish, Michael, Brian C. Mooney, and Nina J. Easton. *John F. Kerry: The Complete Biography by the Boston Globe Reporters Who Know Him Best.* New York: PublicAffairs, 2004.

Pomper, Gerald M. "The Presidential Election: The Ills of American Politics after 9/11." In *The Elections of 2004*, edited by Michael Nelson. Washington, D.C.: CQ Press, 2005.

Maurice T. Cunningham

KING, MARTIN LUTHER, JR.

(1929–1968), civil rights leader, preeminent voice of the post–World War II African American freedom movement. Born in Atlanta, Georgia, the son and namesake of a prominent

Baptist minister, King entered Atlanta's Morehouse College at age fifteen. After graduation he enrolled at Crozer Theological Seminary in Pennsylvania, where he encountered Walter Rauschenbusch's Social Gospel theology, Reinhold Niebuhr's justifications for the use of coercion to combat evil, and MahatmaGandhi's philosophy of nonviolent direct action. Enrolling at Boston University, he earned a PhD in systematic theology (1955). He married Coretta Scott in 1953; they had four children.

In 1954, King was appointed pastor of Dexter Avenue Baptist Church in Montgomery, Alabama. On 1 December 1955, the arrest of Rosa Parks for violating the city's racial-segregation ordinances sparked a bus boycott, and local organizers selected the twenty-six-year-old King to lead it. "It happened so fast," King remembered, "that I did not even have time to think it through." At the boycott's first mass meeting, King delivered a speech that revealed not only his oratorical gifts and his expansive vision of African American liberation, but also a political strategy. Declaring, "the only weapon we have . . . is the weapon of nonviolence," King situated the movement within U.S. civic traditions and Cold War politics. "If we were incarcerated behind the iron curtains of a communistic nation we couldn't do this," he said, "but the great glory of American democracy is the right to protest for right." Underlining the threat that black protest could pose to U.S. foreign policy, King envisioned God proclaiming to the United States: "Be still and know that I am God—and if you don't obey Me I'm going to break the backbone of your power—and cast you out of the arms of your international and national relationships." He concluded with a prophetic call for African American self-affirmation: "Right here in Montgomery, when the history books are written in the future, somebody will have to say, 'There lived a race of people, black people, fleecy locks and black complexion, who had the moral courage to stand up for their rights.'" Nonviolent direct action, Cold War realism, and appeals to what he later called "a sense of somebodiness" among African Americans summed up King's ensuing strategy. After a 381-day bus boycott, a federal district court declared Alabama's bus-segregation statutes unconstitutional, and the U.S. Supreme Court concurred. King told the Montgomery bus boycott story in *Stride toward Freedom* (1958).

Following up this victory, King in 1957 founded the Southern Christian Leadership Conference (SCLC). Based in the black churches, the SCLC led a series of campaigns in southern cities to expose the reality of racism for all to see, with the goal of securing federal civil rights legislation. A self-described reformer, King invoked the Bible, the U.S. Constitution, and the "American dream"—although he declared in 1957 that he "could never accommodate [him]self" to capitalism "because it denies necessities to the many to provide luxuries to the few." Moving to Atlanta in 1960, he became copastor, with his father, of Ebenezer Baptist Church. That fall he was imprisoned following a sit-in at an Atlanta snack bar. John F. Kennedy's intervention to secure his release helped Kennedy solidify the black vote in the November presidential election.

King's strategy failed in Albany, Georgia, in 1962, when shrewd local authorities responded mildly to the demonstrations, but succeeded spectacularly in Birmingham, Alabama, in 1963. As the television cameras rolled, Police Commissioner Eugene "Bull" Connor battled peaceful demonstrators with fire hoses and snarling dogs and imprisoned King, whose "Letter from Birmingham Jail" eloquently summarized his goals and strategy. That August, thousands flocked to Washington, D.C., for an interracial civil rights rally at the Lincoln Memorial, where King delivered his memorable "I Have a Dream" speech. The landmark Civil Rights Act of 1964 resulted directly from these events. Further demonstrations led by King and the SCLC, including one in Selma, Alabama, in 1965, led to the Voting Rights Act of 1965. The Selma demonstrations, which also triggered police violence, culminated in a major demonstration at the capital in Montgomery, where 25,000 protesters heard King's powerful oratory and sang the movement's anthem, "We Shall Overcome."

King's protests were predicated on Cold War realpolitik. America was "battling for the hearts of men in Asia and Africa, he declared, "and they aren't going to respect the United States . . . if she deprives men and women of the basic rights of life because of the color of their skins." Images of violence against protestors, broadcast worldwide, forced the federal government to intervene. The movement that King symbolized brought about the 1964–1965 civil rights legislation, which, along with the Supreme Court's earlier *Brown v. Board of Education* ruling, stands as enduring achievements of a freedom movement that toppled the formal racial caste system in the United States and created a new black sense of self.

By 1965, as King took up the issues of poverty and structural racism in northern cities and began to criticize the Vietnam War, his popularity waned. Young black activists in the Student Non-Violent Coordinating Committee and the Congress of Racial Equality, together with the Nation of Islam leader Malcolm X, urged a more militant approach. The Federal Bureau of Investigation, seizing upon King's sexual indiscretions, sought to destroy him by a campaign of spying, blackmail, and humiliation. On 4 April 1968, as he lent support to striking garbage workers in Memphis, Tennessee, King was assassinated by James Earl Ray, a white racist who was convicted of the crime, although aspects of the killing remain unclear.

The brief career of Martin Luther King Jr., took him to the heights of world leadership, capped by the Nobel Peace Prize (1964), and led him to die fighting for garbage workers, urging a nonviolent revolution of the poor, and denouncing America's military role in Southeast Asia. His legacy as a symbol of nonviolent direct action and progressive social change continues to resonate throughout the world. Martin Luther King Jr., Day is observed as a national holiday on the third Monday in January.

[*See also* **African Americans in Politics; *Brown v. Board of Education;* Civil Rights; Civil Rights Legislation; Congress of Racial Equality; Constitution; Equality; Federal Bureau of Investigation; Kennedy, John F.; Poverty; Segregation;** *and* **Southern Christian Leadership Conference.**]

BIBLIOGRAPHY

Branch, Taylor. *Parting the Waters: America in the King Years, 1954–63*. New York: Simon & Schuster, 1988.

Fairclough, Adam. *Martin Luther King Jr.* Athens, Ga.: University of Georgia Press, 1995.

Fairclough, Adam. *To Redeem the Soul of America: The Southern Christian Leadership Conference and Martin Luther King, Jr.* Athens, Ga.: University of Georgia Press, 1987.

Garrow, David. *Bearing the Cross: Martin Luther King, Jr., and the Southern Christian Leadership Conference*. New York: W. Morrow, 1986.

Lewis, David Levering. *King: A Critical Biography*. New York: Praeger, 1970.

Timothy B. Tyson

KNOW-NOTHING PARTY

The group that would come to be known by this name arose in the 1840s amid nativist sentiment roused by the influx of Irish

Catholics to East Coast cities. The American Republican Party (later simply the American Party) was founded in New York City in 1843; in coalition with the Whigs, it elected a nativist mayor of New York in 1844. Advocating a ban on Catholic and foreign-born officeholders and a 20-year time limit for naturalization, the party made headway in Philadelphia also, sparking anti-Catholic riots. It gained momentum in 1849 when Charles B. Allen founded the secret Order of the Star Spangled Banner in New York. Lodges soon spread to other cities. When questioned, members were instructed to answer "I know nothing," leading the *New York Tribune* to deride them in 1853 as "Know-Nothings."

In the early 1850s, as the Whig Party split over slavery in the territories, a Whig faction that supported the Compromise of 1850, called the Union Whigs, aligned with the American Party. In 1854, the Whig James W. Barker replaced Allen as leader. The party now added to its platform a new theme, pro-Unionism, first enunciated by Thomas Whitney, editor of a nativist periodical called the *Republic.* The nation faced two major threats, Whitney warned: abolitionism and politicized Catholicism. Members now swore to do everything possible to preserve the Union. At a party convention in 1855, when the leadership added a platform plank proclaiming, "Congress ought not to legislate upon the subject of slavery within the Territories," northern delegates opposed to slavery extension bolted, dividing the party. In 1856, the southern Know-Nothings nominated Millard Fillmore for president. The election proved a disaster for the party, however. Amid deep sectional divisions evident in the vote for Democrat James Buchanan and Republican John C. Frémont, Fillmore carried only the slave state of Maryland. The party subsequently disbanded, and organized nativism subsided for a time.

[*See also* **Antislavery Movement; Buchanan, James; Compromise of 1850; Democratic Party; Fillmore, Millard; Immigration Law and Policy: Before 1930; Political Parties; Republican Party;** ***and*** **Whig Party.**]

BIBLIOGRAPHY

Abinder, Tyler. *Nativism and Slavery: The Northern Know Nothings and the Politics of the 1850s.* New York: Oxford University Press, 1992.

Baker, Jean H. *Ambivalent Americans: The Know Nothing Party in Maryland.* Baltimore: Johns Hopkins University Press, 1977.

Billington, Ray A. *The Protestant Crusade, 1800–1860: A Study of the Origins of American Nativism.* Chicago: Quadrangle Books, 1938.

Thomas J. Curran

KOREMATSU v. UNITED STATES

See Japanese American Interment.

KU KLUX KLAN

The most notorious of terrorist groups that arose in the Reconstruction Era to uphold white supremacy and Democratic Party rule in the South. Founded as a social club (kuklos, the Greek word for circle, inspired the name) by six Confederate veterans in Pulaski, Tennessee, in 1866, the Klan soon became a powerful and frightening vehicle of vigilante violence and lawlessness. Racial terrorists from all walks of life adopted the Klan's white hoods and secret rituals to protect their identities and lend an aura of legitimacy to their activities. Their aim was to punish anyone perceived as threatening white supremacy, including assertive black workers, black or white teachers in black schools, and those who violated interracial sexual taboos. The overwhelming focus of Klan violence and intimidation, however, was Republican Party politicians, black and white, and black voters. During the election year of 1868, in Louisiana alone, the Klan and other terrorist groups murdered between 800 and 1,000 people, the vast majority of whom were Republican leaders, political candidates, and others challenging white, Democratic rule. Similar murderous waves across the South kept countless black voters away from the polls. A congressional investigation and anti-Klan state and federal legislation diminished the Klan's influence after 1871, but the movement left a powerful legacy.

Later, historians, novelists, and filmmakers offered racist apologies for the Reconstruction Klan. The most notorious of these, D. W. Griffith's film *Birth of a Nation* (1915), based on Thomas Dixon's 1905 novel *The Clansman*, inspired a second Klan movement. This revived Klan, founded at Stone Mountain, Georgia, by William J. Simmons and later taken over by the Texan Hiram W. Evans, differed markedly from the first. It attracted millions of male and female members from throughout the nation, especially in the Midwest and West, enriching paid recruiters (called Kleagles) as well as Simmons, Evans, and other leaders at the national headquarters in Atlanta. It was racist, but in an era when the institutions of white supremacy faced no serious challenge, race was not the exclusive focus. The second Klan's central message was that white Protestant hegemony was threatened by Roman Catholics, Jews, African Americans, immigrants, Prohibition violation, gambling and other crimes, political corruption, sexual immorality, materialism, and the erosion of religion and traditional family values. This Klan sometimes used intimidation and violence, but most frequently targeted fellow white Protestants who violated traditional morality. Political mobilization, parades, and social events were the Klan chapters' primary activities. By the mid-1920s, the Klan elected its candidates to local office in many communities; dominated politics in Indiana, Colorado, Oregon, Oklahoma, Alabama, and other states; and exerted a strong national influence within both major parties. A motion to condemn the Klan bitterly divided the 1924 Democratic Party convention. The second Klan declined dramatically after 1925 as a result of bitter divisions among Klan leaders, the imprisonment of Indiana "Grand Dragon" D. C. Stephenson on rape and manslaughter charges, and declining faith that the Klan could accomplish its goals.

In the following decades, pockets of support lingered, and racial vigilantes continued to invoke the Klan's name and regalia. During the era of the civil rights movement, a variety of Klan organizations surfaced with newfound support and, like their predecessors of the Reconstruction Era, attacked and terrorized African Americans and racial reformers. As the twentieth century ended, isolated Klan groups, although generally discredited, continued to perpetuate an occasionally violent right-wing subculture.

[*See also* **Democratic Party; Eighteenth Amendment; Immigration Law and Policy before 1930; Progressive Era; Prohibition;** ***and*** **Reconstruction Era.**]

BIBLIOGRAPHY

Chalmers, David M. *Hooded Americanism: The History of the Ku Klux Klan*, 3d ed. Durham, N.C.: Duke University Press, 1981.

MacLean, Nancy. *Behind the Mask of Chivalry: The Making of the Second Ku Klux Klan*. New York: Oxford University Press, 1994.

Trelease, Allen W. *White Terror: The Ku Klux Klan Conspiracy and Southern Reconstruction*. Westport, Conn.: Greenwood Press, 1971.

Leonard J. Moore

L

LABOR'S ROLE IN POLITICS

Organized labor has pressured government for favorable laws and supported sympathetic candidates for public office since American workers first organized to advance their interests. After the Civil War, as trade unions grew, many participated in coalitions that won federal and state laws declaring the legal workday to be eight hours. Some unions worked for the Greenback Party and the Populist Party, which supported the eight-hour day planks in their national 1878 and 1892 platforms, respectively, and for select Democratic and Republican candidates. From the late 1860s through the 1880s, the National Labor Union, the Knights of Labor, and the American Federation of Labor (AFL) all fought to establish federal and state labor agencies. These efforts culminated in 1913 with the creation of a separate U.S. Department of Labor, expected to be "labor's voice in the Cabinet."

Labor leaders disputed political strategy as unionization further strengthened in the early twentieth century. Many miners, machinists, and garment workers urged the need for a broader political agenda and supported an independent labor or Socialist party. But other leaders, especially in the crafts and building trades, favored "pure and simple" unionism and rejected broad political involvement in favor of lobbying for specific laws that directly benefitted unions. Long-time AFL president Samuel Gompers placed top priority on unions' economic power (based on a theory of "voluntarism"). Gompers rejected an independent labor party in favor of opportunistically rewarding labor's friends and punishing its enemies regardless of a candidate's partisan affiliation. In 1902, AFL leaders narrowly defeated a proposal to commit the AFL to socialism. Thereafter, the growing muscle of the crafts unions fortified Gompers's anti–labor party position. The Industrial Workers of the World, a militant union organization, eschewed political engagement in favor of syndicalism. The United States became the only wealthy capitalist democracy without a labor or social democratic party. At the same time, the AFL was a very active lobbyist, consistently pushing for legislation that strengthened unions' bargaining position, established public offices supportive of labor's agenda, and regulated the employment of women and children.

Hostile Republican legislators, along with adverse court rulings, prompted Gompers and other AFL leaders to gravitate toward an informal alliance with the national Democratic Party in the early 1900s. Gompers personally campaigned against the reelection of House Speaker Joseph Cannon (R-IL), who Gompers viewed as "the strategic center to the opposition to labor." The Democratic Party was more welcoming to the AFL because its candidates needed labor's vote to contest the large, industrializing northern states. Federation leaders built an alliance with the Democrats in the Progressive Era that has more or less endured ever since. But the AFL maintained its official position of nonpartisanship because it depended on the support of progressive Republicans, such as U.S. Senator Robert La Follette (R-WI).

Organized labor's political role surged along with union membership during the New Deal. The Roosevelt Administration actively protected unions and built an especially strong alliance with the industrial unions that formed the Congress of Industrial Organizations (CIO), an AFL rival. Although CIO president John L. Lewis grew disaffected from the New Deal and tested independent labor politics as well as a Republican presidential endorsement in 1940, unions and the Democratic Party were firmly allied by Roosevelt's death. Since the New Deal, organized labor has reliably provided armies of campaign workers and sizeable campaign contributions for Democratic candidates.

Union economic and political strength peaked in the 1950s and 1960s. The AFL and CIO merged in 1955 and also merged their political action committees into the Committee on Political Education (COPE), a path-breaking political action committee. Organized labor formed a close and effective partnership with the Democratic presidential administrations and Congressional majorities in the late 1940s, 1950s, and 1960s. George Meany, AFL–CIO president (1955–1980), and Walter Reuther, president of the United Automobile Workers (1946–1970), were major forces in bringing about the reforms of the Great Society.

By the 1970s, economic shifts were cutting away at unionized manufacturing jobs, slowly eroding union membership and organized labor's political strength. The unionization of service workers and public employees enhanced the political strength of these unions, but did not stem the overall decline of unionization, which fell to about one in eight American workers in 2010. According to national exit polls, voters who live in union households have continued to cast about 60 percent of their ballots for Democratic presidential candidates, but the percentage of voters who live in union households declined from nearly 30 percent in 1976 to about 20 percent in 2008. By the late 1970s, the AFL–CIO found that it could not advance some of its top legislative priorities, such as a law allowing "common situs" picketing of an entire worksite because of a dispute with a single contractor. Organized labor had a poor relationship with

Jimmy Carter and an adversarial one with Ronald Reagan. Union leaders were unhappy with some initiatives of the Bill Clinton administration, notably the North American Free Trade Agreement, and were disaffected by the administration of George W. Bush. The administration of Barack Obama disappointed the union leaders' hopes that it would give high priority to reforms making it easier to organize workers.

[*See also* **Great Society; Greenback Labor Party; La Follette, Robert; New Deal;** ***and*** **Populist Party.**]

BIBLIOGRAPHY

Dark, Taylor. *The Unions and the Democrats: An Enduring Alliance*. Ithaca, N.Y.: ILR Press, 1999.

Greene, Julie. *Pure and Simple Politics: The American Federation of Labor and Political Activism, 1881–1917*. Cambridge, UK; New York: Cambridge University Press, 1998.

Robertson, David Brian. *Capital, Labor, and State: The Battle for American Labor Markets from the Civil War to the New Deal*. Lanham, Md.: Rowman & Littlefield, 2000.

David Brian Robertson

LA FOLLETTE, ROBERT

(1855–1925), Progressive Era politician and reformer. Born and raised in Wisconsin, La Follette won election as district attorney of Dane County in 1880. As a Republican congressman between 1885 and 1891, he found himself increasingly at odds with the conservative state leaders of his party, led by Senator Philetus Sawyer. As governor of Wisconsin (1901–1905), he joined the ranks of Republican insurgents, presiding over a reform administration that received national attention and came to be called, in Theodore Roosevelt's phrase, the "laboratory of democracy." Working closely with the economist John R. Commons (1862–1945) and other experts at the University of Wisconsin, La Follette successfully battled for social-reform laws, measures promoting majoritarian democracy such as the direct primary, tax-law changes designed to equalize the tax burden, and new regulatory commissions aimed at bringing railroads and large corporations under control.

In the U.S. Senate from 1906 on, La Follette continued many of the same campaigns he had pursued at the state level, making the "Wisconsin Idea" a blueprint for federal reform. He promoted his ideas through *La Follette's Weekly Magazine* (founded 1909), later the *Progressive*. His hopes for the presidency in 1912 were dashed as William Howard Taft won the Republican nomination and Theodore Roosevelt headed the insurgent Progressive Party ticket. La Follette vocally opposed U.S. participation in World War I and in April 1917 was one of six senators to vote against President Woodrow Wilson's call for a declaration of war, a position that cost him heavily in popularity. In 1924, he ran unsuccessfully for president as the candidate of a new Progressive Party.

La Follette passionately advocated the causes he embraced. Like many Progressives, he believed in a rational, scientific approach to reform. Unlike such leaders as Theodore Roosevelt, who were willing to compromise, he believed, as he asserted in his autobiography, that "in legislation *no bread* is often better than *half a loaf*."

[*See also* **Economic Policy: Regulation; Federal Government, Legislative Branch: Senate; Progressive Era; Progressive Party of 1912; Progressive Party of 1924; Regulatory Agencies, Federal; Republican Party; Roosevelt, Theodore; Taft, William Howard; Taxation;** ***and*** **Wilson, Woodrow.**]

BIBLIOGRAPHY

La Follette, Robert M. *La Follette's Autobiography: A Personal Narrative of Political Experiences,* forward by Allan Nevins. Madison: University of Wisconsin Press, 1960.

Thelen, David P. *Robert M. La Follette and the Insurgent Spirit.* Boston: Little, Brown, 1976.

Allan M. Winkler

LA GUARDIA, FIORELLO

(1882–1947), congressman, mayor of New York City. Born in New York City, La Guardia grew up in the West and moved to Italy. Returning to New York at age twenty-four and earning a law degree from New York University in 1910, he plunged into Republican Party politics. In 1916, he became the first Italian American to be elected to Congress, serving in the House of Representatives until 1932, with interruptions for World War I service in Italy and a brief tenure as president of the New York City Board of Alderman. In 1933, running on the Republican and City Fusion tickets, La Guardia was elected mayor of normally Democratic New York with less than 40 percent of the votes, as two candidates from the scandal-ridden Democratic Party split the rest. He won reelection in 1937 and 1941 with backing from the American Labor Party. After leaving office in 1946 he served as director-general of the United Nations Relief and Rehabilitation Administration.

During his long political career, La Guardia emerged as one of the nation's most prominent advocates of urban liberalism. A one-man balanced ticket (the Episcopalian son of a Jewish mother, he married a Catholic and spoke Italian, Yiddish, German, and Hungarian), the "Little Flower" projected a cosmopolitan Americanism at odds with the rampant nativism and racism of his day. In Congress, he opposed Prohibition, defended labor and immigrants, and sought checks on corporate power, allying with a minority bloc of midwestern progressives. As mayor, he worked to rationalize the sprawling city government and root out corruption, using his close ties to the New Deal to fund a massive expansion of the city's infrastructure and social services. Although never as popular with voters as his Democratic predecessors and successors, La Guardia after his death came to be seen as the political embodiment of modern New York.

[*See also* **Federal Government, Legislative Branch: House of Representatives; Liberalism; New Deal; Prohibition;** *and* **Republican Party.**]

BIBLIOGRAPHY

Kessner, Thomas. *Fiorello H. La Guardia and the Making of Modern New York.* New York: McGraw–Hill, 1989.

Mann, Arthur. *La Guardia: A Fighter against His Times, 1882–1933.* Philadelphia: Lippincott, 1959.

Joshua B. Freeman

LAND POLICY, FEDERAL

Early in the nineteenth century large tracts of land were acquired by the federal government by way of vast territorial acquisitions mostly in the West. The U.S. government developed incentives for private ownership through sales, legislation, and grants since the government was not yet equipped to deal with the ownership and management of these parcels of land.

Federal Land Policy, 1781–1862. Between 1781 and 1802, the U.S. government came into the possession of 225 million acres of public lands. The sources of this bounty were the Treaty of Paris (1783), which established the limits of the new, independent American nation, and the cession by the states of their western land claims. Under the original colonial charters, some colonies (now states) had large western land claims; others had none. The solution was the cession of the claims of the landed states to the new national government. With these cessions (from New York in 1780 and Virginia in 1781 to Georgia in 1802) the government needed to draft a policy for the administration and disposal of what came to be known as the public domain.

The solution was the adoption of the Ordinance of 1785, which would become the foundation of policies for the public domain for the next century. Under the provisions of the Land Ordinance (as it came to be called), before sale the lands would be surveyed into townships six miles square and subsequently by subdivisions of 640 acres, each numbered in an orderly fashion and plainly marked on the ground. Surveying would be done under the direction of the geographer of the United States, with the assistance of a surveyor from each state. The basic principle of survey before sale had been adopted.

Next, the Ordinance established a mechanism for sale of the public lands at publicly advertised auctions. This provision reflected the idea that all citizens of the republic should have an opportunity to purchase; it also addressed the need of the public domain to generate revenue of the new nation. The United States was deeply in debt; the public domain represented one of the most important potential sources of revenue. Lands would be auctioned by whole townships alternately with townships divided into lots. The minimum price was set at a high $1 per acre payable in specie or in land office certificates reduced to specie value. The purchaser also paid the cost of the survey. Payment of one-third was due at the time of sale and the rest within three months. Settlement on the public domain without purchase was forbidden.

Having established a policy of high principles, Congress then proceeded to violate them. In response to the disappointing sales, Congress passed a resolution in the fall of 1787 authorizing the Board of the Treasury to enter into negotiations for the sales of tracts of not less than 1 million acres to large land companies. Congress now contracted with three large groups of speculators, the Ohio Company, the Scioto Company, and John Cleves Symmes Company. The Ohio Company established a settlement at Marietta.

In the government under the new constitution adopted in 1789, secretary of the treasury Alexander Hamilton proposed that land be considered a source of revenue. Congress passed the Land Act in 1796 to facilitate sales. Now, alternate townships would be sold at Pittsburgh or Cincinnati in sections of 640 acres. The price was raised to $2 an acre with credit for one year. The new law also confirmed the principle of survey before sale, and the administration of the law would rest in the hands of the secretary of the treasury. Still, the price was too high, and the credit for one year insufficient. Sales were small.

The Land Law of 1800 represented a dramatic departure from these policies. With William Henry Harrison, the delegate from the Northwest Territory as the key figure, the land system was changed. The price remained a minimum of $2 an acre, but the new law extended credit for up to four years. The minimum size for purchase was reduced to 320 acres. The law established four district land offices in the Northwest Territory. Each had a register in charge of sales and a receiver who handled public monies. The so-called Harrison law coincided with the expansion of the territories and the expansion of the land system. By 1812, fourteen land offices had been established. In the decade from 1801 to 1811, sales of public lands averaged 700,000 acres a year.

With the coming of peace in 1815, immigration to the West surged. This movement of individuals and families found the land system in place. The federal government had embarked on a half century of acquisition of Indian lands that represented an increasingly callous disregard for Indian rights. With the land so acquired, the mechanisms for survey and sale followed. After 1815, the high price of commodities, especially cotton, and the opening of new tracts to sales led to record prices and annual sales. With the rising sales came a parallel rise in the land debt owed the federal government. When the crash in credit and commodities in 1819 ended this first great chapter in the sale of the public domain, creditors owed the federal government $23 million. In response, Congress enacted the Land Law of 1820. This law abolished the credit system and reduced the minimum price to $1.25 an acre. Still, the large debt remained, and between 1821 and 1832 Congress passed 11 relief acts to resolve these obligations.

In opening the public domain, the principle of preemption was employed. The preemption law allowed the individual or settler family to settle on the public domain and later purchase the 160-acre tract with improvements at the minimum price of $1.25 an acre. Before preemption, claims clubs offered a degree of protection from large speculators through intimidation. They were an extralegal device, used with the support of local officials. Urged on by pressure from growing western political strength, Congress passed the first preemption law in 1830, with subsequent extensions in 1832, 1834, 1838, and 1840. In 1841, Congress passed a permanent preemption law.

The next land mark legislation was the Graduation Act of 1854. This act reduced the minimum price of public lands in proportion to the amount of time they had been on the market. Under the new law, the price of tracts on the market for 10 years would be reduced from $1.25 to $1 an acre, with progressive reductions down to lands available for 30 years, now priced at 12.5 cents an acre.

An important law in the distribution of the public domain was the Homestead Act of 1862. The principle of homestead—free land to those who would occupy the tract and place it under cultivation—was an important part of the Republican platform in the election of 1860. Its provisions provided for conveying 160 acres of the public domain free to any citizen (or applicant who declared the intention to become a citizen) who would improve it by continuous residence over five years and pay minimal administrative costs.

The Homestead Act marked the end of the first period of federal land policy. After two generations of increasingly generous laws, Congress had established the principle that the settlement of the public lands by the citizens of the republic was more important than revenue. As part of this policy, lands should be disposed of and settled in small units to insure that small farms were available to the greatest number of people. This policy was reflected in earlier laws reducing the minimum size of the public domain available for purchase (80 acres in 1820, 40 acres in 1832). Free land through the Homestead Act was the ultimate statement of this principle.

Private Land Claims. From the creation of the public domain, issues of its disposal were clouded by a series of claims that dated from previous occupants. These claims—originally associated with the French settlements in Illinois and Indiana—were greatly enlarged by the purchase of Louisiana. Congress responded by creating boards of commissioners to adjudicate these claims. The commissions moved slowly, handicapped by strange documents, no documents, and the hostility of the claimants.

Yet, these claims turned out to be an important dimension of federal land policy. Eventually, they would include the claims assumed by the United States for lands acquired from Great Britain, France, Spain, and Mexico. These covered parts of the future states of Florida, Louisiana, Missouri, Mississippi, California, and New Mexico. All came with serious land title problems. Throughout the nineteenth century, Congress, state legislatures, and federal and state courts remained heavily involved in sorting out these claims (and, where legitimate, their boundaries). Such claims, for example, involved some 9 million acres in California alone. The opportunities for fraud were rampant. The most egregious examples emerged from New Mexico, where a courthouse cabal of unscrupulous lawyers acquired by fraud huge tracts originally given to Mexican people.

Congressional Gifts of Land. From the establishment of the new, independent American nation (and, indeed, even before independence), Congress distributed land to a wide variety of individuals and groups. The reason was simply that this was a world in which the United States lacked money and had lands stretching to the horizon and beyond. So the Congress dispensed land as inducement, payment, and recognition of a national obligation. Between 1789 and 1841, Congress passed and the president signed some 375 laws concerned with the public domain. Most of these acts involved gifts and grants.

For a generation after independence, Congress gave land to individuals. Among the long list of recipients, for example, were grants to George Rogers Clark and his men; to the Marquis de Lafayette for services during the American Revolution; to Meriwether Lewis, William Clark, and the members of the "Corps of Discovery;" and to countless other individuals.

As early as 1776, Congress also granted from 100 to 500 acres (depending on rank) to officers and men who would serve in the continental army for the duration of the war or until discharged. In 1796, twenty years after the first enactment, the federal government allotted a tract of land in Ohio, the U.S. Military District, for location of the Revolutionary War bounties. Congress offered a 160-acre bounty (plus three months' pay) for enlisted men who would serve five years or until discharged. To satisfy these claims, at the close of the war, Congress set aside three tracts of 2 million acres each in Michigan, Illinois, and Arkansas.

To encourage enlistments in the war with Mexico, Congress made each soldier who served twelve months entitled to a 160-acre tract on any open land within the public domain. After the close of the war, beginning in 1850, a series of laws recognized veterans of other conflicts whose service was not covered by previous laws. Finally, an act of 1855 granted 160 acres to any soldier or his heirs who had seen service in any war since 1790. The total of these military bounties was about 74 million acres.

Congress also gave large grants to foster internal improvements of many kinds, including roads, canals, and river navigation. By 1854, Congress had given some 19 million acres to the states in support of internal improvements. Beginning in 1850, Congressional land grants to foster railroad construction in Illinois, Mississippi, and Alabama opened an era of ever larger gifts to railroad companies. Between 1850 and 1857, Congress granted 21 million acres for railroad construction in the Mississippi Valley. But the great land grants were associated with the transcontinental lines. These began with the Pacific Railroad Act of 1862 and over twenty years reached a total of 174 million acres.

Among the many congressional laws that dispersed the public domain, one of the largest in its effect was the Swamp Land Act of 1850.

The idea was that states would make provisions to develop the "swamp and overflowed lands" within their boundaries. With the several extensions, this series of laws eventually conveyed some 65 million acres to fifteen states.

There were continuing grants of public lands to education, beginning with the Ordinance of 1787. Under the ordinance, Section 16 in each township would be given to support public schools. The money from one section in each township was to support public schools. Beginning in 1848, school support was increased to two sections per township and later to three. These large grants for education eventually totaled some 130 million acres of land.

Congress also supported institutions of higher learning with grants of land. The most important of these laws was the Morrill Land Grant Act. Passed in 1862, this law gave every state loyal to the Union 30,000 acres for each representative and senator then in Congress. Under its provisions, sixty-nine land grant colleges were established or supported, with a total of 72 million acres for higher education.

Federal Land Policy, 1862–1904. Between 1862 and 1904, the federal government and its land system distributed free 147 million acres, most of that under the Homestead Act. In these same years, purchasers (under a variety of laws) bought another 611 million acres. The generous terms and free land fostered the settlement of the West in the half century after the Civil War. The movement of individuals and families (in response to these generous conditions) carried them onto the Great Plains. Here, they encountered new weather patterns, in the form of wet and dry cycles that could produce periods of drought. Driven by the century-long dream of land ownership, Americans continued to take up lands under the Homestead Act and lands sold by railroad companies in defiance of experiences on the plains.

Congress passed additional laws to assist in this expansion. The Timber Culture Act of 1873 offered land to individuals and families who would plant trees on 40 acres (later reduced to 10 acres). Next, the Desert Land Act of 1877 offered 640 acres of desert at a low price with the condition of running water for irrigation. This law was grossly abused by cattlemen, speculators, and lumber operators. Both laws recognized the different conditions of the plains, but they were open to exploitation by unscrupulous groups (like so much else in the public domain).

In 1902, the passage of the Newlands Act changed the trajectory of the Homestead Act and federal land policy. The act specified that the proceeds of the sales of the public domain would be used in the future to finance irrigation projects in the West. This was a dramatic recognition of the significance of water in the West and acknowledged that agriculture and its conditions had changed in the most direct kinds of ways.

Yet distribution of lands under the laws governing the public domain continued unabated. In 1909, Congress enlarged the provisions of the Homestead Act to 320 acres in eight western states. More lands were patented under the Homestead Act after 1904 than before that date.

Conservation Movement. In the years after the Civil War, the continuing exploration of the West and the accompanying publicity gave rise to a conservation movement. The most immediate object was the preservation of sites of singular beauty and grandeur. In 1872, Congress set aside a large tract of 2 million acres as Yellowstone National Park. This was the first in a series of national parks. By 1974, Congress had established thirty-eight national parks, covering some 15 million acres.

In a parallel movement, the idea of national forests took hold as part of the conservation movement. After much opposition, in 1891, the first lands were withdrawn from the public domain for national forests. By 1974, thirty-eight national forests had been established, protecting some 15 million acres of the public domain from entry. Almost all of these national forests were in the western states.

The reservation of so much land in the West for conservation purposes gave rise to an opposition movement. In the 1970 and 1980s, drawn together under the banner of "The Sage Brush Rebellion," this group objected that such large reservations in western states restricted opportunities for economic development. Federal land policy is still the subject of lively debate.

Whatever the objections to elements of federal land policy in the late twentieth century, the principles have remained consistent over the two centuries since the establishment of the public domain. It was the policy of the national government to dispose of the public domain in a rapid and orderly fashion and always in the interests of settlement and to encourage the establishment of needed public services.

[*See also* **Harrison, William Henry; Homestead Act; Louisiana Purchase; Morrill Land Grant Act;** ***and*** **National Park System.**]

BIBLIOGRAPHY

Bogue, Margaret B., ed. *The New American State Papers: Public Lands*, 8 vols. Wilmington, DE: Scholarly Resources 1972–1973. The most important collection of documents on federal land policy to1840, with a fine introduction.

Carstensen, Vernon, ed. *The Public Lands: Studies in the History of the Public Domain*. Madison: University of Wisconsin Press, 1963. A collection of articles by the leading scholars of federal land policy with an important introduction.

Donaldson, Thomas. *The Public Domain: Its History with Statistics*. Washington, D.C.: Government Printing Office, 1884. A compendium of the first century of federal land policy.

Feller, Daniel. *The Public Lands in Jacksonian Politics*. Madison: University of Wisconsin Press, 1984. This book describes the influence of politics on the development of public land policy at a crucial moment.

Gates, Paul W. *History of Public Land Law Development*. Washington, D.C.: Government Printing Office, 1968. This is the standard account of the development of federal land policy, written by the most important historian of the public lands.

Gates, Paul W. *The Jeffersonian Dream: Studies in the History of American Land Policy and Development*, edited by Allan G. Bogue and Margaret B. Bogue. Albuquerque: University of New Mexico Press, 1996. A collection of the most influential essays by the most important historian of the public domain.

Gates, Paul W. *Landlords and Tenants on the Prairie Frontier: Studies in American Land Policy*. Ithaca, N.Y.: Cornell University Press, 1973. Nine studies on how federal land policy shaped the economic, political, and social development of prairie lands.

Nelson, Paula. *After the West Was Won: Homesteaders and Town-Builders in Western South Dakota, 1900–1917*. Iowa City: University of Iowa Press, 1986. The final application of the homestead law describes attempts to establish homesteads in the face of great physical and economic hardships.

Oberly, James. *Sixty Million Acres: American Veterans and the Public Lands before the Civil War*. Kent, OH: Kent State University Press, 1990. A definitive account of military land bounty acts from 1775 to 1855.

Rohrbough, Malcolm J. *The Land Office Business: The Settlement and Administration of American Public Lands, 1789–1837*. New York: Oxford University Press, 1968. This book analyzes the organization and operation of the federal land system in the first half century of its operations.

Robbins, Roy M. *Our Landed Heritage: The Public Domain, 1776–1936*. Princeton, N.J.: Princeton

University Press, 1942. Although dated in its interpretations, this book still contains a wealth of material about federal land policy.

Wyatt, William K. *Westward in Eden: The Public Lands and the Conservation Movement.* Berkeley: University of California Press, 1982. This is an analysis of the conservation movement from 1870 to 1970.

Malcolm J. Rohrbough

LANGDELL, CHRISTOPHER COLUMBUS

One of the most influential law professors in American history, Christopher Columbus Langdell's views of the law and of legal instruction reshaped the American law school. A master of contract law, Langdell is remembered not for his scholarship but for the teaching method that has dominated legal education for the past century and a half—the case method of instruction.

Langdell was born on 22 May 1826 in New Boston, New Hampshire, in a Scotch-Irish family of which little is now known, although the family was not wealthy. Christopher worked while a student at Phillips Exeter Academy and while at Harvard College, which he entered in 1848. Finances required him to leave the college without his degree, although he reentered in the law school, which was then an undergraduate program, receiving his bachelor's of laws in 1854. He had been in school much longer than most law students, working as a research assistant for professor Theophilus Parsons, who was then completing his great treatise on contracts. While a student, Langdell was bookish but pleasant, and he became friends with a young chemistry student from a good family, Charles Eliot, who would later have a considerable influence on his career. After graduation, Langdell began practicing in New York, New York, where he was respected but where he grew increasingly disenchanted with the standards of the profession.

In 1869, the then thirty-five-year-old Charles Eliot became the president of Harvard University and committed himself to the reform of Harvard's professional schools. The following year, Eliot named Langdell the Dane Professor of Law. A few months later, the faculty elected him the first dean of a newly reorganized law school. He would serve as dean for a quarter century.

Langdell fervently believed that law is a science, and the principles of law can be extracted from cases in the same way that the principles of chemistry can be perceived in a reaction. He sought for students to be able to perceive these principles through engagement and experimentation with the arguments and opinions from cases. Toward that end, he abandoned the traditional lecture, given as a monolog of principles and illustrations of those principles that was presented by a teacher, talking to passive students. Rather Langdell assigned students to read collections of cases, about which he asked questions, seeking to spur the students to discern the reasons why the facts of cases and arguments of law gave rise to specific results. This dialog, sometimes called Socratic dialog, was the hallmark of the case method of instruction.

His first class, the contracts class of the fall of 1870, followed this pattern. It was not popular. Student enrollment plummeted, and faculty dissatisfaction was high. Many students and faculty left Harvard for Boston University to set up a rival school along the old lines of instruction.

Backed by Eliot, Langdell persevered. He reorganized the school, increasing the length of the standard course of instruction from one to three years. He required new entrance criteria and instituted exams at the end of each year of instruction. He created a graduate degree. He built a robust law library. He also moved away from the recruitment of judges and practicing lawyers as teachers and sought out young graduates who had showed promise in their study. In 1873, Langdell hired one of his own recent graduates as a replacement professor, James Barr Ames. In time, more students came than had left and more faculty were recruited. By the time he stepped down the school was larger than ever, and the instructional and administrative reforms Langdell had instituted were emulated nationwide.

By the mid-twentieth century, Langdell's case method had become the nearly universal approach to U.S. legal education, or at least it seemed so. In reality, the dialog Langdell had standardized and the study of cases he had encouraged no longer worked as he had envisioned. Far from teaching students the natural principles of law as they evolved in the cases, the new form of instruction allowed the generation that followed his own to see in the cases the vagaries of human construction. The cases increasingly demonstrated the reality of human invention rather than the nature of legal science. Yet that change, instituted in part by Langdell's own disciple, his successor as dean, James Barr Ames, was unknown to Langdell himself. He spent the last decade of his life writing in the Harvard law library, his eyesight failing but his mind sharp. He died on 6 July 1906.

[*See also* **Contract, Law of.**]

BIBLIOGRAPHY

Carrington, Paul D. *Stewards of Democracy: Law as a Public Profession*. Boulder, Colo.: Westview Press, 1999.

Kimball, Bruce A. *The Inception of Modern Professional Education: C. C. Langdell, 1826–1906*. Chapel Hill: University of North Carolina Press, 2009.

Langdell, Christopher C. "Teaching Law as a Science, 1886." In *The History of Legal Education in the United States, Commentaries and Primary Sources*, edited by Steve Sheppard, p. 514. Clark, N.J.: The Lawbook Exchange, 2007.

Sheppard, Steve. *Casebooks, Commentaries, and Curmudgeons: An Introductory History of Law in the Lecture Hall*, 82 Iowa Law Review 547, 1997.

Stephen M. Sheppard

LEGAL THEORY, CRITICAL

Sometimes called critical legal studies (CLS), this movement originated at Harvard, Stanford, SUNY–Buffalo, and the University of Wisconsin law schools in the 1970s as a reaction to formalism and other conceptions of law as a science or set of rules. Critical legal theorists instead emphasized law's open-textured, indeterminate nature according to which a judge could just as easily arrive at one result by emphasizing certain precedents as another by highlighting a different set of rules and authorities. These theorists argued that dominant ideologies, principally capitalism, underlie most legal doctrines and rulings.

In the United States, critical scholars such as Duncan Kennedy (Harvard), Morton Horwitz (Harvard), Roberto Unger (Harvard), Mark Kelman (Stanford), Robert Gordon (Yale), and Alan Freeman (SUNY–Buffalo) critiqued American legal institutions in law review articles, books, conferences, and workshops. Some of the movement's principal ideas stem from European social theory, particularly the Frankfurt school, whereas others, such as law's indeterminacy and instrumentalism, show the influence of legal realism.

Many of the main figures were leftists whose formative experiences were in the civil rights and antiwar movements and who were distrustful of tradition, convention, and authority. Unsurprisingly, the movement drew criticism from conservative legal scholars, including those associated with law and economics, as well as from a few traditional liberals who deplored its lack of interest in educating students for jobs in the welfare state and its deconstruction of legal authority. One prominent critic (Paul Carrington) urged that critical legal scholars leave the legal academy, since they could not embrace its articles of faith, and seek positions in other departments such as sociology.

Although critical theory no longer maintains an organizational presence with regular meetings and conferences, its influence remains strong both in the academy and in some sectors of the practice community, such as the National Lawyers Guild. Many scholars today incorporate the movement's teachings, for example, in analyzing tort law or statutory interpretation, and a number of casebooks contain references to indeterminacy, hegemony, and other classic critical ideas.

Critical theory influenced other legal theories including critical race theory, which applies many of its signature notions to the study of race and racism; a law-and-society contingent, which analyzes law in action; radical feminism, which examines patriarchy and women's rights; and queer theory, which challenges sexual orthodoxy. Thus, although many of the founding figures of critical legal theory are nearing retirement, their ideas continue to wield influence over much of American law.

BIBLIOGRAPHY

Kelman, Mark. *A Guide to Critical Legal Studies.* Cambridge, Mass.: Harvard University Press, 1987.

Kennedy, Duncan. *Legal Education and the Reproduction of Hierarchy: A Polemic against the System.* New York: New York University Press, 2004.

Richard Delgado

LESBIAN, GAY, BISEXUAL, AND TRANSGENDER RIGHTS MOVEMENT

The movement to protect lesbian, gay, bisexual, and transgender (LGBT) civil rights emerged in the wake of World War II. Thousands of men and women who had thrived in the military's same-sex worlds began settling in the nation's cities, constructing dynamic social lives that dramatically expanded the previously small homosexual subcultures. They did so, however, just as homosexuality and cross-dressing were becoming increasingly penalized. Federal, state, and local governments began to prohibit homosexuals from working within the civil service, the military instituted an elaborate homosexual-exclusion process, and local police forces began to regularly arrest bar patrons. That combination of an expansive subculture and repressive policing led some to forge a sense of shared identity and community and launch a civil rights movement focused on gay men and lesbians.

The first explicitly political phase of that movement started in Los Angeles in 1950 when several homosexually active men, mostly former Communist and progressive activists, founded the Mattachine Society. Drawing on leftist ideas about oppressed minorities and a new cultural emphasis on psychology and self-expression, they created a network of discussion groups where men and women shared their experiences and constructed a common identity. Mattachine, whose membership peaked in the thousands with groups meeting across southern California and as far east as Chicago and New York, was soon joined by other organizations, including the lesbian-focused Daughters of Bilitis, founded in San Francisco in 1955. This handful of small organizations began to refer to themselves as homophiles.

Homophile activists—typically white and middle-class—were often integrationist in their goals, encouraging other homosexuals to conform to social standards. Nevertheless, over two decades, they helped to fashion a "gay culture," publishing newsletters and creating social forums. In one early achievement, they won a U.S. Supreme Court decision declaring that their publications were not obscene and could be sent through the mail.

During the 1960s, gay activism became somewhat more visible, as homophiles staged small pickets in front of the White House and Philadelphia's Independence Hall to protest federal discrimination. Less explicitly organized bar patrons also took to the streets in several cities in the late 1960s to protest police harassment. Most famously, on 27 June 1969, at New York's Stonewall Inn, patrons refused to disperse after a police raid and instead fought back; street rioting ensued for several days.

Those actions—especially the Stonewall Riots—are seen as marking the emergence of a second phase of LGBT activism, one that was much more aggressive and public and identified as gay liberation. Gay liberation brought thousands more into the movement: whereas there were 50 homophile organizations in 1969, 800 gay liberation groups existed in 1973, and thousands in 1979. Following the lead of other movements, gay liberationists demanded "gay power" and insisted that homosexuals "come out of the closet" by announcing their homosexuality to friends, families, and colleagues. Joining groups like the Gay Activists Alliance, activists around the country interrupted city council meetings and psychiatric conferences, sat in at magazine offices and political campaign headquarters, and marched through the nation's streets. Their actions yielded results: editorial policies were modified, the American Psychiatric Association removed homosexuality from its disease list, and Congress considered antidiscrimination legislation. In fact, by 1976, seventeen states had repealed their laws criminalizing homosexual activity and thirty-six cities had passed antidiscrimination laws.

These political achievements produced a strong backlash. In 1977, singer and orange-juice promoter Anita Bryant led a successful campaign in Florida to overturn Dade County's new nondiscrimination law, and other cities followed. In 1978, Harvey Milk, a gay San Francisco supervisor, was assassinated in the wake of a debate among California voters about whether to allow homosexuals to be public school teachers. The backlash politicized more mainstream gay individuals and the movement adopted more traditional political actions. Lobbying groups began working to elect openly gay politicians and forge formal relationships with various governmental administrations.

During the 1980s, this expanding political energy was devoted to fighting HIV/AIDS. As the disease spread among gay men—appearing clearly in 1981—and the federal government largely failed to respond, gay men and lesbians established social service agencies to support the sick and dying. Organizations like Gay Men's Health Crisis in New York set up hotlines and buddy systems and developed "safe sex" guidelines to offer some direction in the midst of a devastating epidemic. Community members felt especially besieged by governmental indifference: President Ronald Reagan made no major statements about AIDS until 1987, the same year the first AIDS drug finally received Food and Drug Administration (FDA) approval and shortly after the Supreme Court affirmed the criminalization of homosexual behavior. Outraged, activists launched a campaign of aggressive demonstrations. Led largely by ACT UP, the AIDS Coalition to Unleash Power, demonstrators staged sit-ins at Wall Street, the FDA, and pharmaceutical corporations and garnered enough media and governmental attention to yield improved care. That fight galvanized a new cohort of self-identified queer activists and brought greater political influence to the movement. Indeed, in the 1992 presidential campaign, Bill Clinton actively sought the support of LGBT voters, becoming the first presidential candidate to do so.

With that political attention in the 1990s, gay rights were contested in national politics. Clinton, who as a candidate had promised voters that he would repeal the military ban on gay and lesbian soldiers, initiated a Congressional debate in 1993 that ultimately reaffirmed the ban under the name "Don't Ask, Don't Tell." That policy, promoted as more lenient, actually led to an increase in the number of individuals forced out of the service. Same-sex marriage also moved center stage in the 1990s, driven there by couples around the country who sued for the right to marry. A 1991 lawsuit in Hawai'i set off a wave of political activity as many states scrambled to define marriage as exclusively heterosexual and to assert their right not to recognize same-sex marriages performed elsewhere. Clinton and the Congress codified that right in the Defense of Marriage Act (DOMA) in 1996. Despite DOMA, a few states began to offer limited recognition of same-sex relationships, and in 2000 Vermont became the first state to license "civil unions" as a same-sex equivalent to marriage.

The tenor of these debates shifted somewhat in 2003, when the U.S. Supreme Court, in *Lawrence v. Texas,* overturned its 1986 decision and struck down all laws criminalizing consensual adult homosexual sex. As Justice Anthony Kennedy wrote, LGBT individuals "are entitled to respect for their private lives. The State cannot demean their existence or control their destiny by making their private sexual conduct a crime." Building on that decision, the Massachusetts Supreme Court deemed it unconstitutional to deny marriage licenses to same-sex couples and, in 2004, Massachusetts began to allow same-sex marriages. As several municipalities began to follow Massachusetts's example, controversy flared: President George W. Bush endorsed a federal constitutional amendment banning same-sex marriage nationwide and multiple states saw similar proposals on their ballots. Nonetheless, over the next six years, four more states and Washington, D.C., decided to allow same-sex marriages and six others offered equivalent options like civil unions.

The *Lawrence* decision also paved the way for a reevaluation of the ban on military service. Especially after the country became embedded in war in Iraq in 2003, the policy came under increasing scrutiny. In December 2010, Congress repealed the ban and President Barack Obama signed the legislation, declaring "We are not a nation that says, "Don't ask, don't tell.' . . . We are a nation that believes all men and women are created equal."

Not insignificantly, these policy shifts were buttressed by a steady increase in popular representations of LGBT individuals across the 1990s and 2000s. Many high-profile performers—such as Rosie O'Donnell, George Michael, and Ellen DeGeneres—came out publicly, and LGBT characters became regular elements of mainstream films and television. *Will & Grace,* in which two of the four main characters were gay men, was a top-ratings hit on NBC from 1998 until 2006, and by 2010 gay characters were prominently featured on several primetime TV programs.

Beyond marriage and the military, the other major development of the past twenty years has been the emergence of a self-identified transgender movement. The term transgender took hold as a broad label in the 1990s for individuals who, through dress, self-naming, surgery, or some other sense of identity, resisted dominant gender categories. Transgender activists had developed support networks and organizations since the 1950s, and during the 1960s and 1970s some played crucial roles in the public actions of gay liberation. During the 1990s, however, transgender activists began to organize as a distinct faction under the wider umbrella of queer politics. Galvanized in part by the killings of transgender individuals like Brandon Teena, they brought both legislative and media attention to the violence and discrimination that transgender individuals face. Indeed, as the wider movement worked to pass hate crimes legislation that protected LGBT individuals, they increasingly emphasized violence provoked by both sexual orientation and gender expression. When Obama signed expanded federal hate crimes legislation in October 2009, the new law addressed both sexual orientation and gender identity.

Despite the many gains of the 1990s and 2000s, the goals for LGBT activists remain numerous. They emphasize the need for antidiscrimination laws regarding employment and housing, as well as greater protection for LGBT families and young people, whose experiences of bullying and rates of suicide remain shockingly high.

[*See also* **Bush, George W.; Civil Rights; Civil Rights Legislation; Clinton, William J.;** *and* **Obama, Barack.**]

Daniel Hurewitz

LEWIS, JOHN (REPRESENTATIVE)

John Lewis gained a reputation as one of the most fearless student activists during the civil rights movement—he once gave a talk at a mass meeting shortly after having his skull cracked. He served as the chairman of the Student Nonviolent Coordinating Committee (SNCC; 1963–1966) and later became a congressman from Georgia (1987–present).

Born and raised in Pike County in rural Alabama, Lewis was a devout Christian, pacifist, and vegetarian. As a teenager, he was deeply influenced by the radio sermons of Reverend Martin Luther King Jr. John Lewis attended American Baptist Theological Seminary and Fisk University, both in Nashville, Tennessee. As a student, he was drawn to the nonviolent protests sweeping Southern campuses and was a passionate advocate of an interracial "beloved community." At Fisk University, he led sit-ins alongside the heroine of the Nashville movement, Diane Nash.

Lewis emerged as a central leader in civil rights protest in the 1960s. He was one of the first freedom riders, an interracial group who were viciously and repeatedly assaulted as they sought to ride an interstate bus through the South. He was one of the headline speakers at the March on Washington of 1963, and his speech was by far the most critical of the federal government. He helped to organize the Mississippi Freedom Summer of 1964 and was beaten at the front of the "Bloody Sunday" march from Selma to Montgomery in 1965. As chairman of SNCC, he was committed to confronting the worst aspects of segregation directly and provocatively. But Lewis remained close to Martin Luther King Jr., both personally and ideologically, throughout this time, even as many of his fellow students turned toward Black Power. He was ousted as SNCC chairman in 1966 over the question of whether white students could remain in the organization.

After leaving SNCC, Lewis worked in voter registration, including serving as executive director of the Southern Regional Council's influential Voter Education Project. In 1981, he won a seat on the Atlanta City Council. Five years later, he defeated fellow SNCC activist Julian Bond in a bitter primary battle for the U.S. House of Representatives. He went on to win the general election and has held the seat ever since. He has held numerous leadership positions in the House Democratic caucus. Lewis was one of the first senior African American political figures to support Barack Obama's run for the presidency (like most of his black caucus colleagues, he had initially supported Hilary Clinton). At Obama's inauguration, Lewis was seated near to the president on the platform. Television pictures repeatedly focused on the veteran civil rights leader observing the inauguration of a black president on the very site where nearly four decades previously he had demanded, "we want our freedom and we want it now."

[*See also* **Civil Rights; King, Martin Luther, Jr.;** *and* **Obama, Barack.**]

BIBLIOGRAPHY

Carson, Clayborne. *In Struggle: SNCC and the Black Awakening of the 1960s.* Cambridge, Mass.: Harvard University Press, 1995.

Lewis, John, with Michael D'Orso. *Walking with the Wind: A Memoir of the Movement.* New York: Simon & Schuster, 1998.

Stephen Tuck

LIBERALISM

The term "liberalism" is best understood historically as a language of individual rights with widely variant, and sometimes contradictory, political applications. The origins of the American liberal tradition lie in seventeenth- and eighteenth-century English political philosophy. As science, technology, and civil war challenged the organic social order of medieval society, Thomas Hobbes, John Locke, and Adam Smith envisioned new relationships among the individual, the church, and the state. Whereas Hobbes deduced political rights from the harsh conditions of life in a state of nature—"nasty, brutish, and short"—Locke more optimistically redefined civil society as a voluntary social contract among rational individuals. In his view, legitimate authority derived not from monarchs, nobles, or clerics, but from the consent of the governed, insofar as they accurately interpreted God's unchanging natural law. If a regime abrogated the rights to life, liberty, and property, its subjects could overthrow it and choose a new one. Tempering his philosophy's revolutionary implications, Locke stressed fidelity to Christian virtue, but on an individual level only. The state, reduced to a neutral arbiter of economic disputes, would leave matters of faith to individual conscience.

The notion that the state exists primarily to preserve private property emerged as one of free-market liberalism's two core principles; Adam Smith provided the second, arguing in *Inquiry into the Nature and Causes of the Wealth of Nations* (1776) that markets, left alone, function with optimum allocative efficiency. Although Smith cautioned against the excesses of unbridled free enterprise, he insisted that society benefited when the state allowed acquisitive individualism full scope.

In America, the potent union of Lockean and Smithian principles, generally called "classical" or "laissez-faire" liberalism, pervaded Revolutionary Era political texts and formed a central tenet of early national political economy. It also undergirded Thomas Jefferson's idealization of the independent yeoman farmer. Equating large-scale urban manufacturing with poverty and vice, Jefferson favored a rural economy based on agricultural exports and small-scale manufacturing. The frontier's seemingly limitless supply of natural resources, he suggested, guaranteed immunity from the Old World's class struggles and moral corruption. The frontier ethos helped sustain Americans' commitment to Locke's calculus of property and liberty—despite the emergence of evangelical Christianity, labor unionism, and government-sponsored internal improvements, all part of an urban industrial order at variance with Locke's idealized "state of nature."

During the Progressive Era, John Dewey, Herbert Croly, and other reformers redefined liberalism by affixing the term to what was, in fact, a sharp departure from classical liberalism.

Locke, considering labor a form of property, was untroubled by the dehumanizing effects of industrial work. In the new liberal discourse, however, government emerged as the benevolent guardian of individual liberties against laissez-faire capitalism run amok. Thus, the states passed laws shielding children from labor exploitation and small businesses from unfair monopolies. For pragmatists like Dewey, a new science of administrative efficiency would replace the now closed frontier as a guarantor of perpetual progress.

During the Great Depression of the 1930s, Franklin Delano Roosevelt's New Deal accelerated the departure from classical liberalism by shifting emphasis from individual property rights to utilitarian governance on behalf of the public good. Through massive work programs, government sought to restore the economic independence once exclusively provided by property and wealth. World War II hastened the emergence of a managerial ethos that stressed group psychology over individualism. Throughout his presidency, Roosevelt stressed liberalism's secondary dictionary definitions: generous support for those in need and a broad-minded tolerance for diversity, in stark contrast to the rise of totalitarianism elsewhere.

Cast into the realm of political rhetoric in postwar America, liberalism came to represent one side of a partisan debate. Post–New Deal liberals generally opposed socialism but favored the state's heightened role as an active agent for promoting individual well-being and social equality. Conservatives, by contrast, raised the discarded banner of classical liberalism, which in the 1950s enjoyed a brief renaissance as a subject of scholarly debate. In 1955, Louis Hartz construed *The Liberal Tradition in America* as a broad historical consensus about freedom that bred a natural distrust of extremism. Although acknowledging the dangers of conformity, Hartz found no room in a centrist, classless political system for radical ideologies like Communism or messianic leaders like Senator Joseph McCarthy. Political scientists elaborated Hartz's vision of a nonpartisan liberal consensus, portraying municipal governance as an open, self-correcting system of group competition, absorbing the discontent manifested abroad as riot and revolution.

During the 1960s, Lyndon B. Johnson completed liberalism's break from its roots in Lockean individualism. Johnson's Great Society initiatives extended government's advocacy into relationships between parents and children (welfare), patients and doctors (Medicare and Medicaid), and consumers and manufacturers (consumer protection). In Johnson's liberal vision of the good society, the benefits of economic growth accrued to all citizens more fairly, a principle underlying legislation banning discrimination on the basis of race, sex, age, and national origin. But whereas Johnson's support for civil rights alienated many southern Democrats, weakening liberalism's political base, the Vietnam War discredited the notion of liberalism as a humane philosophy and fueled a younger generation's revolt against the Democratic Party's procorporate strategy. The Watergate scandal further eroded trust in government as an agent of change. Faced with a soaring national debt and opposition from a revitalized conservative movement, New Deal–style liberalism lost favor in the 1980s and 1990s, and politicians avoided the term. Blamed for a variety of evils, including an alleged decline of moral consensus, liberals found themselves relying, ironically, on the federal court system—the most undemocratic of government institutions—to continue the pursuit of social justice.

In the late twentieth century, commentators debated whether the so-called crisis of liberalism resulted from its failures or its successes. Those who argued the former position cited such measures as affirmative action (racial preferences to redress past discrimination) as examples of government's excessive infringement of individual rights. Others suggested that the successful civil rights struggle had made the goal of equality in public life part of a new consensus and that liberalism remained salient as a continuing appeal to the public conscience for tolerance and understanding of all racial and ethnic groups in an increasingly diverse society.

The focus on diversity, however, entailed new problems. Should liberalism maintain official neutrality among competing claims for the good, or should it affirm a set of core principles? Building on John Rawls's assertion, in *A Theory of Justice* (1971), that individuals naturally gravitate to a conception of justice, Ronald Dworkin argued that liberal activism derived from "a theory of equality that requires official neutrality amongst theories of what is valuable in life." This argument found favor among advocates of multiculturalism but dismayed communitarians, who argued that liberalism rested on a sense of fixed values shared by all members of a liberal community.

Despite the accrual of competing meanings over its long history, liberalism remains a focal point of Americans' efforts to balance the benefits of capitalism with larger moral and ethical priorities.

[*See also* **Anti-Communism; Civil Liberties; Conservatism; Croly, Herbert; Great Society; Jefferson, Thomas; Johnson, Lyndon B.; McCarthy, Joseph; Medicare and Medicaid; New Deal; Progressive Era; Radicalism; Republicanism; Roosevelt, Franklin Delano;** *and* **Social Policy: Public Welfare.**]

BIBLIOGRAPHY

Appleby, Joyce. *Capitalism and a New Social Order.* New York: New York University Press, 1984.

Dworkin, Ronald. "Liberalism." In *Public and Private Morality,* edited by Stuart Hampshire, pp. 113–143. Cambridge, UK; New York: Cambridge University Press, 1978.

Galston, William A. *Liberal Purposes: Goods, Virtues, and Diversity in the Liberal State.* Cambridge, UK; New York: Cambridge University Press, 1991.

McCoy, Drew R. *The Elusive Republic: Political Economy in Jeffersonian America.* Chapel Hill: University of North Carolina Press, 1980.

Macpherson, C. B. *The Political Theory of Possessive Individualism: Hobbes to Locke.* Oxford: Clarendon Press, 1962.

Ross, Dorothy. "Liberalism." In *Encyclopedia of American Political History,* edited by Jack P. Greene, pp. 750–763. New York: Scribner & Sons, 1984.

Sandel, Michael J. *Liberalism and the Limits of Justice.* Cambridge, UK; New York: Cambridge University Press, 1982.

Andrew Chamberlin Rieser

LIBERTARIANISM

Libertarianism, a political ideology, advocates the freedom of the individual from state interference and is, as such, the antipode of totalitarianism. Unlike welfare liberals and socialists, libertarians defend economic liberties against governmental regulation, taxation, and redistribution; unlike conservatives, they defend personal and civil liberties against censorship, prohibition, and paternalistic laws. In popular parlance "libertarian" describes a loose coalition of theorists and activists who often disagree on fundamental principles as well as on particular policy prescriptions (some even reject the label "libertarian"), but their common dedication to individual liberty makes it feasible to treat them together.

Classical liberalism, the wellspring of libertarianism, has a major source in *Two Treatises of Government* (1689) by John Locke, who declared that the state of nature is governed by a law of nature, "and reason, which is that law, teaches all mankind, who will but consult it, that being all equal and independent, no one ought to harm another in his life, health, liberty, or possessions." In the state of nature man has the right to protect himself and his property against aggressors and to judge and punish them. For the sake of mutual preservation, individuals may relinquish their rights of self-protection and enforcement and put themselves under a government "but only with their own consent." But when a regime egregiously violates their rights, it forfeits the power vested in it by the people who have the right to resume their original liberty and establish a new government. Another important theorist, Montesquieu, in *The Spirit of the Laws* (1784), observed, "Eternal experience shows that all men who have power come to abuse it, and this they will do to the limit of their power." His solution was to limit government by separating its powers into legislative, executive, and judicial branches. "So that none can abuse power, we must arrange, by the disposition of things, that power shall check power." Locke's influence on the American Founders is evident in the Declaration of Independence (1776), drafted by Thomas Jefferson, which affirmed as "self-evident" that all men possess the rights of "life, liberty, and the pursuit of happiness," and that "to secure these rights, governments are instituted among men, deriving their just powers from the consent of the governed." Montesquieu's ideal of limited government also inspired the framers of the U.S. Constitution.

Economics was another important source for classical liberalism. Eighteenth-century French physiocrats such as François Quesnay and A.-R.-J. Turgot held that the economy was governed by natural laws that channel individual self-interest to general prosperity, a process that would be disrupted by positive (i.e., governmental) laws imposing restrictions, for example on free trade. Their watchword "laissez faire" became a synonym for free-market economics. Likewise, Adam Smith's *Wealth of Nations* (1776) explained the benefits of an unrestricted market economy including the division of labor and free trade. An economic actor may make decisions beneficial to his society, although "he intends only his own gain, and he is in this, as in many other cases, led by an invisible hand to promote an end which was no part of his intention.... By pursuing his own interest he frequently promotes that of the society more effectually than when he really intends to promote it." These promarket views were amplified by early economists including David Ricardo, Jean Baptiste Say, and Frédéric Bastiat.

During the nineteenth and twentieth centuries, centralized nation-states gained supremacy, a development promoted by ascendant ideologies of collectivism, nationalism, and socialism, including progressivism in the United States. In reaction, what came to be known as libertarianism assumed a more radical form. Although agreeing in their opposition to statism, libertarians diverge on fundamental principles into two main theoretical branches.

One branch takes utilitarianism as its starting point, following the precedent of Jeremy Bentham's principle of utility, which approves or disapproves of actions according to whether they have as their consequences "the greatest good for the greatest number." This approach appeals to theorists who maintain that libertarianism should be based on "scientific" principles rather than natural rights, which Bentham derided as "nonsense on stilts." A major figure in the utilitarian tradition was John Stuart Mill, who argued in *On Liberty* (1859) "that the only purpose for which power can be rightfully exercised over any member of a civilized community, against his will, is to prevent harm to others. His own good, either physical or moral, is not a sufficient warrant."

In political economy, however, Mill recognized a more expansive role for government and late in life drifted toward socialism. Mill was a bellwether for later economists who endorsed central planning, interventionism, and the welfare state. Opposing this trend, three schools of economics arose, especially in the United States, in the twentieth century. The Austrian School, introduced by Ludwig von Mises in *Human Action* (1949, rev. 1966) and F. A. Hayek in *The Road to Serfdom* (1944), argues that socialism is unworkable and that attempts by government to control markets are self-defeating and also tend to erode political and civil liberties. The Chicago School, including the influential Milton Friedman in *Capitalism and Freedom* (1962) and *Free to Choose* (1980), also defends the free market but emphasizes the role of governmental monetary policy in causing inflations and depressions. The Public Choice School, led by James Buchanan, Gordon Tullock, and Mancur Olson, applies economic analysis to political behavior and contends that many actual laws and regulations fail to promote the public interest because of special interest "rent seeking" and voter apathy and incompetence resulting in "government failure." In addition, the law and economics movement, represented by Ronald Coase, Richard Posner, and Richard Epstein, advances free-market alternatives to laws and regulations expanding the role of government in response to social problems. Despite important methodological differences, these theorists share a commitment to liberty, and many have belonged to the Mont Pelerin Society, founded 1945 "to work out in continuous effort, a philosophy of freedom."

The other major branch of libertarian theory is based on a philosophical theory of rights. An important transitional figure, Herbert Spencer in *Social Statics* (1851) and *The Man versus the State* (1891) argued that from a version of utilitarianism one could deduce a theory of natural rights, which are sanctioned by laws of conduct that necessarily tend to produce the general good and "are to be conformed to irrespective of a direct estimation of happiness or misery." Although viewed as a social Darwinist, Spencer characterized his own position as "true liberalism," concerned with protecting the equal liberty of all individuals against the encroachments of the state. In the mid-twentieth century Ayn Rand defended individual rights in *The Virtue of Selfishness* (1964) and *Capitalism: The Unknown Ideal* (1967) and in her popular novel *Atlas Shrugged* (1957). Unlike Spencer she repudiated utilitarianism and argued that rights must be based in her own philosophy of objectivism, which holds that man's life is the standard of value, that rational self-interest egoism is the proper moral code, and that man has a right to live for his own sake, sacrificing neither himself to others nor others to himself. Hence, "no man may initiate the use of force against others," and force is permitted only in retaliation against those who initiate its use. The ideal society is capitalism, which Rand defined as "a social system based on the recognition of individual rights, including property rights, in which all property is privately owned." Rand's work, succeeded by Robert Nozick's *Anarchy, State, and Utopia* (1974), sparked a neo-Lockean movement among academic philosophers, including John Hospers, Tibor Machan, Eric Mack, Douglas Den Uyl, and Douglas Rasmussen. Recent political philosophers in affinitive traditions include David Gauthier, Loren Lomasky, Jan Narveson, and David Schmidtz.

Libertarians disagree over whether the best system is limited government or anarchy. Early anarchistic libertarians included Lysander Spooner, Benjamin Tucker, and Albert Jay Nock. More recently Murray Rothbard in *For a New Liberty: The Libertarian Manifesto* (1973) and David Friedman in *The Machinery of Freedom: Guide to a Radical Capitalism* (1971) argued for anarchocapitalism, which holds that individual freedom could be effectively protected and enforced by means of private agencies competing in a free market and that a government is necessarily a coercive monopoly violating the rights of those under its control. Although the former claim was criticized by Rand and the latter by Nozick, anarchism attracts many libertarians. Rand and others reject the label "libertarian" owing to its anarchistic connotation, and some would rather be called "classical liberals."

Libertarianism remains primarily an intellectual movement with only indirect impact on electoral politics in the United States. The Libertarian Party, founded in 1971, regularly runs candidates for president and other offices but so far with only slight success. Libertarians have made much greater progress in public policy by promoting incremental reforms in laws and regulations (e.g., the replacement of military conscription by a voluntary military). In addition to the Cato Institute and Reason Foundation, a plethora of national, state, and specialized think tanks has arisen, generating a stream of studies and policy proposals aimed at reducing the power and scope of government by means of privatization and deregulation and expanding the scope of individual choice, self-reliance, property rights, and market transactions. There are also educational or scholarly organizations such as the Institute for Humane Studies, Foundation for Economic Education, Federalist Society, Atlas Society, Ayn Rand Institute, and Ludwig von Mises Institute. Although libertarian ideas have had the greatest impact in the United States, they are also making inroads in other countries via publications, media outlets, Internet websites, and think tanks such as the Institute for Economic Affairs (UK), Fraser Institute (Canada), and numerous local institutes, many assisted by the Atlas Economic Research Foundation.

[*See also* **Constitution; Declaration of Independence;** ***and*** **Libertarian Party.**]

BIBLIOGRAPHY

Ashford, N., and S. Davies. *A Dictionary of Conservative and Libertarian Thought.* London; New York: Routledge, 1991.

Boaz, D. *The Libertarian Reader.* New York: Free Press, 1997.

Doherty, B. *Radicals for Capitalism: A Freewheeling History of the Modern American Libertarian Movement.* New York: PublicAffairs, 2007.

Hamowy, R. *The Encyclopedia of Libertarianism.* Los Angeles: Sage, 2008.

Machan, T. *The Libertarian Reader.* Totowa, N.J.: Rowman and Littlefield, 1982.

Miron, J. A. *Libertarianism from A to Z.* New York: Basic Books, 2010.

Fred D. Miller Jr.

LIBERTARIAN PARTY

Founded in Colorado in 1971, the Libertarian Party became a significant, if somewhat exotic, variation on late twentieth-century antigovernment politics. Dedicated to challenging "the cult of the omnipotent state," the party nominated its first presidential candidate in 1972 on a platform best described as antigovernment fundamentalism. Among other things, it demanded an immediate or eventual end to mandatory taxation; all social welfare and economic subsidies; government funding for education; and any government restrictions on immigration, freedom of speech, drug use, and consensual sex. Later, the party proposed an end to all government regulation of food and drugs and any restrictions on discrimination in housing, employment, or other areas of "private trade." It also adopted a variety of isolationist foreign policy positions.

The party nominated the television producer and children's author Roger MacBride for president in 1976. An articulate former Republican Party activist, he won more than 170,000 votes. In 1980, with growing support in the West and among some intellectuals, the party turned to Ed Clark, who had recently helped lead the popular California property-tax revolt. Clark garnered nearly 1 million votes. The party lost support in the 1980s and 1990s, however, a time of ample opportunity to oppose government power without resorting to a marginal third party. MacBride himself returned to the Republican fold in 1983 and promoted Libertarian ideas in an increasingly receptive mainstream setting. The Libertarian Party itself softened some of its positions but remained committed to private, free-market solutions to social and cultural as well as economic problems. In 1998, it claimed to have elected more than 100 local officials throughout the nation but showed little promise of significant future growth.

[*See also* **Conservatism; Immigration Law and Policy after 1930; Political Parties; Regulatory Agencies, Federal; Republican Party; Social Policy: Public Welfare; Taxation;** ***and*** **Third Parties.**]

BIBLIOGRAPHY

Hazlett, Joseph M. *The Libertarian Party and Other Minor Parties in the United States.* Jefferson, N.C.: McFarland and Co., 1992.

Leonard J. Moore

LIBERTY

Rich and poor, the leaders and the led, from Carolina to New England, almost any group of Revolutionary War–Era Americans, if asked what they were seeking, would almost certainly have used this word—liberty or death, as Patrick Henry put it. A representative collection of late twentieth-century Americans might say "democracy" and have as many different things in mind. The revolutionaries drew on several interlinking patterns of ideas, less distinct for them than for modern analysts looking for roots in different intellectual traditions.

By liberty, the revolutionaries clearly meant, from the beginning of the crisis in imperial relations, the liberties or rights to which all Englishmen, including British Americans, were entitled by birth—that is, by virtue of the traditions, Common-Law decisions, colonial charters, and parliamentary statutes (such as the Magna Carta or the English Bill of Rights of 1689) that eighteenth-century Britons called their "constitution." Trial by jury, security against cruel punishments or warrantless searches, the writ of habeas corpus, freedom of the press, and toleration of dissenting religious faiths were generally agreed to be among these rights. When Americans could no longer claim them as Englishmen and had come to insist on written rather than unwritten constitutions, they wrote them into the states' first declarations of rights and ultimately into amendments to the new federal Constitution.

Between 1765 and 1776, Britons on opposite sides of the Atlantic increasingly differed in their definitions of English rights. As this happened, Americans appealed to the rights of man, which they had long supposed to be closely related to English rights in any case. In doing so, they drew on a long succession of modern natural-law and law-of-nations writers—most famously, John Locke—who taught that it was "sacred," "undeniable," or evident to any inquiring mind that no man was born with a natural right to rule another or to take by force what others had by right: their lives, their property, and their capacity to make their own decisions about the things in which their happiness might seem to consist.

Thomas Jefferson captured much of what the revolutionary generation meant by liberty in the eloquent second paragraph of the Declaration of Independence, including the conclusion that legitimate political authority can only rest on the consent of the governed and that the governed retain a right to withdraw their consent and make their government anew if it threatens the natural rights that governments are instituted to protect.

But liberty in this final sense, for Revolutionary War–Era Americans, meant more than ultimate or tacit consent to whatever sort of government might rule. It meant the right, initially of Englishmen and then of citizens of the American republics, to a representative political system: the right of a people to govern themselves continuously and actively through elections, petitions, and free assemblies. Valuing this participation for its own sake, not merely as a means of protecting their individual rights, they drew on a republican tradition extending back to ancient Greece and Rome. James Madison was plainly using the word in this sense when he wrote in Federalist Paper Number 51 that "justice" or security for fundamental rights was "the end of civil society" and would "ever be pursued until it be obtained, or until liberty be lost in the pursuit." Self-governance, inalienable rights, and ancient, Common-Law protections and procedures were all encapsulated in this potent word.

[*See also* **Bill of Rights; Civil Liberties; Civil Rights; Conservatism; Constitution; Declaration of Independence; Federalist Papers; Jefferson, Thomas; Liberalism; Madison, James;** *and* **Republicanism.**]

BIBLIOGRAPHY

Greene, Jack P., ed. *Colonies to Nation: A Documentary History of the American Revolution, 1763–1789.* New York: W. W. Norton, 1975.

Lance Banning

LIBERTY PARTY

The Liberty Party was organized in Warsaw, New York, in 1839 by abolitionists convinced that they must take their decade-long antislavery propaganda campaign into the polling booth to accomplish their purpose. The party campaigned in two presidential elections, in 1840 and 1844, nominating in both years James G. Birney (1792–1857), a former slaveholder from Kentucky and long-time abolitionist. The party contested a number of local and state races as well. Rooted in New England, upstate New York, and the Western Reserve area of northern Ohio, the Liberty Party drew support largely from Protestant groups opposed to slavery on moral and religious grounds. Party leaders tried to broaden their appeal by stressing in their platform an economic argument against slavery, claiming that wasteful expenditures by slaveholders drained resources from workers and the middle class in the North.

The party fared poorly at a time when deep loyalties to the two major parties, the Democrats and the Whigs, as well as a lack of widespread antislavery sentiment, dominated American political culture. Liberty Party activists also encountered difficulties with other abolitionists who feared that electoral politics would compromise their beliefs. The party drew less than 1 percent of the national vote in the 1840 presidential election and just over 2 percent in 1844. Some historians suggest that its New York State vote in the latter year denied the state to the Whig candidate, Henry Clay, and insured the election of the slaveholder James Knox Polk, but this involves the unlikely assumption that in the Liberty Party's absence, its voters would have cast their ballots for Clay. It is more useful to see the Liberty Party as an early manifestation of a gathering movement that would culminate in the crusades of the Free Soil and Republican parties against slavery's expansion.

[*See also* **Antislavery Movement; Democratic Party; Free Soil Party; Political Parties; Republican Party; Third Parties;** ***and*** **Whig Party.**]

BIBLIOGRAPHY

Sewell, Richard H. *Ballots for Freedom: Antislavery Politics in the United States, 1837–1860*. New York: Oxford University Press, 1976.

Joel H. Silbey

LINCOLN, ABRAHAM

Abraham Lincoln was born on 12 February 1809 in a log cabin near Hodgenville, Kentucky. His mother, Nancy Hanks Lincoln, and his father, Thomas, were from Virginia. In 1816 the family moved to a farm near Little Pigeon Creek, Indiana. Nancy Lincoln died in 1818, and two years later Thomas married Sarah Bush Johnston, whom the Lincoln children loved. In February 1830 the family moved again, this time to Illinois.

As a young man on his own, Lincoln moved to the town of New Salem, Illinois, and worked as a store clerk. When Denton Offut's store went bankrupt, Lincoln enlisted in the Black Hawk War, where he was elected captain of his militia unit. In 1832, when he had lived in New Salem only half a year and was only 23, he announced in the *Sangamo Journal* his candidacy for the Illinois General Assembly as a Whig. He addressed local issues—internal improvements, rising interest rates, and, notable for a man with less than a year's formal schooling, public education, declaring it "the most important subject which we as a people can be engaged in." Lincoln lost this bid, but two years later, after jobs as store clerk, day laborer, postmaster, and surveyor, Lincoln was elected, winning reelection in 1836, 1838, and 1840. Lincoln's antislavery commitment was evident early in his political life as the freshman representative from Sangamon County.

In the meantime the self-taught Lincoln had also been studying law. In 1837 he relocated to Springfield and received his license to practice law. As an attorney, Lincoln and his partners took cases as they came. His legal work in Springfield and touring the circuit gave him a broad following of friends and colleagues interested in supporting his political ambitions. Also helpful to his political future was his marriage to Kentuckian Mary Todd on 4 November 1842. Both Mr. and Mrs. Abraham Lincoln were hard working and ambitious.

In 1846 Lincoln was elected to Congress as a Whig. He opposed the popular Mexican War and, although he avoided debate on the sensitive subject of slavery, he voted numerous times for the antislavery Wilmot Proviso. Lincoln also introduced a bill calling for a referendum to eliminate slavery, with compensation for the slaveholders, from the District of Columbia. Working behind the scenes, Lincoln got backing from Northerners and Southerners, but the bill was dropped quickly when it became public. Following a prior agreement, Lincoln did not run for reelection, and with a growing family (Robert (1843–1926), Edward (1846–1850), William (1850–1862), and Thomas (1853–1871)), Lincoln concentrated on his legal practice.

Passage of the Kansas–Nebraska Act in 1854 brought Lincoln back into the political fracas. The prime proponent of the new act, Senator Stephen A. Douglas of Illinois, introduced popular sovereignty as means of determining slavery's expansion. He called it "the sacred right of self-government," although in his franker moments he said it was to make sure government was "for the benefit of white men and their posterity forever." In reply to Douglas, Abraham Lincoln said of popular sovereignty, "I hate it because of the monstrous injustice of slavery itself. I hate it because it deprives our republican example of its just influence in the world." Lincoln decried equating slaves with other property rights, asserting that slaves were humans and that all humans had rights.

In the political turmoil following the Kansas–Nebraska Act, the Whig Party struggled to become a majority party. Divided between its northern and southern factions, it fell apart. In 1854 Lincoln was still a Whig, but worked with the new Republican Party. The following year he lost a bid to the U.S. Senate, and in 1856 Lincoln campaigned for the Republicans. He emerged the champion of an Illinois Republican Party whose values he had shaped.

Chosen by the Illinois Republican Convention in June 1858 to be their candidate for the U.S. Senate, Lincoln continued to affirm his opposition to slavery. In a speech at Springfield, Illinois, on 16 June 1858, Lincoln declared, "A house divided against itself cannot stand." His opponent, Democrat Stephen Douglas, turned his considerable talents into discrediting him, but Lincoln refuted Douglas's assertion that the U.S. government was "made by the white man, for the benefit of the white man, to be administered by white men." He claimed remarkable privilege for the Declaration of Independence and its implications about race and equality. The Lincoln–Douglas debates presented Illinois and America with two visions of democracy. Douglas and the Democrats proffered pure white supremacy and Abraham Lincoln a more inclusive vision of liberty and democracy.

Lincoln lost the election, but the well-publicized debates brought him attention nationwide and an invitation to speak in New York in February 1860. Addressing a large audience of political leaders and sophisticated easterners at Cooper Union, Lincoln used clear and compelling arguments, and his analysis of slavery and the Founding Fathers moved along conservative lines. The speech struck a resounding chord. Few knew prior to this speech that Lincoln had presidential aspirations, but with its delivery he substantially advanced that goal. In May 1860 Lincoln won the Republican nomination for president. He did not even try to campaign in the southern states, and indeed he garnered almost no votes there. That handicap should have been enough to assure the Republican's defeat. It was of minor consequence, however, because the opposition was split three ways. Lincoln garnered just 40 percent of the vote (versus 29.5 percent for Democrat Stephen Douglas, 18 percent for the southern Democrat John Breckinridge, and 12.5 percent for Constitutional Union Party's John Bell). In the Electoral College, however, that plurality translated into 180 of 303 electoral votes—a thumping victory.

The election of Abraham Lincoln in 1860 signaled that a minority of people from a sectional political party could decide the presidency. Lincoln's antislavery sentiments were fervent and real, and such formulations go far toward explaining why southerners—and a significant cluster of northern Democrats as well—saw Lincoln's elevation to the presidency as a dangerous step. Yet, Lincoln strove repeatedly in 1860 to allay fears that his party aimed at dismantling slavery. "I have no purpose, directly or indirectly," he promised, "to interfere with the institution of slavery in the States where it exists." What Lincoln failed to renounce—as all Southerners noted—was the Republican opposition to slavery's advance in the territories.

Abraham Lincoln's Inaugural Address, given on 4 March 1861, two weeks after Jefferson Davis was sworn in as the Confederacy's first president, pleaded for rationality and calm. He asked the seceding states to reconsider their actions. In only another four years, he pointed out, those dissatisfied might elect a president more to their liking. For all his rational argument, for all his emotional appeals, Lincoln's First Inaugural Address had an iron lining. It makes clear his underlying, nonnegotiable premise that the Union is perpetual and that he would defend it against insurrection.

Although some advocated letting the South go in peace, Lincoln understood that secession would mean the end of the democratic experiment and the end of the best hope for the world. Lincoln's understanding of southern honor cautioned him against striking the first blow. Moreover, time's passage might permit moderates to solve the impasse or at worst force Confederates into the aggressor's role. Secessionists ultimately forced the issue, and on 12 April the South Carolina militia, now constituted as Confederate troops, fired on Fort Sumter. Lincoln responded with a call for 75,000 military volunteers, which gave Confederates the evidence they required: Lincoln meant to coerce the South. Lincoln's call for troops spawned a new wave of secession activity, as many Upper South states joined the Confederacy, decrying the "unjust wanton war" caused by Abraham Lincoln.

Lincoln had to be careful to keep the border states on the Union side. For that reason, he steered clear of slavery and focused on rebellion as the main issue before the nation. His wisdom and forbearance paid off in Kentucky, where Union sentiments outshouted the strains of "Dixie." In Maryland Union troops held 31 legislators until after the November elections when voters elected pro-Union men. Neither did Missouri join the Confederacy, although it was troubled with guerrilla fighting throughout the war and after.

Lincoln recognized the danger of fifth-column organizations on the home front. Southern sympathizers worked to disrupt Federal efforts and intimidate potential Union recruits. "Dark lantern" societies like the Knights of the Golden Circle rallied Confederate loyalists in the North and comforted antiwar politicians like Ohio's Clement Vallandigham. Lincoln's efforts to curb such resistance included dismissing *habeas corpus.* Lincoln was not sympathetic to cries of civil liberty and Republican "tyranny." His job, as he saw it, his one major objective, was preservation of the Union.

To do so he had to win the war. Without victory, naught else would matter. As commander in chief, Lincoln watched over the military situation, sending telegrams, visiting troops, and recommending strategy. Throughout the war he strove to find generals who would be sufficiently aggressive and attack southern forces, rather than holding southern real estate. Lincoln had trouble with his generals until he found the one man, General Ulysses S. Grant, who agreed with him that fighting meant killing. Together they developed the winning line of attack.

With southern states out of Congress, Lincoln easily approved the Republican legislators' agenda. To finance war, Lincoln signed legislation creating national banks and encouraged and signed an internal revenue law. Other legislation included a Department of Agriculture and the Morrill Act, passed in 1862, which allowed states a grant of 90,000 acres and more to establish colleges. Lincoln also signed a far-reaching homestead act, providing a quarter-section (160 acres) of farmland to any household head (including women) at a nominal price ($200). The Pacific Railway Act set the terms for construction of a transcontinental line. In April 1862, Lincoln signed the bill for compensated emancipation in the District of Columbia.

With no quick and easy end to the rebellion, Union recruitment trailed off dramatically. By the autumn of 1862, desperate for men, Lincoln moved from hesitation to boldness on a decision he had been contemplating. He decided to combine two essential aspects of making war. His military problem was to find more soldiers for the ranks. His ideological problem was to articulate a stronger rationale for war—a higher purpose. However moral, complex, and far-reaching this decision, Lincoln understood that the Emancipation Proclamation was a weapon of war. He also understood that emancipation dovetailed with a larger understanding of what was at stake in the war. Moreover, tens of thousands of African Americans had been walking away from slavery as soon as Union forces came close enough. Theirs was a journey toward freedom.

Lincoln and the Union soldiers knew how much the enslaved labor force helped the rebellion. Freedom for that very large minority of southern Americans would hinder the Confederate war effort on the front lines and on the southern home front. In addition, Lincoln wanted to preclude involvement of European countries on the southern side. Finally, northern consensus was building for emancipation because Americans were growing in their own conviction that freedom could no longer include slavery. In July 1862 Lincoln told his cabinet that he had decided to issue an emancipation proclamation. Secretary of State William Seward persuaded him to wait for a Union victory so as not to look desperate. After the battle at Antietam, Lincoln announced his emancipation plan, which was to take effect on New Year's Day 1863.

The proclamation had a major effect on the course of the war. Immediately southerners had to put an even greater emphasis on controlling their slaves, leaving less time and money available for the war effort. Moreover, it ended any question of European intervention. The measure also clarified war aims: the war for the Union was now undeniably a war for freedom. The proclamation also called for allowing African Americans to serve in the Union armed services at a time when manpower needs were critical. Fully 200,000 African American men mustered into Federal service over the next two years.

Rivers of blood continued to flow. In November 1863 at a military cemetery in Gettysburg, President Abraham Lincoln articulated the meaning of the battle, of the war, of the American dream. He called for a "new birth of freedom." In the end, it took many more deaths before the last rebel surrendered. The failures of the battlefield confirmed Lincoln in a simple method of slaughter: if the South could not be outwitted on the battlefield, it could be outbludgeoned. After McClellan's dismissal that fall, Lincoln chose a series of generals he called "fighters" but those closer to the front labeled "butchers." In the spring of 1864, Lincoln brought the relentlessly hard-hitting Grant from the Tennessee front and appointed him the new American lieutenant general to oversee all Union forces.

Confederates knew full well that their main chance for success was Lincoln's political defeat at the polls in November of 1864, and that possibility was real if the Confederacy could prevent Union victory in battle. Lincoln fully expected to lose the election to the Democratic nominee, George McClellan, writing in April of that year, "it seems exceedingly probably that this Administration will not be re-elected." All told, it was the close relationship between the battlefront and the home front that ultimately proved determining, as General Sherman's victory in the Atlanta campaign promised an eventual end to the conflict.

The election of 1864 was not close: Lincoln garnered 2.2 million votes or 55 percent; McClellan won 1.8 million or 45 percent. Confederates, of course, did not vote in this election, nor did most northern African Americans. Some of the northern states authorized a new system of absentee voting so soldiers, widely anticipated to be pro-Lincoln, could cast ballots. Among absentee votes tabulated separately,

Lincoln received 119,754 to McClellan's 34,291. The end of the Confederacy was assured.

In his Second Inaugural Address in March 1865, Lincoln acknowledged that "American slavery" was a national sin and that God gave the punishment of war "to both North and South." The end of war was in sight. Questions would now involve the aftermath of war, the unification of the country, the role of the freed peoples. On 11 April from the White House balcony, Lincoln made some remarks to the gathering crowd, "We must simply begin with, and mould from, disorganized and discordant elements." Earlier Lincoln had called for allowing "the very intelligent, and those who served our cause as soldiers" to vote, and he again spoke about the need for citizenship for the valiant African Americans who fought for the Union. One man in this audience understood perfectly what Lincoln intimated. John Wilkes Booth told his companion, "That means nigger citizenship. Now, by God, I'll put him through. That is the last speech he will ever make." The North lost a hero. African Americans lost an ally for fair and equal opportunity. The South lost a leader who called for charity without malice. By murdering the president, on Good Friday no less, Booth guaranteed Father Abraham's place in history as a beloved martyr for freedom.

[*See also* **Antislavery Movement; Douglas, Stephen A.; Emancipation Proclamation; Grant, Ulysses S.; Kansas–Nebraska Act; Morrill Land Grant Act; Republican Party; Whig Party;** ***and*** **Wilmot Proviso.**]

BIBLIOGRAPHY

Burlingame, Michael. *Abraham Lincoln: A Life*, 2 vols. Baltimore: Johns Hopkins University Press, 2008.

Burton, Orville Vernon. *The Age of Lincoln*. New York: Hill and Wang, 2007.

Burton, Orville Vernon. *The Essential Lincoln*. New York: Hill and Wang, 2009.

Carwardine, Richard J. *Lincoln: A Life of Purpose and Power*. New York: Alfred A. Knopf, 2006.

Donald, David Herbert. *Lincoln*. New York: Simon & Schuster, 1995.

Fehrenbacher, Don E. *Prelude to Greatness: Lincoln in the 1850s*. Stanford, Calif.: Stanford University Press, 1962.

Foner, Eric. *The Fiery Trial: Abraham Lincoln and American Slavery*. New York: W. W. Norton, 2010.

Goodwin, Doris Kearn. *Team of Rivals: The Political Genius of Abraham Lincoln*. New York: Simon & Schuster, 2005.

Guelzo, Allen C. *Abraham Lincoln: Redeemer President*. Grand Rapids, Mich.: W. B. Eerdmans, 1999.

Holzer, Harold. *Lincoln at Cooper Union: The Speech that Made Abraham Lincoln President*. New York: Simon & Schuster, 2004.

McPherson, James. *Abraham Lincoln and the Second American Revolution*. New York: Oxford University Press, 1991.

McPherson, James. *Tried by War: Abraham Lincoln as Commander in Chief*. New York: Penguin Press, 2008.

Neely, Mark E., Jr. *The Fate of Liberty: Abraham Lincoln and Civil Liberties*. New York: Oxford University Press, 1991.

Paludan, Phillip Shaw. *The Presidency of Abraham Lincoln*. Lawrence: University Press of Kansas, 1994.

Thomas, Benjamin P. *Abraham Lincoln: A Biography*. New York: Alfred A. Knopf, 1952.

Orville Vernon Burton

LINCOLN–DOUGLAS DEBATES

A fabled series of political duels, the Lincoln–Douglas debates comprised seven joint appearances during the 1858 U.S. Senate contest in Illinois between the Democratic incumbent, Stephen A. Douglas, and his Republican challenger, Abraham Lincoln. The debates began at Ottawa on 21 August and concluded at Alton on 15 October. They aroused intense state and national interest because they involved the political future of Douglas, probably the nation's most influential Democrat, and because they concentrated on the intensifying sectional conflict over slavery. They are remembered in history for elevating Abraham Lincoln to national prominence.

Both candidates elaborated long-held positions on the issues of slavery in the South, the extension of the institution westward, and race. Lincoln insisted that slavery was a moral wrong that should be placed on a course toward extinction. Although the Constitution obliged Americans to give each state plenary control over slavery within its jurisdiction, he said, citizens were equally obliged by moral principle to prevent slavery from extending its geographical reach. Douglas, refusing to take a position on the morality of slavery, declared that the Union and slavery were compatible institutions; whether a territory adopted slavery was a matter for its settlers to decide—the doctrine known as "popular sovereignty." Lincoln retorted that Douglas's hidden object was to inculcate popular indifference to the injustice of slavery as part of a conspiracy to spread bondage not only throughout the territories but also ultimately into the free states.

Douglas, in turn, asserted that his policy on slavery arose from his belief that the republic was a white man's government in which blacks were entitled only to those privileges that whites chose to extend to them. Lincoln, he alleged, was not only an abolitionist and a reckless inciter of sectional warfare, but also a proponent of racial equality. The power of this last charge was registered in Lincoln's tortured response that the equality he claimed for blacks was compatible with white supremacy and did not extend to the rights to vote, serve on juries, or marry whites.

In the election, the Democrats narrowly prevailed where it mattered: they held control of the Illinois legislature, which proceeded to return Douglas to the Senate. Although Lincoln lost the contest, his respectable showing against Douglas in the debates proved a major step toward a grander prize, the Republican Party nomination for president in the fateful election of 1860.

[*See also* **Antislavery Movement; Civil Rights; Democratic Party; Douglas, Stephen A.; Federal Government, Legislative Branch: Senate; Kansas–Nebraska Act; Lincoln, Abraham; Popular Sovereignty; Presidential Debates;** *and* **Republican Party.**]

BIBLIOGRAPHY

Fehrenbacher, Don E. *Prelude to Greatness: Lincoln in the 1850's*. Stanford, Calif.: Stanford University Press, 1962.

Jaffa, Harry V. *Crisis of the House Divided: An Interpretation of the Issues in the Lincoln–Douglas Debates*. Seattle: University of Washington Press, 1959.

George B. Forgie

LIPPMANN, WALTER

(1889–1974), author, columnist, public-affairs commentator. Born into a wealthy German-Jewish family in New York City, Lippmann graduated from Harvard in 1910. A college socialist who grew more conservative over time, Lippmann epitomized the stresses of twentieth-century American liberalism. Active over more than six decades, he advised Theodore Roosevelt, helped craft Woodrow Wilson's Fourteen Points, aided in drafting John F. Kennedy's inaugural address, and assailed Lyndon B. Johnson's Vietnam War policies.

A founding editor of the *New Republic* magazine in 1914, Lippmann emerged as one of the Progressive Era's leading social theorists with two influential early books. *A Preface to Politics* (1913), reflecting his encounter with

Sigmund Freud's work, examined the irrational aspects of politics. *Drift and Mastery* (1914) explored the transition from premodern to modern society, delineated the interest groups emerging in the new industrial order, and proposed loyalty to scientific method as a unifying force.

World War I soured Lippmann on progressive idealism. His *Public Opinion* (1922) and *The Phantom Public* (1925) criticized the media and advocated intervention by experts to help the masses deal with complex issues. *A Preface to Morals* (1929), his most enduring book, examined the alienation and aimlessness of the postwar "lost generation." Turning once again to journalism, Lippmann wrote a daily column for the *New York Herald Tribune* from 1931 to 1967 and later for the *Washington Post*. Syndicated in more than 200 newspapers and read by some 50 million people, his columns influenced both the political elite and the educated public. Critical of the New Deal in the 1930s, he forsook his neo-Hamiltonianism, with its emphasis on governmental activism, to defend a market-oriented liberalism that some critics mistook for warmed-over laissez-faire ideology. With the rise of totalitarianism abroad, Lippmann abandoned his youthful pragmatism and its attendant relativism. During and after World War II he criticized U.S. Cold War ideology for oversimplifying complex international realities, becoming an articulate exponent of a tough-minded foreign policy "realism." Because he wrote so much, for so long, about so many issues, Lippmann occasionally seemed a man for every season. But a fundamental skepticism and elitism consistently characterized his views of public affairs and foreign policy.

[***See also*** **Croly, Herbert; Johnson, Lyndon B.; Kennedy, John F.; Liberalism; New Deal; Progressive Era; Roosevelt, Theodore; *and* Wilson, Woodrow.**]

BIBLIOGRAPHY

Riccio, Barry D. *Walter Lippmann—Odyssey of a Liberal*. Piscataway, N.J.: Transaction, 1994.

Steel, Ronald. *Walter Lippmann and the American Century*. Boston: Little, Brown, 1980.

Barry D. Riccio

LOCHNER v. NEW YORK

In 1895, New York State passed a law limiting the hours of work for employees in bakeries to 10 hours per day and 60 hours per week. Spearheaded by the bakers' union and tenement-house reformers, this statute reflected the labor movement's long struggle to achieve shorter work hours. In 1902, the Utica bakeshop owner Joseph Lochner was fined for violating the new law. Appealing to the U.S. Supreme Court, Lochner claimed that the statute violated the Fourteenth Amendment guarantee that no person shall be denied life, liberty, or property without due process of law. Voting 5 to 4, the Court in 1905 voided Lochner's conviction and ruled the bakeshop law unconstitutional. Justice Rufus Peckham's majority opinion reasoned that among the liberties protected by the Fourteenth Amendment was "liberty of contract," including the right of the employee and employer voluntarily to contract about the hours of work. A state might interfere with that liberty, Peckham admitted, but only if its regulation fell under the legitimate police powers of the states. Peckham defined the police power narrowly, saying that the bakeshop law was not a reasonable use of the state's power to protect the bakers' health.

Justice Oliver Wendell Holmes Jr. dissented vigorously. Attacking the majority's underlying premise, he argued that the majority had based its decision on laissez-faire economic theory rather than on the Constitution, substituting its own judgment for that of the state legislature.

Lochner became the symbol of laissez-faire constitutionalism and judicial activism. For more than thirty years, critics complained that the Court had erected an insurmountable barrier to economic reform. The "*Lochner* Era" came to an end in 1937, when *West Coast Hotel v. Parrish* rejected the liberty-of-contract doctrine.

[*See also* **Civil Liberties; Conservatism; Constitution; Contract, Law of; Due Process: Legal Cases; Economic Policy: Regulation; Holmes, Oliver Wendell, Jr.; New Deal; Progressive Era; Supreme Court, U.S.;** ***and West Coast Hotel v. Parrish.***]

BIBLIOGRAPHY

Gillman, Howard. *The Constitution Besieged: The Rise and Demise of Lochner Era Police Power Jurisprudence.* Durham, N.C.: Duke University Press, 1993.

Kens, Paul. *Judicial Power and Reform Politics: The Anatomy of Lochner v. New York.* Lawrence: University Press of Kansas, 1990.

Paul Kens

LONG, HUEY

(1893–1935), Louisiana political leader and would-be presidential candidate. A populistic and politically ambitious lawyer from the northern Louisiana town of Winnfield, Long won election to the state railroad commission in 1918. His relentless opposition to corporate privilege, especially the unbridled power of the Standard Oil Company, led to an unsuccessful run for governor in 1924. Fours years later he won the governorship thanks to a folksy style and shrewd maneuvering that disrupted traditional alliances. As governor, Long did what other reformist politicians only talked about: He built roads, schools, and hospitals, and he shifted the tax burden to the corporations and the wealthy. He also organized a statewide machine that all but destroyed the conservative "Bourbon" oligarchy that had controlled Louisiana politics since the end of Reconstruction. Long offered the downtrodden a long-awaited taste of power, but his increasingly ruthless and graft-driven methods polarized the state. Followers regarded him as a populist champion and a political messiah; critics labeled him a demagogue and political gangster. After surviving a 1929 impeachment trial, he won election to the U.S. Senate in 1930.

Long strongly supported Franklin Delano Roosevelt during the 1932 presidential race, but he later became a sharp critic of the New Deal's measured response to the Great Depression. In 1934, after publishing a manifesto entitled *Every Man a King*, Long launched a nationwide "Share Our Wealth" campaign. He used radio broadcasts and high-profile personal appearances to promote his radically progressive tax proposals that he claimed would alleviate unemployment and the maldistribution of wealth. In 1935 he planned a run for the presidency and even wrote a book entitled *My First Days in the White House.* But his insurgent candidacy ended abruptly on 9 September, when he was fatally shot by Dr. Carl Weiss (the son-in-law of Judge Benjamin Pavy, an anti-Long leader) in the Louisiana statehouse in Baton Rouge.

During his brief but remarkable career, Huey Long ruled Louisiana with an iron hand, dispensing economic panaceas and political retribution with a ferocity seldom seen in American politics. The most powerful southern politician of his day, the "Kingfish," as he liked to be called, spawned a political dynasty that influenced state and national politics decades after his death. Immortalized in Robert Penn Warren's novel *All the King's Men* (1946), a semifictional meditation on the temptations of power, this talented but tragically flawed leader left an ambiguous and troubling legacy.

[*See also* **Federal Government, Legislative Branch: Senate; New Deal; Political Parties; Populist Party; Roosevelt, Franklin Delano;** *and* **State Governments.**]

BIBLIOGRAPHY

Hair, William Ivy. *The Kingfish and His Realm: The Life and Times of Huey Long*. Baton Rouge: Louisiana State University Press, 1991.

Williams, T. Harry. *Huey Long*. New York: Vintage Books, 1969.

Raymond O. Arsenault

LOUISIANA PURCHASE

An 1803 agreement by which the United States bought from France that part of France's North American empire roughly defined by the Missouri and Mississippi River watersheds. The deal doubled the size of the nation, creating what Thomas Jefferson termed an "empire for liberty."

French control of the region dated from 1682, when the explorer René-Robert Cavelier, Sieur de La Salle, claimed on behalf of King Louis IX a vaguely defined area he named "Louisiana." Rather than lose the colony to Britain as a result of its defeat in the Seven Years' War, France ceded Louisiana to Spain in 1763. Rising tensions between the United States and Spain led to Pinckney's Treaty (1795), which guaranteed American navigation rights on the Mississippi River and the right to deposit goods for export at New Orleans, through which most of the trade of the western states passed.

In 1801, rumors that Spain had transferred Louisiana back to France alarmed many Americans. Fearing that access to the Gulf of Mexico might be interrupted, some Americans, mostly from the West, called for the territory to be taken by force. To head off this sentiment, President Thomas Jefferson dispatched Robert Livingston of New York and, later, James Monroe to Paris to negotiate the purchase from France of New Orleans and the province of Florida west of the Perdido River.

Meanwhile, Emperor Napoleon Bonaparte, faced with defeat in the French sugar colony of Santo Domingo, decided to sell all of Louisiana to consolidate his forces in Europe. Although their instructions empowered them only to acquire New Orleans and West Florida, Livingston and Monroe jumped at the French offer. Understanding the territorial ambitions of many Americans, they recognized this acquisition as a unique opportunity. On 30 April 1803, American and French negotiators initialed agreements transferring the Louisiana territory to the United States in exchange for $11,250,000. In addition, the United States assumed $3,750,000 in claims of its citizens against France.

The Lewis and Clark expedition of 1804–1806 brought back the first scientific and economic knowledge of a land purchased sight unseen by the United States. The expedition also helped undergird a U.S. claim extending the limits of the Louisiana territory as far west as the Columbia River region and as far south as West Florida and Texas. Spanish objections, first to the legality of France's sale of the territory and then over its boundaries, resulted in a diplomatic dispute with the United States that lasted until the signing of the Adams–Onís Treaty in 1819.

In the long run the United States paid a steep price in blood and treasure for the Louisiana territory. The region saw a series of bitter conflicts with Indians, and the controversial question of slavery in the new lands exacerbated sectional tensions between northern and southern states, leading to both the

Missouri Compromise of 1820 and its eventual repeal in the Kansas–Nebraska Act of 1854. In this respect the Louisiana Purchase can be understood as one of the long-term causes of the Civil War.

[*See also* **Compromise of 1820; Jefferson, Thomas; Kansas–Nebraska Act;** ***and*** **Monroe, James.**]

BIBLIOGRAPHY

Adams, Henry. *History of the United States of America during the Administrations of Jefferson and Madison*, vols. 2 and 3. New York: A. & C. Boni, 1889–1891.

DeConde, Alexander. *This Affair of Louisiana*. New York: Scribner & Sons, 1976.

Labbé, Dolores Egger. *The Louisiana Purchase and Its Aftermath*. Lafayette: Center for Louisiana Studies, University of Southwestern Louisiana, 1998.

William Earl Weeks

M

MacARTHUR, DOUGLAS

(1880–1964), attained the highest rank in the U.S. Army as general of the armies and was appointed by the Philippines as field marshal. The United States, France, and many other nations decorated him for his courage and his military strategy. However, his career was marked by controversy. MacArthur was not disposed to obey orders he found disagreeable and he became a rallying point for the political right. His dispute with President Harry Truman over the Korean War was a defining moment in America's tradition of civilian control of the military.

Graduating first in his class at West Point, MacArthur challenged authority early in his career. In 1914 he was denied a Medal of Honor during the occupation of Veracruz for exceeding his orders. MacArthur was promoted to brigadier general while serving in France in World War I. During the 1920s he became superintendent of West Point, where his reforms angered the faculty, and president of the U.S. Olympic Committee. By 1930 he was appointed Army chief of staff with the rank of general. He became notorious for expelling the "Bonus Army" of World War I veterans, exceeding the instructions of President Herbert Hoover to keep public order by undertaking military action against the marchers.

Under Franklin Roosevelt, MacArthur helped organize the Civilian Conservation Corps to provide public works jobs during the Great Depression, but was distrusted by the president. In 1935 he was sent to the Philippines to organize that nation's rudimentary military. Accused of being unprepared for Japan's assault in December 1941, MacArthur fought a defensive action before escaping to Australia. As Allied supreme commander in the Pacific, he was an architect of war strategy along with Admiral Chester Nimitz. MacArthur accepted Japan's surrender in September 1945 and governed the conquered nation through 1951. Credited with redirecting Japanese institutions toward democracy, MacArthur organized war crimes trials and instituted social reforms while rebuilding the Japanese economy, a postwar success story.

With the invasion of South Korea by North Korean forces in June 1950, MacArthur organized America's military response. Acting under a Security Council resolution, MacArthur became commander of a United Nations' force composed primarily of U.S. and Commonwealth contingents along with contributions from other nations. MacArthur's bold amphibious landing at Inchon temporarily turned the tide of battle, yet his pursuit of an aggressive strategy encouraged China to enter the war. Openly critical of Truman's more cautious policies, MacArthur was relieved of command in April 1951 for insubordination.

The American public viewed MacArthur as a hero for his role in defeating Japan and Truman's decision raised a furious protest. MacArthur was given a tickertape parade in New York City and addressed a joint session of Congress. Although he had long entertained hopes of being drafted as a presidential candidate by the Republican Party, his time had passed. In his last years he played a role in conservative politics and was occasionally consulted by government officials on Asian policy. A magnetic and charismatic personality, MacArthur was also egocentric. He is remembered as a superb military mind yet a man who resisted the chain of command he felt constrained him.

[*See also* **Civilian Conservation Corps; Roosevelt, Franklin Delano;** ***and*** **Truman, Harry S.**]

BIBLIOGRAPHY

Manchester, William. *American Caesar: Douglas MacArthur, 1880–1964*. Boston: Little, Brown, 1978.

Perrett, Geoffrey. *Old Soldiers Never Die: The Life of Douglas MacArthur*. New York: Random House, 1997.

Spanier, John W. *The Truman–MacArthur Controversy and the Korean War*. Cambridge, Mass.: Belknap Press, 1959.

Weintraub, Stanley. *MacArthur's War: Korea and the Undoing of an American Hero*. New York: Free Press, 2000.

Glen Jeansonne and David Luhrssen

MADISON, JAMES

(1751–1836), "Father of the Constitution" and fourth president of the United States. Born in King George County, Virginia, James Madison spent his childhood at Montpelier in Orange County, Virginia. After attending local schools, he entered the College of New Jersey at Princeton in 1769 and graduated in 1771.

Poor health and small stature prevented Madison from participating in the Revolutionary War, but in the summer of 1776, as a delegate to the Virginia Convention, he played a decisive role in altering George Mason's draft of the Virginia Declaration of Rights. Mason had proposed to grant religious dissenters toleration under the law, but Madison persuaded the Convention to make religious freedom a matter of right rather than a mere concession.

Between 1777 and 1779, while advising the governors of Virginia as a member of the Council of State, Madison commenced his friendship with Thomas Jefferson. During the 1780s Madison served in the Continental Congress (1780–1783 and 1786–1788) and the Virginia House of Delegates (1783–1786). In the latter body, he further advanced the goal of religious liberty by ensuring the passage in 1786 of Jefferson's Statute for Establishing Religious Freedom. In the Continental Congress, Madison joined the effort to replace the Articles of Confederation with a new constitutional structure. Madison drafted the "Virginia Plan," which defined the agenda for the Constitutional Convention of 1787 and ultimately became, with modifications, the blueprint for the federal Constitution. Playing an equally prominent role in the ratification process, Madison collaborated with Alexander Hamilton and John Jay on the *Federalist Papers,* writing twenty-nine of the eighty-five essays; led the Federalist forces in the Virginia ratifying convention; and in 1789 headed the campaign to add the first amendments to the Constitution in the form of the Bill of Rights.

Madison served four terms in the U.S. House of Representatives (1789–1797). At first, he cooperated with George Washington's administration, but differences over economic policy and foreign affairs drove Madison into leading the political opposition that coalesced into the Jeffersonian Republican Party. In 1797 Madison and his wife Dolley Payne Todd (whom he had married in 1794) retired to Montpelier. He continued to act as an opposition leader, however, by drafting the 1798 Virginia Resolutions protesting the violations of civil liberties and states' rights embodied in the 1798 Alien and Sedition Acts.

In 1801 Madison became President Thomas Jefferson's secretary of state. In this capacity he served as Jefferson's closest advisor and contributed to both the successes of his administration (such as the 1803 Louisiana Purchase) and its failures (such as the Embargo Acts of 1807–1809). His tenure in the State Department after 1803 was dominated by efforts to protect American neutral trade during the Napoleonic wars (1803–1815). Madison tried, without success, to implement policies of commercial restriction against France and Great Britain as an alternative to armed force and war, an approach he also pursued during his own presidency.

Madison's two terms as president (1809–1817) were troubled ones. He was beset by trade quarrels with France and Great Britain and by a territorial dispute with Spain. By 1810, France had repealed its anti–neutral trade policies, and in the same year Madison seized West Florida from Spain, thereby consolidating U.S. control of the Gulf Coast. With Great Britain, however, his efforts proved unavailing. Madison became the first president to act as commander-in-chief when Congress declared war on Great Britain on 18 June 1812. Madison's purpose in the War of 1812 was to conquer Canada, thereby compelling Great Britain to sign a treaty that guaranteed the neutral rights of U.S. vessels, but the war effort—hobbled by inadequate preparation, bad generalship, untrained troops, and logistical difficulties—was largely ineffective. For Madison the nadir of the conflict came in August 1814 when British forces captured and burned Washington, D.C., forcing Madison and his wife into ignominious flight. Peace with Great Britain was restored under the December 1814 Treaty of Ghent, after which Madison enjoyed the final years of his second administration in tranquility and prosperity. Vivacious and outgoing Dolley Madison, seventeen years her husband's junior, presided as White House hostess during Madison's presidency.

In retirement at Montpelier, Madison assumed the role of elder statesman. He prepared his records of the 1787 Federal Convention for publication, worked to establish the University of Virginia, and made an appearance at the 1829 Virginia Constitutional Convention. Of all the Founding Fathers, none was more important than Madison in conceiving of the possibilities of a national republic. In his protests against the excesses of federalism in the 1790s, however, Madison also contributed ideas that were instrumental in dissolving the Union after his death. Had Madison himself lived until 1861, he probably would not have been altogether surprised at this development.

[*See also* **Alien and Sedition Acts; Articles of Confederation; Bill of Rights; Church and State, Civil Liberties; Separation of; Constitution; Constitutional Convention of 1787; Continental Congress; Federal Government, Executive Branch: State Department; Federal Government, Executive Branch: Presidency, The; Federal Government, Legislative Branch: House of Representatives; Federalist Papers; Federalist Party; Hamilton, Alexander; Jay, John; Jefferson, Thomas; Louisiana Purchase; Political Parties; Republican Party; States' Rights;** *and* **Washington, George.**]

BIBLIOGRAPHY

Banning, Lance. *The Sacred Fire of Liberty: James Madison and the Founding of the Federal Republic.* Ithaca, N.Y.: Cornell University Press, 1995.

Ketcham, Ralph. *James Madison: A Biography.* New York: Macmillan, 1971.

Matthews, Richard. *If Men Were Angels: James Madison and the Heartless Empire of Reason.* Lawrence: University Press of Kansas, 1995.

McCoy, Drew. *The Last of the Fathers: James Madison and the Republican Legacy.* Cambridge, UK; New York: Cambridge University Press, 1989.

Rakove, Jack N. *James Madison and the Creation of the American Republic.* Glenview, Ill.: Scott, Foresman/Little, Brown Higher Education, 1990.

Stagg, J. C. A. *Mr. Madison's War: Politics, Diplomacy and Warfare in the Early American Republic, 1783–1830.* Princeton, N.J.: Princeton University Press, 1983.

J. C. A. Stagg

MANIFEST DESTINY

A term first used in the 1840s to justify U.S. expansion into Texas, Oregon, and Mexico. The Jacksonian journalist John O'Sullivan originated the phrase. The "manifest destiny" of the United States, he wrote in 1845, was "to overspread the continent allotted by Providence for the free development of our yearly multiplying millions." With roots in both evangelical Protestantism and the ideology of republicanism, the logic of the phrase was straightforward: History had a purpose and this design or "destiny" manifested (revealed) itself in specific situations. Providence had clearly designated North America as a stage for demonstrating history's larger trajectory. Armed with this divine mandate, politicians and publicists justified the territorial expansion of the United States into contiguous areas. In the Antebellum Era, the manifest destiny impulse culminated most spectacularly in the appropriation of half of Mexico by means of war (1846–1848). Critics tended to turn manifest destiny into a contested slogan. Although most agreed that the United States was, in fact, invested with some sanctified mission, they argued, for various reasons, that expansion would pervert, not promote, that mission.

Notions of manifest destiny returned when territorial expansionism again beckoned in the late 1890s, but the discourse now took the form of an imperialist Western duty to conquer and/or uplift alien territories that would never become part of the Union. Destinarian thinking remained integral to twentieth-century American politics. Typically, however, it took diametrically opposite forms. Although some argued that the United States, as the carrier of world-historical purposes, had an innate duty to act or intervene in the world to save or regenerate it, others claimed that any such intervention would stain the purity of America's distinctive identity.

[*See also* **Republicanism;** *and* **Texas Annexation.**]

BIBLIOGRAPHY

Merk, Frederick. *Manifest Destiny and Mission in American History*. Westport, Conn.: Greenwood Press, 1963.

Stephanson, Anders. *Manifest Destiny*. New York: Hill and Wang, 1995.

Weinberg, Albert. *Manifest Destiny*. Baltimore: Johns Hopkins University Press, 1935.

Anders Stephanson

MARBURY v. MADISON

In this 1803 decision, the U.S. Supreme Court, speaking through Chief Justice John Marshall, for the first time declared an act of Congress unconstitutional and thus established the precedent for judicial review of legislative acts. The case arose from the appointment of the so-called "midnight judges"—judicial appointments made by President John Adams during the last days of his administration. Adams appointed William Marbury a justice of the peace in the District of Columbia, and his commission was signed by the outgoing secretary of state, John Marshall, but not delivered. When Thomas Jefferson's Republican administration took power, the new secretary of state, James Madison, refused to deliver the commission. Marbury filed suit against Madison in the Supreme Court under Section 13 of the Judiciary Act of 1789, which had established the particulars of the new federal court system. That section, Marbury contended, gave the Supreme Court the right to hear the case and issue a writ of mandamus directing the secretary of state to deliver his commission.

Marshall well knew that an order to Madison to deliver the commission might be ignored, irreparably damaging the authority of the Supreme Court and effectively neutralizing the Federalist Party's strength in the federal judiciary. Marshall began his opinion by stating unequivocally that Marbury deserved the commission and that the Republican administration was wrong in not delivering it. That said, however, Marshall held that the Supreme Court did not have the power to aid Marbury because Section 13 of the Judiciary Act had improperly enlarged the Supreme Court's original jurisdiction (the right to hear a case in the first instance). That jurisdiction had been established by the Constitution itself, Marshall stated, and a federal law in contravention of the Constitution was void.

The notion that courts could strike down acts of a legislature did not originate with Marshall. In both seventeenth-century England and late eighteenth-century America, courts had suggested that legislation that violated "natural law" or the fundamental principles of government might be void. Alexander Hamilton, defending the proposed Constitution in Federalist Paper No. 78, had sketched out the logic of judicial review that Marshall would follow in *Marbury v. Madison.* Marshall, however, established this specific judicial power in the American constitutional system, and although no other federal law was declared unconstitutional until 1857, the Marshall court subsequently reaffirmed in a number of cases its power to consider the constitutionality of federal laws. Marshall's opinion also first articulated the distinction between political questions (in this case, the powers of a coordinate branch of the government), which the court would not resolve, and judicial ones, which were properly its responsibility.

[*See also* **Adams, John; Constitution; Federal Government, Judicial Branch; Federalist Papers; Federalist Party; Hamilton, Alexander; Jefferson, Thomas; Judicial Review;**

Judiciary Act of 1789; Jurisprudence; Madison, James; Marshall, John; *and* Supreme Court, U.S.]

BIBLIOGRAPHY

Clinton, Robert L. *Marbury v. Madison and Judicial Review*. Lawrence: University Press of Kansas, 1968.

Hobson, Charles F. *The Great Chief Justice: John Marshall and the Rule of Law*. Lawrence: University Press of Kansas, 1996.

Paul G. E. Clemens

MARSHALL, JOHN

(1755–1835), fourth chief justice of the United States. Born into the Virginia gentry, John Marshall had little formal schooling. During the Revolutionary War, he saw combat with the Culpepper Minutemen and the Continental army, spent the winter of 1778 at Valley Forge, and came to revere George Washington. He resigned his commission in 1781. This military service reinforced his nationalism.

In 1780, Marshall studied law briefly at the College of William and Mary under George Wythe, one of Virginia's most respected lawyers; passed the bar; and received a license to practice from Governor Thomas Jefferson. In 1782, he was elected to the Virginia House of Delegates. He married Mary Willis Ambler, called Polly, in 1783; they had ten children. Moving to Richmond, Virginia's new capital, Marshall enjoyed an extensive practice and was recognized as the leader of the local bar. As a delegate to the Virginia Convention of 1788, he helped win approval of the new federal Constitution, delivering a noteworthy speech defending the judiciary.

Through the 1790s, Marshall stalwartly supported the Washington and John Adams administrations. In 1797, Adams sent him as an envoy to settle grievances during the Quasi-War with France. There with Charles Pinckney and Elbridge Gerry he became part of the so-called XYZ Affair. Welcomed as a hero upon returning to America in 1798, he was the subject of the famous toast, "Millions for Defense but not a cent for Tribute," and won a seat in Congress in 1799. President Adams appointed him secretary of state in 1800, in which capacity he supervised the federal government's move to Washington, D.C., the new capitol. In 1801, Adams appointed him chief justice of the United States, a post he held until his death in 1835.

Marshall is known as the "Great Chief Justice" because he established the institutional integrity of the U.S. Supreme Court. The Court decided over 1,100 cases in his tenure; he wrote the decisions in over 500—including thirty-six of sixty-two constitutional decisions. Among these were some of the most important precedents in American constitutional law: *Marbury v. Madison* (1803); *Fletcher v. Peck* (1810); *McCulloch v. Maryland* (1819); *Dartmouth College v. Woodward* (1819); *Cohens v. Virginia* (1821); and *Gibbons v. Ogden* (1824).

Marshall's greatness traces to the timing of his appointment, his sociable temperament and engaging personality, and his remarkable ability to get to the heart of issues and express himself with compelling logic. An unwavering nationalist, Marshall believed in a living Constitution, a strong national government, and a vigorous and independent judiciary within the federal system. Defining the role of chief justice through his long tenure, he initiated the practice of the Court's speaking with one majority opinion and regularly suppressed his own views to help his colleagues reach a majority opinion. He dissented only once in a constitutional case, *Ogden v. Saunders* (1827). Although sometimes prone to stating general principles and then making the facts and statutes in a case conform to them, John Marshall was a brilliant jurist who always remained keenly sensitive to the political and economic consequences of the Court's decisions.

[*See also* **Adams, John; Constitution; Dartmouth College Case; Federal Government, Judicial Branch; Federalism; Federalist Party;** ***Gibbons v. Ogden;*** **Jefferson, Thomas; Judicial Review; Jurisprudence;** ***Marbury v. Madison; McCulloch v. Maryland;*** **States' Rights; Supreme Court, U.S.;** *and* **Washington, George.**]

BIBLIOGRAPHY

Beveridge, Albert J. *The Life of John Marshall,* 4 vols. Boston: Houghton Mifflin, 1916–1919.

Hobson, Charles F. *The Great Chief Justice: John Marshall and the Rule of Law*. Lawrence: University Press of Kansas, 1996.

Francis N. Stites

MARSHALL, THURGOOD

(1908–1993), was a civil rights lawyer and Supreme Court justice. Raised in Baltimore, Maryland, which he later described with some exaggeration as the most segregated city in America, Marshall was an indifferent student in college. Knowing that he was barred by law from attending the all-white University of Maryland Law School, Marshall attended Howard University Law School, where he was captivated by the vision of lawyers as social engineers articulated by the school's academic dean Charles Hamilton Houston. He worked for Houston as a research assistant and paralegal, graduating at the top of his class in 1933.

After establishing a law practice in Baltimore and struggling at making a living during the Depression, in 1936 Marshall leapt at the opportunity to move to New York to work with Houston in the National Association for the Advancement of Colored People (NAACP) legal department. After Houston's departure, Marshall led the NAACP's legal department from 1939 to 1961, placing him at the heart of the civil rights struggle in the 1940s and 1950s. Working from a plan developed early in the 1930s, Houston and then Marshall attacked school segregation, initially at graduate schools and universities. In 1950 the attack culminated in three Supreme Court decisions that made it clear to Marshall that the time had come to take on segregation in elementary and secondary schools. This "direct attack" on segregation led to the Supreme Court's decision in *Brown v. Board of Education* (1954). Marshall was the chief strategist for the direct attack, coordinating lawsuits around the country and arguing the most important of the five cases the Court decided.

After 1954 Marshall's time was consumed with largely unsuccessful efforts to desegregate schools in the deep South and with successfully defending the NAACP against attacks on the organization in Texas, Alabama, and elsewhere in the South. He also became one of the leading spokesmen for civil rights until he was displaced in that role by Martin Luther King Jr.

John F. Kennedy's election opened the possibility of an appointment to the federal bench. Tired of the travel associated with his civil rights work, and with two young boys at home, Marshall negotiated an appointment to the federal court of appeals in New York, delayed for eleven months by opposition from segregationist Senator James Eastland of Mississippi. In 1965 Lyndon Johnson named Marshall solicitor-general, in charge of the government's litigation in the Supreme Court, anticipating elevating him to the Supreme Court as the Court's first African American justice. Johnson did so in 1967.

Marshall served on the Supreme Court until his retirement in 1991. Expecting to be part of a solid majority of liberals on the Warren court, Marshall instead quickly found himself a persistent dissenter to the more conservative decisions rendered by the Burger and Rehnquist courts. He wrote major opinions—often in dissent—against the death penalty and developed a distinctive and important doctrinal approach to deciding cases questioning racial, gender, and other forms of inequality.

Writing in 1987 during the nation's celebration of the Constitution's bicentennial, Marshall called the document "defective from the start" because of the support it lent slavery, but he retained his faith in the Constitution throughout his career.

[*See also* **Brown v. Board of Education; Civil Rights; Kennedy, John F.; King, Martin Luther, Jr.; National Association for the Advancement of Colored People;** *and* **Supreme Court, U.S.**]

BIBLIOGRAPHY

Tushnet, Mark. *Making Civil Rights Law: Thurgood Marshall and the Supreme Court, 1936–1961.* New York: Oxford University Press, 1994.

Tushnet, Mark. *Making Constitutional Law: Thurgood Marshall and the Supreme Court, 1961–1991.* New York; Oxford: Oxford University Press, 1997.

Williams, Juan. *Thurgood Marshall: American Revolutionary.* New York: Times Books, 1998.

Mark Tushnet

MAYFLOWER COMPACT

(21 November 1620). The first written framework of government in English America, the Mayflower Compact was an agreement made among the forty-one adult male passengers aboard the *Mayflower* on arrival at Cape Cod. It bound the signers to form a civil government and to obey its laws for their "better Ordering and Preservation," while pledging them to enact "just and equal Laws for the General Good of the Colony."

The compact aimed to legitimize the new government and to prevent disorder, especially among those recruits who were not Pilgrims and who, according to Governor William Bradford, wanted to "use their own libertie." The issue of legitimacy was important, since the settlers lacked a valid charter, having landed several hundred miles north of their intended destination in Virginia. The only recorded copy of the document is in an anonymous account of the voyage called *Mourt's Relation* (1622). Modeled on Puritan church covenants, it contained few specifics about the structure of government and had questionable legal status other than common consent. Nevertheless, it established a government in which people were bound to obey laws voted by the majority of adult males and served as a precedent for more elaborate covenants like the "Fundamental Orders" of Connecticut (1639).

Although the Mayflower Compact is commonly regarded as having embodied the democratic principles of self-government and consent, it was far from establishing an actual democracy of universal adult suffrage. Voting rights, initially limited to adult males, became gradually more exclusive until Plymouth was absorbed by the short-lived Dominion of New England in 1686 and then annexed by the Massachusetts Bay Colony in 1691.

BIBLIOGRAPHY

Bradford, William. *Of Plymouth Plantation, 1620–1647,* edited by Samuel Eliot Morison. New York: Alfred A. Knopf, 1952.

Greene, Jack P., ed. *Settlements to Society 1607–1763: A Documentary History of Colonial America.* New York: W. W. Norton, 1975.

Sargent, Mark L. "The Conservative Covenant: The Rise of the Mayflower Compact in American Myth." *New England Quarterly* 61 (1988): 233–251.

Andrew J. O'Shaughnessy

McCARTHY, JOSEPH

(1908–1957), Republican senator from Wisconsin, notorious "Red-hunter" during the early Cold War years. Born on a dairy farm near Appleton, Wisconsin, McCarthy quit school at age fourteen to raise chickens. He subsequently went bankrupt, returned to high school, crammed four years of work into two terms, and entered Marquette, a Jesuit college in Milwaukee. Earning a law degree in 1935, McCarthy established a small practice before winning a circuit judgeship by frantic campaigning and smearing the incumbent's good name.

At twenty-nine, the youngest judge in Wisconsin, McCarthy raised eyebrows by providing "quickie divorces" to political supporters. The state supreme court also censured him for destroying crucial evidence in a price-fixing case. Although judges were exempt from the draft, McCarthy joined the Marines in 1942 and spent World War II as an intelligence officer in the Pacific. He later claimed to have suffered wounds as a "tail-gunner" when his plane crash-landed under Japanese fire. In fact, his only war injury occurred during a troopship hazing incident, when he fell down a flight of stairs and broke his foot.

In 1946, McCarthy defeated three-term incumbent Robert M. La Follette Jr., a member of Wisconsin's leading political family, in the Republican senatorial primary. The overconfident La Follette barely bothered to campaign; McCarthy never stopped. A few months later, McCarthy buried his Democratic opponent, Howard McMurray, under a mountain of baseless allegations.

As a senator, McCarthy became known for his raucous, erratic behavior. Then, in February 1950, his political career in trouble and his reelection chances looking grim, he told a Republican gathering in Wheeling, West Virginia, that he held in his hand a list of 205 Communists currently "working in the State Department." The claim was preposterous; McCarthy knew nothing about Communists in government or anywhere else. But his aim was publicity, and his timing was right. Americans were alarmed by Soviet aggression in Europe, China's recent fall to Communist rule, Alger Hiss's conviction for perjury, and Russia's successful atomic bomb test. McCarthy provided a simple explanation for these disturbing events. The Communists were "winning" the Cold War, he insisted, thanks to traitors within the U.S. government. The real enemy wasn't in Moscow; it was in Washington, D.C.

When Communist North Korea invaded anti-Communist South Korea in June 1950, McCarthy's message took on special force. In the November elections, Republicans gained five seats in the Senate and 28 in the House. As the 1952 presidential campaign approached, McCarthy grew bolder. He called Secretary of Defense George Marshall a traitor, mocked Secretary of State Dean Acheson as the "red Dean of Fashion," and described President Harry S. Truman as a drunkard, adding, "The son-of-a-bitch should be impeached." During the campaign, McCarthy claimed, falsely, that the Communist *Daily Worker* had endorsed the Democrat Adlai Stevenson for president. And he made the intentional slip "Alger I mean Adlai" in a nationally televised address. So long as his targets were Democrats, leading Republicans were generally supportive. Senator Robert Taft advised: "Keep talking and if one case doesn't work out, proceed with another."

Not only did McCarthy easily win reelection in the Republican landslide of 1952, but four of the Democratic senators he campaigned against lost, including Millard Tydings of Maryland, chair of a Senate committee that in 1950 had labeled McCarthy's charges "a fraud and a hoax." At his peak of influence, McCarthy became chairman of the Committee on Government Operations and its powerful Subcommittee on Investigations. Filling key staff positions with former agents of the Federal Bureau of Investigation and former prosecutors like Roy M. Cohn from New York, McCarthy set out to uncover "Communist influence" in the federal government. His targets included the Voice of America, the Government Printing Office, and the Foreign Service. He even questioned the anti-Communist credentials of President Dwight D. Eisenhower, a member of his own party. McCarthy's hearings did not uncover any Communists. They did, however, ruin numerous careers, undermine government morale, and make America look ridiculous in the eyes of the world.

McCarthy's downfall began with his investigation of "subversive activities" in the U.S. Army. The public got to see him for thirty-six days in the televised Army–McCarthy hearings during the spring of 1954, and the cumulative impression was devastating, as the senator insulted witnesses, attacked fellow senators, and launched crude personal attacks against his critics. A 1954 TV documentary on McCarthy by the respected and influential CBS newsman Edward R. Murrow further eroded his influence. In November, the Senate censured McCarthy for bringing that body into "into dishonor and disrepute." Many linked his censure to an easing of Cold War tensions. The Korean War was over, the Soviet dictator Joseph Stalin was dead, and the radical right was in disarray. His demagoguery no longer effective, McCarthy grew increasingly depressed. He died of alcoholism in 1957, utterly discredited, but the word "McCarthyism" lived on, a reminder of the worst times of the early Cold War.

[*See also* **Anti-Communism; Army–McCarthy Hearings; Communist Party USA; Eisenhower, Dwight D.; Hoover, J. Edgar; House Un-American Activities Committee; La Follette, Robert; Republican Party; Rosenberg Case; Stevenson, Adlai; Taft, Robert;** *and* **Truman, Harry S.**]

BIBLIOGRAPHY

Bayley, Edwin R. *Joe McCarthy and the Press.* Madison: University of Wisconsin Press, 1981.

Fried, Richard M. *Nightmare in Red: The McCarthy Era in Perspective.* New York: Oxford University Press, 1990.

Oshinsky, David M. *A Conspiracy So Immense: The World of Joe McCarthy.* New York; London: Free Press; Collier Macmillan, 1983.

David M. Oshinsky

McCULLOCH v. MARYLAND

Chief Justice John Marshall's memorable phrases and magisterial reasoning make his opinion in this case the classic formulation of the implied powers of the national government and of the relation between the national government and the states. Congress had incorporated the Second Bank of the United States (BUS) in 1816 and given it the power to establish branches in the states without their consent. Maryland imposed a tax on banks issuing notes without state consent, and James McCulloch, treasurer of the Baltimore branch of the BUS, refused to pay. Maryland then sued McCulloch, who, after losing twice in state court, appealed to the U.S. Supreme Court.

The case attracted intense public interest. Many held the BUS, the "Monster," responsible for the Panic of 1819. Further, agricultural depression and debates over slavery in

Missouri were reviving interest in old states' rights arguments. Beginning on 22 February 1819, some of the nation's best lawyers argued the case for nine days. On 17 March, Marshall spoke for a unanimous Court in upholding Congress's power to incorporate the bank and in ruling Maryland's tax unconstitutional.

Maryland's state's rights, strict-construction argument, Marshall said, would retard national growth and turn the Constitution into a "splendid bauble." The people of the United States, not the states, had created the Constitution as their instrument of government and had given the government limited, enumerated powers. It was unimportant that the power to incorporate a bank or anything else was not among those enumerated powers, Marshall argued, because the "necessary and proper" clause of Article I, Section 8, of the Constitution granted the government broad discretion in devising ways to execute its powers. If the end was legitimate and within the scope of the Constitution, he concluded, then "all means which are appropriate, which are plainly adapted to that end, which are not prohibited, but consist with the letter and spirit of the constitution, are constitutional."

The supremacy clause (Article VI) established that the national government was supreme within its sphere. Lawful congressional acts took precedence over state law. States could not threaten or impede the national government in exercising its constitutional power. So, because the power to tax "involved" the power to destroy, Maryland's tax was unconstitutional. The Constitution, Marshall proclaimed, was intended for "ages to come" and must be adaptable to circumstances its framers could not have imagined.

[*See also* **Constitution; Jurisprudence; Marshall, John; State Governments; States' Rights; Supreme Court, U.S.;** *and* **Taxation.**]

BIBLIOGRAPHY

Gunther, Gerald, ed. *John Marshall's Defense of McCulloch v. Maryland.* Stanford, Calif.: Stanford University Press, 1969.

White, G. Edward. *The Marshall Court and Cultural Change, 1815–1835,* vols. III–IV. In *The Oliver Wendell Holmes Devise History of the Supreme Court of the United States.* Cambridge, UK: Cambridge University Press, 1988.

Francis N. Stites

McKINLEY, WILLIAM

Born on 29 January 1843 in Ohio, William McKinley taught at a small school in rural Ohio before joining the Union Army at the beginning of the Civil War. McKinley rapidly advanced in rank and eventually befriended Colonel Rutherford B. Hayes. Hayes awarded the young brevet major with a position on his staff. After the war, McKinley returned to Ohio and pursued a career as a lawyer. He opened a law office in Canton, Ohio, and, under the influence of Hayes, became a leader in the Ohio Republican Party. In 1869, McKinley was elected to his first public office as the Stark County prosecutor. At this time, McKinley met wealthy Ohio industrialist Mark Hanna, who later helped fund and manage his political campaigns.

With such strong political and social connections in Ohio, McKinley pursued his political ambitions. He was elected to the U.S. House of Representatives in 1877 and was appointed to serve on the influential Ways and Means Committee. In that role, McKinley became the leading voice of protectionism and tariff policy, which eventually culminated in the passage of the McKinley Tariff Bill of 1890. The bill raised import taxes on goods such as wool and tin and represented a major victory for the so-called "Napoleon of Protection."

Shortly afterward, McKinley was nominated as the Ohio Republican Party's gubernatorial candidate and won the 1891 election. His stellar career in Congress, his election as governor, and America's general disenchantment with the Democratic Party after the Panic of 1893 easily positioned McKinley for a presidential bid in 1896. McKinley defeated Democrat William Jennings Bryan in both presidential elections in 1896 and 1900.

As president, McKinley sought to elevate America's position in the world through territorial acquisition. In 1898, the brewing diplomatic crisis with Spain over the Cuban colony spilled into war after an investigation concluded that the battleship *USS Maine* stationed in Havana's harbor was destroyed by a Spanish mine. Congress declared war against Spain on 25 April 1898, and three months later the United States possessed many Spanish colonies including the Philippines, Guam, Puerto Rico, and Cuba. McKinley also successfully annexed the Hawaiian Islands, thereby securing American hegemony from the West Coast of the United States to the Pacific Rim. In 1900, McKinley dispatched 2,000 soldiers to China in an effort to quell the Boxer Rebellion and protect American interests. After the rebellion subsided, McKinley directed Secretary of State John Hay to issue a series of notes supporting an independent China and an "Open Door" policy that allowed all countries equal access to China's vast resources.

McKinley's life, however, was cut short when anarchist Leon Czolgosz assassinated him at the Pan-American Exposition in Buffalo, New York, on 6 September 1901. McKinley died eight days later. Nevertheless, McKinley's presidency represents a key moment in diplomatic history as America emerged from the nineteenth century as a major power. McKinley's astute use of presidential authority at home and abroad marked the beginnings of what historians have classified as the modern presidency.

[*See also* **Bryan, William Jennings; Hayes, Rutherford B.;** *and* **Tariffs.**]

BIBLIOGRAPHY

Gould, Lewis. *The Spanish–American War and President William McKinley*. Lawrence: University Press of Kansas, 1982.

Morgan, Howard W. *William McKinley and His America*. Syracuse, N.Y.: Syracuse University Press, 1963.

Matthew C. Sherman

MEDICARE AND MEDICAID

On 31 July 1965, at the Truman Library in Independence, Missouri, President Lyndon B. Johnson signed the Medicare and Medicaid Bill into law. The site was chosen to honor former president Harry S. Truman, who had supported national health insurance during his presidency. The date of the signing preceded by only two weeks the thirtieth anniversary of the 1935 Social Security Act, to which Medicare was attached.

The new law contained three parts that had been put together a year earlier by the House Ways and Means Committee chairman, Wilbur Mills, an Arkansas Democrat. The first part, Medicare, expanded the Social Security Act's old-age pension program. Through wage deductions, employees would contribute to a Medicare trust fund. At retirement, those eligible for Social Security benefits would also receive coverage for hospital care, some surgical care, and nursing-home reimbursements. The original law specified 120 days of hospital benefits and 120 days of nursing-home follow-up benefits. The Medicare program also included general revenue funds for hospital construction, diagnostic equipment purchase, and grants to teaching hospitals for medical education.

A second part of the 1965 law, called Part B, covered visits to physicians. This option had to be selected by eligible individuals on retirement. If this option were chosen, deductions were made from the recipient's monthly Social Security checks. Part B originated as the American Medical Association's (AMA) alternative to Medicare, called Eldercare, which Mills had streamlined and turned into an optional addition to Medicare.

The third part of the bill, Medicaid, funded from general tax revenue, provided health care for the needy poor and others. Administered by the individual states, Medicaid covered a broad range of people, including welfare recipients, persons who were blind or disabled, and low-income elderly citizens who did not qualify for Social Security or whose Medicare benefits had run out. The Medicaid idea had originated in the early 1960s as a Republican alternative to the Johnson Administration's push for a compulsory health insurance plan.

The enactment of Medicare and Medicaid in 1965 culminated three decades of political controversy. Agitation for federal (as opposed to state) health care coverage arose with the passage of the 1935 Social Security Act, which left out any provision for health insurance. Repeated failures over the next two decades to establish a comprehensive national health insurance plan, in large part because of fierce opposition by the AMA, led reformers to try for more limited plans covering the neediest groups. In 1957, advocates of health insurance for the elderly enlisted the support of Representative Aime Forand (D-RI), but the resulting Forand Bill, the direct ancestor of Medicare, failed to win passage. In 1960, President John F. Kennedy made Medicare part of his national agenda. Representative Cecil King (D-CA) and Senator Clinton Anderson (D-NM) sponsored the bill in Congress. After a number of hearings in the House and Senate—and the Democratic landslide in the 1964 elections—Medicare became President Johnson's top priority.

In the years after 1965, Medicare and Medicaid were modified periodically by Congress in an effort to control escalating costs. Changes in 1971 and 1974 instituted a review of standards and costs and tried to eliminate duplication of equipment and hospitals. Revisions in 1983 standardized charges for medical procedures. Both state and federal agencies waged a continual battle to control fraud and abuse in the system. In the 1980s health care discussion turned to the long-term needs of the elderly, coverage for medical catastrophes, and ways to preserve the Medicare system when the large baby-boomer cohort of the population reached retirement age. Health maintenance organizations (HMOs), introduced by the private sector after being enabled by legislation passed by Congress in 1973 as a way to control rising costs, were subsequently included as an option for Medicare and Medicaid recipients. At the end of the century, debate focused on ways to cover the approximately 44 million uninsured Americans and to provide reimbursement to Medicare recipients for expensive pharmaceuticals.

In 2003, under intense pressure from the George W. Bush administration and the American Association of Retired Persons, Congress narrowly passed legislation giving older Americans limited prescription drug benefits under Medicare beginning in 2006. Critics charged that the added benefits (estimated to cost $534 billion in the first decade alone) could bankrupt the system. The critics also targeted the law's failure to regulate drug company prices and its ban on the purchase of cheaper drugs from Canada. By permitting private health care providers to compete with

Medicare by offering lower rates to healthier seniors, critics further charged, the new legislation could in the long run destroy the entire program.

[*See also* **Bush, George W.; Great Society; Health Insurance; Johnson, Lyndon B.; Kennedy, John F.; New Deal; Social Policy: Public Welfare; Social Security; Social Security Policy;** ***and*** **Truman, Harry S.**]

BIBLIOGRAPHY

Berkowitz, Edward. *America's Welfare State: From Roosevelt to Reagan*. Baltimore: Johns Hopkins University Press, 1991.

David, Sheri I. *With Dignity: The Search for Medicare and Medicaid*. Westport, Conn.: Greenwood Press, 1985.

Harris, Richard. *A Sacred Trust*. New York: New American Library, 1966.

Marmor, Theodore. *The Politics of Medicare*. London: Routledge and K. Paul, 1970.

Myers, Robert J. *Medicare*. Homewood, Ill.: R. D. Irwin, 1970.

Stevens, Robert, and Rosemary Stevens. *Welfare Medicine in America: A Case Study of Medicaid*. New York: Free Press, 1974.

Sheri I. David; revised and updated by Paul S. Boyer

MIRANDA v. ARIZONA

A 1966 landmark Supreme Court case involving the rights of arrested persons. Prior to *Miranda,* the "voluntariness" test governed the admissibility of confessions. But determining whether a confession was "voluntary" involved so many variables that the test became extremely subjective. Moreover, trial judges almost always resolved in the government's favor the inevitable disagreements over what tactics police interrogators had utilized. Addressing the shortcomings of the voluntariness test, the Supreme Court in *Miranda* offered a clearer, more manageable alternative.

On the basis of his confession, Ernesto Miranda, an indigent, poorly educated twenty-three-year-old, had been convicted in Arizona of kidnapping and rape. On appeal, the case reached the Supreme Court. Although his two hours of questioning had been comparatively mild, Miranda had not been advised of his right to consult with an attorney or to have a lawyer present before answering any questions. Because the confession was obtained under circumstances the High Court found constitutionally unacceptable, Miranda's conviction was reversed.

The Fifth Amendment provides that no person "shall be compelled in any criminal case to be a witness against himself." The pre-*Miranda* view was that this provision applied only to judicial or other formal proceedings. But in *Miranda,* a 5-to-4 majority led by Chief Justice Earl Warren held that the self-incrimination clause also applied to the informal compulsion exerted by the police during their interrogations after a suspect has been arrested.

In the "interrogation environment," the *Miranda* majority concluded, a suspect typically assumed (erroneously) or was misled by the police into believing that he or she had to answer their questions. Thus, unless "adequate protective devices" were utilized to dispel the anxiety and coercion inherent in police interrogation, no statement obtained from a suspect could truly be the product of a free choice. The adequate protective devices set down by the Court (unless the government adopted other equally effective means) were the now-familiar *Miranda* warnings against self-incrimination and notification of the right to counsel.

In reality, *Miranda* is a much more limited ruling than was at first realized. Its principal weakness (or, depending upon one's viewpoint, its saving grace) is that it permits someone subjected to the inherent pressures of arrest and detention to waive his or her rights without obtaining the advice of counsel. Moreover, *Miranda* permits the police to obtain the waiver of a suspect's rights without the presence of a judicial officer or any disinterested observer and without making any formal record of the "waiver" transaction.

When President Richard M. Nixon, after sharply criticizing *Miranda* during his successful 1968 presidential campaign, appointed four new Supreme Court justices, many thought *Miranda* would be overruled. But this did not happen, and by the 1990s the Supreme Court understood *Miranda*'s limited scope. Further, most empirical studies indicated that it had no significant adverse effect on law enforcement. The police, despite their initial anger, had similarly learned to live with the rule.

To some, *Miranda* remains the "red flag" of the Warren Court's activism in the criminal law area. To others it symbolizes the willingness of the American legal system to treat even the lowliest criminal suspect as worthy of respect and consideration.

[*See also* **Civil Rights; Crime Policy, Federal; Nixon, Richard M.; Supreme Court, U.S.;** ***and*** **Warren, Earl.**]

BIBLIOGRAPHY

Baker, Liva. *Miranda: Crime, Law and Politics*. New York: Atheneum, 1983.

Kamisar, Yale. "Miranda, the Case, the Man, and the Players." *Michigan Law Review* 82 (February 1984): 1074–1092.

Kamisar, Yale. *Police Interrogation and Confessions*. Ann Arbor: University of Michigan Press, 1980.

Leo, Richard A. "The Impact of Miranda Revisited." *Journal of Criminal Law and Criminology* 86 (Spring 1996): 621–692.

Schulhofer, Stephen J. "Reconsidering Miranda." *University of Chicago Law Review* 54 (Spring 1987): 435–461.

Yale Kamisar

MODEL PENAL CODE

First proposed by the American Law Institute (ALI) in the 1930s, the Model Penal Code, or MPC, finally gained sufficient funding to proceed in the 1950s. Animating the code's genesis was a sense that criminal law had failed to stay abreast of modern developments in psychology and the social sciences, leading to a convoluted array of overlapping offenses defined by idiosyncratic elements and terms, some dating back to the middle ages. To correct this, the code's drafters devised a series of clarifications and innovations that states could adopt as they pleased, depending on how far they wanted to go down the road of reform.

Headed by Columbia Law Professor Herbert Wechsler, the MPC Reporters divided the code into a General Part—focused on rules of culpability, conduct, and causation—and a Special Part, focusing on specific offenses such as murder, manslaughter, robbery, and burglary. The MPC also simplified a variety of common law crimes. Instead of battery, aggravated assault, and mayhem, for example, the MPC simply prohibited "bodily injury." Rather than particularized offenses aimed at punishing recklessness like "failure to protect [the] public from attack by wild animals and reptiles," "throwing knives or shooting at human being in course of exhibition," and "negligently furnishing insecure scaffolding," the code simply included a statute prohibiting "reckless conduct."

The code's most controversial innovation was a focus on the treatment of offenders, rather than simply their punishment. According to Wechsler, who outlined the basic "challenge" of a model penal code in 1952, the primary goal of criminal law was to reduce crime by successfully treating present and future offenders. This focus on treatment rankled some criminal law scholars, most notably Henry M. Hart, who maintained that the code should balance its emphasis on offenders with a counteremphasis on "the aims of the good society generally."

Completed in 1962, the MPC exerted an immediate impact on both legal scholarship and state legislation. Criminal law scholars like Sanford Kadish quickly incorporated the MPC into their casebooks, making it a cornerstone of criminal law teaching. Meanwhile, states across the country moved to adopt the code in place of their arcane, often convoluted assemblages of criminal statutes. Yet, even as thirty plus states moved to implement the MPC, no state adopted all of its provisions, nor did states adopt its more radical recommendations. The code recommended that first- and second-degree murder be eliminated on the theory that premeditation and deliberation were false concepts, particularly since most states held that premeditation could be achieved in an instant. Yet, most states stuck with their old definitions of murder, leaving prosecutors the discretion to charge first-degree murder in particularly heinous crimes.

Although the MPC influenced the criminal codes in a majority of American states, localization remained a problem for the remainder of the twentieth century, as subsequent waves of legislators responded to moral panics with additional, often redundant crimes. Indeed, by the close of the twentieth-century criminal law scholars such as William J. Stuntz asserted that the politics behind criminal law were pathological, raising the possibility of a second model penal code project. The potential for such a project remains to be seen.

[*See also* **Crime Policy, Federal.**]

BIBLIOGRAPHY

Dubber, Markus. *Criminal Law: Modern Penal Code.* New York: Foundation Press, 2002.

Wechsler, Herbert. "A Rationale of the Law of Homicide (Parts I & II)." 37 *Columbia Law Review* 701 (1937): 1261.

Hart, Henry M., Jr. *The Aims of Criminal Law.* 23 L. & Con. Prob. 401, 402 (1958).

Anders Walker

THE OXFORD ENCYCLOPEDIA OF
AMERICAN POLITICAL AND LEGAL HISTORY

THE OXFORD ENCYCLOPEDIA OF AMERICAN POLITICAL AND LEGAL HISTORY

Donald T. Critchlow
Philip R. VanderMeer
EDITORS IN CHIEF

VOLUME 2
MONE—ZENG

OXFORD
UNIVERSITY PRESS

OXFORD
UNIVERSITY PRESS

Oxford University Press, Inc., publishes works that further
Oxford University's objective of excellence
in research, scholarship, and education.

Oxford New York
Auckland Cape Town Dar es Salaam Hong Kong Karachi
Kuala Lumpur Madrid Melbourne Mexico City Nairobi
New Delhi Shanghai Taipei Toronto

With offices in
Argentina Austria Brazil Chile Czech Republic France Greece
Guatemala Hungary Italy Japan Poland Portugal Singapore
South Korea Switzerland Thailand Turkey Ukraine Vietnam

Published by Oxford University Press, Inc.
198 Madison Avenue, New York, NY 10016
www.oup.com

The Library of Congress Cataloging-in-Publication Data

The Oxford encyclopedia of American political and legal history / Donald T. Critchlow and
Philip R. VanderMeer, editors in chief.

p. cm.

Includes bibliographical references and index.

ISBN 978-0-19-975461-8

1. United States—Politics and government—Encyclopedias. 2. Political planning—United States—History—Encyclopedias. 3. Law—United States—History—Encyclopedias. I. Critchlow, Donald T., 1948- II. VanderMeer, Philip R., 1947- III. Title.

JK9.O94 2012
320.97303—dc23

2011032748

1 3 5 7 9 8 6 4 2

Printed in the United States of America
on acid-free paper

COMMON ABBREVIATIONS USED IN THIS WORK

AD	*anno Domini,* in the year of the Lord
AH	*anno Hegirae,* in the year of the Hajj
b.	Born
BCE	before the common era (= BC)
c.	*circa,* about, approximately
CE	common era (= AD)
cf.	*confer,* compare
d.	died
diss.	dissertation
ed.	editor (pl., eds.), edition
f.	and following (pl., ff.)
fl.	*floruit,* flourished
l.	line (pl., ll.)
n.	note
n.d.	no date
no.	number
n.p.	no place
n.s.	new series
p.	page (pl., pp.)
pt.	part
rev.	revised
ser.	series
supp.	supplement
USSR	Union of Soviet Socialist Republics
vol.	volume (pl., vols.)

THE OXFORD ENCYCLOPEDIA OF
AMERICAN POLITICAL AND LEGAL HISTORY

M

CONTINUED

MONETARY POLICY

Encompassing two major components, the coining of currency and the creation of a banking system, U.S. monetary policy is as old as the national government itself.

Currency. Following Alexander Hamilton's recommendations, the Coinage Act of 1792 established the dollar as the official unit of account and established a bimetallic standard that defined the dollar in relation to gold and silver. The silver dollar contained fifteen times as much silver as the gold in the gold dollar. Originally the 15 to 1 ratio was close to the prevailing market value, but as market values changed over time, one of the metals became overvalued at the mint price. In the early nineteenth century, silver became overvalued, and its possessors presented silver to the mint for coinage. Gold coins began to disappear from circulation. In 1834 the Treasury adjusted the mint ratio to around 16-to-1, now overvaluing gold. Hence, gold began to replace silver in circulation, causing the latter to be hoarded or exported.

This system whereby the value of the dollar and foreign currencies was defined by their specie (gold or silver) content in turn fixed the value of currencies relative to each other. In other words, a system of fixed exchange rates enabled specie, dollars, and foreign exchange all to be freely convertible. Civil War economic exigencies, however, led Congress to pass the Legal Tender Act of 1862, which provided for the issue of fiat money, commonly know as greenbacks, not convertible into specie at a fixed rate. Market forces determined the value of the greenback (paper) dollar relative to gold and foreign currencies in a system of floating or flexible exchange rates. At one point, greenbacks in New York fell to a gold price as low as 35 cents on the dollar.

To restore the prewar parity between the U.S. dollar and the British pound sterling (the standard for global exchange rates), the post–Civil War American government adopted fiscal policies to deflate prices and bring greenbacks onto a par with gold. The ensuing sharp deflation, which hurt debtors and aided creditors, caused fierce opposition. The Greenback Labor Party (founded in 1874) appealed to debtors and entrepreneurs who wanted to expand the issue of greenbacks, increase the money supply, and raise the price level. Later, the free silver movement advocated the free and unlimited coinage of silver at the old ratio (16 to 1) to accomplish the same ends. Only after a decade of deflation did Congress pass the Resumption Act of 1875 and commit the Treasury to exchange gold dollars and paper dollars at par. On 1 January 1879 greenbacks became freely convertible to gold with fixed exchange rates restored at the prewar parity.

The victims of deflation, however, continued to condemn the gold standard as the congressional "Crime of '73." (In 1873, ancillary to its deflationary policy, Congress had "demonitized" silver by ordering the U.S. Mint to stop making silver coins.) The 1880s and early 1890s remained a period of intense controversy as to the appropriate monetary standard. The election of William McKinley over William Jennings Bryan in 1896 and, subsequently, rising prices stilled the protests of debtors and free-silver advocates. In 1900 the U.S. formally committed itself to the gold standard.

After the financial crises and disruptions of the 1930s and World War II, the United States and its major allies agreed to restore fixed exchange rates at the 1944 Bretton Woods Conference. The dollar, set at a price of $35 per ounce of gold, replaced the pound sterling as the international currency of record. The Bretton Woods system lasted into the early 1970s when domestic inflation prompted President Richard M. Nixon to end fixed exchange rates. Afterward the dollar floated against other currencies, its value determined by the demand and supply of foreign exchange.

Banking. Congress chartered the first Bank of the United States in 1791 as proposed by Alexander Hamilton, who modeled it after the Bank of England. The bank was a combined public and private enterprise with branches in major cities, the authority to issue notes, and a role as a commercial bank as well as the fiscal agent of the government. When the bank's charter came up for renewal in 1811, the recharter bill failed in the Senate after a hotly contested debate about its constitutionality.

Shortly thereafter, however, in 1816, Congress established a second Bank of the United States with charter provisions similar to those of the first. After a rather undistinguished early history, the Second Bank came into its own in 1823 with the appointment of Nicholas Biddle of Philadelphia as director. Biddle actively pursued a policy of pressing state banks to redeem their outstanding banknotes at promised par or face value in specie. Such a policy restrained the temptation of such banks to "overissue" notes, dampened inflation, and increased public confidence in circulating banknotes. During the 1820s Biddle's policy narrowed the range of discounts among state banknotes. This policy promoted soundness and confidence in the banking system but produced discontent in western regions and among individuals desirous of easier credit.

President Andrew Jackson, who vetoed a bank recharter bill in 1832, represented the enemies of Biddle. In his veto message,

Jackson criticized the bank's monopoly status, its domination by financiers and foreigners, and its regulation of economic growth in the West. He even questioned its constitutionality. Jackson resolved to cripple the bank's power by removing government deposits and redepositing them in selected state banks known as "pet banks." Jackson's war against the Second Bank was followed by a speculative boom (with the highest peacetime inflation rate before the 1970s) and an ensuing financial panic and deep depression (1837–1843). After 1836 the federal government withdrew from the banking system altogether, later establishing an independent treasury to administer revenues and their disbursement. This system lasted nearly three-quarters of a century until the establishment in 1913 of the Federal Reserve System.

To replace the circulation of heterogeneous state banknotes with a uniform currency and simultaneously increase the demand for government bonds, the National Banking Act of 1863–1864 established a national banking system. Banks with national charters were allowed to issue banknotes backed by U.S. government bonds. The dominance of national banks proved short-lived. Increasing use of checks and demand deposits made banks' inability to issue notes less of a disadvantage, so that by 1890 the nonnational banks surpassed national banks both in number and in assets. This system of small, independent local banks (as opposed to branch banks) proved particularly vulnerable to financial crises. In the late nineteenth century, financial panics and subsequent suspensions of cash payments by banks became common. A panic in 1907 was the last straw, leading Congress to establish the congressional National Monetary Commission to consider banking reform. The result was the Federal Reserve Act of 1913.

The Federal Reserve System created a central bank to alleviate the problem of recurrent panics. The new institution was to furnish "an elastic currency," smooth seasonal money-market stringencies, and act as the lender of last resort during crises. The law established a decentralized structure that dispersed power and reflected popular and congressional suspicion of the concentration of economic power in Washington or among Wall Street bankers. Twelve regional Federal Reserve Banks operated under a coordinating board in Washington.

In its initial years the new system appeared successful in adjusting seasonal credit flows and smoothing seasonal interest rates. The Federal Reserve, however, failed to avert the Great Depression of the 1930s. Indeed, many economists cite its inaction as the principal factor underlying the severity of the depression. The failure of the Federal Reserve System between 1929 and 1933 led the Franklin Delano Roosevelt administration to propose further reforms. The Banking Act of 1933, known as the Glass–Steagall Act, created the Federal Deposit Insurance Corporation (FDIC) to protect depositors' accounts. Glass–Steagall also divorced investment and commercial banking operations. The Banking Act of 1935 further centralized and extended the power of the Federal Reserve Board, now called the Board of Governors. Thereafter, the Federal Reserve Board had greater power to regulate the money supply and set interest rates.

The high inflation and interest rates of the 1970s created great problems for regulated banks, which were limited as to the loans they could make and the rate of interest they could pay. Depositors thus withdrew funds from banks and redeposited them in unregulated money market mutual funds that offered higher interest rates. The Depository and Monetary Control Act of 1980 partly deregulated commercial banks and savings-and-loan associations, allowing them to offer higher interest rates by making more diverse investments. The ensuing pattern of highly speculative investment led to the savings-and-loan scandal of the 1980s. As the twentieth century ended, however, further deregulation of banking seemed likely.

[*See also* **Bryan, William Jennings; Economic Policy: Banking and Financial Regulation; Federal Deposit Insurance Corporation; Federal Government, Executive Branch: Treasury Department; Federal Reserve Act; Federal Reserve System; Free Silver Movement; Greenback Labor Party; Hamilton, Alexander; Jackson, Andrew; McKinley, William; Nixon, Richard M.; Roosevelt, Franklin Delano;** *and* **Taxation.**]

BIBLIOGRAPHY

Friedman, Milton, and Anna Schwartz. *A Monetary History of the United States, 1867–1960*. Princeton, N.J.: Princeton University Press, 1963.

Hammond, Bray. *Banks and Politics in America from the Revolution to the Civil War*. Princeton, N.J.: Princeton University Press, 1957.

Studenski, Paul, and Herman Krooss. *Financial History of the United States*. New York: McGraw–Hill, 1963.

Temin, Peter. *The Jacksonian Economy*. New York: W. W. Norton, 1969.

Timberlake, Richard. *The Origins of Central Banking in the United States*. Cambridge, Mass.: Harvard University Press, 1978.

White, Eugene N. *The Regulation and Reform of the American Banking System, 1900–1929*. Princeton, N.J.: Princeton University Press, 1983.

John A. James

MONROE, JAMES

(1758–1831), fifth president of the United States. Born in Westmoreland County, Virginia, James Monroe entered the College of William and Mary in 1774, but left two years later to fight in the Revolutionary War. Rising to the rank of lieutenant colonel, Monroe saw active service at Long Island, Manhattan, Trenton, Brandywine, Valley Forge, and Monmouth Courthouse.

Elected to the Virginia House of Delegates in 1782, Monroe soon went to Philadelphia for a term in the Continental Congress (1783–1786). He opposed ratification of the federal Constitution, but was nevertheless elected to the U.S. Senate in 1790. He represented the United States in Paris from 1793 to 1796, but was recalled after disagreeing with the George Washington administration over foreign policy. He served three terms as Virginia governor (1799–1802) before President Thomas Jefferson sent him back to Paris for the final stage of the negotiations for the Louisiana Purchase (1803). Thereafter, until 1807, Monroe was, alternately, U.S. minister in London and Madrid, but he achieved little success. Jefferson rejected a commercial treaty he negotiated with Great Britain in 1806, and in Spain Monroe failed to obtain the Floridas for the United States.

In 1808 Monroe ran unsuccessfully for the presidency. He began another term as governor of Virginia in 1811, but resigned the same year when President James Madison appointed him secretary of state. During the War of 1812 Monroe contemplated resuming a military career but he remained in the State Department while simultaneously serving as secretary of war in the winter of 1812–1813 and again in 1814–1815.

In 1816 Monroe was elected to the first of two terms as president. Winning on each occasion without significant opposition, he presided over the "Era of Good Feelings" following the collapse of the Federalist and Jeffersonian Republican parties. On the domestic front, the Monroe Administration undertook few initiatives. The president played no active role in the debates occasioned by the

Missouri Crisis, although he did ultimately support the measures that resolved the dispute by linking the admission of Maine and Missouri to the Union to the restriction on slavery throughout the remainder of the Louisiana Purchase. In foreign affairs, Monroe's accomplishments were more substantial. He worked closely with his secretary of state, John Quincy Adams, on the negotiations with Spain that produced the 1819 Adams–Onís Treaty granting the United States clear title to the Floridas, establishing the final boundaries of the Louisiana Purchase, and extending U.S. territory to the Pacific. A section of his 1823 annual message, drafted by Adams, warning European powers against intervening in the Americas and opposing the incorporation of South American territory into European colonial empires, was subsequently enshrined as the "Monroe Doctrine," which helped lay the foundation for U.S. diplomatic hegemony in the Americas.

[*See also* **Adams, John Quincy; Compromise of 1850; Constitution; Continental Congress; Federal Government, Executive Branch: Presidency, The; Federal Government, Legislative Branch: Senate; Federalist Party; Jefferson, Thomas; Louisiana Purchase; Madison, James;** *and* **Political Parties.**]

BIBLIOGRAPHY

Ammon, Harry. *James Monroe: The Quest for National Identity*. New York: McGraw–Hill, 1971.

Cunningham, Noble E., Jr. *The Presidency of James Monroe*. Lawrence: University Press of Kansas, 1996.

J. C. A. Stagg

MORRILL LAND GRANT ACT

This 1862 law, which provided land grants to the states for the founding of colleges to teach "agriculture and the mechanic arts," was first introduced in Congress in 1857 by Representative Justin Morrill, a Vermont Whig (later Republican). Morrill was convinced that existing colleges were failing to provide practical education for the nation's farmers and workers, whose productivity might be greatly improved through the diffusion of "useful knowledge." Although Morrill's first bill encountered strong southern opposition and was ultimately vetoed by President James Buchanan, a similar bill was passed in 1862 after southern secession and was signed into law by President Abraham Lincoln.

The Morrill Act entitled each state to a grant of 30,000 acres of federal land for each member of Congress. Funds from the sale of these lands were to be used as a permanent endowment for "at least one college where the leading object shall be, without excluding other scientific and classical studies, to teach such branches of learning as are related to agriculture and the mechanic arts." The states themselves had authority to choose their parcels of federal land, arrange for their sales, and designate the recipients of the income. States chose existing universities (as in Wisconsin), founded new flagship universities (California), or named special agricultural and mechanical colleges (Indiana). Some southern states (which received grants after the Civil War) split the funds among separate agricultural and mechanical (A&M) colleges for whites and blacks.

Most land-grant colleges struggled at first, lacking both students and a body of useful scientific knowledge to teach. Rising demand for engineering education and a surge in high-school graduates, however, eventually caused these institutions to prosper. They were assisted materially by two subsequent acts passed in part because of lobbying efforts by the colleges themselves. The Hatch Act (1887) provided federal funds for agricultural experiment stations, which considerably furthered agricultural science, and the Second Morrill Act (1890) legislated annual federal appropriations.

The Morrill Act shaped American higher education in important respects. It promoted the equal standing of practical and liberal studies; encouraged publicly supported higher education by inducing states to found universities and materially assist their development; and fostered a system of agricultural education, research, and dissemination that ultimately brought useful knowledge to the farmers Justin Morrill had originally sought to help.

[*See also* **Agricultural Policy; Buchanan, James; Education Policy: Higher Education; Land Policy, Federal; Lincoln, Abraham;** ***and*** **Whig Party.**]

BIBLIOGRAPHY

Eddy, Edward D., Jr. *Colleges for Our Land and Time: The Land-Grant Idea in American Education.* New York: Harper, 1957.

Geiger, Roger, ed. "The Land–Grant Act and American Higher Education." In *History of Higher Education Annual.* New Brunswick, N.J.: Transaction, 1998.

Williams, Roger L. *The Origins of Federal Support for Higher Education: George W. Atherton and the Land-Grant College Movement.* University Park: Pennsylvania State University Press, 1991.

Roger L. Geiger

MOYNIHAN REPORT

Originally titled *The Negro Family: The Case for National Action,* the Moynihan Report became the popular name for a White House memo authored by then-Johnson aide Daniel Patrick Moynihan. The report declared that the breakdown of poor African American families was the major problem hindering the advancement of the black community. Upon its release in the summer of 1965, various commentators declared that Moynihan ignored structural barriers to black progress and was "blaming the victim" by holding African Americans primarily responsible for their economic conditions. The backlash against the report played a key role in inhibiting the discussion of cultural factors with regard to black poverty for a generation.

The civil rights movement's success in eliminating the legal barriers to black equality provided the impetus for the report. With the passage of the Civil Rights Act of 1964 and the imminent signing of the Voting Rights Act of 1965, many within the movement began to focus on the need for government action to close the economic gap between blacks and whites. In this context, President Johnson had launched a series of antipoverty initiatives as part of his Great Society programs.

Moynihan, who grew up fatherless in New York City, researched the history of the African American family. Drawing on the works of several academics, including black scholars such as E. Franklin Frazier and W. E. B. Du Bois, Moynihan suggested that the rising number of blacks growing up in single-parent households in urban ghettoes posed the greatest threat to the African American community. Although careful to stress that the legacy of white racism and economic deprivation was responsible for the weak state of poor black families, he emphasized the "tangle of pathology" among this group. The report became a key source for President Johnson's speech at Howard University in June 1965 calling for the country to achieve not only "equality of opportunity" for black Americans, but "equality of result" as well.

Controversy ensued when the report was leaked to the press in August 1965, shortly after the Watts riot in Los Angeles. As the debate over the causes of the riot raged, many commentators viewed the report as the administration's response to this upheaval. Some observers thought Moynihan was suggesting that the problems of poor black families, rather than white racism, were the primary barrier facing African Americans. By this time, Moynihan had left Johnson's staff and, amid the firestorm, the administration disowned the report.

In the two decades after the initial controversy, most scholars shied away from any discussion involving the cultural roots of black poverty. Moynihan would go on to a successful career in public life, working in the Nixon and Ford administrations before serving four terms as a U.S. senator from New York between 1977 and 2001. In the 1990s, some scholars began to revisit the relationship between black family life and poverty, suggesting that the Moynihan Report had been prescient. Others, like William Julius Wilson, were less effusive, although he acknowledged that whereas Moynihan's "presentation certainly lacked elegance . . . it was an attempt to synthesize structural and cultural analyses to understand the dynamics of poor black families and the plight of low-skilled black males"(quoted in Patterson, 2010, p. 213).

[*See also* **Civil Rights; Equality; Great Society; Johnson, Lyndon B.;** *and* **Poverty.**]

BIBLIOGRAPHY

Patterson, James. *Freedom Is Not Enough: The Moynihan Report and America's Struggle over Black Family Life from LBJ to Obama*. New York, Basic Books, 2010. The author provides the best full-length discussion of the report and the debates it has provoked since the 1960s.

Rainwater, Lee, and William Yancey. *The Moynihan Report and the Politics of Controversy*. Cambridge, Mass.: MIT Press, 1967. This book contains the text of the original report as well as contemporary reactions to it.

Robert Fleegler

MUCKRAKERS

Theodore Roosevelt first applied the term "muckrakers" to a group of journalists and writers who exposed corruption in business and government in the early twentieth century. Roosevelt intended the term, borrowed from John Bunyan's *Pilgrim's Progress,* to be somewhat pejorative, but the muckrakers were very influential for a time and provided strong impetus to the ongoing Progressive-Era reform movement.

Around 1902, a number of prominent magazines, including *McClure's, Collier's, Cosmopolitan, Everybody's,* and the *Arena,* began featuring crusading exposés or "muckraking" articles. Some of these pieces were later expanded into full-length books. Among the best known were Ida Tarbell's *History of the Standard Oil Company* (1902); Lincoln Steffens's *The Shame of the Cities* (1904), documenting corruption in municipal government; Samuel Hopkins Adams's *The Great American Fraud* (1906), lambasting the patent-medicine industry; and Ray Stannard Baker's *Following the Color Line* (1908), a pioneering exposé of American racism.

A few muckrakers made their case in works of fiction. Upton Sinclair's *The Jungle* (1906), a fictionalized account of the Chicago meatpacking industry, was the best known of the genre, but David Graham Phillips was perhaps the most prolific of the muckraking novelists. Among his numerous works were *Lightfingered Gentry* (1907), on the insurance industry; *Susan Lenox: Her Fall and Rise* (1908, published in 1917), on prostitution; and many others.

The muckraking spirit also influenced some of the major novelists of the time, although usually in less tractarian form. Frank Norris's *The Octopus* (1901) and *The Pit* (1903); Theodore Dreiser's *The Financier* (1912) and

The Titan (1914); and Jack London's *Iron Heel* (1908) all address the social consequences of unregulated capitalist expansion.

After about 1912, the muckraking movement abated. The public tired of the exposés, some of which seemed sensationalized and overly sordid. But muckraking already had exerted a major impact on the reform movement and would influence the policies of President Woodrow Wilson. Indeed, Ray Stannard Baker became an aide to Wilson and later edited a six-volume collection of Wilson's public papers (1926–1927). Assuming many different forms, the muckraking impulse continued to influence American journalism as the twentieth century wore on.

[*See also* **Progressive Era; Roosevelt, Theodore;** *and* **Wilson, Woodrow.**]

BIBLIOGRAPHY

Brasch, Walter M. *Forerunners of Revolution*. Lanham, Md.: University Press of America, 1990.

Harrison, J. M., and H. H. Stein, eds. *Muckraking*. Philadelphia: Pennsylvania State University Press, 1974.

George H. Douglas

MUGWUMPS

Late nineteenth-century reformers who blamed partisanship for the rampant corruption of Gilded Age politics. By voting independently of party lines, Mugwumps attempted to pressure regular Republicans and Democrats to support civil service reform, lower tariffs, and a hard-money policy based on the gold standard.

In 1884, members of the Republican Party's independent wing rejected their party's presidential candidate, James G. Blaine, to support the Democratic Party nominee, Grover Cleveland. Republican loyalists called the insurgents "Mugwumps," an Algonquian word for "great man," used in this context to deride the bolters' claim to moral superiority.

Most Mugwumps were college-educated business and professional men from New York or New England. Their spokesmen in 1884 were veteran Republicans such as Carl Schurz (1829–1906), a former U.S. senator and cabinet official, and George William Curtis (1824–1892) and E. L. Godkin (1831–1902), editors, respectively, of *Harper's Weekly* and *The Nation*. But younger men such as R. R. Bowker, a New York publisher, and George Fred Williams, a Boston lawyer, did the day-to-day organizational work.

Cleveland's slim victory margin in 1884 seemed to underscore the importance of the Mugwump vote, and Cleveland courted their support by backing civil service reform and lower tariffs. After 1884, some bolters became Democrats and helped revive Democratic strength in New England in the early 1890s. But Mugwump–Democratic cooperation was never wholehearted. Irish-American Democrats and the Mugwumps distrusted each other from the start, and the Democrats' 1896 presidential candidate, William Jennings Bryan, advocated populist programs that the Mugwumps abhorred. The last national campaign in which the Mugwumps figured prominently was the anti-imperialist opposition to U.S. annexation of the Philippines following the Spanish-American War.

[*See also* **Civil Service Reform; Cleveland, Grover; Political Parties; Populist Era;** *and* **Tariffs.**]

BIBLIOGRAPHY

McFarland, Gerald W. *Mugwumps, Morals and Politics, 1884–1920*. Amherst: University of Massachusetts Press, 1975.

Tucker, David M. *Mugwumps: Public Moralists of the Gilded Age*. Columbia: University of Missouri Press, 1998.

Gerald W. McFarland

MULLER v. OREGON

A 1908 U.S. Supreme Court decision granting states the right to regulate the hours of women workers. The case began when laundry-owner Curt Muller, convicted of violating Oregon's ten-hour law for women, carried his appeal to the Supreme Court, arguing that the statute infringed his right to contract freely with his workers. At issue, then, was whether states had the power to intervene on behalf of employees in employment relationships. In *Lochner v. New York* (1905), the Supreme Court had overthrown a New York law regulating the hours of bakers. The opportunity to prepare evidence in defense of the Oregon law fell to Florence Kelley and her research chief at the National Consumers' League (NCL), Josephine Goldmark. The case exemplified Kelley's strategy of using gender-specific means to achieve classwide goals. Goldmark collected extensive evidence to prove that long hours jeopardized women's health and morals, and her brother-in-law Louis Brandeis argued the case before the Court. His famous "Brandeis Brief," a compilation of sociological and medical evidence, persuaded the high court to uphold Oregon's law. Writing for the majority, Justice David Brewer accepted the argument that overwork was injurious to women and that the state bore a responsibility for protecting women "to preserve the strength of the race."

The ruling led many more states to regulate working conditions. It also popularized the practice of introducing sociological and medical data to establish legal claims. This approach, central to the concept that came to be known as "legal realism," helped lay the groundwork for such later landmark decisions as *Brown v. Board of Education*. Although women's organizations supported the *Muller* decision at the time, changes in working conditions and in ideology brought about a reversal of attitude, and in the 1960s and 1970s the National Organization for Women and other feminist organizations successfully campaigned for the removal of gender-specific laws.

[*See also* **Brandeis, Louis;** ***Brown v. Board of Education;*** **Contract, Law of; National Organization for Women; Progressive Era; State Governments; States' Rights; Supreme Court, U.S.;** ***and West Coast Hotel v. Parrish.***]

BIBLIOGRAPHY

Goldmark, Josephine. *Impatient Crusader: Florence Kelley's Life Story*. Urbana: University of Illinois Press, 1953.

Woloch, Nancy. *Muller v. Oregon: A Brief History with Documents*. Boston: Bedford Books of St. Martin's Press, 1996.

Kathryn Kish Sklar

MUNICIPAL JUDICIAL SYSTEM

Municipal judicial systems encompass a variety of courts of limited or special jurisdiction that form the base of the American justice system. They are termed "municipal" courts not because they are in cities, although they often are, but because they oversee the exercise of municipal or, as they are more frequently called, police powers. These are the powers of government—historically left to the cities and states—to regulate the health, safety, morals, and welfare of the population. In contrast to state courts of general jurisdiction, which also exercise police powers, these lower-level courts typically hear and decide cases that result in a fine of less than $1,000 or a jail term of less than twelve months; misdemeanor violations involving traffic, petty larceny, prostitution, and similar criminal acts; and matters covered under municipal ordinances. The initial hearing of some felony charges also occurs in municipal courts. Together they account for 90 percent of all courts in the nation and 80 percent of all litigation.

Modern courts of limited jurisdiction have their roots in the American colonies and more distantly in the judicial institutions and Common-Law experience of England. The first local colonial courts were rough approximations of their seventeenth- and eighteenth-century English counterparts. Most colonies had local judges, usually called justices of the peace or magistrates, who possessed limited legal training, served by appointment of the governor, and handled matters ranging from immoral behavior to economic regulation. These local courts, the forerunners of the modern municipal courts, were also important in reminding the colonists that they were entirely capable of delivering their own brand of justice, independent of their English governors.

This powerful heritage of local legal control carried beyond the ratification of the Constitution and reminds us that the most immediate impact of American law is at the local level. The nineteenth-century justice-of-the-peace courts, for example, operated on a neighborhood basis. The justice was a quasi-paternal figure, often untrained formally in the law, but a local notable who knew the people who appeared before him. Justices of the peace and magistrates, who depended in most cases on the fines and fees assessed on defendants, viewed themselves as semiautonomous figures who managed their own case flows and finances and more often than not held a presumption of guilt about the defendants who appeared before them.

This scheme of local justice, like the rest of the American judicial system, came under growing pressure during the Progressive Era. Since relatively few records of the actions of these courts survive, it is hard to establish their real level of business. It was surely vast, however. By 1900, for example, over 500 separate courts existed in the Chicago metropolitan area alone, more than double the number in 1880. The courts of Kansas City had 5,100 cases on the dockets in December 1903, twice the total from a decade earlier.

As the number of courts and cases grew, so, too, did the work of those courts. European immigration and industrialization, for example, prompted cities and states to criminalize an increasingly broad range of human conduct. Thus, municipal courts typically became the place where judges unfamiliar with immigrant culture and language meted out justice to drunks, petty thieves, and status offenders, such as prostitutes.

The judges were invariably political rather than legal figures. Municipal judgeships were filled in various ways, but whatever the method, the office, especially in light of the court's role as an agent of local social control, had powerful and often pernicious political overtones. These conditions drew the wrath of increasingly organized and professionally oriented municipal bar associations that by 1900 made municipal-court reform a priority.

The leaders of these bar associations preached that justice would only flow from a politically disinterested court system presided over by legal professionals. Businessmen joined the chorus to protest the waste, corruption, and political influence associated with these municipal courts. Chicago in 1900, for example, had fifty-two justices of the peace, whose salaries were paid by the fees of litigants and whose courts suffered from endless delays. The poor who could not afford an appeal were forced to accept the justices' ruling. At the same time, police magistrates, who heard petty criminal cases, were appointed by the mayor, who wielded extensive political influence over the courts.

Faced with these challenges, Chicago's bar and business leaders adopted reform measures that produced the nation's first modern municipal court system. The Illinois legislature in 1904 authorized an amendment to the Illinois Constitution that granted extensive home-rule powers to Chicago, including the authority to establish a unified municipal court. This new court, created in 1905, won broad popular support at the polls after a vigorous campaign. It involved a network of branch courts under a single chief justice. The court had jurisdiction to hear civil complaints, ordinance violations, and misdemeanors and even had preliminary jurisdiction over felonies. The act empowered the chief justice, Harry Olson, to bring a corporate style of management to the courts, including setting a trial calendar, developing civil procedures for the courts, assigning the twenty-seven associate justices to either the civil or the criminal branch, and requiring a monthly reporting of activity. The judges were popularly elected on nonpartisan ballots to six-year terms.

Under Olson's leadership, the Chicago Municipal Court became a national model. Within a decade, Cleveland, Milwaukee, Pittsburgh, Buffalo, New York City, Atlanta, Philadelphia, Birmingham, St. Louis, and Kansas City had adopted the Chicago model. The reformers who fashioned these new courts also embraced a different approach to the relationship of law and society. They expected municipal judges to approach each offender as a social worker might, using knowledge of the person's mental abnormalities, family history, and social experiences to shape appropriate punishments. As a result, a host of new, special-jurisdiction courts developed, including those dealing with juvenile justice, domestic relations, small claims, and public morals.

The promise of Progressive reform, however, was never fully realized. Although the corporate administrative model offered a more effective way to manage case loads, city and state governments often failed to provide funding sufficient to keep pace with rapid population growth. The municipal courts became the subject of increasing complaint because they often provided only assembly-line justice. Whereas the general ethic of American law presumes innocence, by the 1960s the day-to-day practice at the lowest level was a working presumption of guilt, a simple fact of judicial life in heavily overworked local court systems. The Progressive attempt to enlist the voters as a way of eliminating political and partisan influence in the selection of municipal judges fared just as poorly. Turnout in local judicial elections was invariably low; candidates for judgeships were frequently unknown to the electorate. Moreover, outside major metropolitan centers, the tradition of local justice remained strong, especially in the South, where it was so intimately tied to racial control.

Beginning in the 1970s a new reform effort took hold. The National League of Cities pioneered efforts to bring technology to the courtroom, making it possible for judges to administer growing case loads, to settle matters outside the courtroom through mediation and arbitration, and to share information about defendants that would prevent known criminals charged in one court from walking free in another court. Some of the most significant changes took place in California. At the end of the twentieth century, for example, Los Angeles County had the largest municipal justice system in America. It included fifty law enforcement agencies and twenty-four municipal court districts with 300 judges presiding over half a million arrests a year and more than 2 million traffic citations. California in 1995 gave local judges the opportunities to eliminate justice courts altogether and fold them into municipal courts. Moreover, voters in 1998 passed Proposition 220, which authorized the municipal courts to unify with the general-jurisdiction superior courts, if the judges of the two court systems could agree to do so. This unification process transferred many of the tasks formerly performed by the municipal courts to the superior courts and streamlined judicial business overall.

Despite these continuing efforts at consolidation and centralization, the American scheme of municipal justice retains strong local ties, extraordinary diversity, and a compelling role as an agency of social control. That tradition means that these courts are often shaped to fit local circumstances, but it also means that local justice does not mean exactly the same thing everywhere in America.

[*See also* **Crime Policy; Federal Government, Judicial Branch; Jurisprudence; Progressive Era;** ***and*** **State Governments.**]

BIBLIOGRAPHY

Gilbert, Hiram T. *The Municipal Court of Chicago.* Chicago: Author, 1928.

Hall, Kermit L. *The Magic Mirror: Law in American History.* New York: Oxford University Press, 1989.

Jacob, Herbert. *Urban Justice: Law and Order in American Cities.* Englewood Cliffs, N.J.: Prentice Hall, 1973.

Meyer, Jon'a. *"Doing Justice" in the People's Court: Sentencing by Municipal Court Judges.* Albany: State University of New York Press, 1997.

Monkkonen, Eric. *Police in Urban America, 1860–1920.* Cambridge, UK; New York: Cambridge University Press, 1981.

Walker, Samuel. *Popular Justice*, 2d ed. New York: Oxford University Press, 1998.

Willrich, Michael. "The Two Percent Solution: Eugenic Jurisprudence and the Socialization of American Law, 1900–1930." *Law & History Review* 16 (Spring 1998): 63–111.

Kermit L. Hall

MUNICIPAL POLITICS

Over the course of four centuries American municipal politics has adapted to changing ideology, rapid urban growth, burgeoning service demands, and shifting class and ethnic tensions. It has reflected and responded to the many forces transforming America's urban scene.

Emergence of Urban Politics. During the colonial era the structure of local government in the nascent urban centers varied markedly. The municipal corporations of Philadelphia, Norfolk, and Williamsburg were closed corporations, their aldermen serving for life and all vacancies being filled by the remaining officials. The general citizenry had no voice in the selection of municipal officials. In New York City, Albany, and New Jersey municipalities, the mayor and chief legal officer, known as the recorder, were appointees of the royal governor, whereas the electorate chose the aldermen and common councilors. In Boston a town meeting in which all the electorate participated directly was the basic governing body; a board of selectmen was in charge of the day-to-day governance of the community. Nowhere was there universal white manhood suffrage. Property-holding requirements limited the body of voters, although the municipal corporations in the middle colonies could grant freeman status and the accompanying right to vote to those who failed to meet property qualifications. Occasionally, heated contests drew many voters to the polls, but sustained partisan competition did not exist. In most communities a stable body of prosperous citizens held the reins of authority one decade after another.

The American Revolution marked an end to the unrepresentative closed corporations. Henceforth, the urban electorate would select their municipal legislators. Moreover, during the decades following American independence, property-holding and taxpaying requirements gradually disappeared, so that by the mid 1800s universal white manhood suffrage was the rule. Meanwhile, the emergence of national political parties transformed municipal politics, making each election a partisan battleground. As early as the 1790s Federalists and Republicans were vying for power in New York City and Philadelphia.

The rise of a broad suffrage and sustained partisan politics heightened the tensions on election day. In addition, an influx of working-class immigrants, often Roman Catholic, from Ireland and Germany resulted in ethnic, religious, and class conflict. By the 1850s and 1860s critics of municipal government were already complaining of corrupt rings of politicians who exploited working-class and immigrant support to secure power and profit. As the number of public employees and public work projects mounted in the nation's fast-growing cities, opportunities for rewarding supporters through jobs and contracts increased. The most notorious of the much-publicized rings was the Tweed Ring, which robbed New York City's municipal coffers during the late 1860s.

Bossism and Reform. During the late nineteenth and early twentieth centuries the dominant theme of municipal politics was bossism versus reform. Yet this simplistic dichotomy veiled the complexities of urban politics. "Boss" was a label applied indiscriminately to partisan leaders. It referred equally to those who commanded an effective citywide organization, those who wielded clout only in a single ward, and those who attempted to patch together loose coalitions of rival neighborhood leaders and thereby secure victory on election day. Similarly, the "reform" ranks included business leaders dedicated primarily to low taxes, a nonpartisan civil service, and financial probity as well as social crusaders like Cleveland's Mayor Tom Johnson and Toledo's Mayor Samuel Jones, who favored government ownership of public utilities and improved services for working-class urbanites.

The reform crusades produced notable structural innovations in city government. Beginning in Galveston, Texas, in 1901, reformers rallied behind the commission form of government. Under this structure, all executive and legislative authority was vested in a small board of commissioners elected at large, each of whom was responsible for a single branch of municipal service. The commission plan was intended to eliminate rule by neighborhood representatives advocating parochial interests. Moreover, it supposedly would increase accountability. If there was a crime wave, the electorate could express its discontent by voting the commissioner in charge of public safety out of office. By 1915 423 cities had opted to replace the traditional mayor-council form of government with commission rule.

During the second decade of the twentieth century, however, a new reform scheme, the city manager plan, was beginning to supersede the commission alternative. Under the city manager scheme, the city council was expected to hire a nonpartisan professional administrator to manage city government, thus supposedly ensuring expert, efficient operation of municipal services. This plan spread quickly throughout the nation with 448 cities adopting the scheme by 1933. In the years following World War II the number of city manager municipalities soared whereas commission rule waned as a reform remedy.

Although especially popular among smaller cities, the commission and city manager schemes also transformed the emerging metropolises of the southwest. Fast-growing cities such as Dallas, Phoenix, and San Diego embraced reform government, opting for city manager administration and at-large, nonpartisan election of city council members. The result was inordinate power for the business elite who enjoyed citywide clout and limited participation by ethnic minorities and working-class residents who could not voice their frustrations through neighborhood-based representatives. In the late twentieth century, civil rights advocates clashed with these reform regimes and forced the adoption of district election of council members and increased opportunities for minority representation.

Ethnic divisions transformed the power structure in the older cities of the Northeast and Midwest as well as in the West. As the African American share of the central city population increased, black politicians exercised growing power. During the 1970s African Americans Coleman Young of Detroit and Tom Bradley of Los Angeles won the mayor's office, whereas in the 1980s Wilson Goode secured the top position in Philadelphia and Harold Washington became mayor of Chicago. Hispanics likewise were elected mayors, most notably Henry Cisneros in San Antonio, Federico Pena in Denver, and in 2005 Antonio Villaraigosa in Los Angeles. Adjusting to the demands of democracy, municipal politics had progressed along an often difficult road from the self-elected closed corporations of the colonial era to the ethnically diverse metropolises of the twenty-first century.

[*See also* **African American Mayors since 1960; African Americans in Politics; Hispanic Americans;** *and* **Urban Policy: National Policy.**]

BIBLIOGRAPHY

Bridges, Amy. *Morning Glories: Municipal Reform in the Southwest.* Princeton, N.J.: Princeton University Press, 1997.

Callow, Alexander B. *The Tweed Ring.* Westport, Conn.: Greenwood Press, 1966.

Rice, Bradley Robert. *Progressive Cities: The Commission Government Movement in America, 1901–1920.* Austin: University of Texas Press, 1977.

Teaford, Jon C. *The Unheralded Triumph: City Government in America, 1870-1900.* Baltimore: Johns Hopkins University Press, 1984.

Jon C. Teaford

N

NADER, RALPH

(1934–), consumer advocate. Ralph Nader dominated the U.S. consumer movement during the last third of the twentieth century. Born in Winsted, Connecticut, to Lebanese immigrant parents, Nader graduated from Princeton College and Harvard Law School and began his law practice in Hartford. He first came to public attention in 1965 with *Unsafe at Any Speed,* an indictment of the design of the General Motors Corvair automobile and of the automotive industry's more general failure to attend to the "second collision," the impact of occupants with the inside of the vehicle in an accident. This book and Nader's congressional testimony played a key role in passage of legislation in 1966 allowing the federal government to set vehicle-safety standards.

Nader branched out quickly from his initial interest in auto safety, and his efforts resulted in a proliferation of federal consumer-protection legislation during the 1960s and early 1970s, including the 1972 act creating the Federal Consumer Product Safety Commission. Nader also established numerous consumer organizations, including the Center of Auto Safety, Health Research Group, and Public Citizen, Inc., staffed by young activists nicknamed "Nader's Raiders." His legislative influence faded after 1977, following a failed, acrimonious effort to create a federal consumer protection agency.

Nader's determination and idealism elicited both admiration and condemnation. Although his achievements won praise, he was criticized as unwilling to compromise, insensitive to the costs of his consumer-protection initiatives, and excessively beholden to trial lawyers (the latter connection allegedly explaining his antipathy to no-fault auto insurance).

His activist energies undiminished, Nader in the early 1990s campaigned against trade agreements that he believed jeopardized hardwon consumer, environmental, and labor protections. In 1996, he ran as the Green Party's candidate for president, refusing contributions and urging campaign finance reform. He received 685,128 votes. Again the Green Party presidential nominee in 2000, he received 2.7 million votes. Had it not been for Nader's 97,488 votes in Florida, the Democrat Al Gore would almost certainly have carried the state and won the presidency. By 2004, when Nader again ran for president, his earlier reputation for consumer advocacy was eroded by accusations that he had become an ego-driven political spoiler.

[*See also* **Environmentalism; Gore, Albert A., Jr.;** *and* **North American Free Trade Agreement.**]

BIBLIOGRAPHY

Bollier, David. *Citizen Action and Other Big Ideas: A History of Ralph Nader and the Modern Consumer Movement.* Washington, D.C.: Center for the Study of Responsive Law, 1989.

Gorey, Hays. *Nader and the Power of Everyman.* New York: Grosset & Dunlap, 1975.

Robert N. Mayer; updated by Paul S. Boyer

NARAL PRO-CHOICE AMERICA

For over forty years, the National Abortion Rights League (NARAL) has been dedicated to fighting for the basic human rights of women to control and limit their own reproduction. The organization engages in political, social, and legal action to oppose restrictions on abortion and to help to expand access to safe abortions by qualified physicians.

NARAL, originally the National Association for the Repeal of Abortion Laws, was founded in Chicago in February 1969. Lawrence Lader was instrumental in the founding and became the group's first chair. From 1969 to 1973, NARAL, along with other pro-choice groups and physicians, brought the abortion issue to the attention of policy makers. NARAL effectively lobbied state legislatures and by 1971, fourteen states had revised their laws to allow for abortions under certain circumstances.

The greatest changes in abortion laws came from the Supreme Court. On 22 January 1973, the Supreme Court handed down its landmark decision in *Roe v. Wade,* ruling that during the first three months of pregnancy, abortion is a private decision between a woman and her doctor. *Roe* declared a constitutional right to privacy in all reproductive decisions, prompting NARAL to change its name to National Abortion Rights League and to move its headquarters to Washington, D.C., D.C. NARAL's move demonstrated its new emphasis on federal lobbying and policy.

In response to President Ronald Reagan's support of a constitutional amendment banning abortion, NARAL launched the "Abortion Rights: Silent No More" campaign. NARAL, along with Planned Parenthood and the National Organization for Women (NOW), collected 20,000 personal letters from those who had suffered the tragic consequences of illegal abortions before *Roe.* NARAL also led the campaign against the anti-choice nominee to the Supreme Court Robert H. Bork in 1987.

Throughout the 1980s, abortion rights were again threatened by a variety of tactics, from clinic blockades to death threats and clinic bombings. Capping the 1980s was *Webster v.*

Reproductive Health Services of Missouri (1989), which expanded the rights of the states to further restrict abortions so long as they did not impose an "undue burden" on a woman's right to choose. *Webster*'s ruling meant that states could ban abortions in public hospitals and require doctors to conduct fetal "viability" tests before an abortion could be performed. In response to *Webster,* NARAL cosponsored the largest pro-choice demonstration ever held at the time, with an estimated 500,000 supporters marching in Washington, D.C. Also in 1989, NARAL began working with pro-choice legislators to introduce the Freedom of Choice Act (FOCA), which would codify *Roe v. Wade* into federal law.

In 1991, NARAL President Kate Michelman testified before the U.S. Senate on the nomination of anti-choice nominee Justice Clarence Thomas for a seat on the Supreme Court. Michelman discussed her personal hardships in trying to obtain a legal abortion in 1969 after her husband abandoned her and her three small children. Despite the effort, the Senate ultimately confirmed Justice Thomas.

In 1992, NARAL began nationwide lobbying for FOCA and endorsed then-governor Bill Clinton's campaign to become the first pro-choice president. On the 20th anniversary of *Roe,* two days after taking the oath of office, President Clinton issued executive orders that overturned five discriminatory anti-choice policies. Shortly thereafter, President Clinton signed the Family and Medical Leave Act into law, a bill for which NARAL, along with several pro-life groups, had lobbied intensely. From 1994 to 1997, NARAL successfully lobbied for the passage of several pro-choice bills including the Freedom of Access to Clinic Entrances Act (FACE), the Equity in Prescription Insurance and Contraceptive Coverage Act, and the Family Planning and Choice Protection Act.

In 1998, NARAL's legal director testified before the Food and Drug Administration (FDA) Advisory Committee to gain approval for the medical abortion drug RU486. In the midterm elections that year, NARAL helped pro-choice candidates win 97 of 114 races. NARAL launched the *Choice for America* campaign in 1999, which was a multiyear marketing and mobilization drive to reinforce its main pro-choice position. To further reinforce its pro-choice message, NARAL dropped the long form of its name and simply became NARAL Pro-Choice America. In 2004, NARAL cosponsored and helped organize the March for Women's Lives, which drew close to 2 million participants to the National Mall in Washington, D.C.

In 2005, after Michelman's retirement, Nancy Keenan was appointed the new president. Shortly after assuming her new position, Keenan embarked on the "Heartland Tour" to work with community leaders, stakeholders, and policy makers to discuss proactive, pro-choice policies in states, which traditionally were antiabortion. After Michelman's eighteen-year term, Keenan's newness to the multiple issues confronting the abortion debate led her to make gaffs that alienated some of NARAL's members. During the 2006 midterm elections, NARAL invested $2.5 million in a political program to make contributions to congressional races and campaigns to defeat anti-choice ballot proposals. Yet, during the 2006 confirmation hearings for Chief Justice John Roberts, NARAL marginalized many of its members by commissioning a controversial ad seen as a smear campaign against Roberts. The ad featured Emily Lyons, the abortion clinic director who was injured in the Eric Rudolph bombing in 1998. The ad implied that Roberts filed court briefs in support of fringe groups and a convicted bomber, which he did not do. Thus, the ad had to be pulled from national media immediately.

In the 2008 presidential election, Keenan further antagonized members by endorsing

Senator Barack Obama over Senator Hillary Clinton, who had been a longtime supporter of NARAL. Moreover, Keenan announced the endorsement without board approval the Friday before Clinton officially withdrew from the race on Sunday, leaving staunch supporters of NARAL further angered that Keenan did not wait until Clinton officially dropped out of the race. These actions have caused a significant decline in membership and contributions, negatively affecting what was once listed as one of the most powerful lobbying groups in Washington, D.C.

[*See also* **Clinton, Hillary Rodham; Clinton, William J.;** *and Roe v. Wade.*]

BIBLIOGRAPHY

Lee, Jennifer. "Abortion Rights Groups Plans a New Focus and a New Name." *The New York Times*, 4 January 2003. http://www.nytimes.com/2003/01/05/us/abortion-rights-group-plans-a-new-focus-and-a-new-name.html/ (accessed 19 August 2011).

NARAL Pro-Choice America. "History of NARAL Pro-ChoiceAmerica."http://www.prochoiceamerica.org/assets/files/about-naral-history.pdf/ (accessed 5 December 2010).

"NARAL Pro-Choice America." http://www.naral.org/ (accessed 19 August 2011).

O'Connor, Karen. *No Neutral Ground? Abortion Politics in an Age of Absolutes*. Boulder, Colo.: Westview Press, 1996.

Toner, Robin. A Call to Arms by Abortion Rights Groups. *The New York Times*, 12 April 2004. http://www.nytimes.com/2004/04/22/politics/22MARC.html/ (accessed 19 August 2011).

Karen O'Connor and Felicia Fognani

NATIONAL AERONAUTICS AND SPACE ADMINISTRATION

The National Aeronautics and Space Administration (NASA) emerged in 1958 at the height of the Cold War rivalry between the United States and the Soviet Union. In the field of space exploration, the Soviets scored a dramatic coup on 4 October 1957 when they launched Sputnik 1, the first artificial satellite to orbit the Earth, as part of a larger scientific effort associated with the International Geophysical Year. Concerned about the perception that the United States had fallen behind the Soviet Union in technology, Congress established NASA to explore and use space for the benefit "of all mankind."

The new agency's space missions began with Project Mercury to study the possibilities of human space flight. The efforts expanded significantly in 1961 when President John F. Kennedy, responding to perceived challenges to U.S. leadership in science and technology, announced Project Apollo, whose goal was to place an American on the moon by 1970. For the next eleven years this project consumed NASA's energies. Between 1969 and 1972 NASA landed six teams of astronauts on the moon. The first landing mission, Apollo II, achieved success on 20 July 1969, when astronaut Neil Armstrong (1930–) first set foot on the lunar surface, proclaiming to millions of listeners, "That's one small step for [a] man—one giant leap for mankind." Subsequent landings, coming at approximately six-month intervals thereafter, spent more time on the moon and conducted more sophisticated experiments.

NASA went into a holding pattern after Project Apollo. The reusable space shuttle, its major program of the 1970s, first flew in 1981 and by the end of 1985 had made twenty-four flights. During the launch of Challenger on 28 January 1986, however, a leak in the joints of a solid rocket booster detonated the main fuel tank. Six astronauts and high-school social studies teacher Christa McAuliffe died in this accident, the worst in NASA's history. Following the Challenger disaster, the shuttle program experienced a two-year hiatus, while

NASA redesigned the system and revamped its management structure. Space shuttle flights resumed on 29 September 1988. Over the next decade, NASA launched more than seventy accident-free shuttle missions. In November 1998, seventy-seven-year-old John H. Glenn Jr. returned to space for a ten-day mission in the shuttle Discovery, thirty-six years after he flew a mission in Project Mercury in 1962.

In addition to the human space-flight programs, scientific probes were sent to the moon and planets, particularly Mars. The space vehicle Viking landed on Mars in 1976 and the Mars Pathfinder in 1997. The Voyager mission to the outer solar system in the 1970s and early 1980s provided stunning images and data about distant planets and their moons. In the 1990s the Hubble space telescope, initially impaired, began returning exceptional scientific data about the origins and development of the universe; the Magellan mission radar-imaged Venus; and the Galileo probe to Jupiter generated important scientific data.

The effort to develop an international space station, inaugurated in the 1980s with the launch of the first components in 1998, promised a future presence in space and the possibility of renewed exploration of the moon and nearby planets. At the same time, the high cost of space exploration dampened the enthusiasm of some members of Congress, which provided the funding. From the beginning, some critics had argued that NASA's budget might be better spent on social needs at home, but this remained a minority view, as the romance of space continued to exert its allure.

NASA experienced both tragedy and triumph in the early twenty-first century. In February 2003, insulation tiles broke loose from the space shuttle Columbia on launch, damaging a wing. The shuttle ignited and disintegrated on reentry, killing the seven-member crew. Early in 2004, by contrast, NASA landed two unmanned exploratory vehicles on Mars that sent back spectacular photographs and gathered important scientific data. President Bush announced an ambitious plan for manned flights to the Moon and Mars, but in 2009 President Obama responded to criticism of the strategy and cost and canceled the plan. Public reaction forced additional reevaluation of that decision, but the agency's long-term future remained uncertain.

[*See also* **Kennedy, John F.**]

BIBLIOGRAPHY

McDougall, Walter A. *The Heavens and the Earth: A Political History of the Space Age*. New York: Basic Books, 1985.

Launius, Roger D. *NASA: A History of the U.S. Civil Space Program*. Malabar, Fl.: Krieger, 1994.

Roger D. Launius

NATIONAL AMERICAN WOMAN SUFFRAGE ASSOCIATION

The National American Woman Suffrage Association (NAWSA) was founded in 1890, healing the split among the suffrage forces that had occurred in 1869 and joining together the National Woman Suffrage Association (headed by Elizabeth Cady Stanton and Susan B. Anthony) and Lucy Stone's American Woman Suffrage Association. Initially, the new organization failed to make many gains, either at the state or at the national level. This was a conservative era, but the problems were internal as well. The NAWSA's key early leader, Anna Howard Shaw, first as vice president (1892–1900) under Anthony and then as president (1904–1915), was a gifted orator but a poor administrator and strategist and essentially conservative in many of her social views. Thus, in this early period, the NAWSA was sometimes identified with conservative political positions, anti-immigrant pronouncements, and even, among its southern members, racist views. Around 1910, however, a new group of younger, more progressive leaders emerged, mostly in state branches and sometimes influenced by the British militant suffrage leaders. Including Harriot Stanton Blatch of New York, the daughter of Elizabeth Cady Stanton, they introduced such dynamic tactics as parades, rallies, aggressive lobbying, and alliances with working-class groups, and they won notable successes. Before 1910, women could vote in only four states: Wyoming, Utah, Colorado, and Idaho; between 1910 and 1914, six states were added: Illinois, Washington, California, Arizona, Kansas, and Oregon.

Whereas the NAWSA focused on state referenda, the Quaker Alice Paul (1885–1977), closely following the English example, split with the NAWSA in 1913 to found the Congressional Union. Her organization focused on congressional passage of the long-dormant woman-suffrage amendment to the Constitution. In 1916 the Congressional Union regrouped into the Woman's Party and began a campaign to unseat antisuffrage legislators in state elections.

Relations between the much larger NAWSA and the Woman's Party were generally cordial until the war year 1917, when the NAWSA, led by the dynamic and tireless Carrie Chapman Catt, disavowed the militancy of the Woman's Party as members of the latter group picketed the White House; were arrested and jailed; and, embarking on hunger strikes, were force-fed.

The NAWSA strongly supported the war effort during World War I, maintaining a hospital in France and supporting the work of Shaw and Catt on the Women's Committee of the Council for National Defense and of Blatch as an official of the Food Administration. Meanwhile, however, the organization also continued its steady work for woman suffrage, following Catt's "Winning Plan" announced in 1916. This plan involved tight national discipline combined with forceful grassroots agitation to increase the number of states with women's suffrage and to pressure congressmen, senators, and state legislators to support the suffrage amendment in Congress and, later, during the state ratification process. The plan succeeded. The Nineteenth Amendment was passed by Congress in 1919 and ratified in 1920, whereupon the NAWSA became the League of Women Voters.

[*See also* **Anthony, Susan B.; Feminism; Nineteenth Amendment; Progressive Era; Stanton, Elizabeth Cady;** *and* **Woman Suffrage Movement.**]

BIBLIOGRAPHY

DuBois, Ellen C. *Harriot Stanton Blatch and the Winning of Woman Suffrage*. New Haven, Conn.: Yale University Press, 1997.

Flexner, Eleanor. *Century of Struggle: The Woman's Rights Movement in the United States*, 1959, revised ed. Cambridge, Mass.: Belknap Press of Harvard University Press, 1975.

Lois W. Banner

NATIONAL ASSOCIATION FOR THE ADVANCEMENT OF COLORED PEOPLE

Founded in 1909, the National Association for the Advancement of Colored People (NAACP) arose from two American reform traditions, one rooted in white philanthropy and the antislavery movement, the other in various black self-help organizations created in the antebellum free states to promote group solidarity and racial power. In the decades following emancipation, African Americans formed a number of organizations committed to the struggle for equal rights. Among these were T. Thomas Fortune's Afro-American League and Josephine St. Pierre Ruffin's National Federation of Afro-American Women. Other groups, such as Alexander Crummell's American Negro Academy, utilized research and publications to combat theories of black inferiority. These organizations maintained ties with white Progressives and encouraged interracial cooperation toward the goal of a more egalitarian society, one in which African Americans might fully enjoy the benefits of American citizenship—both as individuals and as members of an ethnic community.

In the early twentieth century, Booker T. Washington worked behind the scenes with white Progressives and northern capitalists to encourage a form of industrial democracy for the benefit of black workers and white capital alike. Washington's so-called Tuskegee machine was challenged by the elitist but racially conscious W. E. B. Du Bois, who in 1905 founded the Niagara Movement, which advocated militant propaganda and political activism to achieve black advancement.

The NAACP originated as a philanthropic movement among white Progressives, including Oswald Garrison Villard, Joel Spingarn, William English Walling, and Mary White Ovington. Black "founders" immediately entered its ranks from across the political spectrum, including Du Bois; Mary Church Terrell, a Tuskegee sympathizer; and Ida B. Wells-Barnett, a radical anti-Bookerite. The immediate impetus was the lynching of two African Americans in Springfield, Illinois, in 1908, and the antilynching crusade became a major early focus. Du Bois effectively functioned as the NAACP's voice through his editorship of its monthly magazine, *The Crisis,* until his ouster in 1934 for advocating a degree of voluntary segregation embodying modified socialism within the black community.

From 1934 to the 1960s the NAACP emphasized the legal struggle against de jure racial segregation. After Du Bois's departure, leadership passed to the field secretary Walter White and the chief legal counsel Thurgood Marshall, whose arguments before the U.S. Supreme Court led to the 1954 *Brown v. Board of Education* decision, which outlawed de jure segregation of public schools. Under Roy Wilkins, executive director from 1955 to 1977, the NAACP, through its national office and local branches throughout the country, was active in the struggle for passage of the Civil Rights Act of 1964 and the Voting Rights Act of 1965. It also fought against public acts of defamation and the negative stereotyping of African Americans and other people of color. Indeed, as early as 1915, the NAACP had organized a boycott of D. W. Griffith's racist movie *The Birth of a Nation.*

By the early 1970s, de jure segregation had been at least temporarily eradicated through a combination of court decisions, acts of Congress, and executive orders. Legal barriers to black participation in the electoral processes of the southern states had also been effectively overcome. With these objectives largely achieved, by the early twenty-first century the NAACP continued to search for new ways to define its mission and reinforce its identity as a black-controlled self-help organization. With some 500,000 members in more than 2,000 branches, it remains the nation's oldest, largest, and most influential African American organization.

[*See also* **Antislavery Movement; Civil Rights; Civil Rights Legislation; Du Bois, W. E. B.; Equality; Marshall, Thurgood; Progressive Era;** *and* **Washington, Booker T.**]

BIBLIOGRAPHY

Fox, Mark, and August Meier, eds. *Papers of the NAACP. Frederick,* Md.: University Publications of America, 1981– .

Kellogg, Charles Flint. *NAACP: A History of the National Association for the Advancement of Colored People.* Baltimore: Johns Hopkins University Press, 1967.

Reed, Christopher Robert. *The Chicago NAACP and the Rise of Black Professional Leadership, 1910–1966.* Bloomington: Indiana University Press, 1997.

Wilson J. Moses

NATIONAL CIVIC FEDERATION

The National Civic Federation (NCF), founded in 1900, sought to improve labor–capital relations by finding middle ground between the "socialism" of radical labor unions and the "anarchism" of short-sighted business interests. The founders were Ralph Easley, a midwestern journalist and economist earlier associated with the Chicago Civic Federation, and his wife, Gertrude Beeks Easley, a former director of employee-welfare programs at Chicago's International Harvester company. The NCF was most active from 1900 to 1920. Primarily an organization of prominent business leaders (its first president was the Cleveland, Ohio, business tycoon and Republican Party leader Mark Hanna), the NCF gained credibility and prominence through its alliance with Samuel Gompers and other moderate labor leaders. In promoting harmony between capital and labor, it sought, by extension, to strengthen and legitimate American capitalism. To this end, the federation urged businesses to bargain with trade unions; to offer voluntary benefits to workers (sometimes called "welfare capitalism") as an alternative to radical unionism or state intervention; and to tolerate a limited range of prolabor legislation, such as a ban on child labor and laws requiring compensation of workers injured on the job.

Easley became obsessed with the threat of Communism after the 1917 Bolshevik Revolution and increasingly channeled NCF attention and resources into a campaign against U.S. recognition of the Soviet Union. Neither progressive employers nor moderate unions showed much interest, and business and labor support for NCF evaporated after 1920. Easley's view of labor–capital relations proved increasingly irrelevant amid the bitter antiunion "open shop" campaign waged by many corporations in the 1920s and in the Great Depression and New Deal decade of the 1930s. Gertrude Beeks Easley took over after her husband's death in 1939, but by then the NCF, a relic of the Progressive Era, had drifted into obscurity.

[*See also* **Anarchism; Anti-Communism; New Deal; Progressive Era;** ***and*** **Socialism.**]

BIBLIOGRAPHY

Green, Marguerite. *The National Civic Federation and the American Labor Movement, 1900–1925.* Westport, Conn.: Greenwood Press, 1956.

Weinstein, James. *The Corporate Ideal in the Liberal State, 1900–1918.* Boston: Beacon Press, 1968.

Colin Gordon

NATIONAL EDUCATION ASSOCIATION

The National Teachers Association, founded in 1857, became the National Education Association (NEA) in 1871. Its members met annually to discuss educational issues. By the late nineteenth century, the NEA leadership was dominated by college presidents like Nicholas Murray Butler of Columbia University. Beyond its annual meetings and proceedings, its chief influence came from committees. The Committee of Ten (1893), led by President Charles Eliot of Harvard, recommended four equivalent and thoroughly academic high-school curricula, putting modern subjects on a par with the classics. After 1900, three developments shaped the NEA: the activism of college presidents waned while school administrators came to dominate; women successfully challenged male dominance and occupied offices (including the presidency, with the election of Ella Flagg Young in 1910); and the organization's committees (especially its Commission on the Reorganization of Secondary Education in 1918) endorsed school curricula that emphasized a variety of nonacademic purposes. The organization grew from 2,300 members in 1900 to 53,000 in 1920 and 454,000 by 1950.

By the 1950s, a majority of NEA members were classroom teachers, and the organization faced a challenge from the American Federation of Teachers (AFT). Unlike the NEA, the AFT accepted collective bargaining, and it began to sanction strikes by teachers in the 1960s. The NEA accepted collective bargaining (but not strikes) in 1962, thus becoming more like a union. In the 1960s and 1970s, the NEA achieved two major lobbying goals: federal assistance to elementary and secondary education and the creation of a federal Department of Education. By blending its long-standing emphasis on teacher professionalism and a somewhat reluctant endorsement of collective bargaining, the NEA retained the loyalty of most organized teachers, with 2.2 million members in 1996, compared with 830,000 in the AFT. While the NEA moved toward collective bargaining, the AFT began emphasizing teacher professionalism. This convergence bred serious talk of merger throughout the 1990s.

[*See also* **Education Policy: An Overview.**]

BIBLIOGRAPHY

Murphy, Marjorie. *Blackboard Unions: The AFT and the NEA, 1900–1980.* Ithaca, N.Y.: Cornell University Press, 1990.

Wesley, Edgar B. *NEA: The First Hundred Years. The Building of the Teaching Profession.* New York: Harper, 1957.

Carl F. Kaestle

NATIONAL INSTITUTES OF HEALTH

The National Institutes of Health (NIH) began in the late nineteenth century as a small bacteriological laboratory of the Marine Hospital Service (MHS). By the 1960s, the NIH had become the twenty-first century's major division of the Department of Health and Human Services, which supports basic and clinical health research, primarily through extramural grants to researchers in universities and other nonfederal research institutions. This transformation was the result of able leadership, advances in science, changes in the causes of mortality, interest group and congressional politics, and the general public belief that biomedical research will improve health.

In 1887, a one-person laboratory was established to support the MHS's quarantine mission, using the new science of bacteriology. The size and scope of activities of the Hygienic Laboratory, as it came to be named, increased with the expansion of the MHS into the full range of public health work in the early twentieth century. In 1891, the Laboratory was moved from Staten Island to Washington, D.C. Two 1902 laws broadened the service's public health mission and gave the laboratory regulatory authority over manufacturers of vaccines and antitoxins. A 1912 law changed the name of the laboratory's parent organization to the Public Health Service (PHS) and authorized the PHS "to study and investigate the diseases of man and conditions influencing the propagation and spread thereof."

After World War I, a broad coalition favoring biomedical research—unable to secure funding for a private institute—joined forces with Senator Joseph Ransdell of Louisiana and others to elevate the Hygienic Laboratory to a NIH. By the time the NIH bill finally passed in 1930, more people were dying of chronic diseases than infectious diseases. Growing public fear of cancer led to efforts to create a parallel institute for cancer research. Initially opposed by the PHS, new leadership (Surgeon General Thomas J. Parran Jr., NIH Director Lewis R. Thompson) assisted Congress in establishing the National Cancer Institute (NCI) as part of the PHS in 1937. The NCI became the model for expanding funding for health research through establishing new categorical institutes for the major health problems of public concern. The NCI was a model in other ways. Unlike the NIH, the NCI had authority to provide grants and fellowships to nonfederal researchers, and its advisory council of outside experts had to approve all grants.

During World War II, the wartime Office of Scientific Research and Development (OSRD) conducted a crash program of applied research resulting in the development of radar, the atomic bomb, penicillin, and other impressive advances with practical utility. The work was performed mostly in universities under flexible, grant-like contracts. Parran and other PHS officials helped draft the Public Health Service Act of 1944, which made the NCI part of the NIH, thereby giving the NIH grant-making authority. At the end of the war, the NIH took over a number of OSRD contracts, which were converted to grants and initiated the NIH's extramural grant program.

After World War II, a new force—citizen activists for increased health research funding (most notably Mary Lasker)—joined with sympathetic members of Congress, disease lobbies, and scientists to increase funding and establish a series of new categorical institutes. By 1948 there were institutes for research on mental health, heart disease, and dental health. Over the next twenty years, especially from 1955 to 1968 under Director James A. Shannon, the NIH expanded in number of institutes (nine), range of activities (large research facility construction, research training, and medical education in addition to research projects), and appropriations ($1.6 billion in 1968, up from $52 million in 1950). Biomedical research had steady bipartisan support and was a politically safe way to support health improvement in the absence of national health insurance. Subsequently, additional institutes were established, mostly because of outside pressure from disease lobbies and their congressional allies, resulting in the twenty-seven institutes and research centers of the early twenty-first century. Congress also generally appropriated more than the administration requested, and with rare exceptions, the NIH's budget grew year by year after World War II.

Although the money was appropriated for diseases, most was allocated to researchers on the advice of peer review groups organized by scientific discipline using scientific opportunity rather than disease burden as the primary criterion. Most of the research was basic, not clinical or linked to a specific disease. Scientists fearful of federal control of research were reassured by the emphasis on basic research and by the use of peer review panels to recommend, as well as national advisory councils to approve, grants. However, the focus on basic research led to tensions with supporters in Congress and the public, who wanted more emphasis on turning past research into current cures. The development of successful chemotherapies for leukemia and other childhood cancers occurred when NCI (and NIH) funding growth stalled, after 1967. That stimulated

Mary Lasker and her associates to push for a "war on cancer" by a new independent authority modeled after the National Aeronautics and Space Administration (NASA) and the Manhattan Project. An independent NCI was strongly opposed by NIH leaders. Although the National Cancer Act of 1971 left the NCI in the NIH, the NCI emerged with greater authorities and a much larger budget.

In the 1980s and 1990s, the human genome became a major focus of health research policy, leading to the establishment of an institute for genome research in 1997 in hopes of identifying and eventually repairing the genetic bases of disease. NIH research also played a substantial role in funding discoveries underlying the new industry of biotechnology. Those developments have continued to reinforce the general belief that biomedical research should be expanded substantially. Because of then-favorable federal budget circumstances, a concerted effort was made to double the NIH annual budget from $13.7 billion to $27.1 billion between 1998 and 2003.

As of 2010, NIH was a $31 billion-a-year enterprise, of which 80 percent supported extramural research. It was the largest single funder of biomedical research in the world and accounted for far more publicly supported health research than programs in any other country. NIH had supported the work of more than 120 winners of the Nobel Prize for physiology or medicine and for chemistry, including five scientists in the NIH's intramural program.

[*See also* **Public Health Service, U.S.**]

BIBLIOGRAPHY

Cook-Deegan, Robert, and Michael McGeary. "The Jewel in the Federal Crown? History, Politics, and the National Institutes of Health." In *History and Health Policy in the United States: Putting the Past Back In,* edited by Rosemary Stevens et al., pp. 176–201. New Brunswick, N.J.: Rutgers University Press, 2006.

Drew, Elizabeth. "The Health Syndicate: Washington's Noble Conspirators." *Atlantic Monthly* (December 1967): 75–82.

Harden, Victoria A. *Inventing the NIH: Federal Biomedical Research Policy, 1887–1937.* Baltimore: Johns Hopkins University Press, 1986.

Strickland, Stephen P. *Politics, Science, and Dread Disease: A Short History of United States Medical Research Policy.* Cambridge, Mass.: Harvard University Press, 1972.

Michael McGeary

NATIONAL LABOR RELATIONS ACT

The National Labor Relations Act of 1935, or the Wagner Act (PL 74-198), established the legal framework for unionization and collective bargaining in the United States. The road to the Wagner Act began at the turn of the twentieth century, as courts increasingly used injunctions to stop unionization efforts. Unions lobbied for a legal exemption from these injunctions. The Clayton Act of 1914 attempted to exempt unions from antitrust prosecution and strictly limit court injunctions against peaceful union actions such as meeting, picketing, striking, boycotting, or paying strike benefits. Court decisions such as *Hitchman Coal & Coke Co. v. Mitchell* (245 U.S. 229, 1917) made the Clayton Act protections ineffective. The Railway Labor Act of 1926 established a Railway Labor Board, separate from the courts, that protected collective bargaining and engaged in resolving disputes between employers and the unions representing railroad operating employees. A 1930 court ruling guaranteed that workers could form their own unions through elections, independent of "company" unions created by employers to help control workers. The Norris–LaGuardia Act of 1932, which applied to workers beyond the railroads, limited labor injunctions more strictly and undermined company unions.

When the New Deal's National Industrial Recovery Act (NIRA) of 1933 relaxed antitrust enforcement in favor of "codes of fair competition," the American Federation of Labor (AFL) insisted that that these codes protect independent unions. Section 7(a) of Title I of the NIRA required that each industry's code guarantee that "employees have the right to organize and bargain collectively through representatives of their own choosing," and it required employer compliance with minimum wage and maximum hours provisions in the codes. A National Labor Board, established to implement Section 7(a) and chaired by Senator Robert Wagner (D-NY), could not compel employers or other NIRA administrators to enforce the provision when employers in the auto, steel, and other manufacturing industries established company unions.

In 1934, Senator Wagner proposed a new, stronger National Labor Relations Board (NLRB) to guarantee fair collective bargaining procedures and to enforce provisions of the Clayton and Norris–LaGuardia acts. This new NLRB would serve as a three-member "Supreme Court" for labor relations that would administer elections, investigate charges of unfair labor practices, and mediate labor disputes. The National Labor Relations Act passed the Senate 63 to 12 in May 1935. When the Supreme Court struck down the NIRA later that month, Wagner's National Labor Relations bill won Roosevelt's late endorsement. The House of Representatives passed the bill in June. Several states also passed "little" Wagner acts.

The NLRB under Roosevelt encouraged the organization of industrial unions. By 1947, one-third of the nonagricultural labor force was unionized. A Republican majority in Congress passed the Taft–Hartley Act of 1947 over President Truman's veto. Taft–Hartley expanded employer powers, allowed public supervision of internal union affairs, and, in Section 14b, allowed states to enact laws prohibiting the union shop, or a job that requires a worker to pay union dues as a condition of employment. By 2011, twenty-two states had such "open shop" or "right-to-work" laws.

[*See also* **New Deal; Roosevelt, Franklin Delano;** ***and*** **Taft–Hartley Act.**]

BIBLIOGRAPHY

Bernstein, Irving. *The New Deal Collective Bargaining Policy.* Berkeley: University of California Press, 1950.

Gross, James A. *The Making of the National Labor Relations Board.* Albany: State University of New York Press, 1974.

Tomlins, Christopher L. *The State and the Unions: Labor Relations, Law, and the Organized Labor Movement in America, 1880–1960.* Cambridge, UK; New York: Cambridge University Press, 1985 .

David Brian Robertson

NATIONAL LABOR RELATIONS BOARD

The National Labor Relations Act of 1935 (Wagner Act) established a three-member National Labor Relations Board (NLRB) to interpret and apply the act. As an independent quasi-judicial administrative agency with the power to enforce its rulings, the NLRB decided cases through a formal adversary process and developed a body of binding case law.

After the U.S. Supreme Court ruled the act constitutional in 1937, the NLRB, under chairman J. Warren Madden, initially enforced it vigorously and literally. An unlikely coalition of critics, including business interests, congressional conservatives, old-style union leaders, and even President Franklin Delano Roosevelt, sought to weaken the board, however, and consequently it began to act more cautiously and less decisively on behalf of labor.

The 1947 Taft–Hartley Act further limited the NLRB, restricting it to adjudicative responsibilities and creating the office of general counsel to investigate charges, prosecute complaints, and represent the agency in court proceedings. By the 1990s, the NLRB, headquartered in Washington, D.C., had more than thirty regional offices across the United States.

The NLRB implements statutory language that, although broad, can also be unclear or ambiguous. In carrying out its statutory mandate, the board chooses among alternatives that affect opposed constituencies and that reflect conflicting views of what national labor policy should be. After 1954, when the NLRB had its first Republican-appointed majority and general counsel, case doctrine underwent periodic modification depending on which political party held power. Democrats interpreted Taft–Hartley in ways that encouraged collective bargaining and facilitated union organizing, whereas Republicans focused on provisions in Taft–Harley protecting individual choice and the right to reject collective bargaining.

[*See also* **Federal Government, Judicial Branch; National Labor Relations Act; New Deal; Roosevelt, Franklin Delano;** ***and*** **Taft–Hartley Act.**]

BIBLIOGRAPHY

Gross, James A. *Broken Promise: The Subversion of U.S. Labor Relations Policy, 1947–1994*. Philadelphia: Temple University Press, 1995.

Gross, James A. *The Making of the National Labor Relations Board: A Study in Economics, Politics, and the Law*. Albany: State University of New York Press, 1974.

Gross, James A. *The Reshaping of the NLRB: National Labor Policy in Transition, 1937–1947*. Albany: State University of New York Press, 1981.

James A. Gross

NATIONAL NEGRO CONGRESS

Founded at the height of the Great Depression, the National Negro Congress (NNC) represented the most important Popular Front organization fighting for African American rights in the 1930s.

The NNC grew out of the May 1935 Conference on the Status of the Negro in the New Deal at Howard University, sponsored by the Joint Committee for National Recovery (JCNR). This extraordinary gathering of laborers, activists, writers, and intellectuals established a committee to call for a National Negro Congress, organized by the JCNR's secretary, John P. Davis. Between May 1935 and February 1936, Davis worked to assuage differences within the vast coalition that sought to participate, including Communists, black churches, fraternal organizations, and traditional civil rights groups.

As a result, the founding conference on 14–16 February 1936 in Chicago was attended by more than 800 official delegates representing over 550 organizations. Because of the fragile nature of the coalition, the NNC's first president, A. Philip Randolph, argued it should be a nonpartisan group, promoting unity among race organizations on issues of common concern. In this spirit, the NNC endorsed resolutions attacking lynching and the Ethiopian invasion, supporting black churches and businesses, and calling for unionization of black workers.

Over the next two years, much of the impetus for action through the Congress came at the local level. Chapters in major industrial areas organized protests against police brutality and employment discrimination, successfully integrating both private and public employers. Some chapters placed a strong emphasis on youth issues, as in a push for government-sponsored recreational activities or opposition to racist school textbooks, whereas others provided cultural events for local black communities.

By 1938, however, power shifted to the national office, as the group moved in a more partisan direction. Not only did the Congress endorse specific legislative policies, including the expansion of social security benefits, federal antilynching bills, and fair labor legislation, but also it began endorsing candidates for office. More importantly, the NNC devoted a great deal of time to black union organizing. Its successful coalition with the new Congress of Industrial Organizations (CIO) contributed to a fivefold increase in black unionization between 1936 and 1940.

These labor efforts also laid the groundwork for the group's demise. At the 1940 annual convention a coalition of activists tried to push the NNC to affiliate more closely with labor organizations. Randolph, sensing the group was drifting from its founding goals, resigned the presidency after an impassioned plea for nonsectarianism emphasizing the Congress's original racial mission. Combined with fractures in the "Popular Front" following the Nazi-Soviet Pact of 1939, this spelled the end of the NNC as an effective national group, although it did not formally disband until 1947. Despite its short existence on the national scene, the NNC served as an important precursor to the civil rights coalitions of the 1950s and 1960s, particularly with its emphasis on federal legislative remedies and its collaborations between civil rights groups and organized labor.

[*See also* **Civil Rights;** *and* **Great Depression.**]

BIBLIOGRAPHY

Solomon, Mark. *The Cry Was Unity: Communists and African Americans, 1917–36.* Jackson: University Press of Mississippi, 1998.

Wittner, Lawrence S. "The National Negro Congress: A Reassessment." *American Quarterly* 22, No. 4 (Winter 1970), pp. 883–901.

Thomas J. Edge

NATIONAL ORGANIZATION FOR WOMEN

The first formal organization of the late twentieth-century feminist movement, the National Organization for Women (NOW) was founded in 1966 by reformers frustrated by the government's failure to enforce Title VII of the 1964 Civil Rights Act, which prohibited sex discrimination in employment. Most founders were professional women, union activists, or members of state commissions on the status of women. Under the leadership of its first president, Betty Friedan, and its board chair Kathryn Clarenbach, and with support from the United Auto Workers union, NOW set out "to bring women into full participation in the mainstream of American society in truly equal partnership with men." Seven initial task forces focused action on employment, education, religion, family, mass media, politics, and poverty.

A national membership organization with state and local chapters, NOW grew from 1,000 members in 1967 to 220,000 in 1982. Internal conflicts arose over the Equal Rights Amendment (ERA), abortion, lesbian rights, and the organization's bureaucratic structure. By the late 1970s, facing growing national opposition to feminist gains, NOW concentrated on working for ratification of the ERA, defending abortion rights, and increasing its involvement in electoral politics. Subsequently, NOW targeted violence against women, racism, homophobia, and economic inequity as priority issues. "To eliminate sexism and end all oppression" became NOW's expanded purpose. By the early twenty-first century, with some half a million members in 550 chapters, NOW was the nation's largest feminist organization, a key partner in a women's policy lobby, and an important forum for the ongoing development of feminist ideas.

[*See also* **Civil Rights Legislation; Equal Rights Amendment; Feminism; Lesbian, Gay, Bisexual, and Transgender Rights Movement;** *and* **Woman Suffrage Movement.**]

BIBLIOGRAPHY

Ferree, Myra Marx, and Beth B. Hess. *Controversy and Coalition: The New Feminist Movement across Four Decades of Change.* 3d ed. New York: Routledge, 2000.

Wandersee, Winifred D. *On the Move: American Women in the 1970s.* Boston: Twayne, 1988.

Joyce C. Follet

NATIONAL PARK SYSTEM

In 1872, President Ulysses S. Grant designated 4.2 million acres of public land in Wyoming as Yellowstone National Park. Thus began a vast park system eventually administered by the National Park Service, established in 1916 within the Department of the Interior. By the 1990s, the National Park System (NPS) oversaw 54 national parks and 112 national historic sites and historical parks, along with an array of national memorials, monuments, battlefields, seashores, parkways, scenic trails, and recreation areas.

The origins of the national park idea go back to the earlier growth of urban parks. Starting with New York City's Central Park in 1857, many cities created parks to provide healthful recreation for their residents. This goal, in turn, influenced the wilderness-preservation movement. The first legislation aimed at preserving a wilderness area, California's Yosemite Grant of 1864, setting aside the Yosemite Valley, was explicitly intended to provide healthful leisure for Californians. The valley was protected on the condition that it be kept open to the public. This goal of promoting public relaxation and enjoyment was reflected in the subsequent management of the valley and of Yosemite National Park (1890). The commissioners thinned trees and dredged lakes, for example, to make the valley more "park-like."

From the first, changes in technology profoundly affected the NPS. Transcontinental railroads allowed easier access to parks, and the dry-printing process made possible the mass production of photographs that enhanced park publicity. As the parks became democratized, urban, middle-class tourists arrived in growing numbers. The rise of the automobile and a national highway system brought still more visitors. Managers at Yellowstone, Yosemite, and other parks responded by building more roads, hotels, and tourist facilities.

With more tourists came congestion and many of the problems associated with urbanization. By the 1950s, visitors were voicing unhappiness with park management because of overcrowding. By the 1990s, the parks and sites administered by the NPS were attracting upward of 250 million visitors annually, creating profound tensions between the dual goals of public access and wilderness preservation. However, the founders of the NPS had from the first encouraged citizens to enjoy recreation in a newly "civilized" wilderness. The problems confronting America's NPS at the end of the twentieth century were thus rooted, ironically, in the overwhelming success of the system's original goal: to provide outdoor recreation on a large scale to the American people.

[*See also* **Environmental Policy: An Overview; Environmental Protection Agency; Environmentalism; Federal Government, Executive Branch: Other Departments;** ***and*** **Grant, Ulysses S.**]

BIBLIOGRAPHY

Hays, Samuel P. *Conservation and the Gospel of Efficiency: The Progressive Conservation Movement, 1890–1920.* Cambridge: Harvard University Press, 1959.

Runte, Alfred. *National Parks: The American Experience.* Lincoln: University of Nebraska Press, 1979.

Michelle Lee Park

NATIONAL RECOVERY ADMINISTRATION

A federal agency created under the National Industrial Recovery Act of 1933 and abolished after the Supreme Court held this act unconstitutional in 1935. The agency was modeled on the War Industries Board (WIB), the World War I agency that sought to promote industrial self-government. A similar system, advocates claimed, could end the "destructive competition" allegedly perpetuating the Great Depression. In 1933, as part of his New Deal, President Franklin Delano Roosevelt secured an emergency two-year measure suspending the antitrust laws and authorizing government-recognized industrial organizations to formulate a new regulatory system consisting of codes of fair competition and fair labor practices. Presidential approval made such codes federal law, and where no approvable codes were adopted by industrial sectors, federal authorities were authorized to impose them.

To administer the law, Roosevelt created the National Recovery Administration (NRA) under General Hugh Johnson, a former WIB member. A massive propaganda campaign followed, depicting support for the NRA's codes of fair competition as patriotic and urging citizens to boycott businesses operating without the NRA's official Blue Eagle emblems. Eventually 541 codes were approved, each combining regulation of business practice with a required guarantee of workers' rights to organize and bargain collectively. Despite widespread noncompliance, codification did reduce competition, foster labor and business organization, and largely end child labor. Yet such results failed to bring recovery, and because of this failure a code structure disproportionately fashioned by big businessmen came under severe criticism from smaller businesses, labor, consumers, and political dissidents, many demanding extensive code revision. In 1934 a new administrative board replaced Johnson, but policy conflicts and deadlocks only worsened. By May 1935, when the Supreme Court ruled that the system involved both an unconstitutional delegation of legislative power to the executive branch and an unconstitutional expansion of the government's power to regulate commerce, it had few supporters left. The NRA that lingered on under a six-month extension busied itself mostly with writing official histories of the codification experience.

Historians have generally regarded the NRA as a huge mistake, an unfortunate flirtation with corporatism that, in effect, turned policy making over to big business with disastrous results. Recently, however, scholars have complicated the picture by using the history of the NRA to illuminate patterns of business organization and disorganization, federal administrative structures and incapacities, and liberal ideas concerning planning. Some have also shown that parts of the code structure reflected the demands of small and medium-size rather than big business. In addition, the historical significance of the NRA has become clearer, both as an example of failed corporatism in America and as an unsuccessful experiment that opened the way to more innovative reforms and the new regulatory agencies of the later New Deal.

[*See also* **Antitrust Legislation and Law; Economic Policy: Regulation; New Deal; Regulatory Agencies, Federal; Roosevelt, Franklin Delano;** *and* **Supreme Court, U.S.**]

BIBLIOGRAPHY

Bellush, Bernard. *The Failure of the NRA*. New York: W. W. Norton, 1975.

Brand, Donald R. *Corporatism and the Rule of Law: A Study of the National Recovery Administration*. Ithaca, N.Y.: Cornell University Press, 1988.

Ellis W. Hawley

NATIONAL RIFLE ASSOCIATION

The National Rifle Association of America (NRA) was incorporated in 1871 by William C. Church and other Civil War veterans. Military doctrine of the time emphasized massed rifle fire, downplaying marksmanship. The NRA stressed accurate shooting and promoted competitions at its rifle range. The early NRA focused its efforts on state militia units, and its fortunes varied with their support. In 1880, New York State stopped funding NRA activities, leaving it effectively moribund. The organization revived after the U.S. Congress established the National Board for the Promotion of Rifle Practice in 1903 and in Public Law 149 (1905) allowed members of NRA-approved clubs to purchase guns and ammunition at low cost.

Through the twentieth century, the NRA steadily expanded its scope and membership and broadened its interests to include safety instruction, firearm collecting, hunting, and police training. From the 1960s on, the NRA also devoted increasing attention to firearm-control legislation. It supported laws that punished armed criminals but fought most limits on general gun ownership and use. A lobbying arm, the Institute for Legislative Action, was formed in 1975. At the 1977 annual meeting, a group led by the activist Harlon Carter gained control of the organization. Carter's group increased the membership's role in governance and launched an unyielding campaign against gun control. By 1995, membership exceeded 3 million.

[*See also* **Gun Control.**]

BIBLIOGRAPHY

Davidson, Osha Gray. *Under Fire: The NRA and the Battle for Gun Control*. New York: H. Holt, 1993.

Trefethen, James B. *Americans and Their Guns: The National Rifle Association Story through Nearly a Century of Service to the Nation*. Harrison, Pa.: Stackpole Books, 1967.

David McDowall and Alan Lizotte

NATIONAL RIGHT TO LIFE COMMITTEE

The National Right to Life Committee (NRLC) was formally organized in Detroit on 14 May 1973, after the U.S. Supreme Court ruling on *Roe v. Wade*. The group came together with significant funding and organization from the National Council of Catholic Bishops (NCCB). Although the Catholic Church had long opposed abortions, the NRLC was the first group that made stopping illegal abortions its number one goal. Its mission is the protection of innocent human life, including abortion, euthanasia, and infanticide. In June 1973, the NRLC held a conference in Detroit bringing together activists from pro-life groups around the country to form the largest pro-life organization in the United States. The NRLC maintained such close ties with the Catholic Church that in New York, the committee agreed to collect donations from parishioners during Mass to support it.

The NRLC's first political victory came in the election of pro-life Senator Bob Dole (R-KS) in 1974, who defeated incumbent Congressman William Roy, a doctor who performed abortions. The NRLC was also influential in the passage of the long-controversial Hyde Amendment in 1976, which prohibited Medicaid funds being used for abortions. Once Congress passed the Hyde Amendment, the NRLC began lobbying state legislatures by presenting them with "model" abortion statutes and continued to press Congress to pass an antiabortion amendment to send to the states for their ratification.

In the first presidential race after *Roe,* the well-organized pro-life movement seized the opportunity to make abortion a campaign issue. After first running as a candidate for the Democratic Party, Ellen McCormack, a New York antiabortion activist, ran as a candidate for the Right-to-Life Party and was able to pull Republican voters away from President Gerald Ford. Her single-issue campaign cast the debate as right to life versus murder and women having abortions as a selfish act, jeopardizing the sanctity of the family. McCormack forced the other candidates to confront this issue of abortion head-on. As a result, the 1976 Republican Party added language to their platform, for the first time calling for a Constitutional amendment banning abortion.

NRLC's increased involvement in politics led to the formation of the NRLC Political Action Committee (PAC) in 1979, with a focus of pushing the antiabortion agenda by lobbing and providing support for pro-life candidates. In its first year, the NRLC PAC was a key contributor in the 1980 presidential election of pro-life Republican Ronald Reagan in his defeat of pro-choice president Jimmy Carter. Banding together with an energizing Christian Right and Jerry Falwell's Moral Majority, the NRLC was able to bring in new supporters under a larger social movement umbrella. These groups brought together the antiabortion, anti–Equal Rights Amendment (ERA), anti–gun control, and antiunion movements, which had strong ties in the Deep South. Consequently, Republicans dominated this region in the 1980 election, despite the fact that President Jimmy Carter was a southerner. During the election the Christian Right and the NRLC held two major rallies in Washington, D.C., in support of pro-life candidates. Additionally, eleven Senate seats were won by pro-life candidates, targeted by pro-life groups in the 1980 election.

Throughout the 1980s, the NRLC was active in fighting for pro-life seats in the Supreme Court. In 1981 President Reagan nominated Judge Sandra Day O'Connor, the first woman to serve on the Supreme Court. The NRLC and the Moral Majority attacked her nomination, fearing that she would uphold *Roe* given her past actions as a state legislator. Additionally, during her nomination hearing, O'Connor refused to answer any questions regarding abortion. Despite the NRLC's efforts, the Senate confirmed O'Connor in a 99 to 0 vote. In 1986, the NRLC again had the chance to help bring in a pro-life justice. Against well-organized support, William Rehnquist was appointed chief justice, and pro-life Roman-Catholic Justice Antonin Scalia was confirmed as an associate justice.

The NRLC and the Moral Majority were again active in President Reagan's reelection in 1984. In his second term, the president continued to support the NRLC's pro-life agenda. In a meeting with the NRLC in 1987, he assured members that any program that provided referrals or counseling for abortions as a means of family planning would not be eligible for Title X funds. Additionally, the NRLC endorsed President Reagan's federal task force to promote adoption as an alternative to abortion.

In 1988, President George H. W. Bush was elected to the White House, with the support of the NRLC PAC. In response to a pro-choice rally in 1989, the NRLC organized the Rally for Life '90 in 1990. According to the National Park Services, approximately 300,000 people attended the rally, which President Bush addressed via telephone. In the following year President Bush sent a letter to House Speaker Thomas Foley, vowing that he would veto any legislation that attempted to weaken laws or regulations on abortion.

In the presidential election of 1992, the pro-life movement was unable to reelect President Bush, who lost to the pro-choice Democratic candidate, Governor Bill Clinton. When a federal statute was proposed in 1993 to invalidate the narrow types of state abortion regulations, the NRLC led a strong lobbying campaign against the so-called "Freedom of Choice Act." Just before the nationwide congressional election of 1994, the NRLC led a massive public education and lobbying campaign against President Clinton's health care plan. Ultimately, President Clinton's plan failed, and in the November election, Republicans took majority control of both houses of Congress. Not a single pro-choice candidate was elected, whereas the pro-life movement picked up six new seats in the Senate and forty in the House. The pro-life movement fought hard while Republicans held control of Congress because President Clinton vowed to veto the Partial Birth Abortion Ban Act. When President Clinton vetoed the bill in 1997, Congress was unable to garner the necessary votes to override his veto.

Despite political losses throughout the Clinton presidency, in 1997 *Fortune* magazine named the NRLC the 10th most powerful public interest group in the country and in 1999 the eighth most influential lobbying group in Washington, D.C. The organization had grown to 3,000 chapters in all fifty states and the District of Columbia. Additionally, National Teens for Life and National College Students for Life have been beneficial outcroppings of the NRLC, helping to reach younger members. The NRLC's monthly newsletter is published for nearly 400,000 subscribers. Between 2009 and 2010, the NRLC led a major grassroots movement through the mail and email, encouraging supporters to write to their members of Congress to oppose President Obama's health care plan. The health care plan was seen as a means of promoting abortions by diverting federal funds to perform abortions. The NRLC further flexed its political muscle by writing to Republican members of Congress and reminding them that their vote would factor in the NRLC's scorecard ranking of the legislator, which serves as a major indicator for donors looking to fund and support campaigns.

[*See also* **Bush, George H. W.; O'Connor, Sandra Day; Reagan, Ronald;** ***and Roe v. Wade.***]

BIBLIOGRAPHY

NRLC. "Abortion History Timeline." http://www.nrlc.org/abortion/facts/abortiontimeline.html/ (accessed 11 February 2011).

"NRLC Launches National Grassroots Lobbying Campaign" [press release]. http://www.nrlc.org/press_releases_new/Release012210.html/ (accessed 19 August 2011).

NRLC. "Pro-Life Lawmakers Take Over Key Positions in House." *National Right to Life News* 38(2011).http://www.nrlc.org/news/index.html/ (accessed 19 August 2011).

O'Connor, Karen. *No Neutral Ground? Abortion Politics in an Age of Absolutes.* Boulder, Colo.: Westview Press, 1996.

Karen O'Connor and Felicia Fognani

NATIONAL SCIENCE FOUNDATION

An independent agency within the executive branch of the federal government. Created in 1950, the National Science Foundation (NSF) awards grants and fellowships to institutions and individuals to support scientific research and science education. Its 2000 budget exceeded $3.9 billion. Policy is set by a twenty-five-member board named by the president and approved by Congress. Although the NSF does not itself conduct research, it does maintain several research centers, such as the Kitt Peak National Observatory in Arizona.

The foundation's origins are rooted in two contrasting visions, one articulated by the Democratic senator Harley Kilgore of West Virginia and the other by the scientist Vannevar Bush. Kilgore's proposals, dating from the early 1940s and reflecting his populist belief in broad-based democratic participation in, and government coordination of, science for public purposes, envisioned a central science agency to set research priorities and to support research that would promote economic growth. Bush, head of the World War II Office of Scientific Research and Development, proposed in *Science—The Endless Frontier* (1945) an agency controlled by scientists and dedicated to the support of "basic" science.

By the time President Harry S. Truman signed legislation creating the NSF in 1950, many of the functions envisioned by Kilgore had been assumed by other agencies, such as the Atomic Energy Commission and the National Institutes of Health. In its early years, therefore, the NSF largely confined its grants to basic research. From the first, however, it had to justify its funding policies to a utilitarian-oriented public and Congress.

The Soviets' launch of the *Sputnik* satellite in 1957 led to a substantial boost in the NSF's budget and made it a serious player in research funding, responsible for some 13 percent of all federally supported academic research. But the upheavals of the 1960s prompted President Lyndon B. Johnson in 1968 to sign legislation proposed by Congressman Emilio Daddario (D-CT) that fundamentally altered the agency's mission in the direction of "applied" research. This set a pattern by which the NSF's funding priorities reflected current congressional and public concerns. During the oil crises of the 1970s, high priority went to developing alternative energy technologies. In the 1980s, worried that the United States was losing economic competitiveness, Congress pushed the NSF to support economically relevant research. In the 1980s, too, engineering, which had remained precarious within the NSF's priorities because of its image as a vocational field rather than a basic research field, gained greater representation and status within the foundation.

[*See also* **Atomic Energy Commission; Education Policy: Higher Education; Energy Crisis of the 1970s; Johnson, Lyndon B.; National Aeronautics and Space Administration; National Institutes of Health;** ***and*** **Truman, Harry S.**]

BIBLIOGRAPHY

Kevles, Daniel J. *The Physicists: The History of a Scientific Community in Modern America.* Cambridge, Mass.: Harvard University Press, 1987.

Kleinman, Daniel Lee. *Politics on the Endless Frontier: Postwar Research Policy in the United States.* Durham, N.C.: Duke University Press, 1995.

Daniel Lee Kleinman

NATIONAL SECURITY ACT OF 1947

This measure, signed into law by President Harry S. Truman on 26 July 1947, created four new coordinating agencies: the National

Military Establishment, directed by a secretary of defense; a National Security Resources Board to ensure preparedness for a future war; a National Security Council to advise the president on national security policy; and a director of central intelligence to coordinate the military and civilian intelligence services. The 1947 act reflected the experience of World War II and the subsequent recognition that the institutions shaping American strategic and foreign policy were inadequate for a global power. It originated in President Truman's determination to unify the armed forces before the outbreak of another war. Truman was strongly supported in this effort by General George Marshall and vehemently opposed by Secretary of the Navy James Forrestal (1892–1949), whose objections were fueled by the suspicions that, given the Soviet Union's massive land army, a unified U.S. armed services would be dominated by the army to the detriment of the navy.

But Forrestal also viewed the Soviet Union as a dangerous antagonist and was therefore determined to add a military and intelligence component to American foreign policy, to coordinate means and ends. Seeking a more comprehensive alternative to the army plan, Forrestal commissioned a study to recommend a new national security process. As a result, Forrestal became a major architect of the act.

Debate over the proposed National Security Act continued for two years because of intense opposition within the navy, and among its congressional supporters, to unification of the military services. Disagreements also arose over the position of the director of central intelligence and the agency that would support that position: Military intelligence agencies maneuvered to maintain their own autonomy, and the State Department sought to control the proposed new intelligence agency. In addition, President Truman and his advisers opposed the creation of a statutory National Security Council and worked to weaken what they saw as a threat to the independence of the presidency.

The act that emerged was, consequently, the result of a series of compromises. With the help of congressional supporters, for example, Forrestal weakened the authority of the secretary of defense, thereby undercutting the attempts at unity and enhancing, he hoped, the position of the navy.

In 1949 amendments to the act finally created a Department of Defense that diminished the power of the civilian service secretaries and strengthened the position of the secretary of defense. The amendments also removed the service secretaries from the National Security Council, thus augmenting the State Department's influence within the council.

In the following decade, both the National Security Council and the Central Intelligence Agency grew into formidable agencies; the National Security Resources Board expired; and the Department of Defense, seeking an elusive unity, periodically reorganized itself. The National Security Act created the basic structure of U.S. strategic and foreign policy decision making in the Cold War. It was one of the most significant pieces of legislation passed in the second half of the twentieth century.

[*See also* **Federal Government, Executive Branch: Defense Department; Federal Government, Executive Branch: States Department; Federal Government, Executive Branch: Presidency, The; National Security Council;** *and* **Truman, Harry S.**]

BIBLIOGRAPHY

Caraley, Demetrios. *The Politics of Military Unification: A Study of Conflict and the Policy Process.* New York: Columbia University Press, 1966.

Neu, Charles E. "The Rise of the National Security Bureaucracy." In *The New American State,* edited by Louis Galambos, pp. 85–108. Baltimore: Johns Hopkins University Press, 1987.

Anna Kasten Nelson

NATIONAL SECURITY COUNCIL

The National Security Council (NSC) is one of the most important organizations in the federal bureaucracy when it comes to foreign policy. It consists of three groups: the statutory principals spelled out in the National Security Act of 1947 (the president, the vice president, the secretary of state, and the secretary of defense); the statutory advisers (the director of national intelligence and the chair of the joint chiefs of staff); and the Council staff. The Council's professional staff has ranged in size from only a few people in the early days to upward of 100 in more recent administrations. All but a handful of these aides serve on loan from various executive agencies. The individual who binds the groups together is the "special assistant to the president for national security affairs," a job title established in the Eisenhower administration to designate the overall director of the NSC's staff activities. This title was shortened under President Nixon to "the assistant for national security affairs" or, in common parlance, "the national security adviser." The position has become one of great importance in the government of the United States. Initially, officials viewed the post as little more than a neutral coordinator of information prepared for the president by the government departments and agencies with foreign policy responsibilities. In the early twenty-first century, however, the national security adviser resides at the center of the system for making foreign and defense policy.

The job of national security adviser has stretched from the original task of paper coordinator to one of policy advocate on behalf of the president. Some advisers have become internationally known, notably Henry Kissinger, who in 1973 combined the job with his position as secretary of state. Two advisers, Robert McFarlane and John M. Poindexter, involved the NSC staff in questionable operations during the Iran–Contra scandal of 1987.

A core obligation of the national security adviser is to help ensure that the president hears a range of opinions before making a decision. The adviser is expected to keep the channels of communication open between the White House and the departments and agencies; to make sure that weaker advocates are heard; to dredge new channels, if necessary, in the persistent search for reliable information and policy options to assist the president; and to be alert for malfunctions in the flow of information to, and orders from, the White House. Above all else, the office of the NSC adviser has evolved into the role of "honest broker" to mediate disputes among the cabinet departments, especially between the departments of state and defense. Brent Scowcroft was viewed by many as the quintessential honest broker when he served twice as national security adviser, first under President Gerald R. Ford and later under President George H. W. Bush.

Presidents have understood that the complex issues of foreign and security policy in the aftermath of the Cold War demand an active national security adviser. The goal is have an adviser who can serve as an honest broker, faithfully representing the views and recommendations of NSC principals, while sharing his or her own thoughts with the president; someone who keeps the paper flowing into and out of the Oval Office; and someone who can assist the administration in explaining its foreign policy initiatives to an increasingly demanding public and media.

[*See also* **National Security Act of 1947.**]

BIBLIOGRAPHY

Inderfurth, Karl F., and Loch K. Johnson, eds. *Fateful Decisions: Inside the National Security Council.* New York: Oxford University Press, 2004.

Rothkopf, David. *Running the World.* New York: PublicAffairs, 2005.

Loch K. Johnson

NATIONAL WOMAN'S PARTY

The National Woman's Party (NWP), formed in 1917, had its roots in two earlier organizations. In 1913, two American students, Alice Paul (1885–1977) and Lucy Burns, fresh from "suffragette" actions in London, returned to the United States to revive the nearly defunct campaign for a constitutional amendment to enfranchise women. (American suffragists at the time were focused on winning suffrage through individual state constitutional amendment campaigns.) Paul and Burns formed the Congressional Union (CU), initially a wing of the National American Woman Suffrage Association (NAWSA), but soon a separate and rival organization. The CU's first action was a controversial suffrage parade held in Washington, D.C., on the eve of Woodrow Wilson's first inaugural. It then embarked on a campaign to convince women already enfranchised by state action to vote against Democratic candidates in the 1914 congressional elections; the goal was to force the Democratic Party, which controlled Congress and the White House, to support the suffrage amendment. A similar campaign was mounted for the 1916 elections, at which time a second organization, made up entirely of women voters and named the Woman's Party, was formed. Members tended to be younger, more militant suffragists. Important figures included Mary Beard; Florence Kelley; Harriot Stanton Blatch, the daughter of Elizabeth Cady Stanton; and Alva Belmont, a wealthy New York socialite.

Despite the militants' campaign, Woodrow Wilson, who promised to keep the United States out of the European war, was reelected in 1916. The militants now formed a single organization, the NWP, which abandoned electoral techniques in favor of propaganda and demonstrations. In January 1917, picketing of the White House began. After America entered the war in April, the picketers were arrested; although tried on minor charges, some, including Paul herself, received sentences of up to six months. The resulting publicity so embarrassed the Wilson administration that all charges were dismissed and arrests ceased.

In January 1918, the House of Representatives passed the Nineteenth Amendment to the Constitution, followed sixteen months later by the Senate. By August 1920 the ratification process was complete. The NWP and the NAWSA each claimed that its approach—militant civil disobedience versus law-abiding lobbying—produced the victorious result, but more likely the combination, against the background of wartime politics, was responsible.

After enfranchisement, Paul was determined to keep the NWP an active feminist force. Claiming to have learned from the suffrage struggle the importance of concentrating on a "single issue," she in 1923 committed the NWP to a campaign for another constitutional amendment that would ensure "equal rights before the law" for women and men. However, most postsuffragists objected to this platform, and within a few years the NWP's membership had dramatically decreased. It survived, however, fighting for equal rights nationally and internationally. Paul stayed at the organization's helm until her death in 1977, at which time the campaign for the Equal Rights Amendment was taken up by a younger organization, the National Organization for Women. Formally the NWP still existed at the end of the twentieth century, sustained by its ownership of a headquarters building, the Alva Belmont House, in Washington, D.C., within sight of the White House.

[*See also* **Equal Rights Amendment; Equality; Feminism; National Organization for Women; Nineteenth Amendment; Stanton, Elizabeth Cady; Wilson, Woodrow;** ***and*** **Woman Suffrage Movement.**]

BIBLIOGRAPHY

DuBois, Ellen Carol. *Harriot Stanton Blatch and the Winning of Woman Suffrage.* New Haven, Conn.: Yale University Press, 1997.

Lunardini, Christine A. *From Equal Suffrage to Equal Rights: Alice Paul and the National Woman's Party, 1910–1928.* New York: New York University Press, 1986.

Ellen C. DuBois

NATIVE AMERICAN LAW

See **Indian Law, Federal; and Indian Law, Tribal.**

NAVIGATION ACTS

(1651–1696). The outbreak of the English Civil War in 1642 temporarily cut the American colonies' supply lines to the mother country, leading the colonists to establish commercial relations with the Dutch and French. At the end of the war, England sought to reassert control over the American trade by passing a series of laws that came to be known as the "Navigation Acts."

The first statute, passed by Parliament in 1651 and reenacted in 1660 upon the restoration of the monarchy under Charles II, stipulated that all goods brought into England be imported only in English ships and that "enumerated commodities," such as tobacco and sugar grown in the Americas, be exported only to England or English colonies. The second Navigation Act, passed in 1663 and known as the Staple Act, required that European commodities be exported to the English American colonies only via approved ports in England. A third Navigation Act (1673) set customs duties for the colonies and established a cadre of officers in the colonies to collect them, in the hope of better controlling the flow of enumerated commodities to England and its possessions. A fourth Navigation Act, the 1696 Act of Trade and Plantations, strengthened the machinery of metropolitan control by setting up admiralty courts in the colonies. Together, these statutes summed up seventeenth-century English mercantilist thought by creating an exclusionary imperial commercial system restricted to English and colonial traders and designed to benefit the mother country. Subsequent statutes passed with similar intent, such as the Molasses Act of 1733, exhibited the same mercantilist spirit.

In considering the Navigation Acts and the empire's mercantile regime, British and American historians have divided over two issues. The first is the extent of smuggling to contravene the acts. The surviving evidence seems to confirm the effectiveness of the parliamentary laws, coupled as they were with the threat of prosecution. On the other hand, the evidence is incomplete, since successful smuggling leaves few traces, and the presence of French, Dutch, and Spanish imports in American markets seems too great to be accounted for in any other way.

Whether the Navigation Acts contributed to the ferment that led to the Revolutionary War has engendered more heated debate. Historians long viewed the laws as exploitative and debt-inducing, at least after 1763 when the ministry decided to make the colonists pay for the Seven Years' War. However, Robert P. Thomas in 1965 estimated the burden of the acts in the 1760s and 1770s to be less than 0.5 percent of average annual American income.

So slight a burden, Thomas suggested, could not have caused revolt. Thomas's conclusion, hotly debated at first, eventually became historical orthodoxy. Subsequent scholarship, however, showed that the burden of the acts was not evenly distributed and that they did impose significant costs on certain groups—in particular, tobacco and rice planters, colonial merchants and manufacturers, and artisans and mechanics—actors central to pre-Revolutionary agitation. These groups may have thought the burden intolerable enough to warrant rebellion.

BIBLIOGRAPHY

Harper, Lawrence A. *The English Navigation Laws: A Seventeenth-Century Experiment in Social Engineering.* New York: Columbia University Press, 1939.

Sawers, Larry. "The Navigation Acts Revisited." *Economic History Review* 45 (1992): 262–284.

Thomas, Robert P. "A Quantitative Approach to the Study of the Effects of British Imperial Policy on Colonial Warfare: Some Preliminary Findings." *Journal of Economic History* 25 (1965): 336–355.

David J. Hancock

NEAR v. MINNESOTA

In *Near v. Minnesota,* the U.S. Supreme Court by a 5-to-4 vote declared state gag laws an unconstitutional prior restraint on speech. These laws, enacted in response to the proliferation of yellow journalism in the 1920s, allowed judges to halt the publication of newspapers seen as engaging in malicious, scandalous, or defamatory criticism of public officials.

Near involved a newspaper that had been shut down under Minnesota's gag law for accusing a mayor and police chief of being under the control of a gangster. Instead of addressing the unsettled question of whether defamatory criticism of public officials was protected speech under the First Amendment, the Court concentrated on the means of suppression. Comparing prior restraints and subsequent sanctions, it reasoned that the former posed a far greater danger because it prevented the speech from entering the public realm. Regardless of the content of the speech, the majority ruled, the state must rely on subsequent sanction rather than prior restraint in its efforts at suppression.

The legacy of *Near* is threefold. First, the decision firmly established the freedom of the press against censorship and prior restraint. Second, it applied the First Amendment to the states, thereby curtailing the use of state police power to silence unpopular speech. Third, the Court adopted the marketplace-of-ideas rationale for protecting free speech. This rationale views speech in terms of its social value in a democratic community: enhancing the deliberative process by injecting controversial ideas that might otherwise have been excluded.

[*See also* **Abrams v. United States;** **Bill of Rights;** *and* **Supreme Court, U.S.**]

BIBLIOGRAPHY

Murphy, Paul L. *The Meaning of Freedom of Speech.* Westport, Conn.: Greenwood, 1972.

Patrick M. Garry

NEOCONSERVATISM

Neoconservatism is a faction of American conservatism rooted in the New York Jewish intellectual community. During the 1930s and 1940s, these intellectuals generally had adhered to various schools of Marxism and socialism. At the start of the Cold War, however, many in this group—including Irving Kristol, Daniel Bell, and Nathan Glazer—abandoned socialism for a liberal stance that accepted capitalism and rejected communism, supported continued social reforms at home, and embraced containment abroad. Known as Cold War liberals, they were firmly anchored in the Democratic Party.

Starting in the mid-1960s, several factors led some Cold War liberals to move away from the liberal mainstream. Concerned that the ambitious social programs of President Lyndon Johnson's Great Society rested on weak intellectual foundations, Bell and Kristol in 1965 started the *Public Interest,* a journal dedicated to informing policy discussions with hard data and rigorous analysis. During the next several years, as America's social problems grew and it became clear that many Great Society programs had fallen short of their goals, *Public Interest* developed a comprehensive critique of liberalism's effort to shape the development of a modern society. Many of the social programs, noted frequent contributor Daniel Patrick Moynihan in 1970, "went about this extraordinarily complex task in a fairly simple-minded manner." Although they continued to support maintaining the basic structure of the welfare state, contributors to *Public Interest* during the 1970s became steadily more skeptical of the efficacy of large-scale government reform programs. Indeed, the belief that such programs make problems worse has become one of the hallmarks of neoconservatism.

Another factor was changes at *Commentary* magazine. Founded in 1945 to discuss American Jewish affairs and related issues, *Commentary* during the 1950s became one of the country's leading intellectual journals and a prominent voice of Cold War liberalism. Starting in 1960, its new editor, literary critic Norman Podhoretz, moved *Commentary* to the left. By the late 1960s, however, Podhoretz and many of the magazine's contributors—several of whom, like Bell, Glazer, and Moynihan, already wrote for *Public Interest*—were disturbed by the growing anti-intellectualism and violence of the counterculture and New Left. Starting in June 1970, Podhoretz turned *Commentary* sharply to the right. New York intellectuals long had written in a combative style, but *Commentary* now assaulted its opponents with unrelenting harshness. "The magazine ran articles critical of almost every important aspect of the radicalism of the sixties," Podhoretz later wrote, and uncompromising criticism of 1960s leftism and its lingering effects on American culture remains a prominent theme in *Commentary.* During the next few years, the terms "new conservative" and then "neoconservative" came into use, intended as pejoratives to describe the *Commentary–Public Interest* liberals whom other liberals accused of having moved to the right.

Foreign policy issues also played a major role in the evolution of neoconservatism. The neoconservatives had remained strong anti-Communists and supporters of containment. They were angered by the Democrats' seeming drift toward isolationism in the early 1970s, the Nixon and Ford administrations' policy of détente with Moscow, and what they viewed as the U.S. failure to rebut foreign dictatorships' attacks on Western democracy. Stalwart supporters of Israel, the predominantly Jewish neoconservatives were alarmed by mounting left-wing criticism of Tel Aviv. During the presidency of Jimmy Carter, whom the neoconservatives criticized as dangerously weak in foreign affairs, the neoconservatives broke with the Democrats and joined Ronald Reagan's conservative coalition. Since then, they have remained in the Republican Party and conservative movement and continue to advocate foreign policies that defend U.S. interests—and Israel—without compromise.

Neoconservative influence peaked in the early 1980s. Prominent neoconservatives held important positions in the Reagan administration—political scientist Jeane Kirkpatrick served as U.S. ambassador to the

United Nations, and Podhoretz's son-in-law, Elliott Abrams, was an assistant secretary of state. But neoconservatives outside the government, led by Podhoretz, began to criticize Reagan's policies toward the Soviet Union as too soft and accommodating. Indeed, almost to the moment that the Soviet empire collapsed, *Commentary* insisted that Moscow posed a dire threat to U.S. security. Misunderstanding of the changes in Mikhail Gorbachev's Soviet Union made the neoconservatives appear intellectually rigid and cost them any chance of having influence in the administrations of George H. W. Bush or Bill Clinton—despite the support of some neoconservatives for the moderate Democratic candidate in 1992.

In domestic policy, its adherents' skepticism about government has made many of neoconservatism's arguments indistinguishable from the limited-government positions of other conservatives, albeit with some exceptions. During the 1990s, journalist David Brooks promoted "national greatness" policies, proposing large-scale public projects as a way to heal the political splits caused by cultural conflicts. In foreign affairs, Irving Kristol's son, William, advocated "neo-Reaganite" policies, promoting U.S. hegemony and the spread of democracy. Neither variety of activist policies has found much support on the right, however. Thus, despite their continued prominence in conservative media—especially after William Kristol founded the *Weekly Standard* in 1995—neoconservatives were only marginal figures at the start of George W. Bush's presidency in 2001.

Neoconservatives briefly regained their influence after the terrorist attacks of 11 September 2001. Viewing the threat of Islamic terrorism through the prism of their Cold War experience, the neoconservatives described a threat similar to that of Soviet expansionism. Believing that expanding democracy could defeat this threat, they advocated a neo-Reaganite response and became the leading proponents of invading Iraq, which they saw as the first step toward democratizing the Arab world. The 2003 invasion and the disaster that followed, however, showed that the neoconservatives had had almost no understanding of the situation in Iraq or the implications of the policies they advocated.

In the early twenty-first century the neoconservatives remain on the margins of American politics. They have lost two of their most important platforms—in 2005 *Public Interest* ceased publication and its foreign policy analog, *National Interest,* turned away from neoconservatism. Even sympathetic observers of neoconservatism, such as Benjamin Balint and Justin Vaisse, note that the intellectual level of *Commentary,* now edited by Norman Podhoretz's son John, has declined and that the neoconservatives show little inclination to consider what lessons to draw from their experiences. A new, high-quality journal, *National Affairs,* began publication in 2009, but it remains to be seen whether it will be able to match the prestige of *Public Interest* in an age of infinite competing voices on the Internet and cable television.

[***See also* Conservatism; Democratic Party; *and* Liberalism.**]

BIBLIOGRAPHY

Bloom, Alexander. *Prodigal Sons: The New York Intellectuals and Their World.* New York: Oxford University Press, 1986.

Dorrien, Gary. *The Neoconservative Mind: Politics, Culture and the War of Ideology.* Philadelphia: Temple University Press, 1993.

Ehrman, John. *The Rise of Neoconservatism: Intellectuals and Foreign Affairs, 1945–1994.* New Haven: Yale University Press, 1995.

Fukuyama, Francis. *America at the Crossroads: Democracy, Power, and the Neoconservative Legacy.* New Haven: Yale University Press, 2006.

Heilbrunn, Jacob. *They Knew They Were Right: The Rise of the Neocon*. New York: Doubleday, 2008.
Kristol, Irving. *Neoconservatism: Selected Essays, 1949–1995*. New York: Free Press, 1995.
Podhoretz, Norman. *Breaking Ranks: A Political Memoir*. New York: Harper & Row, 1979.
Vaisse, Justin. *Neoconservatism: The Biography of a Movement*. Cambridge, Mass.: Belknap Press of Harvard University Press, 2010.

John Ehrman

NEOLIBERALISM

Like the term liberalism from which it derives, neoliberalism has distinct meanings and connotations in the United States and abroad. Traditionally speaking, liberalism refers to a set of political ideas that support individual rights, private property, free markets, economic competition, and limited government. European liberals are often contrasted with socialists (and until recently Communists) who call for the state to take a more active role in the economy to correct market failures and redistribute wealth. Until the 1930s, liberalism in the United States was defined in roughly the same way. However, in the hands of Franklin D. Roosevelt, the term underwent a profound change. In response to the Great Depression, Roosevelt redefined liberalism to refer to his view of an active and positive role for the national government. Although his opponent in the 1932 presidential election, Herbert Hoover, protested FDR's use of the word, his complaints fell upon deaf ears. Roosevelt's New Deal program—one that entailed major new laws that committed government to new regulations of business and created the foundations of the American welfare state—was dubbed "liberal." Ever since, liberalism in the United States has meant a left-of-center doctrine that calls for greater state responsibility for managing the economy and society.

After World War II, the positive state received intellectual support from the macroeconomic theories of John Maynard Keynes. According to Keynes, wise fiscal and monetary policies pursued by national governments—especially countercyclical spending—could smooth the fluctuations of the business cycle. Until the 1960s, then, liberalism remained the dominant current of American political thought. In that decade, the social policies of FDR were vastly expanded under President Lyndon B. Johnson. His Great Society program increased government involvement in poor relief, health care, education, and civil rights. The new policies increased the regulation of the private sector, created new bureaucracies, and committed the American state to huge long-term expenditures.

Beginning in the late 1960s, conflict over the advancement of marginalized groups, the Vietnam War, and economic woes put liberalism on the defensive. The challenges to liberalism continued into the 1970s and reached a fever pitch during the presidency of James E. Carter (1977–1981). New groups representing women, gays and lesbians, environmentalists, and the disabled issued some of these challenges. All demanded government provide them with greater attention. In addition, economic conditions in the late 1970s challenged the reigning Keynesian faith. An unprecedented combination of high inflation and high unemployment (called stagflation) led many to believe that American government had become too cumbersome and too expensive. This gave an opening for conservatives to argue that traditional liberal policy prescriptions suppressed economic freedom. Carter's defeat for reelection in 1980 by Republican Ronald Reagan indicated a shift in the national mood.

The term neoliberalism gained currency over the next decade. The "neo" indicated a brand of liberalism closer in its theoretical assumptions to what had existed in the United

States prior to Roosevelt's reinterpretation of the term. Insofar as neoliberalism described a set of ideas held by American conservatives, it pointed to their rejection of Keynesianism and adoption of neoclassical, monetarist, or Austrian School economics emanating from the University of Chicago. Although they differed internally, these economic theories rejected key aspects of the positive state. Neoliberalism thus pointed to efforts to reduce government's reach by cutting taxes and reducing regulations. Although few conservatives described themselves with this term, they emphasized the threats of "Big Government" to liberty and stressed the value of the free market system. These positions were often called "Reaganomics" or "supply-side" economics.

Neoliberalism also found resonances within the Democratic Party. In fact, a renewed appreciation for free market solutions to policy problems began among Democrats during the Carter administration, which initiated a series of deregulatory efforts in trucking, airlines, and telecommunications. The so-called neoliberal faction of the party in the late 1970s and 1980s was usually described as being more attuned to the beneficial aspects of markets than the party mainstream, open-minded on cultural issues, and skeptical about the use of American military might abroad. Colorado Senator Gary Hart's two campaigns for the party's presidential nomination in the 1980s expressed some of these themes. In 1984, Hart ran as the candidate of "new ideas." Although this slogan was vague, what substance it had was based on a skepticism of the various interest groups—labor unions, feminists, environmentalists, and minorities—that pressed for a larger and more intrusive state. After Walter Mondale's defeat of Hart for the Democratic Party's presidential nomination and Mondale's crushing loss to Reagan in the general election, neoliberals gathered in 1985 under the umbrella of the Democratic Leadership Council (DLC). The DLC and its affiliated think tank, the Progressive Policy Institute, continued to develop market-friendly ideas in a number of areas, including health care and poverty relief. Bill Clinton then used the DLC as a launching pad for his successful presidential bid in 1992.

The term neoliberalism has also been adopted globally, especially among critics of America's foreign economic policy. In the 1970s, a group of free market–oriented economists in Latin American—some of them trained at the University of Chicago—began to describe their program as *neoliberalismo*. In response, left-wing critics of market-based reform in developing countries and antiglobalization activists saddled neoliberalism with a derogatory connotation in the 1990s. In their eyes, neoliberalism's policy prescriptions would lead (or were leading) to a withdrawal of government protections, unrestrained competition, and "savage capitalism." Neoliberalism thus became shorthand for the ideological persuasion of an ensemble of international institutions (the International Monetary Fund, the World Bank, and the United Nations) backed by the United States and known colloquially as the "Washington Consensus." According to critics, the policies recommended—free trade, sound money, and use of the dollar as the world's reserve currency—were designed to impose American capitalism and culture to the global south. Today, it is this conception of neoliberalism that is most likely to be invoked in the world's major newspapers.

[***See also*** **Great Society; Johnson, Lyndon B.; Liberalism; New Deal;** ***and*** **Roosevelt, Franklin Delano.**]

BIBLIOGRAPHY

Bear, Kenneth S. *Reinventing Democrats: The Politics of Liberalism from Reagan to Clinton.* Lawrence: University of Kansas Press, 2000.

Hamby, Alonzo L. *Liberalism and Its Challengers: F.D.R. to Reagan*. New York: Oxford University Press, 1992.
Harvey, David. *A Brief History of Neoliberalism*. New York: Oxford University Press, 2005.
Milkis, Sidney M., and Jerome M. Mileur. *The Great Society and the High Tide of American Liberalism*. Amherst: University of Massachusetts Press, 2005.
Steger, Manfred B., and Ravi K. Roy. *Neoliberalism: A Very Short Introduction*. Oxford; New York: Oxford University Press, 2010.

Daniel DiSalvo

NEUTRALITY ACTS

Neutrality acts have been considered by Congress at various times to keep the United States aloof from actual or imminent European wars. When in 1793 France declared war on Britain, the newly appointed French minister to the United States, "Citizen" Edmond Genêt, began to recruit American volunteers and sought to stimulate the revolt of British and Spanish colonists in Canada and Louisiana. In response, Congress in June 1794 passed its first neutrality law, confirming President George Washington's "Rules Governing Belligerents," which prohibited the arming of belligerent vessels within American ports and military recruitment by belligerent powers within U.S. borders.

A different kind of legislation became an issue when World War I broke out. On 11 February 1916, in an effort to crack the British blockade, Germany announced that it would attack enemy merchant ships, endangering citizens of neutral states who might be traveling on such vessels. President Woodrow Wilson believed that travel by neutrals was a neutral right, but some in Congress wanted to ensure America's continued neutrality in the war by eliminating the possibility of provocation. In mid-February 1916, Representative Jeff McLemore (D-TX) introduced a resolution requesting the president to warn Americans not to travel on armed belligerent vessels, and Senator Thomas P. Gore (D-OK) introduced a resolution denying passports—and protection—to Americans seeking passage on such ships. Under pressure from President Wilson, Congress early in March tabled both resolutions.

In the aftermath of World War I, when many Americans became convinced that the United States had entered the conflict because of the Wilson administration's pro-Allied partisanship, Congress enacted various neutrality bills. The Johnson Act of 1934, not technically a neutrality act, prohibited private loans to any government in default of obligations to the U.S. government. In August 1935, in its first general neutrality act, Congress legislated that an arms embargo would become mandatory once the president declared that a war existed between two or more foreign powers. The bill also authorized the president to proclaim that Americans traveling on belligerents' ships did so at their own risk.

In a second neutrality bill enacted in February 1936, Congress extended the existing law by fourteen months while adding a prohibition on loans to belligerents. In 1937, Congress, by overwhelming majorities in both houses, reacted to the Spanish Civil War by enacting a nondiscriminatory embargo designed to minimize U.S. involvement on either side.

In May 1937, Congress passed a third neutrality bill. It retained bans on arms sales, loans, credit, and travel on belligerent ships whenever the president found a foreign or civil war endangering the United States. In addition, the 1937 act banned the arming of all merchant ships trading with belligerents. It gave the president discretionary authority to put the sale of nonembargoed goods on a "cash-and-carry" basis, requiring belligerents to pay at the time of purchase and to transport the goods on their own ships. The act also gave the president discretionary authority to prohibit armed belligerent ships from using American ports.

The neutrality laws of the 1930s proved short-lived. In November 1939, two months after World War II began, Congress repealed the arms embargo. By December 1941, when the United States entered the war, it was already convoying munitions to Britain, making most neutrality legislation a dead letter.

[*See also* **Peace Movements; Washington, George;** *and* **Wilson, Woodrow.**]

BIBLIOGRAPHY

Divine, Robert A. *The Illusion of Neutrality*. Chicago: University of Chicago Press, 1962.

Link, Arthur S. *Wilson*, vol. 4. *Confusion and Crises, 1915–1916*. Princeton, N.J.: Princeton University Press, 1964.

Justus D. Doenecke

NEW DEAL

A period of political, economic, cultural, and social ferment that spanned President Franklin Delano Roosevelt's first two terms in office, the New Deal Era (1932–ca. 1940) takes its name from the slogan that Roosevelt first used in his acceptance speech at the 1932 Democratic National Convention and later adopted to describe his administration. This era saw an unprecedented level of federal intervention to regulate economic life and provide basic welfare to citizens in response to the Great Depression. This redefinition of government in turn facilitated the realignment of both major political parties, the rise of unionism among mass-production workers, demands for progress by women and minorities, and the growth of populist influences in culture and the arts.

Above all, the New Deal Era changed American government. President Herbert Hoover's administration, although more active than any previous government in combating economic depression, remained hostage to the belief that privately coordinated economic action was preferable to government regulation. Hoover's policies proved incapable of halting economic decline or reviving public confidence amid unemployment rates that exceeded 25 percent of nonagricultural workers. In his first hundred days in office, President Roosevelt broke decisively from Hoover's example in favor of experimentation with new government programs. In those early months, Roosevelt pushed fifteen major bills through a compliant Democratic Congress.

The First New Deal. Among the acts of 1933 were such reforms as the Emergency Banking Act, the passage of which was accompanied by a "bank holiday" (the temporary closing of the nation's banks), and the Glass–Steagall Act, which separated commercial and investment banking. Other acts focused on relief: The Federal Emergency Relief Administration dispensed $500 million in aid to the poor; the Civilian Conservation Corps (CCC) put 2 million men to work on environmental projects; the Civil Works Administration provided work relief; and the Home Owners' Loan Corporation refinanced mortgages. A massive construction program, the Tennessee Valley Authority (TVA), built some thirty flood-controlling dams and thirteen power plants that provided cheap electricity to regional consumers. Through the TVA in the South and large public works projects in the West, the New Deal stimulated economic development and urbanization in those regions.

But the most significant programs aimed to restart a floundering economy. The Agricultural Adjustment Administration (AAA) boosted farm prices by reducing production. It paid farmers to take acreage out of cultivation and to reduce livestock herds. The National Recovery Administration (NRA) reinvigorated industry by restraining competitive forces and raising prices. It created industry boards composed of business and government officials who jointly wrote codes that set minimum wages, maximum hours, and price guidelines. The National Industrial Recovery Act (NIRA), the law that created the NRA, also launched a $3.3 billion Public Works Administration that initiated projects from airport construction to school building and protected workers' rights to join a union (through Section 7a of the act).

In 1934, the "First New Deal," as it is often called, came to an end with a flurry of legislation that included the Securities and Exchange Act, which prohibited such abuses as insider trading—a contributor to the stock market crash of 1929. Already it was clear that government would never again be quite the same. The proliferation of "alphabet soup" agencies attracted to Washington a new governing class of lawyers and economists. With "Brains Trust" advisers such as Ben Cohen (a Jew) and Tommy Corcoran (an Irish Catholic), the New Deal reached beyond the conventional Protestant elite for talent. This new governing class experimented with economic planning. The NRA took a step in this direction, as government attempted to boost prices by having consumers patronize companies that complied with NRA codes and displayed "Blue Eagle" logos. In truth, however, no single approach animated Roosevelt's advisers, nor did any one philosophy characterize the president's early initiatives.

Yet by 1935 a host of developments sent the New Deal in a new direction. First, Roosevelt found it increasingly difficult to placate business. Small businesses denounced NRA policies that favored larger competitors. Even big business leaders, who initially supported the NRA, soon chafed under its codes. A powerful business lobby, the American Liberty League, emerged in 1934 to promote anti-Roosevelt candidates.

Meanwhile, the New Deal's effort to make government an instrument of social justice inspired a wide range of activist demands during 1934–1935. In California, the novelist Upton Sinclair nearly won election as governor in 1934 on a left-wing platform. Militant strikes broke out in textiles, trucking, and longshoring, as workers sought to realize the right to organize promised by Section 7a. Democrats unexpectedly augmented their majorities in both houses in the 1934 congressional elections. A mass movement demanding regular government payments to retirees emerged under the leadership of Dr. Francis Townsend. And two skillful demagogues—Father Charles Coughlin and Senator Huey Long—castigated the New Deal's inadequacies. Coughlin, a Catholic priest who hosted a radio program with a fervent national following, called for currency reform. Long, the corrupt boss of Louisiana politics, demanded that the nation "Share Our Wealth" by expropriating vast fortunes and distributing them to all.

Losing business support and facing demands for action from other quarters, Roosevelt's First New Deal was finally undermined by the U.S. Supreme Court's decision in *Schechter Poultry Corp. v. United States,* which declared the NRA unconstitutional. Searching for an alternative program, Roosevelt embraced the ideas of advisers who believed that the fundamental problem of the Great Depression was underconsumption. This thinking corresponded to the new theories of the British economist John Maynard Keynes (although New Dealers had little knowledge of Keynesianism). Legislation launched in 1935, often termed the "Second New Deal," attempted to build purchasing power among the unemployed, industrial workers, the elderly, and others. This demand-side approach represented a departure in fiscal policy, inaugurating what became the Keynesian revolution in the U.S. political economy.

The Second New Deal. Among the programs launched in 1935 were the Works Progress Administration (WPA), a relief program that dwarfed previous New Deal efforts by employing nearly one-third of the nation's jobless. The Emergency Relief Appropriation disbursed some 5 billion dollars in aid to the distressed. The Public Utility Holding Company Act, which broke up the thirteen companies that controlled most of the nation's utilities, drove down electricity prices. The Rural Electrification Act provided federal funds to electrify hamlets and farmsteads. And the Wealth Tax Act increased taxes on corporations and the rich. Together these laws tapped corporate wealth while boosting the incomes of the poorest Americans.

The two most significant pieces of legislation to emerge from the Second New Deal were the Social Security Act (SSA) and the National Labor Relations Act (NLRA). The SSA enrolled a majority of Americans in a federal pension program that guaranteed them retirement income. It also provided funds to the states for unemployment and disability insurance and aid to single mothers of dependent children. The act set the foundation on which the American welfare state was built. The NLRA (or "Wagner Act," after its sponsor, Senator Robert F. Wagner of New York) guaranteed workers' right to organize, prohibited company unions from representing them, and established a National Labor Relations Board to oversee collective bargaining. It opened the door to mass-production unionism.

The legislation of the Second New Deal defined the government's role in American life for the remainder of the century: the New Deal state regulated and stimulated the economy, promoted workers' rights, and offered welfare to the poor. The Second New Deal did not go as far as some supporters hoped (no national health plan was adopted, for example), but its direction was clear. For decades to come, political debate would no longer focus on whether government should intervene to steer the economy and foster social justice, but rather on how and to what extent such intervention should take place.

The New Deal Era also witnessed a shift in U.S. foreign policy away from unilateralism and toward internationalism. In December 1933, announcing a "Good Neighbor Policy" toward Latin America, Roosevelt renounced unilateral military intervention as a tool of American policy in the Western Hemisphere. Although Roosevelt continued to defend perceived U.S. interests in South America, he did so with more restraint than his recent predecessors. Reversing the policy adopted by previous administrations since 1917, the administration also granted diplomatic recognition to the Soviet Union. And, as a depression-fighting tactic, Roosevelt pursued reciprocal trade agreements between the United States and its trading partners that lowered tariffs and facilitated foreign trade.

The New Deal's Domestic Impact. But the impact of the New Deal Era was visible above all in domestic developments, and nowhere more so than in politics. Since the Civil War, the Republican Party had dominated presidential politics. Only two Democrats went to the White House between 1856 and 1932—and neither gained a majority of popular votes in their elections. The New Deal, however, built a powerful Democratic coalition, appealing to urban voters and some previously Republican blocs, including midwestern farmers and African Americans. The Democratic Party emerged from Roosevelt's 1936 reelection as the nation's majority party, a status it would hold for decades.

In his 1936 campaign against Alfred M. ("Alf") Landon (1887–1987), the Republican governor of Kansas, Roosevelt attacked Republicans as "economic royalists" and reactionaries and enthusiastically defended the New Deal's achievements. Voters gave him 61 percent of the popular vote and all but eight electoral votes—the largest electoral landslide in American history. More important, Roosevelt not only swept Democratic strongholds in the "solid South" and urban America, but also won new constituencies to his party. Never before had a president received more unified or enthusiastic support from organized labor. Roosevelt also gained votes from more than 80 percent of the poorest Americans and won a similar majority among first-time voters, most from immigrant stock. Significantly, he also won large majorities among African Americans, breaking black ties to the party of Abraham Lincoln and creating thereafter the Democrats' most loyal voting bloc.

The 1936 New Deal coalition also swept Democrats to large majorities in both houses of Congress and to power in many traditionally Republican statehouses. For more than a generation, the Democratic Party would be seen as the party of reform, government action, and the "common man" (a phrase invoked by Roosevelt in 1932). So well did Roosevelt align the Democrats with such ideas that even long-time third-party protest voters flocked to the Democratic banner.

Ultimately, however, the New Deal Era proved how deeply rooted America's conservative tendencies were. The New Deal's political realignment went only so far. Roosevelt's party also enjoyed the support of powerful business forces, especially those with an interest in promoting consumption-oriented economic policies. Mass retailers, the investment banking houses connected to them, some powerful legal firms, influential building contractors, real-estate developers, and consumer-oriented banks all benefited from the New Deal's political capitalism. Their voices checked the influence of unions and liberals within the party. Similarly, the power of southern Democrats, especially in Congress, blocked the party from moving very far leftward. Entrenched segregationists with years of seniority on powerful committees enacted provisions that weakened key New Deal reforms—for example, exempting agricultural and domestic workers from protection by the SSA or NLRA. When Roosevelt challenged some of these southern conservatives by endorsing their liberal opponents in the 1938 Democratic primaries, the strategy failed. As a result, the Democratic Party emerged from this era divided between hopeful black masses, labor unionists, and liberals on the one hand and die-hard southern segregationists on the other.

Nonetheless, the political shifts of the New Deal Era awakened the hopes of previously subordinated groups in American society. Workers, radicals, blacks, and women alike enjoyed rising expectations.

To no group did the New Deal promise more than to industrial workers. The protection of the right to organize embodied in Section 7a of the NIRA sparked a wave of unionizing efforts in basic industry. That ferment in turn stirred reform within the American Federation of Labor (AFL). Unable to meet the needs of mass-production workers owing to its anachronistic craft structure, the AFL floundered in response to Section 7a. By 1935, a group of union reformers led by John L. Lewis of the United Mine Workers of America demanded that the AFL issue charters to industrial unions to reach mass-production workers. When AFL president William Green balked, Lewis and others formed the Committee for Industrial Organization (CIO).

The CIO sponsored mass organizing drives in the iron and steel, automotive, rubber, and electrical industries that came to fruition in a series of dramatic breakthroughs in 1937. The most important, a sit-down strike in a Flint, Michigan, auto plant, forced General Motors to recognize the CIO's United Automobile Workers union. Shortly thereafter, the U.S. Steel Corporation recognized the CIO. When the Supreme Court unexpectedly upheld the constitutionality of the NLRA in April 1937, the CIO's position was further strengthened. Before the end of the year, Lewis led industrial unionists out of the AFL to institutionalize the CIO as the Congress of Industrial Organizations. Breaking with AFL policies that excluded blacks, women, and most radicals, the CIO forged a new path for American labor. By the end of World War II, the CIO had unionized much of mass-production industry and established itself as a power in Democratic politics.

The rise of the CIO was in part aided by an alliance that developed among unionists, liberals, and radicals. During the Depression, the Communist Party USA grew into the dominant left-wing presence, despite its policy of spurning alliances with the democratic left. In 1935, however, the Communist International, mindful of the threat of fascism, abandoned its previous sectarianism and inaugurated the Popular Front, urging Communists everywhere to ally with liberal, antifascist forces. In America, Communist workers abandoned efforts to build their own unions and instead streamed into the CIO, becoming in many cases its best organizers and rising to positions of leadership in several CIO unions. Although especially important for labor, the Popular Front strategy was broadly influential. Communists entered New Deal agencies (without disclosing their party connections) and joined with liberals in civil rights, peace, and civil liberties efforts. Never before had radicals exerted more influence in government or mainstream political causes—a fact that would haunt liberals during the Cold War when Republicans attacked them as onetime "fellow travelers" of the Communists.

Among the causes that Communists helped advance during this period were African American civil rights. Communists played an active role in publicizing the Scottsboro case, which involved nine black youths dubiously charged with raping two white women in Alabama in 1931. Communists also organized southern black sharecroppers into the Share Croppers Union. (Socialists, meanwhile, founded their own Southern Tenant Farmers Union.) They also helped launch civil rights groups such as the National Negro Congress and the Southern Negro Youth Congress.

The New Deal's own record on civil rights was less luminous. Roosevelt refused to support antilynching legislation for fear of angering powerful southern Democrats, the CCC ran segregated camps, relief programs frequently discriminated against blacks, and nearly all TVA employees were white. Still, the administration did evince solicitude for black concerns. Roosevelt regularly consulted with an informal "Black Cabinet"; he appointed such black leaders as Mary McLeod Bethune to secondary-level administration posts; and Eleanor Roosevelt, the president's wife, championed black demands for equality. In 1939 the First Lady and Secretary of the Interior Harold Ickes (1874–1952) intervened when the Daughters of the American Revolution barred the black opera singer Marian Anderson from performing at their Washington, D.C., concert hall. Mrs. Roosevelt and Ickes arranged for Anderson to sing instead on the steps of the Lincoln Memorial, staging a stirring radio broadcast of the event.

Likewise, although the New Deal did little to advance feminist goals in programmatic terms, women gained increasing influence in government during this period. Molly Dewson, a feminist activist, headed the newly established Women's Division of the Democratic National Committee. Working with Eleanor Roosevelt and other allies, Dewson helped secure appointment of the first women to hold the positions of cabinet secretary (Frances Perkins of the Department of Labor), ambassador, U.S. Court of Appeals judge, and a score of lesser posts. Meanwhile, Eleanor Roosevelt's travels, speeches, syndicated newspaper column, and frequent interventions in policy debates within the administration transformed the role of First Lady.

The New Deal also brought improvements for Native Americans. The long-time reformer John Collier (1884–1968), appointed head of the Bureau of Indian Affairs by Roosevelt, pushed through Congress a series of laws that aided beleaguered Native American communities. These culminated in the Indian Reorganization Act of 1934, which granted Indians rights of self-government and cultural freedom on reservations.

Although such social changes should not be exaggerated, they did encourage an emerging ideal of cultural pluralism among liberals who celebrated America's cultural diversity. This tendency was greatly strengthened by simultaneous developments in music and the arts. Here, too, government played a role. Under the aegis of the WPA in 1935, the Federal Arts Project, the Federal Music Project, the Federal Writers Project, and the Federal Theatre Project were born. These programs employed jobless artists and writers to compose and perform music and plays, to write local histories, to paint murals in public buildings, and more. Such projects encouraged artists to draw upon folk culture and everyday life for themes, making the arts more accessible to the masses.

By the end of the 1930s, American arts and letters had been permeated by a concern for everyday people's struggles. The paintings of John Steuart Curry, the proletarian fiction of John Dos Passos and John Steinbeck—whose novel *The Grapes of Wrath* (1939) celebrated the endurance of Dust Bowl migrants—and the composer Aaron Copland's "Fanfare for the Common Man" all revealed an effort to give voice to the voiceless.

Developments in popular culture reinforced this trend. The New Deal Era saw film and radio gain a vast following. The movies offered the fantasy world of *The Wizard of Oz* and escape into the past with *Gone with the Wind* (both 1939). Radio diverted listeners with the comedy shows of Jack Benny, George Burns and Gracie Allen, and the mildly racist stereotypes of "Amos 'n' Andy." Radio also made mass opinion a force as never before, as Roosevelt's "Fireside Chats" showed. Moviegoers watched newsreels touting the New Deal's efforts, cheered the populist heroes of the director Frank Capra's films, and admired strong women such as Bette Davis and Joan Crawford. Just as the federal government supplanted local, ethnic, or religious institutions unable to care for the Depression's victims, the new mass media partially supplanted their audiences' distinctive subcultures with a national mass culture at once democratic and consumerist.

The New Deal's Demise and Its Legacy. Yet the New Deal that had initiated such vast changes began to fade by 1937, in part because of difficulties created by Roosevelt himself. Frustrated by the Supreme Court's conservative rulings, Roosevelt in early 1937 led a vain effort to expand the number of justices on the court. This transparent attempt to "pack" the court and thereby influence its decisions alienated many of the president's allies and reinvigorated his foes. Later in 1937, worried about deficit spending and assuming that the economy was rebounding, Roosevelt decided to cut back relief programs. The stock market promptly crashed and jobless rates again soared.

Other calamities ensued. Smaller steel companies refused to follow the lead of U.S. Steel, successfully avoiding recognition of the CIO in a bitter 1937 strike that weakened Roosevelt's labor allies. Then, in 1938, conservatives on the House Un-American Activities Committee mounted a damaging investigation into Communist influence in New Deal agencies. These same conservatives ensured that the last great piece of New Deal legislation—the Fair Labor Standards Act of 1938—exempted agricultural workers and set minimum wages at a level that would not hurt low-waged southern industry. Increasingly under attack after 1938, administration liberals retreated from ambitious efforts to restructure the economy and contented themselves with pursuing economic growth policies.

By the time Adolf Hitler's storm troopers invaded Poland on 1 September 1939, unleashing World War II, thc New Deal Era was waning. Conservative and liberal political forces became locked in a stalemate that blocked significant reforms until the United States went to war in December 1941. Only in wartime was Roosevelt able to place the New Deal's central legacy—a powerful regulatory government—on a durable footing. By then, however, those interests that had most resisted the New Deal's changes had regrouped to ensure that their power would not be undermined by the postwar political dispensation.

What is the legacy of the New Deal Era? Historians differ, and their views have shifted over time. During the early Cold War years, most saw the New Deal as the triumph of democracy and liberal capitalism at a time when the future of both looked bleak. By the 1960s, however, revisionists began focusing on the missed opportunities and the conservative achievements of this era, the spread of an entrenched government bureaucracy, and the coopting of militant unionism. The New Deal's failure to address the grievances of minorities and women also received increasing scrutiny. In the last years of the century, however, as the era of "big government" faded, scholars seemed willing to grant that the New Deal Era witnessed a profound broadening of American democracy against great odds. Workers, consumers, and minorities benefited from the developments of this period, even if they gained little direct influence over public policy. Their advances may be the era's most enduring legacy.

[*See also* **Agricultural Adjustment Administration; Agricultural Policy; American Liberty League; Civil Rights; Civilian Conservation Corps; Communist Party USA; Conservatism; Court Packing; Democratic Party; Economic Policy: Banking and Financial Regulation; Equality; Feminism; Hoover, Herbert; Housing Policy, Federal: Home Owner's Loan Corporation; Liberalism; Long, Huey; National Labor Relations Act; National Labor Relations Board; National Negro Congress; National Recovery Administration; Peace Movements; Public Utilities Policy, Federal; Radicalism; Regulatory Agencies, Federal; Roosevelt, Eleanor; Roosevelt, Franklin Delano; *Schechter Poultry Corp. v. United States;* Securities and Exchange Commission; Segregation; Social Policy: Public Welfare; Social Security; Social Security Policy; Socialism; Socialist Party of America; Tariffs; Tennessee Valley Authority;** *and* **Works Progress Administration.**]

BIBLIOGRAPHY

Brinkley, Alan. *The End of Reform: New Deal Liberalism in Recession and War.* New York: Alfred A. Knopf, 1995.

Cohen, Lizabeth. *Making a New Deal: Industrial Workers in Chicago, 1919–1939.* Cambridge, UK; New York: Cambridge University Press, 1990.

Dubofsky, Melvyn, ed. *The New Deal: Conflicting Interpretations and Shifting Perspectives.* New York: Garland, 1992.

Fraser, Steve, and Gary Gerstle, eds. *The Rise and Fall of the New Deal Order, 1930–1980.* Princeton, N.J.: Princeton University Press, 1989.

Hawley, Ellis. *The New Deal and the Problem of Monopoly*; Princeton, N.J.: Princeton University Press, 1966.

Leuchtenberg, William E. *Franklin D. Roosevelt and the New Deal, 1932–1940.* New York: Harper & Row, 1963.

McElvaine, Robert. *The Great Depression.* New York: Times Books, 1984.

Pells, Richard. *Radical Visions, American Dreams: Culture and Social Thought in the Depression Years.* New York: Harper & Row, 1973.

Plotke, David. *Building a Democratic Political Order: Reshaping American Liberalism in the 1930s and 1940s.* Cambridge, UK; New York: Cambridge University Press, 1996.

Sitkoff, Harvard. *A New Deal for Blacks.* New York: Oxford University Press, 1978.

Ware, Susan. *Holding Their Own: American Women in the 1930s.* Boston: Twayne, 1982.

Zieger, Robert H. *The CIO, 1935–1955.* Chapel Hill: University of North Carolina Press, 1995.

Joseph A. McCartin

NEW LEFT

An uprising of students against the dominant policies and cultural mores of American society, the New Left emerged in the early 1960s, peaked at mid-decade, and dissipated in the early 1970s. Arising from the civil rights movement, fears of nuclear war, and socialist movements of the 1930s (the so-called Old Left), the New Left became closely identified with protests against the Vietnam War and related campus uprisings as the 1960s progressed. The spread of left-leaning periodicals, most notably *Liberation, Ramparts,* and *Studies on the Left;* the specter of student protests, black and white; and the formation of leftist organizations, particularly Students for a Democratic Society (SDS), the Student Nonviolent Coordinating Committee (SNCC), and the Congress of Racial Equality (CORE), signaled the emergence of the New Left.

The movement's espousal of "participatory democracy" emphasized widespread popular engagement in political decision making. The slow pace of change, meanwhile, reinforced the New Left's disdain for political liberalism. Although SDS supported the idea of a war on poverty, it found President Lyndon B. Johnson's policies lacking and established its own Economic Research and Action Project, aimed at forging an interracial movement of the poor. Furthermore, although they applauded the Civil Rights Act of 1964, SNCC and other New Left voices condemned Johnson's forces for refusing to seat the Mississippi Freedom Democratic party at the Democratic National Convention that same year.

The New Left gained a devoted following, particularly among college students, through its leadership of the antiwar movement and association with black power advocates and the counterculture. Together, these forces broke down the liberal consensus represented by President Johnson's landslide victory in 1964 and fueled a host of other movements on issues such as feminism and environmentalism. Whether the New Left actually shortened the Vietnam War remains a problematic question, since radical student protests created a backlash among mainstream Americans.

Although it was most prominent on the East and West coasts, on campuses like Columbia and Berkeley, the New Left attracted supporters nationwide, at such institutions as the University of Texas, the University of Wisconsin, and Kent State in Ohio. Moreover, the youth-led rebellions in France, Czechoslovakia, and elsewhere during the 1960s demonstrated that New Left–type protests were not confined to the United States. Convinced that a worldwide revolution was at hand, some New Left students abandoned their initial goals and methods in favor of more traditional Marxist-Leninist tactics. Most prominently, the Weathermen, a violent offshoot of SDS, cast itself as the vanguard of a global struggle against racist imperialism.

Several factors produced the New Left's demise. Increased militancy alienated some movement supporters, while prompting a government crackdown on radical insurgencies. The end of the Vietnam War also took its toll, turning leftist attention and energy to other social and political movements. Paradoxically, some New Right groups adopted the tactics and vocabulary of the New Left in their own crusades of the 1970s and beyond.

Although some scholars present the New Left in a favorable light, as an idealistic movement dedicated to increasing minority rights and ending a disastrous war, others focus more on its excesses, including the defense of terrorism by some and its divisive impact on the Democratic Party and its liberal agenda. Nearly all scholars, however, agree that the New Left played a key role during the 1960s, leaving a powerful legacy of youthful protest and political change.

[*See also* **Antiwar Movements; Black Panthers; Civil Rights; Civil Rights Legislation; Congress of Racial Equality; Democratic Party; Environmentalism; Feminism; Great Society; Johnson, Lyndon B.; Nixon, Richard M.; Poverty; Radicalism; Socialism;** ***and*** **Students for a Democratic Society.**]

BIBLIOGRAPHY

Anderson, Terry. *The Movement and the Sixties*. New York: Oxford University Press, 1995.

Gitlin, Todd. *The Sixties: Years of Hope and Days of Rage*. Toronto; New York: Bantam Books, 1987.

Levy, Peter B. *The New Left and Labor in the 1960s*. Urbana: University of Illinois Press, 1994.

Miller, James. *Democracy Is in the Streets: From Port Huron to the Siege of Chicago*. Cambridge, Mass.: Harvard University Press, 1994.

Sale, Kirkpatrick. *SDS*. New York: Random House, 1973.

Unger, Irwin. *The Movement: A History of the New Left, 1959–1972*. New York: Dodd, Mead, 1974.

Peter B. Levy

NEW YORK TIMES CO. v. SULLIVAN

376 U.S. 254 (1964), argued 6 January 1964, decided 9 March 1964 by vote of 9 to 0; Brennan for the Court, Black, Douglas, and Goldberg concurring. In this case, the Supreme Court for the first time considered the extent to which the constitutional guarantee of freedom of speech and the press limits the award of damages in a libel action brought by public officials against critics of their official conduct. Sullivan, an elected commissioner of the city of Montgomery, Alabama, brought a civil libel action against four black clergymen and *The New York Times* alleging that he had been libeled by statements in a full-page advertisement that was carried in the *Times*. The advertisement, which was entitled "Heed Their Rising Voices," described the civil rights movement in the South and concluded with an appeal for funds.

It was uncontroverted that several statements contained in the text of the advertisement were inaccurate. For example, the advertisement stated that students protesting racial segregation sang "My Country, 'Tis of Thee" on the steps of the Alabama State Capitol, but they had actually sung "The Star-Spangled Banner"; it also said that several students were expelled from school for leading that protest, but they were actually expelled for demanding service at a segregated lunch counter in the

Montgomery County Courthouse on another day; finally, the advertisement claimed that "the entire student body" of Alabama State College protested the expulsions, but only a majority of the students, not the "entire" student body, had protested the expulsions.

The trial judge submitted the case to the jury under instructions that these statements were libelous per se, that falsity and malice were presumed, and that general and punitive damages could be awarded without direct proof of pecuniary loss. Under these instructions, the jury returned a judgment for Sullivan in the amount of $500,000 against each of the defendants.

The Supreme Court reversed, holding that the rule of law applied by the Alabama court violated the First Amendment. At the outset the Court confronted its own past declarations to the effect that libelous utterances are no essential part of any exposition of ideas (*Chaplinsky v. State of New Hampshire,* 1942) and that they are not constitutionally protected speech (*Beauharnais v. Illinois,* 1952). In rejecting these prior declarations the Court explained that, like "the various other formulae for the repression of expression that have been challenged in this Court, libel can claim no talismanic immunity from constitutional limitations"; to the contrary, libel "must be measured by standards that satisfy the First Amendment" (p. 269).

Turning to the task of articulating these standards, Justice William J. Brennan observed in an oft-quoted passage that "we consider this case against the background of a profound national commitment to the principle that debate on public issues should be uninhibited, robust, and wide-open, and that it may well include vehement, caustic, and sometimes unpleasantly sharp attacks on government and public officials" (p. 270). Drawing upon history, the Court analogized the civil law of libel, as applied by the Alabama court, to the Sedition Act of 1798, which had been invalidated "in the court of history" because of the restraint it "imposed upon criticism of government and public officials" (p. 276).

The essential difficulty, Brennan explained, was that "erroneous statement is inevitable in free debate," and even false statements must therefore "be protected if the freedoms of expression are to have the 'breathing space' that they 'need . . . to survive" (pp. 271–272). Thus, the Alabama rule of law could not be "saved by its allowance of the defense of truth," for a "rule compelling the critic of official conduct to guarantee the truth of all his factual assertions" would lead to intolerable "self-censorship." Indeed, under such a rule, "would-be critics of official conduct may be deterred from voicing their criticism, even though it is believed to be true and even though it is in fact true, because of doubt whether it can be proved in court or fear of the expense of having to do so." Such a rule, the Court concluded, "dampens the vigor and limits the variety of public debate" (pp. 278–279).

With these considerations in mind, the Court held that public officials may not recover damages for defamatory falsehood relating to their official conduct unless they can prove actual malice; "that the statement was made with . . . knowledge that it was false or with reckless disregard of whether it was false or not" (pp. 279–280).

New York Times revolutionized the law of libel and, equally importantly, it signaled a critical shift in our general First Amendment jurisprudence. *New York Times* abandoned the traditional approach, which concentrated solely on whether libel was "protected" or unprotected speech, and embraced a more speech-protective analysis, which focused on the danger that actions for libel might deter expression that lies at the very heart of First Amendment concern. By fashioning its First Amendment standards in light of these "chilling" effects, the Court took an important step toward a more sensitive, less formulaic mode of analysis, a mode of analysis that is the hallmark of contemporary First Amendment jurisprudence.

Perhaps the most important question remaining after *New York Times* was whether the privilege it recognized governed only libel actions involving the official conduct of public officials or whether it extended to other persons. In *Curtis Publishing Co. v. Butts* (1967) and *Associated Press v. Walker* (1967), the Court, in a sharply divided set of opinions, extended the *New York Times* holding from public officials to figures such as movie stars, athletes, industrialists, and other individuals who, although they are not officials, are nonetheless well known to the public. In reaching this result, the Court rejected the argument that *New York Times* was premised on, and thus limited by, the analogy to seditious libel. Rather, the Court reasoned that *New York Times* rested on a profound national commitment to uninhibited, robust, and wide-open debate on public issues. The Court therefore concluded that libelous utterances concerning public figures, like libelous utterances concerning public officials, must be governed by the *New York Times* privilege.

Several years later, however, in *Gertz v. Robert Welch, Inc.* (1974), the Court, again sharply divided, recognized an important limitation on the scope of *New York Times,* holding that it did not extend to libel actions brought by private individuals, even where the defamatory statement related to a matter of "public concern." The Court explained that, unlike public officials and public figures, private individuals are usually unable to rebut the libel effectively and they usually have not gone out of their way to seek the public's attention. The Court reasoned that, because private individuals are more vulnerable to injury and more deserving of recovery than either public officials or public figures, they may recover damages for libel merely by showing that the publisher or broadcaster had acted negligently in disseminating the defamatory material.

New York Times and its progeny have been criticized as both overprotective and underprotective of free expression. Some critics maintain that *New York Times* failed adequately to protect the press because its "reckless disregard" standard implicitly authorized highly intrusive inquiries into the thought processes of reporters and editors and because it failed to preclude large and potentially chilling damage awards whenever a jury would find that the press has acted with reckless disregard. These critics, echoing the views expressed by Justices Hugo Black, William O. Douglas, and Arthur Goldberg in their concurring opinions in *New York Times,* argue that the press should have absolute protection against actions for libel. Other critics maintain that *New York Times* gave too much protection to the press and failed to protect the innocent victims of libel. These critics fault *New York Times* for denying innocent victims reasonable compensation for the harm they suffer and for preventing such victims from obtaining a judicial declaration of falsity, which would at least set the record straight.

Several proposals have been offered in recent years in an effort to "cure" these "deficiencies." The most intriguing of these proposals calls for the creation of a new civil action in which the alleged victim of a defamatory falsehood could sue for a judicial declaration of falsity upon waiving the right to sue for damages. The theory is that such an action would reduce litigation costs and enable the victims of libel to vindicate their reputations without intruding into the editorial process or threatening the press with potentially devastating damage awards. Although this approach would avoid some of the problems identified with *New York Times,* it would effectively empower the judiciary to decide on a case-by-case basis whether specific statements made by the press are "true" or "false." It is questionable whether such a relationship between the judiciary and the press would comport with the underlying theory and assumptions of the First Amendment.

New York Times cannot be fully understood without recognizing that it was driven not only by concerns about free expression but also by the unique historical circumstances in which it arose. *New York Times* was, in short, a product of the civil rights movement of the 1950s and 1960s. Like other devices designed to obstruct the civil rights movement, the libel judgment against the *New York Times* and the African American clergymen named in the advertisement was designed to dampen the drive for civil rights. After all, if this Alabama jury's massive damage award could be sustained on the basis of such minor inaccuracies, then no person or institution would be free to challenge racial segregation in the South. *New York Times,* one of most important decisions in the history of the First Amendment, was thus not only a triumph for free expression, but also a triumph for civil rights and racial equality.

[*See also* **Alien and Sedition Acts; Black, Hugo; Civil Liberties; Civil Rights; Douglas, William O.; Jurisprudence;** *and* **Supreme Court, U.S.**]

BIBLIOGRAPHY

Barrett, David A. "Declaratory Judgments for Libel." *California Law Review* 74 (1986): 847–888.

Kalven, Harry, Jr. "The New York Times Case: A Note on 'The Central Meaning of the First Amendment.'" *Supreme Court Review* (1964): 191–221.

Smolla, Rodney A. *Suing the Press.* New York: Oxford University Press, 1986.

Geoffrey R. Stone

NINETEENTH AMENDMENT

Ratified in 1920, the Nineteenth Amendment inscribed women's right to vote into the U.S. Constitution. No other constitutional amendment required such a long, hard-fought struggle. The woman suffrage movement, launched by Elizabeth Cady Stanton at the Women's Rights Convention in 1848 in Seneca Falls, New York, was initially understood to involve a state-by-state process. After the Civil War, in response to the constitutional amendments that granted citizenship to former slaves and established suffrage rights "regardless of race, color or previous condition of servitude," woman suffragists shifted their sights to the federal Constitution. A woman-suffrage amendment was introduced in 1878 by Senator Aaron Sargent of California, but for the next thirty-five years suffrage efforts focused on the state level.

In 1913, however, a new, more concerted drive for a federal amendment was initiated by Alice Paul, a charismatic young woman from Pennsylvania. Paul's followers, first known as the Congressional Union and then as the National Woman's Party, forthrightly challenged Congress and the president to support the amendment; they were soon joined by the National American Woman Suffrage Association, a larger and more moderate group, under the leadership of Carrie Chapman Catt. In 1918 (with President Woodrow Wilson, praising women's contributions to the war effort, finally endorsing the cause), these combined forces won House passage of the amendment; eighteen months later the Senate, less amenable to public pressure, passed the measure. Ratification proved difficult because Democrats from the South, where most blacks were excluded from the franchise, opposed an assertion of federal control over suffrage. After sixteen months, however, the border state of Tennessee ratified the Nineteenth Amendment, bringing the seventy-two-year effort for woman suffrage to a successful conclusion.

[*See also* **Anthony, Susan B.; Civil Rights; Constitution; Elections: Suffrage; Feminism; League of Women Voters; National American**

Woman Suffrage Association; National Organization of Women; National Woman's Party; Progressive Era; Seneca Falls Women's Rights Convention of 1848; Stanton, Elizabeth Cady; Wilson, Woodrow; Woman Suffrage Movement; *and* **Women in Politics since 1920.**]

BIBLIOGRAPHY

Flexner, Eleanor, with Ellen Fitzpatrick. *Century of Struggle: The Woman's Rights Movement in the United States,* enlarged ed. Cambridge, Mass.: Belknap Press of Harvard University Press, 1996.

Lunardi, Christine A. *From Equal Suffrage to Equal Rights: Alice Paul and the National Woman's Party, 1910–1928.* New York: New York University Press, 1986.

Ellen C. DuBois

NIXON, RICHARD M.

(1913–1994), thirty-seventh president of the United States. Born in Yorba Linda, California, to Quaker (Society of Friends) parents who had moved from the Middle West, Richard Milhous Nixon excelled at Whittier College, a Quaker school. A scholarship student at Duke Law School, he graduated third in his class in 1937. Returning to Whittier, he married Catherine (Pat) Ryan in 1940; they had two daughters. After working in the wartime Office of Price Administration, Nixon obtained a naval commission in 1942 and served in the South Pacific during World War II, rising to the rank of lieutenant commander.

Running for Congress as a Republican in 1946, he defeated five-term liberal Democrat Jerry Vorhees. In 1950 he won a U.S. Senate seat from California, defeating the equally liberal Helen Gahagan Douglas. From the first, Nixon generated controversy, as he accused his opponents of Communist leanings. Such tactics earned him a reputation as a ruthless political polarizer who would do anything to win. In 1948 he proposed the Mundt–Nixon bill requiring Communist organizations and individuals to register with the government. On the House Un-American Activities Committee, he effectively ended the career of Alger Hiss by accusing him of Communist connections and espionage in the 1930s. Although many scholars now believe Hiss guilty of the perjury charge for which he was convicted, some liberals never forgave Nixon for bringing down Hiss and using the case to promote his own career. He did not make anti-Communism a major theme after the Hiss case, however, and kept his distance from Senator Joseph McCarthy.

Tapped as Dwight D. Eisenhower's running mate in 1952, Nixon faced charges that wealthy friends had created a secret fund to further his career. In a nationwide television broadcast, Nixon successfully defended himself and salvaged his place on the ticket. The speech is best remembered for Nixon's maudlin declaration that his daughters would keep their cocker spaniel "Checkers," a gift from a supporter.

During eight years as vice president, Nixon campaigned widely for Republican candidates. His reputation as the party's hatchet man related especially to his attacks on Adlai Stevenson, the Democrats' presidential candidate in 1952 and 1956. He also, however, supported educational reform and civil rights; honed his foreign-policy skills; and campaigned for moderate as well as conservative Republicans, broadening his base of party support. His popularity rose after his car was stoned during a 1958 visit to Venezuela and his 1959 "kitchen debate" with Soviet premier Nikita Khrushchev at a U.S. exhibition in Moscow. Although Eisenhower excluded Nixon from his inner circle, gave him few responsibilities, and occasionally humiliated him in public, Nixon upgraded the vice presidency to a more meaningful office than it had been before. Through Eisenhower's various medical crises in 1955–1957, Nixon displayed tact and restraint, presiding over numerous cabinet and National Security Council meetings.

Nixon's party services and "centrist" image assured his presidential nomination in 1960, but his loss to John F. Kennedy created bitternesses—and taught him lessons—he never forgot. Although the press described Kennedy as a "youthful" candidate representing a new generation, Nixon was in reality only four years older. Nixon's more liberal record on social and foreign-policy issues was generally ignored in the media blitz surrounding the charismatic Kennedy, as were Kennedy's womanizing and medical problems. Finally, the one-on-one TV debates with Kennedy taught Nixon that the television tactics he had honed in the 1950s were outmoded. Nixon lost by 112,000 votes—the closest presidential election since 1884. To his credit, he did not challenge the results despite evidence of election fraud in Illinois and Texas.

Returning to private life, Nixon practiced law in New York and wrote a political memoir, *Six Crises* (1961). His defeat in the 1962 California gubernatorial race prompted his much-quoted remark to reporters that they would not "have Nixon to kick around anymore." He tirelessly campaigned for Republican candidates and played a centrist role, especially after the arch-conservative Barry Goldwater's 1964 loss to Lyndon B. Johnson.

Winning the 1968 Republican presidential nomination, Nixon faced a Democratic Party divided over the Vietnam War, shaken by demonstrations at its Chicago convention, and haplessly led by Hubert Humphrey after Johnson's withdrawal. Appealing to a "silent majority" of northern blue-collar workers and southern whites, Nixon campaigned as a "law and order" candidate who would quell domestic protests and end the war. He won by 500,000 popular votes, garnering 301 electoral votes to Humphrey's 191 and George Wallace's 46. He did well in the South, Wallace's home turf.

Publically committing himself to "government reform such as this nation has not witnessed in half a century," Nixon focused on five areas of domestic policy: welfare, the environment, some aspects of civil rights, and executive-branch reorganization. He supported increased Social Security benefits, expansion of the Job Corps, quotas to increase minority access to skilled employment, an innovative plan to replace welfare with a guaranteed annual income for the poor, and creation of the Environmental Protection Agency (1970). On the economic front, he adopted various strategies—including, for a time, Keynesian deficit spending—to combat the inflation and budget deficits inherited from Johnson's efforts to wage the Vietnam War and fund his Great Society programs without raising taxes. Underrated at the time, Nixon's domestic record appears more impressive in retrospect. Pursuing his "southern strategy," Nixon opposed court-ordered school busing and extension of the 1965 Voting Rights Act, urged a slowdown of southern school integration, and unsuccessfully nominated two southern conservatives to the Supreme Court. (He also made four successful Supreme Court appointments: Warren Burger as chief justice, Harry Blackmun, Lewis Powell, and future chief justice William Rehnquist.)

In the global arena, Nixon and his national security adviser (and later secretary of state) Henry Kissinger pursued better relations with America's Cold War adversaries, the People's Republic of China and the Soviet Union. Nixon triumphantly visited China in February 1972, laying the groundwork for later diplomatic recognition, and that May in Moscow signed agreements with the Soviets to reduce the risk of military confrontations and to promote cooperation in science, technology, health, environmental matters, and space exploration. The two powers also signed the Anti-Ballistic Missile Treaty, an interim Strategic Arms Limitation Treaty (SALT I), and a document entitled "Basic Principles of U.S–Soviet Relations." This brief détente anticipated the Cold War's eventual end, but in the short run it foundered in the later 1970s and early 1980s.

A central goal of these initiatives was to improve chances for a favorable Vietnam settlement, but this effort failed. Despite Nixon's strategy of "Vietnamization" and protracted U.S.–North Vietnamese negotiations, the conflict dragged on until 1975, finally ending in a North Vietnamese victory. Elsewhere, the Nixon–Kissinger foreign policy involved geopolitical considerations largely unrelated to economic realities or the interests of the peoples involved. Among other instances, these priorities emerged in the United States' tilt toward Pakistan in its 1971 war with India and in the clandestine use of U.S. power to overthrow the democratically elected leftist government of Salvador Allende in Chile. In the Middle East, Kissinger's shuttle diplomacy produced more show than substance. Overall, Nixon's foreign policy record was mixed at best, despite his unquestioned expertise in this area.

Although hardly photogenic, Nixon employed television in innovative and widely imitated ways, including effective use of prime-time broadcasts, interviews on morning talk shows, speaking live with orbiting astronauts, and assuring satellite coverage of his foreign policy triumphs. These public-relations tactics, coupled with his domestic record and foreign-policy achievements, all but assured Nixon's reelection in 1972. By nominating the antiwar candidate George McGovern, the badly divided Democrats turned the election into a rout. Nixon amassed a plurality of almost 18 million popular votes, and won 520 electoral votes to McGovern's 17.

Nixon's second term proved disastrous. In 1973 came Vice President Spiro Agnew's resignation amid charges of tax evasion and accepting bribes, to be replaced by Congressman Gerald Ford. Far more serious was the Watergate crisis, involving a foiled break-in at the Democratic National Committee headquarters on 17 June 1972 by burglars linked to the White House and the administration's subsequent cover-up of its involvement, including payoffs to the arrested burglars. The break-in was conducted by a secret White House unit, dubbed "the Plumbers," created in 1971 to plug leaks and to harass persons on Nixon's "enemies list." As the media, federal judge John Sirica, Special Prosecutor Leon Jaworski, a special Senate committee, and eventually the House Judiciary Committee conducted investigations, the pressure on Nixon built steadily in 1973–1974, especially after the release of White House tapes with incriminating Oval Office conversations. On 9 August 1974, with impeachment looming, Nixon resigned—the only president ever to do so. The Watergate scandal ultimately resulted in the conviction of twenty men, including not only those directly involved in the burglary, but also such top administration figures as Nixon advisers John Ehrlichman and H. R. (Bob) Haldeman, presidential counsel John Dean, special assistant Charles Colson, and Attorney General John Mitchell. Nixon himself received a full pardon in September 1974 from President Ford. Phoenix-like, ex-President Nixon worked to rehabilitate his reputation by publishing books on foreign policy, for example. As a younger generation arose that did not remember Watergate, the scandal's centrality somewhat faded. (It had never loomed as large abroad as it did domestically.)

Richard Nixon remains one of the most enigmatic and controversial politicians of the post–World War II era. Highly intelligent and a master of politics, he was also consumed by gnawing grievances and a preoccupation with shadowy "enemies." Nevertheless, he ranks without question as one of the most important presidents of the twentieth century.

[*See also* **Agnew, Spiro; Anti-Communism; Blackmun, Harry S.; Burger, Warren; Civil Rights; Eisenhower, Dwight D.; Environmental Protection Agency; Environmentalism; Federal Government, Executive Branch: Presidency, The; Federal Government, Legislative Branch: Senate, Ford, Gerald R.; Great Society; House Un-American Activities Committee; Humphrey, Hubert; Kennedy, John F.; National Security Council; Presidential Debates; Presidential Impeachment; Rehnquist, William; Republican Party; Social Policy: Public Welfare; Social Security; Social Security Policy; Stevenson, Adlai; Supreme Court, U.S.; Wallace, George C.;** *and* **Watergate.**]

BIBLIOGRAPHY

Ambrose, Stephen E. *Nixon: The Triumph of a Politician*. New York: Simon & Schuster, 1987.

Hoff, Joan. *Nixon Reconsidered*. New York: Basic Books, 1994.

Kutler, Stanley. *Abuse of Power*. New York: Free Press, 1997.

Litwack, Robert S. *Détente and the Nixon Doctrine*. Cambridge, UK; New York: Cambridge University Press, 1984.

Moynihan, Daniel Patrick. *The Polities of a Guaranteed Income: The Nixon Administration and the Family Assistance Plan*. New York: Random House, 1973.

Nixon, Richard. *RN: The Memoirs of Richard Nixon*. New York: Grosset & Dunlap, 1978.

Parmet, Herbert. *Richard Nixon and His America*. Boston: Little, Brown, 1990.

Reichley, James. *Conservatives in an Age of Change: The Nixon and Ford Administrations*. Washington, D.C.: Brookings Institution, 1981.

Wills, Garry. *Nixon Agonistes: The Crisis of a Self-Made Man*. New York: New American Library, 1971.

Joan Hoff

NORTH AMERICAN FREE TRADE AGREEMENT

In June 1991, the administration of President George H. W. Bush opened talks designed to achieve a trilateral trade agreement among the United States, Canada, and Mexico. The largely secret negotiations came to fruition in December 1992 with the signing of a 2,000-page agreement by President Bush, Prime Minister Brian Mulroney of Canada, and President Carlos Salinas of Mexico. President Bill Clinton in 1993, after initiating and signing side agreements addressing concerns raised by labor and environmental groups, lobbied vigorously for ratification of the North American Free Trade Agreement (NAFTA). Congress approved the agreement in 1993, and it went into effect in 1994.

Under the terms of NAFTA, tariffs among the three countries were to be gradually phased out. The detailed agreements also reduced nontariff barriers to trade and investment by outlawing preferential treatment of government monopolies and by exempting businesses from many forms of local, state, and national regulation. Disputes arising under NAFTA are referred to a supranational panel of trade officials and lawyers whose hearings are secret.

Some of the largest corporations in Canada, Mexico, and the United States lobbied intensively on behalf of NAFTA, arguing that the treaty would bring widespread prosperity by creating the world's largest free trade bloc. Opposition surfaced in all three countries, however, among those who feared that the agreement would cost jobs and undermine labor organizations, environmental protections, small-scale agriculture, and public-sector service and transportation programs.

[*See also* **Agricultural Policy; Bush, George H. W.; Clinton, William J.; Economic Policy:**

Regulation; Environmentalism; Regulatory Agencies, Federal; *and* Tariffs.]

BIBLIOGRAPHY

Chomsky, Noam. *World Orders Old and New*. New York: Columbia University Press, 1994.

Hossein-Zadeh, Esmail. "NAFTA and Sovereignty." *Science and Society* 61 (Summer 1997): 243–254.

U.S. International Trade Commission. *The Impact of the North American Free Trade Agreement on the U.S. Economy and Industries: A Three-Year Review*. Washington, D.C.: U.S. International Trade Commission, 1997.

Elizabeth McKillen

NORTHERN SECURITIES CASE

A landmark antitrust case. In 1901 three powerful business leaders, J. Pierpont Morgan, James J. Hill, and E. H. Harriman, decided to cooperate rather than compete, forming the Northern Securities holding company, which held the stock of their rival railroad interests in the Northwest. Their action was part of a great wave of corporate mergers that began in 1895 after the Supreme Court ruled that the E. C. Knight Company, a holding company that monopolized U.S. sugar production, did not violate the Sherman Antitrust Act of 1890.

By 1900 state and federal courts had found a variety of monopolistic practices illegal under the Sherman Act and state laws. Yet no holding company was successfully prosecuted until the Theodore Roosevelt administration brought an antitrust action against the Northern Securities Company in 1903. The trial court upheld the government's contention that the creation of the Northern Securities Company violated the Sherman Act. Upon appeal the following year, the Supreme Court upheld this ruling by a 5-to-4 vote. The majority, led by John Marshall Harlan, ruled that the holding company's intent to eliminate competition was illegal. The four dissenters, led by Oliver Wendell Holmes Jr., and Edward D. White, argued that a more flexible standard of reasonableness should have been applied to sustain the combination.

The decision ended the great wave of mergers. Federal officials, some business leaders, their lawyers, and members of the Supreme Court nonetheless concluded that in the future a "rule of reason" should govern merger cases. The Court adopted this doctrine in its *Standard Oil* and *American Tobacco* opinions of 1911. That same year, however, the Court reaffirmed that many monopolistic practices by companies working in collusion were illegal. These remained the prevailing doctrines of American antitrust law thereafter, encouraging an economic order in which both big and small business could prosper.

[*See also* **Antitrust Legislation and Law; Economic Policy: Regulation; Harlan, John Marshall; Holmes, Oliver Wendell, Jr.; Progressive Era; Roosevelt, Theodore; *and* Supreme Court, U.S.**]

BIBLIOGRAPHY

Lamoreaux, Naomi R. *The Great Merger Movement in American Business, 1895–1904*. Cambridge, UK; New York: Cambridge University Press, 1985.

Sklar, Martin J. *The Corporate Reconstruction of American Capitalism, 1890–1916: The Market, the Law, and Politics*. Cambridge, UK; New York: Cambridge University Press, 1988.

Tony A. Freyer

NORTHWEST ORDINANCE

A measure adopted by the Continental Congress, acting under the Articles of Confederation, to provide an orderly system of government leading to statehood for the territory north and west of the Ohio River. In 1789, after ratification of the Constitution, Congress reenacted the ordinance with minor modifications.

When the Revolutionary War began, seven states claimed lands in the Trans-Appalachian West on the basis of their colonial charters or treaties with Native Americans. As the war grew more protracted and costly, these states faced growing pressure to cede the lands to Congress to provide funds (through land sales) to pay war debts and soldiers' pensions. By 1786, Congress controlled most of the Ohio territory.

Congress faced three problems: governing the region, selling the land, and dealing with the numerous Native American inhabitants of the region. Congress was committed to establishing republican governments in the territory and to the formation of states that would join the union on an equal basis with the existing states. Some in Congress also feared that unruly westerners might try to form states independent of the nascent United States. Addressing these concerns, a committee chaired by Thomas Jefferson produced a general statement of principles (often called the "Ordinance of 1784") that recommended moving the western territory toward statehood in stages of increasing self-government.

Congress addressed the land-sale issue in the Ordinance of 1785. It directed that land be surveyed in six-mile-square townships, each containing thirty-six one-mile-square (640 acre) "sections" to be auctioned off for a dollar an acre. One section in each township would be set aside to support education. Most settlers, unable to afford the $640 minimum price, bought farms from land companies and speculators. With land now for sale, Manasseh Cutler, an agent for the Ohio Company (a group of speculators), and others pressured Congress to provide a more specific plan of governance.

The 1787 Ordinance set forth this plan. It called for the eventual establishment of three to five states in the region. Congress would initially appoint a governor and other officials for each future state. When the free adult male population reached 5,000, an elected assembly and an appointed legislative council would jointly elect a nonvoting delegate to Congress. When the territory's population reached 60,000 free inhabitants, the residents could frame a constitution and apply for statehood. The ordinance also included a bill of rights, a pledge that Indian lands would not be taken without Indian consent, encouragement for the development of schools, and a prohibition on slavery. (In fact, slavery persisted in the region, becoming a political issue in Indiana and Illinois territories.)

Early settlement clustered along the Ohio River. Native American groups resisted further incursions, encouraged by the British, who retained troops and fur-trading posts in the region. By 1789, white settlement on lands of the Shawnee, Miami, and other Indian groups led to war. In 1795, an army led by Anthony Wayne (1745–1796) defeated the Algonquian-speaking peoples of the region at the Battle of Fallen Timbers, forcing them in the Treaty of Greenville to surrender their land claims north of the Ohio. Meanwhile the British agreed, in Jay's Treaty, to remove their troops. As settlers poured in, Ohio became a state in 1803, Indiana in 1816, Illinois in 1818, Michigan in 1837, and Wisconsin in 1848.

The Northwest Ordinance left an ambiguous legacy. It established the principle that with territorial expansion would come republican government, although simultaneously reflecting an assumption that Native Americans would make way for new settlers. Although the ordinance prohibited slavery, its persistence in the region underscored Abraham Lincoln's claim, in the Lincoln–Douglas debates, that "not only law, but the enforcement of law" was necessary to prevent slavery's expansion.

[*See also* **Antislavery Movement; Articles of Confederation; Continental Congress; Education Policy: An Overview; Indian Law, Federal; Jay, John; Jefferson, Thomas; Land Policy, Federal; Lincoln, Abraham;** *and* **Lincoln–Douglas Debates.**]

BIBLIOGRAPHY

Onuf, Peter S. *Statehood and Union: A History of the Northwest Ordinance.* Bloomington: Indiana University Press, 1987.

Williams, Frederick D., ed. *The Northwest Ordinance: Essays on Its Formulation, Provisions, and Legacy.* East Lansing: Michigan State University Press, 1989.

Paul G. E. Clemens

NOTES ON THE STATE OF VIRGINIA

The only book authored by Jefferson in his lifetime, the compilation of the *Notes* was initiated in 1780 by a questionnaire about the American states circulated by the secretary of the French legation to members of the Continental Congress. The task of offering answers from Virginia fell to Jefferson, who turned in an initial draft in 1781 but significantly expanded the work through a private publication in Paris in 1785, a French translation of the same year, and its first English publication in 1787. The organization of the *Notes* as a response to a series of questions masks the coherence of Jefferson's scheme to describe American nature, manners, geography, and government and to identify major threats to republicanism and encourage reform. The *Notes* is the only piece of writing we have in which Jefferson wrote for the public in his own voice rather than as a spokesman in an official capacity. Along with Benjamin Franklin's autobiography, it remains perhaps the finest production of the American Enlightenment and secured Jefferson's international reputation as a philosophe.

The *Notes* offered a demonstration of American capacity for independence and self-government, as well as its "hopeful proofs of genius" (Jefferson, 1982, p. 65). On the other hand, the *Notes* never hesitated to emphasize the multiple dangers threatening to undermine the public spirit that could sustain American republicanism. In places, it is a very dark book. But its hope rests on the vastness of American nature—an almost limitless space that invited filling "with people and with happiness" and on the structural reforms Jefferson encouraged to both cultivate public spirit and check the potential for corruption and decline into the indefinite future.

A significant portion of the work responds to the European suggestion, made most prominently by French naturalist Comte de Buffon, that the American climate resulted in a degeneration of American nature. Jefferson's refutation of this theory in the *Notes* was exhaustive, resting on his extensive empirical research compiled in tables listing the height and weight of American animals. Although he explicitly refused to conclude his discussion "in favor of the American species," the tables leave little room for any other conclusion, and his explanation of the list comparing animals unique to each continent suggests that the North American tapir alone outweighed all the quadrupeds in "the whole column of Europeans." This section also contains a complicated defense of American Indians against European aspersions of their barbarism. The Indians, Jefferson suggested, remained in a savage state because of their culture rather than their nature or American climate; his solution was cultural assimilation.

In the *Notes,* Jefferson observed that it was the "manners and spirit of a people which preserve a republic in vigour," suggesting that the cultivation of that spirit must be a central concern of the republican statesman, hence Jefferson's proposals in the book for public education, elimination of primogeniture and entail, religious liberty, and other expansions of individual freedom. This stance—the cultivation of the capacities of citizens by the removal of artificial impediments to their progress and pursuits of happiness—remained Jefferson's default position, which is precisely why his refusal to fully extend it to blacks has seemed so striking a contradiction in the *Notes*. The condemnation of slavery there is the most impassioned passage in all of Jefferson's writing, eliciting contemporary and future praise. John Adams told him that the "Passages upon slavery are worth Diamonds." But the *Notes* also contain the most troubling passages upon the question of race in Jefferson's writing, passages that conclude with Jefferson's "suspicion" that blacks "are inferior to the whites in the endowments both of body and mind" and his insistence upon coupling his proposal for emancipation with a plan for colonization. These passages have been the most controversial of his writings in the most recent assessments of Jefferson's character but they raised objections even in his day. Charles Thomson, whose advice Jefferson had sought, encouraged Jefferson to excise them precisely because they "might seem to justify slavery." The tortured discussion of racial complexities that Jefferson found insurmountable combine in the *Notes* with his warnings against European immigration and encouragement of Indian assimilation to reveal Jefferson's craving for a homogeneity that belied actually existing American variety, a central theme in the *Notes*. Other notable features include Jefferson's lengthy critique of the Virginia Constitution of 1776, a passage noted and, in part, mildly rebuked in Madison's *Federalist* 49.

[*See also* **Continental Congress; Jefferson, Thomas;** *and* **Republicanism.**]

BIBLIOGRAPHY

Ferguson, Robert A. "'Mysterious Obligation': Jefferson's *Notes on the State of Virginia*." *American Literature* 52 (November 1980): 381–406.

Jefferson, Thomas. *Notes on the State of Virginia*, edited with introduction and notes by William Peden. Chapel Hill: University of North Carolina, 1982.

Tucker, David. *Enlightened Republicanism: A Study of Jefferson's Notes on the State of Virginia*. Lanham, Md.: Lexington Books, 2008.

Wilson, Douglas L. "The Evolution of Jefferson's 'Notes on the State of Virginia.'" *The Virginia Magazine of History and Biography* 112 (2004): 98–133.

Brian D. Steele

NUCLEAR POWER

In the aftermath of World War II and the beginning of the widely hailed "atomic age," a plethora of books and articles suggested that the dangers of atomic weapons would be offset, at least partially, by the potential peaceful benefits of nuclear technology. Most of the projected applications, such as atomic automobiles and small reactors to heat and cool individual homes, were hopelessly fanciful. Proposals for building reactors to generate electricity in central power stations were more realistic, but progress was slow, especially with the Harry S. Truman administration's focus on the military uses of atomic energy.

In 1954, Congress passed a law intended to speed nuclear power development. The 1954 Atomic Energy Act made possible for the first time the wide commercial use of atomic energy by ending the government's monopoly of the technology. It assigned the Atomic Energy Commission (AEC) responsibility for both promoting nuclear power and regulating its safety. To the frustration of the AEC and the congressional Joint Committee on Atomic Energy, many utilities refrained from making a major commitment to nuclear power because of the abundance of conventional fuels and because of economic uncertainties and unresolved safety questions about the technology.

Beginning in the mid-1960s, however, nuclear power development experienced a sudden and unanticipated boom. This came about for several reasons, including indications that large nuclear plants could compete economically with coal, the rise of interconnected electrical grids that encouraged the construction of large plants, and intensifying concern about air pollution from fossil-fuel units. The nuclear boom produced a rapid growth not only in the number of nuclear plants but also in the size of individual plants, which in less than a decade grew from small demonstration facilities to behemoths.

The expansion of the nuclear industry took place at virtually the same time as the development of environmentalism as a potent political force. By the early 1970s, nuclear power had become a leading target of environmental activism and the subject of a highly visible and increasingly strident debate. Critics claimed that the technology was neither safe nor necessary; supporters argued that it was both safe and essential for the nation's energy future. At the center of the controversy were the unresolved issues of the likelihood and consequences of a major reactor accident and the effects of exposure to low levels of radiation. As the debate continued, public uneasiness about the risks of nuclear power increased substantially, and by the end of the 1970s orders for new plants had slowed dramatically. The slump in the industry resulted more from inflation and reduced demand for electricity than from antinuclear activism, but the complaints of nuclear opponents strongly influenced public attitudes.

The debate over nuclear power intensified after the most serious accident in a U.S. nuclear power plant occurred at the Three Mile Island station near Harrisburg, Pennsylvania, in March 1979. The accident's severity was caused by mechanical failures and human error, and although only small amounts of radiation were released, the political fallout was heavy. The accident undermined the credibility of the Nuclear Regulatory Commission (NRC) and the nuclear industry, whereas it enhanced that of antinuclear critics.

After the shock of Three Mile Island, the NRC and the nuclear industry focused on a series of issues that had commanded only limited interest before the accident. These were intended to reduce the likelihood of another major accident and, if one did occur, to enhance the ability of the NRC, the utility, and the public to cope with it. At the direction of the NRC, power companies improved plants that were operating or under construction. After a moratorium of more than one year, the NRC resumed issuing operating licenses for completed nuclear units in August 1980. By 1989, it had granted full-power licenses to more than forty reactors, most of which had been under construction since the mid-1970s. No new nuclear power reactors were ordered after 1978, and many earlier orders were canceled.

In 2000, 103 nuclear power plants were operating in the United States, providing about 20 percent of the nation's generating capacity. By that time, the debate over nuclear power had faded as a national issue, although it continued to trigger heated arguments in many local areas where plants were located.

Watts Bar 1, which came online on 7 February 1996, was the last U.S. commercial nuclear reactor to go online. This is often quoted as evidence of a successful worldwide campaign for nuclear power phase-out. However, even in the United States and throughout Europe, investment in research and in the nuclear fuel cycle has continued, and some nuclear industry experts predict electricity shortages, fossil-fuel price increases, global warming and heavy metal emissions from fossil-fuel use, new technology such as passively safe plants, and national energy security will renew the demand for nuclear power plants.

As of March 2010, U.S. regulators were expecting applications to build twenty-six new nuclear power reactors. As of July 2010, fourteen of the new applications were for Westinghouse's AP1000 reactor, which has been criticized on safety grounds; the NRC anticipates completing the overall design certification review for the AP1000 around September 2011. Several license applications filed with the NRC for proposed new reactors have been suspended or canceled. After the 11 March 2011 Tohoku earthquake and tsunami, which severely damaged the Fukushima Daiichi nuclear plant facilities, American and world leaders undertook serious reevaluation of nuclear power as an alternative fuel source.

[*See also* **Antinuclear Movement; Atomic Energy Commission; Energy Policy: Environmentalism; Nuclear Regulatory Commission; Regulatory Agencies, Federal;** ***and*** **Truman, Harry S.**]

BIBLIOGRAPHY

Balogh, Brian. *Chain Reaction: Expert Debate and Public Participation in American Commercial Nuclear Power, 1945–1975*. Cambridge, UK; New York: Cambridge University Press, 1991.

Mazuzan George T., and J. Samuel Walker. *Controlling the Atom: The Beginnings of Nuclear Regulation, 1946–1962*. Berkeley: University of California Press, 1984.

Morone, Joseph G., and Edward J. Woodhouse. *The Demise of Nuclear Energy?* New Haven, Conn.: Yale University Press, 1989.

Rees, Joseph V. *Hostages of Each Other: The Transformation of Nuclear Safety since Three Mile Island*. Chicago: University of Chicago Press, 1994.

Walker, J. Samuel. *Containing the Atom: Nuclear Regulation in a Changing Environment, 1963–1971*. Berkeley: University of California Press, 1992.

J. Samuel Walker; revised and updated by Pearson Bramblett

NUCLEAR REGULATORY COMMISSION

The Nuclear Regulatory Commission (NRC) was created by the Energy Reorganization Act of 1974 to assume the regulatory duties of the Atomic Energy Commission (AEC), which the law abolished. The AEC had become the target of sharp criticism in the public debate over the safety of commercial nuclear power, partly because it had a statutory mandate both to regulate and to promote the nuclear industry. The NRC's responsibilities were limited to regulating the safety of nuclear power and other civilian applications of nuclear energy.

The NRC, headed by five commissioners appointed by the president of United States, began operations in January 1975. Most of its staff members were holdovers from the AEC, but the new agency hoped to dispel the widespread public suspicion of the AEC by demonstrating its toughness as a regulator. This proved difficult, if not impossible. As the public debate over nuclear power safety raged on, former critics of the AEC were not inclined to regard the NRC more charitably. The NRC's efforts to overcome these suspicions were hampered by a serious fire at an Alabama nuclear power plant in 1975, highly publicized allegations that the NRC's radiation-protection regulations and reactor-safety requirements were too lax, and growing concern about nuclear weapons proliferation.

In March 1979, the worst accident in the history of commercial nuclear power in the United States occurred at Unit 2 of the Three Mile Island plant near Harrisburg, Pennsylvania. A series of mechanical failures and human errors uncovered the core of the reactor and melted about half of it. The plant suffered irreparable damage, and the credibility of the nuclear industry and the NRC fared almost as badly. Although very little radiation escaped into the environment, the accident intensified doubts about nuclear power safety and seriously undermined public support for the technology.

In the aftermath of Three Mile Island, the NRC devoted increased attention to a number of issues that the accident highlighted. These included ways in which a series of minor failures could lead to a major accident, the need for improved operator training, better means to assess the probability of reactor accidents, and upgraded emergency preparedness and planning. In the absence of orders for new plants, the agency allocated more of its resources to regulating the safety of existing plants, setting standards for the decommissioning of closed plants, and evaluating the complex and politically sensitive issue of the disposal of radioactive waste materials.

[*See also* **Antinuclear Movement; Atomic Energy Commission; Environmentalism; Federal Government, Executive Branch: Other Departments;** *and* **Nuclear Power.**]

BIBLIOGRAPHY

Okrent, David. *Nuclear Reactor Safety: On the History of the Regulatory Process*. Madison: University of Wisconsin Press, 1981.

Walker, J. Samuel. *A Short History of Nuclear Regulation, 1946–1990*. Washington, D.C.: Office of the Secretary, U.S. Nuclear Regulatory Commission, 1993.

J. Samuel Walker

NULLIFICATION

The origins of the doctrine of nullification lie in the 1790s, when strict construction of the Constitution, states' rights, and hostility to national "consolidation" became the principles of the new Jeffersonian Republican Party. When a Congress dominated by the Federalist Party passed the Alien and Sedition Acts in 1798 to stifle domestic dissent in anticipation of war with France, Republican leader Thomas Jefferson, in his draft of the Kentucky Resolutions, declared "nullification" the "natural right" of a state in response to a federal act deemed unconstitutional. James Madison's complementary Virginia Resolutions asserted that states "have the right and are in duty bound to interpose for arresting the evil" of unconstitutional federal legislation. Exactly how a state could exercise the right of nullification remained unclear.

In response to high import duties adopted by Congress in 1828 and 1832, many citizens of South Carolina ardently embraced ideas of nullification and interposition. A high protective tariff, as distinct from low import duties levied to raise revenue, they had come to believe, represented an unconstitutional tax designed to enrich the industrializing Northeast at the expense of the agricultural South. Moreover, South Carolina's leaders, governing the only state with a population more than half slave, feared that the enhanced federal authority encouraged by the protective tariff could eventually be turned against the institution of slavery. John C. Calhoun, the foremost exponent of nullification theory, repeatedly invoked the language and principles of 1798. As his "Fort Hill Address" of 1831 insisted, "This right of interposition, thus solemnly asserted by the State of Virginia, be called what it may—State-right, veto, nullification, or by any other name—I conceive to be the fundamental principle of our system." A state's right to declare null and void within its borders a federal branch of the solemn constitutional compact among sovereign and independent states, Calhoun concluded, would serve to prevent the creation of a "consolidated" government dictating the agenda of a numerical majority. Once a state convention had vetoed a federal law, the contested legislation could be legitimated only through a constitutional amendment ratified by conventions in the requisite three-quarters of the states. When a South Carolina convention voted in 1832 to nullify the contested tariffs and no other state followed suit, the possibility that President Andrew Jackson, an ardent nationalist, might use military means to enforce federal authority was averted only by a congressional compromise in 1833 that promised lower import duties. Calhoun always portrayed nullification as a process designed to preserve the union, but he himself acknowledged that secession could follow interposition if repeated abuses of the Constitution went uncorrected.

Although the outcome of the Civil War seemed to negate the principle of state sovereignty that underpinned both secession and nullification, in 1956 and 1957 eight southern states, led by Virginia, exhumed the doctrine of interposition against court-ordered school desegregation. The Supreme Court had the final say, upholding a lower court ruling in *United States v. Louisiana* (1960) "that interposition is not a constitutional doctrine. If taken seriously, it is illegal defiance of constitutional authority."

[*See also* **Alien and Sedition Acts; Calhoun, John C.; Constitution; Federalist Party; Jackson, Andrew; Jefferson, Thomas; Republican Party; Segregation; States' Rights; States' Rights Party; Tariffs; Taxation;** *and* **Virginia and Kentucky Resolutions.**]

BIBLIOGRAPHY

Bartley, Numan V. *The New South, 1945–1980.* Baton Rouge: Louisiana State University Press, 1995.

Freehling, William W. *Prelude to Civil War: The Nullification Controversy in South Carolina, 1816–1836.* New York: Harper & Row, 1966.

Shearer Davis Bowman

O

OBAMA, BARACK

Barack Obama is the forty-fourth president of the United States and the nation's first African American chief executive. He was born in Honolulu, Hawai'i, on 4 August 1961. Obama is the son of Barack Hussein Obama Sr., a black African from Kenya, and Ann Dunham, a white American from Kansas. The marriage ended in divorce. In 1967, Obama's mother married an Indonesian man, and the family moved to Jakarta.

Obama returned to Hawai'i in 1971 to live with his maternal grandparents. He attended an academically demanding college preparatory school in Honolulu and went on to Occidental College for his first two college years, completing his education at Columbia University. He graduated in 1983 with a major in political science. As graduation approached, Obama decided to become a community organizer. He found a position with a Chicago church–based organization that involved running job training and tenants' rights programs in a predominately black public housing project. After several years as an organizer, he concluded that he would be better able to serve the poor if he became an attorney. He was accepted by Harvard Law School, which he entered in 1988.

Obama proved to be an outstanding student. In his second year, he was elected president (the equivalent of editor) of the prestigious *Harvard Law Review*. Obama's editorship was noteworthy for his success in working with the editorial board of a wide range of political persuasions, an early sign of the conciliatory leadership style he was to evince in politics. Because he was the first African American to head the law review, his selection was widely reported, and he was awarded a contract for the book that appeared in 1995 with the title *Dreams from My Father: A Story of Race and Inheritance.* Obama graduated from law school in 1991 and returned to Chicago, where he directed a project that registered large numbers of African Americans to vote. He also joined a law firm that specialized in civil rights and taught a popular course in constitutional law at the University of Chicago Law School.

Political Ascent. In 1996, an Illinois state Senate seat representing Chicago's South Side became vacant. Obama ran for it, was elected, and served from 1997 to 2004. For most of this period, he was limited in what he could accomplish, because the senate was under Republican control. The Democrats came to power in 2003, however, and Obama was able to build a substantial record. His signature law ended the practice of coercing confessions in potential homicide cases by requiring the videotaping of interrogations. Undeterred by initial resistance, Obama responded with a campaign of persuasion that won over skeptics of both parties. The bill was passed by a unanimous Senate vote.

Early in 2003, Obama won the Illinois Democratic primary for an open seat in the U.S. Senate. Between the nomination and the general election, he was invited to be the keynote speaker at the Democratic National Convention, an event that transformed his political career. Obama's address electrified the convention, making him an instant political celebrity. Within moments, he had the attention of the noisy delegates. Speaking with pride of his mixed racial heritage, he declared that "there's not a liberal America and a conservative America—there's the United States of America," and "there is not a Black America and a White America and Latino America and Asian America—there's the United States of America." With his newfound visibility, he was elected to the U.S. Senate with a record 70 percent of the vote.

On 10 February 2007, Obama announced his candidacy for the presidency. He was one of three frontrunners for the Democratic nomination. The others were ex–first lady Hillary Clinton and former North Carolina senator John Edwards. By February, Edwards had suspended his campaign after running third in his home state. Meanwhile, Obama opened up a gradually increasing delegate lead over Clinton. The contest continued until June, when Clinton conceded. Obama's Republican opponent was Senator John McCain of Arizona. Their respective running mates were Delaware Senator Joseph Biden and Alaska governor Sarah Palin.

As the candidate of the party that held the White House, McCain was particularly hurt by the unpopularity of President George W. Bush, who had led the nation into an intractable war in Iraq and the most severe economic downturn since the Great Depression. Obama won a decisive victory with 53 percent of the popular vote and an electoral vote margin of ninety-seven. The Democrats also won commanding leads in both houses of Congress.

The Obama Presidency. Obama began his presidency with an inaugural address that alternated between the soaring rhetoric that is standard for such occasions and a straightforward enumeration of his administration's policy agenda. The first major goal for the Obama Administration was to take action against the economic crisis. Within weeks after Obama took office, Congress passed and signed the American Recovery and Reinvestment Act of 2009, a $787 billion economic stimulus. By the final months of 2010, there was evidence that it had contributed to a slight economic upturn, but high unemployment continued into the third year of Obama's first term.

The proposal in Obama's first-year legislative program that had the greatest potential for placing him on the short list of chief executives who have presided over major policy breakthroughs relates to health care. As Obama pointed out in a 10 September 2009 address to a joint session of Congress, the United States had long been the only highly developed nation not to guarantee health care to all of its citizens. Obama stated in general terms the provisions he wanted the health care bill to include, leaving it to the lawmakers to fill in the specifics.

By late 2009, both the House and the Senate had passed health insurance bills that were broadly consistent with his guidelines. The two bills then needed to be reconciled, but several pro-life House Democrats balked at what they viewed as provisions in the Senate bill that would permit government funding of abortions. Obama then broke the logjam by promising to issue an executive order declaring that the bill did not authorize the termination of pregnancies.

Obama's ambitious domestic program did not prevent him from being active in the international sphere. He placed a particular priority on improving relations with the Islamic world. In a 4 June 2010 address at Cairo University, Obama called for "a new beginning between the United States and Muslims around the world" and declared "the truth that America and Islam are not exclusive and need not be in competition." Obama's responses to the two wars he inherited differed. In the case of Iraq, his administration announced that the United States would end its combat mission on 31 August 2010 and concentrate on helping the Iraqi military and protecting civilian and military personnel. In the case of Afghanistan, he presided over an extensive policy review that resulted in a two-stage policy. First, the American troop level would be briefly increased to enable Afghanistan to strengthen its military and political institutions. Then, in July 2011, the United States would begin to withdraw its troops. Neither nation was to be abandoned, but both were to be brought to the point at which they could defend themselves.

The final major legislative enactment before Congress adjourned for the 2010 midterm election was the most sweeping reform of the nation's financial industry since the Great Depression, the Dodd–Frank Wall Street Reform and Consumer Protection Act. This law was designed to reduce the likelihood of the kind of meltdown of the banking system that produced the financial crisis of 2008. It did so by regulating risky banking practices and better monitoring the banking system. Obama signed the bill into law on 21 July 2010.

Obama's strong electoral showing in 2008 led to the election of Democrats from normally Republican districts so it was inevitable that his party would lose seats in the 2010 Congressional election. To his chagrin, the Democrats experienced the greatest seat loss of any presidential party since 1938, losing control of the House of Representatives and losing six seats in the Senate. But despite assertions that Obama had been repudiated by the voters, he scored a number of successes when Congress reconvened for a six-week postelection session. The legislators ratified a controversial nuclear arms reduction treaty and repealed the military's don't-ask-don't-tell policy, which made it necessary for gays to conceal orientation. Obama agreed to the Republicans on an extension of former president George W. Bush's tax cuts for the wealthy in exchange for a number of measures designed to stimulate the economy.

The new Congress convened on 6 January 2011 with the Republicans in control of the House. As Obama put it in his 25 January 2011

State of the Union address, "New laws will only pass with support from Democrats and Republicans." Focusing on policies that in principle might receive bipartisan support, he came out for improving the nation's infrastructure, taking steps that would make industry more competitive, and reducing the national debt. By the time this entry went to press, Obama was preoccupied with events that could not be predicted when he gave his address, most dramatically a wave of protest and governmental transformation in North Africa. It was inevitable that there would be more surprises between his State of the Union address and the 2012 presidential election.

[*See also* Clinton, Hillary Rodham; *and* Democratic Party.]

BIBLIOGRAPHY

Alter, Jonathon. *The Promise: President Obama, Year One*. New York: Simon & Schuster, 2010.

Mendell, David. *Obama: From Promise to Power.* New York: Amistad/HarperCollins, 2007.

Obama, Barack. *Dreams from My Father: A Story of Race and Inheritance.* New York: Times Books, 1995.

Obama, Barack. *The Audacity of Hope.* New York: Crown, 2006.

Remnick, David. *The Bridge: The Life and Rise of Barack Obama.* New York: Alfred A. Knopf, 2010.

Woodward, Bob. *Obama's Wars.* New York: Simon & Schuster, 2010.

Fred I. Greenstein

OBSCENITY AND PORNOGRAPHY

Virtually every society has struggled with the question of what to do about representations of sexual activity. Such material is prevalent because it manifests the tensions that arise between desire and social norms. Artful treatments of sex enhance our understanding of these tensions. But because societies are ambivalent about sexual freedom and are concerned about the impact of degrading sexual depictions on the quality of sexuality, they attempt by law to distinguish proper from improper display or to prohibit display altogether.

This struggle is particularly acute in a liberal democracy, in which the values of liberty and democracy often conflict. Liberal principles hold that all forms of expression should be protected by the First Amendment unless they cause direct, demonstrable harm to others. Although violent erotic materials have been shown in laboratory studies to make males more inclined to commit violence against women, such studies have not demonstrated direct, systematic harm. The liberal approach would limit regulation to protecting minors and the sensibilities of unconsenting adults. Democratic principles, however, endorse the right of majorities to restrain liberty to protect society from potential harm and to support communitarian norms of sexual virtue.

Although the Supreme Court has ratified the imposition of liberal principles in cases involving political or religious speech, it has allowed some measure of community control by holding that the First Amendment does not protect all forms of expression. Expression deemed to possess social value merits protection unless it causes substantial and demonstrable direct harm, whereas less valuable expression is "unprotected." It may be prohibited if the government simply shows a good reason to be concerned about its potential impact. In the seminal 1942 case of *Chaplinsky v. State of New Hampshire,* the Court established the rationale that distinguishes protected and unprotected speech. Obscenity and lewdness, libel, and fighting words are not protected by the First Amendment because "such expressions are no essential part of any exposition of ideas, and are of such slight social value as a step to truth that any benefit that may be derived from them is clearly outweighed by the social interest in order and morality" (p. 572).

Traditionally, American law has used the concept of "obscenity" to draw the line between prohibited and permitted sexual representations. Obscenity is not the same thing as "pornography." Etymologically, obscenity refers to those things considered disgusting, foul, or morally unhealthy. Pornography is broader in meaning, pertaining to depictions of sexual lewdness or erotic behavior. Pornography may not be obscene.

Chaplinsky's rationale for First Amendment protection expressed a traditional notion of moral virtue and a conventional theory of truth as a purely cognitive process. But ensuing decades challenged these assumptions, as moral consensus concerning sexuality gave way to the experimental 1960s and 1970s, and the understandings of depth psychology and emotivist aesthetics supplemented traditional notions of knowledge.

Until 1957, obscenity cases simply dealt with the statutory meaning of obscenity. The absence of constitutional challenge reflected the strength of the moral consensus against obscenity. But as pornographic representations and literature became more available after World War II, the Supreme Court was eventually confronted with a constitutional challenge to suppression of pornography. In *Roth v. United States* (1957), Justice William Brennan held that obscenity is unprotected because it is "utterly without redeeming social importance" (p. 484). Brennan confined obscenity to "material which deals with sex in a manner appealing to prurient interest." He defined prurient interest as either "[h]aving a tendency to excite lustful thoughts" or as a "shameful and morbid interest in sex" (p. 487). He then promulgated the following test for obscenity: "whether to the average person, applying contemporary community standards, the dominant theme of the material taken as a whole appeals to the prurient interest" (p. 489).

Roth's test focused on prurience. Yet prurience was never adequately defined, and the rest of the test provided little guidance as to what is obscene.

In *Jacobellis v. Ohio* (1964), the Court recognized that it had to make its own independent evaluation of the nature of allegedly obscene material in each case. This compelled the Court to create a decidedly more liberal three-part test in the 1966 Fanny Hill case, *A Book Named "John Cleland's Memoirs of a Woman of Pleasure" v. Attorney General of Massachusetts*. Justice Brennan declared that material is obscene if its dominant theme is prurient; it is "patently offensive because it affronts contemporary community standards"; and it is "utterly without redeeming social value" (pp. 419–420). Only the most explicit material could meet the *Memoirs* test, which shifted emphasis from prurience (*Roth*) to patent offensiveness and the presence or absence of even minimal social value. The minimal social value test, in effect, required the prosecution to prove a negative—always a difficult task. Subsequently, the Court began to overturn virtually every obscenity prosecution it encountered unless the material was sold to minors or advertised salaciously (e.g., *Redrup v. New York*, 1967). Concurrently, the availability of progressively explicit materials mushroomed as publishers pushed the new standard to its limits. Antipornography activists reacted by turning pornography and the "permissive" Warren Court into major national issues.

In *Stanley v. Georgia* (1969), the Warren Court ruled that the constitutional right of privacy prohibited punishing someone for using illegal obscenity in the home. But the Burger court refused to carry out the logical implications of Stanley and restored power to communities to control sexual materials. In *Miller v. California* (1973), the Court promulgated a revised test. Material is obscene if its predominant theme is prurient according to the sensibilities of an average person of the community; it depicts sexual conduct in a patently offensive way; and, taken as a whole, it "lacks serious literary, artistic, political, or scientific value" (p. 24).

Miller's reformulation of the social value test made it less likely that otherwise obscene works would slip over the threshold of protection by the spurious inclusion of minimal social commentary. But in another respect, it simply reaffirmed *Memoirs*' implicit emphasis on hard-core pornography, because Chief Justice Warren Burger stated that only hard-core depictions could be designated patently offensive. Burger presented some "plain examples" of such depictions, including "patently offensive representations or descriptions of ultimate sex acts" and "lewd exhibition of the genitals" (p. 25). Nudity alone, or pictures of sexual behavior short of "ultimate acts," is not obscene.

Miller's test is still the linchpin of obscenity doctrine. Courts have become fairly adept at distinguishing hard-core from non-hard-core pornography. Literary works that deal with sexuality are strongly protected, and magazines like *Playboy* and *Penthouse* are substantially secure from constitutional attack.

Problems persist, however. Although *Miller* has resulted in fairly objective adjudication, decisions at the margin are unavoidably subjective. Only a direct-harm approach would alleviate this problem. But the Supreme Court has been unwilling to forsake completely nonliberal values in this area of expression. On the other side of the issue, some conservatives and feminists contend that *Miller* conceded too much to liberalism, crippling the community's ability to curb the spread of all but the most explicit forms of pornography. Obscenity law often delivers less than it modestly promises.

In reaction to these problems, some feminists in the early 1980s advocated making pornography a new exception to First Amendment freedoms. They defined pornography broadly, as the sexually explicit subordination of women, and provided no provision for redeeming artistic or social value. Lower federal courts held this approach unconstitutional (*American Booksellers Association v. Hudnut,* 1984). But the Supreme Court has allowed some hedging of Miller's quasi-liberal approach in specific areas. It has allowed zoning control of nonobscene pornography (*City of Renton v. Playtime Theatres, Inc.,* 1986) and upheld the Federal Communications Commission's decision to limit (not ban) the availability of nonobscene "indecent" expression in broadcasting (*Federal Communications Commission v. Pacifica Foundation,* 1978). In addition, the Court ruled that states may ban knowing distribution of nonobscene pornography made with minors as subjects (*New York v. Ferber,* 1982).

These measures have enhanced the power of democratic controls but (with the exception of child pornography in *Ferber*) have not expanded the domain of the prohibitable. In general, obscenity law maintains a balance between liberal and democratic values that favors liberalism. The Supreme Court could make application of the law easier by adopting a fully liberal standard that reconciled sexual expression with most other expression, but such a reconciliation would be tantamount to the abandonment of democratic control in this highly charged issue.

The rise of the Internet has raised a host of new issues as thousands of websites have made pornography available to minors. The Court has struck down a federal law prohibiting the knowing transmission to minors of indecent or patently offensive messages (*Reno v. ACLU*, 1994) and a federal law that prohibited making images of actual adults or computer-created images ("virtual pornography") that appear to be images of minors engaged in sexually explicit conduct (*Ashcroft v. Free Speech Coalition*, 2002). These laws were not sufficiently limited to protecting minors. But the Court upheld the federal Children's Internet Protection Act, which requires libraries receiving federal funds to use Internet filters to screen out pornography (*United States v. American Library Association*, 2003).

[***See also*** **Burger, Warren; Civil Liberties; Federal Communications Commission; Privacy;** ***and*** **Supreme Court, U.S.**]

BIBLIOGRAPHY

Downs, Donald A. *The New Politics of Pornography*. Chicago: University of Chicago Press, 1989.

MacKinnon, Catherine. "Pornography, Civil Rights, and Speech." *Harvard Civil Rights-Civil Liberties Law Review* 20 (1985): 1–70.

Randall, Richard S. *Freedom and Taboo: Pornography and the Politics of a Self Divided*. Berkeley: University of California Press, 1989.

Donald A. Downs

O'CONNOR, SANDRA DAY

(1930–), first woman justice of the U.S. Supreme Court. A native of El Paso, Texas, O'Connor graduated third in her class at Stanford Law School in 1952, but encountered difficulty in finding employment in the legal profession, which was still largely closed to women. Eventually, after a career in the public sector, including a term as an Arizona state senator and a judgeship on the Arizona Court of Appeals, O'Connor was appointed to the Supreme Court by President Ronald Reagan in 1981.

O'Connor's principal contributions to the Court's constitutional jurisprudence came in the areas of religion and federalism. In *Lynch v. Donnelly* (1984), she outlined an approach to cases involving the First Amendment's establishment clause that focused on when the government could be said to have "endorsed" religion. A decade later, that approach appeared to command a majority of the Court.

In federalism cases, O'Connor ardently defended state sovereignty. Her dissent in *Garcia v. San Antonio Metropolitan Transit Authority* (1985) described the "essence" of federalism as a recognition "that the States have legitimate interests which the National Government is bound to respect." In *New York v. United States* (1992), she led the first Court effort in decades to put teeth in the Tenth Amendment as a substantive limitation on federal power. After initially appearing to endorse a constitutional jurisprudence favored by conservatives during the chief justiceship of Warren Burger, O'Connor moved to a more centrist position during William Rehnquist's tenure as chief justice, often joining majorities in closely divided cases. Despite her status as the first woman justice, she did not play a conspicuous role in gender discrimination cases. On 1 July 2005, O'Connor announced her plan to retire upon the confirmation of her successor. On 19 July, President George W. Bush nominated D.C. Circuit Judge John G. Roberts Jr. to succeed O'Connor. O'Connor expected to leave the Court before the next term started on 3 October 2005. However, Chief Justice William Rehnquist died on 3 September. Two days later, Bush withdrew Roberts as his nominee for her seat and instead appointed him to fill the vacant office of Chief Justice. O'Connor again agreed to stay on the Court until her replacement was confirmed. On 31 October, Bush nominated

Third Circuit Judge Samuel Alito to replace O'Connor; Alito was confirmed and sworn in on 31 January 2006. O'Connor continues to hear cases and has rendered over a dozen opinions in federal appellate courts across the country, filling in as a substitute judge when vacations or vacancies leave their three-member panels understaffed.

[*See also* **Church and State, Separation of; Reagan, Ronald; States' Rights;** *and* **Supreme Court, U.S.**]

BIBLIOGRAPHY

Gelfand, M. David, and Keith Werthan. "Federalism and the Separation of Powers on a 'Conservative' Court." *Tulane Law Review* 64 (1990): 1443–1476.

Huber, Peter. *Sandra Day O'Connor: Supreme Court Justice*. New York: Facts on File, 1990.

G. Edward White; revised and updated by Pearson Bramblett

OKLAHOMA CITY BOMBING

On the morning of 19 April 1995, a huge explosion ripped through the Alfred P. Murrah Federal Building in downtown Oklahoma City. Caused by a lethal mixture of diesel fuel and ammonium nitrate packed into a rental truck parked nearby, the blast spread death and destruction throughout a forty-eight-square-block area, overturning automobiles and damaging 300 buildings. At the time of the explosion, nearly 1,000 people were in the Murrah Building, which housed sixteen federal agencies and a daycare center. The entire north face of the structure collapsed and each of the nine floors received extensive damage. Emergency personnel frantically searched the Murrah Building for survivors. The final human toll numbered 168 killed, including many children, and at least 700 injured.

A short time later, two men were arrested and charged with the bombing. Both had ties to ultra–right wing paramilitary groups that viewed the federal government as an evil force to be confronted and destroyed. Timothy McVeigh, a U.S. Army veteran who planted the bomb, was convicted and sentenced to death. Terry Nichols, his accomplice, was sentenced to life in prison. Evidence suggested that the bombing was timed to coincide with the second anniversary of a raid by the Bureau of Alcohol, Tobacco, and Firearms on the compound of the Branch Davidians, a heavily armed apocalyptic sect in Waco, Texas, led by David Koresh. The raid, in which some 80 Branch Davidians perished when fire of undetermined origin destroyed the compound, had infuriated McVeigh as an example of overweening federal power.

The Oklahoma City bombing stands as the worst act of domestic terrorism in American history. An active survivors' association soon took shape, and the Murrah Building site became a major focus of mourning rituals, including thousands of poems, memorabilia, and teddy bears left at the chain-link fence surrounding the ruin. In October 1998, architectural plans for a permanent memorial on the site were unveiled at a ceremony attended by Vice President Al Gore and other officials. It was completed and opened to the public on 19 April 2000, the fifth anniversary of the bombing.

BIBLIOGRAPHY

Hamm, Mark. *Apocalypse in Oklahoma*. Boston: Northeastern University Press, 1997.

Hansen, Jon. *Oklahoma Rescue*. New York: Ballantine Books, 1995.

Oklahoma Department of Civil Emergency Management. *After Action Report: Alfred R. Murrah Federal Building Bombing, 10 April 1995, Oklahoma City, Oklahoma*.

Serrano, Richard. *One of Ours: Timothy McVeigh and the Oklahoma City Bombing.* New York: W. W. Norton, 1998.

Richard Lowitt

OTHER AMERICA, THE

The Other America: Poverty in the United States (1962) was written by Michael Harrington (1928–1989), a young socialist whose first encounter with poverty had come during the two years he lived on New York City's Lower East Side as part of the Catholic Worker movement, a ministry to the poor founded by Dorothy Day (1897–1980). Harrington became known as "the man who discovered poverty" when his book caught the eye of President John F. Kennedy. Influenced by the book, Kennedy proposed to his advisers shortly before his assassination that the federal government undertake a "War on Poverty."

Harrington's book made two main points. First, poverty was rampant in the United States, with 40 to 50 million victims, despite the prevailing national belief in the "affluent society." "That the poor are invisible is one of the most important things about them," Harrington wrote. "They are not simply neglected and forgotten as in the old rhetoric of reform; what is much worse, they are not seen."

Second, Harrington argued that a "culture of poverty" existed in the United States. Suffering the effects of generations of inadequate education, nutrition, housing, and medical care, the poor lacked both the ability and the aspiration to improve their lot in life. Thus, poverty could not be eliminated either by an expanding economy or by exhortations to the poor to lift themselves up by their own bootstraps. "Society," Harrington concluded, "must help [the poor] before they can help themselves."

[*See also* **Great Society; Kennedy, John F.; Poverty; Social Policy: Public Welfare; Socialism;** *and* **Socialist Party.**]

BIBLIOGRAPHY

Katz, Michael. *The Undeserving Poor: From the War on Poverty to the War on Welfare.* New York: Pantheon Books, 1989.

Patterson, James T. *America's Struggle against Poverty, 1900–1985,* rev. ed. Cambridge, Mass.: Harvard University Press, 1986.

Maurice Isserman

P

PANAMA CANAL

Since colonization by Spain in 1502, Panama's unique and advantageous geographical location has defined its economic, political, and social history. Beginning with Panama's U.S.-supported uprising against Colombia (of which it was a province) in 1903 and the subsequent U.S. completion of a French-begun canal in the early twentieth century, the trajectory of Panamanian politics was for almost a century intimately tied to the foreign policy of the United States. The Isthmian Canal Convention of 1904 granted the United States occupation and control of the ten-mile-wide (sixteen-kilometer) Canal Zone in which the United States maintained six military bases and an infantry brigade.

For most of the twentieth century, Panama exercised essentially no sovereignty over this slice of its country. This situation was begrudgingly accepted by Panamanian leaders since the canal provided a number of economic benefits and served as a useful scapegoat for periodic unrest. Under the original Hay–Herrán Treaty of 1903, the United States paid Panama annual payments for the canal. However, Article 136 of the treaty also stipulated that the United States could intervene militarily in Panama if Washington thought it necessary to maintain order.

A drastic shift in the political landscape occurred following the 1968 military coup by the Panamanian National Guard. The emergent leader, General Omar Torrijos, established a more nationalistic stance vis-à-vis the United States while instituting numerous populist labor, social, and economic reforms. For the next thirteen years, relations with Washington worsened as Torrijos increasingly sought to distance Panama from U.S. hegemony and to acquire full sovereignty over the canal.

President Gerald Ford proposed the turnover of the Panama Canal to Torrijos, and Ronald Reagan found crowds cheering when he attacked the proposal. Reagan declared the proposed turnover threatened national security because it deprived the United States of easy access between the Pacific and Atlantic oceans. Reagan's opposition to a turnover of the canal divided the conservative movement, setting the stage for a subsequent fight in the Carter administration.

Two treaties were negotiated between the United States and Panama in August 1977 to transfer legal title of the American Canal Zone to Panama in 1999. Immediately, the grassroots right in the United States framed the issue as a battle between Wall Street and the American people. Grassroots conservatives maintained that eastern banks in the United States initiated the turnover to protect loans that they had extended to the Torrijos government. The American Conservative Union launched a series of massive mailing campaigns against the treaty. Not all conservatives opposed the return of the canal, including William F. Buckley Jr., founding editor of the *National Review,* and Hollywood actor John Wayne.

Carter drew on probusiness interests to gain support for the treaties, including the U.S. Chamber of Commerce, banks, shipping companies, and larger multinational corporations with investments in Panama. The administration hired F. Clinton White, a Republican strategist, and Lawrence F. O'Brien to lobby the Senate for ratification.

In the Carter administration, an agreement was struck that produced the 1977 Panama Canal treaties, which pledged to turn over the canal to Panama on 31 December 1999. Although most Americans in polls opposed the treaty, the Panama Neutrality treaty was ratified by the Senate in March 1978 by a single vote. The battle over the Panama Canal treaties revealed an insurgent grassroots right that laid the foundations for Ronald Reagan's defeat of Jimmy Carter in the 1980 election.

Torrijos's death in a mysterious plane crash in 1981 drastically altered Panamanian domestic politics and the bilateral relationship with the United States. The ascension to power of former chief of intelligence and longtime Central Intelligence Agency informant, Manuel Noriega, exacerbated the situation. Noriega wielded power as a brutal Machiavellian dictator and transformed the National Guard into his personal praetorian guard, promoted himself to the rank of general in 1983, shredded all semblances of civil rights, and beat and cheated the political opposition into partial submission. The emergence of a Panamanian leadership so potentially antagonistic to the United States and its access to the Canal concerned U.S. policy makers greatly.

In 1984, Noriega permitted the first civilian elections in sixteen years but when it was clear that opposition candidate Arnulfo Arias would win, the vote tabulation was halted and Noriega's hand-picked candidate, Nicolás Barletta, was declared the winner. On the basis of defending democracy, combating drug trafficking, and protecting the integrity of the canal treaties, the United States invaded Panama on the morning of 20 December 1989. Using overwhelming firepower, the United States quickly routed the National Guard and arrested Noriega after a brief standoff at the Papal Nuncio. Following the return of democracy, the American invasion was the catalyst for a dramatic shift in Panama's political structure.

[***See also*** **Buckley, William F., Jr.; Ford, Gerald R.;** ***and*** **Reagan, Ronald.**]

BIBLIOGRAPHY

Clymer, Adam. *Drawing the Line in the Big Ditch: The Panama Canal Treaties and the Rise of the Right.* Lawrence: University Press of Kansas, 2008.

Harding, Robert C. *The History of Panama.* Westport, Conn.: Greenwood Press, 2006.

Harding, Robert C. *Military Foundations of Panamanian Politics.* New Brunswick, N.J.: Transaction, 2001.

Robert C. Harding

PARIS, TREATY OF

One of the greatest triumphs of American diplomatic history, the Peace of Paris (1783) between the United States and Great Britain ended the Revolutionary War and achieved American independence. After the victory of George Washington and his French allies at Yorktown in 1782, the Continental Congress named five commissioners to conduct peace talks with the British in Paris. Only three were able to attend—John Adams, Benjamin Franklin, and John Jay—but their combined talents proved indispensable to the final outcome.

Although the French expected a coordinated diplomatic strategy because of the Franco-American alliance of 1778, the U.S. envoys distrusted European diplomats and pursued their own goals. The results justified their decision. They won from the British recognition of American independence, fishing rights for Americans in Canadian waters, and control of the vast area from the Allegheny Mountains to the Mississippi River. The British negotiators insisted only on language safeguarding Loyalists to the British cause against persecution by state and local governments in the United States. The treaty was officially signed on 3 September 1783, and the Continental Congress gave its approval a few months later. Adams, Franklin, and Jay had achieved the maximum success from the victories that American troops, aided by French strength, had won on the battlefield.

[*See also* **Adams, John; Continental Congress; Franklin, Benjamin; Jay, John;** *and* **Washington, George.**]

BIBLIOGRAPHY

Dull, Jonathan R. *A Diplomatic History of the American Revolution.* New Haven: Yale University Press, 1985.

Morris, Richard B. *The Peacemakers: The Great Powers and American Independence.* New York: Harper & Row, 1965.

Lewis L. Gould

PARTY SYSTEM

In 1966 when Richard P. McCormick published his pathbreaking work, *The Second American Party System,* few historians were familiar with this terminology. The conventional wisdom was that the United States invented modern parties in the 1790s and had had a continuing two-party system since that time. Historians' understanding of political parties focused on a relatively consistent conflict between liberal and conservative parties, setting a cycle of periods of reform led by liberals and periods of conformity dominated by the conservatives. The long-term secular trend was toward an expansion of democracy in the form of the extension of the vote to landless men, the freed slaves, women of both races, and even those over eighteen years of age. This process was disrupted by reformist "third" parties that usually preceded a period of reform. Although the labels of the two major parties did change in the first half of the nineteenth century, the Democrats have contested the Republicans since the Civil War.

McCormick imparted a different conceptualization of party systems. His view of what previously had been called "the Age of Jackson" emerged in the political science literature from the insights of V. O. Key in the 1950s concerning "critical elections." These were the elections that altered not only voter behavior and the people in power, but also the inner workings of the political system. Key's followers, most particularly Walter Dean Burnham, projected a view of American political history that could be best characterized by a generation or more of stasis punctuated by periods of sometimes radical change—a "realignment" in the nature and substance of the two-party conflict. Of course, these scholars considered "third" parties, but "third" hardly tells the story.

Thus, since the 1960s, many political scientists and historians have described U.S. party history in terms of what is called a "realignment perspective." The historians who use these concepts have adopted the methods and modified the "perspective" to fit the traditional story of "ages and eras" and used it in a way to amplify our sense of U.S. party history. The struggle between the Federalists and the Republicans, who constituted the first party system, was essentially different from the contest between the Jacksonian Democrats and the Whigs during the second party system.

Historians who have adopted this realignment perspective have used slightly different terminology referring to a succession of "electoral systems." To a degree these terms are interchangeable since both draw on the Key/Sorauf tripartite conception of American political parties as essentially composed of the party organization, the office-holding elite, and the voters. Partisan change results in the alteration in each of these. Change is not simply in labels but also in the question of development or, perhaps more clearly, the integration of not only parties in the various branches of government, but also the parties' ability to transcend national, state, and local levels. Thus, historians can examine how well developed party systems were by looking not only at electoral results in presidential elections, but also at how integrated they are with the state and local elections and structures.

Until "the Age of Reagan," the American party system seems to have gone through a realignment cycle yielding five or six systems that generally coincide with traditional historians' "ages and eras." The first party system existed in the Jeffersonian era. The two major parties were labeled, generally the Federalists and the Republicans, although there were other labels including "Federalist Republicans" and "Americans" or "American Republicans." The first party system began in the congressional fight over the Jay Treaty in 1795 and petered out after the War of 1812. Perhaps the demise of the Federalists has been overstated by many historians, since they did run local candidates after that date, but for a decade after Monroe's election in 1816 there was a "one-party period" or "era of good feelings."

Historians have questioned how well developed the first party system actually was. There were no party organizational structures. It was basically a "system" that only existed in Congress and primarily on foreign policy matters. There was only a weak connection with the state parties. Thus, little existed upon which to build McCormack's second party system, which eventually developed to a degree that we call the Whigs and Democrats of the 1840 modern parties. There was a certain amount of party organization and a high level of electoral response that reflected partisan behavior.

Historians suggest that the late 1840s represented a period of decay of the second party system. Although partisans on both sides tended to vote for their party's candidates, the antislavery Liberty Party sucked off Whigs, especially in New York in 1844, allowing Democrat James K. Polk, a southern slaveholder, to win. Four years later, defectors from the northern Democracy, as it was called, joined the Liberty men to form the Free Soil Party and gave the presidency to the Whig candidate, Zachary Taylor. In the next election, when many of those Democrats returned to their party, a northern Democrat, Franklin Pierce, won in a three-way race.

Although the Democrats retained the presidency in 1856, the 1850s was a classic period of realignment in which two "third" parties, the nativist American Party and the antislavery Republicans, challenged the Democrats. By 1860 things were more complicated and there was a four-way fight for the presidency. Northern and southern Democrats divided and ran separate tickets. The Americans also split, with most of the northern nativists joining the Republicans to support Abraham Lincoln and the southern Americans becoming Constitutional Unionists. Lincoln won the presidency with slightly less than 40 percent of the popular vote. He received no popular votes in ten of the eleven states that would form the Confederacy.

The Civil War made little change in the party system. In the North Democrats and Republicans confronted each other, presenting contrasting partisan agendas. There was less party conflict in the Confederacy. Following the disruptions of Reconstruction, the third party system finally settled in during the Gilded Age. Although voter turnout remained high, the parties were closely divided, with the Democrats dominant in the South and the Republicans more powerful in the North.

Another critical realignment occurred in the 1890s, which led to what traditional historians call the Progressive Era. This actually meant that the fourth party system had a Republican majority, although the Democrats did elect Woodrow Wilson for two terms. The Progressive Era was followed by another period of complacency. The return to "normalcy" in the 1920s allowed the Republicans to control the presidency and Congress. However, the third-party activity in 1924 and the nomination of a Catholic by the Democrats in 1928 indicate the preconditions for the realignment that occurred in 1832 with the election of Franklin Roosevelt and a Democratic congress.

The New Deal/Fair Deal Era can also be termed the time of the fifth party system. It was disrupted by the popular presidency of the relatively nonpartisan war hero, Dwight D. Eisenhower. However, he had only one Republican Congress to work with and the Democrats regained the presidency in 1960. Thus one might argue that the fifth party system actually continued at least until 1968. Some scholars call the period from 1952 to 1968 the sixth party system. Of course there are scholarly differences and the concept of "realignment" has been attacked on various grounds, particularly that it is overly focused on presidential elections. The "eras and ages" view shared that weakness.

Some political scientists talk about contemporary realignment and dealignment. Where are we at the dawn of the twenty-first century? The New Deal system seemed to have lasted through the modest dealignment of the Eisenhower years until the election of Reagan. Since that time we have had an exchange of Republican and Democratic presidents and gridlock in Congress. There were a few third-party advances. Voter participation has declined from the late nineteenth century and in the number of people calling themselves "Independents" has increased, but at the same time a fierce partisanship of conservative Republicans and progressive Democrats exists. Thus, it is difficult to determine whether a seventh party system exists, although the debate about the role of government and social issues involving abortion and homosexuality has been consistent.

[*See also* **Democratic Party; Federalist Party; Free Soil Party; Liberty Party; Republican Party;** ***and*** **Whig Party.**]

BIBLIOGRAPHY

Chambers, William Nisbet, and Walter Dean Burnham. *The American Party Systems: Stages of Political Development*. New York: Oxford University Press, 1967.

Chambers, William Nisbet. *The First Party System*. New York: Wiley, 1972.

Clubb, Jerome M., William H. Flanagan, and Nancy H. Zingale. *Partisan Realignment: Voters, Parties and Government in American History*. Beverly Hills, Calif.: Sage, 1980.

Kleppner, Paul, et al., eds. *The Evolution of American Electoral Systems*. Westport, Conn.: Greenwood Press, 1981.

Kleppner, Paul. *The Third Electoral System, 1853–1892: Parties, Voters, and Political Cultures*. Chapel Hill: University of North Carolina Press, 1979.

Kleppner, Paul. *Continuity and Change in the Electoral Politics, 1893–1928*. New York: Greenwood Press, 1987.

Levendusky, Matthew. *The Partisan Sort: How Liberals Became Democrats and Conservatives Became Republicans*. Chicago: University of Chicago Press, 2009.

McCormick, Richard P. *The Second American Party System: Party Formation in the Jacksonian Era*. Chapel Hill: University of North Carolina Press, 1966.

Sorauf, Frank J. *Party Politics in America*. Boston: Little, Brown, 1968.

William G. Shade

PATENT AND COPYRIGHT LAW

U.S. patent and copyright law is based on Article 1, Section 8, of the Constitution, which gives Congress the power "to promote the progress of science and useful arts, by securing for limited times to authors and inventors the exclusive right to their respective writings and discoveries." This clause, when drafted in 1787, represented a culmination of legal and economic theory and practice regarding intellectual property going back at least as far as Renaissance Europe, where similar grants of exclusive rights were first recorded. In colonial America, although few patents and no copyrights in the modern sense were granted, practice generally followed English precedents. But whereas in England the Crown granted patents and copyrights as a royal prerogative, in America they were granted at first by colonial legislatures as private acts and later under general statutes enacted by the states.

In 1790, exercising its constitutional authority, Congress enacted the nation's first general patent and copyright statutes, effectively supplanting those of the states. The new statutes spelled out preconditions for the grants, general penalties to be imposed on infringers, and other details. Responsibility for issuing both patents and copyrights was assigned to the executive branch of the new government. The task of interpreting the statutes in disputed cases was left to the courts, whose decisions over the years constitute an enormous body of jurisprudence, much of which has found its way into statutory law. Periodic revisions in this body of law have sought to fine-tune the balance of interests of inventors and authors, patent and copyright owners, and the general public. Most far reaching, perhaps, have been changes to what the statutes specify as patentable and copyrightable subject matter, changes made necessary by the ever unforeseen evolution of technology in new directions.

Through much of the nineteenth century, books or other materials published abroad enjoyed little copyright protection in the United States, and U.S. publishers freely pirated foreign works. The Berne Convention of 1887, updated most recently in 1971 by the Universal Copyright Convention at Paris (accepted by the United States in 1974), helped close this loophole. At the end of the twentieth century, the genetic manipulation of plants and even animal species, as well as the rise of the Internet and online publishing, raised complicated new patent and copyright issues.

[*See also* **Constitution;** ***and*** **Jurisprudence.**]

BIBLIOGRAPHY

Bugbee, Bruce W. *The Genesis of American Patent and Copyright Law*. Washington, D.C.: Public Affairs Press, 1967.

Kendall J. Dood

PATRIOT ACT, THE

On 11 September 2001, terrorists attacked America without warning, killing 2,752 people in New York City alone. On 26 October 2001, President Bush signed into law the USA PATRIOT Act (Uniting and Strengthening America by Providing Appropriate Tools Required to Intercept and Obstruct Terrorism Act of 2001, or USAPA). The USAPA is a comprehensive antiterrorism law.

The USAPA gives law enforcement officials expansive powers and security agencies increased resources to fight terrorism, at home and abroad, including the following: (1) reducing restrictions of law enforcement powers to search telephone, email communications, medical, financial, and other records; (2) reducing restrictions on foreign intelligence gathering within the United States; (3) expanding the secretary of the treasury's authority to regulate financial transactions, particularly those involving foreign individuals and entities; (4) creating new terrorism (related) crimes, such as bulk cash smuggling and attacking mass transportation systems; (5) increasing penalties on terrorism crime; (6) expanding prohibitions against terrorism instruments, such as biological weapons; (7) lifting the statute of limitations on terrorism crimes; (8) requiring background checks for licenses to transport hazardous materials; (9) establishing more procedures to check money laundering; (10) promoting information sharing and coordination of intelligence efforts; (11) providing federal grants for terrorism prevention, antiterrorism training, and preparation and response to terrorist acts; (12) broadening the grounds for denying aliens admission to the United States based on their involvement with terrorism; and (13) allowing the attorney general to ask for the military's assistance during an emergency involving weapons of mass destruction.

USAPA powers were fashioned to alleviate problems besetting the U.S. security system, as revealed by the 9/11 Commission (e.g., the need to coordinate and integrate disparate government efforts in fighting terrorism). The USAPA anticipated the president's National Strategy for Homeland Security (July 2002; i.e., secure the homeland from attack, reduce the nation's vulnerability from attack, minimize the damage from an attack, and recover from an attack quickly).

Operationally, the USAPA is designed to shift the criminal justice paradigm, fix security lapses, and otherwise enhance law enforcement–intelligence capacities. These shifts include the following.

From crime to war metaphor: shifting counterterrorism from "crime" suppression to "war" fighting. Terrorists are no longer treated as criminals entitled to civil liberties but as enemies deprived of human rights.

From liberty to security: shifting from a concern with constitutional rights and civil liberties of citizens to a concern with the security and survival of the state, justified as "no liberty without security."

From reaction to preemption: shifting from a reactive crime-fighting mentality to a proactive terrorism reduction/prevention/interdiction mindset.

From collecting evidence to collecting intelligence: to accurately predict, effectively prevent, and timely interdict terrorist subterranean and subversive activities, information of every kind is necessary.

From competition to collaboration: breaking down the intelligence wall between law enforcement (Federal Bureau of Investigation; FBI) and the intelligence community (Central Intelligence Agency; CIA) so that they can pool investigative resources and share intelligence data.

Legislative History. The USAPA was rushed through Congress in seven weeks with overwhelming support—358 to 68 in the House and 88 to 1 in the Senate—with sunset provisions attached. Throughout the entire USAPA legislative process, neither the Congress nor the White House systematically investigated, judiciously examined, openly debated, and comprehensively considered the relative utilities—necessity and efficacy, costs and benefits, and long-term impact of the act.

The USAPA was fiercely objected to by civil libertarians and nongovernmental organizations (NGOs). In the House, congressmen Dennis Kucinich (D-OH), Ron Paul (R-TX), and John Conyers (D-MI) led the charge against the USAPA. In the Senate, the lone dissenter was Senator Russell Feingold (D-WI). In the public, organizations including the American Civil Liberties Union, the Electronic Privacy Information Center, the American Library Association, the Center for Democracy and Technology, and the Bill of Rights Defense Committee were taking the lead.

The USAPA continues to draw vociferous criticism and fiery protests. Critics have called the act undemocratic and unconstitutional. Many legal, commercial, and political associations and myriads of special interest groups have called for more stringent oversight on the implementation and reauthorization of the act. Finally, grassroots resistance, ad hoc or organized, grew. As of 1 April 2007, there were 410 resolutions upholding civil liberties and rights and against aspects of the USAPA across the country, representing eight states and 402 communities and affecting 85,104,445 people.

Necessity. The USAPA is a controversial piece of legislation. More than a few have commented that the USAPA is not necessary. The events of 9/11 happened not because of a lack of power, but despite it. All pre-9/11 studies and reports indicate that we need more effective leadership, coordination, and administration of counterterrorism programs, not more legal authority. More front-line powers do not automatically translate into effective central leadership nor do they help with interdepartmental cooperation. In fact, the expansion of power without effective control invites the abuse of power, from mission creep to power leaks, and added authority without cooperation leads to jurisdiction disputes and operational chaos.

Utility. More security powers mean fewer citizens' rights. A national security state threatens the sanctity and integrity of our constitutional system of government. The marginal utility of the USAPA in preventing or interdicting 9/11 is speculative at best and nonexistent at worst. The USAPA has the effect of encroaching on the fundamental rights of citizens and violating the foundational constitutional norm of the country. The USAPA has put the nation on a wartime footing with the creation of a police state with an imperial president at the helm, unchecked by Congress and not supervised by the Court.

[*See also* **American Civil Liberties Union; Bill of Rights; Civil Liberties; Civil Rights;** ***and*** **Terrorist Detention Policy.**]

BIBLIOGRAPHY

Wong, Kam C. *The Impact of USA Patriot Act on American Society: An Evidence Based Assessment.* New York: Nova Science Publishers, 2007.

Kam C. Wong

PEACE MOVEMENTS

From the early nineteenth century to the end of the twentieth century, a series of disparate peace movements arose from temporary political coalitions that coalesced around a core group of peace organizations in response to specific national issues. The mobilizing issues have varied—from arbitration and international law to the nuclear-arms race—but all have had in common the goal of replacing warfare with the peaceful resolution of conflict.

The American peace movement started with small, religiously based peace societies in New York and Massachusetts (1815). The pacifist New York group totally renounced war; the Massachusetts organization pursued all forms of peace advocacy. The latter, broader approach also characterized the American Peace Society (1828), whose leaders Alan Ladd and Elihu Burritt advocated international law, a congress of nations, and the arbitration of international disputes. Arbitration and international law attracted some U.S. and English political leaders and by the turn of the century had become the fulcrum for the first large peace coalition. These were the issues of choice for prestigious peace societies founded by businessmen like Andrew Carnegie and directed by intellectuals like Elihu Root, John Bates Clark, and Hamilton Holt.

The outbreak of World War I in 1914 gave currency to the idea of an international security organization. Combined with arbitration, this goal was promoted by the League to Enforce Peace (1915) and became the centerpiece for President Woodrow Wilson's peace policy. But acceptance of Wilson's League of Nations foundered on U.S. political divisions. The established peace movement split on the question of U.S. league membership, a remnant emerging in 1923 as the League of Nations Nonpartisan Association (in 1929 renamed the League of Nations Association, or LNA).

Meanwhile, as U.S. neutrality had become a salient issue in 1914–1917, progressive reformers, Social Gospel ministers, women suffragists, and social workers had created a second peace-movement coalition. Such groups as the Women's Peace Society (1915, subsequently the American Branch of the Women's International League for Peace and Freedom, or WILPF); the pacifist Fellowship of Reconciliation (FOR); the American Union against Militarism; and the American Friends Service Committee (AFSC, 1917) promoted U.S. leadership in peacemaking but opposed intervention in the European war.

With the U.S. declaration of war in 1917, this new constituency shrank to a few uncompromising pacifists like Jane Addams, Emily Green Balch, Dorothy Detzer, Frederick Libby, Kirby Page, Nevin Sayre, and A. J. Muste. After the war they spearheaded a broad, politically active peace movement that, however, promoted contending programs, including arms limitation, outlawry of war, and international organization.

In the 1930s, the threat of renewed European war generated a third coalition, the

Emergency Peace Campaign, that mobilized public and legislative support for neutrality. James T. Shotwell and Clark Eichelberger of the LNA broke with the movement's pacifist wing, however, to campaign for aiding the European democracies and, during World War II, to mobilize a fourth peace coalition that rallied support for the United Nations.

The next peace coalition coalesced around the 1950s campaign to ban atmospheric nuclear tests. Leaders from the FOR and AFSC created the 1957 Committee for a Sane Nuclear Policy (SANE) and the Committee for Non-Violent Action (CNVA), which organized protests such as sailing into Pacific test zones. SANE, with Women Strike for Peace (WSP, 1961), mobilized public opinion and lobbied in Washington, contributing to the 1963 Limited Nuclear Test Ban Treaty.

The largest and most tumultuous of all peace coalitions was the Vietnam-Era antiwar movement. Core peace groups initially included the FOR, AFSC, WILPF, SANE, and WSP. New constituencies were quickly added, including Students for a Democratic Society, Clergy and Laymen Concerned, and business, professional, and civil rights groups. Within this shifting coalition arose tension between the liberals' goal of ending the war and the radical objective of exploiting the war and cultural conflict to promote broader economic and social change. The movement's radical phase peaked in 1968–1970, after which a liberal antiwar constituency became dominant.

When the nuclear-weapons issue again arose in the 1980s, peace groups helped mobilize still another large political coalition: the Nuclear Weapons Freeze Campaign to halt the U.S.–Soviet arms race. Although Congress compromised the freeze proposal and its popular support dissolved after President Ronald Reagan proposed his Strategic Defense Initiative in March 1983, the campaign revived arms-control pressures and strengthened support for détente.

The historian Charles DeBenedetti has aptly described the peace movement as a social reform movement in the area of foreign policy. Indeed, American peace advocates have been integral to a transnational social movement that has interacted with international agencies and national governments to create institutions and procedures that offer alternatives to war.

[*See also* **Antinuclear Movement; Antiwar Movements; Liberal Party; Nuclear Weapons; Radicalism; Students for a Democratic Society;** *and* **Wilson, Woodrow.**]

BIBLIOGRAPHY

Alonso, Harriet Hyman. *Peace as a Women's Issue: A History of the U.S. Movement for World Peace and Women's Right.* Syracuse, N.Y.: Syracuse University Press, 1993.

Chatfield, Charles. *The American Peace Movement: Ideals and Activism.* New York: Twayne, 1992.

DeBenedetti, Charles. *The Peace Reform in American History.* Bloomington: Indiana University Press, 1980.

Howlett, Charles. *The American Peace Movement: References and Resources.* Boston: G. K. Hall, 1991.

Kuehl, Warren F. *Seeking World Order: The United States and International Organization to 1920.* Nashville, Tenn.: Vanderbilt University Press, 1969.

Kuehl, Warren F., and Lynne K. Dunn. *Keeping the Covenant: American Internationalists and the League of Nations, 1920–1939.* Kent, Ohio: Kent State University Press, 1997.

Wittner, Lawrence. *One World or None: A History of the World Nuclear Disarmament Movement through 1953.* In *The Struggle against the Bomb, Vol.* 1 (3 vols.). Stanford, Calif.: Stanford University Press, 1993.

E. Charles Chatfield

PENAL CODE, MODEL

See **Model Penal Code.**

PENSIONS, CIVIL WAR

Often considered a welfare laggard, the United States pioneered generous disability and old-age benefits for Union veterans of the Civil War. This was a break with precedent, because paltry benefits were opened to surviving veterans of the Revolutionary War only in the 1830s. When the South seceded in 1861, however, the federal government needed to recruit an army without the capabilities of a central bureaucracy. To help recruit citizen-soldiers, Congress in February 1862 promised pensions to those disabled "from causes which can be directly traced to injuries received or disease contracted while in military service." Benefits were graded by rank; yet privates as well as officers were eligible, and family dependents of the dead could also apply for aid.

Although the Civil War left millions dead and disabled, pension expenditures initially peaked in the mid-1870s, with fewer than 10 percent of veterans enrolled. Then Congress passed the 1879 Arrears of Pension Act, which promised cumulative pensions from the date of discharge if veterans could prove that later disabilities were service related. Tempted by lump sums often sufficient to finance new homes, tens of thousands discovered latent injuries. A growing backlog enabled U.S. commissioners of pensions to influence close elections by speeding up the processing of applications from swing states.

Responding to southern voters after 1876, Democrats (including the two-time president Grover Cleveland) sought to limit expenditures and trim the rolls. Hard-pressed former Confederate states had to help pay for Union pensions, yet they could afford only hardship aid for Confederate veterans and survivors. Meanwhile, Republicans competed to fund ever more help for the "saviors of the Union" from "surplus" federal revenues generated by protective tariffs.

After capturing both houses of Congress and the presidency in 1888, Republicans in 1890 passed the Dependent Pension Act. Henceforth anyone who had honorably served the Union for ninety days or more could be pensioned when unable to do manual labor. Pension administrators soon decided that veterans met this criterion at age sixty-two. By 1910, some 90 percent of surviving Union veterans—more than a third of elderly men in the North—received benefits that were very generous by the international standards of the day. Expenditures dwindled as the old soldiers died, but as late as the mid-1970s, pensions were still being paid to a few widows who, in their youth, had married aging Union veterans.

[*See also* **Cleveland, Grover; Confederate States of America; Grand Army of the Republic; Republican Party;** ***and*** **Social Policy: Public Welfare.**]

BIBLIOGRAPHY

Glasson, William H. *Federal Military Pensions in the United States*. New York: Oxford University Press, American Branch, 1918.

Skocpol, Theda. *Protecting Soldiers and Mothers*, 1992, Ch. 2, pp. 102–151. Cambridge, Mass.: Belknap Press of Harvard University Press, 1992.

Theda Skocpol

PENTAGON PAPERS

Commissioned by the secretary of defense Robert McNamara in June 1967 to determine what had gone wrong in Vietnam, the research project that came to be called the Pentagon Papers played a critical role in the Vietnam War saga. Completed in 1969, the study comprised forty-seven volumes and more than 7,000 pages of text and government documents analyzing U.S. involvement in Vietnam from World War II forward, especially during the presidential administrations of John F. Kennedy and Lyndon B. Johnson. It raised fundamental policy questions and confirmed antiwar critics' charges of high-level deception and duplicity.

The former Defense Department official Daniel Ellsberg leaked the papers to the *New York Times,* which began to publish them in June 1971, provoking a political and constitutional crisis. Revelations from the Pentagon Papers fueled popular disillusionment with an already discredited war. Obsessed with government secrecy, President Richard M. Nixon sought a court injunction to prevent further publication. In *New York Times Co. v. United States* (1971), the Supreme Court ruled that the government had not met constitutional tests for prior restraint. Large portions of the papers subsequently appeared in the *Times* and other newspapers, as well as in various paperback editions.

The Pentagon Papers had a profound impact in a tumultuous period. Strengthening public and congressional opposition to U.S. involvement in Vietnam, they also initiated an era of aggressive investigative journalism. Their leak provoked a vengeful Nixon to take steps that would culminate in the Watergate scandal and his resignation. The papers remained for many years the basis for much of the scholarship on the Vietnam War.

[*See also* **Johnson, Lyndon B.; Kennedy, John F.; Nixon, Richard M.; Supreme Court, U.S.;** ***and*** **Watergate.**]

BIBLIOGRAPHY

Rudenstine, David. *The Day the Presses Stopped: A History of the Pentagon Papers Case.* Berkeley: University of California Press, 1996.

George C. Herring

PEOPLE v. SANGER

On 16 October 1916, Margaret Sanger (1879–1966) opened America's first birth control clinic behind the curtained windows of a tenement storefront in the Brownsville district of Brooklyn, New York. The clinic registry recorded 464 clients in the few weeks before the police shut the facility down and arrested Sanger and her associates.

Sanger was a visiting nurse among the city's immigrant populations when, upon witnessing a woman's death from an illegal abortion, she vowed to abandon palliative care and claim contraception as a fundamental women's right. In 1914, she was arrested for publishing a pamphlet identifying basic techniques of birth control—a term she coined as a simple way of talking about the still clandestine and delicate subject.

Birth control had been driven underground by obscenity statutes adopted through the efforts of the notorious antivice crusader Anthony Comstock, whose evangelical fervor captivated post Civil War America and led to the adoption by the states and federal government of broad criminal sanctions on sexual speech and commerce, including all materials related to contraception and abortion. Sanger fled to Europe following her indictment, but an elderly Comstock, only weeks before his death, convicted her husband, William Sanger, for distributing the pamphlet. A storm of publicity ensued, effectively ending the country's longstanding reticence over public discussion of sexuality and reproduction. Upon Sanger's return, all charges against her were dismissed.

Sanger staged her second arrest deliberately to test not only the rights of free expression, but also whether prescribing contraception for medical reasons could be protected broadly under Section 1145 of the New York Comstock statute, which allowed physicians to provide condoms to prevent venereal disease. The Brooklyn court refused to hear testimony from a doctor she identified to serve as an expert witness, but her lawyer, J. J. Goldstein, cannily called on the Brownsville mothers to tell their own stories about the health complications of multiple pregnancies.

This was an important legal breakthrough because Sanger as a nurse did not have technical standing to demand clarification of physicians' rights. She was found guilty and jailed for a month. The conviction was upheld on appeal in *People v. Sanger,* a decision rendered on 8 January 1918 by Judge Frederick Crane of the New York Court of Appeals, who affirmed the state's right to prohibit laymen and women from distributing contraceptives.

Crane's opinion, however, did take note of the lower court's evidence by licensing doctors to prescribe birth control on broadly defined medical grounds, the circumstances under which Sanger then built the modern family planning movement. Still hoping for a decision that would also grant this right to nurses, she had Goldstein petition the U.S. Supreme Court to hear the case, but after many postponements of a scheduled hearing, jurisdiction was refused without explanation.

In 1936, Sanger and Hannah Stone, MD, won a second legal victory in *U.S. v. One Package*. The decision of the U.S Second Circuit Court of Appeals in New York voided the federal Comstock law prohibiting interstate commerce in contraception intended for use by physicians and defined birth control as a safe and essential element of modern medical practice.

Local sanctions on family-planning clinics endured in the heavily Catholic states of Massachusetts and Connecticut, however, until 1965, when the U.S. Supreme Court in *Griswold v. Connecticut* established the use of contraception by married Americans as an inherent right. The U.S. Congress finally removed the label of obscenity from contraception in 1970. Two years later, the Supreme Court in *Eisenstadt v. Baird* extended the right of access to contraception to the unmarried.

These decisions opened the door to public subsidy of family planning for poor women at home and abroad. Although family planning today is a global norm, it remains captive to culture war controversies, with opponents now disputing those government expenditures.

[***See also Griswold v. Connecticut.***]

BIBLIOGRAPHY

Chesler, Ellen. *Woman of Valor: Margaret Sanger and the Birth Control Movement in America.* New York: Simon & Schuster, 1992, 2007.

Gordon, Linda. *The Moral Property of Women: A History of Birth Control Politics in the United States.* Urbana and Chicago: University of Chicago Press, 2002.

Katz, Esther, Cathy Moran Hajo, and Peter C. Engelman, eds. *Selected Papers of Margaret Sanger, Volume 1: The Woman Rebel, 1900–1928.* Chicago: University of Illinois Press, 2003.

Katz, Esther, et al., eds. *Selected Papers of Margaret Sanger, Volume 2: Birth Control Comes of Age, 1928–1939.* Chicago: University of Illinois Press, 2006.

Ellen Chesler

PEROT, ROSS

Entrepreneur, independent presidential candidate, and Reform Party founder Henry Ross Perot was born in Texarkana, Texas, in 1930. He attended the U.S. Naval Academy, going on to serve four years in the Navy. In 1957, Perot returned to Texas, where he took a job as a salesman with IBM in Dallas. In 1962, he left the company to begin his own computer services firm, Electronic Data Systems (EDS).

Perot capitalized on the federal government's enormous data-processing needs following

Medicare's establishment in 1965, securing contracts with state medical organizations that brought EDS rapid growth and profits. With revenues skyrocketing from $865,000 in 1965 to over $7.5 million in three years, Perot's company staged one of the most successful public stock offerings of 1968.

In the late 1960s, Perot became deeply interested in the plight of American prisoners of war in Vietnam. Since that time, Perot has worked with veterans' groups, attempted to influence government policy, and proved receptive to conspiracy theories about the existence of living American prisoners years after the end of the conflict. This rendered him open to controversy, as did his efforts to free two EDS employees held captive in Iran in the closing days of the shah's reign in 1978–1979.

General Motors (GM) purchased EDS in 1984. Perot's relationship with GM chief executive officer Roger Smith proved highly fractious, and Perot accepted a sizeable buyout of his interest in the company in 1986.

Perot's greatest influence upon American political life, however, came in 1992. Concerned about the mounting federal budget deficit and an unresponsive government, he promised to mount an independent presidential campaign if volunteers placed his name on ballots in all fifty states. This pledge unleashed a wave of volunteer activity throughout the spring and early summer.

Perot articulated a populist message of returning power to ordinary American citizens, balancing the budget, and setting term limits. He enjoyed considerable support among the electorate, his appeal enhanced by witticisms such as referring to the deficit as "like a crazy aunt we keep deep down in the basement. All the neighbors know she's there but nobody wants to talk about her" (Patterson, 2005, p. 251). As the summer progressed, however, his off-the-cuff speaking style caused negative publicity. Perot withdrew from the race in July and later claimed he was the victim of efforts to sabotage his campaign and his daughter's wedding.

Despite Perot's formal exit, much of his volunteer organization remained intact. By mid-September his name was on all fifty state ballots. Perot reentered the race on 29 September and garnered an invitation to participate in the presidential debates against Republican incumbent George H. W. Bush and Democrat Bill Clinton. Most of his campaign was conducted via paid television programs that allowed Perot to speak directly to viewers. Perot's wealth enabled him to opt out of campaign finance regulations by refusing federal funding. Perot went on to garner 19 percent of the vote, the best finish by a third-party candidate since Theodore Roosevelt in 1912.

Following the 1992 election, Perot established the nonprofit, nonpartisan organization United We Stand America. He was a prominent opponent of the North American Free Trade Agreement (NAFTA) in 1993. He helped found the Reform Party in 1995 and ran as its 1996 presidential candidate, but garnered only 9 percent of the vote and was not invited to participate in the candidate debates. Perot's public profile has been low in recent years. Perot Systems Corporation, founded following the EDS buyout, was sold to Dell in 2009.

[*See also* **Bush, George H. W.;** *and* **Clinton, William J.**]

BIBLIOGRAPHY

Critchlow, Donald T. *The Conservative Ascendancy: How the GOP Right Made Political History*. Cambridge, Mass.: Harvard University Press, 2007.

Patterson, James T. *Restless Giant: The United States from Watergate to Bush v. Gore*. Oxford; New York: Oxford University Press, 2005.

Posner, Gerald. *Citizen Perot: His Life and Times*. New York: Random House, 1996.

Laura Jane Gifford

PIERCE, FRANKLIN

(1804–1869), fourteenth president (1853–1857) of the United States. Pierce was born and reared in Hillsboro, New Hampshire. His father, Benjamin, a Revolutionary War general and later governor of New Hampshire, influenced his son toward a career in Democratic Party politics. After graduating from Bowdoin College, Pierce read law with several jurists and joined the bar in 1827. He first entered politics as a representative in the state legislature and then in 1833 became one of the youngest members of the U.S. House of Representatives. A fervent supporter of Andrew Jackson, Pierce fully embraced the Democratic creed of small government and states' rights. In 1837 he won election to the U.S. Senate. His unexpected nomination as the presidential candidate of a divided Democratic Party in 1852, coming on the forty-ninth ballot, made him the first "dark-horse candidate" in American history. He defeated the Whig Party candidate, General Winfield Scott (1786–1866).

Pierce's presidential significance lies primarily in his failure to achieve the sectional harmony he hoped for. He supported the 1854 Kansas–Nebraska Act, believing that Southerners should be allowed to take their slaves wherever they wished and hoping that leaving the slavery issue to local decision making would end sectional friction. In fact, most of his presidency was preoccupied with the fierce and sometimes violent conflict between proslavery and antislavery settlers in Kansas. Criticizing the newly formed Republican Party as disruptive and sectionalist, Pierce struck most Northerners as a "doughface": a northerner who favored Southern interests. An expansionist, he tried without success to buy Cuba from Spain, but by means of the Gadsden Purchase (1853) he did acquire a sliver of land from Mexico for a southern railroad line. Overall, Franklin Pierce represents that group of northern Democrats sympathetic to Southern positions but whose efforts at sectional compromise proved unsuccessful. As president, he exemplified passive, mid-nineteenth-century chief executives during a time of congressional domination.

[*See also* **Antislavery Movement; Buchanan, James; Democratic Party; Douglas, Stephen A.; Federal Government, Executive Branch: Presidency, The; Federal Government, Legislative Branch: House of Representatives; Federal Government, Legislative Branch: Senate; Jackson, Andrew; Kansas–Nebraska Act;** ***and*** **States' Rights.**]

BIBLIOGRAPHY

Gara, Larry. *The Presidency of Franklin Pierce.* Lawrence: University Press of Kansas, 1991.

Nichols, Roy. *Franklin Pierce: Young Hickory of the Granite Hills.* Philadelphia: H. Milford, 1931.

Jean Harvey Baker

PLESSY v. FERGUSON

An 1896 Supreme Court decision upholding racial segregation. The state of Louisiana in 1890 required railroads to provide "equal but separate accommodations for the white and colored races." The railroads objected to the legislation because of the additional cost it imposed in providing separate cars. The Louisiana law, however, had little to do with economic efficiency; instead, it represented an attempt by white legislators to restrict racial mixing. In response, a group of Creoles and African Americans in New Orleans organized the Citizens' Committee to Test the Constitutionality of the Separate Car Law. In 1892, Homer Plessy, a person who was one-eighth black and therefore appeared to be white, agreed to test the law. Plessy purchased a ticket on a train traveling solely within the state of Louisiana and made sure that the train's conductor understood that he was a "colored" person. When the conductor ordered Plessy from an all-white car, he refused to leave and was arrested. At his trial before Judge John H. Ferguson, Plessy argued that the Louisiana law violated the Thirteenth and Fourteenth amendments to the federal Constitution. The trial judge disagreed, as did the Louisiana Supreme Court, giving Plessy and his supporters the opportunity they wanted to test the meaning of the Thirteenth Amendment's prohibition against slavery and the Fourteenth Amendment's guaranteeing to all citizens "equal protection" of the laws.

Speaking for an 8-to-1 Supreme Court majority, Justice Henry Billings Brown, an admiralty lawyer from Detroit, disposed of Plessy's case in a precedent-setting fashion. Brown found that the Thirteenth Amendment applied only to actions intended to reintroduce slavery and that distinctions resting on color and race by themselves did not constitute slavery. Brown also proclaimed that the Louisiana law's requirement that passengers be separated on the basis of race did not violate the equal protection clause of the Fourteenth Amendment, since both races enjoyed equal facilities.

Brown rested his opinion on two important nonconstitutional assumptions: first, that segregation by race was not a mark of inferiority, and second, that race-mixing enjoyed little public support. To prove his point that separate but equal facilities were acceptable, he cited an 1849 Massachusetts decision, *Roberts v. City of Boston,* that upheld segregation by race in the Boston public schools. According to Brown, as long as the facilities provided were equal, even if separate, the state had satisfied the constitutional burden imposed by the equal protection clause.

Justice John Marshall Harlan, a former slaveholder from Kentucky, issued the lone dissent. Harlan insisted that the Thirteenth Amendment did apply, since segregation was a "badge of servitude" and that, in any case, the "Constitution is color-blind, and neither knows nor tolerates classes among citizens." Harlan's dissent proved prophetic. In 1954, the Supreme Court in *Brown v. Board of Education* overturned the "separate but equal" doctrine written into the Constitution by *Plessy v. Ferguson* and began the process of dismantling legally imposed racial segregation in the United States.

[***See also Brown v. Board of Education;* Civil Rights; Civil Rights Legislation; Constitution; Fourteenth Amendment; Harlan, John Marshall; Segregation; *and* Supreme Court, U.S.**]

BIBLIOGRAPHY

Lofgren, Charles A. *The Plessy Case.* New York: Oxford University Press, 1987.

Kermit L. Hall

PLURALISM

"Pluralism" is discussed here in terms of the pluralist theory of power and the contention about this theory following the publication of Robert A. Dahl's book *Who Governs?*, the most influential work in political science during the 1960s for the study of American politics (Dahl, 1961). However, no one intends to supplant the ordinary language use of pluralism as referring to ethnic, religious, or other forms of diversity within some jurisdiction as one might refer to "pluralism in India."

Dahl's *Who Governs*? was a study of political power in the city of New Haven. This work was sparked by C. Wright Mills' *The Power Elite,* which described political power in America as primarily located in the hands of several hundred persons at the top of major corporations, civilian hierarchies of the national government, and the defense establishment. Mills' evidence consisted mainly of maldistribution of economic resources and the capacity to initiate war and foreign policy action. Dahl argued that political power should be observed by conducting case studies of political action in different issue areas and defined power as changing the process of politics in the direction of one's intentions. Dahl conducted such case studies in the area of urban politics, and he found power to be decentralized and fragmented because different actors had power in different issue areas. Although Dahl himself almost never described findings of fragmentation of power as "pluralist," most political scientists immediately used the terms "pluralist theory of power" and "pluralism" to describe such findings.

Who Governs? set off one of the major academic controversies of its generation, still remembered as "the community power controversy." Other students of community power (especially sociologists) began with a different concept of power, defining power in terms of resources such as money and social status, the answers given by interviewees when queried "who has power in this town?" This school of community power was termed "elitist," to differentiate from "pluralist," whereas other pluralists emerged who published community power studies with findings similar to those of Dahl. After many contrasting publications, no general agreement emerged among political scientists and sociologists as to the nature of community power, and the subject was largely displaced on disciplinary research agendas.

Pluralist studies of various national institutions and national political process actually had more long- impact on political science than studies involved in the community power controversy. Influential studies reported findings of pluralism in the administrative process in general and in the congressional budgetary process in particular, in other forms of congressional decision making, in the limits of presidential power, and in the complexities of federalist interactions. Such research taken together as a body formed an initially persuasive, apparently comprehensive theory of American politics, referred to as pluralism.

Preceding *Who Governs?*, David B. Truman's *The Governmental Process* (1951) was the most influential book in the study of American politics during the 1950s. Truman's basic point was that interest groups and their interaction in political processes is the most important factor in understanding American politics, more important than understanding the rules and structures of political institutions. Truman's so-called "group theory" was briefly the most discussed theory in political science, but was rejected by Dahl and almost all political scientists as an overstatement, although they found value in many of Truman's specific descriptions of political process. A term describing group theory was "a pluralist theory of politics" since Truman focused on the influence of the great plurality of groups in American politics. However, post-1961 observers often missed the point that Truman's pluralism was different from Dahl's pluralism; Dahl found that elections had a much greater impact on important events than the activities of interest groups. Unfortunately in *Who Governs?*, Dahl did not directly compare the relative importance of interest groups and of elections in influencing events, and so later scholars mistakenly attributed Truman's views to Dahl.

Multiple Elite Theory. Around 1970 a veritable barrage of criticism was launched against Dahl's pluralist theory of power. By this time Dahl was interested in comparative democracies, and most other leading pluralist writers ceased defending *Who Governs*? as presenting a comprehensive theory of power. Scholars of American politics and policy often accepted an advance from Dahl's theory of "multiple elitism," accepting Dahl's finding of different power holders in different issue areas, but rejecting his interpretation that such decentralization of power enhanced democracy. Instead, the multiple elitists found that power in particular issue areas was often wielded by elite coalitions specific to that issue area, often coalitions of interest groups, legislative committees, and concerned executive branch agencies. In nonacademic vernacular, such coalitions are called "iron triangles."

The major theorist of multiple elitism was Theodore Lowi Jr., whose *The End of Liberalism* (1979) had great influence over the study of politics and policy in American government. The title referred only secondarily to New Deal liberalism, but mainly symbolized Lowi's contention that the delegation of public authority to private elites, controlling specific policy areas, was steadily undermining democracy and effective government. Numbers of book-policy studies, written independently of Lowi, seemed to confirm the general view of specific elites, each one controlling a specific policy area, as the basic factor in domestic policy-making processes.

The theory of multiple elitism, basically developed from case studies of policy areas, was bolstered by a theory developed from the economics of oligopoly, published as *The Logic of Collective Action* by Mancur Olson Jr., in 1965. Olson argued that it is much easier to organize an interest group having only a few units, such as a few corporations, than it is to organize an interest group seeking to represent widely diffused interests of a large public, such as the consumers of a product. Olson noted that if a public good (such as clean air) is provided, beneficiaries may not contribute to an interest group lobbying to get that public good, since the beneficiary will get the public good anyway, even with no contribution. Hence the public goods lobby will tend to diminish and be dwarfed in power by an opposing producer group lobby, continually organized by a few contributors, substantially profiting from organizing. Olson's theory of collective action bolsters Lowi's multiple elite theory, because Olson developed a compelling logical argument as to why an elite coalition can develop the power to control a particular policy area, whereas the general public would be poorly represented in that policy area.

Neopluralism. However, research published during 1978–1995 convinced many scholars of American public policy that most areas of policy making actually have a more complex pattern of representation, with more groups and other actors having some power than was found by the multiple elitists. Such research may be termed "neopluralism," in that it found fragmented patterns of power similar to Dahl, but accepted that a fraction of policy areas are controlled by special interest elites. Neopluralists find Olson's theory of collective action to be provocative of research, but observe that nevertheless widely shared interests do get organized into lobbies and political entrepreneurs sometimes represent widespread constituencies. Neopluralists are quite clear that fragmented, complex decision making cannot be automatically equated with democratic or fair decision making. Accordingly, neopluralists usually assume that business groups are typically the most powerful in some policy area, although other groups can check or even defeat wealthier groups. Neopluralists are currently developing a theory termed "the politics of attention," descriptive of sharp changes in previously static areas of public policy caused by sudden changes in the foci of public attention from one policy area to another (Jones and Baumgartner, 2005).

Two other uses of "pluralism" must be briefly noted. Sociological pluralism flourished during 1955–1975 as theorists influenced by Alexis de Tocqueville stressed the importance of groups in civil society for protecting democracy when challenged by fascist or communist mass movements (Korhhauser, 1959). Since 1990 political philosophers have used the term pluralism to refer to philosophical writing stressing the importance of enhancing the diversity of modern society and promoting equality for women and various types of minorities (Young, 2000).

BIBLIOGRAPHY

Dahl, Robert A. *Who Governs?*. New Haven, Conn.: Yale University Press, 1961.

Jones, Byron, and Frank R. Baumgartner. *The Politics of Attention*. Chicago: University of Chicago Press, 2005.

Korhhauser, William. *The Politics of Mass Society*. Glencoe, Ill: Free Press, 1959.

Lowi, Theodore J., Jr. *The End of Liberalism*. New York: Norton, 1979.

McFarland, Andrew S. *Neopluralism*. Lawrence: University Press of Kansas, 2004.

Mills, C. Wright. *The Power Elite*. New York: Oxford University Press, 1956.

Olson, Mancur, Jr. *The Logic of Collective Action*. Cambridge, Mass.: Harvard University Press, 1965.

Truman, David B. *The Governmental Process*. Westport, Conn.: Greenwood Press, 1951.

Walker, Jack L., Jr. *Mobilizing Interest Groups in America*. Ann Arbor: University of Michigan Press, 1991.

Young, Iris Marion. *Inclusion and Democracy*. Oxford University Press, 2000.

Andrew S. McFarland

PLURALISM, LEGAL

Legal pluralism emerged as a challenge to state-centric concepts of law. It criticizes the idea that state-made law is the only form of law used to regulate society, offering instead a polycentric or polymorphic concept of law. Early scholars of legal pluralism, such as Lon Fuller, Marc Galanter, John Griffiths, Robert Ellickson, and Lisa Bernstein, highlighted the substantial social impact of nonstatal normative regimes and explored the role played by various private bodies in creating them.

The idea of legal pluralism was also invoked to describe global phenomena, triggering a new wave of literature focusing on "global legal pluralism." Similarly to the national context, this literature challenged the Westphalian emphasis on the state as the exclusive source of norm-making within the international domain, highlighting the increasing influence of nonstatal regimes. Examples include the *lex mercatoria,* the normative orders created by multinational enterprises and global international standard-setting organizations and hybrid initiatives such as the Global Reporting Initiative and the Equator Principles. This phenomenon was studied by various writers including Paul Berman, Ralf Michaels, Oren Perez, Gunther Teubner, and Peer Zumbansen. Finally, the notion of legal pluralism is also used to describe ideological diversity within national legal systems (e.g., the tension between deterrence, corrective justice, and distributive justice in tort law or the tension between religious and secular-liberal commitments in family law). Overall the main focus of the legal pluralism literature has been empirical; it sought to provide a richer picture of the normative orders that exist in society and to highlight the various ways in which these coexisting regimes interact. Normative questions and issues of institutional design received much less attention.

The legal pluralism research program faces several theoretical and empirical challenges. First, the concept of legal pluralism, despite the long scholarly engagement with it, is conceptually imprecise. This vagueness concerns, primarily, the jurisprudential questions of the meaning of law and the (proper) distinction between law and nonlegal normative orders. Resolving these questions is necessary both for delineating the boundaries of "legal pluralism" as a field of study and to gain better understanding of the interaction dynamic between different normative regimes. A second question concerns the normative issue of whether legal pluralism is socially valuable (and in what sense). Some authors have emphasized the risks of legal pluralism, highlighting the potential for regimes—collisions, paralysis, and incoherence—whereas others have pointed out the possible contribution of legal pluralism to the creation of a more democratic, tolerant, and creative society. This discussion also highlights the need to develop more refined theories of interlegality as well as better empirical understanding of the interaction between coexisting legal regimes. These theoretical questions have also been explored by studies of multiculturalism and soft law.

[*See also* **Pluralism;** *and* **State Governments.**]

BIBLIOGRAPHY

Griffiths, John. "What Is Legal Pluralism?" *Journal of Legal Pluralism* 24 (1986): 1–55.

Tamanaha, Brian Z. "Understanding Legal Pluralism: Past to Present, Local to Global." *30 Sydney Law Review* 375 (2008).

Teubner, Gunther. "'Global Bukowina': Legal Pluralism in the World Society." In *Global Law without a State*, edited by Gunther Tuebner, pp. 3–28. Aldershot: UK; Brookfield, Vt.: Dartmouth, 1997.

Twining, William. "Normative and Legal Pluralism: A Global Perspective." *20 Duke Journal of Comparative and International Law* 473 (2010).

Oren Perez

POLITICAL CAMPAIGNING

Colonial Era. Politics before the 1790s was characterized by widespread opportunities for adult white men to vote, a political culture in which the average man deferred to his betters, a lack of organized political factions or parties, and widespread communications through newspapers, pamphlets, and local taverns. During the revolutionary period from 1765 to the 1780s, politics was handled by locally organized organizations such as the Sons of Liberty, which mobilized Patriot efforts to protect their rights as Englishmen, especially their rights to local self-government. The level of political discussion was dramatically higher than before—or since—and produced a commitment to the principles of republicanism, emphasizing civic virtue, opposition to aristocracy, and opposition to all forms of corruption, especially by powerful government officials. The idea of organized political parties was repugnant.

The Party System. In the 1790s Alexander Hamilton proposed a strong national government based on financial interests, whereas Thomas Jefferson opposed it in favor of agrarianism. They each set up protoparties in every state to rally support. They did not take over local parties because none existed. The Jay Treaty of 1794 was a trade agreement with Britain that angered Jeffersonians, who feared republicanism was betrayed. The parties emerged as the two groupings organized supporters at the grassroots level, with the "Republicans," led by Jefferson, losing to the "Federalists" in 1796 but defeating them in 1800. Rhetoric was hot and tempers frayed during this "first party system" but the transfer of power in 1800 was handled peacefully, and indeed there was little political violence in the new nation.

Army Style. As the population grew, new wholesale methods for quickly reaching more voters appeared in the United States for the first time in the world. By the 1820s the great majority of free white men could vote. In the second party system from 1830 to the mid-1850s, two major parties usually controlled elections and government at the county, state, and national levels. Some men ignored politics, but there were no independents. The two parties each formed a loyal "army" of supporters. Nearly all government jobs were distributed on a patronage basis to party workers as their reward for victory. The jobs were prestigious and paid very well. The best way to get a patronage job was to work in the election campaign for the winning party, and volunteers were numerous.

Political parties conceptualized themselves as armies—as disciplined, hierarchical fighting organizations whose mission it was to defeat a clearly identified opponent. When defeated on election day, they knew how to retreat, regroup, and find new leaders to fight again another day. If they won, then the victory was sweet. In an era when many politicians had military experience, structuring the parties along a militaristic chain of command seemed logical enough. Between the days of Alexander Hamilton and his Federalist party in the 1790s and Mark Hanna and his Republicans in the 1890s, there was no national boss. Presidential candidates and their top aides spent a great deal of time organizing their own temporary national infrastructure, which was set up outside the state and national committees. County committees did the real work for the parties, with the state committees largely honorific. The county committees sent delegates to the state convention, where state nominees were selected. In turn the county committees were based on local conventions—mass meetings that were open to any self-identified partisan.

Recruiting Partisans. Partisans were as excited by politics as any sports fan in the early twenty-first century. By 1800 the Jeffersonian Republicans had built a sophisticated system for recruiting troops throughout the country, as well as a correspondence system that state officials and local party activists used to keep in touch. As a Federalist complained, "The jacobins have at last made their own discipline perfect; they are trained, officered, regimented and formed to subordination in a manner that our own militia has never yet equaled." The Federalists began to imitate the new tactics, but were always too aristocratic to appreciate the value of a grassroots movement. The Democratic–Republican caucus in Congress chose presidential candidates for the party, but by the 1830s the national convention was in use. Its delegates were chosen specifically for the task of selecting candidates and anyone who took part in a convention was duty bound to support its nominees. It was possible to bolt a convention before candidates were selected, as the southern Democrats did in 1860 and Roosevelt's supporters did in 1912.

William Jennings Bryan perfected the technique of multiple appeals in 1896, running simultaneously as a regular Democrat, a Silver Republican, and a regular Populist. Voters of all parties could vote for him without crossing their personal party loyalty. Most states soon thereafter banned the same person running on different tickets—one man, one party, one platform became the usual rule (except in New York, where third, fourth, and fifth parties have flourished since the 1830s.)

Turnout Soars after 1824. The basic campaign strategy was the maximum mobilization of loyal partisans. To excite them speakers systematically canvassed their districts, talking up the state and national issues of the day and watching which themes drew the best responses. In such a large, complex, pluralistic nation, the politicians discovered that citizens had a primary loyalty to their own ethnoreligious groups. These groups, furthermore, had distinctive moral perspectives and political needs. The Whigs and Republicans were especially effective in winning support among pietistic and evangelical denominations and later the black church members. The Democrats, on the other hand, did much better among Catholics and other High-Church (liturgical) groups, such as Episcopalians and among men who were not religious and did not want the churches interfering in their lives with laws like Prohibition. Economic issues engaged the voters too, especially the speed and direction of geographical expansion and economic modernization. The Whigs and Republicans aggressively supported modernizing the economy; supporting banks, railroads, factories, and tariffs; and promising a rich home market in the cities for farm products. The Whigs always opposed expansion, as did the Republicans until 1898. The Democrats, meanwhile, talked of agrarian virtues of the yeoman farmer, westward expansion, and how well rural life comported with Jeffersonian values.

Both parties formed local campaign clubs, such as the Wide Awakes where young men paraded in torchlight processions wearing special uniforms and holding colorful banners. By the late century the parties in the Midwest combined to turn out over 90 percent of the eligible electorate in entire states, reaching over 95 percent in 1896 in Illinois, Indiana, Iowa, Michigan, and Ohio. Some counties passed the 100 percent mark not because of fraud but because the parties tracked people down whom the census missed. Fraud did take place in municipal elections in large cities, where the ward-heelers could expect tangible rewards. Apart from some Reconstruction episodes in the South, there was little fraud in presidential elections because the local workers were not in line for presidential rewards anyway. The best way to build enthusiasm was to show enthusiasm. The parties used rallies, parades, banners, buttons, and insignia to display partisanship and promote the theme that with so much strength victory was inevitable. The side that lost was usually surprised and tended to ascribe defeat to preternatural factors, such as bad weather or treachery.

Internal Communications. The parties created an internal communications system designed to keep in close touch with the voters. They set up volunteer organizations in every county and city, and townships or precincts as well, charged with visiting every potential supporter, especially in the critical last days before the election. These workers, of course, comprised the activists who attended conventions and ultimately selected the candidates. This intensive face-to-face networking provided excellent information in both directions—the leaders immediately found out what the rank and file liked and disliked. The function was replaced in the twentieth century by public opinion polls. With the collapse of the biggest city machines after 1940, door-to-door canvassing became less common. It was chiefly used by labor unions, which used local activists to canvass their members. As early as 1964, politicians were using telephone banks to identify supporters and turn them out at the polls on election day.

Partisan newspapers were a powerful party device in the nineteenth century, most of their news was political, most other editors were party activists, and the parties subsidized subscriptions. Thanks to the invention of high-speed presses for city papers and free postage for rural sheets, low-cost newspapers proliferated. In 1850, the Census counted 1,630 party newspapers (with a circulation of about one per voter), and only eighty-three "independent" papers. The party line was behind every line of news copy, not to mention the authoritative editorials, which exposed the "stupidity" of the enemy and the "triumphs" of the party in every issue. Editors were senior party leaders and often were rewarded with lucrative postmasterships. Top publishers were sometimes nominated on the national ticket. In the 1890s the big-city moguls invented yellow journalism, with sensationalism, sports, scandal, and gossip about celebrities that sold 1 million copies a day. The higher the circulation, the higher the advertising rates, as the publishers realized they could make far more profit through advertising to the masses than by peddling politics to the partisans. By becoming nonpartisan they doubled and tripled their advertising base to include the opposition party, as well as women, who read the ads and the features but not the political news. There was less and less political news after 1900, as citizens became more politically apathetic while diverting their partisan loyalties to new professional sports teams and focusing their taste for celebrities more on Hollywood than on Washington. The middle class kept involved by fighting corruption, but the working class—many of them recent immigrants—showed less and less interest in voting after 1900.

Financing Campaigns. Campaigns were financed internally for most of the nineteenth century. Aspirants for office volunteered their services as speaker; wealthy leaders contributed cash, and patronage appointees not only worked for the party but also donated 2 to 5 percent of the salaries. The problem with the system was the winners curse: in a close election, campaign managers promise the same lucrative jobs over and over again. If they lost it made no difference; if they won they faced an impossible task, which was guaranteed to alienate supporters. After civil service reform ratcheted into place late in the century, new revenue sources were needed. Mark Hanna found the solution in 1896, as he systematically billed corporations for their share of the campaign.

Crusades. The most exciting—even passionate—campaign was the crusade. A new body of intensely moralistic politicians would suddenly discover that the opposition was ensconced in power, was thoroughly corrupt, and had plans to utterly destroy republicanism. Americans were profoundly committed to the principle that republicanism could never be allowed to perish from the earth, so crusades roused their emotional intensity. The American Revolution itself had followed this formula, as did Jefferson's followers in 1800. Jackson in 1828 crusaded against the "corrupt bargain" that had denied him the White House in 1824 and again against the Bank of the United States in 1832. Republicans crusaded only once, in their first campaign in 1856 when the Slave Power was the target. In 1872 Horace Greeley, running on a third-party ticket called the "Liberal republicans," rang the charges against Grant's corruption. The most dramatic crusade was that of William Jennings Bryan in 1896, as he identified the gold and moneyed interests as responsible for depression, poverty, and plutocracy. The Tea Party of 2010 identified a bipartisan list of heavy spenders, high taxers, and aloof bureaucrats.

Strategists discovered that the most effective way to squelch crusaders was not to defend the status quo but to launch a countercrusade, attacking the crusaders as crazy extremists. Thus Jefferson was attacked as an atheist, Jackson as a murderer, Fremont as a disunionist, Bryan as an anarchist, Goldwater as a warmonger, and McGovern as a friend of "abortion, acid (drugs), and amnesty (for draft dodgers)."

Advertising Styles. The advertising style of politics replaced the army style in the early twentieth century. The theme now was to reach out to the independent voter, who was seen as a consumer who had a choice to make. The nation's leading advertising man, Albert Lasker, sold Warren G. Harding to the voters in 1920 using the same advertising techniques that had sold hundreds of millions of dollars worth of war bonds. Radio and movies were the new media of the 1920s and 1930s, but did not play a major role in politics. Since the great majority of major newspapers opposed Roosevelt, he used radio to reach his constituents more directly, and his "fireside chats" were so informal it seemed he was a live speaker in the living room quietly talking matters over with them. The voters responded much more enthusiastically to a live speaker than to a detached oratorical speech. Father Coughlin had a weekly radio program that prefigured the talk radio stars of the twenty-first century. The breakthrough came with the television commercial. Even when it was trimmed down to sixty or thirty seconds or even fifteen seconds, the politician could get his name across by constant repetition. By the 1970s, television commercials were the largest expenditure in election campaigns. By the 1990s, candidates for major office were spending millions of dollars on television commercials and spending most of their time in private fund-raising sessions. Other media such as direct mail has special uses, such as raising funds from a small targeted group. The Internet is much cheaper than television, and by the twenty-first century it was gaining an even wider audience. In 2008, the Obama campaign demonstrated that social networking could be an easy way to keep followers updated with campaign tidbits. Every candidate had to have a homepage, where interested voters could explore their biographies and positions on issues. Start-up independent groups, such as the Tea Party in 2010, used the Internet to organize themselves and attract audiences to their rallies.

[*See also* **Party System.**]

BIBLIOGRAPHY

Baumgartner, Jody C. *Modern Presidential Electioneering: An Organizational and Comparative Approach.* Westport, Conn.: Praeger, 2000.

Dinkin, Robert J. *Campaigning in America: A History of Election Practice.* New York: Greenwood Press, 1989.

Jamieson, Kathleen Hall. *Packaging The Presidency: A History and Criticism of Presidential Campaign Advertising.* New York: Oxford University Press, 1996.

Jensen, Richard. *Grass Roots Politics.* Westport, Conn.: Greenwood Press, 1983.

Schlesinger, Arthur, Jr., and Fred Israel, eds. *A History of American Presidential Elections,* 4 vols. New York: Chelsea House, 1971.

Troy, Gil. *See How They Ran: The Changing Role of the Presidential Candidate.* New York: Free Press, 1996.

Richard Jensen

POLITICAL PARTIES

Influenced by the eighteenth century's classical republican intellectual tradition, America's founding fathers were hostile to political parties, believing them to be corrupt advocates of narrow factional interests. Political parties emerged, nevertheless, when Hamiltonians and Jeffersonians, soon Federalists and Republicans, squared off to define the authority of the new federal government in the 1790s. Much was at stake as a multitude of social, economic, and regional interests bred unremitting conflict. As political leaders addressed these issues, they mobilized support across a large landscape to contest regular elections on behalf of different policy initiatives. The Federalists, their strength centered among the social and economic elite of the New England and Middle Atlantic states, advocated a vigorous national government that would guarantee the nation's security and develop its commercial and manufacturing resources. The Republicans, in contrast, were more socially pluralist, wary of federal power, and supportive of economic policies that sustained the nation's dominant agricultural economy.

Political Parties in Antebellum America. With much at stake, the contests between the

Federalist Party and the Jeffersonian Republican Party were intense. But party activities remained limited, intermittent, and ephemeral. Turnout at the polls was low. Few voters were deeply committed to either party, policy disagreements were largely confined to small groups of political leaders, and the antiparty tendencies of the political culture remained influential. Neither party developed extensive organizations to promote its interests, and whatever furor the parties provoked in Congress or state legislatures did not survive for long. As a result, the history of the first parties was brief. The Federalists faded after 1815, whereas the Republicans splintered into factions. What conflict remained in this "era of good feelings" was fragmented and shallowly rooted.

Party politics reappeared in the 1820s with more intensity and staying power. The nation's rapid development reinvigorated battles over the authority of the central government, whereas the expansion of the electorate, which by 1840 encompassed most white males, increased the need to organize voters and draw them into the electoral process. Democrats and Whigs, the respective successors to the Republicans and Federalists, were, like their predecessors, coalitions of social and economic interests united by their commitments to distinct policy perspectives. The Democrats, having elected Andrew Jackson as president in 1828, pushed an agenda favoring limited government. The Whig Party, arising in opposition to Jackson, tended to be more commercially oriented, favoring the use of national power to develop an integrated market economy. Socially, the parties differed on ethnic and religious lines. Historic tensions between Catholics and Protestants, different Protestant denominations, and people of different national background continued to shape political outlooks in the New World and to influence party choice. Party leaders articulated alternative policy agendas so starkly and made the differences between them seem so wide that party loyalists felt they had to participate in partisan warfare for fear of losing their birthright should the other side win. Election campaigns became raucous nationwide extravaganzas, drawing thousands to rallies spiced by debates among candidates and rousing speeches by party heroes. Each party maintained a newspaper network to spread the partisan word. Each energetically brought out the faithful on Election Day. Politics was about parties. Voters loyally followed their party's direction and turned out at the polls in record numbers. Once in office, party representatives worked assiduously to implement their declared policies.

With these developments came a significant ideological shift. Parties were now accepted as necessary. Their authority was great. Still, aspects of the constitutional system, such as the need to amass an absolute majority in the Electoral College to win the presidency, limited the number of parties at the national level. Locally, the major parties used their power to restrict the number of candidates on the ballot. Minor parties never attracted a large vote, their hopes thwarted by most voters' strong partisan commitments. Nevertheless, given the close competition between the two major parties, minor parties were sometimes important in determining electoral outcomes and—in the case of the Liberty and Free Soil parties—in signaling the rise of sectional tensions.

Electoral realignments, sharp political shocks that jolted voters from their partisan moorings and affected the subsequent course of party warfare, occurred at regular intervals after the 1830s. The first of these came in the 1850s. Neither Whigs nor Democrats had spent time discussing sectional matters, but as new territories were acquired, as a campaign against the further spread of slavery took root, and as a bipartisan nativist backlash against Irish Catholic immigration beset the major parties, a new organization, the Republican Party, arose. It brought together antislavery sectionalists and other northern dissenters from the old party system. The Republicans' victory as a sectional party in 1860 led to the South's secession and the Civil War, during which party conflict remained as vigorous as ever in the North. The Republicans won support as the pro-Union party, whereas the Democratic Party suffered because of its adherents' alleged treasonous sympathy for the South. In the Confederacy, party warfare subsided during the war but reappeared with renewed vigor thereafter.

From the Gilded Age through the New Deal Era. Partisan warfare was unusually intense in the postwar decades. The two parties fought to a standstill in some of the closest, best organized, and most partisan elections in American history. Nevertheless, much was changing. With rapid industrialization, a new economic elite of investment bankers and manufacturers sought federal policy support for their efforts, and the Republican Party best embodied the probusiness position. The Democrats, in contrast, were strong in the agrarian South and among urban immigrant laborers put off by the Republicans' traditional hostility to ethnic outsiders. The latter supported the new urban political machines that pushed policy initiatives stressing government's responsibility to protect recent arrivals, the unemployed, and others in need.

Despite the Republicans' industrial tilt, the Democrats did not entirely win over the agricultural and labor sectors. Old party loyalties, Civil War memories, and ethnic antagonisms held thousands to their Republican loyalties. In the Gilded Age and Populist Era, economically marginalized workers and especially Western farmers challenged the existing order through third parties, notably the Greenback Labor and Populist parties. The Democrats behind William Jennings Bryan successfully attracted many of these have-nots in the mid-1890s but were soundly beaten by William McKinley and the Republicans in 1896 in another transforming electoral realignment that solidified Republican control of national politics for a generation.

In the Progressive Era, modernizing economic elites joined forces with the political reformers in a coalition that reinvigorated residual antiparty sentiment and presaged a massive change in American political culture. In the name of unselfish and uncorrupt politics, these antipartisans pushed legislation that weakened party control of the nominating and electoral process, significantly cut off the parties' major source of funds necessary to fight elections (the spoils system), and, in general, made the parties' operations more difficult. This attack had significant long-range consequences. Parties remained influential, but a process of destabilization and decline was underway.

The first third of the twentieth century also brought a major ideological reshuffling of party positions. Within the Democratic Party the rise of urban political groups seeking federal welfare legislation affected its traditional commitment to limited government. The Great Depression of the 1930s provoked a new electoral realignment that, this time, badly hurt the Republicans. Rallying behind Franklin Delano Roosevelt's New Deal, liberal Democrats vastly expanded the federal government's role to make it the guarantor of citizens' social and economic well-being. They were constrained, however, by resistance from the party's southern wing. Southern Democratic opposition also prevented action on civil rights, even as African Americans shed their traditional Republican loyalties in gratitude for Democratic economic policies.

So popular were Democratic policy initiatives from the 1930s onward that some Republicans embraced them in the name of political survival. Although still verbally confrontational, the parties lost some of their polarizing edge as a result. Under President Dwight D. Eisenhower in the 1950s, the Republicans briefly regained national power but with an agenda that accepted many of their rivals' initiatives. Back in power after 1960, the Democrats extended their social legislation, this time including civil rights, with the support of liberal Republicans.

The Declining Influence of Political Parties. The conditions for a partisan realignment again seemed present in the 1960s. Some liberal Republicans did join the Democrats, and many southern whites became Republicans. But the effect of the Progressive Era assault on parties was now increasingly evident, aided by the decline of party-reinforcing mechanisms, such as the fervent campaign rally, as well as by the rise of alternative means of political communication, especially television, which shaped election campaigns in nonpartisan, often antipartisan ways. Party identification weakened as voters grew more unsettled in their behavior, primarily reacting to dramatic crises and to the appeal of charismatic candidates, rather than expressing long-standing party loyalty. Electoral stability declined. The elements necessary for a realignment no longer existed.

Accompanying this voter defection from the party system was a strong popular reaction against the excesses and abuse of federal power identified with the Vietnam War and the Watergate scandals. The antigovernment mood benefited the Republicans in the 1980s behind the conservative Ronald Reagan. The Democrats, charged with policy excesses that produced inflation and violent confrontations over civil rights, fell apart at the polls. The Reagan revolution undid or weakened much of the Democratic policy agenda of the previous era and reinvigorated sharp ideological polarities between the parties. In 1994, the backlash against the Democrats brought in the first Republican-controlled Congress in forty years. But Republican gains were limited, with Democrats winning successive presidential elections in the 1990s. This continued into the next century. Although the Republicans regained the presidency in 2000 and held it in 2004, Democrats remained dominant in Congress most of the time. These divided outcomes suggested that a stable, partisan electoral order no longer existed as the number of voters identifying themselves as independent of either party continued to increase and shift their behavior from election to election. The major parties remained, but shorn of all but their true believers, they became more ideologically rigid and less prone to agree to common solutions to the nation's problems. Coupled with a proliferation of political blogs on the Internet, many of which challenged and denounced parties and their leaders, America's political atmosphere grew more bitter, more cynical, and more rhetorically violent, with the parties less and less able to accomplish much or remain in power long. Whatever role they continued to play, their influence was increasingly problematic in what seemed to be becoming a postpartisan political environment.

[*See also* **Anti-Masonic Party; Civil Service Reform; Communist Party USA; Democratic Party; Elections: Election Law; Elections: Nominating Systems; Elections: Presidential Elections; Elections: Suffrage; Elections: Voting Systems; Federalism; Federalist Party; Free Soil Party; Greenback Labor Party; Libertarian Party; Liberty Party; Municipal Politics; National Woman's Party; New Deal; Party System; Populist Party; Progressive Era; Progressive Party of 1912; Progressive Party of 1924; Progressive Party of 1948; Raza Unida Party; Republican Party; Socialist Party of America; Spoils System; State Governments; States'**

Rights Party; Third Parties; Voting: Voting Behavior; *and* Whig Party.]

BIBLIOGRAPHY

Chambers, William Nisbet, and Walter Dean Burnham, eds. *The American Party Systems*. New York: Oxford University Press, 1975.

Kleppner, Paul, et al. *The Evolution of the American Electoral Systems*. Westport, Conn.: Greenwood Press, 1981.

Maisel, L. Sandy, and William Shade, eds. *Parties and Politics in American History*. New York: Garland, 1994.

McGerr, Michael. *The Decline of Popular Politics, the American North, 1865–1928*. New York: Oxford University Press, 1986.

Milkis, Sidney. *The President and the Parties: The Transformation of the American Party System since the New Deal*. New York: Oxford University Press, 1993.

Nichols, Roy. *The Invention of the American Political Parties*. New York: Free Press, 1967.

Silbey, Joel H. *The American Political Nation, 1838–1893*. Stanford, Calif.: Stanford University Press, 1991.

Wattenberg, Martin. *The Decline of American Political Parties, 1952–1992*. Cambridge, Mass.: Harvard University Press, 1994.

Joel H. Silbey

POLITICAL POLARIZATION

Beginning in the mid-1970s, congressional politics became much more divisive. More Democrats staked out consistently liberal positions, and more Republicans supported wholly conservative ones. Congress began to polarize. Polarization is a term used by pundits, the press, and politicians themselves to describe contemporary American politics. But how do we know, scientifically, that politics has in fact become more polarized over the past thirty years? The basic answer is that changes in polarization can be measured because the members of Congress form overlapping cohorts. The Pennsylvania senate seat once held by the moderate Republican John Heinz was recently held by the conservative Republican Rick Santorum, who in turn was replaced by the liberal Bob Casey. Heinz had served with Arlen Specter. Specter also served with Santorum. Heinz and Specter had similar voting records. In contrast, Specter voted with the liberals (or Democrats) much more frequently than Santorum. Observations like this one form the basis for measuring increases in polarization. Replacements like that of Heinz by Santorum and Santorum by Casey in Pennsylvania or Sam Ervin by John Edwards in North Carolina are the symptoms of polarization.

Political scientists Kenneth Poole and Howard Rosenthal developed a statistical procedure that uses the overlapping cohorts to analyze all the roll call votes in American history from 1789 to 2011. This procedure—known as DW-NOMINATE—can be used to study polarization and ideological change over time. It is based on a simple geometric (spatial) model of voting behavior. Each legislator is represented by one point and each roll call is represented by two points—one for "yea" and one for "nay." These points form a spatial map that summarizes the roll calls. In this sense a spatial map is much like a road map. A spreadsheet that tabulates all the distances between every pair of sizable cities in the United States contains the same information as the corresponding map of the United States. Much like a road map, a spatial map formed from roll calls provides a way of visualizing the political world of a legislature. The closeness of two legislators on the map shows how similar their voting records are, and the distribution of legislators shows what the dimensions are.

The first dimension of the map typically divides the two major parties on the fundamental issue of the role of government in the economy. The second dimension differentiates the members by region, mainly over race and civil rights, but in the latter part of the nineteenth century it picked up regional differences on bimetallism and the free coinage of silver. In the modern era the primary dimension is liberal–moderate–conservative as it is commonly understood and the second dimension captures the conflict over race and civil rights.

Through most of American history there have been two major mass-based political parties. A "left" party represents the less well off and the "right" party represents the somewhat better off. To be competitive both the "left" and the "right" parties had to aim their appeals at people of middling incomes. Because of the nature of the system of representation, both parties have tended to be internally divided over regional issues. For most of U.S. history this regional issue has been concerned with race. These two basic political features of the parties account for the two dimensions of the spatial maps.

The beginning of the modern trend to greater polarization began with a major change in the political parties in the late 1960s. For almost fifty years the United States had a three-political-party system produced by a split in the Democratic Party into its Northern and Southern wings from the late 1930s to the early 1990s. In Congress all three parties easily formed coalitions with one of the others against the third, depending on the issue at hand. The northern and southern Democrats united to organize the House and Senate and thereby seize the spoils due the "majority" party. The northern Democrats and Republicans united to pass the 1964 Civil Rights Act and the 1965 Voting Rights Act and the "conservative coalition" of Republicans and southern Democrats united to block liberal economic (and in the 1970s social) policies.

The demise of this system began with the assassination of President John F. Kennedy in 1963. President Lyndon Johnson proved instrumental in enacting civil rights legislation. The landslide victory over Republican Barry Goldwater in 1964 produced a liberal northern Democratic Congressional majority for the first time since 1936. This destabilized the Democratic coalition. Democrats in the eighty-ninth Congress (1965–1966) no longer required southern support to pass expansive federal programs. These programs along with other redistributive programs initiated by the federal courts—mandatory school busing to alleviate racial disparities in the public schools being the most conspicuous—led to a polarizing backlash in the late 1960s and early 1970s. The effects of this backlash were blunted by the Watergate scandal (1972–1974) and the Republican Party did not fully recover its footing until the 1980 elections.

The old southern Democratic Party has, in effect, disintegrated. Race has been drawn into the liberal–conservative dimension because race-related issues are increasingly questions of redistribution. In addition, the "social/lifestyle" issues are increasingly being drawn into the main dimension of conflict. The end result was that the Democrat and Republican parties became more homogeneous and polarized. Moderates disappeared during the past thirty years. Republicans moved steadily to the right on the liberal–conservative dimension with conservatives replacing more moderate Republicans outside the southern states and conservative Republicans replacing moderate and conservative Democrats in the South. In contrast, the old right flank of the Democratic Party composed mostly of southerners disappeared, leaving a polarized Congress.

At least until the late 1990s the American public did not appear to be polarizing. More recent surveys have shown that activists and voters who are strong party identifiers have polarized as well. The disappearance of moderates has meant increased difficulty for either party to govern effectively.

As of 2011 there is no sign that the polarization has peaked. The last period of such intense polarization was just before World War I. Then the war and the dramatic increase in taxes to pay for it, as well as the success of Progressive Era reforms, lessened tensions and polarization declined for forty years. No resolution of this sort appears likely for this modern period of polarization.

BIBLIOGRAPHY

Abramowitz, Alan I. *The Disappearing Center*. New Haven, Conn.: Yale University Press, 2010.

Fiorina, Morris. *Culture War? The Myth of a Polarized America*. Boston: Longman, 2010.

Poole, Keith T., and Howard Rosenthal. *Congress: A Political–Economic History of Roll Call Voting*. New York: Oxford University Press, 1997.

Poole, Keith T., and Howard Rosenthal. *Ideology and Congress*. New Brunswick: Transaction Publishers, 2007.

Keith T. Poole

POLITICAL REALIGNMENT

The concept of political realignment holds that American history is characterized by rare bursts of electoral change that then largely persist across decades of relative stability. The term also encompasses the idea that the electoral landscape may be reshaped by a gradual realignment of voting groups.

Development. Realignment theory blossomed in the wake of Harry S. Truman's 1948 upset presidential victory. The result of the election jolted students of American politics into rethinking the meaning of the elections of the 1930s and 1940s. The initial breakthrough in the development of realignment theory was made by the journalist Samuel Lubell. His breakthrough was then refined by the political scientist V. O. Key. The capstone to realignment theory was subsequently provided by the social psychologist Angus Campbell.

Lubell's *The Future of American Politics* (1952) focused on the elections of 1932 and 1936 as examples of lasting electoral change. The deepening of the Great Depression gave the Democrats victory in 1932; the successes of the New Deal then resulted in the landslide win of 1936. The election of 1948 demonstrated that the earlier Democratic victories had resulted in enduring electoral change. Additionally, Lubell extended his ideas across historical time, arguing that the Civil War and the depression of the 1890s provided similar examples of crises leading to lasting electoral upheaval. Finally, Lubell added that underlying demographic change—such as the coming of age by the 1930s of the children of immigrants from southern and eastern Europe—additionally contributed to enduring electoral change.

Lubell's work stimulated political scientist V. O. Key, who was also seeking a new understanding of elections over time. In 1955 Key published his seminal article, "A Theory of Critical Elections," in the *Journal of Politics*. In it, he focused on elections which led to lasting new cleavages among the electorate. In 1959 Key contributed another article, "Secular Realignment and the Party System," also in the *Journal of Politics*, which focused on factors such as demographic changes that gradually altered voting patterns.

Key influenced Angus Campbell and his coauthors, who produced *The American Voter* (1960). The contribution of Campbell was twofold. First, Campbell developed the concept of party identification, the idea based upon extensive surveys of individuals that voters typically developed an emotional or psychological attachment to a political party that then often guided their voting choices. In addition, he developed a classification of elections, building on Key's critical elections concept. Realigning elections led to durable shifts among voters, strong enough to change party identification. Maintaining elections essentially reflected existing cleavages. Deviating elections were those—such as 1952 and 1956—when existing party identification essentially remained in place but large numbers of voters cast ballots in a contrary way because of short-run factors. Changes in party identification constituted the crucial factor in determining whether an election or electoral era was realigning.

Application. With the essentials of realignment theory in place by 1960, scholars and political analysts undertook to apply the concept not only to the political past but also to the elections of the 1960s and beyond. The two ventures were not unrelated. Some political historians and political scientists reached back to apply the concept to the elections of 1800 and 1828; this, added to the focus on the 1860s, 1890s, and 1930s, led to the notion of a cyclical periodicity in American politics, with a critical election or critical election era occurring every twenty-eight to thirty-six years. Two of the most influential such expositions were the writer Kevin P. Phillips's *The Emerging Republican Majority* (1969) and the political scientist Walter Dean Burnham's *Critical Elections and the Mainsprings of American Politics* (1970). In the upheaval of the 1960s, fueled by racial conflict and cultural upheaval, Phillips saw a turning from the dominant issues and electoral coalitions shaped by the 1930s to new issues and a new dominant coalition centered on the Sunbelt. Burnham set forth the idea of cyclical periodicity based on the concept that the cumbersome U.S. constitutional system resulted in an accumulation of problems with an eventual crisis leading to a realigning era.

The work influenced a generation of young scholars who focused on potentially realigning elections. A 1964 landslide triggered thought of an enhanced Democratic majority. In 1968, with a sharp reversal for the Democrats, came the conclusion that Republican Richard M. Nixon's narrow victory plus the significant vote for American Independent George Wallace meant the doom of the old Democratic coalition and the birth of its replacement. Nixon's huge landslide win of 1972, in which the 1968 Wallace vote and hence the white South overwhelmingly went Republican, lent credence to the idea of an emerging Republican majority. But problems ensued in terms of realignment theory. Congressional election results were not in sync with presidential returns. The Democrats retained control of both houses of Congress throughout the 1970s. Party identification did not massively shift, leading to the conclusion that the Republican presidential victories of 1968 and 1972 constituted deviating elections. This latter conclusion was then buoyed by the election of Democrat Jimmy Carter to the White House in 1976.

Realignment theory received an encore of sorts with Republican Ronald Reagan's large victory in 1980 accompanied by a Republican takeover of the Senate. Reagan's even larger victory in 1984 accompanied by some shift in party identification in the Republican direction contributed further to the idea of a pro-Republican realignment. The Democrats retook the Senate in 1986, but the victory of Republican George H. W. Bush in 1988 provided evidence to many analysts of at least a Republican presidential realignment. Democrat Bill Clinton's 1992 victory notwithstanding, the Republican takeover of Congress in 1994 was widely interpreted as the culmination of the turn toward the Republicans dating from 1968 and 1980. The length of time between 1968 and 1994 and the fact that Congress remained largely Democratic long after numerous Republican presidential victories led to a lessened emphasis on the idea of quick election change. Instead, increased emphasis was placed on the secular component of realignment theory, especially in terms of the gradual movement of the White South from Democratic dominance to Republican hegemony, first at the presidential level and then at the Congressional level.

Assessment. The apparent difficulties in applying realignment theory to the elections of the 1960s and beyond also led to calls to jettison the concept. Two major alternatives set forth were dealignment and retrospective voting. Analysts focusing on dealignment held that the 1960s had spawned not a realignment strengthening one party in an enduring way but rather a growth of voters who were unaligned with either party—an expansion of independents. If there had been a significant erosion of party identification, if increasing numbers of voters swayed back and forth based on short-run factors, there could be no stable base against which to measure realignment itself. Elections would be determined not by long-standing party loyalties but by current issues and candidates. Dealignment cohered with retrospective voting. If long-term loyalties had eroded, then short-term judgments based on whether the administration in power had performed satisfactorily, especially on the economy, would sway elections. Hence, partisans of retrospective analysis declared that voters rendered a negative judgment on Jimmy Carter in 1980, positive judgments on Ronald Reagan in 1984 and his heir apparent George H. W. Bush in 1988, a negative judgment on Bush in 1992 because of economic recession, and a positive judgment on Bill Clinton in 1996 because of economic prosperity.

Defenders of realignment theory in the late twentieth century, applying their concept to elections dating to the 1960s, held that realignment had occurred but along new lines. Dealignment, they maintained, was realignment by other means. Instead of a dominant new party as in the Civil War era, or the enhanced strength of an existing party as in the 1890s, or a switch in dominance from one party to another as in the 1930s, the pattern of realignment shaped by the 1960s featured greater voter independence. It also demonstrated enduring if gradual shifts in partisan electoral behavior. Certainly, they argued, there could be no denying the massive shift of white Southerners from their historic Democratic allegiance to a strong Republican base of support.

Realignment theory, much criticized since the late 1970s, nonetheless remains in the early twenty-first century a widely used approach to interpreting the American political past. It also continues to be applied contemporaneously, fueling speculation as to the long-term political impact of crises such as the 9/11 attack and the 2008 economic meltdown. Realignment theory's major misuse has been perhaps the most obvious. A concept designed to illuminate the past was turned into an instrument to gauge the realigning potential of current elections—a flawed instrument given that the realigning impact of any election or series of elections can only be determined with the extended passage of time.

[*See also* **Bush, George H. W.; Carter, Jimmy; Clinton, William J.; Nixon, Richard M.; Party System; Reagan, Ronald;** ***and*** **Truman, Harry S.**]

BIBLIOGRAPHY

Campbell, James E. "Party Systems and Realignments in the United States, 1868–2004." *Social Science History* 30 (2006): 359–386.

Mayhew, David R. *Electoral Realignments: A Critique of an American Genre*. New Haven, Conn.: Yale University Press, 2002.

Paulson, Arthur. *Electoral Realignment and the Outlook for American Democracy*. Boston; Hanover: Northeastern University Press; University Press of England, 2007.

Rosenof, Theodore. *Realignment: The Theory That Changed the Way We Think about American Politics*. Lanham, Md.: Rowman & Littlefield, 2003.

Shafer, Byron E., ed. *The End of Realignment? Interpreting American Electoral Eras*. Madison: University of Wisconsin Press, 1991.

Sundquist, James L. *Dynamics of the Party System: Alignment and Realignment of Parties in the United States*. Revised ed. Washington, D.C.: Brookings Institution, 1983.

Theodore Rosenof

POLITICAL SCIENCE

Like other social scientists, American political scientists have long questioned whether their field of study constitutes, or ought to constitute, a coherent discipline. The result has been a vibrant field, but one whose whole is less than the sum of its parts. Although lively and productive, it lacks even a wavering consensus about its proper methodology, theory, or subject matter. What is called "political science" in America is, in fact, an amalgam of philosophy, history, sociology, economics, law, psychology, systems theory, institutional analysis, quantitative analysis, and a dozen other perspectives, all with competing presuppositions and clashing *raisons d'être.*

The problem with defining political science begins with the term itself. In what sense can the study of politics be called a science? The discipline's lineage extends back to Aristotle's *Politics,* which embedded a rich account of political life in a more general "scientific" perspective on the natural and human worlds. Yet Aristotle did not mean "science" in the modern sense nor did he envision the study of politics as something independent of what one might call "moral philosophy." Rejecting Aristotle's approach, the founders of modern political science sought to make the field more "scientific" precisely by distancing it from moral philosophy, focusing instead on the value-neutral, quantitative study of human behavior. David Easton's 1953 definition of politics—"the behaviors or set of interactions through which authoritative allocations (or binding decisions) are made and implemented for a society"—sums up this view. Such behaviorist, realist, or structuralist-fuctionalist approaches largely dominated much of twentieth-century American political science—although outlines emerged as early as the 1780s, in James Madison's Federalist No. 10.

Challenging this approach, conservative traditionalists and admirers of the German refugee scholars Leo Strauss, Eric Voegelin, and Hannah Arendt continued to insist that the study of politics is a fundamentally philosophical and moral undertaking. Marxist, feminist, socialist, and other "engaged" scholars meanwhile rejected the goal of scholarly detachment and value neutrality, espousing a political science openly committed to political goals. Both approaches were amply represented in the discipline at the end of the twentieth century. Indeed, the tension between engagement and detachment lies at the very heart of political science and is unlikely ever to be finally resolved.

Views of political science's proper subject matter have shifted as well. American founders of the discipline, such as Columbia University's John W. Burgess (1844–1931), following their German mentors, focused on the state and other governmental institutions—a natural enough preoccupation for academics who had experienced the breakdown of the American nation-state in the Civil War. But subsequent generations changed and expanded this focus. Scholars such as Charles A. Beard, Arthur Bentley, E. Pendleton Herring, V. O. Key Jr., and David Truman cast aside the legalism and formalism of Burgess's generation, substituting more pragmatic and experimental approaches to American politics, emphasizing extraconstitutional, extralegal, and extragovernmental groups. Writers such as Walter Lippmann, Harold Lasswell, and Charles Merriam explored the influence of psychology, particularly mass psychology, upon modern politics.

Post–World War II social scientists, epitomized by Talcott Parsons, exuded confidence in the application of science to human affairs, yet they were leery of the notion that politics ought to involve public arguments over fundamental values, believing that fanaticism bred by political ideology had in part caused the war. Therefore, they sought to manage social conflict through value-neutral doctrines of functionalism and pluralism, pitting faction against faction in the neo-Madisonian fashion to produce a social equilibrium. Their mantle continued to be carried in the late twentieth century by the advocates of "rational choice" theory. New Left scholars of the 1960s vehemently rejected this value neutrality as both an apology and a prop for the status quo; they sought instead to reinfuse political science with moral purpose. After the 1960s, the study of elections and political institutions had to compete with sympathetic interest in social movements, particularly those of minorities or "subaltern" groups, and in the nongovernmental institutions of "civil society."

Noteworthy in this pattern was the steady retreat from the consideration of the "political" per se. Instead, twentieth-century American political science, particularly after the postwar "behavioral revolution," increasingly reduced politics to the social, the economic, the psychological, or the cultural. Arendt warned against this process, particularly the tendency to conflate the "social" and the "political." Arendt's observations were perhaps borne out by the perceived erosion of the public realm in late twentieth-century America. That problem could not be addressed without reviving an older tradition of reflection on politics, as a distinctive form of human activity involving public deliberation by citizens in public spaces. Try as it may, political science appears unable to escape its normative dimension because that dimension is implicit in the very concept of politics.

[*See also* **Federalist Papers; Lippman, Walter; Madison, James; New Left;** ***and*** **Political Parties.**]

BIBLIOGRAPHY

Burgess, John W. *The Foundations of Political Science.* New York: Columbia University Press, 1933.

Ceaser, James. *Liberal Democracy and Political Science.* Baltimore: Johns Hopkins University Press, 1990.

Crick, Bernard. *The American Science of Politics: Its Origins and Conditions.* Berkeley: University of California Press, 1959.

Ross, Dorothy. *The Origins of American Social Science.* Cambridge, UK: Cambridge University Press, 1992.

Somit, Albert, and Joseph Tanenhaus. *The Development of American Politic Science: From Burgess to Behavioralism.* New York: Irvington, 1982.

Strauss, Leo. *Natural Right and History.* Chicago: University of Chicago Press, 1950.

Wilfred M. McClay

POLK, JAMES KNOX

(1795–1849), eleventh president of the United States. A Jacksonian Democrat and devotee of Thomas Jefferson's agrarian political ideology, Polk was born in Mecklenburg County, North Carolina, and reared in Maury County, Tennessee. Graduating with honors from the University of North Carolina in 1818, he first practiced law and in 1823 won election to the Tennessee legislature. He married Sarah Childress in 1824. Elected to Congress in 1825, he opposed President John Quincy Adams's domestic program of economic development and political consolidation. As chair of the House Ways and Means Committee in Andrew Jackson's first term, he led the Democratic

Party's opposition to federally funded internal improvements and renewal of the national bank's charter. He served two terms (1835–1839) as speaker of the House.

Polk backed the Democrat Martin Van Buren for president in 1836, but Tennessee voted Whig. Determined to regain political control of his state, he won the governorship in 1839. Tennessee again voted Whig in 1840, however, and Polk himself lost gubernatorial bids in 1841 and 1843. In 1844, seeing near-certain Democratic defeat if Van Buren again headed the ticket, the aged Andrew Jackson persuaded the party to nominate Polk, a westerner who, he hoped, would annex Texas while bridging the deepening sectional divide. The first "dark horse" presidential candidate, Polk defeated both the Whig Henry Clay and James G. Birney of the tiny antislavery Liberty Party by a razor-thin plurality. Clay hurt his candidacy by issuing ambiguous statements on Texas annexation, whereas Polk limited his public utterances to a single statement on the tariff. The election revealed a nation almost evenly divided over expansionism, the tariff, immigration policy, and agrarianism versus the market revolution.

As president, Polk pursued five major goals: Texas annexation (already approved by Congress), settlement of the Oregon boundary dispute with Britain, tariff reduction, establishment of an independent treasury, and the purchase of California. In pursuing Texas annexation, Polk first tried diplomacy. He offered to purchase Mexico's northern provinces, not from a belief in so-called Manifest Destiny but from a desire to preserve the agrarian republic. Each new generation of independent farmers, he believed, must find its own rich soil or sink into wage dependency. Mexico, rejecting America's right to annex lands west of the Sabine River, broke diplomatic relations shortly after Polk's inauguration. Polk sought to restore amicable ties, but Mexico's military rulers feared that the loss of Texas would precipitate other provincial uprisings and a further erosion of centralized control. For his part, Polk saw annexation as preferable to a drawn-out defensive border war upholding Texas's sovereignty and its claims to the Rio Grande as its southern boundary. Convinced that Mexico intended to invade Texas and frustrated when Mexico snubbed John Slidell, his diplomatic emissary, Polk ordered Zachary Taylor and his troops to the Rio Grande. On 24 April 1846, a large Mexican force crossed the river and captured an American patrol. Reacting forcefully, Polk on 11 May informed Congress that "war exists by the act of Mexico itself." The resulting war led to U.S. acquisition of Texas, California, and Mexico's other territories north of the Rio Grande.

The British cabinet, meanwhile, had decided to settle the Oregon dispute by accepting a boundary line at the forty-ninth parallel. Contrary to the view of his secretary of state, James Buchanan, Polk had calculated correctly that the British would not go to war over its commercial interests in North America. Polk's diplomatic and military successes failed to bring political consensus at home, however, as the Whig Party blamed him for giving up half of Oregon and denounced the Mexican War as immoral. Polk's expansionist policies postponed the demise of the agrarian republic, but left unresolved the profound economic, religious, and racial issues dividing the nation. Having accomplished his goals, he honored his pledge not to seek a second term. Polk succumbed to cholera at his Nashville, Tennessee, home just three months after leaving office.

[*See also* **Adams, John Quincy; Agricultural Policy; Buchanan, James; Clay, Henry; Immigration Law and Policy: Before 1930; Jackson, Andrew; Jefferson, Thomas; Tariffs; Taylor, Zachary; Taxation;** *and* **Van Buren, Martin.**]

BIBLIOGRAPHY

Quaife, Milo Milton, ed. *The Diary of James K. Polk during His Presidency, 1845–1849*, 4 vols. Chicago: A. C. McClurg, 1910.

Sellers, Charles Grier, Jr. *James K. Polk, Jacksonian*. Princeton, N.J.: Princeton University Press, 1957.

Weaver, Herbert, Wayne Cutler, eds. *Correspondence of James K. Polk*, 9 vols. Nashville, Tenn.: Vanderbilt University Press, 1969–1996.

Wayne Cutler

POPULAR SOVEREIGNTY

Popular sovereignty holds that the power to govern ultimately resides with the people. In the late 1840s the doctrine became an alternative in the political effort to resolve the slavery debate in the United States. As America expanded westward it created new territories, and those territories in turn sought to become states. Each application for statehood threatened to divide the Union, and as the crisis grew, placing the spread of slavery in the hands of territorial residents emerged as a possible solution.

In the early nineteenth century, the majority of Americans lived in the North, creating a precarious balance of free and slave states in Congress. In 1820 the admission of Missouri brought the possibility that slavery could be legislated into extinction when a debate arose as to whether Missouri could be admitted free or slave. The Missouri Compromise resolved the immediate dispute and established a geographical line at 36°30′ below which any new territory seeking admission as a state would come in as a slave state.

The Missouri Compromise functioned for a time, but in the late 1840s America's war with Mexico expanded her borders by an additional 525,000 square miles. When the war began Free Soil advocates tried to prohibit slavery in this new territory. The Wilmot Proviso did not pass, but it sent a clear signal that slavery would have to fight to expand. In 1850 California applied for statehood. The 36°30′ line proved to be unworkable as it became apparent that certain places, like the West, simply would not support slavery. When Congress moved to admit California as a free state, the Southern states objected. The Compromise of 1850 bought a tenuous peace, in part using the notion that the people in the territory could decide whether to seek admission as free or slave.

Conceived by Senator Daniel Dickinson (D-NY) and popularized by Lewis Cass (D-MI), popular sovereignty, in effect, divested Congress of its power over territories by allowing the residents of a territory to decide whether the territory would enter the Union as free or slave. The Compromise of 1850 applied the concept to the New Mexico territory, a region not part of the Union at the time of the Missouri Compromise. In 1854 Senator Stephen Douglas (D-IL) moved to extend popular sovereignty to the Kansas–Nebraska territory. Reasoning that slavery could not exist where it was unwanted, Douglas successfully guided the Kansas–Nebraska Act through Congress, implicitly repealing the Missouri Compromise. The residents of the Kansas territory would determine the fate of slavery there.

The Kansas–Nebraska Act completed the split of the Democratic Party into "Northern" and "Southern" factions. It destroyed the Whigs and laid the groundwork for the Republicans. In 1857 the U.S. Supreme Court decided *Scott v. Sandford* and settled the issue, declaring the Missouri Compromise unconstitutional and holding that Congress had no power to restrict slavery. By then the harsh reality of the rift between North and South had destroyed popular sovereignty as a political tool. Pro- and antislavery factions poured into Kansas trying to dictate the slavery question. Political corruption and violence rendered the electoral process ineffective. Kansas remained a territory until 1861 and a region plagued by violence until after the Civil War.

[*See also* **Compromise of 1850; Free Soil Party; Kansas–Nebraska Act;** ***Scott v. Sandford; and*** **Wilmot Proviso.**]

BIBLIOGRAPHY

Etcheson, Nicole. *Bleeding Kansas: Contested Liberty in the Civil War.* Lawrence: University Press of Kansas, 2004.

Forbes, Robert. *The Missouri Compromise and Its Aftermath: Slavery and the Meaning of America.* Chapel Hill: University of North Carolina Press, 2007.

McArthur, Debra. *Kansas–Nebraska and "Bleeding Kansas" in American History.* Berkeley: Enslow Publishing, 2003.

Mark A. Weitz

POPULATION POLICY

In its first century, the population policies of the United States were indirect but powerful: the federal government subsidized the numerical and geographical expansion of the citizenry by acquiring new territories and removing Indians from them, providing cheap land to settlers and railroads, and welcoming the nearly unlimited immigration of people not of "African descent." The federal system and population-based representation encouraged cities and states to compete for settlers. Still, the founders' "republican" theory of democracy did hold that a rising population was fraught with peril and augured the kind of fully settled, manufacturing-based, and morally decrepit European society from which the colonists had fled. Residual concerns about the social ills of population concentration animated expansionary foreign policy through the Mexican–American War (1846–1848). As Americans rushed pell-mell into the industrial age, however, unease that population growth would undermine the nation's agrarian character faded, and the few lone voices who doubted the inexhaustibility of natural resources were overwhelmed by the exuberant westward expansion and dramatic growth (from 35 million in 1865 to 76 million in 1900) of a prosperous and still seemingly wide-open country.

The Census Bureau's observation after the Census of 1890 that the nation no longer had a discernable "frontier" greatly expanded the number of American "Malthusians"—individuals, inspired by British pastor Thomas Malthus's claims a century earlier that population growth eventually overwhelms natural resources, who wished to arrest population growth. The first third of the twentieth century also saw the heyday of the American eugenics movement, which spuriously sought to engineer a "better" population by encouraging births among the genetically "fit" and discouraging births among the genetically "unfit." Malthusianism and eugenics spurred the 1924 Immigration Act, which severely curtailed immigration to the United States, especially from non-"white" nations of southeastern Europe. In addition, a majority of states passed eugenically inspired laws that banned mixed marriages and/or established compulsory sterilization of state institution residents with perceived mental and sexual defects, among other categories. Between 1900 and the 1970s, over 60,000 Americans were forcibly sterilized.

During the Great Depression, lower birthrates and erroneous predictions of future population decline led some politicians to recommend pro–population growth policies such as payments for every baby. "Reform" eugenicists also sought to encourage growth through profamily welfare state spending. But with a quarter of the nation unemployed, the goal of more births seemed odd to many, and no formal pronatalist policies emerged. Roosevelt's New Deal did initiate a modest program of resettling Americans from distressed farmlands to new towns and homesteads.

After World War II, population growth surged in developing nations because of improvements in health, sanitation, and food production, and "population policy" became synonymous with the quest to halt this growth. Against the backdrop of the Cold War, policy makers feared that rapidly expanding populations would destabilize fragile postcolonial states and drive them into the Soviet sphere. Meanwhile, a small community of conservationists rejuvenated Malthusianism by fusing it to the new field of ecology, suggesting population growth might trigger global environmental collapse. At home, the Baby-Boom, the unexpected and sustained increase in birth rates from 1946 to 1964, further boosted trepidation about population growth, even if the discussion about domestic expansion often centered on amenities such as open space rather than on the prospect of true scarcity. And the prevailing Keynesian economic paradigm supported the notion that a smaller population would be consistent with a healthy economy if the state promoted rising levels of per-capita consumption.

Some population-reduction advocates harbored racist fears of expanding numbers of dark-skinned people, but most were genuinely motivated by philanthropic desires to help the world's poor and to conserve natural resources. In 1952, philanthropist John D. Rockefeller III funded the creation of the Population Council, which helped expand a small prewar community on population experts into a tight-knit issue network led by the Council and the Ford and Rockefeller foundations. Research rather than policy agitation dominated the 1950s, but the population network laid the groundwork for a widespread acceptance of the global overpopulation paradigm and the emergence of state international and domestic population policy in the 1960s.

In 1959, President Eisenhower famously said that the government should have nothing to do with birth control, yet that year's report of the president's Committee to Study the U.S. Military Assistance Program urged federal aid for family planning programs in the developing world. The U.S. Agency for International Development took baby steps in this direction during the Kennedy years. Then, in a sudden five-year burst after Lyndon Johnson promised in his 1965 State of the Union Address to "seek new ways to use our knowledge to help deal with the explosion in world population and the growing scarcity in world resources," the U.S. government erected a significant and still-standing population policy regime by not only providing overseas population assistance but also incorporating family planning into the domestic "War on Poverty." For a brief moment in the late 1960s, more dramatic population-reduction measures seemed imminent when a "zero population growth" movement, inspired by political radicalism and mass environmentalism (and highlighted by Stanford biologist Paul Ehrlich's best-selling "The Population Bomb") rose to the fore. In 1969, President Nixon delivered a special message to Congress on the population crisis, and Congress created the National Commission on Population Growth and the American Future.

Yet the zero population growth movement fizzled as quickly as it emerged. In 1972, Nixon ignored the final report of his population commission, which called for policies, such as abortion rights, that would have encouraged population stabilization, partially because he feared a growing backlash from Catholics. In addition, conservative economists—poised to take charge of the national economic discussion during the downturn of the 1970s—had already rejected Malthusian economics and launched a new celebration of the virtues of population enlargement. In the 1970s, the media and policy makers turned away from population matters because the environmental movement was exhausted and the domestic birth rate bottomed out (before resuming its trajectory as one of the highest in the developed world). The Supreme Court's 1973 *Roe v. Wade* decision and the ascendant culture wars solidified conservative opposition to population policy. Even many liberal groups avoided the issue, fearing its connections to contentious racial politics: critics had long charged that population control targeted minorities, and because skyrocketing immigration accounted for a significant and increasing share of population growth (Congress had reopened the gates in 1965), support for population control was easily branded anti-immigrant. U.S. aid for international family planning programs persisted, but the economic and political consensus behind it frayed. In 1984, the American delegation to a global conference on population famously declared that "in any particular society, population growth is of itself a neutral phenomenon."

The recent stalemate in American politics has produced little change in population policy. Most visibly, Republican presidents have imposed the "global gag rule," which demands that any overseas family planning organization receiving funds from the United States refrains from providing information on abortion, whereas Democratic administrations have rescinded it. In the early twenty-first century, most economists and politicians emphasize that more babies would help fund the massive retirement bill of the baby-boomers. That the nation is headed for a population of 440 million in 2050—and that ever more western-style consumers across the globe threaten the climate—seem almost afterthoughts.

[*See also* **Immigration Law and Policy: After 1930; Immigration Law and Policy: Before 1930; Johnson, Lyndon B.; Nixon, Richard M.;** ***and Roe v. Wade.***]

BIBLIOGRAPHY

Connelly, Matthew. *Fatal Misconception: The Struggle to Control World Population.* Cambridge, Mass.: Belknap Press of Harvard University Press, 2008.

Critchlow, Donald T. *Intended Consequences: Birth Control, Abortion, and the Federal Government in Modern America.* New York: Oxford University Press, 1999.

Hoff, Derek S. *The State and the Stork: The Population Debate and Policymaking in United States History.* Chicago: University of Chicago Press, 2012.

Derek S. Hoff

POPULIST ERA

No historical period conforms precisely to a specific span of years, and the Populist Era is no exception. The events of the 1890s—the time period known as the Populist Era—reflected social and economic pressures, and reactions to those pressures, that had been building for decades. Similarly, the Populist movement itself, a response to long-term political, economic, and social changes, was rooted in earlier agrarian protest movements—the Farmers' Alliance movement of the 1880s, the Granger movement of the 1870s—and even in rural folkways antedating the Civil War.

Populist Politics. The politics of the Populist Era were issue-oriented. Following several decades of weak presidents, corrupt politicians serving corporate interests, and dominance by two parties that often seemed indistinguishable, the Populist Party and Populists generally took a sharply different approach. Whereas both the Republican Party and the Democratic Party usually nominated candidates allied with corporate interests, Populists championed America's workers, small farmers, tenants, and sharecroppers. the dominant parties espoused Social Darwinism, laissez-faire (at least in theory), and governmental passivity, Populists advocated active government intervention in the economy and regulation of trusts and corporations in the public interest. Whereas Presidents Benjamin Harrison, Grover Cleveland, and William McKinley all advocated a sound-money policy to protect creditors and used force to break strikes and unions, Populists favored the unlimited coinage of silver and other measures to increase the money supply and help debtors and opposed the use of troops against striking workers.

The Economy. The 1890s was a decade of depression, unemployment, widespread poverty, and crisis in rural America. In the period after 1870, the rapid settlement of western lands, improved agricultural technology, and the spread of railroads and steamship lines resulted in agricultural overproduction and increased competition in world markets, driving prices down and putting farmers in a harsh credit squeeze. The Panic of 1893, triggered by the failure of a London banking firm, caused many British investors to unload their American stocks, precipitating a stock market crash. The sell-off came just as the high McKinley Tariff of 1890 depressed the agricultural export market. The resulting three-year depression, the worst in American history up to the 1930s, saw soup kitchens, desperate strikes, farm foreclosures, and ragged armies of the unemployed.

Evidence of unrest abounded. In July 1892, strikers at Andrew Carnegie's Homestead Steel Works near Pittsburgh, Pennsylvania, fired on two barges loaded with Pinkerton detectives, killing seven and wounding many more. State militia broke the strike, and a steelworkers' union did not emerge until the 1930s. An 1894 strike at George Pullman's sleeping-car works near Chicago, protesting wage cuts combined with rent increases in Pullman's company town, precipitated a confrontation between the American Railway Union and the General Managers Association, the latter representing twenty-four railroads operating through Chicago. The Cleveland administration, securing a court injunction against the strike, sent in federal troops when escalating violence threatened delivery of the mail. Meanwhile, in the spring of 1894, "Coxey's Army," 300 unemployed workers led by the Ohio Populist Jacob S. Coxey (1854–1951), staged one of the earliest marches on Washington, demanding jobs and relief.

The South and the Great Plains, both Populist strongholds, suffered severe economic deprivation exacerbated by drought in the 1890s. Indeed, the rural South experienced a prolonged economic downturn that extended from the end of the Civil War through the 1930s. Along with agrarian protest, factory workers' discontent in industrialized areas of the South, such as northern Alabama, contributed to the climate of unrest.

Desperate economic conditions were widespread. Some 40 percent of Americans lived in poverty in 1900, a higher percentage than in the Great Depression of the 1930s. No organized social service network, no minimum wage laws, no unemployment insurance, and no federal welfare programs protected the poor. Poverty fell especially hard on the unemployed, marginal farmers, urban immigrants, and other particularly vulnerable groups. African Americans experienced not only high rates of poverty but also the added burden of racism. Jim Crow laws spread across the South in these years, imposing a rigid system of racial segregation. In *Plessy v. Ferguson* (1898), the U.S. Supreme Court upheld racially segregated public facilities, from schools to transit systems. A record of 226 lynchings occurred in 1892, mostly in the South and Southwest. The total number of lynchings from 1889 to 1918 exceeded 2,500, and most victims were African American. Even in the North, de facto segregation and discrimination prevailed. Speaking in Atlanta in 1895, the era's most prominent black leader, Booker T. Washington, urged African Americans to acquire useful vocational skills and to avoid agitation for racial equality.

Society and Culture. Battered by economic crisis and political upheaval, American society and culture also underwent major transformations. The nation's ethnic composition was changing dramatically. Nineteenth-century immigration peaked at 790,000 in 1882, and even during the depression of the later 1890s, between 250,000 and 350,000 newcomers arrived annually. The massive immigrant influx contributed both to desperate overcrowding and appalling conditions in city slums and to a vibrant urban culture of immigrant festivals and social organizations; churches, saloons, dance halls, and beer gardens; and music halls offering vaudeville shows featuring broad ethnic humor and the latest songs from Tin Pan Alley, such as *After the Ball* (1892) and *Only a Bird in a Gilded Cage* (1900).

The "new immigration" from southern and eastern Europe unsettled many native-born Americans of northern and western European ancestry. The increasing numbers of Jews, Catholics, and Orthodox Christians alarmed many American Protestants and gave rise to urgent strategies to convert and assimilate the newcomers. The waves of immigrants placed tremendous pressure on local governments and city services, providing convenient scapegoats for those seeking explanations for municipal corruption, labor unrest, and political radicalism. Blacks moving to cities—although only a trickle compared to the Great Migration ahead—experienced disruption as well. Between 1880 and 1915, 25 to 30 percent of urban black households had a mother but no father present, twice the percentage for rural black families. The economic crisis affected the family life of immigrants and native-born, white and black alike. Across America, unemployed men left home to seek jobs in other cities and even other regions, sometimes abandoning their families in the process. On foot and in freight trains, tramps scoured the country seeking employment or, if not a job, a handout.

Reform Movements. Populism was only one manifestation of a larger reform current in the 1890s that launched the Progressive Era. Through the leadership of Jane Addams and others, settlement houses arose in the immigrant districts of most big cities. The Woman's Christian Temperance Union, under its energetic president Frances Willard, pursued a broad reform agenda, whereas the Anti-Saloon League, founded in 1895, launched a coordinated campaign for national prohibition. Social Gospel advocates like W. D. P. Bliss and Washington Gladden exhorted middle-class churchgoers to apply their Christian principles to the social problems of the new industrial order. Charles M. Sheldon's bestselling Social Gospel novel *In His Steps* (1896) told of an urban congregation that commits itself to reform by posing the question "What would Jesus do?" The British journalist William T. Stead made a similar plea in *If Christ Came to Chicago* (1893). The photojournalist Jacob Riis offered middle-class readers a harrowing picture of slum life in *How the Other Half Lives* (1890), as did the novelist Stephen Crane in *Maggie: A Girl of the Streets* (1893). William Dean Howells addressed urban labor unrest and the economic roots of crime in such novels as *A Hazard of New Fortunes* (1890) and *The Quality of Mercy* (1892), whereas Theodore Dreiser's *Sister Carrie* (1900) portrayed the corrupting effects of city life on an ambitious young woman from the country.

The 1890s saw activist stirrings among middle-class American women, signaling the revival of the woman-suffrage movement and women's broad-scale reform involvement in the Progressive Era. Kate Chopin in *The Awakening* (1899) portrayed the stultifying life of a vivacious young wife in the tradition-bound and patriarchal culture of New Orleans, whereas Charlotte Perkins Gilman explored the effects of women's economic subordination in *Women and Economics* (1898). A vogue for bicycles and bicycling, a prelude to the automobile era just ahead, put many young women as well as young men on wheels in the 1890s.

America and the World. Expansionist fever pervaded the Populist Era, fueled by missionary zeal, a quest for overseas markets, desires for an empire to match those of the European powers, and the jingoism of tabloid newspapers. In *Our Country* (1885), the Reverend Josiah Strong offered a potent array of nationalistic, racial, and religious arguments to awaken Americans to their global destiny. In *The Influence of Sea Power upon History* (1890), Alfred Thayer Mahan urged an expansion of U.S. naval power, including acquisition of the refueling stations that a two-ocean navy demanded. After a series of diplomatic interventions in South America, the decade ended with a major expansion beyond the nation's continental borders: The United States annexed Hawai'i in 1898 and, in the same year, in the aftermath of the Spanish–American War, acquired Cuba, Puerto Rico, Guam, and the Philippines from Spain. An anti-imperialist movement recruited such varied supporters as William Graham Sumner, William James, and Andrew Carnegie, but most Americans approved of the nation's imperial aspirations. In foreign affairs, as in the domestic arena, the last decade of the nineteenth century stands as a kind of curtain-raiser to the twentieth.

The Culture of Populism. The Populist movement unfolded in a rapidly changing society. Many Populists lived in a traditional world that preserved rhythms of life dating to the pre–Civil War Era and earlier. In the small towns of rural America, churches and the village store nourished community life. Cooperative patterns of work, common rites and rituals such as hunting and fishing, land-inheritance customs, and grazing on common lands in the West all encouraged premodern and anticommercial values and patterns of life. But this traditional life was under siege. The spread of railroads brought "drummers" (traveling salesmen), mail-order catalogs, and national magazines whose advertisements offered an array of mass-produced goods. And farm life itself was evolving under the economic pressures posed by expensive new equipment; rising land prices; a global market; and new systems of transporting, processing, and marketing agricultural products.

Threats to traditional folkways from industrialization, business consolidation, commercial agriculture, and the rise of urban-immigrant America spurred the agrarian protest spirit known as Populism. Some historians have seen Populism as a reactionary phenomenon, a last stand for agrarian values before the juggernaut of modernization. Richard Hofstadter, in his influential *Age of Reform* (1955), viewed the Populists as deluded reactionaries who scapegoated Jewish bankers and big-city immigrants, oversimplified complicated economic issues, and romanticized an idealized past of self-sufficient yeomanry.

Certainly Populism had a darker side. One leader, Thomas E. Watson (1856–1922) of

Georgia, soured by his foray into biracial agrarian protest, became a virulent nativist and racist. Yet recent historians generally adopt a more positive approach, viewing Populists as realistic in their analysis of their problems and the remedies they espoused and tolerant by the standards of their time, providing a place for women in their movement—the first American political movement to do so—and even, in the South, for a time making common cause with blacks in a class-based political campaign. The historian Lawrence Goodwyn, in *The Populist Moment* (1978), emphasized the creation of a "movement culture" based on a shared commitment to democratic forms and institutions. From this perspective, Populism appears at heart a cooperative movement, not only in the narrow sense of establishing purchasing-and-marketing cooperatives, but also in the broader sense of seeking to promote cooperation among agrarian communities with similar values, a shared culture, and a remembered past. From the perspective of a century later, Populists can be seen as precariously suspended between two worlds: one of agrarian values and cooperative, grassroots, democratic institutions and the other a modernizing, corporate, impersonal world. The Populists' attempt to adapt to that emerging modern world while preserving as much as possible of their traditional values, folkways, and institutions gave their movement—and the decade that bears its name—its unique character as an epoch in American history.

[***See also*** **Anti-Saloon League; Bryan, William Jennings; Cleveland, Grover; Farmers' Alliance Movement; Feminism; Free Silver Movement; Granger Laws; Granger Movement; Immigration Law and Policy: Before 1930; McKinley, William; *Plessy v. Ferguson;* Populist Party; Poverty; Progressive Era; Prohibition; Regulatory Agencies, Federal; Segregation; Tariffs; Washington, Booker T.;** ***and*** **Woman's Christian Temperance Union.**]

BIBLIOGRAPHY

Fite, Gilbert C. *The Farmers' Frontier, 1865–1900.* New York: Holt, Rinehart and Winston, 1966.

Goodwyn, Lawrence. *The Populist Moment: A Short History of the Agrarian Revolt in America.* New York: Oxford University Press, 1978.

Hahn, Steven. *The Roots of Southern Populism: Yeoman Farmers and the Transformation of the Georgia Upcountry, 1850–1890.* New York: Oxford University Press, 1983.

Hicks, John D. *The Populist Revolt: A History of the Farmers' Alliance and the People's Party.* Minneapolis: University of Minnesota Press, 1931.

Holmes, William F., ed. *American Populism.* Lexington, Mass.: D. C. Heath, 1994.

McMath, Robert C., Jr. *American Populism: A Social History, 1877–1898.* New York: Hill and Wang, 1993.

Palmer, Bruce. *"Man Over Money": The Southern Populist Critique of American Capitalism.* Chapel Hill: University of North Carolina Press, 1980.

Pollack, Norman. *The Populist Response to Industrial America.* New York: W. W. Norton, 1962.

Shaw, Barton C. *The Wool Hat Boys: Georgia's Populist Party.* Baton Rouge: Louisiana State University Press, 1984.

Wayne Flynt

POPULIST PARTY

Popular name for a third party of the 1890s, the People's Party of America. Organized nationally in May 1891 in Cincinnati, Ohio, the Populist Party's first national nominating convention met in Omaha, Nebraska, the following year. There, the party nominated a presidential ticket headed by James B. Weaver of Iowa and James G. Field of Virginia and fashioned what came to be called the Omaha platform, ratified and promulgated on 4 July 1892. To its adherents, this document symbolized a "second declaration of independence," designed to restore the nation to a course they believed had been abandoned in Gilded Age America's headlong rush into a new urban-industrial age in a political environment that placed corporate and financial interests above the general welfare. Thus, Populism came to stand for a politics designed to put the people first.

The Omaha platform emerged from political protests and organizational efforts that had been building since the 1870s among the nation's farmers. Southern and western farm organizations, together with earlier third parties, were especially active in formulating a program aimed at helping America's rural majority. This program, encompassed in the Omaha platform and its accompanying resolutions, called for the national government to exert a new and positive role on behalf of the general welfare and democratic reform. It urged government ownership of all transportation and communication systems; a graduated income tax; immigration restriction; the direct election of U.S. senators and other electoral reforms; and, in a bid for labor support, a shorter work week in industry. Although not without precedents, the call was historically significant in an era when most political leaders envisioned only a limited role for government, apart from government aid to business interests. In the 1892 election (in which Democrat Grover Cleveland defeated Republican Benjamin Harrison), Weaver received just over 1 million votes, or about 9 percent of the total. The party failed, however, to win much support in the South or in urban-industrial districts.

In 1896, the Democratic Party coopted an aspect of the Populists' financial program, the free and unlimited coinage of silver, on behalf of the candidacy of William Jennings Bryan. The Populist Party thus faced a dilemma: either nominate Bryan and support his fight against the gold standard or divide the reform vote and insure the election of Republican William McKinley. In the end McKinley won despite Populist support for Bryan, and the party gradually faded, leaving Populists with only the consoling thought that they had contributed to the conversion of the Democratic Party to the cause of reform.

Throughout, the Populist Party was strongest in Kansas, Nebraska, Colorado, Texas, and North Carolina, although its influence was also felt in other southern and western states. Out of its ranks emerged many talented and colorful figures, among them Ignatius Donnelly of Minnesota; Jeremiah Simpson, William A. Peffer, Mary E. Lease, and Annie Diggs of Kansas; and William V. Allen and William Neville of Nebraska. Among the prominent southern leaders were Thomas E. Watson of Georgia, Marion Butler of North Carolina, and James Harvey Davis of Texas.

From 1891 to 1903, fifty Populist Party candidates, representing sixteen states and one territory, were elected to Congress, where they waged an educational campaign on behalf of the Populist program and spoke out on a wide range of issues, from the economic depression of 1893–1896 to the nation's imperialist expansion. For many, the Populist movement remains a source of inspiration. As one historian has written: "The Populists' message remains as relevant today as in the nineteenth century, and their vision of community still serves as a powerful critique of American society."

[*See also* **Agricultural Policy; Bryan, William Jennings; Farmers' Alliance Movement; Free Silver Movement; Greenback Labor Party; Immigration Law and Policy: Before 1930; McKinley, William; Political Parties; Populist Era; Republican Party;** ***and*** **Third Parties.**]

BIBLIOGRAPHY

Argersinger, Peter H. *The Limits of Agrarian Radicalism.* Lawrence: University Press of Kansas, 1995.

Clanton, Gene. *Congressional Populism and the Crisis of the Nineties.* Lawrence: University Press of Kansas, 1998.

Clanton, Gene. *Populism: The Humane Preference in America, 1890–1900.* Boston: Twayne, 1991.

Goodwyn, Lawrence. *The Populist Moment.* New York: Oxford University Press, 1978.

Hahn, Steven. *The Roots of Southern Populism.* New York: Oxford University Press, 1983.

McMath, Robert C. *American Populism: A Social History.* New York: Hill and Wang, 1993.

Gene Clanton

POSTAL SERVICE, U.S.

For most of its history, the postal service was the nation's largest civilian institution and the federal government's most visible manifestation in Americans' everyday lives. Empowered by the Constitution to "establish Post Offices and post Roads," Congress created a communication network to unite the fragile young nation. Some of the first postal connections, for instance, linked county seats to state capitals and ultimately to Washington, D.C. The Post Office Department itself did not build many roads or operate many long-distance transports. But contracts with private carriers—stagecoach and steamship lines, railroads, trucking firms, and airlines—helped create a nationwide transportation system.

Politics pervaded the Post Office through most of its history. From Andrew Jackson's administration until 1971, the postmaster general customarily served as the president's chief political lieutenant, some having previously headed the party's national committee. Postmasters general dispensed patronage—tens of thousands of local postmasterships and thousands of contracts—throughout the nation. Congress itself set postage rates, often arguing for years over a fraction of a cent for one category or another. Residents of rural areas, and their representatives in Congress, lobbied assiduously for special postal services to reduce their isolation. Rural free delivery (1896) was the most direct response, but postal savings banks (1911–1966) and parcel post (1913) also helped.

Although the postal service facilitated personal correspondence, most material sent by mail was related to the press, business, or commerce. The volume of mail grew from 7 billion pieces in 1900 to 85 billion in 1970. The number of post offices peaked at 76,688 in 1900, dropping to 32,002 in 1970. Between 1926 and 1970, by contrast, the number of postal employees more than doubled to 741,000.

The postal service long maintained a dual relationship with the press. Newspapers and magazines enjoyed free or below-cost postage rates from the 1790s to the 1970s, and vestiges of the subsidies continued even longer. But the very centrality of the postal service also made it the federal government's principal censor of printed material. From the passage of a federal postal censorship act in 1873 through the mid-twentieth century, the Post Office Department, often in tandem with the U.S. Customs Service, barred from circulation printed matter or other materials considered indecent and obscene. The Post Office also suppressed material deemed treasonable or subversive, notably during the abolitionist controversy, the Civil War, World War I, and the Cold War.

The Postal Reorganization Act of 1970 transformed the Post Office Department into the U.S. Postal Service, a quasi-corporate agency. Seeking to rectify the shortcomings of legislative rate making by elevating economic considerations over politics, the act removed rate-making control from Congress and vested it in an independent regulatory body, the Postal Rate Commission.

Although a late-twentieth-century surge in direct-mail marketing increased the volume of parcels and catalogs in the mail stream, new private carriers such as Federal Express and United Parcel Service (UPS), promising faster, more efficient service, aggressively competed with the U.S. Postal Service for this business. At the same time, email messages via the Internet increasingly supplanted the U.S. mails as a favored mode of communication. The future of the postal service in the new era of privatization and electronic information-exchange remained unclear as the twenty-first century dawned.

[*See also* **Censorship; Jackson, Andrew;** *and* **Obscenity and Pornography.**]

BIBLIOGRAPHY

Fuller, Wayne E. *The American Mail: Enlarger of the Common Life.* Chicago: University of Chicago Press, 1972.

John, Richard R., Jr. *Spreading the News: The American Postal System from Franklin to Morse.* Cambridge, Mass.: Harvard University Press, 1995.

Richard B. Kielbowicz

POVERTY

Poverty has always been a serious problem in America. Throughout its history, large numbers of Americans have been unable to purchase food, shelter, and clothing, or to achieve a reasonable standard of living according to the standards of their time. Their poverty has reflected a variety of factors, from sickness, disability, and natural disaster to conditions in the labor market, structural problems of economics or demography, the absence of a social safety net, racial and gender discrimination, and other failures of public policy. Yet public authorities and private charities often have adopted moral definitions of poverty, blaming poor people for their inability to support themselves.

Chronological and Demographic Overview. Expenses for poor relief started to rise in the late eighteenth century. Destitute immigrants crowded nineteenth- and early twentieth-century cities, and homeless children wandered the streets. By any objective measure, half the population of large cities at the end of the nineteenth century—including many who worked full-time—must be counted as poor. The number of poor people, which remained very high in the early decades of the twentieth century, soared during the Great Depression of the 1930s. Although World War II and the postwar prosperity reduced poverty, the ranks of the poor remained far higher in the 1950s than popular images of the period suggested.

Estimates of poverty remain crude for the years before the federal government instituted an official poverty line in the 1960s. However, poverty rates clearly declined from the 1960s until 1973, when they began to rise again. From the mid-1970s to the late 1990s the national poverty rate fluctuated around 14 percent. The recession during the first decade of the twenty-first century led to a poverty rate of 15.1 percent in 2010.

Women, too, have figured disproportionately in the ranks of the poor. Excluded from jobs that paid living wages throughout most of American history, many women depended on men for material support. Indeed, virtually all self-supporting women struggled constantly against poverty. Young women on their own in nineteenth- and twentieth-century cities earned so little that many turned to forms of prostitution to survive. With no public social safety net in place, job opportunities restricted, and wages low, widows, usually left without payments from life insurance, often found themselves destitute. Even in the late twentieth century, a number of factors—including limited work opportunities and low wages, public benefit programs that discriminated by gender, and an increase in the number of female-headed families—kept poverty rates higher among women. In 1960, single mothers headed about 8 percent of all families with children; by 1990 the proportion had increased to 25 percent. Nearly half of all families supported by women were poor.

African Americans have, on average, always been poorer than whites. As slaves, most owned no assets whatsoever. From the post–Civil War Era through World War II, southern planters and state legislatures worked to keep blacks in the South as a low-wage labor force picking cotton and working in domestic service. In 1935, under pressure from southern white politicians, Social Security legislation excluded agricultural and domestic workers, which meant most blacks. In the North before the Civil War, white immigrants often replaced blacks in occupations customarily open to them, such as barbering and catering, and well into the twentieth century, northern employers relegated blacks to the harshest and most poorly paid jobs.

As they migrated to northern cities in the twentieth century, African Americans increasingly concentrated in segregated, high-poverty neighborhoods drained of mortgage capital by banks that practiced redlining—that is, using loan criteria, originally supported by federal government agencies, that defined black neighborhoods as poor credit risks. Unequal educational opportunities in both the North and South combined with racial segregation and job discrimination to reinforce high levels of poverty among African Americans. However, between 1959 and 1974, as a result of the civil rights movement, affirmative action, and expanded education opportunities, the poverty rate for African Americans dropped from 55.1 percent to 30.3 percent. By 2010, Hispanic Americans experienced poverty at about the same rate as blacks—about 26 percent, compared to 27 percent among blacks. Meanwhile whites' poverty rate in 2010 was 9.9 percent. Both Hispanics and blacks suffered from discrimination and the lack of the educational credentials essential for well-paying work.

As for unskilled and semiskilled workers, their experience in nineteenth- and early twentieth-century cities was framed by a combination of low wages, irregular work, and periodic illness, rather than long-term unemployment. In the best of times, they earned barely enough to feed and clothe a family, but seasonal labor demands, as well as shifts in the business cycle, often left them with no work at all. In and out of work, they alternated between bare self-sufficiency and dependence. Work-related accidents and sickness struck ordinary workers and their families frequently and with devastating impact. Because they had little or no insurance, a serious illness could devastate the capacity of families to support themselves; well into the twentieth century sickness, and accidents remained prime causes of poverty.

The working poor, ubiquitous in towns and cities before World War II, became less common as economic growth and trade unions fueled rising wages. By the 1980s, however, as real wages declined, their numbers had started to grow once again. Among families with children and an unemployed household head, the poverty rate rose by nearly half—7.7 percent to 11.4 percent—from 1977 to 1993. In the late twentieth century, chronic joblessness also became a new and widespread source of poverty. As manufacturing disappeared from cities, many people found themselves more or less permanently out of the regular labor force, a problem prevalent especially among young black men. Many had not worked in the regular labor market for a long time, if at all, and their prospects for steady, remunerative work remained dim. With neither jobs nor public assistance sufficient to lift them out of poverty, chronic joblessness defined a large, new component of the urban poor.

Throughout American history, poverty has displayed a rural as well as an urban face. In rural areas, low wages, soil exhaustion, the exploitation of sharecroppers and miners, declining prices of farm commodities, and natural disasters all promoted poverty. Rural poverty in southern Appalachia initially inspired the War on Poverty in the early 1960s and the redesign and vast expansion of the food-stamp program a few years later. Although rural poverty persisted, by the 1970s public attention focused more on urban poverty, especially the concentration and persistence of poverty in inner cities. The number of city census tracts in which the rate of poverty reached 20 to 40 percent increased alarmingly in northern and midwestern cities during the 1970s; in the 1980s it spread to cities in the South and West as well. In the nation as a whole, the number of census tracts with a population at least 40 percent poor rose to 50.1 percent in the 1970s and 54.3 percent in the 1980s.

From the early Colonial Era, public authorities grappled with poverty. Colonial poor laws initially followed British precedents, which included outdoor relief—that is, aid to people outside institutions. Although widely condemned, outdoor relief remained a staple of public policy throughout American history. In the late twentieth century, state-level outdoor relief was called "general assistance," or something similar; at the federal level, it became Aid to Families with Dependent Children, Food Stamps, Supplemental Social Insurance, or what most Americans simply called "welfare." Public authorities also built institutions for the poor, including almshouses (which by the early twentieth century had largely become public old-age homes), hospitals, dispensaries, and orphanages. This combination of outdoor relief and institutional support kept public spending on poverty high and contentious.

Private Charity and Government Responses. A myriad of voluntary associations and private charities also responded to poverty with direct relief, institutions, and advice for the poor. Through the charity organization movement, which flourished in the 1870s and 1880s, private philanthropy unsuccessfully attempted to abolish outdoor relief and rationalize charitable giving across the country. Private charity and voluntary associations never proved capable of meeting the needs of America's poor. Economic depressions—such as the depression of 1893–1896 and the Great Depression of the 1930s—only underlined the limits of the voluntarist approach. Nonetheless, private organizations played an indispensable role in the nation's response to destitution, less as an alternative to government than as a partner. Because all levels of government have always depended on the private sector to operate services or institutions with public money, America's response to poverty has rested on a mixed economy.

The major federal government response to poverty began with the New Deal of the 1930s. For the first time in American history, the federal government provided direct relief, initially through short-term measures such as the Federal Emergency Relief Administration and the Civil Works Administration. Of more lasting importance were the Economic Security Act of 1935, often called the Social Security Act, which instituted unemployment insurance, old-age insurance, and aid to dependent children; the Fair Labor Standards Act of 1938, which regulated working conditions; and the National Labor Relations Act of 1935, also known as the Wagner Act, which established labor's right to bargain collectively. In the 1960s, influenced by Michael Harrington's pathbreaking book *The Other America* (1962), the federal government extended its antipoverty efforts through President Lyndon B. Johnson's War on Poverty, whose programs, notably Head Start and Legal Services, attempted to expand and equalize opportunities and to empower poor people through community action. The Great Society programs of the same era expanded Social Security and other income-related programs, increased public housing, and with Medicare and Medicaid created the first national health insurance. These programs reduced poverty, hunger, and substandard housing and extended health care to millions.

Though poverty arises mainly from objective factors, public discussions often trace it to moral failure or flaws in individual character. Since the early nineteenth century, discussions of poverty have stressed a distinction between the deserving and undeserving, or the worthy and unworthy, poor. Although contradicted by empirical evidence, this moral definition has retained a powerful hold on the way issues of poverty have been addressed in America. In the 1870s it legitimated attempts to abolish outdoor relief; in the 1980s and 1990s it helped justify reductions in public benefits and the passage of a federal welfare bill that ended the poorest Americans' entitlement to public assistance.

The 1980s, 1990s, and beyond proved years of paradox. Homelessness increased, sometimes related to problems of addiction or mental illness; poverty was endemic in many inner-city districts; the share of children living in poverty increased; and the number of factory jobs declined, diminishing the prospects of unskilled or poorly educated youth, especially in the inner cities. Yet public policy rested increasingly on market models that emphasized individual rather than social responsibility. Federal, state, and local governments redesigned programs by reducing funding, tightening eligibility standards for public assistance, and emphasizing sanctions intended to force the dependent poor into the workforce. In the early twenty-first century, were there enough jobs to substitute work for welfare? Would forcing individuals to accept responsibility for their fate motivate them to improve their lives? Answers to these questions promised to reconfigure poverty once again and continue profoundly to affect American society.

[*See also* **Great Society; Housing Policy, Federal: An Overview; Housing Policy, Federal: Public Housing; Immigration Law and Policy: After 1930; Immigration Law and Policy: Before 1930; Medicare and Medicaid; National Labor Relations Act; National Labor Relations Board; New Deal; Social Security; Social Security Policy; Social Policy: Orphanages; Social Policy: Public Welfare;** ***and*** **Welfare Reform Act of 1996.**]

BIBLIOGRAPHY

Brace, Charles Loring. *The Dangerous Classes of New York, and Twenty Years' Work among Them*. New York: Wynkoop & Hallenbeck, 1872.

Hunter, Robert. *Poverty*. New York: Macmillan, 1904.

Katz, Michael B. *The Undeserving Poor: From the War on Poverty to the War on Welfare*. New York: Pantheon, 1989.

Katz, Michael B., ed. *The "Underclass" Debate: Views from History*. Princeton, N.J.: Princeton University Press, 1993.

Mohl, Raymond A. *Poverty in New York, 1783–1825*. New York: Oxford University Press, 1971.

Patterson, James T. *America's Struggle against Poverty, 1900–1994*. Cambridge, Mass.: Harvard University Press, 1994.

Riis, Jacob A. *How the Other Half Lives: Studies among the Tenements of New York*. New York: Charles Scribner's Sons, 1890.

Wilson, William Julius. *When Work Disappears: The World of the New Urban Poor*. New York: Alfred A. Knopf, 1996.

Michael B. Katz

POWELL, ADAM CLAYTON, JR.

Representative Adam Clayton Powell Jr., a leading African American minister and politician from New York, was born in New Haven, Connecticut, on 29 November 1908. He was raised in New York, City, where his father, Adam Clayton Powell Sr., became the pastor of the influential Abyssinian Baptist Church a few months after his son was born. The senior Powell was a prominent civil rights activist and one of black New York's social elite. Powell spent his early childhood in New York's black districts. After a poor performance at the City College of New York, Powell attended Colgate University in upstate New York.

After graduation in 1930 Powell returned to Harlem, where he became an assistant minister in his father's church. The younger Powell was an effective and popular preacher who also become known for his high-profile lifestyle. As economic depression deepened following the stock market crash in 1929, he devoted increasing attention to the economic problems that confronted Harlem's residents. He expanded community social and economic services offered by the church. After the 1935 Harlem Riots he became increasingly outspoken, first in a series of newspapers columns and then through political action organizations on the behalf of black civil rights. In 1937 Powell succeeded his father as the pastor of Abyssinian Baptist Church.

In 1941 Powell entered politics, successfully campaigning for a city council seat as an independent. There he took his battle against discrimination, especially in the New York city schools, to city hall. In 1944 he organized a coalition of Democrats, Republicans, and Communists to win election to a new congressional district in Harlem. Powell became New York's first black congressperson and the second of the two black Democrats in Congress.

Powell was a different sort of congressman from his black colleague William Dawson (D-IL). Never content to work quietly in the background, Powell openly challenged the segregated facilities within the Congress and the city of Washington. Unable to push his legislative agenda, he continued to raise racial issues, especially through what came to be known as the "Powell Amendment," an unsuccessful effort to amend spending legislation to withhold federal funds from any project that supported racial segregation, and became an outspoken advocate of civil rights.

In 1960s Powell experienced both his greatest political success and failure. He was in tune with the reforms of the Kennedy–Johnson years, and seniority made him chairman of the House Committee on Education and Labor, which passed many of the reform measures of the Great Society, including the "Powell Amendment," which was embodied in the Civil Rights Act of 1964. Powell's flamboyant lifestyle and financial dealings caught up with him, and he confronted a series of scandals and accusations of wrongdoing. In 1958 Powell had been indicted, but not convicted of tax evasion. In 1960 he was involved in a libel lawsuit and found in contempt of court for failing to honor the judgment against him. In 1966 a House committee found Powell guilty of financial impropriety and voted to remove him from Congress. After a special election, which Powell won, and a Supreme Court ruling, Powell reclaimed his seat in 1969, but he was stripped of his seniority and fined $25,000. Publically discredited and in failing health, Powell was defeated in 1970 by Charles Rangel. Two years later, Adam Clayton Powell Jr. died in Miami, Florida.

[*See also* **African Americans in Politics; Civil Rights;** *and* **Civil Rights Legislation.**]

BIBLIOGRAPHY

Hamilton, Charles V. *Adam Clayton Powell, Jr.: The Political Biography of an American Dilemma*. New York: Atheneum, 1991.

Haygood, Wil. *King of the Cats: The Life and Times of Adam Clayton Powell, Jr.* Boston: Houghton Mifflin, 1993.

Paris, Peter J. *Black Leaders in Conflict: Joseph H. Jackson, Martin Luther King Jr., Malcolm X, Adam Clayton Powell Jr.* New York: Pilgrim Press, 1978.

Powell, Adam Clayton, Jr. *Adam by Adam: The Autobiography of Adam Clayton Powell, Jr.* New York: Dial Press, 1971.

Ragsdale, Bruce A., and Joel D. Treese. "Adam Clayton Powell, Jr." In *Black Americans in Congress, 1870–1989,* pp. 113–115. Prepared under the direction of the Office of the Historian, U.S. House of Representatives. Washington, D.C.: Government Printing Office, 1991.

Cary D. Wintz

PRAYER IN SCHOOL

Prayer in public schools has been an issue in American public education since its founding in the early 1800s. Early public schooling proceeded on the assumption that education must have a moral basis, one grounded in commonly shared religious values. Initially, religious instruction took the form of Bible reading, prayer, hymn singing, and catechisms, all reflecting an evangelical Protestant perspective. During the 1840s education reformer Horace Mann modified the practices by substituting "universal" religious principles for more doctrinaire elements, thus emphasizing morality over indoctrination. Still, the "nonsectarian" practices reflected a Protestant perspective, and they encountered growing opposition by Catholics and Jews who immigrated to the nation in the nineteenth century. Nationwide controversy over religious exercises erupted following the Civil War when public school districts in several cities—led by Cincinnati—abolished the practices in response to complaints by Catholics and other groups. After the Ohio Supreme Court upheld the action of the Cincinnati school board in 1873, Congress considered several bills to prevent schools from prohibiting prayer and Bible reading, although none passed. Nonsectarian exercises remained common into the twentieth century, particularly in the South and Midwest. However, by midcentury only 40 percent of schools nationwide conducted any religious exercises, despite supportive laws in approximately half of the states.

In 1962 and 1963, the U.S. Supreme Court heard challenges to state policies requiring prayer and Bible reading in the public schools. In the first case, *Engel v. Vitale,* the Court in an 8-to-1 decision struck down the recitation of a prayer approved by the New York Board of School Regents. Although the prayer was nonsectarian in content and student participation was voluntary, the Court held that it was still a religious exercise and violated the Establishment Clause of the Constitution. Interpreting that clause, the Court held that the government "is without power to prescribe by law any particular form of prayer which is to be used as an official pray in carrying on any [government] program." The following year the Court struck down school policies requiring readings from the Bible and the recitation of the Lord's Prayer (*Abington School District v. Schempp*). The justices reaffirmed that school officials must remain neutral with respect to religious matters and could not use religion to promote moral values.

Both decisions caused a public outcry, with critics charging that the Court had "thrown God out of the schools." Congress held hearings on proposed "school prayer" constitutional amendments in 1964, 1966, and 1971, but the proposals were opposed by Democrats and a coalition of religious liberals, secularists, and Jews. The efforts died in congressional committees. New momentum for a school prayer amendment came with the election of President Ronald Reagan in 1980, who endorsed the idea shortly after taking office. Several hearings were held on the "Reagan Prayer Amendment" in 1982–1983, and a floor vote was avoided only by the passage of a 1984 law allowing school children to organize "Bible clubs" during noninstructional times.

The issue of school prayer has remained contentious, in part because the Supreme Court has refused to back down from its earlier holdings. In 1985 the Court struck down a law requiring "moments of silence" for prayer; in 1992 the justices prohibited prayers at public school graduation ceremonies; and in 2000 the Court forbade student-led prayers at school athletic events. As a result, religious conservatives have continued to agitate for a constitutional amendment to allow for school prayer.

[*See also* **Constitution;** ***Engel v. Vitale;*** ***and*** **Reagan, Ronald.**]

BIBLIOGRAPHY

Alley, Robert S. *Without a Prayer: Religious Expression in Public Schools.* Amherst, N.Y.: Prometheus Books, 1996.

DelFattore, Joan. *The Fourth R: Conflicts over Religion in America's Public Schools.* New Haven, Conn.: Yale University Press, 2004.

Green, Steven K. *The Bible, the School, and the Constitution.* New York: Oxford University Press, 2012.

Ravitch, Frank S. *School Prayer and Discrimination.* Boston: Northeastern University Press, 1999.

Steven K. Green

PRESIDENTIAL ASSASSINATIONS

Presidents have frequently been the targets of political violence. From 1832 to the beginning of the twenty-first century, ten presidential incumbents have been the victims of assassinations, attempted assassinations, or physical violence. President Andrew Jackson was the first president to be the victim of an assassination attempt when deranged painter Richard Lawrence tried to kill "Old Hickory" in the U.S. Capitol building. Since the attack on Jackson, approximately one of every five presidents, or 22 percent, has been assaulted by an assassin with the intent to kill or injure. Four of the ten presidents—Abraham Lincoln, James A. Garfield, William McKinley, and John F. Kennedy—fell victim to an assassin's bullet. These four assassinations in America had significant political ramifications because their deaths were used to promote a reformist agenda and expand national authority.

Abraham Lincoln. Before Lincoln was elected as the sixteenth president of the United States, he was made the target of assassination. Threats and poisoned packages arrived daily to his home in Springfield, Illinois. Even a painting by a South Carolinian, depicting the Republican Party's presidential nominee's head in a noose, was delivered to the Lincoln home. With Lincoln's election and the secession of seven Southern states by February 1861, these threats increased and made Lincoln, Republican Party officials, and the president-elect's advisors wary of the president's trip to his inauguration in Washington. These fears proved to be justified. It was discovered midway through Lincoln's journey that a plot was engineered by the Southern-sympathizing terrorist organization the Knights of the Golden Circle to assassinate Lincoln as he transferred trains in Baltimore. The plot, however, was foiled because Lincoln left Baltimore in the middle of the night and arrived in Washington nine hours early. He was safely inaugurated on 4 March 1861.

Lincoln constantly lived under the threat of assassination during the Civil War. To ward off potential assassins, the military and his friends surrounded Lincoln with an infantry and cavalry unit to protect the president. These measures proved to save Lincoln's life because Confederate cavalry units were dangerously close to Washington, D.C., on more than one occasion. After the war, it was learned that the Confederate Secret Service had developed plans to kidnap Lincoln through its extensive network of agents in Maryland and Canada. At the center of one of these cells was the young thespian John Wilkes Booth. Booth initially conspired to capture Lincoln, but after the South fell to the Union in April 1865, his plans changed to murder.

Booth, with coconspirators George Atzerodt and Lewis Powell, planned to cut off the head of the Union through the assassinations of Secretary of State William Seward, Vice President Andrew Johnson, and Lincoln. Their chance came on the night of 14 April 1865. It was well publicized that Lincoln was attending Ford's Theatre to watch Tom Taylor's *Our American Cousin*. Booth knew the hotel intimately because he was in several plays at the theatre. Before the play, Booth meticulously engineered the presidential booth so that he could observe the president during the play and easily facilitate his escape after he shot the president. Powell was assigned the task of killing Seward, and Atzerodt was given Johnson as a target. That evening, Booth walked into the presidential booth and during a moment of laughter in the play shot Lincoln in the back of the head. He stabbed Lincoln's guest, Major Henry Rathbone, and leapt from the presidential booth. Booth later learned that Powell only seriously injured Seward, and Atzerodt did not follow through with the plans. Lincoln died the following morning. Booth escaped from Washington to the Maryland countryside and received help from other conspirators. Those who conspired with him, eight people in all, were arrested within twelve days. They were tried for Lincoln's death at a military tribunal. Four of the conspirators—Atzerodt, Powell, tavern keeper Mary Surratt, and David Herold, were found guilty and executed on 7 July. The other four conspirators, Dr. Samuel Mudd, Edward Spangler, Michael O'Laughlin, and Samuel Arnold, served sentences at Fort Jefferson, a military prison in the Florida Keys. John Surratt, Mary's son, escaped to Canada and later served in the Pontifical Zouaves in Rome. He was arrested and sent back to the United States, but was released after a mistrial.

Lincoln's death had profound political implications. Johnson was the first vice president to ascend to the presidency after the assassination of a president. Since Lincoln was killed immediately after the end of the war, it was viewed that his death was the last cruel act of the South. Ministers from various denominations, using the pulpit on Easter Sunday, one day after Lincoln's death, delivered strong sermons condemning the assassination and urged reprisal against the South. For nearly a year, Republican politicians, building upon this sentiment fostered by ministers, used Lincoln's assassination to promote their own vision of Reconstruction. By the fall of 1866, it became apparent that Johnson and Congress had two competing plans of Reconstruction. This acrimony over Reconstruction continued until it resulted in Johnson's impeachment by the House in 1868. Johnson was acquitted by the Senate, but he became the first president to be impeached.

James A. Garfield. On 2 July 1881, Charles J. Guiteau shot James A. Garfield twice as the president was waiting at the Baltimore and Potomac train platform to escape the summer heat of Washington, D.C. Before Garfield's election, Illinois native and lawyer Guiteau had delivered two speeches in support of Garfield's presidential campaign. He later printed his speech for distribution. His printed speech had very little impact on the outcome election, but Guiteau, who was mentally insane, believed his miniscule act put Garfield in the White House. In the spring of 1881, he harassed the Garfield administration for a position within the State Department. He incessantly visited the White House and the office of Secretary of the State James Blaine, and eventually he was denied access to both places. Guiteau became enraged as entreaties for a patronage position were denied. Guiteau also lost faith in Garfield because of his political battle with former senator Roscoe Conkling (R-NY) over the New York Customs House collectorship. Bewildered by these political revelations, Guiteau believed that Garfield was the enemy of the Stalwart faction and that his death would unite the two Republican factions. He purchased a .44-caliber English Bulldog handgun to kill the president. He also read several newspapers to monitor the president's future trips and plans. By doing so, Guiteau learned that Garfield was leaving in July to spend part of his summer in New Jersey and the remainder of the summer at his home in Mentor, Ohio.

After shooting the president, Guiteau was quickly apprehended by the police. Garfield was transported back to the White House, and over the course of two months a cadre of doctors tried to locate the bullet. Garfield briefly recovered in early September, and his wife, Lucretia, wanted to move him to a resort in Elberon, New Jersey, so that he could leave the muggy heat of Washington, D.C., and enjoy the breeze of the Atlantic Ocean. The trip proved to be too hard on the president, and he died two weeks later on 19 September 1881.

Guiteau's murder trial began on 14 November 1881. Almost immediately, the primary question in the trial was Guiteau's sanity because it meant his imprisonment in an insane asylum or death. His defense team, along with expert witness Dr. Charles Spitzka, an alienist or protopsychologist, claimed that Guiteau was mentally insane. Guiteau, on the other hand, maintained that he purposely killed the president with full and complete knowledge of the ramifications, although his peculiar behavior and rants proved otherwise. With Guiteau's repeated statements of sanity, the prosecution ably convinced the jury that he knowingly murdered the president. He was convicted on 25 January 1882 and was hanged on 30 June 1882.

Much like Lincoln's death, politicians, reformers, and the press capitalized on Garfield's death to promote a political agenda. Since Guiteau continually claimed that he killed the president because he was denied a job, proponents of civil service reform characterized him as a "disappointed office seeker" in their effort to eliminate patronage. Their promotional efforts paid off and resulted in the Pendleton Civil Service Reform Act of 1883, which led to the first significant effort of the federal government to regulate its workforce. The U.S. Civil Service Commission was created to monitor the enforcement of the Pendleton Act.

William McKinley. Following William McKinley's overwhelming election to his second term as president in 1900, Leon Czolgosz fatally shot the president twice at the Pan-American Exposition in Buffalo, New York, on 6 September 1901. Born on 5 May 1873 to Polish immigrants, Czolgosz resided in Michigan. In 1892, he later moved to Cleveland, Ohio, to work at the Newberg Wire Mills. In the aftermath of the Panic of 1893, the owners of the Newberg factory reduced his wages. Czolgosz joined the other employees in a strike and subsequently lost his job. The Panic greatly affected Czolgosz. He became deeply influenced by the ideology of socialism and anarchism after attending several radical meetings. By the late 1890s, Czolgosz had made his political transformation. He read anarchist literature on a regular basis, joined local anarchist groups, and left the Catholic faith. He became intrigued by the assassination of King Humbert I of Italy by New Jersey anarchist Gaetano Bresci on 29 July 1900 and reread newspaper accounts of the assassination.

In the spring of 1901 Czolgosz made several trips to anarchist meetings to acquaint himself with prominent radicals. At one meeting in May, he listened to the passionate speech of renowned anarchist Emma Goldman at the Franklin Liberal Club in Cleveland. Her speech, as Czolgosz later admitted under interrogation 7 September 1901, "set him on fire" and influenced him to kill McKinley.

In August 1901, the White House announced that McKinley planned to attend the Pan-American Exposition in Buffalo. Czolgosz had lived close to Buffalo since late July, and in September he bought a .32-caliber Iver–Johnson pistol to kill the president. On 6 September McKinley held a public reception at the Temple of Music at the Pan-American Exposition. Czolgosz, with a gun wrapped in a handkerchief in his right hand, reached the president and shot him twice. Fairgoers and the three Secret Service officers guarding McKinley pounced on Czolgosz. McKinley died eight days later from complications arising out of the operation to remove the bullet.

Since no federal crime existed making it illegal to attack a president, the assassin was handed to the Buffalo police. Czolgosz admitted that he was an anarchist and was influenced by Emma Goldman. Similar to Guiteau's experience, alienists tried to establish whether Czolgosz was insane. From their inquiries, it certainly appeared that Czolgosz was mentally insane. Nevertheless, Czolgosz continually provided the Buffalo police and the district attorney with rational answers to their questions. He clearly outlined his action as a duty to anarchist doctrines. Czolgosz was subsequently charged with murder and pled guilty at his trial. On 29 October 1901, he was electrocuted at Auburn Prison in New York.

As the third president to die within thirty-six years, McKinley's death led to significant political reforms. Theodore Roosevelt, a well-known reformer, became president. The Immigration Act of 1903, directly in response to McKinley's assassination by a self-proclaimed anarchist, was passed to limit socialists and anarchists from entering the United States and becoming citizens. The act represented the first time that citizenship was restricted on the basis of political beliefs. The Secret Service, which initially was formed in 1865 to prevent the counterfeiting of money, was informally allowed to protect the president. The necessary legislation granting the Secret Service formal authority to guard the president was not enacted until 1907. Furthermore, McKinley's assassination provided politicians and reformers the opportunity to invoke his death while promoting an agenda for Progressive reform. In his message to Congress on 3 December 1901, Roosevelt mourned McKinley's death but blamed it on the terrible social conditions facing the nation.

John F. Kennedy. President John F. Kennedy traveled to Dallas, Texas, on 22 November 1963 to deliver a speech on America's national security to the Dallas Citizens Council. While riding in an open limousine with his wife Jacqueline and Texas governor John Connally and his wife en route to the meeting's location, Kennedy was fatally shot twice in the neck and head. Governor Connally was also shot. Kennedy and Connally were immediately transported to Parkland Memorial Hospital. Connally survived, but the president was declared dead half an hour after the attack. Vice President Lyndon Johnson was sworn in as president aboard Air Force One in Dallas.

The Dallas police, Secret Service, and the Federal Bureau of Investigation (FBI) immediately learned that the gunshots emanated from the sixth floor of the Texas School Book Depository. An Italian-made Carcano rifle was found, and the supervisor told the police that one of his employees, Lee Harvey Oswald, was missing. A manhunt for Oswald began, and Dallas police officer J. D. Tippit found a man matching Oswald's description in a residential area. When approached by Tippit, Oswald fatally shot Tippit four times with a revolver. Oswald immediately fled to a nearby movie theater to hide, but he raised suspicion when he did not buy a ticket. The theater's employees reported the incident to the Dallas police. After resisting arrest and nearly killing another officer, he was arrested at the theater for killing Tippit. Oswald was later charged with Kennedy's murder, and as he was being transferred from the Dallas police headquarters to the county jail, Oswald was shot and killed by Dallas nightclub owner Jack Ruby.

While a nation mourned Kennedy's death, Democratic Party politicians recognized the intrinsic political value of his death in advancing Kennedy and the party's political agenda. Similar to Theodore Roosevelt's speech to Congress in 1901, five days after Kennedy's death, Johnson poignantly stated to a joint session of Congress, "Let us continue." Johnson believed that "we have talked long enough in this country about civil rights. It is now time to write the next chapter and to write it in books of law." Only approving such a measure, Johnson argued, "could more eloquently honor President Kennedy's memory."

Johnson's words conveyed to Congress and the American public that he would carry on Kennedy's vision of reform. Within three years of Kennedy's death, the Democratic Party, with crucial help from Republicans in Congress, was able to secure some of the most important and lasting legislation of the twentieth century. The Civil Rights Act of 1964 outlawed the discrimination of African Americans and women and the segregation of public and private places. One year later, the Voting Rights Act was passed that prevented the use of certain discriminatory practices. African Americans had been disenfranchised for many years, despite their constitutional right to vote. Finally, immigration reform, one of Kennedy's little known goals, was achieved through the passage of the Immigration and Nationality Act of 1965. It eliminated the restrictive National Origins Formula established by the Immigration Act of 1924 and placed all immigrants on an equal footing trying to enter the United States.

[*See also* **Garfield, James; Jackson, Andrew; Kennedy, John F.; Lincoln, Abraham;** ***and*** **McKinley, William.**]

BIBLIOGRAPHY

Fine, Sidney. "Anarchism and the Assassination of McKinley." *American Historical Review* 60 (July 1955): 777–799.

Peskin, Allan. "Charles Guiteau of Illinois: President Garfield's Assassin." *Journal of the Illinois State Historical Society* 70 (1977): 131-136.

Posner, Gerald. *Case Closed: Lee Harvey Oswald and the Assassination of JFK*. New York: Random House, 1993.

Rauchway, Eric. *Murdering McKinley: The Making of Theodore Roosevelt's America*. New York: Hill and Wang, 2003.

Rohrs, Richard C. "Partisan Politics and the Attempted Assassination of Andrew Jackson." *Journal of the Early Republic* 1 (1981): 149–163.

Steers, Edward, Jr. *Blood on the Moon: The Assassination of Abraham Lincoln*. Lexington: University Press of Kentucky, 2001.

Matthew C. Sherman

PRESIDENTIAL DEBATES

In his classic work *The Making of the President 1960,* Theodore H. White described that year's televised debates, the first, as a "revolution . . . born of the ceaseless American genius in technology; its sole agent and organizer had been the common American television set," which permitted "the simultaneous gathering of all the tribes of America to ponder their choice between two chieftains in the largest political convocation in the history of man." White's enthusiasm was not universal. The *New York Times* panned the debates as a "powderpuff performance." The eminent historian Henry Steele Commager called them "televised press conferences" beneath the dignity of the office.

Controversy over the debates' value has continued into the beginning of the twenty-first century, although the debates themselves very nearly did not. Political and legal obstacles prevented further debates until 1976, and they very nearly collapsed in 1980. But debates have become a fixture of the modern presidential campaign, and although candidates are not required to participate in them, even popular incumbents cannot credibly avoid them. In campaigns dominated by paid advertising, the debates are for most Americans the only opportunity to see and listen to the candidates speak extemporaneously and at length.

The 1960 debates between Vice President Richard M. Nixon and Senator John F. Kennedy were historic above all because they were the first ever face-to-face encounters between major-party presidential candidates. Historically, presidential debates had been between surrogates, not the candidates themselves. The televised debates brought the candidates into the living rooms of millions of voters, allowing them to see, hear, and judge them in a way never before possible. An average of 71 million Americans watched each of the four debates. Another 40 million listened to the debates on radio. The debates made television a permanent and important part of American politics, stoking the public appetite for and the modern campaign's emphasis on the image and the sound bite.

Origins of Broadcast Political Debates in the United States. Broadcast political debates in the United States began with radio. Before the 1928 presidential election, the National League of Women Voters sponsored a ten-month series of nationally broadcast debates featuring journalists, scholars, and other politicians arguing on the candidates' behalf. The same year, the Mutual Broadcasting System launched "American Forum of the Air," a regular debate program featuring candidates for lesser national and state offices. In March 1935, the National Broadcast Corporation (NBC) launched "America's Town Meeting of the Air," in which candidates were given twenty minutes to make their case to the listening audience but did not address each other directly. The first nationally broadcast program featuring candidates in face-to-face debate was held on 17 May 1948 between Republican governors Harold Stassen of Minnesota and Thomas Dewey of New York on the question "Shall the Communist Party in the United States be outlawed?" Nearly 900 radio stations across the country carried the program.

Television's growth as a consumer technology in the United States was delayed by World

War II and the Korean War, and household penetration of television sets did not exceed 50 percent until 1956. That year's Democratic presidential nominee, Illinois governor Adlai Stevenson, thought the new medium presented a more cost-effective, informative, and even dignified way of reaching a national audience than the traditional barnstorming tour. In a May 1960 magazine article he urged that presidential candidates be provided, without charge, half-hour blocks of time on television and radio during the final eight weeks of the campaign.

In May 1960, a Senate subcommittee held hearings on Stevenson's proposal in which it called as witnesses several network executives, including Columbia Broadcast System (CBS) president Frank Stanton. Where Stevenson had proposed candidate time, Stanton proposed actual debates. But neither candidate time nor debates were possible, Stanton said, unless Congress suspended a provision of the 1934 Communications Act known as the "equal time" rule. The rule, still in effect, requires broadcast stations that give time to a candidate to provide equal time to all legally qualified candidates for the same office. Congress had amended the law in 1959 to exempt appearances by candidates in "bona fide newscasts, bona fide news interviews, bona fide news documentaries," or "on-the-spot coverage of bona fide news event." Debates did not qualify for any of these exemptions, and broadcasters would not participate in them, Stanton said, if doing so would expose them to lawsuits seeking equal time or demands to be included in the debates from any of the fourteen minor-party candidates running for president in 1960. Congress therefore suspended the equal time rule, but only for 1960 and only for the offices of president and vice president, thus making the Nixon–Kennedy debates possible.

In subsequent elections Congress did not renew the suspension. In 1964 President Lyndon Johnson told Congress he would not debate Republican Barry Goldwater; Richard Nixon, as Republican nominee in 1968 and as president in 1972, said he would not debate his Democratic challengers. The debates resumed in 1976 only after the Federal Communications Commission ruled in 1975 that debates qualified as news programs and were thus exempt from the equal time rule so long as broadcasters did not organize them, as they had in 1960. The National League of Women Voters became the debates' first sponsor.

The political timing for the rule change was fortuitous. The 1976 election was the first after the Watergate scandal had forced Richard Nixon to resign from office. President Gerald Ford trailed Jimmy Carter by more than 30 points and so was the rare incumbent who believed he had nothing to lose by debating. In the second of their three meetings, Ford twice said Poland was not under Communist domination, a gaffe for which he was severely criticized. But he later credited the debates for bringing him from far behind to almost winning the election.

Efforts to institutionalize debates were very nearly scuttled when President Carter, after having committed to debate Republican Ronald Reagan, refused to participate when the League decided to include independent John Anderson. Dozens of other candidates wanted to participate, but only Anderson had significant public support. As a result, the first debate featured only Reagan and Anderson. Afterward the League proposed a debate between Reagan and Carter, to be followed by a third debate with all three candidates. Carter and Anderson accepted but Reagan did not, so the League withdrew the offer. Finally the League arranged a debate between Reagan and Carter after Anderson's public support dropped below the 15 percent the League had earlier established as the required threshold for participation. The single debate between the two major-party candidates was at the time the most-watched program in U.S. television history and led independent voters overwhelmingly to support Reagan, who went on to win the election.

In 1984 President Reagan agreed to debate Democratic challenger Senator Walter Mondale, but again the campaigns ignored the League and independently negotiated terms, dates, and moderators. After the campaign, separate commissions at Georgetown University and Harvard University met to discuss the debates' sponsorship, their format, and how to fairly accommodate third-party and independent candidates. The result was that in the 1988 election the League was replaced as debate sponsor by the Commission on Presidential Debates (CPD), a not-for-profit organization based in Washington, D.C. The Commission has organized all the debates since that time and has been the subject of intense criticism and numerous lawsuits portraying it as an organization whose principal concern is insulating the major parties both from third-party challengers and from serious questioning.

The Commission on Presidential Debates and Its Critics. Typically 200 or more people register as candidates with the Federal Election Commission (FEC) for each presidential election, of whom perhaps a dozen go on to meet the legal qualifications for the office. The policy dilemma is how to permit and encourage candidate debates while not being unfair to minority-party candidates who want to participate in them. In parliamentary systems this dilemma is usually resolved by multiple rounds of voting until only two candidates remain; they then debate, but only if neither candidate enjoys the benefit of incumbency or a large lead in the polls, in which case the advantaged candidate or party often finds some pretext to avoid sharing a stage with a challenger. In the United States, multicandidate debates often take place between candidates of the same party in primary campaigns, but those programs frequently devolve into incoherent and uninformative shouting matches, sometimes with the help of celebrity journalists (or even celebrity actors and musicians) acting as instigators rather than moderators.

In the 1988 election, its first as debates sponsor, the CPD employed three factors to determine an independent candidate's eligibility for participation: evidence of a national organization; signs of national newsworthiness and competitiveness; and indications of national public enthusiasm or concern. On that basis, no independent candidate joined the debates. In 1992, the Commission used the same criteria to reach the same end until 1 October when independent Ross Perot, who had withdrawn from the race in July with 40 percent public support, reentered it. The Commission decided he satisfied the criteria for inclusion and Perot went on to win 19 percent of the popular vote.

Four years later, in September 1996, Ross Perot was running again, but with very low public support, and the Commission excluded him from the debates. The decision puzzled the public and angered the press, especially when Perot went on to win 9 percent of the popular vote. A subsequent report by the FEC found the CPD's criteria legally defensible, despite a report to the contrary by its general counsel who characterized them as "vague," "subjective," and "biased."

In response, the Commission in January 2000 adopted new standards that were virtually identical to those used by the League of Women Voters in 1980, requiring independent candidates to meet the constitutional requirements for presidential eligibility, to be on a sufficient number of state ballots to have at least a mathematical chance of securing an Electoral College majority, and to show support of at least 15 percent of the national electorate as determined by an average of five national public opinion polls (although the League had used eight polls to include John Anderson). The new criteria were more explicitly nonpartisan, although critics continue to urge alternatives. The federal courts have repeatedly upheld the legality of the CPD's criteria, however, and they remain in use today.

Criticisms that the debates are empty political theater are as old as the debates themselves. Before and after the debates, the campaigns spin them for political advantage. Political pundits and journalists scour the candidates' performances looking for the "winner." However, as speech scholars Kathleen Hall Jamieson and David Birdsell have written, political debates in America have been "beset by abusive advocates, fractious crowds and unbearable tedium" since the earliest days of the republic. The arrival of broadcasting in the twentieth century served only to separate debates from other forms of public entertainment, such as parades and picnics.

Research also suggests that voters believe the debates are substantive. They affect the electoral choices of independent voters particularly, and beginning with John Kennedy, candidates themselves have said the debates were critical to their electoral success or failure. Clearly the debates are not and cannot be academic debates in which judges determine the winner based on which side argues a proposition most effectively, on points rather than substance. In presidential debates, the judges are the voters. To the extent the debates determine their choices, the standards they use to evaluate the candidates' performances are as varied as they themselves are. Voters mix objective and subjective reasoning and the "winner" of a political debate can therefore be a matter for enduring dispute. Americans widely believe, for example, that Abraham Lincoln "won" the most famous political debates in American history, his series of seven debates with Stephen Douglas in 1858, as the two men contested a U.S. Senate seat in Illinois. Lincoln lost the election; in addition, in all seven of the Illinois counties where the two men debated, Democrats did better than Republicans on election day.

[*See also* **Federal Communications Commission; Johnson, Lyndon B.; Kennedy, John F.; Nixon, Richard M.;** *and* **Stevenson, Adlai.**]

BIBLIOGRAPHY

"Commission on Presidential debates." http://www.debates.org/ (accessed 24 August 2011).

Farah, George. *No Debate: How the Republican and Democratic Parties Secretly Control the Presidential Debates.* New York: Seven Stories Press, 2004.

Jamieson, Kathleen Hall and David S. Birdsell. *Presidential Debates: The Challenge of Creating an Informed Electorate.* New York: Oxford University Press, 1988.

Kraus, Sidney. *Televised Presidential Debates and Public Policy.* Mahwah, N.J.: Lawrence Erlbaum, 2000.

Newton, Minow, and Craig LaMay. *Inside the Presidential Debates: Their Improbable Past and Promising Future.* Chicago: University of Chicago Press, 2008.

Craig L. LaMay

PRESIDENTIAL IMPEACHMENT

Impeachment is the principal, if not only, means that the Constitution vests in the Congress to address presidential misconduct. The Constitution is designed to make removal through such means difficult. Although many presidents have been threatened with impeachment, only three have actually faced serious prospects of removal through this process—Andrew Johnson, Richard Nixon, and Bill Clinton.

The impeachment proceedings brought against these presidents, along with the pertinent constitutional text, structure, and original meaning of the Constitution, provide the basis for the modern understanding and practice of presidential impeachment.

The constitutional scheme for presidential impeachment was purposefully designed to differ from the existing British system that had prevailed in prerevolutionary America. In the British system the king was not subject to impeachment or removal, but Article II, Section 4, of the Constitution explicitly makes the president, among certain other federal officials, subject to the impeachment process. In addition, Article II of the Constitution expressly narrowed the range of officials subject to the impeachment process from what it had been in England, where anyone who was not a member of the royal family could be impeached. This article explicitly restricts impeachment to "[t]he President, Vice-President and all civil officers of the United States." Furthermore, Article II narrowed the range of impeachable offenses for impeachable officials to "Treason, Bribery, or other high Crimes or Misdemeanors." This phrase was designed to restrict the scope of impeachable offenses to political crimes or "great offenses" or "breaches of the public trust" and thus deviate from the parliamentary practice, which recognized no limit to the grounds for impeachment. The framers made conviction more difficult than it had been in Great Britain, where the House of Lords needed only a bare majority to convict. In contrast, the framers divided the impeachment authority between the House and Senate; gave the House the "sole power to impeach," which required majority approval; and required at least two-thirds concurrence of the Senate for conviction and removal. The framers gave the Senate trial authority because they believed that senators would be better suited and more insulated from majoritarian pressures than House members to make the difficult judgments regarding conviction and removal. Where the British Parliament could impose any punishment upon conviction, including death, Article I limited the sanctions in impeachment trials "to removal from Office, and disqualification to hold and enjoy any Office of honor, Trust, or Profit under the United States." Article II expressly makes the pardon power inapplicable to impeachments in contrast to the king's power to pardon anyone convicted in an impeachment trial.

In contrast to Great Britain, where impeachment was understood to be a criminal proceeding, Article I in pertinent part provides that "the Party convicted [in an impeachment trial] shall nevertheless be liable and subject to Indictment, Trial, Judgment and Punishment, according to law." The framers required the chief justice of the United States to preside over presidential impeachment trials to avoid the conflict of interest that the vice president, who usually presided over the Senate, might have had in presiding over the trial of the one person who stood between him and the presidency. The Constitution further requires senators to be "on oath or affirmation" when sitting in presidential impeachment trials. These requirements underscore the solemnity of such proceedings.

The framers expected the actual scope of presidential impeachment to be refined through practice over time. The House has formally impeached seventeen officials, including two presidents, Andrew Johnson and Bill Clinton, but it has only convicted and removed eight officials, all federal judges. Although a third president, Richard Nixon, resigned before being formally impeached by the House, the proceedings against him as well as presidents Johnson and Clinton have helped to substantially clarify the grounds for presidential removal through the impeachment process.

The subject of the first presidential impeachment trial was Andrew Johnson, who had become president after the assassination of President Lincoln. Johnson clashed repeatedly with radical Republicans in Congress over whether they, or he, should have the final say over Reconstruction policies. The clash came to a head when Johnson fired his war secretary Edwin Stanton without complying with the Tenure of Office Act, which had been enacted over his veto and which required Senate approval prior to a president's dismissing any officials whom he had nominated but the Senate had confirmed. Although the House had previously tried but failed to impeach Johnson on other matters, Johnson's letter to the House announcing his firing Stanton without complying with the Tenure of Office Act made it easy for the House to do what it wanted. In 1867, it quickly impeached him for illegally obstructing Reconstruction and the Tenure of Office Act. Before the Senate, Johnson's lawyers, including former Supreme Court justice Benjamin Curtis, mounted two principal defenses. They argued that the grounds for presidential impeachment were restricted solely to criminal offenses and that removing Johnson for what was nothing more than a policy dispute with Congress would severely weaken the presidency and effectively destroy it as a coequal branch. The latter argument proved to be the stronger and made the critical difference: The Senate vote fell one short of the number needed for conviction. Johnson was acquitted and let Congress generally have its way in his remaining ten months in office. All seven of the Republican senators who crossed party lines to acquit Johnson lost their seats in the next election cycle. Subsequently, Johnson's acquittal has generally been understood to stand for the principle that impeachment should not be used to retaliate against a president for difference of opinion with Congress over policy questions.

Johnson's impeachment trial was also historic for providing the first opportunity for a chief justice to preside over a presidential impeachment trial. Indeed, the chief justice, Salmon Chase, surprised many observers and members of Congress by presiding over the impeachment trial with an iron hand. He declared at the outset his understanding that "the Constitution has charged the Chief Justice with an important function in the [impeachment] trial . . . of the President." In discharging that function, he helped to shape the rules adopted by the Senate to govern the president's impeachment trial, which continue to this day and include the rule he favored that empowered him to rule initially on every procedural issue subject to override by a majority of the Senate. Although the Senate upheld most of procedural rulings and they had generally favored the defense, it overrode his evidentiary rulings seventeen times.

The next president to face the serious prospect of impeachment and removal was Richard Nixon when he became ensnarled in the Watergate scandal a century later. In the course of congressional inquiries into the White House's possible involvement in a burglary of the Democratic national headquarters prior to the general election in 1972, a White House aide revealed Nixon had secretly taped all of his conversations in the White House. When Nixon refused to comply with a judicial subpoena to turn the tapes over to a special prosecutor who was investigating the burglary, the special prosecutor asked the Supreme Court to intervene. In a unanimous ruling, the Court ordered Nixon to turn the tapes over to the special prosecutor. Nixon begrudgingly complied with the order, and the House Judiciary Committee approved three articles of impeachment against him. In August 1974, Nixon resigned from office after congressional leaders assured him of certain impeachment by the House and conviction and removal from office by the Senate.

Because Nixon was not formally impeached, much less removed from office, the significance of the three impeachment articles approved by the House Judiciary Committee remain in some doubt. The first two articles charged Nixon with having illegally ordered the Federal Bureau of Investigation and the Internal Revenue Service to investigate and harass his political enemies, whereas the third article charged that Nixon had failed to comply with a legislative subpoena to turn over the White House tapes. The Committee considered but did not act on a fourth article, which had charged Nixon with income tax fraud. The first two articles are generally thought both to be within the authority of Congress and to provide strong support for the proposition that impeachments may be based on conduct that does not violate some statute but nonetheless is an abuse of power or breach of the public trust. Scholars disagree over the legality of the third article approved by the House Judiciary Committee. Some legal and historical scholars maintain that the article is necessary to ensure a president cannot undermine the impeachment process as a means to hold him accountable for his misconduct. Others suggest that a president, even Nixon, was entitled to refuse to comply with the subpoena on the basis of a good faith claim of executive privilege or the need to maintain the presidency on an equal footing with Congress. The legitimacy of the fourth article that was not approved remained an open question at least until a similar claim arose and was arguably settled in the next presidential impeachment.

In 1998, the House of Representatives initiated impeachment proceedings against President Clinton. The inquiry arose from Clinton's efforts to deflect the plaintiffs in a sexual harassment case filed against him, *Clinton v. Jones,* from using discovery to expose the intimate relationship he had with a White House intern, Monica Lewinsky. Once the plaintiff's lawyers discovered Clinton's misconduct, they passed the information along to the attorney general, who asked for a special tribunal to appoint an independent counsel to investigate further. The independent counsel Kenneth Starr sent the House a report of his findings regarding Clinton's misconduct. Before the House, Clinton argued, without success, that the House had an obligation to do its own fact-finding rather than rely on Starr's report. The Republican majority in the House at the time took the position that the House's function was like that of a grand jury in a criminal proceeding and thus was to inform the Senate of its belief that a trial was needed. The House subsequently, by a straight party-line vote, approved two impeachment articles against Clinton for perjury and obstruction of justice. Before the Senate, Clinton continued to press two other defenses he had pressed with little success before the House. Clinton's lawyers argued that lying under oath about whether he had "sexual relations" with a White House intern and staff member did not rise to the level of an impeachable offense; the other defense was that impeaching a president for personal but not official misconduct in office would transform our system of government into a parliamentary system in which Congress could remove a leader at any time because it did not like his policies. With Chief Justice William Rehnquist presiding and none of the senators challenging any of his procedural rulings, the Senate acquitted Clinton on both articles. Neither article commanded a majority of the Senate. The vote was largely along party lines; only five Republicans crossed party lines to vote for Clinton's acquittal.

Since President Clinton's acquittal, Congress has not initiated impeachment proceedings against any other presidents. For a short time, some members of Congress urged that President George W. Bush and Vice President Dick Cheney should have been impeached and removed from office for allegedly lying to receive congressional approval for a preemptive military attack against Iraq. Congress never acted on their complaints.

[*See also* **Clinton, William J.; Constitution; Johnson, Andrew;** ***and*** **Nixon, Richard M.**]

BIBLIOGRAPHY

Black, Charles. *Impeachment: A Handbook.* New Haven, Conn.: Yale University Press, 1974.

Gerhardt, Michael J. *The Federal Impeachment Process: A Constitutional and Historical Analysis.* Revised ed. Chicago: University of Chicago Press, 2000.

Rehnquist, William H. *Grand Inquests: The Historic Impeachments of Justice Samuel Chase and President Andrew Johnson.* New York: Morrow, 1992.

Stewart, David O. *Impeached: The Trial of President Andrew Johnson and the Fight for Lincoln's Legacy.* New York: Simon & Schuster, 2009.

Michael J. Gerhardt

PRESIDENTIAL PRIMARIES

The Constitutional Convention that met in Philadelphia in 1787 spent more time on deciding how to select the president than on any other subject, but in a nonparty era, no thought was devoted to how the parties would select their nominees. After the new Constitution took effect in 1789, and once the consensus choice, George Washington, had left the scene after the second presidential contest, leaders of the new parties had to improvise a system. Loath as they were to make the president too dependent on Congress, they nevertheless opted to rely on the caucus of party members of Congress.

This method of choosing nominees seemed logical: members of Congress were familiar with the new government, represented a cross-section of the new nation, and knew the likely candidates for high office. The nominees in the early elections included not only national notables like John Adams, Thomas Jefferson, and James Madison, but also state dignitaries such as George Clinton and Charles Coatsworth Pinckney. For several elections, this process produced a series of credible candidates from the large eastern states of Massachusetts and Virginia.

An Expanding Nation. By 1824, the nation was expanding westward, and the eastern tilt of the nominating process began to seem increasingly anachronistic. Within the Democratic-Republican Party, the presidential candidacy of John Quincy Adams of Massachusetts was being challenged by westerners Andrew Jackson of Tennessee and Henry Clay of Kentucky, as well as William H. Crawford of Georgia and John C. Calhoun of South Carolina. New candidates called for new institutions, and Jackson was nominated by a resolution of the Tennessee legislature. When Adams won the vote in the House of Representatives, the Jackson forces suspected that a corrupt bargain had occurred and began preparing for the 1828 campaign.

By this point it became clear that the system needed a new direction, and it came from the small Anti-Mason Party. Taking a leaf from religious bodies, the Anti-Masons in 1831 held the first national party convention in Baltimore. The advantage over the congressional caucus for the Anti-Masons was simple: they had no members of Congress. The ability to send nonmembers to the national convention was also attractive to the other parties because it enabled them to send a more diverse group of activists to their national meeting. The national convention would be an opportunity to select the party ticket (the Twelfth Amendment made it necessary to select a vice presidential nominee) adopt a platform of party principles, and select rules to govern the party. At this time—the mid-nineteenth century—the parties established national committees and congressional organizations, which created an institutional infrastructure. The second national convention was held by the National Republicans in 1831, also in Baltimore. Under Jackson, who was first elected president in 1828, the Democrats held their first national convention, also in Baltimore, in 1835.

The National Convention System. At early national conventions party leaders gave orations, including a keynote address; when nominations were in order, orators gave nominating and seconding speeches and the rules and platform were debated. Nominees did not appear at the convention to accept nominations. Democrats required that their nominees secure two-thirds of the delegates, which led to extraordinarily lengthy fights in the early twentieth century, when the party was closely divided over ethnocultural issues.

The convention system was hardy enough to survive upheavals in the party system. When sectionalism in the 1850s split both the Democrats and the Whigs and almost destroyed the Democrats, they and the new Republican Party continued to use conventions without visible interruption.

There were legendary conventions, perhaps most notably the Democrats of 1896, when the thirty-five-year-old former Nebraska representative William Jennings Bryan galvanized the delegates with his "Cross of Gold" speech or when in the same year delegates who favored silver-backed currency walked out to the strains of "Good Night, Ladies" sung by their gold-standard rivals.

Reforms to the Party System. At this time, reformers of the party system promoted such innovations as the direct primary, direct election of U.S. Senators, and woman suffrage. For national conventions, their preferred reform was direct election of delegates. This occurred first in Florida in 1904 and then in 1908 in Robert M. La Follette's Wisconsin. By 1916, at least twenty-two states conducted primaries, although in other respects the conventions were unaffected. Other innovations of the Progressive Era included bonus votes; heretofore states had received delegate allocations proportional to their Electoral College strength, but the unrepresentative nature of the results—Southern Democrats were overrepresented and Southern Republicans underrepresented—led both parties to adopt allocation schemes that rewarded party performance in elections. Although primaries widened the base of the selectors of delegates, there often was little tie between the candidate preferences of the delegates and those of the people who had selected them. In Harry Truman's pungent expression, primaries were "eyewash."

The most significant reform was the Democrats' abolition of the two-thirds rule. It had led to three unusually long conventions in 1912, 1920, and the unprecedented 103-ballot convention of 1924. So embarrassed were the Democrats that the next time they held a consensual convention and renominated Franklin D. Roosevelt for a second term in 1936, they did away with the rule.

The Democratic conventions of the 1940s and 1950s saw the growing influence of northern blacks pitted against white southern Democrats, resulting in pitched battles among Democrats. This culminated in a walkout by southern delegates when northerners adopted a strong civil rights platform in 1948. Other Democratic conventions in the period worked to reunify the party, often by balancing the ticket between north and south.

The turbulence of the 1960s had a profound effect on the nominating process in both parties. For the Democrats in 1964, Mississippi Freedom Democrats sought greater representation for their racially integrated members, but the Lyndon Johnson–Hubert Humphrey forces agreed to only a token integration of the delegation. Four years later, the grievances spread from African Americans to the mostly white anti–Vietnam War forces. They objected to several entrenched practices of the Democratic establishment, including the secretive nature of the delegate selection process; the lack of relationship between primary votes and delegate preferences; the underrepresentation of young people, women, and minority groups; and the heavy-handed tactics of the managers in the convention hall. One of the last decisions of the 1968 Democratic National Convention was to establish two reform commissions, one for the delegate selection process, which would be chaired by South Dakota senator George McGovern and later by Minnesota representative Donald Fraser, and the other for floor procedures at the convention itself, to be chaired by Michigan representative James O'Hara.

The McGovern–Fraser reforms fell into four categories. The least controversial was greater procedural fairness, including published rules, accessible times and places for delegate selection meetings, and the abolition of proxy voting. A second area, which would occasion the greatest revising and rerevising over the years, was to represent fairly the supporters of different candidates. At a minimum this meant abolition of the unit rule, by which the entire state delegation votes the way the majority of the delegation votes, and winner-take-all procedures. Eventually it also entailed various schemes of proportional representation. The third area, which was the most controversial at the time, was greater representation of women, young people, and members of minority groups.

Although only the Democrats were directly affected by these rules, the Republicans were soon carried in their wake. In some cases, the changes involved state laws that governed the primaries. Even when Republicans were not enthusiastic about these new rules, some saw them as creating a reformed process, whereas others believed that public pressure would soon target them. The reforms created a new era of reformed and more democratic politics, a reaction to the boss-dominated politics that had dominated the conventions of the past.

The McGovern–Fraser reforms seemed to usher in a new era of convention politics, one in which primaries would be central. As a consequence, there was a pronounced increase in the number of primaries. Politicians resistant to the trend saw primaries as the easiest way to conform to the new rules; the 1972 Democratic National Convention refused to seat the Illinois delegation because it was not in compliance with the new rules. By 1980, no fewer than thirty-four Democratic and thirty-five Republican states, with three or four delegates, held primaries. Much scholarship demonstrated that the change was not as abrupt as it seemed because the states had been moving in that direction for some time.

Although the role of party organization seems weakened, most aspirants appealed to the state and local organizations for support. This placed the organization in a prominent role, as before, but not as formal organization—rather as informal networks. Party organization is still important, but less as hierarchical organization, with authority lines going downward, than as horizontal networks among equals who make peer decisions about the viability, attractiveness, and ideological appeal of the various candidates. In 2000, for example, George W. Bush claimed a virtual monopoly of support from other Republicans in this fashion.

Primaries provide us with a rich history of American presidential nominations and numerous templates for aspiring candidates of the future.

[*See also* **Anti-Masonic Party;** *and* **Constitutional Convention of 1787.**]

BIBLIOGRAPHY

Brown, Lara M. *Jockeying for the American Presidency: The Political Opportunism of Aspirants.* Amherst, N.Y.: Cambria Press, 2010.

Cohen, Marty, David Karol, Hans Noel, and John Zaller. *The Party Decides: Presidential Nominations before and after Reform.* Chicago: University of Chicago Press, 2008.

David, Paul T., Ralph M. Goldman, and Richard C. Bain. *The Politics of National Party Conventions.* Washington, D.C.: Brookings Institution, 1960.

Garson, Robert A. *The Democratic Party and the Politics of Sectionalism, 1941–1948.* Baton Rouge: Louisiana State University Press, 1974.

Marcus, Robert D. *Grand Old Party: Political Structure in the Gilded Age 1880–1896.* New York: Oxford University Press, 1971.

Reiter, Howard L. *Selecting the President: The Nominating Process in Transition.* Philadelphia: University of Pennsylvania Press, 1985.

Howard L. Reiter

PRIVACY

Privacy is an expansive American legal concept, yet has no clear legal definition. The word privacy can actually refer to two distinct legal concepts, commonly referred to as "information privacy" and "decisional privacy." Information privacy refers to the body of law surrounding the collection, use, and disclosure of personal information. Decisional privacy refers to the body of law surrounding the freedom to make decisions affecting one's body and family, such as abortion, contraception, sexual activity, child rearing, and cohabitation. Outside of the constitutional disputes focusing on decisional privacy, the term privacy is more commonly associated with informational concerns.

Privacy holds a significant place in American jurisprudence. Fredrick Lane (2009) has observed that the history of America is also the history of the right to privacy. Colonial America offered greater solitude than the crowded cities of Europe. Even in close-knit communities, the colonists could rely on legal protections for the sanctity of one's home and against eavesdropping. The framers of the U.S. Constitution's concerns regarding government invasions of privacy are reflected in the Third, Fourth, and Fifth Amendments in the Bill of Rights, which restrict the quartering of soldiers in homes, government search and seizure, and the compelled disclosure of information, respectively.

The law of privacy in the United States has emerged, in large part, as a response to technology. This is best illustrated in the seminal publication on privacy law in America, a *Harvard Law Review* essay, "The Right to Privacy" by Samuel Warren and Louis Brandeis (1890). The article, a call for a new right to privacy in America, was inspired by the author's perceived dangers of the expansion of gossip newspapers and handheld cameras. The authors were concerned that instantaneous photography would allow a sensationalistic press to invade the privacy of individuals and that these violations were not currently prohibited by law. Thus, they proposed a general "right to be let alone" that could be effectuated through common law, specifically, a tort action.

Warren and Brandeis's proposal took seed in the early twentieth century and was recognized by a number of courts in the United States. However, it was not until Dean William Prosser, principal author of the influential *Restatement of Torts,* synthesized "the right to be let alone" into four privacy torts that this right became canonized. After analyzing relevant case law, Prosser concluded that there were four harms for which the common law provided a remedy in tort: (1) intrusion upon seclusion, (2) public disclosure of private facts, (3) false light or "publicity," and (4) appropriation of name or likeness. Today, a large majority of states recognize most of these torts.

The four privacy torts are only a part of the patchwork of laws involving privacy in the United States. Protections for privacy can be found in other tort laws, federal and state constitutional law, administrative regulations, criminal law, contract law, and evidentiary privileges. Although scholars typically agree that the privacy law is gaining coherence and symbiosis throughout these separate areas, a common conceptualization of privacy remains elusive. Daniel Solove (2008) has observed that privacy has been conceptualized a number of different ways in the law beyond the right to be let alone, including limited access to the self, secrecy, control over personal information, personhood, and intimacy. Solove eschewed a singular conceptualization of the term, proposing that "privacy" is best used as an umbrella term that refers to a diverse group of related things.

The difficulty in prescribing one meaning for privacy in the law is partially because of the many different ways in which privacy can affect individuals, groups, and society as a whole. The media must constantly be mindful of privacy, particularly the four privacy torts, when gathering and publishing information. The government is prohibited from unreasonable search and seizure by the Fourth Amendment as well as federal electronic surveillance law when collecting information. Medical professionals must maintain the confidentiality of medical information. Individuals have privacy interests in their associations with groups and in remaining anonymous while speaking. Custodians of public records must balance the right of the public to access information with the privacy interests of the subjects of the information. Businesses must comply with legislation aimed at curbing misuse of consumer and financial information. Consumers are protected by regulations from the Federal Trade Commission from unfair and deceptive trade practices that threaten consumer privacy. Given the diversity of scenarios that implicate privacy, it is not surprising that the meaning of privacy varies according to context.

There is no scholarly consensus on how to approach privacy from a legal or policy perspective. Although some scholars argue for a market-based approach with little governmental intervention, others believe strong laws are needed to protect the privacy of individuals. A few scholars, such as David Brin, have questioned whether privacy is even possible or necessary in a society that is increasingly under surveillance. Yet most scholars agree that information privacy has never been more significant in American jurisprudence. Information privacy is becoming a legislative priority as more Americans grapple with personal boundaries on the Internet and the proliferation of their personal information online. The ease of publishing, collecting, and storing information via the Internet has diminished the effectiveness of traditional remedies for privacy violations like the four privacy torts.

Regardless of the law's approach to privacy, it is clear that privacy law will trail technology. In an era of great technological innovation, courts and lawmakers will be asked to help draw boundaries surrounding the collection, use, and disclosure of personal information.

[*See also* **Bill of Rights; Constitution;** *and* **Tort, Law of.**]

BIBLIOGRAPHY

American Law Institute, *The Restatement (Second) of Torts*. St. Paul, Minn: American Law Institute Publishers, 1979.

Bok, Sissela. *Secrets: On the Ethics of Concealment and Revelation*. New York: Vintage Books, 1989.

Brin, David. *The Transparent Society: Will Technology Force Us to Choose between Privacy and Freedom?* Reading, Mass.: Addison-Wesley, 1998.
Lane, Frederick S. *American Privacy: The 400-Year History of Our Most Contested Right.* Boston: Beacon Press, 2009.
Solove, Daniel J. *The Digital Person: Technology and Privacy in the Information Age.* New York: New York University Press, 2004.
Solove, Daniel J., and Schwartz, Paul. *Information Privacy Law.* Wolters Kluwer Law & Business: Austin, Texas, 2009.
Solove, Daniel J. *Understanding Privacy.* Cambridge, Mass.: Harvard University Press, 2008.
Warren, Samuel, and Brandeis, Louis D. "The Right to Privacy." *4 Harvard Law Review* 193 (1890).

Woodrow Hartzog

PROCLAMATION OF 1763

The Royal Proclamation of 7 October 1763 is best known for establishing a boundary along the crest of the Appalachian Mountains, separating European and Indian settlement. (This decree also created governments for three colonies newly acquired by Great Britain in the aftermath of the Seven Years' War: East Florida, West Florida, and Canada, which the British now called Quebec.)

The fear of native hostilities—underscored by the uprising known as Pontiac's Rebellion (1763–1765)—encouraged the British to draw this line. It was, however, hardly permanent. The English acknowledged certain Indian claims east of the mountains, whereas pressure from settlers and speculators forced Indians to concede large tracts to the west. Negotiations with the Iroquois, concluded at the Treaty of Fort Stanwix (1768), pushed the boundary of European settlement into present-day West Virginia and Kentucky, and dealings with the Cherokees, Creeks, Choctaws, and Chickasaws led to other modifications. Quarrels among native groups, and among colonists with conflicting claims, helped shape these treaties.

Although squatters ignored the proclamation and colonial leaders such as George Washington believed it would never be enforced, the decree was nevertheless a grievance for the Americans. It led the British to keep a standing army in the colonies to make certain that this border was respected and it symbolized the clash between a British government determined to guide colonial development and the boisterous, expansion-minded colonists.

[*See also* **Indian Law, Federal;** *and* **Washington, George.**]

BIBLIOGRAPHY

Sosin, Jack M. *Whitehall and the Wilderness: The Middle West in British Colonial Policy, 1760–1775.* Lincoln: University of Nebraska Press, 1961.

Marc Egnal

PROGRESSIVE ERA

The Progressive Era takes its name from the Progressive Party of 1912–1924 and from the general feeling both at the time and in subsequent histories that the early years of the twentieth century were focused on a coherent body of democratic reforms that changed important aspects of the American political system. Interpretations of the Progressive Era have undergone many changes. Autobiographies and early histories stressed the return to popular control over political actions and the gradual shift from local to state to national authority. The next generation stressed points of continuity between Progressive reforms and those of the New Deal Era in a presumptive march toward a moderate welfare state.

In the 1950s, historians stressed the "status resentment" of middle-class reformers who, presumably fearing a loss of social power, had enacted laws to preserve an economic system in which they did well. Radical historians subsequently derided the extent of Progressivism's reform achievement and stressed its conservative nature; their successors focused on such matter as professionalization and bureaucratization. The subject remains contentious, but few in the early twenty-first century regard the actual legislative achievements of the Progressive Era as more than tentative first steps toward substantive reform.

Viewed chronologically, the "Progressive Era" normally covers three discrete time periods. Toward the end of the 1880s, a significant number of women and their male allies came to the conclusion that Social Darwinism, the reigning ideology that had justified economic expansion since the Civil War, was inhumane in its effects and un-Christian in its implications. Seeking more meaningful vocational choices than those the order of the day supplied, they pioneered such new professions as social work or reinvented such older ones as teaching and journalism to make them more ethically meaningful. Following the precedents of Toynbee Hall in London, Jane Addams and Ellen Gates Starr opened Hull House in Chicago in 1889, in a quiet way beginning the era with a concrete achievement. The social settlement movement, with its efforts at adult education, public health, political lobbying, and immigrant assimilation, gave women a respectable place in society. When John Dewey, George Herbert Mead, and other academics joined various clergy and a few doctors in associating themselves with settlement houses, Progressivism was essentially under way.

The growing body of reformers soon included such local politicians as Hazen Pingree in Detroit; Samuel M. "Golden Rule" Jones in Toledo, Ohio, and Governor John P. Altgeld of Illinois. As these locations attest, the upper Midwest particularly nurtured the movement. The focus was on "gas and water socialism," that is, requiring de facto monopolies to charge fair prices in the absence of true competition. Municipal transit fares were often popular issues, but water, gas, electricity, and eventually telephone rates all drew attention. Taxation of real estate, an issue that Henry George had made central to California reform activity, was basic. Allied issues included low wage rates, dangerous working conditions, polluted water supplies, and conditions in the schools.

Attention shifted to the national level with the inauguration of Theodore Roosevelt as president in 1901. A former member of the U.S. Civil Service Commission and of the New York City Police Commission, Roosevelt not only knew crime and corruption firsthand, but also was friendly with reform journalists such as Lincoln Steffens. A moderate reformer by temperament, Roosevelt was sympathetic to early efforts at "muckraking" journalism. Steffens, Ida Tarbell, Ray Stannard Baker, and Samuel Hopkins Adams focused public attention on the underworld of contemporary capitalism, and Roosevelt supported efforts to break up large trusts, regulate railways, purify food and drugs, and protect public lands from private exploitation. He rebelled, however, against writers such as Upton Sinclair and David Graham Phillips, whom he felt went overboard in denouncing corrupt business or political behavior.

An aroused public reelected Roosevelt in 1904, enabled William Howard Taft to win in 1908, and carried Woodrow Wilson to the White House in 1912. Taft proved inept, but Wilson managed to lower tariffs; increase economic regulation of business; assist education, agriculture, and labor; and above all enact the Federal Reserve Act, a long overdue measure that proved the most enduring of all Progressive reforms. During these years as well, local reformers adopted "initiative, referendum, and recall" measures enabling voters to initiate legislation, ratify legislative acts, and remove public officials who violated their trust. Certain states, notably California, Oregon, and Wisconsin, proved especially friendly to reform activity.

The outbreak of World War I in 1914 began a slow but inexorable shift from domestic to international preoccupations. At first favoring neutrality, Wilson took America into the war in 1917, an act that, in Wilson's obsessively theological mind, seemed quintessentially Progressive: America could bring its reform mentality to the supreme task of assuring a permanent world peace. Through a series of "covenants" he would conduct a war to end all wars and instill democratic principles everywhere. Wilson's failure to win the kind of peace treaty he sought at Versailles, and the U.S. Senate's repudiation of American membership in the League of Nations, marked the end of the Progressive impulse as a political force.

Early interpretations of the Progressive Era dwelled on political and diplomatic goals, but in reality the movement was a broad-based cultural and even religious phenomenon. Most Progressive leaders came from Protestant and often clerical families; they had learned Christian moral principles from an early age, and they tended to assume that sin was somehow at the core of social problems. Sin implied sinners; sinners needed to repent; and thus the period comes increasingly to look like a massive revival effort, with journalists, professors, lawyers, social workers, and clergy exhorting their audiences in sermons, secular or otherwise. Roosevelt was not simply using rhetoric opportunistically when he twice urged voters at national conventions to "stand at Armageddon" and "battle for the Lord." The era was more a third "Great Awakening" than an "early New Deal."

In fact, the greatest achievements of the Progressive impulse were not legislative at all. "Progressive education," for example, remains a major legacy of the period. Drawing ideas from psychology and pragmatic philosophy, John Dewey supervised a Laboratory School during his years (1894–1904) at the University of Chicago, publishing a number of influential papers consolidating the results. Insisting that traditional methods that stressed sheer memorization and an outmoded morality merely stifled intelligence, he demanded a schooling experience that would be less oriented toward "reading, writing, and 'rithmetic" and more focused on recreating the educational effect of a vanishing rural life. Students needed to work on projects; familiarize themselves with fabrics, carpentry, and crafts; learn about local governments and fire laws, take trips to observe biology and botany in their nature setting; and, in general, use their arms and legs more than their vocabularies. When he shifted to Columbia University in 1904, Dewey founded one of the more forceful institutions in modern life, the Progressive educational establishment, a bureaucracy that in time caused many parents to equate the word "Progressive" with "child-centered" and "undisciplined."

In intellectual life, Progressivism reshaped church and university. Led by George D. Herron and Walter Rauschenbusch, most Protestant denominations developed versions of a Social Gospel closely tied to British and continental socialism. The true Christian had a moral duty to do good in this world rather than withdrawing from society to pursue his or her own salvation. In social science, new graduate schools such as Johns Hopkins and the University of Chicago were soon turning out PhDs intent on social investigation as a prelude to reform. Woodrow Wilson and John Dewey, both with PhDs from Johns Hopkins, offered models of the socially engaged intellectual. At Chicago, sociology was especially strong, as William I. Thomas pioneered in the study of immigration and Robert Park in study of the city. Charles A. Beard at Columbia and

Carl Becker at Cornell were only two of the historians who recast American history in terms of present needs rather than some abstract "scientific knowledge."

In journalism, the muckrakers generated an astonishing number of reform novels. Upton Sinclair took on the meatpacking industry in *The Jungle* (1906) and Brand Whitlock the criminal mentality in *The Turn of the Balance* (1907); David Graham Phillips produced books on one industry in need of moral reform after another. In the arts, Vachel Lindsay was only the most eloquent of several poets who celebrated William Jennings Bryan, three-time reform candidate for president, or William Booth, the Salvation Army general who devoted himself to helping society's outcasts. The painter John Sloan of the "ashcan school" worked for socialist candidates while picturing scenes of urban poverty.

Like Progressives in other arenas, reformers in the arts yearned nostalgically for the moral, natural, God-centered world of their grandparents, creating comparable solutions for contemporary problems. Unlike the modernists of Greenwich Village, who valued the new in and of itself, without reference to Protestant moral values, the Progressives always combined their innovations with nostalgia.

In this context of "innovative nostalgia," the composer Charles Ives looked back to the Revolutionary War, antislavery, and the Civil War to find materials for his radical innovations. He named movements of a *Concord Sonata* after Ralph Waldo Emerson, Nathaniel Hawthorne, the Alcotts, and Henry David Thoreau; the String Quartet No. 1 bears the subtitle *A Revival Service*; and the most innovative piece of all, *Putnam's Camp*, from *Three Places in New England*, fuses tales of the Revolutionary War and a stream-of-consciousness dream sequence with memories of a Fourth of July celebration when two uncoordinated brass bands marched into Danbury, Connecticut, each competing for sonic dominance.

Most famous of all, Frank Lloyd Wright brought Progressive concerns into architecture. From a background of Unitarianism, he adapted the educational ideals of Friedrich Froebel to the concerns of Hull-House and the University of Chicago, fitting easily into the world of Addams and Dewey. Developing a "prairie style" of single-unit construction, usually of houses or churches, he sought in the manner of the transcendentalists to fit his works into nature. Form and function were one; generations of efforts to impose on the landscape, to ornament without regard to useful purpose, went out the window.

Defeated politically in 1920, Progressivism persisted in identifiable ways at least until World War II. It helped shape both sides of the interior foreign policy debates, as Progressive internationalists fought isolationists. Some Progressive moralists resisted the secular and nationalizing tendencies of the New Deal, whereas others adapted with little trouble. In time, the Progressive image became increasingly tarnished. National Prohibition, adopted by the Eighteenth Amendment in 1919, seemed a fiasco, with the effort to remoralize drinking habits eventually leading to more drink and much more crime. Once devoted to moral reform, America turned toward secularism and social democracy in 1933, only to return to at least one strand of the Progressive ethos in the Ronald Reagan years, when issues like the legality of abortion and religion in the public schools focused public debate in ways eerily reminiscent of the years before World War I.

[*See also* **Antitrust Law and Legislation; Bryan, William Jennings; Education Policy: An Overview; Eighteenth Amendment; Federal Reserve Act; Federal Reserve System; Lippmann, Walter; Muckrakers; New**

Deal; Peace Movements; Progressive Party of 1912; Progressive Party of 1924; Prohibition; Pure Food and Drug Act; Reagan, Ronald; Regulatory Agencies, Federal; Roosevelt, Theodore; Taft, William Howard; Tariffs; *and* **Wilson, Woodrow.**]

BIBLIOGRAPHY

Boyer, Paul. *Urban Masses and Moral Order in America, 1820–1920.* Cambridge, Mass.: Harvard University Press, 1978.

Crunden, Robert M. *Ministers of Reform: The Progressives' Achievement in American Civilization, 1889–1920.* New York: Basic Books, 1982.

Davis, Allen. *Spearheads for Reform: The Social Settlements and the Progressive Movement, 1890–1914.* New York: Oxford University Press, 1967.

Dawley, Alan. *Struggles for Justice: Social Responsibility and the Liberal State.* Cambridge, Mass.: Belknap Press of Harvard University Press, 1991.

Frankel, Nora Lee, and Nancy S. Dye, eds. *Gender, Class, Race, and Reform in the Progressive Era.* Lexington: University Press of Kentucky, 1991.

Kloppenberg, James T. *Uncertain Victory: Social Democracy and Progressivism in European and American Thought, 1870–1920.* New York: Oxford University Press, 1986.

Link, Arthur S., and Richard L. McCormick. *Progressivism.* Arlington Heights, Ill.: Harlan Davidson, 1983.

Link, William A. *The Paradox of Southern Progressivism.* Chapel Hill: University of North Carolina Press, 1992.

Rodgers, Daniel. "In Search of Progressivism." *Reviews in American History* 10, No. 4 (December 1982): 113–132.

Robert M. Crunden

PROGRESSIVE PARTY OF 1912

At a time when Britain, France, Denmark, and Germany had more generous welfare states than the United States, the National Progressive Party of 1912 (Bull Moose Party) was founded to advocate for several reforms including old age pension and unemployment insurance, as well as direct democracy ideas about citizen participation in government such as presidential primaries and the direct election of senators. Early in President William Howard Taft's term of office (1909–1913) insurgents within the Republican Party became alienated from Taft (his failure to back tariff reform and his lack of commitment to labor issues). After the Ballinger–Pinchot controversy of 1910, in which Taft fired chief forester Gifford Pinchot for accusing interior secretary Richard Ballinger of dishonesty, Pinchot attacked Taft in the press and attempted unsuccessfully to convince former president Theodore Roosevelt to run against Taft. In the months after the 25 March 1911 Triangle Shirtwaist Fire, Roosevelt aligned himself more closely with New York's labor activists and social justice progressives who wanted the antilabor Taft out. Senator Robert M. La Follette gathered midwestern support for a progressive nomination challenge to Taft, but Roosevelt refused to endorse La Follette's candidacy and finally decided to run against Taft late in 1911.

Because party nominations for president were still based largely on state party caucuses (or district meetings and state conventions) and only fourteen states had adopted nominating primaries with direct voter participation, Taft controlled most state Republican presidential nominating processes. Roosevelt beat Taft in nine of the twelve primaries he entered, but most delegates were chosen by party caucuses and in many states disputed results were common. In June 1912 the Republican National Convention in Chicago began with 252 seats in dispute. The pro-Taft Credentials Committee judged that among the contested seats 238 belonged to Taft. Roosevelt's supporters charged the Credentials Committee with ignoring the primary results and stealing the nomination for Taft. When pro-Taft delegates were seated, Roosevelt supporters called for a third-party challenge. Roosevelt agreed to lead the party, and in close consultation with Pinchot, Paul Kellogg, Jane Addams, and Florence Kelley wrote the Bull Moose platform, which called for strong defense and a larger navy, conservation, public health reforms, woman suffrage, old age pensions, unemployment insurance, the minimum wage, national health insurance, workmen's compensation, the right to collective bargaining, and direct democracy reforms including the direct election of senators, initiative and referendum, and campaign finance reform. The Bull Moosers also advocated the graduated federal income tax and inheritance and a ban on child labor. If the Democrats had nominated the conservative Champ Clark, Roosevelt might have won the November election. After a deadlocked convention with forty-six ballots, the Democrats finally nominated progressive reformer New Jersey governor Woodrow Wilson. In a rancorous four-way race for president, Socialist Party nominee Eugene Debs also defended many progressive social justice ideas, but Wilson, despite his enthusiasm about tax, tariff, and direct democracy reforms, never supported welfare state ideas or a ban on child labor. When the votes were counted Wilson won and Roosevelt came in second, Taft third, and Debs fourth. Despite its defeat, the Bull Moose campaign cast long shadows across American political history as the most successful third-party challenge to the two-party system. Roosevelt continued to work with reformers to build a nationwide third party, a progressive policy institute called the Progressive Social Service, and a congressional delegation to promote the Bull Moose Party Deal.

[*See also* **Debs, Eugene, Roosevelt, Theodore; Taft, William Howard; Third Parties;** ***and*** **Wilson, Woodrow.**]

BIBLIOGRAPHY

Chace, James. *1912: Wilson, Roosevelt, Taft, & Debs—The Election That Changed the Country.* New York: Simon & Schuster, 2004.

Dalton, Kathleen. *Theodore Roosevelt: A Strenuous Life.* New York: Alfred A. Knopf, 2002.

Gable, John. *The Bull Moose Years: Theodore Roosevelt and the Progressive Party, 1912–1916.* PhD dissertation. Ann Arbor, Mich.: University Microfilms, 1972.

Kathleen Dalton

PROGRESSIVE PARTY OF 1924

Wisconsin senator Robert M. La Follette sought the Republican presidential nomination in 1924, but incumbent president Calvin Coolidge swept the first ballot. La Follette, a leading progressive reformer, considered Coolidge and the Democrat's nominee, John B. Davis, equally dedicated to protecting corporate interests rather than serving the needs of average Americans. La Follette declared himself an Independent Progressive and announced his platform, whose planks included a thorough housecleaning of various executive departments of the government, protections for organized labor, revisions to the Versailles Treaty, and nomination and election of the president by direct vote of the people. Perhaps most controversial was the plank that would, by amendment to the Constitution, give Congress the power to pass and validate laws declared unconstitutional by the Supreme Court.

La Follette and his running mate, Senator Burton K. Wheeler (D-MT), were supported by distressed farmers and laborers and other Americans who were impatient with the failure of mainstream politicians to meet the ongoing challenges of the newly industrialized, urbanized nation. The ticket enjoyed early widespread support. La Follette's record, including electoral and tax reforms, environmental protections, and legislation promoting fairness and safety in the workplace, gave credence to his campaign promises to step up efforts to more equitably redistribute the nation's power and wealth. Leading African Americans including W. E. B. Du Bois promoted La Follette, and the ticket also appealed to Jane Addams, Helen Keller, Florence Kelley, and others who urged women to put their newly won votes to the best possible use.

As the campaign progressed, La Follette, who was sixty-nine and suffered from heart disease, staunchly maintained that he had the vitality to serve two terms as president. For strategic reasons, the two major parties both credited him with more support than he really had. The press too presented La Follette as a potential "spoiler" who could force the election into the House. Despite these predictions, La Follette suffered a sharp decrease in support just prior to the election, a fate common to third parties. Many initial supporters came to fear that a third-party vote was a wasted vote, and others were dissuaded by the advent of a more prosperous economy. Mismanaged and poorly funded, the ticket appeared on ballots under four different party labels: Progressive, Socialist, Farmer-Labor, and Independent.

Too radical for conservatives and too conservative for radicals, the La Follette–Wheeler ticket received 4,822,319 of the estimated 28,649,709 votes cast. It took more votes from Davis than from Coolidge and gained most of its support from farmers, union members, and socialists in midwestern and western states. Although La Follette took only Wisconsin in the Electoral College, he received nearly 17 percent of the national vote, more than five times the previous total for a candidate endorsed by the Socialist Party of America. Despite what La Follette considered a humiliating loss, based on dollars spent per vote, the Progressive Party of 1924 was the most successful third-party effort in the twentieth century.

[*See also* **Coolidge, Calvin; Du Bois, W. E. B.; La Follette, Robert;** ***and*** **Socialist Party of America.**]

BIBLIOGRAPHY

Johnston, Scott D. "Robert La Follette and the Socialists: Aspects of the 1924 Presidential Campaign Re-examined." *Social Science* 50 (1975): 69–77.

La Follette, Robert M. "Passive Citizenship Is Not Enough." *American Rhetoric: Online Speech Bank.* http://www.americanrhetoric.com/speechbankm-r.htm/ (accessed 24 August 2011).

Unger, Nancy C. *Fighting Bob La Follette: The Righteous Reformer.* Madison: Wisconsin Historical Society Press, 2008.

Nancy C. Unger

PROGRESSIVE PARTY OF 1948

The Progressive Party was the vehicle for Henry A. Wallace's 1948 independent presidential campaign in 1948, challenging Harry Truman and the Democratic Party. Sentiment for a third party began to grow in late 1946 as the Truman Administration's foreign and domestic policies deeply alienated the left wing of the Democratic Party. The Communist Party USA (CPUSA) did much to encourage such talk and played a significant, although clandestine, role in convincing Wallace to launch a third party instead of challenging Harry Truman for the nomination. Beanie Baldwin, a concealed Communist and ultimately Wallace's campaign manager, coordinated these efforts, but Wallace himself made the final decision. Indeed, it is unlikely the party would have been launched had he not agreed to lead it. By the time Wallace announced his candidacy in December 1947, however, many of the liberals on whose support he had counted had abandoned him, in part because they were wary of the Communist presence around him, but also because they had concluded that supporting a third party would benefit the Republicans. Nonetheless, Wallace threw himself into the campaign, which he called his "crusade for peace." Denouncing Truman as a "warmonger," Wallace insisted that only he could negotiate an end to the Cold War with the Soviets. Skeptics noted that his speeches were long on emotional rhetoric but short on details.

The Progressive Party convention, intended to turn around the flagging campaign, did precisely the opposite. Press coverage emphasized the Communist presence, but the Communists did little to conceal themselves. On the floor, stalwarts insisted the Progressive Party refrain from any criticism of the Soviet Union. When the delegates roared down as "red-baiting" an innocuous platform amendment stating that "it is not our intention to give blanket endorsement of the foreign policy of any nation," voters were left to draw their own conclusions.

Wallace's tour through the South proved the high point of his fall campaign. Refusing to speak to segregated audiences and braving angry, egg-throwing mobs, the Progressive nominee directly confronted southern white racism and in his speeches denounced segregation as "sin." Wallace's courageous performance inspired many African Americans, but won him few votes. By October many non-Communist liberals still lingering in the Progressive ranks had quietly withdrawn. Wallace, however, continued to insist the Progressive Party offered a long-term alternative to the two "Wall Street parties" and quarreled publicly with Baldwin when the latter announced (without consulting Wallace) that the Progressives were withdrawing most of their congressional candidates who were challenging liberal Democrats. The exodus of the liberals made the Communist presence in the Progressive party even more noticeable, particularly at the local level where many of the remaining activists were concealed party members.

In November Wallace received only 1.1 million votes, 37 percent of which came from New York City. The defeat was especially stinging to the Communists. In supporting the Progressive Party, they had lost their influence in the unions and other liberal organizations. Indeed, the persistent tension between liberals and Communists within the Progressive Party demonstrated that the old Popular Front could not be sustained in the new Cold War environment. The Progressive Party would continue on—after 1950 without Wallace—but, politically, it was a spent force.

[*See also* **Communist Party USA; Truman, Harry S.;** *and* **Wallace, Henry A.**]

BIBLIOGRAPHY

MacDougall, Curtis D. *Gideon's Army,* 3 vols. New York: Marzani & Munsell, 1965.

Starobin, Joseph R. *American Communism in Crisis.* Berkeley: University of California Press, 1972. Provides an astute analysis of the Communists' participation in the Progressive Party.

Thomas W. Devine

PROHIBITION

Prohibition, the statutory restriction of the consumption of beverage alcohol, was the younger sibling of a temperance movement that dates from the early days of the republic. Whereas the sale of alcohol had been regulated and taxed since colonial times, the first efforts to prohibit alcohol sales were efforts in the 1830s and 1840s to restrict the licensing of saloons in the wake of the Washingtonian temperance movement. The ineffectiveness of that campaign led Neal Dow, the mayor of Portland, Maine, to press the state legislature to adopt a measure that banned the manufacture and sale of alcoholic beverages in the state. Similar laws were adopted in twelve states in the Northeast and Midwest. These gains were short lived, as the sectional crisis and Civil War overwhelmed other issues and the failures of Reconstruction drained the energies of reform.

Prohibition reemerged in the late nineteenth century as a political force, despite the fact that the two major parties tried to exclude it from partisan campaigns, recognizing the disruptive effect it would have on the delicate political equilibrium of the Gilded Age. The Prohibition Party, founded in 1869, never drew a significant number of votes, but always threatened to act as the spoiler in close elections. Nevertheless, in alliance with the Woman's Christian Temperance Union (WCTU), the revival of the issue resulted in statewide Prohibition campaigns in eighteen states. Many campaigns, particularly in the southern states, resulted in statewide bans on the sale of alcohol, although few restricted personal use. A wave of local option elections dried up counties and towns in otherwise wet states.

The campaigns of the 1880s stalled with the political realignment of the 1890s, but in the early years of the twentieth century reformers turned their sights on the urban saloon. Progressives, businessmen, religious leaders, and opponents of immigration all found in the saloon a source of corruption. The Anti-Saloon League (ASL), founded in 1895, under the leadership of a group of Ohio reformers, took Prohibition back to the political arena. A brilliantly effective lobbying group, the ASL crossed party lines to support prohibitionist candidates and local option campaigns. There were a few successful statewide campaigns, but the real success of the ASL was in supporting local option, a form of Prohibition that posed little threat to private consumption or to the states' rights sensitivities of southern politicians. Nevertheless, the organization's greatest success came at the national level. Despite the reservations of many of its supporters, the ASL was able to help elect a sufficient number of dry members of Congress in 1916 to secure the two-thirds vote needed to submit a Prohibition amendment to the Constitution.

American involvement in World War I provided the best opportunity for prohibitionists. The campaign to conserve grain for food production combined with virulent anti-German rhetoric led to the quick passage of the 1817 Lever Act, prohibiting the distillation of liquor from foodstuffs. Ten days after the end of the war, Congress passed the Wartime Prohibition Act, which banned the sale of alcohol until the end of demobilization. The Eighteenth Amendment was ratified on 16 January 1919, and the Volstead Act, passed later that year, banned the manufacture or sale of virtually all beverage alcohol.

The "Great Experiment" did not last. Changes in middle-class drinking patterns, concern over organized crime and the disregard of prohibition law, and the economic collapse at the end of the decade prompted a vigorous repeal campaign. In 1933 the Twentieth Amendment was ratified, bringing the close to a reform movement as old as the nation.

[*See also* **Anti-Saloon League; Eighteenth Amendment; Reconstruction;** *and* **Woman's Christian Temperance Union.**]

BIBLIOGRAPHY

Blocker, Jack S. *American Temperance Movements: Cycles of Reform*. Boston: Twayne Publishers, 1989.

Pegram, Thomas R. *Battling Demon Rum: The Struggle for a Dry America, 1800–1933*. Chicago: Ivan R. Dee, 1998.

Rumbarger, Jon J. *Profits, Power and Prohibition: Alcohol Reform and the Industrialization of America, 1800–1930.* Albany: State University of New York Press, 1989.

Tyrell, Ian R. *Sobering Up: From Temperance to Prohibition in Antebellum America, 1800–1860.* Westport, Conn.: Greenwood Press, 1979.

James Ivy

PROPERTY RIGHTS

Throughout much of American history the Supreme Court has defended property rights against legislative interference. In assuming this role, the justices have mirrored the values of the framers of the Constitution, who were strongly influenced by the natural law philosophy of John Locke. According to Locke, private property existed under natural law before the creation of political authority. Building on natural law theory, the eighteenth-century Whig political tradition stressed the rights of property owners as a bulwark of freedom against arbitrary government. The framers also emphasized the economic utility of private property. They believed that security of property and contractual arrangements facilitated the development of investment capital and the emergence of a strong national economy. Although some state constitutions contained provisions to protect property rights, in the years immediately following the Revolution many became convinced that state governments could not be trusted to respect property ownership. Accordingly, the delegates to the Constitutional Convention were vitally concerned with the need to safeguard economic interests.

Numerous provisions of the Constitution pertain to economic interests. For instance, the Constitution prohibits Congress or the states from confiscating property through bills of attainder and limits the power of Congress to impose direct taxes. The Constitution also contained several clauses that protected property in slaves. Foremost among the constitutional restrictions on state authority was the contracts clause, forbidding the states from enacting any law "impairing the Obligation of Contracts." Even more important was the Fifth Amendment, which provided that no person should be "deprived of life, liberty, or property, without due process of law; nor shall private property be taken for public use, without just compensation." The Fifth Amendment in effect incorporated into the Constitution the Lockean idea that protection of property was a chief aim of government.

From the outset, federal courts signaled their intention to safeguard existing economic arrangements and to curtail state legislative interference with property rights. In *Champion v. Casey* (1792), one of the first exercises of federal judicial review, a circuit court held that a Rhode Island statute granting an individual debtor exemption from attachments for a period of time was an unconstitutional impairment of contract.

Property Rights and Natural Law. Looking to the precepts of natural law rather than any specific clause of the Constitution, some federal judges adopted the doctrine of vested rights to protect established property rights from legislative impairment. According to this doctrine, property ownership was a fundamental right. Laws that disturbed such rights were void because they violated the principles limiting all constitutional governments. Justice William Paterson articulated this view in the significant circuit court case *Vanhorne's Lessee v. Dorrance* (1795). Observing that "the right of acquiring and possessing property, and having it protected, is one of the natural, inherent and inalienable rights of man" (p. 310), Paterson implicitly linked the doctrine of natural rights with the contracts clause.

Writing a separate opinion in *Calder v. Bull* (1798), Justice Samuel Chase reiterated the vested rights doctrine. "There are certain vital principles in our free republican governments," he observed, "which will determine and overrule an apparent and flagrant abuse of legislative power" (p. 388). Chase maintained that the legislature could not "violate the right of an antecedent lawful private contract; or the right of private property" (p. 388).

The Marshall and Taney Courts. John Marshall, who became chief justice in 1801, dominated the Supreme Court for three decades. As a Federalist, Marshall was sympathetic to property interests and business enterprise. He believed that property ownership both preserved individual liberty and encouraged productive use of resources. The contracts clause emerged as the centerpiece of Marshall Court jurisprudence. Drawing upon the doctrine of vested rights, Marshall fashioned the clause into a powerful bulwark to property interests. His initial step was to broaden the definition of contracts that were entitled to protection under the Constitution. In the landmark case of *Fletcher v. Peck* (1810), Marshall held that a state was constitutionally barred from breaching its contracts. At issue was an attempt by the Georgia legislature to rescind the huge Yazoo land grant. Marshall noted that the terms of the contracts clause "are general, and are applicable to contracts of every description" (p. 137). Likewise, in *New Jersey v. Wilson* (1812) the Marshall Court determined that a tax exemption was a contractual right and hence a state could not revoke such preferred treatment.

A more far-reaching application of the contracts clause occurred in *Dartmouth College v. Woodward* (1819), which held that a corporate charter was a constitutionally protected contract. As corporations grew more numerous and powerful during the nineteenth century, public control of corporations became a major concern. The power of the state to repeal or alter the charter of incorporation suggested one avenue by which regulations might be imposed. The *Dartmouth College* ruling aided corporate enterprise by erecting a constitutional barrier against legislative infringement of existing charters. In a concurring opinion, however, Justice Joseph Story suggested that state legislatures could reserve the right to modify corporate charters when they were issued. The exercise of such a reserved power would not constitute the impairment of contract.

The contracts clause was also a major force in shaping debtor–creditor relations. After ratification of the Constitution, many states continued the practice of enacting debtor-relief measures. Creditors vigorously attacked such laws, arguing that state debtor-relief measures represented an unconstitutional impairment of contract. A challenge to New York's Bankruptcy Act of 1811 came before the Supreme Court in *Sturges v. Crowninshield* (1819). Marshall concluded that New York's law was void because it relieved debtors of the obligation to pay debts contracted before the measure was passed. States could not retroactively discharge contractual obligations. Spurred by economic distress in the wake of the Panic of 1819, many states passed new bankruptcy laws covering only debts incurred after the date of enactment. By a narrow 4-to-3 margin, the Supreme Court sustained New York's revised statute in *Ogden v. Saunders* (1827). The justices held that a law in effect when a contract was made formed part of the agreement. Consequently, the application of bankruptcy laws to posterior obligations did not impair any contract.

The *Ogden* decision marked a watershed in the history of the contracts clause's interpretation. Without retreating from early decisions, the Court was henceforth guided by a more cautious spirit in contracts clause cases. In *Providence Bank v. Billings* (1830), Marshall declared that surrender of a state's power of taxation could not be implied from the grant of a charter incorporating a bank. This ruling established the principle that grants of privileges to corporations must be expressly set forth in their charters.

Reflecting his commitment to economic nationalism, Marshall labored for broad protection of contracts to encourage investment capital. By any standard he achieved considerable success—indeed, the contracts clause figured in more Supreme Court decisions than any other section of the Constitution during the nineteenth century. Despite criticism of some rulings, there was little hostility to Marshall's core belief that the federal courts should safeguard established economic rights.

The political triumph of Jacksonian Democracy brought new attitudes to the Supreme Court. On Marshall's death, President Andrew Jackson named Roger B. Taney as chief justice in 1837. Under Taney's leadership the Court shaped constitutional law to harmonize with the Jacksonian tenets of states' rights, hostility to special privilege, and strict construction of the Constitution. Despite a shift of emphasis, however, the Court did not fundamentally depart from the constitutional principles of the Marshall era. Taney shared Marshall's economic values, especially the need to protect private property and to promote economic growth. To be sure, there were differences between the judicial approaches of Taney and Marshall. Taney limited the reach of the contracts clause and allowed the states greater flexibility to fashion economic policy. This was illustrated by *Charles River Bridge v. Warren Bridge* (1837), in which Taney rejected the notion of implied corporate privilege. He emphasized the principle that corporate grants must be strictly construed, a doctrine that affirmed legislative control over economic policy. Sensitive to the relationship between law and technology, Taney further asserted that recognition of implied corporate privileges would stymie economic progress. To Taney's mind, existing property rights could sometimes be destroyed to make room for innovations and improvements.

The power of eminent domain constituted another limit on the scope of the contracts clause. In *West River Bridge Company v. Dix* (1848) the Court held that the contracts clause did not protect a corporation against the exercise of eminent domain. The justices reasoned that all contracts were subject to the state's paramount power of eminent domain.

The justices, however, enforced the contracts clause in cases involving debtor-relief laws, exemptions from taxation, and banking regulations. In *Bronson v. Kinzie* (1843) the Court heard a challenge to two Illinois statutes that retroactively limited mortgage foreclosure sales and gave mortgagors broad rights to redeem foreclosed property. Writing for the Court, Taney found the Illinois statutes to be an unconstitutional abrogation of contract.

The use of eminent domain to take private property did not receive much attention from the federal courts before the Civil War. The Constitution makes no direct reference to the power of eminent domain, but the Fifth Amendment requires that private property be taken only for public use and upon payment of just compensation. In *Vanhorne's Lessee*, Justice Paterson had concluded that the "despotic power" of taking private property "exists in every government" and that "government could not subsist without it" (p. 311). He stressed, however, that compensation must be paid to landowners and that determination of land value was a judicial, not a legislative, function.

In practice, the takings clause of the Fifth Amendment did not bulk large during the antebellum era. The most significant Supreme Court takings decision in this period was *Barron v. Baltimore* (1833), in which the city of Baltimore sought to increase the access of shippers by undertaking harbor improvements. The city diverted water from the plaintiff's wharf, greatly reducing its value, and the plaintiff claimed compensation for his loss under the Fifth Amendment. Rejecting this contention, the Court held that the Fifth Amendment restricted the federal government but did not apply to the states.

Like the takings clause, the due process clause of the Fifth Amendment played almost no role in the constitutional protection of economic interests before the Civil War. By the mid-nineteenth century, however, federal courts began to wrestle with substantive interpretations of due process. Substantive due process first appeared in federal jurisprudence in the controversial 1857 *Scott v. Sandford* decision. Chief Justice Taney interpreted the due process clause as placing a limitation on the power of Congress to exclude slave property from the territories. The *Scott* ruling was effectively superseded by the Civil War and the Fourteenth Amendment, but the concept of substantive due process was destined for a robust rebirth in a later generation. Hence, the property-conscious jurisprudence of the antebellum era was a precursor of laissez-faire constitutionalism later in the century.

Civil War and Reconstruction. The Civil War compelled the federal government to play an active role in managing the economy. Congress experimented with new methods of public finance. In 1861 it levied the first income tax, a flat tax of 3 percent on income over $800 a year. In addition, the government issued large amounts of paper money irredeemable in gold or silver, popularly known as greenbacks. The Legal Tender Act of 1862 declared such paper money to be lawful tender for all debts and the payment of taxes. The greenback dollars rapidly depreciated in value, and creditors resisted attempts to discharge debts with such currency. Further, in 1864 Congress organized the national banking system and established a uniform currency of national banknotes. A year later Congress placed a heavy tax on state banknotes, effectively driving them out of circulation as currency.

The Supreme Court sustained these fledgling moves toward national regulation of the economy. In *Springer v. United States* (1881) the Court upheld the Civil War income tax as applied to professional earnings. Also significant was the decision in *Veazie Bank v. Fenno* (1869), in which the Court affirmed the power of Congress to tax the notes of state banks. Stressing the importance of securing a uniform currency, the Court refused to scrutinize the motives of Congress in levying such a prohibitive tax. Thus, *Veazie Bank* established that Congress could use the taxing power to regulate or even eliminate particular economic activities.

Far more controversial was the Court's handling of constitutional challenges to the legal tender legislation. In *Hepburn v. Griswold* (1870) the Supreme Court, by a vote of 4 to 3, declared the Legal Tender Act invalid as applied to contracts made before its passage. Speaking for the Court, Chief Justice Salmon P. Chase concluded that the act violated the due process clause of the Fifth Amendment and impaired the obligation of contract in a manner inconsistent with the spirit of the Constitution. Many in business and government feared economic chaos as a result of this ruling. After reargument the Court, in *Knox v. Lee* (1871), overruled *Hepburn* and upheld the constitutionality of the Legal Tender Act with respect to both preexisting and subsequent contracts. The upshot of these *Legal Tender Cases* was judicial recognition of broad congressional power over currency and monetary policy.

Following the Civil War, America experienced an era of enormous economic growth. Spearheaded by the railroads, industrial development and technological innovation proceeded rapidly. Rapid industrialization, however, produced economic dislocation, and not all segments of society benefited from unbridled operation of the market economy. Corporations and property owners looked to the judiciary for protection against governmental regulations. They sought to utilize the Fourteenth Amendment as a shield against state legislation that in their view represented arbitrary and unreasonable interference with economic rights.

The first interpretation of the Fourteenth Amendment came in the Slaughterhouse Cases (1873). During Reconstruction, the Louisiana legislature created a monopoly of the slaughterhouse business in New Orleans. Some New Orleans butchers challenged the Louisiana statute, arguing that the monopoly deprived them of the property right to pursue a trade in violation of both the privileges or immunities and the due process clauses of the Fourteenth Amendment. By a 5-to-4 vote, the Supreme Court rejected this contention and placed a narrow construction on the scope of the privileges or immunities clause. According to the Court, no federally protected right to be free of monopoly existed. In sharp contrast, the dissenting justices saw the amendment as a substantive restraint on state power to regulate the rights of property owners. Attacking monopolies as an encroachment on the right to acquire property, Justice Stephen J. Field argued that the right to pursue a lawful occupation was protected by the Fourteenth Amendment.

The Supreme Court next considered the authority of the states to control private property in *Munn v. Illinois* (1877). At issue in *Munn* was an Illinois statute that set the rate for storing grain in Chicago elevators. The elevator managers assailed this measure as a deprivation of property without due process of law. Upholding the Illinois law, the Supreme Court again adopted a deferential attitude toward state authority to control the use of private property. Speaking for the Court, Chief Justice Morrison R. Waite ruled that "when private property is devoted to a public use, it is subject to public regulation" (p. 130). Whether this public interest doctrine applied to a particular enterprise was considered a matter for legislative judgment. Although recognizing that the owner of property "clothed with a public interest" was entitled to reasonable compensation, Waite declared that the determination of such compensation was a legislative, not a judicial, task. The only protection of property owners against legislative abuse was resort to the political process. Field vigorously dissented, warning that under the *Munn* rationale "all property and all business in the State are held at the mercy of a majority of its legislature" (p. 140).

During the 1880s the Supreme Court adopted a more skeptical posture toward state regulation of property and business. In *Stone v. Farmers' Loan & Trust Co.* (1886) the Court upheld a Mississippi statute that empowered a commission to regulate railroad rates, but it cautioned that such authority was not unlimited. Chief Justice Waite added that "the State cannot require a railroad corporation to carry persons or property without reward; neither can it do that which in law amounts to a taking of private property for public use without just compensation, or without due process of law" (p. 331). In addition, the Court strengthened the legal position of corporations. The justices ruled in *Santa Clara County v. Southern Pacific Railroad* (1886) that corporations were persons within the meaning of the Fourteenth Amendment and thus entitled to protection under the due process clause.

Economic Due Process. In *Mugler v. Kansas* (1887) the Supreme Court went a step further, moving toward a substantive interpretation of the due process clause to safeguard fundamental property rights. This step laid the foundation for the doctrine of economic due process. Although the Court sustained a state measure prohibiting the manufacture and sale of alcoholic beverages as a valid use of the police power to protect health and morals, Justice John Marshall Harlan emphasized that courts could scrutinize the purpose behind state regulation as well as the means employed to achieve the stated ends. Moreover, Harlan insisted that there were "limits beyond which legislation cannot rightfully go" (p. 661).

Economic due process soon became the most important judicial instrument safeguarding property rights and vindicating the principles of laissez-faire constitutionalism. In the 1890s, the Court ruled that utilities were constitutionally entitled to charge reasonable rates and that the determination of reasonableness was a judicial question. This line of development culminated in *Smyth v. Ames* (1898), in which the Court unanimously held that a utility must be allowed a "fair return upon the value of that which it employs for public convenience" (p. 547). The *Smyth* formula required that rates be based on a company's present value and promulgated a complex text to ascertain such value.

In *Allgeyer v. Louisiana* (1897) the Supreme Court also developed an important corollary of economic due process, the liberty of contract doctrine. The Court reasoned that liberty, as protected by the Fourteenth Amendment, encompassed the right to "enter into all contracts which may be proper" to pursue an occupation or acquire property (p. 589). States could not interfere with this contractual freedom, a position that cast a deep shadow over legislative attempts to regulate the terms of employment.

Although laissez-faire constitutionalism became predominant during the 1890s, the Court also recognized that states could lawfully restrict property and contractual rights in appropriate situations under police power. The justices were usually sympathetic to laws that protected the health, safety, and morals of society. In *Holden v. Hardy* (1898), for instance, the Supreme Court by a vote of 7 to 2 upheld a Utah statute limiting work in mines to eight hours a day. Rejecting a challenge based on the liberty of contract doctrine, the Court stressed the unhealthy conditions of mine work and noted that mine owners and their employees did not have equal bargaining power.

Takings. In addition to fashioning the doctrine of economic due process, the Supreme Court enlarged the protection available to property owners under the takings clause of the Fifth Amendment. The Court broadened the definition of a taking in *Pumpelly v. Green Bay Company* (1871), holding that a physical invasion that destroyed the usefulness of land was a taking, although title technically remained with the owner. Further, the Court gave an expansive reading to the just compensation requirement in *Monongahela Navigation Company v. United States* (1893), reiterating that the assessment of an indemnity payment was a judicial, not a legislative, task. Speaking for the Court, Justice David J. Brewer ruled that the owner must receive "a full and exact equivalent" (p. 325) and that the value of property was determined by its profitableness. Even more important, in *Chicago, Burlington & Quincy Railroad Co. v. Chicago* (1897) the justices unanimously held that the just compensation requirement constituted an essential element of due process as guaranteed by the Fourteenth Amendment. Accordingly, the just compensation rule became in effect the first provision of the Bill of Rights to be applied to the states.

At the same time, the Court was cool toward the claim that regulations limiting the use of property represented an unconstitutional taking without compensation. A Kansas law prohibited the manufacture or sale of liquor and ordered the destruction of liquor already in stock. By preventing the use of breweries for their intended purpose, the statute drastically reduced the value of land and equipment to the owners. Stressing that this legislation did not disturb the owner's use of property for lawful activities, the Court in *Mugler v. Kansas* (1887) stated that a restriction on the use of property could not be deemed a taking.

Declining Importance of Contracts Clause. After the Civil War, the contracts clause continued to figure in constitutional policy. Indeed, the Supreme Court expanded the reach of the contracts clause to encompass arrangements made in reliance on judicial interpretation of state law. In *Gelpcke v. Dubuque* (1864) the Supreme Court sustained the validity of a municipal bond issue as a contract that could not be impaired by a changed interpretation of state law. Nonetheless, the Supreme Court contributed to the decline of the contracts clause by diluting the protection afforded by this provision. In *Stone v. Mississippi* (1880), for example, the Court held that a state could forbid the sale of lottery tickets despite the fact that a previous charter granted the right to operate lotteries. This concept of inalienable police power opened the door for state legislatures to interfere with contracts to protect public health and morals.

Income Tax. The Supreme Court narrowly construed congressional taxing authority. Desiring to reduce concentrations of wealth and to enhance federal revenue, Congress in 1894 enacted a second income tax, placing a levy of 2 percent on individual and corporate income over $4,000 a year. Conservatives promptly arranged a challenge to the newly enacted levy in *Pollock v. Farmers Loan & Trust Co.* (1895). Writing for a 6-to-2 majority, Chief Justice Melville W. Fuller held that the tax on income from land was a direct tax not apportioned among the states according to population as required by the Constitution. In addition, the Court unanimously found that the tax on income from municipal bonds was unconstitutional because the federal government could not tax state bonds. The Court was divided 4 to 4 on the validity of the tax on general incomes, and the case was reargued when the absent justice could be present. In the second Pollock decision, a 5-to-4 majority overturned the entire income tax as an unconstitutional direct tax.

The income tax controversy sharply divided both the Court and the nation. As Justice Field's concurring opinion demonstrates, the majority was moved to safeguard property interests against perceived spoliation by the political majority. Field darkly warned of class struggle: "The present assault upon capital is but the beginning. It will be but the stepping-stone to others, larger and more sweeping, till our political contests will become a war of the poor against the rich" (p. 607). The dissenters denied that the income tax discriminated against the wealthy and charged that the majority was frustrating political democracy. (The authority of Congress to tax incomes was expressly established by adoption of the Sixteenth Amendment in 1913. Seeking to defeat a direct challenge to the Pollock decision, Senate conservatives in 1909 proposed a constitutional amendment enabling Congress to tax incomes. They mistakenly calculated that the proposal would fail to win ratification by the states. The Sixteenth Amendment voided the Pollock decision.)

Laissez-Faire and Social Legislation. By 1900 a new industrial and urban society increasingly supplanted the older America of rural communities. Although many Americans prospered during the early decades of the twentieth century, the tremendous economic expansion caused social dislocation. The progressives worked to correct the imbalance of economic power associated with the new industrial order. At the heart of the reform program lay the Progressive insistence upon a more active role for both state and federal governments in regulating the economy and meeting social problems.

Influenced by laissez-faire values, the majority of Supreme Court justices remained leery of economic regulations that altered free-market ordering or infringed on property rights. In the seminal case of *Lochner v. New York* (1905), the Court gave sharp teeth to economic due process by invalidating a statute that restricted working hours in bakeries. Speaking for a 5-to-4 majority, Justice Rufus W. Peckham held that the law violated the liberty of contract as protected by the Fourteenth Amendment. He concluded that the statute exceeded the permissible bounds of state police power. Peckham also expressed broad disapproval of legislation protective of labor. Two dissenters attacked the majority's position from different perspectives. Justice Harlan accepted the legitimacy of the liberty of contract doctrine but argued that the Court misapplied it in this case. Emphasizing that contracts were subject to health and safety regulations, he maintained that long hours of work in bakeries endangered the health of employees. Justice Oliver Wendell Holmes, Jr., went a step further and rejected the laissez-faire interpretation of the Constitution. Holmes articulated a philosophy of judicial self-restraint under which the Court should defer to the right of a political majority to govern.

The *Lochner* decision firmly established the authority of the Supreme Court to review the substance of economic regulations under the due process clause. For the next thirty years the Court closely scrutinized the reasonableness of numerous statutes affecting property rights, treating liberty of contract as the general rule governing economic affairs. State interference with this right under the police power could only be justified in exceptional circumstances, and such restraint could not be arbitrary. To the discomfort of the Progressives, the *Lochner* decision became a symbol of the Supreme Court's commitment to property rights.

Despite the triumph of laissez-faire constitutionalism, the Supreme Court was receptive to laws dealing with obvious health and safety risks even when such regulations imposed heavy costs on property owners or businesses. For instance, the justices upheld the regulation of safety in mines and workmen's compensation statutes that provided for a financial award to employees injured by industrial accidents. The Court also took a deferential view with respect to state supervision of public morals, readily approving laws restricting the operation of lotteries and pool halls and prohibiting the manufacture and sale of alcoholic beverages. Nor did the Supreme Court see any constitutional infirmity with laws to prevent fraudulent business practices.

In *Muller v. Oregon* (1908) the Supreme Court sustained a state law that limited working hours for women in factories and laundries. The Court stressed the special health needs of women and their dependent status as justifying disparate treatment under law. The justices did not see women as equal competitors with men in the marketplace and thus accepted the necessity for protective legislation. Although a qualified victory for reform, *Muller* did not challenge the dominance of economic due process. Moreover, the paternalistic assumptions behind legislation designed to protect women appear suspect to modern eyes.

Notwithstanding this willingness to accommodate some regulation of economic life, the Supreme Court increasingly relied upon the doctrines of economic due process and liberty of contract to safeguard property rights. In general terms, the Court rejected those regulations that it deemed excessive or unwarranted. The contours of such review were imprecise, but the Court tended to look with disfavor on several types of economic legislation: labor laws, anticompetitive measures, and statutes fixing wages and prices.

A majority of the Court believed that government should not intervene in labor–management relations. This attitude was illustrated by a line of cases that struck down both federal and state laws prohibiting so-called yellow dog contracts, which made it a term of employment that employees not belong to labor unions. Although the justices may have held unrealistic notions about the bargaining position of individual employees, allegations of systematic favoritism to business are difficult to demonstrate. In actuality the Supreme Court was committed to the laissez-faire norm of an unregulated market economy. Thus, the justices also invalidated laws that restricted the right to engage in business or that imposed barriers to new enterprises.

The decision in *New State Ice Co. v. Liebmann* (1932) confirmed the Supreme Court's devotion to free-market competition. Oklahoma required a certificate to enter the ice business. The Court emphasized that the practical effect of the certificate provision was to shut out new enterprises and thus foster a monopoly in the existing ice companies. Accordingly, the Court found by a margin of 6 to 2 that the Oklahoma statute unreasonably curtailed the right to engage in a lawful private business in violation of the due process clause.

Legislative attempts to set minimum wages raised novel issues. The justices were loath to accept wage regulation or to expand the category of businesses in which wage or price fixing was constitutional. In *Adkins v. Children's Hospital* (1923) the Supreme Court by a 5-to-3 margin overruled a District of Columbia statute that established a minimum wage for women as an infringement of the liberty of contract. Speaking for the Court, Justice George Sutherland stressed that "freedom of contract is . . . the general rule and restraint the exception" (p. 546). He reasoned that the minimum-wage law arbitrarily cast upon employers a welfare function that belonged to society at large.

The Supreme Court sometimes treated economic rights and other liberties as interdependent. For instance, judicial protection of property rights was instrumental in a successful assault on residential segregation laws. The Supreme Court in *Buchanan v. Warley* (1917) held that such an ordinance restricted the right to alienate property and constituted a deprivation of property without due process.

Congressional taxing powers were also strengthened in the early twentieth century. The Supreme Court approved the use of taxation to regulate or prohibit economic activity that could not be reached directly by Congress under the commerce clause. In *McCray v. United States* (1904) the Court upheld the imposition of a prohibitory tax on yellow oleomargarine. Since the taxing power was not limited to interstate commerce, the McCray decision seemingly permitted Congress to regulate all aspects of the economy.

Any expectations for the broad use of tax authority to achieve regulatory ends were soon dashed. To halt the use of child labor Congress placed a 10 percent tax on the profits of companies employing children. In *Bailey v. Drexel Furniture Co.* (1922) the Court scrutinized the purpose behind the tax measure and held by an 8-to-1 margin that child-labor tax was an unconstitutional infringement on state authority to regulate manufacturing. The result of the *Bailey* ruling was to curtail the use of the taxing power for regulatory purposes.

Further, the Court faced novel questions concerning the protection of property rights under the takings clause of the Fifth Amendment. Urbanization and industrialization created serious land-use problems in the years after 1900. Both the federal government and the states began more vigorously to control the use of land. In *Pennsylvania Coal Co. v. Mahon* (1922) the Court recognized the concept of a regulatory taking where the value of private property was unduly diminished by governmental action. A transfer of title or a physical incursion was unnecessary for a taking to occur. Justice Holmes formulated the crucial inquiry in *Mahon:* "The general rule at least is, that while property may be regulated to a certain extent, if regulation goes too far it will be recognized as a taking" (p. 415).

Another vexing issue was raised by the emergence of zoning as a land-control technique. When traditional nuisance law proved inadequate to cope with urban land-use problems, localities began to enact specific restrictions to safeguard public health and safety. But such regulations restricted an owner's dominion over his land and often impaired its value. Critics argued that zoning represented an unconstitutional interference with the right of owners to make use of their property.

In *Euclid v. Ambler Realty Co.* (1926) the Court, by a 6-to-3 vote, upheld the constitutionality of a comprehensive zoning ordinance that divided a locality into residential and commercial districts, restricting the type of building construction in each district. Reasoning that such limitations served the health, safety, and morals of the public, Justice Sutherland ruled that state police power included the authority to classify land and prevent the erection of commercial buildings in residential areas. The Court stressed, however, that zoning power was not unfettered. In *Nectow v. City of Cambridge* (1928) the Supreme Court struck down a particular application of a zoning ordinance as a deprivation of property without due process.

The regulation of rental practices was also a source of controversy. Citing emergency housing conditions growing out of World War I, a congressional measure established a commission to determine reasonable rents in the District of Columbia and protected a tenant's right of occupancy. In *Block v. Hirsh* (1921) the Supreme Court upheld the validity of the statute by a vote of 5 to 4. Justice Holmes concluded that under the circumstances of a wartime housing shortage, the rental business in the District was cloaked with a public interest justifying temporary regulation.

The New Deal and "Constitutional Revolution." Despite the Great Depression of the 1930s, the Supreme Court remained skeptical about regulation of the economy, particularly about attempts to adjust employment relationships or significantly alter the operations of the free market. Yet President Franklin D. Roosevelt's New Deal program was grounded on the notion that government had an affirmative duty to promote the general social welfare. New Deal liberals worked to remedy economic distress, manage the national economy, control corporate behavior, encourage labor unions, and actively promote the economic interests of the disadvantaged. This social-welfare approach flatly contradicted the insistence on limited governmental activity, marketplace competition, and respect for property rights that were at the heart of laissez-faire constitutionalism.

Among the problems spawned by the Depression was the wholesale loss of homes and farms through foreclosure of delinquent mortgages. At issue in *Home Building & Loan Association v. Blaisdell* (1934) was a Minnesota act imposing a limited moratorium on the foreclosure of mortgages. By a 5-to-4 margin the Supreme Court held that the moratorium did not violate the contracts clause. Chief Justice Charles Evans Hughes ruled that contracts were subject to the reasonable exercise of the state police power, which encompassed the authority to give temporary relief for extraordinary economic distress.

In *Nebbia v. New York* (1934), the justices by a 5-to-4 vote sustained a milk control law as a reasonable means of stabilizing milk prices. The *Nebbia* ruling signaled an important shift away from economic due process and judicial supervision of state regulatory legislation. Speaking for the Court, Justice Owen J. Roberts emphasized that a state could validly "adopt whatever economic policy may reasonably be deemed to promote public welfare" (p. 537). He added, "The Constitution does not guarantee the unrestricted privilege to engage in a business or to conduct it as one pleases" (pp. 527–528).

In 1935 and 1936 the Supreme Court struck down a series of important New Deal measures. In *Schechter Poultry Corp. v. United States* (1935) the justices unanimously overturned the National Industrial Recovery Act as an unconstitutional delegation of lawmaking power to the executive branch. In *Carter v. Carter Coal Co.* (1936) the Court by a vote of 6 to 3 invalidated the Bituminous Coal Conservation Act on grounds that the legislation exceeded the authority of the federal government under the commerce clause.

The Supreme Court also took a restrictive view of congressional power to levy taxes and appropriate money. The Agricultural Adjustment Act authorized the payment of subsidies to farmers in exchange for reducing the amount of their crops. To raise revenue for this scheme, Congress placed a "processing tax" on the first processor of such commodities. In *United States v. Butler* (1936) the justices struck down the processing tax. Writing for the Court, Justice Roberts concluded that the ostensible tax was in actuality a means of regulating agricultural production, a matter reserved for the states under the Tenth Amendment.

Yet another objection to the New Deal centered on the takings clause of the Fifth Amendment. To assist indebted farmers, the Frazier–Lemke Act of 1934 compelled the holders of existing mortgages to relinquish farm property to mortgagors without full payment of the mortgage debt. In *Louisville Bank v. Radford* (1935) a unanimous Supreme Court found the act to constitute an unconstitutional taking of property without compensation.

Never before had the Supreme Court struck down so many acts of Congress in such a short period of time. These judicial setbacks dealt a blow to the New Deal program of economic revival and social reform. In their dogged adherence to laissez-faire constitutionalism, however, the justices were unmindful of the constraints imposed on the Court by political realities. The Court's stubborn defense of property rights precipitated a constitutional crisis. The political climate, combined with the threat of President Roosevelt's court-packing plan, dictated a judicial retreat. In the process, the Court undertook a wholesale reversal of landmark decisions. This abrupt change in the Court's thinking, known as the constitutional revolution of 1937, is best understood within a larger political context.

In *West Coast Hotel Co. v. Parrish* (1937) the justices sustained a Washington State minimum-wage law for women and minors. Speaking for a 5-to-4 majority, Chief Justice Hughes overruled the *Adkins* precedent and effectively repudiated the liberty of contract doctrine. The decision in *West Coast Hotel* marked the virtual end of economic due process as a constitutional norm. Since 1937 the Supreme Court has not overturned any economic or social legislation on due process grounds.

The New Deal judicial revolution also had important implications for governmental regulation of utility rates. In *Federal Power Commission v. Hope Natural Gas Co.* (1944) the Supreme Court abandoned the fair-value standard of *Smyth v. Ames,* ruling that rate-making bodies were not bound to follow any single formula for determining charges. Judicial inquiry was directed only to the impact of the rate order on the regulated industry, not the method of calculation.

The lacerating struggle over the validity of the New Deal program engendered lasting hostility against judicial protection of property rights and had a profound impact on the course of American constitutional history. Once the Supreme Court accepted the New Deal, the justices abruptly withdrew from the field of economic regulation. This reflected a monumental change in the Court's attitude toward property rights and entrepreneurial liberty. The cornerstone of this new constitutional direction was a judicially created dichotomy between property rights and personal liberties articulated in 1938 in *United States v. Carolene Products*. Henceforth, economic regulations would be found to violate the due process clause only when such legislation did not rest "upon some rational basis within the knowledge and experience of the legislators" (p. 152). As a consequence, the Supreme Court virtually eliminated property rights from the constitutional agenda for several decades.

Late Twentieth-Century Developments

Judicial concern for the protection of economic rights, however, never entirely disappeared. By 1970 a more conservative Supreme Court gradually began to revitalize constitution protection of economic rights. This shift became apparent in the late 1970s, when the Supreme Court reinvigorated the long-neglected contracts clause. In *United States Trust Co. of New York v. New Jersey* (1977) the justices, for the first time in nearly forty years, applied the clause to strike down a state law. One year later, in *Allied Structural Steel Co. v. Spannaus* (1978) the Court relied on the contracts clause to void state interference with a private contractual arrangement. During the 1980s the Court seemed to revert to a more restrictive view of the contracts clause. In *Keystone Bituminous Coal Association v. DeBenedictis* (1987) the Court rejected a contracts clause challenge to a Pennsylvania law that prevented enforcement of contractual waivers of liability for surface damage caused by mining. Speaking for a 5-to-4 majority, Justice John Paul Stevens observed that "the prohibition against impairing the obligation of contracts is not to be read literally" (p. 502).

The takings clause of the Fifth Amendment has emerged as the principal bulwark of property rights in contemporary constitutional law. The Supreme Court has virtually eliminated the "public use" requirement as a check on the power of government to appropriate private property by eminent domain. In *Berman v. Parker* (1954) the Court equated the "public use" clause with the police power. The justices insisted that the "concept of the public welfare is broad and inclusive" (p. 33) and concluded that the judiciary should defer to legislative determinations of the need to use eminent domain.

The justices have protected landowners against physical intrusion onto their property by the government. In *United States v. Causby* (1946), for instance, the Court held that regular military flights at low altitude over private land destroyed its value as a farm and in effect appropriated the property. The justices went a step further in *Loretto v. Teleprompter Manhattan CATV Corp.* (1982), ruling that any permanent physical occupation of property, no matter how slight, amounted to a taking.

The justices have been reluctant to invoke the doctrine of regulatory taking and have allowed Congress and the states wide latitude to impose conditions on the use of land. The Court has permitted cities to enact land-use regulations that enhance the aesthetic features of municipal life. In *Penn Central Transportation Co. v. New York City* (1978), the Court, by a 6-to-3 vote, sustained the designation of Grand

Central Terminal as a historic landmark despite the fact that such action prevented the landowner from modifying the building without municipal permission, thereby causing a drastic reduction in its value.

Nonetheless, the Supreme Court took a fresh look at the question of regulatory taking in 1987 and strengthened the position of property owners against governmental authority to reduce the value of their property by regulation. In *Nollan v. California Coastal Commission* (1987) the Supreme Court struck down a land-use regulation for the first time since the 1920s. The case arose when a state agency issued a permit to rebuild a beach house on the condition of the landowner's grant of a public easement across the beachfront. The Court held by a margin of 5 to 4 that the imposition of such a condition constituted a taking because the requirement was unrelated to any problem caused by the development. The *Nollan* decision signaled a heightened degree of judicial supervision of land-use controls. Moreover, in *First English Evangelical Lutheran Church of Glendale v. County of Los Angeles* (1987) the justices ruled that a property owner may be entitled to compensation for the temporary loss of land use when controls are later invalidated. This decision raised the prospect of damage awards against excessive regulations.

This resurgent interest in property rights was also manifest in renewed judicial review of utility rate-making under the takings clause. In *Duquesne Light Co. v. Barasch* (1989) the justices upheld a Pennsylvania rate order and reaffirmed that no particular rate-making method was mandated by the Constitution. Yet the Court emphasized that "the Constitution protects utilities from being limited to a charge for their property serving the public which is so 'unjust' as to be confiscatory" (p. 307).

For a brief period in the 1970s, the Supreme Court flirted with the protection of various government benefits as a type of "new property." The basic question was whether Social Security, welfare benefits, and public employment should be viewed as rights or as privileges subject to withdrawal. Critics charged that the "new property" notion was simply a subterfuge to constitutionalize the welfare state and protect the economic interests of political liberals. In *Goldberg v. Kelly* (1970) the justices, by a vote of 5 to 4, edged toward acceptance of the new property concept. They held that New York City violated due process procedural guarantees by terminating welfare benefits without a prior hearing. Ultimately, however, the Court declined to treat most entitlements under government programs as traditional property rights for the purpose of due process. Instead, the Court preserved a large measure of legislative authority to manage and even eliminate benefit schemes.

By the beginning of the twenty-first century it was apparent that the Supreme Court continued to play a major role in safeguarding economic rights. A return to laissez-faire constitutionalism, however, appears problematic. The Court will more likely strike a balance between popular democracy and the constitutional protection of private property ownership.

[***See also Adkins v. Children's Hospital;*** **Agricultural Adjustment Administration; Bill of Rights;** ***Charles River Bridge v. Warren Bridge;*** **Chase,** ***Salmon;*** **Constitution; Constitutional Convention of 1787; Contract, Law of; Court Packing; Dartmouth College Case; Due Process: Substantive Process; Economic Policy: Regulation; Federalism; Fourteenth Amendment; Harlan, John Marshall; Holmes, Oliver Wendell, Jr.; Income Tax, Federal; Jackson, Andrew; Judicial Review; Marshall, John; Monetary Policy;** ***Muller v. Oregon;*** **New Deal; Roosevelt, Franklin Delano;** ***Schechter Poultry Corp. v. United States; Scott v. Sandford;*** **Sixteenth Amendment; Slaughterhouse Cases; Slavery,**

Laws; State Governments; States' Rights; Story, Joseph; Supreme Court, U.S.; Taney, Roger B.; Taxation; *United States v. Carolene Products; West Coast Hotel v. Parrish;* and Whig Party.]

BIBLIOGRAPHY

Ely, James W., Jr. *The Guardian of Every Other Right: A Constitutional History of Property Rights.* New York: Oxford University Press, 1992.

Hall, Kermit L. *The Magic Mirror: Law in American History.* New York: Oxford University Press, 1989.

Hovenkamp, Herbert. "The Political Economy of Substantive Due Process." *Stanford Law Review* 40 (1988): 379–447.

Kelly, Alfred H., Winfred A. Harbison, and Herman J. Belz. *The American Constitution: Its Origins and Development,* 7th ed. New York: W. W. Norton, 1991.

Kens, Paul. *Judicial Power and Reform Politics: The Anatomy of Lochner v. New York.* Lawrence: University Press of Kansas, 1990.

Newmyer, R. Kent. *Supreme Court Justice Joseph Story: Statesman of the Old Republic.* Chapel Hill: University of North Carolina Press, 1985.

Paschal, Joel Francis. *Mr. Justice Sutherland: A Man against the State.* Princeton, N.J.: Princeton University Press, 1951.

Wright, Benjamin Fletcher. *The Contract Clause of the Constitution.* Cambridge, Mass.: Harvard University Press, 1938.

James W. Ely, Jr.

PUBLIC BROADCASTING

Throughout their history, public radio and television have struggled to survive in a minimally regulated broadcasting system dominated by commercial interests. Although educational radio stations airing instructional programming were prevalent in the 1920s, their numbers plummeted in the 1930s in the face of economic hard times and powerful national commercial radio networks. The limited federal regulatory legislation of the interwar years, primarily the Communications Act of 1934 that established the Federal Communications Commission (FCC), made no explicit provision for educational and nonprofit stations.

This situation remained largely unchanged for the next thirty years despite the FCC's reservation of a small number of radio bands and television channels for nonprofit stations. Then, in 1966, spurred by the FCC's failure to diversify commercial television and reflecting the spirit of President Lyndon B. Johnson's Great Society initiatives, a report by the Carnegie Commission on Educational Television on the state of public broadcasting led to the most significant event in the history of the medium: the passage of the Public Broadcasting Act of 1967. To address congressional concerns about the dangers of both political interference and the creation of a "fourth network," the legislation established a highly decentralized structure under which the newly formed Corporation for Public Broadcasting (CPB) would allocate federal grants to separate national associations of noncommercial television and radio stations—incorporated in 1969 as the Public Broadcasting Service (PBS) and National Public Radio (NPR). These associations would in turn coordinate interconnection among their member stations.

Over the following three decades, federal funding, the number of stations, and the audience for public programming all grew substantially, and the medium solidified its position in American culture. Many programs attracted a large and loyal audience including public radio's news feature *All Things Considered* and Garrison Keillor's variety show *A Prairie Home Companion;* PBS's educational and witty children's show *Sesame Street;* the British drama import *Masterpiece Theatre;* the science series *Cosmos* and *Nova;* and *Eyes on the Prize,* the 1987 series documenting the history of the civil rights movement. Charged with the sometimes contradictory mandate of providing unique, high-quality, and diverse programming to the most varied audience possible while maintaining strict objectivity and balance, public broadcasting faced increasing criticism from both the political left and the right. From the left came charges that women and minorities were underrepresented, that programming catered too much to an elite audience, and that the system had become overly reliant on corporate underwriters. Conservatives complained that the CPB and public-broadcasting networks were overly centralized bureaucracies that reflected a liberal, even left-wing bias and used federal funds to glorify aberrant social practices. The conservative critique came to a head in 1995 when the Republican-controlled Congress called for the phased-in elimination of all federal funding for public broadcasting. However, a widespread show of support (particularly for the beloved *Sesame Street*) defeated this effort.

In the heyday of the major networks' almost exclusive control of the airwaves, public broadcasting clearly provided innovative and influential children's, cultural, and public-affairs programming that was otherwise unavailable. Although public television and radio continued to provide moments of national cultural import, such as Ken Burns's 1990 documentary series *The Civil War*, in the far more diverse and expansive communication environment at the turn of the century, its future remained unclear.

[*See also* **Economic Policy, Federal; Federal Communications Commission; Great Society; Johnson, Lyndon B.;** *and* **Regulatory Agencies, Federal.**]

BIBLIOGRAPHY

Lashley, Marilyn. *Public Television—Panacea, Pork Barrel, or Public Trust?* New York: Greenwood Press, 1992.

Witherspoon, John, and Roselle Kovitz. *The History of Public Broadcasting*. Washington, D.C.: Current, 1989.

Anthony Harkins

PUBLIC HEALTH

This entry contains two subentries: An Overview; and Surgeon General.

AN OVERVIEW

For much of American history, protecting local business figured prominently in public health efforts. During the Colonial Era, smallpox and yellow fever ravaged seaports, paralyzing business activity. Townspeople fled; shops closed; visitors avoided the stricken cities. To revitalize trade, local authorities often published false reports minimizing the danger. They also quarantined ships, established pesthouses (isolation hospitals), introduced short-term sanitary reforms, and experimented with smallpox inoculation. A major vindication of inoculation came during a 1721 Boston epidemic that claimed 900 lives. Cotton Mather championed the procedure, whereas Boston's most prominent physicians opposed it. Smallpox vaccination, developed by the English physician Edward Jenner, became available by 1800.

During the nineteenth century, outbreaks of cholera, especially in 1832–1833, 1849–1850, and 1866, and other epidemic diseases shaped public health practice. As yellow fever devastated southern cities, physicians disagreed about whether it was contagious and how to combat it. Those who supported the broad exercise of government authority sought to quarantine incoming ships, whereas those favoring free trade and individual liberty urged the removal of decaying organic wastes, whose noxious "miasmas," they believed, caused most epidemics. (In 1900 an army medical team led by Dr. Walter Reed at last discovered yellow fever's mode of transmission: the *Aëdes aegypti* mosquito.)

By midcentury, local governments increasingly addressed public health issues. New York City built a municipal water system in 1842. Dr. John H. Griscom's *The Sanitary Condition of the Laboring Class of New York with Suggestions for Its Improvement* (1845) proved highly influential. New York created a permanent Metropolitan Board of Health in 1866, in response to a threatened cholera epidemic, and reformers in other cities soon followed suit. As municipal water and sewer systems replaced backyard wells, cesspools, and privies, outbreaks of cholera, typhoid fever, dysentery, malaria, and typhus diminished. As in the past, local business groups often led these sanitary reforms.

At the federal level, Congress in 1798 had created the U.S. Marine Hospital Service, under a Surgeon General, to care for ailing seamen. The U.S. Sanitary Commission, a volunteer agency headed by Frederick Law Olmsted, worked to improve health and sanitary conditions in Civil War military camps. Meanwhile, the Marine Hospital Service steadily expanded its activities, including a bacteriological research laboratory founded in the 1890s. Renamed the U.S. Public Health and Marine Hospital Service in 1902, it eventually became simply the U.S. Public Health Service (PHS). Early PHS campaigns combated hookworm and pellagra.

With the triumph of the germ theory of disease and the advent of bacteriology in the early twentieth century, the rationale for public health efforts shifted from ridding the environment of miasmas to attacking disease-causing microbes. Public health became professionalized as lay reformers gave way to physicians and scientists. The laboratory became the principal battleground against disease, with impressive results. Vaccines, serums, and tests attacked rabies, diphtheria, typhoid fever, tuberculosis, and, later, yellow fever, poliomyelitis, measles, and whooping cough. The Progressive Era's reform ethos opened new public health vistas, including school vaccination programs, maternal and child care, rural health efforts, medical inspection of immigrants, regulation of nuisance industries, inspection of food processors and providers, and campaigns to reduce infant mortality and tuberculosis. In many of these programs, the federal government played a central role. By World War I, there existed a vast network of governmental public health agencies, supported by the American Red Cross, settlement houses, and other volunteer groups. Although organized medicine, led by the American Medical Association, enthusiastically supported the public health movement, it strenuously sought to limit activities to prevention, not treatment.

As the acute, communicable diseases were defeated, attention shifted to the chronic and degenerative afflictions, especially cancer, diabetes, stroke, and heart disease. Public health workers alerted the public to risk factors they could control, such as obesity; poor nutrition; lack of exercise; and, in the case of venereal disease, unprotected sex. In the 1930s, Surgeon General Thomas Parran lifted the veil of silence surrounding syphilis. Beginning in the New Deal Era, the federal government increasingly funded municipal and state public health programs.

By the late twentieth century, public health efforts at all governmental levels had vastly expanded in size and complexity. In the 1990s the PHS, now a part of the Department of Health and Human Services, included the Surgeon General's Office, with a corps of over 6,000 public health professionals; specialized agencies such as the Indian Health Service, the Food and Drug Administration, the data-gathering Centers for Disease Control, and the research-oriented National Institutes of

Health; and offices addressing such issues as aging, mental illness, minority health, women's health, physical fitness, and the AIDS epidemic. The landmark *Surgeon General's Report on Smoking and Health* (1964) alerted citizens to the hazards of smoking and led to health warnings on cigarette packages, advertising restrictions, congressional investigations, and major legal challenges to the tobacco industry. Other federal bodies addressing public health issues included the Bureau of Prisons, the Environmental Protection Agency, the Consumer Product Safety Commission, the Immigration and Naturalization Service, and the Occupational Safety and Health Administration. Globally, the PHS cooperated with the World Health Organization, a United Nations agency. From small beginnings, public health had emerged as a major governmental responsibility as the twenty-first century dawned.

[*See also* **Environmental Protection Agency; Federal Government, Executive Branch: Other Departments; Immigration Law and Policy: After 1930; Immigration Law and Policy: Before 1930; National Institutes of Health; New Deal; Progressive Era; Public Health Service, U.S.; Public Health: Surgeon General;** *and* **Pure Food and Drug Act.**]

BIBLIOGRAPHY

Brandt, Allan M. *No Magic Bullet: A Social History of Venereal Disease in the United States since 1880.* New York: Oxford University Press, 1985.

Duffy, John. *The Sanitarians: A History of American Public Health.* Urbana: University of Illinois Press, 1990.

Galishoff, Stuart. *Newark, the Nation's Unhealthiest City, 1832–1895.* New Brunswick, N.J.: Rutgers University Press, 1988.

Humphreys, Margaret. *Yellow Fever in the South.* New Brunswick, N.J.: Rutgers University Press, 1992.

Leavitt, Judith Walzer. *The Healthiest City: Milwaukee and the Politics of Health Reform.* Princeton, N.J.: Princeton University Press, 1982.

Rosenberg, Charles E. *The Cholera Years: The United States in 1832, 1849, and 1866.* Chicago: University of Chicago Press, 1962.

Stuart Galishoff

SURGEON GENERAL

In 1870, Congress reorganized the network of locally controlled hospitals of the Marine Hospital Service (MHS) into a centrally controlled service with its headquarters in Washington, D.C. The supervising surgeon administered the MHS and in 1871 Dr. John Woodworth became the first supervising surgeon. He instituted a military model for his staff and made his physicians part of the general service instead of assigning them to a particular facility. In this manner, he created a cadre of mobile, career-service physicians. In 1873, Congress changed his title to supervising surgeon general.

Dr. John Hamilton succeeded Woodworth as supervising surgeon general and under his leadership the MHS gained the authority to administer the national quarantine regulations at sea and on land. In 1887 he established the Hygienic Laboratory (predecessor to the National Institutes of Health) whose researchers applied the new science of biology to public health issues. Dr. Hamilton issued regulations requiring competitive examination for admission to the Commissioned Corps, which the Congress duly authorized in 1889.

Congress significantly expanded the responsibilities of the MHS in 1902 and renamed it the Public Health and Marine Hospital Service (PHMHS) headed by the surgeon general. In 1912, Congress shortened the name of the PHMHS to the Public Health Service (PHS), recognized the PHS as the lead federal public health agency, and established a four-year term for surgeons general. In 1914 Congress extended the mission of the PHS to include occupational and environmental hazards and in 1919 granted the PHS responsibility for veterans' health care.

The Tuskegee syphilis experiment occurred during the tenure of Dr. Hugh Cummings. Initiated in 1930, the study of untreated syphilis in African American males was declared unethical, and the PHS ended it in 1973. In the 1940s, Congress entrusted the PHS with the promotion of civilian public health. Under this new mandate, Surgeon General Dr. Leonard Scheele issued a public recommendation of fluoridation in 1951, elevating the role of surgeon general as a spokesperson on public health issues.

In the 1960s, Surgeon General Dr. Luther Terry, established the Surgeon General's Advisory Committee on Smoking and Health. The Committee's 1964 report found cigarette smoking causally related to lung cancer and chronic bronchitis. The PHS undertook action including the now-familiar surgeon general's health warnings on cigarette packages. In the 1970s, Surgeon General Dr. Julius Richmond led efforts to lessen disparities in health services.

In the 1980s, Surgeon General C. Everett Koop made the anti-tobacco campaign a high-profile effort, releasing a 1986 report on the dangers of passive smoking. As the chief federal spokesperson on AIDS, he released an explicit, non-judgmental, and controversial report in 1986 contributing significantly to providing accurate and comprehensive information on the disease.

Since the 1980s, surgeons general have spoken out on important health issues of the time, including underage drinking, the immunization of children, the adoption of universal health care coverage, comprehensive health education in schools, and promoting healthy lifestyles. The surgeon general continues to act as the primary federal spokesperson on public health.

[***See also*** **National Institutes of Health; Public Health Service, U.S.;** ***and*** **Public Health: An Overview.**]

BIBLIOGRAPHY

History of the Office of the Surgeon General. http://www.surgeongeneral.gov/about/history/index.html (accessed August 24, 2011).

Mullan, Fitzhugh. *Plagues and Politics: The Story of the United States Public Health Service*. New York: Basic Books, 1989.

Stephen E. Randoll

PUBLIC HEALTH SERVICE, U.S.

The U.S. Public Health Service began in 1798 as the Marine Hospital Service (MHS). The original mission focused on the care of sick and disabled seamen, but the following year Congress extended this to cover all navy personnel. The MHS established locally controlled marine hospitals along coastal and inland waterways. Congress centralized hospital administration in the MHS in 1870 under the supervising surgeon, later the surgeon general. In 1871, Supervising Surgeon John Maynard Woodworth created the Commissioned Corps, a cadre of mobile, career-service physicians in uniform assigned to any of the marine hospitals.

Congress enacted the National Quarantine Act in 1878, empowering the MHS to implement immunization programs, quarantine, and disinfection measures to prevent the introduction of contagious and infectious diseases into the United States. Congress later extended the act to prevent the spread of disease among the states. The Commissioned Corps became formalized in 1889, with Corps officers receiving military titles and pay corresponding to Army and Navy grades. By 1902, the MHS carried out the medical inspection of immigrants, such as those coming in at Ellis Island, New York, and assumed many of the quarantine responsibilities formerly carried out by the states. Reflecting these greater responsibilities, Congress changed the name of the service to the Public Health and Marine Hospital Service (PHMHS). In 1912, Congress further extended the authority of the PHMHS, granting the service the authority to investigate human diseases such as tuberculosis, hookworm, and pellagra and oversee sanitation, water supplies, and sewage disposal. Reflecting this broader authority, Congress shortened the name to the Public Health Service (PHS).

The PHS's reputation was severely damaged when it established the Tuskegee syphilis experiment in 1932. Originally intended to be a six-month study of a group of African American men infected with venereal disease in Macon County, Alabama, the experiment left the men untreated. The PHS never told the participants they had syphilis or treated them for it, even after penicillin became the accepted treatment for the disease in 1945. Only in 1972 after news articles exposed the study did the PHS end it. The study increased African American distrust of the government, contributing to rumors among African Americans that the government introduced the HIV virus into the African American community.

The PHS Corps expanded in the 1930s and 1940s to include engineers, dentists, research scientists, nurses, and other health care specialists. In 1953, Congress integrated the PHS into the Department of Health, Education, and Welfare. Later the PHS became part of the Department of Health and Human Services, although the agency operated with a substantial amount of independence. The more than 6,000 active-duty officers of the Commissioned Corps of the PHS continue to fulfill their mission to protect and promote the public health of the United States. These officers work both nationally and internationally to ameliorate disease, sickness, and suffering.

[*See also* **Public Health: An Overview;** *and* **Public Health: Surgeon General.**]

BIBLIOGRAPHY

Furman, Bess. *A Profile of the United States Public Health Service, 1798–1948*. Bethesda, Md.: National Institutes of Health, 1973.

Mullan, Fitzhugh. *Plagues and Politics: The Story of the United States Public Health Service*. New York: Basic Books, 1989.

Williams, Ralph. *The United States Public Health Service, 1798–1950*. Washington, D.C.: Commissioned Officers of the U.S. Public Health Service, 1951.

Stephen E. Randoll

PUBLIC OPINION

Since democratic theory requires leaders to respect "the will of the people" in directing the affairs of the nation, public opinion holds an exalted place in democracies like the United States. It was an essential concept in Enlightenment political thought, and social observers from Alexis de Tocqueville to Walter Lippmann (*Public Opinion,* 1922; *The Phantom Public,* 1925) have noted its importance in America. Most philosophers and scholars writing about public opinion in the United States agree on its role: It embodies the consent of the governed and confers legitimacy on the government. Americans have expressed their opinions on policy issues and political actions, while leaders have sought to know the popular will. Scholars have had a harder time agreeing on a definition of public opinion, however, with both of the terms "public" (or "the public") and "opinion" stirring debate. Contemporary scholars appear to be comfortable defining public opinion as "the aggregated views of large numbers of people in a society on issues central to how that society functions."

Methods for determining public opinion have varied throughout American history. The most basic of these has been electoral: popular referenda on public issues, proposed laws, and enactment of (or changes to) constitutions. Tens of thousands of these have been conducted from the eighteenth century to the present. In the late twentieth century, between 200 and 300 referenda were typically voted upon in each election year. In the eighteenth and nineteenth centuries, less formal means were also employed, including the use of informed observers (notables, public figures, ward heelers in urban political machines), "straw polls" dating from as early as the 1820s, through the first systematic opinion surveys beginning in the late nineteenth century. Although these forms of collecting information on public opinion were reported widely in the press and avidly consumed by an increasingly literate and engaged mass readership, historians generally agree that they were not very accurate and were subject to reporting bias.

In the 1930s and 1940s, scientific polling and the use of probability samples improved methods for collecting information on the public's opinion. Notable in this era were George Gallup's founding of the influential American Institute of Public Opinion (Gallup Poll) in 1935 and the establishment of such university-based survey organizations as the National Opinion Research Center (NORC) at the University of Chicago and the Survey Research Center at the University of Michigan. As regular polls and somewhat more scientific nationwide surveys proliferated, these investigations of the public's "opinion" more accurately reflected society as a whole. Topics expanded from electoral and policy-related issues to include social problems and individuals' consumer tastes, radio and television preferences, and economic behavior. By the end of the twentieth century, the mass media had joined commercial and university-based survey organizations in constantly monitoring (and reporting) public attitudes. Despite ever-present concerns over the ways of manipulating public opinion (including advertising and propaganda), the appetite of both decision makers and the general citizenry for information on what the public "thinks" appeared undiminished.

[*See also* ***Democracy in America****; and* **Lippmann, Walter.**]

BIBLIOGRAPHY

Converse, Jean M. *Survey Research in the United States: Roots and Emergence, 1890–1960*. Berkeley: University of California Press, 1987.

Herbst, Susan. *Numbered Voices: How Opinion Polling Has Shaped American Politics*. Chicago: University of Chicago Press, 1993.

Erik W. Austin

PUBLIC UTILITIES POLICY, FEDERAL

In the early twentieth century three different political perspectives had emerged concerning the regulation of electrical energy. Private power proponents believed that the generation, transmission, and distribution of electricity should be left to market forces. Another group thought that ownership should remain in private hands, but subject to state or federal regulation. A third group believed that only public ownership could guarantee fair electrical rates. Advocates of each position debated legislation regarding regulation of electric energy throughout the 1910s.

Regardless of whether they favored market forces, government regulation, or public ownership, nearly everyone involved the policy debate recognized that the generation, transmission, and distribution of electricity represented a natural monopoly. It made little economic sense to duplicate transmission and distribution systems serving the same community. Multiple dams could not occupy the same site on a river. Through hydroelectric development, the generation of electricity became entwined with the conservation movement early in the twentieth century. Conservationists believed that the nation's rivers and streams should be developed to serve and benefit the most people. Hydroelectricity seemed to offer a nearly inexhaustible energy source that distant population centers could use following the advent of long-distance transmission lines. All parties thought the widespread use of electricity would modernize American industry, business, and the American home.

During World War I, the energy demands of the nation at war underscored the need for a comprehensive electrical utility law that would also promote hydroelectric development. In 1920, President Woodrow Wilson signed the Federal Water Power Act that resulted, in part, in the formation of the Federal Power Commission (FPC) composed of the secretaries of the interior, war, and agriculture. Congress charged the FPC with reviewing applications for hydroelectric projects and issuing fifty-year permits for dam sites. The law also required utilities to pay an annual fee for administrative costs and use of the dam site.

Private power proponents often used the phrase "super power" in the 1920s to describe the interconnection of the nation's electrical grid. Private power executives believed that super power resulted in better rates and improved service. Energy shortages in one area could be alleviated by energy surpluses elsewhere. Additionally, merging smaller systems allowed for the improvement of electrical systems. Public power advocates, however, considered super power nothing more than a monopoly that hampered the widespread use of electricity. Super power, public power advocates argued, resulted in high rates and prevented widespread use of electricity because private utilities would only serve the most lucrative markets. Beginning in 1925, the debate took on new form.

After several years of prodding by Senator George Norris (R-NE) and other progressives, in 1925 the U.S. Senate authorized the Federal Trade Commission (FTC) to investigate several antitrust issues including the electrical utilities (subsequent legislation extended the investigation). Although many progressives considered the FTC probusiness and questioned the agency's impartiality, the FTC did not disappoint Norris and other public power advocates. The investigation, which continued into the 1930s, was especially damaging to private utilities. The FTC found that profit was the main motive for holding companies, which controlled utilities through stock ownership and dominated the generation, transmission, and distribution of electricity. Other findings showed paid propaganda of the utility companies entering into newspaper editorials and college curricula.

The election of Franklin Roosevelt fundamentally altered the American political landscape in many ways, including the regulation of electrical utilities. Numerous laws passed during Roosevelt's presidency influenced the political debate regarding electrical power including the Rural Electrification Act and establishment of the Tennessee Valley Authority and the Bonneville Power Administration. In partial response to the FTC findings, the Public Utility Holding Company Act of 1935 (PUHCA) established the regulatory structure for electrical energy in the United States into the late twentieth century.

The Rural Electrification Act limited the size and influence of holding companies, although it did not abolish them as some desired. Since its passage, private power and public power have coexisted in an uneasy state. The PUHCA divided the country's electrical markets into a series of regional monopolies. At the same time, large-scale publicly owned electrical systems served as "yardsticks" to measure private electrical rates. The ideas of natural monopolies and economies of scale continued to dominate thinking regarding electrical energy for the next forty years.

Beginning in the late 1970s, amid energy shortages, economic uncertainty, and a backlash against "big government," the political landscape began to change. Technological advances allowed for the separation of the generation, transmission, and distribution of electricity. The idea that electrical markets were, by definition, natural monopolies dominated by economies of scale came under question and many consumers and producers began advocating deregulation. In 1978, the Public Utility Regulatory Act (PURPA) required utilities to purchase power from independent generators of electricity. Congress anticipated that the law would promote a diversity of electrical generation resulting in energy independence. Wind and solar energy, as well as electricity from natural gas cogeneration plants, would now enter the energy market. The use of natural gas, which was also deregulated in 1978, meant that small-scale cogeneration turbines could supply electricity to a market independent of the nation's power grid. The development of cogeneration plants marked a stark departure from large-scale generating systems.

In 1992, Congress passed the Energy Policy Act that required the Federal Energy Regulatory Commission (the successor to the FPC) to open the interstate transmission network to wholesale electrical sales. Regardless of who owned the transmission network, any utility could use the system to transmit, or "wheel," electricity. A customer, in theory, could purchase electricity from one generating company and have it delivered to his home by a different utility. The era of a utility serving a defined geographic region had, in theory, come to an end. Although the deregulation of electricity in California became the focus of much attention during the Enron scandal, deregulation occurred in other states into the twenty-first century.

Electrical utility regulation since the early twentieth century has thus gone through three distinct phases. In each phase technological change and public policy debates drove the regulatory debate. Early in the twentieth century initial debates occurred that resulted in the passage of PUHCA in the 1930s. From the 1930s into the 1970s and 1980s, PUHCA was at the core of electrical regulation. Beginning in the late 1970s political change made possible by technological advances resulted in the movement toward deregulation of electrical utilities in the 1990s.

[*See also* **Energy Policy; Roosevelt, Franklin Delano;** *and* **Tennessee Valley Authority.**]

BIBLIOGRAPHY

Bonbright, James C., and Means, Gardiner. *The Holding Company: Its Public Significance and Its Regulation.* New York: McGraw–Hill, 1932.

Brigham, Jay. *Empowering the West, Electrical Politics before FDR.* Lawrence: University Press of Kansas, 1998.

Glaser, Leah. *Electrifying the Rural American West, Stories of Power, People, & Places.* Lincoln: University of Nebraska Press, 2009.

Hirsch, Richard. *Technology and Transformation in the American Utility Industry.* Cambridge, UK; New York: Cambridge University Press, 1989.

Hughes, Thomas. *Networks of Power: Electrification in Western Society, 1880–1930*. Baltimore: Johns Hopkins University Press, 1983.

Nye, David E. *Electrifying America: Social Meaning of a New Technology*. Cambridge, Mass.: MIT Press, 1990.

Jay L. Brigham

PURE FOOD AND DRUG ACT

Signed into law on 30 June 1906 by President Theodore Roosevelt, the Food and Drugs Act—popularly know as the Pure Food and Drug Act—with its companion piece the Meat Inspection Amendment originated the regulatory apparatus that became the Food and Drug Administration. This landmark statute prohibited the "misbranding" of any foodstuff or pharmaceutical offered for sale or their "adulteration" by any ingredient not specified on the label. Congress authorized the Bureau of Chemistry of the Department of Agriculture to enforce the law by testing random specimens for misbranding or adulteration, notifying suspect manufacturers, and granting them a hearing. Only if a manufacturer refused to comply could the bureau turn the case over to a district attorney for prosecution. Convictions carried fines of up to $300 and imprisonment for up to one year, with confiscation of the offending product the ultimate punishment.

Dr. Harvey W. Wiley (1844–1930), chief chemist of the Department of Agriculture from 1883 to 1912, was the moving force behind the law. Wiley publicized the problem by feeding dubious preservatives to volunteers dubbed the "poison squad." For over two decades, Wiley functioned as the chief propagandist, organizer, and strategist for the law and then as its principal enforcer. Public support for such a law grew steadily thanks to a series of reports on harmful and unsanitary meatpacking processes published in muckraking magazines and in Upton Sinclair's 1906 exposé, *The Jungle*. The measure won backing from a broad-based coalition including the National Association of State Dairy and Food Departments, the National Consumers' League, the American Medical Association, and the General Federation of Women's Clubs, joined by some well-established manufacturers seeking to eliminate marginal competitors. Its opponents included the National Food Manufacturers' Association; the National Liquor Wholesale Dealers' Association; and the Proprietary Association of America, the drug industry's lobbying arm. Sponsored by two Republican senators and by two GOP congressmen, and aided by an eleventh-hour endorsement by Roosevelt, the final bill passed both houses by overwhelming margins and stands as a major Progressive Era legislative achievement.

[*See also* **Economic Policy: Regulation; Federal Government, Executive Branch: Agriculture Department; Muckrakers; Progressive Era; Public Health: An Overview;** *and* **Roosevelt, Theodore.**]

BIBLIOGRAPHY

Anderson, Oscar E., Jr. *The Health of a Nation: Harvey W. Wiley and the Fight for Pure Food*. Chicago: University of Chicago Press, 1958.

Young, James Harvey. *Pure Food: Securing the Federal Food and Drugs Act of 1906*. Princeton, N.J.: Princeton University Press, 1989.

John D. Buenker

R

RADICALISM

Radicalism in the United States owes its origins to the so-called Radical Reformation of the sixteenth century and to civil rebellions and millenarian movements reaching far back in human memory. Indian rebellions against European colonizers and transplanted pietist communes offer the clearest precursors of American political radicalism. Thomas Paine's antimonarchical *Common Sense* (1776), the first widely read document with direct bearing upon the fate of the incipient nation, was characteristic in two ways. The revolution Paine helped inspire stopped well short of addressing social class, race, and gender inequities. Yet Paine's continuing attack on wrongful authority nevertheless gained him the enmity of ungrateful American conservatives, forcing him into postrevolutionary political exile. The burden of radicalism had already passed to the direct action of Shays's Rebellion in Massachusetts in 1786, which sought to redress economic privilege. Fifteen citizens received death sentences (two actually were hanged), a small figure compared with the vengeance visited upon the organizers of and participants in a long series of Indian and slave uprisings, real and potential.

Radicalism found new outlets in the early labor movements and the utopian and communitarian movements of the Antebellum Era. Urging shorter hours, free public schools, and free land in the West, early workers' movements ultimately failed, but they did make their mark upon public life and Democratic machine politics. The great reform movements of the mid-nineteenth century—women's rights, antislavery, and spiritualism—began from a different standpoint. Social class as such concerned them less than the vision of universal citizenship and multifaceted social improvement. Meeting in Seneca Falls, New York, in 1848, the first women's rights convention declared a new revolutionary principle for half the human race. Abolitionists likewise demanded the expropriation of wrongfully held human "property." Spiritualism, an often misunderstood link between the various reform movements and a larger population of sympathizers, grew from a rejection of patriarchal Calvinism and a belief in the oneness of the human spirit with nature.

The outbreak of the Civil War eclipsed every movement but war itself—and emancipation of the slaves. African Americans abandoning the plantations helped speed the Union victory, but Republican Party "radicals" finally abandoned African Americans to what W. E. B. Du Bois called "a new capitalism and a new enslavement of labor," establishing a model for global economic expansion. The first American followers of Karl Marx, mostly German immigrants, renewed efforts to create a radicalized labor movement. Swept away in the postwar conservative reaction, socialism arose in different forms following the national railroad strikes of 1877 and reemerged in the labor and populist movements of the 1880s and 1890s.

Intermittently for the next half-century, African Americans, Hispanic Americans, and Asian Americans would find a thin section of socialists and labor radicals ready to address race issues with special urgency. The Knights of Labor briefly mobilized a half-million working people during the mid-1880s. Populism (and its constituent movements known as the Farmers' Alliance) revived multiracial radicalism in other forms, including cooperatives and third-party politics. Socialists struggled in vain to halt the Spanish–American War and the American slaughter of Filipino nationalists. A large and influential Socialist Party found a constituency of working people early in the twentieth century, only to be crushed by the repression of the Woodrow Wilson administration after 1917.

Twentieth-century intellectuals like Du Bois, labor activists such as A. Philip Randolph, and advanced figures within such labor movements as the Industrial Workers of the World (IWW) proposed drastic changes in society's racial orientation as well its economic–political character. A thoroughgoing antiracism emerged in the 1920s when a defeated American left looked abroad to forces shaking the colonial world. American Communists, altogether too closely tied to the Soviet Union but sometimes heroic in their own local circumstances, struggled to build an antiracist movement. In part, they achieved impressive success—at least until the Cold War—in building egalitarian industrial unions and a radical interracial culture.

The Cold War and its concomitant domestic repression chilled radicalism severely. Civil rights radicals, however, never quite as crushed as labor radicals had been, revived the direct-action approach, from the Montgomery bus boycott to the lunch-counter sit-ins to the Black Power movement of the 1960s. The anti–Vietnam War movement; environmentalism; feminism; activism by Indian, Chicano, and Asian American groups; and, still later the gay-rights movement added new dimension to the American radical tradition. But by the 1980s, the hegemonic power of capitalism had overwhelmed resistance in most quarters. Radicalism again consisted, as it had during earlier low periods, largely of support for revolutionary movements abroad and antinuclear protest movements at home. The close of the twentieth century found American radicalism dispersed and institutionally weak. Nevertheless, the partial revival of a weakened and corrupted labor movement, and the appearance of new immigrant populations (most notably from the Dominican Republic and Haiti), with definite radical sentiments, showed signs of reawakening a radicalism damped down by defeat and disappointment.

[*See also* **Antinuclear Movement; Antislavery Movement; Antiwar Movements; Civil Rights;** ***Common Sense;*** **Communist Party USA; Debs, Eugene; Du Bois, W. E. B.; Environmentalism; Farmers' Alliance Movement; Feminism; Goldman, Emma; Lesbian, Gay, Bisexual, and Transgender Rights Movement; Populist Era; Populist Party; Seneca Falls Women's Rights Convention of 1848; Shays's Rebellion; Socialism; Socialist Party of America; Students for a Democratic Society; Third Parties;** ***and*** **Wilson, Woodrow.**]

BIBLIOGRAPHY

Brecher, Jeremy. *Strike!* Boston: South End Press, 1997.

Buhle, Mari Jo, Paul Buhle, and Dan Georgakas, eds. *Encyclopedia of the American Left*. New York: Oxford University Press, 1998.

Buhle, Mari Jo, Paul Buhle, and Harvey J. Kaye, eds. *The American Radical*. New York: Routledge, 1994.

Buhle, Paul, and Edmund Sullivan. *Images of American Radicalism*. Hanover, Mass.: Christopher Publishing House, 1998.

Flacks, Richard. *Making History: The American Left and the American Mind*. New York: Columbia University Press, 1988.

Whitman, Alden, ed. *American Reformers: An H. W. Wilson Biographical Dictionary*. New York: H. W. Wilson, 1985.

Paul Buhle

RANKIN, JEANNETTE

(1880–1973), suffragist, pacifist, first woman elected to the U.S. Congress. Born near Missoula, Montana Territory, the eldest of seven children of schoolteacher Olive Pickering and rancher John Rankin, Jeannette earned a BS in biology from the University of Montana in 1902 and studied social work at the New York School of Philanthropy and the University of Washington. While working in Seattle in 1909, Rankin joined Washington's successful woman suffrage movement. After campaigning for the cause in fifteen states in 1912–1914, she returned home to help win the vote for women in Montana. Elected to Montana's at-large seat in Congress in 1916, Rankin was only four days into her term when she voted (with fifty-six others) against a U.S. declaration of war on Germany. Failing in a reelection bid in 1918, she became a lobbyist and organizer for various peace groups. Throughout her life, Rankin championed two causes she believed were intertwined: women's rights and peace. Female voters, she contended, would counterbalance male militarism and eventually render war obsolete.

In 1940, Rankin returned to Congress and became the only member to vote against a declaration of war against Japan on 8 December 1941. This vote ended her political career; she resumed her efforts for peaceful alternatives to war. In 1968, at age eighty-eight, Rankin led 5,000 women calling themselves the Jeannette Rankin Brigade in marching in Washington, D.C., against the Vietnam War. Rankin died of a heart attack in 1973 while considering a third congressional race to oppose what she saw as the growing risk of another world war.

[*See also* **Feminism; Peace Movements;** ***and*** **Woman Suffrage Movement.**]

BIBLIOGRAPHY

Josephson, Hannah Geffen. *Jeannette Rankin, First Lady in Congress*. Indianapolis, Ind.: Bobbs–Merrill, 1974.

Wilson, Joan Hoff. "'Peace Is a Woman's Job . . .' Jeanette Rankin and American Foreign Policy: The Origins of Her Pacifism." *Montana: The Magazine of Western History* (Winter 1980): 28–41.

Wilson, Joan Hoff. "'Peace Is a Woman's Job . . .' Jeanette Rankin and American Foreign Policy: Her Life Work as a Pacifist." *Montana: The Magazine of Western History* (Spring 1980): 38–53.

Janann Sherman

RAYBURN, SAM

(1882–1961), was one of the most influential members of Congress and speakers of the House of Representatives in American history. Born in 1882 in Tennessee, he moved to Fannin County, Texas, at a young age with his parents and siblings. He attended country schools and then East Texas Normal College. He briefly taught before being elected to the Texas House of Representatives in 1906. While in the Texas House, he attended the University of Texas law school and became a lawyer. Young Sam Rayburn was a protégé of the Texas politician and orator Joseph Weldon Bailey. His political ties to Bailey led to Rayburn's election as speaker of the Texas House of Representatives in 1911. In 1912, he was elected to the U.S. House of Representatives.

Supported by John Nance Garner, an influential Texan in Congress, Rayburn was able to obtain a seat on the Interstate and Foreign Commerce Committee, an important House committee with vast powers to pass regulatory laws. Rayburn was an advocate of railroad regulation because his small farmer constituency was very dependent on railroads for their economic survival. Along with his committee work, Rayburn allied himself politically with John Nance Garner who was advancing in the leadership of the Democratic Party in the House of Representatives, eventually becoming speaker in 1931 and vice president in 1933.

With Democratic control of the House in 1931, Rayburn became chair of the Interstate and Foreign Commerce Committee and in 1933 Rayburn's committee sponsored major New Deal legislation, which included key securities and business regulations. After unsuccessful tries to become speaker, Rayburn was elected majority leader in 1937 and speaker in 1940. He was to serve as speaker from 1940 until his death in 1961 with the exception of the four years when Republicans controlled the House in 1947–1948 and 1953–1954, during which time Rayburn served as Democratic leader of the House. Rayburn led the House during part of the Great Depression, World War II, the Korean War, and the Cold War. He liked to say he served "with" rather than "under" eight presidents—Wilson, Harding, Coolidge, Hoover, Roosevelt, Truman, Eisenhower, and Kennedy.

Rayburn led the House at a time when the seniority controlled the committee system of the House and when conservative Democratic Southerners dominated the leadership of those committees. Often allied with Republicans, this "conservative coalition" stymied progressive legislation, especially civil rights legislation. Rayburn has been criticized for failing to reform the House to break the conservative coalition's power in the House, although he successfully backed an expansion of the Rules Committee, which weakened the conservative coalition's control over the House's agenda.

Rayburn proved remarkably effective in leading the House at a time when conservative committee chairs held power and the speaker held little formal power. He was able to perform the role of a middleman where he balanced the interests of Northern Democratic members of Congress with those of Southern Democrats. It was his ability to balance competing interests that was the source of his success and longevity in House leadership.

[*See also* **New Deal.**]

BIBLIOGRAPHY

Champagne, Anthony. *Congressman Sam Rayburn*. New Brunswick, N.J.: Rutgers University Press, 1984.

Champagne, Anthony, Douglas B. Harris, James W. Riddlesperger Jr., and Garrison Nelson. *The Austin/Boston Connection: Five Decades of House Democratic Leadership, 1937–1989*. College Station: Texas A & M University Press, 2009.

Hardeman, D. B., and Donald C. Bacon. *Rayburn: A Biography*. Austin, Tex.: Texas Monthly Press, 1987.

Anthony Champagne

RAZA UNIDA PARTY

One of the most significant third-party movements in the history of the United States began in south Texas in the spring of 1970 in Zavala County (Winter Garden area). After a strike of Mexican American students at Crystal City High School, protesting discrimination, organizers led by José Angel Gutiérrez formed La Raza Unida Party (LRUP). In April the organization won five positions on the city council and school board. At the same time voters elected LRUP candidates in neighboring counties. Chicano activists from outside Texas were greatly impressed with these achievements, a factor catapulting the LRUP and Gutiérrez into national prominence.

At the LRUP convention in October 1971, delegates decided to field candidates in state-level races. In the 1972 election, Waco lawyer Ramsey Muñiz ran for governor and Alma Canales from Edinburg for lieutenant governor. In the primary elections, the LRUP drew away enough Mexican American voters from the Democrats that conservative Dolph Briscoe defeated Frances "Sissy" Farenthold, a liberal.

By now, the LRUP concept had spread to other areas in such states as Arizona, Colorado, California, New Mexico, Illinois, Wisconsin, and Nebraska. In 1970 Rodolfo "Corky" Gonzales, leader of the Crusade for Justice in Colorado, envisioned a national-level LRUP totally removed from the traditional parties. As a prelude he led an unsuccessful campaign for the top state offices. In a race for the California Assembly during 1971, Raúl Ruiz, LRUP activist, drew enough votes from a Mexican American Democrat that a Republican was elected in east Los Angeles. In September 1972, a LRUP national convention called El Congreso de Aztlán was held in El Paso. At the meeting the pragmatic José Angel Gutiérrez squared off against the more ideological Corky Gonzales for the party chairmanship. Gutiérrez won, provoking a bitter split that could not be bridged.

Nonetheless, the LRUP activists returned to electoral campaigns in their respective states. Raúl Ruiz, for example, hoped to derail the election of another Mexican American Democrat to the State Assembly but was defeated resoundingly. In 1974, a LRUP candidate tried to enter the gubernatorial race but failed to get enough signatures to qualify. That same year, the LRUP lead a failed attempt to incorporate east Los Angeles as a separate city.

In Texas in 1972, the LRUP continued the campaign of Ramsey Muñiz for governor. Muñiz received 6 percent of the vote, allowing Dolph Briscoe only a plurality win over his Republican opponent. In the meantime, LRUP victories in South Texas encouraged Muñiz to run for governor in 1974, but he could not duplicate the 1972 role of spoiler; Briscoe won both the primary and the general contests handily.

Then in 1976 Muñiz was arrested on charges of narcotics trafficking—an incident that dealt a severe blow to the prestige of the LRUP. Regional leaders tried to maintain local power bases but only Gutiérrez succeeded in remaining a political boss in Zavala County. In 1978, the veteran activist Mario Compeán ran for governor, receiving less than 2 percent of the vote. The Republican Bill Clements won. In the meantime, disaffected LRUP members in Zavala County voted José Angel Gutiérrez out of power; in 1982, he left electoral politics for good.

In the rest of the country, the LRUP also died a slow, painful death. After violent clashes with the Denver police department, Crusade for Justice membership declined precipitously. In California, former members turned to Marxist politics or returned to the traditional parties. The ephemeral existence of the LRUP drew dramatic attention to Mexican American politics and politicized a whole generation, a process that has benefitted those who now participate in traditional party activity.

[*See also* **Party System.**]

BIBLIOGRAPHY

García, Ignacio M. *Chicanismo: The Forging of a Militant Ethos among Mexican Americans*. Tucson: University of Arizona Press, 1997.

García, Ignacio M. *United We Win: The Rise and Fall of La Raza Unida Party*. Tucson: MASRC, University of Arizona Press, 1989.

Navarro, Armando. *La Raza Unida Party: A Chicano Challenge to the U.S. Two-Party Dictatorship*. Philadelphia: Temple University Press, 2000.

Navarro, Armando. *Mexican American Youth Organization: Avant-Garde of the Chicano Movement in Texas*. Austin: University of Texas Press, 1995.

Quiñones, Juan Gómez. *Chicano Politics: Reality and Promise, 1940–1990*. Albuquerque: University of New Mexico Press, 1990.

Rosales, F. Arturo. *Chicano! The History of the Mexican American Civil Rights Movement*. Houston, Tex.: Arte Público Press, 1996.

F. Arturo Rosales

REAGAN, RONALD

Ronald Wilson Reagan was the fortieth President of the United States (1981–1989) and a key figure in the conservative movement in America. Reagan was born on 6 February 1911 in Tampico, Illinois, into a lower-middle class family. His father was a shoe salesman and a Catholic and his mother (Nell) was a devout member of the Disciples of Christ church. He had one younger brother. Reagan attended Eureka College, where he majored in economics and sociology, graduating in 1932. He embarked on a career in radio sports casting, which he soon turned into a major movie acting career. The future president starred in over fifty films and served three terms as president of the Screen Actors Guild (SAG). Following a divorce from actress Jane Wyman in 1948, Reagan married actress Nancy Davis in 1952. Nancy Reagan greater affected Reagan's future political career by encouraging his shift to the right.

Beginning as a New Deal Democrat, his experience as SAG president in the late 1940s convinced him that the threat of communism was real. His views on taxation were formed as he observed the disincentive effects of 90 percent marginal income tax rates. From 1954 to 1962, Reagan served as a traveling spokesman for General Electric, speaking to an estimated 250,000 workers at 139 plants about the benefits of the free enterprise system. Reagan also came to believe that his party had abandoned Jeffersonian principles of states' rights and limited government. Although remaining a registered Democrat, he supported Dwight D. Eisenhower for president in 1952 and 1956 and Richard Nixon in 1960. In 1962, Reagan officially became a Republican.

A supporter of the conservative Republican presidential nominee, U.S. Senator Barry Goldwater, Reagan entered the national political scene in 1964 when he made a fund-raising speech for Goldwater that was aired on national television on 27 October 1964. In the speech, Reagan warned about the dangers of creeping socialism at home and aggressive Communism abroad, saying "we have a rendezvous with destiny." The speech catapulted Reagan to the front ranks of conservative figures.

Shortly after the end of the 1964 campaign, a group of conservative California businessmen persuaded a reluctant Reagan to run for governor in 1966. Although widely assumed to be unelectable, he easily defeated San Francisco mayor George Christopher, a moderate Republican, for the GOP nomination. In November, a big midterm election for Republicans nationwide, he beat incumbent Democrat Pat Brown in the general election by approximately 1 million votes (57 to 42 percent) after running a campaign against high taxes, spending, and liberal permissiveness.

As governor of California, Reagan balanced the budget, generally cut taxes (although raising some), and cracked down on student unrest. He was reelected against assembly speaker Jess Unruh in 1970, by a diminished but still healthy margin of half a million votes (53 to 45 percent). He left office in January 1975 when his second term ended.

Road to the Presidency. In 1968, Reagan considered a run for the presidency, but backed away. After leaving the governorship of California, Reagan began planning for a serious campaign for the Republican nomination in 1976 against incumbent president Gerald R. Ford. Despite losing some important early primaries, Reagan came back and nearly deprived Ford of the nomination. Emphasizing limited government, federalism, and a tough anti-Soviet foreign policy, Reagan won ten primaries and 45.9 percent of the vote to Ford's sixteen wins and 53.3 percent. At the start of the Republican national convention, neither man had enough delegates to win the nomination. Leveraging his incumbency, Ford finally prevailed with 1,187 votes to 1,070.

Reagan worked in the following years to build a base for another run. He wrote a column on current events, delivered a syndicated weekly radio commentary, and became actively involved in the campaign to defeat the Panama Canal Treaties. Reagan also formed "Citizens for the Republic," which served as an organizational and fundraising foundation for a new campaign.

By the time the 1980 primaries began, he was widely considered the front runner. Following a setback in the Iowa caucuses, when Reagan was upset by George H. W. Bush, the Californian came back to decisively win the New Hampshire primary. Reagan went on to win crucial primaries in South Carolina, Illinois, Texas, and elsewhere. Overall, Reagan won 60.8 percent of the Republican primary vote nationwide. At the Republican national convention, held in Detroit, Reagan received the GOP nomination with 1,939 of 1,994 delegates. After briefly exploring the possibility of offering the vice-presidential nomination to Gerald Ford, he chose Bush to round out the ticket.

The fall campaign, which pitted Reagan against incumbent Democratic President Jimmy Carter, was a hard-fought contest. Reagan emphasized the issues of double-digit inflation, recession and high unemployment, federal government overreach, and American weakness abroad, which he argued was demonstrated in the ongoing Iranian hostage crisis and the December 1979 Soviet invasion of Afghanistan. Carter emphasized his experience and accused Reagan of extremism. Although polls showed a close race, Reagan seized an advantage in the one presidential debate between himself and Carter, in which he successfully framed the election as a referendum on the state of the nation. On election day, voters delivered a landslide victory to Reagan, who won forty-four states with 489 electoral votes to Carter's six states and the District of Columbia, containing 49 electoral votes. The popular vote was split 51 percent for Reagan, 41 percent for Carter, and 6 percent for Independent candidate John Anderson. At the same time, Republicans gained control of the U.S. Senate and gained thirty-three seats in the House of Representatives.

The Reagan Presidency. At sixty-nine, Reagan was the oldest man to become president. In his inaugural address, Reagan argued that "in the present crisis, government is not the solution, it is the problem." In 1981, with the help of conservative Democrats in the House, he won a package of spending and tax cuts that defined his economic policies. The tax cuts, contained in the Economic Recovery Tax Act of 1981 (ERTA), included a 25 percent across-the-board cut in marginal income tax rates, reduction of the top rate from 70 percent to 50 percent, tax cuts for business investments, and a provision indexing income tax rates to inflation. The cuts in domestic spending totaled $38 billion in fiscal year 1982 and $130 billion from 1982 to 1984.

Reagan also launched a drive against federal regulation, which saw the *Federal Register* decline from about 87,000 pages in 1980 to 53,000 pages in 1988. He generally supported free trade, reduced government barriers to energy production, and backed an anti-inflationary monetary policy. Despite a renewed recession in 1981–1982, Reagan publicly stood behind the Federal Reserve Board's tight-money policy. By 1984, inflation had declined to about 4 percent. The economy began to grow in December 1982 and continued growing through the remainder of Reagan's presidency.

As president, Reagan also promoted a conservative vision of constitutionalism, including conservative appointments to the federal bench, a drive to restore power to the states, and opposition to *Roe v. Wade* and other liberal court decisions. In the social realm, he promoted voluntarism as an alternative to activist government and favored stricter policies against crime and drugs.

Reagan's foreign policy was built around a large defense buildup, support for pro-U.S. governments facing pressure from Soviet-backed forces, and a strategic offensive (outlined in documents such as NSDD-75) aimed ultimately at overthrowing Soviet power. He proposed the Strategic Defense Initiative (a missile defense system); aided anti-Communist guerrillas in Afghanistan, Nicaragua, Cambodia, and Angola; and used military force directly against Soviet clients in Libya and Grenada. Reagan called the Soviet Union an "evil empire" and, in a 1987 speech in Berlin, called on Soviet leader Mikhail Gorbachev to tear down the Berlin Wall. At the same time, Reagan was prepared to negotiate, and when Gorbachev took a conciliatory approach Reagan engaged with him, signing the Intermediate Nuclear Forces (INF) Treaty in December 1987 (largely on American terms) and presiding over a general decline in tensions by the end of his presidency.

Running a campaign focusing on improvements in the nation's economy and international standing since 1980, Reagan was easily reelected in 1984, winning 59 percent of the vote and forty-nine states with 525 electoral votes. His opponent, former vice president Walter Mondale, won thirteen electoral votes. Reagan had contentious relations with Congress after the 1982 midterm elections, when Republicans lost twenty-six seats in the House. Democrats regained control of the Senate in the 1986 midterms.

Reagan's supporters credit him for the 1982–1990 economic recovery, U.S. victory in the Cold War, and a restoration of public confidence in the nation and the presidency. He has continued to serve as a model for many Republican political figures. His critics blame him for an increase in the federal deficit, the costly collapse of the savings and loan industry, and the Iran–Contra affair, which resulted when individuals in the administration secretly sold arms to Iran and sent the proceeds to the anti-Communist Nicaraguan resistance. On balance, polls indicate that a majority of ordinary Americans consider Reagan a good or great president, and his rating among scholars has steadily climbed since 1993. Although there are some dissenters, there is something approaching a consensus among analysts across the political spectrum that Reagan was a highly significant president who shifted policy, changed the political environment, and left a long presidential shadow.

After leaving office, Reagan embarked on a speaking tour, published his memoirs, and spoke at the 1992 Republican national convention, before announcing in 1994 that he was suffering from Alzheimer's disease. After he died on 5 June 2004, an estimated 100,000 people paid their respects at the U.S. Capitol.

[*See also* **Bush, George H. W.; Carter, Jimmy; Constitutionalism; Ford, Gerald R.; Iran–Contra Affair;** *and* **Panama Canal.**]

BIBLIOGRAPHY

Brownlee, W. Elliott, and Hugh Davis Graham, eds. *The Reagan Presidency: Pragmatic Conservatism and Its Legacies*. Lawrence: University Press of Kansas, 2003.

Cannon, Lou. *President Reagan: The Role of a Lifetime*. New York: Simon & Schuster, 1991.

Hayward, Steven F. *The Age of Reagan: The Conservative Counterrevolution, 1980–1989*. New York: Crown Forum, 2009.

Hayward, Steven. *The Age of Reagan: The Fall of the Old Liberal Order, 1964–1980*. Roseville, CA: Forum/Prima, 2001.

Morris, Edmund. *Dutch: A Memoir of Ronald Reagan*. New York: Random House, 1999.

Pemberton, William E. *Exit with Honor: The Life and Presidency of Ronald Reagan*. Armonk, N.Y.: M. E. Sharpe, 1997.

Reagan, Ronald. *An American Life*. New York: Simon & Schuster, 1990.

Wilentz, Sean. *The Age of Reagan: A History, 1974–2008*. New York: Harper, 2008.

Andrew E. Busch

RECONSTRUCTION

The attempt to rebuild and reform the South politically, economically, and socially after the Civil War and to refashion race relations throughout the nation. Historians of the era have focused on four questions: How much change occurred between the antebellum and postbellum eras? Was Reconstruction too radical or too conservative? When did it start and end? How and why did it fail?

Background to Reconstruction. Reconstruction proved as deeply political as the controversies over slavery and secession, and all three followed the same pattern: liberalism triumphed when reactionaries overreached. In 1861, Southern secession freed Republicans from the pressure to compromise to preserve the Union. Over time, the Abraham Lincoln administration and the Republican majority in Congress repealed racist laws, freed secessionists' slaves, enrolled African American troops, and eventually passed the Thirteenth Amendment abolishing slavery throughout the country. Slaves effectively freed themselves by escaping to Union territory, and they fought valiantly against their former masters. The most deadly war in American history destroyed not only slavery but also most of the South's physical and financial capital. Defeated, demoralized, and economically depressed, the South in 1865 seemingly lay helpless before the self-confident, prosperous North, whose activist government, bathed in the moral authority of a patriotic, reformist war, appeared poised to remake what many northerners considered the country's nether region.

The Reconstruction Era: 1865–1877. White Southerners, however, behaved as though the war had settled nothing except the impracticality of secession and the nominal abolition of slavery. After Lincoln's assassination and accession of Tennessee Democrat Andrew Johnson to the presidency, Southern states passed "Black Codes" that denied African Americans the right to vote, serve on juries, testify against whites in court, buy or lease real estate, or refuse to sign yearly labor contracts. Blacks were excluded from public schools, black orphans "apprenticed" to their former owners, and black "servants" required to labor from sunup to sundown for their "masters." White Southerners also demanded that former Confederate officers and politicians be immediately seated in Congress.

But the Republicans who controlled Congress refused to admit the erstwhile rebels, and they took decisive control of Reconstruction. When Johnson vetoed a bill extending the Freedmen's Bureau, which provided food to destitute southerners of both races, supervised labor contracts, and started schools where ex-slaves could be educated and courts where their rights could be protected, Republicans in Congress overrode his action, as they did his veto of a civil rights bill that outlawed the Black Codes and mandated basic legal equality. Over unanimous Democratic opposition, Republicans passed the Fourteenth Amendment, which constitutionalized civil rights by guaranteeing due process and equality before the law for all.

In the critical 1866 election campaign, Johnson demagogically lambasted Congress, Northern Democrats endlessly race-baited, and white southerners rioted in Memphis and New Orleans, killing 89 African Americans in full view of the national press. Northern voters reacted by giving the Republicans a landslide victory, which turned Reconstruction more radical. Ten Southern states were placed under temporary military rule, forced to enfranchise African American men, and granted congressional representation only after they had ratified the Fourteenth Amendment and rewritten their state constitutions to make them more liberal. Because Johnson persisted in trying to subvert the antiracist settlement, he was impeached, almost convicted, and practically rendered powerless.

Although buttressed by federal troops; by the Fifteenth Amendment, which mandated racially impartial suffrage nationally; and by federal jobs with which to reward supporters, the new Republican governments of the South faced three obstacles that ultimately proved insuperable. First, they had to rebuild the Southern infrastructure and satisfy a greatly increased demand for government services, especially education, by raising taxes in a devastated region that after 1873 also faced a severe economic depression. Second, they had to overcome two centuries of ingrained racism and convince one in four white men to vote for the party that had just defeated their section in a bloody war. Third, they had to compete at the polls against opponents willing to use any amount of fraud and violence to win elections and to employ election-law trickery and discriminatory practices to retain power once they gained it. After Northern voters reacted to the economic depression and northern ethnoreligious conflicts by electing a Democratic majority in the House in 1874, the survival of Reconstruction became increasingly problematic. Although Republicans rebounded to win the closest presidential election in U.S. history in 1876, part of the price for settling disputes over the election outcome was the implicit promise to stop using the army to protect Southern Republicans. The Compromise of 1877, as the settlement came to be called, marked what is usually treated as the end of Reconstruction.

Evaluating Reconstruction. Many historians believe that Reconstruction brought profound changes. As slaves, African Americans had worked very intensively, often in large groups or "gangs," under the constant threat of physical punishment. They could not legally marry or learn to read and write. They could be sold or moved against their wills and their families could be broken up. Masters constantly intervened in their lives. After emancipation, blacks first worked in "squads," usually headed by independent black contractors, and gradually convinced landowners to let them reside on small family plots, where they enjoyed a degree of privacy and independence. Through sharecropping arrangements, in which workers were paid a percentage of the value of crops after sale, landowners and workers shared the risk of crop failure and guarded against contract violations by either party. Ex-slaves used their new freedom of mobility to bargain with employers. By 1900, 20 percent of black farm operators owned the land they worked.

The United States was the only large slave society that quickly enfranchised ex-slaves, and the eagerness and skill with which the freedpeople took to politics surprised and dismayed their former masters, who had expected docility and incompetence. Almost unanimously supporting the Republican Party—the party of abolition and enfranchisement—the freedpeople participated in the constitutional conventions of 1867–1868 and elected governments that launched statewide education systems, encouraged railroads, passed civil rights laws, protected the rights of laborers, established orphanages and other public institutions, and mandated universal manhood suffrage. African Americans sat in all Southern legislatures and filled high state posts in Louisiana, Mississippi, and South Carolina. Several, mostly from South Carolina, were elected to the House of Representatives, and two went to the Senate: Hiram Revels and Blanche K. Bruce of Mississippi. Most black males retained the vote until around 1900 when suffrage restrictions adopted by Democratic legislatures and constitutional conventions disfranchised the vast majority of African Americans and many poor whites.

Reconstruction-Era social changes were also striking. Blacks could now legally marry; worship as they wished; form private clubs; receive at least some education at public expense; and often patronize public accommodations such as restaurants, theaters, and railroads on a nonsegregated basis, if they could afford to pay. Absolute racial segregation of public places arrived only toward the turn of the century, and it was a matter of law, not custom.

Despite such transformations, however, historians who stress continuity between the antebellum and postbellum periods point to the persistent, often increased poverty of southern African Americans; the continuation of the plantation system; the survival of many former plantation owners or their sons among the postwar economic and social elite; the eventual disfranchisement and segregation of blacks; and the frequent outbreaks of racist violence, particularly the surge of lynching in the 1890s, which was horrifying enough, although far below the levels of the 1860s and 1870s The change-or-continuity question turns on which comparisons are made: One side emphasizes that post–Civil War blacks were far from being slaves and the other that they were far from being fully equal citizens.

Historians who believe that Reconstruction was too radical contend that more gradual enfranchisement, a stronger Republican alliance with former Southern Whigs, and less vigorous attacks on segregation and discrimination would have led to more lasting change. Critics of the conservative position respond that in the short interval when significant change was possible, radical Republicans had to push for as much reform as they could get and that the former Whigs, who were largely responsible for the 1865–1866 Black Codes, were hardly attractive allies for a party of blacks and poor whites. Those who criticize Reconstruction as too conservative hold that only widespread land redistribution from former masters to former slaves, and perhaps even the extermination of the planter class, would have achieved a true social revolution. Those who reject this position reply that a full-scale radical assault on the Southern order might have frightened Northern voters into ending Republican dominance earlier and hazarded a holocaust of revenge violence. In any event, they suggest that to have given the freed slaves small, undercapitalized farms, most on marginal land, might only have shackled them and the South to even deeper poverty.

If the end of Reconstruction is placed in 1877, then violence, ballot-box stuffing, and the repudiation of the Republicans for mostly economic reasons must figure prominently in explanations of its failure. If Reconstruction is thought to have collapsed a generation later, however, with the imposition of strict segregation and disfranchisement across the South, then a succession of incremental legal changes and their validation by the Supreme Court account better for its demise. The upsurge of civil rights legislation in the North in the 1870s and 1880s and the near passage of the Lodge Elections Bill, a measure strongly attacking fraud in southern congressional elections, in 1890 support the view that Reconstruction extended beyond 1877 and suggest that diffuse northern racism did not account for its waning. Throughout the later nineteenth century, almost all congressional Republicans, but not a single Democrat, supported civil rights measures. Reconstruction, in short, was born, evolved, and died in political struggle.

[*See also* **Agricultural Policy; Antislavery Movement; Civil Rights; Compromise of 1877; Democratic Party; Due Process: Procedural Process; Equality; Fifteenth Amendment; Fourteenth Amendment; Freedmen's Bureau; Hayes, Rutherford B.; Johnson, Andrew; Liberalism; Lincoln, Abraham; Presidential Impeachment; Radicalism; Segregation;** ***and*** **Whig Party.**]

BIBLIOGRAPHY

Carter, Dan T. *When the War Was Over*. Baton Rouge: Louisiana State University Press, 1985.

Foner, Eric. *Reconstruction*. New York: Harper & Row, 1988.

Gillette, William. *Retreat from Reconstruction*. Baton Rouge: Louisiana State University Press, 1979.

Holt, Thomas. *Black over White*. Urbana: University of Illinois Press, 1977.

Jaynes, Gerald David. *Branches without Roots*. New York: Oxford University Press, 1986.

Kousser, J. Morgan. *The Shaping of Southern Politics*. New Haven, Conn.: Yale University Press, 1974.

Perman, Michael. *The Road to Redemption*. Chapel Hill: University of North Carolina Press, 1984.

Richardson, Heather Cox. *The Death of Reconstruction: Race, Labor, and Politics in the Post-Civil War North, 1865–1901*. Cambridge, Mass.: Harvard University Press, 2001.

Wayne, Michael. *The Reshaping of Plantation Society*. Baton Rouge: Louisiana State University Press, 1983.

Woodward, C. Vann. *The Strange Career of Jim Crow*. New York: Oxford University Press, 1974.

J. Morgan Kousser

RECONSTRUCTION FINANCE CORPORATION

The Reconstruction Finance Corporation (RFC; 1932–1957) was a federal lending agency established to provide aid to troubled banks and railroads during the Great Depression but subsequently transformed into the capital bank for the New Deal and the principal funder of World War II mobilization. In operation, it became one of the most elaborate lending complexes in American history, spawning a wide array of specialized subsidiaries, lending approximately $50 billion, and guaranteeing billions more in private loans.

Modeled on the War Finance Corporation of 1918, the RFC was established on 2 February 1932 under legislation sought by President Herbert Hoover after efforts to organize voluntary financial relief had failed. Provided with $500 million in capital and authority to borrow another $1.5 billion, it could extend emergency loans to railroads, banks, and other financial institutions, the hope being that this would thaw money markets and bring the credit expansion needed for economic recovery. Subsequently, in July 1932, the agency was given additional capital and authorized to extend agricultural credits, relief loans to states, and loans for self-liquidating works projects. Initially, its establishment slowed bank failures. But it brought little credit expansion, and it quickly became the subject of intense criticism, primarily for its alleged favoritism to the rich and powerful, its strict security requirements, and its stringent rationing of relief loans. Nor were its loans sufficient to prevent the banking panic of early 1933 and the national bank holiday with which the New Deal began.

The agency's independence and flexibility appealed to President Franklin D. Roosevelt, and under the Emergency Banking Act of 1933 it received new powers to assist in bank reorganization and recapitalization. In addition, it helped to fund new agencies engaged in providing relief, stimulating construction, refinancing mortgages, promoting exports, supporting farm prices, and electrifying rural areas. Under laws in 1934 and 1938, it received and made some use of authority to extend direct loans to businesses having adequate security but unable to secure private loans. By 1935 it had succeeded in restoring financial liquidity and stability. But the continuing hope that such lending could bring the credit expansion needed for economic recovery proved elusive, and as directed by the Texas banker Jesse Jones, it strongly resisted efforts to turn it into a provider of venture capital, profit guaranties, or small business relief.

The RFC's greatest expansion came during World War II. In 1940 it was authorized to lend for defense purposes, and subsequently it proceeded through eight subsidiaries to fund programs for stockpiling strategic materials, developing key war industries, and providing war insurance and defense housing. By war's end it had the reputation of having served the nation well. But after Jones's departure in 1945, it quickly deteriorated into a scandal-ridden, poorly administered bureaucracy with much evidence of political favoritism in the loans being granted. Calls for its abolition proliferated, and in 1953 its lending powers were terminated or transferred to a new Small Business Administration. It then went into a liquidation that was finally completed in 1957.

[*See also* **Hoover, Herbert; New Deal;** *and* **Roosevelt, Franklin Delano.**]

BIBLIOGRAPHY

Dunar, Andrew J. *The Truman Scandals and the Politics of Morality*. Columbia: University of Missouri Press, 1984.

Jones, Jesse H. *Fifty Billion Dollars: My Thirteen Years with the RFC (1932–1945)*. New York: Macmillan, 1951.

Olson, James S. *Herbert Hoover and the Reconstruction Finance Corporation, 1931–1933*. Ames: Iowa State University Press, 1977.

Olson, James S. *Saving Capitalism: The Reconstruction Finance Corporation and the New Deal, 1933–1940*. Princeton: Princeton University Press, 1988.

United States Treasury Department. *Final Report on the Reconstruction Finance Corporation*. Washington, D.C.: U.S. Government Printing Office, 1959.

Ellis W. Hawley

REGULATORY AGENCIES, FEDERAL

The first federal regulatory agency was the Interstate Commerce Commission (ICC). Created in 1887 after decades of controversy over "the railroad problem," the ICC in many ways served as a model for future agencies. Like the ICC, the agencies were established by Congress in response to crises in particular industries (or, occasionally, across industries). Staffed with persons thought to be experts and bipartisan or nonpartisan by law, most were nevertheless plagued by continual controversy.

The ICC found its power limited by the federal courts. In a pattern repeated later with other regulatory commissions, Congress then proceeded to strengthen the original Interstate Commerce Act through a series of laws passed between 1903 and 1940 that, in effect, gave the commission de facto rate-making authority for railroads, pipelines, trucks, and barges. The ICC's staff evolved complicated standards to set rates for passengers and freight carried by diverse modes of transportation over different routes. Its primary principle sought to assure transportation companies a "fair rate of return" on the "fair value of property used and useful" in performing their services. This seemingly simple idea involved the ICC in arbitrary estimates, dubious valuation schemes to determine the "rate base," and unworkable attempts to allocate traffic "fairly" among various modes of transportation.

In reality, American capitalism proved too fluid and complex to lend itself to minute regulatory control as developed by the ICC, and industries under ICC supervision tended to stagnate because entrepreneurial opportunity was too constricted. Not until the deregulation movement of the 1980s and 1990s did some ICC-regulated industries again become vibrant parts of the national economy, by which time the ICC itself had been abolished by Congress.

Economic Regulation. Congress had created nine other federal regulatory agencies to address different areas of the economy. Five agencies were given primarily economic functions and four were assigned social or environmental regulatory duties. The five economic agencies are as follows:

1. The Federal Trade Commission (FTC), created in 1914 and assigned the ambiguous task of maximizing competition in business. The FTC's biggest successes came in presenting to Congress detailed industry studies that prompted important legislation such as the Public Utility Holding Company Act of 1935 and several laws restricting the fixing of retail prices. Since 1935, Congress delegated to the FTC the enforcement of additional business regulation statutes and the FTC promulgated

a number of regulations. The FTC also shares responsibility for civil enforcement of antitrust laws with the Department of Justice. However, the Antitrust Division of the Department of Justice retained the responsibility to bring civil and criminal charges in antitrust matters.

2. The Federal Power Commission (FPC), created in 1920, strengthened in 1930 and 1935, and in 1977 Congress renamed it the Federal Energy Regulatory Commission. The dynamism of the energy sector overwhelmed this agency, and by the 1950s it could not manage its huge caseload effectively. Beginning in the 1960s, a series of reforms alleviated the impossible pressures under which the FPC worked, culminating in the Department of Energy (DOE) Organization Act of 1977, which consolidated various energy-related agencies into a Department of Energy. Congress insisted that a separate independent regulatory body be retained, and the FPC was renamed the Federal Energy Regulatory Commission (FERC), preserving its independent status "within" the department. Congress granted FERC the added responsibility to hear appeals of DOE oil price control determinations and to conduct all "on the record" hearings for the DOE. In 1978, FERC was given additional responsibilities for harmonizing the regulation of wellhead gas sales in both the intrastate and the interstate markets. In 1983, FERC undertook to bring greater competition to both the natural gas and the electric industries. The Energy Policy Act of 2005 expanded FERC's authority to impose penalties on entities that manipulate the electricity and natural gas markets.

3. The Federal Communications Commission (FCC), created in 1934 with jurisdiction over radio, interstate telephone communication, and later television. The FCC was plagued by a fundamental lack of clarity about its proper functions. In the broadcasting industry, it should promote growth, censor content at times, and even potentially rescind the licenses of stations violating FCC policies. As for the telephone industry, in the 1960s the FCC began allowing long-distance companies other than AT&T to offer specialized services. Then, in the 1970s, the FCC allowed other companies to expand their offerings to the public. A lawsuit filed by the Justice Department led to the split of the so-called Baby Bells from AT&T in 1982, breaking up the company's monopoly. In 1984, the FCC enabled all long-distance companies to obtain equal access to the local phone company's customers. During the Reagan administration, the FCC shifted toward a decidedly more market-oriented stance. The administration ended a number of regulations perceived as outdated, including the Fairness Doctrine in 1987. The FCC also took steps to increase competition to broadcasters, fostering broadcast alternatives such as cable television. Congress followed with the Telecommunications Act of 1996, in the wake of the break-up of AT&T. The 1996 legislation attempted to create more competition in local telephone service by requiring incumbent local exchange carriers to provide access to their facilities for competitive local exchange carriers. The development of the Internet, cable services, and wireless services raised questions regarding whether new legislative initiatives are needed, but as of 2011 Congress has not undertaken a major revision of these regulations. In 2006, President Bush signed into law the Broadcast Decency Enforcement Act, increasing the fines tenfold for each violation found by the FCC to violate its decency standards.

4. The Securities and Exchange Commission (SEC), created in 1934 and assigned the task of reviving and policing the nation's Depression-battered capital markets. Compared with other agencies, the SEC achieved remarkable success. It did so by working through allies in the private sector (especially

lawyers, accountants, and officials of organized exchanges), whose interests were aligned by statutes and rulings with the goals the SEC defined as best for the industry and the public. In 2002, Congress enacted the Sarbanes–Oxley Act, setting new standards for all U.S. public boards, management, and public accounting firms. The act contains eleven titles, or sections, ranging from additional corporate board responsibilities to criminal penalties, and requires the SEC to implement rulings on requirements to comply with the new law. In 2006, Congress enacted the Credit Rating Agency Reform Act of 2006 to improve ratings quality by fostering accountability, transparency, and competition in the credit rating agency industry.

5. The Civil Aeronautics Board (CAB), created in 1938 and abolished during the 1980s. The CAB restricted entry into the airline industry, allocated the routes companies flew, standardized prices along these routes, and in general supervised a cartel. Although efforts to determine a fair rate of return made some sense for such "natural monopoly" industries as railroads and electric utilities, it did not for airlines, where entry was easy, competition keen, and business flexibility high. The government's response to the 11 September 2001 attacks included the USA Patriot Act establishing a new Department of Transportation organization, the Transportation Security Administration, which the Act granted broad powers to protect air travel and other modes of transportation against criminal activity.

Social and Environmental Regulation. The four social and environmental regulatory agencies reflected the heightened attention to civil rights, environmental, and consumer issues in the 1960s and 1970s. These agencies are as follows:

1. The Equal Employment Opportunity Commission (EEOC), created in 1964 and charged with administering Title VII of the Civil Rights Act of that year. The EEOC coordinates federal efforts at affirmative action for the employment of women and minorities. It investigates charges of violation, promotes awareness of the law, and publishes statistical reports on employment patterns. Congress extended the Civil Rights Act's protection to include disability with the enactment in 1990 of the Americans with Disabilities Act (ADA). In 2008, Congress added the ADA Amendments Act to grant broader protection to disabled workers and reverse court rulings the Congress deemed too restrictive.

2. The Environmental Protection Agency (EPA), created in 1970 and granted a broad range of responsibilities for the control of air and water pollution and the cleanup of hazardous waste sites. As the largest of all federal regulatory agencies measured by both size of budget and number of employees (over 18,000 by 2010), the EPA has formidable powers. Since 2001, the authority of the EPA has come under increasing criticism, particularly from conservative and business groups opposed to the EPA's position on climate change regulation, but the agency's authority has remained intact.

3. The Occupational Safety and Health Administration (OSHA), created in 1970, headed by an assistant secretary of labor and charged with developing regulations for workplace safety. OSHA's effectiveness suffered from the difficulty of conducting a sufficient number of inspections at the nation's millions of worksites.

4. The Consumer Product Safety Commission (CPSC), created in 1972 to enforce safety standards on potentially dangerous items such as hand tools, lawnmowers, flammable clothing, and children's toys. Its rules are often cited in product liability suits brought by private parties. The Consumer Product Safety Improvement Act enacted in 2008 increased the Commission's funding and enabled the

agency to add new employees by 2013. The CPSC is responsible for regulating the sale and manufacture of more than 15,000 products as of 2011.

In addition to these major regulatory agencies, many other governmental bodies, including the National Highway Traffic Safety Administration, the Federal Aviation Administration, the Food and Drug Administration, the National Labor Relations Board, the Nuclear Regulatory Commission, and the Federal Reserve Board, also have important regulatory responsibilities.

[*See also* **Civil Rights; Civil Rights Legislation; Environmentalism; Environmental Protection Agency; Federal Communications Commission; Federal Reserve System; Federal Trade Commission; Interstate Commerce Act; National Labor Relations Board; New Deal; Nuclear Regulatory Commission; Progressive Era; Public Utilities Policy, Federal; Pure Food and Drug Act;** *and* **Securities and Exchange Commission.**]

BIBLIOGRAPHY

Bernstein, Marver H. *Regulating Business by Independent Commission*. Westport, Conn.: Greenwood Press, 1955.

Hoogenboom, Ari, and Olive Hoogenboom. *A History of the ICC*. New York: W. W. Norton, 1976.

McCraw, Thomas K. *Prophets of Regulation: Charles Francis Adams, Louis D. Brandeis, James M. Landis, Alfred E. Kahn*. Cambridge, Mass.: Belknap Press of Harvard University Press, 1984.

Rosenbaum, Walter. *Environmental Politics and Policy*. Washington, D.C.: CQ Press, 1994.

Vogel, David. "The New 'Social' Regulation in Historical and Comparative Perspective." In *Regulation in Perspective: Historical Essays*, edited by Thomas K. McCraw, pp. 155–185. Boston; Cambridge, Mass.: Harvard University, 1981.

Wilson, James Q., ed. *The Politics of Regulation*. New York: Basic Books, 1980.

Thomas K. McCraw and Stephen E. Randoll

REHNQUIST, WILLIAM

William Hubbs Rehnquist, associate justice of the U.S. Supreme Court and chief justice of the United States (1971–2005), was born 1 October 1924 in Milwaukee, Wisconsin, and died 3 September 2005 in Arlington, Virginia. He served in the Army Air Corps during World War II. He graduated with an AB from Stanford University in 1948, MAs from Stanford and Harvard in 1949 and 1950, respectively, and a JD from Stanford in 1951. He clerked for Supreme Court Associate Justice Robert Jackson in 1952 and 1953, practiced in private practice in Arizona, and then served as assistant attorney general for the Office of Legal Counsel under President Richard Nixon from 1969 to 1971. He was confirmed as an associate justice in 1971 and as chief justice of the United States in 1986. During his tenure as a Supreme Court justice, Rehnquist authored several books for lay readers about the Supreme Court and about legal disputes influential in American political history.

During his tenure on the Supreme Court, Rehnquist embodied in an intellectually serious and judicially effective manner a critique of the Warren Court popular among political conservatives in the 1960s and 1970s. The Warren Court was criticized by scholars on the ground that it was interpreting indeterminate constitutional rights guarantees to impose legislative value judgments on unwilling legislative majorities. Rehnquist carried this academic critique onto the Court by decrying the "notion of a living Constitution."

Although this critique was shared by some subsequent Republican Court appointees, it was rejected by all subsequent Democratic appointees and more than half of substantive Republican appointees. As a result, Rehnquist succeeded only partially in conforming Supreme Court precedent to the critique. For example, in privacy law, the Court never overruled *Roe v. Wade* (1973), which declared a due process right to procure an abortion (*Casey v. Planned Parenthood,* 1992). Yet Rehnquist did author opinions declining to extend due process doctrine further to encompass a general right to commit suicide in *Washington v. Glucksberg* (1996) and *Cruzan v. Director* (1990).

Similarly, Rehnquist never had a Court majority to overrule *Miranda v. Arizona* (1966), a major Warren Court decision ordering law-enforcement officers to notify arrestees of their rights to remain silent and seek counsel. Indeed, Rehnquist wrote a Court opinion declining to overrule *Miranda* in *Dickerson v. United States* (2000). Yet Rehnquist had managed over thirty years to persuade different Court majorities to announce significant limitations on and exceptions to *Miranda*'s holding. By writing a narrow Court opinion refusing to repudiate *Miranda* formally, Rehnquist conserved a generation's efforts to confine it substantively.

Rehnquist changed the course of constitutional law most significantly in the field of federalism. Rehnquist had long supported states' rights, and in the 1970s and 1980s federalism and decentralization became more intellectually respectable than they had been immediately after the civil rights movement. As chief justice, Rehnquist authored significant opinions limiting Congress's ability to abrogate the constitutional sovereign immunity of states in *Florida v. Seminole Tribe of Florida* (1996). He also authored the first two Court opinions since the 1930s limiting Congress's power under the Commerce Clause to regulate in-state activities in *United States v. Morrison* (2000) and *United States v. Lopez* (1995).

[***See also Miranda v. Arizona;* Nixon, Richard M.; *and* Supreme Court, U.S.**]

BIBLIOGRAPHY

Bork, Robert H. "Neutral Principles and Some First Amendment Problems." *Indiana Law Journal* 47 (1971): 1–35.

Kamisar, Yale. "*Dickerson v. United States*: The Case That Disappointed *Miranda's* Critics—and Then Its Supporters." In *The Rehnquist Legacy,* edited by Craig Bradley, pp. 107–128. Cambridge, UK; New York: Cambridge University Press, 2006.

McGinnis, John O. "Reviving Tocqueville's America: The Rehnquist Court's Jurisprudence of Social Discovery." *California Law Review* 90 (2002): 485–571.

Rehnquist, William H. *All the Laws but One: Civil Liberties in Wartime.* New York: Vintage, 2000.

Rehnquist, William H. *Centennial Crisis: The Disputed Election of 1876.* New York: Alfred A. Knopf, 2004.

Rehnquist, William H. *Grand Inquests: The Historic Impeachments of Justice Samuel Chase and President Andrew Johnson.* New York: Morrow, 1992.

Rehnquist, William H. "The Notion of a Living Constitution." *Texas Law Review* 54 (1976): 693–706.

Rehnquist, William H. *The Supreme Court.* New York: Alfred A. Knopf, 2001.

Whittington, Keith E. "William H. Rehnquist: Nixon's Strict Constructionist, Reagan's Chief Justice." In *Rehnquist Justice: Understanding the Court Dynamic,* edited by Earl M. Maltz, pp. 8–33. Lawrence: University Press of Kansas, 2003.

Eric R. Claeys

RELIGIOUS RIGHT

The Religious Right (also known as the Christian Right) is a conservative political movement composed predominantly of evangelical Christians who have allied with other social conservatives in the Republican Party. The movement first gained national attention in the late 1970s, but conservative evangelical political mobilization began with culture wars that developed decades earlier.

The Religious Right's championship of moral laws based on conservative Christian values reflects a long-standing quest on the part of conservative Protestants to fight sexual licentiousness and secularism through moral legislation and to make America a "Christian nation" through politics. In the 1920s, fundamentalist Protestants led political campaigns against alcohol, Catholic politicians, and the teaching of evolution in public schools. In the 1940s, the National Association of Evangelicals lobbied for national restrictions on liquor advertising and defended Bible reading in public schools. In the 1950s, evangelicals such as Billy Graham made anti-Communism a central part of their preaching and cultivated an alliance with President Dwight Eisenhower and the Republican Party based on shared foreign policy goals.

In the 1960s and 1970s, evangelicals became increasingly concerned about the secularization of the country. The development of a national sex education curriculum, the Supreme Court's decisions on school prayer and Bible reading, the proliferation of pornography, and the rise of the feminist movement galvanized evangelicals and led them to unite with Catholics, their inveterate opponents, in launching a new political movement. Evangelicals were slower than Catholics to mobilize against abortion, but by the late 1970s, they began to enlist in the pro-life cause, partly because of the leading of evangelical Presbyterian theologian Francis Schaeffer. At the same time, Southern Baptist singer Anita Bryant's campaign against gay rights in Miami in 1977 sparked a nationwide evangelical anti–gay rights campaign. In 1980, evangelicals secured the Republican Party's support for their positions on abortion, gay rights, and prayer in schools, which were now their central political concerns.

Evangelicals joined the GOP partly because the party was willing to endorse their positions on social issues and the Cold War, but also because they shared conservative Republicans' suspicion of federal regulation, fearing that it would disrupt their enterprises. Some Religious Right leaders entered politics as part of a successful campaign in 1978 to prevent the Internal Revenue Service from denying tax-exempt status to Christian schools it deemed racially discriminatory.

In the 1970s, evangelicals attracted the attention of the Republican Party because of their rising socioeconomic status, rapid growth in the Sunbelt, and control of vast financial resources. Richard Nixon was the first national Republican politician to make a concerted effort to win evangelical votes, primarily through his liaison with Billy Graham. But Ronald Reagan developed an even stronger alliance with the Religious Right, although his administration did not give evangelicals most of the legislation they desired.

Jerry Falwell's Moral Majority, the leading Religious Right organization of the 1980s, mobilized millions of evangelical voters for Reagan, whereas Pat Robertson and Ralph Reed's Christian Coalition developed even closer ties to the GOP in the 1990s. Reed used the Christian Coalition to take over more than one-third of state Republican parties and push the national party to the right on social issues. By the end of the twentieth century, the Religious Right had become a sufficiently powerful interest group within the GOP to prevent the nomination of any presidential candidate who did not share its views on abortion.

The Christian Coalition quickly faded from public view after Reed's departure from the organization in 1997, but other Christian Right leaders, most notably James Dobson of Focus on the Family, continued the fight against gay rights and abortion. Dobson, along with other evangelicals, allied himself with President George W. Bush, who identified closely with conservative evangelical causes. But Bush passed only modest restrictions on abortion, and his administration did little to stop the rapid expansion of gay rights, despite Bush's official—albeit reluctant—endorsement of a proposed constitutional amendment against same-sex marriage. Nearly three-quarters of white evangelicals voted for Republican presidential candidate John McCain and his running mate Sarah Palin in 2008, but many of them were also frustrated with the GOP for failing to effect their agenda.

The Religious Right succeeded in forging a long-term alliance between white evangelicals and the Republican Party, and it also reshaped the nation's political debate by ensuring that abortion, gay rights, and other issues of evangelical concern would remain on the national political agenda. The movement also produced a controversial conservative politicization of evangelical churches, a trend that repelled some evangelicals, particularly those of a younger generation. But despite the publicity that the Christian Right gained, it experienced only limited success in its quest to change national policy, and its polarizing political agenda appealed to only a minority of the electorate.

[*See also* **Anti-Communism; Bush, George W.; Christian Coalition; Eisenhower, Dwight D.; Nixon, Richard M.; Reagan, Ronald;** ***and*** **Republican Party.**]

BIBLIOGRAPHY

Miller, Steven P. *Billy Graham and the Rise of the Republican South.* Philadelphia: University of Pennsylvania Press, 2009.

Williams, Daniel K. *God's Own Party: The Making of the Christian Right.* Oxford; New York: Oxford University Press, 2010.

Daniel K. Williams

REPUBLICANISM

Imported from the civic humanism of Renaissance Italy via the English dissenting tradition, republicanism attracted eighteenth-century Americans who adopted the ideology as a rationale for establishing an independent republic. Americans of the revolutionary generation warmly embraced the republican ideal of civic virtue, historian Gordon Wood argued in *The Creation of the American Republic, 1776–1787* (1969), so that the eventual triumph of a politics of self-interest constituted a profound transformation of values.

Although some historians have characterized quite different ideas as "republican" to distinguish a public-spirited "republicanism" from a selfish "liberalism," such characterizations are problematic. Eighteenth-century American republicans trusted the capacity of autonomous, public-spirited citizens to preserve civic virtue by participating in local politics, so republicanism does represent a clear alternative to the late twentieth century's emphasis on individual rights as the core value in American culture. But beyond the central commitment to civic virtue, historians have disagreed about the republican legacy. Because republicans scorned dependency, celebrated sacrifice for national glory, and feared that change meant decline, they excluded unpropertied workers, women, and slaves from citizenship, advocated military conquest, rejected interest groups of any kind, and prized austerity over economic growth—hardly a program for latter-day American egalitarians or communitarians. But viewed historically, both republicanism and liberalism comprised multiple arguments deployed in changing contexts to solve diverse problems and articulate different ideals, and the discourses of both civic virtue and individual rights must be understood within the overarching context of America's persistent and pervasive religiosity. When the classical Aristotelian idea of man as a political animal and the Italian Renaissance conception of civic virtue are placed within the framework of Augustinian Christianity, republican ideas assume different meanings. When Samuel Adams defined the future American republic as a "Christian Sparta," the qualifier carried enormous weight. Since the central theme of the classical republican tradition, autonomous citizens participating in public affairs, resonated with American ideals and experience and overlapped with the Lockean idea of responsible freedom and the Christian idea of the covenant formed by God's people, Americans could think of themselves simultaneously as republicans, liberals, and Christians, although the first two categories are ours rather than theirs. In the absence of entrenched traditions differentiating people by heredity, social class, or creed, diverse interpretations of these ideas could coexist and loose coalitions could form and dissolve over time.

James Madison in the *Federalist Papers* offered a republican justification for institutions that might produce civic virtue despite the moral and political frailties of the body politic, but Madison's foes, the anti-Federalists, also sought to defend local republican public life by opposing commerce, centralized authority, and the corruption they detected in the Federalist Party gentry. If Jeffersonians invoked civic virtue to legitimate their policies and accused Federalists of scheming to undermine the autonomy of independent craftsmen and farmers, Federalists understood their own call for a strong standing army, stable elites, and the suppression of selfish individualism as a straightforward republican program. As for the Jacksonians of the 1820s and 1830s, whose ranks included slaveholders, craftsmen, and frontiersmen espousing diverse programs, characterizing them simply as "republican" distorts their complex amalgamation of values. Members of the Whig Party, too, considered themselves legitimate heirs of republicanism, thanks to their emphasis on duty, organic unity, and hierarchical order, but neither party succeeded in laying exclusive claim to the republican heritage.

Although Republican terminology survived in the Antebellum Era, meanings and contexts changed. Some Americans began identifying virtue not with citizens as a whole, but with women safely cordoned off from the now poisonous public sphere. Further, whereas John Locke and Adam Smith had conceived of political rights and economic activity within the contexts of religious duty and ethical life, some Americans began thinking of liberty as freedom from restraint. Nevertheless, as William J. Novak shows in *The People's Welfare: Law and Regulation in Nineteenth-Century America* (1996), the states' lower courts continued to enforce the republican doctrine "salus populi"—the people's welfare—by effectively regulating economic activity.

Abraham Lincoln's Republican Party succeeded in part because it was able to revitalize older republican ideals of autonomy and ethical citizenship by linking them with appeals to the property rights of free men and to biblical injunctions against injustice. Champions of the Confederacy likewise stood firmly on the republican principle of autonomous and honorable service to the public good and homage to biblically justified forms of hierarchy. Republican echoes continued to reverberate after the Civil War, although more faintly, as champions of laissez-faire endorsed a new ethos of greed and discarded civic virtue as quaint or counterproductive. Workingmen's parties likewise developed laborers' sense of themselves as a distinctive group with particular interests, thereby helping transform American public life into a contest to satisfy individual desires rather than a cultural project devoted to shaping and channeling those desires toward the common good.

Republican themes persisted in twentieth-century political rhetoric, but they fit poorly into the dominant discourse of rights. Some American progressives, such as John Dewey, Jane Addams, and Herbert Croly, worked to resuscitate the ideal of a public interest emerging from the active participation of all citizens in democratically organized communities. But in the wake of World War I, their pragmatist conception of knowledge as uncertain, and of politics as egalitarian and open-ended, seemed to most Americans shapeless and naive. New Dealers of the 1930s preferred a coalition of different groups attracted to an ill-defined agenda promising prosperity for all. In the late twentieth century, the Democratic Party sometimes tried to refashion the republican ideal by invoking themes of justice and equality, if not civic virtue. But Democrats more often appealed in the language of rights to the interests of particular groups rather than trying to forge a united republican citizenry. Given the absence of resources in republicanism for oppressed groups like African Americans, Indians, Hispanic Americans, and women struggling for equality, such a shift from republican to liberal and religious discourse was hardly surprising.

The Republican Party, by contrast, packaged itself for national consumption by incorporating classical republican themes of its own. Republican candidates denounced centralized power as a source of corruption, deprecated welfare dependency and interest groups, defended hierarchy and patriarchy, honored valor in battle, interpreted cultural (although not economic) change as decline, and claimed to find virtue in austerity—at least for those without tax shelters. Although few American politicians in either party displayed much interest in (or evident familiarity with) civic virtue as the twenty-first century began, Republicans had as legitimate a claim to aspects of the republican tradition as did Democrats, whose vision, it often seemed, had narrowed to the demands of well-organized interest groups.

[*See also* **Adams, John; Calhoun, John C.; Civil Rights; Clay, Henry; Conservatism; Constitution; Constitutional Convention of 1787; Croly, Herbert;** ***Democracy in America;*** **Federalism; Federalist Papers; Jackson, Andrew; Jefferson, Thomas; Liberalism; Lincoln, Abraham; Madison, James; New Deal; Progressive Era; States' Rights; Webster, Daniel; Whig Party;** *and* **Woman Suffrage Movement.**]

BIBLIOGRAPHY

Appleby, Joyce. *Liberalism and Republicanism in the Historical Imagination*. Cambridge, Mass.: Harvard University Press, 1992.

Banning, Lance. *The Sacred Fire of Liberty: James Madison and the Founding of the Federal Republic*. Ithaca, N.Y.: Cornell University Press, 1995.

Kloppenberg, James T. *The Virtues of Liberalism*. New York: Oxford University Press, 1998.

McCoy, Drew R. *The Elusive Republic: Political Economy in Jeffersonian America*. Chapel Hill: University of North Carolina Press, 1980.

Rodgers, Daniel T. "Republicanism: The Career of a Concept." *The Journal of American History* 79 (1992): 11–38.

Sandel, Michael. *Democracy's Discontent: America in Search of a Public Philosophy*. Cambridge, Mass.: Belknap Press of Harvard University Press, 1996.

James T. Kloppenberg

REPUBLICAN PARTY

The Republican Party emerged in the 1850s from a party system torn by political pressures it could not contain. The organizers of the new party brought together formerly hostile groups, including Northern Whigs, antislavery Free Soil Party members, and dissident Democrats—all affected by worsening North–South tensions unleashed by the struggle for control of the Kansas territory—along with nativist Know-Nothings reacting against the flood of Irish Catholic immigrants. Republicans portrayed the Democratic Party as controlled by an expansionist Southern "slavocracy" abetted in the urban North by immigrant votes, and the new party grew rapidly as sectional conflict intensified in the late 1850s. Its opposition to the expansion of slavery and its backing of free labor and federal support for economic development—a reflection of its Whig ancestry—as well as its nativism all won support in the North.

The election in 1860 of Abraham Lincoln, the first Republican president, and the Civil War that followed solidified Republican dominance. The Lincoln administration, in the name of saving the Union, greatly expanded federal power. At first prepared only to restrict slavery, not to abolish it, Republican leaders gradually accepted emancipation both as a war measure and as an expression of the expanded understanding of liberty forged in the heat of conflict.

From the Gilded Age through the 1930s. In the postwar years, Republicans won support in the small-town and rural North by portraying the Democrats as the party of rebellion, a tactic known as "waving the bloody shirt." The Grand Army of the Republic, an association of Union veterans, mobilized votes as a Republican pressure group. Union veterans headed party tickets for decades, starting with Ulysses S. Grant in 1868. Republican orators also continued to appeal to nativists by picturing the Democrats as the party of immigrants. In this era, too, while retaining their support among northern farmers and shopkeepers, the Republicans championed the era's new industrial conglomerates and financial institutions. The party agenda focused on aiding capitalist development through high tariffs, railroad subsidies, and generous support for the nation's economic infrastructure.

Like all political parties, the Republicans experienced factional tensions rooted in regional differences and policy conflicts. Early in the twentieth century, these tensions produced a wrenching split. Progressive Republicans, led by Robert La Follette and Theodore Roosevelt, argued that unbridled industrialization was harming farmers and laborers and promoted policies of social amelioration and corporate regulation. The party's corporate wing, predictably, opposed higher taxation, business regulation, and legislation extending workers' rights. The party split allowed the election and reelection of a Democratic president, Woodrow Wilson, in 1912 and 1916.

The most able Republican leader of the 1920s, Herbert Hoover, first as secretary of commerce and then as president, succeeded for a time in reconciling the party's warring wings. Down to 1929, the Republicans, despite their factionalism, remained sufficiently united to dominate national politics. But the 1929 stock market crash and the ensuing economic collapse ended the party's electoral dominance and threatened its survival. From 1932 to 1952, the Republicans found themselves for the first time a minority in a sea of Democrats, tainted by their association with the Great Depression, Hoover's failed presidency, and their opposition to the New Deal.

Liberal Republicans in the urban Northeast, ignoring conservative charges of "me tooism," demanded action. The party would collapse, they warned, unless it accepted parts of the New Deal's regulative and social welfare program. Most congressional Republicans, however, were from small towns and rural areas, and they followed their leader, Senator Robert Taft of Ohio, in rejecting the New Deal. The factional battle raged for thirty years. Liberal Republicans, led by Wendell Willkie (1892–1944) and New York governor Thomas Dewey (1902–1971), gained control of the party in the 1940s, at least at the presidential level, but failed to win the White House until the election of Dwight D. Eisenhower in 1952. Eisenhower and Richard M. Nixon, the first Republican presidents since Hoover, accepted New Deal programs and insisted that Republicans could be as caring as Democrats in the face of want and despair. In the Nixon years, particularly, support for the welfare state and an active government role in the economy became Republican orthodoxy.

To the party's conservative midwestern wing, all this remained unacceptable despite the anti-Communist Cold War pronouncements of Eisenhower and Nixon. To conservatives, the issues were big government, high taxes, and the strangling of free enterprise in governmental red tape. At first, conservatives made little headway against the liberal wing. Their strength was not in the voter-rich regions of the country. Senator Taft and other conservative Republicans initially welcomed the anti-Communist crusade of Senator Joseph McCarthy of Wisconsin, but when McCarthy attacked prominent Republicans and even the U.S. Army, many members of his own party joined in a 1954 Senate censure vote. When Senator Barry Goldwater of Arizona defeated the governor Nelson Rockefeller of New York to win the 1964 Republican nomination, the result was an electoral disaster, the landslide victory of the Democrat Lyndon B. Johnson.

Amid the urban riots, campus unrest, economic strains, and Vietnam War controversies of the late 1960s, however, Republican conservatism revived. As a Democrat-supported racial revolution turned from expanding civil rights to promoting programs that seemed to favor ethnic minorities and women at the expense of white males and as Democratic candidates became more liberal (or radical, in conservatives' eyes), traditional Democratic voters turned to Republican candidates espousing once-unfashionable conservative positions.

The 1980s and Beyond. Ronald Reagan, a New Dealer turned conservative Republican, won the presidency in 1980 by excoriating the excesses and failures of the welfare state. Reagan also flexed America's Cold War military muscle, challenging alleged Democratic weaknesses on foreign policy. His success underscored the exhaustion of both Democratic liberalism and me-too Republicanism. As Republicans made significant inroads in the white South and in Democratic strongholds of the urban North, the conservative mood within the party hardened. Although conservative Republicans were themselves divided, they clearly controlled the party in the 1980s and 1990s. The emergence of an uncompromising conservatism among highly individualistic entrepreneurs, small shopkeepers, and middle managers typically living and working in the suburbs on the burgeoning Pacific Coast and in the Old South and Southwest (rechristened the Sunbelt) sharpened the party's laissez-faire, antigovernment outlook. The rise of Republican-oriented religious, moral-reform movements such as Jerry Falwell's Moral Majority and Pat Robertson's Christian Coalition and the revival of Republican nativism added new issues—tougher immigration controls, school prayer, pornography regulation, opposition to abortion and gay rights, and other matters of personal and group morality—to the Republican agenda.

Conservative Republicans triumphed electorally in the early 1990s, winning in 1994 control of both houses of Congress for the first time in almost fifty years. Espousing themes of individual responsibility and suspicion of government deeply rooted in the party's history, conservative Republicans—with Democratic support—pushed through a sweeping reform of a federal welfare system dating to the New Deal Era. But new economic and social issues sorely tested Republican unity and promoted internecine warfare, contributing to Democratic presidential victories in 1992 and 1996 and further gains in the 1998 midterm elections.

Republican Divisions over Foreign Policy. Republican divisions were important in the foreign policy arena as well, in long-term conflicts between internationalists and isolationists. President Theodore Roosevelt favored vigorous U.S. engagement in world affairs, but after World War I, Republican isolationists rejected U.S. membership in the League of Nations and generally withdrew from the international arena. Midwestern Republican senators like Taft, Idaho's William Borah (1865–1940), and Arthur Vandenberg (1884–1951) of Michigan opposed U.S. interventionism in the 1930s and, although supporting World War II, reiterated their isolationism after the war. A turning point came in 1947, however, when Vandenberg supported President Harry S. Truman's call for U.S. aid to Greece and Turkey, and a bipartisan approach to foreign policy generally prevailed during the Cold War. But the intraparty split reemerged in the 1990s, as most Republican business leaders supported the global economy and lower trade barriers, whereas other Republicans, such as the TV commentator and sometime presidential candidate Pat Buchanan, espoused protectionism and a more nationalistic economic program.

In the 2000 presidential election, Democrat Al Gore won the popular vote, but George W. Bush, bearing a famous Republican name, narrowly won the Electoral College vote after the Supreme Court resolved the bitterly disputed Florida outcome in his favor. Although Bush had campaigned as a "compassionate conservative," he and Vice President Dick Cheney strengthened the party's historic ties to corporate interests, particularly energy companies, while courting the increasingly active religious right on such hot-button issues as abortion, gay marriage, and Internet pornography. Bush also gave high priority to missile defense, a relic of the Reagan era.

In foreign policy, unlike his internationalistminded father, Bush embraced the unilateralism of neoconservatives in his administration, pursuing an aggressive U.S. policy abroad—especially in the Iraq War of 2003—and showing little interest in coalition building or multinational cooperation on such issues as environmental protection.

The Republican Party under George W. Bush appealed to patriots, religious conservatives, corporate leaders, and entrepreneurs, especially in the South and Southwest. Hispanic voters, increasingly important in U.S. politics, were divided, sharing the party's cultural conservatism but not its favoritism to big business and the rich on tax policies and other economic issues. Under Bush the GOP held little appeal for African American voters and increasingly alienated Republican moderates in New England, the mid-Atlantic states, and elsewhere. Indeed, in 2001 Republican Senator James Jeffords of Vermont left the party and became an independent. Ironically, many traditional Republicans who were suspicious of big government were dismayed by Bush's tolerance for massive federal deficits and his tolerance of vastly expanded federal power in the War on Terror that followed the terrorist attacks of 11 September 2001.

As the nation moved further into the new century, many Americans viewed the Republican Party's conservative wing as too extreme, suggesting the imminence of yet another realignment in the party's ever-shifting balance of power among competing factions.

Bush won reelection in 2004 but the party's extreme conservatism, coupled with a serious economic downturn, led to the election of the Democrat Barack Obama as president in 2008, with large Democratic majorities controlling both houses of Congress. In the first two years of Obama's presidency, however, the Republicans began to bounce back, showing great unity in Congress and by condemning, in their traditional way, what they denounced as the great expansion of federal power under Obama's leadership.

[*See also* **Anti-Communism; Blaine, James G.; Bush, George W.; Christian Coalition; Conservatism; Democratic Party; Eisenhower, Dwight D.; Free Soil Party; Goldwater, Barry; Grant, Ulysses S.; Hoover, Herbert; Know-Nothing Party; La Follette, Robert; Lincoln, Abraham; McCarthy, Joseph; New Deal; Nixon, Richard M.; Progressive Era; Political Parties; Progressive Party of 1912; Reagan, Ronald; Roosevelt, Theodore; Taft, Robert; Tariffs; Taxation;** ***and*** **Whig Party.**]

BIBLIOGRAPHY

Gienapp, William. *The Origins of the Republican Party, 1852–1856*. New York: Oxford University Press, 1987.

Hoff-Wilson, Joan. *Herbert Hoover: Forgotten Progressive*. Boston: Little, Brown, 1975.

Johnson, Donald B. *The Republican Party and Wendell Willkie*. Urbana: University of Illinois Press, 1960.

Lowi, Theodore J. *The End of the Republican Era*. Norman: University of Oklahoma Press, 1995.

Marcus, Robert. *Grand Old Party: Political Structure in the Gilded Age, 1880–1896*. New York: Oxford University Press, 1971.

Parmet, Herbert. *Richard Nixon and His America*. Boston: Little, Brown, 1990.

Patterson, James T. *Mr. Republican: A Biography of Robert A. Taft*. Boston: Houghton Mifflin, 1972.

Silbey, Joel H. *The American Political Nation, 1838–1893*. Stanford, Calif.: Stanford University Press, 1991.

Thelen, David. *Robert M. La Follette and the Insurgent Spirit*. Boston: Little, Brown, 1976.

Joel H. Silbey

ROBERTS, JOHN

John Glover Roberts Jr., is the seventeenth chief justice of the United States. Nominated by President George W. Bush and confirmed by the U.S. Senate in a 72-to-22 vote, Roberts took his seat 29 September 2005. During his confirmation hearings, Roberts notably said, "[J]udges should be like umpires. Umpires don't make the rules; they apply them. . . . But it is a limited role. Nobody ever went to a ball game to see the umpire. . . . I will remember that it's my job to call balls and strikes and not to pitch or bat." This analogy later became emblematic of the view that judges should interpret the law, not make it.

Roberts has already marked his tenure with a number of important decisions. A recurrent theme has been a balance between judicial restraint and constitutional responsibility. For example, in *Boumediene v. Bush* (2008) the Supreme Court held that alien enemy combatants detained at the U.S. Naval Station at Guantanamo Bay, Cuba, have the constitutional privilege of habeas corpus and that the Detainee Treatment Act of 2005 did not provide an adequate substitute for this right. Roberts dissented and criticized the majority for substituting its own judgment for the carefully designed policies of the president and Congress on matters of national security. He concluded that the decision failed to benefit "the American people, who today lose a bit more control over the conduct of this Nation's foreign policy to unelected, politically unaccountable judges."

Chief Justice Roberts has also upheld a strong view of the unitary executive, stressing and the importance of presidential control over the federal bureaucracy for democratic accountability: "One can have a government that functions without being ruled by functionaries, and a government that benefits from expertise without being ruled by experts. Our Constitution was adopted to enable the people to govern themselves, through their elected leaders" (*Free Enterprise Fund v. Public Company Accounting Oversight Board,* 2010).

Roberts has opposed programs that seek "racial balance" by classifying individuals on the basis of race. In *Parents Involved in Community Schools v. Seattle School District No.1* (2007) the Court held that the programs that assigned children to schools on the basis of race violated the Fourteenth Amendment's guarantee of equal protection. Roberts wrote for the Court, "The way to stop discrimination on the basis of race is to stop discriminating on the basis of race."

In an important decision about restrictions on funding for federal elections, the Supreme Court struck down parts of the Bipartisan Campaign Reform Act of 2002 (also referred to as the McCain–Feingold Act) on First Amendment grounds. The chief justice wrote a concurring opinion for *Citizens United v. Federal Election Commission* (2010) to explain why the Court could overrule its earlier decisions. He emphasized that the Court must be able in some circumstances to correct past mistakes to serve the rule of law.

Chief Justice Roberts has also taken a visible role defending the position and authority of the Supreme Court. After President Barack Obama criticized the Court's decision in *Citizens United* during the State of the Union Address, Roberts publicly questioned whether Supreme Court justices should attend what has "degenerated into a political pep rally."

In his judicial opinions as well as in public life, Roberts has not avoided controversy. Some have criticized him for using the rhetoric of moderation but in fact being a "doctrinaire conservative." Although characterizations of his jurisprudence differ, Roberts has sought a principled approach to judging that respects the authority of the president and Congress, but also upholds an important role for the courts in preserving the constitutional balance.

Roberts was born 27 January 1955, in Buffalo, New York. He graduated from Harvard College, *summa cum laude,* and from Harvard Law School, *magna cum laude.* He served as a law clerk for Judge Henry J. Friendly of the U.S. Court of Appeals for the Second Circuit and as a law clerk for then-Associate Justice William H. Rehnquist of the Supreme Court of the United States during the 1980 term. Roberts served as associate counsel to President Ronald Reagan, Office of the Counsel to the President, from 1982 to 1986, and principal deputy solicitor general, U.S. Department of Justice, from 1989 to 1993. From 1986 to 1989 and 1993 to 2003, Roberts practiced law in Washington, D.C. In 2003, President George W. Bush appointed Roberts to the U.S. Court of Appeals for the District of Columbia Circuit, where he served until his appointment as chief justice of the United States in 2005, replacing Chief Justice William H. Rehnquist.

[*See also* **Bush, George W.;** *and* **Supreme Court, U.S.**]

BIBLIOGRAPHY

Baker, Peter. "Obama v. Roberts: The Struggle to Come." *The New York Times*. 17 April 2010.

Toobin, Jeffrey. "No More Mr. Nice Guy: The Supreme Court's stealth hard-liner." *The New Yorker*. 25 May 2009.

Neomi Rao

ROCKEFELLER, NELSON

(1908–1979), liberal Republican governor of New York and U.S. vice president. From the time he was a boy, Nelson Aldrich Rockefeller had set his sights on the presidency. After all, the most politically prominent member of the Rockefeller dynasty mused to reporters, given his family's vast fortune, what else was there to aspire to? He fell short in three attempts (1960, 1964, 1968), but was elected four-term governor of New York (1959–1973) and named vice president (1974–1977) under Gerald Ford. He remains the best-known progressive Republican of recent times; northeastern GOP moderates still are often termed "Rockefeller Republicans."

As the grandson of Standard Oil magnate John D. Rockefeller and Senate chieftain Nelson Aldrich, Rockefeller was advantageously placed for a political career. After college at Dartmouth and work with several family businesses, in 1940 he became Coordinator of Inter-American Affairs (COIAA), bolstering cooperative efforts with Central and South American nations to counter Nazi influence in the western hemisphere. Following service in a variety of other official responsibilities in the Roosevelt, Truman, and Eisenhower administrations, Rockefeller entered electoral politics with an upset victory in the 1958 New York gubernatorial race. Hard-driving, charismatic, and of course immensely rich, Rockefeller immediately became the subject of presidential speculation. His advantages included not only his famous name and wealth but also a reputation for innovative and activist government, an ability to attract talented advisors such as Harvard professor Henry Kissinger, and a sophisticated and technologically advanced public relations operation.

Rockefeller failed to dislodge Richard Nixon in the 1960 Republican primaries, although his challenge to the preconvention platform led to an agreement with Nixon—the so-called "Compact of Fifth Avenue"—that strengthened the civil rights plank. His divorce and 1963 remarriage to Margaretta "Happy" Murphy, who divorced her husband and signed over custody of her four young children, scandalized many Americans and seriously undermined Rockefeller's presidential possibilities. Nonetheless, in 1964 he almost defeated Barry Goldwater in the California GOP primary before exiting the presidential race. Rockefeller came close to stopping Nixon on the first ballot of the 1968 GOP convention, but fell short in his final quest for the Oval Office.

Rockefeller might have attained the presidency had he not been the principal enemy of his party's right wing, even provoking the creation of the Conservative Party of New York to mount candidates against the governor and his political allies. Despite Rockefeller's hard-line stance against Communism and in favor of American involvement in the Vietnam war, conservatives opposed his civil rights efforts and his drive to make New York the model of a high-tax, high-service state and demonized him as a symbol of the eastern establishment. Rockefeller represented a commingling of financial and political power that worried liberals as well, and he alienated many with his punitive laws against the sale and use of illegal drugs and his decision to forcibly suppress a riot at Attica Prison in 1971. As vice president, Rockefeller became frustrated by his inability to play a substantive role in domestic policy. Pressured by conservatives, Ford dropped Rockefeller from the 1976 Republican ticket.

[*See also* **Ford, Gerald R.; Goldwater, Barry; Nixon, Richard M.;** *and* **Republican Party.**]

BIBLIOGRAPHY

Persico, Joseph E. *The Imperial Rockefeller: A Biography of Nelson A. Rockefeller*. New York: Simon & Schuster, 1982.

Reich, Cary. *The Life of Nelson A. Rockefeller: Worlds to Conquer, 1908–1958.* New York: Doubleday, 1996.

Geoffrey Kabaservice

ROE v. WADE

In *Roe v. Wade* (1973), the U.S Supreme Court found unconstitutional state criminal abortion laws dating back to the 1860s and 1870s. By a 7-to-2 vote, announced on 22 January 1973, the court ruled that prohibiting abortion violated a woman's right to privacy in determining whether to carry a pregnancy to term. The Court declared, however, that this right was not "absolute," but balanced against state interests. States were prohibited from interfering with abortion during the first trimester of pregnancy; they were allowed to regulate abortions in the second trimester to ensure the safety of the woman; and they could prohibit abortion in the third trimester to protect fetal life, unless the pregnancy jeopardized the woman's life or health. In a companion opinion, *Doe v. Bolton,* the Court found that policies designed to restrict abortions by reviewing (and often overturning) physicians' recommendations for abortion were unconstitutional because they violated doctors' rights to make medical decisions.

The principal author of both decisions was Justice Harry A. Blackmun (1908–1999). Blackmun's decision derived the right-to-privacy principle (not mentioned in the Constitution) from the due process clause of the Fourteenth Amendment. The two dissenters, Justice Byron White and future chief justice William Rehnquist, criticized the right-to-privacy argument as constitutionally dubious and the trimester approach as arbitrary.

Roe v. Wade grew out of a changing legal and political context. Several states (Alaska, Hawai'i, and New York) had already legalized abortion, and a dozen more had liberalized their laws to make it easier for women to obtain "therapeutic" abortions. (Therapeutic abortions to protect the life of the pregnant woman were always permitted.) The movement toward legalization began in the mid-1950s among physicians and lawyers and by 1970 had won the support of numerous feminist, religious, professional, student, and labor organizations.

Underpinning this support was a heretofore quiet and private tradition of accepting abortion as well as the frightening history of the injury and death of women seeking illegal abortions. During the century of illegal abortion, American women of every class, ethnic, religious, and racial background obtained abortions. By the 1960s, however, low-income and nonwhite women were overrepresented among those who died from illegal abortions. As legal abortions replaced illegal and self-induced abortions, maternal mortality fell and hospital septic abortion wards closed. In 1973, nearly 800,000 legal abortions were performed.

With the legalization of abortion nationwide, the pro-life movement, an antiabortion campaign initially financed by the Catholic Church and fundamentalist Protestants, grew in political power. This volatile issue was used to mobilize voters and swing elections at all levels. By the mid-1990s, 80 percent of all U.S. counties had no abortion providers. The reduced availability of legal abortion was achieved by various means: political pressure; laws, such as those requiring women under eighteen to obtain parental permission; the elimination of state funding for abortions for low-income women; and criminal antiabortion activity, including the bombing of clinics and the murder of abortion providers. Nonetheless, opinion polls found that a growing proportion of the population supported legal abortion.

[*See also* **Blackmun, Harry S.; Civil Rights; Civil Rights Legislation; Feminism; Fourteenth Amendment; Rehnquist, William;**

State Governments; ***and*** **Supreme Court, U.S.]**

BIBLIOGRAPHY

Joffe, Carole. *Doctors of Conscience: The Struggle to Provide Abortion before and after Roe v. Wade.* Boston: Beacon Press, 1995.

Reagan, Leslie J. *When Abortion Was a Crime: Women, Medicine, and Law in the United States, 1867–1973.* Berkeley: University of California Press, 1997.

Leslie J. Reagan

ROOSEVELT, ELEANOR

(1884–1962), First Lady, humanitarian, social activist. Eleanor Roosevelt (ER) was born in New York City into an affluent, aristocratic, troubled family. Eleanor was eight when her mother Anna died and ten when her beloved father Elliott died of alcoholism at the age of thirty-four. She was nurtured and influenced by her maternal grandmother and her paternal uncle, Theodore Roosevelt.

Sent to Allenswood School in England at fifteen, Eleanor was inspired by headmistress Marie Souvestre. ER excelled, debated fiercely, made the first team at field hockey, and emerged a leader. But her grandmother insisted that she return to New York City to perform the debutante ritual of "coming out" when she was eighteen. In 1903, surrounded by friends who founded the Junior League as a smart-set rebellion, including Mary Harriman and Jean Reid, ER taught dancing and calisthenics to the immigrant girls of New York's Lower East Side at their new University Settlement. There she met her mentors and allies, social work pioneers Florence Kelley and Lillian Wald (1867–1940).

Becoming engaged to her fifth cousin Franklin Delano Roosevelt, she introduced him to issues of poverty and struggle, encouraged his Harvard studies, and promoted his ambitions. Their love deepened despite the opposition of his mother, Sara Delano Roosevelt, and they married in 1905. Of their six children, five survived: Anna (1906), James (1907), Elliott (1909), Franklin Jr. (1914), and John (1916). Sara Delano Roosevelt remained a dominant presence in their lives.

In 1910 FDR was elected to the New York State Assembly, and ER flourished in Albany's political climate. She established important alliances with reform politicians, notably Alfred E. Smith, Robert F. Wagner, and Frances Perkins. In 1913 President Woodrow Wilson named FDR assistant secretary of the navy, and their move to Washington was initially happy. But ER's life felt momentarily derailed when she discovered her husband's affair with her social secretary Lucy Mercer. She offered a divorce, but they agreed to carry on—to repair their hearts and protect the children and his career. With FDR's nomination for the vice presidency in 1920, ER campaigned fully for the first time.

During that failed effort, she forged a new partnership with Louis Howe, FDR's primary adviser, who became the bridge between them. Together, they battled to keep FDR interested in public life and promoted his political ambitions during the years of his convalescence from polio. In the 1920s, too, ER became the center of a powerful network of political women in the Democratic Party and the new League of Women Voters. With Esther Lape and Elizabeth Read, ER campaigned for the U.S. membership in the World Court. With three partners, Marion Dickerman, Nancy Cook, and Caroline O'Day, she co-owned Val-Kill, a model furniture factory two miles from the Roosevelts' Hyde Park, New York, home. After her husband's death, she converted Val-Kill into her residence. She also taught history and literature, was coprincipal at New York's Todhunter School, and edited the

Women's Democratic News. By 1928, when FDR was elected New York State governor, ER was the women's political "boss" of the Democratic Party and a bipartisan leader for women's rights and equity.

In 1932 when FDR was elected president, ER's circle was in place to demand patronage, power, and New Deal justice for women. Her work with Mary (Molly) Dewson, secretary of labor Frances Perkins, Ellen Sullivan Woodward, Mary Anderson, Florence Kerr, and Hilda Worthington Smith successfully enlarged the New Deal's scope. With Mary McLeod Bethune, Walter White, and the National Association for the Advancement of Colored People (NAACP), ER battled racial segregation and discrimination. In 1938 she helped launch the Southern Conference on Human Welfare, a network of race radicals dedicated to end the poll tax and all discrimination. In 1939 she resigned from the Daughters of the American Revolution (DAR) when it refused to permit Marian Anderson to perform in the DAR's Constitution Hall in Washington, D.C. Associated Press reporter Lorena Hickok (Hick), ER's intimate friend during the White House years, influenced her career as a writer and encouraged her to hold press conferences for women journalists only and write a daily column, *My Day*.

Although ER generally supported her husband's policies, during the 1930s, they differed on such international issues as the World Court, collective security, and the Spanish Civil War. Journalist, editor, and radio broadcaster, ER was the only First Lady to disagree publicly with her husband. In *This Troubled World* (1938), she offered a point-by-point alternative to FDR's isolationist policies. On domestic issues FDR encouraged his wife to speak out. If she could "warm up" an issue, he would run with it. Their unique partnership allowed each to do more than either could have achieved alone. In the area of housing, for example, ER in 1934 with the support of her network created a model community, Arthurdale, in West Virginia, that became a prototype for other New Deal model communities.

ER lobbied less successfully for refugees fleeing Nazi persecution. In 1940, she became involved in a covert operation headed by Varian Fry that resulted in the rescue of over 2,000 refugees, including Hannah Arendt, Pablo Casals, Marc Chagall, Wanda Landowska, and Alma Mahler. But the State Department had Fry arrested and terminated the operation in 1941. During World War II, ER criticized the incarceration of Japanese Americans and campaigned for women's rights, civil rights, and the survival of New Deal programs.

Distraught by FDR's death on 12 April 1945 in Warm Springs, Georgia (and dismayed to learn that Lucy Mercer had been with him at the end), ER announced her retirement from public life. But President Harry S. Truman appointed her a delegate to the United Nations and she used the opportunity to carry on her vision of the best of FDR's legacy: a New Deal for the world; dignity for all people. She helped create the United Nations Declaration of Human Rights, which passed the General Assembly on 10 December 1948, and spent the rest of her life lobbying for the United Nations, human rights, and nuclear disarmament. In 1961 President John F. Kennedy appointed her chair of his new Commission on the Status of Women, which helped launch the second wave of the women's movement. Her final book, *Tomorrow Is Now*, was published posthumously in 1963. She is buried beside her husband at Hyde Park.

[*See also* **Antinuclear Movement; Civil Rights; Democratic Party; Federal Government, Executive Branch: Presidency, The; Feminism; Japanese American Internment; Kennedy, John F.; National Association for the Advancement of Colored People; New**

Deal; Poverty; Progressive Era; Roosevelt, Franklin Delano; Roosevelt, Theodore; Segregation; Smith, Alfred; Truman, Harry S.; Wilson, Woodrow; *and* Woman Suffrage Movement.]

BIBLIOGRAPHY

Black, Allida M. *Casting Her Own Shadow*. New York: Columbia University Press, 1997.

Black, Allida M., ed. *Courage in a Dangerous World: The Political Writings of Eleanor Roosevelt*. New York: Columbia University Press, 1999.

Cook, Blanche Wiesen. *Eleanor Roosevelt,* Vol. 1, *1884–1933*. New York: Viking, 1992.

Cook, Blanche Wiesen. *Eleanor Roosevelt,* Vol. 2, *The Defining Years, 1933–1938*. New York: Penguin, 1999.

Lash, Joseph P. *Eleanor and Franklin*. New York: W. W. Norton, 1971.

Lash, Joseph P. *Eleanor: The Years Alone*. New York: New American Library, 1972.

Ware, Susan. *Partner and I: Molly Dewson, Feminism, and New Deal Politics*. New Haven, Conn.: Yale University Press, 1987.

Blanche Wiesen Cook

ROOSEVELT, FRANKLIN DELANO

Democrat, president of the United States 1933–1945, led the country to recovery from the Great Depression and victory in World War II.

Early Life and Career. Born 30 January 1882 to James and Sara Delano Roosevelt in Dutchess County, New York, Franklin grew up effectively an only child (he did have an adult half-brother) in a manner characteristic of wealthy families: tutored, traveling; boarding school at Groton, and college at Harvard. He made no great academic or social success at either school, and during his time at Harvard his distant cousin Theodore became president, thus giving Franklin a model of accomplishment he feared he would never achieve: after all at Harvard he failed election to Theodore's club, the Porcellian.

While at college Franklin met and courted his cousin Eleanor Roosevelt, Theodore's niece. With dissimilar characters—he was outgoing and flippant, she focused and earnest—they complemented each other. They became engaged upon Franklin's graduation and were married, with Theodore, the president, giving the bride away, in 1905. Eleanor and Franklin would have five children. After some time at Columbia Law, Franklin passed the bar and began practicing.

In 1910 Franklin Roosevelt entered politics, winning a New York State Senate seat from Dutchess County, a habitually Republican district, as a Democrat. Reelected in 1912, he left his seat to accept an appointment to Woodrow Wilson's administration as assistant secretary of the Navy, the same position Theodore had held when he came to national notice. Franklin held the job through the Wilson presidency, including preparation for and fighting World War I.

In 1920 he ran for the vice presidency on the ticket with James Cox and lost. After ten years of politics Roosevelt had not greatly distinguished himself. With his pince-nez and generally if vaguely progressive policies, he looked and sounded like an offshoot of Theodore Roosevelt or Woodrow Wilson. He had a reputation as a lightweight, a butterfly, and a banterer—the "Feather Duster," his critics sometimes unkindly called him, playing on his initials.

While in Washington, Franklin began an affair with Lucy Mercer, Eleanor's appointments secretary. Eleanor found out in 1918 when she discovered letters between the two. The Roosevelts discussed divorce but decided against it; he pledged to keep away from Mercer. Eleanor and Franklin remained married, but without intimacy or even friendship.

In 1921 Roosevelt contracted polio, which deprived him of the regular use of his legs. He struggled without success to walk unaided. He needed a wheelchair, although he avoided being photographed in it, and made public appearances standing, and even, with the help of leg braces and his son, walking. At the age of forty, he had left love, health, and a considerable degree of ease behind him. In exchange he gained strength and a solitude of spirit, turning inward and learning to depend on himself. He was still a creature of persiflage, but now the surface clearly hid a core whose contents maybe nobody ever knew.

Roosevelt emerged from political hibernation to nominate Governor Al Smith of New York for the presidency at the 1924 Democratic convention and then again in 1928. Both episodes did more for Roosevelt than for Smith: in 1924 the Democrats split bitterly between pro- and anti-Klan forces (the Catholic, immigrant-descended, Prohibition-defying Smith and his allies were anti-Klan) and settled on a disastrous compromise candidate, John Davis. In 1928 Smith received the nomination and endured a drubbing at the hands of Herbert Hoover, whose campaign made liberal use of anti-Catholic, anti-immigrant, antiwet rhetoric and won over some of Smith's old Klan opponents. Meanwhile Roosevelt showed himself capable of standing to give a vigorous speech, limping but unbowed by his illnesses. Smith never quite forgave Roosevelt his support in these failed endeavors or his own successes: Smith lost New York by 100,000 votes to Hoover, whereas Roosevelt won the gubernatorial election to succeed Smith.

As governor, Roosevelt managed New York State at the outset of the Great Depression. He promoted public works projects, secured state funding for unemployment relief, and increasingly castigated President Hoover for his inert response to the crisis, which Roosevelt came to believe would not right itself without government intervention. His positions and policies won him a second term in Albany in 1930.

Even while asking that the federal government do more to right the economy, Roosevelt complained that Hoover was running an unbalanced budget. Although Roosevelt gained political advantage from fretting about federal inaction and overspending alike, there is no reason to believe that he was insincere about either concern, as he continued to express them through 1932 and into his own time in office.

Roosevelt won the Democratic nomination for presidency in 1932 by outflanking Smith and John Nance Garner of Texas, whom he made his running mate. He flew to Chicago to address the convention, marking a first in U.S. political history; presidential candidates traditionally did not appear before nominating conventions. There he pledged "a new deal for the American people," to include public works, agricultural price supports, new mortgage markets, working-hours legislation, securities regulation, freer world trade, reforestation, and repeal of Prohibition, among other goals. He also made clear his belief that evidence of clear action to meet the crisis would be the only way the United States could avoid the rise of "wild radicalism."

The New Deal. In the depths of the Depression, with the jobless rate nearing 25 percent and the federal government denying the need for relief to the unemployed while deploying soldiers to chase veterans from the National Mall for protesting their poverty, Roosevelt handily won the presidency with 472 electoral votes over Hoover's 59. For the last time, a president-elect would have to wait until 4 March to take office (the Twentieth Amendment was ratified during the wait for Roosevelt's inauguration). Hundreds of American banks failed as one-third of a year ticked by. Roosevelt said little, and Hoover did nothing. Hoover tried to get Roosevelt to join him in a statement on economic policy, including a guarantee that Roosevelt would keep the dollar on the gold standard. Roosevelt declined to endorse Hoover's economic record. In the remaining weeks of Hoover's presidency the banks collapsed as depositors withdrew their savings. The Federal Reserve Bank of New York ran low on gold and requested a bank holiday.

On taking office Roosevelt closed the banks and suspended convertibility of the dollar to gold. Slightly over a week later the administration began to open the banks it had found sound. Savers began to return their money. The dollar would never again be convertible to gold, but the administration proved to savers both in America and overseas that the dollar was a safe bet. Gold flowed back into American vaults, increasing the supply of money and credit and easing the economic crisis.

This first New Deal success was largely Roosevelt's doing, as he had long meant to inflate the currency. But New Deal programs did not always owe to Roosevelt: some he either initially opposed, like federal insurance of bank deposits, or accepted reluctantly and nervously, like federal unemployment relief. Still, the New Deal could not have proceeded nor have taken the shape it did—for better and worse—without his guidance.

At first, Roosevelt favored an emergency approach to the economy similar to the one the nation adopted during World War I, when the government worked with industry to fix prices and wages. In 1933, the National Recovery Administration adopted this approach, creating cartels. It may have had some economic success by reversing the expectation of falling prices, but it faltered politically because consumers and corporate managers alike complained about favoritism in its workings. By the time the Supreme Court declared it unconstitutional in 1935, it had already manifestly failed.

Having abandoned price fixing, the federal government would use its powers and spending to rebalance the nation's scales. In the past, as Roosevelt pointed out, the federal government had given public land to banks and railroads, enriching them as they developed the nation. Now, he said, the government would give public money so that other Americans had help similar to that previously enjoyed by the corporations. Groups that had suffered disadvantages previously would have the power to bargain for themselves. Evening up the scales would let government stay out of the price-setting process. The National Recovery Administration and the Wagner Act encouraged workers to unionize, so they could bargain for their own wage increases and benefits; the Works Progress Administration improved roads to rural areas, providing them opportunities for economic modernization; and the Public Works Administration brought hydroelectric power to the West while the Tennessee Valley Authority brought it to the South, permitting industrialization in those regions that had previously had little of it. The Social Security Act, too, gave power to ordinary workers, so that they need not fear unemployment, injury, or old age quite so much; less dependent on their employers, they had that much more security in bargaining for their own advantages.

The New Deal that thus emerged from Roosevelt's negotiation with Congress and effort to accommodate the Supreme Court's reading of the constitution was a careful affair; the government did adjust the workings of the capitalist economy, but to ensure as much as possible a fair field and no favor among bargaining parties, not to set prices itself. Scholars have referred to this strategy as the operation of a "broker state" or the policy of creating "countervailing power."

Throughout the New Deal, Roosevelt advanced his agenda personally, by radio broadcasts known as fireside chats. Americans came to feel they knew their president, wrote to him in record numbers, and believed him to have control of the government. Eleanor acted as his emissary, traveling where he could not and reporting on what she saw.

Roosevelt easily won reelection in 1936. Republicans asked voters to view the contest as a referendum on the New Deal, pointing to the Supreme Court's antagonism to the program's constitutionality. Voters did not share these worries and returned Roosevelt by a record-breaking margin to the White House.

Roosevelt's second term saw New Deal reformism slow. The president took aim at the Supreme Court, asking Congress to permit him to appoint as many as six justices for every one that had not retired by the age of seventy. The bill failed and cost Roosevelt some Congressional support.

Roosevelt himself contributed to the increasing conservatism of the New Deal. He tried to keep federal relief minimal and cut it in 1937—prematurely, because a recession immediately followed. Afterward Roosevelt became explicitly Keynesian, saying that the government should borrow money and spend to reverse economic downturns. He justified the venture in conservative terms, saying that only government action to improve the economy could preserve democracy.

In adopting Keynesianism, as in adopting the earlier strategy of giving groups the power to bargain for themselves, Roosevelt had designed a bigger, more activist federal government by explaining that the government would act in ways calculated to thwart calls for diminished liberties.

The Second World War The New Deal's success in generating peacetime recovery was obscured by the start of World War II, the economic mobilization for which generated economic activity. Roosevelt tried persuading Americans to "quarantine" military aggression in 1937, without success. The advance of fascism changed minds. In 1940, even while he was running for an unprecedented third term, Roosevelt persuaded Congress to begin American sales of munitions to the British and traded destroyers to Britain in exchange for naval bases. Having won reelection, Roosevelt pressed Congress for the Lend-Lease Act to make the U.S. "the great arsenal of democracy." By the end of summer 1941, the nation was waging an undeclared naval war against Germany in the Atlantic.

In August 1941 Roosevelt met Winston Churchill to agree on aims for the yet undeclared war, issuing the Atlantic Charter, which guaranteed basic rights to "all the men in all the lands," a major step toward a universal declaration of human rights.

With the attack on Pearl Harbor and the German declaration of war, Roosevelt enjoyed much greater freedom to act. Despite the Japanese attack, he dedicated the United States to a two-front war, making defeat of the Nazis his primary goal. With Churchill he designed the strategy for invading Africa and then, after an extensive bombing campaign, Europe. At the same time the Navy and Marines advanced westward across the Pacific.

Roosevelt's administration oversaw industrial mobilization for the war, a manufacturing success producing ships and airplanes so swiftly it virtually guaranteed victory. War work returned dignity to a laboring class that had struggled through the Depression. But some home front mobilization was shameful, as when Roosevelt overrode his attorney general and ordered the internment without due process of Japanese Americans—whom the administration deemed insufficiently loyal to live freely in the United States, but loyal enough to wear the uniform of, and die for, their country.

The president continued to press for economic equity, issuing an "economic bill of rights," including the right to a job, a "decent home," and medical care. Congress did not move to make such provision for Americans generally, but did pass the Servicemen's Readjustment Act, or GI Bill, which provided housing and educational benefits to returning veterans.

Roosevelt's health declined during the war. He leaned increasingly on a small circle of friends, including Lucy Mercer Rutherfurd, who had returned to him. He ran for a fourth term and won.

The Postwar World. Roosevelt's decisions shaped the postwar world. He authorized the Manhattan Project to create atomic weapons. He convened the Bretton Woods conference to ensure global economic prosperity and the United Nations conference at Dumbarton Oaks to create a forum for world diplomacy. He also, in January 1945, met Churchill and Soviet Premier Josef Stalin at Yalta, where he conceded the reality of Soviet control in Eastern Europe, although he lied to hide it on his return to the United States and did not take his newly inaugurated vice president, Harry Truman, into his confidence.

On 12 April 1945, Franklin Roosevelt died of a stroke, with the now-widowed Lucy Mercer Rutherfurd at his side.

Victory over Germany came in May and over Japan in August. Subsequent administrations of both parties expanded the New Deal, strengthening Social Security and adding heath care entitlements. Even opponents of these measures had to define their positions in terms of Roosevelt's legacy to Americans of the modern era.

[*See also* **National Recovery Administration; New Deal; Roosevelt, Eleanor; Roosevelt, Theodore; Servicemen's Readjustment Act; Social Security; Tennessee Valley Authority; Truman, Harry S.; Wilson, Woodrow;** ***and*** **Works Progress Administration.**]

BIBLIOGRAPHY

Altschuler, Glenn C., and Stuart M. Blumin. *The G.I. Bill: A New Deal for Veterans*. Oxford; New York: Oxford University Press, 2009.

Borgwardt, Elizabeth. *A New Deal for the World: America's Vision for Human Rights*. Cambridge, Mass.: Belknap Press of Harvard University Press, 2005.

Brinkley, Alan. *The End of Reform: New Deal Liberalism in Recession and War*. New York: Alfred A. Knopf, 1995.

Brinkley, Alan. *Franklin Delano Roosevelt. Oxford: Oxford University Press,* 2010.

Burns, James MacGregor. *Roosevelt*. 2 vols. *The Lion and the Fox* and *The Soldier of Freedom*. Reprint. New York: Mariner Books, 2002.

Kennedy, David M. *Freedom from Fear: The American People in Depression and War, 1929–1945*. New York: Oxford University Press, 1999.

Rauchway, Eric. *The Great Depression and the New Deal: A Very Short Introduction*. Oxford; New York: Oxford University Press, 2008.

Eric Rauchway

ROOSEVELT, THEODORE

(1858–1919), twenty-sixth president of the United States. Born in New York City, Theodore Roosevelt grew up in comfortable circumstances in the wealthy family of Theodore Roosevelt Sr., and Mittie Bulloch Roosevelt. He struggled with asthma and poor eyesight as a child but also showed the determination to excel, love of books, and fascination with the outdoors that marked his life. A graduate of Harvard, he married Alice Lee in 1880. Fascinated with politics, he won election to the New York Assembly in 1881. The sudden deaths of his mother and his wife on the same day in February 1884 left him with a baby daughter, Alice Lee Roosevelt, and a desire to escape New York. He ranched in the Dakotas for several years.

In 1886, Roosevelt married Edith Kermit Carow, a childhood friend, with whom he had five children. He ran for mayor of New York that year, but came in third. Appointed to the U.S. Civil Service Commission in 1889, he served until 1895. In 1897, after two years as the president of New York City's Board of Police Commissioners, he resigned to become assistant secretary of the navy in the administration of President William McKinley. In that office he urged the expansion of the navy and lobbied for war with Spain.

When the Spanish–American War began in April 1898, Roosevelt volunteered. The regiment that he led, known as the Rough Riders, attacked the Spanish in Cuba on 1 July 1898 in a battle that made him a national hero. That fall, running on the Republican Party ticket, he was elected governor of New York State in a close election. An activist governor, Roosevelt spoke out for worker protection, the conservation of natural resources, and the mild regulation of corporations, leading the state's Republican boss, Thomas C. Platt, to conclude that Roosevelt would be less troublesome as vice president. In the absence of credible alternatives, and since he also had the support of western Republicans and younger party members, Roosevelt joined the national Republican ticket in 1900 and campaigned vigorously for McKinley's reelection. He was inaugurated as vice president on 4 March 1901.

On 6 September 1901, McKinley was shot by an assassin; he died eight days later. At forty-two, Roosevelt became the nation's youngest president. He promised to continue McKinley's policies, but his energy, activism, and distinct leadership style soon led him in fresh directions. Taking on corporate America and revitalizing the 1890 Sherman Antitrust Act, he ordered the Justice Department to file what proved to be a successful suit to break up the Northern Securities Company, a railroad conglomerate, early in 1902. He also helped settle a bitter anthracite coal strike later that year on terms that established him as a champion of the "Square Deal" for labor. In foreign policy, he settled an Alaska boundary dispute with Canada and in 1903 secured control of the Panama Canal Zone in a manner that outraged Colombia but pleased most Americans. He pushed construction of the Panama Canal and became the first president to leave the continental United States when he visited the Canal Zone in 1906. Roosevelt's achievements and popularity secured his election to the presidency in his own right in 1904 when he decisively defeated the Democratic nominee, Alton B. Parker. On election night he announced that he would not be a candidate in 1908.

Roosevelt pursued a more activist course in his second term. In foreign affairs, he acted as peacemaker for the Russo-Japanese War in 1905, winning the Nobel Peace Prize for his efforts. His diplomacy facilitated the Algeciras Conference of 1906 that quieted differences between France and Germany over Morocco, and he sent a powerful naval force, the "Great White Fleet," around the world in 1907–1909 as a display of American strength. In Latin America, he proclaimed the Roosevelt Corollary to the Monroe Doctrine, warning European nations against exploiting the troubles of Caribbean countries for military or political advantage.

In domestic affairs, Roosevelt championed railroad regulation through the Hepburn Act, sponsored the Pure Food and Drug Act, and secured meat-inspection legislation, all in a single year, 1906. More reformist as his term progressed, he pushed for corporate regulation, toughened the antitrust laws, and promoted sweeping conservation policies. Although he invited Booker T. Washington to the White House, his peremptory dishonorable discharge of African American soldiers in 1906 because of their purported participation in a shooting incident in Brownsville, Texas, marred his record and reflected his ambiguity on the race issue.

Roosevelt hand-picked William Howard Taft as his successor and helped Taft win the White House in 1908. Upon leaving office, he went on safari in Africa in 1909–1910. Progressive Republicans' increasing unhappiness with Taft's policies, culminating in the Ballinger–Pinchot controversy, led Roosevelt to announce his candidacy for the Republican nomination in 1912. Losing the nomination to Taft after a bruising primary battle and a tumultuous national convention, Roosevelt bolted the Republican Party and ran on the Progressive Party ticket. He spoke out for social justice, but finished second to the Democratic nominee, Woodrow Wilson.

The Progressive Party did not prosper and Roosevelt returned to his Republican roots soon after World War I broke out in 1914. Unhappy with Wilson's neutrality, he urged the country to prepare for war and, if necessary, intervene on the side of the Allies. Roosevelt lost to Charles Evans Hughes in the race for the 1916 Republican nomination. Once the United States entered the war in April 1917, Roosevelt sought to raise a volunteer division to fight in France. Wilson and the army refused. Theodore Roosevelt was the likely candidate for the Republican presidential race in 1920, but he died on 6 January 1919.

A major figure in establishing the presidency in its modern form, TR (a nickname he favored) was both intensely controversial and a political celebrity of vast popularity. A forceful orator and an advocate of the strenuous life (he installed a boxing ring in the White House), Roosevelt with his bushy mustache, pince-nez, and wide, toothy grin was a caricaturist's delight. Vigorous and outspoken, he basked in the limelight: "He wanted to be the bride at every wedding, the corpse at every funeral," a relative commented. A century after he came to the White House, his fame still endured.

[*See also* **Antitrust Legislation and Law; Ballinger–Pinchot Controversy; Civil Service Reform; Economic Policy: Regulation; Federal Government, Executive Branch: Presidency, The; Hepburn Act; McKinley, William; Northern Securities Case; Panama Canal; Progressive Party of 1912; Pure Food and Drug Act; Republican Party; Taft, William Howard; Washington, Booker T.;** *and* **Wilson, Woodrow.**]

BIBLIOGRAPHY

Blum, John Morton. *The Republican Roosevelt.* New York: Atheneum, 1954.

Cooper, John Milton, Jr. *The Warrior and the Priest: Woodrow Wilson and Theodore Roosevelt.* Cambridge, Mass.: Belknap Press of Harvard University Press, 1983.

Gatewood, Willard B. *Theodore Roosevelt and the Art of Controversy: Episodes of the White House Years.* Baton Rouge: Louisiana State University Press, 1970.

Gould, Lewis L. *The Presidency of Theodore Roosevelt.* Lawrence: University Press of Kansas, 1991.

Harbaugh, William H. *The Life and Times of Theodore Roosevelt.* New York: Oxford University Press, 1975.

McCullough, David. *Mornings on Horseback.* New York: Simon & Schuster, 1981.

Lewis L. Gould

ROSENBERG CASE

The early 1950s conviction and execution of Julius and Ethel Rosenberg for providing classified information to the Soviet Union about America's atomic bomb development remain among the most controversial events of the early Cold War. A graduate of the City

College of New York, Julius Rosenberg joined the Communist Party USA, along with his wife Ethel, in 1939. Working for Soviet intelligence during World War II, he provided Russian contacts with the supersecret information he received from well-placed spies at the Manhattan Project's Los Alamos, New Mexico, atomic research facility. Despite clues from Soviet defectors, American authorities did not learn about atomic espionage until 1948, when the Federal Bureau of Investigation, working with code breakers in the U.S. Army, decrypted and interpreted nearly 3,000 messages, called the Venona Cables, between Soviet intelligence agencies in Moscow and spies in the United States. The cables quickly led to David Greenglass, Ethel's brother, who had worked as a machinist at Los Alamos during the war. Greenglass soon implicated Julius Rosenberg—code-named "Liberal" in the Venona Cables—as the leader of an atomic spy ring. Arrested in 1950, against a Cold War backdrop that included the second Alger Hiss trial, the fall of China to Communism, the Korean War, and the 1949 confession of the German-born British scientist Klaus Fuchs that he had spied for the Russians while assigned to Los Alamos, the Rosenbergs were tried and convicted the following year on the charge of conspiracy to commit espionage. Before issuing the death sentence, trial judge Irving R. Kaufman accused the couple of causing "the Communist aggression in Korea, with the resultant casualties exceeding 50,000, and who knows but that millions more innocent people may pay the price for your treason."

The government's case against Julius Rosenberg was far stronger than its case against Ethel. Although she undoubtedly knew about—and may well have supported—her husband's spying, she was not, by any reasonable standard, an active coconspirator. It appears she was arrested to pressure Julius into confessing. This was part of the government's "lever strategy"—a strategy that would lead an unyielding woman directly to her death. When Ethel was arrested, one of the prosecutors said privately that "the case is not too strong against Mrs. Rosenberg," and it grew no stronger as time passed. A death-house questionnaire, prepared by prosecutors should Julius break down at the last moment, included this startling question: "Was your wife cognizant of your activities?"

Despite international protests, the Rosenbergs were electrocuted at New York's Sing Sing prison on 19 June 1953, proclaiming their innocence to the end. By the 1990s, however, the declassification of the Venona files and other documents led all but their most fervent supporters to acknowledge the guilt of Julius Rosenberg and, at least, the partial complicity of his wife. Although the Rosenbergs' crimes were real indeed, millions still remember their executions as a vindictive act of Cold War justice.

[*See also* **Anti-Communism; Communist Party USA;** *and* **Federal Bureau of Investigation.**]

BIBLIOGRAPHY

Haynes, John Earl, and Harvey Klehr. *Venona: Decoding Soviet Intelligence in America.* New Haven, Conn.: Yale University Press, 1999.

Lamphere, Robert J., and Tom Schachtman. *The FBI–KGB Wars: A Special Agent's Story.* New York: Random House, 1986.

Radosh, Ronald, and Joyce Milton. *The Rosenberg File,* 2d ed. New Haven, Conn.: Yale University Press, 1997.

Richard Gid Powers

S

SACCO AND VANZETTI CASE

In May 1920, Nicola Sacco, a shoemaker, and Bartolomeo Vanzetti, a fish peddler, were arrested for the murder of a paymaster and guard in a robbery at a South Braintree, Massachusetts, shoe factory. In a trial marked by flimsy evidence and flawed procedures, they were convicted and sentenced to death. Critical observers recognized at the time that the police, jurors, prosecutors, and judge were responding less to the evidence than to the fact that Sacco and Vanzetti were immigrant Italian anarchists who had evaded the draft in World War I. Their case was set against the backdrop of the Red Scare of 1919–1920, when Americans, fearful that the Bolshevik Revolution could spread to their country and resentful of rising prices, a wave of labor strikes, and a growing immigrant presence, were catapulted into an antiradical, anti-immigrant furor. As Vanzetti himself put it, "The jury were hating us" because it was "a time when there was a hysteria of resentment and hate against the foreigner, against slackers."

The conviction sparked a wave of protest among reformers and radicals, as well as artists, such as Ben Shahn, and writers, including the novelist John Dos Passos and the poet Edna St. Vincent Millay. The future Supreme Court justice Felix Frankfurter wrote a lengthy exposé for the *Atlantic Monthly* in 1927, in which he concluded that Judge Webster Thayer's handling of the case was characterized by "misquotations, misrepresentations, suppressions, and mutilations." A special commission appointed by the governor of Massachusetts, however, upheld the conduct of the trial and dismissed the evidence suggesting the pair's innocence. Both men were electrocuted in August 1927. Historians still debate the guilt of Sacco and Vanzetti, but most concur that the two men did not receive a fair trial and the case stands as an example of the excesses of the post–World War I Red Scare.

[*See also* **Anarchism; Anti-Communism; Frankfurter, Felix;** ***and*** **Radicalism.**]

BIBLIOGRAPHY

Russell, Francis. *Sacco and Vanzetti: The Case Resolved.* New York: Harper & Row, 1986.

Young, William, and David E. Kaiser. *Postmortem: New Evidence in the Case of Sacco and Vanzetti.* Amherst: University of Massachusetts Press, 1985.

Lynn Dumenil

SCALIA, ANTONIN

Antonin Scalia, associate justice of the U.S. Supreme Court (1986–present), was born 11 March 1936 in Trenton, New Jersey. He graduated with an AB from Georgetown University in 1957 and with an LLB from Harvard Law School in 1960. Before becoming a federal judge, he practiced law for six years, taught for twelve years on the law faculties of the universities of Virginia and Chicago, and served in the Nixon and Ford administrations, most notably as assistant attorney general for the Office of Legal Counsel from 1974 to 1977. He was confirmed to the U.S. Court of Appeals for the D.C. Circuit in 1982 and to the U.S. Supreme Court as associate justice in 1986.

In his jurisprudence, Scalia has generally tried to reinvigorate structural constitutionalism and limit individual rights to core guarantees. He has supported the unitary executive, insisting that the president have sole discretion to fire at will special prosecutors investigating executive wrongdoing (*Morrison v. Olson,* 1988). He has argued strenuously against construing constitutional due process guarantees to protect the rights to procure an abortion (*Planned Parenthood v. Casey,* 1992) or to engage in homosexual sodomy (*Lawrence v. Texas,* 2003).

In general, Scalia has reached these results by applying originalism. Indeed, Scalia has shaped originalism, convincing American conservative legal elites to conceive of it as the search not for "original intent" but rather for the "original public meaning" of controlling text (Scalia, 1986; Scalia, "Originalism," 1989; Scalia, 1997). Thus, to ascertain the meaning of the Second Amendment right to bear arms, Scalia searched for the most likely public meaning of the amendment to its intended audience at the time it was ratified (see *District of Columbia v. Heller,* 2009). So understood, originalism separates interpretation from a judge's personal policy preferences. Under the original meaning of the Fifth Amendment Self-Incrimination Clause, police do not need to issue *Miranda* right-of-counsel warnings to arrestees as long as they refrain from coercing confessions from the arrestees (*Dickerson v. United States,* 2000). Under the original meaning of the Sixth Amendment Confrontation Clause, however, courts must let criminal defendants cross-examine adverse witnesses, even when the witnesses are children previously abused sexually by the defendants, the witnesses are terrified to testify in open court, and the defendants will be acquitted without that testimony (*Maryland v. Craig,* 1990). Originalism requires a judge to apply both constructions although one leads to a law-and-order result and the other to a fairness-to-defendants result.

Scalia acknowledges that he is only a "faint-hearted originalist," however (Scalia, "Originalism," 1989), because he tempers his originalism with a competing attachment, to judicial restraint. Judicial restraint seeks to minimize the policy-making discretion judges exercise (see Claeys, 2011; Scalia, "Rule of Law," 1989). Thus, if long-established precedent construes the Necessary and Proper Clause broadly, Scalia will, too (*Gonzales v. Raich,* 2005). In relation to the nondelegation principle (which bars Congress from passing statutes that vest broad policy-making discretion in regulators), although Scalia finds it "difficult to imagine a principle more essential to democratic government," he refrains from supporting a judicial doctrine enforcing it aggressively. Because the doctrine requires context-sensitive determinations about how much discretion legislators may appropriately assign to executive offers or judges, "it is not [a doctrine] readily enforceable by the courts" (*Mistretta v. United States,* 1989).

[*See also* **Constitution; Ford, Gerald R.; Nixon, Richard M.;** ***and*** **Supreme Court, U.S.**]

BIBLIOGRAPHY

Claeys, Eric R. "Obamacare and the Limits of Judicial Conservatism," *National Affairs* 8 (Summer 2011): 56–76.

Rossum, Ralph A. *Antonin Scalia's Jurisprudence: Text and Tradition.* Lawrence: University Press of Kansas, 2006.

Scalia, Antonin. "Common-Law Courts in a Civil-Law System." In *A Matter of Interpretation: Federal Courts and the Law,* edited by Amy Gutmann, pp. 3–47. Princeton: Princeton University Press, 1997.

Scalia, Antonin. "Originalism: The Lesser Evil." *University of Cincinnati Law Review* 57 (1989): 849–865.

Scalia, Antonin. "The Rule of Law as a Law of Rules." *University of Chicago Law Review* 56 (1989): 1175–1188.

Scalia, Antonin. "Speech Before the Attorney General's Conference on Economic Liberties." In Office of Legal Policy, *Original Meaning: A Sourcebook,* p. 106. Washington, D.C.: U.S. Department of Justice, 1986.

Weizer, Paul I. *The Opinions of Justice Antonin Scalia: The Caustic Conservative.* New York: Peter Lang, 2004.

Eric R. Claeys

SCHECHTER POULTRY CORP. v. UNITED STATES

The National Industrial Recovery Act (NIRA), passed in 1933, was President Franklin Delano Roosevelt's major effort to combat the Great Depression. Among other things, the act authorized industry groups, operating through the National Recovery Administration (NRA), to establish codes of fair competition. These codes, subject to presidential approval, affected such matters as wages, hours, working conditions, and methods of competition.

The Schechter brothers, owners of a small Brooklyn slaughterhouse, were convicted of violating the Live Poultry Code on several counts, including selling diseased chicken and filing false sales and price reports. They appealed, and in a unanimous 1935 ruling, the Supreme Court declared the NIRA unconstitutional. Speaking for the Court, Chief Justice Charles Evans Hughes said that the law failed to provide adequate guidance concerning what matters the codes would cover. As a result, the NIRA unconstitutionally delegated legislative power to the executive branch. Hughes further argued that the poultry code violated the commerce clause of the Constitution (Article 1, Section 8). According to past cases, Congress could only regulate intrastate activity having a "direct" impact on interstate commerce. The Schechters' local commercial activity, Hughes noted, was clearly "indirect."

Although Roosevelt accused the Supreme Court of possessing an anachronistic view of the Constitution, he was not sorry to see the unwieldy and unworkable NRA dismantled. Indeed, the *Schechter* decision prompted more careful drafting of New Deal legislation in the future. Although this decision has not been explicitly overruled, later justices abandoned the nondelegation doctrine and the distinction between direct and indirect effects enunciated therein. Some scholars regarded this development as a necessary jurisprudential response to an increasingly complicated world. Others argued, however, that the Court has merely encouraged Congress to renounce its legislative duties.

[*See also* **Economic Policy: Regulation; Jurisprudence; National Recovery Administration; New Deal;** ***and*** **Roosevelt, Franklin Delano.**]

BIBLIOGRAPHY

McCloskey, Robert G. *The American Supreme Court,* 2d ed. Chicago: University of Chicago Press, 1994.

Jeffrey D. Hockett

SCHLAFLY, PHYLLIS

Phyllis Schlafly played an important role in the revival of the political right in America in the 1970s when she formed STOP ERA, a grassroots organization opposed to the Equal Rights Amendment (ERA). The ERA had passed Congress on 22 March 1972 and needed to be ratified by two-thirds of the states to become a constitutional amendment. Schlafly, a conservative activist within the Republican Party, brought other ERA opponents together to prevent ratification of the amendment. Schlafly remained active in conservative circles after the anti-ERA crusade through the establishment of her St. Louis–based organization Eagle Forum, a grassroots organization involved in "profamily" issues.

Schlafly was born in St. Louis, Missouri, on 15 August 1924. She grew up in a modest middle-class, Roman Catholic family in the Great Depression. When her father lost his job in 1930, her college-educated mother went to work as a librarian to support the family, including Schlafly and her younger sister. As valedictorian of her high school class, Schlafly received a full scholarship to a local Catholic college, but then transferred to Washington University in St. Louis where she majored in political science. To pay for tuition she took a full-time night job in a local ordnance plant, testing ammunition. After graduating Phi Beta Kappa in 1944, she accepted a graduate fellowship at Radcliffe College, where she earned an MA in government in 1945.

After Radcliffe, she moved to Washington, D.C., where she worked at the American Enterprise Institute. She then returned to St. Louis at the age of twenty-four to manage a successful campaign for a Republican congressman. While working as a librarian at a local bank, she married thirty-nine-year-old bachelor John F. Schlafly, a local attorney. They moved to Alton, Illinois, across the Mississippi River from St. Louis. They raised a family of three sons and two daughters. She ran unsuccessfully for Congress in 1952 and later in 1970.

In the 1950s and 1960s, Schlafly was active in various anti-Communist causes. She gained national attention as author of the best-seller *A Choice Not an Echo,* self-published in 1964 to promote the candidacy of Barry Goldwater, Jr., a conservative U.S. senator from Arizona. In 1967, she ran for the presidency of the Republican Federation of Women's Clubs. Although she lost this contest, her national network of supporters was mobilized to defeat

ERA ratification. The ERA simply declared, "Equality of rights under the law shall not be denied or abridged by the United States or by any State on account of sex." In organizing to defeat the ERA, Schlafly brought into her movement evangelical Christians, traditional Roman Catholics, and Mormons. This marked the beginnings of the emergence of the Christian Right, which revived the fortunes of the Republican Party that had been severely damaged when Richard Nixon resigned the White House in 1974 in the midst of the Watergate scandal. Schlafly's arguments against ERA made her into a national political figure. As conservative Illinois congressman Henry J. Hyde said, "Without her, I can say without a twinge of doubt, ERA would be part of the Constitution—unquestionably."

Following the defeat of ERA on 30 June 1982, Schlafly and her Eagle Forum became involved in education, antiabortion, immigration reform, and other social issues.

[*See also* **Anti-Communism;** *and* **Equal Rights Amendment.**]

BIBLIOGRAPHY

Critchlow, Donald T. *Phyllis Schlafly and Grassroots Conservatism*. Princeton, N.J.: Princeton University Press, 2005.

Donald T. Critchlow

SCOTT v. SANDFORD

In the 1830s, Dr. John Emerson took his slave, Dred Scott, to the free state of Illinois and then to Fort Snelling, in Wisconsin territory (now Minnesota), where the Missouri Compromise had prohibited slavery. In 1846, Scott sued Emerson's widow to gain his freedom. A Missouri court freed him in 1850, ruling that he had become free while living in Illinois and at Fort Snelling. This decision conformed to a long line of earlier cases in Missouri, other states, and England. In 1852 the Missouri Supreme Court reversed the lower court, and in 1854 Scott took his case to the federal courts, suing his new owner, John Sanford (the name is misspelled "Sandford" in the official report of the case), under the clause in Article 3, Section 2, of the U.S. Constitution that allows a citizen of one state to sue a citizen of another state in federal court. As a "citizen of Missouri," Scott argued, he could sue Sanford, a New Yorker, in federal court. In opposing this suit, Sanford rejected Scott's claim to citizenship "because he is a negro of African descent; his ancestors were of pure African blood, and were brought into this country and sold as negro slaves."

Federal district judge Robert W. Wells ruled that if Scott were free he could sue as a citizen of Missouri. However, on the merits of the case, Wells held that Scott was still a slave. Scott then appealed to the U.S. Supreme Court, where, in an aggressively proslavery majority opinion, Chief Justice Roger B. Taney held that the Missouri Compromise was unconstitutional because it deprived Southerners of their property in slaves without due process of law or just compensation, in violation of the Fifth Amendment. Taney also denied that African Americans could ever be U.S. citizens. Ignoring that free black men in a number of states could vote when the Constitution was ratified, Taney declared that blacks were not included under the word "citizens" in the Constitution. According to him, blacks were "so far inferior, that they had no rights which the white man was bound to respect."

This decision shocked many Northerners, who had long seen the Missouri Compromise as a barrier against the expansion of slavery and a means of accommodating sectional differences. Abraham Lincoln attacked it in his

1858 debates with Stephen A. Douglas and again during the 1860 presidential campaign.

The Lincoln Administration and the Civil War Congress ignored the Dred Scott decision. During the war, Congress banned slavery in the western territories, and the Fourteenth Amendment, ratified in 1868, declared all native-born persons citizens of the United States and of the state in which they lived.

[*See also* **Antislavery Movement; Bill of Rights; Civil Rights; Civil Rights Legislation; Compromise of 1820; Constitution; Douglas, Stephen A.; Due Process: Procedural Process; Fourteenth Amendment; Lincoln, Abraham; Lincoln–Douglas Debates; Slavery, Laws; Supreme Court, U.S.;** ***and*** **Taney, Roger B.**]

BIBLIOGRAPHY

Fehrenbacher, Don E. *The Dred Scott Case: Its Significance in American Law and Politics*. New York: Oxford University Press, 1978.

Finkelman, Paul. *Scott v. Sandford: A Brief History with Documents*. Boston: Bedford Books, 1997.

Paul Finkelman

SEARCH AND SEIZURE

The relationship between American search and seizure law and history reveals complexity because policy imperatives have changed dramatically over time. Consequently, radically different opinions exist about the implications of Anglo-American search and seizure history. Most pertinent are controversies and practices concerning writs of assistance and revenue law enforcement; search warrant jurisprudence and procedure, including the invalidation of general warrants; and struggles regarding the status of protected spaces, including but not limited to the home.

Writs of assistance are often referred to as general warrants because officials claimed wide-ranging search authority under them. Writs, however, were not warrants. Warrants provide search or seizure authority. Writs, technically, did not. Writs, creatures of statute, were documents that required bystanders to help officers, upon demand, in the execution of their duty. Writs were used to justify general searches during enforcement of customs laws, with both British and colonial officers claiming extant search authority under the statutory authority that authorized their commissions. Colonial resistance to the legitimacy of these writs became heated in the 1760s, leading Great Britain to promulgate the 1767 Townshend Act to formally legalize the writs in the colonies. The strategy was mostly unsuccessful because colonial judges often continued to resist issuing the writs, especially unparticularized ones. It is widely accepted that colonial hostility to writs of assistance was one animating cause of the Revolution and a catalyst for the Fourth Amendment.

Judges in Great Britain successfully challenged the monarch's authority to search under general warrants, which further strengthened the colonial movement for greater search protections. In 1763, John Wilkes, an outspoken Parliamentarian, anonymously published a pamphlet critical of King George III and his ministry. The secretary of state, Lord Halifax, deemed this a seditious libel and issued a general warrant calling for a "strict and diligent search for the authors printers and publishers" of the pamphlet (he also issued several other general warrants against other allegedly seditious publications). The warrants did nothing to limit search discretion because they failed to provide any meaningful narrowing instructions. Wilkes and about fifty other search targets launched a litigation campaign and between 1763 and 1769 won trespass lawsuits and significant damages from juries, with British courts ruling such general warrants void. American colonists already esteemed Wilkes because he had steadfastly supported them, and his acclaim only increased after the litigations. The Wilkes dispute was widely publicized in the colonies and is thought to have strongly influenced the Framers and their views about legitimate governmental search authority, such as the invalidity of general warrants and the concomitant prerequisite of particularity for valid warrants, a requirement included in the Fourth Amendment.

Certain aspects of search warrant procedure during the early part of our nationhood are unfamiliar or uncertain. Abundant evidence indicates that probable cause, another Fourth Amendment warrant requirement, was an immature concept that could be satisfied under terms unacceptable today, such as merely being a night-walker or living an idle, vagrant, and disorderly life. Whether judges had a well-established duty to independently assess the adequacy of probable cause prior to issuing search and arrest warrants is debatable. Judges in our early history often may have viewed their role in issuing warrants as largely ministerial, with the validity of the warrant subject to an ex post determination through a trespass action in which the jury had the primary duty of assessing probable cause. The U.S. Supreme Court did not clearly enumerate a strong ex ante judicial sentryship duty until *Nathanson v. United States* (1933) (although it was implicit in *Byars v. United States* (1927)), a duty it felt compelled to reiterate in *Giordenello v. United States* (1958).

Quite unclear in the historical record is how far constitutional search protections extended. The home has been the paradigmatic example of a protected space. But the rhetorical power of the ancient maxim that "a man's house is his castle" has always surpassed the actual protections extended. The first British judicial decision to echo the maxim, *Semayne's Case* (1603), carefully preserved the king's authority to search homes. Since the latter half of the twentieth century, the U.S. Supreme Court has authorized warrantless and even suspicionless searches of homes for many reasons, such as for regulatory purposes (e.g., *Griffin v. Wisconsin* (1987) (probationer's home); *Wyman v. James* (1971) (welfare home inspections)) or when police are engaged in community caretaking (e.g., *Brigham City, Utah v. Stuart* (2006)).

The scope of constitutional search protections for other spaces, as well as what role history should play in defining them, is even less certain. For example, ships would seem to fall outside the Fourth Amendment's textual protections for "persons, houses, papers, and effects" because they could qualify only as "effects," an unnatural reading. Yet, early American statutes extended varying levels of search protections to ships and their contents. What meaning to attribute to this is unclear because the statutes, some promulgated close in time to the Fourth Amendment, may have incorporated constitutional values. More difficult are automobiles and even worse are modern intangibles such as electronic communications.

A great difficulty in using history as a guide to current search and seizure protections is that changing conditions have fundamentally altered guiding imperatives. In the Framers' era, the concern was with protecting against governmental power, and thus search and seizure law was designed to limit governmental discretion. As time advanced and new developments confronted us, such as the move from rural to urban life and the rise of technology that vastly increased the harm one individual can inflict, as well as the interest in surveillance, the concern became assuring adequate governmental power to protect the public from third parties, and thus search and seizure law has moved dramatically in the direction of expanding governmental discretion.

These tensions are only likely to increase, so troubling and difficult search and seizure issues will persist. Additionally, the search and seizure history of other potentially important periods, such as Reconstruction and Prohibition, have more recently begun to be mined, so there may be more history to consider as we struggle to appropriately formulate our Fourth Amendment jurisprudence.

BIBLIOGRAPHY

Amar, Akhil Reed. "Fourth Amendment First Principles." *Harvard Law Review* 107 (1994): 757–819.

Arcila, Jr., Fabio. "The Death of Suspicion." *William & Mary Law Review* 51 (2010): 1275–1341.

Cuddihy, William J. *The Fourth Amendment: Origins and Original Meaning 602–1791*. New York: Oxford University Press, 2009.

Davies, Thomas Y. "Recovering the Original Fourth Amendment." *Michigan Law Review* 98 (1999): 547–750.

Dickerson, O. M. "Writs of Assistance as a Cause of the Revolution." In *The Era of the American Revolution: Studies Inscribed to Evarts Boutell Greene*, edited by Richard B. Morris, pp. 40–75. New York: Columbia University Press, 1939.

Lasson, Nelson B. *The History and Development of the Fourth Amendment to the United States Constitution*. New York: Da Copo Press, 1937.

Maclin, Tracey. "The Complexity of the Fourth Amendment: A Historical Review." *Boston University Law Review* 77 (1997): 925–974.

Sklansky, David A. "The Fourth Amendment and Common Law." *Columbia Law Review* 100 (2000): 1739–1814.

Taslitz, Andrew E. *Reconstructing the Fourth Amendment: A History of Search and Seizure, 1789–1869*. New York: New York University Press, 2006.

Thomas, George C., III. "Time Travel, Hovercrafts, and the Framers: James Madison Sees the Future and Rewrites the Fourth Amendment." *Notre Dame Law Review* 80 (2005): 1451–1518.

Fabio Arcila, Jr.

SECOND AMENDMENT

The Second Amendment reads: "A well regulated Militia, being necessary to the security of a free State, the right of the people to keep and bear Arms, shall not be infringed." These words have generated considerable controversy as part of the broader debate over gun control. Proponents of stricter controls generally contend that the amendment was meant to protect the collective right of states to maintain militia units. Their opponents respond that the amendment was intended to protect an individual right, noting that in the eighteenth century the militia was composed of the entire free white male population, who were expected to muster bearing their own arms.

This lively debate notwithstanding, the Supreme Court has only considered Second Amendment claims in a handful of cases. One reason is that for much of American history there were few regulations concerning firearms ownership. The settlers of colonial America were heirs to the English tradition of distrust of standing armies and professional police forces as dangerous to individual liberty. The English tradition of relying on the armed yeomanry both to enforce laws and to protect the realm from external enemies was reinforced in the colonial era. The need to defend settlements against Native Americans and the armies of other European powers led to the deputization of the entire white population. Colonial statutes required all white men, with few exceptions, to both keep arms and bear them in militia formations. The American Revolution strengthened the traditional suspicion of standing armies and reinforced the view that militias composed of armed citizenry were the best way to guarantee both security and liberty.

Like the rest of the Bill of Rights, the Second Amendment was an attempt to answer the objections of anti-Federalists who charged that the new Constitution would be used to deprive the people of rights traditionally considered among the rights of Englishmen. Statements by the amendment's principal author, James Madison, indicate that he saw the amendment as protecting the arms of the population at large.

The antebellum era brought no Second Amendment cases before the Supreme Court. The few firearms regulations that existed were primarily statutes in the slave states prohibiting African Americans from possessing firearms. Some antebellum state statutes prohibited the carrying of concealed weapons, but those laws were not the subject of Supreme Court scrutiny. The Court's holding in *Barron v. Baltimore* (1833) that the Bill of Rights only limited federal action effectively precluded Supreme Court review of state restrictions. Although the Court did not rule on the amendment before the Civil War, statements by Justice Joseph Story and Chief Justice Roger Taney expressed the then-prevailing view. Story in his *Commentaries on the Constitution of the United States* (1833) offered the opinion that the right to keep and bear arms provided a "strong moral check against the usurpation and arbitrary power of rulers" (pp. 746–747). Taney in *Scott v. Sandford* (1857) listed the right to own and carry arms as one of the rights of citizenship.

The aftermath of the Civil War brought a new dimension to the history of the amendment. The Black Codes, enacted in Southern states immediately after the war, limited the civil rights of the newly freed slaves, including the right to own firearms. These codes helped spur the passage of the Fourteenth Amendment. A number of the framers expressed the view that the new amendment would require the states to honor the Bill of Rights, including the Second Amendment.

Despite this, the Court continued to adhere to the holding in Barron. The two principal postbellum cases involving Second Amendment claims, *United States v. Cruikshank* (1876) and *Presser v. Illinois* (1886), tell us at least as much about the Court's early reaction to the Fourteenth Amendment as they do about the Second. In *Cruikshank*, the Court, in an opinion authored by Justice Joseph P. Bradley, held that the Second and Fourteenth amendments did not give Congress the authority to legislate against private interference with the right to bear arms. The Court in *Presser* declared that the Second Amendment only protected individuals from federal and not state infringement.

The Court thus entered the twentieth century adhering to the view that the Second Amendment only limited federal power. That view, coupled with the virtual absence of federal firearms regulation, left the Court with little to say on the topic. That changed with the violence generated during Prohibition. Responding to the increase in organized crime in the 1920s and 1930s, Congress passed the National Firearms Act of 1934. The act, which provided for taxation and registration of automatic weapons and sawed-off shotguns, generated the principal Second Amendment case, *United States v. Miller* (1939). The unanimous opinion, authored by Justice James C. McReynolds, noted that the Second Amendment did not protect the right of citizens to own firearms that were not ordinary militia weapons. As the defendant in *Miller* had been charged with possession of an unregistered sawed-off shotgun, the Court noted that it had no evidence that such a weapon constituted ordinary militia equipment.

Since *Miller*, the Supreme Court has not directly addressed the issue. Lower federal courts have upheld firearms regulations against Second Amendment claims, sometimes applying the collective rights theory, at other times on the grounds that the amendment does not apply to the states. The Court has not reviewed these decisions. In the 1970s and 1980s a number of justices expressed support for the collective rights view in out-of-court statements or in dicta. More recently, Chief Justice William Rehnquist and Justices Antonin Scalia and Clarence Thomas, also in dicta or in out-of-court statements, appear to have endorsed individual rights readings of the amendment. The right to possess arms has also been listed among the rights of American people in some privacy cases. None of these statements can be viewed as definitive evidence of the Court's position on the issue.

Despite the Court's institutional reticence, a vigorous debate rages in other forums. Since the 1980s the amendment has been the subject of a growing body of literature in law and history journals. This debate has influenced jurists in some lower federal courts. In *United States v. Emerson* (2001), the Fifth Circuit recognized the Second Amendment as an individual right although sustaining a federal statute restricting firearms possession in cases involving domestic violence. In 2002 Attorney General John Ashcroft stated his view that the amendment protected an individual right although leaving broad room for firearms regulation.

It is not clear how much longer the Court can maintain its silence. Although overall restrictions on firearms ownership remain relatively slight, there are a number of fairly restrictive jurisdictions. The battle over gun control has also become a perennial feature of American political life. Widespread firearms ownership coupled with strong demands for stricter gun controls ensures that the debate over the Second Amendment will remain lively; it is a debate that the Supreme Court will ultimately be forced to enter.

[*See also* **Anti-Federalists; Bill of Rights; Civil Rights; Civil Rights Legislation; Constitution; Fourteenth Amendment; Gun Control; Madison, James; Rehnquist, William; Scalia, Antonin;** ***Scott v. Sandford;*** **Story, Joseph;** ***and*** **Taney, Roger B.**]

BIBLIOGRAPHY

Cottrol, R. J., and R. T. Diamond. "The Second Amendment: Toward an Afro-Americanist Reconsideration." *Georgetown Law Journal* 80 (1991): 309–361.

Kates, D. B., Jr. "Handgun Prohibition and the Original Meaning of the Second Amendment." *Michigan Law Review* 82 (1983): 204–273.

Levinson, S. L. "The Embarrassing Second Amendment." *Yale Law Journal* 99 (1989): 637–659.

Malcolm, J. L. *To Keep and Bear Arms: The Origins of an Anglo-American Right.* Cambridge, Mass.: Harvard University Press, 1994.

Robert J. Cottrol

SECRET SERVICE, U.S.

Founded on 14 April 1865 as one of the last executive acts of President Abraham Lincoln, the U.S. Secret Service was created to combat and investigate the burgeoning world of counterfeiters that emerged during the Civil War. Despite this mission occupying the agency's long history, the duties of the Secret Service—as the only investigative federal police agency from 1865 to 1908—gradually expanded to include extralegal functions such as espionage, presidential protection, and the investigation of innumerable crimes against the federal government. With this expansion, the Secret Service and its agents played a critical role in expanding the federal government's authority. The Secret Service's expression of national authority, however, has fallen under the congressional microscope when the agency failed in its mission or abused its powers.

The origins of the Secret Service can be traced to the complexities of the war economy of the Civil War. In the winter of 1862,

Congress passed the Legal Tender Act that allowed the federal government to print nearly $150 million dollars of paper money or so-called "greenbacks" and pay its wartime debts with the printed money, but it also opened the door for enterprising criminals to print and distribute counterfeit money in the Union. At the war's end in April 1865, still one-third of the money in circulation was counterfeited, which posed a significant risk to the economy. As a result, Hugh McCulloch, the newly appointed secretary of the treasury, recommended to Lincoln to establish a special commission to investigate the merits of forming a national police force to prevent and eliminate counterfeiting operations. The commission made its report in April 1865 urging the organization of a police force. Moreover, unlike the Postal Inspection Service and the Federal Marshals that were formed specifically by an act of Congress, the Secret Service was formed through an executive function by the solicitor's office in the Treasury Department, not Congress. Without congressional approval, the agency derived its statutory authority through appropriations bills. The agency's hurried genesis enabled Congress to keep close tabs on the agency, and, most importantly, portended future conflicts over the agency's increasing autonomy and extralegal activities.

Congress seemingly tolerated the agency's increasing autonomy from 1865 to 1874 because its operatives continued to produce satisfactory results, but conflict between Congress and the Secret Service came to a head in 1874. Hiram C. Whitley, Secret Service chief from 1869 to 1874, illegally used the agency's resources and his position in an attempt to frame a troublesome and prominent Washingtonian with a phony crime. Congress led an investigation and urged Treasury solicitor Bluford Wilson to conduct his own investigation. As a result of these inquests, Wilson fired Whitley and all of the operatives. Wilson also sought to tame the agency's increasing autonomy. He changed the function of the chief from detective to administrator, moved the agency's headquarters from New York to Washington, and hired new operatives with previous experience.

For nearly 20 years, the Secret Service and its administration worked to resurrect itself from its fall from grace. The agency employed better tactics to eliminate counterfeiting, worked closely with local and state law enforcement agencies, established offices in nearly every major city in the United States, and maintained a centralized information network. Other government departments recognized the value of the Secret Service and "hired out" operatives to conduct a wide range of investigations on their behalf. Operatives were even employed to infiltrate the Commonweal Army (Coxey's Army) in the spring of 1894 to investigate and report whether the mass of disgruntled marchers posed a threat to the nation's security. Since then, the Secret Service became an integral part of the federal government's regulatory and investigative arm as its agents were used during the Spanish–American War, land fraud investigations, and even thefts committed in the Library of Congress.

These extralegal activities attracted the ire of Congress in 1908. Since 1906, it had been rumored that President Theodore Roosevelt employed the Secret Service to investigate congressman who disagreed with his policies. While such charges may have been embellished by the president's critics, archival evidence does suggest that the president did use the Secret Service for political purposes during the New York mayoral contest of 1903 to watch "certain . . . Republican leaders" and their relationship with Tammany Hall, the Democratic Party machine. Roosevelt also deployed the Secret Service to vigorously investigate frauds committed on the government, even when the culprits were elected officials. In 1905, three congressional lawmakers from Oregon were under investigation for land fraud by a Secret Service officer loaned to the Land Office to conduct the investigation. Because the appropriation laws did not authorize the use of the Secret Service in any other manner except in the prevention of counterfeiting, the House Appropriations Committee found the hiring out of agents unsavory and limited the agency's activities through its appropriation. This spurred a political fight between Congress and Roosevelt, which ended in the president's censure by the House. Out of this conflict, however, the Federal Bureau of Investigation was created.

Near the turn of the century, the Secret Service began protecting the president and the president's family. Beginning in 1894 and as a direct result of labor violence, social unrest, and threats against the lives of President Grover Cleveland and his family, First Lady Frances Folsom Cleveland requested that Secret Service officers be assigned to guard the first family at their private home in Massachusetts. This obviously fell outside the realm of the Secret Service's responsibilities because the agency did not have statutory authority to guard the president. But with this request, the Clevelands institutionalized presidential protection for later administrations. The Secret Service was used to guard William McKinley during and after the Spanish–American War, but the three Secret Service officers assigned to protect the president at the Pan-American Exposition in Buffalo, New York, failed to safeguard his life when anarchist Leon Czolgosz shot the president on 6 September 1901. The agency drew intense criticism for McKinley's murder, but out of his death, Congress temporarily allowed the Secret Service to protect future presidents. The Secret Service also crafted new tactics to ensure the safety of the president and groomed close relationships with other federal agencies in the name of the president's security. The agency operated under arrangement until 1907 when Congress formally approved presidential protection as one of the Secret Service's responsibilities. Congress permanently authorized protection for the president and the president-elect six years later in the agency's yearly appropriations bills. In 1951, after the assassination attempt on President Harry S. Truman by Puerto Rican nationalists, Congress passed legislation that permanently established the Secret Service and defined presidential protection as one of its two major responsibilities. Following the assassination of President John F. Kennedy by assassin Lee Harvey Oswald in November 1963, the agency underwent a major transformation as the Warren Commission, charged with investigating the murder, recommended changes in the agency's protocols. A new training center was established, and new protective procedures were installed. Despite these new practices, twenty years later, President Ronald Reagan was attacked by John F. Hinckley Jr. The Secret Service again amended its protection procedures and established new directives.

The Secret Service's mission expanded from its dual mission of protection and anticounterfeiting after the terrorist attacks in New York City and Washington, D.C., on 11 September 2001. As part of the Patriot Act passed in October 2001, the agency was transferred from the Treasury Department to the new Department of Homeland Security in 2003. The Patriot Act also required that the Secret Service establish electronic crimes task forces throughout the nation. These task forces were specifically designed to secure the infrastructure of the nation's financial systems and detect computer-based crimes. Today, there are twenty-four task forces in existence. Since its transfer to the Department of Homeland Security, the Secret Service has made 29,000 arrests and has seized approximately $300 million dollars in counterfeit money.

[*See also* **Cleveland, Grover; Federal Bureau of Investigation; Kennedy, John F.; Lincoln, Abraham; McKinley, William; Patriot Act, The; Reagan, Ronald; Roosevelt, Theodore;** *and* **Truman, Harry S.**]

BIBLIOGRAPHY

Blaine, Gerald, Lisa McCubbin, and Clint Hill. *The Kennedy Detail: JFK's Secret Service Agents Break Their Silence.* New York: Gallery Books, 2010.

Bowen, Walter, and Harry Neal. *The United States Secret Service.* Philadelphia: Philadelphia Chilton Co., 1960.

Johnson, David R. *Illegal Tender: Counterfeiting and the Secret Service in Nineteenth-Century America.* Washington, D.C.: Smithsonian Institution Press, 1995.

Mihm, Stephen. *A Nation of Counterfeiters: Capitalists, Con Men, and the Making of the United States.* Cambridge, Mass.: Harvard University Press, 2007.

Matthew C. Sherman

SECURITIES AND EXCHANGE COMMISSION

Established by the Securities Exchange Act of 1934, the Securities and Exchange Commission (SEC) was given broad authority to regulate stock exchanges, brokers, and dealers. The previous year, President Franklin Delano Roosevelt had urged Congress to mandate "full and fair disclosure" of all new security issues and to require sellers to provide accurate information. Meanwhile, the Senate Banking and Currency Committee, directed by chief counsel Ferdinand Pecora, uncovered evidence of fraud, corruption, and gross misrepresentation in the buying and selling of securities.

In response, Congress passed the Securities Act of 1933, requiring all companies issuing stock to file with the Federal Trade Commission detailed information regarding their business and financial condition. Barraged with business complaints that the 1933 law was too intrusive, in the 1934 measure Congress limited the law's scope and transferred its administration to the newly created SEC. Five commissioners, with no more than three coming from a single political party, would oversee the new agency. The SEC required stock exchanges and investment companies had to register and provide annual financial reports. For many companies this was the first time financial reports were publicly available. The SEC later gained additional regulatory authority through the Public Utility Holding Company Act (1935), the Investment Companies Act (1940), the Investment Advisers Act (1940), and other measures. In 1977, the SEC mandated an end to fixed broker commissions and, in 1988, gained new authority over stock-index futures. As a quasi-judicial agency, the SEC's decisions can be appealed in federal court.

After the accounting fraud in Enron, Tyco International, and WorldCom, the Sarbanes–Oxley Act of 2002 restored investor confidence by making corporate leaders responsible for their financial statements. The SEC is responsible for ensuring companies follow the new regulations. SEC chairman created the Public Accounting Oversight Board, which served as an external auditor for public companies ensuring the accounting accuracy.

Two oversight failures would taint the SEC's reputation in monitoring the markets. In 2008 Bernard L. Madoff Investment Securities was revealed to be a Ponzi scheme, making it one of the largest cases of financial fraud in history. The SEC investigated Madoff in 1992, but found no evidence of fraud. Since 1999 they had been receiving letters from a whistleblower detailing potential illegal activities, but the SEC declined to investigate.

The SEC was highly criticized during the financial crisis. Chairman Christopher Cox received criticism for not taking part in the Federal Reserve and Treasury Department's efforts to prevent the collapse of Bear Stearns. Their hands-off policy of government regulation was blamed for the unchecked markets for mortgage-backed securities and credit default swaps. In 2008 the SEC prohibited naked short selling to control market volatility.

[*See also* **Economic Policy: Regulation; Federal Trade Commission; Public Utilities Policy: Federal;** ***and*** **Roosevelt, Franklin Delano.**]

BIBLIOGRAPHY

Geisst, Charles R. *Wall Street; A History: From Its Beginning to the Fall of Enron*. Oxford; New York: Oxford University Press, 1997.

Parrish, Michael E. *Securities Regulation and the New Deal*. New Haven, Conn.: Yale University Press, 1970.

Seligman, Joel. *The Transformation of Wall Street: A History of the Securities and Exchange Commission and Modern Corporate Finance*. Boston: Houghton Mifflin, 1982.

John D. Buenker and Andrea Field

SEDITION

Also known as seditious libel, this crime initially covered any "dangerous words" threatening the authority of the state, the sanctity of its laws, or the reputation of its officers. Under the interpretation of seditious libel that emerged during the seventeenth century, judges determined the "law of the case" (whether a statement or publication was seditious), permitted juries to determine only the "facts of the case" (whether the defendant has expressed the words), and disallowed evidence of truth as a defense.

During the eighteenth century, an alternative interpretation emerged. The guarantees of freedom of speech and press, critics insisted, required that juries determine the seditious nature of political statements and that truth constitute a defense. The Federalist Party incorporated these ideas, which had emerged in the 1735 Zenger trial, into the Sedition Act of 1798. Jeffersonians tried under this law, however, found it useless to argue either the nonseditious quality of their words or their truth to Federalist judges and juries. Although some Jeffersonian lawyers argued that the First Amendment barred any federal prosecution for sedition, the Sedition Act expired in 1801 without a Supreme Court ruling on its validity.

Attempts to suppress dissent, especially during wartime, revived debates over the issue of sedition in the twentieth century. The 1918 Sedition Law restricted criticism of U.S. participation in World War I. The Smith Act (1940), passed on the eve of U.S. entry into World War II, made it a crime to advocate or teach the desirability of violently overthrowing the government. The Supreme Court upheld these laws' constitutionality but divided over how they should be applied. The more libertarian justices, building on Justice Oliver Wendell Holmes Jr.'s, dissent in *Abrams v. United States* (1919), insisted that the government could criminalize political speech only if it posed a "clear and present danger" of "substantive" harm to the state. This position, suggesting that speech could not be criminalized solely on the basis of its allegedly dangerous content, remained contested, however, especially when the Court heard cases involving Communist Party members during the 1950s.

Important rulings during the next decade, however, translated the libertarian position into constitutional doctrine. In two 1964 political libel cases (*New York Times v. Sullivan* and *Garrison v. Louisiana*), the Court ruled that the Sedition Act of 1798 had violated the First Amendment's "core meaning"—"a profound national commitment to the principle that debate on public issues should be uninhibited, robust, and wide open." In *Brandenburg v. Ohio* (1969), the Court held that only words intended to incite or produce "imminent lawless action" could, in light of the First Amendment, be the object of criminal sanctions. These decisions effectively denied the legitimacy of prosecuting "dangerous" political discourse, the core notion in the old crime of sedition.

[*See also* **Abrams v. United States; Alien and Sedition Acts; Anti-Communism; Bill of Rights; Censorship; Federalist Party; Holmes, Oliver Wendell, Jr.;** ***New York Times v. United States;*** *and* **Zenger Trial.**]

BIBLIOGRAPHY

Kalven, Harry, Jr. *A Worthy Tradition: Free Speech in America*. New York: Harper & Row, 1988.

Rosenberg, Norman L. *Protecting the Best Men: An Interpretive History of the Law of Libel.* Chapel Hill: University of North Carolina Press, 1990.

Norman L. Rosenberg

SEGREGATION

The southern social, economic, and political system that enforced the separation of races from the post-Reconstruction era to the mid-twentieth century. Racial segregation was also called "Jim Crow," an expression derived from the caricatured portrayal of blacks in antebellum minstrel shows. By the 1890s, however, Jim Crow had come to describe the segregation, social control, and political and economic subjugation of black people in the South. Upheld by the Supreme Court in *Plessy v. Ferguson* (1896) and other decisions, segregation persisted until challenged by the anticolonialist politics of World War II and the postwar civil rights movement.

Whereas C. Vann Woodward's *The Strange Career of Jim Crow* (1955) launched a debate over the origins and nature of racial segregation in the South, comparative studies of segregation in South Africa and the American South by John W. Cell and George Frederickson linked the phenomenon to a broader white-supremacist ideology and demonstrated its variation over space and time. In America, restrictive customs and practices designed to separate the races were first devised by whites of the antebellum North in the 1840s. As the historian Leon Litwack has noted, many abolitionist newspapers used the term "segregation" to describe separate facilities for blacks and whites in Northern cities.

Segregation Imposed. After the Civil War, southern whites unwilling to accept the social and political equality of freedmen adopted the practice of segregation. The earliest postwar southern legislatures passed restrictive laws to maintain the prewar racial hierarchy and secure a cheap labor force perpetually tied to the land. These so-called Black Codes were overturned as radical Republicans took charge of Reconstruction, but in their place arose a system of sharecropping, crop lien, disfranchisement, and violent repression. African Americans struggled against the poverty and degradation born of tenancy and sharecropping, but as northern attitudes shifted, federal troops left, the southern Democratic Party revived, and the Ku Klux Klan and other racist organizations inaugurated a reign of terror, conditions very similar to slavery took root.

Many historians hold that Jim Crow was already so firmly entrenched by custom that the rise of *de jure* segregation in the late nineteenth and early twentieth centuries merely ratified the prevailing situation. The historian Howard Rabinowitz, for example, has found that Baton Rouge, Atlanta, Charlotte, Birmingham, and other Southern cities excluded free blacks from militias, education, and welfare services in the antebellum and immediate post–Civil War Eras. Although radical legislators, Reconstruction officials, and black political leaders favored racially integrated facilities, fears of further antagonizing white Southerners inhibited their efforts, and neither Republicans nor black legislatures proposed constitutional or legislative measures for achieving that goal. Indeed, as black churches, fraternal organizations, and mutual-aid societies proliferated, patterns of voluntary racial separation arose. Government, political, and judicial bodies were often the only integrated institutions in the Reconstruction South.

By the 1880s, however, railroads and streetcars, involving close contact between black and white passengers, became the focus of challenges to segregation. Amid growing racial tensions, exacerbated by urbanization and industrialization, Southern state legislatures enacted railroad separate-car laws that reshaped the region's social and political landscape. Blacks vigorously resisted. Prominent African American business and professional leaders staged boycotts and sued railroads, insisting on equal access, but to little avail. After the U.S. Supreme Court in 1883 sharply restricted the 1875 Civil Rights Act and sanctioned the separate-but-equal doctrine in *Plessy v. Ferguson,* a torrent of segregation laws increasingly regulated all black–white contact throughout the South, banning or sharply restricting black access to public and private facilities including schools, theaters, hotels, parks, libraries, and the like. Simultaneously, employers and labor leaders blocked blacks' access to skilled jobs, limiting them to unskilled, semiskilled, or domestic occupations.

The spread of segregation and deteriorating race relations in the 1890s arose from Southern white fears of racial mixing and miscegenation and from a desire to curb black aspirations for education and property. It coincided with an epidemic of lynchings; antiblack riots in Atlanta, New Orleans, East St. Louis, Tulsa, and other cities; discrimination against black soldiers, as in the Brownsville incident; and the propagation of racist ideas by politicians such as Benjamin Tillman, James K. Vardaman, and Thomas Watson and writers such as Thomas Nelson Page and Thomas Dixon, whose 1905 novel *The Clansman* inspired D. W. Griffith's racist movie *The Birth of a Nation*. The legal imposition of strict racial segregation was also paralleled by a campaign of black disfranchisement through intimidation and terror; state constitutional amendments (in Mississippi, South Carolina, and Georgia); and poll taxes, literacy tests, property and residency requirements, and other devices intended to circumvent the Fifteenth Amendment.

Segregation Challenged. Black southerners responded to these developments in a variety of ways. Some embraced Booker T. Washington's strategy of conciliation, racial uplift, and group solidarity. Others, such as Ida B. Wells-Barnett and W. E. B. Du Bois, advocated militant challenges to the racist assumptions underpinning segregation. Still others, such as Bishop Henry M. Turner (1834–1915) of the African Methodist Episcopal Church, West African chief Alfred Sam, and Marcus Garvey, stressed racial solidarity, ethnic pride, and emigration to Africa. Whereas novelists from Charles Chesnutt (1858–1932) to Langston Hughes, Zora Neale Hurston, and Richard Wright, along with a host of African American ragtime, blues, and jazz musicians, implicitly challenged segregation by underscoring African Americans' cultural contribution to the nation as a whole, millions of Southern blacks voted with their feet by moving north.

Amid black migration northward, the growing importance of the black vote, and the rising political awareness of African peoples worldwide in the 1920s and 1930s, African

Americans fashioned a viable critique of the South's white-supremacist and segregationist ideology. The international and domestic politics that developed from this transformed perspective underlay the Supreme Court's landmark 1954 *Brown v. Board of Education* decision outlawing racial segregation in public schools and fueled the black freedom struggles of the 1950s and 1960s. By 1965 racial segregation had been all but dismantled throughout the South. The promise of economic, social, and political equality in the region—and the nation—however, has yet to be fulfilled.

[*See also* **Antislavery Movement; *Brown v. Board of Education;* Civil Rights; Civil Rights Legislation; Du Bois, W. E. B.; Equality; Fifteenth Amendment; King, Martin Luther, Jr.; Ku Klux Klan; National Association for the Advancement of Colored People; New Deal; *Plessy v. Ferguson;* Poverty; Progressive Era; Reconstruction; Southern Christian Leadership Conference; Trotter, William Monroe;** *and* **Washington, Booker T.**]

BIBLIOGRAPHY

Brundage, William Fitzhugh. *Lynching in the New South: Georgia and Virginia, 1880–1930*. Urbana: University of Illinois Press, 1993.

Cell, John W. *The Highest Stage of White Supremacy: The Origins of Segregation in South Africa and the American South*. Cambridge, UK; New York: Cambridge University Press, 1982.

Levine, Lawrence W. *Black Culture and Black Consciousness: Afro-American Folk Thought from Slavery to Freedom*. New York: Oxford University Press, 1977.

Litwack, Leon F. *Trouble in Mind: Black Southerners in the Age of Jim Crow*. New York: Alfred A. Knopf, 1998.

Rabinowitz, Howard N. *Race Relations in the Urban South, 1865–1980*. New York: Oxford University Press, 1978.

White, Deborah Gray. *Too Heavy a Load: Black Women in Defense of Themselves, 1894–1994*. New York: W. W. Norton, 2000.

Woodward, C. Vann. *The Strange Career of Jim Crow*, 3d ed. New York: Oxford University Press, 1955; rep. 1974.

Robert F. Jefferson

SENECA FALLS WOMEN'S RIGHTS CONVENTION OF 1848

The Seneca Falls Women's Rights Convention, held on 19 and 20 July 1848 at the Wesleyan Chapel in Seneca Falls, New York, was the first convention in the United States specifically called to discuss women's social, civil, and religious rights. Although the published meeting call did not mention women's political rights, the introduction of a resolution demanding woman suffrage was the convention's most contentious and most enduring legacy.

The village of Seneca Falls, located in central New York State, was at the heart of reform politics in the mid-nineteenth century. Many active reformers in the abolition and temperance movements as well as many progressive religious reformers of the Quaker faith also lived in the village and the neighboring town of Waterloo.

On 9 July 1848, Philadelphia Quaker and nationally recognized reformer Lucretia Mott attended an afternoon social gathering with her sister, Martha Wright, at the home of Jane Hunt in Waterloo. Also invited were the Hunts' neighbor, Mary Ann McClintock and Elizabeth Cady Stanton of Seneca Falls. Although Stanton and Mott had discussed holding a women's rights convention several years before, by the end of that afternoon the women began planning such a meeting in earnest to take advantage of Mott's short visit to the area. The group composed an advertisement for the convention, and the unsigned meeting call was published in the local newspaper only a week prior to the first day of the convention. The organizers also sent personal invitations to their own well-established network of reformers, including abolitionist and former slave Frederick Douglass in nearby Rochester.

The first day of the two-day convention was reserved for women speakers and those in attendance amended and adopted the list of grievances and resolutions drawn up in advance by the organizers. The final document, the Declaration of Sentiments, was modeled after the Declaration of Independence and boldly asserted that all men and women were created equal.

The resolutions adopted at the convention were far reaching and ranged from calls for women's control of earned wages to greater equality for women in organized religion. However, it was the ninth resolution, written by Elizabeth Cady Stanton and demanding women's right to the elective franchise, that was the most revolutionary, even within reform circles. Frederick Douglass and Stanton both rose to speak in support of the resolution, and after much debate, the suffrage resolution was passed.

It is estimated that close to 300 men and women attended the Seneca Falls convention, and sixty-eight women and thirty-two men signed the Declaration of Sentiments. Importantly, the majority of those who attended the convention had kinship ties to the newly formed abolitionist Free Soil Party or the Progressive Friends (Quakers) who had recently broken away from the mainstream church over issues of equality between the sexes. The combination of reform politics and commitment to gender equality that were brought together in Seneca Falls resulted in a women's rights movement going forward that focused on women's equal participation as citizens, with women's suffrage as its cornerstone.

[*See also* **Douglass, Frederick; Free Soil Party; Stanton, Elizabeth Cady;** ***and*** **Woman Suffrage Movement.**]

BIBLIOGRAPHY

Wellman, Judith. *The Road to Seneca Falls: Elizabeth Cady Stanton and the First Woman's Rights Convention*. Urbana: University of Illinois Press, 2004.

"Women's Rights National Historical Park." http://www.nps.gov/wori/index.htm/ (accessed 24 August 2011).

Linda C. Frank

SERVICEMEN'S READJUSTMENT ACT

In 1944, during the height of World War II, President Franklin Delano Roosevelt signed the Servicemen's Readjustment Act, designed to enhance the future of the more than 16 million men and women who served in the armed forces. The American Legion had drafted the legislation and lobbied for its passage, calling it "a bill of rights for GI Joe and GI Jane." The "GI Bill of Rights," or "GI Bill," as it is commonly known, authorized payments for tuition, books, and living expenses for up to four years of college or vocational school, low-interest mortgages for homeowners, loans for veterans to buy farms and start businesses, and a "readjustment allowance" of $20 per week while veterans sought employment.

In important ways, the GI Bill shaped the economic and social history of postwar America. More than a million veterans enrolled in colleges in 1946—half of that year's total enrollment. By 1956, almost 10 million men and women had benefited from the law's educational and training provisions. Colleges often made places for male veterans by turning away qualified women, however.

Furthermore, almost 4 million veterans received Veterans Administration loans for houses, spurring the suburbanization process, the postwar baby boom, and record demand for goods and services. The importance of the GI Bill lies not only in its immediate economic and social impact, but also in the fact that its provisions were later extended to millions of veterans of other conflicts, including the Korean and Vietnam Wars.

[*See also* **Education Policy: Higher Education; Housing Policy, Federal: An Overview;** ***and*** **Roosevelt, Franklin Delano.**]

BIBLIOGRAPHY

Bennett, Michael J. *When Dreams Came True: The GI Bill and the Making of Modern America.* Washington, D.C.: Brassey's, 1996.

Olson, Keith W. *The G.I. Bill, the Veterans, and the Colleges.* Lexington: University Press of Kentucky, 1974.

William M. Tuttle Jr.

SHAYS'S REBELLION

The political label "Shays's Rebellion," attached to the rural protest movement of 1786–1787 against the government of Massachusetts, is misleading: the protest was neither directed by Captain Daniel Shays, the Continental army veteran from Pelham, Massachusetts, on whom it was blamed, nor was it unmistakably a rebellion. Dubbed "the regulation" by participants, the movement was triggered by economic distress in the aftermath of independence. Determined to redeem its Revolutionary War debts, Massachusetts imposed heavy taxes, payable in hard money, in the midst of a severe depression in transatlantic trade. With cash scarce, lawsuits for debts mounting, and taxes due, many farmers feared foreclosure and jail and pressed the state for relief. Their program called for paper money and tender laws to ease payment of debts, court reforms and lower salaries for officials to reduce public expenses, and changes in political institutions to bring government closer to the people. From 1784 to 1786 the state legislature, dominated by commercial interests and intent on upholding credit, rejected all these proposals.

The result was an angry protest movement in western Massachusetts that revived the methods and rhetoric that had been used a decade earlier to resist British rule. The movement started with petitions from town meetings, a traditional means of seeking redress; expanded into extralegal county conventions; and escalated into crowd actions, involving hundreds of armed men, that prevented courts from meeting in several counties during the fall and winter of 1786. When Governor James Bowdoin dispatched an army to defend the courts, events reached a climax. On 25 January 1787, Shays led some twelve hundred men in a march on the federal arsenal at Springfield. A burst of cannon fire from defending militia routed the insurgents, leaving four dead on the field; ten days later, General Benjamin Lincoln crushed the remnants of resistance at Petersham. Thus ended what the Massachusetts General Court proclaimed "a horrid and unnatural rebellion."

The Massachusetts uprising dramatized rural unrest throughout the new republic, and though only a minority of dissidents took up arms, it symbolized for conservatives a republic in peril. In their view, ambitious demagogues like Shays, exploiting an unruly people, jeopardized the liberty gained in the Revolution. Nationalists seized upon the specter of Shays to underscore the weakness of the government set out in the Articles of Confederation and to urge support for the Constitution produced by the Philadelphia Convention in 1787. Shays's Rebellion and the Constitution have been linked ever since. The crisis in the countryside illuminates the difficult passage of the new nation to a republican political order.

[*See also* **Articles of Confederation; Constitution; Constitutional Convention of 1787;** *and* **Taxation.**]

BIBLIOGRAPHY

Gross, Robert A., ed. *In Debt to Shays: The Bicentennial of an Agrarian Rebellion*. Charlottesville: University Press of Virginia, 1993.

Szatmary, David P. *Shays' Rebellion: The Making of an Agrarian Insurrection*. Amherst: University of Massachusetts Press, 1980.

Robert A. Gross

SINGLE TAX MOVEMENT

The Single Tax movement was inspired by the plan of the San Francisco journalist and political economist Henry George (1839–1897), first articulated in an 1871 pamphlet and then in *Progress and Poverty* (1879), to return the profits of growth to society by imposing a uniform land tax that would end land monopoly and real-estate speculation. Rising land values, George argued, were created by community development rather than by landlords and real estate speculators who unjustly reaped the benefits of economic growth by paying lower taxes on undeveloped land. The "Single Tax," so dubbed by Thomas Shearman in 1887, proposed that the government appropriate unearned real-estate profits by setting a uniform tax on all land, whether developed or not. George envisioned the Single Tax as a great panacea. Speculators, faced with the prospect of paying high taxes on non-income-producing lands, would be forced to sell or develop their holdings. This would spur the construction of more homes and factories, thereby lowering rents, increasing profits and wages, and alleviating unemployment and urban congestion. Moreover, the Single Tax would generate funds sufficient to eliminate all other taxes and yet leave a surplus that would be returned to citizens in the form of increased public services.

Progress and Poverty became a best-seller, and the Single Tax movement attracted national and international attention during George's trips to England and Ireland in the 1880s and his unsuccessful campaigns for mayor of New York City in 1886 and 1897. Despite George's death in 1897, the movement over the next several decades spread throughout the United States, Canada, Australia, Great Britain, Denmark, and Hungary. The Single Tax was opposed by economists, who thought it unworkable, and by wealthy landowners, churches, and farmers who feared losing their lands or profits. Although the movement declined after the 1920s, a number of Single Tax advocates succeeded in shifting the burden of local property taxes from buildings and improvements to land. In 2000, Single Tax groups still operated in over 22 countries.

[*See also* **Populist Era; Radicalism;** *and* **Taxation.**]

BIBLIOGRAPHY

Adelson, Robert V., ed. *The Critics of Henry George: A Centenary Appraisal of Their Strictures on Progress and Poverty*. Rutherford, N.J.: Fairleigh Dickinson University Press, 1979.

Barker, Charles Albro. *Henry George*. New York: Oxford University Press, 1955.

Steven J. Ross

SIXTEENTH AMENDMENT

This 1913 amendment to the Constitution empowers Congress to "lay and collect taxes on incomes, from whatever source derived, without apportionment among the several states," specifically exempting income taxes from the constitutional mandate governing "direct taxes." Although an 1881 Supreme Court decision had upheld the constitutionality of the Civil War income taxes, a sharply divided Court in *Pollock v. Farmers' Loan and Trust Company* (1895) invalidated the income tax inserted into the 1894 Wilson–Gorman tariff by the Democratic-controlled Congress.

In the years after *Pollock,* a variety of groups and concepts interacted to produce a broad-based consensus in favor of federal income taxation. Increases in government spending mandated a significant flow of revenue, especially if tariff reformers achieved their goal of major downward revision. The West and the South, regarding themselves as colonial regions exploited by the industrial Northeast, embraced the income tax as a weapon to redress the sectional balance. Believing that customs duties and excise taxes fell heaviest on the great mass of workers and consumers, largely missing the huge fortunes accumulated by the principal holders of financial and industrial assets, a growing number of Americans advocated income taxation as a matter of "tax equity." The conviction that taxation should be based on "the ability to pay" and that it should come "from whatever source derived" increasingly united southerners and westerners, economists and tax experts, social reformers, urban machine politicians, organized labor, agrarian groups, socialists, and mass-circulation newspapers and magazines.

The Democratic Party platform of 1908 called for a constitutional amendment to overturn the *Pollock* decision, whereas the Republican presidential candidate William Howard Taft proclaimed that a properly drafted tax bill would be sufficient. In 1909, however, when the Republican leaders in Congress sought Taft's aid to prevent a coalition of Democrats and insurgent Republicans from inserting an income tax into the Payne–Aldrich tariff, Taft proposed both a corporation excise tax and a constitutional amendment. Despite initial denunciations of the amendment as a ploy to defeat the income tax clause of the tariff bill (a charge the Republican leadership freely admitted), the amendment process went forward. Congress proposed the Sixteenth Amendment to the states in Septe-mber 1909, and by February 1913 the ratification process was complete. Every state except Virginia, Florida, Utah, Rhode Island, Connecticut, and Pennsylvania eventually concurred, as political upheavals in several urban, industrial states of the Northeast and Middle West produced unexpected Democratic control of their legislatures. Ratification was staunchly opposed by conservative politicians, both Republicans and Democrats, and by prominent industrialists and financiers.

Urged on by President Woodrow Wilson, majority Democrats swiftly added an income tax to the 1913 Underwood–Simmons tariff. It levied a tax of 1 percent on incomes over $3,000 for single persons and $4,000 for married couples, thereby exempting over 95 percent of Americans. An "additional tax," graduated to 6 percent on income over $500,000, reinforced the concept of taxation according to "ability to pay." Quickly emerging as the federal government's chief source of revenue, the income tax also become a major political battleground between those who viewed it as an instrument for the redistribution of wealth and those who favored lower rates to stimulate economic growth.

[*See also* **Constitution; Income Tax, Federal; Progressive Era; Taft, William Howard; Tariffs; Taxation;** ***and*** **Wilson, Woodrow.**]

BIBLIOGRAPHY

Brownlee, W. Elliott. *Federal Taxation in America: A Short History*. Washington, D.C.: Woodrow Wilson Center Press, 1996.

Buenker, John D. *The Income Tax and the Progressive Era*. New York: Garland, 1985.

John D. Buenker

SLAUGHTERHOUSE CASES

An 1873 Supreme Court ruling interpreting the Fourteenth Amendment. During the Reconstruction Era, the Louisiana legislature granted certain business and political interests a monopoly over the butchering of animals in New Orleans. Before refrigeration technology was developed, private butchering practices created public health problems that properly regulated slaughterhouse monopolies helped to remedy. A group of the city's butchers nonetheless sued, contending that the state law prevented them from freely pursuing their trade.

Defeated in state court, the butchers appealed to the U.S. Supreme Court; their lawyer, John A. Campbell, argued that the monopoly violated his clients' rights under the Fourteenth Amendment's privileges and immunities (due process) clause. The Slaughterhouse cases presented the Court with its first chance to define the meaning of the Fourteenth Amendment, which had originated in the Republican Party's post-Emancipation efforts to grant black freedmen full rights of citizenship. Campbell contended, however, that the privileges and immunities clause protected economic as well as civil rights from state infringement. The Court divided 5-to-4. Justice Samuel F. Miller's majority opinion sustained the monopoly, interpreting the privileges and immunities clause narrowly as a guarantee of only a few civil rights, such as the right to petition, and not as a broad charter of economic liberty. The dissenters, to the contrary, embraced Campbell's theory that the clause guaranteed the right to pursue economic activity free of government regulation.

By 1890 a new Court majority reversed this position, adopting the view that the Fourteenth Amendment's due process clause protected individual and corporate economic rights. The Court's expansion of economic due process limited state and federal regulation of business, especially of large corporations. Not until 1937, in the New Deal Era, did the Court abandon this construction of the Fourteenth Amendment. Meanwhile, Justice Miller's narrow construction of the civil rights amendment guarantee fostered the triumph of racial segregation. It took the civil rights movement following World War II to overcome the consequences of Miller's Slaughterhouse decision and other prosegregation judicial rulings.

[*See also* **Civil Rights; Civil Rights Legislation; Due Process: Procedural Process; Economic Policy: Regulation; Emancipation Proclamation; Fourteenth Amendment; Reconstruction; Segregation;** ***and*** **Supreme Court, U.S.**]

BIBLIOGRAPHY

Benedict, Michael Les. "Preserving Federalism: Reconstruction and the Waite Court." *Supreme Court Review* (1978): 39–79.

Fairman, Charles. *Reconstruction and Reunion, 1864–1888, Part One. History of the Supreme Court*, vol. 6. New York: MacMillan, 1971.

Tony Freyer

SLAVERY, LAWS

In 1860 slave owners were among the wealthiest people in the United States, and the aggregate value of the nation's 3.9 million slaves exceeded the value of any other type of property except real estate. Remembered mostly as a system of racial oppression and economic exploitation that generated enormous wealth and profits for both the master class and the entire American nation, slavery was rooted in America's legal system and its political structure. Slavery emerged as a viable economic institution in early Virginia only after legislation and judicial decisions secured its place in the legal structure. Slavery and the law of slavery did not dramatically affect politics until after the Revolution began. However, from the adoption of the Constitution to the abolition of slavery with the ratification of the Thirteenth Amendment in December 1865, slavery affected the development of constitutional law and national political debate. The relationships between slavery and law can be divided chronologically and topically. This essay exams the legal history of slavery through the following divisions: the colonial origins of slave law, public law and emancipation during the Revolution, the private law of slavery in the antebellum South, criminal law and slavery, and the U.S. Constitution and federal law.

The Colonial Origins of Slave Law. The first blacks to arrive in Virginia in 1619 were treated as indentured servants because there were no laws in British America (or Great Britain) creating or enforcing the status of "slave." Initially Africans were treated like other non-British colonists, subject to discrimination based mostly on not being Christians or not being subjects of the King. Before the 1660s some blacks intermarried with whites, testified in court for and against whites, were baptized, and acquired property. By the 1640s some whites were treating blacks as slaves, and some courts supported the practice. A few laws recognized that Africans were different than Europeans, so a militia law did not require arming Africans (but did not prohibit it either). Starting in 1660 the Virginia legislature began to use the term "slave" and to regulate their status. A 1662 act deviated from English Common Law by providing that children of African women would follow the status of their mothers, rather than their fathers. This meant that the children of white men and slave women would be considered slaves. Thus, from 1662 on white southern men began enslaving their own children. An act of 1667 provided that baptism would not change the status of slaves, thus allowing Anglican clergymen (and later all clergymen) to convert slaves with the support and encouragement of their masters. By the nineteenth century almost every denomination in the South (except Quakers and Mennonites) supported slavery. This religious support of slavery led southern ministers to develop elaborate theological defenses of slavery. Recognizing the brutal nature of slavery—that it could only survive by force—Virginia declared in 1669 that it would not be considered murder if a slave was killed during punishment or while attempting to run away or resist a master. By the early eighteenth century Virginia had developed an elaborate code that banned black testimony in court, prohibited interracial marriage, eliminated private manumission of slaves, presumed all Africans and their children were slaves, supported harsh punishments for slaves, and created a system of slave patrols and other mechanisms to make sure that slaves could not revolt. Most other Southern colonies passed similar laws with minor variations. From 1700 to the Revolution the southern colonies (Maryland, Virginia, North Carolina, South Carolina, and Georgia) vigorously imported new slaves, although they occasionally passed laws to limit importations for economic reasons or for fear that it was unsafe to have too many slaves.

Public Law and Emancipation during the Revolutionary Era. On the eve of the American Revolution slavery was legal, and profitable, in all colonies. The importance of slavery varied, however. The colonies south of Maryland were 40 to 50 percent slave, while Pennsylvania, New Hampshire, and Massachusetts were less than 5 percent. In the period leading to the Revolution Quakers began to agitate for an end to slavery, first within their faith and then for others. Methodists initially opposed slavery, as did many Baptists, but most denominations were unconcerned about human bondage.

As anti-British agitation grew, Northern blacks began to agitate for freedom. By the eve of the Revolution there were significant free black populations throughout New England, New York, and Pennsylvania, although slavery was still legal and economically viable in all those places. During the Revolution numerous northern masters, especially in New England, manumitted their male slaves so they could fight for the patriot cause. In 1778 voters in Massachusetts rejected a proposed state constitution in part because it did not abolish slavery. In 1780 Massachusetts adopted a constitution, largely written by John Adams, which began with the statement "All men are born free and equal." In the Quock Walker (1781) and Mumbet cases (1783) the Massachusetts courts concluded this provision had brought an end to slavery in the state. In 1780 Pennsylvania passed a gradual abolition act, which provided that the future children of all slave women would be born free, thus guaranteeing an end to slavery as the existing slaves died off. By 1804 Connecticut, Rhode Island, New York, and New Jersey had adopted similar laws, while New Hampshire and the new states of Vermont and Ohio ended slavery in their constitutions. In these states free blacks often faced restricted rights, although they could vote in all states except Connecticut and Ohio.

In the years after the Revolution most of the free states allowed southern masters to visit with their slaves, with New York allowing a nine-month and Pennsylvania a six-month sojourn. Meanwhile, a number of southern states accepted the rule that a slave who was brought to a free state became free. This reciprocity broke down in the 1830s, however. In *Commonwealth v. Aves* (1836) the Massachusetts Supreme Judicial Court ruled that slaves brought to that state became instantly free because there was no positive law creating slavery. This ruling was based on the pre-Revolutionary War decision in England, *Somerset v. Stewart* (1772). By the 1850s most Northern states had adopted this rule through statutes or court cases. Meanwhile, starting in the 1830s Southern states began to reject freedom claims based on residence in non-slave jurisdictions. The high point of this jurisprudence came in the 1850s. In *Scott v. Emerson* (1852) the Missouri Court rejected nearly thirty years of precedents in holding that the slave Dred Scott did not gain his freedom, although his master took him to two free jurisdictions—Illinois and the Wisconsin Territory—and kept him there for a number of years. In *Mitchell v. Wells* (1859) Mississippi went further, holding that the slave Nancy Wells was not free, although her master took her to Ohio and formally manumitted her.

The Revolution also affected slave law in the South. Many Southern states revised their criminal codes to reduce the number of capital offenses for blacks and to ban particularly barbaric punishments, such as hamstringing, castration, and other types of mutilation. North Carolina criminalized the intentional murder of a slave. In 1782 Virginia allowed masters to free some slaves within the state, rather than requiring that manumitted slaves move to another state. Between 1782 and 1810 the state's free black population grew by 1,500 percent, from about 2,000 to over 30,000. However, by that date Virginia had once against restricted the right of manumitted slaves to remain in the state. During the Revolution and its aftermath none of the Southern states considered or debated actually ending slavery. St. George Tucker, a professor of law at William and Mary and later a federal judge, drafted an elaborate scheme that would have ended slavery in a century but no one in the legislature would even consider it.

The Private Law of Slavery. Everywhere slavery existed, slaves were considered a form of private property. Some seventeenth-century colonies considered slaves real estate for purposes of taxation, sale, and inheritance. This categorization undermined the economic viability of slavery by allowing slaves to be entailed and transferred to heirs through primogenitorship in the case of intestate succession (if a master died without a will). Slaves were tied to landholdings which initially may have helped families increase assets over multiple generations, but at the same time limited the economic use of slaves. Considering slaves' real estate complicated their sale even during the master's life because of the rules of dower. Under English law a widow had a dower right to use one-third of all the real estate her husband owned during their marriage. This also limited the economic value of slaves. Thus, by the beginning of the eighteenth century all colonies considered slaves personal or moveable property. In legal terminology slaves were chattels, or "things," to be bought, sold, rented, inherited, seized for debt, used as collateral for debts, or gifted.

A significant amount of litigation took place in the South over the sale of slaves. Disputes typically occurred over the behavior or health of a slave. Buyers complained when they purchased a slave who immediately ran away, complaining that the slave was "addicted" to running away, a defect the seller did not disclose. However, modern scholarship suggests that many slaves ran away precisely because they were sold, often trying to return to loved ones at their former residence.

Masters allowed slave couples to "marry," and most masters encouraged unions among their slaves because they would result in children. But no slave state ever recognized the legality of a slave marriage. By definition marriage is a contract, and slaves were legally incapable of entering into a contract. Thus, a master could break up a slave family when it was economically or socially useful to do so. Some legal theorists, like Georgia's Thomas R. R. Cobb, expressed concern about the destruction of slave marriages, but in the end had no solution to the problem. Nor did the Southern clergy have a solution. They urged masters to solemnize slave unions with religious ceremonies, but understood that the sale of one spouse should be considered the functional equivalent of a divorce. From the perspective of Southern whites, slaves had to be considered commodities to be bought and sold at whim of the master or to satisfy the demands of creditors. Louisiana prohibited the public sale of slave children under the age of eight without their mothers, but the law barely affected slave sales or protected slave families. Slave mothers could still be sold away from their children. When slavery ended all Southern states legalized existing slave marriages, but these laws could not repair all the problems created by centuries of slave unions broken by sale, migration, and escape. As late as 1901, in *Irving v. Ford,* Chief Justice Oliver Wendell Holmes Jr., of the Massachusetts Supreme Judicial Court held that the son fathered by a slave who later escaped to Massachusetts had no claim to his father's estate.

The issue of manumission connected public law and private law. Masters were always able to take their slaves to free jurisdictions and emancipate them. For example, shortly after the War of 1812 ended, Edward Coles, who had been James Madison's private secretary, took his slaves to Illinois, where he emancipated them. Most states regulated in-state manumission through statutory regulations. From 1782 to 1806 Virginia allowed masters to free adult slaves, who could then remain in the state. From 1806 to 1852 the state maintained changing and inconsistent policies, allowing manumitted slaves to remain in the state on a case-by-case basis, with county judges or the state legislature making the decision. After 1852 the state completely banned in-state manumissions. Other states followed similar patterns, with upper south slave states—Maryland, Kentucky, Missouri, and Delaware—generally allowing manumissions. However, most of the Deep South states gradually eliminated that option. In *Mitchell v. Wells* (1859) Mississippi's highest court declared that it was the public policy of the state to prohibit, as much as possible, any manumission of slaves. That case involved a slave whose owner (who was also her father) emancipated her in Ohio. But when the master died the Court would not let her inherit his property, claiming that Mississippi considered her to be a slave, even though she had been formally manumitted in Ohio. Heirs often challenged wills that manumitted slaves or distributed property to former slaves. Although rules varied from state to state, before 1820 most Southern states allowed masters to free their slaves during their lifetime or through their wills. In the next forty years this changed dramatically. In *Elder v. Elder* (1833) the Virginia court upheld a will in which slaves were allowed to decide whether to remain in bondage or be sent to Liberia, but in *Bailey v. Poindexter* (1858) the same court disallowed a similar will.

Slaves were often rented, which created numerous contract disputes that were generally dealt with like any other contract dispute. However, because slaves were also people, contract disputes could be complicated. Often owners restricted the use of rented slaves. In the 1840s a Georgia master named Woodbridge rented his slave to a steamboat company, with the explicit restriction that the slave, Ned, would never be allowed in the water. When the boat got stuck on a sandbar Ned jumped overboard with the rest of the crew to help dislodge it. Ned drowned, and Woodbridge won a breach of contract suit, although the ship owner claimed that it was impossible to prevent the slave from jumping overboard. In *Scudder v. Woodbridge* (1846) the Georgia court ruled that if necessary the ship captain should have chained the slave to the deck to keep him out of the water. Such rules impacted the use of slave labor in industry, but protected the owner's property interest.

Criminal Law and Slavery. Although treated as property for some purposes—to be bought, sold, bartered, mortgaged, bequeathed, and gifted—slaves were also capable of committing crimes or being the victims of crimes. In the colonial period most jurisdictions provided savage punishments for slaves who resisted the authority of any white person. Slave rebels were often executed, as were slaves charged with other crimes. Similarly, before the Revolution there were almost no restrictions on the public or private punishment of slaves. During and after the Revolution most southern states eliminated barbaric punishments and significantly reduced the number of capital offenses for slaves.

In the mid-nineteenth century a number of slave states began to seriously consider the way slave criminals were treated. Appellate courts overturned the convictions of slaves who were denied counsel or had their confessions coerced. Some convictions were overturned because indictments were not proper or the description of the accused was inaccurate. In *Dick, A Slave v. Mississippi* (1856) the Mississippi high court overturned a conviction for attempted rape of a white woman because the indictment charged that Dick, a "Negro" slave, had committed the crime, but in fact Dick was a mulatto. The North Carolina court overturned a number of convictions of slaves who had killed whites in self-defense. After an overseer shot the slave Will in the back for no apparent reason, Will ran away. He accidently stabbed and killed the overseer while trying to fend off slaves who had been sent to capture him. In *State v. Will* (1834) the Court reversed Will's conviction, concluding that even a slave had the right to defend himself when his life was threatened. Cases like these established that the trials of slaves would be procedurally fair and sometimes even afford slaves a measure of justice. For example, at least two other slaves in North Carolina won reversals for murder convictions after they killed whites in self-defense or while defending other slaves. But these were the exception. Procedural fairness was undermined by the reality that slaves could never testify against whites, could never serve on juries, and were always subject to the whims of their masters. The criminal law may have given slaves some protections, but in reality most decisions benefitted the master class by protecting their investment.

The same was mostly true for laws and cases punishing whites who harmed slaves. In 1791 North Carolina made the murder of a slave a capital offense, but in *State v. Boon* (1801) the state's highest court concluded the law was unenforceable because of its vagueness. In 1817 a new statute simply told courts to apply Common Law principles to trials of those who murdered slaves. In the next four decades the state Supreme Court would uphold battery and murder convictions of whites who harmed other people's slaves. These cases usually involved third parties who harmed slaves, and the reasoning behind such cases went directly to the need to protect a master's investment in his slaves. In upholding the conviction of a white man who beat up someone else's slave, the North Carolina court noted in *State v. Hale* (1823), "These offences are usually committed by men of dissolute habits, hanging loose upon society, who, being repelled from association with well disposed citizens, take refuge in the company of coloured persons and slaves, whom they deprave by their example, embolden by their familiarity, and then beat, under the expectation that a slave dare not resent a blow from a white man." Only by prosecuting such "men of dissolute habits" could the master class protect its investment in slaves.

Limitations on what masters could do were more problematic. Most states required masters to feed and clothe their slaves, although no one appears to have ever been prosecuted for failing to maintain a slave. Economic self-interest led most masters to provide minimal substance for slaves. But sadistic behavior, or simply short tempers, could lead to horrible results for slaves. Rarely did the courts or legislatures intervene. In *State v. Mann* (1829) the North Carolina court famously held that a master or a renter was free to punish a slave in any manner he chose, short of killing the slave or breaching any statutory ban on certain kinds of punishment. Chief Justice Thomas Ruffin set out a harsh standard for punishment: "We cannot allow the right of the master to be brought into discussion in the Courts of Justice. The slave, to remain a slave, must be made sensible, that there is no appeal from his master; that his power is in no instance, usurped; but is conferred by the laws of man at least, if not by the law of God. The danger would be great indeed, if the tribunals of justice should be called on to graduate the punishment appropriate to every temper, and every dereliction of menial duty."

All slave states accepted Ruffin's analysis and conclusion that masters had to have almost unlimited power to punish their slaves. The one exception was murder. Thus, in *State v. Hoover* (1839) the North Carolina court upheld John Hoover's conviction for brutally murdering his own slave, for which he was hanged. Similarly, in *Souther v. The Commonwealth* (1851) Virginia's court upheld the conviction of a master whose slave died after two days of barbaric punishment. The Court only regretted that it could not impose a great sentence than five years because the jury had convicted Souther of manslaughter, rather than murder. In her book, *The Key to Uncle Tom's Cabin,* Harriet Beecher Stowe devoted an entire chapter to *Souther,* sarcastically calling to "The Ne Plus Ultra of Legal Humanity." "Nobody," she wrote, "could willingly read them [the counts in the indictment] twice." Stowe noted that after Souther served his five-year sentence "there is no law in Virginia to prevent his buying as many more negroes as he chooses, and going over the same scene with any one of them at a future time." Of course Stowe was correct. Southern states never restricted whites from owning slaves and, with only the most minor caveats, never restricted the behavior of masters. In the 1820s two nephews of Thomas Jefferson chopped a slave to death with an axe, but the only witnesses were other slaves and so the two young men went unpunished. This was the harsh reality of slave law.

The Constitution and Federal Law. The U.S. Constitution provided a series of specific protections for slavery. Slavery is in fact the only economic or social institution to receive such protections. Thus, the Constitution, through the Three-Fifths Clause of Article I, gave the slave states extra representation in Congress for their slaves and, by extension, extra votes in the Electoral College. Thomas Jefferson, for example, would have lost the election of 1800 if it had not been for the presidential electors created by counting slaves. Similarly, proslavery legislation, such as the admission of Missouri as a slave state, Texas annexation, and the Fugitive Slave Act of 1850, could not have been passed (or at least not in the form they were adopted) without the congressional votes created through the Three-Fifths Clause. The Constitution specifically prevented an end to the African slave trade before 1808 and did not require it to ever be ended. It is likely that Congress would have ended the trade in the 1790s without this clause. Between 1800 and 1808 about 65,000 slaves were imported from Africa. After 1808 there were some illegal imports but few prosecutions. The powerful Southern block in Congress prevented meaningful interdiction of the illegal African trade before the Civil War. The two domestic insurrections clauses (in Article I and Article IV) led the national government to participate in the suppression of slave rebellions. Congress passed two fugitive slave laws (1793 and 1850) to implement the Fugitive Slave Clause of Article IV. The 1850 law led to enormous conflict between the national government and many Northern communities. Ironically, on the issue of fugitive slaves the South supported a strong national government, while many Northern states argued to protect fugitive slaves from being sent South as well as to protect northern blacks from kidnapping. The overall structure of the Constitution made it impossible to end slavery by normal means because the slave states had a perpetual veto over any Constitutional amendment. The Constitution required that three-fourths of the states ratify an amendment, but the fifteen slave states that existed in 1860 could block an amendment, even in the modern fifty state union. Without secession and civil war there was no constitutional or legal process for ending slavery in the nation.

From the beginning the Supreme Court almost always protected slavery. Commerce clause cases in the 1830s that had nothing to do with slavery nevertheless were affected by the Court's need to protect it. The Court upheld the first fugitive slave law in *Prigg v. Pennsylvania* (1842) and in the process struck down all Northern laws passed to prevent kidnapping of free blacks. This was a real issue. One of the blacks seized by Prigg and subsequently sold to the Deep South was born in Pennsylvania and thus was born a free person. After *Prigg* most Northern states simply refused to cooperate with the return of fugitive slaves, leading to Southern demands for the harsher 1850 law, which created the first federal law enforcement bureaucracy in American history. This law prohibited alleged fugitives from testifying when brought before a judge, suspended the writ of habeas corpus for alleged fugitives (in violation of the very specific provisions of the Constitution involving suspension), and paid judges $5 if they determined the person seized was not a slave, but $10 if the court determined the person was a slave.

In *Dred Scott v. Sandford* (1857) the Supreme Court reaffirmed that slavery was specifically protected by the Constitution and ruled that Congress did not have the power to ban slavery in federal territories. The Court also held that free blacks, even if they were able to vote and hold office in their own states, could never be citizens of the United States. In *Ableman v. Booth* (1859) the Court emphatically upheld the Fugitive Slave Act of 1850 and rejected any attempts by states to prevent kidnapping or in any other way interfere with the return of fugitive slaves.

By the eve of the Civil War slavery was secure in the American legal structure. The national government had no power to touch slavery in the states and the South had a perpetual veto over any constitutional amendment that might threaten slavery. The Three-Fifths Clause had allowed the South to dominate Congress, the Supreme Court, and the presidency since 1788. However, the election of Lincoln changed the political dynamics. Lincoln pledged to prevent the creation of new slave states, and, unlike every other president, had expressed his open hostility to slavery and his belief that human bondage was fundamentally wrong. This led Southern extremists to successfully push for secession. Each state that left the Union expressed its belief that Lincoln threatened slavery and that secession was necessary to prevent an end to slavery. Thus the vice president of the Confederacy, Alexander Stephens, declared that the Confederate Constitution "has put at rest, forever, all the agitating questions relating to our peculiar institution African slavery as it exists amongst us the proper status of the negro in our form of civilization." He asserted that the Confederacy's "foundations are laid, its corner-stone rests, upon the great truth that the negro is not equal to the white man; that slavery subordination to the superior race is his natural and normal condition. This, our new government, is the first, in the history of the world, based upon this great physical, philosophical, and moral truth."

Secession led to civil war, and initially Lincoln believed he had no legal or constitutional power to touch slavery in the states. But after a year of war Congress and the executive branch worked in tandem to dismantle slavery, while the Army implemented many of the changes. Congress ended slavery in the

District of Columbia and the territories, and Lincoln supported generals who emancipated slaves who ran to U.S. Army lines. In the first significant use of an executive order, Lincoln issued the Emancipation Proclamation, ordering an end to slavery in the Confederate states. Congress meanwhile passed and sent on to the states the Thirteenth Amendment, which abolished slavery throughout the nation. In a constitutional innovation the amendment empowered Congress to pass appropriate legislation to secure freedom.

[*See also* **Constitution; Emancipation Proclamation; Fugitive Slave Act;** *and* ***Scott v. Sandford.***]

BIBLIOGRAPHY

Campbell, James M. *Slavery on Trial: Race, Class, and Criminal Justice in Antebellum Richmond, Virginia.* Gainesville: University Press of Florida, 2007.

Fehrenbacher, Don E. *The Dred Scott Case: Its Significance in American Law and Politics.* New York: Oxford University Press, 1978.

Finkelman, Paul. *Dred Scott v. Sandford: A Brief History.* Boston: Bedford Books, 1995.

Finkelman, Paul. *An Imperfect Union: Slavery, Federalism, and Comity.* Chapel Hill: University of North Carolina Press, 1981.

Finkelman, Paul. *Slavery and the Founders: Race and Liberty in the Age of Jefferson.* 2d ed. Armonk, N.Y.: M. E. Sharpe, 2001.

Finkelman, Paul, and Donald R. Kennon, eds. *In the Shadow of Freedom: The Politics of Slavery in the National Capital.* Athens, Ohio: Ohio University Press, 2011.

Franklin, John Hope, and Loren Schweninger. *Runaway Slaves: Rebels on the Plantation.* New York: Oxford University Press, 1999.

Gross, Ariela. *Double Character: Slavery and Mastery in the Antebellum Southern Courtroom.* Princeton, N.J.: Princeton University Press, 2000.

Jones, Bernie. *Fathers of Conscience: Mixed-Race Inheritance in the Antebellum South.* Athens, Ga.: Georgia University Press, 2009.

Morris, Thomas D. *Southern Slavery and the Law, 1619–1860.* Chapel Hill: University of North Carolina Press, 1996.

Schafer, Judith Kelleher. *Becoming Free, Remaining Free: Manumission and Enslavement in New Orleans: 1846–1862.* Baton Rouge: Louisiana State University Press, 2003.

Schafer, Judith Kelleher. *Slavery, the Civil Law, and the Supreme Court of Louisiana.* Baton Rouge: Louisiana State University Press, 1994.

Schwarz, Philip J. *Slave Laws in Virginia.* Athens, Ga.: University of Georgia Press, 1996.

Schwarz, Philip J. *Twice Condemned: Slaves and the Criminal Laws of Virginia, 1705–1865.* Baton Rouge: Louisiana State University Press, 1988.

Tushnet, Mark V. *Slave Law in the American South: "State v. Mann" in History and Literature.* Lawrence: University Press of Kansas, 2003.

Paul Finkelman

SMITH, ALFRED

(1873–1944), governor of New York and Democratic presidential candidate. Smith was born on New York City's Lower East Side. His father was of German and Italian background; his mother was Irish American. Forced by his father's death to quit school early, he supported his family by working in the Fulton Fish Market. Local leaders of New York City's Democratic organization, Tammany Hall, got him a job with the Commissioner of Jurors. Elected to the state assembly in 1903, he served for twelve years, rising to become Speaker. He also cochaired the State Factory Investigating Commission, which was established in response to the Triangle Shirtwaist Company fire of 1911. The commission sponsored numerous bills regulating factory work and established Smith as a champion of the working class.

Needing more income, Smith, now a father of five, became sheriff of New York County in 1915 and president of the New York City Board of Aldermen two years later. Nominated as the Democratic candidate for governor in 1918, he won easily, serving from 1919 to 1920 and again from 1923 to 1928. His strong legislative record as a progressive reformer expanded his political support. Although Smith lost the Democratic presidential nomination at the party's rancorous 1924 convention, he won in 1928, becoming the first Catholic to run for president on a major party ticket. A number of factors—Smith's religion, his stand against Prohibition, and eight years of Republican prosperity—led to his crushing loss to the Republican candidate, Herbert Hoover. In New York, Franklin Delano Roosevelt was narrowly elected governor, winning the post that Smith had vacated.

After losing the 1932 Democratic presidential nomination to Roosevelt, Smith did not seek office again. Embittered by Roosevelt's popularity, he opposed much of the New Deal and even joined the conservative American Liberty League. He was an active Catholic layman and served as figurehead president of the Empire State Building Corporation headed by John Raskob, a prominent Democrat. Popular with audiences and the press for his affability and oratorical skills, Al Smith remains one of New York's most beloved public figures.

[*See also* **American Liberty League; Democratic Party; Hoover, Herbert; Progressive Era; Prohibition;** ***and*** **Roosevelt, Franklin Delano.**]

BIBLIOGRAPHY

Eldot, Paula. *Governor Alfred E. Smith: The Politician as Reformer*. New York: Garland, 1983.

Handlin, Oscar. *Al Smith and His America*. Boston: Northeastern University Press, 1958.

Elisabeth Israels Perry

SMITH v. ALLWRIGHT

321 U.S. 649 (1944), argued 10 and 12 November 1943, reargued 12 January 1944, decided 3 April 1944 by vote of 8 to 1; Reed for the Court, Roberts in dissent. The history of the "white primary" was a game of constitutional chess waged against blacks and the Supreme Court by whites and the Texas legislature. After Reconstruction, a Democratic primary victory assured success in the general election in Texas and throughout the one-party South. Therefore, exclusion of African Americans from primary participation had the practical effect of disenfranchisement.

Initially, in *Newberry v. United States* (1921), the Court concluded that party primary elections were unknown to the framers and therefore were beyond the reach of the Constitution. Two years later, the Texas legislature enacted a statute expressly barring African Americans from voting in a Democratic primary. The Court in *Nixon v. Herndon* (1927) held this measure invalid under the Fourteenth Amendment. The Texas legislature then enacted another statute that authorized the state party executive committee to determine membership qualifications, including race, and again the Court held the statute invalid in *Nixon v. Condon* (1932). Next the Texas legislature repealed all state primary election statutes, anticipating that the Democratic state convention would exclude African Americans, which the Court upheld, in *Grovey v. Townsend* (1935), as "private" discrimination beyond the Constitution.

African American voters were checked until the National Association for the Advancement of Colored People (NAACP) saw an opening in *United States v. Classic* (1941), which held that Congress could regulate primary as well as general elections for federal office. The NAACP sponsored Smith, who brought suit against Texas Democratic Party election officials in a direct challenge on the *Grovey* holding, alleging that he had been unconstitutionally denied a primary ballot because of his race.

Justice Stanley Reed applied the *Classic* reasoning to overrule *Grovey,* and the white primary was checkmated. Since the primary system was an integral part of the state's election procedures, citizens had the right under the Fifteenth Amendment to vote in party primaries free of racial discrimination. The discrimination was not merely "private." First, since state law authorized primary elections and regulated the party's procedures, the party in convention acted as an agent of the state in excluding African Americans. Second, conducting elections was a state function; therefore, the state was responsible for allowing the private racial discrimination.

Justice Owen J. Roberts, who had written for a unanimous Court only nine years before in *Grovey,* dissented on the grounds that the overruling promoted disrespect for the Court and instability in the law. Justice Reed replied that the Court's decision only corrected the earlier misapplication of settled principles. Neither opinion noted that seven of the justices had been appointed by President Franklin D. Roosevelt in that interim.

Constitutional scholars cite *Allwright* as one of the seminal cases in the development of the "public function" concept. Certain activities traditionally and exclusively performed by the government—such as elections—are deemed to be state action under the Constitution even when performed by private actors. This doctrine was extended in *Terry v. Adams* (1953), in which the Court invalidated an unofficial primary held by a private, all-white "club" despite the lack of state regulation of the club.

After *Allwright,* the available methods for reducing African American participation in elections were limited to those directed at individuals rather than groups, such as literacy tests and poll taxes. These methods proved less effective with time. The federal legislative response came in the Civil Rights Acts of 1957, 1960, and 1964, followed by the Twenty-fourth Amendment, which banned poll taxes in federal elections, and especially in the Voting Rights Act of 1965 with subsequent amendments.

The broader significance of this decision lies in the Court's focus on substance over form in determining voting rights. This approach became the conceptual foundation for later landmark civil rights cases involving such matters as racially restrictive covenants, school segregation, and political reapportionment.

[*See also* **Civil Rights; Civil Rights Legislation; Constitution; Fifteenth Amendment; Fourteenth Amendment; National Association for the Advancement of Colored People; Reconstruction, Roosevelt, Franklin Delano; State Governments;** *and* **Supreme Court, U.S.**]

BIBLIOGRAPHY

Elliot, Ward E. Y. *The Rise of Guardian Democracy: The Supreme Court's Role in Voting Rights Disputes, 1845–1969.* Cambridge, Mass.: Harvard University Press, 1974.

Hine, Darlene Clark. *Black Victory: The Rise and Fall of the White Primary in Texas.* Columbia: University of Missouri Press, 1979.

Thomas E. Baker

SOCIALISM

A political ideology that rejects the private ownership of land, factories, and other means of production as well as the wage-labor system and the competitive market economy.

Socialist beliefs and movements, although dizzyingly varied, have generally fallen into four groups: communitarian, revolutionary socialist, democratic socialist, and syndicalist. Communitarianism, which has the longest pedigree, can be traced to eighteenth-century religious movements such as the Shakers, who reacted to a commercializing society by retreating into rural settlements, holding their property communally, and hoping to reform society by example. As antebellum Americans felt the first shocks of the emerging industrial order, some embraced European alternatives to capitalism, from the paternalistic industrialism of Robert Owen to Charles Fourier's utopian blueprints for communal cooperatives.

By the 1860s, having absorbed the work of Karl Marx, most socialists turned from debating how best to withdraw from capitalist society to arguing over how to revolutionize it. Two major streams of thought emerged, both initially espoused in America mainly by German immigrants, who founded a branch of Marx's Communist International in New York in 1872. Orthodox Marxists, committed to overthrowing capitalism through revolutionary class struggle, concentrated on infiltrating labor unions and mobilizing the masses. Democratic socialists, by contrast, sometimes called "Lassalleans," for the German Ferdinand Lassalle, believed that socialism could be achieved peacefully through electoral politics.

Neither group proved notably successful. The revolutionary Marxists, squandering their energies in factional infighting, were rejected by the trade-union movement they assiduously courted. On the electoral front, the Workingmen's Party (1874), renamed the Socialist Labor Party (SLP) in 1877 and led after 1890 by Daniel De Leon, fielded a presidential candidate in 1892, but he won only 21,000 votes. Foreign-language socialist newspapers did little to broaden the movement's appeal. The Socialist Party of America (SPA), founded in 1901 by Eugene V. Debs, Morris Hillquit (1869–1933), Victor Berger (1860–1929), and other defectors from the SLP, never overcame most Americans' tendency to give their racial, ethnic, and religious identity a higher priority than their social class. Neither Debs, the SPA's five-time presidential candidate between 1900 and 1920, nor Norman Thomas, the party's perennial candidate from the 1920s to the 1960s, seriously challenged the major-party nominees.

The final category of socialism, syndicalism, combined the immigrant Marxists' critique of capitalism with the abolitionists' suspicion of government. Whereas Marxists sought to transform the labor movement into a revolutionary force to overthrow the government, syndicalists envisioned a new society emerging from workers' control of the mills and factories. Syndicalism flourished in western mining, lumber, and railroad camps with the founding of the Industrial Workers of the World (IWW, or Wobblies) in 1905. The Wobblies' dramatic strikes; flamboyant leaders; and wealth of songs, lore, and poetry made them a romantic symbol of the syndicalist version of socialism.

Despite its overall failure, American socialism has influenced American thought and culture, particularly in the late nineteenth and early twentieth centuries. Edward Bellamy's novel of evolutionary socialism, *Looking Backward* (1888), which drew upon Laurence Gronlund's *Cooperative Commonwealth* (1884), proved enormously popular. Some prominent Social Gospel advocates espoused Christian socialism, and influential reformist works by socialists, or reflecting socialist ideas, included Henry Demarest Lloyd's *Wealth against Commonwealth* (1894); William Dean Howells's *A Traveler from Alturia* (1894), Upton Sinclair's *The Jungle* (1906); and Jack London's *The Iron Heel* (1907). The socialist magazine the *Masses* (founded 1911) enjoyed considerable Progressive Era influence.

World War I, which brought repression of the antiwar left and the Bolshevik Revolution in Russia—a revolution celebrated by the American socialist John Reed in *Ten Days That Shook the World* (1919)—redrew the contours of American socialism. The Communist Party USA (CPUSA), founded in 1919, ceded control of its affairs to Moscow and, like its Marxist forebears, generally favored doctrinal purity over coalition building. Both the CPUSA and the SPA gained ground early in the Great Depression, but both were eclipsed by the popularity of the New Deal and then by the antiradical climate of the Cold War.

Socialism's fortunes rose with the emergence of the New Left in the 1960s. The leading New Left organization, Students for a Democratic Society, a hybrid of socialist traditions, rejected Marxist dogmatism while it embraced both the communitarian dream and the democratic-socialists' hope for radical social change through a revitalized politics. Socialism's indirect influence resurfaced in the 1960s as well. For example, the socialist Michael Harrington's *The Other America* (1962) helped inspire President Lyndon B. Johnson's War on Poverty. Although the New Left soon faded, its blend of communitarian hopes and democratic-socialist goals remained alive in the late twentieth century. The Democratic Socialists of America, founded by Harrington in 1983 to pursue socialist goals within the Democratic Party, was the latest manifestation of socialism's continuing influence in American life.

[*See also* **Communist Party USA; Conservatism; Debs, Eugene; Johnson, Lyndon B.; Liberalism; New Left; *Other America, The;* Poverty; Progressive Era; Radicalism; Socialist Party of America; Students for a Democratic Society; Third Parties;** ***and*** **Thomas, Norman.**]

BIBLIOGRAPHY

Buhle, Mari Jo, Paul Buhle, and Dan Georgakas, eds. *Encyclopedia of the American Left*, rev. ed. New York: Oxford University Press, 1998.

Buhle, Paul. *Marxism in the U.S.A.: From 1870 to the Present Day*. New York: Verso Books, 1987.

Diggins, John Patrick. *The Rise and Fall of the American Left*. New York: W. W. Norton, 1992.

Egbert, Donald, and Stow Persons, eds. *Socialism and American Life*. Princeton, N.J.: Princeton University Press, 1952.

Isserman, Maurice. *If I Had a Hammer: The Death of the Old Left and the Birth of the New Left*. New York: Basic Books, 1987.

Weinstein, James. *The Decline of Socialism in America, 1912–1925*. New York: Monthly Review Press, 1967.

Timothy Messer-Kruse

SOCIALIST PARTY OF AMERICA

Founded in 1901, the Socialist Party of America (SPA) drew on deep roots of dissent within American society, enjoyed its peak influence during the Progressive Era, and remained a sometimes lively ghost in later years. The Socialist Party's precursors—including abolitionists, women's rights campaigners, agrarian radicals, utopian socialists, and trade unionists—had long proposed alternative social arrangements. Small socialist political organizations, led mainly by German Americans in the post–Civil War decades, played a crucial role in the formation of the American labor movement. But the depression of the 1890s, violent labor struggles, the Populist revolt, and the appearance of newer ethnic immigrants (especially East European Jews) with socialist connections all foreshadowed a major reorientation. A split in the sectarian Socialist Labor Party of 1899 and the emergence of former railroad-union leader Eugene V. Debs in 1900 brought unity within sight.

The SPA's founding convention, held at Indianapolis, Indiana, in 1901, included various elements of the socialist movement, especially small-town and rural socialists—native-born, often middle-aged railroad mechanics, teachers, ministers, and farmers—who carried the educational zeal of earlier times into hundreds of local presses, study clubs, and political campaigns. Because these grassroots activists were unimpeachably "American," immigrant socialists usually ceded them leadership in the movement. By 1912, Oklahoma had become the epicenter of socialist influence, more than 1,000 socialist candidates had been elected nationwide, and Debs garnered 6 percent of the presidential vote.

The labor movement changed dramatically as well. Beginning in 1909, a wave of strikes by unskilled, foreign-born workers shook the confidence of the business classes. The Industrial Workers of the World, launched with socialist assistance in 1905, preached "solidarity" among all working people. Even within the staid American Federation of Labor, headed by antisocialist Samuel Gompers, a number of member unions turned strongly leftward. Buoyed by this energy, the Socialist Party reached a membership of 100,000, including a growing number of foreign-language federations made up of immigrant nationalities.

But the two-party system quickly adjusted itself to the threat of radical outsiders. In many localities where socialists sought election, Republicans and Democrats formed "fusion" tickets with resources beyond the reach of newcomers. Elsewhere, reformers appropriated socialist positions involving municipal issues and honest government. Many disappointed voters fell away from Socialist Party ranks. America's entry into World War I nearly finished off socialism, as the government's crackdown on antiwar activities fell heavily upon socialists and labor radicals.

The Socialist Party never fully recovered from the war. Although Debs received 1 million presidential votes in 1920 while in a federal penitentiary, the party lost more than half of its members. Its remaining appeal owed largely to the charismatic leadership of Norman Thomas, a former Presbyterian minister from New York. A perennial candidate for local, state, and national office, Thomas garnered 800,000 votes for president in 1932. Yet the party faced an uphill struggle as the New Deal borrowed socialist planks (as in the Social Security Act) and won blue-collar workers to the Democratic Party. A shattering division in 1936 between moderates and radicals and the coming of another world war reduced the party to a few thousand members. Nevertheless, loyalists persisted in maintaining a few press organs and running local candidates for office. A handful continued to be elected, generally in nonpartisan races.

[*See also* **Debs, Eugene; Political Parties; Populist Era; Progressive Era; Radicalism; Socialism; Third Parties;** *and* **Thomas, Norman.**]

BIBLIOGRAPHY

Buhle, Mari Jo, Paul Buhle, and Dan Georgakas, eds. *Encyclopedia of the American Left*, rev. ed. New York: Oxford University Press, 1998.

Judd, Richard. *Socialist Cities: Explorations into the Grass Roots of American Socialism*. Irvine: University of California, 1990.

Paul Buhle

SOCIAL POLICY

This entry contains two subentries: Orphanages; and Public Welfare.

ORPHANAGES

Orphanages played a central role in the United States for a century, from the 1830s to the 1930s, caring for orphans and other dependent children for a few months or many years. Like many long-lasting social institutions, orphanages began simply, underwent many transformations as time passed, and were eventually replaced by other policies deemed more modern.

The first orphanages in colonial North America were based on European models. In 1729 nuns in New Orleans founded an orphanage. In 1738 a Lutheran asylum, based on a German orphanage, opened in Ebenezer Colony in Georgia. The New Orleans orphanage lasted more than a century, whereas the orphanage in Ebenezer Colony soon vanished. The Charleston Orphan House, founded in 1790, was a public institution. Over the next four decades orphanages would continue to be opened as cities grew, people flowed into and out of them in ever-growing numbers, and diseases devastated port towns, particularly their more impoverished communities. Opening an orphanage became the common response to the ever-growing number of full orphans (with both parents deceased), half-orphans (with one living parent), and dependent children (with two parents living, but unable to provide them with shelter and food). The vast majority of orphanages were Catholic, a specific Protestant denomination, or broadly Protestant; although they were private institutions, they often received some level of public support, such as public money for land or a building.

By 1830 there were about thirty orphanages in the United States. Over the next three decades orphanages would spread much more rapidly, with more than eighty new institutions founded by 1850 and approximately seventy-five more by 1860. A number of factors led to this increase: an increasingly widespread belief in institutional care in general, support for orphanages in particular, increasing immigration and rapid urban growth, and the spread of wage labor, all of which combined to leave growing numbers of families moving far away from family and vulnerable to injury, death, or the loss of employment. Epidemics regularly hit cities, affecting working-class communities in particular; cholera epidemics in 1832–1833 and 1849–1850 were especially responsible for many children needing care, with dozens of orphanages being built in response.

Individuals, small groups, and churches built orphanages to care for children and to protect their religious and cultural heritage. The Irish built Catholic orphanages to protect Irish children from a broader Protestant society that was hostile to Catholicism; in later decades, Italian Catholics built their own orphanages to protect their children not only from Protestant public welfare officials and public schools, but also from other ethnic groups' Catholic orphanages. Similar issues motivated specific Protestant and Jewish groups.

By the eve of the Civil War, in 1860, there were between 150 and 200 orphanages in the United States. They had become a common, recognized institution that their own communities generally saw as a source of pride. The devastation brought by the Civil War would lead to an increase in private orphanages as well as the development of public orphanages to care for soldiers' orphans and of state institutions designed to care for children whom private institutions did not accept. Pennsylvania established an extensive system of large institutions for needy children of veterans. Michigan established a large state school that effectively served as a short-term orphanage specializing in placing children out in private homes after a relatively brief institutional stay; a number of other states copied Michigan's approach. Ohio, Connecticut, and Indiana established county-based public orphanages. This dramatic increase in direct public involvement in building and managing orphanages, along with religious and ethnic groups' continuing reliance on private orphanages, made orphanages even more commonplace. An 1890 census of orphanages found 563 orphanages in the United States, with a mean population of 84 children per institution.

Even as many new orphanages were being built, however, the seeds of their decline were being sown. Starting in the 1850s, Charles Loring Brace argued against institutional care for children and began sending "orphan trains" of dependent children west to find new homes on farms. By the 1890s, many prominent public officials and charitable leaders were arguing against orphanages as institutional care that raised children in an unhealthy manner. These critics argued for keeping children with their own mothers if possible (since by this time it was clear to everyone that most children in orphanages had at least one living parent) or by placing them in a new private home (called placing out at the time and now known as foster care), rather than relying on orphanages. This viewpoint received the highest possible approval at a 1909 White House Conference on dependent children, which deemed orphanage care a last resort.

The power of the federal government to intervene was limited when it did not actual develop programs of its own, and orphanages served important local needs for a variety of groups. By 1910 there were almost 1,000 orphanages in the United States, and by 1923 there were over 1,300, a number that stayed basically stable into the early 1930s. This growth had been in response to the same sorts of societal problems that had led to orphanage founding for decades. It was also fueled by the arrival of new immigrant groups wanting to build their own orphanages, as well as by the rise of fraternal organizations such as the Masons and Odd Fellows. By 1923 there were eighty fraternal orphanages in the nation.

Although local groups continued to build orphanages, in the 1910s state governments began developing alternative methods of caring for dependent children. By 1920 almost every state had some form of widows' or mothers' pensions that allowed dependent children to remain at home. In the 1920s state governments became more involved in placing children in homes, leading to the professionalization of "placing out" in homes (which orphanages had often done themselves), which gradually turned into foster care, seen as preferable to orphanages. Finally, in 1935 mothers' pensions programs of states were effectively replaced by Aid to Dependent Children, a joint federal–state program that allowed greater number of mothers to keep their children at home.

Although orphanages in the South and Catholic orphanages lasted into the 1950s and 1960s more often than other kinds of orphanages, they too were either changing into institutions for children with needs other than poverty or into foster care agencies. At the same time, many closed. The development of state and federal programs fulfilled the calls of reformers in the 1890s and 1900s to keep children in homes rather than in institutions.

BIBLIOGRAPHY

Cmiel, Kenneth. *A Home of Another Kind: One Chicago Orphanage and the Tangle of Child Welfare*. Chicago: University of Chicago Press, 1995.

Crenson, Matthew A. *Building the Invisible Orphanage: A Prehistory of the American Welfare System*. Cambridge, Mass.: Harvard University Press, 1998.

Hacsi, Timothy A. *Second Home: Orphan Asylums and Poor Families in America*. Cambridge, Mass.: Harvard University Press, 1997.

Zmora, Nurith. *Orphanages Reconsidered: Child Care Institutions in Progressive Era Baltimore*. Philadelphia: Temple University Press, 1994.

Timothy A. Hacsi

PUBLIC WELFARE

The federal government's involvement with public welfare in the United States occurred later than that of other nations. The government funded Civil War pensions, which served as an early form of social insurance for a significant minority of the population. But this initiative was an exception to the general character of American public welfare, which is typified by a narrower range of residual programs. Without family allowances that provide monthly payments for every child, a federal day care system, free education through graduate school, or, until 2010, a national system of health care financing, the role of American public welfare has always been capped at about two-thirds the size of the average European welfare state. Over the last quarter century, pressures have arisen to slash this spending, or if it cannot be cut back, at least to make public welfare programs market-like and ever more conditional on work.

The Limits on Public Welfare. There are many explanations for the comparatively limited nature of U.S. public welfare. Unlike smaller European nations whose class structure descended from feudalism and a landed aristocracy, the United States consisted of a large land mass with a frontier and a more fluid class system. This geopolitical fact dovetailed with the cultural appeal of individualism: in social welfare, it meant that most people were willing to trade the security of a better safety net for the chance that they or their children would be upwardly mobile. In the economy, it gave rise to the oft-stated preference for *laissez-faire* policies and small government. Although corporations have grown in size and the government has assumed a steadily larger economic role, a belief in small government remains the default American political ideology. Moreover, businesses have always worried that generous public welfare programs would erode the work ethic and inflate wages, which would have to be boosted to draw people into the labor force. Last, American political conflicts occur in a federal system, where, in contrast to the parliamentary systems that prevail in most of Europe, checks and balances decentralize power within the federal government, and states' rights obstruct the implementation of national legislation on the local level. When the issue of race and, more broadly, the heterogeneity of the U.S. population, is filtered through this political system, it is no wonder that the comprehensive public welfare systems common in Europe have been so difficult to establish here.

Civil War Pensions: The First Federal Public Welfare Program. The role of public welfare has grown steadily since the early twentieth century. Conventional social welfare histories were used to trace the establishment of a federal role for public welfare to the New Deal and passage of the 1935 Social Security Act, which provided for aid to poor children (welfare), unemployment insurance, and retirement benefits. But as Harvard University sociologist Theda Skocpol explored in *Protecting Soldiers and Mothers* (1992), this narrative is too tidy. Although pensions for civil war veterans began as a relatively small program, it soon consumed a significant portion of all federal revenues—41 percent by 1893. In fact, by 1910, 28 percent of all elderly men and 8 percent of all elderly women received civil war pensions. Hence, even though it may not have been designated as a federal social security program, the federal government was actually providing a form of social insurance to the elderly long before the 1935 Social Security Act.

Yet hopes for the potential of civil war pensions to expedite the passage of a modern social insurance program proved ill-founded. Securing a civil war pension depended not on a bureaucracy with established eligibility guidelines, but on whom you knew—a local politician or well-connected lawyer. With the taint of patronage hanging over this federal program, it became harder rather than easier to enact comprehensive social security legislation. As a consequence, throughout the Progressive Era, the states alone sponsored most public welfare legislation.

The Progressive Era to the New Deal (1890–1932). Workers' Compensation and Mothers' Pensions were the two most important public welfare programs the states established during the Progressive Era. Minnesota, Wisconsin, and New York were the first to enact workers' compensation in 1909, but by 1920, forty-three states had passed laws compensating employees for job-related injuries. Although state courts had originally classified all workers as "independent contractors" who bore the financial risk of on-the-job injuries, the toll of workplace injuries—35,000 workers killed and more than a half-million injured each year from 1888 to 1908—prompted a gradual shift in the law. Once the courts began to award significant damages, employers acquiesced to a system that would compensate employees for their injuries and protect employers from bankrupting lawsuits.

The states also initiated mothers' pensions. Missouri and Illinois were the first, in 1911, but other states soon followed, so that by 1919, a total of thirty-nine had similar programs. By 1931, some 200,000 children in every state except Georgia and South Carolina resided in homes that mothers' pensions helped to support. Although the program was not large and the benefits mostly went to widows, mothers' pensions are often credited with anticipating the Aid to Dependent Children (ADC) provision in the Social Security Act.

When the federal government intervened in public welfare during this period, the interventions were limited, circumscribed, or soon ruled unconstitutional. The first White House Conference on Children was held in 1909; a Children's Bureau was established within the federal government in 1912; the Owen–Keating Law outlawing child labor was passed in 1916, only to have the Supreme Court rule it unconstitutional two years later; and the Sheppard–Towner Act (1921) provided medical care for mothers and infants until it was defunded in 1929. Despite the growing economic role of the railroads and other large companies like Standard Oil and U.S. Steel, their political power combined with that of other businesses to preserve the dominant *laissez-faire* ideology and restrict public welfare interventions to the states.

The New Deal (1933–1945). This associative welfare system based on voluntary charity was ineffective in addressing mass unemployment in the ensuing depression of the 1930s. After the stock market crashed in 1929, 100,000 workers were laid off every week for the next three years, and industrial production fell 54 percent. With the unemployment rate peaking at 25 percent in 1933, President Franklin Roosevelt experimented with a series of cautious interventions. These emergency programs included the National Recovery Administration (1933–1935), which tried to stimulate the economy by granting corporations governmental approval for price fixing; the Federal Emergency Relief Administration (1933–1935), to aid local relief efforts; the Civilian Works Administration (1933–1934) that provided government employment; the Civilian Conservation Corps (1933–1942), which paid young men to develop state parks and conserve forests; the Works Projects Administration (1935–1942), which constructed airports, roads, and buildings; and the Tennessee Valley Authority that introduced dams, electricity, and economic development to much of the Deep South.

The most important of Roosevelt's social welfare measures occurred during the period from 1935 to 1937. Sometimes called the Second New Deal, the legislation of this period set the precedent for federal intervention in public provision. Foremost among this legislation is the 1935 Social Security Act, which provided welfare to poor children through the ADC program; authorized unemployment insurance benefits; and passed a retirement insurance program for the elderly. Two years later, the Roosevelt Administration enacted the Housing Act of 1937, which provided capital funds for public housing projects. The Fair Labor Standard Act of 1938 complemented this constellation of public programs by establishing a minimum wage. And even after enthusiasm for the Second New Deal had faded, the shortage of labor during World War II created a need for the Lanham Act (1943), which, by funding day care provisions in the factories, enabled women to work.

The New Deal broke sharply with the previous history of social welfare provision. But despite its federal auspices, this legislation recognized and often yielded to the rights of states, especially on racial matters. At a time when most African American men in the South were employed in the fields and African American women worked as domestic servants, the original Social Security Act covered neither agricultural nor domestic labor. More evidence of deference to the South appears in both the welfare (ADC) and the unemployment provisions of the act, where authority to determine both the standard of needs and the standard of benefits is granted to the states. Moreover, as Ira Katznelson shows in *When Affirmative Action Was White,* the supposedly universalistic provisions of the Fair Labor Standard Act and the Servicemen's Readjustment Act, or G.I. Bill (for free college tuition and mortgage assistance), were actually designed and implemented to exclude blacks. These concessions were probably necessary because Roosevelt had to compromise with conservative southern Democrats whose seniority gave them control over most of the major congressional committees. As a result, although New Deal legislation aspired to be national and comprehensive, it still could not depart too much from the history that preceded it.

Post World War II to the New Frontier (1946–1960). When the United States emerged victorious from World War II, it triggered a great policy debate about whether the postwar era would extend or recoil from the policies of the New Deal. The Full Employment Act of 1946 was the headline legislation in this debate. With 15 million military personnel demobilizing, labor unions were concerned that in the absence of a war, unemployment would rapidly return to Depression levels. They strongly supported the legislation, because it authorized a government planning agency to ensure full employment. Businesses, however, thought that government involvement in employment policy was "socialistic" and usurped a role usually reserved for the private sector. With the specter of a rising Soviet Union and the Cold War on the horizon, the business community was able to roll back this legislation and convert the government planning board into the president's purely advisory Council of Economic Advisors. The same legislative environment also killed President Harry Truman's efforts to provide government health care.

The New Frontier and the Great Society (1961–1968). Advances in federal social provision did not really reappear on the national agenda until the 1960s. Factors that contributed to its reappearance include the domestic civil rights movement led by Martin Luther King Jr.; civil unrest in many major American cities; the popularity of books like Michael Harrington's *The Other America,* which reminded the electorate that despite the relative prosperity of the postwar years, many Americans continued to live in desperate poverty; and the need during the Cold War to win the hearts and minds of newly independent and unaligned nations by expunging legal segregation from the United States. The resulting flurry of legislation includes the Community Mental Health Act of 1963, which funded community mental health centers; the Civil Rights Act of 1964 outlawing segregation in public facilities; the Food Stamp Act of 1964; federal aid to education (1965); the 1965 Voting Rights Act eliminating the poll tax in the South and guaranteeing universal suffrage; the Medicaid and Medicare laws providing health care for the poor and the elderly, respectively; and a cluster of War on Poverty programs such as Head Start, Model Cities, and the Job Corps. It was the greatest outpouring of social legislation since the Great Depression, but the perception that it was disproportionately beneficial to people of color opened the door to a conservative counterattack.

Conservative Dominance and the Reduction of Social Provision (1968–present). In the 1968 presidential election, Richard Nixon campaigned on the theme that the programs of the Great Society had ignored "the silent majority." Although Nixon began to devolve some services to the states, his legislative initiatives were often more universalistic. His administration raised Social Security benefits by 20 percent and indexed them to inflation (1972); turned the old age, blind, and disabled programs previously administered by the states into the federalized Supplemental Security program (1973); enacted the Comprehensive Employment Training Program (CETA, 1973) to offset jobs lost during the recession of the mid-1970s; and passed the Housing Act of 1974, whose Section 8, now renamed Housing Choice, persists to the beginning of the twenty-first century.

The counterattack on federal social provision did not really gather momentum until the election of President Ronald Reagan in 1980. Americans whose income had begun to stagnate during the 1970s responded positively to Reagan's contention that too much social welfare was hampering the natural productivity of the American economy. Cutbacks to federal social welfare programs then began in earnest. During his two terms, Reagan slashed the Housing and Urban Development budget by 76 percent; reoriented job training from CETA and the public sector to Job Training Partnership Act (1983) and the private sector; cut funding for food stamps outreach; removed almost 500,000 people from the Social Security disability rolls; and encouraged states to experiment with welfare-to-work programs.

Reagan's critique of social welfare generally was particularly devastating to the Aid to Families with Dependent Children (AFDC) welfare program. By the time President Bill Clinton was elected in 1992, his promise to "end welfare as we know it" was one of the cornerstones of his campaign. In the midst of the 1996 reelection campaign, he finally did. AFDC was replaced by Temporary Assistance for Needy Families (TANF), which block-granted the fixed sum of $16 billion to the states, established a lifetime limit of five years for the receipt of public assistance, and required that most welfare clients work. This legislation remains very controversial. It has reduced the welfare rolls—by 66 percent from 1996 to 2008—but in its absence, poverty has risen, and the recession that began in 2008 has been much harder on many families.

The only recent exception to this broad trend of cutting back or placing conditions on the receipt of social welfare is President Barack Obama's 2010 health care bill. It prohibits insurance companies from using a preexisting condition to reject an applicant; permits children to remain on their parents' health insurance until they reach the age of twenty-six; and requires everyone to purchase insurance while subsidizing lower-income families. Conservatives have sharply criticized the bill, because although it preserves the position of private insurance in health care financing, the heightened profile of the federal government in any social welfare initiative still triggers longstanding concerns about its proper role.

[*See also* **Civilian Conservation Corps; Housing Policy, Federal: Public Housing; Medicare and Medicaid; National Recovery Administration; Servicemen's Readjustment Act; Social Security; Social Security Policy; Tennessee Valley Authority;** *and* **Works Progress Administration.**]

BIBLIOGRAPHY

Blau, Joel, with Mimi Abramovitz. *The Dynamics of Social Welfare Policy*. New York: Oxford University Press, 2010.

Harrington, Michael. *The Other America*. Baltimore: Penguin Books, 1962.

Katznelson, Ira. *When Affirmative Action Was White*. New York: W. W. Norton, 2005.

Noble, Charles. *Welfare as We Knew It*. New York: Oxford University Press, 1997.

Skocpol, Theda. *Protecting Soldiers and Mothers: The Political Origins of Social Policy in the United States*. Cambridge, Mass.: Belknap Press of Harvard University Press, 1992.

Joel Blau

SOCIAL SECURITY

The passage of the Social Security Act in 1935 launched the federal welfare state. Without this program, now a central feature of American life, the incomes of most older citizens would fall below the poverty line. By the 1990s, more than a quarter of all U.S. households received monthly old age, survivors, or disability pensions. The enactment of this historic measure was neither sudden nor inevitable. Lawmakers and critics had been debating for decades whether the United States should borrow European models, modify programs from the Progressive Era (such as pensions for the aged poor or corporate gratuities), or continue to rely on traditional forms of relief.

In the depths of the Depression of the 1930s, when more than a quarter of all workers were unemployed, large numbers of middle-class Americans faced dependency in their later years. Older workers were among the first fired, and some hard-pressed corporations reneged on pension promises. Struggling with bankruptcy and lost savings, many families could not provide for their elderly relatives. Charities and state welfare boards ran out of money. States with old-age pensions tightened eligibility requirements, and veterans' benefits were cut.

Something had to be done, but President Franklin Delano Roosevelt, who as governor of New York in 1929 had signed into law the nation's most progressive old-age pension plan, proceeded cautiously. Roosevelt told Congress early in 1934, "I am looking for a sound means which I can recommend to provide at once security against several of the great disturbing factors in life—especially those which relate to unemployment and old age." Building on New Deal strategies, the president wanted to give workers and their families "the security of social insurance." He expected state governments, employers, and workers themselves to join with the federal government in developing a plan built on traditional American practices.

The 1935 act was a complex piece of legislation. Title I provided federal grants to states to pay half the cost of old-age assistance. Titles II and VIII inaugurated an old-age insurance program, whereas Titles III and IX launched an unemployment compensation program. Title IV gave states funds for aid to dependent children. Title V underwrote four different programs for (disabled or not, depending on the program) children and their mothers, especially in rural areas. Title VI increased public health services. Title VII created a Social Security Board to oversee programs and to collect data on the program's impact. Title X provided support for the needy blind. Title XI acknowledged Congress's right to "alter, amend, or repeal any provision of this Act."

Congress radically altered the original provisions of Title II before they even went into effect. Whereas the 1935 act had treated benefits based on employees' contributions as if they were annuities, and thus correlated to wages, the 1939 amendments gave lower-income contributors and their surviving families benefits that were more "adequate" than they had earned. With this change of policy, the system henceforth was tilted toward a welfare model rather than a private-insurance model. Incremental reforms gradually made Social Security broader in coverage and more generous in benefits. Congress increased Title II benefits 77 percent in 1950. Disability provisions were introduced in the mid-1950s. Medicare, which covered hospitalization for Social Security recipients, was added in 1965. Seven years later, Social Security benefits were automatically indexed to reflect changes in the cost of living.

In its formative years, Social Security enjoyed overwhelming popular support. The system ran surpluses as long as the ratio of workers to beneficiaries was high. Republican presidential candidates Alf Landon in 1936 and Barry Goldwater in 1964 criticized the program, but Republicans generally joined Democrats in supporting reforms recommended by Social Security officials and outside experts. By the mid-1970s, however, support for Social Security had become more problematic. Inflation eroded trust funds. Public confidence was shaken by doomsday scenarios. Some predicted intergenerational warfare: They feared that when the millions of baby boomers retired, the cost of their Social Security benefits would place a very heavy tax burden on the younger generation. Congress, spurred by President Jimmy Carter, increased Social Security taxes substantially in 1977. A compromise set of amendments six years later raised the retirement age in the twenty-first century and set a ceiling on benefits not subject to income tax. Such measures were taken to reaffirm the fundamental aims of the original act.

In many ways, Social Security fulfilled Roosevelt's conviction that the measure was "a sound idea—a sound ideal." New Jersey senator Bill Bradley in 1983 called it "the best expression of community that we have in this country today." The value of Social Security benefits in the mid-1990s for an average wage earner who died and left a spouse and two children under eighteen was equivalent to a $322,000 life insurance policy. The program by the mid-1990s paid monthly survivor benefits to 7.4 million Americans, including 2 million children. More than 4 million disabled workers under the age of sixty-five, in addition to 1.7 million of their dependents (including more than 1 million children), received benefits under Social Security's disability program. Monthly benefits averaged about $680; for a disabled worker, spouse, and two children, benefits were roughly $1,100.

For all of its successes, however, Social Security remained under fire as the century ended. Loath to make dramatic changes, politicians were nonetheless frustrated by their inability to reduce the scope of entitlements. Those receiving benefits or who expected to get them shortly were more likely than younger Americans to declare the system financially secure. Many people, moreover, misperceived the program's scope and operations. Some still thought Social Security operated like a private insurance program. Others felt that monthly Social Security checks should be enough to cover basic expenses, obviating the need for private savings or other retirement pensions. As a result, Social Security appeared likely to become even more controversial in the twenty-first century, particularly if Washington's role in delivering human services continued to diminish.

[*See also* **Carter, Jimmy; Goldwater, Barry; Income Tax, Federal; Medicare and Medicaid; New Deal; Poverty; Progressive Era; Roosevelt, Franklin Delano; Social Security Policy;** *and* **Taxation.**]

BIBLIOGRAPHY

Achenbaum, W. Andrew. *Social Security: Visions and Revisions* Cambridge, UK; New York: Cambridge University Press, 1986.

Berkowitz, Edward D., and Kim McQuaid. *Creating the Welfare State: The Political Economy of 20th-Century Reform,* rev. ed. Lawrence: University Press of Kansas, 1992.

Haber, Carole, and Brian Gratton. *Old Age and the Search for Security*. Bloomington: Indiana University Press, 1994.

Pifer, Alan, and Forrest Chisman, eds. *The Report of the Committee on Economic Security of 1935,* 50th Anniversary ed. Washington, D.C.: National Conference on Social Welfare, 1985.

Quadagno, Jill. *The Transformation of Old Age Security: Class and Politics in the American Welfare State.* Chicago: University of Chicago Press, 1988.

W. Andrew Achenbaum

SOCIAL SECURITY POLICY

Since its passage in 1935, the Social Security Act has fostered eleven different welfare programs, some of which are universal and others poverty based. The most popular, expensive, and effective of the programs, Social Security, provides monthly benefits to 35 million retired workers and another 19 million widows, widowers, spouses, disabled persons, and children. When Social Security was enacted in 1935, the elderly were more likely than other age group to be poor. But Social Security has reduced poverty rates for the aged below rates for other ages. Social Security now comprises about 40 percent of income for all older people. Two-thirds receive at least half of their income and one-third receives at least 90 percent of their income from Social Security. It is a particularly important source of income for women and blacks and Hispanics. Over the decades, legislators have expanded the program. Benefits have been extended to wives and widows, eligibility was made gender neutral, and marital requirements for divorcees dropped from twenty to ten years. Legislators have created a benefit formula that is progressive, designed to redistribute from higher-paid to lower-paid workers. As a result, benefits replace 55 percent of income for the lowest earners compared with 28 percent of income for the highest earners. Social Security's financing formula, however, is regressive. It consists of a flat tax of 6.2 percent on earnings, matched by employer, up to the Social Security tax cap of $106,800 in 2010. Earnings above the ceiling are not subject to payroll taxes; thus lower-income earners contribute a higher proportion of their total earnings to Social Security than higher-income earners.

Social Security is regarded as a universal entitlement for contributors and their families and remains overwhelmingly popular with voters. In nearly all polls between 80 and 90 percent of respondents favor a strengthened program. Social Security was often regarded as the third rail, untouchable by politicians, but cost-cutting changes have been made to the program nonetheless. Aware that cohorts come in different sizes, the Social Security Administration purposely began accumulating a trust fund surplus for this pay-as-you-go system to ensure there would be enough funds for aging baby boomers. That surplus is now over $2.6 trillion. By 2037, it is estimated that the surplus will be gone and the amount coming in from workers each month will cover only 78 percent of the payouts. In response, Congress has implemented changes encouraging people to delay Social Security benefits. Beginning in 2003, the age of eligibility for full retirement benefits has been gradually increasing from age sixty-five to age sixty-seven, where it will be in 2027. The age for early retirement remains age sixty-two, but the penalty for taking early benefits, which most men and nearly all women take, has increased from 20 to 30 percent. Similarly, the Social Security earnings test penalizes wages among early retirees. Originally beneficiaries could not earn more than $15 a month without losing their entire benefit. Those rules have been relaxed and currently there is no earnings test for those ages sixty-five and older, but those ages sixty-two to sixty-five lose $1 in benefits for every $2 in earnings after earning $14,000 for the year.

Privatization. Recent debates about Social Security have focused on privatization. After he was reelected in 2004, President George W. Bush made the privatization of Social Security his top domestic priority. The plan most often discussed would have allowed those under age 55 to divert as much as 4 percent of their 6.2 percent Social Security contribution to private accounts. Supporters of some privatization argued that the existing program would soon be fiscally unsustainable and proposed individual accounts that would maximize each person's choice and responsibility. Opponents argued that privatization would make the fiscal situation worse, increase program costs, expand risk for older people and their families, and eliminate many of the features that make the existing program advantageous for lower earners and those who care for children and disabled and older persons.

At the end of 2010, when proponents of Social Security were asking for a 1 percent increase in the Social Security payroll tax to finance benefits for the baby boomers, President Barack Obama and Congress passed a payroll tax "holiday" that reduced the individual payroll tax from 6.2 to 4.2 percent for the year 2011. The impetus was to jump start the economy and create more jobs by putting $120 billion back in consumer's pockets. The government has stated that the funds will be repaid through a transfer of general tax revenues. Opponents argued that Congress may not actually transfer those funds and that the payroll tax holiday may become a permanent reduction. They prefer that Congress address the shortfall with changes that do not reduce benefits. They have asked Congress to raise the Social Security payroll tax by 1 percent for employees and employers. They have also proposed that Congress raise the cap on taxable earnings to at least $180,000 and index it to inflation, increasing the proportion of income that is taxable from 84 to 90 percent. Social Security remains popular with voters, but many legislators are proposing changes aimed at either strengthening or retrenching the program.

Programs Targeting Families. Temporary Assistance for Needy Families (TANF), a poverty-based benefit program, has never been as broadly supported or funded. Initially named Aid to Dependent Children, then renamed Aid to Families with Dependent Children, it was created to help single parents with children. The program grew throughout the 1970s as the courts guaranteed applicants a hearing before being denied benefits. Poverty rates for children declined throughout the 1970s. But as the program grew, so did its opposition. Opponents argued that it undermined family stability and discouraged work. Throughout the 1980s and 1990s, Congress reduced benefits and child poverty rates rose to their current levels of nearly 20 percent. By 1996, Congress replaced the program with TANF, a block-grant program aimed at moving recipients from welfare to work. The Personal Responsibility and Work Opportunity Reconciliation Act (PRWOA), signed by President Clinton, ended federal entitlement to assistance, implemented work requirements, and set a lifetime maximum of five years for benefits. Caseloads dropped by over 60 percent in less than ten years in part because of a stronger economy and in part because of legislative changes. From the peak of 14 million average monthly recipients in 1994, caseloads have averaged around 4.5 million since 2004. Average monthly benefit size has declined as well, with the real dollar value of benefits dropping by over 60 percent between their peak in the late 1970s and the late 1990s. Although many welfare recipients who left the roles entered employment, not all were able to do so because of physical and mental health problems, lack of training, and relatively high unemployment. Women, as well as blacks and Hispanics, are significantly more likely to rely on TANF; thus reductions to these programs have impacted them, and their children, the hardest.

Programs Targeting the Elderly or Disabled. Supplemental Security Income (SSI) was created in 1972 to provide income to poor people at least 65 years old or disabled. SSI benefits are indexed to cost of living but do not raise many older people above the poverty line because maximum federal benefits are equal to about 77 percent of the federal poverty line for single beneficiaries and 87 percent for older couples. Only about one-third of poor older people and only one-half of those who are SSI eligible actually receive benefits. SSI use among those 65 and older has dropped from 10 percent in 1975 to about 3 percent since 2006 because poverty rates have dropped, many see the applications as arduous and humiliating, and the SSI earnings and assets tests have been frozen for decades. Under federal guidelines, the first $65 in earned income, along with an additional $20, is disregarded each month and any additional earned income decreases benefits by $1 for every $2 earned. Unearned income is penalized $1 for every $1. Assets, excluding a house, car, and burial funds under certain conditions, must be below $2,000 for individuals and $3,000 for couples. The modest income disregards have been in place since 1981; the asset maximums have been in place since 1989. Thus SSI's history is mainly one of legislative inactivity. Women, blacks, and Hispanics are significantly more likely to rely on SSI. When poverty-based programs are left unattended, those who rely on them face even more difficult financial circumstances.

Medicare. Since 1965, Medicare has provided universal health care benefits to people who are age sixty-five and older or disabled. Although Medicare provides broad coverage of acute care, other types of health care, most notably long-term care, remain uncovered. Among the frequent legislative moves by Congress, some have emphasized expanding benefits whereas others have emphasized reducing costs. Medicare has four parts, and each is funded differently and involves out-of-pocket expenses for older people including premiums, copayments, deductibles, and amounts over the allowable rate. Medicare Part A, which pays for inpatient hospital stays, skilled nursing care, some home health visits and hospice care, is funded through the 1.45 percent Hospital Insurance tax paid by employees each month and matched by their employers. Part B covers outpatient physician visits and services, preventative services, and home health visits. By federal law, 25 percent of the cost of Part B is funded by beneficiary premiums and the remaining 75 percent is funded by general revenues.

Part C refers to Medicare Advantage, through which beneficiaries forego traditional Medicare and instead enroll in a managed care or health maintenance organization (HMO) program. Part C is funded through premiums and general revenues. In an effort to reduce Medicare costs, legislation passed in 1982, 1997, and 2003 provided subsidies to the private market to lure HMOs and similar provider groups into developing managed care plans. Now called Medicare Advantage, Medicare Part C covers nearly one-fourth of all Medicare recipients. These efforts, however, have been ineffectual in reducing costs. In 2005, the government was paying an extra $546 per enrollee in private plans compared with those in traditional Medicare. The legislation has, however, shifted millions of U.S. tax funds into the profitable managed care market.

Part D, the voluntary prescription drug plan, was enacted by Congress in 2003. Although many older people had prescription drug insurance, about one-fourth did not. Under the new plan, beneficiaries pay an additional monthly premium, and the remaining costs are covered by general revenues and some state payments. Opponents criticized Part D because the legislation agreed not to negotiate pricing with pharmaceuticals and required beneficiaries to select and pay premiums to one private drug plan from a sea of complex and ever-changing private plan options. Beneficiaries then pay a monthly premium, an annual deductible, a copayment, and then the full amount of any costs inside what has been dubbed "the donut hole." Out-of-pocket expenses for prescription coverage alone can exceed $3,000 per year.

Overall Medicare costs began rising dramatically from the moment Medicare was implemented. In 2010, Medicare expenditures reached $504 billion, 15 percent of the Federal budget, 3.5 percent of the gross domestic product (GDP), or nearly $11,000 per beneficiary. Early efforts to control costs led policy makers in 1984 to implement a prospective payment system aimed at reducing unnecessary medical treatment and thereby lowering costs. But any cost reductions were short lived and costs continue to soar. Out-of-pocket expenses for older people rose from 15 percent of annual income in 1965 to 22 percent by 1998. By 2025, out-of-pocket health care expenses are expected to reach 30 percent. The Medicare trust fund is nearly depleted and costs are expected to continue to increase until legislation addresses the entire U.S. health care system.

Medicaid. Since 1965, Medicaid has provided free and comprehensive coverage of health care for nearly 60 million low-income children and parents, people with severe disabilities, the elderly, and Medicare beneficiaries known as "dual eligibles." Currently one-third of U.S. children are covered by Medicaid. Nearly three-fourths of Medicaid recipients receive care through managed care programs. Health care benefits are broad but vary by state. Medicaid has undergone significant legislative changes since the 1970s, some aimed at expanding coverage and others aimed at cutting costs. In 1986 legislation required states to cover children up to age five if the family was below the federal poverty line. States are now required to cover poor children up to age nineteen and children within 133 percent of the poverty line up to age six. The 1998 Medicare Catastrophic Coverage Act required states to cover Medicare premiums and cost-sharing for low-income Medicare beneficiaries (QMBs) with incomes below 100 percent of poverty. In 1996, The PWROA barred Medicaid coverage for five years for legal immigrants who entered the United States prior to 1996 and made it optional for states to cover legal immigrants after the five-year ban. The Balanced Budget Act of 1997 established the State Children's Health Insurance Program (SCHIP), a block grant to states for coverage of uninsured low-income children ineligible for Medicaid.

Medicaid financing is a federal–state partnership in which the federal government matches at least 50 percent in every state and a higher percentage in poorer states, reaching 76 percent in the poorest state. The federal share of Medicaid spending overall averages about 57 percent. States on average spend about 16 percent of their general funds on Medicaid, and Medicaid accounts for about 7 percent of total federal outlays. Medicaid spending in 2010 totals nearly $400 billion. Two-thirds of Medicaid spending is attributable to seniors and people with disabilities, although they make up just one-quarter of all Medicaid enrollees. Medicaid spending continues to spiral upward as legislators strive to expand coverage and reduce costs.

Nearly eighty years after its passage, the Social Security Act remains one of the most important and influential pieces of legislation ever passed in the United States. Details of the programs have changed tremendously but fiscal viability, universal coverage, and entitlement are still vigorously debated in the twenty-first century.

[*See also* **Medicare and Medicaid; Social Policy: Public Welfare;** ***and*** **Social Security.**]

BIBLIOGRAPHY

Baker, Dean, and Mark Weisbrot. *Social Security: The Phony Crisis*. Chicago: University of Chicago Press, 2001.

Béland, Daniel. *Social Security: History and Politics from the New Deal to the Privatization Debate*. Lawrence: University Press of Kansas, 2007.

Blahous, Charles. *Social Security: The Unfinished Work*. Stanford, Calif.: Hoover Institution Press, 2010.

Gordon, Linda. *Pitied but Not Entitled; Single Mothers and the History of Welfare*. New York; Toronto: Free Press; Maxwell Macmillan Canada, 1994.

Katz, Michael. *The Undeserving Poor: From the War on Poverty to the War on Welfare*. New York: Pantheon Books, 1989.

Harrington Meyer, Madonna and Pamela Herd. *Market Friendly or Family Friendly? The State and Gender Inequality in Old Age*. New York: Russell Sage Foundation, 2007.

Moon, Marilyn, with Pamela Herd. *A Place at the Table: Women's Needs and Medicare Reform*. New York: Century Foundation Press, 2002.

Madonna Harrington Meyer

SONS OF LIBERTY

After the British Parliament passed the Stamp Act in 1765, small groups in each colony—generally artisans or intercolonial merchants, joined by a few attorneys, doctors, and teachers—became convinced that only large crowds prepared to act violently could successfully resist the tax. Together they had the contacts and expertise to organize townspeople against the tax. Leaders in Connecticut dubbed their followers "Sons of Liberty." The name spread rapidly, soon coming to stand for everyone who participated in the popular resistance to the Stamp Act. Between August and December 1765, the Sons of Liberty forced stamp distributors to resign, governors to withhold stamped paper, and courts to remain open in defiance of the law. Their efforts prevented enforcement of the act and led to its repeal in March 1766.

British politicians and conservative colonists hoped the Sons of Liberty would disband after repeal. Suspicious of British motives and convinced that liberty was still at risk, however, the Sons remained active and maintained contact with one another throughout the colonies. While persuading voters to purge conservatives from colonial assemblies and replace them with liberty's friends, they strengthened their own popular base by serving the interests of artisans and small merchants.

In every imperial crisis between 1766 and 1774, the Sons of Liberty called forth crowds to bully British officials and American sympathizers, confident that colonial governments could not respond effectively. In the process, they deepened estrangement between the colonists and their British governors and taught the people that government should rest on popular consent. The collapse of royal authority in 1774–1775 and its swift replacement by local committees and provincial congresses reflected a decade's work by the Sons of Liberty.

[*See also* **Republicanism; Stamp Act;** *and* **Taxation.**]

BIBLIOGRAPHY

Countryman, Edward. *A People in Revolution: The American Revolution and Political Society in New York, 1760–1790*. New York: W. W. Norton, 1981.

Maier, Pauline. *From Resistance to Revolution: Colonial Radicals and the Development of American Opposition to Britain, 1765–1776*. New York: Alfred A. Knopf, 1972.

John L. Bullion

SOUTHERN CHRISTIAN LEADERSHIP CONFERENCE

Created in the wake of the Montgomery Bus Boycott in 1957 by Martin Luther King Jr. and his followers, the Southern Christian Leadership Conference (SCLC) coordinated and assisted local organizations working for the full equality of African Americans during the civil rights movement. Initial organizers included Ella Baker, Ralph Abernathy, Fred Shuttlesworth, Joseph Lowery, C. K. Steele, T. J. Jemison, and Bayard Rustin. Animated by King's philosophy of nonviolent direct action and his vision of a mass movement rooted in Christian love and multiracial democracy, the organization conducted leadership training programs, citizen-education projects, and voter registration drives. Along with the Student Non-Violent Coordinating Committee, the SCLC played an integral role in various southern desegregation and voting-rights campaigns, most notably in Albany, Georgia, and Birmingham and Selma, Alabama. These campaigns spurred the passage of the Civil Rights Act of 1964 and the Voting Rights Act of 1965. In addition, the SCLC helped organize the 1963 March on Washington for Jobs and Freedom where King delivered his famous "I Have a Dream" speech.

Following these initial successes, the SCLC experienced a series of setbacks. In 1965 and 1966, as Black Power began to eclipse nonviolent direct action among many activists and organizations, King and the SCLC embarked on an unsuccessful campaign in Chicago.

In 1968, the SCLC planned a Poor People's Campaign to be held in Washington, D.C., with the hope of uniting poor people from all races, ethnicities, and religions. This effort was cut short by King's assassination in Memphis. Following King's death, the SCLC maintained its philosophy of nonviolent direct action, but focused on smaller, local efforts. The organization was further weakened by internal schisms, most significantly the 1972 departure of the Reverend Jesse Jackson (1941–) of Chicago and his followers who had staffed Operation Breadbasket, an SCLC effort directed at economic justice for African Americans. Despite these difficulties, the SCLC remained active in the struggle for racial, social, and economic justice as the twentieth century ended.

[*See also* **African Americans in Politics; Civil Rights; Civil Rights Legislation; Equality;** *and* **King, Martin Luther, Jr.**]

BIBLIOGRAPHY

Fairclough, Adam. *To Redeem the Soul of America*. Athens: University of Georgia Press, 1987.

Garrow, David. *Bearing the Cross: Martin Luther King, Jr., and the Southern Christian Leadership Conference*. New York: W. Morrow, 1986.

Patrick D. Jones

SPOILS SYSTEM

The "spoils system" as a term is derived from the expression "to the victor belong the spoils" as applied to American political practice by Senator William Marcy of New York in a speech he gave in 1832. Marcy was defending President Andrew Jackson's use of government jobs to reward supporters of his administration (patronage). Jackson may not have been quite so blunt in his presentation of the system, but he did use it to his benefit. It would be wrong to suggest that he inaugurated the system, yet it has been associated with him more than any other president. Jackson did rationalize his actions, however, suggesting that he was dismantling what had become an entrenched, aristocratic bastion and opening up the bureaucracy to the "Common Man." The Common Man, he argued, was endowed with common sense and could ably fulfill the demands of these jobs.

Between Jackson and the late nineteenth century, the spoils system evolved into much more than Jackson's symbolic democracy. The adept use of patronage by presidents and their parties made the system a fixture in American politics. It was a means of rewarding party faithful who had helped the party win power. It also filled party war chests through payroll assessments and helped to maintain the prominence of the political party in American politics. By the Gilded Age, however, the spoils system precipitated some egregious examples of corruption and incompetence. Allowing partisan control of government largesse had become a recipe for abuse. Specific skills were needed in many offices and the process of appointment rarely took those concerns into consideration.

By the election of James A. Garfield in 1880, the spoils system had caused a rift even within the majority Republican Party. Agitation for reform in the civil service began as a reaction to blatant corruption in the Grant Administration. Subsequently, President Rutherford B. Hayes removed the New York Customs House collector, Chester Arthur, because he said Arthur's practice of assessing a percentage of his employees' salaries to go into the coffers of the Republican Party, although technically legal, was unethical. This action launched a ferocious battle within the party between Stalwarts—those who supported the spoils system—on the one hand, and reformers—"Mugwumps" and "Half Breeds"—on the other. When a deranged office-seeker shot and killed Garfield in 1881, the issue of reform became preeminent. Ironically, a Democratic senator from Ohio, George H. Pendleton, had introduced a bill to reform the civil service prior to Garfield's demise.

Pendleton suggested that reforming the civil service would actually fulfill the objective Jackson had sought a generation earlier. The bureaucracy had become entrenched and inefficient again, Pendleton argued. It was filled with long-time occupants who had created a *de facto* aristocracy. Pendleton proposed a merit system involving an examination process overseen by a bipartisan Civil Service Commission to ensure that government employees had the skills necessary to do their jobs well. He also sought to outlaw the practice of political assessments which, he said, led to corruption.

Garfield's assassination prompted Congress to reconsider Pendleton's bill. Republicans still balked, but a poor showing in the 1882 elections prompted them to reconsider. In 1883, the Pendleton Civil Service Reform Act passed and the merit system was introduced for approximately 10 percent of all government jobs. Political assessments ended. In a final irony, the Democrats, upset over losing future spoils of office, ousted Pendleton after one Senate term as thanks for his successful work on reform. Nonetheless, his act was the beginning of the end for Jackson's spoils system.

[*See also* **Garfield, James; Hayes, Rutherford B.;** *and* **Jackson, Andrew.**]

BIBLIOGRAPHY

Fish, Carl R. *The Civil Service and the Patronage.* New York: Longmans, Green, 1905.

Hoogenboom, Ari. *Outlawing the Spoils: A History of the Civil Service Reform Movement, 1865–1883.* Urbana: University of Illinois Press, 1961.

Mach, Thomas S. *"Gentleman George" Hunt Pendleton: Party Politics and Ideological Identity in Nineteenth-Century America.* Kent, Ohio: Kent State University Press, 2007.

White, Leonard D. *The Jacksonians: A Study in Administrative History, 1829–1861.* New York: Macmillan, 1954.

Thomas S. Mach

STAMP ACT

To British politicians seeking new sources of revenue after the Seven Years' War, the American colonies seemed an ideal source, for both economic and political reasons. Prosperous and lightly taxed, the colonists could afford to help pay for their defense. They had obviously benefited from the expulsion of the French from Canada and should be willing to assist the Mother Country. With the exception of William Pitt, a popular leader of the parliamentary opposition, no prominent British politician questioned Parliament's right to tax colonists. The principal difficulty in planning American taxation was finding self-enforcing duties that were appropriate for a people accustomed to evading British customs duties by smuggling and bribery.

Stamp taxes in England provided a precedent. To be legally binding, a wide range of legal proceedings and commercial agreements had to be recorded on stamped papers. In 1764, George Grenville, first lord of the treasury, announced plans to impose such a tax in America the next year, inviting in the interim colonial suggestions about specific stamp duties or alternative taxes. Instead, colonial assemblies argued that since Americans were not represented in Parliament, that body could not tax them. Grenville countered by arguing that members of Parliament represented all Britons, not just those who actually elected them. This doctrine of virtual representation was not simply the first response in the constitutional debate; it also signaled the ministry's determination to impose the stamp tax. Parliament passed the legislation, by 249 to 51 in the Commons and unanimously in the Lords. Grenville did agree to the appointment of Americans as stamp distributors, a step he felt would reduce opposition to the tax and encourage ambitious colonists to look to Britain for political jobs and power.

The reaction in America, partially coordinated by resistance groups calling themselves the Sons of Liberty, was immediate and violent. Rioting crowds forced distributors to resign; colonial assemblies coordinated political resistance through the Stamp Act Congress. Governors could not compel the distribution of stamps, and thus the tax did not enforce itself.

The repeal of the Stamp Act in March 1766 was a major defeat for Britain. George III would subsequently claim that retreat on this issue set the stage for rebellion. Without question, the Stamp Act crisis weakened royal authority in the colonies, heightened American suspicions about British policy, and encouraged further resistance.

[*See also* **Sons of Liberty;** *and* **Taxation.**]

BIBLIOGRAPHY

Bullion, John L. *A Great and Necessary Measure: George Grenville and the Genesis of the Stamp Act, 1763–1765*. Columbia: University of Missouri Press, 1982.

Egnal, Marc. *A Mighty Empire: The Origins of the American Revolution*. Ithaca, N.Y.: Cornell University Press, 1988.

Thomas, P. D. G. *British Politics and the Stamp Act Crisis: The First Phase of the American Revolution, 1763–1767*. Oxford, UK: Clarendon Press, 1975.

John L. Bullion

STANTON, ELIZABETH CADY

(1815–1902), women's rights leader and theorist. A favorite child of a prominent and wealthy New York lawyer, Elizabeth Cady attended Emma Willard's girls' school in Troy, New York, graduating in 1832. In 1840 she married a prominent abolitionist, Henry Stanton. She was inspired to focus on women's rights by her own difficulties as a wife and mother (eventually with seven children), by the serious discriminations against women in U.S. society, and by the reform community around her. In 1848, with Lucretia Mott and others, she organized America's first woman's rights convention, in Seneca Falls, New York, where she lived with her family. She drafted the convention's Declaration of Sentiments, an assertion of women's rights modeled on the Declaration of Indepe-ndence. In 1851, along with Amelia Bloomer, editor of the temperance newspaper the *Lily*, she designed and wore the simplified Bloomer dress. (The opposition was so vehement, however, that they gave it up after several years.) That same year she met her lifelong coworker in the women's rights cause, Susan B. Anthony.

In 1863, after moving to New York City, she and Anthony founded the Women's Loyal National League. The organization secured over 300,000 signatures to a petition demanding the abolition of slavery. In 1866 she ran (unsuccessfully) for the House of Representatives, when she discovered that the state's prohibition against women voting did not extend to their holding office. She was the first woman to do so. In 1868 she and Anthony founded a cross-class Workingwoman's Association to improve working conditions for women. That same year they also launched a weekly newspaper, the *Revolution*, which lasted a year and a half. In 1869 they founded the National Woman Suffrage Association, of which Stanton served as president for the next twenty-one years. That same year she began a twelve-year stint as a national lecturer for the New York Lyceum Bureau, becoming one of its most popular speakers.

Stanton was known for her searching intellect, wide-ranging views, and radical positions. Although suffrage and property rights remained central to her women's rights platform, she also favored birth control and liberalized divorce laws—inflammatory issues in her era. She was attracted to communalism, practiced homeopathy and diet reform, critiqued unfair labor practices, and excoriated men for their treatment of women. Far in advance of her times, she saw the abuse of women's bodies in slavery, rape, and confining fashions as central to men's control of women, under a system she occasionally called "patriarchy." Although Stanton strongly supported woman suffrage—and coedited with Anthony a three-volume *History of Woman Suffrage* (1881–1886)—she rejected Anthony's exclusive focus on this issue. In her final decades, she crusaded against religion's oppression of women, writing a *Woman's Bible* (2 volumes, 1895–1898), in which she reworked Bible stories according to women's rights principles. In 1888, along with Anthony, she participated in the founding of the International Council of Women. Her memoirs *Eighty Years and More* appeared in 1898. A long-planned systemic treatise on women's rights remained uncompleted, but her output of speeches and articles were sufficient to make her the preeminent women's-rights theorist of nineteenth-century America.

[*See also* **Anthony, Susan B.; Antislavery Movement; Birth Control; Feminism; Seneca Falls Women's Rights Convention of 1848;** ***and*** **Woman Suffrage Movement.**]

BIBLIOGRAPHY

Banner, Lois W. *Elizabeth Cady Stanton: A Radical for Women's Rights*. Boston: Little, Brown, 1979.

Griffith, Elizabeth. *In Her Own Right: The Life of Elizabeth Cady Stanton*. New York: Oxford University Press, 1984.

Lois W. Banner

STATE GOVERNMENTS

The American scheme of government is a historical paradox. The federal Constitution proclaims the supremacy of the federal government in a theoretically indissoluble Union, but since the inception of the nation, states and cities have performed most of the tasks of day-to-day governance. The states, like the national government, claim their authority based on the will of the people, yet the Constitution is entirely silent on where cities derive their powers. Indeed, the word "city" nowhere appears in the document. Far from being a neat hierarchy of local, state, and national governments, the American scheme of governance has historically mixed and overlapped levels of governmental activity, combined public and private interests, and appealed to often conflicting theories of popular and state sovereignty.

Creating and Defining State Government. Each of the original thirteen states had a colonial antecedent that lacked a well-defined scheme of separation of powers. In most colonies, power rested with the assembly, and the judiciary was often tied to the legislature. The Revolutionary War, however, transformed these colonial appendages into independent states, each with its own form of government that rested, except for Connecticut and Rhode Island, on a constitution.

These new American states bound themselves into a revolutionary alliance that worked first through the Continental Congress and then, beginning in 1781, the Articles of Confederation. Under the Articles, the national government rested upon a compact among the states. The members of the federal Congress were selected by the state legislatures and any amendment to the Articles required the unanimous vote of the states. The Constitution of 1787, however, provided for a popularly based federal republic of enumerated powers in which the nation held sway in a few areas (e.g., making war, controlling commerce, issuing legal tender), but with a high level of dependency on state governments. For example, the framers allotted representatives in Congress based on population, but the state governments were given the task of apportioning these representatives among districts in the states and setting the terms of their election. Each state was guaranteed two senators to be selected (until passage of the Seventeenth Amendment in 1913) by the state legislatures. The president of the United States was elected not by the people but through the states in an Electoral College. Finally, the Tenth Amendment, ratified in 1791 along with the other Bill of Rights amendments, reserved to the states all governmental power not delegated to the national government.

Under this arrangement, state and local governments retained significant powers, most notably the police powers. Through these powers the states (and local governments) provided for the health, safety, morals, and welfare of their citizens. Throughout American history, therefore, whereas the national government has fulfilled high political functions (e.g., national defense, foreign policy, and territorial acquisitions), state and city governments have played decisive roles in matters such as crime and punishment, marriage, family affairs, contracts, property, and all manner of commercial relations.

When the Constitution was written, no legal distinction existed between cities and other corporations. Gradually, however, American law began to recognize such distinction. In *Dartmouth College v. Woodward* (1819), Supreme Court justice Joseph Story crafted an important distinction, defining as public corporations legal entities such as towns and cities that existed for public political purposes only. As a practical matter, city governments developed as if they were the state itself. In *Hunter v. Pittsburgh* (1907), the Supreme Court held that "municipal corporations are political subdivisions of the State created as convenient agencies for exercising such of the governmental powers of the State as may be entrusted to them." States were free to add, withdraw, and modify at their pleasure the powers exercised by cities. In *Community Communications Co. v. City of Boulder* (1982) the high court pithily ruled, "We are a nation not of city-states but of States."

The Evolution of State Government. By the late nineteenth century the states began to develop legal schemes assuring cities a measure of self-government. The Missouri Constitution of 1875, for example, was the first to include a home-rule provision, which was adopted widely. These provisions granted municipalities control over their local affairs in return for a pledge to abide by certain legislative restrictions, the most important of which involved their borrowing power.

Unlike cities, the federal Constitution recognized the states. One of the most profound powers delegated to the national government was the provision in Article IV, Section 4, guaranteeing each state a "republican form of government." Since the Supreme Court's decision in *Luther v. Borden* (1849), the power to assess either the legitimacy or the republican character of a state government has rested with Congress.

Republican government has meant in concrete terms executive, legislative, and judicial branches. Throughout their history, the legislatures have exercised the greatest authority.

In the modern era, except for Nebraska, which has been unicameral since 1934, states have been bicameral, with an upper house composed of members with usually longer terms and larger districts and a more numerous lower chamber with shorter terms and smaller districts. Today, these legislatures average about 180 total members, with New Hampshire's more than 400 legislators topping the list.

Governors have invariably been popularly elected and generally weaker than their counterparts in the White House. Many states, for example, have an "executive department" of government, of which the governor is one of only several elected officials, such as a treasurer, attorney general, superintendent of public instruction, and secretary, any of whom may be from other than the governor's party. Some states also limit the governor's power to commute sentences and pardon convicted criminals.

Populist forces have similarly shaped state judiciaries. State courts form the largest system of justice in America. Over 97 percent of all judges serve on state or local benches. Each state has a system of trial courts, one or more intermediate courts of appeal, and a final appellate court, usually called a supreme court, to decide matters of state law. These courts exercise the great residue of Common Law concerning private transactions as well as interpreting state statute and constitutional law. The relationship between state and federal courts is complex. The state courts have some authority to rule on the federal Constitution, but the federal courts, especially the district courts, hold broad powers to adjudicate questions of state law. Most state judges, moreover, exercise their powers on short tethers. For example, federal judges are appointed by the president with the advice and consent of the Senate and serve during good behavior. In the mid-nineteenth century, however, the states began to rein in the judiciary by electing most of them for limited terms of office. The judges of the highest state appellate courts also exercise the power of judicial review, as do federal Supreme Court justices, but in seven states these judges can also render advisory opinions, a practice prohibited to the Supreme Court under the Constitution.

State government differs from the federal government in another important way: the limits placed on the terms of elected public officials. The practice dates to the Louisiana constitution of 1812, which provided that no governor could serve more than two consecutive terms of four years each. Missouri followed suit in 1821 and Indiana in 1851. (Indiana did permit a former governor to run again after four years out of office.) By the end of the twentieth century, some thirty-eight states limited governors to two four-year terms, and eighteen limited the terms of state legislators, hoping to encourage a citizen legislature free from professional politicians.

The States as Laboratories of Reform. In this and other areas, state governments have been laboratories of the federal system. In fiscal matters, for example, many state governments, unlike the federal government, require a balanced budget and allow the governor a line-item veto. The states are also limited in their authority to tax and to issue bonds. These restrictions reflect the ease with which many state constitutions can be amended. State governments, therefore, have been subjected to direct popular pressures in ways that the federal government has not. For example, the federal equal rights amendment failed to win ratification, yet at least twelve states have adopted just such a provision. Eight other states have adopted constitutional guarantees of a right to privacy.

The Progressive Era was a particularly active period of experimentation for state and municipal governments, with long-lasting consequences. To stem the power of political parties, many states adopted the initiative, referendum, and recall; adopted woman suffrage; established nonpartisan elections for city councils, and provided for home rule by municipal governments. The states were the first to prohibit the sale of alcohol and the first to create nature preserves. The Progressives also accelerated the trend toward greater involvement by the states in economic matters, creating new nonpartisan agencies to oversee labor, business, and health issues on a scientific basis.

The Shifting Balance of State-Federal Power. Since the Civil War two broad trends have shaped the fortunes of state government. First, the power balance between the states and the national government has tilted in favor of the latter. For example, the Civil War Amendments, especially the Fourteenth Amendment, affirmed in law what the war had made plain on the battlefield: the national government was supreme. The new amendments established the primacy of federal citizenship and introduced the concept of state action, which authorized the federal government to override specific measures taken by the states.

Second, as America became more industrialized and population more mobile, political issues became increasingly national and less susceptible to solution by state and local government. Amid the Depression of the 1930s, for example, Congress passed a host of legislation, most of it eventually sustained by the Supreme Court, granting Washington broad powers of economic regulation. By the mid-twentieth century, state law in matters involving consumer transactions and civil rights had been replaced in part by federal law and regulation based on a significantly expanded understanding of the power granted the federal government through the commerce clause of the Constitution (Article I, Section 8).

The federal government impacted state and local governments in another way as well. Among the powers delegated to the national government was the authority to tax and spend for the general welfare. Beginning in 1921, with the Sheppard–Towner Act, Congress has appropriated federal tax dollars to support national programs carried out at the state level. As the twentieth century wore on, these grants grew in importance, comprising in some instances the largest part of a state's budget. These revenues, however, carried with them restrictions on the ways states and cities could expend them. Moreover, Congress increasingly enacted so-called unfunded mandates that require the states to use their own funds to meet federally imposed guidelines on such matters as highway construction, health care, welfare, and education. As of fiscal year 2011, state governments have accrued over 2.9 trillion dollars in state debt. California alone is carrying over $490 trillion in public debt. Florida, Illinois, Massachusetts, New York, New Jersey, Pennsylvania, and Texas each owe at least $100 billion. In each of these states, public employee pensions account for between 8 and 10 percent of total spending. Many states are facing such severe budget shortfalls that their credit ratings have been reduced.

Despite the federal government's broadened powers, the states and (to a lesser extent) local governments retain great vitality. State governments have done so not by reclaiming lost autonomy but by carving out new areas of authority. Through this process, state governments remain, as they were at the nation's founding, the most ubiquitous influence on the day-to-day lives of Americans.

[*See also* **Articles of Confederation; Continental Congress; Constitution; Dartmouth College Case; Economic Policy: Regulation; Federalism; Fourteenth Amendment;**

Municipal Politics; National Civic Federation; New Deal; Popular Sovereignty; Progressive Era; Prohibition; Republicanism; States' Rights; Taxation; *and* Urban Policy: National Policy.]

BIBLIOGRAPHY

Elazar, Daniel J. *American Federalism: A View from the States.* New York: Crowell, 1972.

Elazar, Daniel J. *Cities of the Prairie: The Metropolitan Frontier and American Politics.* Lanham, Md.: University Press of America, 1984.

Frug, Gerald E. "The City as a Legal Concept." *Harvard Law Review* 93, No. 6 (1980).

Hall, Kermit L. "Mostly Anchor and Little Sail: The Evolution of American State Constitutions." In *Toward a Usable Past: Liberty under State Constitutions,* edited by Paul Finkelman and Stephen E. Gottlieb, pp. 388–417. Athens, Ga.: University of Georgia Press, 1991.

Hartog, Hendrik. *Public Property and Private Power: The Corporation of the City of New York in American Law, 1730–1870.* Chapel Hill: University of North Carolina Press, 1983.

Kermit L. Hall; revised and updated by Pearson Bramblett

STATE REGULATION OF COMMERCE

Today's economy is one of enormous complexity and interdependence. Even the smallest businesses may be tied to interstate markets by such commonplace items as the mailbox, the telephone, and the computer. Goods and services routinely cross state lines. Major corporations may have offices, factories, and distribution centers located in dozens of states. Mass media such as radio and television make it possible for businesses to reach a nationwide audience. It is apparent, then, that the modern business world is oblivious to state lines.

Expansion of businesses into interstate markets was not accomplished without some risk. One of these was the risk of multiple tax liability. An inescapable fact of life is that states are quick to tax successful businesses. They are inclined to tax out-of-state businesses more readily and more severely. This is so for a simple reason: taxes are passed by politicians, and politicians prefer to tax those who cannot vote. A tax imposed on an out-of-state business is a politician's dream. Not only does it ensure an influx of tax money into the state's coffers, but also does so with few adverse political consequences.

Exposure to multiple taxation is a harsh reality for businesses with multistate ties. Were the states' tax power unchecked, they could collectively tax out-of-state businesses to the point of extinction. Sadly, the drain on the assets of nonresident businesses and the welfare of communities hundreds of miles distant do not command the states' attention. Their only immediate concern is the tax dollar. The commerce clause, however, is an important historic check on the taxing power.

To understand fully the purposes that underlie the commerce clause, it is useful to sketch some of our country's earliest history. In the days of the American Confederation, there was no national control over commerce. Every state was free to regulate and tax all commerce that crossed its borders. It is therefore no surprise that taxes were laid on commodities as they were transported into and out of each state. Goods were even banned and subject to forfeiture. This practice tended to snuff out the development of a truly interstate commerce and drew a wave of criticism from merchants who wished to exploit out-of-state markets.

Early Cases. The framers of the Constitution resolved to promote interstate commerce by centralizing the power to control commerce.

They first imposed certain limits on the states' power. Henceforth, states were forbidden to lay taxes on imports and exports, to enter into trade pacts, to coin their own money, or to alter retroactively commercial contracts by law. Beyond these specific limits, Congress was vested with a largely undefined power to "regulate Commerce . . . among the several States." In the decades to come, this clause would lay the foundation for national control over commerce and become the source of a body of law that closely circumscribed the states' tax powers.

Early federal cases charted the development of this body of law. One of the country's earliest and most famous tax cases was *McCulloch v. Maryland* (1819). *McCulloch* did not discuss the commerce clause, but it sounded the same themes that would be repeated in subsequent commerce cases. It is, therefore, an appropriate point to start our inquiry. In the aftermath of the War of 1812, Congress formed the Second Bank of the United States as a depository for federal money. Maryland passed a law that taxed certain operations of the bank's Baltimore branch. The bank's cashier declined to pay the tax, and the battle lines were drawn.

Chief Justice John Marshall's opinion in the case is considered by some his greatest state paper. Marshall, in an oft-quoted phrase, commented that "the power to tax involves the power to destroy" (p. 430). Although the states possessed the power to tax, that power could not be used to weaken or destroy the purpose of a federal law. Congress was authorized to form the bank and the states were powerless to interfere with its lawful operations. Marshall concluded forcefully,

> [T]he states have no power, by taxation or otherwise, to retard, impede, burden, or in any manner control the operation of the constitutional laws enacted by Congress to carry into execution the powers vested in the general government. (p. 36)

McCulloch was followed by *Brown v. Maryland* (1827). A Maryland statute required all importers of foreign goods to secure a license for $50. To sell imported goods without a license was made a criminal offense. A Maryland importer, Brown, attacked the statute as a violation of the commerce clause. Marshall's opinion in Brown recognized the states' power to tax but stated that it must yield to the federal commerce power. The purpose of that power was to ensure a robust and unfettered flow of commerce. Marshall posed a simple question: Why would one import goods except to enter them into commerce? Maryland's statute was in effect a penalty on importers who wished to profit from commerce and was thus hostile to federal law.

A question asked in *Brown,* but not authoritatively answered, was whether a tax on sales of goods in interstate commerce would suffer the same fate. The Supreme Court in *Woodruff v. Parham* (1869) answered that question in the negative. The tax involved in *Woodruff* was imposed on all auction sales within the city of Mobile, Alabama. Distinguishing *Brown,* the Court stressed that Mobile's tax was one on sales and was not hostile per se to commerce. Added to that was the fact the tax applied equally to all goods, whether in state or out of state. This focus on discrimination between in-state and interstate commerce foreshadowed future commerce clause analysis.

One of the principles that developed from these early cases was that a tax on interstate commerce was an undue burden on commerce and was void. This proved to be the catalyst for an economic explosion. New industries blossomed. East and West became linked by railroads, waterways, and early telecommunication systems. But this "tax exempt" status was short-lived. States were anxious to ride the wave of economic boom, and they undertook efforts to require interstate commerce to "pay its way." They soon laid taxes based on receipts that a business derived from interstate activity, but they proportioned these taxes to the activity that was actually carried on within the state. These efforts were fueled by the fact that states lend valuable services to out-of-state businesses. Consider a simple example. A trucking company that hauls commodities in interstate commerce will have substantial ties to its home state. It will employ workers there, it will use that state's roads, it will own or lease real property, and it will receive the protection of the state's laws. These kinds of ties, the states contended, were sufficient to justify a tax. By the early twentieth century the federal courts were convinced of such taxes' validity.

One further principle, an anomaly of sorts, persisted. If a business was involved solely in interstate commerce, it was immune from taxation by any state. This led to some absurd results. In cases decided over a thirty-year span, taxes were struck down for the sole reason that no in-state business was carried on. There was widespread unhappiness with these cases and the courts quietly retreated. Taxes were upheld despite the lack of in-state business where states did not purport to tax interstate commerce. And thus the law remained until the 1970s.

Recent Law. Possibly the most important state taxation case in recent history was *Complete Auto Transit, Inc. v. Brady* (1977), overruling cases that immunized interstate commerce from taxation. Little contained in that decision was new. Its importance lay instead in the fact that it synthesized strands of law from earlier cases. For the first time a reader could find, in one place, the questions that must be asked and answered for a tax to survive a commerce clause attack. These questions may be summarized as follows:

1. Nexus. Is the business activity "sufficiently connected" to the state to support the tax?
2. Impact. Does the tax discriminate against interstate commerce?
3. Fairness. Is the tax fairly related to the services provided by the state and is it fairly apportioned?

These questions mark the threefold inquiry that characterizes modern state taxation analysis. Each is traceable to the historic purposes of the commerce clause. Each is in search of balance. To justify a tax on commerce, a state must show that it has a sufficient connection to the business activity that is to be taxed. There are no absolutes, and courts must examine the facts on a case-by-case basis. A tax must also be evenhanded, so that it applies alike to in-state and interstate commerce. States must draft their tax laws to ensure that interstate commerce is taxed equitably. Finally, a tax on commerce must fairly relate to the state's nexus with the business activity. Only when these factors are in proper balance will businesses be fully protected from the evils of multiple taxation.

Recent state taxation cases have attempted to refine these concepts, particularly the concept of nexus. It has not been an easy task. Many cases explore the kind of nexus that an out-of-state business must have before it may properly be taxed. The line they draw is, however, blurry. Does it suffice that the business has an in-state office or facility or that it solicits customers within the state?

Must the tax relate to the business's actual nexus with the state, or is it sufficient that the business has some nexus? Does the analysis of nexus depend, in part, on the kind of tax involved? These questions will continue to shape the future of the commerce clause as a limit on state taxation. In its state taxation cases, the Court has attempted to work a division of national and state responsibility in a way that furthers the framers' vision of the commerce clause.

[*See also* **Capitalism; Interstate Commerce Act; Marshall, John;** ***McCulloch v. Maryland;*** **Regulatory Agencies, Federal;** ***and*** **Taxation.**]

BIBLIOGRAPHY

Jensen, Merrill. *The New Nation*. Boston: Northeastern University Press, 1950.

Nowak, John E., Ronald D. Rotunda, and J. Nelson Young. *Treatise on Constitutional Law: Substance and Procedure*. St. Paul, Minn.: West, 1986.

Tribe, Laurence H. *American Constitutional Law*, 2d ed. Mineola, N.Y.: Foundation Press, 1988.

James B. Stoneking

STATES' RIGHTS

Rooted in the classical republican view that freedom and virtue are incompatible with empire and in anti-Federalist fears of centralized power, the doctrine of states' rights is enshrined in several parts of the Constitution, including the guarantee of each state's equal standing in the Senate (the only provision permanently unchangeable by amendment). The most often cited guarantee of states' rights is the Tenth Amendment. To states' rights supporters, the amendment limits the federal government's powers to those specifically enumerated in the Constitution and reserves all other powers of government (such as the power to create and tax corporations) to the states.

The first major confrontation between defenders of states' rights and the proponents of centralized power came in response to the Federalist Party's Alien and Sedition Acts of 1798. Thomas Jefferson and James Madison, in the Kentucky and Virginia Resolutions, declared the acts unconstitutional and asserted that states, as parties to the constitutional "compact," had the power to protect the liberties of their citizens and "alien friends" from federal acts that violated the compact. Nationalists on the U.S. Supreme Court under Chief Justice John Marshall restricted states' rights (and protected corporations) in such decisions as *Fletcher v. Peck* and *McCulloch v. Maryland,* but the issue remained unsettled.

In the second major confrontation, during the War of 1812, commercially minded New England Federalists convened the 1814 Hartford Convention, which denounced what they considered the dangerous imperialism of the Republicans in Washington and asserted the rights of states to refuse to authorize the conscription and taxation needed to support "Mr. Madison's War."

In the third major confrontation, the nullification crisis of 1828–1832, involving the federal tariff, the doctrine became associated with John C. Calhoun, who had earlier opposed states' rights. Calhoun's major opponent on nullification, President Andrew Jackson, was also inconsistent: Like many Democratic Party leaders, Jackson supported states' rights on most matters. Although states' rights doctrine was increasingly tied to the defense of slavery, some abolitionists invoked it in their efforts to thwart the Fugitive Slave Act of 1850 (e.g., in *Ableman v. Booth,* 1859).

Although South Carolina had stood alone on nullification, proslavery politicians espoused other versions of states' rights doctrine, eventually taking the ultimate step of secession. Their advocacy of the doctrine returned to haunt them as the Confederate States of America struggled for wartime unity and discipline in the fourth major confrontation, the Civil War. In *State Rights in the Confederacy*

(1925), Frank Lawrence Owsley noted the central irony that to defend states' rights effectively, the Confederacy's leaders would have had to crush them.

After the Civil War, opponents of African American rights embraced states' rights. Although the Supreme Court again restricted state power to regulate corporations in the 1880s and 1890s, it supported broad state power to enforce racial segregation. The principal twentieth-century uses of the doctrine were to ward off federal antilynching laws and to defend racial segregation. Opponents of federal economic regulation sometimes invoked the doctrine as well.

After World War II, liberals generally condemned states' rights through a kind of guilt by association with slavery and segregation. With *Brown v. Board of Education* and related decisions, the Supreme Court under Earl Warren brought civil rights law into line with broader nationalistic trends. After the 1960s, the doctrine moved to the margins of American political culture, although conservatives, including Ronald Reagan, invoked it occasionally in rhetorical thrusts at "big government" and the massive federal budget. Subsequently, under William Rehnquist's chief justiceship (1986–), a narrow majority on the Court resuscitated states' rights for some purposes, but it was not clear how durable these decisions would be. Curiously, despite its historical roots in the defense of civil liberties, immigrant rights, and anti-imperialism, late twentieth-century nonconservative opponents of centralized power (governmental and corporate) found little merit in the doctrine.

[*See also* **Alien and Sedition Acts; Bill of Rights;** ***Brown v. Board of Education;*** **Calhoun, John C.; Civil Rights; Civil Rights Legislation; Confederate States of America; Conservatism; Constitution; Economic Policy: Regulation; Federal Government, Legislative Branch: Senate; Federalism; Federalist Party; Fugitive Slave Act; Hartford Convention; Jackson, Andrew; Jefferson, Thomas; Liberalism; Madison, James; Marshall, John;** ***McCulloch v. Maryland;*** **Reagan, Ronald; Rehnquist, William; Republicanism; Segregation; States' Rights Party; Tariffs;** *and* **Warren, Earl.**]

BIBLIOGRAPHY

Antineau, Chester James. *States' Rights under Federal Constitutions*. London; New York: Oceana Publications, 1984.

Mason, Alpheus Thomas. *The States' Rights Debate: Antifederalism and the Constitution*. Englewood Cliffs, N.J.: Prentice Hall, 1964.

David L. Chappell

STATES' RIGHTS PARTY

In 1948, disgruntled southern Democrats, nicknamed Dixiecrats, launched the States' Rights Party. Although conservative, white southern Democrats had for many years decried the Democratic Party's liberal drift and particularly its courting of northern black voters, the support of a moderate civil rights program by President Harry S. Truman and national Democratic Party leaders provided the immediate impetus for the party bolt.

The Dixiecrats initially tried with limited success to convince southern state Democratic parties to oppose Truman's nomination, but the Democrats' convention, meeting in Philadelphia in July, nominated Truman and adopted a pro–civil rights plank. Two days later, a convention in Birmingham recommended that southern Democratic parties put Governor Strom Thurmond (1902–) of South Carolina on their ballots as the official Democratic presidential candidate, along with

Mississippi Governor Fielding Wright as his running mate. Mississippi, Alabama, South Carolina, and Louisiana complied, but when the Dixiecrats proved unable to control other state Democratic parties, they organized a third party and held a convention in Houston that nominated the Thurmond/Wright ticket.

In the fall election, the Dixiecrats failed to garner national support or even regional solidarity for their party, carrying only those four states where the ballots listed Thurmond as the Democratic nominee instead of Truman. Their revolt, however, represented the beginning of the end of the solid Democratic South and revealed the potential divisiveness of the civil rights issue for the New Deal Democratic coalition. Strom Thurmond, rejoining the Republican Party, went on to become one of the longest-serving U.S. senators in American history.

[*See also* **Civil Rights; Democratic Party; Dixiecrats; New Deal; Political Parties; Segregation, States' Rights;** *and* **Truman, Harry S.**]

BIBLIOGRAPHY

Bartley, Numan V. *The New South 1945–1980*. Baton Rouge: Louisiana State University Press, 1995.

Garson, Robert A. *The Democratic Party and the Politics of Sectionalism, 1941–1948*. Baton Rouge: Louisiana State University Press, 1974.

Charles C. Bolton

STEM-CELL RESEARCH

Despite heated late twentieth- and early twenty-first-century controversy, the history of stem-cell research is actually rather old. The term "stem cell" (SC) appeared in 1895 from translators of Claus's zoological textbook, but was first used in a contemporary fashion in 1896; the earliest experiments with SC occurred in 1907; and LeRoy Stevens at Bar Harbor first advanced the concept of potency in 1958 with his cell line strain 129. By 1970, Stevens demonstrated that murine embryonic germ cells have pluripotency, both as cancer and as kinds of SC. In 1975 Mintz and Illmensee in Philadelphia showed that embryonic SC (ES) produce organisms as well as cancers. In 1981 Gail Martin (UCSF) and Martin Evans (Cambridge) isolated ES from mice and in 1985–1992 Brigid Hogan (Vanderbilt) and Peter Donovan (National Cancer Institute (NCI)) identified factors that induce ES cells to differentiate. Nevertheless, the period since the 1990s has been rich in scandal, intrigue, invective, and glorified hope around SC research and therapy (SCRT).

Stem-Cell Distinctions. The crux of recent SC discussions centers on a series of five distinctions. First, SC exist in different potential states. All SC are unspecialized, can become specialized, and can live and divide over long stretches of time. Three kinds of SCs depend upon their degree of specialization, their "potency." Early embryonic stem cells (ES) may become any specific cell type in the body or indeed an entirely separate organism, a clone. These typically come from in vitro fertilization (IVF) procedures. They are totipotent. Somatic stem cells (SS) or "adult stem cells" are already more specific and may only become certain kinds of the more than 200 differentiated cells; they are pluripotent. A final set of stem cells, multipotent cells (MP), comes from fetal cells, cord blood cells, or adult stem cells. They can become any of a more restricted variety of cells. Furthermore, engineered SC may fall anywhere along that spectrum.

Second, stem cells may only differentiate when placed in the right context. Thus extracellular factors, chemicals needed to induce cellular differentiation, must exist either in the Petri dish or in the surrounding tissue for stem cells to achieve their next state of differentiation.

Third, as of the beginning of the second decade of the twenty-first century, human embryonic stem cells may be acquired by removing one or more cells from an early embryo, by amniocentesis of maternal amniotic fluid, or in principle by induction (reengineering) of SS (induced pluripotent cells, iPS).

Fourth, human stem cells are different from animal stem cells. Specifically, the politics associated with animal experimentation are different from those associated with human experimentation. For example, in 1996 Ian Wilmut and his team cloned Dolly the sheep after 277 attempts; mice were cloned the next year. Dogs can now be cloned privately for a significant fee. Human cloning is still deeply divisive.

Fifth, experimentation is different from treatment. At the legal, procedural and ethical levels, American expectations of propriety are often more exacting for research than for therapy and often more exacting for animal than for human research. The therapeutic possibilities of SC research manifested in 1998–2002 when Michel Levesque at Cedar's Sinai reengineered the neuronal stem cells of a person with Parkinson's disease and reimplanted them with significant clinical improvement.

Policy, Politics, and Legal Issues. With those particularities, the history of SC research is rich in policy, politics, and legal issues, both from the top down and from the ground up. Not surprisingly, in the American context, policy and politics have appeared at the local, state, and federal levels; in the executive, legislative, and judicial branches; at the lay and at the expert levels; in religious and secular venues; and in the popular and specialized media. A truly synthetic, holistic, sociocultural analysis has not yet been written.

At a certain level, SC therapy (SCT), the transfer of cells from one organism transplanted into another organism, is technically linked to bone marrow transplants (BMT) from the early to mid-twentieth century. Multipotent cells from the marrow of one person were transplanted into the marrow of another with bone marrow failure, disruption, or cancer. This work dates from the 1930s and 1950s. At the governmental policy level, this narrow-sense SCT led to the Congressional 1984 National Organ Transplant Act and to the nonprofit National Marrow Donor Program in 1990. The horizons of hope offered by more generalized stem-cell therapy are far broader than this. Consequently, the ethical dilemmas and policy implications are also broader.

An augury of these challenges occurred in 1988, when the Ayala family in California announced they would conceive a child to save the life of their seventeen-year old daughter with leukemia; the child, Marrisa-Eve, was born in 1991 and a BMT was performed. This was echoed in 2000 when a Colorado couple created a test-tube baby to save their six-year-old daughter with Fanconi anemia; baby Adam Nash was born and the transplant was completed. The intentionality of procreation, the therapeutic use of harvested cells, and the mutual obligations of families, individuals, and societies remain hotly debated.

At another level, SC science and its marketized technological offspring have emerged at a time of American legacy arguments in policy. The American furor over SCRT can fall along classic political lines involving definitions of life, abortion, and research. However, neoliberal empowerment of individual choice, scientific marketization, and global economic competitiveness equally interface with nationalistic arguments of declining global competitiveness. In that vein, patient demand provokes international competition for therapy (such that developing world physicians offer "stem cell therapy," which American scientists and physicians decry as charlatanism) and of science (hence the cries of American science falling behind that in France, the United Kingdom, and South Korea). Motivations and patterns are thus convoluted.

A simplistic chronological history hinges on other critical moments. In 1998, James Thompson (University of Wisconsin) developed the first ES lines from cells of early embryos. That same year, John Gearhart (Johns Hopkins) derived germ cells from gonadal tissue (primordial germ cells). Subsequent regulated pluripotent SC "lines" come from both sources. The journal *Science* named SC research the 1999 "Breakthrough of the Year." In 2007, Shinya Yamanaka at Kyoto University as well as Thompson's group announced iPS (*Science's* "Breakthrough of the Year" in 2008). That year researchers at Wake Forest and Harvard reported SC in pregnant women's amniotic fluid; researchers at the Whitehead Institute modified skin cells to function like ES; and two independent groups reported creating human ES without harming the embryo. In 2011 Thompson and Yamanaka shared the "American Nobel," the Albany Prize.

With Thompson's celebrity, the opportunity pressures of SC were equally evident in the scandals associated with its research. The rise of global multi- and mass media, especially under the aegis of the Internet, expanded the scope, the volume, and the multivalency of ensuing debates. In November 2001 a Massachusetts company, ACT, claimed to have cloned human embryos without subsequent conclusive evidence; the team had allowed a *48 Hours* TV film crew to publicize their work in 1998. In 2004 South Korean scientists reported cloning human embryos in *Science,* followed by a 2005 streamlining procedure for minimal human egg SC production. That year Gerald Schatten of the University of Pittsburgh, lead author, reported ethical shortcomings for human subjects in the second paper. In December 2005 Seoul National University's internal investigation announced that all of the data from both papers were fabricated; Hwang Woo-suk, the senior researcher for both papers, was charged with fraud.

Research Funding. Funding for the science that generated these successes and failures came from federal, private, and state sources but always at a political price. In 1988 a National Institutes of Health (NIH) panel voted in favor of government funding. In 1990, Congress voted to override a moratorium on government funding of ES research, but President George Bush vetoed it. In 1993 President Clinton lifted a twenty-three-year moratorium on fetal tissue transplant with the NIH Revitalization Act, allowing in vitro fertilization, but also creating the NIH Human Embryo Research Panel for oversight. President Clinton changed his mind the following year after public outcry. Thereafter, Clinton partially restricted funding for SCR. In August 2000 the NIH released federal funding guidelines and the 106th Congress proposed a Human Pluripotent Stem Cell Review Group to support SC research. In February 2001 President George W. Bush requested review of NIH guidelines and placed all funding on hold, then empanelling a new Council on Bioethics chaired by Leon Kass. Following suit, in July 2001 Senators William Frist and Orrin Hatch called for limits followed by Representative Dennis Hastert in the House. Opposition to federal SCR dollars came from a variety of directions, including the practical desire to avoid political and legal interruptions to support (less likely with private monies), the ideological effort to prevent abortions, and the fiscal constraints on limited research funding. Promotion of federal financing hinged on the curative promise of SCT. Federal funding was finally released but only for research upon those lines already created. Research with new lines received no federal support.

In the face of federal funding restrictions, upon which American biomedical research had become so dependent over the previous seven decades, a series of state initiatives attempted to fill the resulting gap. Beginning in 2004 with $9.5 million in New Jersey and $3 billion (over 10 years) from California's Proposition 71, seven more states funded SCR via executive, legislative, and even popular referendum. In May 2007 Governor Arnold Schwarzenegger signed a Californian–Canadian agreement for collaborative funding and research outstripping federal efforts at international collaboration.

As a consequence, at the federal level, in 2005 the U.S. House and Senate passed a bill to mitigate funding restrictions, but President Bush vetoed it in 2006; Congress tried again in 2007 with the same result. In 2009, President Barack Obama signed the Stem Cell Enhancement Bill, relaxing many prior restrictions. Throughout this timeline private, domestic, and international funding expanded; simultaneously, a number of political leaders changed their positions.

Political Issues. The rhetoric of progress, restrictions on scientific freedom, and paradigm shifts are historical tropes heavily deployed in most American political discussions about SCRT. It is hard to imagine a similar furor over SCRT without the "war on cancer." This declaration of war, instantiated in the NCI (formulated in 1937, 1944, and 1971), along with the Human Genome Project, has become a central feature of U.S. biomedical research policy. Coupled with the expansion of scientific marketization, especially in the form of the NIH's translational sciences push of the first decade of the 2000s, this pseudo free marketeering has injected great financial incentives into generating SC "products" and bringing them to market.

A final particularity of SCRT is the timing with the rise of the Disability Rights movement (DR) in the United States and the United Kingdom, mirrored in other developed and developing countries. As some DR critics expound, SCT, if fully realized, will provoke a kind of genocide upon people with many kinds of disabilities, from spinal cord injuries to parkinsonism to cerebral palsy. The result of such heated objections is unusual political antipathies, partnerships, and compromises, such as the extreme backlash against the actor/activist with a spinal cord injury, Christopher Reeve, when he funded SC research.

BIBLIOGRAPHY

Maienschein, Jane. *Whose View of Life?: Embryos, Cloning and Stem Cells.* Cambridge, Mass.: Harvard University Press, 2003.

Monroe, Kristen R., Ronald B. Miller, and Jerome S. Tobias. *Fundamentals of the Stem Cell Debate: The Scientific, Religious, Ethical and Political Issues.* Berkeley: University of California Press, 2008.

Svendsen, Clive N., and Allison D. Ebert, eds. *Encyclopedia of Stem Cell Research.* Thousand Oaks, Calif.: Sage, 2008.

Walton O. Schalick III

STEVENSON, ADLAI

(1900–1965), governor, presidential nominee, ambassador to the United Nations. A grandson and namesake of Grover Cleveland's vice president, Adlai E. Stevenson was born in Los Angeles and reared in Bloomington, Illinois.

He graduated from Yale in 1922, received a law degree from Northwestern University in 1926, and worked as an attorney in Chicago until World War II, when he became a special assistant to the secretary of the Navy. In 1945, Stevenson moved to the State Department, where he helped plan the United Nations and participated in its activities for several years.

Elected governor of Illinois in 1948, Stevenson won a national following with his eloquent speech-making and broad public appeal. As the Democratic presidential nominee in 1952 and 1956, he campaigned as a proud disciple of Franklin Delano Roosevelt and a vigorous opponent of Senator Joseph McCarthy. Soundly defeated in both races by Dwight D. Eisenhower, Stevenson halfheartedly sought the Democratic nomination in 1960, losing to John F. Kennedy.

In 1961, President Kennedy appointed Stevenson ambassador to the United Nations. In that role, he argued strongly against invading Cuba during the 1962 Cuban Missile Crisis, thereby helping Kennedy guide the United States safely through the most dangerous weeks of the Cold War. Stevenson remained at the United Nations until his sudden death in July 1965.

[*See also* **Eisenhower, Dwight D.; Federal Government, Executive Branch: State Department; Kennedy, John F.; McCarthy, Joseph;** ***and*** **Roosevelt, Franklin Delano.**]

BIBLIOGRAPHY

Martin, John Bartlow. *Adlai Stevenson and the World: The Life of Adlai Stevenson*. Garden City, N.Y.: Doubleday, 1977.

Martin, John Bartlow. *Adlai Stevenson of Illinois*. Garden City, N.Y.: Doubleday, 1976.

William L. O'Neill

STONE, HARLAN

(1872–1946), legal educator, lawyer, associate justice (1925–1941), and chief justice (1941–1946) of the Supreme Court. To date, Stone remains the sole university professor ever to serve as chief justice and, along with Democrat Edward White, one of only two chief justices appointed by a president from a different party. A Republican and a professor at Columbia Law School, Stone was appointed an associate justice by President Warren Harding, and Democrat Franklin Delano Roosevelt elevated him to the chief justiceship. As an associate justice, Stone dissented vigorously against the so-called Four Horsemen, a bloc of justices that routinely objected to Roosevelt's New Deal measures. Stone insisted that the judiciary should exercise restraint and recognize the need for the legislative and executive branches to respond to the Great Depression. By the late 1930s, with new appointees on the court, this had become the majority view.

During his brief service as chief justice (the shortest since that of Oliver Ellsworth, 1796–1800), Stone moved his colleagues away from issues of economic regulation and toward matters of civil rights. Stone began the process of developing the implications of footnote four of his most famous opinion, *United States v. Carolene Products* (1938). This celebrated footnote, although upholding the position that courts should generally defer to legislative bodies on economic matters, suggested that laws restricting the rights of racial or other minorities "may call for a correspondingly more searching judicial inquiry." Stone also led the effort to abolish the all-white primary (*Smith v. Allwright*, 1944).

Stone urged the justices to reason cases out at length, a technique markedly different from that of his predecessors. Greater discussion, however, produced more dissent and increased judicial backbiting, neither of which Stone was able to alleviate. Indeed, high levels of dissent on the modern Court date from Stone's tenure as chief justice.

[*See also* **Civil Rights; Economic Policy: Regulation; Fourteenth Amendment; Harding, Warren G.; New Deal; Roosevelt, Franklin Delano; Segregation; *Smith v. Allwright*; Supreme Court, U.S;** ***and* United States v. Carolene Products.**]

BIBLIOGRAPHY

Mason, Alpheus T. *Harlan Fiske Stone: Pillar of the Law*. New York: Viking Press, 1956.

Lief, Alfred, ed. *Public Control of Business: Selected Opinions of Harlan Fiske Stone*. Buffalo, N.Y.: William S. Hein, 1996.

Kermit L. Hall

STORY, JOSEPH

(1779–1845), justice of the U.S. Supreme Court. Born in Marblehead, Massachusetts, Joseph Story graduated from Harvard in 1798, read law with various jurists, and entered the bar in 1801. A Jeffersonian Republican, he served in the Massachusetts legislature and a term in Congress. Story was appointed to the Supreme Court in 1811 by president James Madison, after three other individuals had declined. A close ally of chief justice John Marshall, Story became a strong advocate of federal jurisdiction, economic nationalism, and the role of federal law in protecting property rights and the sanctity of contract. His dissent in *Charles River Bridge v. Warren Bridge* (1837) invoked the contract clause of the Constitution in a failed attempt to sustain an implicitly conferred monopoly in a charter the Massachusetts legislature had given the Charles River Bridge Company. The federal government, Story argued, should protect investors in such projects from politicians' whims—in this case the Massachusetts legislators who had authorized a new bridge to compete with the Charles River Bridge.

Story's most important nationalist decisions were *Martin v. Hunter's Lessee* (1816) and *Prigg v. Pennsylvania* (1841). In the former, he spoke for the Court in ruling constitutional the clause in the Judiciary Act of 1789 allowing the Supreme Court to review state judicial interpretations of the federal Constitution. In *Prigg*, Story found that state personal-liberty laws guaranteeing escaped slaves their freedom violated the Constitution's pledge that the national government would assist in returning escaped slaves. Faced with denunciations by abolitionists, Story resigned. He hoped to return to scholarly writing and teaching, but died before he could do so.

[*See also* **Antislavery Movement; *Charles River Bridge v. Warren Bridge*; Contract, Law of; Federalism; Fugitive Slave Act; Jurisprudence; Madison, James; Marshall, John;** ***and* Supreme Court, U.S.**]

BIBLIOGRAPHY

Newmyer, R. Kent. *Supreme Court Justice Joseph Story: Statesman of the Old Republic*. Chapel Hill: University of North Carolina Press, 1985.

Kermit L. Hall

STUDENTS FOR A DEMOCRATIC SOCIETY

The most influential and best-known political organization of the white New Left during the 1960s. In 1960, Students for a Democratic Society (SDS) emerged from its forerunner, the Student League for Industrial Democracy, a social democratic organization. Inspired by and affiliated with both the civil rights movement and organized labor, SDS sought to design a political strategy to achieve progressive social change in postwar America. In June 1962, 59 members meeting at a labor-union resort in Michigan drafted *The Port Huron Statement,* a political manifesto critiquing American race relations, the persistence of poverty, and America's Cold War role. The principal author was Tom Hayden (1939–), a University of Michigan student. Arguing that these problems reflected the impoverishment of politics, the manifesto called for "participatory democracy," whereby Americans would involve themselves directly in the decisions affecting their lives and communities. The commitment to participatory democracy guided SDS's organizational structure and future political action.

Over the ensuing decade, SDS members participated in civil rights activism, began community organizing in the urban North with the Economic Research and Action Project in 1963–1964, and played a prominent role in the anti–Vietnam War and student movements. Bringing direct action tactics to these movements, SDS sponsored mass antiwar demonstrations in 1965 in Washington, D.C., and at the Democratic Party's 1968 national convention in Chicago, as well as student strikes on college campuses, including a heavily publicized one in 1968 at Columbia University. As protests and media attention intensified, SDS grew to an estimated membership ranging from 30,000 to 100,000. Rapid growth and ideological divisions contributed to conflicts within the organization about strategy and goals. When the fractious 1969 SDS national convention split between the revolutionary Weathermen (a term drawn from a protest song by Bob Dylan) and the neo-Maoist Progressive Labor Party, the organization collapsed. Many former members remained committed to progressive politics, however, through their career choices and participation in later social and community movements.

[*See also* **Antiwar Movements; Civil Rights;** ***Other America, The;*** **Poverty; Radicalism; Socialism;** ***and*** **Socialist Party of America.**]

BIBLIOGRAPHY

Echols, Alice. "We Gotta Get Out of This Place: Notes toward a Remapping of the Sixties." *Socialist Review* 22 (April–June 1992): 9–33.

Miller, James. *"Democracy Is In the Streets": From Port Huron to the Siege of Chicago.* New York: Simon & Schuster, 1987.

Jennifer Frost

SUPREME COURT, U.S.

Article III of the Constitution provides that "the judicial Power of the United States, shall be vested in one supreme Court, and in such inferior Courts as Congress may from time to time ordain and establish." The First Congress created a Supreme Court and lower tribunals in the Judiciary Act of 1789; the three-tiered system, with some modification, remains the basis for the modern federal court system.

Overview. The Judiciary Act created a Supreme Court of six judges, a chief justice and five associate justices. It also created thirteen district courts, one for each state, and an intermediate court of appeals, consisting of the judge for the district court and two justices of the Supreme Court riding circuit. In addition, the act spelled out the jurisdiction of the federal courts and in the very important

Section 25 gave the Supreme Court appellate jurisdiction over federal questions arising in state courts. It is this provision, allowing the Supreme Court to review state court decisions touching on federal questions, that is the key to enforcing Article VI, which makes the Constitution the supreme law of the land.

Since then, the basic structure of the federal judicial system has been modified slightly. Membership of the Supreme Court increased; during the Civil War it reached ten, but afterward it dropped to nine, where it has remained. Judges are appointed for life and serve during "good behavior." The only means for removing a judge is through impeachment. One justice of the Supreme Court, Samuel Chase, was impeached in 1804, but was not convicted.

The Supreme Court hears appeals in cases of original jurisdiction (such as suits between two states) and has appellate jurisdiction from both the state and the federal systems. In the federal system, cases usually originate in a district court and then may be appealed to one of the Circuit Courts of Appeal. From there plaintiffs may appeal to the Supreme Court, but the so-called Judges Bill of 1925 gave the Court almost complete control over its docket, as well as the power to limit the number of cases it accepts for review. That number, which ran in the 150 range in the 1970s, was steadily reduced thereafter, so that by the mid-1990s the Court was giving a full hearing to fewer than 80 cases a year.

The Court will also hear appeals of final decisions from the highest state court if a federal constitutional issue is involved. If the case can be resolved on adequate state statutory or legislative grounds, the Court will not grant review. For a case to be accepted for review, the "rule of four" applies, by which four members of the Court must agree that review is warranted. The Court's caseload consists primarily of two types of litigation, one involving constitutional questions, in which the Court's word is final, and the other involving interpretation of federal legislation, in which Congress can in effect overrule the justices by revising the statute.

The Marshall Court. In its first ten years the Supreme Court enjoyed little popular esteem, and the first chief justice, John Jay, resigned because he believed the Court would never become a coequal partner in government with the legislative and executive branches. That began to change with President John Adams's appointment of John Marshall as chief justice, a position he held from 1801 to his death in 1835.

Marshall established one of the key powers of the Court in *Marbury v. Madison* (1803), in which he ruled a portion of the 1789 Judiciary Act unconstitutional, thus not only claiming for the Court the power of judicial review over federal legislation, but also establishing the Court as the ultimate interpreter of the Constitution. In a series of decisions over the next three decades, Marshall helped to clothe the new government with extensive powers, carrying out the vision enunciated by the Federalists in the 1790s.

The Court gave a broad reading to the contracts clause in *Fletcher v. Peck* (1810) and further expanded its reach in *Dartmouth College v. Woodward* (1819), thus protecting private property interests against state legislative power. In *McCulloch v. Maryland* (1819), Marshall relied on the argument Alexander Hamilton had made in defense of the first Bank of the United States and elevated it to a constitutional rule, that federal creations made under a legitimate exercise of constitutional power are immune from state regulation or taxation. Marshall carried the reach of the commerce power furthest in *Gibbons v. Ogden* (1824), in which he strained the meaning of the federal coastal licensing law to strike down a New York–sponsored steamboat monopoly.

Gibbons marked the high point of the Marshall Court's expansive nationalism. In the next decade the Marshall Court proved more amenable to states' rights interests, as the chief justice fought to blunt growing criticism of the judiciary and moves to restrict its powers over the states. In *Wilson v. Blackbird Creek Marsh Co.* (1829) he ceded substantial power to the states over interstate waterways, and in *Barron v. Baltimore* (1833) the Court ruled that the Bill of Rights did not apply to the states. When the Court did try to limit state powers, as in the Cherokee removal cases (1831 and 1832), Georgia ignored the rulings and President Andrew Jackson supposedly sneered, "The Chief Justice has made his decision; now let him enforce it."

The Taney Court and Beyond. When Jackson named Roger B. Taney chief justice in 1835, many expected the nationalist tone of the Court to change to a more states' rights orientation, and in some cases it did. Taney and his colleagues proved more sympathetic to local interests and in the famous case *Charles River Bridge v. Warren Bridge* (1837) gave the states extensive leeway over commercial regulation and contracts. This decision also represented a shift in sympathy for new entrepreneurial capital as opposed to the more established capitalism favored by the Federalists. In *Cooley v. Board of Wardens* (1852), the Court pronounced a commonsense rule that, although leaving the federal commerce power supreme, nonetheless gave states far greater leeway to act.

But the Taney Court was in many ways as nationalistic as its predecessor, and in a number of cases it reaffirmed or only slightly modified Marshall Court precedents. Moreover, in *Luther v. Borden* (1849), Taney introduced the "political question" doctrine, allowing the Court to evade issues that, in its opinion, belonged more to the realm of politics than law.

Unfortunately, Taney's reputation, as well as that of his Court, is so bound up with its decisions on slavery that much of its other work has been unappreciated. Taney, a firm believer in both slavery and the right of states to protect the institution, went out of his way in *Scott v. Sandford* (1857) not only to uphold slavery, but also to deny the federal government any power to regulate or limit it.

That case wounded the prestige of the Court until after the Civil War, a conflict in which the Court played a very limited role. As in most wars, the justices delayed hearing potentially divisive issues until after the fighting had ended. Although in *Ex parte Milligan* (1866) the Court, now headed by Salmon P. Chase (1808–1873, chief justice 1864–1873), ruled that the federal government could not resort to military tribunals in areas where civilian courts remained open, for the most part the Court endorsed nearly all of the actions taken by Congress and the Executive during the war. Fear that the Court might invalidate some of its Reconstruction measures led Congress to restrict the Court's jurisdiction in some areas, but these restrictions proved temporary and ephemeral. Moreover, in *Texas v. White* (1869), the Court put its imprimatur on congressional Reconstruction and held the secession of the Southern states to have been invalid at all times.

The Court as Protector of Property Rights. By then, national attention had shifted to the great postwar economic expansion underway and the constitutional issues it raised. The Supreme Court is commonly referred to by the name of its chief justice—the Marshall Court, the Taney Court—and in some instances the chief did exert a commanding influence. But the associate justices, the so-called "side judges," also can have great influence—sometimes greater influence than that of the chief. This proved the case in the latter nineteenth century when chief justices Morrison R. Waite (1816–1888, chief justice 1874–1888) and Melville W. Fuller (1833–1910, chief justice 1888–1910) were overshadowed by some of their associates, such as John Marshall Harlan and, above all, Stephen J. Field (1816–1899).

Field and his ideas came to dominate the Court, and his fierce protection of property rights against state regulation of any sort, complete *laissez-faire,* strongly influenced the Court until the 1930s. The new industrialists looked to the courts to protect them from reformers who wanted to regulate private property in the name of the public good or to protect labor from the harsh conditions of mine and factory.

In *Munn v. Illinois* (1877), over a strong protest from Field, Chief Justice Waite held that states could regulate the rates charged by common carriers. But in the next two decades Field won a majority to his view that states had little or no power to regulate rates or to interfere in any way with vested property rights. The notion of the judiciary as the defender of property as against populist efforts to reform through regulation shaped the Court's decisions from the late nineteenth century until 1937. In a strong dissent in *Lochner v. New York* (1905), Oliver Wendell Holmes Jr., sharply criticized the Supreme Court's hostility to worker-protection legislation in the name of property rights; the Constitution, he insisted, "is not intended to embody a particular economic theory, whether of paternalism or of *laissez faire.*" The Court did, in fact, approve some Progressive Era laws protecting women and children, most notably in *Muller v. Oregon* (1908), in which attorney Louis Brandeis, defending Oregon's right to regulate the hours of working women, presented a brief full of sociological data. (Brandeis himself was appointed to the Supreme Court in 1916 by President Woodrow Wilson and confirmed despite fierce conservative—and in some cases anti-Semitic—opposition.) Nevertheless, in *Adkins v. Children's Hospital* (1923), the high court make clear its position that in all circumstances government regulation of the economy would be the exception and *laissez-faire* the rule.

As in the Civil War, World War I again raised the issue of the government's right to limit First Amendment free-speech protections. Writing for the majority in *Schenck v. United States* (1919), Justice Holmes upheld the wartime Espionage Act, but enunciated the principle that only a "clear and present danger" could justify restraints on free speech. In a notable dissent in *Abrams v. United States* (1919), involving the wartime Sedition Amendment, Holmes eloquently called for "free trade in ideas."

The Supreme Court in the New Deal and Civil Rights Eras. When Depression struck in 1929, and especially after Franklin Delano Roosevelt's New Deal began trying to meliorate its effects, reformers hit a stone wall of conservatism on the high court. A bloc of four—Pierce Butler, James McReynolds, George Sutherland, and Willis Van Devanter—opposed any and all reform measures, often securing Owen J. Roberts as their fifth vote.

To remove what he saw as an unwarranted block to popular demands for reform, Roosevelt proposed a bill in February 1937 that would have allowed him to name up to six more justices on the Court. The public reaction to Roosevelt's so-called court-packing plan eventually led Congress to reject it. But the overwhelmingly negative public response to the Court's reactionary stance hastened the retirement of the conservatives and the appointment of justices thoroughly sympathetic to the New Deal and state efforts to reform the economy. After several decades of a cramped view of the commerce clause, Justice Robert Jackson in *Wickard v. Filburn* (1942) gave Congress such an expanded view of that power that it would be a half century before the Court would invalidate a federal law as having exceeded the commerce power.

In fact the Court's agenda had begun to change in the 1920s, as more and more cases involving individual rights rather than property rights came up for review. Louis Brandeis had suggested that the Fourteenth Amendment's due process clause included more than property rights, and by 1926 the incorporation of the protections included in the Bill of Rights into the due process clause had begun. In a series of cases that *de facto* overruled *Barron v. Baltimore,* the Court applied to the states the Constitution's guarantees of freedom of speech and freedom of the press and criminal-procedure protections.

In 1938, in the otherwise obscure case *United States v. Carolene Products,* Justice Harlan Fiske Stone suggested in footnote four that the Court should apply higher standards of review to those issues involving individual rights or affecting discrete and insular minorities. During the 1940s and 1950s, and especially during the chief justiceship of Earl Warren, which began in 1953, the Court began to do this in earnest, first elaborating the meaning of the speech clause (despite some setbacks during the Cold War) and then undertaking to make people of color full citizens. A series of cases led up to the Warren Court's epic decision in *Brown v. Board of Education* (1954) that reversed the holding in *Plessy v. Ferguson* (1896) and other cases that permitted states to impose an apartheid system separating and humiliating blacks. In the years that followed, the Court upheld one challenge after another to laws and customs that segregated people on the basis of color.

The Warren Court did not invent the rights revolution, but many of the most famous cases expanding the meaning of civil rights and civil liberties were decided between 1953 and 1969, when Warren retired. *Mapp v. Ohio* (1961) expanded the protections of the Fourth Amendment, whereas *Gideon v. Wainwright* (1963) and *Miranda v. Arizona* (1966) ensured that all criminal defendants would have attorneys and protected the rights of persons in police custody. *Griswold v. Connecticut* (1965), involving the distribution of birth control information, established a right to privacy, whereas *Reynolds v. Sims* (1964) transformed the American political scene by requiring states to reapportion their legislatures on the basis of "one person, one vote."

The rights revolution once again underscored the Court's coequal role alongside the executive and legislative branches. Not all Americans welcomed this judicial activism, and many conservatives believed the Court had gone too far in its solicitude for minorities and accused criminals. Richard M. Nixon, in the 1968 electoral campaign, promised that if elected he would appoint a "law-and-order" judiciary, and yet the rights revolution continued under Chief Justice Warren Burger (1907–1995, chief justice 1969–1986), thanks in large measure to the skill and influence of Justice William J. Brennan Jr. (1906–1997). The Burger Court handed down one of the most controversial decisions of the twentieth century, *Roe v. Wade* (1973), establishing a woman's right to an abortion, and struck down many legal barriers that had made women second-class citizens. Although it modified some Warren Court rulings, the Burger Court generally confirmed the growing rights consciousness in the country.

Recent Trends. That began to change in 1986, when Burger retired and President Ronald Reagan named William H. Rehnquist (1924–) chief justice and Antonin Scalia to serve alongside him. These two appointments, as well as three others made by Reagan and his successor George Bush, gave the Court a more conservative cast than it had had in fifty years. Whereas some conservatives cheered the efforts to cut back on constitutionally protected rights, others were dismayed. Whatever the lasting effect of the Rehnquist era, it seemed probable that just as the pendulum swung away from conservatism in the 1930s and away from a liberal rights consciousness in the 1970s, this latest effort to push the constitutional balance far in one direction would elicit a countervailing trend in the opposite direction.

For its first 178 years, the Supreme Court consisted exclusively of white males. This changed in 1967 when President Lyndon B. Johnson elevated the African American civil rights leader Thurgood Marshall to the high court. The first woman justice, Sandra Day O'Connor, was appointed by President Ronald Reagan in 1981. She was joined in 1993 by Ruth Bader Ginsburg, a Clinton appointee; 2009 by Sonia Sotomayor and 2010 by Elena Kagan, both appointed by Barack Obama.

The Supreme Court played a central and controversial rolc in the disputed presidential election of 2000. The Democratic candidate Al Gore won the popular vote by comfortable 540,000-vote margin, but the Electoral College outcome depended on the result in Florida, where defective voting machines, confusing ballots, and other irregularities produced a result too close to call. After much maneuvering by both sides, Florida's Republican attorney general prepared to certify George W. Bush as the winner. But the state supreme court intervened, ordering a recount of all ballots rejected by voting machines. On appeal, the U.S. Supreme Court on 12 December 2000, by a 5-to-4 vote, reversed the state court and halted the recount, in effect making George W. Bush president. Four of the five pro-Bush justices had been appointed by Republican presidents Ronald Reagan or George H. W. Bush Raising further questions of partisanship, conservative Justice Antonin Scalia in 2004 refused to recuse himself from a case involving Vice President Richard Cheney despite having accepted Cheney's hospitality on a recent duck-hunting expedition.

In 2002–2004, a closely divided court ruled on a number of key issues. On capital punishment, the Court in *Atkins v. Virginia* (2002) forbade the execution of a mentally retarded person. On First Amendment rights, the justices in 2003 upheld the Children's Online Protection Act requiring libraries to block obscene websites on computers accessible to minors. In a decision hailed by the gay and lesbian rights movement, the Supreme Court in 2003 overturned a Texas law barring consensual sexual relations between same-sex partners. On the separation of church and state, the high court in 2002 upheld a Cleveland "school choice" plan permitting the use of tax dollars to pay the tuition of students attending church-sponsored schools. In 2004, however, the Court barred states from giving tuition aid to seminary students studying for the ministry. The same year, the Court heard a case challenging the phrase "under God" in the Pledge of Allegiance (inserted by Congress in 1954) as a violation of the First Amendment ban on an establishment of religion.

In a key affirmative-action case, the Supreme Court in 2003 upheld the admissions procedures of the University of Michigan Law School designed to enhance racial and ethnic diversity. At the same time, however, the Court rejected Michigan's undergraduate admissions policy involving a point system that gave automatic preference to African American, Hispanic, and American Indian applicants.

The Roberts Court (2005–present) began with the confirmation and swearing in of Chief Justice John G. Roberts on 29 September 2005 and is the current presiding Court.

The Roberts Court is seen as more conservative than the previous Court. The Roberts Court currently consists of Chief Justice Roberts and associate Justices Ruth Bader Ginsburg, Anthony Kennedy, Antonin Scalia, Clarence Thomas, Elena Kagan, Samuel A. Alito, Stephen G. Breyer, and Sonia Sotomayor. Some of the major rulings have been in areas including abortion (*Ayotte v. Planned Parenthood, Gonzales v. Carhart*); antitrust legislation (*Leegin Creative Leather Products, Inc., v. PSKS, Inc.*); the death penalty (*Baze v. Rees, Kennedy v. Louisiana*); the Fourth Amendment (*Hudson v. Michigan*); military detainees (*Hamdan v. Rumsfeld, Boumediene v. Bush*); voting rights (*Crawford v. Marion County Election Board*); the Second Amendment (*District of Columbia v. Heller, McDonald v. Chicago*), and campaign finance (*Citizens United v. Federal Election Commission*)

As it had for more than 200 years, the Supreme Court of the twenty-first century continued to play a central role on a wide range of public-policy issues confronting American society.

[*See also* **Abortion Politics and Policy;** ***Abrams v. United States; Adkins v. Children's Hospital;*** **Birth Control; Brandeis, Louis;** ***Brown v. Board of Education;*** **Burger, Warren; Civil Liberties; Civil Rights; Civil Rights Legislation;** ***Charles River Bridge v. Warren Bridge;*** **Chase, Salmon; Constitution; Court Packing; Dartmouth College Case; Federal Government, Judicial Branch;** ***Gibbons v. Ogden; Griswold v. Connecticut;*** **Harlan, John Marshall; Holmes, Oliver Wendell, Jr.; Jay, John; Jurisprudence; Liberalism;** ***Lochner v. New York; Marbury v. Madison;*** **Marshall, John; Marshall, Thurgood;** ***McCulloch v. Maryland; Miranda v. Arizona; Muller v. Oregon;*** **Municipal Judicial System; O'Connor, Sandra Day;** ***Plessy v. Ferguson;*** **Political Parties; Rehnquist, William; Roberts, John;** ***Roe v. Wade;*** **Scalia, Antonin;** ***Scott v. Sandford;*** **Segregation; States' Rights; Stone, Harlan; Taney, Roger B.;** ***United States v. Carolene Products; and*** **Warren, Earl.**]

BIBLIOGRAPHY

Currie, David P. *The Constitution in the Supreme Court,* 2 vols. Chicago: University of Chicago Press, 1985, 1990.

Hall, Kermit, ed. *The Oxford Companion to the Supreme Court of the United States.* New York: Oxford University Press, 1992.

Schwartz, Bernard. *A History of the Supreme Court.* New York: Oxford University Press, 1993.

Swindler, William F. *Court and Constitution in the Twentieth Century,* 3 vols. Indianapolis, Ind.: Bobbs–Merrill, 1969–1974.

Urofsky, Melvin I., ed. *The Supreme Court Justices: A Biographical Dictionary.* New York: Garland, 1994.

Warren, Charles. *The Supreme Court in United States History,* 2 vols. Boston: Little, Brown, 1926.

White, G. Edward. *The American Judicial Tradition.* New York: Oxford University Press, 1988.

Melvin I. Urofsky and Pearson Bramblett

SWANN v. CHARLOTTE–MECKLENBURG BOARD OF EDUCATION

A 1971 landmark U.S. Supreme Court decision, based on a case arising in North Carolina, that extended to large metropolitan school districts the duty to dismantle de jure (legally established) racial segregation. Crafted by Justice Potter Stewart, the unanimous ruling upheld federal district judge James B. McMillan's countywide busing order. According to the Court, busing schoolchildren to achieve greater racial balance in individual schools is a constitutionally proper remedy in districts burdened by the effects of past or present de jure segregation. Dismissing the North Carolina school board's argument that Judge McMillan's race-based busing order violated the 1964 Civil Rights Act, the Court sanctioned the use of optimal racial percentages and the involuntary transfer of children to schools outside of their neighborhoods.

Swann placed a heavy burden of proof on any school board attempting to demonstrate that racially imbalanced schools did not reflect official policy, but rather resulted from de facto forces. As a result, it became the touchstone of school desegregation litigation in the 1970s and 1980s mandating the use of court-ordered busing programs in hundreds of American cities. The effects of such programs were mixed, leading to meaningful desegregation in some districts and counterproductive "white flight" in others. In many communities, the dictates of the *Swann* decision triggered widespread opposition to "forced busing" among angry parents who demanded a return to traditional neighborhood schools. The opponents of court-ordered busing received a measure of legal relief in the early 1990s when the Court weakened *Swann* by ruling (in *Board of Education v. Dowell*, 1991, and *Freeman v. Pitts*, 1992) that lower courts could suspend busing programs in districts that made a good-faith and "reasonable" effort to desegregate.

[***See also* Brown v. Board of Education; Civil Rights; Civil Rights Legislation; Education Policy: Education in Contemporary America; *and* Supreme Court, U.S.**]

BIBLIOGRAPHY

Schwartz, Bernard. *Swann's Way: The School Busing Case and the Supreme Court*. New York: Oxford University Press, 1986.

Woodward, Bob, and Scott Armstrong. *The Brethren: Inside the Supreme Court*. New York: Simon and Schuster, 1988, pp. 96–112.

Raymond O. Arsenault

T

TAFT, ROBERT

(1889–1953), U.S. senator, Republican party leader, and son of President William Howard Taft. Born in Cincinnati, Ohio, Taft graduated from Yale University, earned a degree from Harvard Law School in 1913, and married Martha Wheaton Bowers the following year. They had four sons.

Taft got his start in politics by serving in the Ohio House of Representatives (1921–1926) and the Ohio Senate (1931–1932). An arch critic of Franklin Delano Roosevelt's New Deal, he won a U.S. Senate seat in 1938 and was reelected in 1944 and 1950. Although strongly opposed to FDR's interventionist foreign policy in the later 1930s, Taft supported the war effort after the attack on Pearl Harbor. Following World War II, he remained skeptical of the so-called bipartisanship in foreign affairs—voting for American membership in the United Nations but opposing the North Atlantic Treaty Organization. Taft also condemned President Harry S. Truman's commitment of American troops to Korea in 1950 without a formal declaration of war, calling the action unconstitutional. In domestic affairs, he coauthored the Taft–Hartley Act (1947), which limited the activities of labor unions, and he encouraged the early Red-hunting activities of his junior Republican colleague Senator Joseph McCarthy of Wisconsin.

Known as "Mr. Republican," Taft was deeply skeptical of federal power, which grew dramatically in the 1930s and after. Running as a conservative, he unsuccessfully sought the Republican presidential nomination in 1940,

1948, and 1952, failing each time to win the support of the more liberal and internationalist Eastern wing of the party. Following President Dwight D. Eisenhower's inauguration in 1953, Taft enjoyed his greatest political success as an effective Senate majority leader. In June of that year, however, rapidly progressing cancer forced him to relinquish his leadership role.

[*See also* **Anti-Communism; Conservatism; Federal Government, Legislative Branch: Senate; McCarthy, Joseph; Republican Party; Taft–Hartley Act;** ***and*** **Taft, William Howard.**]

BIBLIOGRAPHY

Merry, Robert. "Robert A. Taft: A Study in the Accumulation of Legislative Power." In *First among Equals: Outstanding Senate Leaders of the Twentieth Century,* edited by Richard A. Baker and Roger H. Davidson, pp. 163–198. Washington, D.C.: Congressional Quarterly, Inc., 1991.

Patterson, James T. *Mr. Republican: A Biography of Robert A. Taft.* Boston: Houghton Mifflin, 1972.

Gary W. Reichard

TAFT, WILLIAM HOWARD

(1857–1930), twenty-seventh president of the United States, chief justice of the United States. A native of Cincinnati, Ohio, Taft graduated from Yale and the Cincinnati Law School. He married Helen Herron in 1886. After a legal career in Ohio including three years as a superior court judge, he was named solicitor general of the Justice Department in 1890 and became a federal circuit judge in 1892. President William McKinley appointed Taft to head the Philippine Commission in 1900, in which capacity he proved an effective colonial administrator. Three years later, President Theodore Roosevelt appointed him secretary of war. In 1908, having won the Republican nomination for president as Roosevelt's designated successor, Taft defeated the Democratic candidate, William Jennings Bryan.

The rotund and lawyerlike Taft did not enjoy a happy presidency. Lacking Roosevelt's sure political touch, he had poor press relations and gravitated toward the conservative wing of his party in an era of reform. He proved unable to satisfy Republican Progressives who wanted more of the political and economic reform of the Roosevelt years. His mishandling of the Payne–Aldrich Tariff in 1909 alienated advocates of lower customs duties; the Ballinger–Pinchot Controversy over conservation strained his friendship with Roosevelt. Republican losses in the 1910 elections reflected voter unhappiness with the administration.

During his last two years in the White House, Taft unsuccessfully pursued a reciprocal trade agreement with Canada and international arbitration treaties. Meanwhile, his relations with Roosevelt deteriorated. By early 1912, the former president was openly maneuvering to supplant Taft as the Republican nominee. A fierce struggle ensued in which Taft's command of the machinery of the Republican Party enabled him to repel Roosevelt's challenge. Bitter over his defeat, Roosevelt bolted the GOP and started a third party. After a desultory campaign against both Roosevelt and the Democratic candidate, Woodrow Wilson of New Jersey, Taft came in third in the popular vote and won the electoral votes of only Vermont and Utah.

Out of office, Taft taught at Yale Law School and remained active behind the scenes in Republican politics. During World War I he served on the National War Labor Board. He advocated world organization through the League to Enforce Peace. After the Republicans under Warren G. Harding regained the

White House in 1921, Taft became the chief justice of the United States. Happy at last in a position that suited him, Taft presided over the Supreme Court in a harmonious fashion, played a large role in the selection of Supreme Court justices during his tenure, and improved many of the Court's working procedures. His votes on particular cases reflected the conservatism of his later years, especially on such issues as the rights of labor unions and efforts to curb the power of corporations. Taft's presidency had creditable achievements, but his place between Theodore Roosevelt and Woodrow Wilson has consigned him to the ranks of less-than-successful chief executives.

[*See also* **Ballinger–Pinchot Controversy; Bryan, William Jennings; Conservatism; Federal Government, Executive Branch: Presidency, The; Harding, Warren G.; McKinley, William; Progressive Era; Roosevelt, Theodore; Supreme Court, U.S.; Taft, Robert;** *and* **Tariffs.**]

BIBLIOGRAPHY

Gould, Lewis L. *Reform and Regulation: American Politics from Roosevelt to Wilson*, 3d ed. Prospect Heights, Ill.: Waveland Press, 1996.

Pringle, Henry F. *The Life and Times of William Howard Taft*, 2 vols. New York: Alfred A. Knopf, 1939.

Lewis L. Gould

TAFT–HARTLEY ACT

A 1947 labor law passed over President Harry S. Truman's veto. A series of attacks on the National Labor Relations Board (NLRB), particularly the hostile investigation of the board conducted by the Virginia congressman Howard Smith in 1939–1940, created public distrust of the agency and support for amendments to the 1935 National Labor Relations (Wagner) Act, to restore a balance of power between labor and management. A series of postwar strikes in basic industries such as coal, steel, automobiles, and railroads reinforced the public view that unions had become "too powerful." Charges of union corruption; racial discrimination; and, in some cases, Communist domination heightened the antilabor climate. A Republican victory in the 1946 congressional elections gave critics of the Wagner Act sufficient power to change the nation's labor policy. Senator Robert Taft, chairman of the Senate Labor Committee, and the New Jersey congressman Fred Hartley, the new chair of the House Committee on Education and Labor, offered separate bills that Senate and House conferees combined into the Taft–Hartley Bill.

Taft–Hartley expanded the NLRB from three members to five and created an independent NLRB general counsel as the agency's prosecuting arm, replacing the general counsel who had functioned as part of the board. It included the Wagner Act's preamble encouraging the practices and procedures of collective bargaining but now emphasized workers' rights to refrain from such activities. The bill specified unfair union labor practices, established provisions protecting employers' right of "free speech" to resist unionization, authorized the president to intervene in labor disputes by invoking an eighty-day "national emergency" injunction, and required the NLRB to seek injunctions against unions involved in secondary boycotts or jurisdictional strikes. It also required union officials to sign non-Communist affidavits to obtain the law's protection, outlawed the closed shop, and permitted states to prohibit other forms of compulsory union-membership clauses.

Although Taft–Hartley was hardly the "slave labor law" unions claimed it to be, its emphasis on the right to reject collective bargaining, its protection of employee and employer rights against unions, and its listing of specific unfair labor practices by unions did encourage employers to resist unionization and collective bargaining. Yet the core of the Wagner Act survived in Taft–Hartley, so that interpretations of the law's meaning came to depend primarily on which political party held power. The related Landrum–Griffin Act of 1959 further restricted certain boycott and picketing practices by organized labor, although it did give workers who lost their jobs in a strike the continued right to vote in union elections.

[*See also* **Anti-Communism; National Labor Relations Act; National Labor Relations Board; Truman, Harry S.;** *and* **Veto Power.**]

BIBLIOGRAPHY

Gross, James A. *Broken Promise: The Subversion of U.S. Labor Relations Policy, 1947–1994.* Philadelphia: Temple University Press, 1995.

James A. Gross

TANEY, ROGER B.

(1777–1864), chief justice of the United States from 1836 until his death. Taney's reputation has never recovered from the catastrophe of his majority opinion in the *Scott v. Sandford* (Dred Scott) case of 1857. He blighted his considerable accomplishments by his dedication to slavery, but he made lasting and significant contributions to the law of corporations, federal jurisdiction, and state regulatory power.

Born on a tobacco plantation in southern Maryland and educated at Dickinson College in Pennsylvania, Taney was admitted to the Maryland bar in 1799. He served in the state legislature, became a Jacksonian Democrat, and was attorney general of the United States (1831–1833) and secretary of the treasury (1833–1834) in Andrew Jackson's cabinet.

Taney's most important opinions include *Charles River Bridge v. Warren Bridge* (1837), which refused to read an implied grant of monopoly privileges into a corporate charter; *Propeller Genesee Chief v. Fitzhugh* (1851), extending federal admiralty jurisdiction to inland navigable waters; and *Prigg v. Pennsylvania* (1842), a concurrence in which he insisted on complete and exclusive state regulatory authority over all aspects of slavery.

In the Dred Scott ruling, Taney held that no black American descended from slaves could ever be a citizen of the United States and that Congress lacked constitutional power to exclude slavery from the territories. In thus attempting to impose an undemocratic judicial solution on a grave political and moral issue, Taney both degraded the role of the Supreme Court and besmirched his positive contributions to American public law.

[*See also* ***Charles River Bridge v. Warren Bridge;*** **Democratic Party; Economic Policy: Regulation; Jackson, Andrew;** ***Scott v. Sandford;*** **Slavery, Laws;** *and* **Supreme Court, U.S.**]

BIBLIOGRAPHY

Swisher, Carl B. *The Taney Period, 1835–64.* New York: Macmillan, 1974.

William M. Wiecek

TARIFFS

Tariffs have a long premodern history, but in U.S. history they have served two primary purposes: (1) to protect the domestic economy and specific economic sectors from foreign competition and (2) to raise government revenues.

Even before the founding of the United States, British attempts to regulate imperial trade through tariffs and taxes precipitated resistance in the American colonies. Hence, the Constitution of 1789 gave the new federal government control of overseas commerce, and Congress set low tariff rates solely to raise revenue to cover public expenses and obligations. The first secretary of the treasury, Alexander Hamilton, proposed higher tariffs to promote domestic industry but found scant support in Congress.

Between 1816 and 1820, Congress raised some tariffs to protect "infant" industries from British competition, but most imports traded freely. Political party competition and the rise of manufacturing in New England as shipping declined produced a high tariff in 1828, denounced as the "Tariff of Abominations" by agrarians in the South and West who favored a low tariff policy benefiting U.S. agricultural exports. When Congress passed another high tariff in 1832, the South Carolina legislature declared both the 1828 and 1832 tariffs null and void in the state, leading to a states'-rights confrontation—the so-called Nullification Crisis—pitting South Carolina and its political leader, John C. Calhoun, against the Andrew Jackson administration. Over the next three decades, however, Southern and Western congressmen, whose constituents depended on agricultural exports, kept tariffs low and promoted free-trade principles.

The federal government's financial needs during the Civil War and the absence of Southern congressmen led to higher tariffs in the 1860s. From the Civil War through the 1920s, the Republican Party advocated high tariffs to favor domestic industry, protect U.S. workers against low-wage foreign labor, and defend the "American standard of living." When the Democratic Party regained national power in 1913, southern leaders through the Underwood–Simmons Tariff lowered average rates to antebellum levels. The return to Republican dominance in the 1920s restored high rates, however, through the Fordney–McCumber (1922) and Smoot–Hawley (1930) tariffs. These high protective tariffs disrupted international trade and contributed to the Great Depression of the 1930s. To reinvigorate international trade and promote U.S. exports, President Franklin Delano Roosevelt supported the Reciprocal Trade Agreements Act of 1934. This measure authorized the president to negotiate bilateral tariff reductions with America's trading partners. After World War II, twenty-three industrial nations institutionalized reciprocal-trade principles on a multilateral basis in the General Agreement on Tariffs and Trade (1948). Lower tariff rates negotiated under GATT laid the foundation for the reconstruction of the international economy on free-trade principles and fueled the postwar growth of the industrial economies. By century's end, 124 nations belonged to GATT, known after 1995 as the World Trade Organization (WTO). In 1960 and 1964, Congress passed Trade Expansion Acts; they set the stage for GATT negotiations in 1967 that lowered tariffs still further and practically eliminated those on machinery, chemicals, and transportation equipment. In the ensuing decade U.S. exports and imports doubled, pushing merchandise trade, as a share of the gross domestic product, to levels not seen since 1913. Multilateral trade liberalization also enabled the United States to strengthen its anti-Soviet Cold War alliances and bolster its allies' economic health at low political cost.

Because the U.S. economy was the world's most prosperous and productive from 1945 through 1973, the United States allowed many of its allies, including the member nations of the European Economic Union (EU), launched in 1948, to protect their domestic industries and agriculture. By the mid-1970s, however, as foreign competition increased and the U.S.

economy faltered because of rising energy costs, imperiled U.S. industries, especially steel, textiles, and automobiles, petitioned Congress for protection. Textiles obtained the Multi-Fiber Arrangement (1974), by which overseas competitors voluntarily limited their exports. Under pressure, Japan in 1981 "voluntarily" restricted its auto exports to the United States.

Congress also adopted a confrontational strategy to restore "lost competitiveness" and to protect newer American service industries, agriculture, trade-related investments, and intellectual-property rights. The Omnibus Trade and Competitiveness Act (1988) gave the president an array of coercive powers, including quotas, "voluntary" restraint agreements, and domestic subsidies, to wrest concessions from recalcitrant trading partners who used various nontariff barriers to limit imports. The United States also supported the WTO's efforts to combat nontariff barriers to free trade. The 1999 telecommunications agreement between Japan and the United States required the Japanese government to monitor actively Japanese companies that unfairly discriminated against U.S. competition.

The formation of regional preferential tariff systems that discriminated between members and nonmembers challenged GATT's multilateral approach. The European Union (EU) from the beginning circumvented GATT rules. In 1976, for example, the EU set up a preferential tariff system linking former colonies to the European Common Market. The United States conceded the utility of this approach by emulating it. In 1988, Canada and the United States formed a free-trade zone that became the world's largest when Mexico joined in 1994, through the North American Free Trade Agreement (NAFTA). Caribbean nations were invited to participate as well. An Asian trading system centered around Japan, although less formally organized, showed similar regional aspects.

As the century ended, the U.S. effort to eliminate nontariff barriers to trade globalization, coupled with the emerging world information network, had profound political and social implications. Critics warned that a supranational trading authority such as the WTO could arouse nationalism or reinforce a tendency toward rival regional systems. Protesters cautioned that global trading arrangements weakened efforts to protect the environment and workers' rights. U.S. efforts in the 1990s to bring the Communist People's Republic of China into the WTO proved deeply divisive domestically. Supporters of the WTO responded that international political stability would benefit if global economic integration, through the elimination of tariff and nontariff trade barriers, outweighed the attractions of regional trade alliances. Whether the American initiative would lead to a stable and equitable multilateralism in the global environment remained an open question as the twenty-first century began.

[*See also* **Calhoun, John C.; Economic Development; Hamilton, Alexander; Jackson, Andrew; North American Free Trade Agreement; Republican Party; Roosevelt, Franklin Delano;** ***and*** **States' Rights.**]

BIBLIOGRAPHY

Dobson, John M. *Two Centuries of Tariffs: The Background and Emergence of the U.S. International Trade Commission.* Washington, D.C.: The Commission, 1976.

Garten, Jeffrey E. "Is America Abandoning Multilateral Trade?" *Foreign Affairs* (November–December 1995): 50–62.

Irwin, Douglas. "From Smoot–Hawley to Reciprocal Trade Agreements: The Changing Course of U.S. Trade Policy in the 1930's." In *The Defining Moment: The Great Depression and the American Economy in the Twentieth Century,* edited by Michael D. Bordo,

Claudia Goldin, and Eugene N. White. Chicago: University of Chicago Press, 1997.

Johnson, Harry G. *International Trade and Economic Growth*. Cambridge, Mass.: Harvard University Press, 1958.

Low, Patrick. *Trading Free: The GATT and U.S. Trade Policy*. New York: Twentieth Century Fund Press, 1993.

Paul P. Abrahams

TAXATION

The fundamental structure of the American tax system emerged from the extended political crisis that led to the formation of the U.S. Constitution. Its architects struggled with the problems of how to finance the Revolutionary War debts and establish the nation's credit in international financial markets. Consequently, the Constitution gave the new government clear fiscal authority to establish its sovereignty. In the words of Article I, Section 8, Congress had the general power "to lay and collect taxes, duties, imposts, and excises."

The one tax that the new federal government could not enact was a property tax. Property taxation had been the mainstay of local government in the Colonial Era, and after 1775 the newly independent states employed it extensively and worried that the proposed national government might preempt its use. Accordingly, Article I, Section 9, required that Congress allocate direct taxes, like property taxes, to the states in proportion to their population, rather than to the value of their property.

The First Tax Regime, 1789–1861. The financial program of Alexander Hamilton, the first secretary of the treasury, established tariffs, set at low rates, as the major source of the federal government's revenue. Tariff revenues paid off the Revolutionary War debts and financed the Quasi-War with France in the late 1790s and President Thomas Jefferson's war against the Barbary pirates. Tariff revenues, in combination with borrowing and land sales, funded the Louisiana Purchase and allowed presidents from Jefferson through John Quincy Adams to implement an ambitious program of internal improvements. By 1836, tariff revenues had enabled the federal government to retire its debt, and in 1837 customs duties also enabled President Martin Van Buren to distribute surplus revenues to the states for internal improvements.

Before the Civil War, the nation's leaders rarely broke from a reliance on low tariffs. One exception occurred in the early 1790s, when Congress followed the recommendation of President George Washington and Secretary Hamilton and enacted the nation's first excise taxes. These applied to distilled spirits and touched off the Whiskey Rebellion of 1794. The revolt ended significant use of excise taxation until the Civil War.

Congress also experimented with high tariffs from the 1820s until the early 1830s. Protective tariffs were imposed to promote industrialization and to shelter America's high-wage workers and high-cost industries from British competition. But American industries quickly become competitive, and southern planters and western farmers resisted tariffs that increased the price of manufactured goods. Southern politicians, especially in South Carolina, denounced the 1828 tariff legislation as the "Tariff of Abominations" and vowed to overturn it. During the Nullification Crisis of 1832–1833, high tariffs came to symbolize federal power for South Carolinians worried about the future of slavery. Consequently, Congress in 1833 reduced tariffs and in 1846 passed the low Walker Tariff, which paralleled Britain's repeal of the Corn Laws in the same year, another defeat for protectionism. These actions heralded the adoption of free trade throughout the Anglo-American world.

Meanwhile, state and local governments developed revenue systems that relied heavily on property taxes. As the Industrial Revolution gathered force during the 1820s and 1830s, Jacksonian reformers extended property taxation, trying to tax all forms of wealth. By the Civil War, most states had a general property tax designed to reach not only real estate, tools, equipment, and furnishings, but also intangible personal property such as cash, credits, notes, stocks, bonds, and mortgages.

From the Civil War through World War I, 1861–1918. The financial system of the early republic might have remained adequate for at least another generation had not the Civil War created such enormous requirements for capital that Washington had to adopt emergency taxes unprecedented in scale and scope. The wartime government placed excise taxes on virtually all consumer goods, license taxes on a wide variety of activities (including every profession except the ministry), special taxes on corporations, stamp taxes on legal documents, and taxes on inheritances. Each wartime Congress also raised the tariffs on foreign goods. And, for the first time, the government levied a federal income tax—a graduated tax reaching a maximum rate of 10 percent.

Republican Congresses phased out most of the excise taxes after the war and in 1872 allowed the income tax to expire. Republicans, however, maintained the consumption basis of the federal tax system by retaining two elements of the Civil War tax system. First, they kept high tariffs. Until the Underwood–Simmons Tariff of 1913 significantly reduced the Civil War rates, the tariff on dutiable goods often approached 50 percent of their value. By 1872, the tariff again supplied most federal revenues. The high-tariff system of the Civil War Era came to be justified as a means of creating a national market and protecting American industries and their workers. Second, Republicans retained the taxes on alcohol and tobacco products. A buoyant demand for both meant that revenues from these levies produced at least one-third of all federal tax revenues. These taxes appealed to moralists as discouragements to, and punishments for, the consumption of commodities they stigmatized as sinful and threatening to a virtuous social order.

Between the Civil War and World War I, however, the class and sectional tensions created by industrialization increased political pressure for reform of the federal tax system. One result was the enactment in 1894 of a progressive income tax (i.e., a tax whose rates rose as incomes increased). But in 1895 the Supreme Court, in *Pollock v. Farmers' Loan and Trust Co.,* declared this measure unconstitutional because it was a direct tax not assessed in proportion to population. Popular support for progressive income taxation grew, however, and in 1909 congressional reformers from both parties sent the Sixteenth Amendment, legalizing a federal income tax, to the states for ratification. It prevailed in 1913, and Congress forthwith passed a modest income tax.

State and local governments, too, gradually transformed their tax systems. With urbanization, the rising demands for parks, schools, hospitals, transit systems, waterworks, and sewers overwhelmed the long-established system of general property taxation. Traditional self-reporting of property holdings proved especially inadequate for assessing the value of "intangible" property such as stocks and bonds. Accordingly, most local governments focused property taxation on real estate, which they believed could be assessed accurately at relatively low cost. States gradually abandoned property taxation altogether and adopted special taxes to replace the lost revenues. In 1911, Wisconsin adopted the first modern income tax.

World War I expanded the use of income taxation by the federal government. Mobilization required enormous revenue, and President Woodrow Wilson and other Democratic leaders strongly favored progressive income taxes and opposed the regressive general sales taxes preferred by the Republican Party. To persuade Americans to make financial and human sacrifices for World War I, President Wilson and Congress introduced significant progressive income taxation.

The World War I income tax, first enacted in 1916 as a preparedness measure and then expanded under the Revenue Acts of 1917 and 1918, was an explicit "soak-the-rich" levy. Rejecting an approach that would have fallen most heavily on wages and salaries, it imposed the first significant taxation of corporate profits and personal incomes and placed a graduated tax on all business profits above a "normal" rate of return. This "excess-profits" tax actually raised most of the federal government's wartime tax revenues. The wealthiest 1 percent of individuals paid marginal rates as high as 77 percent on their incomes.

Prosperity, Depression, and New Deal, 1918–1941. During the economic expansion of the 1920s, three successive Republican administrations granted substantial tax reductions to corporations and the wealthiest individuals. Secretary of the Treasury Andrew Mellon (1855–1937) argued that the tax cuts would promote economic productivity. In 1921 Republicans abolished the excess-profits tax, dashing Democratic hopes that the tax would become permanent. In addition, Congress made the nominal rate structure of the income tax less burdensome on the wealthy and introduced a wide range of special tax exemptions and deductions, including the preferential taxation of capital gains and oil- and gas-depletion allowances. Nonetheless, the tax system retained most of its soak-the-rich character. Indeed, Secretary Mellon struggled within the Republican Party to defend income taxation against those who wanted to replace it with a national sales tax. He helped persuade corporations and the wealthiest individuals to accept some progressive income taxation and the principle of "ability to pay." This approach, Mellon told them, would defuse radical attacks on capitalists.

During the 1920s, state governments faced growing expenses for schools, highways, and other needs but were reluctant to compete with the federal government for income-tax revenues. Instead, they expanded their use of sales taxes and of various levies such as vehicle-registration fees, license fees, and gasoline taxes designed to make vehicle users pay the cost of highways. During the 1930s, state governments further increased the scope and rates of their sales taxes until, in 1940, they were raising most of their funds by this means.

The Depression of the 1930s produced a new version of the soak-the-rich tax regime. Beginning in 1935, President Franklin Delano Roosevelt and the Democratic Congress responded to threats from the left, particularly Huey Long's "Share Our Wealth" movement, by increasing the taxes on the wealthiest individuals and corporations while adopting regressive payroll taxes to fund the new Social Security system. In 1936, Roosevelt and Congress took the radical step of enacting an undistributed-profits tax—a progressive tax on the profits that corporations did not distribute to their stockholders. This innovation, more than any other New Deal measure, aroused fear and hostility among large corporations. Business seized the political opening created by the recession of 1937–1938 and Roosevelt's faltering political power, and in 1938 and 1939 a congressional coalition of

Republicans and conservative Democrats eliminated the undistributed-profits tax and halted New Deal tax reform.

The Era of Easy Finance, 1941 to 1975. During the mobilization for World War II, Roosevelt sought to finance the war with substantial taxes on corporations and upper-income groups, but opposition to radical war-tax proposals proved too strong. One source of opposition came from a diverse group of military planners, foreign policy strategists, financial leaders, and economists. To mobilize greater resources than during World War I, and to do so more predictably while also reducing inflationary pressures, they favored a general sales tax or an income tax that would produce most of its revenue from wages and salaries. The second source of opposition to Roosevelt's radical wartime tax proposals came from Democrats in Congress and the administration. They worried that anticorporate taxation could cause a postwar slump and even another major depression.

In October 1942, Roosevelt and Congress finally reached a compromise. They dropped a general sales tax, which Roosevelt opposed, and adopted an income tax that was progressive, although not as progressive as Roosevelt wanted. The act substantially reduced personal exemptions, establishing the means for the federal government to acquire huge revenues from the taxation of middle-class wages and salaries. To make the new individual income tax work, the administration and Congress relied on payroll withholding, deductions that sweetened the tax system for the middle class, a progressive rate structure, and the popularity of the war effort. Under the new tax system, the number of individual taxpayers soared from 3.9 million in 1939 to 42.6 million in 1945, and federal income-tax collections over the period leaped from $2.2 billion to $35.1 billion. Mass taxation had become more important than class taxation.

Victory in World War II and postwar prosperity produced a popular, bipartisan consensus for maintaining the wartime tax regime. This consensus meant that Republicans accepted levels of taxation on large incomes and corporate profits that were substantially higher than the prewar rates. Democrats, in turn, largely abandoned taxation as an instrument to mobilize class interests. Instead, adopting the principles of Keynesianism, they used taxation as a means of stabilizing the economy, often giving Keynesian arguments a conservative twist. Presidents John F. Kennedy and Lyndon B. Johnson won bipartisan support for major tax cuts, enacted in 1964, by hawking the same growth-promoting, "supply-side" benefits that Andrew Mellon had urged during the 1920s. Economics as well as politics extended the life of the World War II tax system. Economic growth enlarged the tax base by expanding the economy, and inflation often pushed people into higher tax brackets (a process known as "bracket creep"). The federal government could cut taxes while still funding national defense and creating new domestic programs.

Assaults on Government and "Ability to Pay," 1975–2011. During the late 1970s, however, a stagnant economy began to erode the ability of the tax system to produce revenues. Also, a powerful antigovernment movement emerged. California voters in 1978 passed Proposition 13, which slashed property taxes, encouraging President Ronald Reagan and Congress to make deep cuts in the federal income tax in 1981. However, the Reagan Administration discovered that it had gone too far and that deficit spending had become excessive. The administration then led the way in raising taxes twice, in 1982 and 1984, by reducing "tax expenditures" (the exemptions and deductions embedded in the tax code). In the Tax Reform Act of 1986, President Reagan and a Democratic Congress cooperated in further slashing tax expenditures. They used the new revenues that resulted to lower the highest marginal rates on wealthy individuals and corporations, to remove 6 million low-income Americans from the tax rolls, and to expand the Earned Income Tax Credit, which provided a kind of negative income tax for the lowest-earning tax payers.

The Tax Reform Act of 1986 had strengthened the income tax politically, and during the 1990s it was able to withstand assaults waged by antigovernment forces. In fact, the administrations of both presidents George H. W. Bush (in 1990) and Bill Clinton (in 1993) were able to increase income taxes, as well as other taxes. Those increases, and a strengthening economy during the mid-1990s, enabled the federal government to bring deficits under control.

In the 2000 presidential campaign, George W. Bush took advantage of the projected budget surpluses by calling for major tax cuts. He took a leaf from Reagan's 1981 tax cut but ignored Reagan's subsequent slashing of tax expenditures. In 2001, the Republican Congress responded with a $1.35 trillion tax cut (spread over ten years), which heavily favored taxpayers in the upper-income brackets. In 2003, Congress followed Bush's second call for major tax cuts with similar distributional effects. The flow of tax revenues slowed but government expenses soared, in part because of antiterror wars in Afghanistan and Iraq, the adoption of an expensive prescription drug program within Medicare, and the initiation of a stimulus program to counter the "Great Recession," which began in December 2007. Consequently, the growth of deficits and national debt accelerated.

During the early years of his administration, President Barack Obama favored allowing the wealth-favoring provisions of the Bush tax cuts to expire, but agreed to their continuation, for fear that to do otherwise might inhibit the progress of economic recovery and also because an antitax movement, loosely organized under a "Tea Party" rubric, contributed to Republican capture of the House of Representatives in 2010. However, in April 2011, Obama endorsed a long-term approach to deficit reduction that included a dramatic reduction of those tax expenditures which favored upper-income groups. His call for Americans to honor their historic commitment to the principle of taxation according to "ability to pay" would be tested in the presidential elections of 2012.

[*See also* **Bush, George H. W.; Bush, George W.; Clinton, William J.; Constitution; Hamilton, Alexander; Income Tax, Federal; Jackson, Andrew; Johnson, Lyndon B.; Kennedy, John F.; Louisiana Purchase; Monetary Policy; New Deal; Roosevelt, Franklin Delano; Sixteenth Amendment; Social Security; Tariffs; Taxes: Proposition 13; Taxes: Reagan Tax Cuts; Whiskey Rebellion;** ***and*** **Wilson, Woodrow.**]

BIBLIOGRAPHY

Brownlee, W. Elliot. *Federal Taxation in America: A Short History,* 2d ed. Washington, D.C.: Woodrow Wilson Center Press, 2004.

Steuerle, Eugene. *Contemporary U.S. Tax Policy,* 2d ed. Washington, D.C.: Urban Institute Press, 2008.

W. Elliot Brownlee

TAXES

This entry contains two subentries: Proposition 13; and Reagan Tax Cuts.

PROPOSITION 13

Proposition 13 was a California initiative amending the Constitution of 1879 approved in June 1978. It started an American antigovernment tax revolt. The ballot measure set real estate property values at 1975–1976 market value for tax purposes, limited real estate taxes to 1 percent of the value, limited tax increases to 2 percent per year, provided for a full reassessed value base at sale price for new owners, required a two-thirds vote for legislative tax increases, and made local government tax increases subject to two-thirds approval of eligible voters.

Howard Jarvis and Paul Gann were the architects of this crusade. Jarvis, the chair of the United Organization of Taxpayers, had failed in 1972 to qualify a property tax reform initiative. Gann was active in the Republican Party and organized the People's Advocate, Incorporated, in 1974. In 1977 Jarvis and Gann linked arms and war chests to fight rising property taxes. With the help of Los Angeles Assessor Philip Watson, they drafted Proposition 13. Working with local groups, 1,263,000 people signed up to get the proposition on the ballot. It was the first time that over 1 million Californians had signed up and "Yes on 13" received over $1.5 million for the campaign. About half of the contributions were less than $50. The groundswell of anger on the local level surprised tax-and-spend politicians.

The Sacramento politicians responded with the Property Tax Relief Act of 1978, ballot measure Proposition 8, providing for a 30 percent property tax cut. Democrats, the Parent–Teacher Association, and labor unions declared that the sky was falling and predicted fiscal disaster. The problem was that Sacramento has a massive budget surplus.

Jarvis went on the road accusing state government of wasteful spending, excessive public employee benefits, fat pensions, and union-inflated wages. He gave the media sound bites worthy of the evening news. In the highest voter turnout in an off-year election since 1916, 65 percent approved Proposition 13 and 53 percent rejected Proposition 8. The landslide gave hope to other state movements to cut property taxes.

Far more importantly for California, the Democrats seized the moment to send state tax revenues to cities, counties, and school districts in a massive bailout. This, in turn, enabled the creation of statewide unions that lobbied Sacramento for fatter salaries, larger benefits, and job security in return for filling the Democratic Party treasury from union dues. It was an ideal liberal world until the costs of the system outran tax revenues.

Proposition 13 also spawned an initiative business with the increasingly stupefied voters progressively sequestering tax funds for special interests and reducing the significance of the legislature. By 2011 the state was at least $25 billion in deficit with reading scores declining, the infrastructure in decay, and the Democratic Party holding sway in Sacramento.

[*See also* **Taxation.**]

BIBLIOGRAPHY

Allswang, John M. *The Initiative and Referendum in California, 1898–1998*. Stanford, Calif.: Stanford University Press, 2000.

Schrag, Peter. *Paradise Lost: California's Experience, American's Future*. Berkeley: University of California Press, 2004.

Gordon Morris Bakken

REAGAN TAX CUTS

The Economic Recovery Tax Act (ERTA) of 1981 was the largest tax cut in American history. It immediately lowered the top marginal personal income tax rate from 70 to 50 percent, provided cumulative tax reduction of 23 percent phased in over three years for other income bands, mandated indexing of personal income taxation to inflation, liberalized the depreciation allowance (the so-called 10-5-3 allowance), and increased the business investment tax credit.

The measure drew inspiration from several sources. Since his conversion to conservatism in the 1950s, Ronald Reagan regarded high personal taxes as the means for a confiscatory state to fund government. Adding an economic rationale in the stagflation-hit 1970s, he claimed that tax cuts were also necessary to boost individual enterprise. Meanwhile, the supply-side doctrines of economists like Robert Mundell and Arthur Laffer indicating that enhancement of individual incentive was the agency of economic growth challenged Keynesian belief in aggregate demand management. Popularized by *Wall Street Journal* columnist Jude Wanniski, their ideas won the support of Republican Congressman Jack Kemp (New York), who persuaded the GOP House leadership to back a three-year, across-the-board, 10-10-10 income tax cut. With Republican senators joining the cause, William Roth (Delaware) agreed to co-sponsor Kemp's bill in 1978. Although the GOP initially lacked the votes to enact Kemp–Roth, it gained Reagan's support in return for Kemp's agreement not to seek the Republican presidential nomination in 1980. Meanwhile, corporate lobbyists, who had secured supply-side additions in the Revenue Act of 1978, persuaded the 1980 Republican platform committee to adopt depreciation and further business allowances.

Based on Kemp–Roth, the Reagan administration's tax-cutting bill was subject to congressional add-ons, some of which benefited special interests. However, the most significant amendment, proposed by GOP Senator William Armstrong (Colorado), was the inflation indexing of personal tax rates to eliminate the automatic increase in revenues generated by bracket creep.

Influenced by Laffer-curve theory that tax reduction would broaden the economic base, Reagan was discomfited by the explosion of the deficit from 2.6 percent gross domestic product (GDP) in fiscal year (FY) 1981 to 6.0 percent in FY 1983. This expansion was primarily caused by the severe recession of 1981–1982, but ERTA's large revenue costs underwrote large deficits into the recovery cycle. Some Democrats suspected that Reagan had deliberately engineered this outcome to defund the liberal state. This was unlikely since it put him under pressure to rescind the last personal tax cut installment. Relenting to raise some business and other taxes as antideficit measures in 1982 and 1983, he held firm to protect the tax benefits that were the core of Reaganomics.

Whether ERTA generated strong postrecession economic recovery is a matter of dispute. Conservatives see it as proof of the supply-side pudding and liberals as the source of growing income inequality and prosperity-threatening deficits. However, it indubitably redefined the Republican agenda. Formerly the party of balanced budgets, the GOP became the party of low taxes in the Reagan era.

[*See also* **Conservatism;** *and* **Reagan, Ronald.**]

BIBLIOGRAPHY

Collins, Robert. *More: The Politics of Economic Growth in Postwar America*. New York: Oxford University Press, 2000.

Domitrovic, Brian. *Econoclasts: The Rebels Who Sparked the Supply-Side Revolution and Restored American Prosperity*. Wilmington, Del.: ISI Books, 2009.

Iwan Morgan

TAYLOR, ZACHARY

(1784–1850), twelfth president of the United States. Born in Virginia and reared in Kentucky,

Taylor acquired plantations and many slaves in Louisiana. Joining the army in 1808, he fought with distinction in the War of 1812. Placed in command of western forts, he honored Indian treaties; prevented white settlement of Indian lands; and during the Seminole wars in Florida, refused to return to their owners escaped slaves living with the Seminoles.

Although opposed to Texas annexation, Taylor in January 1846 was ordered by President James Knox Polk to advance to the Rio Grande River. A Mexican attack on a unit of his army in April led to the Mexican War. Winning battles against numerical odds, he became a national hero, nicknamed "Old Rough and Ready." As the Whig Party's presidential candidate in 1848, he defeated Democrat Lewis Cass. Although a slave owner, Taylor as president defended the interests of slavery opponents. He angered fellow southerners by refusing to oppose the Wilmot Proviso banning slavery from territories acquired from Mexico. He also opposed southern efforts to extend slavery by filibustering expeditions to seize Cuba from Spain. His administration's principal foreign-policy achievement was the Clayton–Bulwer Treaty.

Seeking to defuse the bitter sectional controversy over the newly acquired territories, he supported statehood for California and New Mexico on the understanding that they would themselves decide the slavery issue. With his support, California voted to become a free state. Slaveholding Texas, however, claimed most of New Mexico. Taylor's threat of military intervention may have prevented Texas from seizing New Mexico by force. When southern legislators combined Henry Clay's compromise proposals into a single "Omnibus Bill," Taylor opposed it as an effort to advance Texas's New Mexico claims. The Omnibus Bill eventually failed, and the amended parts that did pass, as the Compromise of 1850, generally conformed to Taylor's views. He did not live to see this outcome, however, having died on 9 July 1850 after a brief illness caused by gastroenteritis complicated by poor medical treatment. Vice President Millard Fill-more succeeded him.

[*See also* **Antislavery Movement; Clay, Henry; Compromise of 1850; Federal Government, Executive Branch: Presidency, The; Fillmore, Willard; Political Parties; Polk, James Knox; Texas Annexation; Whig Party;** *and* **Wilmot Proviso.**]

BIBLIOGRAPHY

Hamilton, Holman. *Zachary Taylor, Soldier of the Republic*. Indianapolis: Bobbs–Merrill, 1941.

Hamilton, Holman. *Zachary Taylor, Soldier in the White House*. Indianapolis: Bobbs–Merrill, 1951.

Smith, Elbert B. *The Presidencies of Zachary Taylor and Millard Fillmore*. Lawrence: University Press of Kansas, 1988.

Elbert B. Smith

TEAPOT DOME SCANDAL

One of the most sensational scandals in American political history took its name from the site of a naval oil reserve in Wyoming that in 1922 was leased by Secretary of the Interior Albert B. Fall to the oilman Harry F. Sinclair. This and a similar lease of the Elk Hills, California, reserve to Edward L. Doheny were possible because Fall, an advocate of private development, had recently persuaded President Warren G. Harding to give him jurisdiction over the reserves and had won the navy's agreement by stipulating that oil royalties could be used to expand above-ground storage facilities. Conservationists objected strongly, and the secrecy surrounding the deal aroused suspicions of favoritism and bribery, especially when Fall began improvements on his New Mexico Ranch. The Senate voted to investigate, and in late 1923, after Harding's death and Fall's departure from the Cabinet, Senator Thomas J. Walsh began an inquiry.

As the story unfolded in subsequent governmental investigations and court cases, Fall had received $409,000 from the two oilmen, partly as unsecured, interest-free loans and partly through the assignment to him of $233,000 in government bonds. The leases would probably have been made without these incentives, but as the evidence of fraud mounted, they were canceled. Fall, convicted of accepting bribes, was sentenced in 1929 to a year in prison and fined $100,000. Sinclair and Doheny were acquitted of criminal charges, although Sinclair did serve short jail sentences for contempt of Congress and contempt of court.

Teapot Dome entered American political folklore as the symbol and major example of Harding Era corruption, and as late as 1928 revelations about those involved and their connections with Republican Party financing continued. Thanks, however, to Harding's death, President Calvin Coolidge's success in winning public trust, and revelations connecting leading Democrats to Doheny, the scandal failed to shake Republican dominance. Teapot Dome's long-range significance lay less in its political fallout than in its relationship to conservation policy. Its roots were in the fierce conservation battles of the William Howard Taft and Woodrow Wilson administrations, and conservationists made good use of the scandal to overturn the prodevelopment actions of 1921–1922, secure creation of a Federal Oil Conservation Board, and return the oil reserves to naval control.

[*See also* **Coolidge, Calvin; Conservative Movement; Environmentalism; Harding, Warren G.; Republican Party; Taft, William Howard;** *and* **Wilson, Woodrow.**]

BIBLIOGRAPHY

Noggle, Burl. *Teapot Dome: Oil and Politics in the 1920s.* Baton Rouge: Louisiana State University Press, 1962.

Werner, M. R., and John Starr. *Teapot Dome.* New York: Viking Press, 1959.

Ellis W. Hawley

TENNESSEE VALLEY AUTHORITY

Established in May 1933 during the frenzied first 100 days of the New Deal, the Tennessee Valley Authority (TVA) sought to revitalize one of America's poorest regions. At the time, the farms and small towns in the seven states that bordered the nearly impassable Tennessee River and its tributaries presented a bleak checkerboard of weather-beaten shacks lacking electricity, crumbling churches, and one-room schools.

President Franklin Delano Roosevelt was not the first public official who sought to harness the Tennessee River's power and address the valley's crippling poverty, but his vision surpassed anything previously imagined. Proposing the TVA to Congress, Roosevelt declared: "It is time [for] national planning for a complete river watershed involving many States and the future lives and welfare of millions." Under agency heads Arthur E. Morgan (1878–1976) and then the Chicago lawyer David E. Lilienthal (1899–1981), the TVA built sixteen dams to prevent spring floods and limit soil erosion, supplied the valley with cheap electricity and recreational facilities, provided farmers with inexpensive fertilizer, and established a model community of neatly placed modern homes. Like most TVA programs and, indeed, most New Deal programs, this model community was racially segregated. Indeed, the TVA's insistence on local control, or "grassroots democracy," meant that discriminatory political and social structures often remained in place, even while the agency fought to eradicate poverty.

For supporters and critics, TVA symbolized the best and worst of the New Deal. Roosevelt's opponents saw it as a frightening instance of government excess; some even denounced it as "creeping socialism." New Dealers, however, pointed to the project as a shining example of government action at its best. For the first time, thanks to TVA, recalled one enthusiast, "the poor and dispossessed of America could imagine a new kind of world, a life based on brotherhood and mutuality." A particularly strong supporter was Senator George W. Norris (1861–1944) of Nebraska, a long-time advocate of public power development. TVA's massive Norris Dam near Knoxville was named in his honor.

The TVA's legacy proved mixed. Within a decade the agency transformed an unpredictable river into a manageable waterway providing vast amounts of hydroelectric power to thousands of isolated rural homes. Malaria, once endemic in the area, was virtually eliminated. The TVA's accomplishments, moreover, eventually including nuclear power, laid the groundwork for industrial development and economic expansion in the Tennessee Valley. But that progress did not end economic inequities or racism or redistribute political power. As the twentieth century ended, the TVA survived, its spectacular dams a major tourist destination. But it survived simply as another big power company, no longer as a model of visionary government planning.

[*See also* **New Deal; Nuclear Power; Roosevelt, Franklin Delano;** *and* **Segregation.**]

BIBLIOGRAPHY

Hargrove, Erwin C., and Paul K. Conkin, eds. *TVA: Fifty Years of Grass-Roots Bureaucracy*. Urbana: University of Illinois Press, 1983.

McCraw, Thomas. *TVA and the Power Fight, 1933–1939*. Philadelphia: Lippincott, 1971.

Bryant Simon

TERRORIST DETENTION POLICY

In the years since the 11 September 2001 terrorist attacks, the United States has captured and detained hundreds of al-Qaeda members and other suspected terrorists, most famously at Guantanamo Bay, Cuba. These detainees are often held for lengthy periods of time and in many cases the government has no plans to charge them with any crime. Three aspects of this detention program deserve further attention: (1) the legal authority to detain terrorism suspects; (2) the sources of and justifications for detention; and (3) the mechanisms by which detainees may challenge the government's decision to hold them.

Legal Authority for Detention. The Supreme Court has held that the Authorization for Use of Military Force (AUMF), which became law on 18 September 2001, authorizes the president to detain at least some suspected terrorists. The AUMF does not expressly approve detention; it simply authorizes the president to "use all necessary and appropriate force" against the "nations, organizations, or persons he determines" were involved in the 9/11 attacks. In *Hamdi v. Rumsfeld* (2004), the Court concluded that the AUMF implicitly authorizes detention. Detention "is so fundamental and accepted an incident to war as to be an exercise of the 'necessary and appropriate force' Congress has authorized the President to use." The Court emphasized that the president may detain American citizens (such as Hamdi himself) as well as foreign nationals.

More controversially, some have suggested that the president has an inherent authority to detain suspected terrorists even in the absence of congressional authorization. This power is said to derive from his constitutional status as commander in chief of the armed forces, among other sources. The George W. Bush administration took this position in *Hamdi* and elsewhere, but the administration of Barack Obama has not publicly embraced it.

It remains uncertain whether the president has the same power to detain a person who is captured on U.S. soil. The Supreme Court has sent conflicting signals. *Hamdi* emphasized that the detainee in that case was "captured in a *foreign* combat zone." Yet a 1942 case, *Ex parte Quirin*, upheld the detention and military trial of eight German saboteurs who were taken into custody in the United States. In *Padilla v. Hanft* (2005), the U.S. Court of Appeals for the Fourth Circuit concluded that domestic capture is "irrelevant." There is no difference, the court reasoned, "between an enemy combatant captured abroad . . . and an enemy combatant who escaped capture abroad but was ultimately captured domestically."

Who, specifically, may be detained? Different officials have answered the question in different ways.

On 13 November 2001, President Bush issued a military order broadly authorizing the detention of three types of people: (1) al-Qaeda members; (2) those who participate in international terrorism against the United States; and (3) those who knowingly harbor either. In *Hamdi*, the Supreme Court interpreted the AUMF as allowing detention of "individuals who fought against the United States in Afghanistan as part of the Taliban" or al-Qaeda. (The Court was silent about the permissibility of detaining other persons in other circumstances.) A 2009 court filing by the Obama administration articulated a more expansive standard than the *Hamdi* court: people are detainable if they have substantially supported al-Qaeda and the Taliban, including in parts of the world other than Afghanistan. This issue—who is subject to detention?—is hotly contested in the ongoing Guantanamo cases.

Sources and Justifications. Government officials typically have justified detention on law-of-war grounds (i.e., as captured enemy combatants, suspected terrorists are subject to detention for the duration of the hostilities). It may be more accurate to say that counterterrorism detention is a hybrid form of detention. The models from which it draws include military sources, as well as the world of intelligence and the criminal justice system.

For instance, the U.S. government asserts a need to detain suspected terrorists to prevent them from participating in future attacks. In other words, detention keeps one's adversaries from returning to the battlefield. To the extent that its goals include prevention and incapacitation, counterterrorism detention thus draws on the law of war; the government holds captured al-Qaeda figures for similar reasons that it held captured Japanese soldiers during World War II.

The American detention system also has intelligence roots. The government sometimes wishes to interrogate suspected terrorists it has captured. These detainees, it is said, might have important information about al-Qaeda's plans, and questioning them could help disrupt future attacks. The government thus holds and questions detainable terrorists for much the same reason it held and questioned Soviet spies during the Cold War—to increase its storehouse of intelligence information.

In addition, counterterrorism detention has features of the criminal justice system. The decision to detain a given person typically is based on a judgment that he is somehow blameworthy. The detainee is believed to have performed some act—such as providing support to a terrorist organization or participating in an attack—that is prohibited by law. In this respect, counterterrorism detention resembles criminal detention, which typically occurs only after a person is convicted of (or at least indicted for) a crime. Military detention, by contrast, usually implies no judgment of blameworthiness. In World War II, captured German soldiers were not held for having violated the laws of war, but simply to prevent them from returning to the battlefield.

Mechanisms for Reviewing Detentions. As of this writing, the principal mechanism by which suspected terrorists may obtain review of the government's decision to detain them is to petition a federal court for a writ of habeas corpus. (The "great writ" of habeas corpus is an ancient device by which prisoners may challenge their detentions.) The story of how detainees gained the right to habeas review is as follows.

Initially, the judiciary played a relatively minor role in reviewing terrorism detentions. That started to change in 2004, when the Supreme Court ruled in *Rasul v. Bush* that detainees at Guantanamo Bay had the right under the federal habeas corpus statute to seek judicial review of their detentions. *Rasul* was a statutory decision, not a constitutional one.

The Bush administration responded by creating an administrative review mechanism for Guantanamo detainees. Panels of military officers called combatant status review tribunals (CSRTs) were charged with determining whether a given captive was in fact an enemy combatant and thus subject to detention. Detainees had the right to introduce exculpatory evidence and they could cross-examine government witnesses. They also received assistance from "personal representatives" who would help them present their cases to the CSRTs. Detainees were not, however, given access to lawyers, nor were they allowed to see classified information that was being used against them. And CSRT rules also allowed the government to use hearsay evidence, as long as it was deemed relevant and helpful.

At this time, Congress enacted the Detainee Treatment Act of 2005 (DTA). As relevant here, the DTA barred federal courts from engaging in habeas review of terrorism detentions. The law did, however, provide for at least some judicial review; it authorized a federal appellate court to determine whether the CSRT procedures were followed in particular cases, as well as whether those procedures are constitutional. In *Hamdan v. Rumsfeld* (2006), the Supreme Court held that the DTA's restrictions did not apply to habeas petitions that had already been filed when the law went into effect. This prompted Congress to enact another law, the Military Commissions Act of 2006, which among other things restricted habeas review for all detainees, including those with pending petitions.

The stage was now set for *Boumediene v. Bush* (2008). That landmark decision held, first, that certain terrorism detainees have a constitutional right to seek writs of habeas corpus. In so doing, the Court used a "functional approach" to determine when aliens who are held outside the United States will enjoy constitutional habeas rights. The relevant factors are the aliens' citizenship, the processes used to classify them as enemy combatants, where they were captured, where they are incarcerated, and any "practical obstacles" to judicial review. Detainees at Guantanamo, the Court concluded, pass the test. *Boumediene* further held that the CSRT system was not an adequate substitute for habeas review. According to the Court, CSRTs suffered from a number of defects, including limits on the detainees' ability to present exculpatory evidence, the absence of legal counsel, and the use of hearsay. In the wake of *Boumediene,* there is no longer any question that federal judges have jurisdiction to hear detainees' habeas petitions.

One critical issue that remains concerns *Boumediene*'s geographic scope: Is the right of habeas corpus limited to Guantanamo Bay, given its unique circumstances, or does it also extend to other facilities elsewhere in the world? In *Al Maqaleh v. Gates* (2009), the federal district court in Washington, D.C., held that detainees at Bagram Airfield in Afghanistan have a constitutional right to habeas review. The following year, that decision was reversed by the U.S. Court of Appeals for the D.C. Circuit, which concluded that habeas does not extend to Bagram detainees.

[***See also*** **Crime Policy, Federal; Federal Government, Executive Branch: Department of Justice;** ***and*** **Judicial Review.**]

BIBLIOGRAPHY

Hafetz, Jonathan. *Habeas Corpus after 9/11*. New York: New York University Press, 2011.

Wittes, Benjamin. *Detention and Denial*. Washington, D.C.: Brookings Institution Press, 2011.

Yoo, John. *War by Other Means*. New York: Atlantic Monthly Press, 2006.

Nathan Alexander Sales

TEXAS ANNEXATION

From the 1820s to the 1830s there were halfhearted attempts to buy Texas from Mexico. Impatient with Washington ineptitude, Texans took matters into their own hands. Already chafing under the Mexican government's attempt to establish centralized control over all of its departments and angered by its abolition of slavery, they declared their independence in 1836. Texas revolutionaries achieved a semblance of independence when, under duress, General Santa Anna signed a treaty that brought the fighting between the Texas rebels and the Mexican Army, which was to withdraw across the Rio Grande, to an end. Andrew Jackson agreed to recognize formally the republic on 1 March 1845. Preoccupied with a depression that began in 1837, his successor Martin Van Buren would go no further.

After years of ingenious and cautious maneuvering, John Tyler, who had assumed the presidency after the death of William Henry Harrison, signed a treaty of annexation with the Texas republic in early April 1844. The president sent it along to the Senate later that month. In an atmosphere charged with political ambitions and ideological convictions, the Senate deliberated the merits of Tyler's treaty and territorial expansion. Fearing that premature and rapid expansion would preclude progress and promote social degeneration, the Whigs stood solidly against Tyler's treaty of annexation. Joined by a handful of Free Soil Democrats, they killed the treaty.

Despite the Whigs' best efforts, Texas annexation became an issue in the presidential campaign of 1844. Democrats ran James K. Polk on a platform that called for the "reannexation" of Texas and the "reoccupation" of Oregon. Although historians have made much of the connection between slavery (or antislavery) and the Texas issue, the divisions between Democrats and Whigs and within the electorate over the measure were both principled and defined by the ideologies of both parties. Individual liberty, most Democrats believed, was incompatible with overcrowding, exhausted lands, and wage dependency. Believing that personal autonomy and true freedom depended on land ownership and economic independence, expansionists maintained that the addition of thousands of square miles of territory to the Union addressed the single most consequential prerequisite of republican freedom.

Whigs feared that a Democratic empire based on unchecked territorial growth would undermine the evolution of American civilization. As the population grew increasingly nomadic, there would develop a distaste for peaceful, civilizing occupations. Their individual capacities and that of the nation would remain undeveloped. Some in the party raised the danger of slavery extension in their opposition. The party's opposition to annexation, however, remained rooted in the fear that they would promote the widespread bondage of whites by enslaving millions to the degraded conditions of a primitive, colonial economy.

Polk, riding this new, powerful issue of expansion, defeated the Whig party nominee Henry Clay. Believing that the election was a referendum on Texas annexation, President Tyler urged Congress again to take up the measure. Bypassing the treaty ratification process (which requires a two-thirds majority in the Senate), Congress annexed Texas as a state by a joint resolution, with simple and fairly slim majorities in both Houses. Tyler signed the bill on 1 March 1845.

[***See also*** **Antislavery Movement; Jackson, Andrew; Polk, James Knox;** ***and*** **Tyler, John.**]

BIBLIOGRAPHY

Hietala, Thomas R. *Manifest Design: Anxious Aggrandizement in Late Jacksonian America.* Ithaca, N.Y.: Cornell University Press, 1985.

Silbey, Joel. *Storm over Texas: The Annexation Controversy and the Road to Civil War.* New York: Oxford University Press, 2005.

Wilson, Major L. *Space, Time, and Freedom: The Quest for Nationality and the Irrepressible Conflict, 1815–1861.* Westport, Conn.: Greenwood Press, 1974.

Michael A. Morrison

THINK TANKS

The think tank emerged in 1916 as a uniquely American political institution—one that housed academics and public policy experts outside of the state who nevertheless sought to influence government policy making through policy research and writing. The first such institution, the Institute for Government Research (founded in 1916), and the second, the Institute for Economics (founded in 1922), merged in 1927 to form the Brookings Institution—the largest think tank still in existence. While undergoing distinct changes and new permutations from 1916 onward, the institution itself formed and continues to exist at the beginning of the twenty-first century as bodies of self-conscious elites who see themselves as counterposed to more democratic, bottom-up political movements.

The Nonpartisan Ideal. Brookings and its scholars, from the 1920s through the mid-1950s, saw itself as committed to a nonpartisan ideal. The institution and its scholars, taking its cue from Progressive Era reformers, saw themselves as a technocratic elite, one that could rise above democratic partisan politics of the late nineteenth and early twentieth centuries. Think-tank inhabitants at Brookings viewed themselves and their institution as necessary in a country that lacked a strong state—they were needed as a bulwark against the political disorder inherent in turn-of the-century America. They would plan policy, help implement it, and contain political activism within elite spheres. As such, the think tank, from its very inception in the Brookings Institution, was distinctly suspicious of democracy, distrustful of party politics, and deferential to areas of perceived expertise in American society. As Donald Critchlow (1985) has correctly observed, the founders of the modern-day think tank at Brookings saw "nonpartisanship" as "a political strategy," one developed "by an elite group of social scientists, mostly economists, and businessmen who sought to undermine the existing control of the government by political parties." In other words, think tanks would house academics (such as Brookings first president Harold Moulton) and would be funded by corporate or business interests (such as its namesake Robert Brookings) in the name of a technocratic elite managing, or at the very least guiding, the workings of the state.

Given that this "nonpartisan ideal" emanated from such conservative forces and conservative impulses, it is unsurprising that much of Brookings' research and advocacy took on conservative overtones and established the institution of the think tank as one that was inherently conservative in orientation. Unlike many progressive reformers of the same period, Brookings and its inhabitants rarely called for state intervention in the economy. This antistatism was seen most predominantly in the institution's campaign against Roosevelt's New Deal in the 1930s and against Truman's Fair Deal in the 1940s. During this period, Brookings' inhabitants saw themselves as defenders of the market economy against unnecessary government intervention by Keynesian social engineers. Its scholars advocated against the National Resources Planning Board, full-employment bills, national health insurance, and social security—among other state interventions into the economy. In doing so, Brookings came to be seen by liberals not as nonpartisan, but as reliable defenders of the conservative business interests that financially supported it.

The Partisan Turn. When Harold Moulton retired as president of Brookings in 1952, Brookings, as well as the institution of the think tank more generally, entered a distinctly new phase. Although think tanks and their inhabitants were still profoundly suspicious of the "messiness" of democratic activism and in favor of technocratic expertise as the primary mover of state policy, the institutions themselves became more partisan in orientation. Brookings led the way as Moulton and his staff were replaced by a group of younger economists more in line with the Keynesian consensus of the period. As such, Brookings, throughout the 1950s and 1960s, came to be distinctly identified with the Democratic Party and the Democratic presidencies of John F. Kennedy and Lyndon Johnson. It was during these years that Brookings came to be seen as a "government-in-waiting" for the Democratic Party as it funneled policy planners into Democratic presidential and congressional staffs. Such a partisan turn led Johnson, at Brookings's fiftieth anniversary in 1966, to declare, "You are a national institution, so important to, at least, the Executive branch—and I think the congress and the country—that if you did not exist we would have to ask someone to create you."

This liberal technocratic turn by Brookings led to think tank counterresponses from both the right and the left. In particular, conservatives and Republicans began to see the think tank as an institution that would be particularly amenable to conservative activism. The first such think tank was the American Enterprise Association, founded in 1943 by Lewis H. Brown, president of the Johns Manville Corporation. Brown brought together corporate funders and intellectuals to produce political and policy analysis explicitly opposed to the dominant Keynesian consensus of the time. The institution faltered for some time until it was taken over in 1953 by William J. Baroody, who changed the name of the institution to the American Enterprise Institute (AEI) in 1962. Initially, Baroody successfully remade the organization as one dedicated to scrupulously providing empirical analysis of policy that was up for debate to members of congress. However, Baroody, himself a conservative, began to remake the organization as a conservative counterpoint to Brookings in the 1960s and 1970s. At first, this meant providing numerous policy staffers for Barry Goldwater's unsuccessful 1964 presidential run. However, from the late 1960s and into the 1970s, there was an explicit reorientation of AEI under Baroody into a conservative policy producer and Republican government-in-waiting.

In this regard, AEI—and other conservative think tanks like the Heritage Foundation, which formed in 1973—saw themselves as explicit conservative counterpoints to a "liberal elite" composed of the media, academia, liberal foundations, and liberal technocratic think tanks like Brookings. Such a repositioning saw a drastic increase in the funding of conservative think tanks by conservative and corporate interests who rightly saw the institutions as ones that would support their programmatic agenda and antistatist sensibilities. Although there were successful left-oriented think tanks during this same period, such as the Institute for Policy Studies (established in 1963), which tried to use the think tank to promote grassroots democratic action against technocratic liberalism and technocratic conservatism, the institution itself was most effectively utilized by conservatives from the 1970s to the beginning of the twenty-first century.

Conservative Consensus. From 1980 onward, the think tank as an institution was most effective in creating an elite conservative consensus within the state and the modern media landscape. First and foremost, and in much the same way liberal technocrats from Brookings took up residence in the Johnson administration, conservative technocrats from AEI and Heritage took up key policy-making positions within the Reagan administration. Likewise, congressional staff positions and key judiciary appointments were also drawn from these same conservative think tanks. As a result, the state itself became more conservative and conservative think tanks helped draw up key legislation passed during the Reagan era. However, beyond this conservative shift within the state itself, the charge leveled by conservative think tanks of a liberal institutional bias within the government, the media, foundations, and think tanks like Brookings began to create a shift to the right within the wider elite political culture of the 1980s and 1990s. In short, the charge of bias emanating from conservative think tanks created a shift within the institutions under critique to the right—in effect, these institutions began to police themselves for "liberal bias." Thus, the Brookings Institution began to hire more conservatives to defend themselves against the charge of liberal bias. Likewise, prominent foundations such as the Ford Foundation began giving grants to conservative think tanks like AEI. Finally, and most importantly, conservative think tanks became the "go to" institution for reporters who needed the conservative view of a policy debate. In all of these ways, think tanks were integral from 1980 to the present in creating a rightward shift within elite policy making and political circles.

Additionally, this rightward shift was exacerbated in the 1990s as the decade witnessed the rise of the conservative-oriented, but Democratically aligned, think tank. Think tanks such as the Democratic Leadership Council (with its policy arm the Progressive Policy Institute) saw themselves as a counterweight to the "interest group" structure of the Democratic Party. With the support of President Clinton, they were able to advocate for and pass key conservative policies such as the North American Free Trade Agreement (NAFTA) and welfare reform.

Post 9/11. In the wake of the attacks of 11 September 2001, the think tank was one of the key institutions involved in pushing a militarized U.S. foreign policy. First and foremost, conservative think tanks such as AEI were integral in promoting a militarized foreign policy both within the media and inside the Bush administration. Second, Brookings helped create a liberal justification for such a militarized response in Afghanistan and Iraq. In doing so, think tanks helped to create an elite consensus in which military interventions in Afghanistan and Iraq were seen as a justified response to the attacks.

[*See also* **Conservatism;** *and* **Democratic Party.**]

BIBLIOGRAPHY

Critchlow, Donald T. *The Brookings Institution, 1916–1952: Expertise and the Public Interest in a Democratic Society*. DeKalb: Northern Illinois University Press, 1985.

Blumenthal, Sidney. *The Rise of the Counter-Establishment: The Conservative Ascent to Political Power*. New York: Union Square Press, 2008.

Phillips-Fein, Kim. *Invisible Hands: The Businessmen's Crusade against the New Deal*. New York: W. W. Norton, 2010.

Ricci, David M. *The Transformation of American Politics: The New Washington and the Rise of Think Tanks*. New Haven, Conn.: Yale University Press, 1993.

Rich, Andrew. *Think Tanks, Public Policy, and the Politics of Expertise*. Cambridge, UK; New York: Cambridge University Press, 2004.

Smith, James A. *The Idea Brokers: Think Tanks and the Rise of the New Policy Elite*. New York; Toronto: Free Press; Collier Macmillan Canada, 1991.

Jason Stahl

THIRD PARTIES

Compared with the party system of virtually any other country, American third parties occupy a unique niche. In countries with multimember systems such as proportional representation, minor parties often wield significant power, providing the legislative seats that help determine which coalition will govern; even in first-past-the-post systems, third parties may dominate regionally or locally (e.g., the Liberal Democrats in Britain or the Communists in parts of Italy). However, in the United States, with both a first-past-the-post system and nationwide presidential elections, third parties have failed to play a major role in governing, with few exceptions, for 150 years.

The long-term dominance of the two major parties is reflected in the term "third party," which has been used to refer to parties other than the two major parties since at least 1852 ("The Pittsburgh Platform," 1852). More recently it has come to refer to independent candidacies as well. For the purposes of this article, third parties are defined as those groups in a two-party system that run candidates for office but are themselves not one of the two major parties. Defining third parties in this way includes parties and candidacies that differ radically both in their longevity and in their sources. Some parties, like the Prohibition Party, have run presidential candidates in every election since 1872 without ever receiving as much as 3 percent of the vote. On the other hand, the most successful third party since the Civil War, Theodore Roosevelt's Bull-Moose Party, which was a close second to the Democrats in 1912, barely existed four years later.

Third parties have very different sources. At one end of a spectrum, parties may emerge from preexisting interest groups, like the antiabortion Right to Life Party. At the opposite end of the spectrum we find the parties of Ross Perot, Theodore Roosevelt, John Anderson, and George Wallace, in which the party revolves around the candidate in terms of both issues and personality.

Although recognizing differences among third parties, some scholars, such as Rosenstone, Behr and Lazarus, contend that what is most important are "the commonalities the movements share. Most prominently, they are all expressions of dissatisfaction with the major parties." Although that is undoubtedly true, it is still useful to categorize third parties, and many scholars have done so. The political scientist V. O. Key argued that a "party can best be comprehended in the light of its place in the total political structure." Based on the differential effect of each on the party system, Key distinguishes between "those [third parties] formed to propagate a particular doctrine," many of which have attracted small votes, but stayed around for multiple elections, and a transient third-party movement marked by a "rapid rise [and significant vote] and equally rapid decline." Key argues that the first set of parties is "effectively outside the [party] system," whereas the second is "intimately connected with it"

R. Harmel and J. Robertson draw a similar distinction in dividing parties into "contender parties" and "promoter parties." Contender parties are often initiated by individual candidates as a vehicle for their presidential candidacies (e.g., George Wallace and Ross Perot). They are heavily focused on a positive electoral outcome, and they have a potential to attract significant support. Promoter parties, on the other hand, have few illusions about winning. As Benjamin Bubar, presidential candidate of the Prohibition Party in both 1976 and 1980, observed, "We have a political message that we think America needs. We're not going to the White House and we may not win, but we're having an impact."

Contender parties differ among themselves as well. Some are formed around a single candidate running for office (usually president). These are referred to as "independent candidacies." Others run candidates across a wide range of offices in an attempt to control all levels of government. Prior to 1924, most significant third-party efforts (Populists, Bull-Moose) ran candidates for Congress and at the state level as well as at the presidential level. But beginning in 1924 with the La Follette Progressives and continuing through the beginning of the twenty-first century, those third parties attracting 5 percent of the vote or more for president have run few if any candidates for lower office. Our discussion will not differentiate between independent candidacies and party candidacies and will focus primarily on national elections.

Challenges to Overcome. We must start with the fact that no third party has supplanted a major party in more than 150 years. This failure implies that barriers to third-party success are strong. Identifying those barriers is important to understanding the life cycle of third parties, the conditions under which new third parties emerge, and the levels of success that third parties achieve. Explaining ease of third-party entry and success are the foci of most of the third-party literature.

Although one might think that entry and success are very strongly related, this is not the case. Since 1876, the number of parties on at least two states' ballots for president and the percentage of total presidential vote for all third parties have not been closely related. In 2008, eleven parties on the ballot in two or more states received a total of 1.6 percent of the total vote, but in 1912, with only four third parties qualified in two or more states, the third-party vote totaled 35.0 percent.

Barriers to Third-Party Formation. Since running candidates for office is the criterion that distinguishes interest groups from parties, and since being on the ballot is essential to running candidates, it is not surprising that ballot access has received prominent attention. Ballot access became a significant formal hurdle after the introduction of the Australian ballot, which was in place in almost every state by 1892. Prior to the Australian ballot parties printed their own ballots, so the number of party ballots was unlimited. However, under the Australian ballot reform, states, now responsible for printing official ballots, had to determine rules to get on the ballot so the ballot could be printed before the election. These requirements generally stipulated the number of eligible voters required to sign petitions supporting the third-party candidacy. Ballot access requirements were fairly easy to meet in the early years of the Australian ballot. By 1924, however, requirements had become much more stringent; and between 1924 and the George Wallace campaign of 1968, requirements for number of petitions, format, and date of filing further increased in difficulty.

Since 1968 third parties have become much more successful in getting on the ballot. The reasons for this are twofold. First, some of the most egregious requirements for ballot access were thrown out by the courts. Legal challenges to some of the most unreasonable ballot access laws by George Wallace in 1968, Eugene McCarthy in 1972, and John Anderson in 1980 eliminated many of these requirements. Whereas Wallace had needed around 1,700,000 valid signatures to get on all fifty states' ballots, Ross Perot (with an electorate half again as large) needed only 695,000.

Another factor easing the effects of ballot access requirements is that the explosion in technology computers, emails, and social networking sites has made it far easier for groups and parties to organize and mobilize. These developments explain how third parties have achieved increased ballot access success over the past twenty-five years, even as the number of required signatures has remained steady or even slightly increased in some states. As a result, problems associated with presidential ballot access, although real, appear less problematic at the beginning of the twenty-first century than at any extended time in American history.

As a result of these factors, in every election since 1972 the number of third parties qualifying for the ballot in presidential elections in two or more states has been higher than in any year between 1872 and 1968.

A second major barrier to third-party formation, especially for contender parties, is the electoral system (i.e., the Electoral College and the first-past-the-post system). Although the electoral system has been a problem for third parties because of the "wasted vote" effect (reluctance to vote for the preferred party if it has no chance of winning), it also impacts third-party formation by affecting the willingness of potential candidates and activists to commit themselves to the effort. Even a potential candidate like Michel Bloomberg, with a clear desire to run for president in 2008, significant support in the electorate, and bottomless financial resources, was scared away by the challenge.

Explaining Third-Party Electoral Success. When third parties obtain a place on the ballot, their problems in terms of attracting voters are just beginning. Third parties are always underfunded relative to the major parties (with the possible exception of Ross Perot in 1992); they do not get the same level of media coverage, and in the fifty-two years since the inception of debates, third parties have been excluded from major candidate debates in all but one election, (Ross Perot in 1992) and only in rare instances have they attracted nationally prominent figures to run.

Even more important, the fact that typically 90 percent of Americans either identify with or lean toward one of the two major parties makes a third party's success dependent on rejection of both parties by a large numbers of voters. But this is an unusual occurrence. Most commonly, when things are going badly and the incumbent party is rejected, the other major party picks up support. For third-party success, more is required: the nonincumbent party must also be rejected.

Of course, major party failure is necessary but not sufficient for third-party emergence. Although it provides the opportunity for third-party success, it does not guarantee it. The quality of third-party candidates and the ability of those candidates to rally discontent around the party or candidate are also crucial to success. It is for this reason that in times of major party failure some third parties do extremely well, others fail to improve their showings from previous elections, and sometimes no third party emerges to seize the opportunity. Therefore, we must identify both strong push factors that provide the opportunity for third-party success and pull factors that convert the potential for protest into actual votes for the third party—a "push–pull" model of third-party support.

Systemic push factors favoring third-party success In most cases push factors have emerged from economic, political, and social change—particularly when these challenges included the emergence of new issues not easily assimilated by the current party system (most notably slavery and the emergence of the Republican Party), dislocation of sufficiently large groups to form the basis of a third-party challenge (economic difficulties of farmers giving rise to the Populists), and demands for policies that are more extreme than either major party had endorsed (race and the emergence of George Wallace's American Independent Party).

Ballot petitions as an opportunity for activist mobilization Although ballot access requirements present a challenge for small third parties, they also provide an opportunity for contender parties with significant popular appeal to use the ballot petition effort to expand their visibility, as well as their eventual vote, through the successful mobilization of campaign activists. The difficulty of collecting petitions is often (especially among twentieth-century third parties) caused by a lack of organization and activists, both of which must be created by third parties for them to be successful in the general election. Getting on the ballot creates a tangible goal around which third-party supporters can rally and helps create an activist base for the campaign. The Perot campaign developed after Perot demanded his supporters get him on the ballot in all fifty states. It created a huge outpouring of grassroots support and an activist base developed around this goal (with almost no central direction).

Factors favoring third-party success: individual level To understand the ways in which these third-party opportunities translate into third-party success, we must focus on individual voter decision making and determine the conditions under which voters will consider/vote for third parties.

Under a first-past-the-post-system with two major parties, a voter will normally select the major party that is closest on issues of greatest concern to the voter. Only if a voter is distant from both major parties on perceived relevant issues will a third party be considered. Yet, even if distant from a party on issues, the voter might be relatively closer to one party. Since any third party is unlikely to win, this means there is a strong incentive to select the closer major party because it will result in preferred policy/incumbents. On the other hand, if both major parties are distant on issues, the third party might have greater appeal. In this case, because the voter is indifferent to the two major party candidates, a vote might be cast for a third party as a means of expressing issue preference and protest against the two major parties. Similarly, in an election where one party is almost certain to win, a single vote is unlikely to affect the outcome, and voters are also freed to cast third-party votes without cost.

The Dynamic of Third Parties. If third parties have not won the presidency or displaced one of the major parties in almost a century and a half, then under what conditions and in what ways do they affect the political system? And what happens to an influential third party after its initial showing?

The historian Richard Hofstadter emphasized the short life span of electorally successful third parties, writing that "third parties are like bees; once they have stung, they die." As Hofstadter suggests, with the exception of the Perot/Reform Party, every party earning more than 6 percent of the vote since the Civil War—the Populist, Bull-Moose, Progressive, American Independent, and Anderson campaigns—was a spent force by the next presidential election.

But like bees, which leave their stinger in their victim, third-party success grabs the attention of the major parties and forces them to respond. And it is this response—"adopting the third party's rhetoric if not the core of its program"—that allows the two-party system to co-opt the third-party constituency and thereby kill the third party. This process of third-party success, major party attention, response, and third-party supporter response to the major parties' attention has been labeled "the dynamic of third parties." The dynamic requires three conditions to be met:

1. A third-party movement must have a large and identifiable issue constituency from which it receives a substantial vote.

2. One or more major parties must make a bid for this support by tailoring their own positions to better reflect those of the third party's supporters.

3. The third party's supporters must respond to the bid by moving their support toward the major party or parties making the bid.

The Perot candidacy of 1992 provides an excellent example of this process. In 1992, both major parties and their candidates failed to engage a set of issues important to a large number of voters: governmental reform, a serious commitment to balance the budget, and economic nationalism (especially concerns about free trade). On this set of issues Perot supporters were far more extreme than either major party. The success of Perot's appeal on these issues helped earn him 18.9 percent of the vote. After the election, Newt Gingrich and John Kasich (over the opposition of more establishment Republicans) courted Perot. By the 1994 midterm elections, the Republicans had adopted the "Contract with America." With its heavy rhetorical emphasis on reform and no mention of either abortion or free trade, it was a clear appeal to Perot supporters. Perot's supporters responded by giving the 1994 Republican House candidates two-thirds of their vote, compared with just half in 1992. The demise of the party began, and by 2000 it was more sideshow than party. Clearly, the Perot campaign, like that of other successful third parties, had not simply been the bee that stung and died, but the bee that left its stinger in the political system.

Conclusion. We write off the possibility of third-party success at our peril. In the final edition of his masterful text on parties, V. O. Key opines, "Students of the topic seem to agree that the day of the third party, at least in presidential elections is done." Ironically, he wrote this in the election year preceding the

1968 Wallace campaign that ushered in a spate of major third-party candidates (in four of the next eight elections, a third party would earn more than 6 percent of the vote—as many as had done in the preceding hundred years). The number of parties on the ballot in two or more states more than doubled from the pre-1964 era to the post-1964 era.

The extreme candidate-centered nature of the third parties that have emerged since 1964 probably explains some of Key's failure of prognostication, but he also failed to consider that when major parties ignore issues or fail to engage those on a particular side of important issues, they create opportunities for entrepreneurial candidates. Technological advances have allowed third parties to form quickly and to overcome the legal impediments to ballot access. This ability extends even to small-vote third parties, which have achieved ballot access more frequently than in the past.

Third-party success looks rather meager if we focus on the ability of a third party to become a permanent part of the party system by either displacing a major party or establishing itself as a significant and consistent vote-getter at the highest (i.e., presidential or congressional) level. However, if we think of third parties as mechanisms to identify large issue constituencies the major parties ignore, raise those issues in an election campaign, and, when successful, influence one or both of the major parties to respond, then their important and influential role in the American party system is clear.

ACKNOWLEDGMENT

I would like to thank Chris Nemacheck and Abby Rapoport for many useful suggestions on this article. The article draws heavily on a lengthier piece found in *The Oxford Handbook of Parties and Interest Groups.*

[*See also* **Elections: Election Law; Elections: Nominating Systems; Elections: Presidential Elections; Elections: Voting Systems; Party System;** ***and*** **Voting: Voting Behavior.**]

BIBLIOGRAPHY

Harmel, R., and J. D. Robertson. "Formation and Success of New Parties: A Cross-National Analysis." *International Political Science Review* 6 (1985): 501–523.

Hofstadter, Richard. *The Age of Reform.* New York: Alfred A. Knopf, 1955

Key, V. O. *Politics, Parties and Pressure Groups.* New York: Crowell, 1964.

Mazmanian, David. *Third Parties in Presidential Elections.* Washington, D.C.: Brookings Institution, 1974.

"The Pittsburg Platform." *The American Whig Review* 94 (1852): 366–374.

Rapoport, R. B. "Winning Isn't Everything: Third Parties and the American Two-Party System." In *The Oxford Handbook of American Political Parties and Interest Groups,* edited by Sandy L. Maisel, Jeffrey Berry, and George Edwards. New York: Oxford University Press, 2010.

Rapoport, R. B., and W. J. Stone, *Three's a Crowd: The Dynamic of Third Parties, Ross Perot and Republican Resurgence.* Ann Arbor, Mich.: University of Michigan Press, 2005.

Rosenstone, S. J., R. L. Behr, and E. H. Lazarus. *Third Parties in America.* Princeton, N.J.: Princeton University Press, 1996.

Sundquist, James. *Dynamics of the Party System.* Washington, D.C.: Brookings Institution, 1983.

Winger, R. "Approximately 690,000 Signatures Needed for 2008 Presidential Candidate. *Ballot Access News Blog,* 2006. http://www.ballot-access.org/2006/11/25/approximately-690000-signatures-needed-for-2008-presidential-candidate/ (accessed 13 September 2011).

Winger, R. "The Importance of Ballot Access." 1994. http://www.ballot-access.org/winger/iba.html (accessed 19 February 2009).

Ronald B. Rapoport

THOMAS, NORMAN

(1884–1968), Socialist Party leader and six-time socialist candidate for president (1928–1948). Born in Marion, Ohio, Norman Thomas attended Princeton University and Union Theological Seminary and was ordained as a Presbyterian minister in 1911. He joined the Socialist Party after supporting the socialist and labor leader Morris Hillquit for New York City mayor in 1917.

A spiritual heir to the nineteenth-century moralistic reformers, Thomas derived his appeal from the ethical–moral perspective and the intense moral revulsion to human suffering that he brought to social, economic, and international problems. A pacifist during World War I, Thomas dropped his pacifism during the Spanish Civil War (1936–1939). He continued to find war morally abhorrent, however, a view that led him to oppose aid to the allies before World War II. This position served him well when he later critically supported that conflict and also in his postwar efforts for world peace, disarmament, and opposition to the Vietnam War.

As a socialist, Thomas criticized President Franklin Delano Roosevelt's policies because Thomas envisioned a cooperative society and not the reformed capitalism of the New Deal. He edged away from socialist orthodoxy after World War II, but never lost his belief in the incompatibility of a just economy and the profit system.

Thomas's historical importance lies with his moral vision. Achieving no socialist goals, he nevertheless moved masses of people to protest the denial of civil rights, civil liberties, and material security to millions of their brothers and sisters.

[*See also* **Antiwar Movements; Civil Liberties; Civil Rights; Debs, Eugene V.; New Deal; Radicalism; Socialism;** *and* **Socialist Party of America.**]

BIBLIOGRAPHY

Swanberg, W. A. *Norman Thomas: The Last Idealist.* New York: Scribner & Sons, 1976.

Warren, Frank A. *An Alternative Vision: The Socialist Party in the 1930s.* Bloomington: Indiana University Press, 1974.

Frank A. Warren

TOBACCO SUITS

Although tobacco use dates to the colonial period, the first tobacco suit against a cigarette company in the United States did not emerge until the 1950s. Beginning with *Pritchard v. Liggett & Myers Tobacco* in 1954, plaintiffs sued tobacco companies on theories fraud, negligence, and breach of warranty. Yet, tobacco companies prevailed for almost five decades, arguing that injuries were not a foreseeable consequence of smoking cigarettes. From 1954 to 1994, Big Tobacco spent over $500 million in legal fees. Despite success in the Courts, however, rumblings of future defeat began to emerge as early as 1964, when the Surgeon General issued a report claiming that smoking constituted a potentially serious "health hazard," was potentially linked to lung cancer, and warranted federal regulation.

In 1965, Congress enacted the Federal Cigarette Labeling and Advertising Act requiring that cigarette manufacturers inform the public of negative health effects caused by smoking both in advertisements and on packaging. The act proved a boon to Big Tobacco, providing producers with a defense against subsequent charges that they deceived the public about the potential harmfulness of cigarettes. More threatening to cigarette manufacturers was a trend in tort law toward making sellers strictly liable for damage that their products caused buyers, particularly if those products were defective. Although cigarette manufacturers fended off early suits brought on this theory by claiming that there was nothing wrong, technically, with their product, the Supreme Court shattered such defenses in 1993 when it held that producers could nevertheless be found guilty on fraud and conspiracy charges. Codified in Section 402(a) of the Second Restatement of Torts in 1965, strict liability theory spawned a wave of litigation in the 1990s, spurred by a federal government inquiry into the addictiveness of tobacco, something that the industry had long denied.

By 1996, a smoker plaintiff had made headlines by winning a $750,000 verdict against Brown & Williamson Tobacco Corporation in Florida, prompting tobacco companies to begin settling claims in Mississippi, Florida, and Texas. By 1998, forty-six states had joined a master settlement agreement (MSA) in which cigarette companies agreed to stop targeting youth and consented to paying $206 billion to forty-six states over the next three decades. Accelerating the industry's willingness to settle was the revelation that cigarette companies like Brown had known of tobacco's cancer-causing effects for decades, meanwhile conspiring to keep such information from the public. Leaked documents, known simply as the "Cigarette Papers," began turning public opinion against the industry.

Tobacco litigation reached a peak in 2000, when R. J. Reynolds lost a class action suit to 500,000 Florida residents, ultimately agreeing to pay $144 billion in damages. Since then, juries have proven less willing to punish tobacco manufacturers, leading to a string of defeats for plaintiffs suing cigarette manufacturers during the first decade of the twenty-first century.

[*See also* **Public Health: An Overview.**]

BIBLIOGRAPHY

Sirabionian, Andrei. *Why Tobacco Litigation Has Not Been Successful in the United Kingdom: A Comparative Analysis of Tobacco Litigation in the United States and the United Kingdom,* 25 Nw. J. Int'l L. & Bus. 486 (2005).

U.S. Department of Health, Education, & Welfare. *Smoking and Health: Report of the Advisory Committee to the Surgeon General of the Public Health Service.* Public Health Service Publication No. 1103. Washington, D.C.: U.S. Public Health Service, Office of the Surgeon General, 1964.

Anders Walker

TORT, LAW OF

Torts is the law governing a private (civil) wrong, other than breach of contract, for which a court will provide a remedy in the form of an action for damages. Modern torts grew out of the old English claim for trespass, whether to land, property, or person, and did not distinguish between negligence and intentional conduct. As society became more sophisticated and more industrialized, the law of torts evolved. In the United States torts was not recognized as a distinct branch of law until the second half of the nineteenth century. The first treatise on torts was in 1859, with the first law school class devoted to the separate study of torts not coming until 1870. However, once established, the law of torts evolved rapidly not only because of the increase in the types of cases giving rise to liability, but also because of the evolution of how the judicial profession began to look at the notion of fault.

Early Development. The law of torts has been evolving for well over 300 years almost exclusively as a creature of case law and judicial interpretation. Almost every American law student is familiar with *Scott v. Shepard* 96 EER

525 (1773), the famous squib case used to teach concepts of remoteness and intervening causes. When America became a nation and began to develop is own judiciary, it embraced such concepts as caveat emptor, or "buyer beware," first laid down by Justice John Marshall in *Laidlaw v. Organ,* 15 U.S. 178 (1817). The doctrine barred consumers from recovering for defects in products and remained the law throughout the nineteenth century.

American tort law remained a combination of English law and older American jurisprudence until the early twentieth century when American jurists began to develop a distinctly American Common Law of torts. No one figured more prominently in the early development of a uniquely American tort law than Benjamin Cordoza. Although an associate justice of the U.S. Supreme Court from 1932 to 1938, it was as a judge on New York's highest court, the New York Court of Appeals, that Cordoza made his most enduring contribution to the development of American tort law. Appointed in 1914, Cordoza served for eighteen years during a period of rapid industrial development that forced American jurists to adopt old concepts to new and expanding fact situations. Cordoza pushed the evolution of tort concepts such as assumption of risk, duty of care, products liability, and forseeability of harm. Decisions like *Palsgraf v. Long Island Railroad Co.,* 162 NE 99 (1928), and *McPherson v. Buick Motor Co.,* 111 NE 1050 (1916), stand as landmark decisions in negligence and products liability tort law.

Although Cordoza and the early development of American tort law are important, the most significant changes in torts would have to wait until after World War II. Although jurists continued to be an important force in the development and application of Common Law torts in America, the post–World War II era saw the intervention of government into the field of torts. It is this codification of tort liability into state and federal statute that has become associated with tort law.

The Tort Law Revolution. Prior to World War II, government regulation of tort liability was almost nonexistent and took the form of basic worker's compensation laws. Early laws like the Pure Food and Drug Act imposed government regulation but did not create private causes of action. Interestingly, government's first significant intervention into the field of torts was to allow private citizens to sue government entities and employees for negligence. The Federal Tort Claims Act of 1946, 28 USC 1928, led the way and most states followed suit with legislation that waived sovereign immunity for torts in certain situations. By the 1950s jurists began to look at tort law as more than simply issues of proximate cause, duty, and foreseeability. The judiciary looked beyond merely restoring people to where they had been prior to injury or loss from negligence or intentional conduct. The courts saw tort law as a tool to deter negligent conduct and motivate manufacturers to make safety and quality a priority, and both state and federal law began to reflect this doctrinal shift. The 1964 Civil Rights Act brought with it significant federally based tort actions for intentional deprivation of property or life interests and the 1965 Restatement of Torts reflected important changes in consumer protection and products liability law.

By the early 1970s state legislatures had taken significant steps to limit the harsh consequences of contributory negligence. Prior to the enactment of comparative negligence statutes, injured parties could not recover if their negligence contributed to any degree in their own injury or loss. Comparative negligence statutes not only allowed for the allocation of liability between tortfeasors, but also most jurisdictions allowed an injured party to recover as well if he was not more than 50 percent responsible for his injuries or damage. Beyond comparative negligence, torts expanded the concept of duty into areas where it had never existed. Courts across America began to impose liability on persons who occupied a special relationship to others. Psychiatrists, schools, common carriers, landlords, and business owners found themselves subject to special duties owed to their patients, students, tenants, and employees created both by an evolving judicial theory and by statutory enactments.

The net effect of this tort revolution was to bring American tort law from a system of "buyer beware" to one of "vendor beware." In a very real sense many aspects of society became safer. Businesses, workplaces, public and private transportation, and the providers of professional services, particularly medicine, came to operate under a legal system that imposed heightened duties both to be aware of potential dangers and to take affirmative steps to either warn or remove those dangers. Under Common Law a person was responsible for his own conduct, but not for the conduct of others. Not only did these special relationships create unique duties, but also the law of vicarious liability developed so as to make employers responsible for the conduct of their employees and principals responsible for the acts of their agents in dealings with other parties. However, with this heightened duty of care and expanded ability of private citizens to recover monetary damages in court for negligence and intentional conduct came consequences that were overlooked. In the zeal to protect people from harm and give them the ability to hold the wrongdoers responsible, tort law in America created a highly litigious society and significantly drove up the cost of doing business.

The Backlash. In the late 1980s huge billboards began to appear in parts of the Texas Rio Grande Valley pleading, "Thou Shall Not Sue Thy Neighbor." Located in extreme south Texas, the region had become a hotbed of plaintiff's litigation with record verdicts. For some people, Hidalgo County, Texas, had become the symbol of a tort system that was out of control. Business withdrew from or refused to go to the region. Insurance premiums for certain professions and business skyrocketed, making the cost of doing business prohibitive. In 1992 the infamous McDonald's hot coffee case made headlines when a seventy-nine-year-old woman won almost $3,000,000 for a cup of coffee that spilled and burned her. Although the verdict was subsequently reduced to around $500,000, the verdict became the rallying cry for a tort reform movement that was already gathering momentum. McDonald's actually had a history of coffee-related injuries and was far from blameless. The plaintiff sustained third-degree burns and some scarring. However, the notion that spilled coffee merited such a huge award did not sit well with a segment of the population that saw tort law as synonymous with a "windfall."

What would become a counterrevolution in tort reform did not occur overnight. Critics of the new reforms trace their genesis to the Ronald Reagan years. Then U.S. attorney general Edwin Meese formed the Tort Policy Working Group, partly in response to what became known as the liability insurance crisis of the 1980s. Meese saw a direct connection between the failure of insurance companies and the increasing number and amount of plaintiffs' verdicts. Some experts argued that it was the decreasing interest rates of the 1970s and 1980s that brought insurance company investment returns down and large verdicts were not responsible for the crisis. Regardless, Meese's working group saw the effects of earlier reforms as the culprit, specifically the growth of strict liability fault, broader notions of causation, and uncapped damage verdicts. The working group made concrete recommendations that focused on three main areas: (1) making it more difficult for injured parties to get to court, (2) making it more difficult to prevail as a plaintiff once in court, and (3) limiting both the amount of damages and the attorney's fees that could be recovered. All three areas would become the subject of tort reform in the 1990s.

Tort Reform in the 1990s. The concerns articulated in the 1980s became the basis of a second wave of tort reform in the 1990s that continues to define American tort law today. One of the most prevalent reforms put caps or limits on punitive damage claims and reduced the incentive for lawyers to take tort cases on a contingency fee basis. Contingency litigation allowed people with little or no financial means access to the courts, often with high-quality legal representation. But the arrangement depended on uncapped damages and a key aspect of the counterrevolution in tort reform has been the limiting of punitive damages, particularly in areas like medical malpractice. In addition, mandatory mediation and early dispute resolution have made tort cases less attractive for lawyers working on a contingency fee basis. One of the most effective methods has been the advent of mandatory arbitration, particularly in consumer product cases. Arbitration tends to undermined plaintiffs' ability to recover by limiting damages in a nonjury forum that is more corporate defendant friendly and provides limited grounds for appeal. Arbitration clauses have become standard in most consumer retail contracts and case law over the past twenty years has reinforced the strength of an arbitration clause if either party to a dispute chooses to invoke the process.

Tort reform also made cases more difficult to win. Plaintiffs in products cases now find liability not so "strict." In many jurisdictions medical malpractice victims find they have to overcome procedural requirements that require sworn medical expert testimony to support their claim even before they file or within a short period of time thereafter. Failure to meet the procedural requirements operates as a bar to continuing the case. Capping potential damage awards not only keeps many plaintiffs out of court, but also, for those who do prevail, winning has become far less lucrative. The limitations on punitive damages are significant. By 2007, forty-five of fifty-one jurisdictions either restricted punitive damages or no longer recognized them. Most of the post–World War II reforms, particularly those that came in the 1960s and 1970s, have been curtailed. Proponents of the counterrevolution argue that tort law is now more balanced, whereas opponents of the changes see the pendulum as having swung too far in the other direction. Those opposed to the restrictions on the ability of victims to recover in tort point to another culprit: the U.S. Supreme Court.

The Supreme Court as a Proponent of Tort Reform. Traditionally the U.S. Supreme Court has had little influence in the evolution of tort law in America. A legal field based on state common law and state and federal statutory law provided little opportunity for the Supreme Court to exert its influence. Although few people point to the U.S. Supreme Court as the instigator of tort reform in the 1980s, some legal scholars argue the Court under Chief Justice William Rehnquist readily supported the movement once it gained momentum. Opponents of the new reforms point to a general hostility toward litigation, particularly plaintiffs' damage suits, that pervades the Supreme Court decisions of that time.

The Rehnquist court consistently limited private remedies for plaintiffs unless clearly articulated statutory language established a private right of action. In constitutional rights cases, most particularly cases brought under 42 USC §1983, the expansion of state immunity and an increased difficulty in proving attorney's fees served to make plaintiff's cases more difficult to bring and to prove. The Court also supported state efforts to limit or eliminate punitive damages and showed a willingness at both the state and the federal level to enforce arbitration clauses. Finally, the Rehnquist court's philosophical shift toward "states' rights" saw a revival of the doctrine of sovereign immunity, making it more difficult to sue political subdivisions.

The Future of Tort Law. Tort law will always be an integral part of American jurisprudence. The debate is therefore not whether tort law exists, but rather how it is structured. Opponents of the post–World War II reforms argued that the shift in the law undermined a basic tenant of American life and culture: the free enterprise system. Free enterprise is the driving force behind the American economy, and the strength of the economy benefits everyone. However, invention and industry bring inherent risks and over time those risks were placed almost completely on the people and businesses that made life more enjoyable and the economy grow. By the late 1970s opponents of consumer-based reforms saw a system that ceased to be a vehicle to compensate victims for harm and injury, but had evolved into a system that had become almost criminal in its retribution and almost socialist in its effort to redistribute wealth. The proponents of the counterrevolution contend that reform simply placed balance into a system that had become woefully skewed toward consumers and plaintiffs to the detriment of business and the economy.

Opponents of the post-1980s tort reform see a more sinister force at work. Reforms that have limited access to courts and the ability of the injured to recover have done more than upset the balance between free enterprise and consumer protection; they have undermined basic democratic ideals. A key tenant of democracy is accountability, and the current state of tort law in the early twenty-first century has left corporate America unaccountable for its actions. Although this may be an exaggeration of the state of American tort law, some areas have clearly been severely restricted. The American Law Institute's Third Restatement of Products Liability provides an obituary for such things as strict liability in product design and "failure to warn" cases and the almost total immunity enjoyed by prescription drugs. The law also recognizes the willingness to leave consumers to the effects of their own vices when it comes to inherently unsafe products like drugs, alcohol, and cigarettes.

The problem lies in striking a balance. The state of tort law since the beginning of the twentieth century represents more of a reaction to perceived shortcomings in the system than an effort to balance competing interests. The goal is to continue to challenge the status quo and the beliefs that underlie the law. Perhaps one of the greatest inventors of all time, Orville Wright, said it best: "If we all worked on the assumption that what is accepted as true were really true, there would be little hope of advance." The evolution of American tort law seems to fit this maxim well. The current state of the law and the beliefs that support it may not represent what is best. Each side of the debate must continue to challenge the law as it exists, with the goal toward striking a balance that neither unfairly punishes business nor unjustly denies those who have been harmed the opportunity to be made whole.

[*See also* **Jurisprudence;** ***and*** **Supreme Court, U.S.**]

BIBLIOGRAPHY

Balkin, Jack M., and Sanford Levinson. *Understanding the Constitutional Revolution,* 87 Va. L. Rev. 1045 (2001).

Kaufman, Andrew. *Cardozo*. Cambridge, Mass.: Harvard University Press, 1998.

Roederer, Christopher J. "Democracy and Tort Law in America: The Counter-Revolution." http://works.bepress.com/christopher_roederer/1/ (accessed 29 August, 2011).

Siegel, Andrew. *The Court against the Courts: Hostility to Litigation as an Organizing Theme in the Rehnquist Court's Jurisprudence,* 84 Tex. L. Rev. 1097 (2006).

White, George Edward. *Tort Law in America: An Intellectual History*. New York: Oxford University Press, 1985.

Mark A. Weitz

TRADE POLICY

This entry contains two subentries: An Overview; and Fair Trade.

AN OVERVIEW

Trade policy consists of the rules and procedures a government uses to regulate commerce between its society and other countries. The Constitution gives Congress primary authority over U.S. trade policy and leaves the president a more modest role. Article I, Section 8, empowers Congress to set and collect taxes and duties and regulate commerce with other nations, whereas Article II, Section 2, allows the president, with the advice and consent of the Senate, to negotiate treaties, some of which may pertain to trade. Since trade affects someone in nearly every state and Congressional district, members of Congress have guarded their trade policy authority from the expanded presidential power found in such areas as national security.

Trade policy in the United States has centered on debates over foreign access to the American market, with businesses and workers producing items that compete with imports seeking limits on trade, whereas retailers, consumers, and those who use imports in their production process argue for free trade (commerce confronting few governmental attempts to inhibit imports and exports). The protectionist and nationalist labels are used to refer to those who want to limit trade, whereas those wishing to promote it are referred to as liberals. Typically, governments limit trade with tariffs (taxes on imports); quotas (quantitative limits on imports); and safety, health, and other regulations that obstruct foreign commerce.

Early U.S. Trade Policy. At independence, trade figured prominently in the debate over the type of society various founders aspired to create. Thomas Jefferson, Benjamin Franklin, and Thomas Paine believed free trade and low tariffs were keys to the agrarian society essential for democracy. Moreover, government-regulated trade was associated with the British commercial controls that sparked the American Revolution. Alexander Hamilton, however, advocated trade restrictions to promote the economic development needed for a high standard of living and national security. In his 1791 *Report on Manufactures,* Hamilton urged an approach later labeled import substitution industrialization (ISI). ISI places high tariffs on imports to encourage local production. Since new businesses typically have higher prices resulting from startup costs, steep tariffs are needed to increase the prices of imports to attract customers for local goods. As local producers become efficient and prices drop, the need for tariffs disappears.

For three decades after independence liberals prevailed, and tariffs were used to provide revenue for the federal government. After the War of 1812, however, attitudes shifted, Hamilton's views became dominant, calls for American manufacturing increased, and higher tariffs were introduced in 1816. Reinforcing the desire for local industry was Henry Clay's promotion of an "American system" that envisioned restricting imports and using commercial interactions among the states to build a national identity. This fostered resentment among those wishing to purchase cheaper imports and contributed to the divisions that led to the Civil War.

The Nationalist Period. Economic growth was rapid after the Civil War. By the 1890s several American industries were vastly outproducing their international competitors. Since tariffs during this period averaged 44 percent, many politicians, especially Republicans, asserted that high tariffs led to prosperity. Protectionists argued domestic producers had a right to the U.S. market and that imports should not be allowed to undermine the sale of American goods. Moreover, Republicans insisted that high tariffs contributed to a peaceful foreign policy by keeping Europe and its conflicts at a safe distance from the United States. Reflecting a growing faith in science, many Republicans championed "scientific tariffs" to guarantee that trade barriers would prevent imports from undercutting the prices of American products. To gather information for calculating tariffs, the Tariff Commission (renamed the International Trade Commission (ITC) in 1974) was established in 1882 to investigate trading practices in other countries.

Although protectionist Republicans dominated trade policy between 1870 and 1930, Democrats offered an alternate view emphasizing lower prices for consumers by reducing tariffs. In addition, such Democratic leaders as Cordell Hull of Tennessee insisted that the Republican depiction of trade as contributing to conflict was inaccurate, arguing that trade made countries less likely to fight because war might mean economic ruin. The Democratic message appealed to small farmers and workers who usually could not compete with the established interests supporting the Republicans. The American experience in World War I also belied the Democratic portrayal of how trade affects conflict because continued trading with the belligerents was what led to submarine attacks on U.S. ships and entry into the war.

The end of World War I caused a drop in the European demand for U.S. goods. Combined with an overproduction of agricultural products, the effect was devastating for farmers. Throughout the 1920s farms across the country were abandoned as their owners went bankrupt. By 1929 farmers needed help, and with Republicans in control of Congress and the White House, increasing the tariff on agricultural imports was the perceived remedy. Congressional consideration of a new trade bill, however, quickly led to a process in which industry after industry demanded and received a tariff increase. The Tariff Act of 1930 (known as the Smoot–Hawley Tariff) set the average tariff at the highest level since the Tariff of 1828 (the Tariff of Abominations). The near collapse of stock prices in October 1929 while the new tariff was crafted, as well as the onset of the Great Depression as it became law, created the impression that high tariffs contributed to the crash, paving the way for a new approach to trade policy.

The Liberal Trading System. When Franklin D. Roosevelt won the 1932 election he appointed Cordell Hull, a prominent trade liberal, secretary of state, the cabinet office responsible for trade negotiations. Realizing Congress would not pass a law reducing tariffs and believing that increased trade would alleviate the depression, Hull called for legislation to allow the president to bargain with other countries to lower trade barriers. Reciprocity would guide the process, with the United States lowering tariffs on selected products if another country would make an equivalent tariff reduction for U.S. exports. Hence, the United States would gain export markets in exchange for increasing its imports. Since bargaining would be with one country at a time and the focus was on specific products (autos, clothing, steel, shoes, etc.), such negotiations would eliminate protection gradually and only for goods that could withstand foreign competition. The United States could create jobs by exporting, while still protecting many products. Moreover, Hull only asked Congress to try his plan for three years.

Congress agreed to Hull's proposals and passed the Reciprocal Trade Agreements Act (RTAA) in 1934. This law allowed the president to negotiate as described above and to proclaim new tariffs for the products involved. The RTAA gradually reduced U.S. tariffs and was continually renewed through the 1960s. This law also allowed the United States to participate in the General Agreement on Tariffs and Trade (GATT). Created in 1947–1948, the GATT established rules for managing trade and reduced trade barriers by sponsoring negotiations among dozens of countries. Known as rounds, these talks lowered tariffs and set international procedures for handling unfair trade, protecting local producers, and adjudicating disputes. Thus, between 1934 and 1974, average U.S. tariffs dropped from over 50 percent to below 10 percent.

As U.S. imports increased after World War II, Congress changed two features of the RTAA approach to trade. The first reflected the concern that the State Department was treating trade as secondary to national security. To prevent this, Congress demanded the appointment of a special trade representative (STR) to handle trade negotiations when President Kennedy proposed the Trade Expansion Act of 1962. Initially given ambassadorial rank, in 1974 the STR was renamed the U.S. trade representative and placed in the cabinet. The second change came in the Trade Act of 1974 when the fast-track system (later labeled Trade Negotiating Authority) was created. Whereas the RTAA authorized the president to reduce U.S. tariffs by proclamation after reciprocal negotiations, fast track allowed the president to negotiate with a Congressional promise to vote on agreements within a specified time period with no amendments.

The culminating events in the liberal era occurred between 1985 and 1994 when the World Trade Organization (WTO) and the North American Free Trade Agreement (NAFTA) were set up. The WTO resulted from the Uruguay Round (1986–1994) of GATT negotiations. In the Uruguay Round, the U.S. goals were expanding trade in services (banking, insurance, etc.) and agriculture and securing rules to protect intellectual property and foreign investments. The United States made progress on every issue but agriculture, where the European Union (EU) hesitated to negotiate over its common agricultural policy (CAP). In 1990, complexities relating to the services, intellectual property, foreign investment, and trade dispute settlement regulations led Canada to call for the creation of the WTO to administer the agreements. Although initially skeptical, the United States became a charter member of the WTO in 1995.

NAFTA involved two stages of negotiations. First, in the early 1980s Canada requested talks because of concerns over protectionism directed at Canadian goods. Since over half of its exports are sold south of the border, the U.S. market is vital to Canada. With the Reagan Administration receptive to eliminating U.S.–Canadian trade barriers, bargaining began in early 1986 and concluded in late 1987. The legislatures of both countries approved a deal in 1988 abolishing all tariffs over ten years. The second stage began in June 1990 when Mexico requested a similar agreement. President George H. W. Bush agreed to negotiate because it would mean new business, especially for U.S. telecommunications and services firms, and the United States could tap into Mexico's energy industry. Canada joined the negotiations in 1991. In 1992, the three countries agreed to drop their trade barriers over a fifteen-year period.

NAFTA sparked public and Congressional controversies because some feared jobs would be lost if businesses relocated in Mexico where workers had fewer rights and were paid less, and others noted that pollution might increase if Mexico failed to enforce its laws. When he took office, President Clinton renegotiated NAFTA to establish procedures to protect workers' rights and prevent environmental degradation. Even with these modifications, the 1993 Congressional vote of approval was close.

The United States negotiated additional free-trade agreements with fifteen countries between 1985 and 2009. In general, those with developing societies met resistance paralleling the Mexican deal. The arrangement with five Central American countries and the Dominican Republic (known as CAFTA-DR) was among the most controversial. Workers' rights and the environment generated such concern that the agreement barely passed Congress in July 2005 despite the inclusion of labor and environmental provisions.

Recent Trade Policy. When the Cold War ended several factors slowed the post–World War II march toward freer trade. These included Congressional and public perceptions that trading partners such as Japan and China did not adhere to established trading norms and that imports were undermining such American industries as autos, steel, textiles, electronics, and furniture, with hundreds of thousands of jobs disappearing in just a few years. Japan and China were accused of manipulating their currencies to gain trade advantages, providing inappropriate governmental assistance to targeted industries, and confronting U.S. exports with unfair barriers. China also was charged with violating human rights and selling replicated American goods at cut-rate prices, costing U.S. firms untold business.

Amid these controversies Congress refused to extend the president's fast-track authority in 1994. This hindered President Clinton as he negotiated China's entry into the WTO and as he tried to ignite new WTO talks (later known as the Doha Round) to further open trade in services and agriculture. Nonetheless, the United States and China forged a deal that Congress passed in 2000 establishing normal trade relations and allowing China to enter the WTO. The United States also set up the African Growth and Opportunity Act (AGOA) in 2000 to promote development by giving African countries special access to U.S. markets.

In November 2001, the United States helped open the WTO-sponsored Doha Round. From the start, these negotiations were plagued by disagreements over agriculture, services, protecting intellectual property, and clashes among the United States, the European Union, and newly assertive developing countries. Although Congress granted President George W. Bush fast-track negotiating authority in 2002, that authority expired in 2007. The talks broke off in the summer of 2008.

[*See also* **Constitution; North American Free Trade Agreement;** *and* **Tariffs.**]

BIBLIOGRAPHY

Destler, I. M. *American Trade Politics*. Washington, D.C.: Institute for International Economics, 2005.

Dryden, Steve. *Trade Warriors: USTR and the American Crusade for Free Trade*. New York: Oxford University Press, 1995.

Eckes, Alfred. *Opening America's Market: U.S. Foreign Trade Policy since 1776*. Chapel Hill: University of North Carolina Press, 1995.

Goldstein, Judith. *Ideas, Interests, and American Trade Policy*. Ithaca, N.Y.: Cornell University Press, 1993.

Kaplan, Edward. *American Trade Policy, 1923–1995*. Westport, Conn.: Greenwood Press, 1996.

Rhodes, Carolyn. *Reciprocity, U.S. Trade Policy, and the GATT Regime*. Ithaca, N.Y.: Cornell University Press, 1993.

Rothgeb, John. *U.S. Trade Policy: Balancing Economic Dreams and Political Realities*. Washington, D.C.: CQ Press, 2001.

Schattschneider, E. E. *Politics, Pressures, and the Tariff*. New York: Prentice Hall, 1935.

John M. Rothgeb Jr.

FAIR TRADE

Fair trade refers to an international exchange between ethically minded developed world consumers and developing world producers. Historically, the first instances of American fair trade referred to domestic trade. Both meanings share many similarities. In both systems a network of producers, retailers, and (increasingly) consumers cooperate to establish mutually assured prices and quality production standards. Advertising campaigns and labeling requirements help define the in-group of fair traders and identify defectors or rival groups. To keep pace with changes in production methods and price levels, these contracts require constant revision and negotiation; simultaneously, they enable long-term planning and facilitate collective bargaining. Generically speaking, these market-based networks present an alternative to extreme market competition and emphasize value-added attributes of ethical consumption, like improved trade conditions or environmental sustainability efforts.

In the early twentieth century, Americans debated the ethics of mass production and corporate consolidation. Department and chain stores began to replace traditional specialty shops because they were able to purchase large quantities of goods at regular intervals and receive quantity discounts. Chain stores often practiced "loss leader advertising"—selling a brand name good at a loss and making up the loss in other markups. Consequently, specialty producers and retailers organized to combat low-cost retailers and unfair trade practices. The American Fair Trade League (AFTL) altered the U.S. political economy through grassroots efforts, facilitating "fair trade" networks between producers and retailers using existing trade associations. These networks assured customers of brand quality and service standards, while bolstering locally owned independent retailers.

California enacted the first fair trade law, which legalized manufacturer price-setting policies and ensured their enforcement, in 1931. An amendment two years later made the price policies enforceable against nonsigners to the sales contract. In the throes of Great Depression price deflation, fair trade laws spread across the states as a means to stabilize retail prices. In 1936, the U.S. Supreme Court in *Old Dearborn Distributing Co. v. Seagram-Distillers Corporation* upheld the state fair trade laws as a legitimate protection for small manufacturers and retailers. The following year the U.S. Congress passed the Miller–Tydings Act, which legalized fair trade agreements in interstate trade, if conducted between two fair trade states, by exempting them from antitrust prosecution. In 1941, forty-five states had fair trade laws.

Following World War II, state fair trade laws came under attack. In the 1950s, the laws were contested by corporations' intent to offer brand name goods at discount prices. By 1956, eight state supreme courts overturned statutes and eliminated manufacturer price setting. By 1975, twenty-five states and the federal government had repealed the fair trade laws.

Beginning in the 1940s, international development groups and faith-based organizations began purchasing handicrafts from developing world producers in the global south at above-market prices to resell directly to ethically minded consumers in the developed world. These alternative trade organizations (ATO) expanded direct sales networks through the 1960s and 1970s. By the 1980s, ATOs consolidated efforts and created product certification and labeling rules. Groups such as Fairtrade Labelling Organizations International (FLO), an umbrella group for twenty national initiatives, focused on harmonizing labeling efforts and developing producer organizations and communities. Fair trade goods include coffee, bananas, tea, cocoa, sugar, honey, fruits and vegetables, dried fruits, juices, rice, wine, nuts, oilseeds, fresh cut flowers, ornamental plants, cotton, and sports equipment.

[*See also* **Tariffs;** *and* **Trade Policy: An Overview.**]

BIBLIOGRAPHY

Drezner, Daniel. *U.S. Trade Strategy: Free Versus Fair.* New York: Council on Foreign Relations, 2006.

"Fairtrade Labelling Organizations International (FLO)." *2004/2005 FLO Annual Report.* http://www.fairtrade.net/ (accessed 30 August, 2011).

Grether, Ewald T. *Price Control under the Fair Trade Laws.* New York: Oxford University Press, 1939.

Lyon, Sarah, and Mark Moberg. *Fair Trade and Social Justice: Global Ethnographies.* New York: New York University Press, 2010.

Raynolds, Laura T., Douglas Murray, and John Wilkinson, eds. *Fair Trade: The Challenges of Transforming Globalization.* New York: Routledge, 2007.

Laura D. Phillips

TRADING WITH THE ENEMY ACT

This 1917 World War I measure, passed by Congress on 6 October 1917, aimed to prevent the Central Powers (Germany and its allies) from obtaining supplies and money. Enacted in a time when trade involved not only commodities but also credits sent by new technologies such as the telegraph, the law regulated and punished a range of trade with the enemy. For instance, it authorized the president to supervise foreign exchange, gold, and property in the United States and defined as an enemy any nation, neutral, or political agent doing business with the Central Powers and their sympathizers. Congressional liberals feared that such sweeping coverage could stigmatize aliens in America as disloyal, but proponents cited English and U.S. case law to validate the comprehensive controls. The act bolstered the wartime British blockade of Germany.

Successive administrations progressively broadened the law's application. A 1933 amendment under the Emergency Banking Act expanded the president's power to impose controls during national domestic crises such as the Great Depression. This led to an open-ended status during subsequent international contests including World War II, the Cold War, and the Persian Gulf War, when the law provided the legal justification for consumer controls, export restrictions, and economic sanctions against designated enemies. The National Emergencies Act of 1977, a post–Watergate effort to curb executive power, terminated all additions to the act since 1933 and provided for congressional oversight of the measure in the future. Emergencies were more precisely defined to limit the law's scope in domestic policy and diplomacy.

[*See also* **Federal Government, Executive Branch: Presidency, The.**]

BIBLIOGRAPHY

U.S. Congress, House Subcommittee on International Trade and Commerce of the Committee on International Relations. *Trading with the*

Enemy: Legislative and Executive Documents Concerning Regulation of International Transactions in Time of Declared National Emergency, 94th Cong., 2d sess., 1976.

Ellings, Richard J. *Embargoes and World Power: Lessons from American Foreign Policy.* Boulder, Colo.: Westview Press, 1985.

Thomas W. Zeiler

TROTTER, WILLIAM MONROE

(1872–1934), civil rights activist, newspaper editor, integrationist. Born in Ohio, William Monroe Trotter spent most of his life in Boston. A Phi Beta Kappa graduate of Harvard, he belonged to a class of northern, middle-class African Americans whose backgrounds included college education and a profession. Along with W. E. B. Du Bois, Ida B. Wells-Barnett, and the novelist Charles Chesnutt, he was part of what Du Bois called the "Talented Tenth," which insisted upon equal rights for African Americans and challenged the racial leadership of Booker T. Washington and his accommodationist platform.

In 1901, Trotter and his wife, Geraldine L. Pindell, founded the *Boston Guardian,* an African American newspaper devoted to the cause of racial integration. Two years later, Trotter gained national attention in the so-called "Boston Riot" by publicly confronting Washington at a local church. Trotter's actions and editorials made him a central figure in the Niagara movement, a series of annual meetings of African American leaders held at Niagara Falls, New York, beginning in 1905, and Trotter's own National Equal Rights League, which competed unsuccessfully with Du Bois and the National Association for the Advancement of Colored People (NAACP) for the allegiance of integrationists, black and white.

Trotter again made headlines by criticizing the racial policies of President Woodrow Wilson and by meeting with presidents Warren G. Harding and Calvin Coolidge to protest racial segregation in the federal government. In the 1920s, he tried to connect his organization to Marcus Garvey's movement and the African Blood Brotherhood. The death of his wife, combined with financial problems and waning national influence, shadowed Trotter's final years. He spent his life and fortune pushing the nation to recognize African Americans as full citizens.

[*See also* **Civil Rights; Coolidge, Calvin; Du Bois, W. E. B.; Equality; Harding, Warren G.; Racism; Segregation;** ***and*** **Washington, Booker T.**]

BIBLIOGRAPHY

Fox, Stephen R. *The Guardian of Boston: William Monroe Trotter.* New York: Atheneum, 1970.

Lewis, David Levering *W.E.B. Du Bois: Biography of a Race.* New York: H. Holt, 1993.

Gregory Mixon

TRUMAN, HARRY S.

(1884–1972), thirty-third president of the United States. Born in the farm village of Lamar, Missouri, 120 miles south of Kansas City, to John A. and Martha Ellen Truman, the future president spent his earliest years on a succession of farms until 1890, when his family, including a sister and younger brother, moved to Independence. Graduating from high school in 1901, Truman worked in Kansas City banks until 1906 when he became a farmer on his grandmother's land near Grandview, Missouri. With America's entry into World War I in 1917, he enlisted in a field artillery regiment and saw action in France. Mustered out in 1919, he operated a haberdashery in Kansas City until 1922.

Truman's political career began with his 1922 election to a three-person county court from the rural, eastern part of Jackson County, which included Independence. In effect he was a county commissioner, as the office generally was known in the Middle West. Defeated in 1924, he was elected presiding judge in 1926, a post he held for eight years. In this position he undertook to construct roads suitable for the automobile era. This led him to encounter the political boss of Kansas City, Thomas J. Pendergast. Truman cooperated in an arrangement whereby Pendergast supporters received county jobs, but the boss allowed Truman to manage the road program without graft.

Elected as a Democrat to the U.S. Senate in 1934 with Pendergast support and tens of thousands of fraudulent votes in Kansas City, Truman at the outset was considered "the senator from Pendergast" and treated as such by President Franklin Delano Roosevelt. Gradually he made a name for himself as (so he put it) a workhorse and not a show horse; his fellow senators came to admire him. Reelected narrowly in 1940, after Pendergast's imprisonment for income-tax evasion, Truman formed a committee to investigate wartime production. It proved so effective that he was chosen as Roosevelt's running mate in 1944, in place of the sitting vice president, Henry A. Wallace. He became president upon Roosevelt's death on 12 April 1945.

President Roosevelt had not been close to his vice president and had told him almost nothing about foreign relations. Yet, as luck would have it, foreign affairs dominated Truman's presidency. The new president did know about the nuclear weapons program, although not in detail. His decision to authorize the atomic bombing of Hiroshima and Nagasaki (1945) was the most controversial of his presidency. His second major involvement in foreign relations was the series of measures—the Truman Doctrine (1947), the Marshall Plan (1947), the Berlin Blockade and Airlift (1948–1949), and the formation of the North Atlantic Treaty Organization (1949)—by which the United States strengthened the nations of western Europe against the eastern bloc led by the Soviet Union. These measures, which included declarations of support for nations threatened by Communism, economic aid, opposition to a Soviet takeover of the western sectors of Berlin, and a military alliance, strengthened the U.S. position in the Cold War confrontation with the Soviet Union. After the Soviet Union's successful test of an atomic bomb in 1949, Truman authorized a U.S. program to develop the hydrogen bomb.

Truman's third major action, intervention in the Korean War on 25 June 1950 as part of a United Nations police action, forestalled North Korea's takeover of South Korea. The task proved unexpectedly difficult. When, after an initial retreat before the North Korean attack, the UN forces under General Douglas MacArthur went on the offensive, crossed the thirty-eighth parallel, and penetrated far into North Korea, the troops of Communist China in November 1950 attacked and nearly defeated MacArthur's overextended troops. The Chinese intervention created a military crisis, resolved early the next year by the U.S. Eighth Army under General Matthew B. Ridgway. When MacArthur pushed his own strategic proposals to the point of insubordination, Truman dismissed him in April 1951. After a long stalemate, a truce was signed in Korea in 1953, shortly after Truman left office.

On the domestic front, Truman managed reconversion of the economy after World War II, despite strikes and inflation. The new president gradually brought the cabinet departments and bureaucracy under his control—a lesson he had learned, albeit on a small scale, in county government. But the Cold War, especially the Korean War, bedeviled his domestic policy. In 1947, as Cold War alarms brought fears of domestic subversion, he initiated a loyalty-review program to ferret out federal workers suspected of disloyalty. It turned up a minuscule number of employees who were alleged security risks.

A bright spot in an otherwise modest domestic record was his championing of civil rights for African Americans. When Congress refused to pass civil rights legislation, Truman did what he could by executive action. He created a Fair Employment Board within the U.S. Civil Service Commission and by a historic executive order of July 1948 established procedures for desegregating the military. The services dragged their feet, but the Korean War crisis sped the process of integration.

In the 1948 election, Truman's civil rights activism gave rise to a third party in the South, the States' Rights, or Dixiecrat, Party. His electoral chances dimmed further with a challenge on the left from Henry A. Wallace's Progressive Party of 1948. Nevertheless, confounding the experts, Truman and his running mate, Senator Alben Barkley of Kentucky, won one of the great upset victories of American political history, narrowly defeating his Republican challenger, New York governor Thomas E. Dewey (1902–1971).

In 1949, Truman proposed to Congress the Fair Deal, a package of legislative reforms and civil rights proposals designed to continue and extend the New Deal. The Fair Deal got nowhere, and Truman's second term was beset by accusations of corruption, by the bloody conflict in Korea, and by the anti-Communist crusade of Senator Joseph McCarthy. Truman hated McCarthy but did not give sufficient attention to the senator's name-calling and accusations.

Stepping aside in 1952, Truman endorsed the Democratic candidate Adlai Stevenson, who lost heavily to the Republican Dwight D. Eisenhower. Returning to Independence, Truman composed his memoirs, arranged construction of a presidential library, and participated in Democratic causes until ill health curtailed his activities in the mid-1960s.

Truman's presidency has come to be seen as highly successful, principally in foreign policy, with domestic policy mostly a holding action. The low points were probably Truman's 1947 loyalty program and his failure to respond forcefully to Senator McCarthy's crusade. But the administration's successes abroad far outweighed the domestic failures. Often underrated in his own day, Truman has become one of the most admired holders of the presidency.

[*See also* **Anti-Communism; Civil Rights; Civil Rights Legislation; Democratic Party; Dixiecrats; Federal Government, Executive Branch: Presidency, The; House Un-American Activities Committee; Liberalism; MacArthur, Douglas; McCarthy, Joesph; Roosevelt, Franklin Delano; States' Rights; Stevenson, Adlai;** *and* **Wallace, Henry A.**]

BIBLIOGRAPHY

Ferrell, Robert H. *Harry S. Truman*. Columbia: University of Missouri Press, 1994.

Hamby, Alonzo L. *Man of the People*. New York: Oxford University Press, 1995.

McCullough, David. *Truman*. New York: Simon and Schuster, 1992.

Truman, Harry S. *Memoirs*, 2 vols. Garden City, N.Y.: Doubleday, 1955–1956.

Robert H. Ferrell

TYLER, JOHN

(1790–1862), tenth president of the United States. A Virginian, John Tyler attended the College of William and Mary, studied law, and served in the House of Burgesses, the U.S. House of Representatives, and as governor of

Virginia (1825–1827) before beginning a distinguished career in the U.S. Senate in 1827.

At first, the rising Jacksonians in Congress looked to Tyler as an ally. By the early 1830s, however, antipathy for President Andrew Jackson's governing style and a strict belief in states' rights led Tyler to join a handful of discontented Democrats in bolting to the fledgling Whig Party. In 1836 the Democratic-controlled Virginia legislature demanded that the maverick Tyler resign his Senate seat.

In 1840, when the Whigs nominated the northerner William Henry Harrison for president, they sought a southerner with less nationalistic views to balance the ticket. Tyler accepted the vice presidential nod, expecting to play a small role in the administration. Harrison's sudden death one month into his term thrust Tyler into the presidency. Derided as "His Accidency," Tyler found himself adrift politically. His states' rights ideas clashed with the nationalist Whigs in Congress, led by the master politician Henry Clay, who sent bills to the new president expecting Tyler simply to comply with his wishes. When Tyler issued two successive vetoes, the Whig congressional caucus wrote him out of the party and all but one of his inherited cabinet members resigned.

Tyler then latched onto the Texas annexation issue as a means of resurrecting his career. Although both parties wished to avoid the Texas question and the brewing conflict over slavery, Tyler saw it as an opportunity to defend both the South and states' rights. He negotiated an annexation treaty and waited for southern Jacksonians to assist in its ratification. The Democrats heeded the call in 1844 by nominating James Knox Polk, an ardent annexationist. Bypassing the ratification process that would have required a two-thirds majority for Tyler's treaty, Congress simply admitted Texas by resolution in February 1845, just days before Tyler left office. In 1860, Tyler served on a futile peace commission during the secession crisis. He later supported Virginia's secession and was elected to the Confederate House of Representatives, but died before he could take office.

[*See also* **Clay, Henry; Confederate States of America; Democratic Party; Federal Government, Executive Branch: Presidency, The; Harrison, William Henry; Polk, James Knox; States' Rights; Texas Annexation;** *and* **Whig Party.**]

BIBLIOGRAPHY

Chitwood, Oliver Perry. *John Tyler, Champion of the Old South.* New York: Russell & Russell, 1939.

Morgan, Robert J. *A Whig Embattled: The Presidency under John Tyler.* Lincoln: University of Nebraska Press, 1954.

Eric D. Daniels

U

UNITED STATES v. CAROLENE PRODUCTS

Decided in 1938, *United States v. Carolene Products* marked an important step in the history of civil rights in the United States. Despite an initial interest in rights following the Civil War, the Supreme Court abandoned the issue after Reconstruction, turning its attention instead toward the protection of business. The question of rights emerged again following World War I, as religious, racial, and ethnic minorities—together with Communists—confronted a wave of xenophobia, pushing the Court to reconsider questions of free speech, assembly, and the right to vote. In an unlikely case involving a 1923 federal law preventing the sale of watered-down, or "filled" milk, the Court suggested in Footnote 4 of its opinion that more rigid scrutiny might be warranted in cases where laws infringed on minority rights.

Specifically, the Court articulated several specific types of state regulation that might warrant closer scrutiny, including legislation that infringed on "the first ten amendments" along with regulations restricting "political processes which can ordinarily be expected to bring about repeal of undesirable legislation." The Court also included restrictions on the right to vote, the dissemination of information, the right to assemble, and "interferences with political organizations." Most importantly, however, the Court indicated that racial minorities might warrant judicial protection, either from legislation aimed directly at them or from legislation that tended to "curtail the operation of those political processes ordinarily to be relied upon to protect . . . discrete and insular minorities." Although the Court had already begun to expand free speech protections to the states prior to *Carolene Products,* Footnote 4's mention of "discrete and insular minorities" proved a watershed in constitutional theory. Over the course of the remainder of the twentieth century, Footnote 4's stature would continue to grow as its mention of discrete and insular minorities came to be applied not only to African Americans, but also to Asians, Latinos, illegitimate children, and women.

[*See also* **Civil Rights;** *and* **Regulatory Agencies, Federal.**]

BIBLIOGRAPHY

United States v. Carolene Products. 304 U.S. 144 (1938). Footnote 4.

Anders Walker

UNITED STATES v. E. C. KNIGHT CO.

156 U.S. 1 (1895), argued 24 October 1894, decided 21 January 1895 by vote of 8-to-1; Fuller for the Court, Harlan in dissent. In early 1892, the American Sugar Refining Company, the corporate successor to the Sugar Trust, acquired all of the stock of its leading competitors. The company thereby secured control of almost all sugar refining in the United States, and the federal government soon filed a civil challenge under the newly enacted Sherman Antitrust Act of 1890.

In its first decision interpreting the act, the Supreme Court affirmed the lower court's dismissal of the government's suit. Chief Justice Melville W. Fuller declared that the key question was whether a monopoly of manufacturing could be suppressed under the Sherman Act. He stressed the power of each state to protect the lives, health, property, and morals of its citizens and noted that this power encompassed the regulation of practical monopolies within the state's borders. In Fuller's view, although the Constitution granted Congress exclusive authority to regulate activities that constituted commerce among the several states, activities not belonging to interstate or foreign commerce fell exclusively within the jurisdiction of state police power.

The Court conceded that the ability to control the manufacture of an article involved simultaneous control over the article's subsequent disposition in interstate commerce and further agreed that combinations to control manufacturing might tend to restrain interstate trade. The Court declared, however, that this was an insufficient basis for congressional regulation because these were not direct but merely indirect or incidental effects on interstate commerce. The Court insisted upon a sharp distinction between manufacturing and commerce and stated that a producer's intention to distribute its products in other states subsequent to their manufacture provided no basis for the exercise of congressional Commerce Clause power. If indirect effects on interstate commerce could justify a federal challenge to the sale of manufacturing stock and the acquisition of refineries, the Court declared, Congress would have sweeping power to regulate the details of not only manufacturing but also "every branch of human industry" (p. 14) whenever ultimate interstate distribution was contemplated. The states simultaneously would be denied any police power authority over these matters within their own borders. The Court declared that Congress had framed the Sherman Act in the light of these "well-settled principles" (p. 16) and that the government's suit therefore exceeded the scope of the act.

Justice John Marshall Harlan dissented. He believed that the Sherman Act constitutionally could reach combinations like the one challenged in this case. Harlan declared that such dominating combinations had the object and ability to control not only manufacturing but also the price at which manufactured goods were sold in interstate commerce and therefore should be deemed to affect interstate commerce directly. Accordingly, he believed, Congress could seek to remove such combinations because they constituted unreasonable restraints of interstate trade. In Harlan's view, if Congress was not empowered to deal with such threatening interstate combinations, Americans would be left unprotected because individual states would not have sufficient power to control them effectively.

Scholars have differed concerning the origins and impact of the Court's decision. Some scholars, for example, see the decision as largely the product of a politically conservative Court majority fearful of extensions of federal government power. In recent years, an increasingly prominent alternative view has been that the majority genuinely sought to preserve substantial state regulatory authority over the in-state operations of corporations in the ultimately unrealized expectation that the states would use those powers effectively to block monopolistic combinations.

Some maintain that the Court's decision helped pave the way for the great merger waves that began in the late 1890s, which dramatically increased the levels of economic concentration in the United States. Yet the Court strongly supported the application of the Sherman Act in a series of other major cases soon after the *Knight* case was decided. Doctrinally, the Court's limited conception of the scope of federal commerce authority, and particularly its direct–indirect effects test, retained validity until the late 1930s, when it was finally rejected by the Court in favor of a much more expansive view of federal power.

[*See also* **Antitrust Legislation and Law; Harlan, John Marshall; State Regulation of Commerce;** *and* **Supreme Court, U.S.**]

BIBLIOGRAPHY

McCurdy, Charles W. "The Knight Sugar Decision of 1895 and the Modernization of American Corporation Law, 1869–1903." *Business History Review* 53 (1979): 304–342.

James May

UNITED STATES v. NIXON

In this landmark decision, the U.S. Supreme Court rejected the claim by President Richard M. Nixon that he possessed an absolute privilege that protected all forms of presidential communications. The basis for the case was the ongoing dispute over the White House tapes that implicated the president in the attempted cover-up of the break-in to the offices of the Democratic National Committee at the Watergate building. In the course of the Senate Watergate Committee investigations, it was revealed that the president had installed a taping system in the White House that captured all internal discussions and would possibly bring to light the level of presidential involvement in the scandal. As the special prosecutor subpoenaed the tapes, a legal battle ensued over whether a president may be forced to turn over to the courts any materials that would reveal private discussions within the White House.

In oral argument before the court, Nixon's lawyer, James St. Clair, argued that the courts had no right to reach into the private deliberations that occur in the Oval Office. St. Clair reasoned to the justices that there may be certain types of internal deliberations that require confidentiality and that the quality of advice that presidents receive would be undermined if there always existed the possibility of disclosure. For example, he added, what if the president were considering the appointment of a new justice to the U.S. Supreme Court? In that case the president would want the candid, confidential opinions of his advisers, which would not be possible if those persons believed that anything they said could be publicly disclosed. But Justice Thurgood Marshall inquired of St. Clair whether such internal deliberations should be revealed if, for example, one of the president's advisers had solicited a bribe from a possible court nominee. Marshall's point was unarguable in the context of the *Nixon* case. Although traditionally there is some protection for presidential communications, in cases of criminal investigations the need for information outweighs secrecy.

The Supreme Court unanimously rejected Nixon's claim that he possessed an absolute and unqualified executive privilege that protected him from disclosing the White House tapes. Nonetheless, the Court decision was not a repudiation of the principle of executive privilege. Indeed, the court affirmed the constitutional standing of executive privilege, when used for legitimate purposes, but not to cover up evidence of criminal activity. Nixon had argued for the complete independence of the executive branch from the reaches of the judiciary. In its decision, the Court not surprisingly reaffirmed its own authority to determine what the law is and to challenge the presidential exercise of power in cases where the chief executive overreaches his authority. Nixon's claim that only the president can determine the scope and limits of his own authority was historically and legally indefensible.

The White House tapes revealed that the president himself had participated in an attempt to cover up criminal acts, particularly when he had instructed a White House aide to use the Central Intelligence Agency (CIA) to divert the investigation of the Federal Bureau of Investigation (FBI) into the Watergate break-in. When the Court rejected the president's claim of privilege, Nixon released the tapes on 5 August 1974. Three days later he announced his resignation from office, effective 9 August 1974.

[*See also* **Executive Privilege; Nixon, Richard M.;** *and* **Watergate.**]

BIBLIOGRAPHY

Fisher, Louis. *The Politics of Executive Privilege.* Durham, N.C.: Carolina Academic Press, 2004.

Friedman, Leon, and William F. Levantrosser, eds. *Watergate and Afterward: The Legacy of Richard M. Nixon.* Westport, Conn.: Greenwood Press, 1992.

Jeffrey, Harry P., and Thomas Maxwell-Long, eds. *Watergate and the Resignation of Richard Nixon.* Washington, D.C.: CQ Press, 2004.

Rozell, Mark J. *Executive Privilege: Presidential Power, Secrecy and Accountability,* 3d ed. Lawrence: University Press of Kansas, 2010.

Mark J. Rozell and Mitchel A. Sollenberger

URBAN POLICY

This entry contains two subentries: Department of Housing and Urban Development; and National Policy.

DEPARTMENT OF HOUSING AND URBAN DEVELOPMENT

In 1965, President Lyndon Johnson signed the law establishing a new cabinet department, Housing and Urban Development (HUD), which expanded upon, and replaced, the Housing and Home Finance Agency (HHFA) and absorbed its two core units, the Federal Housing Administration (the FHA, which insures mortgages made by approved lenders) and the Public Housing Administration (the PHA, now the Office of Public and Indian Housing). Johnson appointed HHFA director Robert Weaver as the first HUD secretary, thus making him also the first African American cabinet appointment in U.S. history. Since Weaver, there have been fourteen additional HUD secretaries, including Shaun Donovan, appointed by President Barack Obama in 2009.

The PHA provided loans and grants to build rental housing for low-income families and individuals, at rates below market value, and owned and managed by local housing authorities (the federal government itself does not have the authority to use eminent domain for the purposes of building and managing public housing). The establishment of HUD brought with it an additional form of low-income housing assistance, subsidies for apartments rented on the private market; known as "Section 8" after 1974, it is now called the Housing Choice Voucher Program.

By the time of HUD, the government's role in housing had been well established, and it had played no small role in increasing the national home ownership rate from 44 to 55 percent between 1940 and 1950 (and to 68 percent by 2000). The Housing Acts of 1949 and 1954 vastly increased the amount of federal money that went to mortgage guarantees (extending them to rural areas as well), traditional public housing, and, in the parlance of the times, "slum clearance." FHA-backed mortgages went disproportionately to new suburban communities, from which minorities were systematically excluded by various means, whereas inner-city locations received more than their share of high-rise public housing, which in many cases created worse environments than the "slums" they replaced.

Some of the inequities in housing were addressed by the 1968 Fair Housing Act. More recently, the Housing Opportunities for People Everywhere (HOPE VI) program, created in 1992, provides funding for the demolition of "distressed" public housing (in many cases traditional high-rises) and for housing alternatives that lower the geographic concentration of poverty. HOPE VI funds were used, for instance, for the purpose of demolishing the Robert Taylor Homes in Chicago (once the largest public housing project in the country and notoriously crime-ridden) and for relocating former residents.

In 1970, the Emergency Home Finance Act created Freddie Mac in response to the monopoly enjoyed by Fannie Mae in the secondary mortgage market. This act required the HUD secretary to oversee Fannie Mae's portfolio. In 1984 the Secondary Mortgage Market Enhancement Act strengthened HUD's regulatory power and authorized Fannie Mae to purchase lien mortgages. Further regulatory reform came with the Financial Institutions Reform, Recovery, and Enforcement Act (1989), which strengthened HUD oversight over Fannie Mae and Freddie Mac. In 1992, the Federal Housing Enterprise Financial Safety and Soundness Act furthered regulatory reform by creating the Federal Housing Enterprise Oversight Office without HUD oversight. This act sought to ensure that both Freddie and Fannie were adequately capitalized and imposed housing goals for affordable housing in central, rural, and underserved cities. In 1993 HUD mandated that a percentage of Fannie Mae business be targeted to low- and moderate-income, underserved, and special affordable housing. HUD secretaries under William Clinton and George W. Bush continued to increase these percentages of Fannie Mae loans to low-income applicants, which rose to over 50 percent under the Bush administration. Oversight of Freddie Mac and

Fannie Mae was transferred to the independent Federal Housing Finance Agency after the financial crisis that began in 2007.

[*See also* **Housing Policy, Federal: An Overview; Housing Policy, Federal: Fannie Mae; Housing Policy, Federal: Federal Housing Administration; Housing Policy, Federal: Public Housing;** *and* **Johnson, Lyndon B.**]

BIBLIOGRAPHY

Hays, R. Allen. *The Federal Government and Urban Housing: Ideology and Change in Public Policy*. Albany: State University of New York Press, 1985.

Pritchett, Wendell E. *Robert Clifton Weaver and the American City: The Life and Times of an Urban Reformer*. Chicago: University of Chicago Press, 2008.

Willman, John B. *The Department of Housing and Urban Development*. New York: Praeger, 1967.

Wolman, Harold. *Politics of Federal Housing*. New York: Dodd, Mead & Company, 1971.

Richardson Dilworth

NATIONAL POLICY

Since the New Deal of the 1930s, liberal commentators, urban experts, and big-city mayors have lamented the lack of a coherent federal urban policy. Under President Franklin Delano Roosevelt, the federal government launched numerous employment and public works programs to restart the economy. Much of the funding for these programs went to large cities. Urban reform advocates believed this was a sign that the federal government recognized the pivotal role of the cities in the life of the nation and would take responsibility for their fate. This did not happen. Since that time champions of a greater federal role in urban affairs have sought to promote a national urban policy. Such a policy would intentionally, comprehensively, and coherently focus federal resource on maintaining and enhancing the prosperity of the country's cities.

Advocates for a national urban policy maintain that cities—not the suburbs and not the countryside—are the key to the national economic and social development. The big cities generate most of the country's economic activity and most of its innovations. If the cities falter, then the nation falters.

Those opposed to a national urban policy argue that targeting government resources on specific types of places is discriminatory and inefficient. The federal government should not favor an urban way of life over a suburban way of life, for example. Moreover, people and businesses, not the government, should decide where they wish to locate. Left to their own calculations, households and firms will pick the most cost-efficient locations. In short, the market will determine whether the United States is an urban, suburban, or even rural nation.

Prior to the New Deal, the federal government left urban matters to the states. Cities are not mentioned in the U.S. Constitution and a famous court case in 1868 had established the precedent that cities fell under the purview of state governments. Even during the Progressive Era, when urban problems were at the center of national debate, reformers and elected officials turned to city governments for solutions, not to the federal government. The federal government, however, did not totally neglect cities. The Census Bureau in 1880 published *Social Statistics of Cities* and in 1892 Congress appropriated $20,000 to be given to large cities for the study of slum conditions. The federal government also attended to local affairs through the Department of Commerce. Then-secretary Herbert Hoover supported an expansion of local city planning and zoning initiatives through his 1921 Advisory Commission on City Planning and Zoning. Publication of the Standard Zoning and Enabling Act of 1924 allowed state and municipal governments to design their own zoning laws and ordinances. Direct involvement in urban issues prior to the 1930s, however, was rare.

The concern with urban slums and the inadequate housing that defined them had much to do with the urban-based, New Deal public works programs. Roosevelt embraced an economic policy that sought to stimulate demand through employment-generating programs. Moreover, with almost one-third of the labor force unemployed and mortgage foreclosures a common occurrence, low-rent housing was desperately needed. Clearing slums would create jobs and free up low-cost land for new homes; building housing would create even more jobs. The Reconstruction Finance Corporation in 1932, the National Industrial Recovery Act in 1933, and the Housing Act of 1937 all provided funds. These programs boosted local economies and helped the working class withstand the Depression.

Public housing and other federally funded public works did not satisfy big-city mayors. Unemployment, mortgage foreclosures, and declining retail sales were not their only problems. Faced with shrinking property values and increasing numbers of property owners in tax arrears, tax revenues were falling dangerously below expenditures and municipal governments were courting bankruptcy. The mayors wanted fiscal relief and they wanted it given directly via unrestricted grants to city governments. To this end, they formed the U.S. Conference of Mayors in 1933 to lobby the federal government. Their efforts were in vain. Roosevelt was focused on the national economy.

The major hope for a federal commitment to the cities was the National Resources Planning Board. Established in 1933, its mission was to think strategically about national problems. It gave rise to the Research Committee on Urbanism, which produced a famous report: "Cities—Their Role in the National Economy" (1937). The report called for a national planning board, a federal research unit, and regional planning. These were ideas around which a national urban policy could seemingly be crafted. The report, however, carried little political weight, and, as attention turned to the war in Europe and the country emerged from the Depression, city problems became less pressing.

The end of World War II brought renewed interest in the cities, particularly with regard to the continuing problem of the slums, housing shortages, and declining commercial property values. Housing advocates and real estate interests lobbied aggressively for federal programs to eradicate slums and rejuvenate the downtowns. The Housing Act of 1949 subsequently provided appropriations for public housing and for local redevelopment authorities to clear slums and redevelop the now-vacant land. Over 800,000 public housing units were built and 2,000 redevelopment projects were financed in 1,200 cities. The city's major problems were being addressed. Slum clearance, however, often exacerbated overcrowding and deterioration elsewhere in the city and public housing concentrated poverty. Reinvestment in the downtown only materialized, if at all, years after the sites were cleared and then did little to keep the city from losing businesses and households to the suburbs.

At the same time, the federal government was supporting programs that seemed to harm cities. Limited-access highways under the 1956 National Interstate and Defense Highway Act were intended to relieve congestion in the downtowns and enable suburbanites to commute to the city for work, shopping, and entertainment. Instead, they drew even more households from the central cities to live in the suburbs. Federal mortgage insurance under the Federal Housing Administration

(FHA; 1934) program and the Servicemen's Readjustment Act (G.I. Bill; 1944) disproportionately targeted suburban construction and bypassed—"red-lined" in the critical commentary—the cities. Federal tax regulations favored new construction rather than renovation, a further disadvantage for built-up cities. If there were a federal urban policy, it was unclear whether it favored or penalized urban life.

Through the 1950s, a number of bills were submitted in Congress to establish a federal agency to coordinate urban initiatives and counteract the cross-purposes at which the current array of programs worked. A cabinet-level department would also give greater visibility to urban affairs in national politics. The Housing and Home Finance Agency had been created in 1947 to do the former, but big-city advocates deemed it insufficient. Not until 1965 did President Lyndon Johnson sign into law the Department of Housing and Urban Development (HUD). This cabinet-level agency would advocate for the cities and coordinate federal urban initiatives.

A year before HUD came into existence, President Johnson launched his War on Poverty to target federal resources on places with concentrated poverty. The War on Poverty centered on local Community Action Agencies and their efforts to coordinate public programs in poor neighborhoods. Many, but not all of them, were in the cities. A few years later, the Demonstration Cities and Metropolitan Development Act designated 153 distressed neighborhoods for additional assistance under the Model Cities program. These and similar federal initiatives, as well as Johnson's efforts with regard to civil rights and fair housing, had a major impact on cities. This period of federal involvement in urban affairs ended with two events: President Johnson's creation in 1968 of the Urban Institute, a federally funded "think tank" on cities, and the passage during the Nixon Administration in 1970 of the National Urban Policy and Community Development Act (1970) that required the federal government to "assume responsibility for development of a national urban policy" and committed HUD to produce a national urban policy report every two years.

Under President Richard Nixon, Congress in 1972 passed the General Revenue Sharing program that distributed unrestricted monies to state and municipal governments. It also created a number of block-grant programs that gave local governments discretion over the use of designated federal funds. The most important of these was the Housing and Community Development Act (1974) that combined seven federal urban programs into one. It provided annual community development block grants (CDBG) to municipalities, which could then be allocated among a variety of efforts to aid poor communities. The grants supported neighborhood-based organizations and were crucial for the evolution of non-profit, neighborhood-based, community development corporations. President Nixon also established a White House Office of Urban Affairs in 1969 to advise him on urban issues and to develop a national urban policy.

Before taking office in 1977, President Jimmy Carter established a cabinet-level Urban and Regional Policy Group to draft an urban policy statement. During his administration, attention to specifically urban concerns increased. HUD, for example, launched an innovative program—Urban Development Action Grants (UDAG)—to subsidize urban redevelopment projects, something that had been lost with CDBG. Between 1977 and 1980, the program gave out approximately 700 grants to nearly 400 cities. Advocates of a national urban policy were further buoyed by the possibility that Carter would order a major federal commitment. His 1978 National Urban Policy Report declared, "A principle aim of national policy should be to enable urban communities to become economically self-sufficient." Among its proposals were the UDAG program, increased funding for CDBG, and extra grants for economic development initiatives in urban areas. The Carter administration also floated the idea of a National Development Bank that would subsidize redevelopment and economic development projects and issued executive orders encouraging federal departments to locate facilities in central cities and conduct urban and community impact analyses of all major federal initiatives. The rhetoric, however, greatly exceeded the performance. The secretary of HUD Patricia Harris told the press that "federal programs should not be a panacea for the ills of the cities. The most essential ingredients of urban progress are local and state leadership activity in concert with private-sector resources."

National debate thus turned away from urban policy. Signaling this shift were the reports produced in 1980 by the President's Commission for a National Agenda for the Eighties. The Commission argued that the role of the federal government "should be to assist communities in adjusting to redistributional trends." The national economy, it wrote, "should take precedence over the competition for advantage among communities and regions."

Consequently, when Ronald Reagan became president in 1981, the move away from federal responsibility for the cities was already underway. The prevailing policy experts argued for focusing on people and not places, enhancing the national economy to help areas in distress, and (starting in the 1990s) shifting away from big cities as the core of urban policy to a concern with metropolitan areas. During Reagan's two terms, most of the urban programs launched under Jimmy Carter were dismantled and HUD was relegated to a policy afterthought. Reagan's administration did support a federal enterprise zone program to target grants and tax and regulatory relief to depressed local economies, but the legislation did not pass. (Numerous states, however, adopted the idea.) George H. W. Bush, who followed Reagan into the Oval Office, was not as aggressive in cutting urban programs but neither did he attend to the cities.

William Clinton reinvigorated HUD during his presidency (1993–2001) and obtained the passage of the Empowerment Zone and Enterprise Communities Program (1993) that channeled funds to economic development in designated localities, including rural areas and a small number of big cities. His administration's first national urban policy report (1995) noted the cities' role in the life of the nation but then proclaimed that "American metropolises are the engines of the national economy." Its guiding principles were to link families with work, leverage private investment, "promote solutions that are locally crafted and implemented," and affirm traditional values of hard work and self-reliance. None of these principles committed the federal government to cooperate with cities to solve their problems. The Clinton administration, like the Reagan and Bush administrations before it and the George W. Bush administration after, made the national economy their top priority.

Upon entering office in 2009, President Barack Obama created the White House Office of Urban Policy to coordinate federal urban programs and attend to national urban policy. Like previous efforts at interagency and intergovernmental coordination, it was minimally funded and had little legal authority over other federal agencies. The Obama administration also created the Sustainable Communities Initiative in 2009 to coordinate programs among HUD, the Department of Transportation, and the Department of Environmental Protection. This was another coordination effort, however, and, like the related

Choice Neighborhoods Initiative to help distressed neighborhoods, was small in scale. As part of the efforts to pull the economy out of a severe recession, Congress extended the Neighborhood Stabilization Program (2009), which channeled funds to distressed neighborhoods faced with home foreclosures. Beyond this, Congress had no interest in national urban policy.

From the 1930s until the late 1970s, the federal government addressed, albeit inconsistently, urban problems and did so with a variety of programs. After, successive national administrations ignored cities or treated them with indifference. In fact, from 1980 through the first decade of the twenty-first century, the cities were marginalized in policy debates. Even Democratic administrations, normally responsive to urban constituencies, seldom accompanied a pro-urban rhetoric with an integrated array of targeted programs. By 2009, "urban" no longer meant "big city" in the national policy discourse. Its place was taken by "metropolitan area." Cities had been downgraded to only one component of integrated urban regions and the country was no closer to a national urban policy.

Consequently, the history of national urban policy in the United States is a history of a policy that never quite existed. Regardless of whether the country was led by a Republican or a Democrat or which party controlled Congress, no federal administration has adopted a comprehensive, coherent, and targeted set of programs focused on the problems of cities, their residents, and their governments. Instead, the history is filled with promising efforts: public housing and urban redevelopment just after World War II, the War on Poverty in the 1960s, and the rhetoric of the Carter administration in the late 1970s. Yet, if one relaxes the criteria that a national urban policy be coherent, noncontradictory, directly focused on cities, and publicly acknowledging cities as the centers of national life, then the federal government has had a national urban policy. That policy, however, has been unacknowledged, incoherent, and often unintentional.

[*See also* **Carter, Jimmy; Clinton, William J.; Hoover, Herbert; Housing Policy, Federal: Public Housing; Johnson, Lyndon B.; New Deal; Nixon, Richard M.; Reconstruction Finance Corporation;** ***and*** **Servicemen's Readjustment Act.**]

BIBLIOGRAPHY

Biles, Roger. *The Fate of Cities: Urban America and the Federal Government, 1945–2000.* Lawrence: University Press of Kansas, 2011.

Gelfand, Mark I. *A Nation of Cities: The Federal Government and Urban America, 1933–1965.* New York: Oxford University Press, 1975.

Graham, Otis. *Toward a Planned Society: From Roosevelt to Nixon.* New York: Oxford University Press, 1976.

Robert Beauregard

V

VAN BUREN, MARTIN

(1782–1862), eighth president of the United States. Born in Kinderhook in New York's Hudson Valley, Martin Van Buren attended the local school and took a traditional path into public life, clerking for a judge. While he worked as a lawyer, his true profession became politics. By his early thirties he had twice won election to the state senate.

Settling in Albany, Van Buren zestfully joined the factional battles that marked New York politics in the 1820s. Active in the so-called Albany Regency opposed to Governor DeWitt Clinton, he won election to the U.S. Senate in 1821 and reelection in 1828. In the Senate he supported state-financed improvements and opposed the Bank of the United States, positions consistent with Andrew Jackson's politics. In a rapid series of changes he resigned his Senate seat and was elected governor of New York (1828), but resigned in 1829 to become Jackson's secretary of state, a post he filled successfully. In 1831 Jackson appointed him ambassador to Great Britain, but the Senate failed to confirm him. He was elected vice president in 1832, replacing John C. Calhoun, who had resigned amid political and personal differences with Jackson. A master of the spoils system in New York, he urged the patronage system on Jackson as well. Winning the 1836 Democratic presidential nomination, he defeated the Whig William Henry Harrison and three other Whig candidates.

As president, Van Buren sought to keep the Democratic Party's northern and southern wings united amid rising antislavery agitation.

He opposed ending slavery in the District of Columbia and any federal interference with slavery in the territories. Despite the clamor of southerners, however, he opposed the annexation of Texas, fearing war with Mexico. His wife Hannah having died in 1819, his daughter-in-law Angelica Van Buren served as White House hostess.

The severe depression of 1837 defined Van Buren's presidency. Rather than proposing public relief measures or increasing the money supply, Van Buren sought to protect government deposits from unstable and speculative state banks. His independent treasury bill proposed to create a central repository for federal funds and the government's financial transactions. Congress did not pass this bill until 1840, however, and repealed it in 1841.

Ridiculed as "Martin Van Ruin" and "Van, Van, a used-up man," Van Buren lost the 1840 election to Harrison and retired to New York. He reemerged in 1848, however, as the presidential candidate of the Free Soil Party, pledged to "free soil, free labor, free speech [an allusion to congressional efforts to block antislavery petitions], and free men." He came in a distant third behind the Whig Zachary Taylor and the Democrat Lewis Cass. Witty and charming, Van Buren also had a reputation for political manipulation captured in his nickname, "the Sly Fox." He understood the importance of organized political parties and pursued politics as a career, not simply an avocation.

[*See also* **Calhoun, John C.; Civil Service Reform; Democratic Party; Federal Government, Executive Branch: Presidency, The; Federal Government, Legislative Branch: Senate; Fillmore, Millard; Free Soil Party; Harrison, William Henry; Jackson, Andrew; Spoils System; Taylor, Zachary;** ***and*** **Texas Annexation.**]

BIBLIOGRAPHY

Cole, Donald B. *Martin Van Buren and the American Political System.* Princeton, N.J.: Princeton University Press, 1984.

McCormick, Richard P. *The Second American Party System.* Chapel Hill: University of North Carolina Press, 1966.

Remini, Robert. *Martin Van Buren and the Making of the Democratic Party.* New York: Columbia University Press, 1959.

Jean Harvey Baker

VETO POWER

Derived from the Latin term meaning "I forbid," the veto traces back to the Roman Republic of the sixth century BCE British monarchs long exercised an absolute veto over acts of Parliament, but waning monarchical authority eroded this power. The last royal veto over a parliamentary act occurred in 1707. The Crown continued to veto colonial legislation in America, however, and the first two complaints lodged against George III in the Declaration of Independence were his arbitrary vetoes of American laws.

Experimentation with allowing vetoes by governors in South Carolina (1776) and New York (1777) opened the door to a presidential veto, provided for in Article I, Section 7, of the Constitution. This qualified power, reversible by a two-thirds vote in both houses of Congress, significantly enhanced presidents' roles in the legislative process. The pocket veto, not subject to override, is used when congressional adjournment prevents a bill's return.

The years down to 1865 saw only fifty-nine presidential vetoes, but they exploded thereafter, because of escalating executive involvement in legislative matters, as well as presidential opposition to runaway Civil War pensions and other private-benefits legislation. President Grover

Cleveland was especially prolific in vetoing private pension bills.

The veto remained a highly effective power in the late twentieth century, with only about 7 percent of all vetoes successfully overridden by Congress. Modern presidents who relied too heavily on a veto strategy, however, such as Gerald Ford and George H. W. Bush, suffered politically for what was seen as an overly negative and reactive approach in dealing with Congress.

[*See also* **Bush, George H. W.; Cleveland, Grover; Constitution; Federal Government, Executive Branch: Presidency, The;** *and* **Ford, Gerald R.**]

BIBLIOGRAPHY

Spitzer, Robert J. *The Presidential Veto: Touchstone of the American Presidency*. Albany: State University of New York Press, 1988.

Watson, Richard A. *Presidential Vetoes and Public Policy*. Lawrence: University Press of Kansas, 1993.

Robert J. Spitzer

VIRGINIA AND KENTUCKY RESOLUTIONS

The Kentucky and Virginia Resolutions (1798–1799), secretly drafted by Thomas Jefferson, then the sitting vice president, and James Madison, respectively, cannot be understood apart from the intense political factionalism dividing the young nation during the John Adams administration. Federalists and Republicans disagreed about the legitimate extent of federal powers, and they used partisan newspapers to wage a war of words against one another. This political infighting gave rise to some the most controversial laws passed in the early Republic: the Alien and Sedition Acts of 1798. Republicans viewed those four acts, particularly the Alien Friends Act and the Sedition Act, as blatant political moves and grievous infringements on citizens' rights. Jefferson, a veteran partisan himself, insisted that the Federalist-backed acts grossly violated the Constitution and, in the case of the Sedition Act, the First Amendment.

On the heels of congressional passage of these acts, Jefferson returned to Virginia determined to fight them through the state legislatures. He drafted a list of eight resolutions that both rebuked the Federalist laws and articulated a Republican understanding of constitutional principles built around the compact theory of government. Jefferson maintained that when the states ratified the Constitution they entered into a coequal agreement and retained every power not expressly granted the federal government. When Congress exceeded its delegated powers, "a nullification of the act is the rightful remedy" to be pursued by the states. Jefferson intended his draft for the North Carolina legislature, whereas his friend James Madison penned a resolution for Virginia. But things did not go according to Jefferson's plans. His version instead surfaced in Kentucky, where legislators moderated his interpretation, including the matter of nullification.

In his proposal, Madison pointedly rejected Jefferson's nullification theory. The disagreement over state authority to veto federal law marked a rare and sharp divide in an otherwise harmonious political partnership that spanned half a century. Echoing Kentucky, the Virginia legislature denounced the Alien and Sedition Acts as unconstitutional. Virginia also advanced the theory that federal authority was "limited by the plain sense and intention of the instrument constituting the compact" and could not exceed those powers "enumerated in that compact." Virginia, as did Kentucky, appealed to other state legislatures for solidarity: "the General Assembly doth solemnly appeal to the like dispositions of the other states, in confidence that they will concur with this commonwealth in declaring, as it does hereby declare, that the acts aforesaid, are unconstitutional."

The other states did not concur. Indeed, no state endorsed Kentucky or Virginia's resolutions and several condemned them. Vermont's legislature pronounced the documents, even in their moderated forms, "dangerous in their tendency" and "unconstitutional in their nature." But the ideas persisted. In 1832, 1861, and 1954, states' rights advocates used Jefferson's draft of the Kentucky Resolutions to argue the legitimacy of nullification, secession, and interposition.

[*See also* **Alien and Sedition Acts; Jefferson, Thomas; Madison, James;** ***and*** **States' Rights.**]

BIBLIOGRAPHY

Cornell, Saul. *The Other Founders: Anti-Federalism and the Dissenting Tradition in America, 1788–1828.* Chapel Hill: University of North Carolina Press, 1999.

Elkins, Stanley, and Eric McKitrick. *The Age of Federalism: The Early American Republic, 1788–1800.* New York: Oxford University Press, 1993.

Constantine Gutzman, K. R. "The Virginia and Kentucky Resolutions Reconsidered: 'An Appeal to the Real Laws of Our Country.'" *Journal of Southern History* 66 (August 2000): 473–496.

Transcriptions of the documents are available at http://avalon.law.yale.edu/subject_menus/18th.asp (accessed 31 August 2011).

Lorri Glover

VIRGINIA DECLARATION OF RIGHTS

The first written enumeration of the rights of citizens and the fundamental principles of government in the newly independent United States. In May 1776, the acting revolutionary government of Virginia officially dissolved the colony's former royal government and created a committee to draw up a declaration of rights and a constitution for the new state. The Virginia Declaration of Rights, passed on 12 June 1776, profoundly influenced other state declarations of rights and the federal Bill of Rights.

Drafted by George Mason (1725–1792), a wealthy planter and political leader, the declaration set forth principles such as popular sovereignty, the separation of powers, freedom of the press, freedom of religion, trial by jury, and security from unreasonable searches and unjust punishments. Most importantly, the declaration grounded these rights not in the traditional liberties of British citizens or in the common law, but in a conception of natural law and social contract. The first article stated "that all men are by nature equally free and independent, and have certain inherent rights, of which, when they enter into a state of society, they cannot, by any compact, deprive or divest their posterity," including life, liberty, property, the pursuit of happiness, and safety.

Although this language echoed that of John Locke and prefigured that of Thomas Jefferson's Declaration of Independence, it was also designed to meet the exigencies of eighteenth-century Virginia. The convention added the phrase "when they enter into a state of society" to insure that the promises of equality and right contained in the declaration did not apply to slaves, who were not considered party to a social contract reserved for politically enfranchised male citizens. Thus, in addition to establishing the supremacy of natural law and popular sovereignty in American political thought, the Virginia Declaration of Rights also foreshadowed the compromises on slavery embodied in the Declaration of Independence and the federal Constitution.

[*See also* **Bill of Rights; Civil Liberties; Civil Rights; Constitution; Declaration of Independence; Jefferson, Thomas; Popular Sovereignty;** ***and*** **Republicanism.**]

BIBLIOGRAPHY

Billings, Warren. "'That All Men Are Born Equally Free and Independent': Virginians and the Origins of the Bill of Rights." In *The Bill of Rights and the States: The Colonial and Revolutionary Origins of American Liberties,* edited by Patrick T. Conley and John P. Kaminski, pp. 335–369. Madison, Wisc.: Madison House, 1992.

Rakove, Jack N. *Declaring Rights: A Brief History with Documents.* Boston: Bedford Books, 1998.

Randolph Scully

VIRGINIA STATUTE FOR RELIGIOUS FREEDOM

Thomas Jefferson wrote the Virginia Statute for Religious Freedom, which was enacted by the Virginia General Assembly, the legislature, on 16 December 1785. It was not the first declaration of religious freedom in the Commonwealth of Virginia. The Virginia Declaration of Rights, written by George Mason, had declared in June of 1776 that "all men are equally entitled to the free exercise of religion, according to the dictates of conscience; and that it is the mutual duty of all to practise Christian forbearance, love, and charity towards each other." Yet Mr. Jefferson's statute took these broad principles; gave them a robust preface in reason, history, civics, and theology; and made them specific prohibitions on the power of the state:

> [N]o man shall be compelled to frequent or support any religious worship, place, or ministry whatsoever, nor shall be enforced, restrained, molested, or burthened in his body or goods, nor shall otherwise suffer on account of his religious opinions or belief, but that all men shall be free to profess, and by argument to maintain, their opinions in matters of Religion, and that the same shall in no wise diminish, enlarge or affect their civil capacities.

Although initially enacted as a statute (and the whole statute is still in force as Section 57-1 of the Virginia Code), the portion of the statute quoted here was also enacted in 1830 into the Constitution of Virginia, now Article 1, Section 16.

For much of the nineteenth and twentieth centuries, the statute was interpreted narrowly. It was employed as one basis for voiding a grant by will that depended on its beneficiary not marrying outside her church, and it protected against favoritism among Christian groups. Interpretations of the statue lacked the breadth of limitations that Jefferson expressed in the text. Thus, it was not sufficient to prevent a prosecution of a cave tour guide under the Sunday closing laws in 1922.

The statute remains in force in Virginia as of 2011, and its significance has grown, parallel with the broader understanding of the federal First Amendment freedoms of religion. The Virginia statute has been applied from time to time by the Virginia courts to strike down legislation and judicial judgments, such as in *Jones v. Commonwealth of Virginia,* 185 Va. 335 (1946), in which two juvenile delinquents were ordered to attend religious instruction. Likewise, religious observance could not be a requirement in a child visitation order in 1991, as expressed in *Carrico v. Blevins,* 12 Va. App. 27 (1991).

The greater meaning of the Virginia statute is not, however, as a tool for the commonwealth courts in Virginia. It was a model for the prohibition against religious tests for office in Article 6 of the Constitution. It was a direct influence on James Madison in composing the prohibitions against an established church and the protection of the free exercise of religion in the First Amendment.

Thomas Jefferson considered the drafting and enactment of the statute one of his greatest achievements. Famously, he instructed its mention, along with the founding of the University of Virginia and the drafting of the Declaration of Independence, as his legacy to be inscribed on his tombstone.

[*See also* **Jefferson, Thomas.**]

BIBLIOGRAPHY

Peterson, Merrill D., and Robert C. Vaughan. *The Virginia Statute for Religious Freedom: Its Evolution and Consequences in American History*. Cambridge, UK: Cambridge University Press, 2003.

Rogosta, John A. *Wellspring of Liberty: How Virginia's Religious Dissenters Helped Win the American Revolution and Secured Religious Liberty*. New York: Oxford University Press, 2010.

Stephen M. Sheppard

VOTING

This entry contains three subentries: Ethnocultural Voting; Retrospective Voting; and Voting Behavior.

ETHNOCULTURAL VOTING

Ethnocultural voting models relate the combination of ethnicity and religion to the partisan behavior of voters, stressing the importance of group solidarity. The weak version of the model says that social factors incline voters to vote the same way as the rest of their group. These factors include social interactions with other members of the group, which is especially important for new arrivals, isolated or segregated groups, and those who have not fully assimilated and are still speaking a foreign language. Since they live in the same communities and often follow the same occupations, they share common political interests with other members of the group. The group may have a special interest in foreign policy. The ethnocultural voting effect is in addition to any class affects and is usually stronger, so a middle-class Catholic would vote more like an unskilled Catholic laborer than like a middle-class Protestant.

Politicians who are not members of the group seek out these ethnocultural groups and their leaders, making specific appeals—sometimes even speaking a few words of the language—and the members respond with their votes. A group might be especially unpopular, such as Mormons or blacks, and become the target of attack. Group members will band together and vote in solidarity to defend themselves. At the time of the heaviest immigration into the United States from the 1840s to the 1920s, ethnic solidarity, typically overlapped with religious membership, was highly salient to many voters.

In the Colonial Period as well, some groups were segregated physically or linguistically, such as the Germans in Pennsylvania and the Dutch in New York, whereas others, such as the Scotch-Irish, were geographically segregated on the frontier and developed a sense of group identity that promoted political homogeneity and their rallying behind leaders such as the Dutchman Martin Van Buren and the Scotch-Irish leader Andrew Jackson. Catholics comprise many different ethnic groups, but they were all the target of anti-Catholicism in the north from the 1840s into the 1920s. Under the leadership of the Irish Catholics, the different Catholic groups displayed political solidarity behind the Democratic Party, which protected them from Whigs, Know-Nothings, and hostile Republicans. They rallied to Al Smith in 1928, registering their womenfolk to vote for the first time. The last great Catholic rally was on behalf of John F. Kennedy in 1960. After Kennedy's historic win, the need for solidarity to demonstrate the legitimacy of Catholics in the White House ended; Catholics after 1968 split their votes about 50–50. Indeed, Catholics in 2004 were more likely to vote for Protestant George W. Bush than for Catholic John Kerry. Groups therefore can lose their solidarity, especially if it is based on a sense of inferiority imposed by outsiders.

Since the 1930s, Jewish voters have displayed high levels of political solidarity, with voting support at the 80 or 90 percent levels for liberal Democrats. This pattern continued even after 1980, when conservative Republicans made a deliberate effort to demonstrate very strong foreign policy support for Israel. Blacks voted Republican from the 1860s to the 1930s by overwhelming margins, largely because the Republicans were much more willing to protect them from their racist enemies than was the Democratic Party. Although the blacks in the South could not vote, they continued their loyalty to the GOP. That changed in the 1930s, when Franklin Roosevelt's New Deal made a systematic effort to attract black voters in northern cities. Black ward machines, as in Chicago for example, switched parties overnight, became a central component of the Democratic coalition, and were rewarded with jobs on federal relief programs. The transition in the South was slower, but the identification of the civil rights movement with the Democratic Party of Lyndon Johnson solidified their support at the 90 percent level. It was not so much a matter of following the leaders as it was individual black voters making their own choices. In the Democratic primaries of 2008, a majority of black leaders supported Hillary Clinton and watched in amazement as 95 percent of their constituents rejected their advice and voted for Barack Obama.

The strong form of the ethnocultural model applies to voting behavior in the nineteenth century and involves a more complex interaction between religiosity and public policy. The model divides religious voters into two groups, the pietistic or evangelical on the one hand and the liturgicals on the other. (An additional third of the voters had no particular religious affiliation and were not affected.) The pietistic voters were moralistic protestants, energized by the revivals of the Great Awakening and committed to the belief that it was their Christian duty to purify the nation, especially in preparation for the second coming of Jesus Christ. Pietistic moralists were organized by Methodist, Congregational, Baptist, Disciples, and Presbyterian ministers to support the antislavery and Prohibition movements. In the north, the pietistic Protestants formed the bedrock of the Republican Party.

In the South, social forces pushed the white Scalawag Republicans into the Democratic Party during the 1870s, so that voting followed a strict black–white divide. The other major religious grouping, slightly smaller but growing faster because of immigration, comprised the liturgicals, especially Catholics, Episcopalians, Mormons, and German Lutherans, who sought religious salvation through the priestly and sacramental structures of their churches. They rejected the notion that government, rather than the church, should set moral standards. They had a minority group identification and felt threatened by what they call the puritanism of the pietists. Led by the Irish Catholics and by the Episcopalians, the liturgicals rallied to the Democratic Party in opposition to abolitionism and prohibition. The Germans also defended the foreign language culture of their parochial schools against Republican nativists. The large German-American element came under hostile pressure in World War I and felt betrayed by both parties. It resolved its political crisis by abandoning the German language, while Americanizing its Catholic and Lutheran church services. Although the old pietistic-liturgical differential faded away in the twentieth century, a somewhat similar ethnocultural coalition has emerged since 1980. It involves a mobilization of the "religious right," with Catholics and fundamentalists uniting in opposition to secularism, tolerance of abortion, and homosexuality. They have found a congenial home in the Republican Party.

[*See also* **Voting: Retrospective Voting;** *and* **Voting: Voting Behavior.**]

BIBLIOGRAPHY

Jensen, Richard. *The Winning of the Midwest: Social and Political Conflict, 1888–1896*. Chicago: University of Chicago Press, 1971.

Kleppner, Paul. *The Third Electoral System, 1853–1892: Parties, Voters, and Political Cultures*. Chapel Hill: University of North Carolina Press, 1979.

Richard Jensen

RETROSPECTIVE VOTING

The retrospective voting model was developed, and has been principally applied, by political scientists, although some historians have adapted it as well. It maintains that voters are more prone to cast ballots on the basis of retrospective judgments of party or elected official performance than on party or candidate prospective promises. As a result, party identification is the product of previous party identification mitigated by current judgments of party performance. The retrospective voting model emerged largely as a reaction to the work of political scientists who saw the lack of "responsible party government" in America whereby, ideally, parties advocate specific policy blueprints and then elect candidates committed to the implementation of said policies. The prevailing literature portrayed party identification as unrooted in policy goals or coherent ideology. The retrospective voting model's proponents, by contrast, contend that voters are not "irresponsible" if they lack knowledge of, or direction on, specific policy details. On the contrary, they can be considered rational in either crediting or blaming incumbent parties for the state of affairs. And whereas political scientists have utilized the model to challenge the notion that party identity is irrational, a few historians have deployed it to explain how, why, and under what circumstances voters' party allegiances are not statically tied to class, ethnic, racial, or religious identity.

The impact of retrospective voting behavior in contemporary politics is evident in the National Election Studies (NES) survey data in presidential elections. Between 1980 and 2000, support for the incumbent party among voters who believed that the economy had improved over the past year ranged from 58 to 86 percent. Among those who thought the economy had worsened, support for the incumbent party ranged from only 21 to 39 percent (Abramson et al., 2003). *The New York Times* exit polls reveal that in 2000 and 2008, roughly 60 percent of voters whose financial situation had improved over the previous year supported the party of the incumbent president; that figure jumped to 66 percent in 1996 and 80 percent in 2004 in elections in which the incumbent president ran for reelection. Conversely, in 2004 as many as 79 percent of voters whose financial condition had worsened over the past year voted against the party of the incumbent president. The disparity in support for candidates based on the change in financial condition question in presidential elections since 1996 has been as great as that produced by religious differences and more pronounced than divisions based on sex, age, geography, education, level of urbanization, and (once one takes into account the asymmetrical nature of their influence) race and income. Only ideology (liberal versus conservative) and normal party identity produced consistently sharper divisions in voting behavior than the change in financial condition question.

The model is a good predictor for voter behavior when policy ends (such as victory in a war or a booming economy) are clearly understood in terms of successes or failures and the means to achieving them are complex. It is less useful as a predictive model when there is significant division over policy ends (such as gay marriage or capital punishment) and when positions on such issues can be articulated in uncomplicated "pro" and "con" terms. It is least useful when both the means and the ends of policy are controversial, such as the government's role in such areas as health care, immigration, and global warming (Abramson et al., 2003). Although even long-term party identification can be altered as a consequence of changed assessments of party performance, the model is especially relevant in explaining the behavior of swing voters, such as Independents, marginal partisans, and voters who participate irregularly.

The difficulties facing historians who use the retrospective voting model are daunting. Not only are polling data not extant prior to the 1930s, but also not until the 1970s did exit polls consistently gather responses to questions involving retrospective judgments. In addition, historians are hampered by the need to substitute their own appraisal of whether the past policies possibly subjected to retrospective evaluation were successful. In some elections, such as those following severe economic downturns (as in 1896 and 1932), the desire of voters to punish the party in power is self-evident. But in other cases, policy success or failure is less clear-cut. Take for example, the 1848 presidential contest. That year, Democrats showered praise on their party for promulgating the Mexican War, a foreign policy success in that the United States gained a vast expanse of territory without a huge loss of blood or treasure. But many voters, in both the North and the South, were uneasy with the sectional conflict the Mexican cession was already producing. Whigs won the election that year, but the extent to which retrospective voting appeals outweighed other factors is unclear.

Some historians have made creative use of the model. One study of politics tied oscillating Whig party fortunes in elections held in between 1836 and 1840 to changing economic conditions, specifically applying the model and associated theories to explain why new voters were mobilized and why preexisting voters either switched party allegiances or dropped out of the active electorate. It also attributed William Henry Harrison's presidential election to the desire of voters to punish the incumbent Democrats, rather than the result of campaign hoopla as conventionally argued (Holt, 1985). Another study used the model to tie shifting levels of Republican Party strength during the Civil War to the success of the Union army. It also situated retrospective voting within the confines of the multitiered federal system of government and politics—showing how incumbent parties were more vulnerable to negative evaluations of their performance when they controlled both the federal and the state governments than when they controlled only one or the other (Renda, 1997).

The future applicability of the model in political science depends on how well it can be integrated with and compared with alternate theories of voter behavior. Multivariate analysis of raw, individual-level survey data can determine the extent of retrospective voting compared with prospective issue voting, and it can locate which demographically or otherwise categorized voters are most likely to vote retrospectively.

[*See also* **Voting: Voting Behavior.**]

BIBLIOGRAPHY

Abramson, Paul, John H. Aldrich, and David W. Rohde. *Change and Continuity in the 2000 and 2002 Elections*. Washington, D.C.: CQ Press, 2003.

Fiorina, Morris. *Retrospective Voting in American National Elections*. New Haven, Conn.: Yale University Press, 1981.

Holt, Michael F. "The Election of 1840, Voter Mobilization, and the Emergence of the Second American Party System: A Reappraisal of Jacksonian Voting Behavior." In *A Master's Due: Essays in Honor of David Donald*, edited by William J. Cooper Jr., Michael F. Holt, and John McCardell. Baton Rouge: Louisiana State University Press, 1985.

Renda, Lex. *Running on the Record: Civil War-Era Politics in New Hampshire*. Charlottesville: University Press of Virginia, 1997.

Lex Renda

VOTING BEHAVIOR

In 1790 the new nation formed its first political party, the Federalist Party—indeed the first party for voters instead of parliamentarians. Treasury secretary Alexander Hamilton had an ambitious agenda and he sought out voter support by forging a nationwide coalition of like-minded nationalists, using his network of treasury agents to bring together friends of the government, especially merchants and bankers in the new nation's dozen major cities. Subsidized newspapers kept the voters informed. In foreign affairs the Federalists opposed the radicalism of the French Revolution, pushed through Congress the highly controversial Jay Treaty that improved commercial relations with Britain, and fought an undeclared Quasi War with France. Federalists enacted the Alien and Sedition Acts to undercut support by immigrants for Jeffersonian opponents, organized into the Republican–Democrat Party. The opposition, led by Thomas Jefferson and James Madison, opposed Hamilton on all points and was especially fearful that the British connection would overwhelm republicanism in America. The Republican Party had elite planter support in the South and worked harder than the Federalists in finding plain folk who agreed with its principles. The Federalist leadership distrusted the public—even their own voters—and favored national power over state power. Republicans turned to voters with a localistic outlook and a fear of business and bankers. In the end, the nation synthesized the two positions, adopting Jeffersonian democracy and a strong Hamiltonian nation state. Just as importantly, American politics by the 1820s accepted the two-party system whereby rival parties stake their claims before the electorate, where opposition is considered legitimate and necessary and where the loser peacefully turns over the government to the winner.

In the 1830s and 1840s the Democrats and Whigs represented distinct coalitions of voters. They were closely matched and spent enormous effort tracking down men not especially interested in public affairs, enlisting them in the partisan army, and making sure they turned out on election day. The Whigs as the party of modernization attracted voters with a modern psychological outlook. This outlook was future oriented and enthusiastic for progress, seeing science, technology, and expertise as the solutions to all of society's problems. They stressed economic progress with national markets, factories, cities, canals, port facilities, and especially railroads and banks. The modernizers concentrated in the cities and small towns—those farmers with modern attitudes moved to town. By the 1830s, the American economy was on the verge of takeoff. Bankers, entrepreneurs, industrialists, merchants, cotton planters, and commercial farmers eagerly joined with the Whigs. Modernizers dreamed of education as a way to uplift society and help individuals improve themselves; the spirit of Horace Mann and Ralph Waldo Emerson was among them. Traditionalists were not adverse to getting rich, but they reckoned that true wealth came from working the land—the wealthy among them were often land speculators. They feared that modernization would create a new class of powerful aristocratic wealth holders who would be able to subvert democracy with their money. Like Jefferson, they felt that true republican virtue could not be nurtured in the city because it was a den of corruption and duplicity. The attitude attracted unskilled workers, traditional craftsmen, and backwoods farmers to the Democrats and in the form of "agrarianism" was a powerful force among voters into the early twentieth century. The towns and cities drew the modernizers and were Whig strongholds, especially those in New England. The traditional outlook of the Democrats proved more favorable to building and maintaining enthusiastic loyalty to strong party leaders and bosses. Strong ethnocultural behavior was evident in Protestant New Englanders, British, and Roman Catholics on the traditional side. Irish Catholics, with a strong sense of group solidarity and respect for hierarchical structures, were highly effective at building local and citywide organizations inside the Democratic Party.

The Whig victory in 1840 demonstrated several basic principles of voting behavior. First, the party in power nationally takes the blame for an economic depression. Thus the Democrats were hurt in 1840 and 1896, the Republicans in 1932 and 1958, and the Democrats again in 2010. In hard times, the majority party voters are disheartened, and the opposition is energized. On the other hand, boom times and prosperity do not generate gains for the party in power because the people give themselves the credit.

Southern Politics. During Reconstruction in the South, from 1863 to 1877, Yankee reformers, supported by the strong arm of President Ulysses Grant, tried to provide a semblance of equal rights for blacks, public schools for all children, and railroads to modernize the economy. To protect their gains they used the U.S. Army and disfranchised their chief opponents. These efforts were not well received by the conservatives, who fought back with violence. The Republican coalition self-destructed through factionalism, thus splitting the large black vote between white Carpetbaggers and white Scalawags and allowing the conservatives (calling themselves "Redeemers") to recapture control of every southern state. The successful counterattack peeled off the white Republicans—the Scalawags—one by one and intimidated the most vulnerable black voters. The era highlighted the worst features of Southern politics: racial hatred, race riots, massive corruption, repeated military intervention, fraudulent elections, routine coercion, systematic vote fraud—and even assassination and terrorism from the Ku Klux Klan (KKK). Federal troops reduced the level of violence and closed down the KKK, but the Army disliked police and political work; it refused to stuff the ballot boxes, for example. Politics appeared in a deeply pessimistic electorate that combined bitter nostalgia for the Lost Cause, desperate hopes for an equalitarian future, and an economy that after the great economic depression of 1873 could not get moving. The permanent disenfranchisement of black voters came later (1890 to 1910) and permitted the South to recover its domestic tranquility at the expense of equality and democracy. Elections in the 1900–1964 era were decided in the all-white Democratic primaries. The blacks became, at best, second-class citizens. Their only political voice came through representation at the Republican national committee, driblets of federal patronage, and an occasional spokesman such as Booker T. Washington who had the ear of national leaders. Disfranchisement techniques, like the poll tax, which was an optional dollar that was paid only if a white man wanted to vote, removed a large fraction of most traditional backwoods white voters. The rednecks, hillbillies, and crackers sometimes fought back, as seen in a card in a weekly newspaper in rural Mississippi in 1891 that called on poor whites to rally at the polls at the upcoming primary election:

> Primary on the 25th.
> And the "rednecks" will be there.
> And the "Yaller-heels" will be there, also.
> And the "hayseeds" and "gray dillers," they'll be there, too.
> And the "subordinates" and "subalterns" will be there to rebuke their slanderers and traducers.
> And the men who pay ten, twenty, thirty, etc. etc. per cent on borrowed money will be on hand, and they'll remember it, too.

The South's small towns became dominant in southern politics into the 1960s as the local merchants, landowners, businessmen, and professionals formed courthouse rings. Voting was a matter of helping friends and neighbors, with personalized groupings that rarely reached far or persisted long. Only in Virginia did a machine—the Harry Byrd Organization—dominate state affairs for a long stretch. There were occasional successful counterattacks based among poor white voters by demagogic leaders. Huey Long and George Wallace dreamed of a national coalition of voters, but failed to provide the necessary infrastructure to corral their supporters into an actual political party.

The civil rights revolution of the 1960s not only liberated the blacks, but also freed the southern whites from their confines. The blacks could now vote, moving at the 90+ percent level into the Democratic Party. The rural white districts had long been stagnant to the detriment of urban areas, but the Supreme Court solved that with its redistricting decisions. The local courthouse cliques had maintained a one-party South by projecting fearful images of a Republican takeover. Now it was all over; the federal government supervised elections, the blacks were all voting, and the new middle-class suburban-based Republican organization was growing fast. The Republicans won presidential elections using the same issues of economics and foreign policy that worked in the North. Reagan in 1980 added a new element—Fundamentalist white voters; previously they had been passive Democrats. Now they were marched to the polls in nineteenth-century army style by their own ministers, looking to the GOP to roll back abortion, secularization, and homosexuality. By the 1990s, Dixie Republicans started to capture the state legislatures and state offices, and by 2012 much of the South was solidly Republican, with occasional metropolitan enclaves of Democrats comprising blacks, Hispanics, or students.

McKinley and the Progressive Era. Changes in the rules of the game in the late nineteenth century settled the voting status of three controversial groups—Chinese, African Americans, and Mormons. The first two groups were excluded from the political arena; the Mormons were brought inside.

In 1896 William McKinley systematically broadened the Republican base by reaching out to traditional ethnic blocs, especially Catholics and Germans. The old divisive prohibition issue was on hold. McKinley therefore had an opportunity to concentrate on the traditionalist voters who comprised about a third of the northern electorate and were a core element in the Democratic base. He realized they could be moved because they had been harassed by attacks on Catholicism, the German language, parochial schools, and prohibition campaigns; they were frightened by free silver and disquieted by the explicitly evangelical religious tone of the agrarian leader William Jennings Bryan, who crusaded in blasphemous language against a "Cross of Gold." McKinley's legions of local workers made sure the target audience heard his message: jobs, sound money, no more Prohibition, no more use of the government by one ethnic group to insult another. McKinley broadened the concept of equal rights to men and fair play for all ethnic and religious groups inside the system. All would share in the new prosperity that high tariffs and sound money (gold) promised, and no group would be punished or left behind. The strategy proved successful in 1896, as McKinley swept all the northern cities but one and dramatically reduced the Democratic pluralities in its ethnic strongholds. Many Germans, however, were upset at McKinley's aggressive foreign policy with respect to Cuba, Hawai'i, and the Philippines, and they moved back toward the Democrats in 1900. Meanwhile, the Democrats were trying to enlarge their base by absorbing poor farmers who comprised the Populist vote. However, the Populist nomination of Bryan in 1896 had the effect of destroying the third-party movement and discouraging its grassroots activists, most of whom refused to join their local Democratic parties. The populist third-party option for voters in the South and West disappeared permanently.

The Progressive Movement changed the rules of the game to purify the democratic process and weaken the forces of corruption. The secret ballot came to most states around 1890. The voting behavior of blacks in the South virtually ended with the disfranchisement of all but a handful of leaders. After a fierce campaign, women won the right to vote in 1920, and male politicians started paying attention. Issues thought to be of special importance to women, especially world peace, Prohibition, schools, and health care, shot up in the political agenda, and both parties made aggressive efforts to turn out new voters. In 1928, Democratic ethnic groups for the first time made sure their women voted for Al Smith and against Prohibition. Apart from issues of war and peace, the attitudes and votes of women closely resembled that of their menfolk. Progressives made a systematic effort to strengthen the political power of the voters by reducing the power of political bosses to dictate party tickets. They shifted the election of senators into the public arena, set up primary elections whereby voters could choose the candidates, and imposed controls on campaign spending. Perhaps their most important success came with Prohibition because the saloon base of local machine activism was wiped out. As a result, voting became increasingly voluntary and less central. Baseball and boxing displaced political gossip. After 1896 national elections were dominated by the Republicans, so campaigns were much less intense and less effort was made to turn out the electorate. The need for mobilization of the party's rank and file gave way to advertising, which was used to reach independents and undecided voters. The overall turnout fell steadily.

Franklin Roosevelt's New Deal Coalition. Franklin Delano Roosevelt (FDR) exerted a magnetic appeal to the cities, pulling into his coalition the ethnics who loved the labor unions, relief jobs, and beer—and sense of hope—provided by their charismatic hero. Taxpayers, small businessmen, and the middle class voted for Roosevelt in 1936 because he turned the economy around, but they dropped him when the recession of 1937–1938 seemed to belie his promises of recovery. Roosevelt discovered an entirely new use for city machines in his three reelection campaigns. Traditionally, local bosses minimized turnout so as to guarantee reliable control of their wards and legislative districts. FDR's support was not strong in the suburbs, towns, and rural areas, so he needed massive big-city majorities. With Harry Hopkins his majordomo, Roosevelt used the Works Progress Administration (WPA; 1935–1942) as a national political machine. Unemployed men could get one of the millions of WPA jobs regardless of their voting, but tens of thousands of well-paid supervisory jobs served as prizes awarded by the local Democratic organizations. Eighty-two percent of the 3.5 million voters on relief payrolls during the 1936 election voted for Roosevelt. The burgeoning labor unions rolled out 80 percent of their membership for FDR. The president had comparable landslides among Irish, Italian, Slavic, and Jewish voters. In the nation's 106 cities with populations over 100,000 70 percent of the voters supported FDR in 1936, compared to 59 percent of voters elsewhere. He did not need the supermajorities that year. However, in 1940 Roosevelt's reelection depended on his margin in the same cities. In the North, cities with populations over 100,000 gave Roosevelt 60 percent of their votes, whereas the rest of the North favored Wendell Willkie, 52 to 48 percent; the big city machines provided FDR with his critical Electoral College margin.

Voters during World War II displayed a sense of national unity and low interest in competitive politics—the nadir came when only 2 percent of the electorate voted for city officers in Corpus Christi, Texas, in 1942. One permanent innovation was the extension of the federal income tax from 10 percent of the electorate to 90 percent. "Tax-tax-tax, spend-spend-spend, elect-elect-elect," a slogan attributed to Hopkins, worked as long as few voters paid federal taxes or when the spending was for the war effort. By 1946 dissatisfaction with high taxes had soured the fast-growing middle class because the relief element that FDR had counted on now had real jobs, and with the jobs came payroll deductions. The New Deal coalition worked best when charismatic FDR was running; in off years it had trouble rallying its poorly educated core members to the polls. Harry Truman miraculously revived the coalition briefly in 1948, but it did not stand a chance against a war hero of the stature of Dwight Eisenhower. Lyndon Johnson labored to restore the old coalition, using Kennedy's martyrdom as a rallying cry, but in practice he splintered Democrats into permanently hostile camps based on issues of war, race, and urban violence. Republicans seized the opening by promising lower taxes and control of crime. The last trump card for the New Dealers was organized labor, but many members resented Johnson's favoritism toward the blacks. After 1970 union membership and influence fell steadily, until by 2011 the Republicans were able to launch devastating attacks on public sector unions, trying to destroy their economic and political power.

Contemporary Period. The European ethnic groups came of age after World War II. The younger cohort, their views broadened by wartime service, no longer needed machine help to get a good job. They relocated to suburbs outside the machine's purview, and one after another the old machines collapsed by 1952. The ethnics still bore a grievance over Catholics being blocked from the presidency and rallied to John F. Kennedy in 1960, as the last remnants of militant anti-Catholicism threw their votes to Richard Nixon. Victory in 1960 proved the last hurrah for Catholics.

By 1968 many were turning to Nixon on cultural and war issues and Catholics have been divided 50–50 ever since. Ronald Reagan pulled many of the working-class social conservatives into the Republican Party as "Reagan Democrats." Of the old ethnocultural blocs, the black and Jewish voters remained reliably Democratic, and Hispanics leaned Democratic; every other ethnocultural group broke 50–50 or favored the Republican Party, the Grand Old Party (GOP).

Parties over the years have experimented with every new communications device to reach voters. Some techniques that were once effective have faded away, including all-day barbecues, parades, and party club houses. From the 1790s to the 1950s newspapers were powerful tools, but that medium weakened and indeed collapsed after 2000. The two-hour in-person rally by a candidate remains important in early primaries or caucus states such as New Hampshire and Iowa, but in general elections they serve only as media events that can be covered at no cost by local television. Magazines, radio, pop music, and the movies attract enormous audiences, but have never worked well for reaching voters. Television, on the other hand, immediately seized the attention of voters to become the dominant political medium in the 1950s. Television's pervasiveness forces candidates to raise millions just for media buys to match the opposition's barrage of thirty-second visuals. The parties have used telephoning for last-minute turnout appeals and direct mail and websites for fund-raising, but otherwise these media have not been not been efficient methods to reach voters. Whether Twitter and Facebook or smart phones and tomorrow's new gadgets will close the gap between the polls and the people remains to be seen.

[*See also* **Voting; Ethnocultural Voting;** *and* **Voting; Retrospective Voting.**]

BIBLIOGRAPHY

Baumgartner, Jody C. *Modern Presidential Electioneering: An Organizational and Comparative Approach*. Westport, Conn.: Praeger, 2000.

Dinkin, Robert J. *Campaigning in America: A History of Election Practice*. New York: Greenwood Press, 1989.

Jamieson, Kathleen Hall. *Packaging the Presidency: A History and Criticism of Presidential Campaign Advertising*. New York: Oxford University Press, 1996.

Jensen, Richard. *Grass Roots Politics*. Westport, Conn.: Greenwood Press, 1983.

Kleppner, Paul. *The Third Electoral System 1853–1892: Parties, Voters, and Political Cultures*. Chapel Hill: University of North Carolina Press, 1979.

Keyssar, Alexander. *The Right to Vote: The Contested History*. New York: Basic Books, 2000.

Melder, Keith E. *Hail to the Candidate: Presidential Campaigns from Banners to Broadcasts*. Washington, D.C.: Smithsonian Institution Press, 1992.

Reichley, James A. *The Life of the Parties*. New York; Toronto: Free Press; Maxwell Macmillan Canada, 2000.

Troy, Gil. *See How They Ran: The Changing Role of the Presidential Candidate*. New York; Toronto: Free Press; Maxwell Macmillan Canada, 1996.

Troy, Gil, et al., eds. *History of American Presidential Elections, 1789–2008*. New York: Facts on File, 2011.

Richard Jensen

W

WALKER'S APPEAL

David Walker's *An Appeal to the Coloured Citizens of the World* (1829), a seminal work of black nationalist doctrine, called for violent resistance against slavery and white supremacy. Evoking a spirit of race pride, the pamphlet challenged all African Americans to overcome their apathy and rise up in defense of their rights and freedoms. Walker (1785–1830), born free in Wilmington, North Carolina, moved to Boston in 1827. There he opened a second-hand clothing store and worked as an agent of the *Freedom's Journal,* the first black weekly newspaper. Walker privately published his pamphlets, scholars believe, and clandestinely transported them to southern ports with the aid of northern seaman.

Divided into a preamble and four articles, Walker's *Appeal* culled ideas from the Declaration of Independence, the U.S. Constitution, and the Bible. It denounced slavery as antithetical to the precepts of Christianity and republicanism, refuted notions of black inferiority proffered by Thomas Jefferson, and sharply attacked the American Colonization Society.

Walker's pamphlet evoked fear and insecurity throughout the South and prompted legislative measures to thwart the circulation of "seditious" documents. In the North, few white abolitionists publicly endorsed the apocalyptic themes of Walker's writings. Although no slave uprisings were tied directly to Walker's effort, his pamphlet continued to confound the slave South and inspire generations of black nationalist thinkers.

[*See also* **American Colonization Society; Antislavery Movement; Civil Rights; Constitution; Declaration of Independence;** ***and*** **Sedition.**]

BIBLIOGRAPHY

Aptheker, Herbert. *"One Continual Cry": David Walker's Appeal to the Colored Citizens of the World (1829–1830)*. New York: Humanities Press, 1965.

Hinks, Peter. *To Awaken My Afflicted Brethren: David Walker and the Problem of Antebellum Slave Resistance*. University Park: Pennsylvania State University Press, 1997.

Stuckey, Sterling. *Slave Culture: Nationalist Theory and the Foundations of Black America*. New York: Oxford University Press, 1987.

Bobby Donaldson

WALLACE, GEORGE C.

(1919–1998), Alabama governor, presidential candidate. A 1942 graduate of the University of Alabama Law School, Wallace was elected to the Alabama House of Representatives in 1946 and elected a circuit judge in 1953. A racial moderate until he lost a 1958 gubernatorial bid to an ultrasegregationist, Wallace vowed that he would "never be out-niggered again." Elected governor in 1962 as the civil rights movement gained momentum, he pledged "Segregation now! Segregation tomorrow! Segregation forever!" In 1963, however, after fulfilling a pledge to "stand in the schoolhouse door" at the University of Alabama, he stepped aside to allow the enrollment of black students. His segregationist stance won strong support among whites in his state and beyond. In 1964 he challenged Lyndon B. Johnson in the Democratic Party's Wisconsin, Indiana, and Maryland presidential primaries, winning more than a third of the votes. Barred from a further consecutive gubernatorial term in 1966, he was succeeded by his wife, Lurleen.

As the presidential candidate of his American Independent Party in 1968, Wallace drew 10 million votes, half from outside the South, and carried five states. His running mate was the retired Air Force general Curtis LeMay, former head of the Strategic Air Command. Regaining the Alabama governorship in 1970, he entered the Democratic presidential primaries in 1972 (with President Richard M. Nixon's secret support), pledging to restore law and order, end court-ordered school busing, and "get tough with protesters." He made strong showings throughout the South and Midwest, including victories on 16 May in Michigan and Maryland.

The day before, however, an unemployed drifter shot and critically wounded Wallace at a rally in Maryland, leaving him permanently paralyzed below the waist. He retired in 1979 but regained the governorship in 1982, winning significant black support after repudiating his earlier racism. A major political figure of the 1960s and 1970s, Wallace helped shape the agenda of social conservatism and white backlash that would dominate the politics of the 1980s.

[*See also* **Conservatism; Democratic Party; Johnson, Lyndon B.; Nixon, Richard M.;** ***and*** **Segregation.**]

BIBLIOGRAPHY

Carter, Dan T. *The Politics of Rage: George Wallace, the Origins of the New Conservatism, and the Transformation of American Politics*. New York: Simon & Schuster, 1995.

Frady, Marshall. *Wallace*. New York: World Pub Co., 1968.

Dan T. Carter

WALLACE, HENRY A.

Henry Agard Wallace was an Iowa farm journalist who became secretary of state, vice president, and secretary of commerce for Franklin Delano Roosevelt. After clashing with Harry S. Truman over foreign policy, Wallace became a third-party candidate for president in 1948.

Wallace was born on a farm in central Iowa on 7 October 1888. After graduating from Iowa State College of Agriculture in 1910, he worked for the family business, a newspaper aimed at Iowa farmers titled *Wallaces' Farmer*. He became editor of the paper in 1921 when his father, Henry Cantwell Wallace, became the secretary of agriculture for Warren G. Harding. He went to Washington himself twelve years later to accept the same position from Franklin Delano Roosevelt.

Like many Iowans of the early twentieth century, Wallace was raised a Republican. However, the agricultural depression that plagued the Midwest during the 1920s and the additional misery of the Great Depression turned him toward support for Roosevelt. He gradually became identified with the most progressive members of Roosevelt's "New Deal" cabinet. His duties included leading the Agricultural Adjustment Administration and otherwise providing federal assistance to American farmers.

During the late 1930s, Wallace aspired to higher political office and devoted more time to foreign affairs, especially to international cooperation. His faith in government solutions to problems often clashed with that of conservative southern congressmen within the Democratic Party. However, during the Democratic National Convention in 1940, Roosevelt threatened to decline his nomination for president unless Wallace was his running mate. Wallace was inaugurated vice president on 20 January 1941.

Wallace promoted Roosevelt's policies during World War II. He traveled to the Soviet Union in 1944, where he infamously declared that Siberian miners were well provided for. In fact, they were prisoners, and Wallace had been duped by a counterfeit village. Roosevelt was unwilling to give Wallace the same support at that year's Democratic National Convention, and as a result Harry S. Truman replaced him on the Democratic ticket.

Roosevelt made Wallace the secretary of commerce in 1945, and he continued after Roosevelt's death. He used this position to speak for openness toward the Soviet Union, even as Truman and others in his administration were pursuing tougher negotiations. In September 1946, he delivered a speech in New York that directly contradicted Secretary of State James F. Byrnes. Truman subsequently demanded Wallace's resignation.

After this, Wallace worked with a variety of liberal organizations to form the Progressive Party, which nominated him for president in 1948. He hoped to attract the disenchanted from both parties and to provide new support for social democracy and international cooperation. Communist Party involvement in the campaign severely damaged Wallace. He received only 2.37 percent of the popular vote. After his defeat, he increasingly distanced himself from his previous pro-Soviet statements and from the party itself. After fighting broke out in Korea in 1950, Wallace became even more openly supportive of the administration's foreign policy.

Wallace was diagnosed with amyotrophic lateral sclerosis (ALS, or Lou Gehrig's disease) in November 1964. He died in a Danbury, Connecticut, hospital on 18 November 1965, at age seventy-seven.

[*See also* **Agricultural Adjustment Administration; New Deal; Progressive Party;** *and* **Roosevelt, Franklin Delano.**]

BIBLIOGRAPHY

Culver, John C., and John Hyde. *American Dreamer: The Life and Times of Henry A. Wallace*. New York: W. W. Norton, 2000.

White, Graham, and John Maze. *Henry A. Wallace: His Search for a New World Order*. Chapel Hill: University of North Carolina Press, 1995.

John J. Fry

WAR POWERS ACT

Adopted by Congress in 1973 over President Richard M. Nixon's veto, this resolution stemmed from legislators' perception that Presidents Lyndon B. Johnson and Nixon had abused the Constitution's war-making powers during the Vietnam War. The act required the president to consult with Congress "in every possible instance" before introducing armed forces "into hostilities or into situations where imminent involvement in hostilities is clearly indicated by the circumstances." It also required the president to report any such deployments to Congress within forty-eight hours and stipulated that if within sixty days Congress refused to endorse the president's use of force, the troops must return home—with a thirty-day extension to assure a safe withdrawal. The resolution also permitted Congress to force the withdrawal of U.S. troops from a region at any time by majority vote, without presidential recourse to a veto. In 1983 the Supreme Court invalidated this provision, ruling that only a congressional joint resolution, subject to a presidential veto, could force a withdrawal.

The War Powers Act did not work as its proponents anticipated, since presidents failed to notify Congress of troop deployments that would start the 60-day clock. Yet it remained in force, a potential check on the president's authority to deploy U.S. military force abroad.

[*See also* **Constitution; Federal Government, Executive Branch: Presidency, The; Federal Government, Legislative Branch: An Overview; Johnson, Lyndon B.; Nixon, Richard M.; Supreme Court, U.S.;** *and* **Veto Power.**]

BIBLIOGRAPHY

Fisher, Louis. *Presidential War Power*. Lawrence: University Press of Kansas, 1995.

Glennon, Michael J. *Constitutional Diplomacy*. Princeton, N.J.: Princeton University Press, 1990.

Loch K. Johnson

WARREN, EARL

(1891–1974), governor of California, chief justice of the U.S. Supreme Court. Reared in Bakersfield, California, Warren received his undergraduate and law degrees from the University of California at Berkeley. In 1925, he married Nina Meyers; the couple had six children. Warren slowly ascended the political ladder in California—as district attorney of Alameda County (1920–1938), attorney general (1938–1942), and governor (1943–1953). During World War II, he actively supported the incarceration of Japanese Americans in detention camps. Known as a political moderate, Warren ran as the Republican Party's candidate for vice president in 1948, on a ticket headed by Thomas E. Dewey, and then sought the Republican presidential nomination in 1952, losing to Dwight D. Eisenhower. The following year, President Eisenhower appointed him chief justice of the United States.

As chief justice, Warren was less concerned with technical constitutional issues than with the ethical imperatives of the Constitution: equality, procedural fairness, and a broad range of rights associated with American citizenship. In *Brown v. Board of Education* (1954), the Supreme Court overruled *Plessy v. Ferguson* (1896) and unanimously held that segregated public schools deprived black students of the equal protection of the laws. In *Baker v. Carr* (1962), the Court, overruling earlier precedent, rejected the doctrine that the apportionment of legislative districts was beyond the scope of judicial review. In *Griswold v. Connecticut* (1965), ruling unconstitutional a Connecticut statute banning the use of contraceptives, the Court discovered a "right of privacy" in the Constitution, despite the absence of any textual language codifying such a right. In *Miranda v. Arizona* (1966), the Court held that the Fifth Amendment's protection against self-incrimination required police to give a precise set of warnings to suspects being interrogated in their custody. Warren was in the majority in all of these decisions, writing both *Brown* and *Miranda*.

Some commentators have celebrated Earl Warren's judicial activism, whereas others have viewed it with alarm. Few, however, have doubted his enormous impact upon some of the most important social and political issues of his time.

[***See also Baker v. Carr; Brown v. Board of Education;* Civil Rights; Constitution; Eisenhower, Dwight D.; *Engel v. Vitale;* Equality; *Griswold v. Connecticut;* Japanese American Internment; Judicial Review; Jurisprudence; *Miranda v. Arizona;* Republican Party; *and* Supreme Court, U.S.**]

BIBLIOGRAPHY

Schwartz, Bernard. *The Unpublished Opinions of the Warren Court*. New York: Viking, 1987.

White, G. Edward. *Earl Warren: A Public Life*. New York: Oxford University Press, 1982.

G. Edward White

WASHINGTON, BOOKER T.

(1856–1915), Booker Taliaferro Washington was the preeminent black political leader of the late nineteenth and early twentieth centuries and champion of industrial education for millions of African Americans just one generation out of slavery. Born a slave on a farm in Hales Ford, Virginia, in Franklin County, Virginia, his family moved to Malden, West Virginia, after the Civil War, where Washington worked as a child laborer in the salt industry and coal mines.

After graduating from Hampton Institute in 1875, Washington returned to Malden, where he taught school. In 1881 he took the position of principal for a new normal school planned for Tuskegee, Alabama, in the heart of Alabama's Black Belt, about forty miles from Montgomery.

From virtually nothing, Washington built Tuskegee Normal and Industrial Institute into a showcase for uplifting poor, uneducated blacks and providing them with a basic education, training in trades, and schooling in agriculture for the many black sharecroppers that made up the bulk of the population of Macon County, Alabama.

Washington's success as an educator attracted national attention and he was able to gain the financial support some of the nation's wealthiest industrialists and philanthropists, including Andrew Carnegie of U.S. Steel, Julius Rosenwald of Sears, Roebuck & Company, H. H. Rogers of Standard Oil, and many others. Tuskegee Institute became Washington's base of operations for a far-flung network of black supporters in cities and towns across America through organizations that he created or fostered, including the National Negro Business League and the Afro-American Council. Washington secretly owned stock in black newspapers and otherwise subsidized the black press to further his agenda.

His speech before the Cotton States and International Exposition in Atlanta, Georgia, in 1895 gave him national and international fame and solidified his position as the most powerful leader among African Americans after the death of Frederick Douglass that same year. In his Atlanta address, Washington offered a solution to the vexing race problems that continued to dominate American politics even after the end of Reconstruction. In Jim Crow America, Washington offered a bargain: If blacks were able to get an education, get jobs, earn a decent living, and eventually be able to buy their own homes, they would not agitate for civil and political rights.

Washington, like most blacks active in politics, was a Republican, and his advice on a southern strategy for the party was sought by several presidents, most notably Theodore Roosevelt and William H. Taft. Washington and Roosevelt had a complex relationship with mutual benefits to both men. Roosevelt turned to Washington for advice on political appointments for both whites and blacks. When Roosevelt had Washington to dinner in the White House in 1901 it caused a national scandal and both men subsequently had to be more circumspect in their contacts.

By 1903 Washington's conservative leadership was openly challenged by Harvard-trained W. E. B. Du Bois, William Monroe Trotter, and others who argued that without political and civil rights blacks would never gain an economic foothold in American society. Du Bois proposed that the race be led by a "Talented Tenth" of well-educated, politically active blacks who would openly challenge Jim Crow laws.

Washington remained the most powerful black leader despite growing criticism, but after 1903 he spent as much time fighting the growing chorus of critics within his own race. By 1909, the year the National Association for the Advancement of Colored People (NAACP) was founded, Washington's leadership was waning. The inauguration of Woodrow Wilson in 1913 spelled the end of his role as an adviser to presidents.

[*See also* **African Americans in Politics; Du Bois, W. E. B.; Roosevelt, Theodore;** ***and*** **Taft, William Howard.**]

BIBLIOGRAPHY

Harlan, Louis R. *Booker T. Washington: The Making of a Black Leader, 1856–1901*. New York: Oxford University Press, 1972.

Harlan, Louis R. *Booker T. Washington: The Wizard of Tuskegee, 1901–1915*. New York: Oxford University Press, 1983.

Harlan, Louis R., and Raymond W. Smock, eds. *The Booker T. Washington Papers,* 14 vols. Urbana: University of Illinois Press, 1972–1989.

Norrell, Robert J. *Up from History: The Life of Booker T. Washington*. Cambridge, Mass.: Belknap Press of Harvard University Press, 2009.

Smock, Raymond W. *Booker T. Washington: Black Leadership in the Age of Jim Crow*. Chicago: Ivan R. Dee, 2009.

Smock, Raymond W., ed. *Booker T. Washington in Perspective: The Essays of Louis R. Harlan*. Jackson: University of Mississippi Press, 1988.

Washington, Booker T. *Up from Slavery*. Garden City, N.Y.: Doubleday & Co., 1901.

Raymond W. Smock

WASHINGTON, GEORGE

(1732–1799), commander-in-chief of the Continental army during the American Revolution, first president of the United States. He was born at his father's estate, Wakefield, in Westmoreland County, Virginia, the eldest son of Augustine Washington and his second wife, Mary Ball Washington. Coming from a family of middling rank, he received little formal education, but soon developed a penchant for self-improvement and an ambition to better himself. During his early youth his greatest influence was his older half brother Lawrence Washington, the master of Mount Vernon, whose marriage into the influential Fairfax family brought him into the first rank of Virginia society. The time young George spent with his brother and his brother's friends fueled his ambition and brought him a coterie of influential friends. By the time he was twenty, he had become surveyor for Culpeper County, traveled with his ailing brother to Barbados, and, after Lawrence's death in 1752, succeeded not only to his estate at Mount Vernon but also to his brother's position as adjutant of the Northern Neck and Eastern Shore of Virginia.

Washington chose the military as his route to advancement, and the encroachment of the French on Virginia's frontiers provided the opportunity. He acted as emissary to the French forces for Governor Robert Dinwiddie in 1753 and served as lieutenant colonel of Virginia's military forces during the unsuccessful Fort Necessity campaign in 1754, as well as a volunteer aide-de-camp with General Edward Braddock's disastrous 1755 campaign against the French at Fort Duquesne. Assuming command of the Virginia Regiment in the fall of 1755, he spent the next four years defending Virginia's western frontier, constructing forts, making military and financial arrangements with the colonial government in Williamsburg, negotiating with England's allies among the Indian tribes, and gaining invaluable experience in command. Eager for promotion, greedy for land, and often critical of his superiors to the point of insubordination, the brash young Washington little resembled the later mature statesman.

Retiring from the regiment in December 1759, he married the wealthy young widow Martha Custis (1731–1802) and established himself as a squire at Mount Vernon. They had no children. Backed by Martha's great personal fortune, he managed his plantation and its slave laborers, served on local vestries and in the House of Burgesses, and acquired substantial land holdings. With other Virginia planters he engaged in land speculation on the Virginia–North Carolina frontier and in the Ohio Country. He also gradually rectified the character defects he had displayed as a young regimental commander. By the time he was elected to the First Continental Congress in 1774, he had already become a prominent figure in Virginia and a leader in the political activities that would lead to the break with England. Both because of his previous military experience and because of the delegates' wish to draw Virginia into the war, Congress appointed Washington commander-in-chief of the American army in June 1775.

Throughout the Revolutionary War he struggled with a lack of supplies, men, support from Congress and state governments, and his own lack of military genius. The Boston siege of 1775–1776 was successful, in part because of Washington's administrative ability, but in 1776 he faced what was probably the insurmountable challenge of defending New York against British attack. Unable to hold the city, he managed the evacuation adroitly, regrouping his forces at White Plains. Although not a master tactician, he occasionally displayed flashes of brilliance. Among his successes were the battles of Trenton and Princeton at the end of the New Jersey campaign, 1776–1777, and his ability to hold his small rag-tag army together through the Philadelphia campaign and the winter of 1777–1778 at Valley Forge. After the Monmouth campaign, June–July 1778, Washington's role in military operations took second place to the war in the South until, in the spring and summer of 1781, in collaboration with the French, he embarked on the southern campaign that culminated in the surrender of General Cornwallis at Yorktown. At the end of 1783 he gave up his commission to Congress and returned to Mount Vernon, where he hoped to retire. Instead Mount Vernon became a mecca for Americans honoring the military leader who had become an icon of integrity and patriotism. Swarms of visitors sought Washington's opinion on every conceivable subject. Both at home and abroad, he symbolized the new republic. In 1787 he served as president of the Constitutional Convention.

Although he accepted the office with considerable misgivings, George Washington was elected president of the United States in February 1789 and reelected in 1792. In office, Washington used his extraordinary administrative abilities to construct an efficient civil service, and under his leadership, the fiscal policies of Treasury Secretary Alexander Hamilton brought financial stability to the new nation. Asserting the power of the new federal government, he mobilized and personally led a militia force of tax-resisting frontiersmen during 1794 against the Whiskey Rebellion. In foreign affairs his administration succeeded in maintaining U.S. neutrality as war erupted between France and England in 1793 and in normalizing diplomatic relations with England by means of Jay's Treaty (1794). A combination of negotiations and military operations brought peace to the country's frontiers. By the end of his second administration his political faith in the new nation was shaken by the growing factional disputes between the Federalist Party, which Washington supported, and Democratic Republicans led by Thomas Jefferson and James Madison. Always obsessive concerning his reputation, he left office embittered by attacks on his policies. In a precedent-setting farewell address (September 1796) he deplored the rise of political parties, explained his decision not to seek a third term, and warned against "permanent alliances" with other nations.

Whatever the criticism of his administration, George Washington's contributions to the creation and development of the new republic were indispensable and unparalleled, a fact the American public clearly understood. His place as an American icon was secure. Retiring to Mount Vernon in March 1797, he resumed the life of a Virginia planter, returning to public life briefly as lieutenant general and commander of the army during the Quasi-War with France in 1798–1799. Washington died at Mount Vernon, 14 December 1799, and was buried on the estate.

[*See also* **Adams, John; Constitutional Convention of 1787; Continental Congress; Federal Government, Executive Branch: Presidency, The; Federalist Party; Hamilton, Alexander;** *and* **Whiskey Rebellion.**]

BIBLIOGRAPHY

Abbot, W. W., et al., eds. *The Papers of George Washington,* 45 vols. to date. Charlottesville: University of Virginia Press, 1982–.

Ferling, John. *The First of Men: A Life of George Washington.* Knoxville: University of Tennessee Press, 1988.

Flexner, James T. *George Washington,* 4 vols. Boston: Little, Brown, 1965–1972.

Longmore, Paul K. *The Invention of George Washington.* Berkeley: University of California Press, 1988.

Schwartz, Barry. *George Washington: The Making of an American Symbol.* New York: Collier Macmillan, 1987.

Smith, Richard Norton. *Patriarch.* Boston: Houghton Mifflin, 1993.

Dorothy Twohig

WATERGATE

A political espionage and cover-up case that began during the 1972 presidential campaign and eventually caused President Richard M Nixon's resignation. The name derives from the Washington, D.C., residential and office complex that was the site of the break-in that triggered the entire episode.

Nixon Administration Illegalities. The constitutional crisis known as Watergate resulted from President Nixon's obsession with his political "enemies" and his resolve to win reelection by the largest possible margin. In 1970, amid massive protests against the Vietnam War, Nixon authorized extensive surveillance of antiwar groups by the Central Intelligence Agency (CIA), the Federal Bureau of Investigation (FBI), the National Security Agency, and even the Internal Revenue Service. In 1971, Nixon staff members recruited a team of ex-FBI and CIA sleuths, nicknamed "the Plumbers," to trace the leaks that had led to the publication of the Pentagon Papers, a hoard of government documents detailing Vietnam War planning. Among other illegal activities, the Plumbers stole the confidential psychiatric records of Daniel Ellsberg, the Pentagon staff member who had released the documents, in an effort to discredit him.

As a natural extension of these tactics, Nixon's reelection campaign manager (and head of "CREEP," the Committee to Re-Elect the President), the former attorney general John Mitchell, in March 1972 approved "Operation Gemstone," a blueprint for "dirty tricks" aimed at undermining potential Democratic nominees. The break-in at the headquarters of the Democratic National Committee (DNC) in the Watergate building on the night of 17 June 1972 was part of Gemstone; its objective was to plant wiretaps on DNC telephones. Those who staged the break-in made crucial mistakes, however, and were arrested by municipal police. Apprehended were four Cuban nationals and a former CIA employee, James McCord, whose address book implicated G. Gordon Liddy and E. Howard Hunt of the Plumbers' unit.

Journalistic, Judicial, and Legislative Inquiries. Although Democratic nominee George McGovern tried to make the break-in a campaign issue, the media dismissed it as a mere "caper," and it did not impede Nixon's landslide victory in November. Two *Washington Post* reporters, Robert Woodward and Carl Bernstein, continued to probe the case, however. They later revealed that an unidentified source they labeled "Deep Throat" told them early on that Mitchell and top White House aides John Ehrlichman and H. R. Haldeman were involved not only in the break-in but also in a subsequent cover-up operation. In January 1973, Federal District Judge John Sirica convicted the four Cuban defendants, along with McCord and White House operatives Liddy and Hunt, and ominously suggested that Congress investigate further. In fact, McCord had revealed to Sirica details of the conspiracy, including large payoffs from White House sources to the Watergate defendants to buy their silence. In February, the Senate established the Select Committee on Presidential Campaign Activities, whose charge included investigation of the break-in. Democrat Sam Ervin of North Carolina was appointed chair, with Republican minority leader Howard Baker of Tennessee serving as vice chair.

The administration's denials of any involvement began to unravel in March, when White House counsel John Dean III testified in court that Ehrlichman and Haldeman, and perhaps Nixon himself, had ordered a cover-up of the White House connection with the break-in. In late April, Nixon announced the resignations of Ehrlichman, Haldeman, and Dean, further fanning public suspicions. Within weeks, the president yielded to pressures for a neutral investigator to conduct a nonpolitical inquiry, permitting the Justice Department to appoint the Harvard law professor Archibald Cox as special prosecutor. Cox launched his investigation just as the Senate committee's hearing got under way in mid-May. The "Watergate hearings," televised over fifty-three days extending into November, attracted enormous public and media attention.

A major breakthrough in the Senate investigation occurred on 16 July 1973, when White House assistant Alexander Butterfield revealed the existence of a system for tape-recording conversations in the president's Oval Office. Both Cox and the Senate committee pressed Nixon to release tapes of several key conversations, but he refused, invoking "executive privilege." On 20 October 1973, Nixon ordered Attorney General Elliott Richardson to fire Cox. After Richardson and Deputy Attorney General William Ruckelshaus both refused the order and resigned, Solicitor General Robert Bork ousted Cox. This episode, dubbed the "Saturday Night Massacre," escalated the worsening crisis. In August and October, respectively, CREEP official Jeb Magruder and John Dean had pleaded guilty to obstruction of justice and other charges. The resignation of Vice President Spiro Agnew on 10 October (after pleading no contest to tax evasion charges unrelated to Watergate) added to the sense of constitutional crisis. The Senate committee concluded its hearings in November (although its final report did not appear until mid-1974), but the drama continued in the courts.

Impeachment Hearings, Nixon's Resignation, and Aftereffects. Throughout early 1974, Nixon continued to resist subpoenas for the tapes. In March, a federal grand jury indicted seven more administration figures for conspiracy, obstruction of justice, perjury, and other charges. Those indicted included Mitchell, Ehrlichman, Haldeman, and White House special counsel Charles Colson, with the president named an "unindicted coconspirator." Nixon agreed in late April to release edited transcripts, but his strategy backfired as even the sanitized transcripts increased public outrage. On 24 July 1974, the U.S. Supreme Court ruled unanimously that Nixon must release the relevant tapes. The tapes revealed Nixon's intimate involvement in all phases of the cover-up and provided the "smoking gun" that investigators had been seeking. The Judiciary Committee of the House of Representatives had already commenced impeachment hearings. After the panel voted positively on four articles, impeachment was inevitable and a Senate vote for the president's removal seemed likely. Facing defeat, Nixon resigned on 9 August 1974; he was succeeded by Gerald Ford, Agnew's replacement as vice president. Ford's pardon in September saved the former president from prosecution but also contributed to Ford's defeat in the 1976 election.

Except for Nixon himself, nearly all the major figures implicated in the break-in and cover-up eventually served prison sentences. Mitchell, Ehrlichman, and Haldeman each served terms of eighteen months or more—among the longest of any of the conspirators. Most of the highest-profile figures in the case, however, later earned substantial royalties from books about their involvement and commanded large fees on the lecture circuit. Watergate-related legal skirmishes continued for more than two decades, as Nixon and the executors of his estate battled to prevent public release of all White House tapes.

Conventional wisdom both at the time and later held that the outcome of Watergate proved that the "system works." Yet, had it not been for the persistence of Woodward and Bernstein, the determination of Judge Sirica, and the disclosure of the White House tapes, attempts to conceal official involvement in the break-in might have gone undetected. Historians continue to debate whether the episode was a bizarre aberration or a logical outgrowth of the massive expansion of presidential power and the official preoccupation with secrecy and "national security" in Cold War America. The institutional impacts of the crisis—in addition to Nixon's resignation—were obvious and significant: The War Powers Act (1973), the Federal Election Campaign Amendments (1974), the Ethics in Government Act (1978), and the Presidential Records Act (1978) all grew directly out of the unraveling of the Watergate conspiracy.

[*See also* **Agnew, Spiro; Democratic Party; Executive Privilege; Federal Bureau of Investigation; Federal Government, Executive Branch: Presidency, The; Federal Government, Judicial Branch; Ford, Gerald R.; Nixon, Richard M.; Pentagon Papers; Presidential Impeachment; Republican Party; Supreme Court, U.S.;** *and* **War Powers Act.**]

BIBLIOGRAPHY

Emery, Fred. *Watergate: The Corruption of American Politics and the Fall of Richard Nixon*. New York: Times Books, 1994.

Kutler, Stanley. *The Wars of Watergate: The Last Crisis of Richard Nixon*. New York: Alfred A. Knopf, 1990.

Lukas, J. Anthony. *Nightmare: The Underside of the Nixon Years*. New York: Viking Press, 1976.

Schudson, Michael. *Watergate in American Memory: How We Remember, Forget, and Reconstruct the Past*. New York: Basic Books, 1992.

Sussman, Barry. *The Great Cover-Up: Nixon and the Scandal of Watergate*. Arlington, Va.: Seven Locks Press, 1992.

Woodward, Bob, and Carl Bernstein. *The Final Days*. New York: Simon & Schuster, 1976.

Gary W. Reichard

WATER POLICY

Water policy reflects the larger federal–state relations and patterns in the United States. The early days of water resource policy in the United States reflected a more state-based Federalism because the federal government deferred to states in matters of water allocation. State governments own, manage, and regulate water. Although water rights differed in eastern and western states, the federal government's involvement in water in the nineteenth century pertained largely to the U.S. Corps of Army Engineers in the regulation of navigable waterways. In the twentieth century, the federal government became involved in reclamation and, in the mid-twentieth century, in regulating water quality. Water quality regulations and species protection added a regulatory focus to federal water management. The result is a bifurcated policy system in which states largely dictate water quantity issues, as they had since our nation's beginning, and federal actions, through legislation and critical legal decisions, around water quality issues.

With the federal government the largest landowner in the American West and much of the climate arid or semiarid, conflict over scarce water resources is often unavoidable. As a result, the American West is characterized by a unique history and Federalism story and faces its greatest challenges today to multijurisdictional cooperation. We precede with caution, recognizing the challenges and debates surrounding both water and Federalism in U.S. history.

Early Days of Federal–State Relations.

State-based Federalism characterized the nineteenth century as states led in canal building and flood control, with water issues resolved primarily at state and local levels. Historically, federal activities focused on discovery, as illustrated by Lewis and Clark's expeditions along the Columbia and John Wesley Powell's journeys along the Colorado River. Through congressional legislation, the federal government consistently deferred to customs of early pioneers and gold miners that allocated water based on prior appropriation. Under the prior appropriation doctrine, the first to appropriate water, or the senior diverter, took the first share, followed by junior appropriators, ensuring the maximum amount of water was diverted regardless of any detrimental impacts on the ecosystem.

By the end of the nineteenth century, with the most easily dammed and diverted small streams utilized, many westerners realized the limits of local efforts and sought federal government assistance in constructing large storage projects on western rivers. The Reclamation Act of 1902 authorized federal funds and constructed reservoirs and water distribution facilitation in sixteen western states, overseen by the Reclamation Service, with federal loans being paid by the farmers. The law increased the scope and extent of federal involvement in western water development. Section 8 of the act protected state water rights; accordingly, the priority dates of water rights for reclamation projects are set in accordance with the law of the state where the waters are diverted for the project.

Until the early twentieth century, western states largely ignored federal authority to use water for its own purposes. This changed in 1908 when the U.S. Supreme Court recognized the concept of federal reserved rights in the *Winters v. United States* case (207 U.S. 564), confronting the traditional state-based Federalism and allocation system that had characterized development throughout the West. But building from the earlier reclamation projects, the federal government would become a major player in water resource development. The New Deal's momentum, combined with the Great Depression and climatic events, including the drought and flooding in some parts of the United States, launched new water development projects across the United States. Federal agencies like the U.S. Bureau of Reclamation and the U.S. Army Corps of Engineers received commensurate powers to implement national water management and development goals and successfully romanced state and local authorities with pork projects. Many of the projects associated with the New Deal Era were multipurpose dam projects, encompassing reclamation, flood control, power generation, and recreational interests, thereby cutting across many areas of state law and resulting in federal–state conflict. Political scientist and Federalism scholar Daniel Elazar refers to this era as "crisis-oriented centralism"—an era in which the federal government became a dominant party in the American federal system.

In the postwar era, western states became concerned that the federal government was encroaching upon western water resources. Western states, under the leadership of Senator Patrick McCarran of Nevada, opposed the Department of Justice regarding western water rights and succeeded in countering it with passage of the McCarran Act in 1952. With this legislation, the federal government waived sovereign immunity and consented to be joined in state general adjudication proceedings, making state courts the forum for federal water claims. Fearing potential loss of water allocation, or even worse a federal regulatory approach to determine and administrate water rights, states representatives determined to adjudicate water rights on their own.

Despite calls for greater management of water resources by states, in 1963 with *Arizona v. California* (373 U.S. 546) the U.S. Supreme Court extended the reserved rights doctrine to include other federal reservations, such as wildlife refuges, and maintained that the intention of the United States was to reserve sufficient water to meet the needs of all reservations in the future as well as at the time they were created. With this decision, the U.S. Supreme Court revived the *Winters* doctrine of 1908. Considering the potential of large Indian reserved water rights claims on rivers, it sent shock waves through the American West. Federal reserved rights would become the major exception to the historic policy of federal deference to state water law.

The Modern Era of Federal–State Relations. Over the years, the federal courts have interpreted and clarified the federal reserved rights doctrine in a number of decisions. Today, federal reserved rights can be asserted on most lands managed by the federal government, including Indian reservations, wildlife refuges, recreation areas, and national forests, and require all reserved water rights claims to be submitted in the state's adjudication process that quantifies and prioritizes water rights. As an alternative to litigation, settlements with tribes have been instrumental in resolving many of these conflicts in the past two decades and, importantly, serving as key forums for federal–state water policy discussions.

Beyond these rights, however, environmental legislation of the 1960s and 1970s institutionalized environmental values in federal resource management, including water management. With legislation, such as the Clean Water Act (CWA) and the Endangered Species Act, attention was drawn to other values, including fish and wildlife concerns, recreation, wetland protection, and quality control. As the federal government demanded massive improvements in municipal sewage treatment from the states, it allocated vast sums of money to pay for these improvements. States became key implementers of policy, playing a central role in permitting and enforcement activities under the CWA. The CWA was the first environmental law to place heavy burdens on local government. The CWA represented the first time that state actions had ever been subject to such complete federal control. As one of the most important and best known environmental laws in the United States, the Endangered Species Act has impacted water development in several cases across diverse watersheds in the West by restricting and limiting new water development projects and also limiting the exercise of established water rights based on the state prior appropriation doctrine. For some, the emerging "cooperative Federalism" served to accommodate political change by financially compensating state and local officials for "federal intrusions." Others deemed it "coercive cooperation." By the mid- to late-1980s, the Reagan administration, however, would signal a marked federal withdrawal of funding for water resource activities like sewage treatment plants, water development projects, dam safety programs, and water data collection (Bell and Johnson, 1991).

As an alternative to growing centralized resource management and to mitigate some of the conflict stemming from federal environmental legislation, greater formalized collaboration between federal government and states emerged in the 1990s. In some cases, this was realized in new large-scale collaborative institutional arrangements that reflect greater attention to stakeholder involvement, agency coordination, and program integration at the watershed and basin level, a sentiment strongly endorsed by the Western Water Policy Review Advisory Commission's review of federal activities and performance in western states in the late 1990s. Although the federal government can be seen as a "facilitator" of cooperation today, it is often the force of federal law, like the Endangered Species Act and the CWA, and the threat of litigation that propels restoration and collaboration efforts.

Since the 1990s, many federal agencies, including the U.S. Bureau of Reclamation and U.S. Army Corps of Engineers, the major water project construction agencies in the United States, have implemented grant programs for environmental restoration. Following their shift in mission to one of "no new water projects" in 1987, the U.S. Bureau of Reclamation also initiated "Water 2025," a forum to address water scarcity issues and prevent conflict in the American West. In addition to collaboration, this initiative emphasizes conservation, efficiency, market approaches, technology, and interagency cooperation. Adopted under the George W. Bush administration in 2003, it promises deference to state water laws and argues that states have the maximum authority to make water allocation decisions, causing one commentator to note its "scarcity of federal action items." The Challenge Grant Program of Water 2025 provides a 50–50 cost share program in which the Bureau of Reclamation forms partnerships with local water districts. The agency also engages in a number of collaboration programs like the adaptive management experiment restoration and controlled flood policies of the Glen Canyon Dam on the Colorado River and a host of more small-scale collaborative restoration efforts with other federal agencies, nongovernmental organizations (NGOs), and state and local partners with varying degrees of funding, community involvement, monitoring, and maintenance and, thereby, varying degrees of effectiveness.

Conclusion. Federal–state relations around water reveal an ebb and flow, characterized by varying degrees of leadership, initiative, and capacity. Like water policy more broadly in the United States, western water policy is highly decentralized, fragmented, and multi-jurisdictional. Our nation's early days reflect a practice of deference to states in terms of water allocation decision making. Regulatory policies of the 1960s and 1970s, to better account for water quality and species protection, then served to bifurcate a water policy system with federal actions centering largely on quality issues. Along the way, a diverse set of actors and interests have come to play a role in water policy and management, including environmental NGOs, industry, and agricultural stakeholders active in every branch of the federal government, along with commensurate state and local actors.

As a result, water policy making today is highly fragmented with multiple agencies managing narrow components or constituencies, such as river preservation, water quality protection, hydropower, or flood control. Patterns of competition between federal resource agencies give way to conflict within federal programs and across watersheds. Horizontal fragmentation makes it such that one governmental entity alone cannot solely manage a particular river basin or watershed. In the past two decades, collaboration has been embraced as a way to overcome some of this fragmentation.

History informs us that the governmental response is often reactionary: devastating floods give way to flood control policies, dramatic species declines result in restoration efforts, and severe degradation in waterways trigger pollution controls. This does not bode well for new challenges—like those around infrastructure and compliance costs that states face under federal legislation. Facing wastewater treatment and drinking water infrastructure improvements and anticipating water shortages in the coming years, many states are demanding increased financial assistance, greater flexibility in complying with federal environmental laws, better coordinated federal action, and consultation on federal and tribal water rights. Water infrastructure funding under the recent American Recovery and Reinvestment Act of 2009 takes a small step in this direction by offering funding to a diverse set of federal agencies to be allocated to states for wastewater and drinking water treatment projects (Copeland and Carter, 2009). Ultimately, however, although the nature of federal–state interactions may vary, we can be sure that it will continue to reflect the complex nature of both Federalism and water in the American West.

[*See also* **Environmental Policy: Clean Water Act; Regulatory Agencies, Federal;** ***and*** **State Governments.**]

BIBLIOGRAPHY

Bell, Craig D., and Norman K. Johnson. "State Water Laws and Federal Water Uses: The History of Conflict, the Prospects for Accommodation." *Environmental Law* 21 (1991): 63–64.

Copeland, Claudia. *Water Quality: Implementing the Clean Water Act.* Washington, D.C.: Congressional Research Service, 2002. RIB89102

Copeland, Claudia and Nicole T. Carter. *Water Infrastructure Funding in the American Recovery and Reinvestment Act of 2009.* Washington, D.C.: Congressional Research Service, 2009. R40216

Gerlak, Andrea K., and Tanya Heikkila. "Comparing Collaborative Mechanisms in Large-Scale Ecosystem Governance." *Natural Resources Journal* 46, No. 3 (2006): 657–707.

Holmes, B. H. *A History of Federal Water Resources Programs, 1800–1960.* Washington, D.C.: U.S. Department of Agriculture, 1972.

Lieber, Harvey. *Federalism and Clean Waters: The 1972 Pollution Control Act.* Lexington, Mass.: Lexington Books, 1975.

Maass, Arthur. *Muddy Waters: The Army Engineers and the Nation's Rivers.* New York: Da Copo Press, 1951.

Andrea K. Gerlak

WEBSTER, DANIEL

(1782–1852), lawyer, politician, orator, secretary of state. Born in Salisbury, New Hampshire, Webster graduated from Dartmouth College (1801), entered the bar in 1805, and practiced law in Portsmouth, New Hampshire. Gaining national recognition for his argument before the U.S. Supreme Court in *Dartmouth College v. Woodward* (1818), he eventually argued more than 170 cases before the high court, including such landmarks as *Gibbons v. Ogden* (1824). He helped determine the nation's constitutional and economic direction by upholding property rights and the federal government's authority over interstate commerce.

A celebrated public speaker, he established the tradition of commemorative oratory in the United States. Active in the Federalist and later the Whig Party, Webster served in Congress as a representative from New Hampshire (1813–1817) and Massachusetts (1823–1827) and then as senator from Massachusetts (1827–1841, 1845–1850). A conservative, he spoke for his business constituents. Like New England's merchants and shippers, he initially supported low tariffs and opposed the Embargo Act and the War of 1812 for disrupting trade. By the 1820s, however, as mills and factories arose in the region, he advocated high protective tariffs. In 1830 he engaged in a notable series of debates with the South Carolina senator Robert Y. Hayne, who, in opposition to the high tariff of 1828, championed states' rights and nullification. On the contrary, said Webster, the Constitution had created a perpetual union of one people: "Liberty *and* union, now and forever, one and inseparable!" In 1850, however, he outraged abolitionists by endorsing the Fugitive Slave Act as part of a sectional compromise.

Webster served two noteworthy terms as secretary of state (1841–1843 and 1850–1852). In 1842 he negotiated the Webster–Ashburton Treaty, which improved relations with Great Britain. He fashioned U.S. policy toward Asia by formulating a statement of America's position toward Hawai'i (1842), inaugurating the first diplomatic mission to

China (1843), and initiating Matthew C. Perry's 1851–1852 voyage to Japan.

[*See also* **Antislavery Movement; Compromise of 1850; Dartmouth College Case; Federal Government, Executive Branch: State Department; Federal Government, Legislative Branch: Senate; Federalist Party; Fugitive Slave Act; *Gibbons v. Ogden;* Supreme Court, U.S.; Tariffs;** *and* **Whig Party.**]

BIBLIOGRAPHY

Baxter, Maurice G. *One and Inseparable: Daniel Webster and the Union.* Cambridge, Mass.: Belknap Press of Harvard University Press, 1984.

Shewmaker, Kenneth E., ed. *Daniel Webster: "The Completest Man."* Hanover, N.H.: Dartmouth College, 1990.

Kenneth E. Shewmaker

WELFARE REFORM ACT OF 1996

The Republican-controlled Congress and Democratic president Bill Clinton combined forces in 1996 to enact this sweeping welfare reform legislation. Among other important provisions, the Personal Responsibility and Work Opportunity Reconciliation Act replaced the sixty-year-old Aid to Families with Dependent Children program with the Temporary Assistance for Needy Families (TANF) program. The new program had the strongest work requirements in the history of welfare, a five-year time limit on welfare receipt, financial sanctions against recipients who did not meet work requirements, and much greater flexibility for states in operating their TANF program. The basic federal and state funding mechanism also changed. Rather than open-ended federal dollars that were available for all who qualified for benefits, the federal government gave states a fixed block grant. Often overlooked, the legislation also made deep changes in curtailing welfare for noncitizens, ending welfare benefits for drug addicts and alcoholics, allowing religious organizations to receive federal funding, and simplifying federal day-care programs and increasing funding. The legislation was estimated to save about $54 billion in federal spending over seven years.

After the legislation was enacted, the welfare rolls declined by more than half, never-married single mothers—those most likely to be on welfare before the 1996 reforms—boosted their work rates by 40 percent in just four years, and child poverty fell substantially. The poverty rates among children in female-headed families and black children fell to their lowest levels ever. Most analysts believe that the decline in child poverty was attributable to increased employment by poor mothers, expansion of government programs that provided financial help to working low-income families, and the millions of jobs generated by the American economy between 1996 and 2001.

The legislation was severely criticized by the American left for abandoning poor mothers and children. Critics predicted that many welfare mothers would not be able to work successfully and would not have enough resources to support their children. The doom and gloom predictions have mostly proven false, but evidence does suggest at least two problems with the reforms. First, Census Bureau data show that there has been an increase in single mothers with no cash welfare and no earnings, which implies that they and their children are at risk for living in deep poverty. Second, it is now clear that the TANF program left many poor mothers eligible for benefits uncovered during and following the Great Recession that lasted from December 2007 until June 2009. Even so, increased coverage by other programs, especially food stamps, prevented an increase in child poverty during the recession.

Despite these problems, the 1996 welfare reform legislation stands as a landmark in American social policy and signals a seminal change that brings work to the center of social policy by time-limiting benefits and making them contingent on work.

[*See also* **Clinton, William J.;** *and* **Social Policy: Public Welfare.**]

BIBLIOGRAPHY

Collins, Jane L., and Victoria Mayer. *Both Hands Tied: Welfare Reform and the Race to the Bottom in the Low-Wage Labor Market.* Chicago: University of Chicago Press, 2010.

Grogger, Jeffrey, and Lynn A. Karoly. *Welfare Reform: Effects of a Decade of Change.* Cambridge, Mass.: Harvard University Press, 2005.

Ron Haskins

WEST COAST HOTEL v. PARRISH

Supreme Court case (1937) reversing a series of anti–New Deal decisions and upholding the constitutionality of legislation regulating the economy. The case involved a 1913 Washington State statute establishing a minimum wage of $14.50 for a forty-eight-hour week. A chambermaid, Elsie Parrish, who had been paid $12 weekly by the West Coast Hotel in Seattle, Washington, sued her employer for the difference. The case was argued before the Supreme Court in December 1936. Parrish's attorneys asked the Court to overrule precedents, such as *Adkins v. Children's Hospital* (1923), that had held minimum-wage laws unconstitutional. In his 5-to-4 majority opinion, Chief Justice Charles Evans Hughes dismissed the notion of freedom of contract, holding that under their constitutional police powers, states had the authority to regulate wages and hours in the public interest. Despite a spirited dissent by Justice George Sutherland on behalf of the conservative justices, a thirty-year era of conservative, antireform judicial activism—going back to *Lochner v. New York* (1905), which struck down a New York law regulating the maximum hours of bakery workers—had come to an end. Not for many decades would the Supreme Court again overturn either a federal or a state law regulating the economy.

The *West Coast Hotel* decision has sometimes been seen as the Court's efforts to forestall President Franklin Delano Roosevelt's 1937 "court packing" plan. The chronology of the case, however, makes clear that although the decision was not announced until late March 1937, after FDR had publicized his scheme, the justices' vote on the case antedated Roosevelt's announcement.

[*See also* **Court Packing; Economic Policy: Regulation;** ***Lochner v. New York; Muller v. Oregon;*** **New Deal;** *and* **Supreme Court, U.S.**]

BIBLIOGRAPHY

Bauer, Judith. *The Chains of Protection: The Judicial Response to Women's Labor Legislation.* Westport, Conn.: Greenwood Press, 1978.

Leonard, Charles A. *A Search for a Judicial Philosophy: Mr. Justice Roberts and the Constitutional Revolution of 1937.* Port Washington, N.Y.: Kennikat Press, 1971.

Melvin I. Urofsky

WHIG PARTY

When President Andrew Jackson won reelection in 1832, soundly defeating a divided field of challengers, antiadministration leaders recognized the need for a new opposition party to challenge the Democrats. The National Republican Party, represented by Henry Clay of

Kentucky and Daniel Webster of Massachusetts, no longer garnered widespread support. The newly formed Anti-Masonic Party, led by Thurlow Weed and William Seward in New York and Thaddeus Stevens in Pennsylvania, represented an organized but narrowly focused group. Coming together in 1834, the founders of the new party dubbed themselves the Whigs, opposing "King Andrew" as the English Whig Party had opposed James II in the Glorious Revolution, and later George III.

Born of political opposition to Jackson, the early Whigs struggled to define a more positive party platform. The Democrat Martin Van Buren's presidential victory in 1836 gave them ample time to consolidate their party. With the Panic of 1837 as a backdrop, they articulated a program for economic recovery. Most Whigs embraced Clay's American System, calling for high protective tariffs, federally subsidized internal improvements, and a national bank. (Despite Clay's prominence as a Whig congressional leader, he never managed to win the presidency.) Although accused of being the party of elite businessmen, Whig candidates in fact won votes among all economic groups, giving them a rough parity of electoral power with the Democratic Party.

Whigs criticized the growth of executive power, a development they associated with Jackson's use of civil-service patronage. Many who came from an evangelical Protestant background encouraged groups fostering moral reform. Whigs also vehemently opposed U.S. territorial expansion during and after the Mexican War. What brought Whigs together, however, was not a rigid set of policies. Indeed, when they won the presidency in 1840 and 1848, electing the military heroes William Henry Harrison and Zachary Taylor (both of whom died soon after taking office), their candidates had run without a formal platform. Rather, party members united around a common worldview and a shared vision of the nation's future. Their conservative temperament emphasized individual self-control and the harmony of collective interests. So long as the populace preserved republican virtues, Whigs saw hope in an emerging industrial nation.

Whatever their foresight, the Whigs ran aground in the 1850s when they confronted the divisive slavery issue. Although Whigs had previously bridged northern and southern interests, differences over the Compromise of 1850 tore the party asunder as many of its supporters defected to the recently formed nativist Know-Nothing Party. Despite their collapse as an electoral force in 1854, Whigs and Whig ideas continued to influence American politics through the emergent Republican Party. Indeed, the first Republican president, Abraham Lincoln, like many others in the new party, had spent much of his career as a Whig.

[*See also* **Clay, Henry; Compromise of 1850; Conservatism; Harrison, William Henry; Jackson, Andrew; Know-Nothing Party; Political Parties; Republicanism; Republican Party; Tariffs; Taylor, Zachary;** ***and*** **Van Buren, Martin.**]

BIBLIOGRAPHY

Holt, Michael F. *The Rise and Fall of the American Whig Party*. New York: Oxford University Press, 1999.

Howe, Daniel Walker. *The Political Culture of the American Whigs*. Chicago: University of Chicago Press, 1979.

Eric D. Daniels

WHISKEY REBELLION

An uprising in western Pennsylvania by settlers protesting a federal excise tax on distilled whiskey, the Whiskey Rebellion took place in

1794. Although similar protests erupted elsewhere, western Pennsylvania became the flash point because it was where the federal government tried to enforce the tax by legal coercion and military intimidation.

A tax on whiskey at the still was part of Secretary of the Treasury Alexander Hamilton's program, enacted in 1790–1791, to fund federal and state debt. But the excise measure roused anger in the cash-poor backcountry, particularly because it taxed large distillers at a lower rate, forcing small, seasonal distillers either to absorb the added cost or to charge more to their customers, many of whom were small farmers and rural laborers. As backcountry protests, intimidations, and stonewalling erupted from Georgia to Pennsylvania, halting tax collections, President George Washington and Hamilton, mindful of Shays's Rebellion in western Massachusetts in 1786, decided in the summer of 1794 on a forceful response. Because of western Pennsylvania's proximity to the federal capital at Philadelphia, it was selected as a test case. As federal marshals served court orders requiring noncomplying distillers to appear in federal district court in Philadelphia, several thousand armed men defiantly gathered near Pittsburgh. In August and September, Washington called up thirteen thousand militia and ordered them into western Pennsylvania. With Washington and Hamilton personally leading the troops, along with the Revolutionary War hero Henry Lee, organized resistance collapsed. Two ringleaders convicted of treason were pardoned by Washington.

For the first time under the new Constitution, the central government had marshaled impressive power to uphold federal authority. Although in fact the government never effectively collected the whiskey tax, which was repealed in 1802, Federalists could nevertheless plausibly claim that the new nation had demonstrated its determination to enforce the law against defiant citizens. This display of Federalist power, however, also stirred resentments that helped elect Thomas Jefferson president in 1800.

[*See also* **Federalist Party; Hamilton, Alexander; Shays's Rebellion; Taxation;** ***and*** **Washington, George.**]

BIBLIOGRAPHY

Elkins, Stanley, and Eric McKitrick. *The Age of Federalism.* New York: Oxford University Press, 1993. See in particular Chapter 10, pp. 451–488.

Slaughter, Thomas P. *The Whiskey Rebellion: Frontier Epilogue to the American Revolution.* New York: Oxford University Press, 1986.

Roger H. Brown

WHITE CITIZENS' COUNCILS

The Citizens' Council movement began in Mississippi two months after the U.S. Supreme Court's May 1954 decision in *Brown v. Board of Education.* Inspired by Thomas P. Brady's "Black Monday" speech, Robert B. Patterson, a plantation manager in Leflore County, rallied more than a dozen white men in nearby Indianola to organize resistance to racial integration. A subsequent, larger public meeting resulted in the formation of the Indianola Citizens' Council. Other local councils soon emerged, and in October 20 groups publicly formed the Association of Citizens' Councils in Mississippi with Patterson as executive secretary. Reflecting an emphasis on local autonomy, the state association had a loose structure. Similar organizations soon developed across the South. Strong and influential councils emerged in Louisiana and Alabama, with smaller, less effective groups in the other Deep South states; in the upper South from

Arkansas to North Carolina, segregationists had difficulty establishing Citizens' Councils or affiliated groups. In April 1956 representatives from eleven southern states formed the Citizens' Councils of America. Some adopted the name White Citizens' Council, although the original Mississippi groups did not, and others did not even use the name Citizens' Council.

The Mississippi councils in October 1955 began publishing a monthly newspaper, originally *The Citizens' Council* but later shortened to *The Citizen;* other state groups also generated publications supporting segregation. In April 1957 the Mississippi organization started the Citizens' Council "Forum" for fifty radio stations and a dozen television stations in the South. Propagandizing for "racial integrity and states' rights," the councils advocated white supremacy, opposed interracial marriage, supported orthodox Christianity, resisted increasing federal authority, and denounced communist influences.

The Citizens' Councils had their greatest appeal to whites in each state's Black Belt, the area with the highest concentrations of African Americans. The councils were sometimes referred to as the "uptown" or "country club" Ku Klux Klan because they officially shunned violence and sought to attract responsible, respectable whites, especially from the corporate and political leadership in each community. Particularly in Alabama, Louisiana, and Mississippi, the councils had an oppressive effect on public discussion and wielded significant influence over political leaders. In Mississippi, for example, the Citizens' Councils received aid from state appropriations through grants from the State Sovereignty Commission. In general, support for the councils increased in response to threats to the racial status quo; during crises over segregation membership grew, but as tensions eased, enthusiasm waned. A negative program of opposition and resistance proved difficult to sustain.

As southern whites accepted token compliance with the *Brown* decision and slowly yielded to the apparent inevitability of integration, the Citizens' Council's popularity declined. From a maximum strength in the late 1950s of perhaps 200,000 members, the Citizens' Councils shrank into insignificance by the mid-1960s, but they persisted for another two decades. *The Citizen* ceased publication in 1988, and the Citizens' Councils of America finally disbanded in 1990; some remnants of the organization migrated to the Council of Conservative Citizens.

[***See also* Brown v. Board of Education*; and* States' Rights.**]

BIBLIOGRAPHY

Carter, Hodding, III. *The South Strikes Back.* Westport, Conn.: Negro Universities Press, 1959.

McMillen, Neil R. *The Citizens' Council: Organized Resistance to the Second Reconstruction, 1954–1964.* Urbana: University of Illinois Press, 1994.

Charles W. Eagles

WHITE PRIMARY CASES

The "White Primary cases" were a series of cases litigated in the U.S. Supreme Court involving repeated efforts by the Texas Democratic Party to restrict the right of blacks to participate in the political process.

The first White Primary case, *Nixon v. Herndon* (1927), dealt with a Texas statute that provided that no blacks could be "eligible to participate in a Democratic party primary election." Nixon sued, alleging that the statute violated his rights under the U.S. Constitution. Justice Oliver Wendell Holmes Jr., writing for the Court, held that the statute was a direct infringement of Nixon's right to equal protection of the laws under the Fourteenth Amendment.

Texas responded by passing a new statute that gave the State Executive Committee of each party the power to "determine who shall be qualified to vote or otherwise participate" in the political party. The Democratic Party's Executive Committee then adopted a resolution limiting participation in its primaries to whites. Nixon sued, and in *Nixon v. Condon* (1932), the Supreme Court again struck down the statute under the Fourteenth Amendment. The new statute, the Court reasoned, made the executive committees of each party "organs of the State itself," which could not discriminate between white and black citizens anymore than could the Texas legislature.

Undaunted, the Texas State Democratic Convention passed a resolution that only whites were eligible to vote in its party's primaries. This time, those seeking to exclude blacks won, because the Court could not find "state action" in the resolution adopted by the Democratic Convention. The Convention's actions, the Court concluded in *Grovey v. Townsend* (1935), were the actions of a private party that was free to exclude blacks from membership.

But this was not the last word. In a case decided several years after *Grovey, United States v. Classic* (1941), the Court held that a party's political primary was "an integral part of the procedure for the popular choice" of elected officials. This gave new hope to those challenging white primaries. Excluding blacks from the primaries, *Classic* suggested, could be a violation of their right to vote under the Constitution, because the primary was part of the overall state system of electing candidates. A primary was not simply private affair: it was fulfilling a state function.

In *Smith v. Allwright* (1944), the Court, relying on *Classic,* found that the exclusion of blacks from the state primary did indeed violate blacks' right to vote under the Fifteenth Amendment. No longer could the Court treat the primary as a "mere refusal by a party of party membership"; instead, the party was "an agency of the State in so far as it determines the participants in a primary election." The Court extended the reasoning of *Smith* further in *Terry v. Adams* (1953), where it held that the actions of the "Texas Jaybird" Party in excluding blacks from its primaries likewise violated the Fifteenth Amendment.

The white primary cases are still the subject of academic debate, especially the rulings in *Smith* and *Terry*. Interpreted broadly, they stand for the proposition that political parties are not private associations, but instead "organs of the State itself"—a potentially breathtaking expansion of the state action doctrine, one whose exact contours remain obscure. Some have suggested (with some plausibility) that the cases are best read as *sui generis*: representing an important milestone in the pre-*Brown* civil rights movement but with limited applicability outside of that context. However broadly or narrowly read these cases, they point to the ambiguous status of political parties in the American system of government: not quite purely private associations, but not wholly instruments of the state, either.

[*See also* **Civil Rights; Democratic Party; Fifteenth Amendment; Fourteenth Amendment; Holmes, Oliver Wendell, Jr.;** ***Smith v. Allwright; and*** **Supreme Court, U.S.**]

BIBLIOGRAPHY

Issacharoff, Samuel, Pamela S. Karlan, and Richard H. Pildes. *The Law of Democracy.* New York: Foundation Press, 2007.

Hine, Darlene Clark. *Black Victory: The Rise and Fall of the White Primary in Texas.* Columbia; London: University of Missouri Press, 2003.

Katz, Ellen. "Resurrecting the White Primaries." 153 *University of Pennsylvania Law Review* 325 (December 2004).

Lowenstein, Daniel Hays. "The Associational Rights of Major Political Parties: A Skeptical Inquiry." 71 *Texas Law Review* 1741 (1993).

Chad W. Flanders

WILMOT PROVISO

Introduced on 8 August 1846, as an amendment to President James K. Polk's request for an appropriation of $2 million to pay for any territorial cession made by Mexico to end the two-month-old war with that nation, the Wilmot Proviso provided that as an express and fundamental condition for any acquisition of territory from that Republic, "neither slavery nor involuntary servitude shall ever exist in any part of said territory." In one parliamentary stroke the twin questions of territorial expansion and slavery restriction were joined. As a Whig editor observed at the time, the amendment "brought to a head the great question which is about to divide the American people."

Free-state resentment and alienation from what they believed to be a pro-South Polk administration lurked behind the proviso. Yet northern Democrats supported it as a means to allay growing opposition in the North to the Mexican conflict and the prospective expansion of slavery into the Southwest. But the appeal of the proviso went deeper. Supporters of the proviso denied that Congress had the power to legalize slavery, a creature of state and local laws, in any territory directly under federal jurisdiction. Moreover, they concluded that the Union itself rested on the principle of individual freedom. Extending slavery would contradict that basic principle. To these restrictionists, the question was not whether black slaves would become free (as abolitionists demanded), but whether white men and women would remain free.

Southerners agreed that Congress's power over slavery was limited: it could not restrict the spread of slavery. To do so would violate the due process clause of the Fifth Amendment. If individual liberty constituted one of the primary objects of the American political system so, too, did the principle of equality: the equality of slaveholders under the Constitution and of the slave states within the Union. Restriction, they contended, would reduce southern citizens—slaveholders and nonslaveholders alike—to a second-class, degraded status. And, as they saw it, the history of the American Revolution was one of a struggle by British colonists against the oppression of inferiority. The proviso, then, not only marked an abandonment of the principles of the Revolution and a violation of the Constitution, but also signaled the beginning of another struggle between a tyrannical majority and an abused minority.

Although the House of Representatives passed the appropriation bill in a vote along sectional lines with Wilmot's amendment, the Senate failed to act on Polk's request before Congress adjourned. In the next session, when the president asked for $3 million to end the war and acquire territory as the price of peace, both the Senate and the House rejected the slavery restriction amendment—with voting again along sectional lines. But Wilmot's proviso—the restriction of slavery into the West—would be the political issue that would be debated and divide the American people in the North and South in the coming decade, lead to the formation of the Republican Party, secure Lincoln's election, and be the rationale for secession of the South.

[*See also* **Antislavery Movement; Civil Liberties; Civil Rights;** ***and*** **Polk, James Knox.**]

BIBLIOGRAPHY

Foner, Eric. "The Wilmot Proviso Revisited." *Journal of American History* 56 (1969): 262–279.

Morrison, Chaplain W. *Democratic Politics and Sectionalism: The Wilmot Proviso Controversy.* Chapel Hill: University of North Carolina Press, 1967.

Morrison, Michael A. *Slavery and the American West: The Eclipse of Manifest Destiny and the Coming of the Civil War.* Chapel Hill: University of North Carolina Press, 1997.

Michael A. Morrison

WILSON, WOODROW

(1856–1924), twenty-eighth president of the United States. Thomas Woodrow Wilson, the son of a Presbyterian clergyman, was born in Staunton, Virginia; raised in Georgia and South Carolina; and educated at Davidson College (1873–1874) and the College of New Jersey, later Princeton University (1875–1879). He attended the University of Virginia Law School, was admitted to the Georgia bar in 1882, and practiced law briefly in Atlanta. In 1883 he began graduate study in history and political science at Johns Hopkins University, receiving his PhD in 1886. His first book, *Congressional Government* (1885), served as his dissertation.

In 1885 Wilson married Ellen Axson (1860–1914); they had three daughters. Wilson taught at Bryn Mawr College and Wesleyan University, and in 1890, having published a second book, *The State*, returned to Princeton as a professor. His work on public administration, begun in the late 1880s, opened a new field of study. In 1902 he was named president of Princeton.

In that position, Wilson implemented reforms to strengthen the institution academically and proposed to abolish private eating clubs on campus. The suggestion angered alumni but earned Wilson praise as an opponent of privilege. In 1910 New Jersey's Democratic Party bosses invited him to run for governor, believing that his reputation as a reformer would make him popular but that his political inexperience would enable them to control him. They were wrong on the second count. Winning the election, Wilson worked closely with both Democratic and Republican reformers to change state laws in ways that helped bring New Jersey into the mainstream of the national Progressive Movement.

The Early Presidential Years. On the strength of his New Jersey record, Wilson captured the 1912 Democratic presidential nomination and, thanks in part to Theodore Roosevelt's Progressive Party insurgency, won the election. Again he moved quickly, calling Congress into special session to consider his program. In 1913 he signed into law the Underwood Act reducing the tariff and implementing the first federal income tax under the Sixteenth Amendment to the Constitution. He played a key role in shaping the Federal Reserve Act, which reformed the banking and currency systems. In 1914 he signed the Federal Trade Commission Act and the Clayton Antitrust Act to regulate big business practices and encourage competition. Over the next two years, among other reforms, Wilson supported legislation to promote agricultural education, extend credit to farmers, begin a federal highway system, curtail child labor, and establish the eight-hour day for railroad workers. On racial matters, Wilson shared the prejudices of his time and region, and racial segregation intensified during his administration.

In foreign relations, Wilson at first tried to apply the same principles that shaped his domestic program. Just as he hoped to free Americans from domination by powerful corporations, he envisioned liberating Mexico and the Caribbean from military tyrants and foreign economic domination. His efforts proved largely unsuccessful, however. Well-intended interventions in Mexico, the Dominican Republic, and Haiti aroused anti-Americanism and often substituted one form of military government for another.

World War I. The outbreak of World War I in Europe in August 1914 confronted Wilson with his greatest challenge. Both the Allies and the Central Powers tried to cut off the flow of American products to the other side. The British blockade of Germany, enforced with surface vessels, cost Americans money, but the German blockade, implemented by U-boats (submarines), killed innocent people. On 7 May 1915, 128 Americans died when a U-boat torpedoed the British liner *Lusitania* off the Irish coast. Wilson demanded that the Germans change their policy. Early in 1916, after sinking another passenger vessel, Germany agreed to halt such attacks. On the strength of this pledge and his strong domestic record, Wilson won reelection in November 1916, running on the slogan "He Kept Us Out of War."

As the situation grew more dangerous, Wilson proposed on 22 January 1917 that the belligerents accept a "peace without victory" restoring the prewar status quo. Neither side proved interested, and the Germans, having earlier decided on a last great effort to win, now announced a policy of unrestricted U-boat warfare. Wilson broke off diplomatic relations with Germany on 3 February and on 2 April asked Congress for a declaration of war.

As the administration struggled with the task of military mobilization and production, it also rallied homefront support for the war through posters, speeches, and bond drives and suppressed dissident voices by means of postal censorship and the Espionage Act (1917) and Sedition Amendment (1918). A wave of intolerance swept the nation and German Americans were harassed and antiwar activists arrested. Socialist Eugene V. Debs and others went to jail for writing and speaking against the war.

Addressing postwar issues, Wilson in January 1918 proposed a statement of Allied war aims, the so-called Fourteen Points. With the signing of an armistice on 11 November 1918, the president announced that he would personally head the American delegation to the peace conference in Paris.

The Versailles Treaty and the League Fight. Hailed by ordinary Europeans as a savior, Wilson found the Allied leaders tough negotiators. He proposed self-determination for European minorities, freedom of trade, and an international organization to keep the peace. They wanted security and revenge. Although the Treaty of Versailles (signed in June 1919) was criticized by the Germans as too severe and by the Allies as too lenient, it did create the League of Nations, which Wilson hoped would secure permanent peace.

When Wilson presented the treaty to the Senate in July 1919 he faced an even tougher fight. Many senators feared that League membership would force the United States to put its armed forces under international command. Wilson argued that the universal nature of the organization would make war impossible, but although he received the 1919 Nobel Peace Prize for his work on the League, he could not win Senate ratification, in part because he adamantly rejected any changes in the League covenant. After an exhausting and futile speaking trip on behalf of the treaty, Wilson suffered a massive stroke on 2 October 1919. A few weeks later the Senate rejected the treaty. Paralyzed and embittered, Wilson served out the remainder of his term as an invalid. Increasingly querulous and emotionally fragile, he was largely isolated from outside contact by his second wife, Edith Galt, whom he had married in December 1915. In late 1919 and early 1920, Wilson's attorney general, A. Mitchell Palmer, and young J. Edgar Hoover of the Justice Department's countersubversion division, exploiting a Red Scare that swept America after the 1917 Bolshevik Revolution in Russia, organized a series of raids and deportations of alleged radicals and Communists, including Emma Goldman. Wilson, leaving the White House in March 1921 as Republican Warren G. Harding took office, lived in seclusion in Washington until his death in 1924.

Assessment. Wilson followed in Theodore Roosevelt's footsteps in enlarging the power of the presidency in an urban-industrial age. His domestic record exemplified the emergence of an activist federal government and dramatically demonstrated how much a president, by focusing public opinion on issues and working closely with Congress, can accomplish. In foreign policy he wielded America's immense economic and military might and served notice that the United States had arrived as a major power with a distinctive global vision. Many Americans shared that vision, even if they were not yet ready to accept permanent obligations to achieve it. Wilson's tragedy was that his own intransigence played a major role in his failure to achieve his loftiest vision, American membership in the new world organization for which he had labored so tirelessly.

[*See also* **Anti-Communism; Antitrust Legislation and Law; Antiwar Movements; Debs, Eugene; Democratic Party; Economic Policy: Regulation; Education: Higher Education; Federal Government, Executive Branch: Presidency, The; Federal Government, Legislative Branch: Senate; Federal Regulatory Agencies; Federal Reserve Act; Goldman, Emma; Harding, Warren G.; Hoover, J. Edgar; Political Parties; Progressive Era; Progressive Party of 1912; Progressive Party of 1924; Roosevelt, Theodore;** *and* **Sixteenth Amendment.**]

BIBLIOGRAPHY

Baker, Ray Stannard. *Woodrow Wilson: Life and Letters*, 8 vols. Garden City, N.Y.: Doubleday, Page, & Co., 1927–1939.

Blum, John M. *Woodrow Wilson and the Politics of Morality*. Boston: Little, Brown, 1956.

Clements, Kendrick A. *The Presidency of Woodrow Wilson*. Lawrence: University Press of Kansas, 1992.

Heckscher, August. *Woodrow Wilson*. New York: Scribner & Sons, 1991.

Link, Arthur S. *Wilson*, 5 vols. Princeton, N.J.: Princeton University Press, 1947–1965.

Link, Arthur S., et al., eds. *The Papers of Woodrow Wilson*, 69 vols. Princeton, N.J.: Princeton University Press, 1966–1994.

Kendrick A. Clements

WOMAN'S CHRISTIAN TEMPERANCE UNION

The Woman's Christian Temperance Union (WCTU) coordinated a mass movement in late-nineteenth-century America opposed to the sale and consumption of alcohol. More broadly, the organization sought to bring gendered concepts of morality to bear upon the issues and conduct of late nineteenth- and twentieth-century politics.

Activists from the Woman's Crusade (1873–1874) founded the WCTU while meeting in Cleveland, Ohio, in November 1874. By the end of the decade the organization included nearly 1,200 local unions with 27,000 members, and by 1890 approximately 150,000 women were in its ranks. Native-born, northern, white, middle-class women predominated, although women from all regions, races, and classes joined; not all members were

Protestant, although founders framed the organization's mission in evangelical terms.

During the WCTU's earliest years, members practiced political nonpartisanship. They encouraged drinkers to sign a total abstinence pledge, visited jails and almshouses, held prayer meetings, campaigned to end the use of communion wine, promoted temperance education in schools, and hosted public speakers. Especially during charismatic leader Frances Willard's presidency (1879–1898), the WCTU took up a varied political agenda. With the slogan "Do Everything," the WCTU advocated for kindergartens, prison reform, purity in the arts, age-of-consent legislation, antiprostitution work, workers' rights, peace, and women's education, as well as prohibitory legislation. An efficient national organization facilitated this work; Willard and an executive committee of officers oversaw various departments directed by superintendents. Autonomous state organizations supervised diverse local unions, many of which engaged in social action projects.

Willard insisted upon the connection between Prohibition and suffrage, advancing a "home-protectionism" political philosophy. Women's involvement in electoral politics, she argued, was an extension of their domestic responsibilities. Many WCTU members found that their pursuit of suffrage, in turn, was inextricably tied to the matter of partisanship.

The WCTU evolved into a nearly partisan organization, joining forces with the Prohibition Party as the Prohibition Home Protection Party in 1882. Members who doubted the wisdom of this alliance formed the new Non-Partisan Woman's Christian Temperance Union, led by Iowa attorney J. Ellen Foster. The WCTU and the Prohibition Party worked together until Willard's death, after which the WCTU formed a closer relationship with the Anti-Saloon League of America (ASLA), a male-dominated, single-issue pressure group. The ASLA borrowed many lobbying techniques originated by the WCTU and other women's organizations, including large public conventions, pamphlet publishing, petition circulation, personal contact with legislators, and testifying before congressional committees. With the ASLA, the WCTU campaigned for an interstate commerce law banning the shipment of liquor into dry states, the Webb–Kenyon Act, and the national prohibition amendment.

During the Prohibition era, the WCTU lobbied for state and federal enforcement and a narrower range of political issues. Membership declined as Prohibition lost credibility, and the emergence of anti-Prohibition women's organizations such as the Women's Organization for National Prohibition Reform undermined the connection among femininity, temperance, and morality that the WCTU had soldered together. The WCTU's headquarters are located in Evanston, Illinois, and the organization continues to publish *The Union Signal* as its national organ.

[*See also* **Anti-Saloon League; Prohibition;** *and* **Woman Suffrage Movement.**]

BIBLIOGRAPHY

Bordin, Ruth. *Woman and Temperance: The Quest for Power and Liberty, 1873–1900*. Philadelphia: Temple University Press, 1981.

Foster, Gaines. *Moral Reconstruction: Christian Lobbyists and the Federal Legislation of Morality, 1865–1920*. Chapel Hill: University of North Carolina Press, 2007.

Tyrrell, Ian. *Woman's World/Woman's Empire: The Woman's Christian Temperance Union in International Perspective, 1880–1930*. Chapel Hill: University of North Carolina Press, 1991.

Zimmerman, Jonathan. *Distilling Democracy: Alcohol Education in America's Public Schools, 1880–1925*. Lawrence: University Press of Kansas, 1999.

Lisa Andersen

WOMAN SUFFRAGE MOVEMENT

The first formal demand for equal political rights for women was made by Elizabeth Cady Stanton in 1848 at the Seneca Falls Convention in Seneca Falls, New York. Initially woman suffrage was controversial, even among the radical pioneers of the women's rights movement, because electoral politics was held in low repute and partisanship was considered fundamentally male. The Civil War and the abolition of slavery, however, moved questions of citizenship and enfranchisement to the forefront of the national political agenda. By 1866, suffrage had become the foremost demand among women's rights activists.

At war's end, Stanton, Susan B. Anthony, Lucy Stone, and other woman suffrage leaders expected that white women would win the vote along with freedmen and freedwomen in a single, comprehensive act of universal enfranchisement. Yet the Republican authors of the Fifteenth Amendment refused to include "sex" along with "race, color, or previous condition of servitude" as federally prohibited grounds for disenfranchisement. Disagreeing over how to proceed, the woman suffrage forces in 1869 formed two rival organizations, the National and the American Woman Suffrage Associations. In a final effort to secure the vote as part of postwar Reconstruction, the National Woman Suffrage Association, led by Stanton and Anthony, advanced a daring constitutional argument, claiming that because women had been made national citizens by the Fourteenth Amendment, they already possessed the franchise, the defining right of citizenship. The U.S. Supreme Court in *Minor v. Happersett* (1875) rejected this argument: although women were indeed citizens, the Court declared, voting was a privilege, not a right.

Although stalled constitutionally, the movement gained many adherents. In the 1880s, Frances Willard's Woman's Christian Temperance Union endorsed woman suffrage as the best means to control liquor and protect the home. By 1890, woman suffrage, originally a radical demand among a small group of reformers, had gained respectability among middle-class American women. That year, the two rival organizations merged, forming the National American Woman Suffrage Association (NAWSA). With respectability, however, the suffrage movement, forged in the fires of the antislavery crusade, became increasingly conservative and racist in its arguments. African American women, who well knew the power of the vote, formed their own woman suffrage societies.

The constitutional upheavals of the Reconstruction Era had left unresolved the question of whether the states or the federal government controlled the right to vote. Through the late nineteenth and early twentieth centuries, woman suffrage advocates concentrated on particular states. The first breakthroughs came in the West, where the democratic politics of radical populism opened up political space for the enfranchisement of women. The territorial legislatures of Wyoming and Utah enacted woman suffrage provisions in 1869 and 1870, respectively, and retained these provisions through the process of becoming states (although Congress, reflecting anti-Mormon sentiment, objected strongly in the case of Utah). In 1893 a majority of Colorado's male voters approved a woman suffrage provision to their state constitution; Idaho followed in 1896, Washington in 1910, and California in 1911. By 1912, women had full voting rights in ten states, all west of the Mississippi River. But in 1915, voters in four heavily urbanized eastern states with large immigrant populations—New Jersey, New York, Pennsylvania, and Massachusetts—decisively defeated woman suffrage referenda. At this point, the suffrage movement's strategy shifted back to amending the federal Constitution.

By the first decade of the twentieth century, as the Progressive reform movement flourished, the suffrage movement itself was also changing. Heavy immigration, urbanization, an expanding female labor force, and rising numbers of college-educated women altered both the composition and the tactics of suffragism. New organizations oriented toward wage-earning women arose in New York and San Francisco. Women college graduates also flooded into the movement. These new suffragists took to the streets, organizing mass parades, automobile caravans, and soapbox speaking. Carrie Chapman Catt, alert to new trends but cautious about innovations, consolidated these changes within the NAWSA.

In 1913, Alice Paul formed a second national organization, the Congressional Union, to pursue more aggressively a woman suffrage constitutional amendment. Determined to use the voting women of the ten "suffrage states" as a lever in national politics, these militants in 1916 urged western women to vote against President Woodrow Wilson on the grounds that he was against woman suffrage. After the United States entered World War I in April 1917, the Congressional Union switched to tactics of public protest. They picketed the White House, carrying signs denouncing Wilson. When many were arrested, they insisted that they were political prisoners and engaged in civil disobedience. Meanwhile, the moderates of the NAWSA concentrated on congressional lobbying. In 1920 the combination of approaches, along with the transformations of World War I, finally led to the passage and ratification of the Nineteenth Amendment to the Constitution. Seventy-two years after Seneca Falls, national woman suffrage had been achieved.

[*See also* **Anthony, Susan B.; Feminism; Fifteenth Amendment; Fourteenth Amendment; Nineteenth Amendment; Populist Era; Progressive Era; Reconstruction; Seneca Falls Women's Rights Convention of 1848; Stanton, Elizabeth Cady;** ***and*** **Woman's Christian Temperance Union.**]

BIBLIOGRAPHY

DuBois, Ellen Carol. *Feminism and Suffrage: The Emergence of an Independent Women's Movement in America, 1848–1869*. Ithaca, N.Y.: Cornell University Press, 1978.

Flexner, Eleanor, and Ellen Fitzpatrick. *Century of Struggle: The Woman's Rights Movement in the United States*. Enlarged ed. Cambridge, Mass.: Harvard University Press, 1996.

Kraditor, Aileen S. *The Ideas of the Woman Suffrage Movement, 1890–1920*. New York: Columbia University Press, 1965.

Wheeler, Marjorie Spruill, ed. *One Woman, One Vote: Rediscovering the Suffrage Movement*. Troutdale, Ore.: NewSage Press, 1995.

Ellen C. DuBois

WOMEN IN POLITICS SINCE 1920

The passage of the Nineteenth Amendment in 1920 is seen by some scholars as the "great divide" in American women's politics. They argue that with the constitutional right to vote, women entered a new political era as partisan integration divided the massive coalition of suffragists and women reformers who came together in the final drive for the Nineteenth Amendment. Scholars who see continuity in women's political activism before and after 1920 argue that partisan integration has a longer history, reaching back into the mid-nineteenth century, and that women's separate political organizations continued to be important to women's political activism throughout the twentieth century. Most scholars agree that any discussion of women's politics must include both electoral and nonelectoral activism.

Partisanship, the Women's Voting Bloc, and Political Parties. American women, whether they could vote or not, supported political parties and worked in political campaigns since the mid-nineteenth century. After 1920, they concentrated their efforts on establishing equality in partisan organizations. Male partisan leaders' fears that women would vote as a bloc on what were known as "women's issues," including maternal and infant health care initiatives, educational and work-place reforms, prohibition laws, and anticorruption efforts, led parties to vie for the loyalties of women voters. Subsequent debates over the Equal Rights Amendment, first submitted to Congress in 1923, and protective labor legislation highlighted divisions among women voters and limited women's influence in parties and with legislatures for the next fifty years. Despite these limitations, individual women successfully lobbied for and introduced important legislation for women. The Equal Pay Act was proposed by Democratic Representative Edith Green in 1955 and was enacted in 1963.

Renewed concerned about a women's voting bloc appeared in the 1980s, as polls on voter turnout and voting patterns revealed what was now called a "gender gap," with women showing greater support for Democratic candidates. In the 2010 election, more women (51 percent) voted for Republican candidates for the House of Representatives. The women's vote continues to be of great interest to political parties because since 1980 women have voted at higher rates than men and comprise a greater proportion of the population.

After 1920, partisan women sought equal representation on national, state, and local committees and to increase the numbers of women delegates. To secure their partisan influence, they also maintained separate women's divisions and clubs. The Women's Bureau of the Democratic National Committee was established in 1916 and it was reconstituted as the Women's Division in 1922. At the same time, the Women's National Democratic Club was established. The Women's Division was abolished in 1953, whereas the Club, an entity independent of the party, still exists.

Republican women created the Women's National Executive Committee in 1919 and it became the basis of the Women's Division of the Republican National Committee. The National Federation of Republican Clubs was established in 1937, first as an arm of the Republican National Committee and then, after the abolition of the Women's Division, as an independent entity called the National Federation of Republican Women. In 1924, black women organized separately into the National League of Republican Colored Women. In the 1980s, both national parties abolished divisions based on race or ethnicity.

In 1920 the Democrats and in 1924 the Republicans required equal representation on their national committees and at the national conventions. Despite the 50–50 rules, women did not have significant influence in either party. Numbers of female delegates to national conventions fluctuated as both parties rewrote their rules. In general, the Democrats have adhered to the quota system, whereas the Republicans have advised states to endeavor to have equal representation.

Although women have served as chairs of different committees within the Democratic National Committee since the 1920s (for example, Lena Springs chaired the Democratic National Convention's Credentials Committee in 1924), the first woman to chair the Democratic National Committee (Jean Miles Westwood) was elected in 1972; two women have subsequently served in this position. The first (and as of 2011 the only) woman chair of the Republican National Committee (Mary Louise Smith) served from 1974 to 1977.

After 1920, the most influential women's organizations were the National League of

Women Voters, founded out of the National American Woman Suffrage Association and the Women's Joint Congressional Committee. The National Women's Political Caucus, established in 1971, is a bipartisan effort that seeks to influence political parties and advance women's electoral progress.

In 1910, Colorado became the first state to require equal gender representation on state party executive committees. By 1928, eighteen states had adopted the 50–50 rule but as late as 1947 eight states had no significant degree of equal representation.

The first three state women legislators were elected in Colorado as Republicans in 1894, and by the end of the nineteenth century sixteen women had served in state legislatures. When the federal woman suffrage amendment was ratified by the states in 1920, twenty-five women were members of eleven state legislatures. In 1928, Iowa became the last state to change it laws to allow women to run for the state legislature and in 1936 Louisiana became the last state to elect its first woman to the state legislature. By 1931, 146 women were serving in state legislatures. In 1933, Minnie Davenport Craig, Republican of North Dakota, became the first woman to serve as speaker of the House in any state, whereas in 1983 Vesta Roy, Republican of New Hampshire, was the first president of a state Senate.

The numbers of women in state offices increased slowly between 1920 and 1970. In 1972, when the ERA passed Congress, the percentages of state women legislators increased dramatically. In 1971, women comprised 4.5 percent of state legislators. In 1981, they comprised 12 percent and in 1995 20 percent. The year 1992 became known as the "Year of the Women" because of the number of women who ran, and won, local, state, and national contests. In 2008, there were 1,265 Democratic women and 518 Republican women state legislators. Viewed as percentages, 31 percent of Democratic and 16 percent of Republican state legislatures were women.

The first Native American state legislator was Cora Belle Reynolds Anderson, elected as a Republican in Michigan in 1924. The first African American woman state legislator was Republican Minnie Buckingham Harper, who was appointed in 1928 by West Virginia's governor to succeed her deceased husband. New Mexico elected the first Latina legislator in 1930, the Republican Fedelina Lucero Gallegos. Hawaiian Democrat Patsy Takemoto Mink, in 1962, was the first Asian American woman to be elected; Mink went on to serve in the U.S. Congress.

Women's importance as campaign workers was noteworthy by 1928. By the 1940s, women were the majority of grassroots party workers and, although only a few individual partisan women had influence at the local level, their collective presence contributed to a greater acceptance of women's partisan and electoral activism.

Women Running for President and Women in Office. In 1964, Margaret Chase Smith of Maine became the first woman to be nominated for president at a major party convention. In 1972, Shirley Chisholm ran for president in the Democratic primaries, won over 150 delegate votes, and provided aspiring women politicians with an important role model. At the same 1972 Democratic convention, Frances (Sissy) Farenthold of Texas came in second in the balloting for the vice presidential nomination. Geraldine Ferraro of New York was the first woman to run on a national major party ticket when, in 1984, she was selected as Democrat Walter Mondale's vice presidential running mate. Sarah Palin of Alaska was the first woman on the national Republican ticket, running with John McCain in 2008. Since 1988, a number of women have sought support for a presidential run and in 2008 Hillary Clinton was the first woman to run in every state primary and caucus.

The first woman elected to the U.S. Congress was Jeannette Rankin, a Republican from Montana, who served from 1917 to 1919. Four women served in the House between 1921 and 1923; one succeeded her deceased father and the other her husband, establishing a trend that would become known as the "widow's succession." Alice Robertson, Republican of Oklahoma, became the first woman to preside over the House Chamber in 1922 and the next year Mae Ella Nolan, Republican of California, became the first to chair a House committee. Patsy Mink, the first woman of color in Congress, served from 1965 to 1977 and from 1990 to 2002. The first black woman was Shirley Chisholm, Democrat of New York, who served from 1969 to 1983.

Democrat Rebecca Latimer Felton of Georgia, who became the first woman in the U.S. Senate when she was appointed in 1922, served only one hour before relinquishing her seat as planned to a male colleague. Democrat Hattie Caraway of Arkansas, initially appointed to succeed her late husband, was the first woman elected to the U.S. Senate (1931), the first to chair a Senate committee (1933), and the first to preside over the Senate Chamber (1943). Republican Margaret Chase Smith of Maine, who entered the House in 1940 after her husband's death, was elected to the U.S. Senate in 1948. In 1978, Nancy Landon Kassebaum, a Kansas Republican, was the first woman Senator who did not follow the widow's succession.

Between 1949 and 2011, twelve women members of the U.S. House were elected by their party peers in the Democratic Caucus to leadership positions: ten as secretary, one as vice chair, and one, Nancy Pelosi of California, as whip, leader, and speaker of the House, making her the highest-ranking woman in congressional history. The Republican Conference also elected twelve women in the same years. Two women—Margaret Chase Smith, in the 90th, 91st, and 92nd Congresses, and Deborah Pryce, in the 108th Congress—served as chair. Lynn Martin was the first of eight women vice chairs, elected in the 99th and 100th Congresses. Kay Bailey Hutchinson was elected vice chair and later policy committee chairwoman. Five women have been elected secretary, two of whom also served as vice chairs and one, Pryce, also served as chair. Of the totals for both Democrats and Republicans, eighteen of the women were members of the House and six of the Senate.

A total of twenty-six women, eighteen Representatives and eight Senators, have chaired congressional committees. The first in the House was Mae Ella Nolan, in 1921, and the first in the Senate, in 1933, was Hattie Wyatt Caraway. As of 2010, 260 women have served in Congress, with the most significant increase occurring during the 1992 "Year of the Women."

The first three women governors were part of the widow's succession. Nellie Tayloe Ross of Wyoming and Miriam "Ma" Ferguson of Texas were elected in 1924, whereas Lurleen Wallace of Alabama was elected in 1967. Ella T. Grasso, elected Governor of Connecticut in 1974, was the first woman governor who did not succeed a husband. Two years after the 1992 "Year of the Woman," thrity-four women ran for governor but only one won her race. Thirty-four women have served as governors.

In 1933, President Franklin Roosevelt appointed Frances Perkins as Secretary of Labor, making her the first woman to serve in a presidential cabinet. Since 1933, twenty-five women have served in the Cabinet. Roosevelt also appointed the first woman to a major diplomatic post when Ruth Bryan Owen became minister to Denmark.

During the New Deal, participation in parties became an avenue for appointed office. This was true for Perkins and Owen, but also for the Democratic Women's Division head Molly Dewson, who was appointed to the Social Security Board in 1937.

Over the course of the twentieth century, American women were more actively involved in partisan politics and slowly increased their numbers and influence as candidates and officeholders at the local, state, and national levels.

[*See also* **Clinton, Hillary Rodham; Equal Rights Amendment; Ferraro, Geraldine; National Woman's Party; Nineteenth Amendment; O'Connor, Sandra Day; Rankin, Jeanette;** ***and*** **Woman Suffrage Movement.**]

BIBLIOGRAPHY

Andersen, Kristi. *After Suffrage: Women in Partisan and Electoral Politics before the New Deal*. Chicago: University of Chicago: 1996.

Carroll, Susan. *Women as Candidates in American Politics*. Bloomington: Indiana University Press, 1985.

Chamberlin, Hope. *A Minority of Members: Women in the United States Congress*. New York: Praeger, 1973.

"Center for American Women and Politics, Eagleton Institute of Politics, Rutgers University." http://www.cawp.rutgers.edu/ (accessed 2 September 2011).

Freeman, Jo. *A Room at a Time: How Women Entered Party Politics*. Lanham, Md.: Rowman & Littlefield, 2000.

Gustafson, Melanie, Kristie Miller, and Elisabeth Israel Perry. *We Have Come to Stay: American Women and Political Parties, 1880–1960*. Albuquerque: University of New Mexico Press, 1999.

Office of the Clerk, U.S. House of Representatives. "Women in Congress." http://womenincongress.house.gov (accessed 9 September 2011).

Rymph, Catherine E. *Republican Women: Feminism and Conservatism from Suffrage through the Rise of the New Right*. Chapel Hill: University of North Carolina Press, 2006.

Tilly, Louise, and Patricia Gurin, eds. *Women, Politics and Change*. New York: Russell Sage Foundation, 1990.

Ware, Susan. *Partner and I: Molly Dewson, Feminism, and New Deal Politics*. New Haven, Conn.: Yale University Press, 1987.

Melanie Gustafson

WORKS PROGRESS ADMINISTRATION

One of the most prominent of the New Deal agencies, the Works Progress Administration (WPA) was established in 1935 as an ambitious and wide-ranging federal jobs program. Harry Hopkins, an advocate of federally funded employment for the jobless, was appointed by President Franklin Delano Roosevelt in 1934 to head the WPA's immediate predecessor, the Civil Works Administration (CWA), a limited work-relief program operating under the Federal Emergency Relief Administration. Its funds exhausted, the CWA ceased operations after only a few months.

The WPA, funded under the 1935 Emergency Relief Appropriations Act, differed from the CWA by seeking to provide employment on necessary projects rather than merely make-work tasks—to replace relief with real jobs. WPA undertakings included such diverse activities as building and road construction, day-nursery work, bookbinding, a federal theater project, a writers' project, research for the Library of Congress, the creation and maintenance of parks and recreational facilities, and many other forms of blue- and white-collar employment. Jobs were of limited duration and usually paid prevailing wages. All told, the WPA employed some 8.5 million people.

The WPA—along with the entire New Deal—encountered considerable opposition from conservatives in Congress. In 1939 the

Dies Committee, headed by Congressman Martin Dies of Texas, investigated alleged Communist influence in the agency, focusing on the Federal Theater Project, which was terminated that year.

Renamed the Work Projects Administration in 1939, the WPA became increasingly involved in defense work; by late 1941, 40 percent of its workers were employed in defense projects. After the United States entered World War II, war work and military service drastically reduced unemployment and in 1942, Roosevelt declared that the WPA had "earned an honorable discharge." It was disbanded on 30 June 1943.

[*See also* **Hopkins, Harry; New Deal;** *and* **Roosevelt, Franklin Delano.**]

BIBLIOGRAPHY

Badger, Anthony J. *The New Deal.* Basingstoke, UK: MacMillan, 1989.

Kurzman, Paul S. *Harry Hopkins and the New Deal.* Fairlawn, N.J.: R. E. Burdick, 1974.

Kenneth Franklin Kurz

Y

YICK WO v. HOPKINS

The Fourteenth Amendment of the U.S. Constitution provided unprecedented protections for individual rights by prohibiting states or persons acting under color of state law from abridging an individual's life, liberty, or property interest. However, early interpretations of the amendment, beginning with *The Slaughterhouse Cases* in 1873, narrowly construed its application to the states. By 1883 a series of U.S. Supreme Court decisions upheld state-sponsored monopolies, the denial of access to public facilities, and public transportation, all in the face of challenges under the Fourteenth Amendment.

In 1885 Yick Wo, a Chinese immigrant living in San Francisco, violated the city's laundry ordinance by failing to secure a license and was arrested. Charged with a misdemeanor and fined $10, Yick Wo refused to pay and remained in jail, whereupon his attorney filed a writ of habeas corpus with the U.S. Supreme Court. Hopkins, the local sheriff, became the named defendant in a case that pitted the city of San Francisco's assertion of a valid exercise of its police power to protect the health and welfare of its citizens against the allegations of Yick Wo that the ordinance violated the Fourteenth Amendment because it discriminated against the Chinese.

The laundry ordinance corresponded with the 1882 Chinese Exclusion Act and reflected efforts by the government on all levels to curb Anglo fears of a growing and significant Chinese presence in California. By 1880 half of the Chinese living in California resided in

San Francisco and most lived and worked in wooden buildings. Yick Wo had owned and operated a laundry since 1861, but was denied a license when he applied, despite passing a health and safety inspection in 1884. Yick Wo provided statistical evidence that the statute was combined with other local ordinances to frustrate Chinese immigration. The ordinance gave the Board of Supervisors absolute authority to restrict laundries to buildings of brick or stone. Only one Chinese laundry owner received a license in 1885, apparently by oversight, whereas Yick Wo and 200 other Chinese applicants were denied.

In a unanimous opinion, unique for its time, the Supreme Court found the exercise of police power to be excessive and discriminatory. The ordinance was class-based legislation that the Fourteenth Amendment clearly prohibited. The Court held that the Fourteenth Amendment was not confined to the protection of citizens, but applied to all persons regardless of race and that the police power had to be applied narrowly and in good faith. The Court had extended the reach of the Fourteenth Amendment farther than ever before. A law, neutral on its face, failed to pass Constitutional scrutiny regardless of intent based on statistical data that showed its discriminatory effect.

The tragedy of the case lies in the fact that subsequent law did not build upon the decision but undermined it. The social and political environment of the nineteenth century did not embrace the modern notion of individual rights. Subsequent decisions returned to the trend that began with *Slaughterhouse,* including the landmark decision in *Plessy v. Ferguson* and its sanctioning of "separate but equal." The debate over whether the Fourteenth Amendment applied to the states continued well into the twentieth century.

[*See also* **Chinese Exclusion Cases; Civil Liberties; Civil Rights; Fourteenth Amendment; *Plessy v. Ferguson*; *and* Slaughterhouse Cases.**]

BIBLIOGRAPHY

Goldstein, Lawrence. *Inherently Unequal: The Betrayal of Equal Rights by the Supreme Court, 1865–1903.* New York: Walker & Co., 2011.

Park, John. *Elusive Citizenship: Immigration, Asian Americans and the Paradox of Civil Rights.* New York: New York University Press, 2004.

Shih-shan, H. T. *The Chinese Experience in America.* Bloomington: Indiana University Press, 1986.

Yick Wo v. Hopkins. 118 U.S. 356 (1886).

Mark A. Weitz

YOUNG AMERICANS FOR FREEDOM

Young Americans for Freedom (YAF) was formed in September 1960 in Sharon, Connecticut. About ninety young people attended the conference and adopted a set of principles known as the Sharon Statement, an elucidation of the principles of conservatism set forth in the magazine *National Review*. Included were a defense of free market economics, belief in God and in the Judeo-Christian religion, and strong anti-Communism.

YAF grew out of a number of groups actively organizing conservative students on college campuses in the 1950s. Many students greeted the arrival of *National Review* and its young editor, William F. Buckley Jr., as a spark for activism against liberal college professors and in favor of a political conservatism. Young conservatives were most excited about Barry Goldwater, whose March 1960 book *Conscience of a Conservative* embodied the principles of anti-Communism, free market economics, and traditionalism young conservatives endorsed. They fought for him as vice president at the 1960 Republican Convention. After Henry Cabot Lodge was selected instead, young conservatives organized YAF to fight for conservative causes.

Over the course of the next two decades, YAF members served as cadres for conservatism, supporting Goldwater in the 1964 election, protesting against Communism, and fighting against the New Left on campus. Many leading figures in the political organization of conservatism during the 1970s, such as Richard Viguerie, Howard Phillips, and Paul Weyrich, were directly members of, or fellow travelers in, YAF.

At its peak in the late 1960s YAF members assumed a pro–Vietnam War stance at home, organized protests against companies like Firestone Tire and Rubber Company (which sold rubber to Communist countries like Romania, which in turn manufactured vehicles for the Vietnamese Communists), and battled against the New Left and antiwar students on campus. At a time when the 1960s New Left and antiwar students were more prevalent on college campuses, YAF held its own and by the end of the 1960s the group claimed a membership of 80,000 students.

With conservatism developing into a more powerful force in national politics, YAF steadily declined throughout the 1970s. YAF sponsored the Conservative Political Action Conference (CPAC) beginning in 1974, but by the time of Ronald Reagan's election in 1980, YAF was seriously diminished as an active force in American politics. The organization still exists, however, and although it never again reached the membership heights it saw in the 1960s, YAF continues to fight for conservative principles embodied in the Sharon Statement.

[*See also* **Anti-Communism; Buckley, William F., Jr.; Conservatism;** *and* **Goldwater, Barry.**]

BIBLIOGRAPHY

Schneider, Gregory L. *Cadres for Conservatism: Young Americans for Freedom and the Rise of the Contemporary Right.* New York: New York University Press, 1999.

Thorburn, Wayne. *A Generation Awakes: Young Americans for Freedom and the Creation of the Conservative Movement.* Ottawa, Ill.: Jameson Books, 2010.

Gregory L. Schneider

YOUNGSTOWN SHEET AND TUBE CO. v. SAWYER

343 U.S. 579 (1952), argued 12–13 May 1952, decided 2 June 1952 by vote of 6 to 3; Black for the Court, Frankfurter, Douglas, Jackson Burton, and Clark concurring, Vinson, Reed, and Minton in dissent. This decision rejected the argument that President Harry S. Truman had inherent constitutional authority to issue an executive order seizing private steel mills in 1952.

Apprehensive that an impending strike by steelworkers would harm the country's participation in the United Nations' police action in Korea, President Truman issued an executive order instructing Secretary of Commerce Charles Sawyer to seize and operate the nation's steel mills. Secretary Sawyer directed the companies' presidents to operate the facilities in compliance with government regulations. The president immediately gave Congress formal notice of his action, but Congress took no action. Although the seizure lacked statutory authority, Truman took the view that his action was valid under the powers invested in him as president and commander in chief. He relied upon the many historical precedents of executive seizure without the consent of Congress.

The steel industry argued that the purpose of the Labor Management Relations Act of 1947 (Taft–Hartley Act) was to allow the parties to arrive at a settlement and to permit Congress to become involved if collective bargaining was unsuccessful. The fact that Congress had specifically rejected a seizure provision during the debate of this act could only be interpreted as a prohibition against executive seizure.

The opinions of the justices reflected the two polar interpretations of the first clause of Article II of the Constitution: "The executive Power shall be vested in a President of the United States."

Justice Hugo Black, writing for the Court, held that inasmuch as Congress could have directed the seizure of the steel mills, the president had no power to do so without an express prior congressional authorization. Black insisted that each of the popular branches must be left to carry out its duties according to the original constitutional understanding. The power exercised by Truman was clearly a law-making task that properly belonged only to Congress.

Concurring, Justice Felix Frankfurter suggested that long-standing executive practices, with the silent acquiescence of Congress, might provide an additional gloss on the executive powers. Justice William O. Douglas concurred, observing that Congress has the power to pay compensation and is the only branch able to authorize a lawful seizure.

Justice Robert Jackson also concurred and distinguished constitutional situations in which presidential powers fluctuate: strongest with a congressional authorization, weakest against a congressional prohibition, and uncertain alongside a congressional silence. Jackson concluded that the president acted unconstitutionally because Congress had refused to authorize the seizure.

Justice Harold Burton concurred because Congress had prescribed specific procedures exclusive of seizure. Justice Tom Clark, who as attorney general had earlier advised Truman, concurred because the president's authority to act in times of national emergency was subject to the limitations expressly prescribed by Congress.

Chief Justice Fred Vinson dissented, joined by Justices Stanley Reed and Sherman Minton, and surveyed the elements of the emergency: the Korean military involvement, the importance of steel as a war material, and the impasse in the labor negotiation. Presidential emergency action had been allowed in the past, and the dissent concluded that the president acted constitutionally.

This decision, especially Justice Jackson's concurring opinion, has provided an important precedent for resisting subsequent claims of presidential inherent authority in areas such as impoundment, executive privilege, electronic surveillance, national security, and the "war on terror." The holding has come to be generally understood as an interpretive effort to restrain the executive branch within a proper separation of power.

[*See also* **Black, Hugo; Constitution; Douglas, William O.; Frankfurter, Felix; Taft–Hartley Act;** *and* **Truman, Harry S.**]

BIBLIOGRAPHY

Marcus, Maeva. *Truman and the Steel Seizure Case—The Limits of Presidential Power,* rev. ed. Durham, N.C.: Duke University Press, 1994.

Rehnquist, William H. *The Supreme Court,* rev. ed. New York: Alfred A. Knopf, 2001.

Westin, Alan F. *The Anatomy of a Constitutional Law Case,* rev. ed. New York: Columbia University Press, 1990.

Thomas E. Baker

Z

ZENGER TRIAL

In 1733, John Peter Zenger, a German immigrant, launched the first opposition newspaper in the American colonies. His *New York Weekly Journal* vigorously attacked New York's royal governor William Cosby. Among the chief backers of this paper were Lewis Morris, whom Cosby had recently removed as chief justice of the colony. Zenger's paper relentlessly attacked Cosby, using sarcasm, innuendo, and allegory to ridicule the overbearing, greedy, and politically inept governor and his chief advisers. The *Weekly Journal* was also the first American publication to reprint numerous essays by the leading English libertarian philosophers of the period, including *Cato's Letters,* essays written by John Trenchard and Thomas Gordon that would heavily influence the ideology of the American Revolution a generation later.

After several futile attempts to persuade a grand jury to indict Zenger, Governor Cosby arranged for his arrest in November 1734. When the grand jury once again refused to indict Zenger, the colony's attorney general, Richard Bradley, charged the printer with seditious libel. Zenger was initially represented by James Alexander and William Smith, two prominent New York attorneys who were also among the chief backers of the *Weekly Journal,* but the new chief justice, James DeLancey, disbarred them when they challenged the legitimacy of his appointment. DeLancey then selected a pro-Cosby lawyer, John Chambers, to defend Zenger. Chambers planned a traditional defense, in which Zenger would have denied publishing the allegedly libelous newspapers. When the case came to trial, however, Zenger was represented by Andrew Hamilton of Philadelphia, the most prominent attorney in British America. Defying the prevailing rules of libel law, Hamilton argued that his client should be acquitted because what he had published about the governor was, in fact, true. Although apparently guilty under the accepted understanding of libel law, Zenger was acquitted by the jury in August 1735.

Zenger's acquittal did not change the Common Law of libel, but it did set a powerful political precedent: Zenger was the last colonial printer prosecuted by royal authorities. In 1736 Zenger published *A Brief Narrative of the Case and Tryal of John Peter Zenger*, in which Hamilton, writing anonymously, recounted the events of his famous libel trial and reiterated his argument that newspapers should be free to criticize the government so long as what they wrote was true. Frequently reprinted in England and America, the *Brief Narrative* helped shape the political culture that led to the Revolutionary War and the subsequent adoption of the Bill of Rights.

[***See also*** **Bill of Rights; Censorship; Civil Liberties;** ***and*** **Sedition.**]

BIBLIOGRAPHY

Buranelli, Vincent, ed. *The Trial of John Peter Zenger*. New York: New York University Press, 1957, reprint 1985.

Finkelman, Paul, ed. *A Brief Narrative of the Case and Tryal of John Peter Zenger, Printer of the New York Weekly Journal*. Union, N.J.: The Lawbook Exchange, 2000.

Paul Finkelman

TOPICAL OUTLINE OF ENTRIES

This topical outline presents an overview of the encyclopedia, with entries listed under the following subject categories:

Activist Organizations: Political/Legal
Activist Organizations: Social/Economic
Concepts, Ideologies, and Movements
Court Cases
Documents
Events and Eras
Government Agencies, Departments, and Programs
Issues and Policy
Laws
Parties and Groups
Biographies

Activist Organizations: Political/Legal

America First Committee
American Anti-Slavery Society
American Civil Liberties Union
American Liberty League
Anti-Saloon League
Bonus Army
Christian Coalition
Grand Army of the Republic
Institute of Pacific Relations
NARAL Pro-Choice America
National American Woman Suffrage Association
National Association for the Advancement of Colored People
National Organization for Women
National Rifle Association
National Right to Life Committee
Sons of Liberty

Activist Organizations: Social/Economic

American Colonization Society
American Farm Bureau Federation
American Indian Movement
Black Panthers
Congress of Racial Equality

Concepts, Ideologies, and Movements

Court Cases

Documents

Events and Eras

Government Agencies, Departments, and Programs

Issues and Policy

Laws

Parties and Groups

Biographies

Agnew, Spiro
Anthony, Susan B.
Baruch, Bernard
Black, Hugo
Blackmun, Harry A.
Blaine, James G.
Brandeis, Louis
Brown, John
Bryan, William Jennings
Buchanan, James
Buckley, William F., Jr.
Bunche, Ralph J.
Burger, Warren
Burr, Aaron
Bush, George H. W.
Bush, George W.
Calhoun, John C.
Cannon, Joseph
Carson, Rachel
Carter, Jimmy
Chase, Salmon
Cheney, Richard
Clay, Henry
Cleveland, Grover
Clinton, Hillary Rodham
Clinton, William J.
Coolidge, Calvin
Croly, Herbert
Daley, Richard J.
Davis, Jefferson
Debs, Eugene
Douglas, Stephen A.
Douglas, William O.
Douglass, Frederick
Du Bois, W. E. B.
Eisenhower, Dwight D.
Ferraro, Geraldine
Field, David Dudley
Fillmore, Millard
Ford, Gerald R.
Frankfurter, Felix
Franklin, Benjamin
Garfield, James
Garnet, Henry Highland
Goldman, Emma
Goldwater, Barry
Gore, Albert A., Jr.
Grant, Ulysses S.
Hamilton, Alexander
Hanna, Mark
Harding, Warren G.
Harlan, John Marshall
Harrison, Benjamin
Harrison, William Henry
Hayes, Rutherford B.
Hearst, William Randolph
Holmes, Oliver Wendell, Jr.
Hoover, Herbert
Hoover, J. Edgar
Hopkins, Harry
Houston, Sam
Humphrey, Hubert
Jackson, Andrew
Jay, John
Jefferson, Thomas
Johnson, Andrew
Johnson, Hiram
Johnson, Lyndon B.
Kennedy, Edward
Kennedy, John F.
Kennedy, Robert
Kerry, John
King, Martin Luther, Jr.
La Follette, Robert
La Guardia, Fiorello
Langdell, Christopher Columbus
Lewis, John
Lincoln, Abraham
Lippmann, Walter
Long, Huey
MacArthur, Douglas
Madison, James
Marshall, John
Marshall, Thurgood
McCarthy, Joseph
McKinley, William
Monroe, James
Nader, Ralph

Nixon, Richard M.
Obama, Barack
O'Connor, Sandra Day
Perot, Ross
Pierce, Franklin
Polk, James Knox
Powell, Adam Clayton, Jr.
Rankin, Jeannette
Rayburn, Sam
Reagan, Ronald
Rehnquist, William
Roberts, John
Rockefeller, Nelson
Roosevelt, Eleanor
Roosevelt, Franklin Delano
Roosevelt, Theodore
Scalia, Antonin
Schlafly, Phyllis
Smith, Alfred
Stanton, Elizabeth Cady
Stevenson, Adlai
Stone, Harlan
Story, Joseph
Taft, Robert
Taft, William Howard
Taney, Roger B.
Taylor, Zachary
Thomas, Norman
Trotter, William Monroe
Truman, Harry S.
Tyler, John
Van Buren, Martin
Wallace, George C.
Wallace, Henry A.
Warren, Earl
Washington, Booker T.
Washington, George
Webster, Daniel
Wilson, Woodrow

DIRECTORY OF CONTRIBUTORS

Lisa Andersen
Department of Liberal Arts, The Juilliard School
Woman's Christian Temperance Union

Fabio Arcila Jr.
Touro College Jacob D. Fuchsberg Law Center
Search and Seizure

Gordon Morris Bakken
Department of History, California State University, Fullerton
Taxes: Proposition 13

Carl L. Bankston III
Department of Sociology, Tulane University
Immigration Law and Policy: After 1930

Robert Beauregard
Graduate School of Architecture, Planning, and Preservation, Columbia University
Urban Policy: National Policy

William C. Berman
Department of History, University of Toronto
Clinton, William J.

Roger Biles
Department of History, Illinois State University
African American Mayors since 1960; Daley, Richard J.

Joel Blau
School of Social Welfare, Stony Brook University
Social Policy: Public Welfare

Joseph Blocher
Duke Law School
District of Columbia v. Heller

Nicholas D. Bloom
Department of Social Sciences, New York Institute of Technology
Housing Policy, Federal: Public Housing

William H. Brackney
Director of Acadia Center for Baptist and Anabaptist Studies, Acadia Divinity College
Antislavery Movement

Pearson Bramblett
Department of History, Saint Louis University
Antiwar Movements; Education Policy: An Overview; Environmental Protection Agency; Federal Government, Executive Branch: Agriculture Department; Federal Government, Executive Branch: Defense Department; Federal Government, Legislative Branch: An Overview; Federal Government, Legislative Branch: Senate; Nuclear Power; O'Connor, Sandra Day; State Governments; Supreme Court, U.S.

Jay L. Brigham
Morgan, Angel & Associates, LLC
Public Utilities Policy, Federal

Eric Burin
Department of History, University of North Dakota
American Colonization Society

Orville Vernon Burton
Department of History, Clemson University
Lincoln, Abraham

Andrew E. Busch
Department of Government, Claremont McKenna College
Reagan, Ronald

Vincent J. Cannato
Department of History, University of Massachusetts, Boston
Ferraro, Geraldine; Housing Policy, Federal: Fannie Mae; Housing Policy, Federal: Federal Housing Administration; Housing Policy, Federal: Home Owners' Loan Corporation

Christopher Capozzola
Department of History, Massachusetts Institute of Technology
Committee on Public Information

Thomas J. Carty III
Department of Social Sciences, Springfield College
Kennedy, John F.

Anthony Champagne
Department of Political Science, University of Texas, Dallas
Rayburn, Sam

Ellen Chesler
The Roosevelt Institute, New York City
People v. Sanger

William R. Childs
Department of History, Ohio State University
Energy Policy

Eric R. Claeys
George Mason University School of Law
Rehnquist, William; Scalia, Antonin

Andrew F. Coffey
Virginia Polytechnic Institute and State University
Disaster Policy, Federal

Douglas B. Craig
School of History, Research School/Social Sciences, Australian National University, Canberra
American Liberty League

Donald T. Critchlow
School of Historical, Philosophical, and Religious Studies, Arizona State University
Environmental Policy: Clean Air Act; Environmental Policy: Endangered Species Act; Equal Rights Amendment; Schlafly, Phyllis

Maurice T. Cunningham
Department of Political Science, University of Massachusetts, Boston
Kerry, John

Sean P. Cunningham
Department of History, Texas Tech University
Goldwater, Barry

Rebecca Schoff Curtin
Independent Scholar
Anti-Miscegenation Laws

Kathleen Dalton
Phillips Academy, Andover
Progressive Party of 1912

Donald A. DeBats
Flinders University, Adelaide
Elections: Voting Systems

Jefferson Decker
Department of American Studies, Rutgers University
Conservatism, Legal

Richard Delgado
Seattle University School of Law
Legal Theory, Critical

Thomas W. Devine
Department of History, California State University, Northridge
Progressive Party of 1948

Richardson Dilworth
Department of History and Politics, Drexel University
Urban Policy: Department of Housing and Urban Development

Daniel DiSalvo
Department of Political Science, City College of New York
Neoliberalism

Brian Domitrovic
Department of History, Sam Houston State University
Federal Deposit Insurance Corporation

Ian Dowbiggin
Department of History, University of Prince Edward Island
Assisted Suicide Policy

Robert L. DuPont
President, Institute for Behavior and Health, Inc
Drug Control Policy, Office of National

Charles W. Eagles
Department of History, University of Mississippi
White Citizens' Councils

Thomas J. Edge
Bowling Green State University
National Negro Congress

John Ehrman
Independent Scholar, Virginia
Neoconservatism

Paul Escott
Department of History, Wake Forest University
Davis, Jefferson

Michael R. Fein
Department of Humanities, Johnson & Wales University
Interstate Highways

Andrea Field
School of Historical, Philosophical, and Religious Studies, Arizona State University
Federal Reserve System; Securities and Exchange Commission

Paul Finkelman
Albany Law School
Slavery, Laws; Zenger Trial

Price V. Fishback
Department of Economics, University of Arizona
Fellow-Servant Rule (Tort)

Chad W. Flanders
Saint Louis University School of Law
Bush v. Gore; White Primary Cases

Robert Fleegler
Department of History, University of Mississippi
Moynihan Report

Matthew L. M. Fletcher
Michigan State University College of Law
Indian Law, Federal; Indian Law, Tribal

Felicia Fognani
American University
NARAL Pro-Choice America; National Right to Life Committee

Andrew K. Frank
Department of History, Florida State University
American Indian Movement

Linda C. Frank
Department of History, University of California, Los Angeles
Seneca Falls Women's Rights Convention of 1848

John J. Fry
Department of History, Trinity Christian College
Wallace, Henry A.

R. Sam Garrett
Department of Government, American University
Campaign Finance Reform

Michael J. Gerhardt
School of Law, University of North Carolina, Chapel Hill
Presidential Impeachment

Andrea K. Gerlak
Institute of the Environment, University of Arizona
Water Policy

Laura Jane Gifford
Department of History, George Fox University
Perot, Ross

Lorri Glover
Department of History, Saint Louis University
Virginia and Kentucky Resolutions

Steven K. Green
College of Law, Willamette University
Prayer in School

John Robert Greene
Department of History, Cazenovia College
Ford, Gerald R.

Fred I. Greenstein
Department of Politics, Princeton University
Obama, Barack

Melanie Gustafson
Department of History, University of Vermont
Women in Politics since 1920

Timothy A. Hacsi
Department of History, University of Massachusetts, Boston
Social Policy: Orphanages

David E. Hamilton
Department of History, University of Kentucky
Agricultural Policy; American Farm Bureau Federation

Robert C. Harding
Department of Political Science, Spring Hill College
Panama Canal

Madonna Harrington Meyer
Department of Sociology, Syracuse University
Social Security Policy

Woodrow Hartzog
Cumberland School of Law at Samford University
Privacy

Ron Haskins
Center on Children and Families, The Brookings Institution
Welfare Reform Act of 1996

Ellis W. Hawley
University of Iowa, Emeritus
Hoover, Herbert; Reconstruction Finance Corporation; Teapot Dome Scandal

David L. Herzberg
Department of History, State University of New York, Buffalo
Federal Government, Executive Branch: Other Departments

Stephen Hess
The Brookings Institution
Cartoons, Political

Jeffrey D. Hockett
Department of Political Science, University of Tulsa
Court Packing; Frankfurter, Felix

Dirk Hoerder
School of Historical, Philosophical, and Religious Studies, Arizona State University
Immigration Law and Policy: Before 1930

Derek S. Hoff
Department of History, Kansas State University
Population Policy

Williamjames Hull Hoffer
Department of History, Seton Hall University
Administrative State

Daniel Hulsebosch
New York University School of Law
Kent's Commentaries

James Ivy
Department of English, Trinity University
Anti-Saloon League; Prohibition

Glen Jeansonne
Department of History, University of Wisconsin, Milwaukee
John Birch Society; MacArthur, Douglas

Richard Jensen
Department of History, Montana State University Billings
Political Campaigning; Voting: Ethnocultural Voting; Voting: Voting Behavior

Loch K. Johnson
Department of International Affairs, University of Georgia
National Security Council; War Powers Act

Troy R. Johnson
American Indian Studies Program, California State University, Long Beach
Alcatraz, Occupation of

Geoffrey Kabaservice
Independent Scholar, Virginia
Rockefeller, Nelson

Benjamin Kleinerman
James Madison College, Michigan State University
Executive Power

J. Morgan Kousser
Division of Humanities and Social Sciences, California Institute of Technology
Elections: Election Law; Reconstruction

Thad Kousser
University of California, San Diego
Initiative and Referendum

Michael E. Kraft
Department of Political Science, University of Wisconsin, Green Bay
Energy Crisis of the 1970s

Larry D. Kramer
Stanford Law School
Constitutionalism, Popular; Judicial Review

Roy Kreitner
Tel-Aviv University, Israel
Contract, Law of

Charles A. Kromkowski
Department of Politics, University of Virginia
Elections: Suffrage

Craig L. LaMay
Northwestern University
Presidential Debates

Matthew Gordon Lasner
Hunter College
Housing Policy, Federal: An Overview

Marc Leepson
Department of History, Lord Fairfax Community College
Flag, U.S.

Stuart Leibiger
Department of History, La Salle University
Adams, John

Allan J. Lichtman
Department of History, American University
Elections: Presidential Elections

Kriste Lindenmeyer
Department of History, Rutgers, The State University of New Jersey
Keating-Owen Child Labor Act

Kyle Longley
School of Historical, Philosophical, and Religious Studies, Arizona State University
Gore, Albert A., Jr.

David Luhrssen
Lecturer, University of Wisconsin, Milwaukee
John Birch Society; MacArthur, Douglas

Thomas S. Mach
Department of History and Government, Cedarville University
Spoils System

Matthew J. Mancini
Department of American Studies, Saint Louis University
Democracy in America

Jerry W. Markham
Florida International University Law School
Economic Policy: Banking and Financial Regulation

Robert Mason
Department of History, University of Edinburgh
Agnew, Spiro

Joshua H. Mather
Department of History, Saint Louis University
Federal Government, Executive Branch: Other Departments

Gary L. McDowell
Jepson School of Leadership Studies, University of Richmond
Constitutional Law

Andrew S. McFarland
Department of Political Science, University of Illinois, Chicago
Pluralism

Michael McGeary
Institute of Medicine of the National Academies
National Institutes of Health

Paul Charles Milazzo
Department of History, Ohio University
Environmental Policy: An Overview

Fred D. Miller Jr.
Department of Philosophy, Bowling Green State University
Libertarianism

Iwan Morgan
Institute for the Study of the Americas, University of London
Budget, Federal; Taxes: Reagan Tax Cuts

Michael A. Morrison
Department of History, Purdue University
Texas Annexation; Wilmot Proviso

Don Toshiaki Nakanishi
University of California, Los Angeles, Emeritus
Asian Americans

Karen O'Connor
Department of Government, American University
NARAL Pro-Choice America; National Right to Life Committee

Phillip Payne
Department of History, St. Bonaventure University
Coolidge, Calvin; Harding, Warren G.

Oren Perez
Faculty of Law, Bar-Ilan University, Israel
Pluralism, Legal

Alan Petigny
Department of History, University of Florida
Busing, School

Laura D. Phillips
Postdoctoral Research Associate, Brown University
Trade Policy: Fair Trade

Frances Fox Piven
Department of Political Science, Graduate Center, City University of New York
Great Society

Keith T. Poole
Department of Political Science, University of Georgia
Political Polarization

Juan Gómez-Quiñones
Professor of History, University of California, Los Angeles (UCLA)
Hispanic Americans

Stephen E. Randoll
Department of History, St. Charles Community College
Health Insurance; Public Health: Surgeon General; Public Health Service, U.S.; Regulatory Agencies, Federal

Neomi Rao
George Mason University School of Law
Roberts, John

Ronald B. Rapoport
Department of Government, College of William and Mary
Third Parties

Eric Rauchway
Department of History, University of California, Davis
Roosevelt, Franklin Delano

Howard L. Reiter
Department of Political Science, University of Connecticut
Presidential Primaries

Lex Renda
Department of History, University of Wisconsin, Milwaukee
Voting: Retrospective Voting

Patrick S. Roberts
School of Public and International Affairs, Virginia Polytechnic Institute and State University
Disaster Policy, Federal; Homeland Security, Department of

David Brian Robertson
Department of Political Science, University of Missouri, St. Louis
Labor's Role in Politics; National Labor Relations Act

Greg Robinson
Department of History, Université du Québec à Montréal
Japanese American Internment

Malcolm J. Rohrbough
Department of History, University of Iowa
Land Policy, Federal

Kermit Roosevelt III
University of Pennsylvania School of Law
Cooper v. Aaron

F. Arturo Rosales
School of Historical, Philosophical, and Religious Studies, Arizona State University
Raza Unida Party

Theodore Rosenof
Department of History, Mercy College
Political Realignment

John M. Rothgeb Jr.
Department of Political Science, Miami University, Ohio
Trade Policy: An Overview

Mark J. Rozell
Department of Public Policy, George Mason University
Environmental Policy: Clean Water Act; *United States v. Nixon*

Nathan Alexander Sales
George Mason University School of Law
Terrorist Detention Policy

Joshua Salzmann
Department of History, University of Illinois, Chicago
Hepburn Act

Clinton Sandvick
Department of History, University of Oregon
Economic Policy: Medical Regulation

Walton O. Schalick III
Waisman Center, University of Wisconsin-Madison
Stem-Cell Research

Calvin Schermerhorn
School of Historical, Philosophical and Religious Studies, Arizona State University
Garnet, Henry Highland

Gregory L. Schneider
Department of Social Sciences, Emporia State University
Bush, George W.; Conservatism; Young Americans for Freedom

Charles Seligson
Independent Scholar
Kent's Commentaries

William G. Shade
Department of History, Lehigh University, Emeritus
Party System

Stephen M. Sheppard
University of Arkansas School of Law
Due Process: Legal Cases; Langdell, Christopher Columbus; Virginia Statute for Religious Freedom

Matthew C. Sherman
Institute for Political History
McKinley, William; Presidential Assassinations; Secret Service, U.S.

David J. Siemers
Department of Political Science, University of Wisconsin-Oshkosh
Anti-Federalists

Brooks D. Simpson
School of Historical, Philosophical, and Religious Studies, Arizona State University
Grant, Ulysses S.

James Allen Smith
Rockefeller Archive Center
Foundations, Philanthropic

Jason Scott Smith
Department of History, University of New Mexico
Civilian Conservation Corps

Raymond W. Smock
Department of History, Shepherd University
Washington, Booker T.

Mitchel A. Sollenberger
Department of Political Science, University of Michigan, Dearborn
United States v. Nixon

Jason Stahl
Department of Postsecondary Teaching and Learning, University of Minnesota
Think Tanks

Timothy Stanley
Department of History, Royal Holloway College, University of London
Kennedy, Edward

Brian D. Steele
Department of History, University of Alabama, Birmingham
Jefferson, Thomas; *Notes on the State of Virginia*

Christopher H. Sterling
George Washington University, Washington, D.C.
Federal Communications Commission

Robert Surbrug Jr.
Department of Liberal Studies, Bay Path College
Antinuclear Movement

Joshua C. Tate
Southern Methodist University Dedman School of Law
Blackstone, William, Influence of

Jon C. Teaford
Department of History, Purdue University
Municipal Politics

Stephen R. Thomas
Ohio Dominican University
Cheney v. U.S. District Court; Economic Policy: Deregulation, 1970 to Present

Timothy N. Thurber
Department of History, Virginia Commonwealth University
Cheney, Richard

Gil Troy
Department of History and Classical Studies, McGill University
Clinton, Hillary Rodham

Stephen Tuck
Pembroke College, Oxford
Lewis, John (Representative)

Mark Tushnet
Harvard Law School
Marshall, Thurgood

Nancy C. Unger
Department of History, Santa Clara University
Progressive Party of 1924

Philip R. VanderMeer
School of Historical, Philosophical, and Religious Studies, Arizona State University
Johnson, Hiram

Irene Morris Vásquez
Department of Chicana/o Studies, California State University, Dominguez Hills
Hispanic Americans

Anders Walker
Saint Louis University School of Law
Affirmative Action: Legal Aspects; *Brown v. Board of Education;* Model Penal Code; Tobacco Suits; *United States v. Carolene Products*

Amy C. Wallhermfechtel
Department of History, Saint Louis University
Education Policy: Higher Education

Alan Ware
Worcester College, Oxford University
Elections: Nominating Systems

Clive Webb
Department of History, University of Sussex
Dixiecrats

Mark A. Weitz
Weitz Morgan PLLC
Popular Sovereignty; Tort, Law of; *Yick Wo v. Hopkins*

Daniel K. Williams
Department of History, University of West Georgia
Abortion Politics and Policy; Religious Right

Cary D. Wintz
Texas Southern University
African Americans in Politics; Powell, Adam Clayton, Jr.

Kam C. Wong
Department of Criminal Justice, Xavier University
Patriot Act, The

Robert F. Zeidel
Department of Social Science, University of Wisconsin, Stout
Cannon, Joseph

Aharon Zorea
Department of History, University of Wisconsin, Richland
Crime Policy, Federal; Federal Government, Judicial Branch

Directory of Contributors to the *Oxford Companion to United States History*

Paul P. Abrahams
Professor Emeritus of History and Humanities, University of Wisconsin, Green Bay
Tariffs

W. Andrew Achenbaum
Professor of History and Dean, College of Humanities, the Arts, and Communication, University of Houston
Social Security

Willi Paul Adams
Professor of North American History, John F. Kennedy Institute for North American Studies, Free University of Berlin, Germany
Common Sense

Margo A. Anderson
Professor of History, University of Wisconsin, Milwaukee
Census, Federal

Raymond O. Arsenault
John Hope Franklin Professor of Southern History, University of South Florida, St. Petersburg
Long, Huey; *Swann v. Charlotte–Mecklenburg Board of Education*

Erik W. Austin
Director of Archival Development, Inter-University Consortium for Political and Social Research, University of Michigan, Ann Arbor
Public Opinion

Jean Harvey Baker
Professor of History, Goucher College
Democratic Party; Pierce, Franklin; Van Buren, Martin

Ross K. Baker
Professor of Political Science, Rutgers University
Baker v. Carr; Federal Government, Legislative Branch: House of Representatives

Lois W. Banner
Professor of History, University of Southern California, Los Angeles
National American Woman Suffrage Association; Stanton, Elizabeth Cady

Lance Banning
Professor of History, University of Kentucky, Lexington
Liberty

Doron Ben-Atar
Associate Professor of History, Fordham University
Embargo Acts

Michael Les Benedict
Professor of History, Ohio State University, Columbus
Fourteenth Amendment; Johnson, Andrew

Charles C. Bolton
Director, Center for Oral History and Cultural Heritage and Associate Professor of History, University of Southern Mississippi
States' Rights Party

Shearer Davis Bowman
Associate Professor of History, University of Texas, Austin
Kansas–Nebraska Act; Nullification

Paul S. Boyer
Merle Curti Professor of History, University of Wisconsin-Madison
Education Policy

Alan Brinkley
Allan Nevins Professor of History, Columbia University
Employment Act of 1946

Kathleen M. Brown
Associate Professor of History, University of Pennsylvania
Bacon's Rebellion

Roger H. Brown
Professor Emeritus of History, American University
Hartford Convention; Whiskey Rebellion

W. Elliot Brownlee
Professor of History, University of California, Santa Barbara
Taxation

John D. Buenker
Professor of History and Ethnic Studies, University of Wisconsin, Parkside
Pure Food and Drug Act; Securities and Exchange Commission; Sixteenth Amendment

Paul Buhle
Visiting Associate Professor of American Civilization, Brown University
Radicalism; Socialist Party of America

John L. Bullion
Professor of History, University of Missouri, Columbia
Committees of Correspondence; Sons of Liberty; Stamp Act

Randolph B. Campbell
Regents Professor of History, University of North Texas, Denton
Houston, Sam

Stanley W. Campbell
Professor Emeritus of History, Baylor University
Fugitive Slave Act

Dan T. Carter
Educational Foundation University Professor, University of South Carolina
Wallace, George C.

Nicholas Casner
Professor of History, Boise State University
Burr, Aaron

John Whiteclay Chambers II
Professor of History, Rutgers University
Conscientious Objection

David L. Chappell
Associate Professor of History, University of Arkansas, Fayetteville
States' Rights

E. Charles Chatfield
H. Orth Hirt Professor of History, Emeritus, Wittenberg University
Antiwar Movements; Peace Movements

Gene Clanton
Emeritus Professor of History, State University of Washington, Pullman
Populist Party

Christopher Clark
Conscription

Paul G. E. Clemens
Professor of History, Rutgers University
Dartmouth College Case; Hamilton, Alexander; Northwest Ordinance

Kendrick A. Clements
Professor of History, University of South Carolina
Wilson, Woodrow

Jerald A. Combs
Professor of History, San Francisco State University
Jay, John

David Conrad
Professor Emeritus of History, Southern Illinois University, Carbondale
Agricultural Adjustment Administration

Blanche Wiesen Cook
Distinguished Professor of History, John Jay College of Criminal Justice, City University of New York
Roosevelt, Eleanor

David T. Courtwright
Professor of History, University of North Florida, Jacksonville
Drugs, Illicit

Francis G. Couvares
Professor of History and American Studies, Amherst College
Censorship

Donald T. Critchlow
Founding Editor, Journal of Policy History
Birth Control

James L. Crouthamel
Professor Emeritus of History, Hobart & William Smith Colleges
Hearst, William Randolph

Robert M. Crunden[±]
Progressive Era

Thoma s J. Curran
Associate Professor of History, St. John's University
Know-Nothing Party

Wayne Cutler
Research Professor of History, University of Tennessee, Knoxville
Polk, James Knox

Matthew Dallek
Independent Scholar
Affirmative Action: Politics of Affirmative Action

Eric D. Daniels
Department of History, University of Wisconsin-Madison
Fillmore, Millard; Free Soil Party; Tyler, John; Whig Party

Sheri I. David
Professor of History, Northern Virginia Community College
Medicare and Medicaid

Robert A. Divine
George W. Littlefield Professor Emeritus in American History, University of Texas, Austin
Johnson, Lyndon B.

Justus D. Doenecke
Professor of History, New College of the University of Southern Florida
America First Committee; Neutrality Acts

Bobby J. Donaldson
Assistant Professor of History and African American Studies, University of South Carolina
Walker's Appeal

Kendall J. Dood
Independent Scholar
Patent and Copyright Law

George H. Douglas
Professor of English, University of Illinois, Urbana-Champaign
Muckrakers

Ellen C. DuBois
Professor of History, University of California, Los Angeles
Anthony, Susan B.; National Woman's Party; Nineteenth Amendment; Woman Suffrage Movement

Lynn Dumenil
Professor of History, Occidental College
Sacco and Vanzetti Case

Diane D. Edwards
Independent Scholar
Indian Health Service

Marc Egnal
Professor of History, York University, Toronto
Proclamation of 1763

Candace Falk
Editor/Director, Emma Goldman Papers, University of California, Berkeley
Goldman, Emma

Carol Faulkner
Assistant Professor of History, State University of New York, Geneseo
American Anti-Slavery Society; Emancipation Proclamation

Daniel Feller
Professor of History, University of New Mexico
Jackson, Andrew

Robert H. Ferrell
Professor Emeritus of History, Indiana University, Bloomington
Truman, Harry S.

Paul Finkelman
Chapman Distinguished Professor of Law, University of Tulsa
Charles River Bridge v. Warren Bridge; Gibbons v. Ogden; Scott v. Sandford; Slavery Laws; Zenger Trial

Roger A. Fischer
Professor Emeritus of History, University of Minnesota, Duluth
Harrison, William Henry

Joyce C. Follet
Public Historian, Sophia Smith Collection, Smith College
National Organization for Women

George B. Forgie
Associate Professor of History, University of Texas, Austin
Douglas, Stephen A; Lincoln-Douglas Debates

Joshua B. Freeman
Associate Professor of History, Queens College, City University of New York
Debs, Eugene V.; La Guardia, Fiorello

Tony A. Freyer
University Research Professor of History and Law, University of Alabama, Tuscaloosa
Antitrust Legislation and Law; Northern Securities Case; Slaughterhouse Cases

Jennifer Frost
Assistant Professor of History, University of North Colorado
Students for a Democratic Society

Stuart Galishoff
Professor of History Emeritus, Georgia State University
Public Health: An Overview

Patrick M. Garry
Director, Center for Constitutional Studies
Civil Liberties; *Near v. Minnesota*

Roger L. Geiger
Professor of Higher Education, Pennsylvania State University
Morrill Land Grant Act

William Gillette
Professor of History, Rutgers University
Fifteenth Amendment

Steven M. Gillon
Carol Elizabeth Young Professor and Dean of the Honors College, University of Oklahoma, Norman
Humphrey, Hubert

Walter Goodman
Critic, The New York Times
House Un-American Activities Committee

Colin Gordon
Associate Professor of History, University of Iowa, Iowa City
National Civic Federation

Lewis L. Gould
Eugene C. Barket Centennial Professor Emeritus in American History, University of Texas, Austin
Ballinger–Pinchot Controversy; Paris, Treaty of; Roosevelt, Theodore; Taft, William Howard

Henry F. Graff
Professor Emeritus of History, Columbia University
Federal Government, Executive Branch: Presidency, the

James Grant
Editor, Grant's Interest Rate Observer
Baruch, Bernard

Dean Grodzins
Visiting Scholar, Charles Warren Center for Studies in American History, Harvard University
Brown, John

James A. Gross
Professor of Industrial and Labor Relations, Cornell University
National Labor Relations Board; Taft–Hartley Act

Robert A. Gross
Forrest D. Murden Jr. Professor of History and American Studies, College of William and Mary
Shays's Rebellion

Kermit L. Hall
Provost and Vice Chancellor for Academic Affairs, North Carolina State University
Engel v. Vitale; Field, David Dudley; Municipal Judicial System; *Plessy v. Ferguson;* Stone, Harlan; Story, Joseph; State Governments

Richard F. Hamm
Associate Professor of History and Public Policy, State University of New York, Albany
Eighteenth Amendment

David J. Hancock
Associate Professor of History, University of Michigan, Ann Arbor
Navigation Acts

Anthony A. Harkins
Instructor in History, Iowa State University, Ames
Public Broadcasting

Ellis W. Hawley
Professor Emeritus of History, University of Iowa, Iowa City
Federal Trade Commission; Hoover, Herbert; National Recovery Administration; Reconstruction Finance Corporation; Teapot Dome Scandal

George C. Herring
Alumni Professor of History, University of Kentucky, Lexington
Pentagon Papers

Jeffrey D. Hockett
Associate Professor of Political Science, University of Tulsa
Black, Hugo; *Schechter Poultry Corp. v. United States*

J. David Hoeveler
Professor of History, University of Wisconsin, Milwaukee
Buckley, William F., Jr.

Joan Hoff
Director, Contemporary History Institute and Professor of History, Ohio University
Nixon, Richard M.

William F. Holmes
Professor of History, University of Georgia, Athens
Free Silver Movement

Ari Hoogenboom
Professor Emeritus of History, Brooklyn College and the Graduate School and University Center, City University of New York
Civil Service Reform; Interstate Commerce Act

Daniel Walker Howe
Rhodes Professor of American History, Oxford University
Clay, Henry

Daniel Hurewitz
Department of History, University of California, Los Angeles
Lesbian, Gay, Bisexual, and Transgender Rights Movement

John C. Inscoe
Professor of History, University of Georgia, Athens; Editor, Georgia Historical Quarterly
Compromise of 1820

Maurice Isserman
William R. Kenan Jr. Professor of History, Hamilton College
Other America, The

John A. James
Professor of Economics, University of Virginia, Charlottesville
Monetary Policy

Robert F. Jefferson
Assistant Professor of History and African American World Studies, University of Iowa, Iowa City
Segregation

Richard Jensen
Professor Emeritus of History, University of Illinois, Chicago
Hanna, Mark; Voting: Voting Behavior

T. Christopher Jespersen
Assistant Professor of American Diplomatic History, School of International Affairs and Development, Clark Atlanta University
Institute for Pacific Relations

Loch K. Johnson
Regents Professor of Political Science, University of Georgia, Athens
War Powers Act

Robert David Johnson
Associate Professor of History, Brooklyn College, City University of New York
Federal Government, Executive Branch: State Department

Patrick D. Jones
University of Wisconsin-Madison
Southern Christian Leadership Conference

William Jordan
Instructor in History, Philips Exeter Academy, Exeter, New Hampshire
Du Bois, W. E. B.

Carl F. Kaestle
University Professor and Professor of Education, History, and Public Policy, Brown University
National Education Association

John P. Kaminski
Director, the Center for the Study of the American Constitution, University of Wisconsin-Madison
Articles of Confederation; Bill of Rights; Constitution; Constitutional Convention of 1787; Federalist Papers

Yale Kamisar
Clarence Darrow Distinguished University Professor of Law, University of Michigan Law School, Ann Arbor
Miranda v. Arizona

Michael B. Katz
Sheldon and Lucy Hackney Professor of History, University of Pennsylvania, Philadelphia
Poverty

Paul Kens
Associate Professor of Political Science and History, Southwest Texas State University, San Marcos
Lochner v. New York

Ben Keppel
Associate Professor of History, University of Oklahoma, Norman
Bunche, Ralph

Richard B. Kielbowicz
Associate Professor of Communications, University of Washington, Seattle
Postal Service, U.S.

Daniel Lee Kleinman
Associate Professor of Rural Sociology, University of Wisconsin-Madison
National Science Foundation

James T. Kloppenberg
Professor of History, Harvard University
Equality; Republicanism

Peter B. Knupfer
Associate Professor of History, Kansas State University, Manhattan
Compromise of 1850

Daniel J. Kevles
Koepfli Professor of the Humanities, California Institute of Technology
Carson, Rachel

Harvey Klehr
Andrew W. Mellon Professor of Politics and History, Emory University
Communist Party USA

J. Morgan Kousser
Professor of History and Social Science, California Institute of Technology
Reconstruction

Kenneth Franklin Kurz
Independent Scholar
Works Progress Administration

Walter LaFeber
Marie Underhill Noll Professor of American History, Cornell University
Iran-Contra Affair

Roger D. Launius
NASA Chief Historian, National Aeronautics and Space Administration
National Aeronautics and Space Administration

Mark H. Leff
Associate Professor of History, University of Illinois at Urbana-Champaign
Income Tax, Federal

David W. Levy
David Ross Boyd Professor of History, University of Oklahoma, Norman
Croly, Herbert

Peter B. Levy
Associate Professor of History, York College
New Left

Alan Lizotte
Professor of Criminal Justice, State University of New York, Albany
Gun Control; National Rifle Association

David S. Lovejoy[±]
Glorious Revolution in America

Richard Lowitt
Professor of History (ret.), University of Oklahoma, Norman
Oklahoma City Bombing

John Majewski
Economic Development

Robert N. Mayer
Professor of Family and Consumer Studies, University of Utah, Salt Lake City
Nader, Ralph

Joseph A. McCartin
Associate Professor of History, Georgetown University
New Deal

Wilfred M. McClay
SunTrust Chair of Excellence in Humanities and Professor of History, University of Tennessee, Chattanooga
Political Science

Stuart McConnell
Professor of History, Pitzer College
Grand Army of the Republic

Brendon McConville
Associate Professor of History, State University of New York, Binghamton
Continental Congress

Thomas K. McCraw
Isidor Straus Professor of Business History, Harvard Business School
Economic Policy: Regulation; Regulatory Agencies, Federal

David McDowall
Professor of Criminal Justice, State University of New York, Albany
Gun Control; National Rifle Association

Robert S. McElvaine
Elizabeth Chisholm Professor of Arts and Letters and Professor of History, Millsaps College
Bonus Army; Hopkins, Harry

Gerald W. McFarland
Professor of History, University of Massachusetts, Amherst
Mugwumps

Elizabeth McKillen
Associate Professor of History, University of Maine, Orono
North American Free Trade Agreement

Timothy Messer-Kruse
Assistant Professor of Labor History, University of Toledo
Socialism

Leonard J. Moore
Associate Professor of History, McGill University, Montreal
Ku Klux Klan; Libertarian Party

Richard Moran
Professor of Sociology, Mount Holyoke College
Capital Punishment

H. Wayne Morgan
George Lynn Cross Research Professor of History Emeritus, University of Oklahoma
Blaine, James G.; Bryan, William Jennings; Garfield, James; Hayes, Rutherford B.

Gregory Mixon
Assistant Professor of History, University of North Carolina, Charlotte
Trotter, William Monroe

Wilson J. Moses
Professor of American History, Pennsylvania State University, University Park
National Association for the Advancement of Colored People

Victor S. Navasky
Publisher and Editorial Director, The Nation
Kennedy, Robert

Anna Kasten Nelson
Distinguished Adjunct Historian in Residence, American University
National Security Act of 1947

David K. Nichols
Associate Professor of Political Science, Montclair State University
Federal Government, Executive Branch: An Overview

Ronald L. Numbers
Hilldale and William Coleman Professor of the History of Science and Medicine, University of Wisconsin-Madison
Health Insurance

Barbara B. Oberg
Lecturer in History, Princeton University
Declaration of Independence; Franklin, Benjamin

Alison G. Olson
Professor of History, University of Maryland, College Park
Albany Congress

William L. O'Neill
Professor of History, Rutgers, The State University of New Jersey
Stevenson, Adlai

John Opie
Distinguished Professor of History Emeritus, New Jersey Institute of Technology
Homestead Act

Andrew J. O'Shaughnessy
Associate Professor, University of Wisconsin, Oshkosh
Mayflower Compact

David M. Oshinsky
Board of Governors Professor of History, Rutgers, The State University of New Jersey
Army-McCarthy Hearings; McCarthy, Joseph

Bruce Palmer
Professor of History, University of Houston, Clear Lake
Farmers' Alliance Movement

Michelle Lee Park
Independent Scholar
National Park System

Donald L. Parman
Professor of History, Purdue University
Dawes Severalty Act

Herbert S. Parmet
Distinguished Professor Emeritus of History, City University of New York
Bush, George H. W.; Executive Privilege

James Lal Penick Jr.
Professor Emeritus, University of Alabama, Birmingham
Conservation Movement

Elisabeth Israels Perry
John Francis Bannon Professor of History and American Studies, Saint Louis University
Smith, Alfred

Richard Gid Powers
Professor of History, College of Staten Island, City University of New York
Anti-Communism; Federal Bureau of Investigation; Rosenberg Case

Walter F. Pratt Jr.
Associate Dean and Professor of Law, Notre Dame Law School, Notre Dame, Indiana
Holden v. Hardy; Insular Cases

Francis Paul Prucha
Professor Emeritus of History, Marquette
Bureau of Indian Affairs

Patrick Rael
Assistant Professor of History, Bowdoin College
Douglass, Frederick

Leslie J. Reagan
Associate Professor of History and Medical Humanities, University of Illinois, Urbana-Champaign
Roe v. Wade

Steven L. Rearden
Joint History Office, Washington, D.C.
Federal Government, Executive Branch: Defense Department

Merl E. Reed
Professor Emeritus of History, Georgia State University
Fair Employment Practice Committee

William J. Reese
Professor of Educational Policy Studies and Professor of History, University of Wisconsin-Madison
Education Policy: Education in Contemporary America

Gary W. Reichard
Associate Vice President for Academic Affairs and Professor of History, California State University, Long Beach
Eisenhower, Dwight D.; Taft, Robert; Watergate

Harold C. Relyea
Specialist in American National Government, Congressional Research Service, Washington, D.C.
Freedom of Information Act

Lex Renda
Associate Professor of History, University of Wisconsin, Milwaukee
Anti-Masonic Party

Leo P. Ribuffo
Society of Cincinnati George Washington Distinguished Professor of History, George Washington University, Washington, D.C.
Carter, Jimmy

Barry D. Riccio
Associate Professor of History, Eastern Illinois University
Lippmann, Walter

Leonard L. Richards
Professor of History, University of Massachusetts, Amherst
Adams, John Quincy

Andrew Chamberlin Rieser
Assistant Professor of History, St. Cloud State University
Liberalism

Norman K. Risjord
Professor Emeritus of History, University of Wisconsin-Madison
Federalist Party

Ruth Rosen
Professor of History, University of California, Davis
Feminism

Norman L. Rosenberg
DeWitt Wallace Professor of History, Macalester College
Abrams v. United States; Alien and Sedition Acts; Sedition

Steven J. Ross
Professor of History, University of Southern California, Los Angeles
Single-Tax Movement

Richard C. Sawyer
Teacher of Science and Mathematics, Newton Senior High School
Federal Government, Executive Branch: Agriculture Department

Roy V. Scott
Professor Emeritus of History, Mississippi State University
Granger Laws; Granger Movement

Randolph Scully
University of Pennsylvania, Philadelphia
Virginia Declaration of Rights

Terry L. Seip
Associate Professor of History, University of Southern California, Los Angeles
Freedmen's Bureau

Christopher Sellers
Associate Professor of History, State University of New York, Stony Brook
Environmental Protection Agency

Janann Sherman
Assistant Professor of History, University of Memphis
Rankin, Jeannette

Kenneth E. Shewmaker
Professor of History, Dartmouth College
Webster, Daniel

Joel H. Silbey
President White Professor of History, Cornell University
Buchanan, James; Liberty Party; Political Parties; Republican Party

Bryant Simon
Assistant Professor of History, University of Georgia, Athens
Tennessee Valley Authority

James F. Simon
Martin Professor of Law, New York Law School
Douglas, William O.

Kathryn Kish Sklar
Distinguished Professor of History, State University of New York, Binghamton
Muller v. Oregon

Theda Skocpol
Victor S. Thomas Professor of Government of Sociology, Harvard University
Pensions, Civil War

Elbert B. Smith
Professor Emeritus of History, University of Maryland, College Park
Taylor, Zachary

Richard D. Sonn
Associate Professor of History, University of Arkansas, Fayetteville
Anarchism

Allan Burton Spetter
Professor of History, Wright State University
Harrison, Benjamin

Robert J. Spitzer
Distinguished Service Professor of Political Science, State University of New York, Cortland
Veto Power

J. C. A. Stagg
Professor of History and Editor in Chief of the Papers of James Madison, University of Virginia, Charlottesville
Madison, James, Monroe, James

Anders Stephanson
Associate Professor of History, Columbia University
Manifest Destiny

Jesse Stiller
Historian, Office of the Comptroller of the Currency, Department of the Treasury, Washington, D.C.
Federal Government, Executive Branch: Treasury Department

Francis N. Stites
Professor Emeritus of History, San Diego State University, California
Marshall, John; *McCulloch v. Maryland*

Shelton Stromquist
Professor of History, University of Iowa, Iowa City
Greenback Labor Party

Daniel E. Sutherland
Professor of History, University of Arkansas, Fayetteville
Confederate States of America

William R. Tanner
Professor Emeritus of History, Humboldt State University
Internal Security Act

Athan G. Theoharis
Professor of History, Marquette University
Hoover, J. Edgar

Daniel J. Tichenor
Assistant Professor of Political Science, Rutgers, The State University of New Jersey
Federal Government, Executive Branch: Department of Justice; Federal Government, Executive Branch: Other Departments

William Vance Trollinger Jr.
Associate Professor of History, University of Dayton
Christian Coalition

Mark Tushnet
Carmack Waterhouse Professor of Constitutional Law, Georgetown University Law Center
Civil Rights; Civil Rights Legislation; Federalism; Marshall, Thurgood

William M. Tuttle Jr.
Professor of History and American Studies, University of Kansas, Lawrence
Servicemen's Readjustment Act

Dorothy Twohig
Associate Professor Emeritus of History, University of Virginia, Charlotte; Editor-in-Chief Emeritus, Papers of George Washington
Washington, George

Timothy B. Tyson
Associate Professor of Afro-American Studies, University of Wisconsin-Madison
King, Martin Luther, Jr.

Melvin I. Urofsky
Professor of History and Public Policy, Virginia Commonwealth University, Richmond
Supreme Court, U.S.; *West Coast Hotel Company v. Parrish*

William L. Van Deburg
Professor of Afro-American Studies, University of Wisconsin-Madison
Black Panthers

J. Samuel Walker
Historian, U.S. Nuclear Regulatory Commission, Washington, D.C.
Atomic Energy Commission; Nuclear Power; Nuclear Regulatory Commission

Samuel Walker
Professor of Criminal Justice, University of Nebraska, Omaha
American Civil Liberties Union

Eric H. Walther
Professor of History, University of Houston
Calhoun, John C.

Frank A. Warren
Professor of History, Queens College, City University of New York
Thomas, Norman

William Earl Weeks
Lecturer in History, San Diego State University, California
Louisiana Purchase

Wyatt C. Wells
Assistant Professor of History, Auburn University
Federal Reserve Act; Federal Reserve System

Simon Wendt
Congress of Racial Equality

G. Edward White
University Professor and John B. Minor Professor of Law and History, University of Virginia, Charlottesville
Harlan, John Marshall; Holmes, Oliver Wendell, Jr.; Jurisprudence; O'Connor, Sandra Day; Warren, Earl

William M. Wiecek
Congdon Professor of Public Law and Legislation, Syracuse University College of Law, and Professor of History, Maxwell School, Syracuse University
Brandeis, Louis; Church and State, Separation of; Taney, Roger B.

Carolyn Williams
Associate Professor of History, University of North Florida
Amistad Case

R. Hal Williams
Professor of History, Southern Methodist University
Cleveland, Grover

Garry Wills
Cultural Historian and Adjunct Professor of American History, Northwestern University
Gettysburg Address

Allan M. Winkler
Professor of History, Miami University, Oxford, Ohio
La Follette, Robert

Wendy Wolff
Historical Editor, Senate Historical Office, Washington, D.C.
Federal Government, Legislative Branch: An Overview; Federal Government, Legislative Branch: Senate

C. Vann Woodward±
Historian
Compromise of 1877

Donald Worster
Hall Distinguished Professor of History, University of Kansas
Environmentalism

Thomas W. Zeiler
Associate Professor of History, University of Colorado, Boulder
Trading with the Enemy Act

Directory of Contributors to *The Oxford Companion to the Supreme Court of the United States*

Thomas E. Baker
Professor of Law, Florida International University College of Law
Smith v. Allwright; Youngstown Sheet and Tube Co. v. Sawyer

Herman Belz
Professor of History, University of Maryland, College Park
Constitutionalism

Philip Bobbitt
Director of the Center for National Security Law, Columbia Law School
Constitutional Interpretation

Robert J. Cottrol
Professor of Law, of History, and of Sociology, Harold Paul Green Research Professor of Law, George Washington University Law School, Washington, D.C.
Second Amendment

Donald A. Downs
Professor of Political Science, Law, and Journalism, University of Wisconsin-Madison
Obscenity and Pornography

James W. Ely Jr.
Professor of Law and History and Milton R. Underwood Chair in Free Enterprise, Vanderbilt University School of Law
Adkins v. Children's Hospital, Property Rights

Mark A. Graber
Professor of Law and Government, University of Maryland
Constitutional Interpretation

Kermit L. Hall[±]
President, University at Albany, State University of New York, and Professor of History
Engle v. Vitale; Ferraro, Geraldine; Municipal Judicial System; *Plessy v. Ferguson*; State Governments; Stone, Harlan; Story, Joseph

Richard F. Hamm
Associate Professor of History, University at Albany, State University of New York
Debs, In re

Peter Charles Hoffer
Research Professor of History, University of Georgia
Due Process: Substantive Process

Wythe Holt
University Research Professor of Law, University of Alabama Law School
Judiciary Act of 1789

Harold M. Hyman
Professor of History, Emeritus, Rice University
Chase, Salmon

Wayne R. LaFave
David C. Baum Professor of Law, Emeritus, University of Illinois, Urbana-Champaign
Katz v. United States

James May
Professor of Law, Washington College of Law, American University
United States v. E. C. Knight Co.

Michael W. McCann
Griswold v. Connecticut

Jeffrey B. Morris
Professor of Law, Touro Law Center
Burger, Warren

Walter F. Pratt Jr.
Associate Dean and Professor of Law, University of Notre Dame Law School
Holden v. Hardy

Thomas O. Sargentich
Professor of Law, Washington College of Law, American University
Due Process: Procedural Process

Geoffrey R. Stone
Harry Kalven, Jr. Distinguished Service Professor of Law, University of Chicago Law School
New York Times Co. v. Sullivan

James B. Stoneking
Wheeling, West Virginia
State Regulation of Commerce

Stephen L. Wasby
Professor of Political Science, Emeritus, Nelson A Rockefeller College of Public Affairs and Policy, University at Albany, State University of New York
Blackmun, Harry A.

John R. Wunder
Professor of History, University of Nebraska, Lincoln
Chinese Exclusion Cases

±(***deceased***)

INDEX

N

P

Q

R

V

W

X

Y